ORIGINS: BRAIN AND SELF ORGANIZATION

Edited by
Karl Pribram
Radford University

LEA

1994

LAWRENCE ERLBAUM ASSOCIATES, PUBLISHERS
Hillsdale, New Jersey   Hove, UK

Lawrence Erlbaum Associates, Inc., Publishers
365 Broadway
Hillsdale, New Jersey 07642

Library of Congress Cataloging in Publication Data

```
Origins : brain and self organization / edited by Karl Pribram.
      p.    cm.
   Includes bibliographical references and index.
   ISBN 0-8058-1786-7
   1. Neuropsychology--Congresses.  2. Self-organizing systems--
Congresses.   I. Pribram, Karl H., 1919-    .
QP360.O735  1994
612.8'2--dc20                                      94-27940
                                                      CIP
```

Books published by Lawrence Erlbaum Associates are printed on acid-free paper, and their
bindings are chosen for strength and durability.

Printed in the United States of America

10 9 8 7 6 5 4 3 2 1

TABLE OF CONTENTS

ACKNOWLEDGEMENTS

The contributions from Sam Leven, Walter Morris and the New College of Global Studies of Radford University are gratefully acknowledged. Without them, the conference would not have been possible. I also want to express my gratitude to Harold Szu and Paul Werbos for help in organizing the conference. Special thanks go to Shelley Bechard who shepherded the manuscript to publication.

FOREWORD

This, the second Appalachian conference on neurodynamics, focuses on the problem of "order", its origins, evolution and future. Central to this concern lies our understanding of time. Both classical and quantum physics have developed their conceptions within a framework of time symmetry. This has led to notions such as Feynman's, which are portrayed in his famous diagrams as time arrows pointing in opposite directions "from time to time". DeBeauregard has challenged this conceptualization, proclaiming instead that it is causality that becomes reversed, not time itself.

My own view as a biologist steeped in time asymmetry, is that all such interpretations, despite their mathematical rigor, are nonsense. My views stem from those proposed by Dirac, who noted that the Fourier transform describes a reciprocal relationship between formulations describing spacetime and those describing a spectral domain. The spectral, holographic-like, domain has enfolded space and time---and thus causality. A new vocabulary (such as talking in terms of spectral density, needs to be applied to fully understand the coherence/correlational basis of phenomena observed in this domain. The Einstein, Podolsky & Rosen proposal, Bell's theorem and the like, lose their "mystery" when conceived as operations taking place in the spectral domain. However, we are unskilled and unused to thinking in such terms which make these phenomena appear strange to us.

One of the reasons for strangeness is that most phenomena are observed to take place in a domain that partakes to one extent or another of both spacetime and spectrum. Hilbert gave formal structure to this "intermediate" domain and Heisenberg applied it to a formulation of quantum physics. It was Gabor who extended this application to the communication sciences, and thus to the classical scale of operations. Nonetheless, to emphasize the relation to quantum physics, Gabor named the maximum density with which a signal could be transmitted without loss of fidelity, a "quantum of information".

Both biological and engineering applications of Gabor's insight have vindicated the usefulness of thinking about this hybrid (space time/spectrum) domain. In image processing (such as magnetic resonance imaging - MRI) which is based on "quantum holography" and in understanding visual processing by the brain, Gabor functions have played a major role during the past two decades. Many of these applications were presented in the proceedings of Appalachian I: New Directions in Neural Networks: Quantum Fields and Biological Data.

These contributions to understanding do not, however, completely resolve the issue of the irreversibility of time. Most of the formalisms describe linear or quasilinear processes and practically all of them are invertible. What is needed is a strongly non-linear, irreversible conceptualization in which time symmetry becomes irrevocably broken. Ilya Prigogine has provided such a conceptualization and I asked him to review for us his most recent insights to keynote Appalachian II. Prigogine, in his application, introduces formally the concept of "possibilities" which goes well beyond the much touted inherent probabilistic aspect of quantum physics. Two consequences emerge from "possibilities" and both have played a major role in the development of non-linear dynamics (or Chaos Theory as it is usually called---turbulence theory, I believe, would better reflect what the theory is about). One consequence, emphasized by the Santa Cruz group, notes that what appears to be random at any moment, may have deterministic roots. In a sense this insight is also given in holography: any spread function that transforms spacetime into a spectral representation, produces an order which appears random but which, by way of the inverse transform, again appears recognizably orderly.

The second consequence emerging from "possibilities" is to me the more interesting: It is Prigogine's demonstration that temporarily stable orders can be formed out of apparent chaos. These stabilities far from equilibrium are the stuff that life is made of. My interest lies in how the brain becomes involved in such orderings of psychological processes. To this end, Appalachian II was convened.

The contributors to Section I sketch the broad outlines within which inquiry can begin. None of these contributions would ordinarily be subsumed under headings such as learning and memory: yet by providing refreshingly new approaches to the problem of the evolution of order, these contributors frame not only the remaining papers in this volume, but also indicate the directions that need to be taken in subsequent conferences, which will address learning and memory more directly.

Werbos provides a global perspective; Shaw, Kadar and Kinsella-Shaw, in a beautiful presentation, bring us a perspective of how to approach intentional dynamics in psychology. Gyr fills out this perspective with regard to self-reference.

MacLennan prepares the ground for understanding the continual switch between discrete and continuous and again discrete processing in the brain, processing which at a particular level, is delineated by Hagen, Jibu and Yasue. Bak and Game indicate how self organization can occur in such processing domains.

In continuation of an interest explored in Appalachian I and in keeping with the theme of the current conference, Section II is composed of papers addressing the issue of how information becomes transmitted in the nervous system. Signal transmission (in distinction to order construction) is performed by way of nerve impulses, by "spike trains" as they are colloquially known. Time series analyses are needed to decipher the code by which "information", a pattern, originating in one part of the brain becomes available to another and Cariani reviews the field for us and adds insights of his own. In keeping with the theme of the conference, the question addressed by Min Xie is whether spike trains recorded from non-stimulated, anesthetized preparations show evidence of a basic deterministic process, or whether such spike trains are truly stochastically random. As far as the evidence Xie, King, and Pribram present, stochasticity is basic, leaving order to be imposed by resonance with the order constructed by processes operating at the synaptodendritic level which are "sampled" by the axons from which recordings are made. A model of stochastic resonance processing, and the importance of "noise" in such models, becomes evident in the papers by Levine; by Segundo and his collaborators; and by Longtin; several excellent contributions and by Bulsara; and one that takes this model a step further by Petr Lansky. What can be accomplished when such models are networked is presented by Farhat and his group, and by Szu and his collaborators.

Section III is devoted to how patterns are constructed at the synaptodendritic level of processing and how such pattern construction relates to image processing. Central to this set of papers is an understanding of the receptive field properties of the dendritic network and how they are demonstrated in the laboratory, a topic developed by our group at the Center for Brain Research and Informational Sciences (King, Xie, Zheng, Pribram).

Eugene Sokolov pursues this line of research with respect to color vision and Vadim Glezer with respect to the perception of visual pattern. One of the issues that needs to be addressed is how, in a distributed process, different spatial locations become synchronously activated. Varela and his colleagues show that such synchronization occurs in the superior colliculus; Bressler demonstrates the dynamics of self organization of such synchronicities at the cortical level; and Erwin applies the results obtained to radar pattern recognition.

Section IV deals with the control operations which operate on image processing to construct entities such as visual and auditory objects such as phonemes, described in a beautiful contribution by Fowler. Manfred Clynes does the same for musical phrases as auditory objects. With regard to his initial mysteries of mystery, I wish he would acknowledge "Brain and Perception" and acknowledge the related presentations in Appalachian I and II some of which he attended. But once he gets going on temporal entities, the going is provocative and substantial. In an important paper Goodale and Milner show that the so called dorsal pathway from the visual cortex to the parietal lobe, as described by Glezer, does not deal so much with <u>where</u> some entity is located (its place) but rather <u>how</u> the entity is to be manipulated (used). Bolster continues this line of investigation with respect to attention: the non-primary sensory-motor cortices (parietal, frontal and temporal lobe) are shown to be uniquely involved in organizing the operations of visual scan (defined as post-eye-movement processing) necessary to controlled aspects of attention. Crawford focuses on the frontal of these cortices in her presentation, showing how disattention, necessary to the control of distraction, operates. Werbos summarizes the section and the conference with the same grand sweep with which he inaugurated it. In a very real sense, as Werbos' contribution shows, the conference itself is an exercise in self-organization.

A caveat: in reading these proceedings, do so in the spirit in which they were presented: progress reports to a workshop. The aim was to bring us together to exchange ideas. Some of these ideas were fairly well worked out; others were in their infancy. As a result, one of the most rewarding aspects of the conference is that it fostered lasting interactions. At the time of going to press, a conference on consciousness has taken place at the University of Arizona--many of the protagonists had met initially at Appalachian I and II. In Prague, in the Czech Republic, two workshops have been organized, one on spike trains and one on brain and biophysics; again contributors to Appalachian I and II have served as seeds to crystalize these meetings.

Karl H. Pribram

Professor Emeritus, Stanford University
James P. and Anna King University Professor
and Eminent Scholar, Commonwealth of Virginia

Radford University
Radford, Virginia 24142

I. ISSUES

Chapter 1

Mind and Matter: Beyond the Cartesian Dualism

Ilya Prigogine

Mind and matter

Beyond the Cartesian dualism

Abstract

As stated by Penrose : "... it is our present lack of understanding of the fundamental laws of physics that prevent us from coming to grips with the concept of "mind" in physical or logical terms.". This difficulty is related to the survival in present day physics of the Cartesian dualism. The usual formulation of the laws of physics implies time symmetry and determinism, while life and the brain need an evolutionary approach and imply the appearance of "novelty".

The author presents a brief summary of the work of his school on the generalization of laws of nature to include irreversibility and probability.

In this view laws of nature are associated to "possibilities" and no more to "certitudes". This generalization applies to well-defined dynamical systems such as chaotic systems and classes of Poincaré non-integrable systems.

The mathematical formulation of this generalized form of dynamical laws is in terms of complex and irreducible spectral representations in appropriate functional spaces. These terms are explained in the text where a simple example (the Bernoulli shift) is presented in detail.

I

It is a great priviledge to participate in this conference organized by my friend Karl Pribram. I feel somewhat uneasy as I have really nothing to contribute from the point of view of neurophysiology. All what I can do is to make some general remarks on the situation of the problem of the brain in respect to our concepts in theoretical physics. In the book by Roger Penrose "The Emperor's New Mind", we read : "... it is our present lack of understanding of the fundamental laws of physics that prevent us from coming to grips with the concept of "mind" in physical or logical terms."

I believe that Penrose is right and moreover the reason for this difficulty is the survival in present day physics of the Cartesian dualism. In this dualism, we have on one side the physical world which obeys fundamental determinstic laws of nature in which future and past play a symmetrical role. In short, matter behaves like an automaton. On the other hand it is difficult to believe that our mind also behaves like an automaton. This seems to be incompatible with one of the main aspects of the human mind which is creativity. We could even not imagine human existence without the distinction between past and future. How then to bridge the Cartesian dualism ? This is obviously a fundamental and difficult problem. In fact, we have carried from the 19th Century two contradictory descriptions of nature. One in terms of time reversible "laws of nature" of which Newton's law is the simplest example, on the other hand the evolutionary view of thermodynamics. This leads to the well-known time paradox which is with us since the time of Boltzmann more than a hundred years ago. The solution of the time paradox is not only a problem of great importance for physics proper but also for our very view of nature and for the meaning we may give to "laws of nature". What makes our period so interesting from this point of view is, I believe, that we begin to have the tools necessary to overcome the time paradox and therefore also the Cartesian duality. This is of course a vast problem and in this short lecture I shall be only able to make a few general remarks. For more details the reader can refer to the papers quoted in the appendix.

I like to distinguish three periods in the history of the time paradox. The first is the discovery that there <u>was</u> indeed a time paradox. The second refers to the resurgence of the time paradox over the last decades. The third period corresponds to what I believe is the gradual overcoming of the time paradox and to a new formulation of laws of nature, a formulation which includes irreversibility

II

The first period is associated with Boltzmann's attempt to derive a microscopic theory of entropy. As is well known, Boltzmann was defeated as the result of devastating criticisms. Einstein has often repeated, "Time (as associated to irreversibility) is an <u>illusion</u>." But over the last decades, we have witnessed the birth of nonequilibrium physics and chemistry. We now begin to understand the <u>constructive</u> role played by irreversibility. Matter

4

in nonequilibrium conditions displays new, fundamental properties. There appears a new form of coherence as exemplified in periodic chemical reactions or in nonequilibrium spatial structures (such as the Turing structures). It is no more possible to releguate the arrow of time to the realm of "illusions". Also, life is only possible in nonequilibrium conditions. To deny the arrow of time would make life and ourselves an "illusion".

The emergence of nonequilibrium sciences marks in my view the second stage in the history of the time paradox.

But as a result of these developments, we unavoidably come to a clash with the traditional formulations of the laws of physics. The prototype of a law of physics is provided by Newton's classical dynamics. As mentioned, Newton's laws are deterministic and time symmetric. This remains true in quantum mechanics, where again the Schrödinger equation is deterministic and time-reversible. How then to understand the emergence of the arrow of time in the world around us?

The usual way out is to associate irreversibility to approximations introduced in classical or quantum mechanics. But how to associate non equilibrium structures which are currently observed to <u>approximations</u> of fundamental laws. It seems to me that the only possibility is as I mentioned to proceed with an extension of dynamics both for classical and quantum systems, to include irreversibility.

This means that we have to extend the concept of laws of nature. In classical dynamics the central object is the trajectory. A trajectory is time reversible. If any extension of the formulation of laws of physics is possible it will be on the level of ensembles of trajectories; that is, in terms of probability distributions ρ

Before going to statistical ensembles let us consider quantum mechanics. Here we deal with wavefunctions which satisfy Schrödinger's equation

$$it \frac{\partial \psi}{\partial t} = H\psi \tag{1}$$

where H is the Hamiltonian operator. The formal solution of this equation is (we take t = 1)

$$U_t = e^{-itH} \tag{2}$$

U_t is the evolution operator. What means then to "solve" a quantum mechanical problem. In short we have to find the eigenfunctions $|u_n>$ and the eigenvalues, E_n, of the Hamiltonian operator

$$H|u_n> = E_n|u_n> \qquad (3)$$

To solve this eigenvalue problem we have to specify the "space" (that is the type of functions) on which operator U_t acts. Since von Neumann we associate to the operators of quantum mechanics a Hilbert space. This is essentially the usual Euclidian vector space extended to an infinite number of dimensions. A basic role is played by the scalar product (we consider a single variable x).

$$\langle f|g \rangle = \int_D f^x(x)g(x)dn \qquad (4)$$

and the norm $|f|$

$$|f|^2 = \int_D f^x(x)f(x)dx \qquad (5)$$

In short, the Hilbert space is a space associated to "nice" functions which are square integrable. In this space the eigenvalues E_n of H (which is a self-adjoint operator) are real. Moreover, we can express H, and as a result also U_t, in terms of the eigenfunctions. Using the bra-ket notation as for the scalar product (4) we have

$$H = \Sigma |u_n> E_n < u_1| \qquad (6)$$

$$U_t = e^{-iHt} = \Sigma |u_n> e^{-iE_nt} < u_n| \qquad (7)$$

In quantum mechanics, the laws of nature are expressed through the spectral decomposition of the evolution operator U_t. Indeed, to calculate $\psi(t)$ once we have $\psi(0)$ it is now sufficient to write :

$$|\psi(t) = U_t|\psi(0) = \Sigma |u_n> e^{-iE_nt} <u_n|\psi(0)> \qquad (8)$$

Note the appearance of the scalar product $u_n|\psi(0)$. The essential feature is that the <u>spectral decomposition is real</u>. That means that the eigenvalues of H are real. As a result the eigenvalues of the evolution operator have modulus 1. This corresponds to time reversible rotations. To include irreversibility we would need <u>complex spectral representations</u>. If we would have $E_1 = \alpha_1 - i\beta_1, \beta_1$ this would lead to the damping factor $e^{-\beta_1 t}$ and symmetry between past and future would be destroyed. Part of our program will be therefore the derivation of complex spectral representations.

III

Before doing so, let us emphasize that classical or quantum mechanics is formulated in terms of individual trajectories or wave functions. But since Gibbs and Einstein there is a second formulation in terms of ensembles characterized by a distribution function ρ. This second formulation is also in terms of a spectral representation of the corresponding evolution operator. Here the basic equation is the so called Liouville equation for ρ (in quantum mechanics it is the von Neumann equation, ρ is then the density matrix).

$$i\frac{\partial \rho}{\partial t} = L\rho \rightarrow \rho_t = e^{-iLt}\rho_0 = U_t \rho_0 \qquad (9)$$

Again we can (at least in principle) determine the spectral decomposition of L (which is a self-adjoint operator) and of U_t. We again obtain a <u>real</u> spectral representation in Hilbert space. The transition to the statistical description does <u>not</u> introduce any form of irreversibility (this would need some supplementary approximations, such as coarse grained distributions, ...).

But there is a second aspect. The spectral representation used in the traditional statistical theory is "reducible". That means that the results obtained by the statistical theory are equivalent to those obtained by the study of trajectories or wavefunctions. For example, let us express $\rho(\omega)$ as the superposition of trajectories with a weight function $\rho(\omega_0)$. We have to identify

$$\rho(\omega) = \int d\omega_0 \delta(\omega - \omega_0)\rho(\omega_0) \qquad (10)$$

Here ω_0 and ω are elements of the phase space and we suppose that $\rho(\omega)$ belongs to the Hilbert space. We may apply the evolution operator U_t either to each trajectory (represented by the δ-function) or directly to $\rho(\omega)$. The result is the same. Going to statistical formulations which are reducible does not introduce any new element into dynamics. The first formulation of dynamics (in terms of trajectories or wavefunctions) is equivalent to the second one.

Our program is therefore to introduce a third formulation of dynamics in which the evolution operator U_t is associated to <u>a complex and irreducible spectral representation</u>.

Note the following points :

1) We do not introduce a "new" evolution operator. In this sense our formulation is not "new" in the sense that quantum mechanics is new in respect to classical theory.

2) This extension is only possible for some classes of dynamical systems (such as chaotic systems or non-integrable systems, see below). These are precisely the systems where one observes irreversible processes.

3) As we shall see this extension is only possible by extending the action of the evolution operator to more general function spaces than the Hilbert space.

Still this extension gives a new meaning to laws of physics. Not only so they include time symmetry breaking at the fundamental level but they introduce also a basic probabilistic element. Now laws of nature express <u>no more certitudes but only possibilities</u>.

In the frame of this short article, I would like first to present a simple example and then make some general comments. This example corresponds to the "Bernoulli shift". In this shift, we double the value of a number every second, keeping its value in the interval between 0 and 1

$$x_{n+1} = 2x_n \qquad (\text{mod } 1) \qquad\qquad (11)$$

Let us write the number in the form

$$x = \frac{u_{-1}}{2} + \frac{u_{-2}}{2^2} + \frac{u_{-3}}{2^3} + \ldots \quad , u_i = 0 \text{ or } 1$$

As is well known, two neighboring "trajectories" diverge exponentially (the Lyapounov exponent is log 2). The successive numbers observed by iterations fluctuate in the interval 0 to 1. For this reason, it is necessary to go to a probabilistic description. In this description, the probability distribution, $\rho_n(x)$, is transformed into a new probability distribution $\rho_{n+1}(x)$ through the operator U called the "Perron-Frobenius" operator. This operator is the evolution operator for the Bernoulli map.

$$\rho_{n+1}(x) = U \rho_n(x) \qquad\qquad (12)$$

The Perron-Frobenius operator plays here the same role as the evolution operator U_t in the ensemble formulation we considered in section III. In this simple case, the explicit form of the Perron-Frobenius operator is

$$U\rho_n(x) = \frac{1}{2}\left[\rho_n\left(\frac{x}{2}\right) + \rho_n\left(\frac{1+x}{2}\right) \right] \qquad\qquad (13)$$

The basic problem is the determination of the spectral representation of the Perron-Frobenius operator. It is here that some important results have been obtained over the last years (references at the end of the article). It is easy to determine the right eigenfunctions of the Perron-Frobenius operator U. They are the Bernoulli polynomials $B_n(x)$ which satisfy the equation

$$UB_n(x) = \frac{1}{2^n} B_n(x) \qquad (14)$$

The eigenvalue associated with the Bernoulli polynomials of degree n is 2^{-n}. This number is closely connected to the value of the Lyapounov exponent. This result is very satisfactory. The higher the degree of the polynomial, the more rapid its decay. After a sufficient number of iterations, the distribution function reduces to a constant that corresponds to the invariant measure associated with the Bernoulli shift.

Note that we deal with a <u>complex</u> spectral representation in the terminology of section III (using a continuous time label t we will have the eigenvalues $e^{-t\,log\,2}$) But the main point is that we have to go out of the Hilbert space. Indeed, the difficulties with the Hilbert space start with the adjoint operator U^+, whose explicit form is given by the equation,

$$U^+f(x) = f(2x) \quad 0 \leq x \leq \frac{1}{2}$$

$$= f(2x-1) \quad \frac{1}{2} < x \leq 1$$

It can be easily verified that this operator is isometric (it conserves the scalar product) and can only have eigenvalues of modulo one in the Hilbert space. But U^t has indeed eigendistributions in <u>generalized</u> spaces. In this example, the eigendistributions are simply derivatives of the delta function $\delta(x)$,

$$\tilde{B}_n(x) = \frac{(-1)^{n-1}}{n!} \left[\delta^{(n-1)}(x-1) - \delta^{(n-1)}(x) \right] \qquad (16)$$

with

$$\delta^{(n)}(x) = \frac{d^n}{dx^n} \delta(x) \qquad (17)$$

Using these distributions we have

$$U^+ \tilde{B}_n(x) = \frac{1}{2^n} \tilde{B}_n(x) \qquad (18)$$

(Note that the right eigendistributions of U^+ are the left eigendistribution of U). We obtain in this way a complete and orthonormal set of eigendistributions

$$\langle \tilde{B}_n | B_m \rangle = \delta_{nm} \leftrightarrow \sum_{n=0}^{\infty} (|B_n\rangle\langle\tilde{B}_n|) = 1 \qquad (19)$$

The spectral representation of the Perron-Frobenius operator becomes

$$U = \sum_{n=0}^{\infty} (|B_n\rangle\frac{1}{2^n}\langle\tilde{B}_n|) \quad \text{and} \quad U^+ = \sum_{n=0}^{\infty} (|\tilde{B}_n\rangle\frac{1}{2^n}\langle B_n|) \qquad (20)$$

Let us write the expression of the distribution function in terms of our complete set of eigendistributions

$$\rho_m(x) = U^m \rho(0) = \sum_{n=0}^{\infty} \left(\frac{1}{2^n}\right)^m |B_n\rangle\langle\tilde{B}_n| \rho_0\rangle \qquad (21)$$

This is the simplest example known to me of a <u>complex and irreducible</u> spectral representation which corresponds to our new formulation of laws of nature. Indeed, consider the scalar product

$$\langle \tilde{B}_n | \rho_0 \rangle = \int_0^1 dx \tilde{B}_n(x)\rho_0(x) \qquad (22)$$

The $\tilde{B}_n$ being singular distributions [see 16], $\langle \tilde{B}_n | \rho_0 \rangle$, has only a meaning together with a class of test functions (for example, polynomials). We cannot apply our results to single trajectories $\delta(x-x_0)$ as the scalar product $\langle \tilde{B}_n | \delta \rangle$ would then be ill-defined. That is precisely what we meant by an <u>irreducible</u> spectral representation. Note that in this case, the appearance of a broken time symmetry is trivial, as the Bernoulli shift implies a priviledged direction of time; if we would instead of multiplying divide by 2, we would have the point attractor $x = 0$.

We have considered a highly simplified example. Similar results are found for large classes of chaotic maps that are real dynamical systems. There is however an additional element in dynamical systems. Because of the time symmetry of the initial equations (i.e. Newton or Schrödinger equations) the evolution operator is also time symmetric. This leads to the <u>group</u> symmetry of the evolution operator $U(t)$,

$$U(t_1)U(t_2) = U(t_1 + t_2) \tag{23}$$

whatever the sign of t_1 and t_2. This is no more so for complex representations of $U(t)$. Then the group is split into two semi-groups corresponding each to a well defined time ordering. In one of the semi-groups we have damping, or approach to equilibrium in <u>our future</u> (this corresponds to terms such as $e^{-\gamma t}$ which vanish for $t \to +\infty$) the other to damping in <u>our past</u> with $e^{+\gamma t}$ which vanish for $t \to -\infty$, and diverge for $t \to +\infty$. This splitting is only possible in generalized functional spaces (for more information see the papers quoted in the references).

Complex irreducible spectral representations are also found in another class of dynamical systems. That is the class of large Poincaré systems (non-integrable systems with continuous spectrum). Note that large Poincaré systems are essential in most of the "interesting" questions of modern physics, such as scattering, interaction between matter and light, interaction between fields, problems in statistical mechanics or cosmology.

We may consider the simple example of scattering. The usual theory (classical or quantum) applies to "<u>transitory</u>" scattering. Particles collide and disappear at infinity. But in addition to transitory scattering, there are other situations corresponding to "<u>persistent</u>" scattering where all the time new particles appear from infinity and are scattered. That is the typical situation in statistical mechanics. Transitory scattering can be treated by traditional methods. However, persistent scattering leads to probability distributions which are singular. As a result we have again to go beyond Hilbert space and we obtain, as for chaotic systems a complex irreducible spectral representation.

Transitory scattering corresponds to integrable systems. There are invariants of motion. But these invariants decay in the case of persistent scattering. Moreover they decay through diffusive-type processes (similar to Fokker-Planck processes in classical theory, or to processes described by the Pauli equation in quantum theory). These diffusive processes introduce irreversibility at the fundamental dynamical level. They limit the validity of trajectory dynamics in classical physics or of wavefunction dynamics in quantum physics, as they require a description on the statistical level. Recent computer simulations have shown a complete agreement with the predictions of our spectral theory, both for classical and quantum systems. We can now see the elementary diffusive processes that lead to irreversibility in our macroscopic world.

The time paradox is closely related to what often has been called the quantum paradox. In short, the quantum paradox arises from the fact that in addition to the Schrödinger equation we need a second mechanism (the so called "collapse" of the wavefunction) to describe a number of phenomena such as, for example, the approach of quantum dynamical systems to equilibrium. However, this collapse of the wavefunction is outside the traditional quantum theory as wavefunctions are conserved by the Schrödinger equation. In the past, many interpretations of the quantum paradox have been proposed but so far as I know, all these interpretations have remained on the verbal level recovering simply the usual equations. Our approach leads to modifications of classical and quantum mechanics which have already been tested in simple situations such as scattering (see references). In conclusion, far from being an artifact, or the result of our approximations, irreversibility requires a suitable extension of the laws of physics. It is only in this way that we may reach a consistent view of the nature we observe. It is indeed a striking fact that we observe in nature both highly disordered systems, such as the famous black-body radiation and highly ordered systems, such as living systems including the brain. This distinction is made possible by the fact that disordered systems correspond to thermodynamic equilibrium, while these ordered systems corresponds to far-from-equilibrium conditions.

The arrow of time is the basic unifying element of nature. All arrows of time point in the same direction: your future is also my future, the future of the sun is also my future. In this view there is no more place for the Cartesian dualism. The various situations we observe in nature correspond to the various possibilities included in our formulation of the laws of nature.

This of course does not lead to a specific theory of the brain but it shows that the main characteristics of the brain, such as complexity, time asymmetry and creativity are general features of nature which are present in the brain to a degree unknown elsewhere.

We already mentioned that laws of nature for unstable dynamical systems express possibilities and no more certitudes. This is quite natural. After all how could we imagine the world shortly after the big-bang. It would likely to be as a child who can become a lawyer or an artist or a teacher but not all at the same time. It seems to me that there is no other reasonable alternative. If really the universe would be deterministic this conference I have the pleasure to attend, would have been preprogrammed at the big bang. We cannot even imagine how this information could have been included in the elementary particles present in the universe at this moment.

The traditional view of nature emphasized stability and equilibrium but then biology and human history appeared outside "normal" physics. This was the point of view expressed by the great biologist Jacques Monod. Today we see instability, fluctuations and irreversibility on all levels. This requires new tools and new concepts which make possible the transition from the dualistic classical world to a more unified description. We are only at the beginning. I can only hope that this lecture will give a feeling for what is involved here.

References

Maps

H. H. Hasegawa & W.C. Saphir, "Unitarity and Irreversiblity in Chaotic Systems" Phys. Rev.A 46 (1992) 7401

H. H. Hasegawa & D.J. Driebe "Transport as a Dynamical Property of a Simple Map" Physics Letters A 168 (1992) 18

H. H. Hasegawa & D.J. Driebe "Intrinsic Irreversibility and the Validity of the Kinetic Description of Chaotic Systems", submitted to Phys. Rev. E (1993)

I. Antoniou & S. Tasaki "Generalized Spectral Decompositions of Mixing Dynamical Systems" (review paper) International Journal of Quantum Chemistry Vol. 46 (1993) 425-474

I.A. Antoniou, Z. Suchanecki & S. Tasaki "Deterministic Diffusion, De Rham Equation and Fractal Eigenvectors" Physics Letters A 179, (1993), 97-102

I.A. Antoniou, Z. Suchanecki & S. Tasaki "Ergodic Properties of Piecewise Linear Maps on Fractal Repellers" Physics Letter A 179, (1993), 103-110

I.A. Antoniou, S. Tasaki & Z. Suchanecki "Spectral Decomposition and Fractal Eigenvectors for a Class of Piecewise Linear Maps" Chaos, Solitons and Fractals (1994) to appear

Poincaré Systems

T. Petrosky & I. Prigogine "Alternative Formulation of Classical and Quantum Dynamics for Non-Integrable Systems" Physica A 175 (1991) 146-209

T. Petrosky & I. Prigogine "Quantum Chaos, Complex Spectral Representations and Time-symmetry Breaking" to appear in Chaos, Solitons and Fractals

T. Petrosky & I. Prigogine "Poincaré Resonances and the Limits of Trajectory Dynamics" PNAS 90 (1993) 9393-9397

T. Petrosky & I. Prigogine "Poincaré Resonances and the Limits of Quantum Dynamics" Physics Letters A182 (1993) 5-15

Chapter 2

Self-Organization: Reexamining the Basics and An Alternative to the Big Bang

Paul J. Werbos

Self-Organization: Reexamining the Basics and An Alternative to the Big Bang

Paul J. Werbos
Room 675, National Science Foundation[1]
Arlington, Virginia, USA 22230
pwerbos@note.nsf

This paper provides a basic, simplified overview of the field of self-organization, stressing those parts of the field -- like thermodynamics and nonlinear systems dynamics -- where there really does exist a coherent, unifying mathematical theory. At the same time, it points towards some basic unanswered questions in this field, and suggests a variety of heresies which merit further research. For example, the paper will conclude with a "caricature model" of cosmology, suggesting how life and order could have evolved in the universe without any need for a Big Bang or for the exogenous mechanisms used in some of the classical alternatives to the Big Bang. Another paper presented at this conference by Ilya Prigogine (discussed in more detail below) takes a position on this issue , which I regard as even stronger (if more tactful): it argues that the basic phenomenon of time-forwards evolution, which underlies life and order, can be deduced entirely from local microscopic effects, without any need to invoke assumptions such as the Big Bang, or special initial conditions, or the special kinds of field effects exemplified in my caricature model.

I have tried to make this paper as simplified as possible, for the sake of interdisciplinary cooperation, which will be crucial to progress in this field. However, I have also tried to include the key mathematical and logical points -- in simplified form -- which underlie the discussion, in the later part of some subsections; these details are essential, in my view, because the literature on this field has become so complex that many scientists become too accustomed to relying on blind faith or on assumptions justified by footnotes to other sources, which cite other sources, and so on... on trails which do not always support the strong beliefs of later authors.

One participant at this conference complained that this paper goes too far in stating (and appearing to support) the views of orthodox mathematical physics which, in his view, have become a great straitjacket to modern science, reducing everyone's openness to new empirical data. Lerner[1] has made similar points, which I do not fully agree with. Nevertheless, the pure empiricist should note that the mathematical heresies described in this paper -- if pursued by future researchers -- could loosen that straitjacket to a significant degree. The caricature model here is emphatically <u>not</u> a grand unified, comprehensive mathematical theory; it is intended purely as a minimalist starting point, designed to encourage <u>the new experiments</u> which would in fact be crucial to achieving a higher degree of precision in a realistic manner.

The paper will begin by discussing what self-organization <u>is</u>, in general terms. Next, it will describe certain basic types of system important to the field. Finally it will summarize classical views (and misconceptions), modern views, and some new heresies, in that order. All five sections will identify fundamental questions for future research. The technical appendix will provide some new ideas in classical stability of particular importance to control theory and artificial neural networks: i.e., new methods for constructing Liapunov functions. Definitions of a few key terms are collected at the end, as an aid to the nonspecialist.

---

[1]The views herein are those of the author, developed on personal time, and do not represent NSF in any way.

WHAT IS SELF-ORGANIZATION?

Self-organization is the study of the way in which systems made up of simpler elements, governed by simple dynamical principles, spontaneously develop organization or patterns or order at a higher level. Self-organization is one of the most important fundamental topics in all of science and engineering, because it provides a kind of glue to connect and unify our knowledge across different levels of aggregation. This section will discuss the role of self-organization as a key unifying component of basic research in general.

In the scientific establishment and in Congress, considerable fuss has been made about the role of "basic scientific research" and the billions of dollars being spent on basic research. Yet, when we get down to fundamentals, all of our science has been built on the efforts to answer only four truly basic questions:

1. What is _reality_? I.e., what are the underlying phenomena -- like matter and energy -- which define our cosmos, and how do they work?

2. What is the _universe_ -- how big is it, where does it come from, and what is it evolving to?

3. What is _life_? Why and where does it exist, and how does it work?

4. What is _mind_ or _intelligence_?

Only a tiny percentage of the funding for "basic" scientific research is directed towards systematic, strategic efforts to find new and deeper answers to these questions. The vast bulk of our efforts seem to be ruled by mental inertia, by people studying issues like ,"What is the 18th spectral line of the 17th isotope of the 88th element?" As Kuhn points out[2], there is a great need for such "normal science," but normal science _by itself_ is not enough to find answers to these questions in an efficient manner.

There is an analogy here to artificial intelligence (AI): reasoning strategies based on _forwards induction_ (like normal science) build up from what is currently known; _backwards induction_ starts from long-term goals or questions, and works its way _backwards_ from these questions, to find a chain of reasoning which can answer these questions. It is well-known in AI that forwards induction by itself works very poorly when the questions to be answered are highly complex and not well-structured in advance. For the four questions above, it is clear that _backwards_ induction -- _strategically_ motivated efforts -- will be crucial to any real progress in the future.

According to conventional wisdom, question number one -- concerned with physics -- is the only area where knowledge is truly unified and scientific (albeit incomplete). Only in physics do we have relatively simple and precise underlying principles, which are used to deduce a wide variety of predictions, applied to a very wide variety of experiments and to engineering. Yet even in physics, the phenomenon of mental inertia has become very common, perhaps as a side effect of the very success of the field in political organization, government-based funding and professional image-building. At last year's Radford conference, I presented a new heresy related to the Quantum Field Theory (QFT) foundations of physics[3-6], based on key concepts in self-organization discussed below.

Just in the last few years, neural network researchers have developed new mathematics which, in my view, begins to put question number four on a physics-like scientific basis[7,8]. More precisely, there is new mathematics which can encompass the central issues in building a brainlike intelligent system, in a unified manner, with a clear link to past and future empirical work on the brain. This was all extreme heresy when it was first proposed[7], but it is now well-established through engineering applications[9,10]. New government initiatives have been announced, to support the neuroscience-engineering collaborations required to follow through on the resulting opportunities.

Question number three is the one which calls directly for a theory of _self-organization_. It calls for a body of mathematical theory (and applications) which explains how life and order evolve, through the operation of simpler underlying laws of nature like those discussed by physicists.

No such unified body of theory exists at present, for the field of self-organization as a whole. Unified, precise concepts certainly do exist, but they do not begin to encompass the range of systems and issues which are necessary to really understanding phenomena such as life. If one were optimistic, one might say that the theory of self-organization today is comparable to the field of AI and neural networks thirty years ago: a heterogenous field, unified by a common question, composed of a few great continents of organized but limited designs, surrounded by lots of islands of suggestive examples and ideas which have yet to be unified into anything like a general theory.

The field of artificial life[11] is full of such islands, and is similar to the field of artificial neural networks thirty years ago; unfortunately, it is difficult to summarize that field, and I will not try to do so here. The fields of thermodynamics and nonlinear system dynamics -- great continents within the field of self-organization -- are far larger and far more unified than those islands; therefore, I will focus mainly on them. It is true that the islands may seem at first to be more relevant to the issue of life -- in all of its complexity -- than the continents now do; however, the continents provide the element of mathematical unity and generality which will be crucial to really understanding the phenomena discussed on the islands. For the truly creative mathematician, the absence of an all-encompassing theory here should not be discouraging; it suggests that question three -- unlike one and four -- is a good place to seek a fundamentally new paradigm -- if, in fact, a unified approach is at all possible here.

Several authors have suggested that the theory of self-organization or the theory of complexity might be the key to understanding intelligence in the brain. Certainly the phenomena of chaos and heat flow, etc., play an important role in the brain, but generic self-organization is not enough to yield intelligence directly. The phenomenon of intelligence requires a very special, very rare kind of underlying system dynamics -- like the dynamics of neurons -- which exists on earth only as the result of billions of years of natural selection. In any event, a generic theory of self-organization or of complexity does not yet exist. Usually, in the neural network field, the term "self-organization" is a loose synonym for "unsupervised learning" or for adaptivity in general.

Question number two above depends heavily on questions number one and number three. Considerable efforts have been made, in recent years, to unify physics and cosmology, in a mathematical way, by developing a unified theory of the Big Bang[12,13]. Observations from astronomy have played a significant role in fine-tuning the Big Bang models, but the assumption that the Big Bang must have happened relies heavily on an assumption about self-organization -- the assumption that the existence of life requires that something like a Big Bang must have happened. This paper will suggest an alternative to that assumption which, I hope, could stimulate more empirical research and a wider variety of mathematical theories.

TYPES OF SYSTEMS OR "RULES"

Self-organization, as defined above, studies how different types of underlying system dynamics -- the microscopic "rules" or "laws" of nature -- result in different patterns of order (like life) at a more macroscopic level. Before I can discuss the link from system rules to the resulting order, I must first discuss the most important types of system rules which have been studied:

1. Lagrangian systems, a type of conservative (energy conserving) system. Our universe itself is a Lagrangian system, according to all current credible theories of physics.

2. Dissipative systems, which are like conservative systems, but leak energy to the outside.

3. Open systems, which input energy (and perhaps matter) from the outside, as well as dissipating it.

4. Time-symmetric systems, whose "rules" look the same whether we look at them forwards or backwards in time.

Lagrangian Systems and Energy Conservation

Virtually every serious model in physics in this century has assumed that the universe is a Lagrangian system. This view achieved its strongest formulation in the field theory of Einstein. Quantum Field Theory (QFT) still assumes that the universe is a Lagrangian system, but there are some qualifications which I will discuss below.

For the sake of the mathematical reader, I will give a worked-out example here; however, I hope that the main ideas will be clear even without following the equations.

In Einstein's view, everything in the universe is made up of force fields -- fields whose intensity varies from point to point across three-dimensional space. Thus the state of the universe at any time is fully specified when we specify the intensity of each force field at each point in space. If there are n force fields, of intensity ϕ_1 through ϕ_n, we may consider these n numbers as a vector $\underline{\phi}$; thus the state of the universe at any time t is specified by specifying $\underline{\phi}(\underline{x},t)$ across all points $\underline{x}$ at time t.

Crudely speaking, when we say that the universe is a Lagrangian system, we are saying that the <u>universe itself</u> acts like a utility maximizer. We are saying that the universe seems to have a kind of utility function, $\mathcal{L}$, and that it tries to maximize the sum of $\mathcal{L}$ across all future time. In physics, $\mathcal{L}$ is called a Lagrangian function.

More precisely, the value of $\mathcal{L}$ at any point $\underline{x}$ is assumed to be a function of $\phi(\underline{x},t)$ and of the derivatives of ϕ at the point $\underline{x}$ at time t. When the <u>current</u> state of the universe is specified, at the current time t_0, then the universe will choose its later states ($\phi(\underline{x},t)$ for $t \triangleright t_0$) so as to maximize or minimize the sum of $\mathcal{L}$ over all future time, across all space.

These ideas by themselves are not enough to specify a theory of how the universe works. We still need to guess how large n is and, more importantly, come up with a theory for what the function $\mathcal{L}$ is. However, once we specify these two pieces of information, <u>we can deduce everything else mathematically</u>. Furthermore, if the universe is a Lagrangian system, this implies that there is another function of ϕ, called $\mathcal{H}$ -- the mass-energy density, which is <u>conserved over time</u> (i.e., its total value across all space does not change from one time to the next). For some possible choices of $\mathcal{L}$ -- <u>but not all choices</u> -- the function $\mathcal{H}$ will be <u>positive-definite</u>; this basically means that $\mathcal{H}$ can never be negative at any point in space. (When $\mathcal{H}$ is positive-definite, we can rule out the possibility that $\mathcal{H}$ will grow larger and larger, without limit, in one region of space, as it grows more and more negative in another.)

A common kind of Lagrangian, with n=1, in a one-dimensional space x, would be something like:

$$\mathcal{L} \;=\; \tfrac{1}{2}\left(\frac{\partial \phi}{\partial t}\right)^2 \;-\; \tfrac{1}{2}\left(\frac{\partial \phi}{\partial x}\right)^2 \;+\; f(\phi) \;\;, \tag{1}$$

which physicists would write in a more condensed notation:

$$\mathcal{L} \;=\; \tfrac{1}{2}(\partial_t \phi)^2 \;-\; \tfrac{1}{2}(\partial_x \phi)^2 \;+\; f(\phi) \tag{2}$$

To work out the dynamic laws of the universe, as implied by any <u>particular</u> Lagrangian, we simply plug that Lagrangian into the Lagrange-Euler equation, a generalized equation which applies to <u>all</u> Lagrangian systems (explained further in [14] and [15]):

$$\textit{For all i:} \quad \partial_t\left(\frac{\delta \mathcal{L}}{\delta(\partial_t \phi_i)}\right) \;+\; \partial_x\left(\frac{\delta \mathcal{L}}{\delta(\partial_x \phi_i)}\right) \;=\; \frac{\delta \mathcal{L}}{\delta \phi_i} \tag{3}$$

The $\delta\mathcal{L}/\delta...$ derivatives represent the derivatives of the function $\mathcal{L}$ with respect to the things which appear in the function $\mathcal{L}$. Thus in equation 2, the derivative of $\mathcal{L}$ with respect to $\partial_t \phi$ is simply $\partial_t \phi$. When we plug equation 2 into equation 3, we arrive at the following equation, which specifies how ϕ changes over time <u>in the theory</u> specified by equation 2:

$$\partial_t(\partial_t \phi) \;-\; \partial_x(\partial_x \phi) \;=\; f'(\phi) \tag{4}$$

Equation 4 is a classical wave equation, the kind of equation used to describe radio waves, sound waves, etc.

Likewise, to figure out the formula for the conserved mass-energy, we plug in the $\mathcal{L}$ of our choice into the Hamiltonian equation (for the case n=1):

$$\mathcal{H} \;=\; \dot{\phi}\left(\frac{\delta \mathcal{L}}{\delta \dot{\phi}}\right) \;-\; \mathcal{L} \;\;, \tag{5}$$

which in the example of equation 2 yields:

$$\mathcal{H} \;=\; \tfrac{1}{2}\dot{\phi}^2 \;+\; \tfrac{1}{2}(\partial_x \phi)^2 \;-\; f(\phi) \tag{6}$$

20

Note that $\mathcal{H}$ is positive definite in this example, if the function f is positive definite. The quantity which is constant or conserved over time is simply the sum, at each time, over all space, of $\mathcal{H}$:

$$Total\ Mass-Energy \quad = \quad H(t) \quad = \quad \int \mathcal{H}(x,t)\,dx \qquad (7)$$

Conventional physical theories generally assume that $\mathcal{H}$ is positive definite, but there are notions of "false vacuum"[16] which begin to put that assumption into question; generally, the mathematics is easier when we assume that $\mathcal{H}$ is positive definite, but there is no apriori reason to assume that it must be. On the other hand, there is very good empirical evidence that mass-energy is in fact conserved. I am unaware of any theorem which says that energy-conserving systems must be Lagrangian systems, but with continuous field theories I am not aware of any workable alternatives.

Perhaps the most important true Lagrangian field theory is the "already unified" field theory of John Wheeler[17], which unified Maxwell's Laws and Einstein's general theory of relativity. More recent related concepts have been developed by Penrose[18] and others[19].

In QFT, the search for the true Lagrangian of the universe still continues, but there is more than just a Lagrange-Euler equation involved. In fact, there are three or four different versions of what we should do with the Lagrangian and of what it means[13]. Generally speaking, most of these versions require us to assume the existence of extra spatial dimensions, and additional "quantization" and "regularization" assumptions. At last year's conference, however, I showed[3] that we can replicate all the main features of QFT, starting from a purely Einsteinian Lagrangian theory, without such additional assumptions, so long as one is very careful not to throw in assumptions about time-forwards causality which do not emerge from the Lagrangian theory itself. Most physicists would recognize this claim as extreme heresy; the discussion of time-symmetric systems below will try to explain the basics of how it makes sense nevertheless.

Dissipative Systems

Even if the universe as a whole is a conservative, Lagrangian system, the systems which exist within our universe can input or output energy.

Classically, a dissipative system is just like a conservative system, except that there are additional terms in the dynamic equations which insure that energy will always be dissipated away, out of the system, until the system reaches some kind of minimum energy equilibrium. For example, consider the damped pendulum shown in Figure 1.

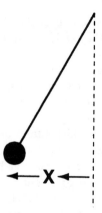

Figure 1. The Damped Pendulum

In the figure, x represents the gap between the pendulum and the center line, and $\dot{x}=v$ is the velocity of the pendulum. So long as x is small, the pendulum is governed by the equation:

$$\ddot{x} = \dot{v} = -ax - bv \tag{8}$$

The term "-bv" represents the effect of friction. Without the friction term, this would be a classical, Lagrangian system. In fact, it would be an example of a "harmonic oscillator," a simple model system used over and over again throughout physics. However, when we <u>add</u> the friction term to this conservative system, we guarantee that velocity and energy will always be dissipated away, until the velocity reaches zero. Friction guarantees that the system will move towards a definite, stable equilibrium point -- the unique point where x=v=0.

In the literature on chaos, the term "dissipative" has acquired a slightly different meanings, which is somewhat less precise[20]. To understand that alternative definition, one must first understand the concept of phase space, which is discussed in the next major section.

Open Systems

Open systems are like dissipative systems, but more general. They may input <u>and</u> output both matter and energy from the outside. As an example, consider the Continuously Stirred Tank Reactor (CSTR), shown in Figure 2.

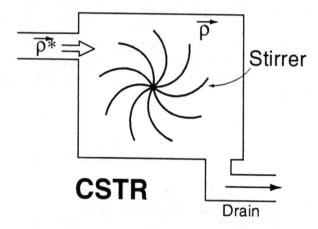

Figure 2. The Continuously Stirred Tank Reactor (CSTR)

The CSTR example plays a fundamental, all-pervasive role in chemical engineering. McAvoy has compared it to the role of the harmonic oscillator in physics. (See chapter 10 of [9] for examples of artificial neural networks used to control both CSTR models and real-world chemical plants.)

To specify the state of a CSTR at any time, we simply need to specify the concentrations of the various chemicals in the tank. Suppose that there are n chemicals, c_1 through c_N. Let ρ_i represent the density or concentration of the chemical c_i. To specify the state of the tank at time t, we need to know the N numbers, $\rho_1(t)$, $\rho_2(t)$, ... , $\rho_N(t)$, which we can think of as a vector, $\rho(t)$.

The CSTR receives an <u>input</u> flow of these chemicals from the outside, indicated by the pipe on the upper left of Figure 2. The input stream is usually assumed to be a constant flow, going at a rate c (controlled by some valve). The input stream contains the same chemicals as the tank, and the concentrations of chemicals in the input stream forms another vector, $\rho^*(t)$. The volume of fluid going out the drain is usually equal to the inflow rate, but the composition of what goes out the drain is simply the same as what is in the tank ($\rho(t)$). The process of stirring insures a uniform concentration of all chemicals throughout the tank, so that we don't have to worry about concentrations varying from point to point in the tank (thereby complicating and confusing the mathematics).

Open systems like Figure 2 can only exist as a <u>subset</u> of our universe. Even then, most thermodynamicists would say that the influx of matter and energy can only continue for a finite time. However, the notion of a CSTR with a sustained influx and perfect stirring is still a mathematically interesting and tractable problem, close enough to real systems that it has enormous practical value.

Years ago, many people became excited by the idea that <u>open systems</u> (like the earth, if the sun would shine forever) could develop and sustain life forever, even if closed systems could not. They concluded that the study of open systems might be crucial to our understanding of life, even if life itself -- like the sun -- must eventually die out in our universe.

Time-Symmetric Systems

The flow of time is a central issue -- perhaps the central issue -- in the study of self-organization. Several versions of the idea exist in science: time as a coordinate axis, no different from coordinates in space; time as the dimension which defines causality; time as the driving gradient along which life evolves; and time as a ruler of human thought and action. A clearer understanding of self-organization -- and even of physics itself [3-6] -- requires a deeper understanding of the relations between these various aspects of time.

A good place to start is by understanding the concept of time-symmetric systems.

In physics, a system is called time-symmetric (or T-symmetric) if the rules which govern that system look exactly the same when viewed in the forwards time direction or in the backwards time direction. In other words, if we captured the evolution of the system forwards in time on a movie film, and then played the movie backwards, the backwards movie should seem to be governed by exactly the same rules; there would be no difference between forwards or backwards.

In mathematical terms, we can test for time-symmetry by plugging in "-t" instead of "t" wherever "t" appears (explicitly or implicitly) in the system equations, and looking to see if the new version of the equations is the same as the old version. For example, consider the simple wave equation back in equation 4:

$$\partial_t(\partial_t\phi) \;=\; \partial_x(\partial_x\phi) \;+\; f'(\phi) \tag{9}$$

When we replace "t" by "-t," the only term which might be affected is the one on the left, which does contain "t." Indeed:

$$\partial_{-t} \;=\; \frac{\partial}{\partial(-t)} \;=\; -\frac{\partial}{\partial t} \;, \tag{10}$$

which would reverse the sign of our "∂_t" operator. But there are two ∂_t operators on the left in equation 9; multiplying the leftmost term by two minus signs, we end up with the term unchanged. Thus equation 9 is totally and perfectly T-symmetric.

On the other hand, consider equation 8, the equation for a damped pendulum, which we may write as:

$$\partial_t(\partial_t x) \;=\; -ax \;-\; b(\partial_t x) \tag{11}$$

The term on the far right -- the friction term -- contains only one "∂_t"; thus when time is reversed, we end up with the equation:

$$\partial_t(\partial_t x) \;=\; -ax \;+\; b(\partial_t x) \tag{12}$$

Equation 12 is very different in its behavior from equation 11. This is what we should expect; if we take a movie of a pendulum slowly winding down to a stop, we know that we would see something quite different (physically impossible, in everyday terms!) when we run the movie backwards.

Based on these two examples, one might guess that Lagrangian systems are time-symmetric while dissipative systems are not. But the first part of this guess would be very wrong. It is easy enough to postulate a Lagrangian which is asymmetric with respect to time, by including terms based on first-order time derivatives. High energy physicists use such terms routinely, in describing fields called fermion fields or spinor fields[14,19,20]. Today's grand unified theories of physics (including the superstring theories) generally are T-symmetric; however, physicists have known for decades that there is a class of nuclear reactions -- the "superweak interactions"[21] -- which do not fit the T-symmetric models, and suggest a likelihood of T-symmetry violations. (More precisely, the existing forms of QFT -- which assume CPT asymmetry, as I will discuss below -- requires that T symmetry must be violated somewhere, in order to explain the experiments already done.) The superweak effects appear extremely small at present, but they may be the tip of a huge iceberg. In system dynamics, it is well-known that small feedback terms -- which appear inconsequential over small time intervals -- may exert large and decisive cumulative effects on the global state of a large system; the superweak effects, tiny though they are, might be a reflection of such small but decisive terms. (After the presentation of this paper at Radford, one participant stated that Weinberg of Harvard -- a major developer of unified theories -- may be developing a new model to cover superweak interactions; however, no information was available yet on the details. In any event, more empirical information would be essential to really understanding these interactions.) Even the existing theory predicts symmetry violations 100 times greater, in experiments now being set up for B mesons, than in the experiments reported so far.

High energy physics generally <u>does</u> require "CPT symmetry." To test for CPT symmetry, we switch t with -t, and we <u>also</u> switch <u>x</u> with -<u>x</u> and reverse the charges of all particles/fields. There are no known violations of CPT symmetry in any physical experiment at this time. Some physicists have assumed that CPT symmetry <u>must</u> be true, apriori, because they don't know how to make the mathematics of QFT work without absolute and perfect CPT symmetry. (Likewise, the whole elaborate apparatus of superstring theory rests entirely on trying to solve other problems in the mathematics -- without any empirical support whatsoever for any of the complexity.) Einsteinian field theory does <u>not</u> require CPT symmetry; therefore, the mathematics in [3-6] should make it possible to relax the assumption of CPT symmetry, <u>if</u> there were ever any empirical reasons to do. Still, even in my new approach, CPT symmetry currently appears to be a very natural and compelling assumption.

<u>Many researchers believe that the central problem in self-organization is to explain why time seems to run forwards, in such an absolute asymmetric way, while at the same time being so absolutely symmetric at the microscopic level.</u> Most people explain this by assuming that macroscopic causality (and life) is a temporary aberration, due to unusual starting conditions in our universe -- the Big Bang. The later part of this paper will suggest some alternative possibilities, related in part to recent work by Prigogine[23] as summarized by Prigogine at this conference.

Time-symmetry is also the key to my new reformulation of QFT. Because QFT describes the <u>underlying</u>, <u>microscopic</u> dynamics of our universe, and does not yet account for superweak interactions, there is no <u>need</u> or <u>justification</u> for assuming anything but T-symmetry as yet at that level.

In past decades, dozens of serious scientists -- including Einstein, Wiener, Von Neumann and DeBroglie -- made strenuous efforts to "explain" QFT as the statistical outcome of a deeper, underlying theory -- a theory of the universe as an Einsteinian Lagrangian system. Those efforts failed, and cast doubt on the whole idea. (However, some of DeBroglie's ideas may yet prove useful in the future.) Von Neumann even proved some theorems suggesting that such an explanation might be impossible. Actually, Von Neumann only proved that it would be impossible to replicate a range of predictions from QFT <u>which had not been tested experimentally</u>. But Bell, Shimony and others designed an <u>actual experiment</u> -- performed several times since 1974 or so [13,24] -- which could never be reconciled with what they called "local causal hidden variable theories."

Bell's theorem actually provides the key needed to overcome these difficulties. The key to Bell's Theorem was the assumption of <u>time-forwards</u> causality. DeBeauregard[13] has shown that QFT itself can only explain Bell's Theorem <u>because of the way it assumes time-symmetry</u> in the flow of causality in the experimental system. In retrospect, this whole episode in physics seems amazingly clumsy. Top scientists, in trying to compute the <u>statistical</u> implications of <u>time-symmetric</u> Lagrangians and dynamics, have generally <u>added</u> an assumption of <u>time-forwards</u> causality -- taken from personal intuition rather than the Lagrangians -- in order to simplify their calculations. The apparent failure of Einsteinian theories was <u>not</u> due to the theories themselves -- theories which <u>in no way</u> implied time-forwards causality -- but to an <u>extraneous</u> assumption which was thrown in when calculating the supposed predictions of these theories. The essence of my reformulation is simply to account for this problem, by going back to calculate the statistics in a more consistent manner. This is still far from trivial, but it does replicate all the main features of QFT, including renormalization, Fock space effects, interference, and so on, to an uncanny degree. (For more details and other issues, see [3-6].) This is <u>not</u> to say that I have constructed a grand unified theory on this basis; rather, I have provided a mathematical starting point which future researchers may use to develop such a theory. This, in turn, still leaves open the puzzle of causality at the macroscopic level.

Prigogine's new paper[23] suggests an alternative formalism for calculating what QFT calculates, which also starts from a purely Einsteinian Lagrangian basis, and provides another way to eliminate the need for apriori quantization assumptions and the like. It is conceivable that the two formalisms, though quite different, are mathematically equivalent, in much the same way that the Schrodinger and Heisenberg formalisms are now known to be equivalent; however, this has yet to be proven.

CLASSICAL CONCEPTS OF SELF-ORGANIZATION

Starting from the wide array of possible systems, discussed in the previous section, how can we deduce how these systems will actually behave at the macroscopic level? What kinds of life or order will they give rise to?

Prior to the mid-1970's, most scientists focused their attention on two kinds of behavior which can emerge, in equilibrium, in a dynamical system: simple, static, stable equilibrium, and states of total disorder or randomness. When behavior of this sort was proven to emerge in certain important systems, many scientists extrapolated this result, and made statements which appeared to suggest that <u>all possible systems</u> - including our own universe, whose dynamic laws are still unknown -- must culminate in a lifeless state, either totally static (like a Big Crunch) or totally random (like a Heat Death). At this conference, Prigogine provided some very strong warnings about such extrapolation or speculation.

This section will discuss some of the key concepts which emerged from this early research, and some of its extensions (and extrapolations). First it will illustrate the basic concepts related to stable equilibrium -- concepts are still the mainstay of control engineering today. Next it will describe the basic mathematics of particle "scattering" (i.e., collisions between particles) and statistics based on scattering. Finally, it will discuss a few extensions and extrapolations.

Static Stable Equilibrium and Related Concepts

The pendulum with friction, shown in Figure 1 above, is a classic example of a system which moves towards a simple, static equilibrium. No matter what state the pendulum start out in, it will move towards the state where x=v=0. It will never reach that state <u>exactly</u>, but as time goes on, it will move closer and closer.

The pendulum is a very simple kind of system, which can be described by only two variables, x and v, which vary continuously with time. Systems like this can be totally described by a <u>phase plane</u> picture, like the one shown in Figure 3.

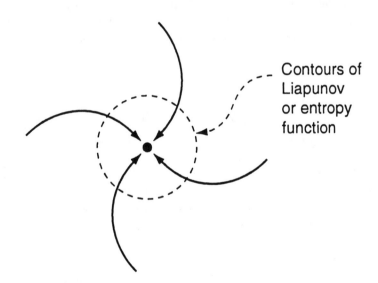

Contours of
Liapunov
or entropy
function

Figure 3. Phase Plane Picture For a Simple Static Equilibrium

In Figure 3, each point in the plane represents a possible state of the system; the two coordinates of the point are simply the values of x and v in that state. The solid curves with arrowheads represent how the system evolves over time, starting from any point on any of the curves. In this example, all arrows lead inwards towards a <u>single point</u> -- the static, stable equilibrium point.

This same notion of a point equilibrium can be applied to more complex systems as well. The phase-plane picture of a system defined by n variables (for n>2) cannot fit on a two-dimensional piece of paper, but we certainly can think about what it looks like. Still, the difficulty of drawing or imagining phase-plane pictures in more than two dimensions was one of the reasons why it took so many years before people developed more advanced concepts in system dynamics. (Difficulties in visualizing time-symmetric causality have also been a problem.)

Even today, the vast bulk of research in control engineering (even with neural networks!) focuses on the effort to achieve a stable point equilibrium, of this classical variety. Yet several researchers [20,25] have shown that other approaches to control are possible, based on ideas like stable <u>regions</u> or points revisited on a regular schedule. Advanced neural net control designs, based on optimization methods[7,9], should be able to learn such unconventional control strategies, when such strategies can improve engineering performance over time.

Figure 3 illustrates another key concept from classical theory: the concept of a <u>Liapunov function</u>. Even for a simple pendulum, the Liapunov function is a function of two variables, x and v; therefore, the only way to show it on paper is by drawing its <u>contour lines</u>, like the dashed circle surrounding the stable equilibrium. You can think of Figure 3 as a kind of map, where each contour line (only one shown) indicate how "high" each point is, in terms of the Liapunov function.

But what <u>is</u> a Liapunov function? A Liapunov function may be defined as <u>any</u> function such that the solid curves <u>always</u> point <u>downhill</u>, <u>except</u> at the stable point, which is the lowest point on the map. (The lines need not point <u>directly</u> downhill; they need only point in some direction which goes down, which reduces the level of the Liapunov function.) Once we know that a system has this kind of Liapunov function, we know that it has a stable point equilibrium.

The usual entropy functions of thermodynamics may be viewed as a <u>special case</u> of Liapunov functions (with their sign reversed): the entropy functions always increase, until the system reaches equilibrium. Energy, by contrast, is usually <u>not</u> a Liapunov function, except in special cases, like our simplified model of a pendulum with friction.

Even when systems do have a stable point equilibrium, it can be difficult to find a Liapunov function, to prove stability. Even today, most people rely mainly on cleverness and guessing here. (It reminds me of how people solved algebraic equations prior to Newton's method!) Certain neural network designs -- the adaptive critic methods [7,9] -- offer the hope of <u>adapting</u> or <u>numerically locating</u> Liapunov functions, because they combine to a mathematical function (the Jacobian function J) which is known to be a Liapunov function for a very broad class of systems; however, a great deal of work would be required to turn this into a working computer-based tool. Some mathematical details of this possibility are discussed in the technical Appendix of this paper

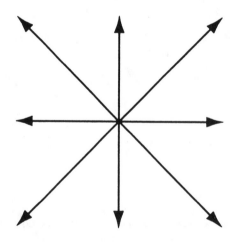

Figure 4. Phase Plane Picture of an Unstable System

Figure 4 illustrates the classical opposite to Figure 3: an unstable, divergent system which simply "blows up."

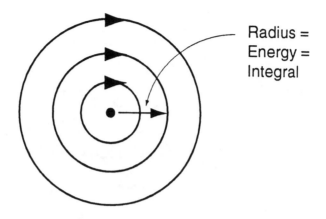

Figure 5. Phase Plane Picture of a Conservative System

Figure 5 illustrates a third classical picture: the conservative system (like the pendulum <u>without</u> friction). Energy-conserving systems cannot approach a universal, stable point equilibrium, because states of one energy level cannot evolve into a state at a different energy level. States of higher energy can <u>dissipate</u> their extra energy, as in the pendulum, in a <u>dissipative</u> system only. (If all possible states had the same "energy," it would be meaningless to say that energy is conserved.) Therefore, when energy or any other "integral" (conserved quantity) is conserved, the regions of phase space representing different energy levels are totally disconnected from each other. There could be stable points or oscillations <u>within</u> a given energy region, but no curves moving towards that point from states of higher or lower energy. In Figure 5, the circles each represent different energy levels; for example, they could represent the swings of a frictionless pendulum, starting off at different distances x from the center.

Scattering: the Classical Model

The classical scattering model begins from ideas about collisions between particles in free space, but it ends up being a fundamental tool in modern chemistry.

In classical, pre-Einsteinian physics, people often thought of the universe as a collection of particles -- simple particles or atoms or molecules -- moving around in free space. In this view, the laws of physics boiled down to predicting what will happen when different types of particle collide with each other, with what probability. Curiously enough, modern QFT has largely returned to this view[13,26]. Modern QFT focuses most of its attention on calculating <u>scattering probabilities</u> (or <u>cross-sections</u>), for different types of particles. These calculations are very complex, because they involve complex field effects in the zone of interaction between particles, but the final result is simply a set of scattering probabilities which are all we observe at the macroscopic level. (Several aspects of QFT which go beyond this will be discussed below.)

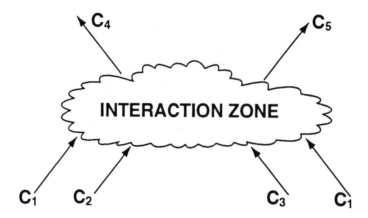

Figure 6. The Concept of Scattering

The notion of scattering or particle collision is illustrated by the example in Figure 6. From the underlying laws of physics or chemistry, we may know that 2 particles of chemical number 1 (c_1), one particle of c_2 and one particle of c_3 may collide and recombine to form particles c_4 and c_5. When the four particles come together, we may know that there is a certain probability of this happening. (Other types of collision may also be possible -- such as c_1 and c_2 colliding alone -- but let us just consider one type of collision at a time, for now.) Our problem, in thermodynamics, is to figure out what kinds of results these microscopic collisions will lead to, for the universe as a whole.

As a simple approximation, we may assume that these particles are distributed all across space, in a uniform, random sort of way, such that we don't have to worry about what happens in any specific location. We simply want to know <u>how many</u> of these particles there will be, for each type of particle, per volume of space. More precisely, we want to know, for each possible particle type, c_i, what will be its density, $\rho_i(t)$, measured in terms of particles per unit of space, at each time t, starting from a known initial density.

To figure this out, look back at Figure 6, and use some intuition. If the density of ρ_1 and ρ_2 is held constant, but the density of ρ_3 is cut in half, then the rate of four-way collisions will be cut in half. Likewise, cutting ρ_2 in half would also cut the frequency in half. Cutting ρ_1 in half would cut the frequency by a factor of 4, because <u>two</u> c_1's are needed for each collision. Putting this together, we would expect that the frequency of collisions (the rate of reaction) would simply be proportional to:

$$\rho_1 * \rho_2 * \rho_3 * \rho_1 = \rho_1^2 \rho_2 \rho_3 \tag{13}$$

Now <u>if the underlying laws of the universe are T-symmetric</u> -- as discussed at length above -- we <u>must</u> assume that this kind of collision could happen just as easily <u>in reverse time</u>, whenever a c_4 particle collides with a c_5 particle in free space. The rate of reverse collisions would be proportional to $\rho_4\rho_5$, and there must be the <u>same likelihood</u> of a backwards reaction as a forwards reaction, allowing for what the densities are. (As a practical matter, in chemistry, elementary reactions are symmetric only with respect to an <u>equilibrium</u> mixture, which will be explained in the discussion of equation 24 below.)

Translating this example into formal language, we would say that the chemicals c_1 through c_5 obey the following <u>reaction equation</u>:

$$2c_1 + c_2 * c_3 \leftrightarrow c_4 + c_5 \; , \tag{14}$$

where the double-headed arrow represents a two-way reaction. We would say that ρ_1, for example, obeys the dynamical equations:

$$\dot{\rho}_1 \; = \; - \, 2R \tag{15}$$

$$R \; = \; k(\rho_1^2 \rho_2 \rho_3 \, - \, \rho_4 \rho_5) \; , \tag{16}$$

where R is the rate of the reaction, at the current time t, and where k is a rate constant. Equation 15 basically says that the reaction uses up two particles of c_1 per collision, and equation 16 is based on equation 13 and our discussion of the reverse collisions. It is interesting that equations 15 and 16 are not themselves time-symmetric, even though they describe statistics of a time-symmetric reaction. (One might hope, at first, that equation 15 -- the conventional kind of equation used in chemistry -- explains very easily how time-forwards statistics can emerge spontaneously in a system whose underlying physics is time-symmetric; however, this is not the case. Our derivation of equations 15 and 16 implicitly assumed that: (1) the densities ρ may start out, at some initial time t, at values different from their long-term equilibrium values; (2) time-forwards causality applies forwards from that time t. The next section of this paper will discus this general issue in more depth.)

More generally, we may consider reaction equations:

$$m_1 c_1 \, + \, ... \, + \, m_N c_N \; \leftrightarrow \; n_1 c_1 \, + \, ... \, + \, n_N c_N \; , \tag{17}$$

where there are N particle types in existence in the universe, and where m_i will typically be zero for most particle types in any particular reaction. (In other words, most reactions involve only a handful of the particle types.) For each such reaction, the rate of reaction will equal the forward collision rate minus the backwards rate, such that:

$$R \; = \; k \left(\prod_{i=1}^{N} \rho_i^{m_i} \, - \, \prod_{i=1}^{N} \rho_i^{n_i} \right) \; , \tag{18}$$

where the large pi refers to a product. Equation 18 is simply the obvious generalization of equation 16. The net change in each ρ_i based on this reaction will simply be:

$$\dot{\rho}_i \; = \; (n_i \, - \, m_i)R \tag{19}$$

For a realistic system of particles or chemicals, we must assume that several reactions, like equation 17, are taking place in parallel. In that case, the total value of $\dot{\rho}_i$ will simply equal the sum of $(n_i-m_i)R$, for each reaction, summed over all the reaction types. Systems of this sort are easy to simulate on a personal computer, even in a spreadsheet.

Is it possible for such a simple, approximate model of particle statistics to yield interesting dynamic effects? For example, if we assumed a universe with very strange sorts of particles, such as negative energy particles, could one generate strange reaction equations leading to interesting dynamics here? Would the existence of negative energy states blow up the universe (as some have feared)?

What if we assumed some variation across space, such as two reaction chambers connected by some kind of diffusion of particles? Such a system could be represented by creating two variables for each chemical c_i, ρ_i^A and ρ_i^B , the densities in the two reaction chambers A and B; we can assume the usual reactions within each reaction chamber, and simply add N simple reaction equations to represent the diffusion process:

$$\rho_i^A \; \leftrightarrow \; \rho_i^B \qquad for \; i=1,N \tag{20}$$

In general, none of these interesting complications changes the basic picture. Simple reaction systems like those above always have a stable point equilibrium. This can be seen by considering the simple Liapunov function:

$$L \; = \; \sum_i (\rho_i \log \rho_i \, - \, \rho_i) \tag{21}$$

It is a straightforward exercise in calculus to prove that this is in fact a Liapunov function for <u>all</u> these reaction systems; one need only calculate $\dot{L}$, plugging in equations 18 and 19 into the result, to verify that $\dot{L}$ is always negative, except at equilibrium points, where it is zero. (Recall that ρ_i can never be negative in these systems.) It is also a straightforward exercise to see that L has a <u>global</u> minimum when ρ_i equals 1, for <u>any</u> chemical c_i. <u>Note that this global minimum</u> does not even depend on the details of the reaction equations! This model provides very powerful support for the view that realistic universes do in fact approach a stable equilibrium, in a very strong way.

In order to approach reality, of course, we must account for some additional complexities here -- though they do not change the basic picture. The two main complications of importance to the classical picture are: (1) the role of mass-energy; (2) the existence of multiple energy levels for each particle type. Readers with less interest in the mathematical details can move on to the next subsection, without losing the basic idea.

Mass-energy does not appear <u>explicitly</u> in equation 17, but it is represented implicitly. If the mass-energy of each particle, c_i, is E_i, then the conservation of mass-energy effectively requires that total mass-energy be unchanged by the reaction:

$$\sum_{i=1}^{N} m_i E_i = \sum_{i=1}^{N} n_i E_i \; , \qquad (22)$$

<u>for every reaction</u> in the system. In vector notation, this may be expressed equivalently as:

$$\boldsymbol{E} \cdot (\boldsymbol{n} - \boldsymbol{m}) = 0 \qquad (23)$$

In fact, <u>any</u> vector $\boldsymbol{E}$ which obeys equation 23 for all reactions will automatically be a conserved integral of this system. When a system of reactions does obey one or more conservation laws, then the system will <u>not</u> evolve towards the global minimum of the Liapunov function unless, by chance, the system <u>starts out</u> at the same energy level as that global minimum belongs to. The system will always evolve towards the unique, stable equilibrium <u>within</u> the set of points that have the same energy etc. If there is a set of integrals, $\underline{E}^{(1)}$ through $\underline{E}^{(M)}$, then it is straightforward to prove that the equilibrium points (points where $\dot{\rho}=0$) are defined by:

$$\rho_i = \exp(-\theta_1 E_i^{(1)}) * \exp(-\theta_2 E_i^{(2)}) * \ldots * \exp(-\theta_M E_i^{(M)}) \; , \qquad (24)$$

where the constants θ_1 through θ_M can be any real numbers (positive or negative), and can be thought of as something like the "temperature" of the particular state. (The θ's must be the same, of course, for all the different chemicals in any one particular state.) For every possible state of the system, $\underline{\rho}$, whether an equilibrium state or not, there will always exist a "temperature level" ($\underline{\theta}$) which matches the energy levels of that state.

The discussion above assumed a finite number of particle types. In actuality, in physics, scattering probabilities are calculated as a function of particle <u>type</u>, <u>velocity</u> and <u>spin</u>. If we think of each c_i as representing a particular <u>combination</u> of particle type, velocity and spin, then the equations above still make sense, but they assume an infinite number of combinations c_i, because the speed of a particle can be anything between zero and the speed of light. This, in turn, limits the possible values of the temperature parameters θ in equation 24. For example, if a system starts out with a <u>finite</u> energy density at time 0, and if the energy values vary from 0 to $+\infty$, then it is <u>impossible</u> for the temperature to be negative, because a negative temperature would represent an infinite energy density. Systems like this still approach a strong equilibrium, despite the infinite number of combinations c_i, in essentially finite time. However, if we allow energy to vary between $-\infty$ and $+\infty$, we could generate an unstable kind of system in which higher energy levels become more and more populated as time goes on, even starting from a very simple initial state. Most physicists would consider this kind of situation highly nonphysical and implausible, but one never can be certain apriori. (Such situations could cause a breakdown in the assumption of spatial uniformity.)

As a practical matter, when there are infinite possible energy levels for each kind of particle, it is usually more convenient to <u>write</u> the reaction equations in terms of simple particle types, and to account for the energy-level effects indirectly in the dynamic equations. In chemistry, for example, one typically adds entropy terms to equations like equation 19. Because of such effects, many chemical reactions in the real world tend to go in one direction, at ordinary temperatures and pressures; however, this does <u>not</u> violate the underlying principle of time-symmetry, when all the various flows are accounted for.

Extensions and Extrapolations of the Classical Ideas

The scattering model described above is central to classical thermodynamics, but it is not, of course, the whole thing.

Most classical textbooks actually stress the work of Carnot, who proved very strong and rigorous limits to the efficiency of heat engines -- mechanical systems based on expansion and compression and chemical reactions like combustion. Many, many people confuse the narrow but rigorous work of Carnot with the more general Second Law of thermodynamics. For example, with small heat engines like automobile engines, Carnot's laws (applied to realistic operating temperatures for such engines) yield a limit of about 38% efficiency, even under optimal operating conditions (which are rare in actual driving). A few years ago, I saw a satire in one of the major energy newsletter, in which Senator Kennedy was portrayed as trying to pass an amendment to Carnot's Laws, to permit higher efficiency in automobiles. In actuality, small fuel cells -- an alternative way to get energy out of hydrocarbons -- have shown to get efficiency close to 100%, far more than Carnot's limits permit, because they are not heat engines. In testimony before Marilyn Lloyd's committee in the House, in the summer of 1993, Philip Haley of General Motors testified that 60% efficiency has been achieved in a certain class of fuel cells, which does appear suitable for automotive use, and is also capable of high efficiency under a wider variety of operating conditions, at 80-100 degrees Celsius. (Designers of coal-fired powerplants usually understand the difference between Carnot's Laws and the Second Law; however, even some world-class automotive experts confuse "T delta S" energy losses -- related to the Second Law -- with the much larger heat losses explained by Carnot. The need for high temperatures even to reach 38% efficiency in heat engines leads to serious problems with NOx emissions -- due to the combustion, in effect, of nitrogen in the air -- which is a crucial form of air pollution.)

The Second Law in its general form has been a source of great confusion, as noted by Prigogine at this conference. Many people have drawn the conclusions that: (1) all possible systems -- including our universe (whose dynamic laws are still unknown!) -- will converge to a maximum of entropy; (2) entropy is a measure of disorder, which can be maximized only when all life or order ceases. It is obvious that these conclusions go too far, because it is easy enough to draw up hypothetical, model systems which do not converge to a simple state of disorder. However, I will try to give at least some of the flavor of what has led to such sweeping extrapolations.

After the great success of Carnot and of the scattering model, it was natural for mathematicians to try to generalize their results to all possible systems. Among the results of this effort were new theorems with the following sort of flavor: Suppose that we try to be more rigorous, and study the dynamics of probability distributions for states of the universe, instead of just distributions for individual particle types. Suppose that we happen to live in a universe which converges to a unique probability distribution $P_0(\{\phi(x)\})$. (In the formal literature, P_0 is usually presented as an "invariant measure.") The function P_0 indicates the equilibrium probability for each possible state of the universe, $\{\phi(x)\}$; I have inserted curly brackets $\{\}$ around $\phi(x)$, to remind you that a state of the universe is defined only when we know the set of values of ϕ across all points in space. After we know the function P_0, we can define the following entropy function:

$$S = \sum_\phi \left(\log Pr(\{\phi(x)\},t)\right) P_0(\{\phi(x)\})) \quad , \tag{25}$$

where the sum is taken over all possible states of the universe, and where Pr represents the current probability distribution for possible states of the universe, at the current time t. Under certain assumptions, it can be proven that S is a Liapunov function (with sign reversed); in other words, it can be proven that S will increase until it reaches its maximum. This is just a fancy way of saying that the actual probability distribution will gradually approach the equilibrium probability distribution.

Theorems of this sort are essentially just tautologies. They assume the existence of an equilibrium probability P_0. The theorems become more powerful if we add the additional assumption that, in equilibrium, the values of the field at any point in space will be statistically independent of the values at any other point. (When we say that two numbers are statistically independent of each other, this is like saying that they are not correlated with each other in any way.) This assumption tells us that:

$$\begin{aligned} P_0(\{\phi(x)\}) &= P_0(\phi(x_1), \phi(x_2), \ldots, \phi(x_i), \ldots) \qquad \textit{(all points x)}\\ &= P_0(\phi(x_1)) P_0(\phi(x_2)) \ldots P_0(\phi(x_i)) \ldots \end{aligned} \tag{26}$$

If we take the logarithm of both sides of this equation, we can see that it lets us write the entropy, in effect, as something like:

$$\log Pr(\{\phi(x)\}) = \sum_x \log Pr(\phi(x)) \; , \tag{27}$$

the <u>sum</u> of entropy across all points in space. This is called a <u>local</u> entropy function. If we <u>assume</u> statistical independence, then, we can <u>deduce</u> a local entropy function, which in turn tells us that the equilibrium state will be "disorderly" in the sense that there will be no order or correlation connecting different points in space. But once again, this is only a tautology! There is absolutely no guarantee that entropy functions, as defined in equation 25, must be local in the general case.

As a practical matter, many physicists have proven more restrictive theorems about entropy, of greater substantive importance than these general theorems. However, many efforts were also made in the 1970's to develop local entropy functions for <u>open systems</u>. Based in part on the <u>hope</u> that such efforts could be or had been completely successful, many scientists concluded that interesting patterns of order -- such as chemical oscillations -- would be impossible even in <u>open systems</u>[27]. This was a very curious hope, since it would appear to rule out the possibility of life on earth even in past history, let alone the long-term future. This is one more example of the need for all scientists -- even the very best scientists -- to work somewhat harder than they normally do to escape from the confines of "groupthink"[7,28] -- a pervasive problem which is not unique to science.

MODERN CONCEPTS OF SELF-ORGANIZATION

Since the late 1970's, the field of self-organization has gone through something of a revolution. A few key elements of the revolution have been:

1. Prigogine's theory of "dissipative structures" -- a rigorous theory which allowed for the possibility of chemical oscillations.

2. A vast expansion in the study of chemical oscillations, both empirical and theoretical.

3. The modern theory of nonlinear systems dynamics, including "chaos theory" and the like.

4. A greater appreciation of <u>spontaneous symmetry breaking</u> (SSB), which leads to forms of order or orientation in systems which appear, at first, to preclude such orientation.

5. A deeper understanding of <u>solitons</u> or solitary waves, ordered states which can emerge even in classical, Lagrangian systems.

Prigogine's theory was undoubtedly motivated in part by <u>empirical</u> work -- work starting from Belousev and Zhabotinsky in Russia -- actually demonstrating chemical oscillations. Prigogine's theory won him both the Nobel Prize, and a general perception that he is the leading thermodynamicist alive today. For a reasonable, popular account of Prigogine's theory and related ideas, see [29].

This section will discuss points 2 through 5 above, in that order, with comments both on the Big Bang and on Prigogine's most recent work, particularly in the section on SSB.

Chemical Oscillations

Work on chemical oscillations began with <u>physical experiments</u> showing how simple, closed systems -- starting out in a bland state far away from equilibrium -- can demonstrate beautiful patterns of oscillation and order <u>on the way</u> to their eventual equilibrium. Later on, <u>open systems</u> were developed, based on CSTRs (defined above), which demonstrated <u>sustained oscillations</u>. Some of these systems demonstrated beautiful color patterns, and were so easy to set up that they were suitable for high school chemistry labs. Several papers on these topics -- complete with big, impressive color photographs -- appeared in <u>Scientific American</u> in the 1970's and 1980's. The early oscillators were essentially discovered by accident, but Epstein et al[27] later developed a more systematic procedure for finding or designing such systems. Later research has found all kinds of fascinating phenomena in these systems, such as complex spatial patterns [30] and chaos[31].

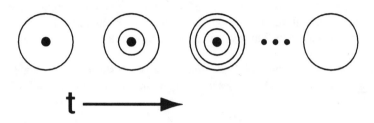

Figure 7. Schematic Picture of the Belousev-Zhabotinsky (BZ) Reaction

Figure 7 illustrates the classical BZ reaction. It shows a round bowl, viewed from overhead, at different times t. Before the reaction starts, one pours and mixes a certain set of chemicals into the bowl. Except for the choice of chemicals, there is no special order or pattern. Then, the reaction starts to take place, typically around a nucleus (like the dark circle in the middle of the leftmost picture). Waves of reaction spread out from the nucleus, as in Figure 7. The waves are red and blue, and usually form much more interesting patterns than this simple black-and-white drawing can show. Finally, after a time, the reaction goes to completion, and the contents of the bowl settle down into a static, pattern-free equilibrium (as in the far right).

The BZ reaction is today's paradigm for the nature of life and order in our universe. The Big Bang provides the initial reaction chamber and chemicals; life evolves as a set of patterns in the intermediate stage; and, finally, everything settles down into eternal death. Epstein, among others, has pointed out that chemical oscillations and cycles are truly fundamental to the functioning of the cells of living systems.

As a practical matter, even if we accept this paradigm, it is a major challenge to develop the details and the mathematics to the point where they describe life in our universe in a more detailed, less metaphorical way. Life on <u>earth</u> is not like a BZ reaction vessel, because it depends primarily on a relatively steady influx of energy from the sun. Thus the CSTR paradigm is a more relevant description, in practice, of what has happened here for the past few billion years. Also, the mathematics of the CSTR is far more tractable, in a sense, because the patterns and the order can exist as long-term phenomena.

In order to make this paper more self-contained, I was hoping to include a simple, simulated example, implemented as a spreadsheet on a personal computer, so that almost anyone could replicate it and study it more carefully. My real goal (which <u>has</u> been achieved) was to show that stable oscillations could be achieved in a simple <u>energy-conserving</u>, <u>closed</u> system based on reactions which are <u>not all time-symmetric</u>; however, in order to achieve this goal, I planned to start out from the "easier" task of generating oscillations in a truly classical system, based on equations 18 and 19, with additional terms to represent an influx of new material, as in the classic CSTR model. More precisely, I tried to develop a hypothetical system based on three chemical types (N=3) and two symmetric reactions, such that each chemical c_i would be governed by the equation:

$$\dot{\rho}_i = (n_i^{(1)} - m_i^{(1)})R_1 + (n_i^{(2)} - m_i^{(2)})R_2 + c(\rho_i^* - \rho_i) , \qquad (28)$$

where $n_i^{(1)}$ and $m_i^{(1)}$ are the coefficients n_i and m_i for the first chemical reaction, where $n_i^{(2)}$ and $m_i^{(2)}$ are the coefficients for the second reaction, where the reaction rates R_1 and R_2 are each calculated using equation 18, where $c\rho_i^*$ is the influx of chemical c_i coming in from the input pipe, and where $c\rho_i$ is the flow of chemical c_i going out down the drain pipe. To locate suitable values for the parameters n_i, m_i, k, c and $\underline{\rho}^*$, I planned to use Epstein's systematic design procedure.

This plan did not work. In fact, it is very difficult -- perhaps even impossible -- to generate oscillations in a very simple, totally symmetric system, even with the addition of a steady influx term. The oscillations observed empirically in chemical systems are consistent with modern physics, which is time-symmetric at a fundamental level, for the ordinary forces which dominate thse reactions; however, these empirical oscillations are far more complex, underneath, than equations 18 and 28. For example, Gyorgyi et al [32] have proposed an 80-reaction mechanism to describe what is really going on in the BZ reaction. The classic model of Boissonade and DeKepper can be expressed as a simple two-equation system[33], which has often been used in simulations; however, its relation to equations 18 and 28 is far from obvious, at least to the mathematician, even when the assumption of symmetry is relaxed. The more complex Oregonator system[34] can be reduced to a three-equation system, but it still involves 5 one-way reactions in addition to nontrivial influx and outflux assumptions. In more complex systems, phenomena like oscillation and chaos are far easier to find (even if they were misinterpreted as mere instability in the premodern literature) [35].

In the end, I was able to simulate oscillations on a spreadsheet -- surprisingly violent oscillations -- by simulating the one-way reactions as follows (based on equation 18 but without the backwards reaction term):

$$2\rho_p + \rho_h \rightarrow 3\rho_p \tag{29}$$

$$\rho_h + \rho_f \rightarrow 2\rho_h \tag{30}$$

$$\rho_c \rightarrow \rho_f , \tag{31}$$

with rate parameters (k) of 1, .45, and .045, respectively, and with initial conditions $\rho_f=0.5$, $\rho_h=0.3$ and $\rho_p=0.2$. The letters f, h and p stand for flora, herbivore and predator -- reflecting the inspiration provided by classical population biology [35]. Whatever the limitations of this example, the reader should be able to simulate it very easily. (In fact, my children enjoyed playing with this simulation on the spreadsheet.) It is easy to see that this system conserves a very simple measure of "mass-energy":

$$E = \rho_f + \rho_h + \rho_p \tag{32}$$

Similar examples have appeared in the past, but I am not personally aware of any with precisely the same characteristics; on the other hand, I am not a chemist.

The remainder of this subsection will give the technical details of my experience here. The nonmathematical reader could skip to the next section without loss.

The first step in Epstein's procedure is to locate chemical systems capable of bistability -- systems capable of two stable equilibria, for certain values of the flow and rate parameters. Epstein also asks that we focus on autocatalytic systems -- systems, for example, where some of the reactions have $n_i>m_i>0$ for some chemical c_i. To implement this in the simplest way possible, I began by looking at a CSTR system with only two chemicals and one reaction:

$$3c_1 + 4c_2 \leftrightarrow 4c_1 + 3c_2 \tag{33}$$

To keep the system at one degree of freedom, without any loss of generality in describing the long-term dynamics, I restricted the CSTR influx and the initial values to:

$$E = \rho_1 + \rho_2 = \rho_1^* + \rho_2^* = 1 \tag{34}$$

To find the flow parameters which produce bistability, I simply set up a graph in Quattro with the curves on it: (1) the graph of ρ_1 production from the chemical reaction (equation 33) as a function of ρ_1, recalling the $\rho_2=1-\rho_1$; (2) the graph of net ρ_1 consumed as a function of ρ_1, based on the influx and outflux. Since the latter was just a straight line, it was easy enough to adjust its slope (c) and its intercept (ρ_1^*) to make it cross the other curve in three places. Still, equation 33 is disturbingly complex, and the resulting bistability too brittle to fit well with Epstein's later steps.

As an alternative, I then found a nicer bistability in the system:

$$c_1 \; + \; 2c_2 \; \rightleftharpoons \; 2c_1 \; + \; c_2 \tag{35}$$

$$c_1 \; + \; c_2 \; \rightleftharpoons \; 2c_3 \tag{36}$$

When I use a rate k of 1 for both equations, and $\rho_1^* = 0$ and $\rho_2^* = .999$, I found that there would be bistability for a range of c (the influx rate) from .08 to .25. When I repeated this analysis for different rates k for equation 35, then the range of bistability for c would also change. The two curves (high c and low c), plotted as a function of k, seemed to converge very nicely, as in the "X" plots of Epstein. But, at the point of intersection, they did not lead to oscillation; instead, they led to a loss of bistability (for large k), or to the bottom of the physically acceptable range (k=0).

In order to understand these difficulties, and improve my chances of finding oscillations, I then looked more closely at the literature on nonlinear system dynamics. Bar-Eli[36], citing [37], discusses four different ways in which oscillations could show up suddenly, as system parameters are changed. The two most basic (and common) involve "Hopf bifurcations," which are discussed more completely by Abed and DeClaris[25], who cite [38] as a primary source. (See also [39], who cites [40]. See [41] for a more recent and colorful source based on the extensive experience of Japanese electronic engineers.)

To understand these bifurcations, one simply cannot avoid some use of matrix analysis. One must consider the properties of the Jacobian matrix (which should not be confused with the Jacobi function), defined by:

$$J_{i,j} \; = \; \frac{\partial \dot{\rho}_i}{\partial \rho_j} \tag{37}$$

In ecology, this matrix has sometimes been called the "community matrix" [35], because it describes the incremental impact of species number j on the rate of growth or decline of species number i.

To look for a Hopf bifurcation, one simply looks for a stable equilibrium point where the Jacobian contains two imaginary eigenvalues, $i\lambda$ and $-i\lambda$. For a simple system with two degrees of freedom, this requires that the trace of the Jacobian be zero. (Even in higher dimensions, the trace of J equals the divergence of the flow, a quantity of some importance.) With the simple Boissonade and DeKepper model, it is very easy to solve for such a bifurcation, using exact algebra; this, in turn, suggests that the Epstein mechanism may be a way of locating that type of oscillation, where it exists. (This is interesting, insofar as Bar-Eli states that most chemists tend to expect a more complex type of bifurcation.) To analyze equations 28, 35 and 36, one can also try to solve for such a point, solving for the equilibrium values of ρ_1 and ρ_2 and the values of ρ^{1*} and ρ_2^* required to zero the trace, as a function of k, c, etc.; however, across a wide range of c and k, the required values for <u>r</u> and $\underline{\rho}^*$ are unacceptable (<0). The attempt to solve directly for Hopf bifurcations is a very powerful computational tool in locating oscillations, but in this case it appears to suggest that oscillations cannot exist -- a suggestion supported by a very large number of simulations. By contrast, for equations 29-31, it is easy to solve algebraically for an equilibrium point with the trace of J equal to zero; that was how I picked the values .45 and .045 (out of a range of equally good parameters). The very first simulation led to strong oscillations.

Two other diagnostic tools were very useful in these runs: (1) the determinant of the Jacobian; and (2) the <u>derivatives</u> of the trace and determinant with respect to all the adjustable parameters, calculated by generalized backpropagation [7]. A Hopf bifurcation typically does <u>not</u> lead to oscillations when the determinant goes to zero along with the trace (though counterexamples can be designed, dependent on extreme bad luck). When only the determinant goes to zero, the system can become very unpredictable; it may bifurcate into two nearby branches, or it may "jump" a finite distance to a totally different solution, or any number of other things may happen. When the traces approaches zero, in a two-degree-of-freedom system, and the determinant does not, one may be sure that the eigenvalues of J have large imaginary components; typically, this implies the existence of strong but damped oscillations on the stable side of the Hopf bifurcation.

Nonlinear System Dynamics and Chaos

The field of nonlinear system dynamics has advanced far beyond the simple idea of stable equilibrium points versus total disorder. As an example, the concept of chaos has become very widely known [42], though commonly misunderstood.

The concept of <u>attractor</u> is fundamental to this field. A stable equilibrium point is one example of an attractor. Instead of settling down to one point, some systems settle down to some kind of fixed oscillation, or "limit cycle, like some of the systems discussed in the previous subsection. In phase space, these systems settle down into a kind of elliptical orbit (or a warped elliptical orbit), travelling around and around forever. (In simple spreadsheets, it is easy to plot part of the phase plane diagram, by using the XY plot option on the simulated values of the system variables.) Whenever the system starts out somewhere in the neighborhood of that orbit, it moves steadily closer and closer to the orbit.

Limit cycles are a second example of an attractor. Attractors may also be higher dimensional spaces, like the surface of a doughnut. In recent years, people have discovered stable attractors of <u>fractal dimension</u> -- something like 2½-dimensional spaces -- even for very reasonable-looking dynamic systems. These are called <u>strange attractors</u>. Strange attractors are not the same thing as chaos, though they often exist in association with chaos [20].

The concept of <u>chaos</u> refers to systems which are very stable on one level, but very unstable at another. A chaotic system always converges to a stable attractor, which usually has a small number of dimensions. <u>Within the attractor itself</u>, however, the system is essentially divergent. If you look at two different starting points on the attractor, very close to each other, you will see them diverging further and further away from each other with increasing time. This is called "sensitive dependence on initial conditions." For a readable but serious introduction to chaos and its applications, see [43]. For a deeper, physics-oriented survey, stressing the phenomenon of chaos in conservative systems, see [44].

Conventional studies of chaos focus on <u>low-dimensional</u> attractors. Between the realm of conventional chaos and the realm of total disorder, there is another realm which I think of as "turbulence." The physicist Kadanoff has done substantial work on turbulence, using both supercomputer simulations and experiments with liquid helium. Intuitively, if a physical system exists in a volume which is R atoms by R atoms by R atoms, then <u>conventional</u> chaos would imply that it settles down to a system with k degrees of freedom (i.e., a k-dimensional attractor); <u>disorder</u> implies that it retains kR^3 degrees of freedom, because all the atoms are independent of each other; <u>turbulence</u> would imply that it settles down to an attractor with something like $kR^{\frac{1}{2}}$ degrees of freedom, or kR, or something of the sort. Turbulent systems have very many degrees of freedom, even when they settle down, but they are still very far from total disorder.

The concept of self-organized criticality, discussed by Per Bak at this conference, can be seen as an example of "turbulence" in this sense. Bak's model of evolution seems highly abstract, but its predictions are very interesting. In particular, his model suggests that the extinction of the dinosaurs might have been due to something like a breakthrough in the evolution of other species, instead of a cosmic catastrophe. There is a fascinating match between his theory and some early suggestions by George Gaylord Simpson that the evolution of the neocortex, among small mammals, might have had a huge impact upon the biosphere. I would propose that we should look more carefully at the possibility that the evolution of the neocortex might have been the real cause of the extinction of the dinosaurs.

The study of turbulent dynamics has been limited by the extreme complexity of the mathematics. It is hoped that the techniques given in [4,5] (starting out from concepts given in [45]) will someday be of use here.

In general, the search for dynamical systems which generate chaos or turbulence is critical to our understanding of life. Living systems are clearly not static equilibria, nor are they states of total disorder; they are clearly a form of chaos or turbulence. Even today, most people believe that chaos or turbulence are possible only in open systems; that belief, in turn, reinforces the belief in the Big Bang.

Spontaneous Symmetry Breaking (SSB): The Iron Rod

Spontaneous symmetry breaking (SSB) is one of the most important forms of self-organization. People have known about SSB for a very long time, but only recently have they begun to appreciate its real importance. Weinberg and Salam have used SSB to unify our understanding of electricity and magnetism with a large part of nuclear reactions [21], and their work is now part of the "standard model" of physics. SSB is also central to the "grand unified theories"[46] of mainstream physics. This paper will argue that SSB might be even more important still than is realized at present; for example, it may play a crucial role in permitting life to exist in this universe.

36

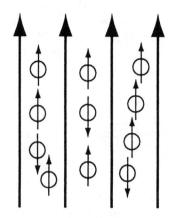

Figure 8. The Iron Magnet: An Example of SSB

Figure 8 describes the magnetization of an iron rod, one of the two classical examples of SSB. When an iron rod is hot enough, it will have no magnetism,, at the macroscopic level. Each atom in the rod is a tiny magnet, but the atoms bounce around at high velocity, constantly colliding and changing their direction, so that they all point in different directions at random. When the rod cools down, however, a kind of bandwagon effect takes over. Different atoms start to line up with their neighbors, until the rod as a whole develops a magnetic orientation (the large arrows in the figure). Even after the rod is magnetized, the movement of the atoms will shift some of them to the opposite orientation for short periods of time, as shown in the figure.

Notice what is going on here. The underlying dynamic laws which govern the individual atoms and the magnetic fields are <u>totally symmetric</u> with respect to space. There is no difference at all between the "up" direction and the "down" direction, so far as these laws are concerned. The microscopic laws are up/down-symmetric. Nevertheless, the <u>macroscopic</u> system which obeys these laws still develops a <u>strong orientation</u> with respect to space. It develops a strong a persistent orientation towards the "up" direction, in this example. A system which is totally symmetric at the <u>microscopic</u> level becomes totally <u>asymmetric</u> and <u>oriented</u> at the macroscopic level.

Could this same phenomenon explain the <u>macroscopic</u> orientation of our universe in time, despite the underlying time symmetry? This theoretical possibility should not be rejected out of hand. At this conference, Prigogine cited some new theorems he and Petrosky have proven [23] suggesting very strongly that a wide range of universes would in fact <u>spontaneously</u> develop a time orientation -- a form of SSB. Whether these theorems really have that effect in our particular universe or not, the possibilities here need to be studied very carefully. If they really do lead to a spontaneous breaking of time-symmetry, as claimed, then they would totally eliminate the need for a Big Bang as a mechanism to explain life and order. (Other motivations for the Big Bang will be discussed in the next major section of this paper.)

An interesting variation of this possibility is that CPT symmetry might be broken by SSB in our universe (or in large regions of it), while asymmetry with respect to T might be part of the underlying laws of physics. The CPT breaking would mainly be a matter of making us see lots of matter but very little antimatter in our universe Starting from there, the T asymmetry could generate the real "arrow of time" that underlies life as we know it -- as I will discuss further in the final section of this paper.

Note that the kind of system shown in Figure 8 does not fit the classical statistical model of random scattering across space. The macroscopic field provides a kind of global interaction effect. This may not be a necessary consequence of SSB, but it still is an important possibility. When QFT is used to analyze systems like the iron rod, one generally uses solid-state physics or tools borrowed from solid-state physics, rather than the pure scattering methods stressed in high-energy physics. The implications of this have yet to be fully understood.

SSB may also be directly relevant to social and biological phenomena. For example, the English language is a very useful tool in communication, but no one believes that every last detail of English grammar and spelling represents some kind of preordained optimal solution. The evolution of language, like the evolution of magnetism, depends heavily on local units lining up with (conforming to) their neighbors and creating a bandwagon effect [7].

It is even conceivable that the unique roles of DNA and protein molecules on earth is due to SSB to some extent; thus, it is conceivable that a different set of molecules could have emerged from evolution, if the initial conditions on earth had been slightly different. We will never know the answers to questions like this is our research is based only on empirical observation of the life we have now on one planet. A number of researchers [11,47] have begun to exploit very different sources of information, in trying to understand the dynamics of life; however, all of this work is only in its infancy, and new efforts to unify the various strands of thought could be very useful.

Solitons and Solitary Waves

Solitary waves were first discovered by empirical observation, by people staring at water waves in a canal in Scotland more than a century ago [48]. Over several decades, mathematicians specializing in the study of water waves gradually developed a basic understanding of this phenomenon [49]. Only in the last two decades have people begun to appreciate their widespread importance for engineering [50] and biology. As an example, the propagation of nerve impulses along the axon is usually modeled as a solitary wave. Hameroff, in the previous Radford conference, described how solitons propagating along microtubules inside the nerve cell may also play a crucial role, such as the implementation of backpropagation. (See [7] for a brief summary of the literature and an explanation of the importance of this point.)

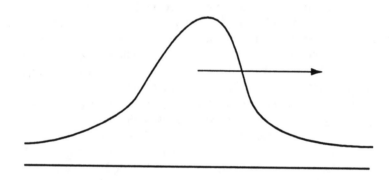

Figure 9. Picture of a Solitary Wave

Figure 9 illustrates the basic idea. In a linear system, an isolated wave like the one shown in Figure 9 would quickly disperse, giving rise to a totally disordered kind of equilibrium. But in a nonlinear Lagrangian system, such a wave could sometimes continue moving along indefinitely, without any change in shape. In certain very special systems, these solitary waves will maintain the exact same shape and speed even after they collide with each other (although the interaction zone would be more complex, of course); mathematicians have developed a very elaborate theory of solitons [51], of solitary waves in that sort of special system (Physicists often use the word "soliton" more loosely, to refer to the broad class of solitary waves.) Solitary waves are generally defined as stable patterns which retain their shape exactly, but may move around at a constant velocity.

In general, solitary waves represent a very interesting kind of order which emerges even in a classical Lagrangian system.

There are some very difficult mathematical challenges in trying to discover whether any given dynamical system can generate solitary waves or solitons. One curious method seems to mimic the Big Bang ideas: build a computer model of the system; start the system out with a huge energy impulse at one point in space; then watch what comes flying out of that initial explosion. But this is only a computational tool; it has nothing to do with astrophysics.

HERESIES: SOME CRITICAL OPPORTUNITIES FOR THE FUTURE

Every major new development in the field of self-organization has started out as a heresy. This section will describe some new opportunities or challenges of that sort. In particular, it will make three basic points, in order, in three subsections:

1. That patterns, order and even life may be possible in time-symmetric, closed Lagrangian systems, even without any spontaneous symmetry breaking (SSB). The word "life" has often been defined in a way which would make this a logical contradiction, but I will suggest that a broader view of life is more appropriate.

2. That life as we know it -- which is inherently asymmetric with respect to time -- may be possible in asymmetric, energy-conserving systems (which could, in fact, be regions within a greater time-symmetric cosmos affected by SSB).

3. That one can construct an image of our own universe -- a "caricature model" -- which provides an alternative to the Big Bang, and opens up empirical questions that can actually follow through on point 2.

The first two hypotheses call for mathematical and computer research, because they are hypotheses about what is possible, in general, for well-specified mathematical universes. The third is mainly an empirical issue; the most pragmatic researcher may want to jump directly to the final section. Nevertheless, a full development of the field of self-organization would require an ability to answer all of these questions, and to unify the mathematical and empirical strands of research.

This paper does not in any way question the importance of research into open systems in biology. To understand the evolution of life on earth as we know it, the open-systems approach is clearly the right starting point, because it reflects the primary role of light from the sun in powering the process of natural selection. But this leaves open the question of how the earth fits into the larger universe, and the possibility of life as we do not know it. Insights from a more general theory might well improve our understanding of classical open systems as well -- if such a theory can ever be developed.

Could Life Exist in Time-Symmetric Lagrangian Universes?

Could chaos, turbulence or life exist on a sustained basis in a conservative, time-symmetric Lagrangian universe?

The issue of chaos is a good starting point here, because it is easier to analyze than life as such, and life itself may be seen as a special case or extension of chaos. Also, the study of chaos in time-symmetric systems is a good warmup exercise, in overcoming the natural tendency to always assume time-forwards causality, unconsciously, even where that assumption is inappropriate.

Conventional wisdom suggests that chaos can only exist in dissipative systems; this would certainly preclude the possibility of chaos in time-symmetric Lagrangian systems. However, the conventional wisdom here is based on finite-dimensional systems, such as $\dot{x}=f(x)$ or $\ddot{x}=f(x)$, where x is a finite-dimensional vector which varies over time but not over space. The conventional wisdom is usually justified by appeal to a special definition of the word "dissipative"[20], related to flows in phase-space; furthermore, it is known [44,p.14] that classical Hamiltonian systems cannot satisfy this definition of "dissipative." Hamiltonian system are roughly the same as Lagrangian systems, so that this does appear to rule out chaos in finite-dimensional Lagrangian systems. Nevertheless, many sources also say that one of the first known examples of chaos was the simple three-body system under Newtonian gravity [44, Appendix A]. Certainly there are phenomena like classical chaos or stochasticity observed in Lagrangian systems which are very similar to chaos [44,p.63].

Chaos can occur far more easily when we account for the fact that fields vary over space and not just over time. In [6], I analyzed the issue of chaos in time-symmetric Lagrangian universes, accounting for variations over space, from a mathematical point of view. At least in theory, there seems to be strong reason to expect the existence of "chaotic solitons" or "chaoitons," patterns which remain stable and localized in space, like classical solitons, but which cycle through a complex attractor, like chaotic systems. In effect, chaoitons are to solitary waves what chaotic systems and the like are to stable point attractors. In the usual formulations of chaos theory, which do not account for fields varying over space as such, it is more difficult to generate chaos in a conservative system, because there is no way for higher-energy states to dissipate energy, as they would have to do in order to settle down into a lower-energy attractor; however, when there are spatial dimensions, energy can simply move away to other parts of space, on out to infinity. Stability based on this principle can apply at the same time to the forwards and backwards time directions. For near-term mathematical research issues, see [6]. In [4,5], I proposed that the neutron and proton might be chaoitons. As this paper goes to press, I have heard indications that Dr. Bogolubsky of the Joint Institute for Nuclear research in Dubna, Russia may have demonstrated the existence of time-varying objects which fit my definition of "chaoiton," for a simple model field theory.

Is there a possibility, then, of life itself, in addition to chaos, in such a universe? Conventional authors have sometimes even defined life as a time-forwards process based on DNA molecules and amino acids. Such definitions would tell us that partially silicon-based life, for example, is impossible simply by definition; however, semantic exercises of this sort are simply a way of covering up our fundamental ignorance about wha might evolve on other planets, under different physical conditions. The issues of what might evolve in a truly time-symmetric environment are part of the same intellectual challenge here.

Usually, when we think of natural selection, or we think about small but critical feedback effects, we think of a time-forwards process. We may think of living systems as a kind of attractor for a simple dynamical system, moving forwards in time.

On the other hand, recall that Lagrangian systems are a very special type of dynamical system. They are based on some kind of optimization process. This may be an important clue to understanding their macroscopic behavior. There is an analogy here to a phenomenon in economics, called "turnpike theorems." Certain economists have spent considerable effort trying to describe the optimal path for highly complex systems. For a wide variety of initial conditions and terminal conditions, they find that the same intermediate states can emerge as part of the optimal solution. (The analogy they give is to turnpikes: regardless of where you start driving from and where you want to go, if the distance is long enough, the fastest route will probably take you to the turnpike. This analogy is not as good for biology as for economics, but the mathematical insight is still valid.) If we interpret natural selection as this kind of emergence or crystallization process -- even in the time-forwards case -- then we should expect that the phenomenon could also occur in a time-symmetric world, or even in a time-symmetric niche in our own universe (if such could exist).

It is conceivable that the phenomenon of intelligence could also be understood better in this approach, and extended to the time-symmetric case. Intelligence as we know it seems to be best understood as a kind of approximate optimization system[7]. If the universe is somehow "trying" to optimize something, we should not be surprised that it creates subsystems which explicitly calculate optimal paths. (This may sound a bit too anthropomorphic, but -- as in the idea of Lagrangian systems itself -- the anthropomorphic metaphor can be useful, if we remember its limitations.) Intuitively, the solution to a constrained optimization problem (as in the Bryson and Ho formulation of Lagrange-Euler dynamics[15]) may involve the use of a distributed control architecture, where intelligent living systems serve as nodes in the system. It is interesting but difficult to imagine what intelligence in a time-symmetric universe might look like; it would certainly not be made up of the usual time-forwards Turing computers or model neurons, but it might have some connection to ideas about quantum computing which have begun to emerge in recent years.

Life in a time-symmetric universe might be similar to life as we know it from a mathematical viewpoint, but it would have very serious differences on a concrete level. For example, the processes of death and birth look very different when viewed in reverse time. What would substitute for birth and death? Would life itself appear to form a kind of vast web, across space and time, with phenomena like "loose ends" replacing both life and birth? Would it generate local causality gradients, on its own, at least along strands of the web which go between its periphery and the "center" (or central skeleton)? Would the phenomenon of learning follow these local causality gradients? Clearly, we would need to do a lot of mathematical work before being able to simulate such possibilities. Furthermore, we would have to be very careful to avoid inserting the assumption of time-forwards causality, unintentionally, into such simulations.

Many mathematicians have stated that the effort to prove Fermat's Last Theorem has led to very important and valuable advances in mathematics, far more important than the theorem itself. In a similar way, the effort to understand these kinds of phenomena may be very useful, even though our own universe does not appear to be completely time-symmetric. If, in fact, our universe is a hybrid or intermediate case, which is not causally time-symmetric but not perfectly time-forwards either, then we may need to understand both the time-symmetric and time-forwards extremes before we can understand the hybrid.

Could Life Persist in a Closed, Asymmetric Universe?

To explain the kind of life that we see on earth -- life which is clearly <u>asymmetric</u> -- we clearly have to assume that this life evolved in an <u>asymmetric</u> environment, either because of asymmetric laws of physics or because of SSB (which creates the appearance of asymmetry). Thus the question which is relevant for our kind of life within the universe as a whole is as follows: in a closed Lagrangian universe, which is <u>not</u> time-symmetric, could chaos and life evolve and continue indefinitely?

As in the time-symmetric case, a logical place to start is to display simple patterns of order -- oscillations, and then later chaos -- in this kind of system. In the section on chemical oscillations above, I have shown a simple example of this phenomenon. That example is truly a baby-like starting point, but it is at least a significant step in showing that energy-conserving closed classical systems can generate interesting patterns. Energy conservation in scattering equations does not necessarily imply that such equations could result from a Lagrangian system, or that the quantity conserved in scattering would match the Hamiltonian of the Lagrangian system. (In fact, the empirical data for our universe really involves energy conservation and the like, more than the Lagrangian property as such.) Clearly, there is more work to be done, to develop and understand more complex examples. The simple model of oscillation in equations 29-31 reminds me of the popularized version of neural networks found in [52]: that work was hopelessly too elementary to be a model of intelligence, but it was a crucial starting point for the community, in coming to appreciate the more complex and relevant theory which had given rise to it[7]. In this case, however, I am hoping that the reader, rather than myself, will uncover the deeper aspects of this issue.

Intuitively, the real issue here is as follows: could a simple term or terms in the dynamic equations of our universe play the same role, for the universe as a whole, that uniform radiation from the sun does for the earth? Personally, I would expect the answer to be "yes," but the challenge here is to prove the answer, and to develop its implications. The most important task, however, is the empirical task, which the next section will address.

An Alternative to the Big Bang

This section will provide a simple "caricature" model, which is intended to encourage the empirical work and further theorizing which will be needed before anyone can develop a final verdict on the Big Bang theory. The emphasis is on the word "caricature," rather than the word "model."

The deepest and strongest reason to believe the Big Bang theory has been the belief that no other mechanism was available to explain order and life in our universe. Up until now, this paper has questioned that belief at a theoretical level. The caricature model gives us a more concrete example of how we could get order and life in the long-term, without a Big Bang. The caricature model is <u>not</u> intended as an all-encompassing theory of everything, but <u>only</u> as a minimal example of some important mechanisms we need to study empirically. In all likelihood, empirical studies will eventually lead us to something much more complicated than the caricature model itself.

What is the empirical evidence for and against the Big Bang, if we truly ignore the issue of explaining life and order (which has very much colored people's interpretation of other evidence)?

The first classical piece of evidence is the widespread <u>redshift</u> from distant galaxies and galaxy-like objects. It is well-known that the colors of any object turn red, when that object moves away from us. Decades ago, Hubble showed that objects further away from us tend to be shifted more towards the red; this seems to suggest a general pattern of expansion or explosion in the universe. On the other hand, more careful and more recent work by Arp and others[53] has shown that the pattern of redshifts is far more complex. There are other sources of very high redshifts, which are well established by the best experts in optical phenomena [54-7], but generally rejected by astronomers because of their apriori commitment to the classical explanation. Furthermore, there are anomalies even in the usual redshift patterns[58]. By and large, normal redshifts do tend to be proportional to the distance from earth, but the caricature model will suggest an alternative possibility for the cause.

The strongest piece of evidence for the Big Bang is said to be the low level microwave radiation reaching the earth from all parts of the sky. This microwave radiation follows the usual distribution of energies which one would expect from <u>any</u> thermodynamic system in equilibrium at the temperature of 3 degrees Kelvin. Actually, all of the well-worked-out versions of the Big Bang theory require that the radiation <u>not</u> be uniform. In 1992, there was great public excitement when NASA's COBE experiment reported variations on the order of 0.000001 from one part of the sky to another; however, this was still far less than the variation expected by Big Bang theories at the time[1]. Given the pressure of this data, some theorists have been creative enough to add some additional mathematical assumptions (epicycles?), which have brought some of the Big-Bang models back into consistency with the data.

41

Significant interactions and fields in deep, intergalactic space are an <u>alternative</u> way to generate low-level radiation, which would naturally approach a black-body equilibrium over many billions of years, and would naturally tend to be more uniform in its point of origin; the high degree of observed uniformity is a more natural and unavoidable prediction in this alternative class of theory.

Lerner has recently published a book[1] describing a wide range of problems with the Big Bang theory, which have not received sufficient attention. Lerner's accounts of global field effects -- related in a sense to SSB -- are extremely interesting. Lerner does hurl some strong and unjustified criticism at mathematicians and mystics and Republicans -- criticisms which may offend many readers for good reason -- but this does not lessen the seriousness of the questions he raises. The work of Arp, Hoyle, Lerner and others has not disproved the Big Bang theory, but it does indicate enough doubt that we are justified in trying to develop and test some alternative possibilities.

The caricature model is a minimal alternative, based on seven reaction equations and five types of "particle." <u>Unlike</u> the simplified system of equations 18-19, this system assumes that each type of "particle" requires one additional number to characterize it -- a velocity or energy level, or a particle number. The five types of particle are "Hydrogen" (H), "Helium" (He), neutrino (ν), photon (γ) and scavenger (s). Nothing is known or assumed about the detailed properties of s -- whether it is really only one particle type or more, whether it has positive mass-energy, or whether it would allow the possibility of supporting life in deep space. (An interesting option is that s might be a kind of "hole" in a "false vacuum," which could have bounded energy and therefore avoid some of the difficulties mentioned in connection with equation 24 above.) Likewise, there is no assumption (or requirement) that there be any oscillation or chaos in the mix of particle types <u>at this level</u>. In conventional QFT, some of these possibilities -- while plausible -- would suggest some important possibilities for instability over large regions of the universe[16]; it is not yet known whether the alternative formulations discussed above would support these suggestions.

In the model, a star is simply an H particle with a large particle number. A dead star or dark matter is an He particle with a large particle number. Other elements, like carbon, are not treated explicitly, because we already know a lot about the formation of planets and so on, <u>starting</u> from stars and hydrogen in space; the challenge here is to model the continued existence of active stars.

The caricature model begins with three chemical-like reactions, representing (in caricature-like fashion) the well-known effects of gravity and nuclear fusion (and related galaxy-forming effects):

$$H(n) \quad + \quad H(m) \quad \leftrightarrow \quad H(n+m) \quad + \quad \gamma \tag{38}$$

$$He(n) \quad + \quad He(m) \quad \leftrightarrow \quad He(n+m) \quad + \quad \gamma \tag{39}$$

$$H \quad \leftrightarrow \quad He \quad + \quad \gamma \quad + \quad \nu \tag{40}$$

These are all <u>time-symmetric</u> reactions, as is well-known from physics.

The model requires two additional reactions, to eat dark matter (dead stars, etc.) and put new hydrogen into deep space:

$$H(n) \quad (+s) \quad \leftrightarrow \quad H(m) \quad (+s) \tag{41}$$

$$He(n) \quad (+s) \quad \leftrightarrow \quad He(m) \quad (+s) \tag{42}$$

Note the <u>testable hypothesis</u> that protons can decay, with some very low probability which is nevertheless significant on astronomical time scales. Actually, many grand unified theories share this properties, often requiring a more dramatic decay. (In fact, the more dramatic predictions have been disproven empirically; one might expect reformulated GUTs to be possible based on a quieter form of proton decay, as above.) Dr. Per Anders Hansson, a consultant to the British scientific establishment, has reported informally that experiments to measure such decay rates may now be feasible, in light of modern high-precision nanotechnology[22]. Note that equations of this general sort would not create hydrogen so much as redistribute it. <u>After</u> time symmetry is broken, by later equations, these two equations by themselves result in a net consumption of energy from the s particles in forwards time.

Finally, to generate the crucial time-asymmetry -- the driving force -- the model would include two one-way equations:

$$s + \gamma \rightarrow s + \gamma \qquad (\gamma \text{ of } \underline{lower} \text{ energy}) \qquad \textbf{(43)}$$

$$s + \nu \rightarrow s + \nu \qquad (\nu \text{ of } \underline{lower} \text{ energy}) \qquad \textbf{(44)}$$

Equation 43 -- which is assumed to occur at a very low rate, just enough to explain the normal distance-related redshifts of astronomy without attributing them to a Doppler effect. Equation 44 -- a somewhat stronger reaction -- would be used to explain the "missing neutrino" problem -- a fundamental, unexplained problem in today's astronomy. The "cost" of equation 44, in terms of Occam's Razor, is zero, because any complete theory of physics has to include something new to account for the missing neutrinos. Given that neutrinos are associated with weak nuclear reactions, which in turn are relatively close to the superweak interactions, it is very reasonable to have a moderate time-asymmetry in that particular equation. Equations 41 to 44 all stand in for a wide range of possible alternatives, and all suggest a variety of related experiments under different conditions. For example, high-precision experiments have been attempted (but not far enough to be conclusive) on distance-related redshift effects, even on earth, though a larger distance base might allow higher precision measurements. High precision neutrino detectors, such as the KARMEN project at Rutherford Appleton [22], might be useful as part of new experiments related to equation 44.

Some physicists have proposed that the missing neutrinos from the sun might be explained by assuming that neutrinos spontaneously mutate into other forms of neutrinos. Lately, I have heard some scientists argue that the <u>total</u> neutrino count from the sun is too low, ruling out this theory, while others think it may still be plausible. A time-asymmetric mutation of neutrinos could be part of a more detailed system implementing the basic ideas here, but that is only one of many, many possibilities.

Even equation 43 may not be quite so speculative as it appears at first. Even in conventional QFT, physical photons are <u>not</u> considered identical to the pure, idealized "bare photons" which appear in the usual Lagrangians; rather, they are held to be a <u>mixture</u> of bare photons, electron/positron pairs, and so on. This results from "renormalization effects" in the mathematics, effects which have been well-proven experimentally[14,26]. (See [4,5] for a more physical interpretation of these effects.) Furthermore, in today's standard model of physics, photons and neutrinos are very closely related to each other; these close relations should be accounted for in any correct, complete renormalization[21]. <u>If</u> one revised the equations for the neutrino, in a crude, direct way, to replicate the high <u>observed</u> rate of energy loss between the earth and the sun, one should also go back and recalculate the propagation equations for the photon. Even a very tiny correction might be enough to replicate the kind of red shift we see from distant spiral galaxies; after all, the observed energy loss per meter of distance travelled by the neutrino is many orders of magnitude larger than the usual red shifts. Nevertheless, I have not yet done these calculations, and the results may well be highly sensitive to one's choice between equally plausible starting points. Furthermore, the close link between photons and neutrinos also suggests that unknown phenomena which affect neutrinos directly might well affects photons directly in any case, simply as a matter of symmetry.

To understand this system, it is crucial once again to break free of the usual time-forwards way of thinking. It is crucial that a small time-forwards feedback effect, provided by the last two equations, can nonetheless lead to large-scale implications.

Equation 44 is the key mechanism which generates the arrow of time, in this model. By gobbling up neutrinos emerging from stars in <u>forwards</u> time, it prevents the phenomenon of fusion from occurring in the <u>reverse</u> time direction. This is what makes stars form and "burn" in forwards time only. That in turn is responsible for life as we know it on earth, in this model.

References

[1] E.J.Lerner, *The Big Bang Never Happened*, Expanded Edition. Random House, 1992.
[2] T.S.Kuhn, *The Structure of Scientific Revolutions*, U. of Chicago Press, 1962.
[3] P.Werbos, "Bell's theorem: the forgotten loophole and how to exploit it," in [13].
[4] P.Werbos, "Chaotic solitons and the foundations of physics: a potential revolution," *Applied Mathematics and*

Computation, Vol. 56, p.289-340, July 1993.

[5] P.Werbos, "Quantum theory, computing and chaotic solitons," *IEICE Transactions on Fundamentals*, Vol.E76-A, No.5, p.689-694, May 1993.

[6] P.Werbos, "Chaotic solitons in conservative Systems: can they exist?," *Chaos, Solitons and Fractals*, Vol. 3, No.3, p.321-326, 1993.

[7] P.Werbos, *The Roots of Backpropagation: From Ordered Derivatives to Neural Networks and Political Forecasting*, Wiley, 1993.

[8] P.Werbos, "The brain as a neurocontroller: some new hypotheses and experimental possibilities," updated version, in this volume.

[9] D.White and D.Sofge, eds, *Handbook of Intelligent Control: Neural, Fuzzy and Adaptive Approaches*, Van Nostrand, 1992.

[10] P.Werbos, "Elastic fuzzy logic: a better fit to neurocontrol and true intelligence", *Journal of Intelligent and Fuzzy Systems*, Vol.1, No.4, 1993.

[11] C.Langton, ed., *Artificial Life* (Santa Fe Volume VI), Addison-Wesley, 1989.

[12] S.Hawking, *A Brief History of Time: From the Big Bang to Black Holes*,Bantam,1988.

[13] M.Kafatos, ed., *Bell's Theorem, Quantum Theory and Conceptions of the Universe*. Kluwer, 1989.

[14] F.Mandl, *Introduction to Quantum Field Theory*, Wiley, 1959.

[15] A.Bryson and Y.Ho, *Applied Optimal Control: Optimization, Estimation and Control*, Hemisphere, 1975.

[16] S.Coleman and F.DeLuccia, "Gravitational effects on and of vacuum decay," *Phys. Rev. D*, Vol.21, p.3305-15, June 1980.

[17] R.Adler, M.Bazin and M.Schiffer, *Introduction to General Relativity*, McGraw-Hill,1965.

[18] R.Penrose and W.Rindler, *Spinors and Space-Time*, Cambridge U.Press, Corrected Edition, 1987.

[19] M.Carmelli, *Classical Fields: General Relativity and Gauge Theory*, Wiley, 1982.

[20] C.Grebogi, E.Ott and J.Yorke, "Chaos, strange attractors and fractal basin boundaries in nonlinear dynamics," *Science*, Vol. 238, p.632-637, 30 October 1987

[21] J.Taylor, *Gauge Theories of Weak Interactions*, Cambridge U. Press, 1976.

[22] Private communication, Dr. Per Anders Hansson, Dec. 8, 1993.

[23] T.Petrosky and I.Prigogine, "Quantum chaos, complex spectral representations and time-symmetry breaking," *Chaos, Solitons and Fractals*, forthcoming.

[24] J.Horgan, "Quantum philosophy," *Scientific American*, Vol.267(1), p.94-104, July 1992.

[25] E.Abed and N.DeClaris, "Analytical and geometric problems in nonlinear system modeling and stability," in R. Kalman, Marchuk, and Viterbi, eds., *Recent Advances in Communication and Control Theory*, New York: Optimization Software Inc., 1987.

[26] C.Itzykson and Zuber, *Quantum Field Theory*, McGraw-Hill, 1980.

[27] I.Epstein, K.Kustin, P.De Kepper and M.Orban, "Oscillating chemical reactions," *Scientific American*, 248(3), p.112-123, 1983.

[28] I.Janis, *Victims of Groupthink*, Houghton Mifflin, 1973.

[29] I.Prigogine and I.Stengers, *Order Out of Chaos*, Bantam, 1984.

[30] Zs. Nagy-Ungvarai, J.Tyson, S.Muller, L.Watson and B.Hess, "Experimental study of spiral waves in the Ce-catalyzed Belousev-Zhabotinsky reaction," *J. Phys.Chem.*, Vol. 94, p.8677-8682, 1990.

[31] Z.Noszticzius, W.McCormick and H.Swinney, "Use of bifurcation diagrams as fingerprints of chemical mechanisms," *J. Phys. Chem.*, Vol. 93, p.2796-2800, 1989.

[32] L.Gyorgyi, T.Turanyi and R.Field, "Mechanistic details of the oscillatory Belousev-Zhabotinsky reaction," *J. Phys.Chem.*, Vol. 94, p.7162-7170, 1990.

[33] C.Hocker and I.Epstein, "Analysis of a four-variable model of coupled chemical oscillators," *J.Chem.Phys.*, Vol. 90 (6), p.3071-3080, March 1989.

[34] H.Krug,L.Pohlmann, and L.Kuhnert, "Analysis of the modified complete Oregonator accounting for oxygen sensitivity and photosensitivity of Belousev-Zhabotinsky systems," *J.Phys.Chem.*, Vol. 94, p.4862-4866, 1990.

[35] R.May, *Stability and Complexity in Model Ecosystems*, Princeton U. Press, Second Edition, 1974.

[36] K.Bar-Eli and M.Brons, "Period lengthening near the end of oscillations in chemical systems," *J. Phys. Chem.*, Vol. 94, p.7170-7177, 1990.

[37] A.Andronov, A.Vitt and S.E.Khaikin, *Theory of Oscillators*, Pergamon, New York, 1966.

[38] J.Casti, *Nonlinear System Theory*, Academic Press, Orlando, Florida, 1985.

[39] W.Zhang, *Synergetic Economics: Time and Change in Nonlinear Economics*, Springer, 1991.

[40] S.Chow and J.Hale, *Methods of Bifurcation Theory*, Springer, 1982.

[41] T.Matsumoto, M.Komuro, H.Kokubu and R.Tokunaga, *Bifurcations: Sights, Sounds and Mathematics*, Springer-Verlag, 1993.

[42] J.Gleick, *Chaos: The Making of a New Science*, Penguin, 1988.

[43] T.Mullin, ed., *The Nature of Chaos*, Oxford U. Press, 1993.

[44] A.J.Lichtenberg and M.A.Lieberman, *Regular and Chaotic Dynamics*, Second Edition, Springer-Verlag, 1992.

[45] G.Nicolis and I.Prigogine, *Self-Organization in Nonequilibrium Systems: From Dissipative Structures to Order Through Fluctuations*, Wiley, 1977.

[46] J.Wess and Bagger, *Supersymmetry and Supergravity*, Princeton U. Press, 1983

[47] L.Margulis and L.Olendzenski, eds, *Environmental Evolution: Effects of the Origin and Evolution of Life on Planet Earth*, MIT Press, 1992.

[48] Scott Russell, J., 1844. *Report on Waves*. Brit Assoc. Rep.

[49] G.Whitham, *Linear and Nonlinear Waves*, Wiley, 1974

[50] A.Scott, F.Chu and D.McLaughlin, "The soliton, a new concept in applied science," *Proceedings of the IEEE*, Vol. 61(10), 1973

[51] G.Eilenberger, *Solitons*, Springer-Verlag, 1983.

[52] D.Rumelhart and J.McClelland, eds, *Parallel Distributed Processing*, Volume I, MIT Press, 1986.

[53] H.Arp, G.Burbidge, F.Hoyle, J.Narlikar and N.Wickramashinge, "The extragalactic universe: an alternative view," *Nature*, Vol.346, p.807-12, Aug. 1990.

[54] E.Wolf, *The Red-Shift Controversy and a New Mechanism For Generating Frequency Shifts of Spectral Lines*, Technical Bulletin of the National Physical Laboratory, New Delhi, India, October 1991.

[55] E.Wolf, "Towards spectroscopy of partially coherent sources," in R. Inguva, ed., *Recent Developments in Quantum Optics*, Plenum Press, New York, 1993.

[56] E.Wolf, "Influence of source correlations on spectra of radiated fields," in J.W. Goodman, ed., *International Trends in Optics*, Academic Press, 1991.

[57] D. James and E.Wolf, "A class of scattering media which generate Doppler-like frequency shifts of spectral lines," submitted to *Physical Review Letters*, 1993.

[58] H.Arp, "The Hubble relation -- differences between galaxy types SB and SC," <u>Astrophysics and Space Science</u>, Vol. 167(2), p.183-219, 1990.

[59] R.K.Brayton and C.H.Tong, "Constructive stability and asymptotic stability of dynamical systems," *IEEE Transactions on Circuits and Systems*, Vol. 27, November 1980.

[60] A.N.Michel, N.R.Sarabudla and R.K.Miller, "Stability analysis of complex dynamical systems: some computational methods," *Circuits, Systems, Signal Processing* (Birkhauser Boston), Vol. 1, No. 2, 1982.

[61] A.N.Michel, B.H.Nam and Vijay Vittal, "Computer generated Lyapunov functions for interconnected systems: improved results with applications to power systems," *IEEE Transactions on Circuits and Systems*, Vol. 31, no,2, February 1984.

[62] A.N.Michel and R.K.Miller, "Stability analysis of discrete-time interconnected systems via computer-generated Lyapunov functions with applications to digital filters," *IEEE Transactions on Circuits and Systems*, Vol. 32, No.8, August 1985.

[63] A.Barto, R.Sutton and C.Anderson,"Neuronlike elements that can solve difficult learning control problems," *IEEE Transactions on Systems, Man and Cybernetics*, Vol. 13, No. 5, 1983.

[64] P.Werbos, "Consistency of HDP applied to a simple reinforcement learning problem," *Neural Networks*, Vol. 3, October 1990.

[65] G.W.Whitehead, *Homotopy Theory*, MIT Press, 1966.

[66] P.Werbos, "Supervised learning," *WCNN93 Proceedings*, Erlbaum, 1993.

[67] W.Miller, R.Sutton and P.Werbos, eds.,*Neural Networks for Control*, MIT Press, 1990.

APPENDIX. NEW METHODS FOR THE AUTOMATIC CONSTRUCTION OF LIAPUNOV FUNCTIONS

This technical appendix will present some new ideas in stability theory, mentioned briefly in the section on classical approaches to self-organization. It will address two closely related ideas in classical control theory, in order: (1) Given a nonlinear dynamical system, $\underline{\dot{x}}=\underline{f}(\underline{x})$, with an equilibrium point $\underline{x}_0$, to find a Liapunov function which proves stability about $\underline{x}_0$, either globally or over a large region, if the process is in fact stable; (2) Given a nonlinear dynamical system, $\underline{\dot{x}}=\underline{f}(\underline{x},\underline{u})$, influenced by control variables $\underline{u}$, to find a controller $\underline{u}=A(\underline{x})$ which results in global (or regional) stability about a desired point $\underline{x}_0$. (The new ideas were designed to handle more general problems[9], but this appendix will address only these two problems.)

More precisely, this appendix will discuss new approaches to the <u>automatic construction</u> of a Liapunov function (and controller) to solve these problems. With very few exceptions [59-62], the classical approaches to these problems all require that a human being simply <u>guess</u> both the Liapunov function and the controller -- something which works very well in the linear case, but only rarely in the nonlinear case. There is an analogy here to the state of the art in solving algebraic equations before Newton: people depended very heavily on using massive amounts of ingenuity to locate closed-form solutions to algebraic equations. Nowadays, closed form solutions are still very useful when they are available, but for practical applications, we routinely rely on equation-solving systems which use methods of successive approximation based on computers. My goal here is to encourage the same kind of alternative approach available to classical stability analysis and control.

A few authors in the control field have occasionally suggested that they have fixed "general" Liapunov functions for "general" nonlinear controllers. However, global stability in the general case is not such a trivial issue. Stability is often easy for simple regulator systems, which require no real intelligence or planning in the controller. For a simple test problem, which helps illustrate the limits of controllers which do not incorporate a deep understanding of dynamics, consider the bioreactor test problem in Appendix A of [67].

In classical control theory, there is essentially only one established method for the automatic construction of Liapunov functions: the method of Brayton and Tong[59], generalized somewhat by Michel et al[60,61]. (Zhubov and others have described techniques for constructing Liapunov functions which are not "automatic" in the sense that they do not lead to specific computer algorithms; for example, Zhubov requires the solution of PDE, which do enter into my discussion below, but we do not have an exact procedure to solve nonlinear PDE in the general case[60].) Brayton's method has been useful in a few practical applications[61,62], but it is limited in several important ways:

1. As one would expect, we can only prove stability for systems which are in fact stable -- which have a Liapunov function (unknown), $V(\underline{x})$, with $V(\underline{x}_0)=0$. It is also necessary that the system be <u>smooth</u> in some sense, related to the Lipshitz condition. One might formalize this by requiring that there exists a characteristic length λ such that $|\underline{x}-\underline{y}|<\lambda$ implies that $|\log V(\underline{x})/V(\underline{y})|<K$, for some K.
2. The computational cost of the method is essentially proportional to adr^{d-1}, where a is a measure of the cost of some matrix comparison operations, d is the dimensionality of the vector $\underline{x}$, and r is the ratio between the size (diameter) of the region under study and the characteristic length λ.
3. The method makes a "worst case" assumption about the interactions of the Jacobians at different points $\underline{x}$ as the process evolves over time.
4. So far as I know, there is no complete rigorous theory which formally verifies stability after a finite number of points have been explored.

The first of these limitations is essentially unavoidable. The second -- the high computational cost -- is important in practice, and has been stressed very heavily by Michel et al [61], who have found ways to stretch the method a little in a few special cases. The fourth limitation could probably be overcome relatively easily, through further theoretical work. The third limitation, however, has not received enough attention: i.e., <u>when</u> the Brayton method proves stability, one may be sure that a process is stable, but there is no reason at all to believe that the method would in fact locate a Liapunov function for "most" stable well-behaved nonlinear system.

To explain this point, I need to explain the essence of how the Brayton method works. Essentially, Brayton argues that a dynamical system looks like a linear system, $\underline{\dot{x}}=J(\underline{x})\underline{x}$, where $J(\underline{x})$ is the Jacobian matrix at the point $\underline{x}$. In effect, the dynamical system generates $\underline{x}(t+dt)$ by multiplying $(I+J(\underline{x})dt)$ by $\underline{x}$. If we can proves that long products like $(I+J_1dt)(I+J_2dt)...(I+J_ndt)\underline{x}$ always stay within some fixed, bounded region, for <u>any</u> matrix J_i which equals J($\underline{y}$) for some point $\underline{y}$ in that region, then we may be sure that the process cannot possibly blow up. In effect, this method allows for the possibility that the system encounters any possible sequence of Jacobian matrices, as it moves through state space. This is very much a worst-case assumption. There are many stable systems which achieve stability because the dynamics in one region -- which appear quite unstable -- automatically push the system into other regions, which are stable. (In the simulations on chemical systems described in this paper, I encountered this phenomenon over and over again, to my great frustration; this happened, for example, when I modified the coefficients in equation 30 to match those of equation 29.) Brayton's method would not demonstrate the global stability of such systems.

This appendix will discuss several related approaches to constructing Liapunov functions. The simplest approaches try to overcome the third limitation above, while maintaining the status quo on the three other limitations. The more radical approaches address the issue of computational cost as well. All of these approaches depend heavily on the use of approximate dynamic programming or adaptive critics, which are explained at length in [9].

The link between constructive Liapunov functions and dynamic programming can be understood at two levels -- intuitively, or formally.

Intuitively, the only way to find a Liapunov function in the general case is to start from the neighborhood of the equilibrium point (where V($\underline{x}$)≈0) and working backwards along the orbits of the process, setting higher values for V as one works one's way back. One would follow the usual dynamic programming approach of backwards movement from the end point, and incrementing the V function as one increments the J function in dynamic programming. (Henceforth, when I refer to J, I will be referring to the Jacobi function J of dynamic programming, rather than the Jacobian matrix J.)

More formally, the Hamilton-Jacobi-Bellman equation[15] reduces to the following equation in this case:

$$\frac{dJ(\underline{x}(t))}{dt} = U(\underline{x}(t)) \quad, \tag{45}$$

where we may require that U be positive definite and that it approach zero as $\underline{x}$ approaches $\underline{x}_0$. This requirement on J is equivalent to the requirement that J be a Liapunov function! In fact, we have a two-way equivalence here. Thus finding a Liapunov function is equivalent to solving a dynamic programming problem.

There is no way to actually solve the Bellman equation exactly for a generalized, continuous nonlinear system. Therefore, to develop general methods to construct Liapunov functions, we must use general-purpose approximations to dynamic programming instead. The most effective approximations to dynamic programming[9] make use of "critic networks" or "critic functions," which try to approximate the function J($\underline{x}$) or to approximate its gradient, $\underline{\lambda}(\underline{x})$. More precisely, these methods require that the user specify a critic function, $\hat{J}(\underline{x},W)$ or $\underline{\hat{\lambda}}(\underline{x},W)$, which is capable of approximating a wide variety of possible functions J or $\underline{\lambda}$, depending on the value of the weights or parameters W; these methods then provide ways of adapting or estimating the set of weights W. Many choices for the function $\hat{J}$ have been used in the literature; most papers describe $\hat{J}$ as an "artificial neural network," but this is often little more than a semantic convention.

To use these methods in constructing a Liapunov function, one can proceed as follows. First, instead of specifying a single function $\hat{J}(\underline{x},W)$, specify a sequence of functions $\hat{J}_1(\underline{x},W_1)$, $\hat{J}_2(\underline{x},W_2)$,....$\hat{J}_i(\underline{x},W_i)$,...$\hat{J}_\infty$, of ever-increasing complexity, with the property that the minimum approximation error (i.e. the minimum over W_i of $|J-\hat{J}|$) goes to zero as i goes to infinity. Pick an arbitrary "utility" function U such as:

$$U(\underline{x}) = (\underline{x} - \underline{x}_0)^T Q(\underline{x} - \underline{x}_0) \quad, \tag{46}$$

where Q is some positive-definite matrix. (Q could simply be set to I, or to any other "natural metric" for the system.) For any given i and cutoff U_{min}, we can use adaptive critic methods to try to solve the Bellman equation using the critic function $\hat{J}_i$ for the set of points $\underline{x}$ such that $U(\underline{x}) > U_{min}$; to define the boundary conditions -- the values of J where $U=U_{min}$ -- one may use the simple linearized approximation:

$$V(\underline{x}) = (\underline{x} - \underline{x}_0)^T W(\underline{x} - \underline{x}_0) \tag{47}$$

$$WA + A^TW = Q , \qquad \qquad (48)$$

where A is the Jacobian matrix at the point $\underline{x}_0$, and where equation 48 -- the Liapunov equation -- must be solved to find the matrix W. (Note that equation 48 is just a linear equation in the elements of W.)

This last procedure only gives us an <u>approximation</u> to the relevant dynamic programming problem, and to a J which is a true Liapunov function; however, a good enough approximation to a Liapunov function should also be a Liapunov function and, by increasing i and decreasing U_{min}, we are guaranteed to have an approximation as good as we like.

To try out this procedure in a simple case, such as a two-dimensional system, one might choose $\hat{J}$ to be a simple lookup table. In other words, one may simply slice up the relevant region of two-dimensional space into a set of square cells, and simply assign a single value of $\hat{J}$ to approximate J in each square. Approximations to dynamic programming of this sort have been very popular in the past -- generally on an ad hoc basis -- and they are also the basis of the original Barto, Sutton and Anderson algorithm[63].

Unfortunately, the square or rectangular approaches will not work here. As an example, consider the following simple process, to be analyzed in (x,y) coordinates, which I define for convenience in polar coordinates (with θ defined in radians):

$$\dot{\theta} = 1 \qquad \qquad (49)$$

$$\dot{r} = -kr , \qquad \qquad (50)$$

where k is 0.01 or 0.001. This process has a stable equilibrium at the origin. However, <u>no matter how small</u> the squares, the points within any square generally flow into <u>three</u> other squares. Assuming the worst (as is required in formal proofs of stability), knowledge of the flows from square to square still permits the possibility of <u>divergence</u>. Formally speaking, there exist flows from squares of lower $\hat{J}$ to higher $\hat{J}$, no matter how small the squares, for any reasonable method of assigning values of $\hat{J}$. (Again, the formal proof that such approximations cannot work really depends on the fact that the square-to-square flows appear to permit divergence;

one need only consider the problem of how to assign $\hat{J}$ values along the squares in such a divergent path, to see that a Liapunov function in this scheme is impossible.)

To make the original approach work, we need to use critic networks which allow a good approximation to the <u>gradient</u> of J, not just to J itself. This can be done quite easily in the two-dimensional case, by dividing up the plane into <u>triangles</u>, rather than <u>squares</u>. For example, one can easily divide the plane up into equilateral triangles (in the usual hexagonal sort of tiling), or one can simply split each of the square tiles in the usual arrangement into two triangles; one an simply draw in the diagonal line from upper-left to lower-right, within each square. One an try to estimate a value for J explicitly at each <u>vertex</u>, and use linear interpolations within each triangle to approximate J. For systems which obey a kind of proportional Lipshitz condition in the <u>derivatives</u> of J, we can be certain that such an approximation scheme allows us to get arbitrarily lose to the true derivatives as the triangles become smaller. If J is a well-behaved Liapunov function, for which the direction of flow is never orthogonal to the gradient of J (i.e., there exists an angle θ_{min} such that the angle between these vectors never exceeds $(\pi/2)-\theta_{min}$), this guarantees that the approximation to J will itself be a Liapunov function, eventually, as the triangles become smaller and smaller. To generalize this to n dimensions, one need only arrive at a tiling scheme made up of solids with n+1 vertices. Strictly speaking, the procedure here is also equivalent to approximating J as a weighted sum of continuous basis functions; for the split square tiling, for example, the equivalent basis functions are functions which look like triangular wedges in cross-section, with square-shaped contours rotated 45 degrees from the original squares.

It is one thing to prove that a Liapunov function <u>exists</u>, within a set of approximating functions. It is another thing to provide an explicit learning rule, and to prove that this learning rule will eventually <u>find</u> the relevant Liapunov function.

The obvious learning rule to use here is Heuristic Dynamic Programming (HDP), which I first proposed in print in 1977, for another application, and which is discussed at length in [9]. (The original Barto, Sutton and Anderson "method of temporal differences"[63] is the special case of HDP where $\hat{J}$ is a lookup table and U equals zero throughout.) In this approach, we would somehow sample points $\underline{x}$ throughout the region of interest; for the sake of efficiency, we would probably want to sample just the enters of each triangle, and begin sampling at the enter, and gradually work our way outwards. (Even random sampling, however, should eventually converge.)

At each sampled point $\underline{x}$, we can call on the system model available in the computer to evaluate $\underline{f}(\underline{x})$. We an find some h small enough that $\underline{x}+h\underline{f}(\underline{x})$ is still within the triangle, but perhaps lose to the edge. Following the procedure in [9], we would then adjust the weights W such that $\hat{J}$ approximates $\hat{J}(\underline{x}+h\underline{f}(\underline{x}),W)+hU(\underline{x})$. In this case, the "weights" are simply the estimates for J at the vertices of the triangle; I would conjecture that convergence is guaranteed <u>if</u> we limit ourselves to adjusting the estimated value of J on that vertex which is furthest "upstream", based on $\underline{f}$. This approach is essentially a special case of the total gradient approach described in [64], which was <u>inconsistent</u> in the general case, with a learning rate of 1. I would further conjecture that the partial gradient approach, with an appropriate choice of learning rates, would also converge efficiently to the right answer. The challenge to future research is either to prove these conjectures, or provide minor variations which would allow such a proof. In a similar way, one could apply DHP [9] -- a more powerful method -- to the same kind of problem. One alloyed try to estimate $\underline{\lambda}$ at each vertex, and again use linear interpolation in-between. This would have the advantage that it allows an exact fit to the usual quadrati Liapunov approximation in the innermost triangle.

The methods described above still have unacceptable costs, as n grows very large. Thus it is crucial to develop more radical approaches, as I will discuss below. Before doing so, I would like to comment on the n-dimensional generalization of the triangle-tiling approach, if only for the sake of curiosity and esthetic completeness.

The main problem in specifying this generalization is to specify a way to slice up or "tile" n-dimensional space into regular locks which have only n+1 vertices each. There are many, many ways to do this. One might expect that excellent methods might be found in the literature on crystallography or on the interface between geometry and topology[65]. However, those are large and difficult bodies of literature; for now, I find it easier just to spell out two relatively simple techniques. Both techniques are n-dimensional generalizations of the simple idea of tiling the plane into squares, and then splitting the squares in half to generate triangles.

In the first alternative, we begin by choosing some unit of length, and then splitting up the region of interest into n-dimensional hypercubes of that size. Then, we split each hypercube into pieces, as follows. If the cube is a unit cube, based on the origin, define each piece as the convex hull of the following n+1 points: $\underline{0}$, $\underline{e}_i$ (for some i between 1 and n), $\underline{e}_i + \underline{e}_j$ (for the same i, for some j, not equal to i, between 1 and n), $\underline{e}_i + \underline{e}_j + \underline{e}_k$ (for the same i and j, for a new k not equal to i or j, and still between 1 and n), ... , $\underline{1}$. Because there are n! choices for the sequence of integers i,j,k,... , there will be n! different pieces. A simple change of coordinate axes (translation and change of scale) extends this procedure to any arbitrary hypercube.

A second alternative -- suggested by Elizabeth Werbos, my 13-year-old daughter -- would probably have better computational properties, because the pieces are less "gerrymandered" in appearance. More tiles are required per cube, but, because the tiles are more compact, one could probably afford to use larger cubes. In the three-dimensional case, she proposes that we first split the cube into six pieces; for each of the six faces of the cube, we cut out the pyramid stretching from that that face to the center of the cube. Then we can slice each pyramid into four pieces, by splitting the square face along its two diagonals (and extending each slice up to the top of the pyramid). The overall effect is to split the cube into 24 pieces, each containing a perfect corner vertex, linked to edges of similar size (0.5 and 0.7). The n-dimensional generalization is straightforward: i.e., slice the n-dimensional hypercube into 2n pieces, one from each face; further split each piece into 2(n-2) subpieces, by slicing each face from <u>its</u> center to <u>its</u> faces; subdivide each of the latter faces into 2(n-4) pieces, and so on.

The methods described above are very broad, and require much more development. Nevertheless, all of that effort would be merely a first step towards what is needed in practice: methods with much lower computational cost. The methods described above would essentially cost something on the order of r^d, which is similar to the preexisting methods. If the <u>only</u> available information about the function $\underline{f}$, aside from our ability to evaluate it at selected points, is a conventional Lipshitz kind of assumption, then it is intrinsically impossible to prove stability at less than a very large computational cost, as d and r grow large. However, the work of Barron at Yale has shown that true neural networks, such as multilayer perceptrons, have the ability to approximate general functions with far fewer hidden nodes, as the dimensionality of the problem grows, than simple lookup or basis-function networks. Halbert White, of UCSD, has shown that MLPs can also approximate derivatives to an accuracy as great as one might like. The obvious approach, then, is to use HDP or DHP (or even GDHP) on an MLP or on new kinds of hybrid networks [65] instead of a basis function network. Using the approaches given in [9], <u>one can use these methods to derive a controller</u>, as well as prove the stability of the result. (Note, however, that the full working versions of DHP, GDHP and the related Gradient-Assisted Learning method, which directly minimizes errors in the derivatives of output, are all covered by a pending patent at BehavHeuristics, Inc., of College Park, Maryland.)

This approach would presumably yield a Liapunov function at a much smaller computational cost; however, the challenge to research lies in proving rigorously that one has in fact found a Liapunov function after one has.

How can one rise to this challenge? One approach would be to use symbolic methods like those used in AI to prove the relevant inequalities. When the critic networks are taken from a relatively simple, restricted set of functions (as with particular types of neural networks), such inequalities may be much easier to handle than they are in the general case.

Another approach is simulation. Even today, the "proofs" of stability in practical systems typically have two parts: (1) rigorous proofs for linear approximate models of the underlying nonlinear plant; (2) lots and lots of simple simulations of entire time-paths, based on more realistic nonlinear models. Narendra, in a 1990 NSF workshop, gave an example of a system which is "provably stable" in this conventional approach. The linear system -- based on the kinds of approximations commonly used in industry today -- was provably stable, assuming he validity of the approximations, based on theorems which Narendra himself originated over a decade ago. However, in realistic simulations of the nonlinear plant, it actually could blow up. He demonstrated a neural network controller directed developed on the nonlinear model, for which he then had no proof of stability, but which never blew up the plant, over many, many simulations.

Given the limitations of this conventional approach to stability analysis, neural networks could possibly make a significant improvement even when an exact approach is not possible. For example, one can use neural networks or hybrid networks[66] to approximate the nonlinear behavior of the plan as accurately as possible. Given a neural network plant model, symbolic reasoning about Liapunov functions may be much easier than it would be if any general algebraic expression were permitted. This is far better than simply using a linear model!

Alternatively, one might simply use these methods as a way to improve the numerical efficiency of the simulation process. One can sample states underline{x} at random, to prove that the Liapunov property is maintained near all points, instead of having to sample complete trajectories of the system. (Brute force simulation is numerically similar to the old Widrow blackjack design, which is well understood to be less efficient than the more modern critic designs.) As with drug testing, the goal may be to develop a kind of statistical bound on the degree of risk, based on some kind of optimized sampling.

This work, if pursued further, offers the hope of building workable general-purpose computer programs able to develop provably stable controllers for general, realistic nonlinear plants whenever stable control is in fact possible.

GLOSSARY OF A FEW BASIC TERMS

Attractor: Many dynamical systems gradually settle down into a fixed, stable equilibrium state or to a stable set of possible states. Each state may be thought of as a point in phase space. An attractor is simply a connected set of points in phase space which the system is attracted to (i.e. converges towards). In many practical applications, a system may have more than one "attractor," when the attractor points are not all connected to each other. There is no consensus on the exact details of the definition. (See [44], page 461.)

Bifurcation: A phenomenon which sometimes occurs when the underlying parameters which define a dynamical system are changed. (For example, we can experiment with different values of the parameter c in equation 28.) A small change in such a parameter can sometimes lead to an abrupt change in the system dynamics, such as a shift from having a simple static equilibrium to having two different stable equilibria; this is a basic form of bifurcation. More examples are given and cited in the 2½ pages which follow equation 32.

Causality: An intuitive concept -- like temperature (see definition) -- which, unlike temperature, has yet to be understood as a purely derived effect from the underlying system dynamics. See the discussion which follows after equation 12. The puzzle of causality, in different forms, permeates the rest of the paper.

Chaos: Chaos refers to the situation where a dynamical system converges to a stable attractor, but behaves in an unpredictable, divergent sort of way within the attractor. See the next subsection after equation 37. See also the definitions of oscillation and strange attractor.

Conservative system: A system which contains one or more "integrals" -- nontrivial quantities which, like energy, remain constant as the system evolves over time. See Figure 5.

CPT symmetry: See the discussion which follows equation 12.

Critical point: An equilibrium point, a point where $\underline{\dot{x}}=\underline{f}(\underline{x})$. Also sometimes called a "singular point." Papers using this terminology often refer as well to the "stable manifold" of such a point (the set of points which flow in towards the point) and the "unstable manifold" of the point (the set of points which points near to the equilibrium flow into).

Dissipation: See Figure 1.

Divergence: See Figure 4.

Energy: In modern thinking, the word "energy" is normally used as a shorthand for "mass-energy," as defined in equation 5 -- a quantity which is absolutely conserved, a quantity whose total value across all space does not change over time. Even in pre-Einsteinian thinking, equation 5 was used as the standard definition of energy. Under certain conditions (as in Figure 1), physical energy may serve as a Liapunov function for approximate models of simple physical systems embedded with a larger conservative universe.

Entropy: A particular type of Liapunov function, normally applied to probability distribution. See the discussion of equation 25. (In information theory, "entropy" refers to a measure of information content or noise -- a different concept, but based on the same equation.) Equation 21 might also be considered an entropy function

Integral: See the definition of conservative system.

Jacobian: Because Jacobi was a very creative mathematician, his name is associated with at least two very different concepts -- the Jacobian matrix (defined in equation 37), and the Jacobian function J (exemplified in equation 45, and discussed further in [8]).

Lagrangian function or system: See the discussion of equation 1.

Liapunov function: A function used to prove the stability of a dynamical system. For any stable dynamical system, a Liapunov function is a function of the system variables which always decreases over time, as the system variables evolve over time, except at the stable equilibrium point (or set of points), where the function reaches its minimum value. See Figures 3 and 4.

Oscillation: A regular, periodic behavior over time -- neither static (as in stable point equilibria) nor chaotic. As the parameters of a system are changed (see the definition of "bifurcation"), there is a kind of standard progression from static equilibrium, to oscillation, to bifurcations within the oscillation, to chaos, to turbulence, and, finally, to thermodynamic disorder. In actuality, there are several different routes to chaos[20], and many variations on this progression.

Phase plane: See Figure 4.

QFT: Quantum field theory, a refined version of quantum mechanics developed in the 1950's by (primarily by Feynman and Schwinger), which is currently viewed as the foundation for all of physics. QFT has yet to have an operational, empirical impact on gravitational physics (though quantum gravity is a major field of research); however, it has had a pervasive impact on the other domains of physics, except at the level of very gross engineering approximations.

Soliton: See the discussion of Figure 9.

SSB: See the discussion of Figure 8.

Strange attractor: A kind of attractor (see the definition of attractor). Ordinary attractors are simple, compact geometric shapes, such as a point, an ellipse, or a surface. Strange attractors are nonordinary attractors -- attractors which typically have fractal dimensions. Strange attractors are typically associated with chaos, but there are

51

exceptions [20].

Temperature: In everyday life, we think of temperature as a physical sensation in our bodies. But in physics, temperature is <u>derived</u> as a secondary quantity, useful in describing the dynamics of a system which does not "know" about temperature in the usual, intuitive sense. Temperature is simply the parameter θ, in equation 24, which does with energy. (In other words, if $\underline{E}^{(1)}$ represents energy, then ρ_1 is temperature.)

Time and time-symmetry: See the discussion surrounding equation 9.

Chapter 3

Modelling Systems with Intentional Dynamics:
A Lesson from Quantum Mechanics

Robert Shaw, Endre Kadar, Jeffrey Kinsella-Shaw

(under review for Human Movement Sc

Modelling Systems with Intentional Dynamics:
A Lesson from Quantum Mechanics

Robert Shaw, Endre Kadar, and Jeffrey Kinsella-Shaw[*]

Center for the Ecological Study of Perception and Action
The University of Connecticut

> "Perception is virtual action" (Henri Bergson)
> "Action is virtual perception" (The Authors)

1.0 Introduction: The Goalpath Navigation Problem

For ecological psychology it has been suggested that the perceiving-acting cycle should be the smallest unit of analysis. We would like to amend this suggestion. It now seems to us that the smallest unit of analysis must be *the perceiving-acting cycle situated in an intentional context.* What this means is the main topic of this paper.

To situate the perceiving-acting cycle under intentional constraints is to identify a space-time context in which the actor selects a goal [1], and then selects from all causally possible paths those that are potential goalpaths, and from these the actual goalpath to follow. The generic problem, therefore, is how best to describe *the action* of an organism. A successful *action* (henceforth defined as *a goal-directed behavior*) minimally entails selecting a (distal) target and moving over a space-time path in an intended manner to that target. This implies that the distal target and the future goal-state of the actor must make their presence felt in the information and control accompanying its current state. Thus somehow the distal must logically condition the proximal, so that the actor's changing relationship to the intended final condition acts to re-initialize (update) the actor's current condition. This is what it means for a space-time path to be *a goalpath.*

A careful consideration of these requirements suggests that *a field of control-specific information* must exist in which the actor and the intended goal both participate. Furthermore, this field of control-specific information must at the same time and in the same place be *a field of goal-relevant control.* Hence each space-time locale in the field is characterized by both an information value and a control value. Such values that go together in this dual fashion are said to be *conjugate information-control values.* The relationship between the energy controlled and the information

---

[*] Also of Haskins Laboratories, New Haven, CT

[1] We take *goalpath* knowledge to comprise both target information and manner determination—that is, specification of where the target is located in space-time and determination of the best manner of approaching it. (See Shaw & Kinsella-Shaw, 1988, for details)

detected with respect to the goal is said to be *adjoint* by nature—something all creatures are born into because of evolutionary design. When this adjoint relationship, however, leads to successful goal-directed behavior (something that often has to be learned), then the adjoint relation of information to control is said to have become *self-adjoint*. [2]

One recognizes in this problem of goal-directedness the need for what the Würtzburger ('imageless thought') School of psychology called a 'determining or organizing tendency' (Einstellung). We call this Einstellung, when augmented with a boundary condition, *an intention* because it is the goal-sensitive, agentive function (a *cognitive operator*, if you will) which determines goal-selection and organizes the dynamics under a 'control law' designed to serve the intention. [3]

The existence of such a field of conjugate values, in which information and control might become self-adjoint, would explain how everywhere that the animal might venture there are opportunities for acting toward the goal in an intended manner (excluding, of course, those places and times where the target is occluded or barriers block its accessibility). *We shall show that such an information-control field has a natural interpretation in an adjoint information/control theoretic formulation of quantum mechanics.*

As a step toward this field theoretic model, we postulate an *intentional process* which acts (as an Einstellung) to set up a perceiving-acting cycle (along the lines discussed by Kugler & Turvey, 1987, and Shaw & Kinsella-Shaw, 1988). The actions that the perceiving-acting cycle *might generate* over space-time define the causally possible family of goalpaths. Here intention, defined as a cognitive operator, tunes the perceiving-acting cycle by directing both the attention and the behavior of the actor toward the goal. A coherent account of this intention-driven dynamics would remove the mystery of how actors maintain informational contact with their goalpaths; namely, they do so by direct perception when the goal is detectable, or otherwise, when not detectable (say, over the horizon), they must navigate either by *indirect perception* or by direct perception *plus dead reckoning*. For humans, indirect perception may be achieved, as Gibson (1979) suggests, by means of verbal instructions, or by use of a map (with target coordinates specified), perhaps, drawn or remembered. As nautical navigators discovered, however, a map alone is not adequate; one also needs a compass to determine directions at choice-points, and a chronometer to satisfy a schedule of departure and arrival times if contact with the goalpath course is to be maintained.

---

[2] In this paper we will discuss the role of adjointness and self-adjointness in perceiving and acting in an intentional context. We will not discuss, however, the nonlinear learning or 'insight' process by which adjointness becomes self-adjointness. That will have to await further developments of the theory of intentional dynamics. But see Shaw & Alley, 1977, and Shaw, Kadar, Sim, & Repperger, 1992, for initial thoughts on learning.

[3] By relating intentional dynamics to this central concept of the Würtzburger school of act psychology, we underscore Gibson's (1979) acknowledgment that ecological psychology has a close historical tie to this school because both oppose the elementarism of the structuralists and emphasize process.

Hence the approach proposed in this paper can be summarized as *a field of conjugate information-control values, with paths being generated by a perceiving-acting cycle which is motivated and guided by intention as a field process.* This account contrasts sharply with more traditional accounts. Let's consider the contrast:

Since animals presumably do not use navigation tools, then they (like humans without benefit of maps, compass, and clocks) must rely on direct perception *plus dead reckoning* to perform the same navigation functions. Traditional psychology assumes, not unreasonably, that under such circumstances they direct themselves by 'cognitive maps' (where intended goals are somehow attentionally distinguished from non-goals). The evidence for the existence of cognitive maps, one might argue, is the actor exhibiting a 'sense of direction' at choice-points, and a 'sense of timing' which keeps the actor on schedule in arriving at and departing from sub-goals. Here the cognitive modelling strategy proceeds by positing internal mechanisms that internalize the map, compass, and chronometer functions. Regardless of either the truth or usefulness of such internal constructs, the success of the internal state modelling strategy is predicated on a successful actor's having access to goal-specific information and goal-relevant control along the goalpath. The field notion also putatively captures the sense of the *social invariance* of the information and control opportunities which

(a) allows an observer to see which goal an organism is most likely pursuing, and

(b) allows different organisms to compete for the same goal.

Hence one may debate whether the field of information and control manifests itself *internally* (as cognitive psychologists maintain), *externally* (as behaviorists have maintained), or *dually* (as we ecological psychologists propose), but the field's existence is without question, being assumed by all parties alike. (See Shaw & Todd, 1980; Shaw & Mingolla, 1981; and Shaw, Kugler, & Kinsella-Shaw, 1991, for a comparative description of these alternative approaches).

Regardless of whether navigation is achieved by direct or indirect perception, the actor's control process must maintain invariant contact with the intended goal over some dynamically developing course of action—a potential goalpath. Consequently, a theory is needed for what constitutes goalpaths, and how they are recognized, selected, and followed. We assume that a goalpath is *generated*, as a segment of a worldline in space-time, by the actions of the perceiving-acting cycle engaged by the organism. Before considering the details of how this engagement is to be formally characterized, we consider the general intuitions that underwrite the intentional dynamics approach to this problem.

1.1 Modelling Systems that Exhibit Intentional Dynamics

Intentional dynamics *inter alia* faces two problems:

First, how is the perceiving-acting cycle comprising a dual relationship between information and control to be formally described? In Section 2 an answer is proposed from the perspective of a variant on optimal control theory called *adjoint systems theory* (Shaw, Kadar, Sim, & Repperger, 1992).

Second, how is the field of conjugate information and control values available to the perceiving-acting cycle to be made formally explicit? Here we borrow from quantum mechanics the image of a particle being involved in measurements as it moves through a field toward an attractor.[4]

The goal of Section 3 is to provide the generic mathematical description of an organism with a complex interior, being driven by internally produced forces and guided by externally available information onto a goalpath toward a future goal-state. This image of a complex animate 'particle' exhibiting intentional dynamics in a field of information and control replaces the standard image of a particle with a simple interior, being driven by outside forces onto a 'least action' path that is indifferent to any future goal state.

Given an actor at some space-time location who intends to connect with an accessible target at some other space-time location, then there will exist a family of causally possible goal-paths. This set is bounded in space-time by the maximum rates of causal action allowed by the (e.g., locomotory) capabilities of the agent who intends the goal. For convenience, we call such a bounded region of goalpath possibilities, an Ω-*(omega) cell* —a construct of *ecological physics* which falls between the cosmological scale and the quantum scale (Shaw & Kinsella-Shaw, 1988). At each moment, along each path there is a certain amount of energy the agent must control if the action is to be in the goal's direction. The amount of control is perceptually specified at each of these points on each goalpath by goal-specific information. What form does this specification take?

This question poses, in part, a version of the so-called 'inverse dynamics' problem for psychology (Shaw, Kugler, & Kinsella-Shaw; 1991), whose solution has been discussed elsewhere (see Saltzman & Kelso, 1987; Shaw, Flascher, & Kadar, *in press*). But since the agent could be on any one of a number of paths, then some perspectivally weighted information and

---

[4] Strictly speaking there is no attractor as a minimum on a physical manifold located solely in either the environment or the organism (construed as exterior and interior fields, respectively) that can be the goal of the action, in the full meaning of the term. Rather the attractor dynamics governing goal-directedness must be defined on the *ecological quotient manifold* (exterior degrees of freedom/interior degrees of freedom) where the flow of generalized action is located (see Shaw, Flascher, & Kadar, *in press*). To our knowledge, there is no discussion of this fact in the literature where goal-directed behavior is attributed to dynamics on a physical attractor basin. The solution called for must be much more abstract. It must be defined over organism and environment, rather than either alone. Hence it must be an ecological physics manifold.

control quantity must be available at each point on each possible path. Quantum physics (as discussed in Section 3) offers us a lesson on how to do such weighting.

In Section 2, in preparation for the quantum field treatment, we show how, even in classical physics, a single quantity exists as *an inner (scalar) product* of information and control which is defined at each point along the goalpath (Shaw, Kadar, Sim, & Repperger, 1992). We offer the following intuition as to what this means: From the internal frame of the actor, one might think of the control-specific information as a wave crest that accompanies the moving agent at each point along the goalpath—from initial to final condition. Let's call this a 'knowledge wave' since it embodies all the dynamical knowledge about the goal (namely, where it is and how to get there) available to the actor as an acting perceiver.

Alternatively, from an external frame of a scientific spectator, one might think of the 'knowledge wave', as it moves over the distribution of possible paths, as specifying at each point, on each path, the likelihood that a perceiving-actor, who intends the goal, will be found there. *Hence intentional dynamics assumes that well-intentioned, normally competent actors will tend to go where goal-specific information is most likely to be found and goal-directed control is most likely to be achievable.* Our aim in this paper is to show that the existence of such a 'knowledge wave' is by no means fanciful under the conception of intentional dynamics, as developed by us in earlier papers—although such a dynamical construct as a 'knowledge wave' has not before been introduced. Consequently, all the mathematics that follow are designed to explicate this intuitive interpretation. Our aim will be to show that *when the knowledge wave embodies information and control that are only adjoint with respect to the goal, then the actions taken can at most be relevant but unsuccessful. However, when they are self-adjoint, then the actions are, by definition, both relevant and successful.* [5]

Before mathematically developing this new explanatory construct, let's consider the current status of the theory of intentional dynamics that has emerged over the past five years or so. The purpose of the next section is twofold: To clarify what one might mean by the claim that *actions must be situated in an intentional context* and to give an overview of the problems that a theory of the intentional dynamics of such situated actions must face. We also indicate the extensions to the theory proposed by the current effort.

1.2 Intentional Dynamics: An Overview

In earlier work we proposed representing the perceiving-acting cycle of an actor as a continuous (Lie) group of complex involutions. This approach draws its inspiration and borrows its mathematical techniques from classical mechanics (e.g., Goldstein, 1980). The virtue of the

---

[5] This notion of self-adjointness has been developed elsewhere under the guise of reciprocities of an intentional system (Shaw, Kugler, & Kinsella-Shaw, 1991).

continuous group representation is that it allows one to characterize the 'intentional' action of systems as the 'flow dynamics' of a *generalized Hamiltonian* action potential which follows paths dictated by a 'least action' principle. We have called this generalized approach *intentional dynamics* and attempted to clarify the notion of the new action potential as follows (Shaw, Kugler, & Kinsella-Shaw, 1991):

For a flow to exist [over a goalpath], there must be a force. A *force* can be defined as *the gradient of some potential*. In some sense a goal can be said to exert an *attractive force* on the system. The sense we suggest is as *some kind of* potential difference between the endpoints of a goal-path. For this to be more than mere metaphor, we must find some way of allowing the interior gradient of the organism's metabolic potential to interact with the exterior force field of the environment. This can only take place through the detection of perceptual information which, in turn, must guide the controllers of the neuro-muscular actuators. Hence the relevant potential difference, or *goal-gradient*, can only be defined over an interior (metabolic) potential relating the initial state of intending the goal to the final state of arriving at the goal. This gradient must also reflect the difference between a system's current manner of behavior *where it is* and the desired manner of behavior *where it wants to be*.

The trick is to get the interior gradient and the exterior gradient linearly superposed so that their resultant is the desired goal-gradient. But this raises another problem. What kind of strange potential is the goal-gradient to be defined over? What is this superposed potential that is neither solely energy nor solely information but both? We call the resulting potential a *generalized action potential*. Whatever this generalized potential is, it is what flows in bi-temporal directions, between the interior and exterior frames, over the perceiving-acting cycle. Furthermore, it is also what must be *conserved* under the intentional dynamics of any system when successfully seeking a goal (pp. 595-596).

In Shaw, Kugler, & Kinsella-Shaw (1991), we proposed a way that this 'trick' of superposition might take place. Furthermore, it was shown how such a generalized action potential might exist, as well as how such a quantity might be conserved (under the Liouville theorem) as a fundamental dynamical invariant of intentional systems.

On the other hand, this 'classical' approach failed to make clear how a particular goalpath is selected by the system from all causally possible goalpaths; rather we described mathematically only how the perceiving-acting cycle might move down *which ever* goalpath was selected. As in the original paper by Shaw & Kinsella-Shaw (1988), the 'extraordinary boundary conditions' posed on a dynamical system by the selection of a goal are not defined, only assumed. In the present paper we seek to remedy this problem. Here we offer an explicit mathematical description of how an actor's intention to pursue a goal automatically does two things: *First, the intention to act imposes the 'extraordinary' information and control boundary conditions on the action taken, and, second, the action selects if not the actual goalpath, then the most probable one to be followed.*

Furthermore, we need to show how getting the appropriate mathematical description of the generalized action potential assigns a probability value to each path in the distribution of potential goalpaths. The probability value provides a *likelihood estimate* of the path being selected by the perceiving-acting cycle as the 'best' route to the goal, given the confluence of environmental and biomechanical constraints. 'Best' here means the practicable compromise between the mathematically ideal and the physically achievable, what can be thought of as the *tolerably suboptimal path* (Shaw, Flascher, & Kadar, *in press*). But how are information and control to be coupled to form a perceiving-acting cycle that can select such a goalpath?

Between the moment of the intent to pursue a goal and the successful attainment of the goal, there exists a functionally defined, space-time region in which the intentional dynamics of the actor is well-defined. In four dimensional geometry any dynamical process is represented by an event which develops over a worldline segment. To understand intuitively the geometry in which goal-directed actions take place, one might first build a geometry for events (Shaw, Flascher, & Mace, *in press*). For example, Figure 1 shows the standard light cone from the Minkowski rendition of special relativity. (Here the third spatial dimension is omitted). The backward temporal cone, called *the domain of (causal) influence*, indicates all those events [6] in the past that might causally affect the event at the origin (vertex). By contrast, the forward temporal cone, called *the domain of (causal) dependence*, indicates all those events in the future that might be affected by the event at the origin.

(Insert: *Figure 1: A Minkowski Light Cone*)

The standard light cone is not adequate for depicting goal-directed behaviors since its worldlines are unbounded. Instead, we need a new four-dimensional geometry in which the worldlines representing goal-directed actions are bounded by endpoints. Figure 2 depicts this new geometry. Imagine, for sake of illustration, that you are given the task of spinning a turntable manually through four successive half-turns (4 x 180°). The kinematics of this goal-directed action is shown below.

---

[6] In space-time there are point-events and worldline paths for ongoing processes. Here we considered events to be finitely bounded segments of worldlines.

(Insert: *Figure 2: An Ω-cell Geometry for a Goal-directed Action*)

The Ω-cell's four dimensional geometry is a *lattice* structure, and therefore has three possible partitions (see Figures 2 and 3): the maximum partition, or *least upper bound*, noted by Ω-cell = ω_{max}, the minimum partition, or *greatest lower bound*, noted by α-cell = ω_{min}, and the intermediate partitions, noted simply by ω-cell = ω Thus, in general, any form of goal-directed behavior will have a lattice structure within the geometry of the Ω-cell as indicated by

$$\Omega\text{-}cell = \omega_{max} \geq \omega \geq \omega_{min} = \alpha\text{-}cell.$$

In the turntable task, the Ω-cell partition corresponds to the overall intention of rotating the turntable through $720°$; the ω-cell partition corresponds to the subgoals of rotating through two full rotations ($2 \times 360°$); and the α-cell partition corresponds to the four $180°$ ballistic rotations (below which no choice-points are possible). A similar analysis generalizes to any goalpath with any number of partitions.

(Insert: *Figure 3: A Schematic Ω-cell Showing its Nested Partitions*)

An *econiche* for an organism (or species) is defined by *how* it lives in its habitat. *Affordances* present opportunities for action since they are possible goals. The character of an econiche is determined by its affordance structure. Indeed, an econiche *is* its affordance structure. *Effectivities* correspond to the means required to carry out a control law by which an affordance goal is realized (what Gibson, 1979, referred to as *a rule for the perceptual control of action*). The repertoire of effectivities possessed by an organism determines what kind of actor it is. Indeed, an actor *is* its effectivity repertoire. In this sense, an ecosystem is the union of the affordance structure of an econiche and the effectivity system of an actor (or species of actors). A *situation* refers to *where* the relevant causal and informational constraints for an action exist. An *occasion* refers to *when* the need or value motivating the action is felt. An *effectivity* is brought to bear on an affordance goal when the actor *intends* to act so as to satisfy a motivating need or value.

All these ingredients (need or value, affordance goal, effectivity means, and intention, together with the implied forces to be controlled and information to be detected) must become a coherent unit of analysis if the intentional dynamics of an entailed action is to be understood. The theoretical construct under which all this comes together as an organized whole is, of course, *the Ω-cell.*

An organism's life as an actor is a 'tiling' of space-time by a concatenation of Ω-cells whose partitions parse the worldline of the actor from birth to death. Intentions are choices of affordance goals which functionally create the Ω-cells to be entered and hopefully crossed. The crossing requires the 'assembling' of an effectivity to engage, direct, and tune the appropriate perceiving-acting cycle to the exigencies of the task situation. The α-cell partitions of an Ω-cell represent the tolerance limits on information detection and energy control—below which a kind of Heisenberg uncertainty is encountered. The ω-cell partitions designate those choice-points in control where a bifurcation set of possible paths exists. Here the actor, given an up-date on perceptual information, can alter the manner of approach to a sub-goal without abandoning the global goal defining the parent Ω-cell. These are the minimal constituents that must be captured in any theory of the intentional dynamics underwriting goal-directed actions. These intuitions are made formally explicit in Section 2 and 3.

Although functionally defined, Ω-cells have an objective reality. They determine the boundaries on behaviors which are tolerant of the same goal (i.e., target plus manner). Such nonlocal goal constraints have the same ontological status as forces in physics, for which evidence is also only functionally defined as a relationship between masses and their observed accelerations (direction and speed). The tolerance class of goalpaths (i.e., each being a velocity field) are parametric (manner) variants whose underlying invariant is their common goal-directedness. Where the *affordance goal* determines the final condition which constrains the resultant direction of the paths, the *effectivity* chosen determines which of the possible goalpaths within the Ω-cell is to be followed. Hence, in the case of a successful goal-directed behavior, an affordance goal—a functional property of the environment— is always complemented by an effectivity— a functional property of the actor. The intention, as a cognitive attunement operation, brings the necessary control and information to bear on the biomechanics of the actor. So long as the intention remains invariant, and *ceteris paribus*, the actor is perceptually guided down the goalpath.

Others have attempted to explain goal-directed behavior, but without the Ω-cell construct to consolidate the 'common fate' or 'determining tendency' of the variant but goal tolerant paths, little mathematical progress was possible (Ashby, 1952; 1956; Sommerhoff, 1950; Weir, 1984; Rosen, 1985). By building our theory of intentional dynamics around this fundamental concept, we show how the perceiving-acting cycle might be situated in an intentional context.

In the next section, we show how the perceiving-acting cycle can be modelled as a set of adjoint differential equations. Here the Ω-cell makes its appearance indirectly under the guise of a famous theorem regarding adjointness in control theory—the Kalman Duality theorem (Kalman, Englar, & Bucy, 1962). Finally, in Section 3, we show how the Feynman path integral approach (a version of quantum mechanics) can be combined with a generalized form of the Kalman Duality theorem. By doing so, we endeavor to obtain a complete and coherent account of the intentional dynamics by which a perceiving-actor 'knows' how to select the 'best' goalpath from among all possible alternatives.

2.0 The Classic Adjoint Systems Approach to the Perceiving-acting Cycle

Let us begin by anticipating what this section will show. A perceiving-acting system might be represented by a pair of dual differential equations—with one equation representing the system's control of energy and its adjoint equation representing its detecting of information. The pair of such equations are said to be *temporally dual* when *self-adjoint* because the original system exhibits a flow of time-forward control over *the same space-time path* that its adjoint system exhibits a counter-flow of time-backward information. Figure 4 portrays schematically the self-adjoint relationship proposed for information and control equations. Note how these quantities 'flow' in opposite temporal directions—with each endpoint doing double duty, serving as a repellor for one quantity and an attractor for the other quantity.

(Insert: *Figure 4: Temporal Self-adjointness of the Information and Control*)

2.1 The Differential Approach to Adjoint Systems

The original control system equations are represented by a set of simultaneous differential equations written in matrix form, called *a state vector differential equation* as follows:

$$\dot{x}(t) = A(t)x(t) + B(t)u(t) \text{ with } x(t_0) \text{ specified,} \tag{2.1}$$

which includes: (a) the derivative of a column matrix, $\dot{x}(t) = dx/dt$, representing *the rate of change of state of the system;* (b) an $n \times n$ square matrix, $A(t)$, which with another column matrix consisting of n-state variables, $x(t)$ (called *the original state-vector)* represents *the system to be controlled*; and (c) an $n \times p$ matrix, $B(t)$, which with a $p \times 1$ matrix of inputs, $u(t)$, represents *the control vector* which sends the system into a new dynamical state configuration. Thus the vector (matrix) difference equation depicted in eq. (2.1) relates the rate of change of state of the system to the current state of the system and the current input signals. This differential equation is inhomogeneous and, therefore, represents a nonautonomous system because of the existence of $B(t)u(t)$—a time-dependent control (forcing) term. We want to solve this equation to see if the specified control vector will send the system from a given initial state at $x(t_0)$ to an intended final state at $x(t_f)$ over an intended goalpath (defined by the intended manner of approaching the intended target).

The solution to this system, called *the steering function*, is given by the inhomogeneous integral equation

$$x(t) = \Phi(t,t_0)\, x(t_0) + \int_{t_0}^{t} \Phi(t,s)\, B(s) u(s)\, ds$$

$$\tag{2.2}$$

where $\Phi(t, t_0)$ and $\Phi(t, s)$ are the state-transition (or fundamental) matrices of the free (autonomous) system given by

$$\dot{x}(t) = A(t)\, x(t_0) \tag{2.3}$$

defined over the interval $[t_0, t_f]$. Associated with the system depicted by eq. (2.1) is an observation vector $y(t)$, an m component vector which satisfies

$$y(t) = H(t)\, x(t) \tag{2.4}$$

where $H(t)$ is an $m \times m$ matrix relating the observation vector $y(t)$ to $x(t)$.

Before presenting the associated adjoint equations of information, one should note that the notion of adjointness is strongly dependent on the given space within which it is defined. Here the adjoint system is presented without any generic definition being given. (However, a specific definition is given in Appendix A.)

If the system of control equations is real, the adjoint system associated with eqs. (2.1, 2.4) is given by

$$\dot{\alpha}(t) = A^T(t)\, \alpha(t) + H^T(t)\, v(t) \tag{2.5}$$

and

$$z(t) = B^T(t)\, \alpha(t) \tag{2.6}$$

$\alpha(t)$ is specified and eqs. (2.5, 2.6) are integrated backwards in time. The superscript $'T'$ indicates matrix transpose (or its conjugate in the complex case). One can now define the dual properties of system eqs. (2.1, 2.4; 2.5, 2.6), such as, *complete controllability* and *complete observability*, by which the role of action and perception in a goal directed (intentional) behavior can be modeled. In addition, one can also define the *inner product operator*, the means by which perceptual information can be scaled to the control of action.

2.2 Controllability, Observability, and the Inner Product Operator

Definition: The action of the system, represented by eqs. (2.1, 2.4), is *completely controllable* if there exists some input $u(t)$ which takes the system from any initial state $x(t_0)$ to any other state $x(t_f)$ in a finite length of time $t_f > t_0$. This property holds if the following matrix is nonsingular for some $t_f > t_0$:

$$W(t_0, t_f) = \int_{t_0}^{t_f} \Phi(t_f, t) \, B(t) B^T(t) \, \Phi^T(t_f, t) dt \ . \tag{2.7}$$

The measure of complete controllability is related to the minimum amount of control energy $u(t)$ necessary to transfer $x(t_0)$ to $x(t_f)$ in t_f-t_0 seconds.

Of interest to determining the optimality of the control is the degree to which the amount of work done approaches the minimum. For this one needs an equation defining minimum energy:

$$\text{Min } E = x^T(t_f) W^{-1}(t_0, t_f) \, x(t_f) \ . \tag{2.8}$$

Small values of $W(t_0, t_f)$ imply little controllability, since large amounts of energy are required to transfer $x(t_0)$ to $x(t_f)$ and conversely.

Perceptual information guides action; hence a duality must exist between the energy required for control and the information that provides the measure of control. Such a measure is guaranteed by the duality of complete controllability to complete observability. This condition is defined next.

Definition: A system's state path is said to be *completely observable* if it is possible to determine the exact value of $x(t_0)$ given the values of $y(t)$ in a finite interval (t_0, t_f) where $t_0 < t_f$. . The original system represented by eqs. (2.1, 2.4) is completely observable if the following matrix is positive definite for some $t_f > t_0$:

$$M(t_f, t_0) = \int_{t_0}^{t_f} \Phi^T(t, t_0) H^T(t) \, H(t) \, \Phi(t, t_0) dt \ . \tag{2.9}$$

It is important to note that there is a close relationship between these system properties. A system is completely controllable if and only if its dual (adjoint) is completely observable. (See Lemma 1 in Shaw & Alley, 1985; Shaw, Kadar, Sim, & Repperger, 1992, p. 21.)

Analogous to the case of minimum energy, one can ask what happens to information when the system successfully achieves control of action with respect to some goal. Given the duality of complete observability with complete controllability, then whenever energy is minimized information must be maximized. Thus, the measure of complete observability is related to the maximum amount of perceptual information as follows:

$$\text{Max Info} = y^T(t_f) \, M^{-1}(t_f, t_0) \, y(t_f). \tag{2.10}$$

We have now arrived at the famous Kalman Duality Theorem:

The Kalman Duality Theorem: Complete observability is dual with complete controllability.

Corollary: Therefore if energy is minimized, then information must be maximized.

The last item of interest is the inner product of the original system with its dual, for it provides a global measure of the amount of control exercised as compared to the amount of information detected over the task interval.

Definition: Inner Product Operator is a bilinear function defined over any pair of elements
(*x* and *y*) of a vector space

$$\langle x, y \rangle = x^T y .$$

(2.11)

Using the above definition, the inner product over the states of the original system and its adjoint happens to be a dynamical invariant. In other words $\langle x, \alpha \rangle = x^T \alpha = c$ (a constant).

These results may be further generalized. They can be extended to systems with hereditary influences, sometimes called *systems with retardation, or time lag*. (For further details consult Shaw & Alley, 1985; Shaw, Kadar, Sim, & Repperger, 1992).

2.3 The integral approach

It is well known that all differential equations can be formulated as integral equations. Using the operator notation, the inverse relationship between the differential equations and integral equations is made even more transparent. For this reason, and for its simplicity, the operator formulation is used. Let us consider the following second order differential equation as an exemplary case.

$$L[y] = p(x) \, y '' + q(x) \, y' + r(x) \, y = g(x)$$

(2.12)

where L denotes the second order differential operator

$$L = p(x) \, d^2/d^2x + q(x) \, d/dx + r(x), \quad \text{that is } L : y(x) \rightarrow g(x).$$

(2.13)

From the operator formulation naturally emerges the idea of using the inverse L^{-1} operator to find the solution of a particular differential equation. The inverse operator will be an *integral operator*

$$L^{-1}[g(x)] = \int_a^b G(x, t) \, g(t) \, dt .$$

(2.14)

Recall the eq. 2.1 (here rearranged) for the actor's control system

$$\dot{x}(t) - A(t)x(t) = B(t)u(t) \text{ with } x(t_0) \text{ specified} .$$

(2.15)

Using the differential operator notation this takes the form $L[x(t)] = B(t)u(t)$,

The solution given by integrating the above differential equation (eq. 2.2) was (shown rearranged)

$$x(t) - \Phi(t, t_0)\, x(t_0) = \int_{t_0}^{t} \Phi(t, s)\, B(s)u(s)ds. \tag{2.16}$$

From this specific example, we can see the role played by the Greens function by going to a generic form: The G kernel function is called *the Green's function of the operator L*. For the given control equation, the inverse operator takes the form,

$$L^{-1}[B(t)u\,(t)] = \int_{t_0}^{t} \Phi(t, s)\, B(s)u(s)ds\ . \tag{2.17}$$

Here the $\Phi(t, s)$ plays the role of the G kernel .[7]

Consequently, the right hand side of eq. 2.14, the integral part, represents the superposition of the intrinsic, quantized influences localized within the scope of system's law, as expressed in the integral form. That is why the Green's function is often called the *influence function* (Greenberg, 1971). Unfortunately, in practical application there are severe difficulties with this technique (see Appendix A).

2.4 Self-adjoint System Equations

Why is the adjoint system not adequate as a way of modelling the perceiving-acting cycle? Because adjoint system equations have terms representing sources of extrinsic influence. We need to make a transition from *adjoint systems* with extrinsic influences to a stronger form of adjoint systems, namely, to *self-adjoint systems*. To achieve the self-adjoint form, however, one must not only get rid of the extrinsic sources of influence but satisfy certain symmetry conditions as well. Self-organizing systems are *conditionally isolated*; that is, they sometimes act solely in accordance with intrinsic constraints because they are *self-adjoint*. (But take care, the physics of adjoint systems as compared to self-adjoint systems is complicated. Here we have used a simplified approach. For a full discussion of the issues, see Santilli, 1978; 1983).

Definition: A system is *self-adjoint* if it coincides with its adjoint.

---

[7]   The Greens function technique provides a method for 'absorbing' a forcing function. We can indeed find a G function for the given L and g, such that $L(G) = \delta(x'-x)$, where δ is the *Dirac delta function*, then the solution $y(x)$ of the equation $L(y) = g(x)$ will be $y(x) = L^{-1}[g(x)] = \int G(x', x)\, g(x')dx'$. To illustrate: given a differential equation, where $g(x)$ is a forcing term on the otherwise homogeneous, $L[y] = 0$ equation, $G(x', x)\, g(x')dx'$ now replaces the extrinsic forcing term.

How one might obtain the self-adjoint equations for a conditionally isolated system? They may be obtained using Greens function technique and selecting the proper transformations (Santilli, 1978; 1983). Shaw & Alley (1985) formulated the information and control relationships between an organism and its environment as a dual pair of dual integral equations (See Table I). These are self-adjoint integral equations because they have symmetric kernels. The 2 x 2 symmetry of these kernels represents the bi-directional propagation of information and control over the actor's perspective and the environment's perspective (see Table II). In psychological terms, these have been identified as *propriospecific* (organism referenced) and *exterospecific* (environment referenced) forms of information and control. And in addition to these, one can also identify their interaction terms (see Shaw, Kugler, & Kinsella-Shaw, 1991).[8]

(Insert: *Table I: The Integral Equations Representing the Perceiving-acting cycle*)

(Insert: *Table II: The Adjoint Operators Representation of the Perceiving-acting Cycle*)

2.5 Why a Quantum Approach is Preferred over the Classical Approach

So far we have presented only one half of the "story", namely, we discussed dual adjoint systems rather than the dual pair of dual systems. The need for the four component subsystem equations suggests that the underlying structure is the *complex involution group*. This is one of several motivations that lead us from the classical adjoint-control theory to the complex Hilbert spaces and the quantum theory of psychological ecosystems thereby entailed.

Another motivation for moving to a quantum mechanical interpretation of intentional dynamics can be understood from Feynman's attempt to answer a problem with the classical approach raised by Poincaré (1905/1952). In Chapter VII of *Science and hypothesis* and echoed by many others ever since, Poincaré remarks in passing that the assumption of the *principle of least action* by which one passes from force-based mechanics to a potential (energy)-based mechanics involves an offense to the mind:

> "The very enunciation of the principle of least action is objectionable. To move from one point to another, a material molecule, acted upon by no force, but compelled to move on a surface, will take as its path the geodesic line—i. e., the shortest path. This molecule seems to know the point to which we want to take it, tp foresee the time it will take to reach it by such a path, and to know how to choose the most convenient path. The enunciation of the principle presents it to us, so to speak, as a living and free entity. It is clear that it would be better to replace it by a

---

[8] These integral equations are directly related to the differential equation approach to adjoint systems by Shaw, Kadar, Sim, & Repperger, 1992).

less objectionable enunciation, one in which, as philosophers would say, final effects do not seem to be substituted for acting causes" (p. 128-129).

If one replaces the word 'molecule' with the word 'actor', then hardly a better description of a system with intentional dynamics is to be found anywhere. But here it seems inappropriate, for it amounts to anthropmorphizing inanimate particles. The danger that the variational approach to mechanics might tempt theorists to anthropomorphize particles is still recognized today. Feynman, who developed a version of quantum mechanics which addresses this issue expressed this problem:

> "It isn't that a particle takes the path of least action but that it smells all the paths in the neighborhood and chooses the one that has the least action by a method analogous to the one by which light chose the shortest time" (Feynman, Leighton, & Sands, 1968; p. 9, chpt. 19). [9]

Our goal in the following sections is to show how a move to a quantum mechanical approach removes the 'offense to the mind' that concerned Poincare' and others. It does so by making plausible the thesis that behaviors of particles follow probabilistic waves rather than having a simple location on a force gradient. Through constructive and destructive wave interference the set of possible trajectories of the particle coalesces around the classical path of least action, indicating, not where the particle is, but where it is most likely to be found. The outcome of this move to quantum field theory is that the particle is constrained to the path observed, making it unnecessary for the particle to select its own path. Here, however, determinism (simple location and certainty) is traded off in favor of a tolerable degree of indeterminism (distributed location and uncertainty).

Formally, we need to provide the generic mathematical description of an organism with a complex interior, being driven by internally produced forces and guided by externally available information onto a goalpath toward a future goal-state. This image of a complex animate 'particle' exhibiting intentional dynamics in a field of information and control replaces the standard image of a particle with a simple interior, being driven by outside forces onto a 'least action' path that is indifferent to any future goal state.

The move to the quantum mechanical approach, vis a vis the Feynman path integral, provides a way to conceptualize how a particle 'selects' the classical stationary path (up to Planck's constant). We shall use this technique to explain how an actor having access to a field of information and

---

[9] Also consider the more recent quote: " The mechanism by which the particle selects the physical trajectory of stationary action is not at all clear. The initial velocity is *not* given, so that the particle will not 'know' in which direction to start off and how fast to go. It is not clear how the particle can 'feel out' all trajectories and 'choose' the stationary one. It should be kept in mind that classical physics does not recognize any path other than the stationary path. Thus, out of a whole set of 'nonphysical' paths, introduced *a priori*, the classical principle of stationary action selects a unique physical trajectory through some mechanism which is not readily apparent" (Narlikar & Padmanabhan, 1986; p. 12)

control selects the goalpath it does. Only here, the global field constraints express, to a large extent, the intention of the actor rather than just the forces imposed on the 'particle' by the environment. The actor, through detection of information about an intended affordance goal, selects the boundary conditions (the Ω-cell) for the field by which it controls its action, by means of the effectivity engaged. The field is the bounded Einstellung ('determining tendency' plus boundary conditions) authored by the actor's intention, under the appropriate affordance-effectivity compatibility condition.

The inanimate particle, on the other hand, has to take whatever field that nature hands it. Put differently: The relevant wave which coalesces around the 'animate particle' is not merely a focus of global forces that completely controls its actions, but rather a knowledge wave, consisting of information as well as forces that allows it informed control. In more psychological terms, this explains how intentional dynamics can situate the perceiving-actor in an intentional context (an Einstellung = an Ω-cell). [10]

3.0 Quantum Mechanical Approach to Intentional Dynamics

The new strategy, which we propose to adopt, originates from a unique approach to quantum mechanics suggested by P.A.M. Dirac and developed by Richard Feynman (Feynman & Hibbs, 1965). This new approach, called *the Feynman path integral*, involves the formulation of the quantum mechanical behavior of particles in terms of *generalized, or distribution, functions* (Schwartz, 1950, 1951). Distribution functions (e.g., Dirac delta function or Heaviside function) are defined only under integrals. The Feynman distribution function[11] is defined under a special class of integrals that describe the sum over all possible path histories that a given particle *might have had*!

Our thesis is that perceiving-acting systems follow paths chosen from among a family of possible paths in the same manner that Feynman particles do. There is a major difference, however. For systems that are not just causal, as particles are, but are both causal and intentional, as perceiving actors are, then we must not only sum over their possible path histories but, dually, over their possible future paths as well. This is the way that controllability (i.e., causal) and observability (i.e., intentional) are represented under the Feynman path integral approach. By

---

[10] Let's be clear about what claims we are making about the ontological status of the 'knowledge wave' field that is encompassed by the Ω-cell and set up by the actor's intention. It is not objective in the sense of being *in* the environment; nor is it subjective, in the sense of being a cognitive 'map' or other mental construct. Surely, this field is causally supported by both neurodynamical and physical processes, and structured by psychological processes—the 'determining tendencies' (e.g., values, needs, beliefs, etc.) of the actor. In this sense, it is functionally defined at an *ecological scale* which comprises all these processes.

[11] In the equation for the Feynman path integral, the distribution function, Dx(t), replaces the ordinary d(x). See eq. (3.33). Later, in dualizing the path integral for the purposes of intentional dynamics, Dx(t) will be interpreted as Dx[t] which is to be interpreted as being simultaneously Dx(+t) and Dx(-t), that is, as running in both temporal directions over all paths in the distribution.

dualizing this distribution function to express the temporal bi-directionality of information and control, the Ω-cell is automatically and necessarily obtained.

It is well-known that all the properties of quantum mechanics can be derived from either the Schrödinger wave equation approach, the Feynman path integral approach, or Heisenberg's matrix approach. The formal relationship of the differential approach and the integral approach to quantum mechanics is the same as the relationship of self-adjoint differential equations and the symmetric kernel integral equations.[12] (We shall be interested, for reasons that will become apparent later, in comparisons of only the first two approaches.) In other words, the differential (wave) equation and the (path) integral equation approaches provide formally equivalent descriptions. There is, however, an important difference between the two approaches. In the first case, the differential wave equation is a generalization of Newton's laws giving a *step-by-step* development of a particle's path in a manner that confounds dynamics and initial conditions. In the second case, the path integral approach is a generalization of Hamilton's variational approach giving a *path-by-path* account of a particle's possible histories, but in a manner that allows dynamics and initial conditions to be separated. [13]

Hence if the conditions that initialize (or finalize) a path are to be studied independently of the dynamic laws by which the path unfolds (causally by control or anticipatorily by information), then it is advisable to assume the path integral approach and to derive the wave equation applications from it. In this way, the probability amplitudes might still be of service, as we shall see, and one avoids loss of separation of boundary conditions from the dynamics. That is, it allows the boundary conditions on intentional dynamics, the Ω-cell, to be treated as a separate but related problem.

3.1 The Differential Approach to the Adjoint Quantum Mechanical Model

Thus, depending on the problem, we can use either of the two methods in formal analysis. However, to make clear the modelling lesson to be learned from quantum mechanics, and how quantum mechanics relates to the adjoint systems approach, the differential approach proves

---

[12] It should also be noted that there is a formally analogous relationship between the Hermitian (self-adjoint) matrix approach of Heisenberg's matrix mechanics and the adjoint differential equation approach of Schrödinger's wave mechanics.

[13] Though mathematically equivalent, the wave equation and path integral equation are not physically equivalent. The function $\psi(x, t)$ depends both on the dynamics and on the initial condition $\psi(x_1, t_1)$. As shown in eq. (3.1), there is no way to separate these two aspects of a physical description. Narlikar & Padmanabhan (1986) explain it this way: "There exist physical situations in which we would like to study dynamics of the system without committing ourselves to any particular initial conditions. The kernel is the most suitable for such cases, since [eq. 3.4] clearly separates out the initial conditions from the dynamics. In short, the kernel is independent of the initial conditions and represents the dynamics while the wave function $\psi(q, t)$ depends on both the dynamics and the initial conditions" (p.25). (Equation numbers are for the current paper.) Also, where no wave equation can be constructed that is independent of end-points, a path integral can be. (See Feynman & Hibbs, 1965, for the construction of such a path integral.

simpler and more convenient. Most importantly, adjointness belongs to properties in the Schrödinger equations that are more transparent. To illustrate this point, examine the Schrödinger equation (3.1) for a particle moving in one dimension in a potential field and then compare eq. (3.2) With it's (complex) adjoint in eq.(3.3.):

$$-\frac{h}{i}\frac{\partial \psi}{\partial t} = -\frac{h^2}{2m}\nabla^2 \psi + V\psi$$

(3.1)

This equation is one specific form of the general Lagrangian

$$\frac{h}{i}\frac{\partial \psi}{\partial t} = H\psi \quad \text{or equivalently} \quad ih\frac{\partial \psi}{\partial t} = H\psi$$

(3.2)

where H represents an operator, called the *Hamiltonian* operator. Similarly, their complex conjugate (adjoint) equations

$$\frac{h}{i}\frac{\partial \psi}{\partial t} = H^*\psi \quad \text{or equivalently} \quad -ih\frac{\partial \psi}{\partial t} = H^*\psi$$

(3.3)

can also be formulated. (Note: The '*' is used in quantum mechanics to denote complex conjugacy.) For the Schrödinger equation, the generic form of the associated integral equation will be (see more detailed discussion in Section 3.5)

$$\psi(x_2, t_2) = \int K(x_2, t_2; x_1, t_1)\, \psi(x_1, t_1)\, dx$$

(3.4)

where

$$K(x_2, t_2; x_1, t_1) = \int_?^? e^{(i/h)S[x_2, t_2; x_1, t_1]}\, Dx(t)$$

(3.5)

This equation provides the standard way to show the equivalence of the differential and the path integral approaches. By simple differentiation in (+t) time yields the Schrödinger equation. (For ease of presentation, the derivation of the dual Schrödinger equation is suppressed; it should be clear, however, that it is obtained in parallel fashion from the dual version of eqs. 3.4 by differentiation with respect to -t.)

The differential operator of the (dual) Schrödinger equation is defined on the wave functions as their solutions. The nature of the equation implies that the Schrödinger differential operator maps solutions into other solutions, that is the domain and the range of the operator consists of wave functions only. This implies that, technically speaking, unlike what is usually the case, the integral equations are not more difficult to handle than the differential equations. (The discussion of how the adjoint equation relates to observation/measurement will be discussed later).

Obviously, these quantum equations (eqs. 3.1, 3.2, 3.3) generalize the form of the classical core eq. (2.3) of the dual system of linear differential eqs. (2.1-2.6) that were used in the adjoint control approach. However, there are two major differences: the treatment of both the forcing functions and the boundary conditions will be much simpler in quantum mechanics.

Consider the role of forcing functions. In the classic case $x(t) = A(t) x(t)$ is called a *free system* meaning that it is *autonomous*. The generic form of control eq. (2.1), however, contains an extrinsic $B(t)u(t)$ term. By contrast, in the Schrödinger equation, there is no extrinsic term, that is, the extrinsic forcing components are formally not separated. Rather the forcing factors are automatically absorbed into the H operator.[14] Nevertheless, this strategy is not without cost, for the Hamiltonian operator can take rather complicated forms.[15] Regarding the boundary conditions similar arguments can be made.

3.2 Controllability, Observability, and the Inner Product in Quantum Mechanics

As in classical adjoint systems (Section 2.1), an inner product can also be defined on the space of the wave functions in the usual way. But here we must take a different route to interpreting observability and controllability. The fundamental problem here is that the Hamiltonian cannot be separated into an *informing* part and a *controlling* part.[16] This is the price paid for the simplicity of adjointness in quantum mechanics, as compared to classical adjoint systems theory, where control and information could be separated. In other words, only a weaker form of the Kalman Duality theorem holds in quantum theory. Furthermore, it assumes an implicit rather than an explicit form. Thus, although the discussion of information and control in the quantum case must differ from the classical case, the key to the adjointness property in both cases is the *inner product* concept. For these reasons, we begin our discussion with the inner product operator.

---

[14] In cases where the system can be conceived as an almost isolated one (with H_0 Hamiltonian), and there is a weak interacting component (with small H_{int}), then the Hamiltonian of this system can be written as a sum of the two parts $H = H_0 + H_{int}$. Even from this splitting, it has to be transparent that any external influence which changes the system, is modelled with a sudden absorption by using an additive interactive component.

[15] As a simple example of this fact, consider a charged particle moving in a magnetic field.

$$-\frac{\hbar}{i}\frac{\partial \psi}{\partial t} = -\frac{1}{2m}\left(\frac{\hbar}{i}\nabla\psi - \frac{e}{c}A\right)\cdot\left(\frac{\hbar}{i}\nabla\psi - \frac{e}{c}A\right)\psi + e\phi\psi \qquad (3.4)$$

where e is the charge, c is the velocity of light, A is a vector potential, and ϕ is a scalar potential. Even for this rather simple case, the Hamiltonian is quite complicated; namely,

$$H = -\frac{1}{2m}\left(\frac{\hbar}{i}\nabla\psi - \frac{e}{c}A\right)\cdot\left(\frac{\hbar}{i}\nabla\psi - \frac{e}{c}A\right) + e\phi$$

[16] Even if, under strong simplifying assumptions, one could separate the Hamiltonian for a single particle in a field, for a particle with a complex interior this will not be possible.

In the classical case the inner product is a *bilinear form* over two finite dimensional vector spaces that is formally a finite sum. By contrast, in the Hilbert space of quantum mechanics, defined over continuous functions, the inner product operator takes an integral form.

Definition: Let f and g be two probability amplitude (wave) functions, then $\int g(x) * f(x)\, dx$ is called the *inner product* of f and g.

The inner product operator is closely tied to a given quantum mechanical system, that is, to its Hamiltonian. How can we unpack this inner product operator to reveal observability and controllability as separate factors? Unpacking the inner product operator will have profound implications for how one interprets the perceiving-acting cycle as situated in an intentional context. The intentional context will be modelled by the Hamiltonian of the system, while the perceiving (observability aspect) and the acting (controllability aspect) will be represented by operators with special properties being required. The tight relationship between perceiving and acting will be revealed as operators that are self-adjoint, that is, the same.

Assume that perception involves a *meter* and that action involves an *effector*, then this self-adjointness property implies that such mechanisms are but different aspects of the same operator. Though the idea is not fully developed here, self-adjointness suggests a possible formal characterization of the construct of a 'smart perceptual device'—a kind of ecological (inner product) operator (Runeson, 1977). Here an actor's capacity for acting (an effectivity) and metering are unified under the intention to discover some characteristic property (an affordance) of the local environment, as in wielding a visually occluded implement to determine its length and its suitability for use in some task (Solomon & Turvey, 1988; Turvey, 1989).

In quantum mechanics one does not have to worry about the specific conditions under which the self-adjointness (hermiticity property) requirements are satisfied. (Primarily, one is concerned with identifying the Hamiltonian of a system). In quantum mechanics the Hamiltonian is always Hermitian.

Definition: An *operator* H is called *Hermitian*, or *complex adjoint* if

$$\int (Hg) * f\, dx = \int g * (Hf)\, dx \tag{3.6}$$

holds with the property that any f and g converge to zero at infinity.

Replacing f and g with ψ in eq. (3.6), that is substituting the solution of the Schrödinger wave equation into f and g, we get

$$\int (H\psi) * \psi\, dx = \int \psi * (H\psi)\, dx \tag{3.7}$$

If ψ satisfies eq. (3.2)[17] then from eq. (3.7) it follows by a substitution

$$\int \frac{\partial \psi*}{\partial t} \psi \, dx + \int \psi* \frac{\partial \psi}{\partial t} dx = \frac{d}{dt} \int \psi*\psi \, dx = 0$$

(3.8)

This important result shows that the inner product is time independent for a solution of eq. (3.2).

In the control theoretical framework, the perception-action system was formally modelled by dual differential equations expressing the observability–controllability conditions. In quantum mechanics, the control of action is expressed in terms of the Schrödinger equation of motion. Its dual process, the detection of information, is identified in quantum mechanics as measurement. This is not unusual, for the perceptual system has been treated as a measurement device before (e.g., Rosen, 1978; Bingham, 1988; Shaw, 1985). What kind of measuring process is perceiving and how does it relate to controlling? We discuss these issues next.

An analogy can be constructed between the influence of a scientist's measurement on the motion of an inanimate particle along its trajectory (in the laboratory frame of reference) and the influence of information detection on the perceptual control of an actor's (self-)motion along its goalpath (in the Ω-cell frame of reference). This analogy holds but with qualification so that measurement *of* the particle becomes perception *by* the 'particle' and extrinsic control becomes informed self-control. Therefore, with certain requisite modifications, the mathematics of quantum measurement can be extended to the case of a complex particle exercising self-control from the case of a simple particle subject to extrinsic control.

In classical quantum mechanics, the measurement process is limited to a short period of time. But for perception (and control) within an intentional context (Ω-cell) the process is continuous between boundary conditions (intent to target at either the α, ω, or Ω scale, as shown in Figure 3). Measurement (and therefore perceptual) information can be represented in the Schrödinger equation of control. The Hamiltonian for the simple particle can be generalized to include a component representing the influence of information on the control of motion (Shaw, Kugler, & Kinsella-Shaw, 1991). How might this be done? Information can be conceived as a field, and the goal for a given task can be modelled as an attractor in the information field (Kugler, Shaw, Vicente, & Kinsella-Shaw, 1990). (But see footnote 4 for qualification). As our simple example, consider again a charged particle moving in a magnetic field. (See footnote 14.) In the formulation for this problem, an external field can influence the form of the control equation without changing the generic form of the Schrödinger equation. Because of their duality, this suggests that the

---

[17] In quantum mechanics, unlike the classical adjoint systems approach, time-reversal cannot be modelled simply by the adjoint system, rather, as proven by Wigner (1932), the correct time-reversal transformation sets $T\psi(t)$ equal to its complex conjugate so that $T\psi(t) = \psi*(-t)$ rather than setting it to the simpler adjoint, $T\psi(t) = \psi(-t)$.

information field can be modelled within the quantum mechanical framework in a similar fashion. Using the (dual) Schrödinger wave function to characterize the perceiving-acting cycle as a 'knowledge wave', contrasts sharply with the traditional view of it as negative feedback control (Smith & Smith, 1987).

To appreciate the modelling strategy for introducing observability (and hence controllability) into quantum mechanics, consider the nature of measurement in quantum mechanics more closely. Assume a measuring device M measures a property G of a moving particle. Property G is called *an observable*. More specifically:

Definition: An *observable* is a Hermitian quantum mechanical operator G.

Definition: The *expectation value*, $< >$, of G in the state f is defined by the integral

$$<G> = \int f(x) *Gf(x)dx = \int (Gf(x))*f(x)dx. \tag{3.9}$$

Definition: A *measurement* is the expectation value of an observable G.[18]

Practically speaking, the measuring device must complete the measurement in finite time. One of the most interesting aspects is that measurement changes the wave function of the 'otherwise freely moving particle' to be measured. Formally, one can show that if the wave function of the incoming particle is $f(x)$, then the measuring equipment modifies the kernel K of the amplitude

$$f(x_2, t_2) = \int K(x_2, t_2; x_1, t_1) f(x_1, t_1) \, dx \tag{3.10}$$

by making it equal to $K_{exp}(x_2, t_2, x_1, t_1)$ in the course of measurement starting at $t = t_1$, $x = x_1$, and ends at $t = t_2$, $x = x_2$. The inner product of f and K_{exp} that is $\int K_{exp}(x_2, t_2, x_1; t_1) f(x_1, t_1) \, dx$, gives the amplitude to arrive at x_2 at the outset of the equipment.

$$f_G(x_2, t_2) = \int K_{exp}(x_2, t_2; x_1, t_1) f(x_1, t_1) \, dx \tag{3.11}$$

Using Feynman's notation (Feynman & Hibbs, 1965), the probability function associated with the property G will be

$$P_G(x_2, t_2) = | \int K_{exp} (x_2, t_2, x_1, t_1) f(x_1, t_1) \, dx |^2 \tag{3.12}$$

where $f(x)$ is the wave function to be measured, $K_{exp}(x_2,x)$ is the kernel for the experimental apparatus, and x_2 is the position arrived at by particles with property G. This result, however, depends on experiment (including the measuring equipment and experimental conditions, such as

---

[18] Since G can be measured it must be real, that is G must be a Hermitian (complex conjugate) operator.

duration of measurement, etc.). To find the kernel of another experiment, another form, $K_{exp'}$ (x_3, x) is needed:

$$P_G(x_3, t_3,) = |\int K_{exp'}(x_3, t_3, x_1, t_1) f(x_1, t_1) dx|^2 \tag{3.13}$$

Since the same property G is measured in each experiment, $P(G)$ should be the same for any incoming wave function(x) within an unimportant constant phase factor $e^{i\delta}$. It follows that

$$K_{exp}(x_2, t_2, x_1, t_1) = K_{exp'}(x_3, t_3, x_1, t_1) = g(x) \tag{3.14}$$

so that one obtains an experiment-independent form of the kernel. This independent function, $g(x)$, is called the *characteristic function* of the property G. One can now refer to the quantum mechanical analogue of observability used in classical adjoint control system. Notice that the integral in eq. (3.13), generally, yields a complex number for the measured amplitude. Furthermore, if the measurement is expressed as a G transformation on the incoming wave function f, than eq. (3.13) can be written in the simplified form

$$P(G) = |\int f(x)^* G f(x) dx|^2. \tag{3.15}$$

The integral will be real if the G operator of the observable is Hermitian. (Compare this result with the required positive definiteness for M in eq. 2.9). This provides the basis for requiring G to be Hermitian operator

Knowing the limitation of measurement in quantum mechanics due to the uncertainty principle, one should not expect a definition of *complete observability*. Nevertheless, a more general definition, called *maximal observability*, can be formulated. This suggests that there may only be an approximate generalization of the Kalman Duality theorem to quantum mechanics. We are not yet clear whether there is a *mini-max* duality between eqs. (3.16) and (3.16a) as there is in the classical adjoint systems case (Section 2.2). This possibility should be ascertained.
Definition: G property is *maximally observable* in a quantum mechanical measuring system if G is Hermitian and

$$P(G) = \int f(x)^* G f(x) dx \rightarrow \max \tag{3.16}$$

Here G must be a close approximation to the generalized Hamiltonian of the system defined over the Ω-cell. Having the intrinsic adjointness of the quantum mechanical equations and the equations of a measuring system, the corresponding definitions for controllability may also be formulated. This can be done by the appropriate variational principle. In quantum mechanics the variational principle is called *the Rayleigh-Ritz method*. It states that if H is the Hamiltonian of the system with E_0 as the lowest energy state value, then for any f the following condition holds:

$$E_0 \leq \int f(x)^* \, Hf(x) \, dx \, / \int f(x)^* \, f(x) \, dx \tag{3.17}$$

This form is not really helpful for our purpose. The fundamental problem faced is that here one wants to split the Hamiltonian into *an informing* and *a controlling part*.[19] In other words, here one must pay the price for the simplicity of the quantum mechanics as compared to the classical approach, where the control and information parts were given in separate equations. Imagine, for example that we need to provide a field to control the path of a particle. Then the controllability can be defined on the basis of the Hamiltonian, which includes the 'control field'. Unfortunately, the measurement (observation) will change the Hamiltonian of the system. Consequently, it is not possible to isolate the control part of the new Hamiltonian. There is a kind of tautological limit on what one can do to separate control from information in the quantum case. One can take a control perspective or an information perspective on the actor's generalized Hamiltonian but there is but one quantity. Hence these control and information seem quite tautological. To get around the tautological nature of the control versus the measurement problem, it seems to us that one can do no better that to consult Feynman & Hibbs' (1965) discussion of the issue. In their discussion, this tautological nature of information and control is simply a strange property of the characteristic function.

They initiate the discussion with the following question: What is the relationship between *f* and *g*? Before answering this question, one must ask: What should the *state function f* be to have the property *G*? To find a particular state function, *F*, for a given experimental apparatus *i* with a given characteristic function *g*, one has to solve

$$\int K_{exp} \, (x_i, \, x) \, F(x) \, dx = \delta(x_i - x). \tag{3.18}$$

This equation has the well-known solution $K^*_{exp} \, (x_l, x)$ for $F(x)$. Here $K^*_{exp} \, (x_i, x)$ is the complex conjugate of $K_{exp} \, (x_i, x)$. Consequently,

$$F(x) = K^*_{exp} \, (x_i, x) = g(x). \tag{3.19}$$

That is, $g(x)$ gives us the wave function of a particle having the property G with probability 1. Furthermore, if the particle is in state $f(x)$ the amplitude that it can be found in a state $g(x)$ is

$$\psi(G) = \int g(x) \, {}^*f(x) dx = \Phi[g(x)] \tag{3.20}$$

---

[19] Here one might expect the duality property (under a Greens function) of the time-forward Feynman propagator and the time-backward Dyson propagator, might be useful ways to represent controlling and informing, respectively. Unfortunately, the problem is more complex than this, for one must have coupling of information and control over internal and external frames of reference. Recall the quote in Section 1 from Shaw & Kinsella-Shaw (1988). These issues, however, have been touched upon algebraically (but not explored analytically) in Shaw, Kugler, & Kinsella-Shaw (1991).

Having outlined the major point of Feynman & Hibbs' discussion (1965, pp. 96-108), they conclude:

"We might say loosely: The probability that the particle is in the state $g(x)$ is $|g(x) f(x)dx|^2$. This is all right if we know what we mean. The system is in the state $f(x)$, so it is not in $g(x)$; but if a measurement is made to ask if it is also in $g(x)$, the answer will be affirmative with probability

$$P(G) = |\int g^*(x) \ f(x) \ dx|^2 = \rho[g(x)] \tag{3.21}$$

A measurement which asks: Is the state $g(x)$? will always have the answer yes if the function actually is $g(x)$. For all other wave functions, repetition of experiment will result in yes some fraction P (between 0 and 1) of the tries. This is a central result for the probabilistic interpretation of the theory of quantum mechanics.

For all this we deduce an interesting inverse relationship between a wave function and its complex conjugate. In accordance with the interpretation . . . [see eq. 3.20], $g^*(x)$ is the amplitude that if a system is in position x, then it has the property G. [Such a statement is put mathematically by substituting a δ function for $f(x)$ [see eq. 3.20]. On the other hand, $g(x)$ is the amplitude that if the system has the property G, it is in position x. (This is just a way of giving the definition of a wave function.) One function gives the amplitude for: If B, then A. The other function gives the amplitude for: If A, then B. The inversion is accomplished simply by taking the complex conjugate. Equation [3.21] can be interpreted as follows: The amplitude that a system has the property G is (1) the amplitude $f(x)$ that it is at x times (2) the amplitude $g^*(x)$ that if it is at x, it has property G, with this product summed over the alternatives x." (Feynman & Hibbs, 1965; pp. 108-109. Numbering on equations refer to equations in the current paper.)

The gist of this section can be interpreted as the quantum version of what Gibson called *a rule for the perceptual control of action* (1979). For the measuring process (detection of goal-specific information) to be successful (in controlling action), the g characteristic function (affordance goal property) of the environment has to be a complex conjugate of the state function f (the effectivity property) of the actor. The measurement procedure specifies a characteristic function (goal-specific information) which will be a real extrinsic constraint. For the measuring process to be successful, the free particle should modify its state function as a result of measurement. More specifically, in order to have a good measurement (high probability) the self-adjointness (or complex conjugacy) of the characteristic function and the state function of the moving particle should be properly set up. The calibration includes the boundary conditions (the Ω-cell) within which the device executes its measurement.

In the quantum mechanical example of a moving charged particle in the magnetic field, the focus was on the measurement problem. Actually, both the action of the particle and the measuring process are equally important, even though the role of action is essentially implicit in the discussion. (This is in keeping with Gibson's being a perceptual psychologist who was at heart an action psychologist.) This is the natural consequence of the fact that the particle is not an intentional system which can set its own goal parameters. In the case of a living organism the focus should be on the goal-directed action which is guided by perception. That is, the focus should be on the intentionally selected goal specific action guided by perception.

For an organism moving toward an intended goal, and perceiving (measuring) its state relative to the goal (which is given by the characteristic function), the task is to move so as to maintain its self-adjointness. This self-adjointness is achieved by the actor observing a rule for the perceptual control of action; namely, in the language of quantum theory: 'Move so that the wave function of motion is the complex conjugate of the characteristic function given by the perceptual measurement!'; and, in the language of intentional dynamics: 'Move so as to perceive what you need to perceive if you want to satisfy your intention of maintaining your goal (that is, completing your intentional task)!' (See Section 3.5 for further discussion).

In the above discussion, intentional dynamics assumes that the property G is an approximation of the generalized Hamiltonian that must be defined over the whole Ω-cell. This compact theoretical formulation may be both too brief and too ambitious. For it requires perfect knowledge of all the observables with regard to the given Hamiltonian—something usually not known explicitly. Nevertheless, it seems clear that a quantum theoretical framework for intentional dynamics may be in the offing. Final judgment should be suspended until empirical examples have been thoroughly worked out. (Note: There are other observables defined with respect to the Ω-cell of intentional dynamics, and additional conditions from quantum mechanics to be satisfied. These are discussed in the Appendix B).

To complete the parallel presentation of the quantum approach to the classical case (Section 2), the integral equations of quantum mechanics formulated by Feynman must be introduced. We do so in the next section.

3.4 Feynman Path Integral Approach

The equivalence of the Feynman path integral formulation and the conventional presentation of quantum mechanics by the Schrödinger differential equations is discussed in several books. The translation between the two languages can easily be found in the literature. For instance, the detailed analysis of the transition from the path integral to the Schrödinger differential equation can be found in Feynman's book (Feynman & Hibbs, 1965). The most common way to do the translation is to differentiate the equation of the path integral so as to derive the Schrödinger equations. Obviously, the derivation is invertible. The inverse direction of translation can also be done by simply reversing the derivation steps. However, here we present the translation from the differential approach to the path integral approach for two reasons:

First, because certain important aspects of the path integral formulation help us understand more about the usefulness of the quantum mechanical technique in intentional dynamics. Second, because it is important to show the role of Green's function and its generalization for the quantum mechanics. Partly, because the self-adjoint formulation in control theoretical framework (Shaw, Kadar, Sim, & Repperger, 1992) naturally offered the Green's function as a candidate to understand formally, and perhaps also empirically/physically the underlying deeper processes.

Following the same steps of the above construction of integral equations as inverse ones to the differential equations, the derivation begins with writing the Schrödinger equation. Next, one must find the corresponding Green's function that will be the kernel of the integral equation associated with the Schrödinger equation. Finally, it must be shown how one can obtain the Feynman path integral formulation from the Greens function.

For the Schrödinger equation, the generic form of the associated integral equation will be

$$\psi(x_2, t_2) = \int K(x_2, t_2; x_1, t_1) \, \psi(x_1, t_1) \, dx \tag{3.22}$$

This equation provides the standard way to show the equivalence of the differential and the path integral approaches. By simple differentiation in time, it yields the Schrödinger equation. (Again, to keep the presentation simple, we suppress the dual version of these equations). [20]

We need to point out that the differential operator of the Schrödinger equation is defined on the wave functions as their solutions. As mentioned earlier, the Schrödinger differential domain of the operator the domain and range of the operator consists only of wave functions. Consequently, the inverse operator can be written in the form eq. (3.22) with the boundary condition

$$K(x_2, t_2; x_1, t_1) = 0 \quad \text{for } t_2 < t_1 . \tag{3.23}$$

The Green's function of the Schrödinger equation will be the kernel of the integral eq. (3.22) as it can easily be seen by comparing eq. (2.21) with eq. (3.22). The Green's function represents a local (infinitesimal) influence resulting in displacement. The kernel $K(x_2, t_2; x_1, t_1)$ of the Schrödinger equation can be given explicitly as

---

[20] The original, time forward equation is given by eq. 3.31. The dual equation then is $\psi(x_1, t_1) = \int K(x_1, t_1; x_2, t_2) \, \psi(x_2, t_2) \, dx$. The dual kernel to eq. 3.33 (antipropagator) is

$$K(x_2, t_2; x_1, t_1) = \int e^{(i/h)S[x_2, t_2; x_1, t_1]} \, Dx(t)$$ As a short hand for both the original and the dual equations,

one might replace the usual path distribution functional, $Dx(t)$ with $Dx[t]$ meaning that the distribution is temporally bi-directional, i. e., is both $Dx(+t)$ or $Dx(-t)$.

$$K(x_2,\, t_2;\, x_1,\, t_1) = \int e^{(i/\omega)S[x_2,\, t_2;\, x_1,\, t_1]}\, D x(t) \tag{3.24}$$

Eq. (3.24) is Feynman's path integral representing integration over all the possible paths between $(x_2,\, t_2,)$ *and* $(x_1,\, t_1\,)$. (Again, consult footnote 19). The kernel is also called *the amplitude with respect to its endpoints*. Figure 5 illustrates the way in which a classical (stationary action) path can be obtained from the distribution, $Dx[t]$, by constructive and destructive wave interference. Traditionally, the divisor in the exponential term, $\omega = h$. This shows that the width of the uncertainty region around the classical path has the width of Planck's constant, h. For generality, however, (explained below), this constant is replaced with a variable ω. Since this is key to understanding the origins of the 'knowledge wave', let's consider this process in more detail.

(Insert Figure 5: *Emergence of the 'Knowledge Wave' within the Ω-cell*)

We ask: How does a particle (or an actor) get from an initial point (intent) to a final (target) point? In the classical approach, although the principle of least action picks out the path, it is not clear how the particle is constrained to that path. Also, in conventional formulations of quantum mechanics, no definite path is possible because of uncertainty. Hence the path concept is deemed useless. Feynman's insight was to appreciate the positive import of this problem; namely, if a unique path is not possible, then *all possible paths are allowed!* Furthermore, he showed how the classical path could be recaptured: Weight each path by the factor $e^{iS/h}$ including the classical path. Feynman then showed that each path is more or less in dynamical phase with the other possible paths. Thus they each contribute to the sum of amplitudes which is greatest in the vicinity where the classical path is to be found by variational techniques. More particularly, the classical path is distinguished by making the action, S, stationary under small changes of path: thus close to this path the amplitudes tend to add up constructively, while far from it their phase factors tend to cancel because of destructive wave interference. The path integral approach essentially gives a 'global' formulation to classical field theory, and for our purposes, to intentional dynamics.

To enrich the intuition on the meaning of the path integral, consider how it may be extended to a concatenation of path distributions (e.g., a sequence of ω-cells):

Amplitudes for events occurring in succession can be expressed in the form

$$K(x_2,\, t_2,;\, x_1,\, t_1) = \int_c K(x_2,\, t_2,;\, x_c,\, t_c)\, K(x_c,\, t_c,;\, x_1,\, t_1)\, dx_c \tag{3.25}$$

where the integration means summing over all $x_c\, t_c$ points, that is the total amplitude to go from $(x_1,\, t_1\,)$ to $(x_2,\, t_2)$ is the sum of the product $K(x_2,\, t_2,;\, x_c,\, t_c)\, K(x_c,\, t_c,;\, x_1,\, t_1)$ taken for all possible (x_c, t_c) The concatenated Ω-cell partitions, shown Figures 2 and 3, provide cases where the 'chain' rule of kernel products applies. It is important to recognize that the Feynman path integral is defined from initial (or final) point to a moving current point, which acts as a parameter that distributes action (S) over the paths moment to moment. Thus, the partitions depicted in Figures 2 and 3 arise dynamically as a function of the perceiving-acting cycle branching at different choice-points while leaving the overall intention (Ω-cell) invariant (For example, consider a predator who must change direction in order to continue tracking a dodging prey.).

(Insert: *Figure 6: Showing the Range of Scales for the Weighting Function in the Feynman Path Integral.*)

In the weighting function, *exp (iS/ω)* (eq. 3.24), over the Feynman distribution, $Dx(t)$, or $Dx(-t)$, the scale used in physics is $\omega = h$ (Planck's constant). This weighting function can be generalized to ecophysics and applied to intentional dynamics. By replacing h with a variable scaling factor corresponding to α or ω, where $h \leq \alpha \leq \omega \leq \Omega$, one can have graded partitions of uncertainty (tolerance) around the classical stationary path. The existence of a variable scaling factor expresses mathematically Kugler & Turvey's (1987) claim the that action system can be variably quantized. Also, the total action (S) associated with these path partitions can be expressed as a product of kernels of the Feynman path integral as defined by eq. (3.25).

3.5 The Analogy Between Ecological Laws and Quantum Mechanical Laws

Classical mechanical laws apply to predict events: Given the appropriate initial conditions (i.e., the mass and layout of three balls A, B, and C) so that if $event_1$ occurs (e.g., ball A strikes ball B), then $event_2$ (i.e., ball B strikes ball C) necessarily (lawfully) follows. Traditionally, psychological laws have been assumed to take the same causal form: Given the appropriate initial conditions (i.e, normal organism with proper learning history, attending to stimulus, and so forth), then if $event_1$ occurs (a stimulus event), then $event_2$ (a certain response) probably (lawfully) follows . Here, as Skinner (1977) suggests, the stimulus, although not truly a force, acts like a force, and the control 'law' (next state function), although not truly a law, acts like a law to move the organism into its next state from which it emits the observed behavior. If the state transition is associative, then this form of law fits a *stimulus-response* behaviorism; however, if the state transition involves *a representation*, or *symbol*, then this form of law fits cognitive psychology (Fodor & Pylyshyn, 1988). This classical law form, however, fits neither quantum phenomena nor ecological psychology phenomena (e.g., intentional dynamics); rather, they both take a different law form.

It is generally agreed that quantum mechanical laws do not predict events with absolute certainty, as deterministic classical laws are supposed to; rather they predict only the probability that subsequent observations (measurements) will follow from previous observations (measurements) if, as discussed earlier, a certain self-adjoint (complex conjugate) relationship holds between a state function and characteristic properties of the situation (Wigner, 1970). As indicated, ecological psychology require laws that operate similarly.

Consider a rule for the perceptual control of action (Gibson, 1979), say, as formulated from the perspective of a prey engaged in a prey-predator competition. 'If you (the prey) intend to escape the predator, whose image is expanding in your optic array, then intend to move so as to make the predator's image contract!' Here, analogous to the quantum law formulation, the law relates a previous observation (information) to a subsequent observation. The quantum mechanical interpretation of intentional dynamics gives the following generic reformulation of a rule for action: "If you (the actor) intend following one of the acceptable goalpaths (i.e., in a congenial Ω-cell distribution) having intended characteristic property g' (positive affordance value), then stop applying the old state function, f (an inappropriate effectivity), which generates unacceptable paths (i.e., in a uncongenial Ω-cell distribution) having the unintended characteristic property, g (negative affordance value), and begin applying a new state function, f' (an appropriate effectivity)!'

(insert *Table III: A Comparison of Law Forms*)

Table III compares the different laws discussed. Both forms of the classical law form (I and II) relate event to event, while the quantum-type law form (III and IV) relate information to information through a function that is the complex conjugate of the characteristic property of that information. In the quantum case, a state function does so, while in the intentional dynamics case, a path function (an effectivity) does so.

4.0 Conclusion

In the adjoint information/control theory (Shaw, Kadar, Sim, & Repperger, 1992), perception was formally construed as *observability* and the action as *controllability* (Kalman, Englar, & Bucy, 1962). This traditional law approach treats control systems as an analytic extension of classical mechanics, formulated in terms of ordinary differential equations, or, alternatively, as an extension of variational mechanics, formulated in terms of functional (Volterra) integrals. It was argued that although these mathematics are quite appropriate, up to a point, they have certain inherent limitations for modelling perceiving-acting systems which exhibit intentional dynamics (e.g., prospective control). The self-adjointness property is a merit of this traditional approach, but alone it is not sufficient. Rather the classical variational approach to defining the goalpath of the perceiving-acting cycle has inherent shortcomings because of the mathematical physics it inherits from classical mechanics. These three shortcomings are most prominent:

(1) it does not give an account for how a 'particle' selects a stationary path;

(2) it does not provide a principled way to handle the tolerance limits on detection and control in following a path; and

(3) it provides no way to embed the perceiving-acting cycle in an intentional context.

Self-adjointness is a natural property of Hilbert space and so is inherited by quantum mechanics. Hence, it was argued that the perceiving and acting in intentional contexts might have a natural description in quantum mechanics so that these three shortcomings are overcome.

To the above complaints we gave the following remedies:

(1)* The Feynman path integral provides a physical motivation for the claim that the path that a 'particle' elects necessarily emerges very close to the classical (stationary action) path. Figure 5 shows that the quantum action distribution is constant to the first order in the vicinity of the classical path (dark strip given by constructive wave interference), while outside this region the dynamical phase oscillates so erratically that the corresponding amplitudes of the other possible paths are washed out (by destructive wave interference).[21]

(2)* The tolerance limits around the path represents the fallibility of control of information detection by intentional 'particles' and Planck's constant range of Heisenberg uncertainty around the path of inanimate particles (Figure 5). The tolerance range for 'particles' exhibiting intentional dynamics is variable, depending on the nature of the task, the degree of certainty of the intention held, scale of information and control resolution, and the number of interpolated choice-points. Regardless of these details, however, the weighting function in the kernel, $e^{iS/\omega}$ (where ω ranges from h to Ω) which propagates the path, unites intentional dynamics with quantum physics *vis a vis* the Feynman path integral and provides access to the Schödinger wave function—the 'knowledge wave' in the case of particles exhibiting intentional dynamics. An important goal of ecological physics has been to provide a continuous link between psychology and physics (Shaw & Kinsella-Shaw, 1988). This link is now forged by this variable weighting factor, ω, for it shows how psychology, through intentional dynamics, can be continuous with physics when a constant scale factor is allowed to become a variable one.

(3)* The perceiving-acting cycle becomes situated in an intentional context when it is embedded in an Ω-cell. Here not only is generalized action conserved under successful goal-directed behaviors but intention acts as a kind of implicit 'steering function' (prospective control) so

---

[21] The Feynman integral is difficult to handle numerically because the trajectories, far from the classical trajectory having complex exponentials, oscillate rapidly (i.e., they have a negative definite metric). To allow for numerical approximations, a bridge from quantum mechanics to statistical mechanics can be built by rotating time t into an imaginary direction by the operation (a Wick rotation) $t \rightarrow i\tau$. This has the effect of dampening the wildly oscillating exponential, $e^{iS/\omega}$, and turning it into an exponentially decreasing function, $e^{i-S/\omega}$, which behaves more like classical weighting functions (i.e., with a positive definite metric). Multiplying through by $-it$ acts holomorphically to counter-rotate the solutions to this path integral back onto the original metric (Aitchison & Hey, 1989).

that the actor (who is well-intentioned) can ride the crest of a dual (information and control) 'knowledge wave'. The symmetric kernel of the dual Feynman path integral, as defined over *Dx[t]*, is called a *propagator* because it generates all the knowledge (remembered history and anticipated future) that may exist for a 'particle' (actor). Consequently, it is the core equation for intentional dynamics as it is for quantum physics and provides the attractor dynamics needed to explain goal-directed behavior.

Perhaps, the chief failure of classical physics, and inherited by the classical adjoint control theory is to make room for goalpaths that are possible but not pursued. In the classical approach, the only path which exists is the path actually followed by a particle, in accordance with the principle of least action. For intentional systems, where choice behavior must be real, paths intended but not followed must be as real as paths that nature defines by least action. This requirement of intentional dynamics, like that of quantum mechanics, calls for a dramatic change in scientific philosophy.

Like quantum mechanics, intentional dynamics, needs a physics of *possibilism* and not just of actualism (Turvey, 1992). Fortuitously, where classical physics does not allow for such possibilism to underwrite choice behavior, the newer view of quantum physics based on the Feynman path integral does. The implications for the philosophy of psychology are immense. Under the classical approach to perceiving and acting in intentional contexts, one had to posit nonobservable constructs, such as unconscious inference, magically acquired memories or cognitive maps, and so forth, to underwrite the choice set from which actual choice-behaviors emerge.

By contrast, from an ecologized version of the Feynman path integral, a field of information and control, is shown to emerge. By differentiating this integral, a Schrödinger-like 'knowledge wave' arises to illuminate the actor's goalpath choices—a goalpath distribution whose width is automatically scaled to the abilities of the actor by an intrinsic weighting function. If so, then the intentional control of the focus of attention, by which the actor finds its way, is explained.

In summary, our aim in this paper was to show that measurement in quantum mechanics could be extended to the Ω-cell to model the perceiving-acting cycle in an intentional context and to show that the existence of the so-called 'knowledge wave' is by no means fanciful. We have provided arguments in favor of both of these claims. How does this approach relate to other attempts to use quantum mechanics in psychology?

If, as we suspect, the internal mechanisms for perception, action, and cognition (e.g., intentional focusing of attention) under the auspices of this approach are to be replaced by ecological operators on a quantum-like field theory, one must wonder if any help from neurodynamics for such mechanisms is in the offing. Apparently so.

It is worth noting in this regard that variations on quantum mechanics have been used to model figural processing (Pribram, 1991), as well as audition (Gabor, 1946), at two distinct constituent scales in the analysis of brain processes: the macroscale of information processing in the brain and at the nanobiological scale of the microtubular processes of the cortex (Hammeroff, 1987). At the more macro scale, the neurodynamics that support visual and auditory perception have been framed in terms borrowed from quantum microphysics. More specifically, the activity at the level of the dendritic microprocesses has been modelled as a quantum field, where Pribram has hypothesized quantum or patch holographical processes to occur and 'signals' are ". . . better conceived of as Gabor-like elementary functions--*quanta rather than bits of information*" (Pribram, 1991, p.271). Where the above approach represents an extrapolation from quantum microphysics to neurodynamics, our efforts represent an attempt to develop a quantum macrophysics appropriate to intentional dynamics at the ecological scale. Where brains provide the boundary conditions for the former approach, the Ω- cell does for the latter (see Shaw, Kinsella-Shaw, & Kadar, *in preparation*).

We have surveyed the promise of the quantum mechanical approach to modelling the perceiving-acting cycle in an intentional context and found many ways that these mathematics might be appropriate. We have also discovered problems that must be overcome if the complex nature of the interaction of information and control is to be understood. Obviously, much further work is required.

References

Aitchison, I. J. R. & Hey, A. J. G. (1989). *Gauge theories in particle physics*. Bristol, England: Adam Hilger

Ashby, W. R. (1952). *Design for Brain*. London: Chapman & Hall.

Ashby, W. R. (1956). *Introduction to cybernetics*. London: Chapman & Hall.

Bingham, G. P. (1988). Task-specific devices and perceptual bottleneck. *Human Movement Science, 7*, 225-264.

Feynman, R. P., & Hibbs A. R. (1965). *Quantum mechanics and path integral s*. New York: McGraw-Hill Book Company.

Feynman, R. P., Leighton, R. B., & Sands, M. (1968). *The Feynman lectures in physics*, vol. II, Reading, MA: Addison-Wesley Pub. Co.

Fodor, J. A. & Pylyshyn, Z. (1988). Connectionism and cognitive architecture: A critical analysis. *Cognition (Special issue), 28*, 3-71.

Gabor, D. (1946). Theory of communication. *Journal of the institute of electrical Engineers, 93*, 429-441.

Gibson, J. J. (1979). *The ecological approach to visual perception*. Boston: Houghton Mifflin.

Goldstein, H. (1980). *Classical mechanics*. Reading, MA: Addison-Wesley.

Greenberg, M. D. (1971). *Application of Greens functions in science and engineering*. Englewood Cliffs, NJ: Prentice-Hall.

Hammeroff, S. R. (1987). *Ultimate computing: Biomolecular consciousness and nanotechnology*. Amsterdam: North-Holland Press.

Kalman, R. E., Englar, T. S., & Bucy, R. S. (1962). Fundamental study of adaptive control systems. ASD-TR-61-27, 1.

Kugler, P. N., Shaw, R. E., Vicente, K. J., & Kinsella-Shaw. J. M. (1990) Inquiry into intentional systems I: Issues in ecological physics. *Psychological Research, 52*, 98-121.

Kugler, P. N. & Turvey, M. T. (1987). *Information, natural law, and the self-assembly of rhythmic movement: theoretical and experimental investigations*. Hillsdale, NJ: Erlbaum.

Narlikar, J. V., & Padmanabhan, T. (1986). Gravity, gauge theories, and quantum cosmology. Dordrecht: D. Reidel Publishing Co.

Poincare, H. (1905/1952). *Science and Hypothesis*. New York: Dover Publications, Inc. (a reprint of the Walter Scott Publishing Company, Limited translation).

Pribram, K. H. (1991). *Brain and Perception: holonomy and structure in figural processing*. Hillsdale, NJ: Lawrence Erlbaum Associates.

Rosen, R. (1978). *Fundamentals of Measurement and representation of natural systems*. New York: North-Holland Scientific Publisher.

Rosen, R. (1985). *Anticipatory systems: Philosophical, mathematical, and methodological foundations*. New York: Pergamon Press.

Runeson, (1977). On the possibility of "smart" perceptual mechanisms. *Scandinavian Journal of Psychology, 18*, 172-179.

Saltzman E., & Kelso, J. A. S. (1987). Skilled actions: A task dynamic approach. *Psychological Review, 94*, 84-106.

Santilli, R. M. (1978). *Foundations of Theoretical mechanics I: Birkhoffian generalization of Hamiltonian mechanics*. New York: Springer-Verlag.

Santilli, R. M. (1983). *Foundations of Theoretical mechanics I: Inverse problem in Newtonian mechanics*. New York: Springer-Verlag.

Schwartz, L. (1950, 1951). *Theorie des distributions*. Vols. I and II. Paris: Herman and Cie.

Shaw, R. E. (1985). Measuring information. In W. H. Warren & R. E. Shaw (Eds.), *Persistence and change* (pp. 327-345). Hillsdale, NJ: Lawrence Erlbaum Associates.

Shaw, R. E., & Alley, T. R. (1985). How to draw learning curves: Their use and justification. In T. D. Johnston & A. T. Pietrewicz (Eds.), *Issues in ecological study of learning* (pp. 275-443). Hillsdale, NJ: Lawrence Erlbaum Associates.

Shaw, R. E., Flascher, O. M., & Kadar, E. E. (in press). Ecological pi numbers: Measuring the fit of dynamic wheelchair activities to environmental layout. In J. Flach & P. Hancock (Eds.). *The ecological approach to human factors*. Hillsdale NJ: Lawrence Erlbaum & Associates.

Shaw, R. E., Flascher, O. M., & Mace, W. M. (1992). (in press). Dimensions of event perception. In W. Prinz & B. Bridgeman (Eds.) *Handbook of Perception*. Berlin: Springer-Verlag.

Shaw, R. E., Kadar, E. E., Sim, M., & Repperger, D. W. (1992). The intentional spring: a strategy for modeling systems that learn to perform intentional acts. *Journal of Motor Behavior, 24(1)*, 3-28.

Shaw, R. E. & Kinsella-Shaw, J. M. (1988). Ecological mechanics: a physical geometry for intentional constraints. *Human Movement Science, 7*, 155-200.

Shaw, R. E., Kugler, P. N., & Kinsella-Shaw, J. M. (1990). Reciprocities of intentional systems. In R. Warren & A. Wertheim (Eds.), *Control of self-motion* (pp. 579-619). Hillsdale, NJ: Lawrence Erlbaum Associates.

Shaw, R. E. & Mingolla, E. (1982). Ecologizing world graphs. *Behavioral and Brain Sciences, 5*, 648-650.

Shaw, R. E., & Todd, J. (1980). Abstract machine theory and direct perception. *Behavioral and Brain Sciences, 3*, 400-401.

Skinner, B. F. (1977). The experimental analyses of operant behavior. *Annals of the New York Academy of Sciences, 291*, 374-385.

Smith, T. J. & Smith, K. U. (1987). Feedback control systems of human behavior. In G. Salvendy (Ed.), *Handbook of human factors* (pp. 251-309). New York: John Wiley & Sons.

Solomon, H. Y., & Turvey, M. T. (1988). Haptically perceiving the distances reachable with hand-held objects. *Journal of Experimental Psychology: Human Perception & Performance, 14*, 404-427.

Sommerhoff, G. (1950). *Analytical biology.* London: Oxford University Press.

Strang, G. (1986). *Introduction to applied mathematics.* Wellesley, MA: Wellesley-Cambridge Press.

Turvey, M. T. (1992). Affordances and perspective control: An outline of the ontology. *Ecological Psychology, 4(3),* 173-187.

Weir, M. (1984). *Goal-directed behavior.* London: Gordon and Breach Science.

Wigner, E. P. (1932). *Nachr. Akad. Wiss. Göttingen, Math. Kl. IIa, 31,* 546.

Wigner, E. P. (1970). Symmetries and reflections: Scientific essays. Cambridge, MA: M.I.T. Press.

Appendix A: Constructing Green's Functions

There are several difficulties in constructing a Greens function for a given differential equation. First of all, the inverse does not necessarily exist. This shortcoming can be redeemed in many cases by some transformation. Even if the inverse exists, its construction is usually more difficult than finding solutions by using a properly chosen conventional trick. However, if the inverse exists, then the problem is equivalent to the task of finding or constructing the kernel, the Green's function of the integral equation (See e.g. $G(x, t)$ in eq. [2.14]). There is more than one way to construct the Green's function associated with a differential equation. Each method may have corresponding physical meaning. Here we presented the one which is the easiest and the most revealing in terms of using the adjointness we have already introduced in our paper. Here we just further refine the basic concepts.

Definition: $L*$ differential operator is *formally adjoint* to L if L and $L*$ are associated with the following equation

$$\int f^*(x)\, Lg(x)\, dx = [...] + \int f(x)\, L^* \, g(x)\, dx \tag{A.1}$$

Definition: L is *formally self-adjoint* if $L = L^*$.

Definition: $L*$ differential operator is *adjoint* to L if the associated differential equations of L has homogeneous boundary conditions, that if the eq. (A.1) takes the simple form

$$\int f^*(x)\, Lg(x)\, dx = \int f(x)\, L^* \, g(x)\, dx. \tag{A.2}$$

or using the inner-product notation

$$(f,\, g) = \int f(x)\, {}^*g(x)dx \tag{A.3}$$

eq. (A.2) takes the form

$$(Lf, g) = (f,\, L^*g). \tag{A.4}$$

The key step to achieve the adjointness is to recognize the importance of elimination of the boundary terms in eq. (A.1). The very same idea leads us to the Green's function (Greenberg, 1971; pp. 22-26). If we find a G function for a given g, for which

$$L^*(G) = \delta(x'-x) \tag{A.5}$$
$$G(a,\, x) = G(x',\, b) = 0 \tag{A.6}$$

91

where δ is the Dirac delta function, then the solution of the equation $L(y)=g(x)$ can be written in the form

$$y(x) = \int G(x',\ x)\ {}^*g(x')dx' \tag{A.7}$$

To illustrate the meaning of this seemingly pure formal trick we can imagine an arbitrary physical problem associated with a differential equation, e.g. eq. (2.12), where $g(x)$ is a forcing term on the otherwise autonomous system, represented by the homogeneous $L[y]= 0$ equation. We can realize that

$$G(x',x)\ {}^*g(x')dx' \tag{A.8}$$

represents a local concentrated influence of the forcing term. Consequently, the right hand side, the integral part, of eq. (2.21) represents the superposition of the localized/quantized influences. That is why the Green's function is often called the influence function.

Appendix B: Minimal Requirements for Quantum Mechanical Observables

Having now provided a generic quantum theoretical framework, two questions naturally emerge:

a) How can an observable be conserved (i.e., be a dynamical invariant)?

b) How can a conserved quantity be found?

To provide the fundamental ideas for answering the first question, a simplifying assumption is needed. Assume a time independent Hamiltonian H. Let F be an observable in the state ψ. If its value, $<F>$ conserved, that is constant, then its time derivative

$$\frac{d}{dt}\langle F \rangle = \frac{d}{dt}\int \psi^* F \psi\,dx = \int \frac{d\psi^*}{dt} F\psi dx + \int \psi^* F \frac{d\psi}{dt}\,dx. \tag{B.1}$$

should be equal to zero. Using the complex conjugate Schrödinger equation

$$-ih\frac{d\psi^*}{dt} = (H\psi)^* = \psi^* H. \tag{B.2}$$

eq. (A.1) takes the form

$$\frac{d}{dt}\langle F \rangle = \frac{i}{h}\int \psi^*(HF{-}FH)\psi dx. \tag{B.3}$$

The integral is vanishing if and only if the commutator of H and F, $HF-FH = [H, F]$, is vanishing, [22] that is

$$[HF-FH] = \bar{0} \rightarrow \frac{d}{dt}\langle F \rangle = 0.$$

(B.4)

The vanishing of the commutator was trivially true for the case when for the observable operator F was the complex conjugate of the Hamiltonian, $F = H^*$. The vanishing of the commutator obviously provides us a less strict requirement for the observable, but it still requires the full knowledge of H.

Regarding the second question concerning the discovery of conserved quantities, one can further weaken the required conditions as follows:

The solution for the second issue is implicit in the first problem. Namely, if we have an operator U which commutes with H and is invertible, then

$$HU - UH = 0 \; \rightarrow HU = UH \; \rightarrow H = U^{-1}HU.$$

(B.5)

If U is time independent then eq. (B.5) shows that U is a symmetry operator of the Schrödinger equation.

Definition: U is a symmetry operation of a differential operator L if for any ψ solution of L $U\psi$ is also a solution of L.

For the Schrödinger equation if U is a symmetry operator and ψ is a solution then

$$ih\frac{d(U\psi)}{dt} = HU\psi.$$

(B.6)

For U is not time dependent,

$$ih\frac{d\psi}{dt} = U^{-1}HU\psi,$$

(B.7)

There is, however, an additional physical requirement for the U transformation. In our conceptual framework this means that the inner product invariance postulate is an intrinsic requirement for quantum mechanics. The U transformation is admissible if the normalization of the wave function is not changing with the application of U, that is if

---

[22] If H and G commute then we can choose the eigenfunctions that they will be common eigenfunctions of H and G
$$H\psi = E\psi$$
$$F\psi = f\psi.$$

$$\int \psi^* \psi \, dx = \int_{?}^{?} (U\psi)^* U\psi dx = \int \psi^* U^\dagger U\psi dx \; . \tag{B.8}$$

It follows that $U^\dagger U = UU^\dagger = I.$, meaning U has to be a unitary transformation. Clearly, the unitary transformations and also the antiunitary (see the time reversal transformation below) transformation play important role in our theoretical analysis due to the inner product invariance postulate.[23]

---

[23] The complex rotation $U = eieF$ *provides* us an interesting connection between the certain unitary and Hermitian transformations. The operator F is called the generator of U and it is the observable connected to U if U is not Hermitian. H. Weyl (The theory of groups and quantum mechanics, Dove, New York, 1950, pp. 100,214) considered this kind of rotation transformations while investigating the electric charge $<Q>$, as a conserved quantity. This type of transformations are called gauge-transformation of the first kind. Gauge invariance, in quantum mechanics, means that the gauge transformation of a solution would be another solution of the Schrödinger equation.

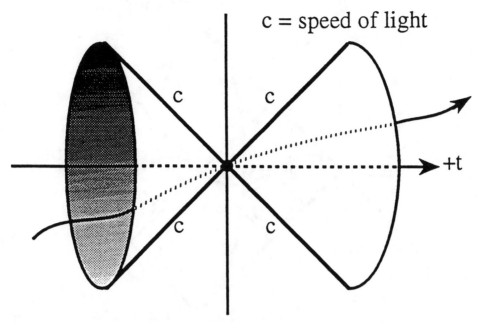

c = speed of light

A Minkowski Light Cone

Figure 1: A Minkowski Light Cone. An unbounded worldline passes through an origin.
Imagine all possible worldlines converging on the origin from the past that might be occupied
by an actor. These are all the events that the actor might have perceived as well as all the past
events that might have causally affected him. Also, imagine all the worldlines diverging from
the origin toward the future. These are all the possible events that may originate from the
actor—actions or information—to affect future events.

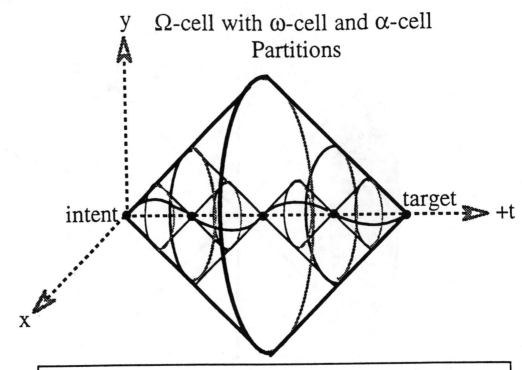

y Ω-cell with ω-cell and α-cell Partitions

intent   target   +t

x

Note: The goalpath corresponds to a point on an object rotating through one 720° Ω-period, or two 360° ω-periods, or four 180° α-periods.

Figure 2: An Ω-cell Geometry for a Goal-directed Action. Here we see that the worldline segment representing a goalpath is bounded by the point of intent and the target point. In between these endpoints are other points, called *choice-points*, at which sub-goals for subordinate actions are determined. The four ballistic half-turns of the turntable are represented as the points parsing the sinusoidal curve generated over space-time by the rotation event. (The accelerations and decelerations are not depicted).

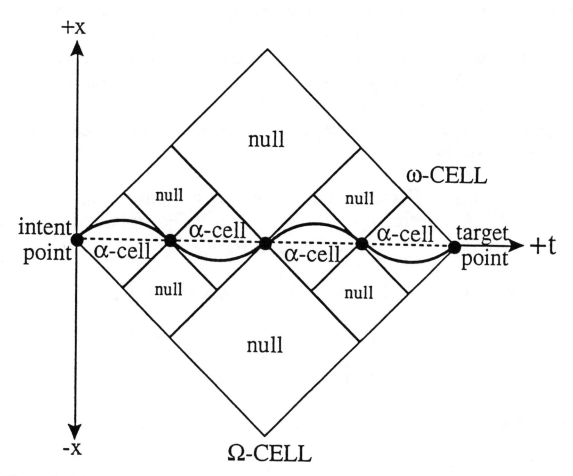

Figure 3: A Schematic Ω-cell Showing its Nested Partitions.

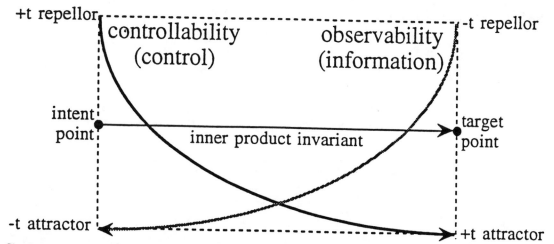

Schematic Representation of Temporal Self-adjointness of
Information and Control over Goalpath

Figure 4: Temporal Self-adjointness of the Information and Control. The dual paths denote the complementary conjugate values of information and control at each point along a goalpath traversed by a perceiving-acting system. There exists an inner-product invariant so that the *generalized action* quantity (defined as the inverse flow of information and control) is conserved. As one quantity increases, the other decreases, so that the bi-temporal integrals always sum to yield the same total amount of generalized action over a given goalpath. If the path is not a goalpath, then this quantity will not be conserved.

$$\text{Organism Perspective} \qquad \text{Environment Perspective}$$
$$\text{(Action)} \qquad\qquad\qquad \text{(Perception)}$$
$$\text{Energy (control)}(+t)$$

$$y(t) = k\,x(t) + \int_0^t K_O(t,s)\,x(s)\,ds \qquad x(t) = k\,y(t) + \int_0^t K_E(t,s)\,y(s)\,ds$$

$$\text{Equation I} \qquad\qquad\qquad\qquad \text{Equation II}$$

$$\text{Information (detection)}(-t)$$

$$x^*(t) = k\,y^*(t) + \int_0^t K_O^*(s,t)\,y^*(s)\,ds \qquad y^*(t) = k\,x^*(t) + \int_0^t K_E^*(s,t)\,x^*(s)\,ds$$

$$\text{Equation III} \qquad\qquad\qquad\qquad \text{Equation IV}$$

Table I: The Integral Equations Representing the Perceiving-acting cycle. This system of adjoint equations are the solutions to the differential equations discussed in Section 2 (See Shaw & Alley, 1985, for discussion).

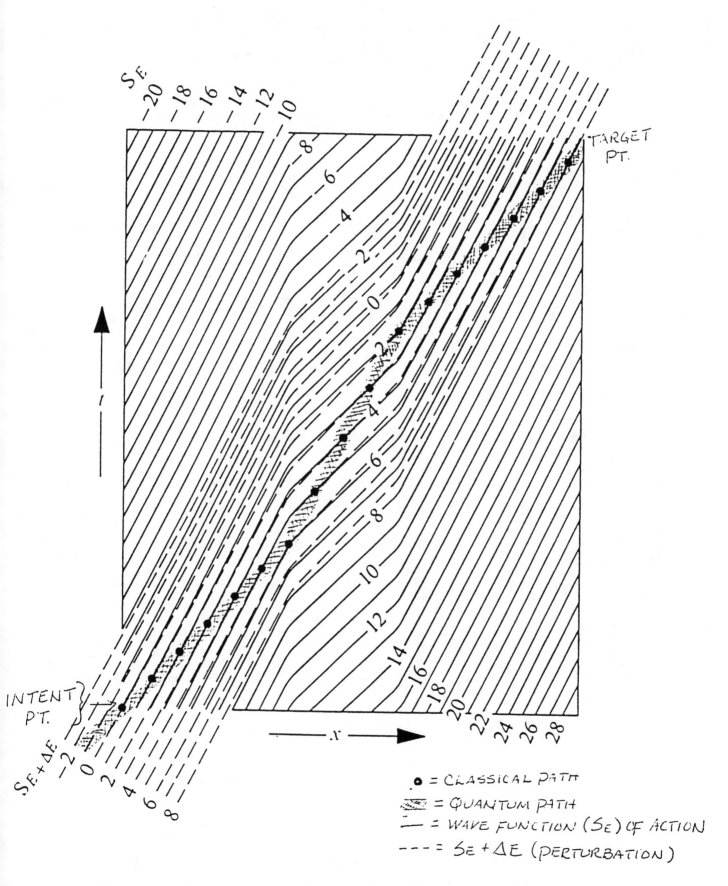

S_E
20 18 16 14 12 10 8 6 4 2 0 2 4 6 8 10 12 14 16 18 20 22 24 26 28

TARGET PT.

INTENT PT.

$S_E + \Delta E$
2 0 2 4 6 8

x

● = CLASSICAL PATH

▨ = QUANTUM PATH

— = WAVE FUNCTION (S_E) OF ACTION

--- = $S_E + \Delta E$ (PERTURBATION)

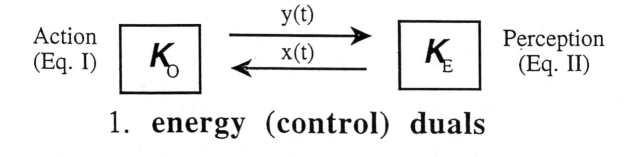

1. energy (control) duals

2. information (observation) duals

Table II: The Adjoint Operators Representation of the Perceiving-acting Cycle. Note the correspondence to Table I.

Figure 5: Emergence of the 'Knowledge Wave' within the Ω-cell. (INSERT HERE).

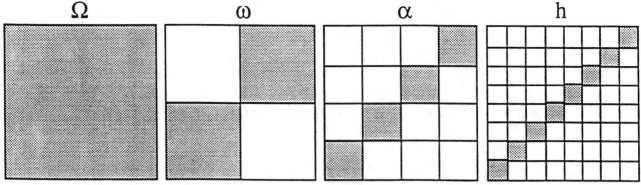

Figure 6: Showing the Range of Scales for the Weighting Function in the Feynman Path Integral.

KIND OF LAW	FORMULATION
I. Classical mechanics	$event_1$—(mechanical law)—>$event_2$
II. Classical psychology	stimulus—(association law)—>response
III. Quantum mechanics	$observation_1$—(QM law)—>$observation_2$
IV. Intentional dynamics	goal-info.—(effectivity)—>goalpath info.

Table III: A Comparison of Law Forms

Chapter 4

Psychophysics: The Self-Referent Holonomic Observer-Observed Relation

John Gyr

PSYCHOPHYSICS:

THE SELF-REFERENT HOLONOMIC OBSERVER-OBSERVED RELATION

John W. Gyr, Ph.D.

Psychiatrische Universitätsklinik

Bern, Switzerland

Abstract

At issue is the observer-observed relation, here concieved of as a quantum **self-referential** constructive reefferent-reafferent, assimilation-accommodation, or cognitive-peripheral perceptual process in which no term can be defined independently of any other. In quantum physics such self-reference can be found, for example, in the suggestion by d'Espagnat (1983) that consciousness and physical reality are like reflections in two opposed mirrors. In such a model the Cartesian duality of mind and matter is overcome.

Self-reference in perception can be dealt with by going to Pribram's (1991) **quantum mechanical brain theory**, and to quantum physical extensions thereof by Gyr or Wolf which hypothesize holonomic **interference** of a reefferent-reafferent (Gyr et al., 1979) or an assimilation-accommodation (Piaget, 1971) type.

Pribram deduces that the **spatiotemporal** constancy characterizing the perception of form as well as the transformational spectral information of global tacit perception – the »grammar« and »semantics« of figural processing – are **computed self-referentially** in quantum mechanical brain of a motorically active perceiver. This sensory perception capacity can be compared to a pinhole camera system in which there is a transformation of waves into points in space and vice versa. The camera itself remains macroscopic, however.

The holonomic extension proposed in this paper by Gyr or by Wolf (1984, 1988), based on the parallel worlds interpretation of quantum mechanics, suggests that the pinhole camera itself also is a micro system which represents the observer's motoric. It can **interfere** holonomically with the sensory in brain, thereby causing self-referentially the production of two, this time **sensorimotor mirror image** spacetime-spectral constellations – the socalled **offer** and **echo waves**. One such constellation is what could be called an **assimilation or reefference perception** system in which, as it were, the semantics of the camera and the grammar of the picture bleed-over into each other. Specifically, the spacetime information of the sensory world transforms to general motoric spectra and vice versa. The other quantum mirror image constellation evolving is an **accomodation or reafference perception** system in which spacetime structures of the motoric transform back and forth to spectral information from the sensory world. Here the grammar of the camera and the semantics of the picture bleed-over into each other.

Modulated assimilation-accommodation and reefference-reafference of the above kind define a positive number mathematically and they constitute what Wolf means by **consciousness**. They formulate a new empirical discipline: **Psychophysics**, which synthesizes the cognitive and the peripheral, mind and matter.

The bearing which Psychophysics has on chaos theory is that consciousness, as defined, may be seen as an attractor. The system assumes a closed concrete nonconscious Reality to underlie the many concretely conscious perceptual realities which latter are derivable through offer – echo wave modulation in parallel worlds. With each such modulation the supporting nonconscious Reality remains intact. There is no collapse of the wave function.

I. Introduction

Of concern are visual perception processes which are founded on a reciprocal connection existing between the observer and the observed. Selected will be those perceptual theories which zero in on the relation between reefference and reafference (e.g. Gyr et al., 1979), on cognitive and peripheral perceptual factors (Pribram, 1991), or on the relation of assimilation and accommodation (Piaget, 1971). In all three instances reference is made to the fact that perception is (motorically) active rather than passive, and that observers select and even construct their perceptual worlds while at the same time resonating to, but never purely copying, it. This is the gist of Piaget's theory, while the reefference-reafference model specifies the existence not only of inward directed reafferent feedback but also of outward going reefferent feedforward: resonance and expectation. Perception is thus conceived to be a process from the inside-out and the outside-in.

The puzzling feature of each of these theories is the apparent impossibility to define the terms in which they are stated independently of each other: accommodation and assimilation, reefference and reafference appear to be complementarities or mirror images, in a quantum theoretical sense. Given the fact that Pribram (1991) has already proposed a quantum approach to the observed, sensory part, of perception this opens up the legitimacy of the question whether the observer-observed, or the motor-sensory, relation as a whole could not also be put on a quantum mechanical footing, thereby offering the chance to resolve the complementarity of inside-out and outside-in rigorously and opening up the exciting possibility of a quantum psychophysics.

In the traditional quantum physics used by Pribram (1991) the observer's motoric is not part of a (micro) system which includes only the sensory. However, there is a newer, socalled **Parallel Worlds Interpretation** of quantum mechanics (Wolf, 1988), in which the total observer becomes part of the quantum wave. Whereas the former, traditional, theory can therefore not be a model for observer-ovserved or sensory-motor perception, the latter theory might.

Indeed, this newer quantum base to perception makes it possible to formulate the sensory-motor relation as a quantum (holonomic) interference between the sensory and the motor which, through modulation, ends in the familiar and complementary reefferent-reafferent or assimilation-accommodation constellations. These are each other's quantum mirror image and, being the terms of a product, they form a positive, measurable, mathematical number which defines consciousness. This explains why consciousness as an event does not also necessitate the collapse of the wave function (Wolf, 1984, 1988). (The meaning of holonomic is related to that of holographic, both of which will be explained later in the paper).

II. Observer-Excluded Conventional Quantum Theory: Pribram's Model for Sensory Perception

Pribram's (1991) notion of figural precessing as the computation in brain of spacetime perceptual constancies over groups of (motor produced) frequential inputs is predestined for the quantum theoretical point of view in which spacetime and frequency are central and complementary events. In the view of quantum mechanics an infinity of spacetime (form) configurations are transformable into each other on the basis of different groups of spatial frequencies. Actually, Pribram prefers talking not of frequency, which enfolds both waves and particles, but of the **spectrum** representing the sites of intersection among wave fronts of varying amplitudes.

What makes the above transformations of spacetime into spectrum and vice versa possible is the fact that, thanks to the work of Gabor (Pribram, 1991), a mathematical space has been formulated in which spacetime constrains spectral computation. It is precisely this feature which allows for the transformation in brain of form into spectral data and vice versa. The age old riddle of, on the one hand, the spatio-temporal nature of perception manifest in object constancy and, on the other, the phenomenon that the infinite variety of form has an internal semantics and membership in a family of tacid perception is elegantly solved. The first represents the world of possible energies and determinate positions; the second that of possible positions and determinate energies. Quantum theory permits unity in identity and identity in unity.

To justify using quantum theory as a model for a neuropsychology the following behavioral and neuropsychological features are stressed by Pribram. In order to have a perceptual system, central characteristics of which are described in terms of movement, motorically active perceivers must be assumed who transform their optic arrays. Moreover, there must be a **motor-sensory correspondence** if such a system is to manifest coherence. The Pribram sensorimotor perception model involves an interaction between the sensory input registered by the retina and the so-called cognitive, motor-related, components at the level of the primary visual cortex. A central part of the theory is the claim that what occurs between retina and primary visual cortex is not filtering but an operation appropriate for a neuropsychological Hilbert-space which can be regarded as the quantum mechanical reality behind the Gabor elementary function. The Hilbert-space describes for classical quantum theory the socalled collapsing of the Schroedinger wave into a particle or wave event when observation takes place. Generalizing this notion to the neuropsychological realm, Pribram states that cortical and putamen stimulation results in smaller receptive fields, whereas frontal cortex and caudate stimulation produces the opposite. In the limit the former will produce a maximum shift in the Gabor function toward the frequency/spectral coordinate, a function described in Fourier terms. In the eyes of Pribram it is thus that the brain's perceptual apparatus functions like a quantum mechanical system, a system for which perceptual constancy, as was seen, holds no great mystery.

The consideration of one further step in the Pribram argument will suffice for the present purpose. Of concern is his assumption of motor-sensory correspondence in perception which was mentioned earlier. I.e. if the motor-produced change of retinal input is to be an essential feature of the holonomic edifice, then a correspondence between the sensory system outlined above and the motor system must be presumed. Pribram handles this requirement through the notion of projections between the visual system and the precentral motor systems in brain. For the latter he also proposes spectral-spacetime encoding and cites previous work which would support such a contention (Bernstein, 1967; Pribram, Sharafat & Beekmann, 1984).

The projection of the sensory system into the motor systems and vice versa is supposed to ensure that the coordinates established in the one area are also to be found in the other. As shown in the next section, it is precisely this notion of projection which can be expanded and replaced by the idea of sensorimotor quantum interference or modulation.

To conclude, the sensory perception capacity in Pribram's theory involves fundamentally a back and forth between spectral and spatiotemporal features in a Gabor space. As such, the sensory perception capacity can be compared with a pinhole camera system in which the pinhole is the position Fourier transform of the wave information contained in the light waves, but in which the camera itself, in the traditional quantum manner, functions as a macroscopic observer, without having a motor capacity that is quantum theoretically explicitly integrated with the business of 'taking a picture'.

III. Observer-Included Quantum Theory: a Model for Sensorimotor Perception

Here the quantum nature of the somatic motor system per se (peristriate and prestriate cortices) and the theoretically rich happenings evolving out of the potential holonomic interference between motor and sensory spectral-spacetime systems within the motor-sensory couplet are considered. This interference is the main theme of the present section.

It was indicated earlier that in order to have a quantum model which includes the observer's motoric one has to switch from traditional quantum theory to the socalled Parallel Worlds Interpretation. Only in the latter does the observer become part of the quantum wave. To explain what the parallel worlds view is it should be recalled that the calculation of an electron's behavior is based on the probability which that behavior has in the pool of all potential behaviors of all electrons consti-tuting a set of (interfering) waves. In traditional wave mechanics the assumption of such waves is a purely mathematical convention. In parallel worlds theory the waves are real. In fact all of a potentially infinite number of electrons and spectra are assumed to exist in actual parallel worlds of waves which run parallel to or which interfere with each other. As actually existing systems of observer-observed interactions the events which they portray thus also take on actual, to wit, psychophysical meaning. This difference between the traditional wave mechanical and the parallel worlds approach is clearly illustrated by the following discussion.

Even within classical quantum theory, there exists a model (Cramer, 1986) of how the **observation** of quantum events comes about which does involve the modulation between two interfering waves within the Schroedinger equation. As will be seen, these two interfering wave systems can be conceptualized in terms of an interference taking place within the motor-sensory couplet as referred to above. However, Cramer does not concretize these waves psychophysically and thus remains loyal to the orthodox interpretation. Specifically, Cramer (1986) states that manifestation, observation, of spectra or spacetime occurs when hypothetical socalled past-to-future directed **offer** waves representing wave or particle possibilities interfere with and are modulated by time-inversed mirror image **echo** waves directed from future to past. As indicated, this routine creation through modulation of with-time offer waves and negative-time echo waves in classical quantum theory is actually an **ad hoc** mathematical procedure which has no intrinsic physical, let alone psychophysical meaning (Wolf, 1988).

The offer wave-echo wave scenario for the observation of spectral or of particle events, attains a special, inherently **psychophysical** sense, in which observer and observed cease to exist as independent entities, when the parallel worlds interpretation (Wolf, 1984, 1988) of quantum physics, respectively a truly self referential reefferent-reafferent or an assimilation-accommodation theory of perception based on such a model, is

111

used.

In these theories the motor system, which Pribram (1991) states is needed to produce sensory spectra and sensory spacetime constancies, interferes holonomically with the sensory system. As will be explained in detail in section IIIA, if interference is successful, the two quantum mirror image waves already discussed will occur: the offer and the echo wave. Specifically, they are mirror image hybrid **combinations** of sensory and motor waves, whereby **sensory** spacetime becomes complementarilly linked to **motor** spectra in the offer wave, and sensory spectra and motor spacetime in the echo wave.

The two events represented by the offer and echo waves are precisely what is needed to accomodate the interferential nature of the motor-sensory or reefference-reafference theory of perception of concern in this paper. To wit, the Wolf-Cramer theory really looks at perception in terms of **expectation** and of **resonance** by an active, deciding observer. That is, observation involves both feedforward and feedback. In this sense, the feedforward process from past to future is represented by the offer wave: the observer is looking for a receiver event. Time-symmetric with this is the time reversed future to past feedback or echo wave: observers are themselves receivers of peripheral events. When these two waves »shake hands« there is consciousness and the experience of NOW. This is when to imagine the future is to imagine the past, is to imagine the future..., etc.

Anticipating the yet to be given formal definition of

holonomic interference, the quantum-derived concepts defined by Pribram (1991) which were presented in Section I would suggest the offer wave to be **motor spectra** or **motor semantics** becoming linked complementarilly to 'objective' **sensory spacetime** or **sensory grammar**. As it were, the 'music' (spectra) of the motoric, through their pattern of interference, determine the spacetime nature of the sensory. (The motoric 'looks for a sensory receiver event'). It is past-to-future feedforward. This can also be thought of as semantic motor (spectral) knowledge of the spacetime sensory world and as a definition of Piagetian (1971) assimilation, (thus putting Piaget's theory on a holonomic footing). Such a quantum formulation resolves the mysteries inherent in the Piagetian idea of 'motor knowledge' (of the sensory world). It also defines reeffence or the process whereby motor events are involved in providing hypotheses about to-be-ecpected sensory signals.

On the other hand, the echo wave is the process whereby specific spatiotemporal motor acts are implicit in stored general sensory spectra or sensory semantics. The 'music' of the sensory, through its pattern of interference, determines the spacetime nature of the motoric and allows for the conclusion that »there must have been a specific preceding motor act«. Respresented here is a future-to-past feedback. The semantics of the sensory world put their stamp on actual motor behavior, and of course vice versa, which is the quantum equivalent of Piagetian **accommodation**. This also defines reafference.

Parenthetically, if the moudlation of offer and echo waves

is sucessful, and thus past-to-future and future-to-past become mirror images of each other, then there is only a relative PRESENT. This is consciousness.

The parallel-worlds interpretation of quantum physics is the only extant formal theory of the self-referential unity of the observer and the observed. Inasmuch as perception is here formulated in terms of the parallel-worlds interpretation of quantum physics, the traditional psychological debate about the greater or lesser contribution of the observer in perception is mute.

Summarizing, whereas in Pribram's case there is as it were a macroscopic pinhole camera system receiving and organizing the spectrum-to-particle-to-spectrum-to-particle transformations of its sensory input, in the sensory-motor interference case the camera interacts holonomically with the sensory input. The above will now be taken up in some technical detail.

IIIA. Traditional Holographic Interference in Quantum Physics

As indicated already, the term holonomic refers to the nature of the Gabor space (Pribram, 1991). It denotes a property of that space whereby spacetime and spectrum are both embedded in the space, such that spacetime considerations constrain spectral computation. On the other hand, for the conceptualization of holographic interference only a simpler Fourier either-or duality between spacetime and spectrum is needed. Although Pribram's (1991) and the present model assume

114

the additional complexity of the Gabor space, the holographic model for the interference within the sensory-motor couplet will, for reasons of simplicity, be presented here instead.

Any hologram can be regarded as an instance of the cross interference or addition of two or more spectrum-spacetime processes. In a conventional hologram the first wave-particle multiplication occurs when a laser beam, modified by traversing a transluscent object, strikes a photographic plate. The second, the **holographic multiplication**, takes place when the above **information wave** and a socalled **reference beam** that does not traverse the object both strike the photographic plate. In this case each wave's energy is multiplied not only by its own spatiotemporal complement but also by that of the other beam.

Because of the importance of holographic interference to everything that is to follow, the relatively simple formalism which Wolf (1984) uses to discuss the topic is introduced to enhance comprehension. Consider first the energy of the already mentioned socalled information wave, the laser beam that traverses a translucent object. It can be expressed as [IW], the brackets denoting the fact that it is represented by a complex number representing both amplitude and phase. Being an instrument of observation, the eye or photographic plate must record the energy of [IW]. As noted earlier, in quantum mechanics this is represented by the multiplication of [IW] with its spatiotemporal complement or, in the language of complex numbers, by its complex conjugate denoted by [IW]*. The latter as Wolf puts it, is the backward form, that is to say the quantum mechanical mirror image of the information wave itself. In brief, the information wave can be written as [IW] [IW]*. Similarly, the second or socalled reference wave can be written as [RW] [RW]*.

The complex number times complex conjugate number discussed above in a simplified form defines a Gabor space. It was seen already that the latter represents the back and forth between spectral events and spatiotemporal particle events. Consider this phenomenon a little bit in depth. Using the language of parallel worlds (Wolf, 1988), spectrum may be considered to result from, or to inhere in, the overlap of an infinity of seperate particle worlds thus producing a cloud or spectral event. The particle picture, on the other hand, can be imagined to inhere in an infinite overlap of possible spectrum cloud patterns. Complex number and complex conjugate number represent these two mirror image processes and when multiplied produce linked complementary spectral and particle events.

When information and reference wave interfere holographically, the multiplication of complex number with complex-conjugate number ([RW]*+[IW]*) x ([RW]+[IW]) produce the following:

$$[RW]^*[RW] + [RW]^*[IW] + [IW]^*[RW] + [IW]^*[IW]$$
term 1   term 2   term 3   term 4

III.B <u>Interference between Sensory and Motor Systems in Perception</u>

In line with the previous notation, let the sensory and the

116

motor systems be represented by [SW] [SW]* and [MW] [MW]*, respectively. Interference between the sensory and the motor system will generate products similar to the four terms computed earlier. These four terms represent four spacetime-spectrum coordinate systems. They are

$$[SW]^*[SW] + [SW]^*[MW] + [MW]^*[SW] + [MW]^*[MW]$$

    term 1   term 2   term 3   term 4

A closer inspection and comparison of terms 1 through 4 reveals the following. Terms 1 and 4 each contain a linkage of the complementarities spectrum and spacetime. Terms 1 and 4, respectively the sensory and the motor systems, are independent of each other in the interference expression above. In it the sensory is thus distinguished from the motor in the conventional way.

This picture changes radically when terms 2 and 3 are inspected and compared. The interference between the sensory and the motor system in terms 2 and 3 produces an indeterminacy between these two systems. This changes the way one has to conceptualize them, much like the indeterminancy between spacetime and frequency in traditional quantum physics changed fundamentally the picture physicists had had of the physical world.

Term 2 is the offer wave as discussed previously. In it there is a complementarity between motor spectrum and sensory spacetime characteristics. To partially repeat what was stated earlier in greater detail, infinite motor covariance or motor

117

memory or motor semantics is implicit in, and is the quantum mirror image of, the spatiotemporal sensory world. It is also a quantum translation of what Piaget (1971) must have meant by assimilation or what is meant by reefference.

Term 3 is the echo wave. In it there is a complementarity between spatiotemporal motor acts which are implicit in, or which are the quantum mirror image of, memories of sensory covariances or sensory spectra. This is the quantum equivalent of Piaget's accommodation or of reafference.

Terms 2 and 3 mirror beautifully the complex happenings occurring in observer-observed interaction. They capture the self-reference existing between motoric and sensory experiences, to the point where each looses its individual identity.

Terms 2 and 3 result from a successful modulation. To repeat, according to Wolf (1988) such a modulation or multiplication defines conscious perception. They can be said to be the forms of two Gabor processes, as defined by Pribram. They are each other's quantum mirror image. In this new domain, of what one can call psychophysics, any intrinsic separateness not only of the sensory and the motoric but also of spatiotemporal realms and of their infinite covariance disappears. The present theory attains an effective synthesis between the observer's 'subjective mind' and observed 'objective matter', a topic which is also of neuropsychological concern to Pribram (1991) but is left by him without a specific formal quantum mechanical resolution.

IV. Psychophysics and Chaos

Producing a determinable positive number — an attractor — requires consciousness, a »handshake« between a world in which the sensory has the function of a grammar against a background of motoric semantics, and a world which is its mirror image. This consciousness elicits the awareness of NOW. In principle, if all possible past to future and future to past waves were »married« to each other, a universal NOW experience would engulf the observer and all distinctions of future and past would disappear.

Quantum theoretically, those offer-echo wave systems »shake hands« and bundle into groups which have highest and high probability. They become bundles of related parallel universes.

As quantum physics states, whenever waves coincide events occur, i.e. something physical appears. But, as seen above, the sensorimotor holonomic view suggests that something intelligent, is also present, indeed something **psychophysical** or conscious occurs. Everything outside momentary parallel worlds bundles remains undifferentiated in the chaos of the vacuum. **It remains unconscious.** In all of this an observer is required.

References

Bernstein, N. (1967) **The coordination and regulation of movement.** New York: Pergamon.

Cramer, J.G. (1986) The transactional interpretation of quantum mechanics. **Review of Modern Physics,** 58 (3).

d'Espagnat, B. (1983) **Auf der Suche nach dem Wirklichen.** Berlin, Heidelberg, New York: Springer.

Gyr, J.W. (1988) Complementarities between the sensory and the motor system in holonomic sensorimotor perception theory. **Gestalt Theory,** 10 (4), 266-273.

Gyr, J.W., Willy, R. & Henry, A. (1979) Motorsensory feedback and geometry of visual space: An attempted replication. **Behavioral and Brain Sciences,** 2, 59-94.

Piaget, J. (1971) **Biology and knowledge.** Chicago: University of Chicago Press.

Pribram, K.H. (1971) **Languages of the brain.** Englewood Cliffs (N.J.): Prentice Hall.

Pribram, K.H. (1991) **Brain and perception: Holonomy and structure in figural prcessing.** Hillsdale, New Jersey: Lawrence Erlbaum.

Pribram, K.H., Sharafat, A. & Beekman, G.J. (1984) Frequency encoding in motor systems. In Whiting, H.T.A. (ed.), **Human motor actions — Bernstein reassessed.** Amsterdam: North-Holland, 121-156.

Wolf, F.A. (1984) **Star wave: mind, consciousness, and quantum physics.** New York: Macmilla.

Wolf, F.A. (1988) **Parallel universes.** New York: Simon & Schuster.

Chapter 5

Continuous Computation and the Emergence of the Discrete

Bruce MacLennan

Continuous Computation and the Emergence of the Discrete

Bruce J. MacLennan
Computer Science Department
University of Tennessee, Knoxville
`MacLennan@CS.UTK.edu`

Over many years I have searched for the point where myth and science join. It was clear to me for a long time that the origins of science had their deep roots in a particular myth, that of *invariance*.

— Giorgio de Santillana

INTRODUCTON

In this paper I'll address the emergence of the discrete from the continuous, first in mythology and psychology, then in cognitive science and artificial intelligence. This will provide a context for considering some continuous neural processes that can result in (approximately) discrete behavior.

Many traditional cosmologies begin with a separation of the primordial *massa confusa* into opposites. For example, Euripedes said,

> And the tale is not mine but from my mother, how *Ouranos* (Sky) and *Gaia* (Earth) were one form; and when they had been separated apart from each other they bring forth all things, and gave them up into the light: trees, birds, beasts, the creatures nourished by the salt sea, and the race of mortals. (fr. 484, *Melanippe the Wise*)

This separation, which is often associated with the creation of recognizable *things*, corresponds to the emergence into the world of the faculty of *discrete categorization*. With definite properties come definite things, and conversely the definiteness of things seems to depend on definite oppositions. Early philosophers enumerated many oppositions (e.g., hot/cold, dry/wet, light/dark, straight/curved, odd/even), but in myth they are often equated to the opposition most salient to all people: male/female. Thus the primordial separation creates a god and a goddess, whose subsequent union creates the world of things (though they retain their separate identities). In an editor's forward [30] Alan Watts observes that this process is reflected in an ancient series of images:

The images represent, respectively, the undifferentiated matrix, the male seed in the cosmic womb, polarization into opposites, and the cosmos as a complex system of polarities.

Discrete categories are very comfortable, for they bring a sense of security: everything either *is* or *isn't*. This is captured by Aristotle's Law of the Excluded Middle, which applies to every space that is topologically discrete: there is *nothing* in the middle, between the points of the space, and there are no matters of degree; two points are either identical or as different as they can be. It is significant that the Greek word *chaos* originally referred to a *gap* and, specifically, to the primordial gap between earth and the heavens [10]; and indeed the categorizing mind finds only chaos in the grey areas between categories.[1] The Pythagoreans were quite explicit about the role of the gap in creating discrete things, including the integers. Stobaeus reported that they said:

> The void (*kenon*) distinguishes the natures of things, since it is the thing that separates and distinguishes the successive terms in a series. This happens in the first instance in the case of numbers; for the void distinguishes their nature. (DK 58B 30)

Another traditional theme in many common accounts of creation is the efficacy of the spoken word in beginning the creation of things; this perhaps reflects the close connection between language and the conceptual faculty.

There is also an old tradition that wisdom comes with the transcending of categories. This is a familiar theme in many Eastern traditions, such as Taoism, but we also find it in the West. For example, Heraclitus recognized that categories are often relative and contextual (DK 22B 9, 13, 37, 58, 59–61). He also recognized the importance of the continuum that unifies the opposition:

> The teacher of most is Hesiod; they are sure he knows most, who did not recognize Day and Night — for they are one. (DK 22B 57)

That is, Hesiod considered the goddesses Day and Night to be different — an archetypal opposition — and failed to acknowledge their underlying unity, for they are just the extremes of a cycle [32]. Heraclitus also stressed that the *harmonia* (structure) of the world results from a flow between opposites:[2] "through opposing currents existing things are made a *harmonia*" (Diogenes Laertius 9.7). Thus, from a deeper perspective, reality is a *structured flow* rather than a discrete structure. Furthermore, the wise realize that this law governing the macrocosm applies equally to people:

> Those speaking with sense need to rely on what is common to all, as a city on its laws — and with much more reliance. For all human laws are nourished by one, the divine.[3] (DK 22B 114)

The message seems to be that we do not have a simple dichotomy between a chaotic continuum and a structure of discrete parts. The third alternative is a *structured continuum* (*harmonia*), which result from a flow between opposites. This is the law of the macrocosm, but also the law of the microcosm, that is, the principle by which an organism's behavior can move in conformity with the universal process.

Similarly, in Jungian psychological theory, the process of conscious individuation results in a personality that is "firm in its flexibility" [4]. This process corresponds to the *coniunctio oppositorum* of spiritual alchemy, which is primarily a union of male and female, but symbolically a reunification of all the opposites [8]. Thus the evolution from an initial undifferentiated state to an inflexible discrete state is superseded by a flexible reintegration of the units that preserves their differentiation. Specifically, an individualized personality requires the unification of the subconscious mind, which is intuitive, synthetic and flexible, but opaque, with the conscious mind, which is transparent, rational and analytic, but rigid. The resulting "conscious spontaneity" combines the light of the conscious mind with the intuitive flow of the unconscious, and so in alchemy it is symbolized by the "fiery water" that results from a conjunction of elemental fire

---

[1]In the Babylonian creation myth, the creation of the organized world does not begin until Enlil (the air god) creates a gap between An (Heaven) and Ki (Earth). In one scholar's reading of the text, the gap is created by an act of cognition, for it is effected by the god Mummu, whose name means "mind," "reason" or "consciousness" [29].

[2]'Harmony' is not the primary sense of ancient Greek *harmonia*, which refers to a continuous structure obtained by joining discrete parts.

[3]There is a three way pun in the Greek between "with sense" (*xun noōi*), "what is common" (*tōi xunōi*) and "laws" (*toi nomōi*) [9]. The nominalized adjectives in this translation reflect the (apparently) intentional ambiguities of Heraclitus' maxim.

(illuminating but rigid and disintegrative conscious rational thought) and elemental water (veiled but flowing and integrative subconscious intuition).

In artificial intelligence, cognitive science and epistemology, we are presently in the progress of recapitulating this evolution. The half century that ended about 1980 was the heyday of discrete knowledge representation; it showed the capabilities of symbolic cognitive models, but also their limitations. Connectionist knowledge representation, as embodied in neurocomputation, promises to fill in the gaps of discrete knowledge structures, providing flexibility while retaining differentiation and structure. That is, by allowing (approximately) discrete symbolic representations to emerge from continuous neurocomputational processes, connectionism will provide a basis for flexible symbolic processing.

In this paper I will discuss several simple, neurally plausible mechanisms by which approximately discrete structures can emerge from continuous computational processes. The goal is to better understand how brains manipulate approximately discrete symbols, as in language and logic, without losing the flexibility of the underlying neural processes.

CONTINUOUS COMPUTATION

What is Computation?

One might suppose that the answer to this question is obvious, but it becomes problematic when one looks for computation in places other than manufactured computers, such as in the brain, and one considers kinds of computation that are less familiar than digital computation, such as analog computation. Indeed, a forthcoming issue of the journal *Minds and Machines* is devoted to the question "What is Computing?" in the context of psychology and philosophy, and exhibits a variety of opinions on the matter. I'll briefly summarize my position, which is presented in more detail elsewhere [21, 26].

The meaning of "computation" is more apparent if we consider the use of the term before it became widely recognized that computers can manipulate nonnumerical data. Then, computation meant doing arithmetic by means of physical procedures. These procedures included the arrangement of written figures in tableaux (as in long division), the position of beads in an abacus or similar "digital" device, and the position of scales in a slide rule, nomograph or similar "analog" device. Here already we can see the essential characteristics of computation, which still hold.

First, the purpose of computing is to operate on *abstract objects*. Originally numbers were the only objects manipulated, but once it became apparent that computers could be used for nonnumerical computation, the manipulable abstract objects were extended to sets, sequences, tuples, Boolean (truth) values, formulas, and many other types of data. In spite of the fact that many of these data types are nonnumerical, they are *mathematical* in the sense that they are *precisely defined* and *abstract* (i.e., "formal" in the sense that they are nonmaterial).

Second, because abstractions do not exist physically, computation must be accomplished by the manipulation of physical surrogates. Examples of these surrogates are the written digits of manual arithmetic, the beads of an abacus, and physical position on a slide rule or nomograph. Even "mental computation" (e.g., mental arithmetic or algebra) displays this characteristic, though less obviously, since the digits or other signs are represented by physical states in the brain that are manipulated with little regard for their meaning (see following).

Third, computation is a mechanical procedure, which depends on reliably determinable physical properties of the surrogates (i.e. computation is "formal" in the sense that it depends on the form but not the meaning of the surrogate objects). For example, manual arithmetic can be carried out without concern for the meaning of the digits. This, of course, is the property that permits automatic computation, but even in the days before computing machinery, it allowed sophisticated calculations to be carried out by skilled, but mathematically ignorant, human "computers," who were organized in large scale parallel arrays for scientific computations and simulations.

Finally, we observe that throughout most of the history of computation, both discrete ("digital") and continuous ("analog") surrogates have been used. For example, in ancient Greece we find both the abacus (discrete) and the use of geometric devices and constructions (continuous). The recent history of computers,

124

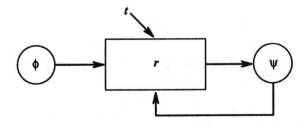

Figure 1: A Process

which has been dominated by discrete computation, biases us against continuous computation, but that is a serious mistake if our concern is computation in the brain (and probably even if our interest is limited to computer technology [12, 16, 17]).

I have argued elsewhere [26] that the difference between analog and digital computation has nothing to do with a supposed analogy, possessed by the former but not the latter, between the physical and abstract systems. On the contrary, both kinds of computation depend on a systematic correlation — an analogy — between the states and processes of the physical and abstract systems, as is explained below. For this reason I will use the terms *discrete* and *continuous* computation instead of "digital" and "analog" computation, which might be misleading.

In summary: *Computation is the physical realization of an abstract process for the purpose of manipulating abstract objects.*

Computation in General

Since computation accomplishes an abstract process through the medium of a surrogate physical process, it's necessary to say precisely what is meant by *process*. To stress the parallels between discrete and continuous computation, the definitions will be stated as far as possible in "topology-neutral terms," that is, in terms inclusive of both discrete and continuous computation.

The future behavior of a process is completely determined by its *input* (the independent variables) and its *state* (the dependent variables).[4] In the case of a discrete process the state comprises one or more variables with values chosen from discrete spaces (e.g., integers, Booleans or floating-point numbers). In the case of a continuous process, the state might be a discrete set of continuous-valued variables or a continuum of continuous values, as in a physical field (the latter actually being a special case of the former). The input to a process may be discrete or continuous in the same way as the state.[5]

The moment-to-moment behavior of a process is determined by a law that relates its state changes to the present state and input; this law is itself permitted to change in time. Specifically, let $\psi(t)$ be the state and $\phi(t)$ be the input, both at time t. Then $\psi'(t)$, the new state at time t, is given by $\psi'(t) = r[t, \psi(t), \phi(t)]$, where the state transition function r is the law determining the process (Fig. 1). For a discrete-time process, the new state is given at the next time step $\psi'(t) = \psi(t+1)$; for a continuous-time process, the new state is given at the next instant, $\psi'(t) = \psi(t+\mathrm{d}t)$. A consequence of this is that the law r takes the form of (generalized) difference equations for a discrete process and (generalized) differential equations for a continuous process.[6]

Having said what a process is, we consider what it means for a physical process to realize an abstract process. In brief a realization is a homomorphism from the physical system to the abstract system. Roughly, a realization is a systematic correspondence between the states of the two systems and between the state changes of the two systems, such that the behavior of the abstract system is recoverable from that of the physical system. I'll explain this more carefully (Fig. 2).

---

[4]For simplicity I'm restricting attention to *deterministic* processes; though nondeterministic processes are also important, they are not relevant to the present discussion.

[5]In principle, hybrid discrete/continuous systems are possible, but they are subject to restrictions imposed by other properties, such as continuity.

[6]This applies even for states containing nonnumerical variables, since generalized difference equations can be defined over any discrete space, and in this sense any digital computer program is a set of generalized difference equations [13]. Generalized differential equations can be defined over Banach spaces.

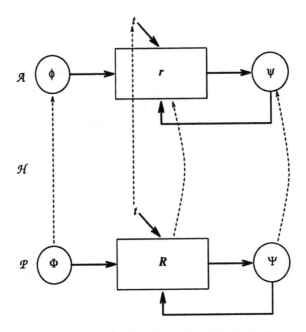

Figure 2: Physical Realization of an Abstract Process

Let $\mathcal{A}$ be an abstract (mathematical, formal) system with a transition operator $r : \mathbf{R} \times \mathcal{S} \times \mathcal{I} \to \mathcal{S}$, where $\mathcal{S}$ is the state space, $\mathcal{I}$ is the input space, and $\mathbf{R}$ is the time continuum. Similarly the physical system $\mathcal{P}$ has the transition operator $R : \mathbf{R} \times \tilde{\mathcal{S}} \times \tilde{\mathcal{I}} \to \tilde{\mathcal{S}}$. Then we say that $\mathcal{P}$ is a realization of $\mathcal{A}$ if there is a homomorphism $\mathcal{H} : \mathcal{P} \to \mathcal{A}$; a homomorphism is a mapping that preserves some, though not necessarily all, of the mapped system (see below for specifics). This is because an abstract system is an abstraction of reality, and so the abstract objects will in general have many fewer properties than real (physical) objects. Thus a homomorphism $\mathcal{H} : \mathcal{P} \to \mathcal{A}$ maps some of the physical properties of $\mathcal{P}$ into abstract properties in $\mathcal{A}$, but others, irrelevant to the computation, are ignored. To specify the homomorphism more precisely we must consider the equations of the two systems:

$$\psi'(t) = r[t, \psi(t), \phi(t)],$$
$$\Psi'(t) = R[t, \Psi(t), \Phi(t)].$$

The homomorphism $\mathcal{H} : \mathcal{P} \to \mathcal{A}$ actually comprises four homomorphisms, $\mathcal{H}_\mathrm{s} : \mathcal{S} \to \tilde{\mathcal{S}}$ on the state spaces, $\mathcal{H}_\mathrm{i} : \mathcal{I} \to \mathcal{I}$ on the input spaces, $\mathcal{H}_\mathrm{r}$ on the transition maps, and $\mathcal{H}_\mathrm{t}$ between time in the two systems, though usually the distinction is clear and the subscripts are omitted. Thus we write $\psi = \mathcal{H}\{\Psi\}$, $\phi = \mathcal{H}\{\Phi\}$ and $r = \mathcal{H}\{R\}$. Figures 3 and 4 show two simple examples of realizations.

We can now state the condition that must be satisfied for the physical system $\mathcal{P}$ to realize the abstract system $\mathcal{A}$. Since a homomorphism preserves structure,

$$\psi' = \mathcal{H}\{\Psi'\} = \mathcal{H}\{R(t, \Psi, \Phi)\} = \mathcal{H}\{R\}(\mathcal{H}\{t\}, \mathcal{H}\{\psi\}, \mathcal{H}\{\phi\}) = r(\mathcal{H}\{t\}, \mathcal{H}\{\Psi\}, \mathcal{H}\{\Phi\}).$$

That is, the mapping is a homomorphism if

$$\mathcal{H}\{\Psi'\} = r(\mathcal{H}\{t\}, \mathcal{H}\{\Psi\}, \mathcal{H}\{\Phi\}). \tag{1}$$

Notice that in Eq. 1 time in the abstract system $\mathcal{H}\{t\}$ need not correspond to time in the physical system t; if they do, $t = \mathcal{H}\{t\}$, then we have a *realtime* system. If they are not the same, then we must distinguish the "simulated time" of $\mathcal{A}$ from the time required for its realization in $\mathcal{P}$. (However, we still require $\mathcal{H}_\mathrm{t}$ to be monotonic so that time proceeds in the same direction in the abstract system and its realization.)

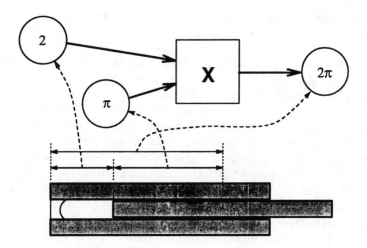

Figure 3: Realization of Continuous System

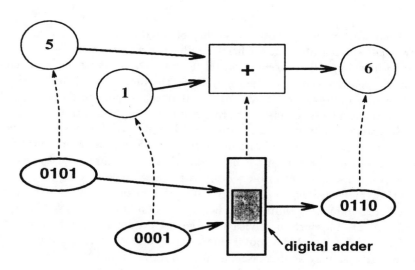

Figure 4: Realization of Discrete System

Computation in Brains

I've suggested defining computation as the physical realization of an abstract process for the purpose of manipulating abstract objects. The phrase "for the purpose of manipulating abstract objects" is essential, since every physical process is the realization of some abstract process — in fact, of many, since any mathematical model of a physical process is realized by it. Therefore it is critical that the purpose of the physical manipulations be to realize an abstract process. We may use a desktop computer for a space heater, a slide rule for a straight edge, or an abacus for a rattle, but these physical processes are not computation.[7]

By referring to purpose, the proposed definition of computation has been made inherently teleological. This is perhaps not a problem when we're dealing with manufactured devices, such as slide rules and desktop computers, for their purposes are often stated explicitly. On the other hand, if we are interested in *natural computation*, that is, computation in naturally occurring systems, such as the brain, then the teleological condition becomes problematic; certainly teleological definitions are suspect in the natural sciences.

Since my concern here is the brain, I can evade the general problem of teleological definitions and adopt a pragmatic solution, for in the context of biology the purpose and function of systems is often identifiable. We can objectively attribute purposes to hearts, lungs, stomachs, eyes without running the risk of inviting too many ghosts into our machines. So also for systems in the brain, and if a brain system can be shown to be accomplishing a basically mathematical task (i.e., an abstract process), then we may call it computational (contra Searle [26, 34]). While identifying computational brain systems is important to cognitive neuroscience, it is also central to psychological and philosophical debates about whether cognition is computation; for example, Searle has stressed that his Chinese Room Argument applies only to computational systems, and Harnad often reminds us that a robot cannot be purely computational, since it must interact with the physical world [5].

In fact I doubt there are many purely computational modules in the brain or elsewhere in organisms. Nature is far too opportunistic, it seems, to miss the chance of making a biological system serve multiple purposes.

Simulacra

A central theoretical construct underlies both the theory of (digital) computation and the use of symbolic (i.e. discrete) knowledge representation in artificial intelligence and cognitive science; it is the idea of a *calculus*, which is an idealized model of *discrete formal systems*. By isolating the essential characteristics of discrete information representation and processing systems, the idea of a calculus unifies investigations in all of these fields. I've argued elsewhere [19, 23, 24, 25] that connectionism lacks an analogous construct, and that this lack hinders our understanding of the range, limits and possibilities of connectionist knowledge representation. In an attempt to remedy this situation, I've proposed the *simulacrum* as a theoretical construct embodying the essential characteristics of *continuous* information representation and processing.

Just as a *calculus* comprises *formulas*, made of *tokens*, that are manipulated by *discrete processes* that can be defined by *rules*, so also a *simulacrum* comprises a *state*, made of *images*, that is transformed by *continuous processes* that can be defined by *graphs*. By "image" I mean, roughly, any element of a continuum, so for example, a single real number is an image, as is a vector of numbers, or a *field* (a spatially continuous distribution of numbers) [11, 14], such as a visual image. (I do not intend, however, that this term be restricted to perceptual images; it includes motor images and various internal representations, of arbitrary abstractness and complexity, so long as they are drawn from a continuum.)

In mathematics, the *graph* of a function is the set of all its input-output pairs; in the simplest case it defines a curve in two dimensions, but it could also be a more complex surface or shape. It is analogous to a rule in that, in its most basic form, it defines an input-output relation by ostension, by showing the output

---

[7]This may seem a frivolous point, but the question of whether, for example, the jostling molecules in my wall could be said to be computing, arises in the context of philosophical debate, such as Searle's Chinese Room Argument [34, 35]. Putnam has used a similar argument [33].

resulting from each input. However, just as discrete computation systems allow rules to be abbreviated and combined in various ways, so also we may abbreviate and combine graphs for continuous computation.

We have identified a number of postulates satisfied by all simulacra, which we list here for completeness (detailed discussions and justifications can be found elsewhere [19, 24]):

Postulate 1 *All image spaces are path-connected metric spaces.*

Postulate 2 *All image spaces are separable and complete.*

Postulate 3 *Maps between image spaces are continuous.*

Postulate 4 *Formal processes in simulacra are continuous functions of time and process state.*

Postulate 5 *Interpretations of simulacra are continuous.*

For the purposes of this paper, an intuitive understanding of simulacra is sufficient.

INVARIANCES

Behavioral Invariances

As suggested by de Santillana's remark, which heads this paper, the concept of *invariance* is fundamental to science.[8] It is also the basis for our perception of a world of stable objects [31, Ch. 5], since the parts of an object retain an invariant relation to one another under transformations, such as rotation and translation, but their relations to the background are not invariant. Invariance also underlies category or concept formation, since we can say that an organism recognizes a category when it responds invariantly to all individuals belonging to that category.[9] For example, if a monkey, when hungry, always responds to a banana by eating it, then we can say that it recognizes the category *banana* (in the context of being hungry). Because the notion of invariance is so important, in this section I will characterize it in general terms, appropriate to continuous knowledge representation, and in the next section I'll consider several simple, biologically plausible mechanisms by which organisms can extract invariances from their environments.

I will be defining "invariance" in terms of the input-output behavior of a system. The goal of these definitions will be questions such as: In what ways can I transform the input to the system, but leave its output invariant? If I transform the input to a system in certain ways, is there a corresponding transformation of the output? The resulting definitions are *behavioral*, but they are not *behavioristic*. First, the system whose input-output behavior is in question need not be an entire organism. For example, we might consider the translation or scale invariance of a particular module in the visual system. Nevertheless, I think it is important to ground cognitive terms, such as *category* or *concept*, in the behavior of the whole organism in its natural environment (i.e. an ecological approach), and many of my examples will relate to an organism's behavior, since they are easier to understand. Thus I may take as an example of invariant behavior: "if a hungry monkey sees a banana (any banana) at location $\mathbf{x}$ in its visual field, then it responds by grabbing the banana at $\mathbf{x}$."

The preceding example illustrates that invariance may depend on the history, or prior state, of the system. (If the monkey isn't hungry, it may not grab the banana.) In the context of our general model of processes (Fig. 1), we must take account of invariance in the face of variation of the internal state as well as variation of the input. In these cases, the transition function of the process (r in Fig. 1) will be treated as a system without memory (state), since this simplifies the analysis, but does not limit its applicability to the more general case. Since in such a case the "input" to the transition function $S(\psi, \phi)$ comprises both the internal state of the system ψ and the input proper ϕ, I will use the term *cause* to refer to the current state/input

---

[8] As also suggested by his remark, invariance is a *myth*: that is, although it's not literally true, it contains an important truth.

[9] Mathematicians may be confused by my use of the term *category*, which, throughout this paper, will refer to a psychological construct also known as a *concept* or *universal*. Some of the objects discussed here will be mathematical categories, but that's coincidental.

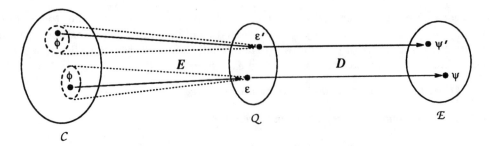

Figure 5: Factoring the Transition Map

pair (ψ, ϕ), since this comprises (by hypothesis) everything that can affect the future state of the system. Similarly, I will call the "output" of $S(\psi, \phi)$ its *effect*, since it comprises the new state as well as whatever external behavior (output proper) the system exhibits. Thus we will be considering invariances in maps $S : \mathcal{C} \to \mathcal{E}$ from a space $\mathcal{C}$ of causes to a space $\mathcal{E}$ of effects.

An invariance rarely holds over the entire space of causes to a system. For example, a hungry monkey may in general respond to a banana in a way that is invariant with the size of the banana image, but there must be limits to this scale invariance, since too small an image will not be visible, and too large an image will not be recognizable as a banana (the visual field will be filled with yellow). Thus we must in general specify some *range* $\mathcal{R}$ of causes over which an invariance holds. In actual practice it may be very difficult to describe the range of an invariance, but for theoretical purposes all we need to know is that the invariance holds over some $\mathcal{R} \subseteq \mathcal{C}$.[10]

Effect Equivalence

The simplest invariance is when certain changes to the cause leave the effect unchanged. For example, we might suppose that a mouse flees whenever it sees a cat, but that changes in the color or size of the cat do not alter its response. In formal terms, the cause may be changed from φ to φ' but the effect ψ remains the same, $S(\varphi) = \psi = S(\varphi')$. Looked at the other way, we can ask what class of causes results in a given effect. Thus, for each effect ψ there is a class of causes φ such that $S(\varphi) = \psi$ (in mathematical terms, this class in the *inverse image* of the effect, $S^{-1}[\psi]$), and so each effect (in the range under consideration) has an associated *effect-equivalence class* of causes. Thus there is a basic category structure observable in the behavior of every system (though some of the categories might be singleton, i.e., contain only one cause). The effect-equivalence classes represent categories of causes that differ only in behaviorally irrelevant properties (in the range under consideration).

By a well-known theorem in mathematics, any function $S : \mathcal{C} \to \mathcal{E}$ can be "factored" into a composition of two functions, $S = D \circ E$ (Fig. 5). The first function, $E : \mathcal{C} \to \mathcal{Q}$, maps causes into their effect-equivalent classes, or into any other space in a one-to-one relation with these classes (e.g., a space of "symbols" for the classes[11]). This intermediate space is called the *quotient space*, $\mathcal{Q}$. The second map, $D : \mathcal{Q} \to \mathcal{E}$, takes an effect-equivalence class (or its surrogate) into the corresponding effect, so $S(\varphi) = D[E(\varphi)]$. Because the equivalence map E eliminates all effect-irrelevant differences, the effect-map D establishes a one-to-one relation between equivalence classes and their effects (since, by construction, no two effect-equivalence classes have the same effect).

The effect-equivalence classes constitute the most basic invariance in the behavior of a system. It can, in principle, be determined by observing the cause-effect relationships of the system, though in practice we can get only an approximation, since determining the entire invariance would require observing an infinite number of cause-effect pairs. In principle, however, we do not have to look inside the system to discover this invariance. The quotient space would seem to be an ideal locus for understanding the emergence of

---

[10]Furthermore, continuity requires that $\mathcal{R}$ have an indefinite boundary; that is, although the invariance holds absolutely within $\mathcal{R}$, it must also hold approximately for causes arbitrarily near to $\mathcal{R}$ but outside of it. This topic is addressed later.

[11]Note, however, that this space of "symbols" must be a continuum (if it has more than one point), since it is the continuous image of a continuum (by the simulacra postulates). Thus any such surrogates for the effect-equivalence classes are not symbols in the familiar, discrete sense.

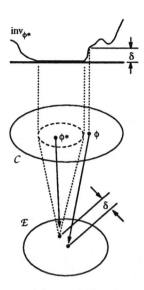

Figure 6: Indefinite Effect-equivalence

invariances through self-organization.

By definition, all causes within a effect-equivalence class lead to the same effect. However, since all maps on simulacra are required to be continuous (by postulates 3 and 4), we know that there are causes outside of the equivalence class whose effects are arbitrarily close to those inside (Fig. 6). Thus it is more accurate to think of effect-equivalence classes as having indefinite boundaries, and to think of invariance as a matter of degree rather than an absolute property. Thus:

Definition The *indefinite equivalence class* of a cause φ^* is:

$$\mathrm{inv}_{\varphi^*}(\varphi) = \delta[S(\varphi^*), S(\varphi)],$$

where δ is the metric (distance measure) on the effect-space.

Thus inv_{φ^*} will be 0 for all members of the (definite) effect-equivalence class of φ^*, for which the invariance is absolute, and will increase gradually as behavior becomes non-invariant outside the effect-equivalence class.[12] Quantifying the degree of invariance is important when addressing the emergence of invariant behavior through adaptation and learning, since the invariances appear gradually.[13] Nevertheless, the following discussion is couched in terms of absolute invariance, since the extension to degrees of invariance is straight-forward.

Transform Invariance and Object Perception

An especially important kind of invariance occurs when a system responds the same to a stimulus in spite of it being transformed in some systematic way. For example, a banana may be recognized as a banana in spite of its image being rotated, translated and scaled. Also a melody may be recognized even though it has been changed in absolute pitch. Invariance under various kinds of transforms is the basis for our perception of stable *objects* in the world [31, Ch. 5]. For example, contextual information may allow a monkey to reliably select the larger of two objects regardless of their relative placement, and hence the relative size of their retinal images [38]. Such an instance of *size constancy* shows that the animal is perceiving absolute size, which is a property of the object itself as opposed to its appearance (sensory image). A complex of

---

[12]Note that inv_{φ^*} is analogous to a fuzzy set, though for the usual fuzzy sets the membership function is 1 for full members and decreases to 0 as their membership decreases. There are a several simple ways, which are described elsewhere [25], for converting our indefinite equivalence class into a standard fuzzy set.

[13]Other traditionally absolute mathematical properties, such as being a group or being orthogonal, must also be redefined as matters of degree, so that we may, for example, discuss the gradual emergence of orthogonality or group structure.

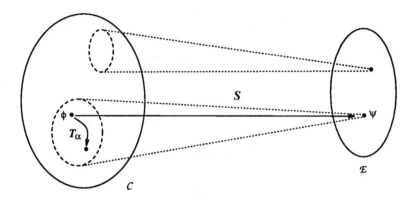

Figure 7: Transform Invariance

properties invariant under transformation is what constitutes a collection of phenomena as a perceptual *entity*. Different classes of transformations lead to different kinds of entities. For example, invariance under rigid body transformations, such as translations, rotations and scalings, leads to perception of physical objects. Invariance under absolute pitch transformation leads to perception of melodies, for a melody (as opposed to an absolute pitch sequence) can be defined as that entity that is invariant under change in absolute pitch.

We will consider transformations mapping causes into causes, which depend, in most cases, on a parameter that controls the change effected by the transform. For example, a rotation has a scalar parameter determining the angle of rotation, and a translation has a vector parameter determining the direction and distance of translation. I'll write $T_\alpha(\varphi)$ for a transformation, of type T (e.g. translation) and parameter α, applied to cause φ. In accord with postulate 3 of simulacra, $T_\alpha(\varphi)$ is required to be continuous in both α and φ. Observe that the parameter often varies in time, $\alpha = \alpha(t)$, as the organism moves, thus generating a continuous trajectory $T_{\alpha(t)}(\varphi)$, which is a rich source of information for separating entities from the environment [31, pp. 93–98]. *Variation is necessary to detect invariance.*

My present goal is to characterize transform invariant behavior, without any discussion of mechanisms for achieving it or by which it may emerge. Possible mechanisms by which a system could develop transform invariances, and thus come to perceive a class of entities, will be presented later ("Self-organization").

> **Definition** A system S is *invariant with respect to transformation T*, or *T-invariant*, whenever, for each allowable cause φ, the set of all allowable transforms of it, $T_\alpha(\varphi)$, are effect-equivalent for S (Fig. 7).

Therefore, for all allowable φ and α,

$$S[T_\alpha(\varphi)] = S(\varphi).$$

(As usual, invariances cannot in general be expected to be universal, so we must specify some range over which the invariance holds. Also, although a system may be simultaneously invariant under several kinds of transforms T_α, U_β, ..., for simplicity I'll consider just one.)

We can get additional insight into transform invariance by factoring S in the same way we did before (Fig. 8). The effect-equivalence classes $\varepsilon = E(\varphi)$ capture all aspects of the causes that are relevant to behavior, and discard all aspects that are not. This is accomplished by the equivalence map E which identifies all behaviorally-indistinguishable causes, thus abstracting only what is relevant to behavior, which is represented by the members of Q. It remains for the second part of the system to map, one for one, these behaviorally relevant abstractions to their effects, $D(\varepsilon) = \psi = S(\varphi)$.

When this analysis is applied to a transform invariant system (Fig. 8), we see that, within the allowable range, E "projects out" all of the effects of the transforms, and passes on the constant entity representing all transformed causes. That is, if $\varepsilon = E(\varphi)$, then for all allowable α, $E[T_\alpha(\varphi)] = \varepsilon$. Thus the elements $\varepsilon \in Q$ represent the entities recognized by the system: those and just those aspects of the causes that are constant under the transformations and affect the behavior of the system. For example, suppose a moderately hungry monkey responds to ripe fruit by smacking its lips, to unripe fruit by wrinkling its nose, and to other things by ignoring them. Then, for stimuli in the appropriate range, the space Q will represent only the fruitness

132

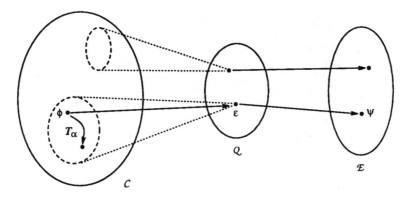

Figure 8: Factored Transform-invariant System

and ripeness of the stimuli, since all other characteristics, including the location, size, orientation, and kind of the fruit, are discarded by the equivalence map E. As a result, an entity $\varepsilon \in Q$ is an abstraction representing a particular degree of fruitness and ripeness.

Since the "entity space" Q is the nexus of the system's behavior, we might expect that this behavior can be described by rules expressed in terms of the entities $\varepsilon \in Q$. This can be done, but only to a limited degree. To see the method, pick an abstract entity $\varepsilon \in Q$. We know that the effect-map D yields a unique effect $\psi = D(\varepsilon)$ for this entity and for just this entity. Further suppose that, over some range, S is T-invariant; thus, if φ is any cause corresponding to ε, then we know that all of its allowable transforms, $T_\alpha(\varphi)$, also correspond to ε. As a consequence, the following rule expresses the behavior of S on all the transforms of φ:

$$T_\alpha(\varphi) \Rightarrow \psi.$$

We can interpret the rule as follows: "If the cause matches $T_\alpha(\varphi)$ for some α (in the appropriate range), then produce the effect ψ."

We cannot assume that the above rule expresses the behavior of the system S over the entire equivalence class leading to ψ, since S may be invariant with respect other properties besides T. However, if it is invariant to only T, or, equivalently, if all the members of the effect-equivalence class are mutually transformable via T, then the above rule completely captures the behavior of S on that equivalence class, and we call it *the rule corresponding to ε*. In this case the cause φ is said to *generate* the entire equivalence class.

Rules are normally expected to be finite in size, and this will be the case provided that the transform T and applicable range of parameters α are understood. Then the rule can be completely specified by exhibiting the particular concrete image φ, a generative cause, and ψ, the corresponding effect. For example, if we understand $\mathsf{rotate}_\theta(\varphi)$ to rotate φ counterclockwise by θ, then the behavior of mapping a square, in any orientation, to a circle, is completely and finitely specified by the rule:

$$\mathsf{rotate}_\theta(\square) \Rightarrow \bigcirc.$$

The question now arises of whether the behavior of a system that is only T-invariant can be completely specified by a finite sequence of rules of the form $T_\alpha(\varphi_k) \Rightarrow \psi_k$. Each such rule completely expresses the behavior of the system over an equivalence class, but it's easy to see that these rules cannot capture all of the system's behavior. This is because the quotient space Q is a continuum (since it is the continuous image of the image space C, which is a continuum by postulates 1 and 2), and so there is an uncountable number of $\varepsilon \in Q$. Since all these ε are necessary to the behavior of S, no finite number of rules, nor even a countably infinite number of rules, corresponding to these ε can suffice to express S. The rules accurately describe the behavior of the system over their corresponding equivalence classes, but they say nothing about its behavior on the rest of the space. On the other hand, just as an irrational number can be approximated arbitrarily closely by fractions, so also (by postulate 2) the behavior of S can be approximated arbitrarily closely by longer and longer lists of rules.

This result, which shows the irreducibility of a continuous process to rules, corresponds to observations of expert behavior, which cannot be completely captured by finite rules; situations falling in the "cracks

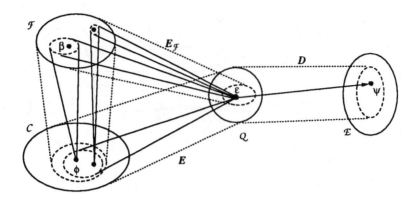

Figure 9: Structural Invariance with One Component

between the rules" are either unspecified, or must be filled in by some arbitrary — and ultimately inexpert — interpolation rule [3].

Structural Invariance

Our analysis so far has treated causes and effects as wholes. Therefore, the entities in the quotient space are likewise abstractions of the entire cause, which reflect behavior invariant with respect to any change in the cause. For example, if we think of the system as an animal, then a cause φ comprises all of the stimulus and the animal's internal state, and the corresponding entity $\varepsilon = E(\varphi)$ is treated as an indivisible abstraction of the stimulus + state, which is the unique abstraction corresponding to its effect.

Although this approach captures the holistic character of an animal's response to the current situation, it's often illuminating to analyze behavior in terms of one or more components of the cause. For example, we might take the stimulus to comprise two figures, a banana and a tree, and the ground on which they appear. Then we would consider invariances with respect to changes in the particulars of the banana as an independent component of the cause. Likewise, we might analyze the internal state as a feeling of hunger on a background of other internal perceptions, and consider invariances with respect to just this component of the state. We would expect such behavior to be describable in terms of abstractions, such as *banana* and *hunger* corresponding to the components of the cause, and abstract relations among these components. In other words, the cause may be analyzed into a number of components in some relation to one another, in which case the entities and effects might be similarly analyzed. In this section, I'll consider the general approach to these *structural invariances*.

Suppose $\beta \in \mathcal{F}$ is concrete image, say, a banana image, and $C : \mathcal{F} \to \mathcal{C}$ is a map that puts a figure on a specific ground, so $C(\beta)$ is a complete cause, which includes β as a component. Factor the system map as before, $S = D \circ E$, where $E : \mathcal{C} \to \mathcal{Q}$ and $D : \mathcal{Q} \to \mathcal{E}$. Now define $E_{\mathcal{F}} : \mathcal{F} \to \mathcal{Q}$, a map from figures to entities, by $E_{\mathcal{F}} = E \circ C$. Each entity $E_{\mathcal{F}}(\beta)$ abstracts all and just the characteristics of the figure β that, in the context provided by C, influence the effect; the corresponding equivalence class of particular figures is $E_{\mathcal{F}}^{-1}[\varepsilon]$ (Fig. 9).

Notice that the same space $\mathcal{Q}$ accommodates the abstractions of the figures in $\mathcal{F}$ and the causes in $\mathcal{C}$. This is because, for a fixed ground or context, the 1-1 relation between abstract figures and effects corresponds to the 1-1 relation between abstract causes and effects. Since the entities in $\mathcal{Q}$ are completely abstract, they may be thought of as abstract figures or abstract causes, as we like, though the figure equivalence map $E_{\mathcal{F}}$ may not be capable of generating all the entities in $\mathcal{Q}$. For example, suppose that, in a given context, a certain monkey will smack its lips at a banana but wrinkle its nose at a mango. Then, if $C(\beta)$ is the operation of putting a particular piece of fruit in this context, then the entities in $\mathcal{Q}$ generated by the figure equivalence map $E_{\mathcal{F}}$ correspond to the abstractions *banana* and *mango* (and all the borderline cases in between), and the corresponding effect-equivalence classes $E_{\mathcal{F}}^{-1}[\varepsilon]$ in $\mathcal{F}$ are classes of particular pieces of fruit. These same entities in $\mathcal{Q}$ may be viewed as abstractions of complete causes including the fruit as a component, and the corresponding effect-equivalence classes $E^{-1}[\varepsilon]$ in $\mathcal{C}$ are classes of complete particular causes. There may

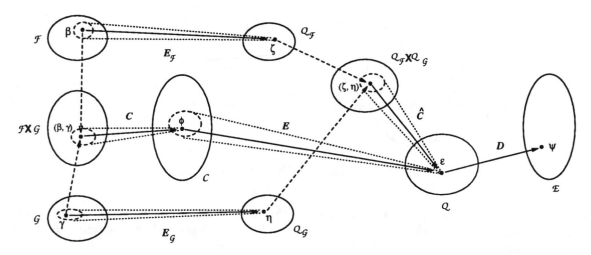

Figure 10: Structural Invariance with Two Components

also be entities $\varepsilon \in Q$ with corresponding equivalence classes $E^{-1}[\varepsilon]$ of causes that are not results of $C(\beta)$, and so do not have corresponding classes of figures.

Commonly, structural invariances involve two or more components of the cause, for example, behavior may be invariant to changes in several figures, or to changes in the background as well as the figures. We'll consider the case of structural invariances involving two components, and the general case will be clear.

Suppose that $\beta \in \mathcal{F}$ and $\gamma \in \mathcal{G}$ are two images, which might correspond to two components of a cause, or to a figure and ground within a cause. Next consider any function $C : \mathcal{F} \times \mathcal{G} \to \mathcal{C}$, which assembles the components β and γ into a cause $C(\beta, \gamma)$. For example, if β is a particular banana image and γ is a particular background image, then $C(\beta, \gamma)$ might place them in a particular context (e.g., relative position) to yield a composite image of that banana on that background.

Our goal then is to characterize the invariant behavior of a system $S : \mathcal{C} \to \mathcal{E}$ in terms of equivalence classes of images in $\mathcal{F}$ and $\mathcal{G}$. To accomplish this, define two quotient classes $Q_\mathcal{F}$ and $Q_\mathcal{G}$ as follows: define two images $\beta, \beta' \in \mathcal{F}$ to be effect-equivalent provided that they always yield the same effect, that is, for all allowable $\gamma \in \mathcal{G}$, $S[C(\beta, \gamma)] = S[C(\beta', \gamma)]$. Then, as before, let $Q_\mathcal{F}$ be the space of all such equivalence classes (or any surrogates in a 1-1 relation to them), and let $E_\mathcal{F} : \mathcal{F} \to Q_\mathcal{F}$ be the equivalence map from a particular figure β to the abstraction $E_\mathcal{F}(\beta)$ representing all and just those properties that can influence the effect $S[C(\beta, \gamma)]$. Thus, if S is a monkey who responds invariantly to banana images in any context, then the equivalence class corresponding to this response will be an abstraction of all banana images, independent of their context. Exactly the same construction can be applied to $\mathcal{G}$, yielding a corresponding effect-equivalence space $Q_\mathcal{G}$ and equivalence map $E_\mathcal{G} : \mathcal{G} \to Q_\mathcal{G}$.

One might suppose that the abstract causes in Q correspond one-to-one with pairs of abstraction in $Q_\mathcal{F} \times Q_\mathcal{G}$, but this is not to case. To see why, suppose that a monkey grabs a banana if it's either on a tree or a dish, but grabs a mango only if it's on a tree. Since the response to bananas is sometimes different from that for mangos, both abstractions must be in $Q_\mathcal{F}$; likewise, since the response to things in trees and in dishes differ, they must be distinct members of $Q_\mathcal{G}$. Therefore, the abstract space $Q_\mathcal{F} \times Q_\mathcal{G}$ must represent (at least) the four possibilities: banana/tree, banana/dish, mango/tree and mango/dish. Nevertheless, three of these combinations map to the same effect. Therefore, to describe the behavior of the system in terms of the abstractions in $Q_\mathcal{F}$ and $Q_\mathcal{G}$ it's necessary to have a second map $\hat{C} : Q_\mathcal{F} \times Q_\mathcal{G} \to Q$ which maps pairs of abstract components into the corresponding abstract causes (Fig. 10). It turns out that such a map always exists; the effect of $\hat{C}(\varepsilon, \eta)$, for $\zeta \in Q_\mathcal{F}$ and $\eta \in Q_\mathcal{G}$, is equivalent to (1) replacing the abstractions ζ and η by any concrete instances β and γ, such that $E_\mathcal{F}(\beta) = \zeta$ and $E_\mathcal{G}(\gamma) = \eta$, (2) composing these into a concrete cause $\varphi = C(\beta, \gamma)$, and (3) finding the corresponding abstract cause, $\varepsilon = E(\varphi)$.[14]

In summary, if some or all of the causes in $\mathcal{C}$ are a result of a mapping on the images of component spaces $\mathcal{F}_1, \ldots, \mathcal{F}_n$, then there are corresponding abstract spaces $Q_1, \ldots, Q_n$, which represent all and just the

_____

[14]Mathematically, $\hat{C} = S \circ C \circ (F_\mathcal{F} \times F_\mathcal{G})$, where $F_\mathcal{F} : Q_\mathcal{F} \to \mathcal{F}$ is any right-inverse of $E_\mathcal{F}$, and $F_\mathcal{G} : Q_\mathcal{G} \to \mathcal{G}$ is any right-inverse of $E_\mathcal{G}$. By definition of Q, the choice of right-inverses does not alter $\hat{C}$.

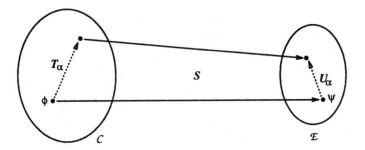

Figure 11: (T_α, U_α)-Transformation-Preserving Behavior

distinctions of the component spaces that can influence the effect. There is also an operation $\hat{C}$ which takes n-tuples of these entities into the corresponding effect-equivalence classes, which determine the system's behavior. Thus the behavior can be described at the abstract level (provided we know the corresponding equivalence classes).

Transformation-Preserving Systems

Next we consider invariances in which there is a systematic relationship between variations in the causes and effects. For example, a monkey may respond to a banana at a particular location in its visual field by reaching toward a *corresponding* location in its motor field. More precisely, in *transformation-preserving systems* the effect is not invariant under changes to the cause; rather the effect varies systematically with variation of the cause. What is invariant is the *relationship* between between transformations of the cause and transformations of the corresponding effect. In this sense it is a higher order of invariance than those hitherto considered. For example, if α is a vector in space, then T_α might be the scaling and translation of a visual image that results from moving the corresponding object. Likewise U_α might be the corresponding change in joint positions to reach an object whose position has been changed by α.

> **Definition**   Suppose, as usual, that $S : C \to \mathcal{E}$ is the system under consideration. Further suppose that for $\alpha \in \mathcal{P}$ a parameter space, $T_\alpha : C \to C$ is a transformation on the cause space, and $U_\alpha : \mathcal{E} \to \mathcal{E}$ is a transformation on the effect space. We say S is (T_α, U_α)-*transformation preserving*, or (T_α, U_α)-*preserving*, provided, for all allowable parameters $\alpha \in \mathcal{P}$ and causes $\varphi \in C$,

$$S[T_\alpha(\varphi)] = U_\alpha[S(\varphi)]. \tag{2}$$

See Fig. 11, which depicts (T_α, U_α)-preserving behavior.

The transformations T_α are an algebra under composition, that is, they are a set having some algebraic structure when their actions are combined. For example, translations form a commutative group, since (1) translations can be done in any order ($T_\alpha \circ T_\beta = T_\beta \circ T_\alpha$), (2) there is an identity translation ($T_0(\varphi) = \varphi$), (3) each translation has an inverse translation ($T_\alpha \circ T_{-\alpha} = T_0$), and (4) translation is associative ($T_\alpha \circ [T_\beta \circ T_\gamma] = [T_\alpha \circ T_\beta] \circ T_\gamma$). (Indeed, any set of transformations closed under composition is a monoid, i.e., satisfies properties 2 and 4.) Similarly, rotation and scaling are commutative groups, the most common algebraic structure. From this perspective we can interpret Eq. 2 in a different way, since it implies a relation between the algebraic structures of the cause and effect transformations. For example, from the commutativity of the cause transformation ($T_\alpha \circ T_\beta = T_\beta \circ T_\alpha$) and Eq. 2 we can conclude

$$U_\alpha \circ U_\beta \circ S = U_\beta \circ U_\alpha \circ S. \tag{3}$$

We *cannot* conclude from this that the effect transformation is commutative ($U_\alpha \circ U_\beta = U_\beta \circ U_\alpha$), but Eq. 3 tells us that the effect transformation is commutative on those effects that can be produced by the system. This is reasonable, since Eq. 2 does not in any way constrain the behavior of U_α on elements of $\mathcal{E}$ not generated by S. This is an example of the *directly induced algebraic structure* of the effect transformations.

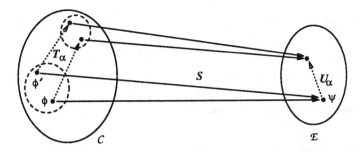

Figure 12: Equivalence Preserving Transformation

Conversely, if the effect transformations commute ($U_\alpha \circ U_\beta = U_\beta \circ U_\alpha$), then we can conclude that

$$S \circ T_\alpha \circ T_\beta = S \circ T_\beta \circ T_\alpha,$$

which does not say that the cause transformations commute, but that the system's behavior is invariant under any differences that result from commuting the cause transformations T_α and T_β. This is an example of the *inversely induced algebraic structure* of the cause transformations. Analogous results hold for other algebraic properties, such as associativity and the existence of identity and inverse transformations.

In the preceding cases we defined, for given cause transformations T_α and effect transformations U_α, what it means for a system to be (T_α, U_α)-transformation preserving, and we saw the conditions under which algebraic properties of the cause transformations are induced in the effect transformations, and vice versa. Now we consider the conditions under which a cause transformation T_α induces an effect transformation U_α such that a system is (T_α, U_α)-preserving, and conversely the conditions under which an effect transformation U_α induces a cause transformation T_α such that a system is (T_α, U_α)-preserving. To this end we will need the following definition:

> **Definition (Equivalence preserving)** For a system $S : \mathcal{C} \to \mathcal{E}$, a transformation $T_\alpha : \mathcal{C} \to \mathcal{C}$ is *S-equivalence preserving* if, for all allowable causes $\varphi, \varphi' \in \mathcal{C}$ and all allowable transformation parameters $\alpha \in \mathcal{P}$, $S(\varphi) = S(\varphi')$ implies $S[T_\alpha(\varphi)] = S[T_\alpha(\varphi')]$.

In other words, if two causes are indistinguishable to the system, then their transformations must also be indistinguishable (Fig. 12). For example, a transformation that magnifies an unnoticeable difference into a noticeable difference would not be preserved by the system, which loses essential information.

It will also be useful to define a generalized notion of an inverse mapping:

> **Definition (Effective Inverse)** Let $S : \mathcal{C} \to \mathcal{E}$ be any mapping, and factor it as usual into a surjection (onto-map) $E : \mathcal{C} \to \mathcal{Q}$ and an injection (1-1 map) $D : \mathcal{Q} \to \mathcal{E}$ such that $S = D \circ E$. Let $C : \mathcal{E} \to \mathcal{Q}$ be any left-inverse of D and let $F : \mathcal{Q} \to \mathcal{C}$ be any right-inverse of E; that is, $C \circ D = $ I and $E \circ F = $ I); these are guaranteed to exist. Then the *effective inverse of S* (relative to C and F) is $S^\star = F \circ C$.

An effective inverse satisfies the following properties (readers may notice some similarities to the Moore-Penrose pseudoinverse):

$$\begin{aligned} S \circ S^\star \circ S &= S, \\ S^\star \circ S \circ S^\star &= S^\star. \end{aligned}$$

That is, $S^\star \circ S$ is an "effective identity" for domain elements of S, and $S \circ S^\star$ is an "effective identity" for the range elements of S.

> **Proposition (Forward-induced Transformation)** For any system $S : \mathcal{C} \to \mathcal{E}$, if the cause transformation $T_\alpha : \mathcal{C} \to \mathcal{C}$ is S-equivalence preserving, then S is (T_α, U_α)-transformation preserving for $U_\alpha = S \circ T_\alpha \circ S^\star$, where $S^\star$ is any effective inverse of S.

Proof: It is necessary to show that for all allowable φ and α, $S[T_\alpha(\varphi)] = U_\alpha[S(\varphi)]$. By hypothesis,

$$U_\alpha[S(\varphi)] = S\left(T_\alpha\{S^\star[S(\varphi)]\}\right) = S[T_\alpha(\varphi')],$$

where $\varphi' = S^\star[S(\varphi)]$ is some φ' such that $S(\varphi') = S(\varphi)$. Therefore, since T_α is S-equivalence preserving, $S[T_\alpha(\varphi')] = S[T_\alpha(\varphi)]$. Hence, $U_\alpha[S(\varphi)] = S[T_\alpha(\varphi)]$. $\Box$

Thus, "well behaved" transformations of the cause space induce corresponding transformations on the effect space.

Proposition (Backward-induced Transformation) For any system $S : \mathcal{C} \to \mathcal{E}$ and effect transformation $U_\alpha : \mathcal{E} \to \mathcal{E}$, the system S is (T_α, U_α)-transformation preserving for $T_\alpha = S^\star \circ U_\alpha \circ S$, where $S^\star$ is any effective inverse of S. Further, T_α is S-equivalence preserving.

Proof: It is is required to show $S[T_\alpha(\varphi)] = U_\alpha[S(\varphi)]$ for all allowable φ and α. By hypothesis,

$$S[T_\alpha(\varphi)] = S\left(S^\star\{U_\alpha[S(\varphi)]\}\right).$$

Let $\psi = U_\alpha[S(\varphi)]$, so $S[T_\alpha(\varphi)] = S[S^\star(\psi)]$. By definition $S^\star(\psi)$ is some φ' such that $S(\varphi') = \psi$. Therefore,

$$S[T_\alpha(\varphi)] = S(\varphi') = \psi = U_\alpha[S(\varphi)].$$

Next it is required to show that T_α is S-equivalence preserving. Therefore suppose $S(\varphi) = S(\varphi')$. Observe:

$$
\begin{aligned}
S[T_\alpha(\varphi)] &= S\left(S^\star\{U_\alpha[S(\varphi)]\}\right)\\
&= S\left(S^\star\{U_\alpha[S(\varphi')]\}\right)\\
&= S(\varphi''),
\end{aligned}
$$

where $\varphi'' = S^\star\{U_\alpha[S(\varphi')]\}$ is some φ'' such that $S(\varphi'') = U_\alpha[S(\varphi')]$. Hence,

$$S[T_\alpha(\varphi)] = U_\alpha[S(\varphi')] = S[T_\alpha(\varphi')],$$

since S is (T_α, U_α)-transformation preserving. $\Box$

Thus *any* transformation on the effect space will induce a corresponding "well behaved" transformation on the cause space.

SELF-ORGANIZATION

Emergence of Discrete from Continuous

Discrete knowledge representation and processing systems are (superficially, at least) very good at manipulating mathematical and logical formulas, and similar discrete structures, according to precise rules; they have been less successful at subsymbolic processes, such as perception, recognition, association, control and sensorimotor coordination. In contrast, connectionist approaches are well-suited to subsymbolic tasks, but there has been doubt about how well they can operate at the symbolic level. This naturally suggests hybrid architectures, with symbolic tasks accomplished by discrete (digital) computation and subsymbolic tasks by continuous (analog) computation.

This is not the way the brain works, however, for in the brain discrete, symbolic processes emerge from underlying continuous, subsymbolic processes. There is reason to believe that this is not just an accident of biological intelligence, but that this underlying continuity imparts to the emergent symbolic processes the flexibility characteristic of human symbol use [16, 17]. The problem is then to understand how approximately discrete representations and processes can emerge from continuous representations and processes.

It is an oversimplification to treat language as a discrete system. For example, although we accept the space between written words without question, anyone who has done continuous speech recognition knows that we cannot depend on spaces in the sound stream. Furthermore, in ancient Greek, when written language was not considered an autonomous means of expression, but was viewed as a visual representation of the sound stream, we find words run together without intervening spaces, just the way we speak. Seneca claimed that Latin writers sometimes separated words because there was a *difference in speech rhythm* between Greek and Latin speakers, namely, that Latin speakers left a pause after each word [37]. Havelock [6] points out that the alphabet was in use in Greece for 300 years before Greek had a word for 'word'. Apparently the concept of a word, as a discrete, indivisible unit of the sound stream is not so obvious as we now take it.

In summary, the phenomenological salience of the word is partially a result of our use of an alphabetic writing that separates words, and of the cultural practices that go along with it, such as dictionaries, indices, and word-oriented reading instruction [37]. Nevertheless, the concept of a word is neither illusory nor arbitrary, since as a matter of fact speakers tend to treat certain segments of the sound stream as units, and it is the recurrence and semi-independence of these segments that form the basis of the 'word' idea. Therefore, it seems that the emergence of approximately-discrete, symbolic processes from the underlying continuous, subsymbolic processes will be illuminated by considering the self-organization of processes for recognizing recurring parts of images (such as words in the sound stream).

The Dendritic Net as a Linear System

In the remainder of this paper I will consider several simple examples of self-organization based on so-called Hebbian learning rules, which are more accurately termed correlational learning rules. I have concentrated on correlational mechanisms because (1) there is more biological evidence for correlational learning than for other processes, and (2) correlational learning tends to be fast, and so may better account for rapid learning in people and other animals.

My first example shows how correlational learning in the dendritic net can lead to the self-organization of recursive, matched filters for spatiotemporal patterns. The end result is that dendritic nets can "resonate" when presented with signals that match those that have previously triggered a learning signal. This can be shown through linear systems analysis, which, I have argued elsewhere [22], is a good model of dendritic interactions; here I will take the model for granted and summarize the analysis.

We analyze the electrochemical dynamics of dendritic nets in terms of three spatiotemporal fields of time-varying electrochemical quantities distributed over the synapses and ephapses of the dendritic net. The input field ϕ at times t, $\phi(t)$, represents computationally relevant variables determined externally to the net; it comprises the variables $\phi(z,t)$ at interaction sites z (typically synapses and ephapses).[15] The output field $\omega = \omega(t)$ represents computationally relevant variables $\omega(x,t)$ that affect processes external to the dendritic net, but not internal to it. The state field $\psi = \psi(t)$ represents those computationally relevant variables $\psi(y,t)$ that are determined internally to the net and whose direct effects are confined to the net. Some of these variables will correspond to physical quantities, such as ion currents and neurotransmitter concentrations; others are introduced for mathematical convenience and represent, for example, derivatives of physical quantities. Since, we have argued, dendritic information processing approximates a linear process [22], the dendritic process can be described by the equations:

$$\omega(t) = E\phi(t) + G\psi(t),$$
$$\dot{\psi}(t) = D\phi(t) + F\psi(t).$$

The matrices D, E, F and G are essentially fixed fields representing the (linear) coupling strengths between the computationally relevant quantities. For example, E_{yz} represents the coupling strength from input variable $\phi(z,t)$ to state variable $\psi(y,t)$; that is, if $\phi(z,t)$ varies by δ and everything else is held constant, then $\psi(y,t)$ will vary by $E_{yz}\delta$.

To analyze the system we take the Laplace transform of the state evolution equation:

$$s\Psi(s) - \psi(0) = D\Phi(s) + F\Psi(s),$$

where $\Psi(s) = \mathcal{L}\{\psi(t)\}$ and $\Phi(s) = \mathcal{L}\{\phi(t)\}$ ($\mathcal{L}\{\}$ being the Laplace transform). This equation can be solved

---

[15] I will be systematically vague about whether the interaction sites form a continuum or a discrete set, and so, for the most part, the analysis will be independent of the denseness of the set of interaction sites. Integration over a set of sites reduces to summation if the sites are a discrete set.

for $\Psi(s)$, the Laplace transform of the state:

$$\Psi(s) = R(s)[D\Phi(s) + \psi(0)],$$

where the transformed transition matrix is given by $R(s) = (sI - F)^{-1}$. To find out the *forced response* of the system (its response with no energy in the initial state), set $\psi(0) = 0$. Then the Laplace transform of the system's output is then given by:

$$\Omega(s) = E\Phi(s) + GR(s)D\Phi(s).$$

If we define the *transfer function matrix*,

$$H(s) = E + GR(s)D,$$

then we can see the relation between the input and output in the transform domain: $\Omega(s) = H(s)\Phi(s)$. When this matrix product is expanded and transferred back to the space-time domain, it becomes a superposition of convolutions ($\star$), which we may write:

$$\omega(x, t) = \sum_z h_{xz}(t) \star \phi(z, t).$$

That is, the signal $\omega(x, t)$ at output site x is given by the sum of each input signal $\phi(z, t)$ convolved with $h_{xz}(t)$, where the *impulse response* $h_{xz}(t)$ is the signal we see at output site x when an impulse is injected into input site z (all other input sites being clamped to 0).

Self-organization of Recursive Matched Filters

It's well known that for normalized signals ζ and ϕ, the inner product $\langle \zeta, \phi \rangle$ is maximized when $\zeta = \phi$; this makes it a simple basis for neural network pattern matching.[16] It's also well-known that the inner product is the final value of reverse convolution:

$$\langle \zeta, \phi \rangle = \zeta(T - t) \star \phi(t)|_{t=T}. \tag{4}$$

Therefore, if a linear system has an impulse response that is the time-reverse of the pattern, $h(t) = \zeta(T - t)$, then it will function as a pattern matcher for ζ, since its output will be maximized by (normalized) signals matching ζ. Such a system is a *matched filter* for ζ.[17]

Since the dendritic tree of a neuron is an approximately linear system, we can conclude that it's a matched filter for the pattern that is the reverse of its impulse response. If the threshold at the axon hillock is a little less than the norm of this pattern, then the neuron will generate an action potential only when its spatiotemporal input signal is sufficiently similar to the pattern. There are several ways that a dendritic net could self-organize into a matched filter for a given pattern signal [22]; just one will be considered here.

Our goal is a network that self-organizes into a linear filter with impulse response $h(t) = \zeta(T - t)$. To accomplish this, expand $\zeta(T - t)$ in a generalized Fourier series in terms of a complete orthonormal set of basis functions ϱ_k over the interval $(0, T)$:

$$\zeta(T - t) = \sum_{k=0}^{\infty} c_k \varrho_k(t),$$

The coefficients c_k needed to implement the filter are given by the integral,

$$c_k = \int_0^T \zeta(T - t)\varrho_k(t)dt, \tag{5}$$

---

[16]The requirement for normalization might seem to be biologically unrealistic, but Sokolov [36] has shown that in the rhesus monkey color is coded by constant-length vectors; previous work by Sokolov and his colleagues indicates that in humans color is likewise coded by position on the surface of a four-dimensional hypersphere [7, 28].

[17]The time T, which is measured from the time when the input signal begins to add energy to the filter, defines the effective duration of the pattern.

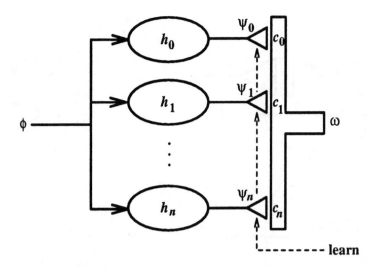

Figure 13: Adaptive Recursive Filter in Dendritic Net

which is just the final $(t = T)$ value of the convolution:

$$c_k = \zeta(t) \star \varrho_k(t)|_{t=T} \, .$$

That is, coefficient c_k is the output signal, at time T, of a linear filter with impulse response $\varrho_k(t)$.

Figure 13 shows a possible neural implementation of this self-organizing filter. The input signal $\phi(t)$ is distributed to a bank of linear filters h_k, each of which has an impulse response equal to one of the basis functions, $h_k(t) = \varrho_k(t)$. (Since the input signal is band-limited, only a finite number of the basis functions need to be represented.) The graded outputs $\psi_k(t)$ of these filters are passed through synapses onto a common neuron, which sums the transmitted signals to produce the output signal $\omega(t)$. When the input signal is the pattern to be learned, $\phi(t) = \zeta(t)$, then the required coefficients will be available presynaptically at time T, $c_k = \psi_k(T)$. Therefore, if some "learning signal" (indicated by "learn" in Fig. 13) causes this presynaptic activity to determine the efficacy of its synapse, then the coefficients c_k will become the connection weights (as shown in Fig. 13). The result is a filter matched to the pattern ζ:

$$h(t) = \sum_{k=0}^{n} c_k h_k(t) = \zeta(T - t),$$

There are several possible sources for the learning signal. It could, of course, be some kind of global reinforcement signal indicating the salience of recently received signals. Another interesting possibility is that it results from an *antidromic electrotonic pulse* in the postsynaptic neuron. This occurs when the postsynaptic neuron generates an action potential, for the sudden depolarization causes an electrical pulse to spread backward from the axon hillock out into the dendrites, where it is efficiently transferred into the dendritic spines [22]. It seems plausible that this pulse on the postsynaptic side could trigger changes in the synapse so that its efficacy reflects the graded activity on the presynaptic side. Therefore, if several adaptive filters of this kind converged on a single neuron, then the firing of that neuron could cause the filters to adapt to the input pattern, thus tuning the neuron to the particular set of patterns that caused it to fire.

It remains to say a few words about the filter bank h_k, which must implement the basis functions ϱ_k. This is not so difficult as it might appear. For example, to implement the familiar trigonometric basis:

$$\varrho_0(t) = 1, \quad \varrho_{2k}(t) = \cos(2\pi kt/T), \quad \varrho_{2k-1}(t) = \sin(2\pi kt/T),$$

it's sufficient to implement the differential equations:

$$\begin{aligned}
\ddot{\varrho}_{2k} &= \dot{\phi} - \nu_{2k}^2 \varrho_{2k}, \\
\dot{\varrho}_{2k-1} &= \phi - \nu_{2k-1}^2 \int \varrho_{2k-1} \mathrm{d}t,
\end{aligned}$$

141

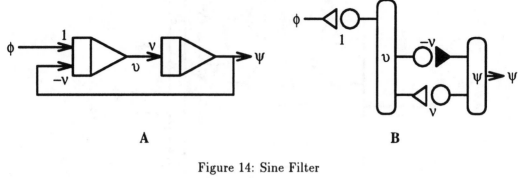

Figure 14: Sine Filter

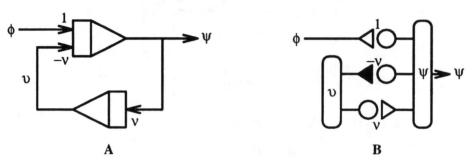

Figure 15: Cosine Filter

where $\nu_k = 2\pi k/T$. These differential equations are implemented by the biologically plausible dendritic nets shown in Figs. 14 and 15. It may seem unlikely that the correct coefficients, $\nu_k = 2\pi k/T$ ($k = 0, 1, 2, \ldots$), which determine the resonant frequencies, would occur in a biological system, but the relationship $\nu_k = k\nu_1$ could result from a simple growth process. Furthermore, simulation experiments have shown that it is not necessary to have an accurate orthonormal basis, and filter banks with randomly chosen coefficients ν_k often do quite well.

Figures 16–20 show results from a simulation of this self-organizing filter. Figure 16 shows the initial impulse response $h(t)$ with randomly initialized coefficients c_k. The training pattern $\zeta(t)$, normalized for ease of comparison, is shown in Fig. 17. The training pattern is input to the filter, and the presynaptic activities at time $T = 500$ msec. are transferred to the coefficients, $c_k = \psi_k(T)$. The result is that the filter has adapted to the pattern, as seen from its new impulse response shown in Fig. 18 (normalized and time-reversed for ease of comparison), which is very similar to the training pattern (Fig. 17). We can also see the self-organization of the filter by comparing its response to the pattern before and after adaptation (recall that a matched filter produces maximum positive output at time T — ideally an impulse — for the signal to which it is matched). Figure 19 shows the response to the pattern $\zeta(t)$ before adaptation; note that the output at time $T = 500$ msec. is quite negative. On the other hand, Fig. 20 shows that after adaptation the filter's response to the same signal is positive and approximates an impulse at time T.

Nonlinear Correlational Learning

One way a system can adapt to algebraic invariances, such as symmetry groups, is to learn an arbitrary nonlinear mapping, given samples of the input and corresponding targets (images of correct completion). Therefore, suppose $\mathcal{I}$ is the space of input images and $\mathcal{O}$ is the space of output and target images; our problem is to learn an arbitrary $S : \mathcal{I} \to \mathcal{O}$. This is easily accomplished if we know a *complete* set of functions $\xi_k : \mathcal{I} \to \mathcal{O}$, $k = 1, 2, \ldots$, since then, by definition, every such S can be represented (in at least one way) by a linear combination of the ξ_k. However, the representing functions need not be normalized or even orthogonal, so the representation may not be unique and cannot be calculated by simple inner products. (These characteristics are typical of some wavelet representations, such as Gabor wavelets [15].) Fortunately,

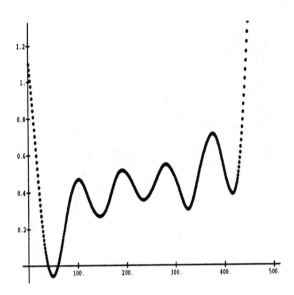

Figure 16: Initial Impulse Response (Random Coefficients)

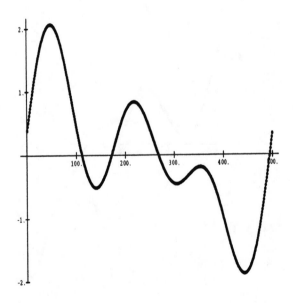

Figure 17: Example Training Signal (Normalized)

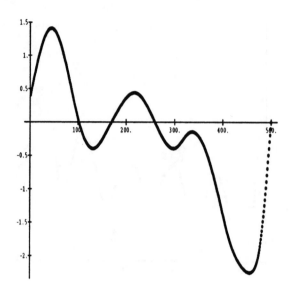

Figure 18: Final Impulse Response (Normalized and Reversed)

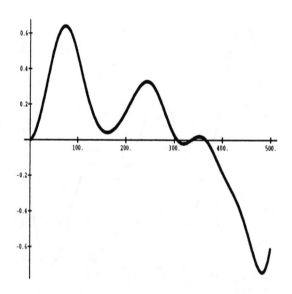

Figure 19: Initial Response to Pattern Signal

144

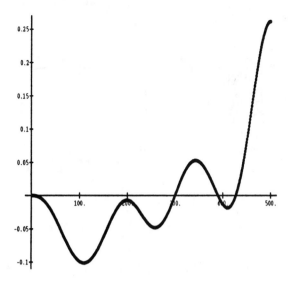

Figure 20: Final Response to Pattern Signal

complete sets of neurally plausible functions are not hard to find; various sorts of radial basis functions, which coarse-code the input space, are examples. Since we require completeness but not orthogonality or normality, the functions can often be generated randomly.

Therefore, suppose we have a complete set of functions $\xi_k : \mathcal{I} \to \mathcal{O}$, $k = 1, 2, \ldots$; then any $S : \mathcal{I} \to \mathcal{O}$ can be written (in at least one way) as a linear combination $S = \sum_k c_k \xi_k$.

Our task is to learn the coefficient vector $\mathbf{c}$ that will give some desired behavior S.[18] Suppose the transformation to be learned is exemplified by the (spatiotemporal) input-output pairs $\phi^j \mapsto \zeta^j$. For the least-squares solution, define as usual the $\mathcal{L}_2$ error as a function of the coefficients: $E(\mathbf{c}) = \sum_j \|\delta^j\|^2$, where $\delta^j = \zeta^j - S(\phi^j)$. To find where the error is minimized, set the derivative to zero:

$$0 = \mathrm{d}E/\mathrm{d}c_k = \sum_j \langle \delta^j, v_k^j \rangle, \tag{6}$$

where $v_k^j = \xi_k(\phi^j)$. Since the error is quadratic in the coefficients and the representation is complete we know that the global minimum is $E = 0$ (possibly degenerate) and that there are no local minima. Since $\delta^j = \zeta^j - S(\phi^j)$ we separate the summation:

$$\sum_j \langle \zeta^j, v_k^j \rangle = \sum_j \langle S(\phi^j), v_k^j \rangle. \tag{7}$$

Define the pattern vector $z_j = \zeta^j$ and the representation matrix $U_{kj} = v_k^j$. Then the left-hand side of Eq. 7 is given by:

$$a_k = \sum_j \langle z_j, U_{kj} \rangle,$$

which we abbreviate $\mathbf{a} = U\mathbf{z}$. The right-hand side of Eq. 7 can be expanded to $\sum_{ji} c_k \langle v_i^j, v_k^j \rangle$, which can be expressed in terms of the matrix:

$$B_{ij} = \sum_k \langle U_{ik}, U_{jk} \rangle,$$

which we abbreviate $B = UU^{\mathrm{T}}$. Now Eq. 7 can be expressed by the equation $\mathbf{a} = B\mathbf{c}$ and we can solve directly for the optimal coefficients, $\mathbf{c} = B^{-1}\mathbf{a}$. Of course, since the representation is only complete, the coefficients may be underdetermined, because there may be many equally good solutions.

---

[18]Corresponding techniques have been used for training radial basis function networks [1, 27].

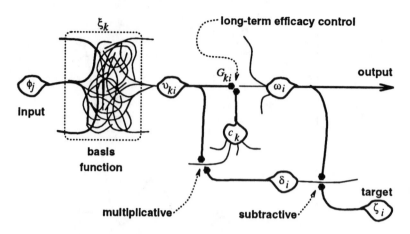

Figure 21: Neural Implementation of Nonlinear Correlational Learning

To avoid the necessity of inverting the B matrix, we can use gradient descent; since there are no local minima it cannot get trapped. From Eq. 6 we know

$$dE/dc_k = \sum_j \langle \delta^j, v_k^j \rangle,$$

which we abbreviate $dE/d\mathbf{c} = U\boldsymbol{\delta}$. For gradient descent we set $\dot{\mathbf{c}} = -\eta dE/d\mathbf{c}$, for learning rate η, so that $\dot{E} = (dE/d\mathbf{c})\dot{\mathbf{c}} = -\eta\|dE/d\mathbf{c}\|^2 \le 0$.

The effect of the gradient descent rule can be seen by expanding B^{-1} in a Neumann series:

$$B^{-1} = I + (I - B) + (I - B)^2 + \cdots,$$

which converges provided $\|I - B\| \le 1$. Therefore,

$$\mathbf{c} = \mathbf{a} + (I - B)\mathbf{a} + (I - B)^2\mathbf{a} + \cdots.$$

To see the relation to gradient descent, observe $\dot{\mathbf{c}} = -\eta U(\mathbf{z} - \mathbf{c}U) = -\eta(\mathbf{a} - U\mathbf{c}U)$. Since $U\mathbf{c}U = B\mathbf{c}$,

$$\dot{\mathbf{c}} = -\eta(\mathbf{a} - B\mathbf{c}). \tag{8}$$

Therefore, gradient descent will compute successive approximations to the Neumann series, $\mathbf{c}_k = \sum_{j=0}^{k}(I - B)^j\mathbf{a}$, if we choose $\mathbf{c}_0 = \mathbf{a}$ for the initial coefficient vector, and $\mathbf{c}_{k+1} = \mathbf{a} + (I - B)\mathbf{c}_k$, which is gradient descent (Eq. 8).

Fig. 21 shows a neurally-feasible implementation of the gradient descent process. The representation functions ξ_k are computed by fixed dendritic networks on the left; as noted previously, completeness is a rather weak property, and an appropriate set of functions, such as radial basis functions, can be computed by randomly generated networks. The resulting field ω is compared with an image ζ of correct completion to generate the difference field δ. Multiplicative synapses combine the difference fields with the intermediate fields v_k to control the long-term efficacy coefficients $G_{ki} = c_k$.

Orthogonal Representation of Discrete Categories

Next I'll consider a simple mechanism by which a system can self-organize so that discrete stimulus classes are represented orthogonally. A basic hypothesis is that (approximately) discrete categories are a consequence of the need for discrete responses (e.g., fight or flight), which in turn are often dependent on discreteness in the environment, as encountered. For example, suppose green lizards are good to eat but blue lizards are poisonous, and that all lizards in the environment are distinctly green or distinctly blue. Under these circumstances we expect discrete categories. On the other hand, if greenish lizards are pretty good to eat and blue ones are not so good, and if the lizards in the environment come in all shades between green and blue, then we expect graded categories, since whether or not we eat a lizard will depend on its exact shade as well as contextual factors, such as our hunger.

I will consider the consequences of a correlational learning rule operating on a simple kind of three-layer network. The input field ϕ is coarse-coded by an intermediate field $v(\phi)$. The coarse-coding neuron v_κ responds most strongly to an input $\phi = \kappa$. For convenience I will assume that all these neurons have a receptive field profile θ with radius of support r; thus $\theta(\lambda) = 0$ for $\|\lambda\| > r$. Therefore, the activity of a coarse-coding neuron is given by $v_\kappa(\phi) = \theta(\kappa - \phi)$. The output field ω is simply a linear combination of the coarse-coded input, $\omega_\lambda = \int G_{\lambda\kappa} v_\kappa \mathrm{d}\kappa$, which is abbreviated $\omega = Gv$.

Next consider the consequences of correlational learning in the interconnection field G, which will result from a correlation of the coarse-coding field $v(\phi)$ and the target response field $R(\phi)$. Thus, $\dot{G}_{\lambda\kappa} = R_\lambda(\phi) v_\kappa(\phi)$, which is the outer product, $\dot{G} = R(\phi) \wedge v(\phi)$. If $\phi(t)$ represents the time sequence of stimuli and $R[\phi(t)]$ the corresponding targets, then the interconnection field after time T will be:

$$G(T) = G(0) + \int_0^T R[\phi(t)] \wedge v(\phi)\mathrm{d}t.$$

If T is sufficiently long, then stimulus ϕ will appear with its stationary probability $p(\phi)\mathrm{d}\phi$, and the limiting interconnection field is

$$G^\infty = c \int_S R(\phi) \wedge v(\phi)p(\phi)\mathrm{d}\phi,$$

where c is a scale factor determined by the learning duration.

Suppose we have n disjoint classes of stimuli $C_1, \ldots, C_n \subset S$ and that these classes are "sufficiently separated" (in a sense to be made clear shortly). Furthermore, let $\mu_k(\phi)$ be the probability density of ϕ in C_k, that is, μ_k is a fuzzy membership function for C_k. Clearly, then

$$G^\infty = c \sum_{k=1}^n \int_S R(\phi) \wedge v(\phi)\mu_k(\phi)\mathrm{d}\phi.$$

Now, to see the effect of discrete target responses, suppose the target response $R(\phi)$ is a constant ϱ_k for all $\phi \in C_k$. In this case,

$$G^\infty = c \sum \varrho_k \wedge \int_S v(\phi)\mu_k(\phi)\mathrm{d}\phi.$$

That is, $G^\infty = c \sum \varrho_k \wedge \varepsilon_k$, where $\varepsilon_k = \int_S v(\phi)\mu_k(\phi)\mathrm{d}\phi$.

It's easy to see that ε_k is the convolution $\theta \star \mu_k$; that is ε_k is the category membership function μ_k "blurred" by the coarse-coding function θ. This blurring has a maximum radius r. Therefore, if the original membership functions were separated by at least $2r$ then the blurred functions ε_k will still be disjoint (i.e. have nonoverlapping support). Under these conditions it's straightforward to show that the ε_k are orthogonal fields; that is, $\langle \varepsilon_j, \varepsilon_k \rangle = 0$ for $j \neq k$. In summary, coarse-coding results in an orthogonal representation if each of the discrete responses is associated with stimuli that are sufficiently unambiguous.[19]

It's also easy to see that the network has self-organized to behave correctly, that is, to produce response ϱ_k for stimuli in C_k. For, suppose $\phi \in C_k$, then the output is $Gv(\phi) = c \sum \varrho_k \langle \varepsilon_k, v(\phi) \rangle$. Now observe that $\langle \varepsilon_k, v(\phi) \rangle = \langle \theta \star \mu_k, v(\phi) \rangle$ is nonzero, since θ spreads μ_k. Conversely, for all $j \neq k$ we know $\langle \theta \star \mu_k, v(\phi) \rangle = 0$, since μ_j is separated from μ_k by at least $2r$. Therefore the output elicited by $\phi \in C_k$ is the correct response ϱ_k, scaled by its "fuzzy" category membership. Note that $\langle \varepsilon_k, v(\phi) \rangle$ amounts to a fuzzy intersection of ε_k (the blurred category) and $v(\phi)$ (the singleton ϕ blurred by coarse coding).

Metric Correlation and Group Invariances

Some of the most important invariances respected by perceptual and motor systems are *algebraic invariances*, especially *group* invariances. While it is true that some of these mechanisms are innate and have evolved

---

[19]If there is some ambiguity, as a result of coarse-coding or noise, then the representation will be correspondingly only approximately orthogonal.

through "blind variation and selective retention" [2], others are learned, and so we need to consider more systematic mechanisms by which such invariances may emerge. One of the attractions of correlational and convolutional methods (such as holography) is that they simultaneously accomplish translation-invariant pattern recognition in parallel with pattern location [31, Ch. 5]. For example, if ζ is a pattern and ϕ is an image, which may contain instances of ζ, the the correlation $\zeta \otimes \phi$ will be an image with "bright spots" wherever the pattern occurs in the input image ϕ, with the location of the spot showing the location of the pattern instance, and the "brightness" of the spot indicating the closeness of the match (by the Euclidean metric). The result of the correlation is reminiscent of the so-called "what" and "where" channels in primate vision (the occipitotemporal and occipitoparietal pathways). There is no mystery about how the correlation (or convolution) accomplishes this: it simply forms, in parallel, inner products between ϕ and every possible translation of ζ.

Although translation invariance is important, there are many other transformations for which we would like a system to respond invariantly, while simultaneously indicating how the input has been transformed. Therefore, in this section I will generalize the familiar correlation operation so that it works on arbitrary transformations and metrics.

As discussed above, the speech stream is essentially continuous, and, to a first approximation, words are segments of the sound stream that can be treated as discrete units, that is, relocated as wholes. Conversely, recurrence of the same signal in a variety of contexts is evidence that it is a meaning unit, often a word. Therefore, we suspect that one component of language learning is the detection of such recurrences. However, a word will rarely recur exactly; it will be transformed in duration, pitch, amplitude, etc., or by the context of surrounding sounds. This suggests metric correlation as a mechanism for the self-organization of a word-recognition system [18].

The familiar correlation attempts to match one signal to all possible translations of another signal, and returns a signal showing how well these matched. The correlation of images φ and ψ is defined:

$$[\varphi \otimes \psi]_\alpha = \int_\Omega \varphi(t - \alpha)\psi(t)\mathrm{d}t.$$

The structure of this is more apparent when we realize that $\varphi(t - \alpha)$ is φ translated to the right by an amount α. Therefore we introduce the operator T_α to mean a rightward translation by α, and rewrite the correlation:

$$[\varphi \otimes \psi]_\alpha = \int_\Omega T_\alpha\varphi(t)\psi(t)\mathrm{d}t.$$

It is then apparent that the correlation is the inner product of the translated image $T_\alpha\varphi$ and the image ψ. So we write it that way:

$$[\varphi \otimes \psi]_\alpha = \langle T_\alpha\varphi, \psi\rangle.$$

The significance of the inner product is that it measures the similarity of normalized images. Therefore we write $\sigma(\varphi, \psi) = \langle\varphi, \psi\rangle$ to emphasize that its purpose is to measure similarity:

$$[\varphi \otimes \psi]_\alpha = \sigma(T_\alpha\varphi, \psi).$$

Thus, in general terms, the value of the field $\chi = \varphi \otimes \psi$ at a point α is the similarity to ψ of the α-translate of φ.

The common correlation can be generalized to other classes of transformation (rotation, scaling, perspective distortion, etc.) as well as to other measures of similarity or dissimilarity. If T is any parameterized class of transforms and σ is any similarity metric, then define $\sigma(\varphi \lhd_T \psi)$, the *metric correlation* with ψ of all T-transforms of φ, by:

$$[\sigma(\varphi \lhd_T \psi)]_\alpha = \sigma(T_\alpha\varphi, \psi).$$

Sometimes it is easier to work in terms of difference rather than similarity, in which case we write:

$$[\delta(\varphi \lhd_T \psi)]_\alpha = \delta(T_\alpha\varphi, \psi),$$

where δ is a (difference) metric. When the metric or transform is clear from context it will be omitted; thus in general $\varphi \lhd \psi$ is the metric correlation of all transforms of φ with ψ. Sometimes it is more convenient to consider the metric correlation of φ with all T-transforms of ψ, so we write:

$$[\rho(\varphi \rhd_T \psi)]_\alpha = \rho(\varphi, T_\alpha\psi),$$

where ρ is either a similarity or difference metric. Clearly, $\varphi \lhd \psi = \psi \rhd \varphi$. Finally we define the operator which correlates all T-transforms of φ with all U-transforms of ψ:

$$[\rho(\varphi \, \diamondsuit_{T,U} \, \psi)]_{\alpha,\beta} = \rho(T_\alpha \varphi, U_\beta \psi).$$

Notice that the correlation field resulting from this operation is indexed over two parameter spaces. These operations satisfy many simple identities, most of which are obvious, and so omitted.

It is often useful to consider metric correlations under multiple transformations. For example, if X_α for $\alpha \in \mathcal{E}^2$ (2D Euclidean space) is a translation by α, and R_β for $\beta \in S^1$ (a topological circle) is a rotation through an angle β, then $T_{\alpha\beta} = X_\alpha R_\beta$ is a rotation followed by a translation (the order doesn't matter; they commute). Thus $(\varphi \lhd \psi)_{\alpha\beta}$ measures the correlation between ψ and the α-translation, β-rotation of φ.

Often the transformations applied to images have algebraic structure; frequently they form a topological group. In these cases the metric correlations inherit the structure; for example, if the transformations are an abelian group:

$$(T_\alpha \varphi \lhd \psi)_\beta = (\varphi \lhd \psi)_{\alpha+\beta} = (\varphi \lhd \psi)_{\beta+\alpha} = (T_\beta \varphi \lhd \psi)_\alpha.$$

The reader may suppose that metric correlations are computationally too expensive to have much significance to cognitive processing, but this need not be so. First observe that they are not much more expensive than the usual (inner product) correlations. Second, the limited precision of neural computation (one or two digits) will limit the number of transforms to be computed in parallel to a dozen or so, for each real parameter. A combination of two transforms might require several hundred to be computed (in parallel).

CONCLUSIONS

I have argued that the foundation of expertise and skillful behavior is knowledge represented as a *structured continuum* as opposed to a discrete structure. The reason is that continuous knowledge representation permits more flexible behavior and avoids failures due to brittleness. As a consequence it is crucial that we understand the principles of continuous representation so that they can be applied in artificial intelligence and neuroscience. To this end I have compared and contrasted continuous ("analog") and discrete ("digital") computation, and have suggested a theoretical framework (*simulacra*) for continuous representations.

This theoretical framework was used to characterize several kinds of *invariance* that occur in natural and artificial systems, including *effect equivalence*, *transform invariance*, *structural invariance* and *transform preservation*. Included as special cases are psychologically significant invariances, such as symmetry groups and other algebraic invariances involved in object perception. Several ways of quantifying *degree of invariance* were noted *en passant*, since quantification is a necessary prerequisite to understanding the emergence of algebraic structure in perceptual and cognitive processes.

I reviewed several simple mechanisms, based on correlational learning, that lead to the emergence of invariances. These included (1) the self-organization of matched filters for spatiotemporal signals by means of approximately linear processes in dendritic nets, (2) the approximation of nonlinear functions by bases that are complete but not necessarily orthogonal, and (3) the emergence of orthogonal representations through coarse coding. Finally, I proposed *metric correlation*, a generalization of the familiar correlation and convolution operations, which accomplishes transform invariant pattern recognition. The foregoing is only a hint, however, of what is needed: a comprehensive theory of the means by which (approximately) discrete representations may emerge from continuous processes to form the structured continua that are the foundation of skillful, intelligent behavior in the world.

References

[1] D. S. Broomhead & D. Lowe, "Multivariable Functional Interpolation and Adaptive Networks," *Complex Systems*. vol. 2, pp. 321–355, 1988.

[2] D. T. Campbell, "Blind Variation and Selective Retention in Creative Thought as in Other Knowledge Processes," in: Gerard Radnitzk & W. W. Bartley, III (Eds.), *Evolutionary Epistemology, Theory of Rationality, and the Sociology of Knowledge*, pp. 91–114.

[3] H. L. Dreyfus & S. E. Dreyfus, *Mind Over Machine: The Power of Human Intuition and Expertise in the Era of the Computer*, New York: Free Press, 1986.

[4] M.-L. von Franz, *Alchemy: An Introduction to the Symbolism and the Psychology*, Toronto: Inner City Books, 1980, pp. 166, 238, 264.

[5] S. Harnad, "Grounding Symbols in the Analog World with Neural Nets: A Hybrid Model," *Think*, vol. 2, pp. 12–20, 74–77, June 1993.

[6] E. A. Havelock, E. A. *The Literate Revolution in Greece and its Cultural Consequences*, Princeton: Princeton University Press, 1982, p. 8.

[7] Ch. A. Izmailov & E. N. Sokolov, "A Semantic Space of Color Names," *Psychological Science*, vol. 3, pp. 105–110, 1992.

[8] C. G. Jung, *Psychology and Alchemy*, Bollingen Series XX, second ed., tr. R. F. C. Hull, Princeton: Princeton University Press, 1968, pp. 327–330.

[9] C. H. Kahn, *The Art and Thought of Heraclitus: An Edition of the Fragments with Translation and Commentary*, Cambridge: Cambridge University Press, 1979, pp. 43, 117–118.

[10] G. S. Kirk, J. E. Raven & M. Schofield, *The Presocratic Philosophers*, second ed, Cambridge: Cambridge University Press, 1983, pp. 36–37.

[11] B. J. MacLennan, "Technology-Independent Design of Neurocomputers: The Universal Field Computer," in *Proceedings, IEEE First International Conference on Neural Networks* (June 21–24, 1987), Vol. III, pp. 39–49.

[12] B. J. MacLennan, "Logic for the New AI," in J. H. Fetzer (Ed.), *Aspects of Artificial Intelligence* (pp. 163–192). Dordrecht: Kluwer, 1988, p. 189

[13] B. J. MacLennan, *The Calculus of Functional Differences and Integrals* (Technical Report CS-89-80), Knoxville: Computer Science Department, University of Tennessee, 1989.

[14] B. J. MacLennan, *Field Computation: A Theoretical Framework for Massively Parallel Analog Computation; Parts I – IV*, University of Tennessee, Knoxville, Computer Science Department Technical Report CS-90-100, February 1990.

[15] B. J. MacLennan, *Gabor Representations of Spatiotemporal Visual Images*, University of Tennessee, Knoxville, Computer Science Department technical report CS-91-144, September 1991.

[16] B. J. MacLennan, "Flexible Computing in the 21st Century," *Vector Register*, vol. 4, 3, pp. 8–12, 1991.

[17] B. J. MacLennan, *Research Issues in Flexible Computing: Two Presentations in Japan* (Report No. CS-92-172). Knoxville: University of Tennessee, Computer Science Department, September 1992.

[18] B. J. MacLennan, *Image and Symbol: Continuous Computation and the Emergence of the Discrete*, University of Tennessee, Knoxville, Department of Computer Science Technical Report CS-93-199, December 18, 1992 (revised August 5, 1993).

[19] B. J. MacLennan, "Characteristics of Connectionist Knowledge Representation," *Information Sciences*, vol. 70, pp. 119–143, 1993.

[20] B. J. MacLennan, "Visualizing the Possibilities" (review of Johnson-Laird & Byrne's *Deduction*), *Behavioral and Brain Sciences*, vol. 16, 2, pp. 356–357, 1993.

[21] B. J. MacLennan, "Grounding Analog Computers," *Think*, vol. 2, pp. 48–51, 74–77, June 1993.

[22] B. J. MacLennan, "Information Processing in the Dendritic Net," in: Karl Pribram (Ed.), *Rethinking Neural Networks: Quantum Fields and Biological Data*, pp. 161–197. Hillsdale, NJ: Lawrence Erlbaum, 1993.

[23] B. J. MacLennan, "Field Computation in the Brain," in: Karl Pribram (Ed.), *Rethinking Neural Networks: Quantum Fields and Biological Data*, pp. 199–232. Hillsdale, NJ: Lawrence Erlbaum, 1993.

[24] B. J. MacLennan, "Continuous Symbol Systems: The Logic of Connectionism," in: D. S. Levine and M. Aparicio IV (Eds.), *Neural Networks for Knowledge Representation and Inference*, pp. 83–120. Hillsdale: Lawrence Erlbaum, 1994.

[25] B. J. MacLennan, "Image and Symbol: Continuous Computation and the Emergence of the Discrete," in: Vasant Honavar and Leonard Uhr (Eds.), *Artificial Intelligence and Neural Networks: Steps Toward Principled Integration, Volume I: Basic Paradigms; Learning Representational Issues; and Integrated Architectures*, New York: Academic Press, in press.

[26] B. J. MacLennan, "Words Lie in Our Way," *Minds and Machines*, to appear.

[27] J. Moody & C. Darken, "Learning with Localized Receptive Fields," in: D. Touretzky, G. Hinton & T. Sejnowski (Eds.), *Proceedings of the 1988 Connectionist Models Summer School*, San Mateo: Morgan Kaufmann, 1989, pp. 133–143.

[28] G. V. Paramei, Ch. A. Izmailov & E. N. Sokolov, "Multidimensional Scaling of Large Chromatic Differences by Normal and Color-deficient Subjects," *Psychological Science*, vol. 2, pp. 244–248, 1991.

[29] S. Parpola, "The Assyrian Tree of Life: Tracing the Origins of Jewish Monotheism and Greek Philosophy," *Journal of Near Eastern Studies*, vol. 52, 2, pp. 161–208, July 1993.

[30] J. W. Perry, *Lord of the Four Quarters: Myths of the Royal Father*, New York: Braziller, 1966.

[31] K. H. Pribram, *Brain and Perception: Holonomy and Structure in Figural Processing*, Hillsdale: Lawrence Erlbaum, 1991, ch. 5.

[32] R. A. Prier, *Archaic Logic: Symbol and Structure in Heraclitus, Parmenides, and Empedocles*, The Hague: Mouton, 1976, ch. 3.

[33] H. Putnam, *Representation and Reality*, Cambridge: MIT Press, 1988, pp. 94–103, 121–125.

[34] J. R. Searle, "Is the Brain a Digital Computer?" Presidential Address, *Proceedings of the American Philosophical Association*, 1990.

[35] J. R. Searle, *The Rediscovery of the Mind*, Cambridge: MIT Press, 1992, pp. 208–209.

[36] E. N. Sokolov, "Vector Coding in Neuronal Nets: Color Vision," these proceedings.

[37] J. P. Small, "Historical Development of Writing and Reading," *Psycholoquy*, 92.3.61. reading.10.small, 1992.

[38] L. Ungerleider, L. Ganz & K. H. Pribram, "Size Constancy in Rhesus Monkeys: Effects of Pulvinar, Prestriate and Infero-temporal Lesions," *Experimental Brain Research*, vol. 27, pp. 251–269, 1977.

Index Terms

analog computation
categories
categorization
computation, analog vs. digital
computation, definition
continuous computation
convolution, *see also* correlation, metric
correlation, metric
correlational learning
entity
filter, matched
group
Hebbian learning, *see also* correlational learning
invariance
object perception
orthogonal representation
simulacrum
symmetry group
transformation
transformation-preserving system

Chapter 6

Consciousness and Anesthesia:
An Hypothesis Involving Biophoton Emission in the
Microtubular Cytoskeleton of the Brain

Scott Hagan, Mari Jibu, Kunio Yasue

Consciousness and Anesthesia: An Hypothesis Involving Biophoton Emission in the Microtubular Cytoskeleton of the Brain

Scott Hagan
Department of Physics, McGill University
Montréal, Québec, H3A 2T8 Canada

Mari Jibu
Department of Anesthesiology, Okayama University Medical School
and
Research Institute for Informatics and Science
Notre Dame Seishin University
Okayama 700, Japan

Kunio Yasue
Research Institute for Informatics and Science
Notre Dame Seishin University
Okayama 700, Japan

October 5, 1993

Abstract

Laser-like long-range coherent quantum phenomena resulting from the instantiation of superradiance and self-induced transparency take place in microtubules of the cytoskeletal network. By taking into account the often neglected interaction between the electric dipole of water molecules confined within a microtubule and the quantized electromagnetic field, it is shown that microtubules play the role of non-linear coherent optical devices. Unlike laser phenomena, superradiance is a specific quantum mechanical ordering phenomenon with characteristic time much shorter than that of thermal interaction, so microtubules may be thought to form an ideal optical network free from both thermal noise and loss. Such a superradiant optical network in cytoskeletal microtubule structure may provide us with a new understanding of holographic brain activity, biophoton emission and the origin of anesthesia.

1 Introduction

In the mid 1960's the advent of optical holography heralded a new departure in the understanding of the relationship between brain, memory and perception. The resistance of aspects of memory and perception to relatively extensive brain damage indicated that memory storage and perceptual processing are distributed procedures. Before the mathematical development of Gabor's holographic equations became available (Gabor 1948), it was difficult to imagine how such a distributed process might be described.

Over the next three decades computer programs inspired by holography were developed, reflecting some of the associative characteristics of the parallel distributed processes that constitute the essence of holographic optical procedures. These *connectionist* or *neural network* procedures made it possible to simulate *in vitro* many perceptual and mnemonic processes and to explore the extent and limitations of the simulations.

It was recognized that an unmodified holographic metaphor was an inappropriate model for brain processing because its spread function is unlimited (infinite). Data from neurophysiological experiments showed that the cortical function modelled by holography is better represented by a sinusoid limited by a Gaussian envelope – a mathematical formulation put forward by Gabor (1946; 1968) to measure the maximum efficiency with which a telephone message could be sent across the Atlantic cable. Gabor used the same equations used by Heisenberg to describe units in microphysics and, therefore, called the unit of communication a "quantum of information." The possibility confronting brain science is therefore to probe the mechanisms that lead to the processing of quanta of information by the brain.

The Gabor function, or something qualitatively similar, describes the functional receptive fields of cortical neurons when they respond to sensory stimulation. These receptive fields are products of densely interconnected dendrites and axons that bring in the results of remote stimulation. The question arises as to how this synapto-dendritic field becomes configured by a sensory input. The possibility to be explored in the current paper is that the configuration results from subneuronal physical processes taking place in the dendritic cytoskeleton and at membrane surfaces served by this cytoskeleton.

Our theoretical speculations stem from those originated by Ricciardi and Umezawa (1967). Without reference to any specific neurophysiological data, these theoreticians developed an hypothesis about the way the insights of quantum physics might be applied to understanding brain activity. They suggested that each brain cell is characterized by spatially-distributed quantum mechanical degrees of freedom whose physical properties can be understood by quantum field theory, not only as it applies to elementary particles but, as well, to condensed matter physics (Umezawa, 1993).

According to Ricciardi and Umezawa (1967), memory storage involves a phase transition from a less-ordered vacuum state to one more ordered. Memory is stored as an ordered vacuum state created by a phase transition induced by a sensory process. Then, assuming that this ordered vacuum state produces spontaneous symmetry breaking, it can be concluded by the Nambu-Goldstone theorem that during recall long-range correlation waves with zero minimum energy requirement are created. (Ricciardi and Umezawa, 1967; Umezawa, 1993)

At about the same time, Fröhlich (1968) proposed a similar idea with more explicit empirical foundation for biological cells in general. Focusing on a thin layer just beneath the cell membrane, he pointed out the possibility that energy can be stored without thermal loss in this two-dimensional region in terms of coherent dipolar wave propagations. That is, biological molecules beneath the cell membrane with dipolar vibrational activity may manifest a globally coherent mode of dynamics so that the thin layer could be seen as a biological superconducting medium or a biological plasma effectively isolated from thermal environments. Today, the existence of such a coherent dipolar wave propagation is well verified by experiments and it is frequently called a Fröhlich wave (Webb, 1980; Webb and Stoneham, 1977; Webb et al., 1977; Neubauer et al., 1990; Grundler and Keilmann, 1983). It appears in a frequency region between 10^{11} and $10^{12} sec^{-1}$ called the Fröhlich frequency. It can be concluded that energy supplied to biological cells with a magnitude equal to the Fröhlich frequency times the Planck constant may not be completely thermalized but stored in a highly ordered fashion.

Fröhlich waves are not restricted to the thin layer just beneath the cell membrane. Dipolar oscillations maintained by non-localized electrons trapped in the one-dimensional chain of protein molecules as well as hydrogen bonds recurring therein may manifest a collective mode which can be considered as a Fröhlich wave propagating in a one-dimensional medium. This fact triggered an extensive investigation of a fine dynamical network structure of protein filaments in the cytoplasm called the *microtrabecular lattice* Davydov (1979) provided a theoretical framework for dipolar solitary wave propagation along the one-dimensional chains of protein molecules such as the protein filaments. The mode of solitary wave propagation is known in quantum field theory to carry energy without loss due to thermalization, and is called the Davydov soliton or dipolar soliton.

About ten years later, Umezawa together with two colleagues, Takahashi and Stuart, refined their hypothesis to include processing among brain cells (Stuart et al., 1978; 1979). The system is composed of two kinds of spatially-distributed degrees of freedom subject to quantum dynamics. The first one is called the corticon field and the second one, the exchange boson field. The two fields interact to realize a typical quantum dynamical system with a spontaneous symmetry breaking mechanism. This refinement provided a theoretical model of non-local memory storage and retrieval. Jibu and Yasue (1992A; 1992B; 1993A; 1993B) presented a physically realistic picture of the system of corticon and exchange boson fields, and proposed to call the new quantum field theoretical framework for understanding the brain description originated by Umezawa and his colleagues, *Quantum Brain Dynamics* (QBD). QBD corticon and exchange boson fields are conceived as the dipolar vibrational field of protein molecules distributed 1) along protein filaments of cytoskeletons; 2) along extra neuronal matrices of glia; and 3) of water molecules filling in and among neural and glial cells.

Inspired by these results incorporating quantum theoretical methods into the investigation of brain cells and general biological cells initiated by Ricciardi and Umezawa (1967) and Fröhlich (1968) in the 1960's, several physicists began in the 1980's to consider the biological cell as an essentially quantum dynamical system with macroscopic order in which energy transfer no longer suffers from thermal loss (Del Giudice et al., 1983; 1985; 1986; 1988; Sivakami and Srinivasan, 1983). On the other hand, several brain scientists and medical scientists also became interested in the possibility of investigating the fundamental processes of brain functioning from the microscopic point of view of quantum physics. They focused especially on a specific cytoskeletal structure called the microtubule (Hameroff, 1987). Embedded densely within the fine dynamical network of protein filaments in the cytoskeletal structure are hollow cylinders made of protein molecules, 25 nanometers in diameter, called microtubules. Not surprisingly, the theoretical investigation from the physicist's point of view included an idea applicable to understanding the fundamental processes taking place in microtubules. First, Fröhlich's coherent polarization waves may exist in a thin layer of ordered water just inside and outside the microtubule which may carry information along the microtubule. Second, the formation of such a microscopic cylindrical structure of microtubule-associated proteins may be understood by the concept of self-focussing of electromagnetic energy in a typical biological system with ordered water. Just like the Meissner effect operating in superconducting media, electromagnetic energy would be confined inside filamentous regions which gather the microtubule-associated proteins around the filamentous regions, producing microtubules.

An interesting and exciting investigation was proposed by Hameroff (1974) in which microtubules were thought to act like "dielectric waveguides" for photons; that is, quantum dynamical modes of electromagnetic radiation. Indeed, living tissue does transmit light more readily than non-living material. It is verified by experiments with mammalian brains that the temporal poles and hippocampus manifest the maximum light penetration rate. This evidence led Hameroff to consider the microtubules as waveguides for photons. Furthermore, he proposed that cytoplasmic interference of certain coherent sources from and among multiple microtubules may lead to a holographic information processing mechanism (Hameroff, 1974). Literally "hardwired" holographic patterns stored in cytoplasmic sol-gel states of the microtrabecular lattice densely interconnecting multiple microtubules govern the propagation of either charge carriers or conformational waves in each microtubule. The totality of these information carriers through many microtubules therefore reflects the cytoskeletal hardwired hologram, and suggests the revival of the holographic brain theory, now in terms of quantum neurodynamics (Pribram, 1966; 197; 1991; Margenau, 1984; Marshall, 1989; Eccles, 1986; Beck and Eccles, 1992).

Although Hameroff could finger two key concepts in understanding cytoskeletal brain activity from the point of view of quantum physics, that is, microtubules as waveguides for photons and as holographic information processors, there has been no theoretical investigation of these concepts by physicists. Holography is based on interference of radiant energy, i.e. of photons. And now the microtubule has been conceived as a waveguide for photons. Naively, the question arises:

> Why do we not look for the *literal* possibility of holography in terms of coherent photons within the cytoskeletal structure of microtubules?

The reason seems clear. Even though the microtubule plays the role of waveguide for photons, no active device for coherent photon generation needed to realize optical holography has been found in any microscopic biological structure.

In the present paper, we propose a new quantum theoretical framework in which the microtubule can be shown to bear a rich, ordered and systematic property so that two typical forms of cooperative quantum dynamics called superradiance and self-induced transparency are realized therein. Namely, it is suggested that the quantum dynamical system of water molecules confined inside the microtubule manifests a specific collective dynamics called superradiance by which the microtubule can transform any incoherent, thermal and disordered molecular or atomic energy into coherent photons. Furthermore, it will also be shown that such coherent photons once created by superradiance penetrate perfectly along the cylinder axis of the microtubule as if the optical medium inside it were made transparent by the propagating photons themselves. This is a purely quantum theoretical phenomenon called self-induced transparency.

Both superradiance and self-induced transparency are key concepts in understanding the cooperative physical activity of the system of microtubules in the cytoskeletal structure which lead to "quantum optical" neural holography. Not only brain cells but also general biological cells may potentially be thought to contain a microscopic but extensive coherent optical supercomputer like the famous HAL 9000 of space ship *Discovery* with holographic memory manipulation (Clarke, 1968).

This hypothesis provides two byproducts. The first is that superradiance and self-induced transparency of microtubules may be understood as the origin of the weak coherent photon emission from living matter known as biophoton emission. The second is that anesthetic molecules may drastically change the collective properties of water molecules inside the microtubule and may result in the breakdown of self-induced transparency in the microtubule. In other words, we can speculate that anesthesia results from the blocking of the cooperative physical activity of the system of microtubules due to the opacity to superradiant photons induced by anesthetically disordered water molecules inside the microtubule. This is a theoretical prediction that can be verified by measuring the change in the penetration rate of photons into the mammalian brain due to the anesthesia.

2   Superradiance in Microtubules

A typical microtubule in the cytoskeletal structure of a brain cell or any general biological cell is a hollow cylinder about 25 nanometers in diameter whose wall is a polymerized array of protein subunits ("tubulins"). Its length may vary from tens of nanometers to microns, and possibly further to meters in nerve axons of large animals. For the purpose of simplifying the physical formulation, we idealize the microtubule as a hollow cylinder with radius r_{MT} and length l_{MT}. Their real values would be $r_{MT} \approx 12$ and $l_{MT} \approx 10^2$–10^3 in nanometers. We denote the spatial region inside the microtubule cylinder by V and restrict our discussion to quantum mechanical dynamics taking place in the region V.

Let us introduce a Cartesian system of coordinates O_{xyz} with the xy-plane parallel to one of the two ends of the microtubule cylinder so that the origin O coincides with the center of the end cap. The z-axis lies naturally along the longitudinal center axis of the microtubule cylinder. Then, any position in the region V can be labelled by giving its coordinates $r = (x, y, z)$.

The spatial region V inside the microtubule is not empty, but is likely to be filled with water molecules. Of course, there may also be a sparse population of other molecules, but we consider the ideal case in which the existence of molecules other than those of water can be neglected. We will return later to a consideration of the more realistic case in which we have impurities such as anesthetic molecules among the water molecules. Most probably the density of water confined inside the microtubule cylinder remains almost constant. Therefore, we fix the total number of water molecules inside the region V to be, say N.

Let the index j, running from 1 to N, denote the fictitious number labelling the N water molecules in question. The position of a typical water molecule, say the jth molecule is given by coordinates $r^j = (x^j, y^j, z^j)$. A water molecule has a constant electric dipole, and so it can be seen as a quantum mechanical spinning top with an electric dipole moment. The average moment of inertia and electric dipole moment of a water molecule are estimated to be $I = 2m_p d^2$ with $d \approx 0.82 \mathring{A}$ and $\mu = 2e_p P$ with $P \approx 0.2 \mathring{A}$, respectively. Here, m_p denotes the proton mass and e_p the proton charge.

Due to the electric dipole moment μ, the water molecule interacts with the quantized electromagnetic field in the spatial region V. Although the water molecule has many energy eigenstates as a quantum mechanical spinning top so that it can exchange energy between the quantized electromagnetic field in many different values, we restrict our discussion to the most likely case in which only the two principal energy eigenstates take part in the energy exchange. This coincides with the conventional two-level approximation for describing the energy exchange between atoms and the quantized electromagnetic field in laser theory.

Then one sees immediately that the quantum dynamics of the j-th water molecule can be aptly described by a spin variable $s^j = \frac{1}{2}\sigma$, such that σ is a vector composed of the Pauli spin matrices denoting the three components of the angular momentum for spin $\frac{1}{2}$. Let ϵ be the energy difference between the two principal energy eigenstates of the water molecule. Its real value is $\epsilon \approx 200cm^{-1}$ (Franks, 1972). Then, the Hamiltonian governing the quantum dynamics of the j-th water molecule is given by ϵs_z^j, and so the total Hamiltonian for N water molecules becomes

$$H_{WM} = \epsilon \sum_{j=1}^{N} s_z^j \ . \tag{1}$$

This Hamiltonian has two energy eigenvalues, $-\frac{1}{2}\epsilon$ and $\frac{1}{2}\epsilon$, reflecting the fact that only the two principal energy eigenstates with energy difference ϵ are taken into account.

Now, let us consider the quantized electromagnetic field in the spatial region V. It is convenient to describe the quantized electromagnetic field in terms of an electric field operator $\boldsymbol{E} = \boldsymbol{E}(r, t)$. Let us assume for simplicity that the electric field is linearly polarized, obtaining $\boldsymbol{E} = eE$, where e is a constant vector of unit length pointing in the direction of linear polarization. Then, the quantized electromagnetic field in question is described by a scalar electric field $E = E(\boldsymbol{r}, t)$ governed by the usual Hamiltonian

$$H_{EM} = \frac{1}{2} \int_V E^2 d^3r \ . \tag{2}$$

Next, we consider the interaction between the quantized electromagnetic field and the totality of water molecules by which they can exchange energy in terms of creation and annihilation of photons. Let us divide the electric field operator into positive and negative frequency parts

$$E = E^+ + E^- \ . \tag{3}$$

Then, the interaction Hamiltonian of the quantized electromagnetic field and the totality of water molecules becomes, in the dipole approximation

$$H_I = -\mu \sum_{j=1}^{N} \{E^-(r^j, t)s_-^j + s_+^j E^+(r^j, t)\} \ , \tag{4}$$

where

$$s_\pm^j = s_x^j \pm i s_y^j \ . \tag{5}$$

The total Hamiltonian governing the quantum dynamics of the electromagnetic field, the dipolar vibrational field of water molecules, and their interaction is given by

$$H = H_{EM} + H_{WM} + H_I \ . \tag{6}$$

Since the spatial region V inside the microtubule cylinder can be viewed as a cavity for the electromagnetic wave, it is convenient to introduce the normal mode expansion of the electric field operator $E = E^+ + E^-$, obtaining

$$E^\pm(\boldsymbol{r}, t) = \sum_{\boldsymbol{k}} E_{\boldsymbol{k}}^\pm(t) e^{\pm i(\boldsymbol{k} \cdot \boldsymbol{r} - \omega_{\boldsymbol{k}} t)} \ . \tag{7}$$

Here, $\omega_{\boldsymbol{k}}$ denotes the proper angular frequency of the normal mode with wave vector $\boldsymbol{k}$. As we are primarily interested in the ordered collective behavior among the water molecules and the quantized electromagnetic field in the cavity region V, we introduce collective dynamical variables $S_{\boldsymbol{k}}^{\pm}(t)$ and S for water molecules by

$$S_{\boldsymbol{k}}^{\pm}(t) \equiv \sum_{j=1}^{N} s_{\pm}^{j}(t) e^{\pm i(\boldsymbol{k} \cdot \boldsymbol{r}^{j} - \omega_{\boldsymbol{k}} t)}, \tag{8}$$

and

$$S \equiv \sum_{j=1}^{N} s_{z}^{j}. \tag{9}$$

Then, the total Hamiltonian (6) becomes

$$H = H_{EM} + \epsilon S - \mu \sum_{\boldsymbol{k}} (E_{\boldsymbol{k}}^{-} S_{\boldsymbol{k}}^{-} + S_{\boldsymbol{k}}^{+} E_{\boldsymbol{k}}^{+}). \tag{10}$$

It seems worthwhile to note here that this total Hamiltonian for the system of N water molecules and the quantized electromagnetic field in the region V inside the microtubule cylinder is essentially of the same form as, not only Dicke's Hamiltonian for the laser system but also that of Stuart, Takahashi, and Umezawa for Quantum Brain Dynamics (Dicke, 1954; Stuart et al., 1979). Therefore, it can be expected that each microtubule in the cytoskeletal structure of brain cells manifests not only the memory printing and recalling mechanism in QBD but also a laser-like coherent optical activity. The former is not surprising as Jibu and Yasue (1992A; 1993A; 1993B) have developed a physical picture of QBD in terms of water molecules and protein filaments. Hence, we will not discuss this in the present paper. On the other hand, the latter seems highly surprising because it may open a completely new picture of the fundamental process of brain functioning, drastically different from the conventional one. Namely, in addition to the usual pathway conduction of neural impulses in terms of transmembrane ionic diffusions among nerve cells, the brain system may possibly use another but much more microscopic and elaborated fundamental physical process in terms of coherent photon emission and transfer in the microtubule in some ways similar to an optical computer with lasers, optical fibers and other optical devices. It is this very surprising possibility that we will discuss throughout the present paper.

It is difficult to look for a physical instantiation of laser devices in brain cells even though the microtubule may manifest the same quantum dynamical behavior, in terms of water molecules and the electromagnetic field, as is governed by the Hamiltonian of a typical laser system. This is because we must initially pump up the majority of water molecules to the higher energy eigenstate by certain incoherent but high intensity light. In actual artificial laser devices, for example, the initial pumping is provided by xenon flash lamps. In other words, the laser system cannot emit coherent photons without some pumping mechanism. We can hardly expect the existence of such a pumping light in the brain.

Fortunately, a physical inspection of the form of the total Hamiltonian (10) reveals that it manifests a dynamical symmetry property not evident in the ground state and so the resulting quantum dynamics is known to involve certain long-range order creating phenomena due to spontaneous symmetry breaking (Stuart et al., 1979). The spatial dimension of this long-range order, that is, the coherence length l_c can be estimated to be inversely proportional to the energy difference ϵ, obtaining $l_c \approx$ hundreds of microns. Among these long-range order creating phenomena we may find a specific one in which the collective dynamics of the majority of water molecules inside the microtubule cylinder V can give rise to cooperative spontaneous emission of photons without any pumping light. Any incoherent and disordered energy distribution among the water molecules due to the macroscopic thermal dynamics of the polymerized array of protein subunits (i.e., tubulins) forming the wall of microtubule cylinder can be gathered collectively into coherent and ordered dynamics ready to emit coherent photons cooperatively. This laser-like process of coherent photon emission without pumping light was first introduced by Dicke (1954) and is called superradiance.

Let us investigate the superradiance in the microtubule cylinder V starting from the total Hamiltonian (10). We assume for simplicity that only one normal mode with a specific wave vector, say k_0, has a proper angular frequency ω_{k_0} resonating to the energy difference ϵ between the two principal energy eigenstates. Namely we have

$$\epsilon = \hbar \omega_{k_0} \, , \tag{11}$$

and all the other normal modes are neglected. In the conventional laser theory, this is known as a single-mode laser. What we are going to analyze may thus be considered to be a single-mode superradiance in the microtubule.

Since we have only one normal mode with wave vector k_0, we may omit all the wave vector indices of the dynamical variables. Then, the total Hamiltonian (10) becomes

$$H = H_{EM} + \epsilon S - \mu(E^- S^- + S^+ E^+) \, . \tag{12}$$

The corresponding Heisenberg equations of motion for the three collective dynamical variables, S and $S^\pm$, for water molecules and the two variables, $E^\pm$, for the quantized electromagnetic field are given by:

$$\frac{dS}{dt} = -i\frac{\mu}{\hbar}(E^- S^- - S^+ E^+) \, , \tag{13}$$

$$\frac{dS^\pm}{dt} = \pm i\frac{2\mu}{\hbar} S E^\mp \pm i\frac{\epsilon}{\hbar} S^\pm \, , \tag{14}$$

and

$$\frac{dE^\pm}{dt} = \pm i\frac{2\pi\epsilon\mu}{\hbar V} S^\mp \, . \tag{15}$$

Because of the short length of the microtubule cylinder ($l_{MT} \approx 10^2$–10^3 in nanometers), the pulse mode propagating along the microtubule cylinder in the direction of the z-axis stays in the cavity region V only for a short transit time $t_{MT} = \frac{l_{MT}}{c}$, where c is the speed of light. As this transit time of the pulse mode is much shorter than the characteristic time of thermal interaction due to the disordered environment, the system of water molecules and quantized electromagnetic field in this single-mode superradiance is free from thermal loss and can be considered a closed system described by the Heisenberg equations of motion (13)-(15). Furthermore, the time derivative of the dynamical variables $E^\pm$ of the quantized electromagnetic field can be approximated by $\frac{E^\pm}{l_{MT}}$ in the case of a pulse mode propagating along the longitudinal axis of the microtubule. Equation (15) then yields

$$E^\pm = \pm i \frac{2\pi\epsilon\mu l_{MT}}{\hbar V} S^\mp . \tag{16}$$

This means that a pulse mode of the quantized electromagnetic field in the microtubule cylinder cavity follows the collective dynamics of water molecules inside the microtubule. In other words, once a collective mode with long-range order is created in the dynamics of water molecules due to spontaneous symmetry breaking, coherent emission of pulse modes of the quantized electromagnetic field follows. This is the mechanism of superradiance.

The last question is whether such a collective mode can be realized in the dynamics of water molecules starting from incoherent and disordered initial conditions. Notice that such an incoherent and disordered initial dynamical configuration of water molecules is due to the interaction between water molecules and thermally disordered states of the conformational dynamics of tubulins. The onset of this collective mode can be seen by rewriting the three Heisenberg equations for the collective variables of water molecules (13) and (14) by the substitution (16). Namely, we have

$$\frac{dS^\pm}{dt} = \beta S S^\pm \pm i\epsilon S^\pm \tag{17}$$

and

$$\frac{dS}{dt} = -\beta S^+ S^- , \tag{18}$$

where $\beta = \frac{4\pi\epsilon\mu^2 l_{MT}}{\hbar^2 V}$. These are coupled nonlinear differential equations for noncommuting operators S and $S^\pm$ subject to certain commutation relations, and it is not so easy to find their solutions. However, if we regard these equations as ordinary coupled nonlinear differential equations for classical (i.e., commuting) dynamical variables, we can find special solutions with respect to any incoherent and disordered initial conditions. They are known as a semi-classical approximation of the quantum dynamical system of superradiance (Agarwal, 1971). A straightforward calculation yields that the intensity of coherent photon emission in the microtubule cylinder due to superradiance can be given in this approximation by

$$I = \frac{\hbar^2}{(4t_R\mu)^2} sech^2 \frac{t - t_0}{2t_R} , \tag{19}$$

where $t_R = \frac{c\hbar^2 V}{4\pi\mu^2\epsilon N l_{MT}}$ and $t_0 = t_R \ln 2N$ denotes the life time and delay time of the superradiance, respectively. Notice that the intensity of superradiance is proportional to N^2 and its delay time is inversely proportional to N. These facts are characteristic of a long-range order-creating process involving N water molecules.

163

We have found that the quantum collective dynamics of water molecules and a quantized electromagnetic field inside the microtubule cylinder manifests the long-range cooperative phenomenon of superradiance in which collective excitation of water molecules can be induced by incoherent and disordered perturbations due to the macroscopic thermal dynamics of protein molecules forming the wall of the microtubule cylinder. This fact ensures that each microtubule in the cytoskeletal structure of brain cells, that is, neurons and astrocytes, may play an important role in the optical information processing regime of brain functioning as a superradiant device which converts the macroscopic disordered dynamics of water molecules and protein molecules into the long-range ordered dynamics of water molecules and a quantized electromagnetic field involving a pulse mode emission of coherent photons. In other words, each microtubule might function as a coherent optical encoder in a dense microscopic optical computing network in the cytoplasm of each brain cell, if such a network is realized in actual cytoplasmic structure. This last point is far from evident and deserves to be discussed in the following section.

3   Self-Induced Transparency in Microtubules

We have shown the possibility of a completely new mechanism of fundamental brain functioning in terms of coherent photon emission by superradiance in microtubules. Unlike a laser, superradiance is a specific quantum mechanical ordering process with a characteristic time much shorter than that of thermal interaction. Therefore, microtubules may be thought of as ideal optical encoders providing a physical interface between 1) the conventional macroscopic system of classical, disordered and incoherent neural dynamics in terms of transmembrane ionic diffusions as well as thermally perturbed molecular vibrations and 2) the yet unknown microscopic optical computing network system of ordered and coherent quantum dynamics free from thermal noise and loss. As Feynman (1985) proposed, the optical computing network is the most realizable quantum mechanical computer among many possibilities such as a superconducting computer. However, it is not clear whether the pulse-mode coherent photons created in the microtubule cylinder by superradiance can be safely transmitted, preserving its long-range coherence. It seems most likely that even coherent photons emitted by superradiance will lose immediately their coherence and long-range order due to the noisy thermal environment. In any case, we require some quantum dynamical mechanism to maintain the coherent transmission of photons in the as yet unknown microscopic optical computing network in brain cells. In this section, we will show that it is again the microtubule in the cytoskeletal structure of brain cells which provides us with such a mechanism.

Let us suppose that the pulse-mode coherent photons are created in a small segment of the microtubule cylinder by superradiance. Then, those photons propagate along the longitudinal axis of the microtubule cylinder, that is, the z-axis. If the region V inside the microtubule cylinder were maintained at vacuum, they would transmit through the region just as they do along a waveguide. However, the region is filled up with water molecules, and it is not evident that the pulse-mode coherent photons can be safely transmitted through the region without absorption or loss of coherence.

For the purpose of describing the transmission of pulse-mode coherent photons through the region inside the microtubule cylinder, it is convenient to work in a semi-classical approximation for which the long-range ordered dynamics of water molecules is described by quantum mechanics while the electromagnetic field is described classically. This approximation becomes reliable when the intensity of the pulse-mode coherent photons is large, and this is indeed the case for superradiant emission (Feynman et al., 1957).

Let us consider the Maxwell equation for the scalar electric field $E = E(z, t)$, representing pulse-mode coherent photons propagating along the z-axis coupled to the collective dynamical variables $S^\pm$ of water molecules inside the microtubule cylinder,

$$\frac{\partial E^\pm}{\partial z} + \frac{\partial E^\pm}{\partial t} = \mp i \frac{2\pi\epsilon\mu}{\hbar V} S^\mp .$$
(20)

This equation is valid under the condition that the collective dynamical variables $S^\pm$ are slowly varying, that is,

$$\frac{\partial S^\pm}{\partial t} \ll i\omega S^\pm .$$
(21)

Then, taking expectation values of the quantum mechanical variables in this Maxwell equation and the Heisenberg equations of motion (13) and (14), eliminating all the expectation values of those variables referring to water molecules, and introducing new variables for the scalar electric field by

$$\theta^\pm(z, t) = \frac{2\mu}{\hbar} \int_{-\infty}^{t} E^\pm(z, u) du ,$$
(22)

we can obtain dynamical equations for the electromagnetic field in the region V inside the microtubule cylinder

$$\frac{\partial^2 \theta^\pm}{\partial\tau\partial\zeta} = -\sin\theta^\pm .$$
(23)

Here, $\tau = \sqrt{\frac{2\pi\epsilon\mu^2 N}{\hbar^2 V}}(t - \frac{z}{c})$ and $\zeta = \sqrt{\frac{2\pi\epsilon\mu^2 N}{\hbar^2 V}}\frac{z}{c}$. This is a typical nonlinear partial differential equation called the sine-Gordon equation, and several exact solutions are obtained by means of the inverse scattering method for soliton equations (Ablowitz et al., 1974).

The most interesting solution of the sine-Gordon equation (23) gives rise to an explicit form of the time evolution of the scalar electric field E in the region V inside the microtubule cylinder

$$E = \sqrt{\frac{2\pi\epsilon N v_0}{V(c - v_0)}} \, sech \sqrt{\frac{2\pi\epsilon\mu^2 N v_0}{\hbar^2 V(c - v_0)}} (t - \frac{z}{v_0}) .$$
(24)

This is a soliton solution and tells us that the pulse-mode photons propagate along the dielectric waveguide of the microtubule cylinder filled up with water molecules with a certain constant speed v_0 less than the speed of light in vacuum c. It is important to note that the pulse form of the soliton solution is kept unchanged due to the nonlinearity of the sine-Gordon equation.

al., 1981; 1988). Although reliably recorded experimentally, no theoretical explanation of the mechanism of biophoton emission from a physical point of view has been proposed.

After elaborating a quantum theoretical framework for the fundamental physical process of not only brain cells but also general living cells in terms of the superradiance and self-induced transparency of microtubules, we are now in a better position to claim that biophoton emission is an experimental realization of our quantum theoretical framework. We will discuss this issue in a forthcoming paper.

Before closing our exposition of this new quantum theoretical approach to the coherent optical activities of microtubules in the cytoskeletal structure of living cells, we wish to speculate about the mechanism of anesthesia (Allison and Nunn, 1968; Franks and Lieb, 1982; Halsey, 1976). The fundamental mechanism of anesthesia is not as yet known. There have been many attempts to obtain the proper theoretical framework for anesthesia, but most of them are formulated from the macroscopic point of view of chemistry, molecular biology or statistical physics. An exception is the model of Jibu and Yasue (1992B; 1993A; 1993B). With the understanding that the long-range ordered mode of Goldstone bosons may take part in intracellular and intercellular quantum signal transfer, the model proposes that anesthetic molecules break down the propagation of Goldstone bosons.

In the present paper we have suggested more realistic pathways for quantum theoretical signal transfer in terms of pulse-mode coherent photons propagating along the dielectric waveguides of microtubules in the cytoskeletal structure of brain cells and other living cells. Furthermore, each microtubule may play the role of an ideal optical encoder, converting the macroscopic informational signals in the regime of the classical neural dynamics of transmembrane ionic diffusions and thermally perturbed molecular vibrations, into microscopic informational signals in the more elaborated regime of long-range ordered quantum dynamics of water molecules and the quantized electromagnetic field inside the microtubule cylinder. These two fundamental properties of the microtubule maintain systematized optical signal processing units which persist against incoherent and disordered perturbations due to their thermal environments. In other words, systematization in brain cells and other living cells cannot be broken in any way other than by annihilating the quantum theoretical long-range order in the cytoskeletal structure of microtubules filled with and surrounded by water molecules.

It seems most likely that the hydrophilic part of the anesthetic molecule gathers around the electric dipoles of water and protein molecules. The long-range ordered collective quantum dynamics of water molecules and the quantized electromagnetic field in microtubules would be directly inhibited by the anesthetic because the quantum mechanical collectivity of the water molecules is lost in the presence of anesthetic molecules and both superradiance and self-induced transparency no longer function. The microtubule waveguides for coherent photon signals lose their perfect transparency, becoming shaded in the presence of the anesthetic impurity. Although this might not be the single, unitary mechanism of anesthesia, it could be a major component of a full explanation of anesthetic processes because the reversal of anesthesia by increased pressure can be explained:

> The quantum mechanical collectivity of water molecules lost in the presence
> of anesthetic molecules will be restored by increased pressure and both su-

We have found that microtubules play the role of dielectric waveguides and that pulse-mode coherent photons propagate through them as if they were perfectly transparent. This phenomenon is termed self-induced transparency and known to be a typical non-linear effect in quantum optics (McCall and Hahn, 1967). The microtubule may be an ideal microscopic optical device for use as a perfectly transparent pathway for pulse-mode photons, free from thermal noise and loss. Combined with superradiance, this self-induced transparency of the microtubule allows us to postulate that the brain constitutes a dense assembly of microscopic and elaborated optical computing networks of microtubules in the cytoskeletal structure of brain cells. Coherent photon emission and transfer in each microtubule are ensured by superradiance and self-induced transparency, characteristic features of long-range ordering phenomena in quantum dynamics.

Both superradiance and self-induced transparency may be essential to the cooperative physical activity of systems of microtubules in the cytoskeletal structure of single cells and among many cells. Thus biological systems in general and the brain in particular may utilize a quantum level holographic information system (Hameroff, 1987; Pribram, 1991).

4 Outlook for Biophotons and Anesthesia

We have developed a new quantum theoretical framework in which the microtubule is shown to bear a rich, ordered and systematic property so that two typical cooperative quantum dynamics called superradiance and self-induced transparency are realized. Although we have especially focused on the cytoskeletal structure of microtubules in brain cells, our new framework can be equally applied to that in general biological cells as long as they contain microtubules. Of course, the microtubule is a universal structure in living matter and it is difficult to imagine a biological cell so ill-generated as to contain no microtubules. Therefore, not only brain cells but also general biological cells may now be considered to contain microscopic yet extensive coherent optical computer networks. A naive question arises here.

> Can the pulse-mode coherent photons emitted by and transmitting along the microscopic optical network of microtubules in the cytoskeletal structure of any kind of living cell be observed?

This depends on whether our current technology can detect such weak coherent photons leaked from living cells. This is made extremely difficult due to the strong incoherent background thermal emission of disordered photons.

The recent rapid development of coherent photon technology however, has opened up the possibility. By using high-sensitivity photon detectors designed for probing proton disintegration events in high energy physics and by eliminating the background of thermally disordered photons using a computer, surprising phenomena have been observed in which weak but coherent photons are certainly emitted from living cells including human bodies, animals and plants. This is called biophoton emission (Chwirot, 1986; Popp et

perradiance and self-induced transparency will resume. The more condensed the nonlinear optical medium becomes, the more frequently such quantum mechanical cooperative phenomena of coherent photons take place.

Acknowledgements

The authors wish to thank Professors H. Umezawa, Y. Takahashi, L. M. Ricciardi and C. I. J. M. Stuart for providing us with a quantum theoretical framework for living matter. They also wish to thank Professors K. H. Pribram and S. Hameroff for active collaboration.

References

Ablowitz, M. J., Kaup, D. J., Newell, A. C. and Sequr, H., 1974, The inverse scattering transform – Fourier analysis for nonlinear problems. Stud. Appl. Math. *53*, 249-315.

Agarwal, G. S., 1971, Master-equation approach to spontaneous emission III: many-body aspects of emission from two-level atoms and the effect of inhomogeneous broadening. Phys. Rev. *A4*, 1791-1801.

Allison, A. C. and Nunn, J. F., 1968, Effects of general anesthetics on microtubules: a possible mechanism of anaesthesia. The Lancet *2*, 1326-1329.

Beck, F. and Eccles, J. C., 1992, Quantum aspects of brain activity and the role of consciousness. Proc. Natl. Acad. Sci. USA *89*, 11357-11361.

Chwirot, W. B., 1986, New indication of possible role of DNA in ultraweak photon emission from biological systems. J. Plant Physiol. *122*, 81-86.

Clarke, A. C., 1968, *2001: A Space Odyssey* (Polaris Productions, Inc.).

Del Giudice, E., Doglia, S. and Milani, M., 1982, A collective dynamics in metabolically active cells. Phys. Lett. *90A*, 104-106.

Del Giudice, E., Doglia, S. and Milani, M., 1983, Self focusing and ponderomotive forces of coherent electric waves: a mechanism for cytoskeleton formation and dynamics, in: *Coherent Excitations in Biological Systems*, H. Fröhlich and F. Kremer (eds.) (Springer-Verlag, Berlin).

Del Giudice, E., Doglia, S., Milani, M. and Vitiello, G., 1985, A quantum field theoretical approach to the collective behavior of biological systems. Nucl. Phys. *B251*, 375-400.

Del Giudice, E., Doglia, S., Milani, M. and Vitiello, G., 1986, Electromagnetic field and spontaneous symmetry breaking in biological matter. Nucl. Phys. *B275*, 185-199.

Del Giudice, E., Preparata, G. and Vitiello, G., 1988, Water as a free electric dipole laser. Phys. Rev. Lett. *61*, 1085-1088.

Dicke, R. H., 1954, Coherence in spontaneous radiation processes. Phys. Rev. *93*, 99-110.

Eccles, J. C., 1986, Do mental events cause neural events analogously to the probability fields of quantum mechanics? Proc. R. Soc. Lond. *B227*, 411-428.

Feynman, R. P., 1985, Quantum mechanical computers. Optics News *11*, 11-20.

Feynman, R. P., Vernon Jr., F. L. and Hellwarth, R. W., 1957, Geometrical representation of the Schrödinger equation for solving maser problems. J. Appl. Phys. *28*, 49-52.

Franks, N. P. and Lieb, W. R., 1982, Molecular mechanisms of general anesthesia. Nature *300*, 487-493.

Franks, F., 1972, *Water: A Comprehensive Treatise* (Plenum, New York).

Fröhlich, H., 1968, Long-range coherence and energy storage in biological systems. Intern. J. Quantum Chem. *2*, 641-649.

Gabor, D., 1946, Theory of communication. J. Inst. Elect. Engin. *93*, 429-441.

Gabor, D., 1948, A new microscopic principle. Nature *161*, 777-778.

Gabor, D., 1968, Improved holographic model of temporal recall. Nature *217*, 1288-1289.

Grundler, W. and Keilmann, F., 1983, Sharp resonances in yeast growth: nonthermal sensitivity to microwaves. Phys. Rev. Lett. *51*, 1214-1216.

Halsey, M. J., 1976, Mechanisms of general anesthesia, in: *Anesthesia Uptake and Action*, E. I. Eger (ed.) (Williams and Wilkins, Baltimore).

Hameroff, S. R., 1974, Chi: a neural hologram? Am. J. Chi. Med. *2*, 163-170.

Hameroff, S. R., 1987, *Ultimate Computing: Biomolecular Consciousness and NanoTechnology* (North-Holland, Amsterdam).

Jibu, M. and Yasue, K., 1992A, A physical picture of Umezawa's quantum brain dynamics, in: *Cybernetics and Systems Research '92*, R. Trappl (ed.) (World Scientific, Singapore).

Jibu, M. and Yasue, K., 1992B, The basics of quantum brain dynamics, in: *Proceedings of the First Appalachian Conference on Behavioral Neurodynamics*, K. H. Pribram (ed) (Center for Brain Research and Informational Sciences, Radford University, Radford, September 17- 20).

Jibu, M. and Yasue, K., 1993A, Intracellular quantum signal transfer in Umezawa's quantum brain dynamics. Cybernetics and Systems: An International Journal *24*, 1-7.

Jibu, M. and Yasue, K., 1993B, Introduction to quantum brain dynamics, in: *Nature, Cognition and System III*, E. Carvallo (ed.) (Kluwer Academic, London).

Margenau, H., 1984, *The Miracle of Existence* (Oxbow Press, Woodbridge).

Marshall, I. N., 1989, Consciousness and Bose-Einstein condensates. New Ideas in Psychology *7*, 73-83.

McCall, S. L. and Hahn, E. L., 1967, Self-induced transparency by pulsed coherent light. Phys. Rev. Lett. *18*, 908-911.

Neubauer, C., Phelan, A. M., Keus H. and Lange, D. G., 1990, Microwave irradiation of rats at 2.45 GHz activates pinocytotic-loke uptake of tracer by capillary endothelial cells of cerebral cortex. Bioelectromagnetics *11*, 261-268.

Popp, F. A., Li, K. H., Mei, W. P., Galle, M. and Neurohr, R., 1988, Physical aspects of biophotons. Experientia *44*, 576-585.

Popp, F. A., Ruth, B., Bohm, J., Bahr, W., Grass, P., Grolling, G., Rattenmeyer, M., Schmidt, H. G. and Wulle, P., 1981, Emission of visible and ultraviolet radiation by active biological systems. Collect. Phenomena *3*, 187-214.

Pribram, K. H., 1966, Some dimensions of remembering: steps toward a neuropsychological model of memory, in: *Macromolecules and Behavior*, J. Gaito (ed.) (Academic Press, New York).

Pribram, K. H., 1971, *Languages of the Brain* (Englewood Cliffs, New Jersey).

Pribram, K. H., 1991, *Brain and Perception* (Lawrence Erlbaum, New Jersey).

Ricciardi, L. M. and Umezawa, H., 1967, Brain and physics of many-body problems. Kybernetik *4*, 44-48.

Sivakami, S. and Srinivasan, V., 1983, A model for memory. J. Theor. Biol. *102*, 287-294.

Stuart, C. I. J. M., Takahashi, Y. and Umezawa, H., 1978, On the stability and non-local properties of memory. J. Theor. Biol. *71*, 605-618.

Stuart, C. I. J. M., Takahashi, Y. and Umezawa, H., 1979, Mixed-system brain dynamics: neural memory as a macroscopic ordered state. Found. Phys. *9*, 301-327.

Umezawa, H., 1993, *Advanced Field Theory: Micro, Macro, and Thermal Physics* (American Institute of Physics, New York).

Webb, S. J., 1980, Laser Raman spectroscopy of living cells. Phys. Rep. *60*, 201-224.

Webb, S. J. and Stoneham, M. E., 1977, Resonances between 10^{11} and 10^{12} Hz in active bacterial cells as seen by laser Raman spectroscopy. Phys. Lett. *A60*, 267-268.

Webb, S. J., Stoneham, M. E. and Fröhlich, H., 1977, Evidence for coherent excitation in biological system. Phys. Lett. *A63*, 407-408.

Chapter 7

Self-Organization and Pavlov's Dogs. A Simple Model of the Brain

Dimitris Stassinopoulos, Per Bak, Preben Alstrom

March 18, 1994

Self-Organization and Pavlov's Dogs. A simple model of the Brain

Dimitris Stassinopoulos and Per Bak

Brookhaven National Laboratory

Department of Physics

Upton, NY 11973, USA

Preben Alstrøm

The Niels Bohr Institute

Department of Physics

Copenhagen 2100, Denmark

Abstract

We have constructed a simple model of the brain. The model consists of a set of randomly connected neurons. Inputs and outputs are also connected randomly to a subset of neurons. For each input there is a set of output neurons which must fire in order to achieve success. A signal giving information as to whether or not the action was successful is fed back to the brain from the environment. The connections between firing neurons are strengthened or weakened according to whether or not the action was successful. The system learns, through a self-organization process, to react intelligently to input signals, i.e., it learns to quickly select the correct output for each input. If part of the network is damaged, the system relearns the correct response after a training period. We simulated Pavlov's experiment by suddenly changing the correct response for a certain input signal. The system continues its old response for an extended period until it eventually learns the new correct response.

How does the brain work?

Two points of view as to where to look for the "secret" are often expressed:

1) The truth is in the detail. The brain consists of neurons. Once we understand the mechanism of the single neuron, we understand in principle everything. Thus, we must put emphasis on measuring the properties including the flow of chemicals, electrical potentials and pulses etc. at the synapses, axons etc. This traditional view has been very successful in science, most noticeably in particle physics where all matter has been reduced to a few quarks and gluons.

2) The truth is in the complexity. The brain has billions of neurons, each connected to thousands of other neurons. Once you have enough neurons, properly connected, intelligent behavior emerges by some magic. It has even been said that the brain must necessarily be so complicated that it can not possibly be understood by the brain. How then can we possibly generate a theory which deals with all these elements? Even to write down the map of the brain would require libraries of books.

Let us look into these two point of views. Let us compare with the way we would "understand" a man-made object, namely a computer.

First, following the strategy of looking into the details, we would take the computer apart and study its smallest parts. We would measure the characteristics of the transistors, that is, how the various currents and potentials depend on each other. We would have to understand the quantum mechanical properties of the materials, silicon etc, on which the transistor is based. Clearly, this will lead nowhere. Without any idea about the function that the transistors perform, no insight emerges. The computer engineer couldn't care less about how the transistor works - it is irrelevant for his purposes.

Second, although it is a popular view that a computer works because of its vast number of circuits, it is not so. The world's largest computers work the same way as the smallest pocket calculator. It simply has more storage, more processors, more input-output devices etc.

Thus, neither of the two points of views are useful for the computer, and most certainly they are not correct for the brain either. In order to understand the computer, one has to understand the principles by which the elements are put together. Whether the elements are of one type or another, whether they are of electrical, optical, or mechanical nature is irrelevant as long as they perform the correct function, that is for instance to carry out a simple logical operation such as an "AND" or "OR" logical operation on two bits. One does not have to explain the complete system with its myriads of connection to understand the computer. The truth is not in the intricacies. A computer is basically a simple device, sending numbers or bits from one location to another, and performing trivial operations with pairs of those numbers.

The same, we argue, goes for the brain. The goal must be to understand the principles by which the neurons interact. This doesn't mean that the study of the hardware, such as the flow of Ca^{++} and Na^+ ions at the synapses and axons, is irrelevant, in the same sense that the feasibility of constructing transistors is not irrelevant for the computer, but simply that this study can be decoupled from a general study of the mechanisms of the brain.

There is, however, one major conceptual difference between understanding the computer and understanding the brain. The computer was built by design. An engineer put together all the circuits etc. and made it work. In other words, with no engineer, we have no computer. However, there is no engineer around to connect all the synapses of the brain. One might imagine that the brain is ready and hard-wired at birth, with its connections formed by biological evolution and coded into the DNA. This does not make any sense. Evolution is efficient, but not that efficient. The amount of information contained in the DNA is vastly insufficient to specify all neural connections. The structure has to be *self-organized* rather than by design.

Thus, in order to understand the brain, we must understand the principles by which it organizes itself, presumably through its interaction with the environment. In order to be biologically feasible, those principles have to be simple and robust. In analogy with the computer, once those principles are understood there might be little qualitative difference between the smallest lobster brain and the human brain. If we are lucky, the difference is quantitative rather than qualitative. This "evolutionary" conjecture has not gained much acceptance; not because of lack of plausibility but because it failed to meet the immediate challenge it raises: to prove by demonstration the existence of such a simple and plausible model.

Conventional attractor neural network models (For reviews see Amit[1] and Hertz et al[2]) work in two modes: a learning mode where the strengths of the neural connections are computed and a retrieving mode where the network recognizes input signals, i.e., provides the same pattern for several similar input patterns. More advanced models use complicated back-propagation algorithms which continuously update the connections by a computation not performed by the neural network itself. These models have been important in constructing technologies for pattern recognition, and emphasis has been on maximizing their capacity for learning, without regards to questions raised in realistic modelling of brain function. From its birth, a real brain is "on its own" in an environment that constantly changes with no outside agent to turn switches between learning mode and retrieval mode.

Recently, Alstrøm and Stassinopoulos[3] addressed some of these points in a new class of neural networks, denoted *adaptive performance networks*. The central idea is the introduction of a global evaluative feedback signal, a dynamic threshold, and a reinforcement rule with no need of further computation. Here, we address the question of how can we get intelligent behaviour not through engineering but through self-organization. We shall demonstrate that this type of network can be trained to react "intelligently" to external sensory signals.[4] In a fashion analogous to the behaviorist techniques used in the training of animals we introduce our system with a set of external signals each of which rewards a specific action. The system learns to recognize all signals and choose the corresponding rewarding action. "Learning" and "retrieving" are two aspects of the same dynamical process. It must be. Individual neurons don't know what is globally going on; they perform their thing automatically, without concern to whether they contribute to a learning or a retrieving task. Only an outside observer is able to identify what is going out as learning or retrieving by inspecting its behavior.

The goal of any scientific theory or model is to capture the essential elements of experiments or observations in nature. Here we wish to model intelligent behavior at its simplest. To be concrete, consider the situation in which a system provides food to a "monkey" if the correct button is pressed. Which button is correct depends on whether a red or a green light is on. We call the two inputs "1" and "2", respectively. This signal, which is shown to the monkey, is all the information the monkey has in order to Figure out which is the right button at every instant. The monkey learns the correct reaction after a "learning" period of trial and error. If the outside world changes, i.e., the "correct" buttons are switched, the monkey should be able to modify its behavior. The monkey is able to learn progressively more complicated patterns. The ability of a model to mimic this process of learning "intelligent" responses (leading to satisfaction) to outside signals is denoted "artificial intelligence."

We start by visualizing our model-brain in its embryonic state: a network of neurons with random connections. Little genetic information is needed to construct such random networks. Sensory signals are fed into the brain randomly. The neural output, such as stimulation of muscle fibers, is also sent randomly. The environment responds to the action directed by the brain's output by rewarding (or not rewarding) it. The result is fed back to the brain through a global signal, which could be a change in the level of a hormone or an increase in the blood-sugar content. There is no mechanism by which the information can be fed back selectively to the individual neurons.

In our picture the interplay with the environment is essential in organizing the brain's ability to explore and become more experienced, allowing it to react intelligently. In order to represent this, our model interacts with the "outer world" in three different ways (Fig. 1). There is i) an input signal giving information about the state of the outer world; ii) a resulting action by the system toward the environment; iii) a global feedback signal indicating whether this action was successful or not in accomplishing the goal. Our model is necessarily grossly oversimplified; its sole purpose is to demonstrate certain simple general principles.

We have studied two network topologies: a layered one and a random one. In the latter model, both *inputs*, *outputs*, and *internal connections* are completely random. N neurons are each connected randomly to C other neurons. The neurons can be either in a firing state, $n_i = 1$, or a non-firing state, $n_i = 0$. The input to the i'th neuron from other neurons is $h_i = \sum J_{i,j} n_j$, where the summation is over the C interacting neighbors. Initially, the j's are randomly chosen in the interval $0 < J < 1$. The neuron fires if the input exceeds a threshold T. The interactions with the environment are implemented as follows.

i) The sensory signal is represented by an additional contribution, h' to the input signal of a number of random neurons. These various branches can be thought of as different features of the input signal such as sound, shape, color, smell, position, size, etc. Different inputs are represented by different sets of random input neurons (see Fig. 1).[6] ii) The output signal is the firing state of a set of randomly selected output neurons. For each input signal, the action is considered successful if one or more specific but randomly selected neurons, belonging to the set of output neurons, are all firing. iii) If the action is successful, a positive reinforcing signal $r << 1$ is fed back to all firing neurons. If the action is unsuccessful a negative signal is fed back. The reinforcement modifies all connections between firing neurons $J_{i,j} \rightarrow J_{i,j} + [rJ_{i,j}(1 - J_{i,j}) + h]n'_i n_j$, where n'_i denotes the state of the i'th neuron at the next time step and h is a random noise between $-h_0$ and h_0. The inputs are normalized, $J_{i,j} \rightarrow J_{i,j} + J_{i,j}/\sum_j J_{i,j}$.

Thus, if the action is successfull, all connections between firing neurons are reinforced, whether or not they participated in delivering the correct output; if the action is unsuccessful, the connections between firing neurons is weakened.

In addition to the above input-output functions, the model has a global control mechanism for the activity (Alstrøm and Stassinopoulos) for the total number of firing output neurons, A. It is important that this be kept to a minimum. If A exceeds a value A_0 the threshold T is reduced, while if A is smaller than A_0 the threshold is increased, $T \rightarrow T + \delta \text{sgn}(A - A_0)$. Thus, if there is no output, or the output is too low, the system is "thinking", that is its sensitivity is increased until an appropriate output is achieved. If the system is "confused", i.e., there is too much output, the sensitivity is lowered. Modulatory chemicals released into the brain help performing this function for the real brain, in addition to participating in the formation of the synapses, the J's discussed above.

At each time step the system is updated in parallel following the algorithm above. The performance P of the network is defined as the average success rate over 250 successive time steps. Figs. 2-7 show the results for a number of different tasks.

In the layered version, the neurons are arranged in rows, with each neuron firing to the three nearest neighbors in the next row. Inputs are random, but output neurons are

178

those in the bottom row. At each time step the system is updated in parallel following the algorithm above.

First, the "monkey" experiment defined above was simulated. A layered network with 256 neurons was studied, with $C = 3$ ($\eta_0 = 0.01, r = 0.1$). Two input signals, each with 16 random input neurons, were chosen. For each input, a pair of output cells was defined in the bottom row. The input signals were switched every 2000 time steps (or when complete success, meaning that the selected output neurons were active while all other neurons were not, has been achieved over 250 consecutive steps). Figure 2a shows the performance versus time. First, there is a period which we can identify as a learning period in which the success rate is low and oscillating. Eventually the networks locks into a state where success is obtained very quickly in response to the switching of inputs. In this phase, the system reacts intelligently to the input signal. It switches quickly back and forth between the two correct outputs. The transition from the learning phase to the retrieval phase is quite abrupt. We emphasize that no outside switch was activated at this point. Figure 2b shows a similar curve for the random-topology case. Again a sharp, self-organized transition from a learning mode to a retrieval mode is observed.

What happens inside the network during the learning phase? Through a complicated self-organization process, the system creates internal contacts or connections between selected parts of the input signal and the correct output cell(s). The process can be thought of as the formation of a river network connecting output with input. When the output is incorrect, the river flow is reduced at existing connections. When the flow is correct, the flow is reinforced. When there is too little output, the river beds are widened.

The state of the system after completion of the learning phase cannot be calculated by means of a simple algorithm. (The synapses are formed by self-organization rather than design). The "fast" dynamical switching between one connection pattern and another under switching of the outside signal in the "retrieval" phase following the long learning phase is quite complicated. Figure 3a,b shows the firing patterns for the "1" and "2" responses. Figure 4 shows a movie of the switching process from the "1" response to the "2" response. The switching from "1" to "2" and back takes place through eleven intermediate steps. We doubt that any engineer would come up with such a solution. If we were free to construct the network "by design" we could obviously come up with a much simpler and efficient solution. The memory lies in the conservation of parts of the river beds from previous correct connections.[7]

The system has self-organized into a state where the change of "water supply" at random positions causes a fast conversion to the correct output. In the learning phase the system is very sensitive to the relative small changes in input - in that sense it is chaotic. No such dynamical switching takes place in conventional neural networks where connections are essentially hard-wired in the retrieval mode.

Figure 5 shows the response to "damage" of the network. After ~150000 time steps, a block of 30 neurons was removed from the network. After a transient period the network has relearned the correct response, carving new connections in the network. In other words, instead of using some features of the input signal the system learns to use other features. Think of this as replacing "vision" with "smell." The memory is distributed and robust,[8] as it should be in order to represent real brain function. The new firing patterns are shown in Figure 3c,d.

Figure 6 shows the situation where a third input (and corresponding pair of output cells) was added after the first two responses had been learned. After a transient period where the system is confused and the success rate is low, the network eventually learns the three appropriate responses.

Finally, we have simulated a situation analogous to Pavlov's famous dog experiment. Before serving the food, Pavlov would present the dog with a signal, such as ringing a bell. The dog learns to respond correct to this signal, it salivates. Next, Pavlov would ring the bell, but not serve any food. The action, salivating, which before led to success is now unsuccessful, or at least a wasted effort. We consider a situation with two inputs "1" and "2", each consisting of a signal sent to 8 random input cells. Think of "1" as representing the ringing of the bell, and "2" the vision of the food. In the beginning, we let the correct response be the same, that is the correct response is to fire the cells #10 and #15 of the bottom row. The system learns to react correctly to the switching of the two inputs as before (Figure 7). After a few more time steps we "cheat" the system by changing the correct input of the "1" signal to be the triggering of output cells #7 and #12. For a long transient period the "dog" keeps triggering the wrong output cells, 10 and 15, until it finally learns the correct response. Actually, we performed one run where the dog never learned the new responce after the switching of feedback signal. It is difficult to teach old dogs new tricks.

A brain working according to the principles illustrated here requires a minimum of biological complexity - it is a relatively simple organ without much structure. Little information is needed to construct the simple network with essentially arbitrary connections. The correlations that control the switching behavior of the system hint to the fact that 'it is not only the well developed "riverbeds," and where most of the activity takes place, that are important for the function of the network but also the relatively silent regions in between.'

In conclusion, we have constructed a simple model simulating aspects of brain function. The build-up of the $J_{i,j}$ landscape is due to a self-organization process. We suggest that simple robots performing "intelligent" tasks can be constructed following the principles outlined here.

The work done at Brookhaven National Laboratory was supported by the U.S. Department of Energy, Division of Materials Science, Office of Basic Energy Sciences under Contract No. DE-AC02-76CH00016.

References

1. Amit, D. J. *Modelling Brain Function: The World of Attractor Neural Networks* (Cambridge University Press, Cambridge, 1989).

2. Hertz, J., Krogh A., & Palmer, R. G. *Introduction to the Theory of Neural Computation* (Addison-Wesley, Redwood, 1991).

3. Alstrøm, P. & Stassinopoulos, D., submitted to Phys. Rev. Lett. (1994).

4. Stassinopoulos, D. & Bak, P., submitted to Nature (1994).

5. McCulloch, W. S. & Pitts, W. Bull. Math. Biophys. 5, 115 (1943).

6. The original AS-model[3] is "blind" in the sense that it operates with a fixed input signal at the upper layer.

7. A more detailed study of the dynamics of this learning mechanism is in progress.

8. To check for robustness we tested the performance of the system when signals were presented randomly and for an arbitrary duration of time.

Figure Captions

Figure 1. Block diagram of brain model. Each signal is represented by random inputs to a number of neurons. For each signal, here red or green, there is a combination of one or more output neurons (shaded circles) which must fire in order to achieve success. The environment feeds back a signal indicating whether or not success was achieved. a) Layered network; b) Random network.

Figure 2. a) Performance vs. time for layered system with two input signals which are switched every 2000 time units or when the system is consistently successfull. After a training period during which the network self-organizes, the system enters an intelligent state with fast switching between the correct outputs. b) Same for random network; the two input signals are presented for 5000 time units unless consistent success has occured.

Figure 3. Firing patterns for "1" input (a) and "2" input (b) in the fast switching mode. The input cells for "1" and "2" are black and dark gray respectively, and the firing cells are light gray. For the "1" input, output cells 10 and 15 of the bottom row must be triggered simultaneously to achieve success; for the "2" input the output cells 7 and 12 must be triggered. c,d) The same as above but in the case where the system has relearned the correct response after removal of a block of 30 neurons (shaded area).

Figure 4. Movie showing the "fast" switching between the "1" response and the "2" response. The transition from "2" to "1" takes place through five complicated steps and back to "1" through an additional six steps.

Figure 5. Performance for the layered system, but with 30 neurons damaged after 150000 time steps. The system has relearned the correct response after 210000 time steps.

Figure 6. Same system as shown in Figure 2a, with a third input added after 150000 steps. After a confused learning period, the correct output for all three inputs is learned after 450000 time steps.

Figure 7 Pavlov's dogs. In the beginning the correct response to two different input signals (Ringing a bell, and vision of food) is the same. This is learned after a few thousand time steps (arrow A). After 40000 time steps (arrow B) the correct response to one signal is altered, i.e., the reaction of the system is supposed to switch when the input signals are switched. For a long transient period the system triggers the wrong output, mostly the cells which were originally correct. Eventually, after 170000 time steps, the system learns the new correct reaction.

Figure 1a

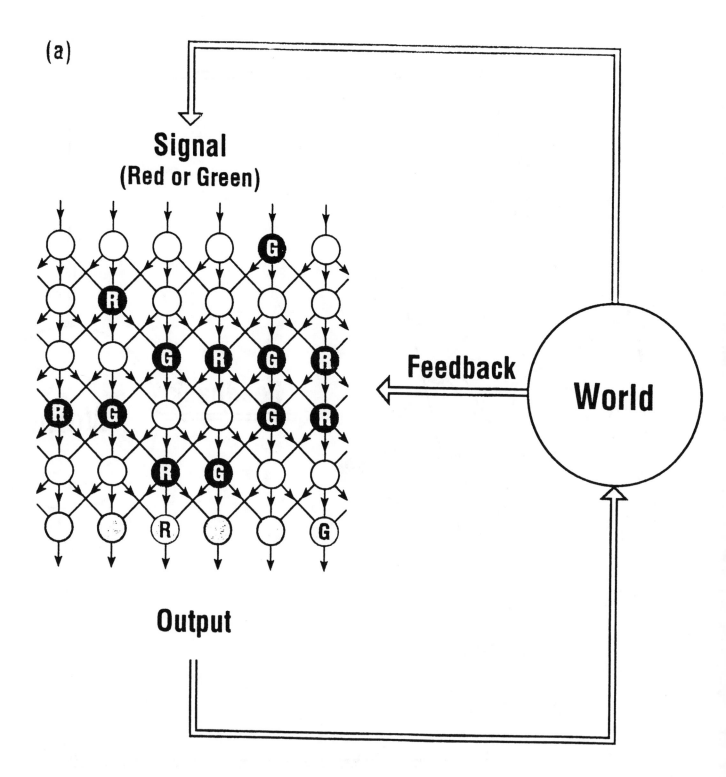

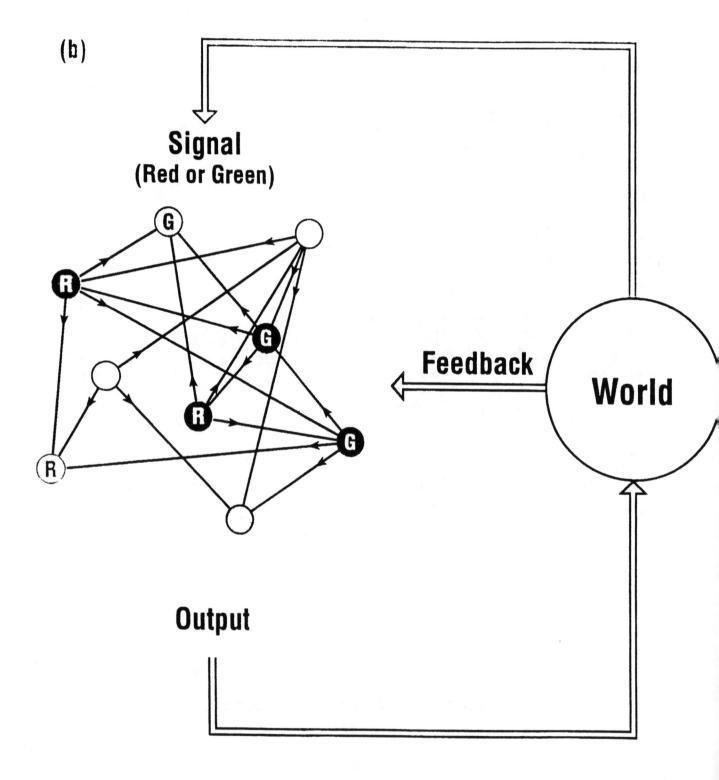

(b)

Signal
(Red or Green)

Feedback

World

Output

Figure 2a

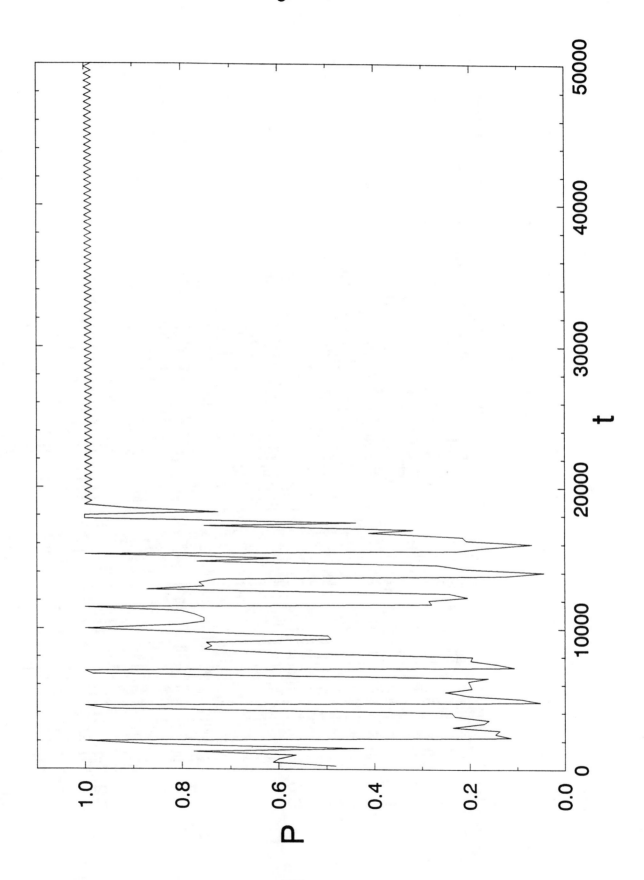

Figure 2b

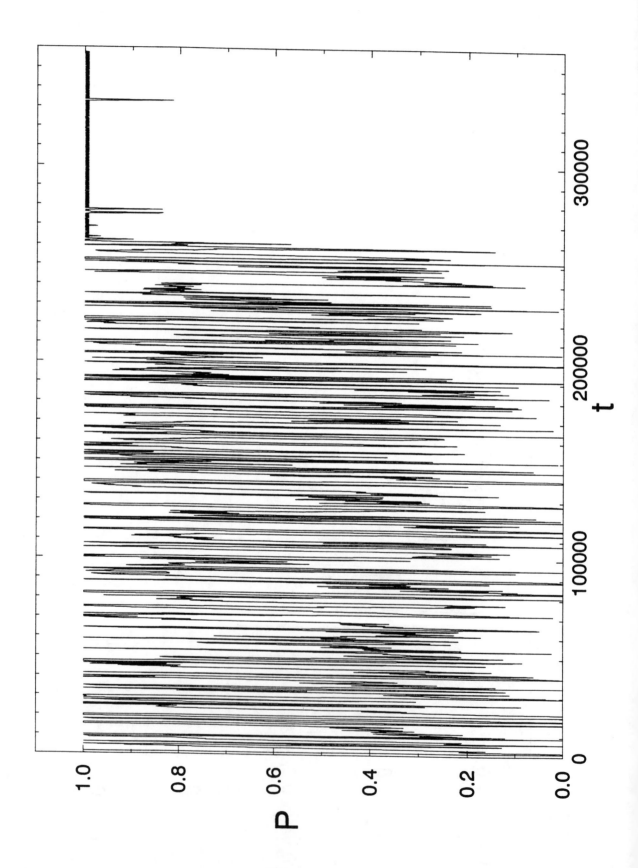

Figure 3

(a)

(b)

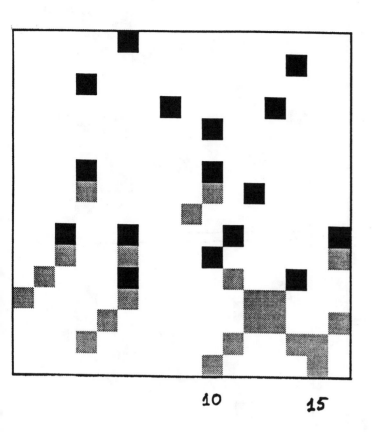

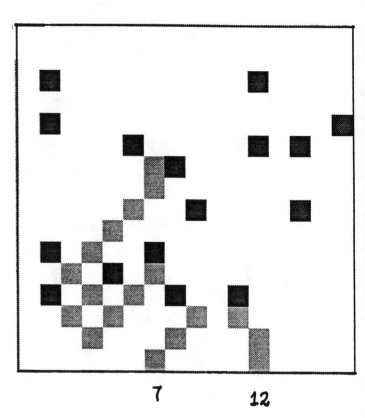

10 15

7 12

(c)

(d)

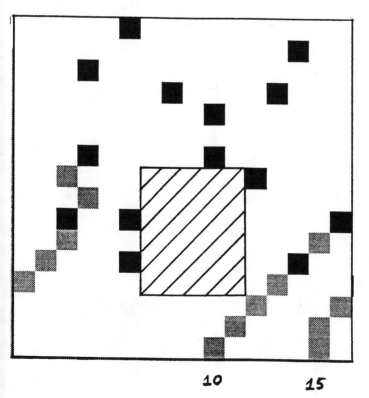

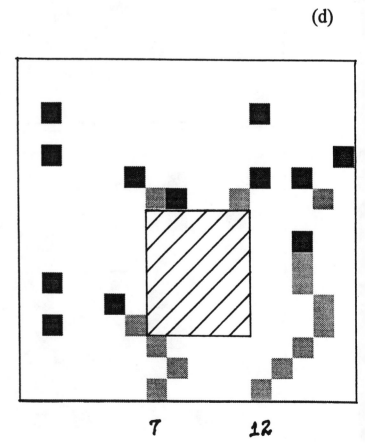

10 15

7 12

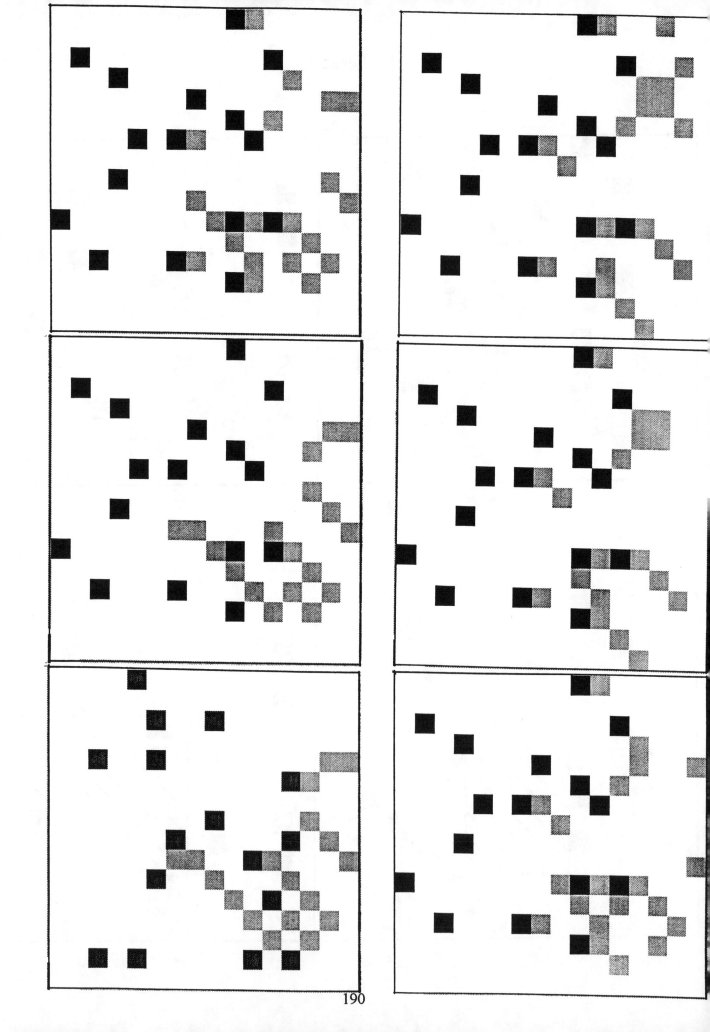

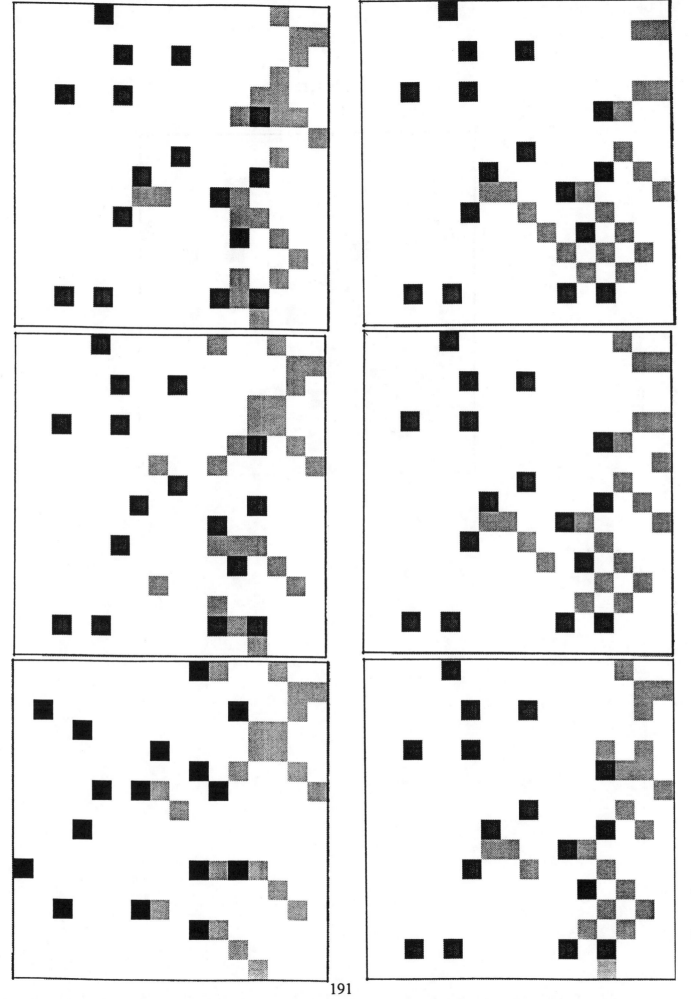

191

Figure 4

Figure 4

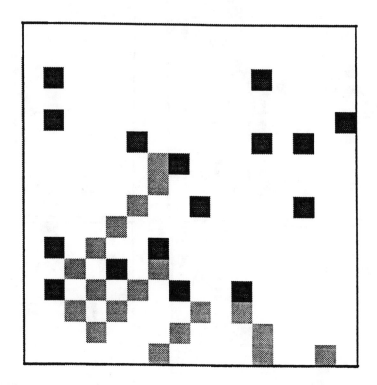

Figure 5

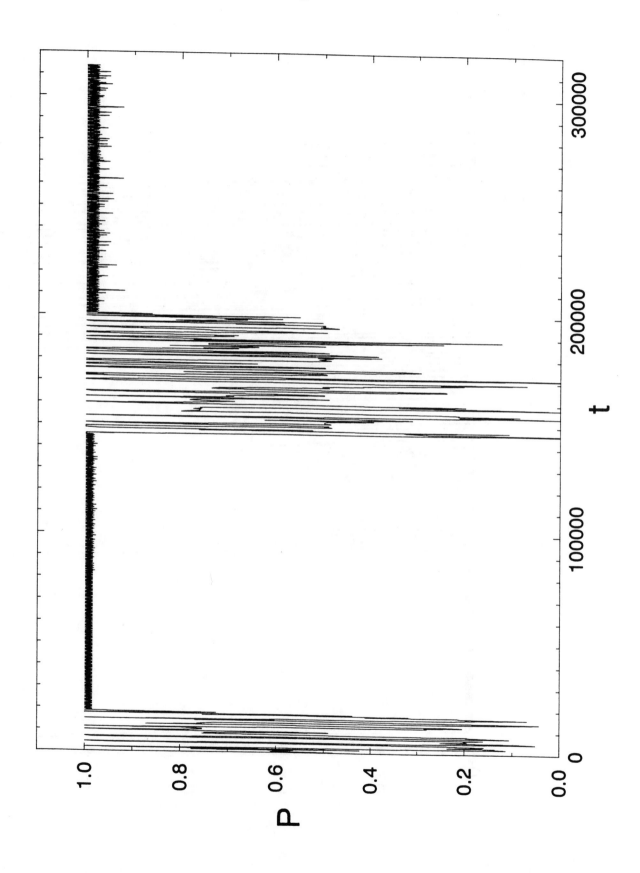

Figure 6

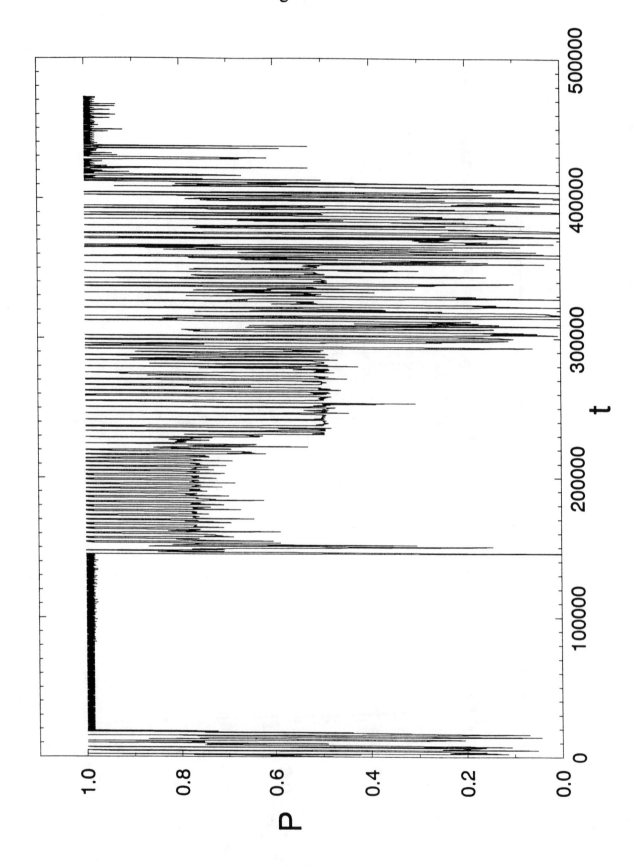

Figure 7

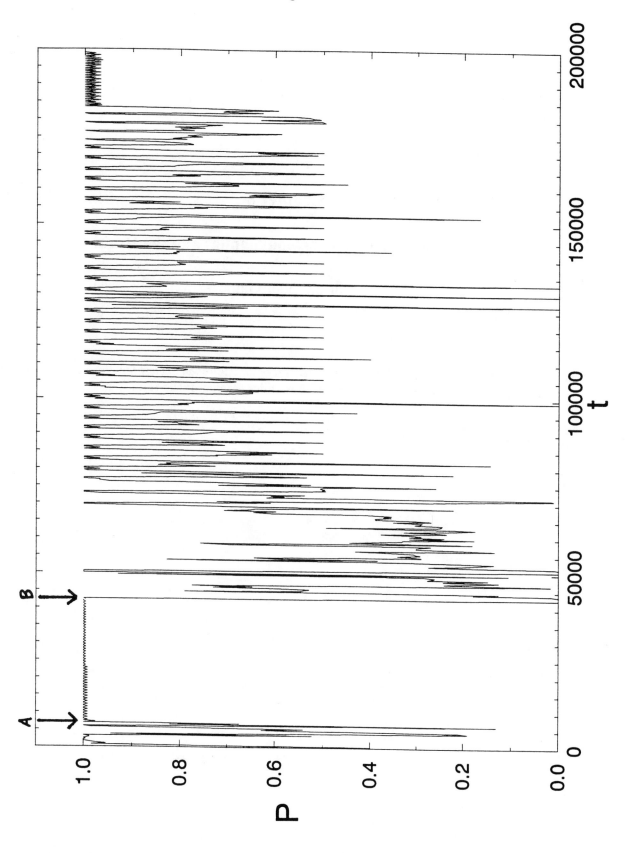

Chapter 8

Non-Equilibrium Thermodynamics and the Brain

Christopher Game

This chapter is reprinted from the *Conference Proceedings of the Australian Society for Biophysics*, Volume 3, pp. 15-29. Copyright © 1979 by Australian Society for Biophysics. Reprinted with permission.

Modified from *Proceedings of the Australian Society for Biophysics*, 3 (1979) 15-20: An invited lecture to the 3rd Annual Meeting of the Society, held at the Flinders University of South Australia, on 31 August - 2 September 1978.

NON-EQUILIBRIUM THERMODYNAMICS AND THE BRAIN

C.J.A. Game

Department of Human Physiology and Pharmacology,
University of Adelaide

Introduction

Physics has a relatively well organised conceptual basis; neurophysiology is not so advanced in this way, but has a large body of observations.

It is the purpose of this paper to explore some relationships between the ideas of physics and those of neurophysiology. The plan is to state some general principles of neurophysiology in an abstract way, so as to display their similarity to ideas used in physics to study critical phenomena.

We may compare an integrative nervous system with a physical system near a critical point. Critical states are in fluctuation dominated regimes, and are characterised by long range correlations. The integrative action of the nervous system depends upon cooperative activity of neurones, described by long range correlations between nerve cells throughout the brain and spinal cord. Besides the long range of the correlations, there is a richness of variety of correlation patterns. The need to consider high order correlation patterns is also felt in the study of physical systems far from equilibrium.

General Principles

Some general principles of neurophysiology are (1) Sherrington's principle of reciprocal innervation; (2) Hughlings Jackson's doctrine of levels; (3) a principle of critical development; (4) lability of consciousness.

(1) Sherrington's principle of reciprocal innervation may be seen as a rule to guide the interpretation of experiments. A coordinated movement is defined as one in which the motor units which contribute to the purpose of a movement are excited, while those which do not are inhibited. In order to specify a coordinated movement it is necessary to specify its purpose to the animal. Sherrington's principle may then be stated: every normal movement is coordinated.

The most elementary example of a coordinated movement, which Sherrington (1906) elucidated many years ago, and has now been studied with more refinement, is that of the flexor-extensor antagonism in the limbs. The flexors tend to bend the leg whereas the extensors tend to straighten it. In the most elementary movements, its is purposeful to bend the leg, or to straighten it, but not to hold it rigid with both sets of muscles contracting at once. Such a movement pattern is said to occur by reciprocal innervation.

Neuronal connections are known which can exert this type of reciprocal innervation (Miller & Scott, 1977). These connections are illustrated in an abbreviated diagram, which shows only a few neurones to indicate the pattern for hundreds of neurones. The motor neurones in the lumbosacral spinal cord can be divided into two sets, the flexors and the extensors, on the basis that Ia primary afferent fibres of flexors make monosynaptic excitatory contacts onto flexor motor neurones, but not extensor motor neurones; while Ia primary afferent fibres of extensors make monosynaptic excitatory contacts onto extensor motor neurones, but not flexor motor neurones. Associated with the flexor motor neurones are cells in the ventral horn which we may call flexor Ia interneurones. The flexor Ia interneurones can inhibit the extensor Ia interneurones and the extensor motor neurones. And vice versa for extensor Ia interneurones. If we imagine a general excitation to be acting on all the cells, we can see how these inhibitory connections would work. A slight fluctuation of increased firing by a flexor Ia interneurone would inhibit many extensor Ia interneurones and thus remove inhibition of other flexor Ia interneurones, thus enhancing their firing rate; positive feedback would occur and soon all the flexor Ia interneurones would be firing more rapidly and keeping the extensor Ia interneurones in an inhibited state. Or a fluctuation could have flipped the system the other way. These nervous connections thus have a flip-flop property.

This is a simple example of a type of mechanism which must account for all coordinated movement. The brain and spinal cord do not normally give mixed and conflicting output signals, but instead make a clearcut decision and execute it. This is what Sherrington called integrative action. Denny-Brown (1962) has continued Sherrington's thinking, speaking of conflicting effects being resolved in a competitive organisation, and showing how it is concordant with Jackson's doctrine of levels.

(2)   Hughlings Jackson's doctrine of levels is not so easy to state or discuss. This reflects a gap in the conceptual repertoire of neurophysiology. As Jackson (1932) stated it, the doctrine of levels seems intuitively appealing, but we lack the skill to state it in terms concordant with the language of physics. If Jackson's intuition could be stated suitably, we would have a powerful tool to aid our analysis of the integrative activity of the nervous system. It is part of the purpose of this paper to contribute to such a statement of Jackson's doctrine of levels. It may be that a clear enough statement would allow rejection of the doctrine as false, but would allow its replacement by some other related proposition which would be true.

Jackson says: "The lowest level ... represents all parts of the body most nearly directly ... The middle level represents all parts of the body doubly indirectly ... The highest level ... represents all parts of the body triply indirectly ... The highest centres re-re-represent the body ... They are centres of triply compound coordination ... The scheme is, not, as I have in some former papers erroneously said, the morphological divisions, into spinal cord, medulla oblongata, pons varolii, cerebral hemispheres, and cerebellum. It is (a different type of) anatomical division ... To give an account of the anatomy of any centre is to give an account of the parts of the body it represents and of the degree of indirectness in which it represents them".

Denny-Brown (1962) writes of the "principle of the refinement of movement by successive levels of differentiation of adequacy of stimulus for a given reaction ... The increasing complexity of motor performance at successively higher levels of integration is related, not to the provision of more and more detailed patterns of neuronal pathways to individual muscles, but to increasing complexity of the afferent mechanisms." He had in mind especially the disturbances of function arising from localised lesions of the brain.

The lesion of function arising from the action of general anaesthetics is well known to occur in stages which are more or less universal in their progression from impairment of thought and feeling down to impairment of elementary rhythmical activities like breathing.

Jackson rejected a morphological hierarchy in favour of one more abstractly defined, by degrees of indirectness of representation. We may compare his idea with the use in physics of the dynamics of correlations (Prigogine, 1963). To describe the character of departures from equilibrium, a sequence of correlation patterns of progressively higher order is used. Jackson's lower level activities are those which could be described by lower order correlation patterns amongst neurones. Higher level activities are those which need also higher order correlations for their description. The lower order activities would include a smaller class of coordinated movements. At each level of integrative activity a class of purposes for movements can be recognised. For example, avoidance of potentially nocuous stimuli requires a higher order of correlations in its description than does a mere withdrawal from an actually nocuous stimulus. And tactile exploration of nearby objects requires a higher order of correlations in its description than does a mere extensor thrust of the legs to bear the weight of the body.

We now have a picture of the integrative activity of the nervous system as a hierarchy of multistable levels. The lowest level is the single molecule sodium gate of the excitatory synaptic receptor: each gate is either open or shut. The next level is the single neurone: each neurone is either firing an impulse or waiting below threshold. The next level is the elementary bistable spinal reciprocal innervation we have considered already. At a higher level, Denny-Brown (1962) has described cerebral cortical organisation in terms of a reciprocity between exploring and avoiding reactions, normally bistable, but abnormally, in athetosis, showing unstable or ergodic drifts between the two extremes. At a higher level still, we may regard the leading of thought by the left cerebral hemisphere and of feeling by the right as a bistable system.

(3)   The nervous system can learn, and adapt its integrative activity after lesions. These abilities can be stated abstractly as a principle of critical development: the growth and metabolism of the nervous system tend to increase the variety of possible coordinated movements. Of course this does not contradict the second law of the thermodynamics, because the nervous system is an open system through which matter and energy flow, and they can carry away entropy.

(4)   Walshe (1972) has offered a sharp discussion of consciousness. Consciousness is labile, like the fluctuation-dominated critical states of physical systems.

Physiologists often think in terms of self-regulating negative-feedback systems. The brain is the regulating device, and the body is the regulated load. For example, body temperature is regulated in man to about 37°C. We may call this temperature the set-point or target of the regulation.

Thermodynamics and Statistical Mechanics

The fantastic complexity of the activity of the brain makes its detailed modelling an enormous task. Even if we knew every detail of every molecular movement of the active brain, we would be very far from an understanding of the behavioural and psychological significance of the activity. Higher levels of decription are needed to make the picture comprehensible. Thermodynamics, and its companion subject statistical mechanics, are the means that physicists have used to make links between the molecular pictures and macroscopically comprehensible pictures of the dynamics of relatively simple physical systems. Neurophysiology may also contemplate an attempt to make links between its various levels of description.

The statistical mechanical model of the brain as a thermodynamic system is an attempt to bridge the gaps between the detailed picture of the motions of single transmitter molecules and receptor molecules, single synapses, single neurones, . . . , single phonemes, single syllables, single words, single sentences, . . . , and single selves. Specifically, thermodynamics is concerned with systems for which there can be defined a unique scalar local temperature which is a parameter of certain Gaussian or Poisson distributions. The temperature is defined by a limit of a sequence of measurements obtained by the use of successively more ideal thermometers. In systems adequately described by the canonical local equilibrium distributions, microscopic variables are of no interest because they simply represent chaotic movements of molecules; only macroscopic variables are of interest.

But it is of no use to neurophysiologists to consider the brain as a macroscopic furnace which produces heat to keep the heart and liver warm, nor can we find appreciable work output to account for the brain's consumption of metabolites. Nor is it of use to us to consider the microscopic movements of individual molecules of the brain. Neurophysiologists need variables that are some way between macroscopic and microscopic. A knowledge of the complete circuit diagram of the brain would not be comprehensible from a physiological viewpoint without some scheme for reducing the number of variables.

Statistical mechanics may be a guide here (Balescu, 1975; Yvon, 1969; Zubarev, 1974).Two ideas may be useful: one is the occurrence of disorder not fully defined by absolute temperature, and the other is the renormalisation group approach to the problem of reducing the number of variables at critical states.

Thermal entropy can be usefully defined for gases by use of Boltzmann's statistical formula in terms of the one-particle reduced distribution of momenta. For more general non-equilibrium dissipative systems, the Brussels school have shown the existence of a unique generalisation of the Boltzmann entropy. But this entropy does not express all the unpredictability of the system; the Gibbs statistical entropy does express it all, but requires the full many-particle distribution function.

The unpredictability of the nervous system is obviously dependent on high order correlations contained in the full many-particle distribution function. This corresponds with the need to describe high level integrative activity in terms of high order correlations between neurones.

Critical States

Statistical mechanics also makes use of the idea of a progression of scales of coordination. States in which the same coordinative mechanism leads to changes of the same form, on a progression of scales, are recognised as critical states. The most parsimonious principle of evolutionary development would suppose that the evolving brain uses the same principle at each step, up though its hierarchy of levels of coordination.

The renormalisation group approach (Pfeuty & Toulouse, 1977) to the problem of reducing the number of variables for a critical state is to make a caricature "Hamiltonian" to express the most relevant properties of the system. The caricature is given convenient symmetries which enable the problem to be tackled. It would be radical to postulate that the brain and spinal cord were spatially homogeneous, but possibly helpful as a first approximation. It could be postulated that each part of the nervous system worked according to a universal pattern like that of the spinal flexor-extensor mechanism we have considered. The idea of repeated re-representation could be interpreted as a multiplication of the variety of coordinated movements arising from interconnections between parts of the nervous system. Each part of the system multiplies the possible effects of the other parts.

A crucial assumption of the renormalisation group approach is that of scale invariance. For the brain this could be interpreted as a correspondence in form between the threshold of the single neurone, the threshold of the flexion-extension reflex pattern, and perhaps more generally for thresholds between modes of activity led by either left (thinking) or right (feeling) hemispheres.

To keep the system at the critical point, with the caricature "Hamiltonian" expressing singular properties, the metabolic structures of the brain would need to stabilize the system near threshold, like the structure described by Thom (1975) for the potential surface $V = x^2y + y^4/4$. This surface has the property that each particle which rolls slowly from an area uphill of the critical point will actually reach the critical point. A small fluctuation may then send it rolling down either of two valleys. Correspondingly a stimulus may impinge upon the nervous system, and set up signals which propagate until a decisive state is reached, when a coordinated movement is selected and executed. The metabolism of the brain and spinal cord have to trim the surface continually, lest the critical property be dissipated, and the particle usually fail to reach the critical point, and the lability of the system be lost.

Another physical approach to critical states sees them as states which lie just on special marginal junction-points between different phases.

The marginal junction-point approach is also of interest to neurophysiologists considering human behaviour. We need to have rapid access to our joy and sorrow, our sharing and our anger. We must steer between sleep and epilepsy, between contemplation and action. It may be possible to regard such physiological states as phases, comparable with the crystalline, nematic, smectic, glassy, liquid, plasma, and gaseous states of simple physical systems.

Within the class of glassy states, statistical mechanics recognises multiple equilibrium states, all of nearly the same energy, but mutually inaccessible at a low and fixed temperature; the classical ergodic hypothesis is not fulfilled by such multiple equilibrium states. Glassy states have been proposed as statistical mechanical models of brain activity. If we lower our mental temperature too far, we become fixed in a rut of inflexible behaviour. On the other hand, too high a mental temperature scrambles our purposes, makes us uncoordinated, and fragments our will. We need a critical mental temperature.

The brain can be seen as a system that may allow propagation and transformation of signals from afferent inputs to efferent outputs. Because of this flow, the brain is not in equilibrium. Non-equilibrium critical states are recognised in statistical mechanics. Percolation is an example. Critical percolation occurs when the packing of the solid grains is just loose enough to permit a trickle of fluid flow through the packed solid medium. Perhaps the brain works best when its afferent input is just critically able to influence its motor output, subject to the critical filtering action of the accumulated grains of knowledge of past experience. If we do not say enough, or if we say too much, in response to what we hear, we may be in trouble.

It has been proposed as a general principle of physical evolution, that natural systems tend to approach critical states, determined by the very dynamical nature of the systems themselves [1].

The brain seems to have built into it a tendency to find its own critical state, the state in which it has available to it the widest possible variety of coordination [2]. This may be the neurophysiological criterion of good.

SUMMARY

Some abstract properties of the activity of the nervous system are stated for comparison with some physical ideas. The properties are:

(1)   cooperativity amongst many small elements, giving thresholds,
(2)   structure arising by repeated re-representation,
(3)   tendency to increase the number of types of cooperative states possible,
(4)   fluctuations dominate.

The unpredictability of interest is not thermal, but may be expressed by a non-thermal entropy, which is important far from equilibrium. The unpredictability may arise as the metabolism of the brain maintains a critical state with a certain type of topology.

REFERENCES

Bak P and Chen K. Sci Am, Jan 1991: 26-33.

Bak P and Chen K. Self-organised criticality. Scientific American, January 1991; 26-33.

Balescu, R. (1975) Equilibrium and Non-equilibrium Statistical Mechanics. Wiley-Interscience, New York.

Denny-Brown, D. (1962) The Basal Ganglia and their Relation to Disorders of Movement. Oxford University Press, London.

Game CJA (1979) Non-equilibrium thermodynamics and the brain. Proc Aust Soc Biophys 3:15-20.

Jackson, J.H. (1932) Selected Writings of John Hughlings Jackson. Vols. I & II. Ed. James Taylor. Hodder and Stoughton, London.

Miller, S. and Scott, P.D. (1977) The spinal locomotor generator. Exp. Brain Res.30, 387-403.

Pfeuty, P. and Toulouse, G. (1977 trs. by G. Barton) Introduction to the Renormalisation Group and to Critical Phenomena. Wiley-Interscience, London.

Prigogine, I. (1963) Non-equilbrium Statistical Mechanics. Wiley-Interscience, New York.

Sherrington, C.S. (1906) The Integrative Action of the Nervous System. Yale University Press, New Haven.

Thom, R. (1975 trs. by D.H. Fowler) Structural Stability and Morphogenesis, An Outline of a General Theory of Models. W.A. Benjamin, Reading, Massachusetts.

Walshe, F.M.R. (1972) The neurophysiological approach to the problem of consciousness, in Scientific Foundations of Neurology. Eds. M. Critchley, J.L. O'Leary, B. Jennett. William Heinemann, London.

Yvon, J. (1969 trs. by H.S.H. Massey) Correlations and Entropy in Classical Statistical Mechanics. Pergamon, Oxford.

Zubarev, D.N. (1974 trs. by P.J. Shepherd) Non-equilibrium Statistical Thermodynamics. Consultants Bureau, Plenum, New York.

II. SPIKE TRAINS AND NETWORKS

Chapter 9

As If Time Really Mattered:
Temporal Strategies for Neural Coding of Sensory Information

Peter Cariani

As if time really mattered:
Temporal strategies for neural coding
of sensory information

Peter Cariani

Eaton Peabody Laboratory of Auditory Physiology
Massachusetts Eye and Ear Infirmary
243 Charles St, Boston, MA 02114 USA
eplunix!peter@eddie.mit.edu

CC-AI, 1995, Vol. 12, No. 1-2,
Special Issue on Self Reference in Biological and Cognitive Systems,
L. Rocha Editor

Abstract

Potential strategies for temporal neural processing in the brain and their implications for the design of artificial neural networks are considered. Current connectionist thinking holds that neurons send signals to each other by changes in their average rate of discharge. This implies that there is one output signal per neuron at any given time (scalar coding), and that all neuronal specificity is achieved solely by patterns of synaptic connections. However, information can be carried by temporal codes, in temporal patterns of neural discharges and by relative times of arrival of individual spikes. Temporal coding permits multiplexing of information in the time domain, which potentially increases the flexibility of neural networks. A broadcast model of information transmission is contrasted with the current notion of highly specific connectivity. Evidence for temporal coding in somatoception, audition, electroception, gustation, olfaction and vision is reviewed, and possible neural architectures for temporal information processing are discussed.

1. The role of timing in the brain

The human brain is by far the most capable, the most versatile, and the most complex information-processing system known to science. For those concerned with problems of artificial intelligence there has long been the dream that once its functional principles are well understood, the design and construction of adaptive devices more powerful than any yet seen could follow in a straightforward manner. Despite great advances, the neurosciences are still far from understanding the nature of the "neural code" underlying the detailed workings of the brain. i.e. exactly which information-processing operations are involved.

If we choose to view the brain in informational terms, as an adaptive signalling system embedded within an external environment, then the issue of which aspects of neural activity constitute the "signals" in the system is absolutely critical to understanding its functioning. It is a question which must be answered before all others, because all functional assumptions, interpretations, and models depend upon the appropriate choice of what processes neurons use to convey information. The role of the time patterns of neural discharges in the transmission and processing of information in the nervous system has been debated since the pulsatile nature of nervous transmission was recognized less than a century ago. Because external stimuli can be physically well-characterized and controlled, the encoding of sensory information has always played a pivotal role in more general conceptions of neural coding.

2. Coding by average discharge rate

With the advent of single cell recording techniques in neurophysiology, it was generally assumed that neural information is encoded solely in the average neural discharge rates of neurons (Adrian 1928). This notion of a average discharge rate code, sometimes called the Frequency Coding principle[1], has persisted and forms the basis for virtually all neural net design (Feldman 1990) and almost all neuroscientific investigations concerned with information processing (Barlow 1972).

While there is much accumulated experimental evidence to support such a principle in many systems, it does not necessarily follow that only average rate codes are used in the nervous coding. From the advent of modern electrophysiology, there were always other conceptions of how sense information could be transmitted (Troland 1921; Troland 1929; Wever & Bray 1937; Boring 1942; Wever 1949). Many other types of codes produce signals which co-vary with average rates, and these other coding schemes may actually contain much higher quality information than average discharge rates. In the auditory nerve, for example, stimulus periodicities below a few kHz are much more precisely represented by interspike interval statistics than by discharge rates (Goldstein & Srulovicz 1977), but because both interval patterns and discharge rate patterns are observed together, it is difficult to determine directly which kinds of codes are functionally operant. However, since rate-coding has become the default assumption of practicing neuroscientists, the burden of proof generally falls on the alternatives.

The principle of rate coding has a number of wide-ranging ramifications in the way that neural networks, both wet and dry are conceptualized. A mean rate code entails some time window over which spikes are counted, and depending upon the system, this window is usually thought to be on the order of tens to hundreds of milliseconds or more. Long integration windows can present problems in sensory systems where coherent, detailed percepts can be generated with short stimulus durations (e.g. tachistoscopically presented images, tone bursts). The meaningful use of an average discharge rate is also stretched when only a handful of spikes are discharged within an integration window, as often occurs in cortical neurons.

Rate coding goes hand in hand with the doctrine of "specific nerve energies," as it was laid out by Müller and Helmholtz (see discussion in (Boring 1933; Boring 1942)). The principle asserts that specific sensory modalities have specific types of sense receptors. Consequently it is by virtue of connection to a given type of receptor that a given neuron is interpreted to be sending a signal related to a particular quality (a visual signal as opposed to a smell). Helmholtz through his study of the cochlea elevated this principle to also include quality differences within a sense modality. Thus, in Helmholtz's view, because particular auditory nerve fibers are connected to receptors at specific places on the cochlear partition, and hence have different frequency sensitivities, they signal different pure tone pitches by virtue of their connectivity. Coding exclusively by average discharge rate necessitates this kind of "labelled line" or "place" coding because there is no other means internal to the spike train itself for conveying what kind of signal it is (e.g. a taste vs. a sound; the semantics of the message). While the doctrine of specific nerve energies does not mandate that average rate be the signal encoded in the spike train (e.g. see the discussion of Troland's resonance-frequency theory of hearing (Boring 1942)), it has generally been taken on faith that sensory coding could be accomplished solely by rate-place codes. Unless temporal patterns are immediately obvious and impossible to ignore, looking elsewhere into coding alternatives has generally been regarded by neuroscientists as wasted effort.

---

[1]"Frequency" has two meanings, one associated with a rate of events, the other associated with a particular periodicity of events. Frequency Coding implies the former meaning.

In tandem with exclusive use of rate codes, it has often been assumed that here is no usable temporal structure in spike trains, i.e. spike trains can be functionally described as a Poisson process with one independent parameter, the mean rate of arrivals. As a result, in many higher-level models of neuronal networks, the temporal dynamics of spike generation are ignored in favor of mean rates or discharge probabilities. One far reaching consequence of these high level functional descriptions is that the neural output signal in any given time period is conceived as a scalar quantity. This effectively rules out the multiplexing of signals in the time domain, which would require a finer grained representation of time and a different (e.g. Fourier) interpretation of the signal. Since only one output signal can be sent from each neural element, multiple input signals converging on a given element must be converted into one output signal. An analogy could be made to a telegraph network which recieves messages from a hundred stations, but can only transmit one message to all of its hundred connecting stations. Each additional signal must compete with all others at each node. In contrast, a station which has several frequency bands available can process meaningful information in one or two bands and relay the other messages unchanged.

Even the assumption that all postsynaptic neurons receive the same message can be called into question, since conduction blocks in different branches of axon trees can filter the spike trains that arrive at the respective synapses (Bittner 1968; Raymond & Lettvin 1978; Waxman 1978; Raymond 1979; Wasserman 1992). Instead of one informationally-passive output line fanning out to send the same signal to all postsynaptic elements, a branching structure is created which sequentially filters the signals. Thus the shift from scalars to multidimensional signalling and the inclusion of axonal operations can drastically the functional topology of the network, and with it the flexibility of infomation processing.

Largely because of the ordering in cortical maps of retinotopic positions, cochleotopic positions, and somatotopic positions, it has long been assumed that the cortex is a spatial pattern processor. This view of cortical structures was crystallized in a set of far-reaching and of provocative papers by David Marr (Marr 1970; McNaughton & Nadel 1990; Marr 1991). In these papers Marr proposed general information processing mechanisms for the major cortical structures in the brain: the cerebral cortex, the hippocampus ("archicortex") and the cerebellar cortex.

While it seems abundantly clear that spatially ordered maps are functionally very important, there is no inherent reason why the cortex must be *only* a spatial processor, why it cannot also be structured so as to effect time-space transformations (Pitts & McCulloch 1947). Alternative time-place architectures, such as those first articulated by Licklider (Licklider 1951) and Braitenberg (Braitenberg 1961; Braitenberg 1967) take advantage of spatial orderings to perform computations in the time domain. After a long period of relative neglect, the recent discoveries of neuronal synchronies in the visual cortex have brought various time-place models back into more general consideration (e.g. (Reitboeck et al 1988; Pabst et al 1989; Baldi & Meir 1990; Singer 1990)), but these models are still more the exception than the rule.

From the belief that the cortex is exclusively a spatial processor it follows that all information which is not place coded in sensory peripheries (e.g. time patterns in somatosensory and auditory systems) must eventually converted into the common language of the cortex, spatial excitation patterns. Thus whatever time patterns might exist in sensory peripheries, so this line of thinking runs, there must be a temporal feature detectors which will realize time-to-place transformations somewhere in the pathway. This transformation allows temporal features to be processed along with other place-coded forms of information by a common cortical architecture. An alternative, however, is to use a cortical spatio-temporal processing architecture capable of handling both types of information, taking advantage of temporal order in its spatially organized input channels when it is available. In this way all information might not need to be transformed into spatial excitation patterns and a mixture of spatial and temporal coding could then be utilized at all levels.

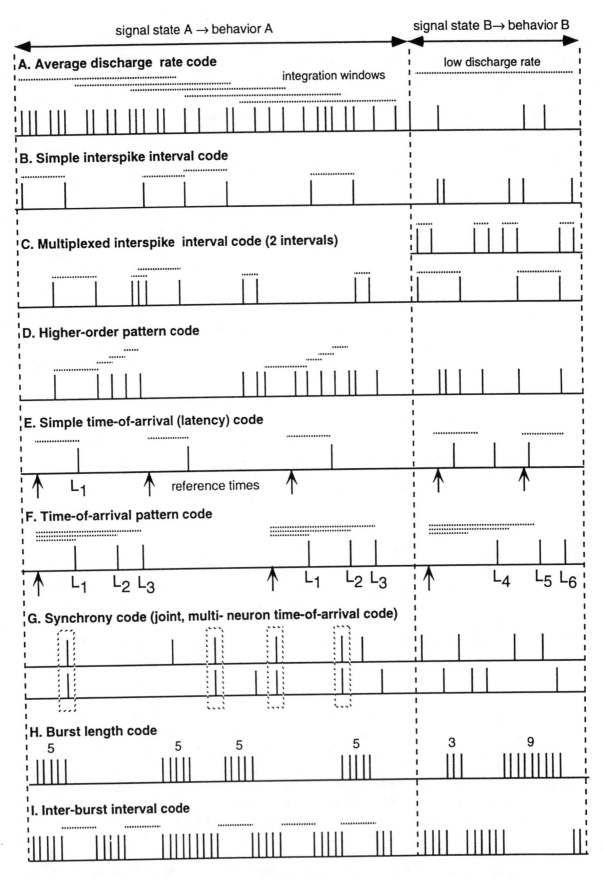

Figure 1. Some possible neural pulse codes.

In summary, because of the twin postulates of specific connectivity and coding by discharge rate , almost all connectionist networks assume that time can be completely ignored, i.e. that all processing operates on spatial rather than spatio-temporal patterns of excitation (Barlow 1972; Arbib 1989; Feldman 1990; Churchland 1992). These two assumptions together with variable synaptic weighting form the basis of virtually all neural network models now in currency (e.g. (Rosenblatt 1958; Selfridge 1958; Kabrisky 1966; Grossberg 1980; Hopfield 1982; Edelman 1987; Marr 1991) to list a few). The only exceptions have been adaptive time-delay networks ((MacKay 1962; Tank & Hopfield 1987; Mozer 1993)), whose temporal processing capabilities are only now beginning to be appreciated and developed more fully.

Although spatially-based neural nets have proven useful in an enormous array of applications, it does not immediately follow that the brain must code by average discharge rate scalars and process information by discharge rate integration. Since neural nets are finite state automata, given enough elements and processing steps, they can replicate any observed natural regularities or behavioral patterns. While this is extremely useful from a modelling perspective, the protean nature of the simulation also present pitfalls to the unwary. When we see that a complex and mysterious natural function can be realized with a computer program or neural net,. lacking viable alternative explanations, it is easy to be seduced into believing that this is the way that nature does it. Thus observations must always be used to test the validity of models, not the other way around.

Related to the difficulties of average rate coding mentioned above, there are some inconsistencies between the view of the cortex as a spatial pattern processor and the observed behavior of its elements. Some researchers have noted that the discharge statistics for cortical pyramidal cells are more consistent with coincidence detection than rate integration as the operational primitive for cortical information processing (Abeles 1982a; Abeles 1982b; Windhorst 1988; Abeles 1990; Softky & Koch 1992)). In this light, it is conceivable that new kinds of neural net architectures based on temporal coincidence operations will be needed before we finally have artificial networks that function at all like those of our brains.

3. Possible alternatives to average rate codes

Other kinds of neural coding schemes besides those based on average discharge rates are possible, and diverse examples of neural timing patterns have been found in nautre (Perkell & Bullock 1968). In general any property of a spike train which covaries with some property of a stimulus can be used to transmit information about that stimulus. While a given spike train over some time interval has but one average discharge rate, there are a very large number of temporal patterns that are possible with the same number of spikes. Some of these codes are potentially more efficient at conveying information than average discharge rates (MacKay & McCulloch 1952). Still more codes are possible if the joint discharge patterns of multiple neurons are considered.

The many different coding schemes in the time domain range from simple interspike interval codes to more complex temporal pattern codes, latency and history-dependent codes. Examples of many codes are shown in Figure 1. The spike trains on the left contain patterns that would be recognized as encoded "signals" while those on the right for the most part are examples of patterns that would either be interpreted as different signals or as the absence of signals. A synchrony code between two neurons is shown as a simple example of a population code, a coding scheme which requires the joint activity of multiple neurons to transmit information. In the late 1960's and early 1970's there were a number of significant efforts to systematically describe a wide array of possible neural codes (Bullock 1967; Morrell 1967; Mountcastle 1967; Perkell & Bullock 1968; Uttal 1973). A large catalog of hypothetical and observed coding schemes can be found in the appendix of Perkel & Bullock, 1968.

3.1 Signs and codes

It is useful to make the distinction between signs and codes (Uttal 1973), which is really the distinction between an observed regularity of nature and an observed regularity which is involved in some identifiable functional role. Signs are the correlates of stimulus qualities. Codes are the functional organizations that actually utilize a particular set of signs to effect a perceptual discrimination. Thus all codes employ signs, but not all signs are necessarily involved in codes (functionally they would be "epiphenomena"). The problems of identifying when a natually-occurring physiological process realizes a "coding relation" or subserves "information processing" is a fundamental problem for theoretical biology (Pattee 1969; Cariani 1989).

To show that a given pattern of activity is a sign one must 1) show that the requisite information needed to effect a particular sensory discrimination or behavior is present in the characteristic patterns of neural activity that constitute the sign, and 2) that the particular sensory discrimination or behavior occurs when the sign is present and does not occur when it is not present. To show that a given pattern of activity is a code rather than a sign one must further show that the particular sign is sufficient by itself to cause the sensory discrimination or behavior to take place. This is a test of whether the system as a whole functionally relies on the particular form of the sign to make the perceptual or behavioral discrimination. In general it is much easier to ascertain whether the requisite information needed to encode a particular stimulus property is present in the discharge patterns of a given neural population than it is to determine whether the rest of the brain actually utilizes information encoded in that form to modify its behavior. One notable exception to this rule is the use of electrical stimulation: in several cases (e.g. (Young 1977; Eddington et al 1978; Covey 1980; Emmers 1981; Di Lorenzo & Hecht 1993; Mountcastle 1993) it has been shown that a particular time patterns of electrical stimulation evoke behavior similar to that of a natural stimulus. All of these cases are strongly suggestive of temporal coding mechanisms. For electrical stimulation both conditions (1) and (2) are likely to be met if it can be assured that the electrical stimulation is in fact inducing the particular pattern of neural activity that constitutes the sign and that the electrical activity is not evoking the behavior through some other set of nonspecific mechanisms or side effects that would not be present under natural stimulation.

3.2 Scalar vs. multidimensional signalling

It should be emphasized that these coding schemes are not mutually exclusive; they are complementary. Because of the non-exclusive nature of many of these coding schemes evidence in favor of one code is not necessarily evidence against another code. Thus the existence of neurophysiological data correlating a given stimulus property with average discharge rates is not necessarily inconsistent with the existence of a temporal code for that property. Indeed, in many cases it can be the case that the accumulated, coarser-grained observations of average discharge rates can be explained by complex, underlying time patterns of excitation and inhibition.

This complementarity of signalling modes also permits multiplexing. A given neuron conveying a spike train may synapse upon many other neurons so that a given spike train could be interpreted by one group of neurons in one way (e.g. by reading off the average rate of discharge), by a second group in a completely different way (e.g. by distinguishing particular temporal patterns), and by a third group in yet a third way (e.g. by examining the time of arrival of the first spike in a burst). In such a case the spike train would be conveying several signals at once; many kinds of information would be multiplexed in the single spike train. Thus depending upon the nature and diversity of the receiving neural assemblies, a spike train can convey several semi-independent signals at the same time. One of the advantages of temporal codes over mean rate codes is this capacity to convey higher dimensional signals rather than one, scalar signal (the mean rate).

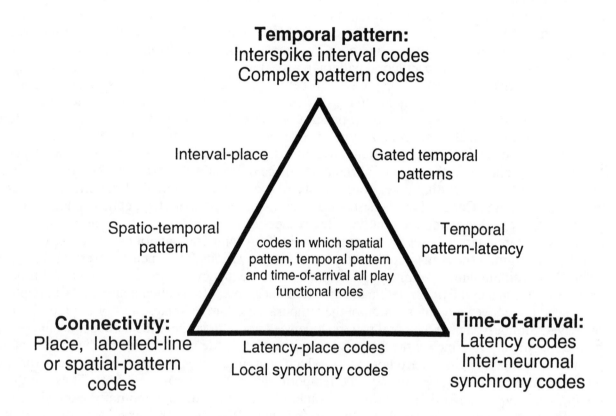

Figure 2. A space of possible neural codes.

Multidimensional signalling can also enhance the reliability of information transmission through the simulatanous use of different kinds of codes. Informational redundancy thus can be achieved not only by sending the same information over different lines using the same code, but also by sending the same information using different codes. Central processors could receive information about stimulus intensity not only by mean discharge rates in afferent channels, but also by the latencies of incoming spikes and the regularities of interspike interval patterns in those channels.

3.3 A space of possible neural codes

What determines how a given spike train is to be interpreted? Is a particular spike train signalling the presence of a pungent odor or a tap on one's back? A high-pitched tone or part of a visual scene? The type of information conveyed can be differentiated by 1) *where* it came from (which neurons produced it -- the place principle), 2) *what* characteristic form it takes (characteristic modality- or quality-specific temporal patterns), and 3) *when* it arrived relative to some reference time (characteristic latency). Conceptually, all neural pulse codes can be classified according to three sets of properties: those relating to the differential connectivity of neurons ("place" or spatial pattern codes), those relating to temporal patterns within spike trains, and those relating to precise time-of-arrival of spikes. Each general type of code can be based on the activity of single neurons or on patterns of activity of populations of neurons. These three different dimensions of pulse codes can be depicted in the form of a triangular space of possibilities. (Figure 2). Each vertex is an archetype for each coding type: connectivity or place coding, temporal pattern coding, and arrival time coding. Connectivity is described in terms of the pattern of synaptic connections in a given system of interest and the relative effectiveness of each synapse in eliciting discharges in each post-synaptic target (a set of "synaptic weights"). A temporal pattern can be described by a Fourier spectrum, a set of magnitude and phases for the various frequencies present in the spike train. Here a single interspike interval is a quantum of frequency information. An arrival time is described in terms of the time relative to some reference time, often called a latency. A pure place code need not convey any information in the temporal structure of spike trains or in precise times of arrival. Similarly, a pure temporal pattern code need not rely on specific neural connectivities or on the specific arrival times of the temporal patterns. And a code which relies on the latency of an event (e.g. a burst of spikes) need not rely on which neurons convey the event nor on the particular temporal patterning of the event (e.g. the temporal microstructure of the burst). Thus the three coding archetypes are orthogonal to each other; hence they are not mutually exclusive, but complementary, and can be combined in various ways. In general the term "temporal coding" includes both temporal pattern codes and time-of-arrival codes, i.e. any code which does not rely on particular neurons with specific connectivities to convey a message .

Associated with each kind of code are the processing elements best suited to produce and interpret it. A set of information processing elements should be capable of both generating the coded form (encoding) and interpreting signals sent in the coded form (decoding).

Generally speaking, rate codes can be generated and interpreted by populations of elements having long integrative time constants, place codes by populations of elements having very specific connectivities and a broad range of synaptic efficacies, temporal pattern codes by populations of elements with highly tuned intrinsic temporal resonances (e.g. recurrent conduction times or recovery kinetics), and time-of-arrival codes by populations of elements with sharply differentiated temporal windows (e.g. coincidence detectors, adaptive control of conduction times).

3.4 The many ways to send a message

To make these distinctions more concrete, we could imagine ourselves in an isolated room with a panel of 10 lights and 10 telegraph keys before us. Another group of people are sitting in a similarly outfitted room far removed from ours. Each telegraph key is connected in 1-to-1 fashion to a particular light in the other room and depressing a key causes the corresponding light in the other room to flash momentarily. The lights can be either on or off at each instant, and the faster they flicker the brighter they appear. With this setup there are many ways that a signalling system could be set up so that messages could be passed from one room to another.

The two groups could decide that particular lights were reserved for signalling special events and that any pattern or number of flashes would signal that this event had occurred. This would be a binary, "labelled line" scheme. It be could decided that the rate of flashes (or the perceived brightness) of each light would signal the measured intensity of a different sensory property. One light would signal temperature, another loudness, another degree of bitterness, and so on. If the lights were arranged systematically to signal different properties arranged in a continuum (e.g. light wavelength, sound frequency) the pattern of lights could convey a spectrum. The rate of flashing of each light would signal the relative intensity of a stimulus parameter within some specified range. In all of these schemes the particular connectivity between the telegraph keys in one room and the lights in another would be critical, but the timing of the lights would be irrelevant. These codes are all therefore purely place codes. Depending upon the complexity of the light patterns, each group would require a device for reading the spatial brightness patterns and deciding what the message was. The longer the time that the device could read each light, the more flashes that could be sent, and the finer would be the resolution of stimulus intensities. Optimally this device would have a long time to count the number of flashes. In a large network consisting of many such groups care would need to be exercised to guarantee that all of the wiring connections remained stable over time.

The groups could devise a code for sending messages in the temporal patterns of the light flashes. Particular rhythms of lights would signal different events. The simplest such scheme would assign particular intervals between flashes to particular stimulus parameters, and different stimulus properties could be represented by intervals spanning different time scales. Alternately, more elaborate patterns of flashes could be sent in which the kind of information would be encoded in one part of the pattern and its magnitude in another. These would all be purely temporal pattern codes, and these codes would be unaffected by rearranging the wiring between the two rooms or by changing the transmission time between the two rooms. Thus it would be irrelevant which lights carried the rhythms or exactly when the flashes arrived, so long as the appropriate pattern was conveyed. Rather than a spatial pattern analyzer, the groups would instead need a device that could recognize rhythms to correctly decode incoming messages. Here it would help to have processing elements that themselves had intrinsic temporal properties. Because the identity of the signal channel is contained in the signal itself (as in radio), this scheme is highly adapted for broadcasting messages in a large network of interacting groups.

The two groups could also send messages by the time of arrival of flashes relative to a reference event. One group would send an initial message, and the second group would send a return message at some prearranged time after the first message. The return time of the second message (its latency) would signal the nature of the event which had occurred. A flash returning 9 seconds after the initial message might mean rain, 10 seconds snow, 11 seconds sunny weather. The number of lights flashing at the appointed time could signal an intensity, so that the temperature could be conveyed by the number of flashes returning at 50 seconds, the humidity the number at 51 seconds, and so on. Such a code would be impervious to rearrangements of the wires, although a change in the transmission time between the two stations would completely alter the message which was received. Here each group would need some kind of resettable clock. This scheme would be useful in large networks where the transmission times between groups are stable and heterogeneous (they are different distances apart or conduction velocities differ), where the response return time (or reverberation time) could signal which stations are replying.

217

Combinations of these codes could also be arranged. Groups could decide that a temporal pattern of flashes in one light might mean something different from the same pattern in another light (interval-place code). Or that a pattern of flashes in one light must be accompanied by another pattern in another light, so that a complex spatiotemporal pattern is conveyed (spatiotemporal pattern code). If the transmission velocities of the wires are different, then a message could depend upon both the time of arrival of a flash and which light was activated (latency-place). Similarly, a temporal pattern arriving at one time after a reference event might connote something different from that same pattern arriving much later (gated-temporal pattern code).

3.5 Sensory representations

A sensory map is formed by an ensemble of elements which represent information using combinations of two or more codes whose parameters are systematically ordered in some way. Usually this is cast in terms of a spatially-coded parameter ("place") vs. some other parameter (e.g. average rate, latency, preferred delay). Four sensory maps are schematized in Figure 3; obviously other (e.g. spatially-distributed "mosaics") representations are possible. Although the coding schemes are cast in terms of auditory representations, all of these strategies are possible in any spatially ordered array of sensory neurons where there is some time structure present in individual channels. For many modalities, the one dimensional tonotopic axis would become a two-dimensional map. Thus tonotopic position would be homologous to somatotopic position in somatoception and retinotopic position in vision.

The rate-place scheme (Fig. 3A) is the most familiar -- a central representation is formed by spatially organized differences in firing rates. The role of the sensory cortex in these schemes is to recognize complex spatial patterns relay these recognitions to higher centers, and finally, via motor cortex, to motor outputs. Three general difficulties for rate-place coding as the sole representational vehicle are the dynamic range problem, the pattern recognition problem, and the multiple object problem.

The "contrast degradation" problem arises because the discharge rates of primary sensory neurons tend to saturate at higher stimulus levels and the spatial excitaton patterns become broader. Spatial excitation patterns therefore should be less well delineated (lower "contrast") for moderate and high levels than at levels just above threshold, where discharge rates increase more rapidly with increasing intensity. However, for psychophysical discrimations (e.g. pitch), the opposite is usually the case -- moving from threshold to moderate levels, discrimination steadily improves and levels off. While peripheral compensatory mechanisms (e.g. cochlear efferents), ranges of thresholds (e.g. different spontaneous rate classes), and particular connectivities for threshold classes may theoretically allow the entire dynamic range to be encoded by mean rates, signal-to-noise ratios still change in the wrong direction with level unless very specific compensatory connectivity patterns are assumed.

The pattern recognition problem arises because extremely subtle and complex spatial patterns must be extracted to account for percepts such as periodicity pitch or visual texture discriminaton. A 200 Hz click train, for example, elicits the same pitch as a 200 Hz tone, even if the lower frequency components of the click train are masked with low frequency noise (so that one cannot hear them separately). although the click train consists of many harmonics spaced equally in frequency and covering the entire frequency map. Frequency separations by themselves are not what the putative central spatial processor uses because shifting all freuqencies by a constant amount results pitches not equal to the frequency spacings. However the central processor operates, it must perform analysis on frequency ratios. Thus to deduce the 200 Hz fundamental from a spatial frequency map, it is necessary to simultaneously extract and compare all of the frequency ratios of the peaks

Four neural schemes for encoding spectral information

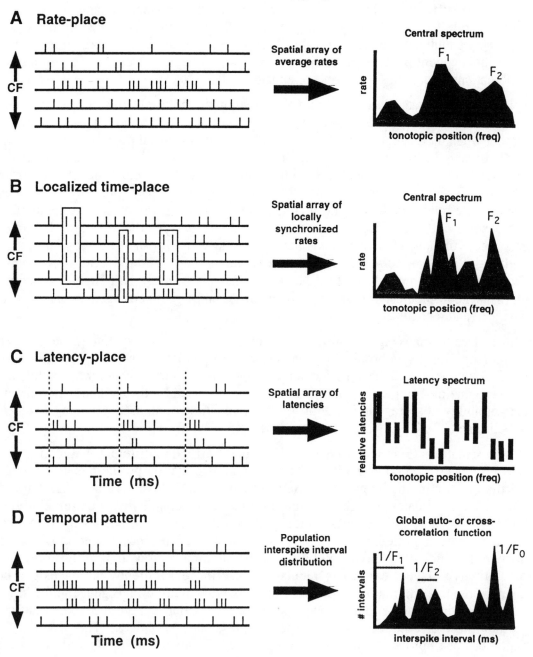

Figure 3. Four general neural schemes for encoding acoustic spectra. Left: hypothetical spike trains of the auditory nerve. Right: central auditory representation. A. Place-based coding scheme using average discharge rates. B. Place-based coding scheme using synchronization between spatially adjacent channels. C. Latency-place representation. Vertical bars in the relative latency map indicate range of latencies in each frequency channel. Shorter latencies with smaller variances signal higher intensities. D. Global temporal pattern coding through population interspike interval statistics. These schemes are not mutually exclusive, and could potentially be combined within the same neural processing structures.

of excitation and to compute what the common fundamental frequency would be. This would demand an extremely powerful, subtle, and elaborate spatial processor.

While it appears that sufficiently large connectionist networks can handle any one pattern recognition task by brute force, it is not yet clear whether these networks could simultaneously handle all of the many simultanous pattern recognition tasks required of a single cortical field. And as the number of independent perceptual qualities to be discriminated increases, the problem of associating combinations of qualities increases combinatorically.

Yet a third difficulty for pure rate-place coding involves segregating multiple objects represented in the map, what von der Malsberg has called the "superposition catastrophe." This problem is especially apparent when there are multiple "transparent" auditory or visual objects in the auditory (Handel 1989)(Bregman 1990) or visual scene (Bruce & Green 1985). Each element in the processing array responds to parts of one or the other object or even combinations of parts from both objects.In order to segregate and recognize the objects, it is necessary (possibly through an iterative process) to determine which elements go together to encode a given object. As the number of objects increases (visual surfaces, voices in a cocktail party), the problem becomes combinatorically more difficult. One can postulate an extensive library of stored spatial pattern templates, but this also involves very elaborate representation, storage, and retrieval mechanisms. If the channels have internal temporal structure, however, channels with similar temporal structures (temporal patterns, synchronicities, or common movements) can be grouped together, and objects can then be separated and recognized.

The localized time-place scheme (Fig. 3B) utilizes local correlations within a spatial map to sharpen the central spatial map. Since synchronization tends to improve as levels increase, the signal-to-noise ratio improves with level and the dynamic range problem is ameliorated somewhat. While the complexities of recognizing complex spatial patterns are not reduced by this scheme, the scheme does permit the possibility of segregating multiple objects in the time domain by grouping channels by common synchronies.

Latency-place representations (Fig. 3C) use the relative time-of-arrival in different spatial locations in order to encode intensity and other qualities. The contrast degradation problem is ameliorated because for virtually all stimuli, latencies shorten with increasing level. This makes latency distributions attractive candidates for the encoding of stimulus intensities over extremely wide ranges (Stevens 1971). As absolute latencies decrease, so do the variances of latency distributions. Latency differences can be amplified more centrally by lateral inhibition, since earlier impulses can excite inhibitory units which can deliver inhibition to surrounding regions before those regions receive their (relatively delayed) excitatory inputs (manuscript ref). Latency variances can be detected by using temporal summation properties of cells with many convergent inputs, since excitatory inputs all arriving nearly simultaneously (small latency variances) produce more transient depolarization than those arriving at different times (large latency variances). The precision of latency estimation can be improved by increasing the number of convergent inputs. Latency-place mechanisms appear to be involved in a wide variety of sensory processes: electroception, vision (motion perception, Pulfrich illusion), and stimulus localization in auditory, somatosensory, olfactory and gustatory systems (see below).

Coding by temporal pattern distributions over a population of neurons is yet another possibility (Fig. 3D). Interspike intervals are perhaps the simplest temporal patterns, but distributions of more elaborate pattern types could also be employed to encode perceptual qualities. If the responses of sensory receptors follow the fine time structure of a stimulus, then periodicities in the stimulus waveform will also be found in the spike trains of primary sensory neurons. The resulting distribution of intervals across a neural population essentially forms an autocorrelation-like

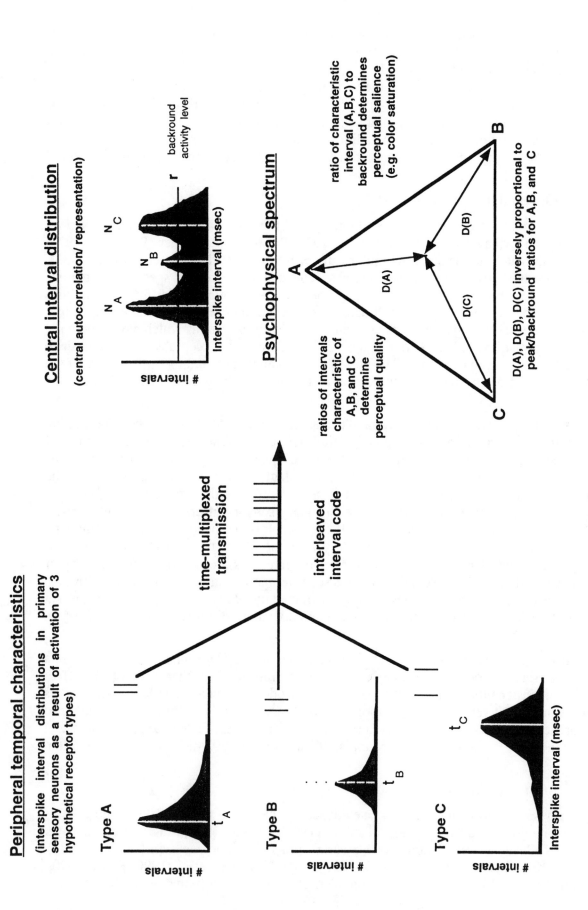

Figure 4. How ratios of temporal pattern primitives can encode a multidimensional perceptual space (e.g. color, taste, smell, timbre). While a simple interspike interval code is illustrated here, more complex temporal pattern primitives could be used to form a central temporal spectrum. The perceptual space or psychophysical spectrum has the same dimensionality as the number of independent temporal pattern primitives.

221

representation of the stimulus, which contains the same information as would be present in a power spectrum. Temporal pattern codes are generally not faced with the contrast degradation problem because higher stimulus levels impress upon more primary sensory neurons the temporal form of the stimulus. As in latency coding, the variability of spike initiation times is reduced with increasing level, and since the absolute timing of intervals related to threshold crossings of the stimulus waveform is more precise, then interspike intervals will more precisely reflect intervals between peaks in the stimulus waveform. In addition, as intensity increases, stimulus time patterns are impressed upon more of the population and the relative proportion of temporally structured activity increases.

3.6 Neural codes and perceptual qualities

One of the central goals of neuroscience is to understand the relationship of neural activity to human perceptual and behavioral capacities (Boring 1933; Boring 1942; Teuber 1959; Uttal 1973; Uttal 1988) and ultimately to the structure and texture of human experience itself (Boring 1933). What is the relationship between a particular coding scheme and the perceptual space of distinctions that it subserves? Any perceptual distinction must be realized through the differential activity patterns of the nervous system. Thus each dimension of perceptual quality should be related to a dimension of neural activity. Since codes have been defined as sign systems which have functional roles, every code at the level of the entire organism should make a perceptual difference. Since codes themselves have structure, it should be possible, given an understanding of the nature of the codes employed, to correlate spaces of perceptual distinctions with spaces of neurally encoded distinctions.

Ratio codes and central spectra are relatively simple strategies for constructing a space of perceptual qualities through the activity of a population of neurons (Figure 4). One needs only three types of receptors to encode a continuous two dimensional space of qualities (e.g. a space of colors). This is accomplished by taking ratios between the respective degrees of excitations produced by the three receptors. Usually the degree of excitation is taken simply as the average discharge rates associated with the respective receptors and their primary sensory afferents, but characteristic temporal patterns can also serve the same role. If the receptors themselves have different time courses of activations or their associated primary afferent fibers have different conduction velocities, then different characteristic time patterns and latencies are produced by the receptor populations in proportion to their excitation. Once a set of temporal pattern or latency primitives is established, a space of perceptual qualities can be constructed by taking the ratios between them at some higher station. The number of distinguishable temporal pattern primitives thus determines the dimensionality of the quality space.

One of the intriguing properties of temporal codes is that the tuning of resonances in elements in a network can in effect introduce new temporal pattern primitives into that network, in effect increasing the dimensionality of the quality space being encoded. On an abstract level, this process of dimensional increase is related to the addition of new observables to a scientific model, hence to systems-theoretic definitions of emergence (Rosen 1985; Cariani 1989; Pattee 1989; Ferenandez et al 1991; Helighen 1991; Kampis 1991b; Kampis 1991a; Cariani 1992a; Cariani 1992b; Cariani 1993).

4. Evidence for temporal codes in sensory systems

In virtually every sensory system there is some evidence for the role of temporal discharge patterns for conveying complex stimulus qualities: olfaction (Gesteland et al 1968; Macrides & Chorover 1972), gustation (Covey 1980; Di Lorenzo & Swartzbaum 1982), nocioception (Emmers 1981), somatoception (Keidel et al 1960; Mountcastle et al 1969; Morley et al 1990; Rowe 1990), electroception (Bullock 1982; Carr et al 1986a; Carr et al 1986b; Hopkins 1988; Heiligenberg

1991; Carr 1993), vision (Chung et al 1970; Festinger et al 1971; Kozak & Reitboeck 1974; Richmond et al 1987; Kozak et al 1989; Bialek et al 1991; McClurkin et al 1991a; McClurkin et al 1991b; Wasserman 1992).

It is not necessarily surprising that this should be the case. In sensory systems with receptors capable of following the stimulating waveform (i.e. audition, vibration perception), action potentials are created at threshold crossings and hence their timings directly reflect stimulus periodicities. In sensory systems where there are no periodicities to be followed (e.g. the chemical senses) or those whose frequencies are too high to follow (e.g. color vision), different classes of receptors can have different time courses of activation and recovery. In these systems characteristic temporal patterns can arise through the interplay of receptor activation times and lateral inhibitory interactions. The lateral inhibitory interactions are driven by latency differences. Those channels most sensitive to the stimulus will have shorter latencies, so that excitation will precede lateral inhibition. Those channels which are least sensitive will have the longest latencies, and lateral inhibition will precede excitation. The time course of lateral inhibition can also interact with the activation kinetics of different receptor types to produce temporal patterns which contain information concerning the ratios of excitations of the different receptors. From this perspective, the noted structural similarity of the olfactory bulb and the retina (Shepherd 1970; Szentagothai & Arbib 1972) may be due to their common functions in the generation of characteristic stimulus-dependent temporal relationships between the various neural elements. Once temporal pattern primitives are established, a space of perceptual qualities within each modality can be established by taking the ratios between them (via temporal correlation).

4.1 Somatoception: vibration perception

The perception of vibration is one of several cutaneous qualities that also include temperature, pressure, and pain. Human beings can distinguish between different vibratory frequencies in the range of 5-1000 Hz (Morley et al 1990). In the somatosensory system there is considerable accumulated evidence that temporal patterns of mechanical vibration of the skin are encoded in corresponding temporal patterns of primary somatosensory afferents (Mountcastle et al 1969; Morley et al 1990; Johnson & Hsiao 1992; Mountcastle 1993). Tactile primary sensory nerve fibers consist of three classes, rapidly-adapting (RA) fibers, slowly-adapting (SA) fibers, and fibers associated with Pacinian corpuscle (PC) receptors. Of these three classes, two are responsive to vibratory stimuli. RA fibers are excited by vibration frequencies in the 5-100 Hz range, while PC fibers are excited in the 30-1000 Hz range, and together these two classes of fibers are thought to cover the human range of vibration perception.

Because all fibers of a given class (RA, SA, PC) have similar frequency tunings, a simple place code for vibration frequency in which each fiber conveys information about a different narrow frequency band appears unlikely. The only other obvious spatial mechanism for encoding the frequencies of vibratory patterns would be an across-neuron pattern code which estimated vibration frequencies by comparing discharge rates between RA and PC afferents. Low vibration frequencies should recruit relatively more RA fibers, evoking higher discharge rates in each fiber, while higher vibration frequencies should recruit relatively more PC fibers, thereby evoking higher discharge rates in that population. One of the consequences of ratio coding, however, is that the amplitude of a one frequency stimulus should change the perceived frequency of the stimulus as the recruitment of one group of fibers saturates and the other slowly increases. (Morley et al 1990) used 30 Hz and 150 Hz vibratory stimuli with different amplitues to test the ratio coding hypothesis psychophysically, and their findings do not appear to be consistent with a ratio code. Further evidence in favor of temporal codes as opposed to ratio pattern codes for flutter perception is that different frequencies of electrical microstimulation of the hand "elicit changes in the subjective sense of frequency" (Mountcastle 1993).

The temporal patterns of the vibratory stimulus are evident in the temporal discharge patterns of units at all stations in the ascending somatosensory pathway: primary sensory fibers, dorsal column nuclei units, and somatosensory cortex neurons (Mountcastle 1993). While patterns of first-order (successive) interspike intervals are gradually disrupted by jitter and intervening spikes as the pathway is ascended, all-order (nonsuccessive) interspike intervals related to stimulus periodicities persist into the somatosensory cortex. From Mountcastle's experiments in alert monkeys, it appears that differences in all-order interspike intervals (rather than differences in discharge rates) are used to discriminate between two vibration frequencies. From the neurophysiological evidence for temporal coding and psychophysical evidence against ratio codes, it therefore currently appears "that temporal patterning of impulse activity remains the major candidate code for pitch perception, at least over a substantial part of the vibrotactile frequency bandwidth" (Morley et al 1990).

4.2 Audition

In the auditory system, neural time codes are thought to be involved in both auditory localization and in the encoding of sound qualities such as pitch, timbre, and phonemic identity. The literature on the timing of neural discharges in the auditory system is extensive, so only a fraction of the many phenomena involved can be discussed here.

In many vertebrates, interaural time differences are used effectively to estimate the azimuthal position of sound sources. A general mechanism for utilizing interaural time differences for localization uses two neural pathways, one from each ear (Jeffress 1948). Each path originates in a specific frequency region of the cochlea and the spikes in each of these frequency channels have precise and reliable latencies (relatively low jitter) relative to the stimulus. The two pathways converge on an array of coincidence detectors in the brainstem, and a range of relative delays between the two pathways are supplied by varying the length of one of the pathways (and hence its conduction time). Those coincidence detectors with the relative delay between the two pathways will discharge the most, hence interaural time differences are converted by means of a latency code into a spatial pattern of excitations (place code). In addition to the spatial patterns which are generated, the time patterns of coincidences are preserved, so that the outputs of such coincidence arrays will also contain time patterns which are common to both ears. These time patterns may be responsible for the binaural "periodicity pitches" heard when continuous noise presented to one ear is delayed by a few milliseconds and presented to the other ear. Similarly, when two harmonically-related pure tones having a common fundamental are presented to separate ears, the low pitch of the fundamental can be heard.

Auditory localization by means of time differences is most highly developed in barn owls and bats, two kinds of flying animals which hunt prey in darkness. Acoustic echolocation ("sonar"), used by bats and some aquatic mammals, involves the measurement of time delays between an emitted sound and its returning echo, and can support very elaborate representations of distant three dimensional surfaces (Simmons 1990). Comparing relative times of arrival of a stimulus to receptors positioned at different body points is a general strategy which can be utilized by many other diverse sense modalities such as touch, taste, and smell (von Bekesy 1963; von Bekesy 1964a; Bower 1974).

The ability of temporal discharge patterns to convey information concerning pitch and other qualities, has long been appreciated by physiologists and theorists of the auditory system (Troland 1929; Wever & Bray 1937; Wever 1949; Kiang et al 1965; Rose et al 1967; Brugge et al 1969; Rose et al 1971; Goldstein & Srulovicz 1977; Evans 1978; Delgutte 1980). It has been argued that the quality and robustness of interspike interval information for representing stimulus components below 4-5 kHz is superior to rate-place representations and is more consistent with human levels of

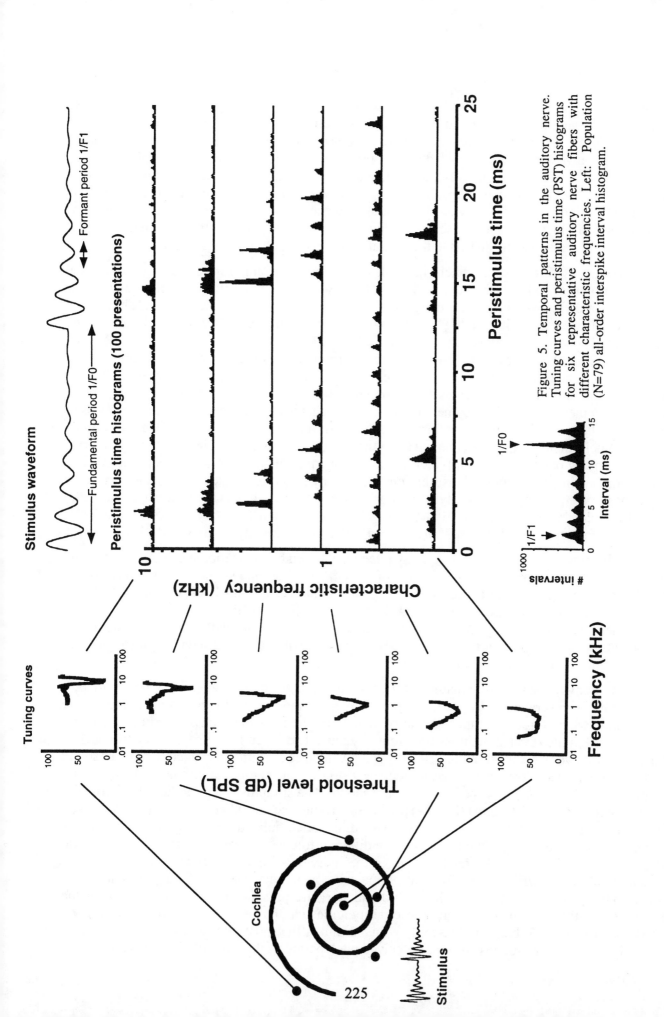

Figure 5. Temporal patterns in the auditory nerve. Tuning curves and peristimulus time (PST) histograms for six representative auditory nerve fibers with different characteristic frequencies. Left: Population (N=79) all-order interspike interval histogram.

performance (Srulovicz & Goldstein 1977; Srulovicz & Goldstein 1983; Javel et al 1988). Although most auditory theorists, in the tradition of Helmholtz, have retained a spatial, spectral pattern approach to central (i.e. cortical) representations of complex stimuli, purely spectral pattern theories must invoke very sophisticated central processors to recognize periodicity pitches, pitch shifts, musical intervals (e.g. octave relations), and spectral shapes over a large range of stimulus intensities and background conditions. Interestingly, these phenomena are described very simply in terms of all-order interspike interval distributions of the auditory nerve, which are essentially the autocorrelation functions of response spike trains. Thus stimulus periodicities can be the form of temporal autocorrelations in addition to the spatially-encoded spectral representations.

The phenomenon of "periodicity pitch" has long been a testing ground for various psychophysical models and neural coding schemes. With very few exceptions, periodic waveforms evoke low pitches (50-500 Hz) associated with their fundamental frequencies (F0). These pitches have been variously called "periodicity pitch", "virtual pitch", "repetition pitch", "the pitch of the missing fundamental", or "musical pitch."(Small 1970; de Boer 1976; Evans 1978; Nordmark 1978). Such pitches are reliably heard even if there is no energy present at F0 or if the frequency region of the fundamental is masked with noise (Licklider 1954). Periodicity pitches can be produced by broadband stimuli, such as click trains and amplitude modulated noise, with frequency components too close together to be resolved by neural rate-place mechanism (and especially at higher levels or in noise). These stimuli with their unresolved spectral patterns, however, produce amplitude modulations in many frequency channels, and these modulations create clear interspike interval patterns in many parts of the auditory nerve array. Modern temporal theories for periodicity pitch have combined interspike interval distributions from many frequency regions of the auditory nerve to produce pooled interspike interval distributions from which the pitch is then extracted (Licklider 1951; Licklider 1956; Licklider 1959; Moore 1982; Van Noorden 1982; Lyon 1984; Lyon 1991; Ghitza 1992);(Lazzaro & Mead 1989; Meddis & Hewitt 1991b; Meddis & Hewitt 1991a)).

These global temporal models for periodicity pitch were tested by the author and Bertrand Delgutte by recording the temporal discharge patterns of more than a thousand single auditory nerve fibers in Dial-anesthetized cats (Cariani & Delgutte 1992a; Delgutte & Cariani 1992; Cariani & Delgutte 1993). The all-order interspike interval distributions of individual fibers of many characteristic frequencies were summed together to construct an estimate of the population interval distribution for the entire auditory nerve array. A diverse set of stimuli with variable fundamental frequencies were constructed to investigate many complex pitch phenomena.

In order to convey the pervasive nature of the temporal patterning in the auditory nerve array, a "neurogram" of several auditory nerve fibers is shown in Figure 5. To the left is the stimulus and the cochlea, which through its mechanical properties implements band-pass filtering in which a given "place" in the spiral structure is preferentially tuned to a given frequency. As a consequence the auditory nerve fibers innervating hair cells at a given place are similarly tuned (i.e. lower sound pressures are needed at the "characteristic frequency" to generate additional discharges than at other frequencies). The tuning curves of six fibers are shown. The stimulus is a periodic waveform with a fundamental period of 12.5 ms (F0=80 Hz) and one resonance period at 1.6 msec (F1=640 Hz, a "single formant vowel"). Inspecting the corresponding peristimulus time histograms of each fiber at right, one can see that the time patterns in the different frequency channels are different. Several discharge periodicities can be readily seen in the individual channels, related to the stimulus fundamental period 1/F0 and the formant period 1/F1, as indicated above. Thus many intervals corresponding to stimulus periodicities 1/F0 and 1/F1 are present in the time structure of the discharges in the array of fibers, and these periodicities can be seen in the population interval distribution (Figure 5, bottom center). For this stimulus the most common interspike interval (1/F0=12.5 msec) corresponds with the perceived pitch period of the stimulus (12.5 msec).

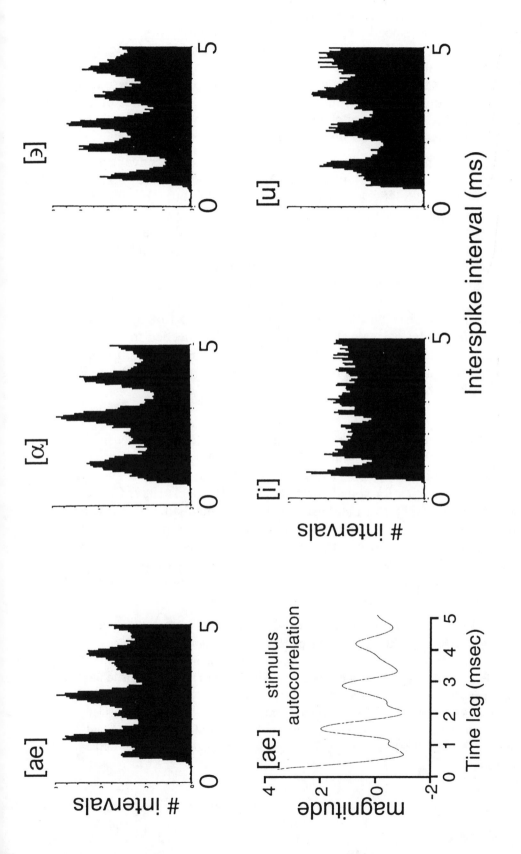

Figure 6. Above: Auditory nerve population autocorrelation histograms (all-order interspike intervals) for 5-formant synthetic vowels. Each histogram represents data from 50-90 auditory nerve fibers (~100,000 spikes) distributed over many characteristic frequencies. The most similar vowels [ae] (as in cat) and [ɑ] as in father have correlations of .82, while all other inter-histogram correlations are below .14. Bottom left: Stimulus short term autocorrelation function for vowel [ae].

For the vast majority of periodic complex stimuli presented (click trains, vowels, AM and QFM tones, AM noise, equi-amplitude harmonic tone complexes, Shepard-Risset "continuously ascending pitch staircases) it was found that 1) the pitch heard by human listeners corresponded to the most common interspike interval in the auditory nerve (the aggregate interval distribution), and 2) that the salience of the pitch heard corresponded to peak-to-background ratio in the population interval distribution. Thus it was found physiologically what had been predicted in global temporal models (Meddis & Hewitt 1991b; Meddis & Hewitt 1991a) , that the aggregate interspike interval distribution of the auditory nerve can account for a great deal of the psychophysics of periodicity pitch: the pitch of harmonic tone complexes with "missing fundamentals", the pitches of click trains, amplitude modulated noise, pitch shift and pitch ambiguity as found with inharmonic AM tones, and pitch dominance of lower harmonics over higher ones.

It has also been known that interspike intervals of single auditory nerve fibers can convey spectral information suitable for recognizing speech (Delgutte 1980; Voigt et al 1982) (Srulovicz & Goldstein 1977; Srulovicz & Goldstein 1983; Secker-Walker & Searle 1990). but it has only been more recently that global temporal models have been developed for this purpose (Lyon 1984; Ghitza 1988; Ghitza 1992). Aggregate interspike interval distributions in a simulated auditory nerve array have been shown to yield high quality, noise-resistant spectral representations sufficient for speech recognition (Ghitza 1992). Physiological experiments have similarly shown that the population interval distribution of the auditory nerve is sufficient to discriminate vowels and in many cases to identify the two single vowels present in a concurrently presented vowel pair (Cariani & Delgutte 1993). The interval distributions characteristic of several 5-formant synthetic vowels are shown in Figure 6. Here only intervals shorter than 5 msec are needed to identify a vowel, and the response population interspike interval distributions resemble the autocorrelation functions of their respective vowel stimuli. Thus it appears that a common temporal code for pitch and vowel identity exists in the auditory periphery.

4.3 Electroception

Several groups of fish have evolved the capacity to sense changes in electric fields in their immediate vicinity. Some fish passively sense changing nearby electric fields, some generate their own weak, electric fields and sense the pattern of field potentials over their body surface, and some use these generating and sensing capacities for social communication (Bullock 1982; Carr et al 1986a; Carr et al 1986b; Hopkins 1988; Heiligenberg 1991). The mechanisms by which electroceptive fishes construct a spatial representation from very small differences in field potentials involve comparisons of spike latencies from different parts of the fish's body (Carr et al 1986a; Carr et al 1986b). The pathways by which spikes are conveyed from the electroceptors to more central structures which do the time comparisons utilize electrical synapses (gap junctions) which produce less jitter than chemical ones.

"In gymnotoform fish, T-type receptor afferents mark the timing of the zero crossing, or phase, of a sinusoidal signal by firing a single spike at a fixed latency within each cycle of the signal. This information is coded for many points on the body surface, and it is relayed in the same form and in somatotopic order, by the spherical cells of the electrosensory lateral line lobe, to lamina 6 of the torus semicircularis in the midbrain. A network within lamina 6 compares the arrival times of spike from pairs of points on the body surface, and *small cells* at a location in lamina 6 representing a given point A on the body surface modulate their rate of firing in accordance with the difference between the timing of the signal in A and some other area, B. The firing of these small cells is irregular and longer locked to individual cycles of the sinusoidal signal." (Heiligenberg 1991)

Thus, in electroception it is believed that a latency-place code is converted to a place code in which various combinations of body points are represented, although the functional organization of this place-based electroceptive map for external space is still not well understood.

4.4 The chemical senses

In the chemical senses of taste and smell, hypotheses for neural coding have generally assumed labelled line or across-pattern theories of sensory quality. Simple place coding hypotheses have encountered several difficulties. Each receptor responds to many different types of stimuli, each receptor apparently responds to a different stimulus set, and these sets do not appear to be ordered in any obvious way in order to code some perceptual dimension. This makes labelled line codes extremely unlikely -- one would need a neuron for each combination of molecular species present, and stimulus generalization would be quite problematic. "Across-pattern" codes might be hypothesized: combinations of ideosyncratic receptors are adaptively wired together so that specific combinations signal particular stimulus qualities. However, in both gustatory and olfactory systems the receptors turn over, and this poses problems for place- or connectivity-based coding of taste and odor qualities.

"The cells making up the taste bud have limited life spans. Radioactive labelling shows that they die and are replaced by new cells...As a cell goes through its life cycle, it appears to move from the edge to the center of the taste bud. Since the nerve fibers do not move, receptor cells are presumably innervated by different nerve fibers as they change location. This poses a problem for stable quality perception. The population of receptor cells that synapse with a single fiber at various times should have the same sensitivities in order to ensure that a stimulus always evokes the same neural signal."(Bartoshuk 1988)

"Perhaps the most intriguing aspect of the constant turnover of olfactory receptor neurons is the ability of olfactory receptor neurons to achieve perceptual constancy. There is good evidence for a number of species of an ability to make consistent responses to a given odorant over periods of time that rival (and even surpass) the lifespan of the receptor neuron. If this is the case then the olfactory system must be able to produce a consistent response to a given odorant even though most, if not all, receptor neurons have been replaced and the newly formed cells have made synaptic contacts within the olfactory bulb." (Mair 1986)

One solution for this problem of perceptual constancy might be through temporal pattern coding of tastes and smells. Both receptor systems have a number of structural features that could give rise to different time course of receptor activation and both systems have lateral inhibitory connections (Bartoshuk 1988; Cain 1988) that could generate patterned phase relations between different types of neurons. Here a relatively small number of temporal pattern primitives could encode independent perceptual dimensions, and their relative ratios would form the continuum of perceptual qualities that are experienced (see the discussion of color coding below).

Despite nearly complete omission in the standard textbooks and reviews (e.g. (Bartoshuk 1988)) there is considerable evidence in favor of a temporal pattern code for taste (Di Lorenzo & Hecht 1993):

"In the study of the neural code for gustation in the central nervous system, the temporal patterns of responses to taste are most often ignored. Typical measures of taste responses account for the overall amount of neural activity evoked by a tastant but do not reflect the temporal arrangement of spikes during the response. These measures would be adequate descriptors if the total number of spikes associated with a given response were equally distributed within the response interval; however, that is almost never the case. Instead, most taste responses are characterized by variations in the rate of firing. The time course and magnitude of these variations defines the temporal pattern of a response. Given numerous reports that different taste stimuli appear to evoke distinctive temporal patterns of response in a number of taste-related neural structures and that similar-tasting stimuli evoke similar temporal patterns of response (Fishman

1957; Scott & Erickson 1971; Ogawa et al 1973; Ogawa et al 1974; Perotto & Scott 1976; Funakoshi & Ninomiya 1977; Covey 1980; Scott & Perotto 1980; Nagai & Ueda 1981; Di Lorenzo & Swartzbaum 1982; Pritchard & Scott 1982b; Pritchard & Scott 1982a; Bradley et al 1983; Yamamoto et al 1984; Travers & Norgren 1989), it is not surprising that several investigators have suggested that this feature of the neural response may contain important, if not essential, information about taste stimuli."

Perhaps the most direct evidence that temporal neural patterns have functional significance and underlie the perception of tastes come from electrical stimulation experiments (Covey 1980; Di Lorenzo & Hecht 1993). In the mammalian gustatory system, three primary sensory nerves convey information from the taste buds to the nucleus of the solitary tract (NTS), which is the first nucleus in the ascending gustatory pathway. The three primary sensory nerves are the chorda tympani/greater superficial petrosal, glossopharygneal, and vagus, which are, respectively, branches of cranial nerves VII, IX, and X. In these experiments the responses of neurons in the NTS of a rat, are recorded when particular tastants are applied to the tongue. The temporal response patterns of the NTS neurons are then digitized and fed into a stimulating electrode situated in either the chorda tympani or the NTS of another rat and the behavior of the rat is observed. The control is application of a pulse train of equally spaced pulses with the same average pulse rate. Since rats have highly stereotyped orofacial behavioral responses to different tastants ("acceptance" or "rejection" licking behaviors or a neutral "jaw snap"), the behavioral responses serve as a reliable indication of how the rat perceived the electrical stimulus. When a given temporal pattern normally associated with a perception of sweetness and evoking an "acceptance" licking behavior was used to electrically stimulate the chorda tympani (Covey 1980) or the NTS (Di Lorenzo & Hecht 1993), rats exhibited all of the behavioral signs associated with a sweet tastant. Analogously, rejection behaviors were elicited by bitter tastants and their corresponding temporal patterns of electrical stimulation. When the control temporal patterns, uniform pulse trains, were used for electrical stimulation, no such behaviors were observed. (It has been found that electrical stimulation of individual taste buds can evoke particular tastes (von Bekesy 1964b) and that different buds have different electrical frequency response curves, but this is prior to the lateral inhibitory interactions that may be in part generating the temporal patterns observed by (Covey 1980), so that the two sets of results are not necessarily contradictory). Since electrical stimulation indiscriminately stimulates all neurons in a region without regard to their connectivities, thereby removing spatial cues, these experiments are strong evidence that temporal discharge patterns by themselves are capable of conveying gustatory quality.

Despite relatively little attention given to analysis of temporal response patterns in the olfactory system, some early experiments gave indications that the responses could be temporally complex and highly dependent on the history of stimulation (Gesteland et al 1968). Although electrical stimulation experiments with recorded spike trains have not yet been attempted in the olfactory system, there is a fair amount of evidence for temporal discharge patterns characteristic of particular odor types (Macrides & Chorover 1972; Macrides 1977; Meredith & Moulton 1978; Meredith 1981)

One difficulty with a temporal pattern theory of odor quality has been that the observed temporal patterns can change with changing stimulus concentrations and may be somewhat dependent upon cycles of air inhalation (sniffing). The discussion is complicated by the difficulty of the experiments themselves and weaknesses in many of the methods commonly used to search for temporal patterns. The relative underdevelopment of temporal coding hypotheses and the analytical methods needed for their validation/falsification is a serious and pervasive problem in research in all sensory systems, including audition. As a consequence, one must be extremely careful not to rule out whole coding schemes on the basis of incomplete analyses in the existing literature.

In general, temporal pattern hypotheses in olfaction have not conceptualized in terms of time patterns in individual spike trains, but as changes in firing rates over time. A typical way that unit responses are analyzed (in olfaction and elsewhere) is to sum together response spike trains of many stimulus presentations to form a peristimulus time (PST) histogram. PST histograms are then analyzed for time patterns. If the temporal patterns in question are not rigidly locked to the stimulus, then much of the timing information that might be present is destroyed. This method also presents problems if the time patterns in individual spike trains are interleaved (as (Emmers 1981) reportedly found for nocioception) or not synchronized to inhalation cycles. It may be, for example, that the crudeness of the analytical methods only allows temporal patterns to be seen when neural populations have been synchronized. When stimuli are presented asynchronously with respect to inhalations, the temporal patterns may be interleaved or jittered with respect to each other (perhaps depending upon the immediate history of the unit (Gesteland et al 1968)) and therefore would not be visible in the PST histograms.

4.5 Pain

In a series of papers and a monograph (Emmers 1969; Emmers 1970; Emmers 1976; Emmers 1981), Raimond Emmers has reported a complex spike interval code for pain and several other sense modalities: touch, temperature, nocioception, and taste. The code, which he observed at the level of the thalamus, consists of an initial burst followed by a modality specific interval, then by several other intervals of a different, characteristic duration (as in Figure 1D). Under natural stimulation, he found these patterns interleaved with each other, so the analytical methods typically used by investigators would almost certainly miss them. Applying electrical stimulation, he was able to evoke the behavioral signs for pain when the correct temporal patterns were induced. When external pain stimuli were applied, he was able to achieve analgesic effects with electrical stimulation that disrupted these characteristic patterns. Unfortunately, his work has been largely ignored, he has retired, and there have been no reported replications or followups to this interesting work.

4.6 Vision

Historically vision has been regarded as the archetypal sensory modality, and one where time plays little or no role. Outside of the Gestaltists and the Gibsonians, vision has usually been conceptualized in static terms, where layers of successive "feature detectors" operate on localized spatial retinal patterns, and the retinal image is progressively reconstructed at higher and higher levels of abstraction (e.g. (Marr 1982); see discussion in (Uttal 1988)). Motion, however, appears to be essential for vision (Ditchburn & Ginsborg 1952), and moving images would be expected to set up coherent time patterns in ON and OFF units of the retina. While temporal structure in the optic nerve is much less well understood than that in the auditory nerve, it is known that retinal ganglion cells, unlike the auditory nerve, exhibit temporally correlated discharges (Mastronarde 1989), so that cross-neuron time patterns are a possible coding mechanism (see especially the work of (Bialek et al 1991) on the use of temporal correlations in insect vision). There is also some psychophysical evidence that several aspects of vision (color, texture, form) may utilize temporal codes, although no comprehensive temporal theory of vision based on these principles has been yet proposed.

One of the advantages of temporal coding is that it permits the multiplexing of visual information. In the late 1960's, Jerry Lettvin and co-workers (Chung et al 1970) found that information concerning conditions of illumination could be transmitted the interspike interval statistics in the dimming fibers of the frog's optic nerve (see also (Wasserman 1992)). They observed different sets of interspike intervals which corresponded to different levels, types and time courses of illumination, and combinations of various intervals occurred together depending upon light level

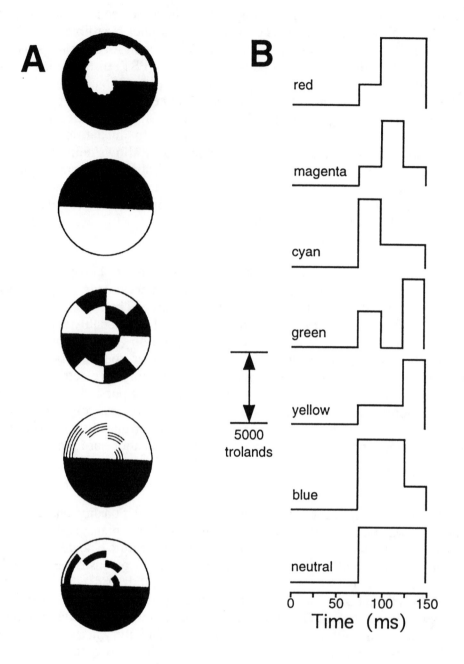

Figure 7. A. Rotating disk patterns used by Fechner (top two), Helmholtz (middle), and Benham (bottom two) to induce subjective colors. B.Temporally-modulated illumination patterns produce characteristic flicker colors (redrawn from Festinger, Allyn & White, 1973). Electrical stimulation of the retina using these patterns produces phosphenes of the corresponding colors (Young, 1977). The existence of these characteristic temporal patterns is highly suggestive of a temporal code for color.

and other factors. Thus their experiments serve as an example of the multiplexing of visual information in interspike interval distributions of the frog optic nerve.

More recent investigations in primate visual systems have found evidence for multiplexing of information concerning visual form and color (Richmond et al 1987; Richmond et al 1989; McClurkin et al 1991a; McClurkin et al 1991b). In these experiments images consisting of a set of black and white squares aranged in different configurations (i.e. 2-D spatial isoluminant, Walsh patterns) are presented to an awake monkey and the temporal discharge patterns of visual neurons are recorded. Temporal patterns in the response spike trains are then extracted using using principal component analysis and the informational content of the temporal patterns is assessed (i.e. how well can the stimulus that was presented be predicted from temporal or average rate patterns of discharge. In all regions of the visual system studied, lateral geniculate, primary visual cortex, and inferior temporal cortex, the response time patterns contained considerably more information than the average discharge rates. More recent work suggests the same is true for color (McClurkin et al 1993). Other investigators analyzing spike trains in single units of the visual cortex have found joint interval patterns ("precisely replicating" spike triplets) present in numbers significantly greater than random process models would predict. (Strehler & Lestienne 1986; Lestienne & Strehler 1987).

There is a substantial literature on the psychophysics and physiology of "subjective color" -- colors induced by achromatic temporal patterns (the Prevost-Fechner-Benham effect or Benham's Top (Benham 1894; Benham 1895)). Several patterns which evoke these colors are shown in Figure 7A. In these patterns, weakly saturated colors are seen around the edges of the black areas. For the colors to be seen there must be a particular phase relationship between the three different sectors of the disk (black, white, line pattern). Any color can be induced by the appropriate temporal pattern of luminance changes, as shown in Figure 7B (Festinger et al 1971), and television shuttering devices have been built to evoke colors with with appropriately flickered black and white images (the Butterfield Color Encoder) (Sheppard 1968). Perhaps even more strikingly, when the characteristic temporal patterns are induced via electrical stimulation of the retina, humans see phosphenes of the corresponding color (Young, 1975). Since electrical stimulation presumably excites all retinal cells to fire in the same temporal pattern, this is strong evidence in favor of a temporal code for color.

Physiological studies of the optic nerve (Kozak & Reitboeck 1974; Kozak et al 1989) , lateral geniculate (Young & De Valois 1977) and visual cortex (Richmond et al 1989) show characteristic temporal patterns when colored stimuli are presented. Underlying the traditionally cited response patterns of color opponency (as manifest in discharge rates) may be relative timings of various excitatory and inhibitory events (van Esch et al 1988). From this perspective, the Benham top induces the appropriate temporal responses characteristic of each color in the retinal ganglion cells, by inducing the temporal patterns that would normally be produced by lateral interactions between different types of (inhibitory and excitatory) retinal cells (von Campenhausen 1969; Festinger et al 1971; von Campenhausen 1973; Jarvis 1976; Adamczak 1981; Zrenner 1983; Tritsch 1992; von Campenhausen et al 1992). It is thus conceivable that the distribution of interspike intervals or some higher order time pattern in a particular patch of visual cortex determines the color perceived in the corresponding visual region. Since each patch is connected to other patches by horizontal connections, time patterns in one patch can interact with those of other patches, and the color perceived in one stimulus region can be influenced by those in surrounding regions.

Temporal coding may also apply to visual texture, since characteristic texture percepts can also be reliably induced by particular flicker patterns (Wilson 1960; Fiorentini & MacKay 1965; Perkell & Bullock 1968; Young et al 1975; Richmond et al 1989). There are also a host of temporal illusions in motion perception and binocular depth perception (Pulfrich effect) that point to a role for neural discharge latencies in the coding of motion and binocular disparity.

That particular temporal patterns can mimic the effects of particular colors and spatial patterns is very suggestive of the presence of generalized time-place cortical transformations that could also potentially underlie many other illusions such as periodicity pitch. As the Gestaltists held, the cortex may be the site of complex interactions between dynamic, two-dimensional spatiotemporal patterns mediated by horizontal connections (Siegel & Read 1993), and flicker stimuli may serve to mimic some of the two-dimensional "standing wave" patterns that would be evoked by regular, textured stimuli.

5. Processing strategies for discriminating temporal patterns

One of the barriers to more serious consideration of temporal coding alternatives has been the relative underdevelopment of information processing strategies which can handle time patterns. The remainder of this paper will outline some of the possibilities for the general kinds of computations that could be performed using temporal information and the kinds of neural architectures that could conceivably realize these computations. While this is an initial, highly speculative excursion, eventually, one would want to specify the models more precisely and test them against known anatomical constraints and physiological behaviors.

What kinds of representations could be computed? One of the great advantages of temporal codes is that correlations between patterns can be implemented by the convergence of axons carrying the patterns onto coincidence detectors (Figure 9)(Longuet-Higgins 1989). If there are a range of relative delays available in a neural subpopulation, either through conduction delays or intrinsic oscillatory periods, then all lags in the cross-correlation function can be computed by that subpopulation by temporal coincidence. This is markedly simpler than a similar computation using spatially-coded patterns.

If all of the the delays are present within a given sensory channel (e.g. an auditory frequency channel or a retinal position channel), then the time patterns in the channel can be correlated with themselves to form an autocorrelation function. As discussed above, global temporal autocorrelations in the auditory nerve are effective for representing pitch (Licklider 1951; Licklider 1955; Licklider 1959; Lyon 1984; Lazzaro & Mead 1989; Meddis & Hewitt 1991b; Meddis & Hewitt 1991a; Slaney & Lyon 1991; Cariani & Delgutte 1992a; Cariani & Delgutte 1992b; Delgutte & Cariani 1992; Slaney & Lyon 1993) and speech (Palmer 1988; Meddis & Hewitt 1990; Ghitza 1992; Palmer 1992; Cariani & Delgutte 1993).

In the auditory system if a global interspike interval distribution can be computed over an entire auditory map and analyzed, then the percepts of periodicity pitch, musical intervals, and spectral shapes can all be subsumed into one general processing scheme. Because intervals intrinsically carry harmonic structure (e.g. octave relations), many form invariances (musical intervals, fusion of chords) naturally fall out of such a representation. Interestingly, in vision, autocorrelation functions which operate on spatial intervals have proven effective in modelling texture perception (Uttal 1975; Uttal 1988). Since auto- and cross-correlations on place-based excitation patterns have been proposed for universal information processing operations (Reichardt 1961; Kabrisky 1967; von der Malsburg & Schneider 1986), such universality would also be a property of similar functions implemented in the time domain.

Where might such functions be computed? Since the computation of all perceptual Gestalts involve assembling information across large portions of a sensory map, a high degree of connectivity across tonotopic regions ("lateral" or "horizontal" connections) must be present in the anatomical substrate. In the auditory case, the computation subserving a percept such as periodicity pitch or

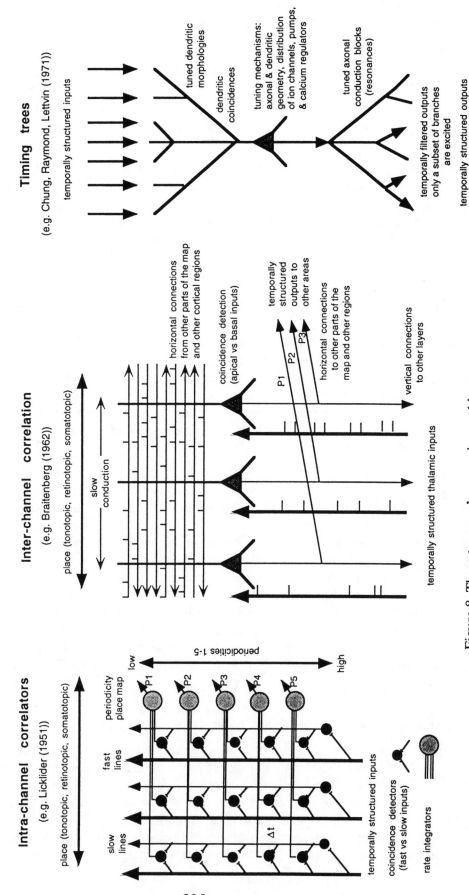

Figure 8. Three temporal processing architectures

Intra-channel correlators

(e.g. Licklider (1951))

place (tonotopic, retinotopic, somatotopic)

periodicity place map

periodicities 1-5

low / high

slow lines

fast lines

Δt

temporally structured inputs

coincidence detectors (fast vs slow inputs)

rate integrators

Inter-channel correlation

(e.g. Braitenberg (1962))

place (tonotopic, retinotopic, somatotopic)

slow conduction

horizontal connections from other parts of the map and other cortical regions

coincidence detection (apical vs basal inputs)

temporally structured outputs to other areas

horizontal connections to other parts of the map and other regions

vertical connections to other layers

temporally structured thalamic inputs

Timing trees

(e.g. Chung, Raymond, Lettvin (1971))

temporally structured inputs

tuned dendritic morphologies

dendritic coincidences

tuning mechanisms: axonal & dendritic geometry, distribution of ion channels, pumps, & calcium regulators

tuned axonal conduction blocks (resonances)

temporally filtered outputs only a subset of branches are excited

temporally structured outputs

vowel identity requires the merging of information from all parts of the frequency map. The primary auditory cortical fields are the first stations in the ascending auditory pathway which generally meet this requirement, since the cerebral cortex contains many horizontal fiber systems coursing through the apical dendrites of its principal (pyramidal) cells (Ramon y Cajal 1894/1990; Lorente de No & Fulton 1933/1949; Gilbert 1983; Imig & Morel 1983; Braitenberg 1986; Ts'o et al 1986; Braitenberg & Schüz 1991; Gilbert & Wiesel 1992). Lesion and ablation studies in animals and humans also suggest that the auditory cortex may be necessary for discrimination of complex acoustic patterns, such as speech and periodicity pitch (Dewson III 1964; Symmes 1966; Whitfield 1980), though not for discrimination of simple tones (Elliot & Trahoitis 1972).

How much temporal information reaches the cortex from sensory peripheries? Unfortunately, in no sensory system has the form and quality of temporal information available to the primary sensory cortices yet been properly characterized. Even in the auditory system, where the temporal patterns present in the auditory nerve have been well described, the time patterns present in primary auditory cortices are poorly understood. Spike latencies for stimulus onsets can be quite precise, with jitters comparable to those found in the auditory nerve (Phillips et al 1991). There is evidence that stimulus periodicities up to several hundred Hz (Goldstein et al 1959; Kiang & Goldstein 1959; Steinschneider et al 1980; Schreiner et al 1983; Phillips 1989; Mäkelä et al 1990; Langner 1992) and perhaps up to 1 kHz (de Ribaupierre et al 1972).are present in primary auditory cortex, so that periodicity pitch could potentially be temporally coded at the cortical level. These periodicity limits should be taken as lower ones, because the recording and analytical methods used (gross potentials, synchronization indices, first order intervals, post-stimulus time histograms) are not powerful enough to detect jittered, desynchronized, or complex temporal patterns. Until more powerful analytical methods are utilized (e.g. autocorrelation, power spectra, joint interval statistics), more elusive temporal patternings (such as those found elsewhere: (Covey 1980; Emmers 1981; Lestienne & Strehler 1987; Richmond et al 1989; Bialek et al 1991; Mountcastle 1993)) cannot be ruled out.

How might global correlation functions be computed in the cerebral cortex? Temporal information could be stored in the resonance patterns of networks with recurrent connections (Greene 1962; McCulloch 1969). Alternately, information could be stored in temporal correlations using adaptively tuned delay lines, coincidence detectors, and/or sets of filters (MacKay 1962; Longuet-Higgins 1969; Longuet-Higgins 1987; Longuet-Higgins 1989). Adaptively tuned conduction blocks in axon trees could potentially parse out particular periodicities from spike trains, thereby implementing temporal pattern recognition in a single neuron (Chung et al 1970; Raymond & Lettvin 1978; Pratt 1990). Learning could be built into various timing nets by adaptively altering conduction times (MacKay 1962) or by strengthening synapses corresponding to particular sets of existing delays, or by tuning membrane properties of pacemaker neurons (Torras i Genis 1985). Currently time delays are being incorporated into discrete neural networks to recognize warped symbol sequences and time-varying patterns (Tank & Hopfield 1987; Mozer 1993). Of these general alternatives, the three possible temporal processing architectures depicted in Figure 8 will be discussed in greater depth.

6. Temporal processing in a single axon tree

An elegant theory of the single neuron as a multiplexing temporal processing element has been proposed which utilizes the temporal properties of axonal conduuction to perform temporal analysis on spike trains (Chung et al 1970; Raymond & Lettvin 1978; Waxman 1978; Pratt 1990; Wasserman 1992). Since the beginnings of single neuron electrophysiology, it has been known that not all action potentials travelling down the axon trunk invade all terminal branches, and that the times between successive discharges (interspike intervals) can determine whether or not a given action potential will be propagated down a given axon branch. In some invertebrate motor systems conduction failures or "blocks" have been demonstrated to play important functional roles. In the crayfish, spike trains with different interspike interval compositions travel down different branches of an axon tree to independently control different muscles of the claw (Bittner 1968; Perkell & Bullock 1968).

Conduction blocks are related to the time that it takes for thresholds to return to normal after an action potential. (Raymond 1979) found that a many kinds of axons showed triphasic threshold recovery curves in which each action potential is followed in turn by a refractory phase, a "superexcitability phase", and a depression phase. During superexcitability, the membrane is slightly easier to re-excite than when it is at rest. In different axons, axon branches, and cell bodies, superexcitability culminates at different recovery times, milliseconds to seconds after the last action potential. The axon is therefore more sensitive to spike trains with intervals that coincide with the superexcitability peak, selecting particular temporal patterns from incoming spike trains to be propagated further on. Different axon branches with different threshold recovery time courses could "parse" incoming spike trains in different ways, so that particular interspike interval distributions could excite different sets of postsynaptic neurons (or muscles, as in the crayfish). The timing and strength of superexcitability phases in axon branches have also been observed to be activity-dependent and independently modifiable (Carley & Raymond, 1987), so that the effective connectivity between neurons might be adaptively modified by mechanisms which do not directly involve changes in synaptic efficacy. Artificial neural networks using pulse-interval temporal parsing trees based on these concepts have been investigated by (Pratt 1990).

Since general anesthetics disrupt the superexcitable recovery phase, it is conceivable that their concomittant effects on consciousness might be due to the removal of conduction blocks which normally play the role of "decoding" temporal patterns (Butterworth IV et al 1989). Thus when general anesthetics are applied, membrane tunings are lost, the temporal coherence of neural activity is disrupted, and the functional integrity of the network is destroyed.

7. Temporal autocorrelation architectures

Perhaps the best articulated neural architecture for processing temporally structured information is still J. C.R. Licklider's autocorrelation-based periodicity-to-place scheme ((Licklider 1951; Licklider 1959)). This architecture was originally developed to account for periodicity pitch in the auditory system, and forms the basis for a number of current autocorrelation-based models (Meddis & Hewitt 1991b; Slaney & Lyon 1991; Slaney & Lyon 1993), physiological studies(Cariani & Delgutte 1992b), and analog VLSI implementations for pitch (Lazzaro & Mead 1989). The scheme utilizes the temporal structuring of discharges present in the auditory nerve by performing an autocorrelation analysis in each channel. In Licklider's formulation this was realized through conduction delays and coincidence detectors, but it could also be achieved using cellular "intrinsic oscillations," where cells discharge more frequently and/or more coherently in response to particular stimulus periodicities(Møller 1974; Frisina et al 1990; Kim et al 1990). Within each frequency channel is a set of delays corresponding to a set of "periodicity" channels. This creates a two-dimensional periodicity vs. "place" map. By summing the outputs from corresponding periodicity channels in different frequency bands, the pitch of a stimulus could be computed by taking the periodicity band with the highest summed activity. This processing architecture thus has the advantage of readily explaining periodicity pitch, the phase insensitivity of the auditory system, and the fusion of place and temporal representations into a unified percept (Licklider 1951; Licklider 1954; Goldstein et al 1959; Kiang & Goldstein 1959; Licklider 1959; Simmons 1990; Simmons et al 1990).

On the other hand, such a network requires specific anatomical structures -- precisely tuned delays or cellular oscillations ranging from 2-15 msec. Unfortunately, no obvious anatomical structures

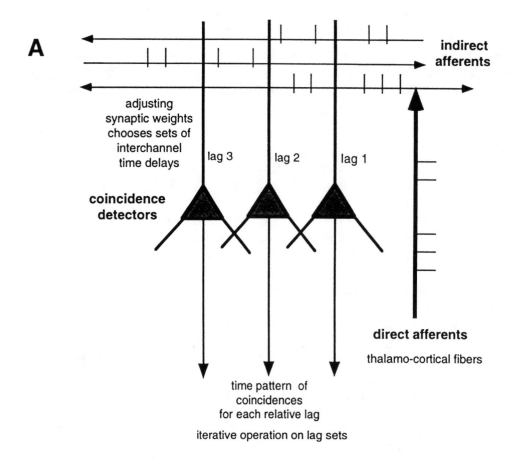

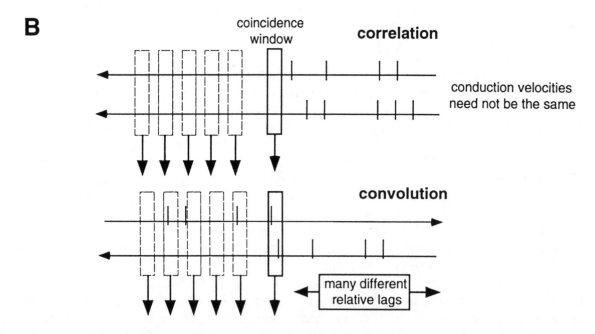

Figure 9. Simple schematics for computing temporal correlations of spike trains using delay lines and coincidence detectors. A: Computation of three lag terms of a cross-correlation function of three spike trains. The relative temporal relations between the inputs are different for each coincidence detector, so that a population of detectors covers many combinations of relative delays. By adjusting synaptic weights, a set of relative delays can be chosen so as to recognize a given spatiotemporal pattern. B: Computation of a correlation and convolution between two spike trains.

subserving delay lines (like those found in the brainstem for the computation of interaural time differences) have been found. Many cells with varied "intrinsic oscillations" are present in the cochlear nucleus, but their tunings are relatively broad (an octave or more). This does not correspond well with the stability and accuracy of periodicity pitch judgements (with errors of a few percent). In contrast, as in the auditory nerve these cochlear nucleus units typically show many interspike intervals corresponding precisely to the fundamental period of the stimulus.Thus at the level of the cochlear nucleus, an interval code still appears more promising for periodicity pitch than one based on average rates and periodicity detectors.

If a temporal-to-place transformation were taking place, one would also expect such maps to be present at higher stations. While there is some possibility that delay maps of bats ((Simmons 1990; Simmons et al 1990; Suga 1990)) might be homologues to periodicity maps in other mammals, no maps spanning the full range of periodicity pitches (50-500 Hz) have been found thus far (Schwartz & Tomlinson 1990; Sheich 1991).

8. Temporal cross-correlation architectures

From an anatomical and physiological point of view, the basic features of Braitenberg's time-based architecture for computing auto- and cross-correlations in the cerebellum (Braitenberg 1961; Braitenberg 1967; Freeman & Nicholson 1970) might be well suited for transposition to the cerebral cortex. Here, pyramidal cells perform the role of detecting coincidences between direct thalamic inputs and indirect (delayed) inputs from local interneurons, association fibers, and commissural fibers (Figure 9A). These latter inputs come from the massive set of horizontal fiber systems that make up the superficial layers of the cortex. Depending upon the relative directions of spike train propagation, an array of coincidence elements can compute correlations or convolutions (Figure 9B)(Longuet-Higgins 1989). Many relative delays could be supplied by many mechanisms: 1) differences in the cortical distances between two pyramidal cells, 2) differences in conduction velocity of horizontal fibers 3) multiple synaptic delays 4) reverberating loops of different lengths (a delay and its multiples), and 5) tuned intrinsic recovery kinetics of pyramidal cells.

The many intra- and inter-channel delays in the net permit a coincidence detector at each delay node to compute the auto- or cross-correlation term for a specific lag. Thus a population of coincidence elements embedded in a system of relative delays can compute global auto- and cross-correlation functions. Local inhibitory neurons would play the role of penalizing non-coincidences, so that unstructured inputs tend to inhibit the cell (Figure 10, top). Horizontal fiber systems of different orientations Additional connectivities between different regions having longer delays might be supplied by dispersive, reciprocal, cortico-cortico and cortico-thalamic links.

Since the output of each coincidence detector also has temporal structure, global cross-correlation operations could be iterated by passing the results of one layer of coincidence detections down (or up) to another layer (Figure 11, cf. (Travis 1988)). Such iterations could provide a temporal sieve through which predominant periodicities could be extracted. Various degrees of global interaction can also be implemented. Depending upon the length and distribution of synapses on horizontal fibers, local cross-correlations could be computed with short systems of horizontal fibers, while more global cross-correlations could be computed with longer systems having more far-flung synapses.

In audition, a temporal cross-correlation network would be capable of computing a global correlation function similar to the population autocorrelation functions which can support the discrimination of periodicity pitch and vowel identity. Many auditory form invariances which are related to frequency ratios (the octave, chords, periodicity pitch, musical consonance) are directly explained by the inherent harmonic structure of interspike intervals. Pairs of spike trains containing

Recurrent network of temporal pattern cross-correlators

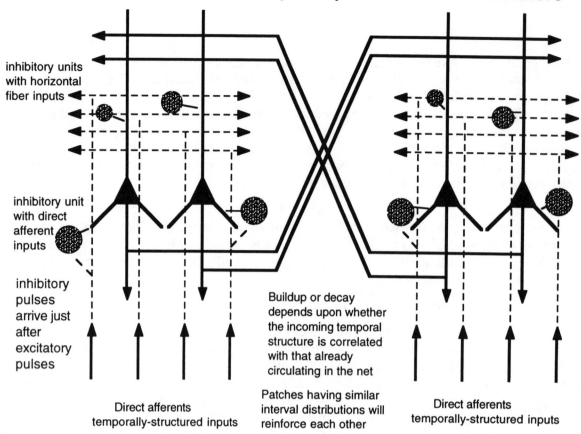

inhibitory units
with horizontal
fiber inputs

inhibitory unit
with direct
afferent
inputs

inhibitory
pulses
arrive just
after
excitatory
pulses

Buildup or decay
depends upon whether
the incoming temporal
structure is correlated
with that already
circulating in the net

Patches having similar
interval distributions will
reinforce each other

Direct afferents
temporally-structured inputs

Direct afferents
temporally-structured inputs

Two dimensional lateral delay net

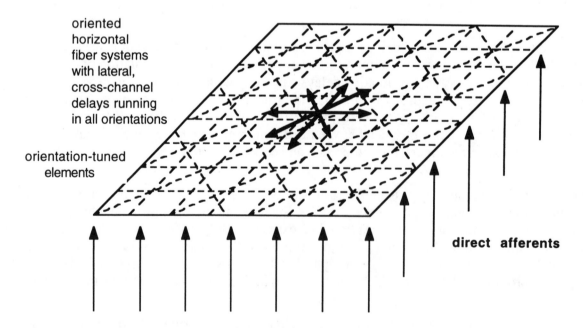

oriented
horizontal
fiber systems
with lateral,
cross-channel
delays running
in all orientations

orientation-tuned
elements

direct afferents

Figure 10. (Top) Network of temporal pattern cross-correlators with local inhibitory elements and recurrentconnections. Inhibition arrives at the pyramidal cell very slightly after excitatory inputs so that non-coincident arriving pulses have the net effect of inhibiting the cell. (Bottom) Two dimensional lateral delay net.

240

intervals related by simple, low integer ratios (i.e. 1:2 octave, 2:3 fifth, 3:4 fourth) will be more highly correlated than those whose intervals have some other relationship. If the delays involved are long enough, rhythm and higher order temporal structure can be analyzed with the same correlative operations that would be utilized for periodicity pitch (Boomsliter & Creel 1962). The analysis of longer-term temporal patterns would open the door to the analysis of the slower time patterns associated the perceptual qualities of other sensory modalities: colors, tastes, smells, pains, and vibratory textures. Longer reverberatory times would also allow slower temporal patterns to circulate in the network, to be correlated with those which are entering at any given moment. Memory-facilitated operations would thus consist of the "broadcast" of characteristic temporal sequences throughout various networks, thereby increasing the correlations of incoming temporal patterns that were similar in some respect to the memory generated sequence.

Temporal cross-correlational operations could conceivably also play a role in vision. Texture discrimination is similar to the discrimination of different musical chords in that both can be described in terms of either power spectra (of spatial frequencies) or autocorrelation functions (of spatial intervals).

> "A current interpretation of the role of frequency channels in vision is that local, but not global, Fourier analysis is performed. On this view patches of the visual image are analyzed into about half a dozen frequency bands at about twenty different orientations. There would be several thousand such patches in the whole visual field, and they would subtend a fraction of a degree in the fovea, and several degrees in the periphery. The result of the analysis would correspond to coefficients of some hundred sinusoids and cosinusoids of differing frequency and orientation for each patch, and the range of frequencies covered would vary with eccentricity and size of the patch. This scheme is a tentative one, but it is consistent with much of the psychophysical and neurophysiological evidence....In vision, the comparable advantage may be that the spatial frequency components represent a description of 'texture' which applies to the whole of each patch. This would be a step beyond a point-by-point description, just as the cochlea goes beyond a moment-by-moment of sound pressure." (Woodhouse & Barlow 1982).

An autocorrelation-based alternative to an array of spatial frequency detectors is to represent the distributions of spatial intervals in various directions for each retinotopic point. If one can compute a local *spatial* interval distribution (spatial autocorrelation function) for several orientations, then one has a processing scheme which explains a large part of the psychophysics of the discrimination of texture and the recognition of dotted forms (Uttal 1975; Uttal 1988). However, spatial distances can be transformed into temporal patterns by either a scanning process (Pitts & McCulloch 1947), by saccades (Reitboeck et al 1988), or by propagation through horizontal fiber systems which cross retinotopic maps at various angles (Figure 10, bottom)(Pabst et al 1989). Lateral inhibitory connections at lower stages of visual processing could also serve the same purpose. Thus instead of arrays of spatial frequency detectors (which, like the "periodicity detectors" in the cochlear nucleus have overly broad tuning) the spatial intervals might be encoded in the time patterns of discharges at each retinotopic point.

One advantage of this strategy is that the harmonic structure of the resulting time intervals can then be used to compute ratios of spatial intervals. While musical chords are perceptually characterized by ratios of sound frequencies and remain similar when all frequencies are shifted upward by a constant factor, textures are perceptually characterized by ratios of spatial frequencies and remain recognizably similar under different magnifications. Invariance of form under different magnifications is of obvious importance to the recognition of objects which are seen at different distances. In this context, it is of interest to note that in auditory frequency maps, being roughly logarithmic, a constant distance or conduction time corresponds to a constant frequency ratio, and in the visual cortex, being also roughly logarithmic (Schwartz 1980; De Valois 1990), a constant distance or conduction time corresponds to a constant spatial ratio. This conceptual ground,

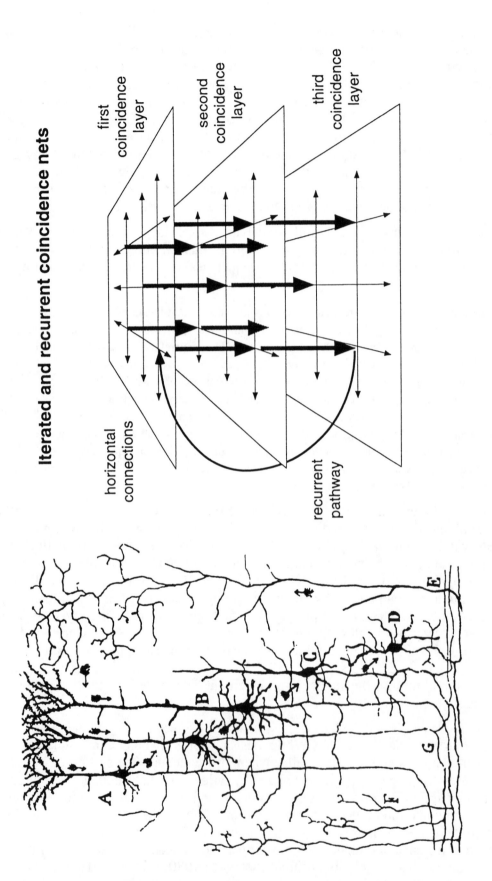

Iterated and recurrent coincidence nets

first coincidence layer

second coincidence layer

third coincidence layer

horizontal connections

recurrent pathway

Figure 11. Iteration of temporal correlation operations in adjacent cortical layers. Left: Camera lucida drawing from Ramon y Cajal (1894). Caption: The probable direction of current flow and the pattern of axodendritic connections between cells in the cerebral cortex. A: small pyramidal cell; B. large pyramidal cell; C and D: polymorph cells; G: an axon that bifurcates in the white matter. Right: schematic for successive temporal cross-correlation operations in a given cortical patch. Ascending connections permit recurrent correlation operations. It is hypothesized that successive correlation operations on temporally structured inputs could function as a temporal sieve, extracting predominant periodicities in a given region from many interacting spike trains.

concerning perceptual invariances and "the exchangeability of time and space," was, of course, originally covered long ago (Pitts & McCulloch 1947): "Octaves span equal cortical distances, as on the keyboard of a piano.").

Two existing texture discrimination models (Reitboeck et al 1988; Pabst et al 1989) convert spatial intervals into time (interspike) intervals. These models use precise neural synchronicities to bind perceptual elements together into wholes (so as to explain the findings of Gray & Singer (Singer 1990)), but absolute synchronicities may not be necessary if local interval distributions can be cross-correlated in networks with many possible delays. Since spatial autocorrelation functions could be directly implemented in running interspike interval distributions of each cortical patch, spatial frequency representations potentially subserving many form invariances (e.g. translation, rotation, magnification) (Reitboeck & Altmann 1984; Gardenier et al 1986; Vol et al 1989) may be realizable in the time domain by asynchronous delay/coincidence mechanisms.

The asynchronous neural delay nets proposed here could perform discriminative functions by selectively strengthening synapses representing different sets of relative lags. In such a scheme adaptive synaptic modification effectively chooses which delays (hence, which correlations) are relevant to detect a given temporal pattern. In this context cortical "assimilation" of stimulus rhythms during conditioning (John 1967) may reflect an ongoing strengthening of specific sets of interneural delays in the wake of a temporally patterned input. Since characteristic temporal patterns are the output of such an array, synaptic modification in coincidence nets can also serve to adaptively generate temporally structured outputs. Since the hippocampus and the cerebellum are also organized along the same general cortical plan (horizontal fiber systems, principal cells with oriented dendritic trees, local inhibitory interneurons), analogous asynchronous adaptive timing operations could also perhaps be envisioned for those structures as well.

9. Higher order resonances

Ultimately, one would want to embed adaptive timing nets tuned for particular sensory tasks in a larger framework in which all specialized nets are connected to each other via recurrent pathways. Cortical anatomy shows a plentiful abundance of such recurrences (Ramon y Cajal 1894/1990; McCulloch 1947). Each recurrent pathway has its own reverberation time, and cortical physiology shows an abundance of reverberations and slow oscillations(Chang 1959; Gerard 1959; Walter 1959b; Walter 1959a; Basar 1990). The particular reverberation times between a particular cortical region and each of all other regions might produce characteristic sequences of returning signals. A temporally-structured message is broadcast to other nodes, facilitating the processing of similarly structured temporal patterns in the other nodes, and evoking a response from every other node which has its own characteristic pattern and return time. By this organization, complex, global resonances would be set up in the network which could be switched, depending upon the history of the network and its inputs (Greene 1962). It is then not such a leap to connect this perspective with theories of interacting cognitive nodes in which each node has its own time course of activation and extinction (MacKay 1987).The notion of dynamic organization as a set of global resonance patterns is an old one common to both theories of life and of neural networks: (Lotka 1924/1956; McCulloch & Pitts 1943; McCulloch 1969; Eigen 1974))(Rashevsky 1948; Hebb 1949; Maturana 1970; Katchalsky et al 1972; Maturana & Varela 1973; Powers 1973; Varela 1979; Pattee 1982; Kampis 1991b; Rosen 1991). In the words of Ernst Mach:

"What is true of the pendulum is true of every vibrating body. A tuning fork, when it sounds, also vibrates. It vibrates more rapidly when its sound is higher; more slowly when it is deeper. The standard A of our musical scale is produced by about four-hundred and fifty vibrations per second.

"...We strike as many [differently tuned] forks as we will, the fork tuned to A is perfectly indifferent to their notes; it is deaf, in fact, to all except its own; and if you strike three, four, five, or any number whatsoever, of forks all at the same time, so as to make the shocks which come from them ever so great, the A fork will not join in the vibrations unless another fork A in the collection struck. It picks out, in other words, from all the notes sounded, that which accords with it.

"The same is true of all bodies which can yield notes. Tumblers resound when a piano is played, on the striking of certain notes, and so do window panes. Nor is the phenomenon without analogy in different provinces. Take a dog that answers to the name "Nero." He lies under your table. You speak of Domitian, Vespasian, and Marcus Aurelius Antonius, you call upon all the Roman Emperors that occur to you, but the dog does not stir, although a slight tremor of his ear tells you of a faint response of his consciousness. But the moment you call "Nero" he jumps joyfully towards you. The tuning fork is like your dog. It answers to the name A."(Mach 1865)

Acknowledgments

The opinions expressed herein are solely my own. I would like to thank Nelson Kiang for many insight-provoking discussions and for the use of his excellent library, Professor Frederick Werner for his kind encouragement, and Bertrand Delgutte for his experimental and experiential wisdom. The auditory experiments cited were supported by N.I.H. DC00038 and DC00119.

References

Abeles, M. Local Cortical Circuits. An Electrophysiological Study. Berlin: Springer-Verlag, 1982a.

Abeles, Moshe. "Role of the cortical neuron: integrator or coincidence detector." Israel Journal of Medical Sciences 18 (1982b): 83-92.

Abeles, Moshe. Corticonics. Cambridge: Cambridge University Press, 1990.

Adamczak, Wolfgang. "The amacrine cells as an important processing site of pattern-induced flicker colors." Vision Research 21 (1981): 1639-1642.

Adrian, E.D. The Basis of Sensation. London: Christophers, 1928.

Arbib, Michael A. The Metaphorical Brain 2: Neural Nets and Beyond. New York: John Wiley, 1989.

Baldi, P. and R. Meir. "Computing with arrays of coupled oscillators: an application to preattentive texture discrimination." Neural Computation 2 (1990): 458-471.

Barlow, H.B. "Single units and sensation: a neuron doctrine for perceptual psychology." Perception 1 (1972): 371-392.

Bartoshuk, Linda M. "Taste." In Stevens' Handbook of Experimental Psychology. Volume 1: Perception and Motivation, ed. Richard C. Atkinson, Richard J. Herrnstein, Gardner Lindzet, and R. Duncan Luce. 461-499. New York: Wiley-Interscience, 1988.

Basar, E. "Chaotic dynamics and resonance phenomena in brain function: progress,, perspectives, and thoughts." In Chaos in Brain Function, ed. Erol Basar. 1-30. Berlin: Springer-Verlag, 1990.

Benham, C. E. "The artificial spectrum top." Nature, Lond. 51 (1894): 200.

Benham, C. E. "The artificial spectrum top." Nature, Lond. 2 (1895): 321.

Bialek, W., F. Rieke, R. R. van Stevenink, and Warland de Ruyter D. "Reading a neural code." Science 252 (28 June 1991): 1854-1856.

Bittner, G.D. "Differentiation of nerve terminals in the crayfish opener muscle and its functional significance." J. Gen. Physiol. 51 (1968): 731-758.

Boomsliter, Paul and Warren Creel. "The long pattern hypothesis in harmony and hearing." Journal of Music Theory 5 (1962): 2-31.

Boring, Edwin G. The Physical Dimensions of Consciousness. New York: Dover, 1933.

Boring, Edwin G. Sensation and Perception in the History of Experimental Psychology. New York: Appleton-Century-Crofts, 1942.

Bower, T. G. R. "The evolution of sensory systems." In Perception: Essays in Honor of James J. Gibson, ed. Robert B. MacLeod and Herbert Pick Jr. 141-152. Ithaca: Cornell University Press, 1974.

Bradley, R. M., H. M. Stedman, and C. M. Mistretta. "Superior laryngeal nerve response patterns to chemical stimulation of sheep epiglottis." Brain Research 276 (1983): 81-93.

Braitenberg, V. "Functional interpretation of cerebellar histology." Nature 190 (1961): 539-540.

Braitenberg, Valentino. "Is the cerebellar cortex a biological clock in the millisecond range?" Prog. Brain Res. 25 (1967): 334-346.

Braitenberg, V. "Two views of the cerebral cortex." In Brain Theory, ed. G. Palm and A. Aertsen. 81-96. Berlin: Springer Verlag, 1986.

Braitenberg, V. and A. Schüz. Anatomy of the Cortex. Statistics and Geometry. Vol. 18. Studies of Brain Function, ed. V. Braitenberg. Berlin: Springer Verlag, 1991.

Bregman, Albert S. Auditory Scene Analysis: The Perceptual Organization of Sound. Cambridge, MA: MIT Press, 1990.

Bruce, Vicki and Patrick Green. Visual Perception: Physiology, Psychology and Ecology. London: Lawrence Erlbaum Associates, 1985.

Brugge, J.F., D.J. Anderson, J.E. Hind, and J.E. Rose. "Time structure of discharges in single auditory nerve fibers of the squirrel monkey in response to complex periodic sounds." J. Neurophysiol. 32 (1969): 386-401.

Bullock, T.H. "Signals and neural coding." In The Neurosciences: A Study Program, ed. G.C. Quarton, T. Melnechuck, and F.O. Schmitt. 347-352. New York: Rockefeller University Press, 1967.

Bullock, Theodore Holmes. "Electroception." Ann. Rev. Neurosci. 5 (1982): 121-70.

Butterworth IV, J.F., S.G. Raymond, and R.F. Roscoe. "Effects of halothane and enflurane on firing threshold of frog myelinated axons." J. Physiol. (London) 411 (1989): 493-516.

Cain, William S. "Olfaction." In Stevens' Handbook of Experimental Psychology. Volume 1: Perception and Motivation, ed. Richard C. Atkinson, Richard J. Herrnstein, Gardner Lindzet, and R. Duncan Luce. 409-459. New York: Wiley-Interscience, 1988.

Cariani, Peter. "Emergence and artificial life." In Artificial Life II. Volume X, Santa Fe Institute Studies in the Science of Complexity, ed. C.G. Langton, C. Taylor, J.D. Farmer, and S. Rasmussen. 775-798. Redwood City, CA: Addison-Wesley, 1992a.

Cariani, Peter. "Some epistemological implications of devices which construct their own sensors and effectors." In Towards a Practice of Autonomous Systems, ed. F. Varela and P. Bourgine. 484-493. Cambridge, Massachusetts: MIT Press, 1992b.

Cariani, Peter. "To evolve an ear: epistemological implications of Gordon Pask's electrochemical devices." Systems Res. (in press) (1993):

Cariani, P. and B. Delgutte. "Interspike interval distributions of auditory nerve fibers in response to variable-pitch complex stimuli." Assoc. Res. Otolaryng. (ARO) Abstr. (1992a):

Cariani, P and B. Delgutte. "The pitch of complex sounds is simply coded in interspike interval distributions of auditory nerve fibers." Soc. Neurosci. Abstr. 18 (1992b): 383.

Cariani, P. and B. Delgutte. "Interspike interval distributions of auditory nerve fibers in response to concurrent vowels with same and different fundamental frequencies." Assoc. Res. Otolaryng. (ARO) Abstr. (1993):

Cariani, Peter A. "On the Design of Devices with Emergent Semantic Functions." Ph.D., State University of New York at Binghamton, 1989.

Carr, Catherine, E., Walter Heiligenberg, and Gary J. Rose. "A time-comparison circuit in the electric fish midbrain. I. Behavior and physiology." J. Neuroscience 6 (1 1986a): 107-119.

Carr, Catherine, E., Leonard Maler, and Barbara Taylor. "A time-comparison circuit in the electric fish midbrain. II. Functional morphology." J. Neuroscience 6 (5 1986b): 1372-1383.

Carr, Catherine E. "Processing of temporal information in the brain." Annu. Rev. Neurosci. 16 (1993): 223-243.

Chang, Hsiang-Tung. "The evoked potentials." In Handbook of Physiology: Neurophysiology. Volume II., ed. John Field, H.W. Magoun, and Victor E. Hall. 299-313. Washington, D.C.: American Physiological Society, 1959.

Chung, S.H., S.A. Raymond, and J.Y. Lettvin. "Multiple meaning in single visual units." Brain Behav Evol 3 (1970): 72-101.

Churchland, Patricia S. and Sejnowski, Terrence J. The Computational Brain. Cambridge: MIT Press, 1992.

Covey, Ellen. "Temporal Neural Coding in Gustation." Ph.D., Duke University, 1980.

de Boer, E. "On the "residue" and auditory pitch perception." In Handbook of Sensory Physiology, ed. W.D Keidel and W.D. Neff. 479-583. 3. Berlin: Springer Verlag, 1976.

de Ribaupierre, Francois, Moise H. Goldstein Jr., and Grace Yeni-Komshian. "Cortical coding of repetitive acoustic pulses." Brain Research 48 (1972): 205-225.

De Valois, RL. and De Valois, K.K. Spatial Vision. Oxford: Oxford University Press, 1990.

Delgutte, B. "Representation of speech-like sounds in the discharge patterns of auditory-nerve fibers." J Acoust Soc Am 68 (1980): 843-857.

Delgutte, B. and P. Cariani. "Coding of the pitch of harmonic and inharmonic complex tones in the interspike intervals of auditory nerve fibers." In The Processing of Speech, ed. M.E.H. Schouten. Berlin: Mouton-DeGruyer, 1992.

Dewson III, James H. "Speech sound discrimination by cats." Science 144 (1964): 555-556.

Di Lorenzo, Patricia M. and Gerald S. Hecht. "Perceptual consequences of electrical stimulation in the gustatory system." Behavioral Neuroscience 107 (1993): 130-138.

Di Lorenzo, P.M. and J.S. Swartzbaum. "Coding of gustatory information in the pontine parabrachial nuclei of the rabbit: Temporal patterns of neural response." Brain Research 251 (1982): 244-257.

Ditchburn, R. W. and B. L. Ginsborg. "Vision with a stabilized retinal image." Nature 170 (1952): 178-94.

Eddington, D. K., W.H. Dobelle, D. E. Brackman, M. G. Mladejovsky, and J. Parkin. "Place and periodicity pitch by stimulation of multiple scla tympani electrodes in deaf volunteers." Trans. Am. Soc. Artif. Intern. Organs XXIV (1978):

Edelman, Gerald M. Neural Darwinism: The Theory of Neuronal Group Selection. New York: Basic Books, 1987.

Eigen, Manfred. "Molecules, information, and memory: form molecular to neural networks." In The Neuroscienes: A Third Study Program, ed. F. O. Schmitt and F. G. Worden. Cambridge: MIT Press, 1974.

Elliot, D.N. and C. Trahoitis. "Cortical lesions and auditory discrimination." Psychol. Bull. 77 (1972): 198-222.

Emmers, Raimond. "Modality coding of lingual afferents in the cat thalamus." In Olfaction and Taste. Proceedings of the Third Symposium., ed. Carl Pfaffman. 517-526. New York: Rockefeller University Press, 1969.

Emmers, Raimond. "Modifications of sensory modality codes by stimuli of graded intensity in the cat thalamus." Brain Research 21 (1970): 91-104.

Emmers, Raimond. "Thalamic mechanisms that process a temporal pulse code for pain." Brain Research 103 (1976): 425-441.

Emmers, Raimond. Pain: A Spike-Interval Coded Message in the Brain. New York: Raven Press, 1981.

Evans, E.F. "Place and time coding of frequency in the peripheral auditory system: some physiological pros and cons." Audiology 17 (1978): 369-420.

Feldman, Jerome A. "Computational constraints on higher neural representations." In Computational Neuroscience, ed. Eric L. Schwartz. 163-178. Cambridge: MIT Press, 1990.

Ferenandez, Julio, Alvaro Moreno, and Arantza Etxeberria. "Life as emergence: The roots of a new paradigm in theoretical biology." World Futures 32 (2-3 1991): 133-150.

Festinger, Leon , Mark R. Allyn, and Charles W. White. "The perception of color with achromatic stimulation." Vision Res. 11 (1971): 591-612.

Fiorentini, A and D.M. MacKay. "Temporal factors in pattern vision." Quart. J. Exp. Psychol. 40 (1965): 282-291.

Fishman, I. Y. "Single fiber gustatory impulses in rate and hamster." Journal of Cellular and Comparative Physiology 61 (1957): 588-618.

Freeman, J. A. and C. N. Nicholson. "Space-time transformation in the frog cerebellum through an intrinisic tapped delay line." Nature 226 (May 16 1970): 640-642.

Frisina, R.D., R.L. Smith, and S.C. Chamberlain. "Encoding of amplitude modulation in the gerbil cochlear nucleus: I. A hierarchy of enhancement." Hearing Research 44 (1990): 99-122.

Funakoshi, M. and Y. Ninomiya. "Neural code for taste quality in the thalamus of the dog." In Food intake and chemical senses, ed. Y. Katsuki, M. Sato, S.F. Takagi, and Y. Oomura. 223-232. Tokyo: University Park Press, 1977.

Gardenier, P.H., B.C. McCallum, and R.H.T. Bates. "Fourier magnitudes are unique pattern recognition templates." Biological Cybernetics 54 (1986): 385-391.

Gerard, R. W. "Neurophysiology: an integration (molecules, neurons, and behavior)." In Handbook of Physiology: Neurophysiology. Volume II., ed. John Field, H.W. Magoun, and Victor E. Hall. 1919-1965. Washington, D.C.: American Physiological Society, 1959.

Gesteland, R.C., J.Y. Lettvin, W.H. Pitts, and S.H. Chung. "A code in the nose." In Cybernetic Problems in Bionics, ed. Hans L. Oestereicher and Darrell R. Moore. 313-322. New York: Gordon and Breach, 1968.

Ghitza, O. "Auditory neural feedback as a basis for speech processing." In IEEE 1988 International Conference on Acoustics, Speech, and Signal Processing in New York, New York, , 1 - 4, Year.

Ghitza, O. "Auditory nerve representation as a basis for speech processing." In Advances in Speech Signal Processing, ed. S Furui and M.M. Sondhi. 453-485. New York: Marcel Dekker, 1992.

Gilbert, Charles D. "Microcircuitry of the visual cortex." Ann. Rev. Neurosci. 6 (1983): 217-47.

Gilbert, Charles D. and Torsten N. Wiesel. "Receptive field dynamics in adult primary visual cortex." Nature 356 (12 March 1992): 150-152.

Goldstein, J. L. and P. Srulovicz. "Auditory-nerve spike intervals as an adequate basis for aural frequency measurement." In Psychophysics and Physiology of Hearing, ed. E.F. Evans and J.P. Wilson. London: Academic Press, 1977.

Goldstein, M. H., Jr., N.Y.S. Kiang, and R.M. Brown. "Responses of the auditory cortex to repetitive acoustic stimuli." J. Acoust. Soc. Am. 31 (1959): 356-364.

Greene, Peter H. "On looking for neural networks and "cell assemblies" that underlie behavior. I. Mathematical model. II. Neural realization of a mathematical model." Bull. Math. Biophys. 24 (1962): 247-275, 395-411.

Grossberg, Stephen. "How does a brain build a cognitive code?" Psychological Review 87 (1980): 1-51.

Handel, Stephen. Listening. Cambridge: MIT Press, 1989.

Hebb, D. O. The Organization of Behavior. New York: Simon & Schuster, 1949.

Heiligenberg, Walter. "The neural basis of behavior: a neuroethological view." Annu. Rev. Neurosci. 14 (1991): 247-67.

Helighen, Francis. "Modelling emergence." World Futures 32 (2-3 1991): 151-166.

Hopfield, J. J. "Neural networks and physical systems with emergent collective computational abilities." Proc. Nat. Acad. Sci. 79 (1982): 2554-2558.

Hopkins, Carl D. "Neuroethology of electric communication." Ann. Rev. Neurosci. 11 (1988): 497-535.

Imig, Thomas J.. and Anne Morel. "Organization of the thalamocortical auditory system in the cat." Ann. Rev. Neurosci. 6 (1983): 95-120.

Jarvis, J.R. "On Fechner-Benham Subjective Color." Vision Research 17 (1976): 445-451.

Javel, E., J.B. Mott, N.L. Rush, and D.W. Smith. "Frequency discrimination: evaluation of rate and temporal codes." In Basic Issues in Hearing, ed. H. Duifhuis, J.W. Horst, and H.P. Wit. 224-225. London: Academic Press, 1988.

Jeffress, L. A. "A place theory of sound localization." J. Comp. Physiol. Psychol. 41 (1948): 35-39.

John, E. R. "Electrophysiological studies of conditioning." In The Neurosciences: A Study Program, ed. Gardner C. Quarton, Theodore Melnechuk, and Francis O. Schmitt. 690-704. New York: Rockefeller University Press, 1967.

Johnson, K.O. and S.S. Hsiao. "Neural mechanisms of tactual form and texture perception." Annu. Rev. Neurosci. 15 (1992): 227-250.

Kabrisky, Matthew. A Proposed Model for Visual Information Processing in the Human Brain. Urbana, Ill.: University of Illinois, 1966.

Kabrisky, Matthew. "A proposed model for visual information processing in the brain." In Models for the Perception of Speech and Visual Forms, ed. Weiant Wathen-Dunn. 354-361. Cambridge: MIT Press, 1967.

Kampis, George. "Emergent computations, life, and cognition." World Futures 32 (2-3 1991a): 95-110.

Kampis, George. Self-Modifying Systems in Biology and Cognitive Science. Oxford: Pergamon Press, 1991b.

Katchalsky, Aharon Katzir, Vernon Rowland, and Robert Blumenthal. Dynamic Patterns of Brain Cell Assemblies. Neurosciences Research Program, 1972. Neurosciences Research Program Bulletin Vol. 12, No. 1.

Keidel, W. D., U. O. Keidel, and N.Y.S. Kiang. "Peripheral and cortical responses to mechanical stimulation of the cat's vibrissae." Arch. Int. Physiol. 68 (1960): 241-262.

Kiang, N.Y.S. and M.H. Goldstein Jr. "Tonotopic organization of the cat auditory cortex for some complex stimuli." J. Acoust. Soc. Am. 31 (1959): 786-790.

Kiang, N.Y.S., T. Watanabe, E.C. Thomas, and L.F. Clark. Discharge Patterns of Single Fibers in the Cat's Auditory Nerve. Cambridge: MIT Press, 1965.

Kim, D.O., J.G. Sirianni, and S.O. Chang. "Responses of DCN-PVCN neurons and auditory nerve fibers in unanesthetized decerebrate cats to AM and pure tones: Analysis with autocorrelation/power-spectrum." Hearing Research 45 (1990): 95-113.

Kozak, W.M. and H.J. Reitboeck. "Color-dependent distribution of spikes in single optic tract fibers of the cat." Vision Research 14 (1974): 405-419.

Kozak, W.M., H.J. Reitboeck, and F. Meno. "Subjective color sensations elicited by moving patterns: effect of luminance." In Seeing Contour and Colour, ed. J.J. Kulikowski Dickenson, C.M. 294-310. New York: Pergamon Press, 1989.

Langner, Gerald. "Periodicity coding in the auditory system." Hearing Research 60 (1992): 115-142.

Lazzaro, John and Carver Mead. "Silicon modeling of pitch perception." Proceedings of the National Academy of Sciences, USA 86 (1989): 9597-9601.

Lestienne, R. and B.L. Strehler. "Time structure and stimulus dependence of precise replicating patterns present in monkey cortical neuronal spike trains." Brain Research 43 (1987): 214-238.

Licklider, J.C.R. "A duplex theory of pitch perception." VII (4 1951): 128-134.

Licklider, J.C.R. ""Periodicity" pitch and "place" pitch." Journal of the Acoustical Society of America 26 (1954): 945.

Licklider, J.C.R. "Information Theory." In Symposium on Information Theory in Royal Institute, London, September 12-16, 1955, edited by clin Cherry, Academic Press, 253-268, Year.

Licklider, J.C.R. "Auditory frequency analysis." In Information Theory, ed. C. Cherry. 253-268. London: Butterworth, 1956.

Licklider, J.C.R. "Three auditory theories." In Psychology: A Study of a Science. Study I. Conceptual and Systematic, ed. Sigmund Koch. 41-144. Volume I. Sensory, Perceptual, and Physiological Formulations. New York: McGraw-Hill, 1959.

Longuet-Higgins, H.C. "The non-local storage and associative retrieval of spatio-temporal patterns." In Information Processing in the Nervous System, ed. K.N. Liebovic. New York: Springer Verlag, 1969.

Longuet-Higgins, H.C. Mental Processes: Studies in Cognitive Science. Cambridge, Mass.: The MIT Press, 1987.

Longuet-Higgins, H.C. "A mechanism for the storage of temporal correlations." In The Computing Neuron, ed. R. Durbin, C. Miall, and G. Mitchison. 99-104. Wokingham, England: Addison-Wesley, 1989.

Lorente de No, Rafael and John Farquhar Fulton. "Cerebral cortex: architecture, intracortical connections, motor projections." In Physiology of the Nervous System, ed. John Farquhar Fulton. 288-330. III ed., Vol. New York: Oxford University Press, 1933/1949.

Lotka, Alfred J. Elements of Mathematical Biology. New York: Dover, 1924/1956.

Lyon, R.F. "Computational models of neural auditory processing." In IEEE International Conference on Acoustics, Speech, and Signal Processing (ICASSP) in San Diego, March, 1984, Year.

Lyon, Richard F. "CCD correlators for auditory models." In Proceedings of the 25th Asilomar Conference on Signals, Systems, and Computers in Pacific Grove, California, November 4-6, 1991, IEEE Computer SocietyYear.

Mach, Ernst. "The fibers of Corti." In Popular Lectures (1894), New York: Dover, 1865.

MacKay, Donald G. The Organization of Perception and Action. New York: Springer-Verlag, 1987.

MacKay, D.M. "Self-organization in the time domain." In Self-Organizing Systems 1962, ed. M.C. Yovitts, G.T. Jacobi, and G.D. Goldstein. 37-48. Washington, D.C.: Spartan Books, 1962.

MacKay, D.M. and W.S. McCulloch. "The limiting information capacity of a neuronal link." Bull. Math. Biophys. 14 (1952):

Macrides, F. "Dynamic aspects of central olfactory processing." In Chemical Signals in Vertebrates, ed. D. Muller Schwartze and M. M. Mozell. 207-229. 3. New York: Plenum, 1977.

Macrides, Foteos and Stephan L. Chorover. "Olfactory bulb units: activity correlated with inhalation cycles and odor quality." Science 175 (7 January 1972): 84-86.

Mair, R. G. "Ontogeny of the olfactory code." Experientia 42 (1986): 213-223.

Mäkelä, J.P., G. Karmos, M. Molnar, V. Csepe, and I. Winkler. "Steady-state responses from cat auditory cortex." Hearing Research 45 (1990): 41-50.

Marr, David. "A theory for cerebral neocortex." Proc. Roy. Soc. London, B. 176 (1970): 161-234.

Marr, David. Vision. San Francisco: W. H. Freeman, 1982.

Marr, David, ed. From the Retina to the Neocortex: Selected Papers of David Marr. First ed., Boston: Birkhäuser, 1991.

Mastronarde, David N. "Correlated firing of retinal ganglion cells." TINS 12 (2 1989): 75-80.

Maturana, Humberto. "The biology of cognition." In Autopoiesis and Cognition, ed. Humberto Maturana and Francisco Varela. 42. Dordrecht, Holland: D. Reidel, 1970.

Maturana, Humberto and Francisco Varela. "Autopoiesis: the organization of the living." In Autopoiesis and Cognition (1980), ed. Humberto Maturana and Francisco Varela. 42. Dordrecht, Holland: D. Reidel, 1973.

McClurkin, John W., Timothy J. Gawne, Lance M. Optican, and Barry J. Richmond. "Lateral geniculate neurons in behaving primates. II. Encoding of visual information in the temporal shape of the response." J. Neurophys. 66 (3 1991a): 794-308.

McClurkin, John W., Timothy J. Gawne, Barry J. Richmond, Lance M. Optican, and David Lee Robinson. "Lateral geniculate neurons in behaving primates. I. Responses to two-dimensional stimuli." J. Neurophys. 66 (3 1991b): 777-793.

McClurkin, J. W., J. A. Zarbock, and L. M. Optican. "Neurons in primate visual cortex multiplex information about red/green, blue/yellow, and black/white opponencies using temporal codes." Neurosci. Abstr. 19 (2 1993): 1576.

McCulloch, Warren S. "Modes of functional organization of the cerebral cortex." Federation Proceedings 6 (1947): 448-452.

McCulloch, W.S. "Of digital oscillators." In Information Processing in the Nervous System, ed. K.N. Leibovic. 293-296. New York: Springer Verlag, 1969.

McCulloch, W.S. and W. Pitts. "A logical calculus of the ideas immanent in nervous activity." In Collected Works of Warren S. McCulloch, ed. Rook McCulloch. 115-133. 5. Bulletin of Mathematical Biophysics, 1943.

McNaughton, Bruce L. and Lynn Nadel. "Hebb-Marr networks and the neurobiological representation of action in space." In Neuroscience and Connectionist Theory, ed. Mark A. Gluck and David E. Rumelhart. 1-64. Hillsdale, NJ: Lawrence Erlbaum Associates, 1990.

Meddis, R. and M.J. Hewitt. "Modeling the perception of concurrent vowels with different fundamental frequencies." J. Acoust. Soc. Am. (1990):

Meddis, R. and M.J. Hewitt. "Virtual pitch and phase sensitivity of a computer model of the auditory periphery. I. Pitch identification." Journal of the Acoustical Society of America 89 (1991a): 2866-2882.

Meddis, R. and M.J. Hewitt. "Virtual pitch and phase sensitivity of a computer model of the auditory periphery. II. Phase sensitivity." Journal of the Acoustical Society of America 89 (1991b): 2883-2894.

Meredith, M. "The analysis of response similarity in single neurons of the goldfish olfactory bulb using amino-acids as odor stimuli." Chem. Senses 6 (1981): 277-93.

Meredith, Michael and David G. Moulton. "Patterned response to odor in single neurones of goldfish olfactory bulb: Influence of odor quality and other stimulus parameters." J. Gen Physiol. 71 (1978): 615-643.

Møller, A. R. "Responses of units in the cochlear nucleus to sinusoidally amplitude-modulated tones." Exp Neurol (45 1974): 104-117.

Moore, B.C.J. Introduction to the Psychology of Hearing. Second edition ed., London: Academic Press, 1982.

Morley, J.W., J.S. Archer, D.G. Ferrington, M.J. Rowe, and A.B. Turman. "Neural coding of complex tactile vibration." In Information Processing in Mammalian Auditory and Tactile Systems, 127-140. Alan R. Liss, Inc, 1990.

Morrell, F. "Electrical signs of sensory coding." In The Neurosciences: A Study Program, ed. G.C. Quarton, T. Melnechuck, and F.O. Schmitt. 452-469. New York: Rockefeller University Press, 1967.

Mountcastle, Vernon. "The problem of sensing and the neural coding of sensory events." In The Neurosciences: A Study Program, ed. G.C. Quarton Melnechuk, T., and Schmitt, F.O. New York: Rockefeller University Press, 1967.

Mountcastle, Vernon. "Temporal order determinants in a somatosthetic frequency discrimination: sequential order coding." Annals New York Acad. Sci. 682 (1993): 151-170.

Mountcastle, V.B., W.H. Talbot, H. Sakata, and J. Hyvärinen. "Cortical neuronal mechanisms in flutter-vibration studied in unanesthetized monkeys. Neuronal periodicity and frequency discrimination." J. Neurophysiol. 32 (1969): 452-485.

Mozer, Michael C. "Neural net architectures for temporal sequence processing." In Predicting the Future and Understanding the Past, ed. A. Weigend and N. Gershenfeld. Redwood City, CA: Addision-Wesley, 1993.

Nagai, T. and K. Ueda. "Stochastic properties of gustatory impulse discharges in rat chorda tympani fibers." J. Neurophys. 45 (1981): 574-592.

Nordmark, Jan O. "Frequency and periodicity analysis." In Handbook of Perception, Vol. IV, Academic Press, 1978.

Ogawa, H., M. Sato, and S. Yamashita. "Variability in impulse dischrages in rat chorda tympani fibers in response to repeated gustatory stimulations." Physiology and Behavior 11 (1973): 469-479.

Ogawa, H., S. Yamashita, and M. Sato. "Variation in gustatory nerve fiber discharge pattern with change in stimulus concentration and quality." J. Neurophysiol. 37 (1974): 443-457.

Pabst, M., H.J. Reitboeck, and R. Eckhorn. "A model of preattentive texture region definition based on texture analysis." In Models of Brain Function, ed. Rodney M.J. Cotterill. 137-150. Cambridge: Cambridge University Press, 1989.

Palmer, A.R. "The representation of concurrent vowels in the temporal discharge patterns of auditory nerve fibers." In Basic Issues in Hearing, ed. H. Duifhuis, J.W. Horst, and H.P. Wit. 244-251. London: Academic Press, 1988.

Palmer, A.R. "Segregation of the responses to paired vowels in the auditory nerve of the guinea pig using autocorrelation." In The Auditory Processing of Speech, ed. Schouten. 115 - 124. Berlin: Mouton de Gruyter, 1992.

Pattee, Howard H. "How does a molecule become a message?" Developmental Biology Supplement 3 (1969): 1-16.

Pattee, Howard H. "Cell psychology: an evolutionary view of the symbol-matter problem." Cognition and Brain Theory 5 (1982): 325-341.

Pattee, Howard H. "Simulations, realizations, and theories of life." In Artificial Life. Volume VI, Santa Fe Institute Studies in the Science of Complexity, ed. C.G. Langton. 63-78. Redwood City, CA: Addison-Wesley, 1989.

Perkell, D.H and T.H. Bullock. Neural Coding. Neurosciences Research Program, 1968. Neurosciences Research Program Bulletin Vol. 6, No. 3.

Perotto, R.S. and T.R. Scott. "Gustatory neural coding in the brain." Brain Research 110 (1976): 283-300.

Phillips, D.P. "Timing of spike discharges in cat auditory cortex neurons: implications for encoding of stimulus periodicity." Hearing Research 40 (1989): 137-146.

Phillips, Dennis P., Richard A. Beale, and John F. Brugge. "Stimulus processing in the auditory cortex." In Neurobiology of Hearing: The Central Auditory System, ed. R. A. Altschuler. 335-365. New York: Raven Press, 1991.

Pitts, W. and W.S. McCulloch. "How we know universals: the perception of auditory and visual forms." Bulletin of Mathematical Biophysics 9 (1947): 1947.

Powers, WIlliam. Behavior: The Control of Perception. New York: Aldine, 1973.

Pratt, Gill. "Pulse Computation." Ph.D., Massachusetts Institute of Technology, 1990.

Pritchard, T.C. and T.R. Scott. "Amino acids as taste stimuli: I. Neural and behavioral attributes." Brain Research 253 (1982a): 81-92.

Pritchard, T.C. and T.R. Scott. "Amino acids as taste stimuli: II. Quality coding." Brain Research 253 (1982b): 93-104.

Ramon y Cajal, Santiago. New Ideas on the Structure of the Nervous System in Man and Vertebrates. Translated by Neely and Larry W. Swanson. Cambridge: MIT Press, 1894/1990.

Rashevsky, Nicholas. Mathematical BIophysics. Chicago: University of Chicago Press, 1948.

Raymond, S.A. "Effects of nerve impulses on threshold of frog sciatic nerve fibres." J Physiol (London) 290 (1979): 273-303.

Raymond, S.A. and J.Y. Lettvin. "Aftereffects of activity in peripheral axons as a clue to nervous coding." In Physiology and Pathobiology of Axons, ed. S.G. Waxman. New York: Raven Press, 1978.

Reichardt, Werner. "Autocorrelation, a principle for the evaluation of sensory information by the central nervous system." In Sensory Communication, ed. Walter A. Rosenblith. 303-317. New York: MIT Press/Wiley, 1961.

Reitboeck, H.J. and J. Altmann. "A model for size- and rotation-invariant pattern processing in the visual system." Biol. Cybern. 51 (1984): 113-121.

Reitboeck, H.J., M. Pabst, and R. Eckhorn. "Texture description in the time domain." In Computer Simulation in Brain Science, ed. R.M.J. Cotterill. Cambridge, England: Cambridge University Press, 1988.

Richmond, B.J., L.M. Optican, and T.J. Gawne. "Neurons use multiple messages encoded in temporally modulated spike trains to represent pictures." In Seeing Contour and Colour, ed. J.J. Kulikowski and C.M. Dickenson. 705-713. New York: Pergamon Press, 1989.

Richmond, B.J. , L.M. Optican, M. Podell, and H. Spitzer. "Temporal encoding of two-dimensional patterns by single units in primate inferior temporal cortex. I. Response characteristics. II. Quantification of response waveform III. Information-theoretic analysis." J. Neurophysiology 57 (1 1987): 132-178.

Rose, J.E., J.F. Brugge, D.J. Anderson, and J.E. Hind. "Some possible neural correlates of combination tones." J. Neurophysiol. 34 (1971): 769-793.

Rose, J.E., J.R. Brugge, D.J. Anderson, and J.E. Hind. "Phase-locked response to low-frequency tones in single auditory nerve fibers of the squirrel monkey." J. Neurophysiol. 30 (1967): 769-793.

Rosen, Robert. Anticipatory Systems. Oxford: Pergamon Press, 1985.

Rosen, Robert. Life Itself. New York: Columbia University Press, 1991.

Rosenblatt, Frank. "The perceptron: a probabilistic model for information storage and organization in the brain." Psychological Review 65 (1958): 386-406.

Rowe, Mark. "Impulse patterning in central neurons for vibrotactile coding." In Information Processing in Mammalian Auditory and Tactile Systems, 111-125. Alan R. Liss, Inc, 1990.

Schreiner, Chr., J.V. Urbas, and S. Mehrgardt. "Temporal resolution of amplitude modulation and complex signals in the auditory cortex of the cat." In Hearing-- Physiological Bases and Psychophysics, ed. R. Klinke and R. Hartmann. 169-175. Berlin: Springer-Verlag, 1983.

Schwartz, Dietrich W.F. and R.W. Ward Tomlinson. "Spectral response patterns of auditory cortex neurons to harmonic complex tones in alert monkey (Macaca mulatta)." J. Neurophys. 64 (1 1990): 282-298.

Schwartz, E. L. "Computational anatomy and functional architecture of striate cortex: A spatial mapping approach to spatial coding." Vision Research 20 (1980): 645-699.

Scott, T.R. and R. P. Erickson. "Synaptic processing of taste-quality information in thalamus of the rat." J. Neurophysiol. 34 (1971): 868-884.

Scott, T.R. and R.S. Perotto. "Intensity coding in pontine taste area: gustatory information is processed similarly throughout rat's brainstem." J. Neurophysiol. 44 (1980): 739-750.

Secker-Walker, H.E. and C.L. Searle. "Time-domain analysis of auditory-nerve-fiber firing rates." J. Acoust. Soc. Am. 88 (3 1990): 1427-1436.

Selfridge, O. G. "Pandemonium: a paradigm for learning." In Mechanization of Thought Processes: Proceedings of a Symposium Held at the National Physical Laboratory, November, 1958, 513-526. London: H.M.S.O., 1958.

Sheich, Henning. "Auditory cortex: comparative aspects of maps and plasticity." Current Opinion in Neurobiology 1 (1991): 236-247.

Shepherd, G. M. "The olfactory bulb as a simple cortical system." In The Neurosciences: A Second Study Program, ed. F. O. Schmitt. 539-552. New York: Rockefeller University Press, 1970.

Sheppard, Joseph .J. Human Color Perception: A Critical Study of the Experimental Foundation. New York: American Elsevier, 1968.

Siegel, Ralph M. and Heather L. Read. "Temporal processing in the visual brain." Ann. N. Y. Acad. Sci. 682 (1993): 171-178.

Simmons, James A. "A view of the world through the bat's ear: The formation of acoustic images in echolocation." In Neurobiology of Cognition, ed. P. D. Eimas and Al. M. Galaburda. 155-199. Cambridge: MIT Press, 1990.

Simmons, James A., Cynthia Moss F., and Michael Ferragamo. "Convergence of temporal and spectral information into acoustic images of complex sonar targets perceived by the echolocating bat, Eptesicus fuscus." Journal of Comparative Physiology A 166 (1990): 449-470.

Singer, W. "Search for coherence: a basic principle of cortical self-organization." Concepts in Neuroscience 1 (1 1990): 1-26.

Slaney, Malcolm and Richard F. Lyon. "Apple Hearing Demo Reel." Cupertino, CA: Apple Computer, Inc., 1991.

Slaney, Malcolm and Richard F. Lyon. "On the importance of time -- a temporal representation of sound." In Visual Representations of Speech SIgnals, ed. Martin Cooke and Beet Steve. London: John WIley & Sons Ltd, 1993.

Small, A.M. "Periodicity pitch." In Foundations of Modern Auditory Theory, ed. J.V. Tobial. 3-54. I. New York: Academic Press, 1970.

Softky, W. and C. Koch. "Cortical cells do not perform temporal integration of small EPSP's." Soc. Neurosci. Abstr. 18 (1992): 740.

Srulovicz, P. and J.L. Goldstein. "Central spectral patterns in aural signal analysis based on cochlear neural timing and frequency filtering." In IEEE in Tel Aviv, Israel, , 4 pages, Year.

Srulovicz, P. and J.L. Goldstein. "A central spectrum model: a synthesis of auditory-nerve timing and place cues in monaural communication of frequency spectrum." J. Acoust. Soc. Am. 73 (4 1983): 1266-1276.

Steinschneider, Mitchell, Joseph Arezzo, and Herbert G. Vaughan Jr. "Phase locked cortical responses to a human speech sound and low frequency tones in the monkey." Brain Research 198 (1980): 75-84.

Stevens, S. S. "Sensory power functions and neural events." In Principles of Receptor Physiology, ed. W.R. Loewenstein. 226-242. Berlin: Springer-Verlag, 1971.

Strehler, Bernard L. and Remy Lestienne. "Evidence of precise time-coded symbols and memory of patterns in monkey cortical neuronal spike trains." Proc. Nat. Acad. Sci. 83 (1986): 9812-9816.

Suga, Nobuo. "Cortical computational maps for auditory imaging." Neural Networks 3 (1990): 3-21.

Symmes, D. "Discrimination of intermittent noise by Macaques folllowing lesions in the temporal lobe." Exp. Neurol. 16 (1966): 201-214.

Szentagothai, John and Michael A. Arbib. Conceptual Models of Neural Organization. Neurosciences Research Program, 1972. Neurosciences Research Program Bulletin Vol. 12, No. 3.

Tank, D. W. and J.J. Hopfield. "Neural computation by concentrating information in time." Proc. Natl. Acad. Sci. USA 84 (1987): 1896-1900.

Teuber, Hans-Lukas. "Perception." In Handbook of Physiology: Neurophysiology. Volume II., ed. John Field, H.W. Magoun, and Victor E. Hall. Washington, D.C.: American Physiological Society, 1959.

Torras i Genis, Carme. Temporal-Pattern Learning in Neural Models. Vol. 63. Lecture Notes in Biomathematics, Brain Theory Subseries, ed. S. Levin. Berlin: Springer-Verlag, 1985.

Travers, S. P. and R. Norgren. "The time course of solitary nucleus gustatory responses: Influence of stimulus and site of application." Chemical Senses 14 (1989): 55-74.

Travis, Bryan J. "A layered network model of sensory cortex." In Computer Simulation in Brain Science, ed. R.M.J. Cotterill. 119-147. Cambridge, England: Cambridge University Press, 1988.

Tritsch, Mark F. "Fourier analysis of the stimuli for pattern-induced colors." Vision Res. 32 (8 1992): 1461-1470.

Troland, L.T. "The enigma of color vision." Am. J Physiol. Optics 2 (1921): 23-48.

Troland, L.T. "The psychophysiology of auditory qualities and attributes." 2 (1929): 28-58.

Ts'o, Daniel Y., Charles D. Gilbert, and Torsten N. Wiesel. "Relationships between horizontal interactions and functional architecture in cat striate cortex as revealed by cross-correlation analysis." <u>J. Neuroscience</u> 6 (4 1986): 1160-1170.

Uttal, W.R. <u>The Psychobiology of Sensory Coding</u>. New York: Harper and Row, 1973.

Uttal, W.R. <u>An Autocorrelation Theory of Form Detection</u>. New York: Wiley, 1975.

Uttal, W.R. <u>On Seeing Forms</u>. Hillsdale, NJ: Lawrence Erlbaum, 1988.

van Esch, A. , van 't Veld, and J.J. Koenderinck. "A temporal red-green opponent mechanism." <u>Biol. Cybern.</u> 58 (1988): 329-355.

Van Noorden, L. "Two channel pitch perception." In <u>Music, Mind and Brain</u>, ed. M. Clynes. 251-269. New York: Plenum, 1982.

Varela, Francesco. <u>Principles of Biological Autonomy</u>. New york: North Holland, 1979.

Voigt, H.F., M.B. Sachs, and E.D. Young. "Representation of whispered vowels in discharge patterns of suditory-nerve fibers." <u>Hearing Res.</u> 8 (1982): 49-58.

Vol, Ilia A., Marina B. Pavlovskaja, and Valerija M. Bonarko. "Similarity between Fourier transforms of objects predicts their experimental confusions." <u>Perception & Psychophysics</u> 47 (1 1989): 12-21.

von Bekesy, Georg. "Interaction of paired sensory stimuli and conduction in peripheral nerves." <u>Journal of Applied Physiology</u> 18 (6 1963): 1276-1284.

von Bekesy, Georg. "Duplexity theory of taste." <u>Science</u> 145 (3634 1964a): 834-835.

von Bekesy, Georg. "Sweetness produced electrically on the tongue and its relation to taste theories." <u>Journal of Applied Physiology</u> 19 (6 1964b): 1105-1113.

von Campenhausen, C. "The colors of Benham's top under metameric illuminations." <u>Vision Res.</u> 9 (1969): 677-682.

von Campenhausen, C. "Detection of short time delays between photic stimuli by means of pattern induced flicker colors (PIFCs)." <u>Vision Res.</u> 13 (1973): 2261-2271.

von Campenhausen, C., K. Hofstetter, M.F. Schramme, and M.F. Tritsch. "Color induction via non-opponent lateral interactions in the human retina." <u>Vision Res.</u> 32 (5 1992): 913-923.

von der Malsburg, Ch. and W. Schneider. "A neural cocktail party processor." <u>Biol. Cybernetics</u> 54 (1986): 29-40.

Walter, Grey. "Intrinsic rhythms of the brain." In <u>Handbook of Physiology: Neurophysiology. Volume II.</u>, ed. John Field, H.W. Magoun, and Victor E. Hall. 279-298. Washington, D.C.: American Physiological Society, 1959a.

Walter, Grey. <u>The Living Brain</u>. New York: Norton, 1959b.

Wasserman, Gerald S. "Isomorphism, task dependence, and the multiple meaning theory of neural coding." In <u>Biological Signals</u>, Karger, 1992.

Waxman, S.G. "Regional differentiation of the axon: A review with special reference to the concept of the multiplex neuron." In <u>Physiology and Pathobiology of Axons</u>, ed. S.G. Waxman. New York: Raven Press, 1978.

Wever, Ernest Glen. <u>Theory of Hearing</u>. New York: Wiley, 1949.

Wever, Ernest Glen and Charles W. Bray. "The perception of low tones and the resonance-volley theory." <u>J. Psychol.</u> 3 (1937): 101-114.

Whitfield, I. C. "Auditory cortex and the pitch of complex tones." <u>J. Acoust. Soc. Am.</u> 67 (1980): 644-647.

Wilson, J.P. "Perceptual anomalies associated with a single contour." <u>Nature</u> 187 (1960): 137.

Windhorst, Uwe. <u>How Brain-Like is the Spinal Cord? Interacting Cell Assemblies in the Nervous System</u>. Berlin: Springer-Verlag, 1988.

Woodhouse, J. M. and H. D. Barlow. "Spatial and temporal resolution and analysis." In <u>The Senses</u>, ed. H. D. Barlow and J. D. Molton. Cambridge: Cambridge University Press, 1982.

Yamamoto, T., N. Yuyama, T. Kato, and Y. Kawamura. "Gustatory responses of cortical neurons in rats: I. Response characteristics." <u>J. Neurophysiol.</u> 51 (1984): 615-635.

Young, R.A. "Some observations on temporal coding of color vision: psychophysical results." <u>Vision Research</u> 17 (1977): 957-965.

Young, R.A. and R. De Valois. "Temporal-chromatic interactions in monkey visual system." <u>Association for Research in Vision and Opthamology (ARVO)</u> (1977):

Young, R.S.L., R.E. Cole, M. Gambel, and M.D. Rayner. "Subjective patterns elicited by light flicker." <u>Vision Research</u> 15 (1975): 1291-1293.

Zrenner, Eberhart. <u>Neurophysiological Aspects of Color Vision in Primates. Comparative Studies on Simian Retinal Ganglion Cells and the Human Visual System</u>. Vol. 9. Studies of Brain Function, ed. V. Braitenberg. Berlin: Springer-Verlag, 1983.

Chapter 10

Are Neural Spike Trains Deterministically Chaotic or Stochastic Processes?

Min Xie, Karl Pribram, Joseph King

Are Neural Spike Trains Deterministically Chaotic or Stochastic Processes ?

the Dynamics of Spontaneous Neural Interspike Intervals

Min Xie, Karl Pribram, and Joseph King

Center for Brain Research and Information Science
and Department of Psychology
Radford University, Radford, VA 24142

Abstract

Before examining neural interspike intervals to see how they might encode information, an essential question that has first to be answered is whether, under the unstimulated condition, the apparent randomness of the neural firing pattern reflects deterministic chaos or a stochastic process. Here, we use short term predictability and the structure of the prediction residual to determine the dynamic characteristics of interspike intervals. As demonstrated in given computer simulations, unlike stochastic processes, deterministic chaos is highly predictable in the short term by linear and / or nonlinear prediction techniques. Interspike intervals recorded from somatosensory cortex and hippocampus were, thus, analyzed by using the same techniques. The results show that the neural spontaneous interspike intervals are poorly predictable in the short term, and the models that best fit the interspike intervals are linear (AR or ARMA) stationary processes. Therefore, the pattern of neural spontaneous firing can be characterized as stochastic rather than deterministically chaotic.

I. Introduction

One of the most pervasive enigmas regarding brain function is how information becomes transmitted from one location to another. In view of the fact that nerve impulses are *per se* more or less all or none in character, attention has been focused on the pattern of interspike, i.e. inter impulse, intervals as the carriers of information. A good deal of evidence has accrued to the effect that in an anesthetized unstimulated brain, the interspike intervals recorded from single neurons in a variety of locations are essentially random in their distribution. Models of the interspike process have therefore been constructed upon the assumption that this randomness reflects a stochastic process. Stochastic resonance models [1, 2, 3] and stochastic resonance with noise models [4] have been especially fruitful in simulating actual data obtained from spike trains. However recording randomness does not in itself insure that a process is stochastic. Recently a surge of interest has developed for the possibility that the behavior of spike trains, though random, could be generated by a deterministic nonlinear process which results in chaos. The current project sets out to test whether deterministically chaotic or stochastic processes best characterizes the patterns of interspike intervals recorded from hippocampus and from somatosensory cortex in the lightly anesthetized rat.

Deterministic chaos is defined as a process which can be described precisely by a deterministic dynamic function. This deterministic function generates an 'unpredictable' bounded stable state [5]. The 'unpredictability', here, reflects the fact that the system is not periodic, quasi-periodic, or at equilibrium, i.e. converges onto a point attractor. The definition highlights two important considerations: The first is that the generator of the behavior is deterministic, even though the behavior currently displays randomness. The second consideration is that the observed randomness is not due to noise or interference from outside the system under observation; rather, the apparent randomness is due to the internal properties of system, i.e. its internal dynamics. Furthermore, to be chaotic, its randomness must reflect the fact that the system is sensitive to initial conditions, small perturbations, and the numerical errors caused by finite data length.

There is no widely accepted definition for stochastic processes. Any process will be called stochastic if its behavior is unpredictable from available past information. Instead of being generated by a determining function, the randomness of a stochastic system is due to possible interference from outside of the system under observation, improper selection of observations, or lack of knowledge about its coding structure. This ambiguity must not be reducible by improving precision of measurement and / or computation. For example, the trajectory of the orbit of Uranus was confusing before Neptune was discovered. The unpredictability in the trajectory of Uranus could not be reduced by just increasing the precision of measurement and computation. Once the interference from Neptune was taken into account, the trajectory became predictable. Thus, the similarity between chaotic and stochastic systems is that both of them currently display random behavior; the major difference is that chaotic randomness is due to an internally determinable generator while stochastic randomness is not.

Furthermore as a result of the operation of a deterministic generator, the trajectory of a chaotic process is structured while that of the stochastic process is not. The structure imbedded in the trajectory will therefore be reflected in its prediction error (residual). Ideally, this error reduction is unbounded when the frequency and precision of measurement and computation are improved. This unbounded characteristic of the reduction of the residual is one of most important measurements characterizing the chaotic process. In a stochastic system, the autocorrelation function of the residual after all the past information has been removed is a delta function. Also, in a stochastic system the variance of the residual will be much larger than that of the computational error, and can not be significantly reduced by increasing the rate of measurement and improving the prediction techniques.

II. Short term prediction in a chaotic process

According to the above, to distinguish a chaotic process from a stochastic one, the current output of a chaotic process must be predictable from immediately previous observations. This characteristic is called short term forward predictability. The characteristics of the prediction error (residual) is an important measure of the unknown process. Therefore, short term prediction becomes the key to determining whether an unknown process is chaotic or stochastic. When the variance of the residual has been minimized, the structure of the process becomes exposed, thus, whether the autocorrelation function of the residual is bounded or not can help to determine if the process is chaotic or stochastic. This section will describe and discuss some linear and nonlinear techniques used in short term prediction. These techniques will, in subsequent sections, be used in the computer simulations. The purpose of this section and the later computer simulations is to demonstrate, in the final section, that short term prediction is a useful tool in analyzing the dynamic properties of an unknown process such as those displayed by spike trains recorded from brain.

In nonlinear system analysis, the infinite series expansion of a general nonlinear function $f(x)$ is useful. If all the derivatives of the nonlinear function $f(x)$ exist, the function $f(x)$ can be written as the following infinite series (the Taylor expansion), expanded at $x=x_0$.

$$f(x)=f(x_0)+\frac{df}{dx}\bigg|_{x=x_0}(x-x_0)+\frac{1}{2!}\frac{d^2f}{dx^2}\bigg|_{x=x_0}(x-x_0)^2+\cdots+\frac{1}{k!}\frac{d^kf}{dx^k}\bigg|_{x=x_0}(x-x_0)^k+\cdots \qquad (1)$$

where $\dfrac{d^kf}{dx^k}\bigg|_{x=x_0}$ is the value of the kth derivative of nonlinear function $f(x)$ with respect to x evaluated at the point $x=x_0$. Clearly, if $\Delta x=|x-x_0|$ is small enough, or x is near x_0, then, $\Delta x^k \approx 0$, for all $k \geq 2$. In equation (1), the sum of the terms of the second-degree and higher-degree of $(x-x_0)$ are negligible compared with the sum of the first two terms, thus, $f(x)$ in the vicinity of x_0 can be represented as following linear form

$$f(x) \approx f(x_0)+\frac{df}{dx}\bigg|_{x=x_0}(x-x_0); \qquad (2)$$

for $\Delta x=|x-x_0|<\delta <<1$.

Equation (2) is the linear approximation of nonlinear function $f(x)$ within the vicinity of x_0.

The first derivative $\dfrac{df}{dx}\bigg|_{x=x_0}$, the slope of linear approximation representation of $f(x)$, is a function of x_0. If x is a function of time t, and t is discretized by a sampling operation, i.e. $t=n\Delta t$, $n=0$, 1, 2,$\cdots$, and $x(n)=x(n\Delta t)$, the dynamic trajectory $y(t) = f(x,t)$, at $t=(n+1)\Delta t$, can be derived from equation (2) by

$$\begin{aligned}y(n+1)&=f(x_n,n\Delta t)+f'(x_n,n\Delta t)(x_{n+1}-x_n)\\&=y(n)+f'(x_n,n\Delta t)(x_{n+1}-x_n)\end{aligned} \qquad (3)$$

where $x_n = x(n\Delta t)$, and $f'(x_n, n\Delta t) = \dfrac{df}{dx}\Big|_{x=x_n}$. The derivative $f'(x_n, n\Delta t)$ in equation (3) is time varying. Thus, a nonlinear function $y(t)=f(x,t)$ can be treated as a time varying linear dynamic equation proposed in equation (3).

This approximation usually works if x_{n+1} is close enough to x_n, or, equivalently, if $\Delta x = |x_{n+1} - x_n|$ is small enough in which case higher degree terms can be negligible. Therefor, to get a good approximation, the sample period Δt has to be small enough to satisfy the condition that $\Delta x^k \approx 0$, for all $k \geq 2$.

Equation (3) can be rewritten as a difference equation, i.e.

$$y_{k+1} = y_k + f_k'' x_{k+1} + f_k' x_k \tag{4}$$

which is a first order autoregressive moving average process (ARMA(1,1)) for a one dimensional dynamic system (single variable system). More generally, a nonlinear multidimentional dynamic equation (multivariable dynamic equation) $Y = F(X, t)$ can be represented approximately as a linear time varying ARMA($p.q$) process. Based on the dynamic model been constructed, the immediately future state y_{k+1} can be predicted by using the present and previous observations.

There are many different linear prediction methods, such as the autoregressive process (AR), the moving average process (MA), and the autoregressive moving average process (ARMA) [6]. Sometimes the "seasonal" model is also useful in predicting the behavior generated by a combination of slow and fast dynamics. All these estimators are called linear parametric estimators; they assume that the unknown system can be described by a linear difference equation, a discrete form of a linear differential dynamic function. The advantage of the linear estimator is its simplicity. These techniques have been well developed and successfully implemented in solving practical problems. The disadvantage of the linear estimator is that chaotic dynamics are strongly nonlinear and thus require a high sampling rate or frequency of observation. Meanwhile, the tracking rate of the linear estimator, known as the convergence rate, must be faster than that of the unknown dynamics.

To handle the above problem, a piecewise linear model can be realized by using a sliding data window for parameter estimation. The narrower the sliding window is, the shorter the linear pieces, and the faster the estimator can track. However, the tracking accuracy of the estimator is related to the variance of estimation, which is related to the total number of samples obtained. If, in a noisy situation, the sliding data window is too narrow, the variance of the estimation will be increased dramatically. The prediction error will contain a great deal of estimation error caused by noise. Therefore, the linear techniques are limited to those slow dynamic processes, mostly continuous cases. For fast chaotic dynamics, especially the discrete chaotic process, nonlinear techniques are needed to get good results. These techniques are usually more sophisticated than the linear techniques and also more computational intensive.

Unlike the linear parametric estimation techniques, the nonlinear methods are usually strongly related to the nonlinear model selected. If the structure of a dynamic function is known, and there are only a few unknown parameters in the function, then the least squares methods can be used to estimate these parameters. However, if the structure of the dynamic function is unknown, the reconstruction of the dynamics from previous observations will be more difficult than the linear methods.

One of promising nonlinear modeling methods is to assume that the nonlinear dynamic function, $y=F(X)$, can be decomposed as a linear combination of a set of basis functions, i.e.

$$y = F(\mathbf{X}) = \sum_{i=1}^{N} \lambda_i \Phi_i(\mathbf{X}) \tag{5}$$

where $\Phi_i(\mathbf{X})$, $i = 1,2,...N$, are called basis functions, and λ_i ; $i=1,2,...N$, are the coefficients or weightings assigned to the basis. The present output of the dynamic is $y(t)$, and the set of previous observations called the input vector becomes $\mathbf{X} = \{x_1, x_2, ..., x_n\}$. The function $F(\cdot)$ defines a projection from the input domain to the output domain. Once the basis is selected, given a set of sample input vectors and their outputs, the unknown function can be reconstructed by estimating the parameters in equation (5). The estimated function gives the 'best fit' to the given samples, and a 'reasonable estimation' in the region between samples.

The success of the method is very much dependent on the selection of basis functions. Here, a radial basis function interpolation network (RBF network) [7, 8] is chosen as a nonlinear estimator to predict the behavior of the unknown process. The idea of radial basis function interpolation is to use the radial basis function as the basis in equation (1), such as a Gaussian function defined by

$$\Phi_i(\mathbf{X}) = e^{(\frac{\|\mathbf{X}-\mathbf{C}_i\|}{\sigma_i^2})} \tag{6}$$

where $C_i = [c_1, c_2, ...c_n]$ is the center of base $\Phi_i(\mathbf{X})$; σ_i is the expansion parameter of $F_i(\mathbf{X})$; and, $\|\mathbf{X}-\mathbf{C}_i\|$ is the Euclidean distance from $\mathbf{X}$ to the center $\mathbf{C}_i$. To simplify the problem, σ_i, $i=1,\cdots,N$ are usually selected as the same constant value for the basis, which are equal to the maximum expansion of the input dynamic region. The center position C_i is selected according to the location of samples. A robust method referred to as orthogonal least square (OLS) [9] can be used to select the center from the input vectors and to compute the weighting coefficients. The interested reader can obtain the details of technique from the listed references.

III. Computer simulations

The computer simulations are designed to demonstrate the performances of linear and nonlinear methods in predicting the chaotic process, especially, to expose the characteristics of the residual, which is important in determining the dynamic properties of an unknown process. The examples are all chaotic processes. One is a continuous dynamic process generated by the Lorenz equation, and the other is the discrete process generated by the Henon equation. Both the linear and nonlinear techniques are tested in the computer simulation.

In the first computer experiment, the Lorenz equation is defined by

$$\begin{cases} \dfrac{dx}{dt} = \sigma(y - x) \\[2mm] \dfrac{dx}{dt} = xz + \alpha x - y \\[2mm] \dfrac{dz}{dt} = xy - \beta z \end{cases} \tag{7}$$

where α, β and σ are constants. Chaotic solutions of the Lorenz equation are presented when $\alpha = 28$, $\beta = 8/3$, $\sigma = 10$ [10]. The Lorenz equation is a third order nonlinear differential equation whose phase plane is three dimensional with variables of $x(t)$, $y(t)$, and $z(t)$. Figures (1a) and (1b) give the phase plane plot of the Lorenz equation and the trajectory of $x(t)$.

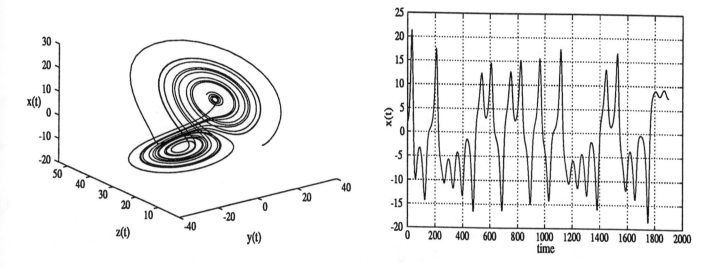

Figure 1. (1a) the trajectory of the Lorenz equation; (1b) the time waveform of x(t) variable

In the simulation, a third order autoregression (AR) forward estimator was used to perform a one step forward prediction. The parameters of the AR model were continuously estimated by the Burg algorithm [11] with a sliding window of 100 data points. The estimated trajectory shows (Figure 2a) a good match to the real trajectory (Figure 1b). The variance of the prediction error $e(t)$ is about 5.4794×10^{-5}. Studying the prediction error $e(t)$ (Figure 2b), its autocorrelation functions are not a delta function (Figure 3a). It has a relative long tail slowly cut at about a time lag $= 40$, which indicates that the prediction error contains information about the past which could be further removed by the predictor. Moreover, comparing $e(t)$ with the original dynamic trajectory $x(t)$, we can find that the prediction error shows a structure identical to that in $x(t)$.

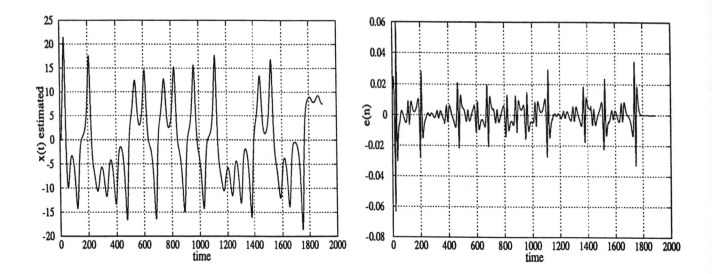

Figure 2. (2a) the forward prediction of x(t) by using the Burg algorithm. (2b) the residual of the Burg estimation.

To further explore the structure of the residual, we plot the normalized residual together with the normalized Euclidean distance which is measured from the trajectory position $[x(t),y(t),z(t)]$ to the hyperbolic point of the Lorenz equation (Figure 3b). The diagram shows that the closer the trajectory is to the hyperbolic point, the larger the prediction error will be after immediately passing the vicinity of this special point. The fact that the hyperbolic point is an unstable equilibrium point which separates the attractors and their dynamic basins (in the phase space) brings about the uncertainty of chaos. Like an ideal rigid ball dropping on the top of an ideal needle, the closer the ball approaches to the center of the needle, the more sensitive its trajectory is to its initial conditions and perturbations. To determine exactly a future trajectory, infinite precision of measurement and computation are required. That is, if we can make our estimator infinitely accurate, the prediction error reduction becomes unbounded. As noted, this is important in distinguishing a chaotic from a stochastic process.

The same Lorenz trajectory is used to test the nonlinear prediction model. The total number of bases used in equation (5) is 20. The variance of the prediction error is 3.2485×10^{-6}, which is about 20 times lower than that obtained with a linear predictor. Comparing the residual obtained with the nonlinear estimator (Figure 4a) to that of the linear one(Figure 3a), there are some similarities; however, the residual of the nonlinear estimator is much smaller than that of the linear predictor. Furthermore, the autocorrelation function of the nonlinear prediction error (Figure 4b) shows a long tail, which suggests that the information contained in the residual is still attributable to the history of its processing. This indicates that the prediction error can be further reduced by improving the numerical precision and the performance of the estimation. This also is important evidence that an unknown trajectory is chaotic.

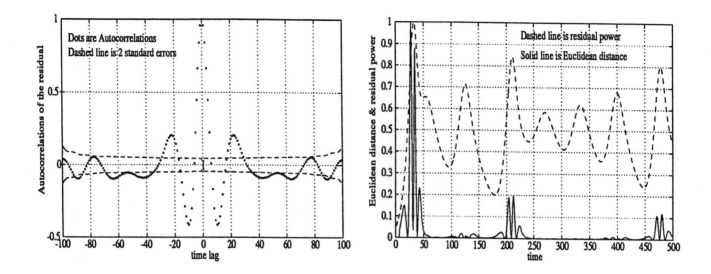

Figure 3. In (3a), the dots are estimated autocorrelation coefficients of the residual by using Burg algorithm, and, the dashed lines are the ± 2 times standard devination of the estimation.. In (3b), the solid line is the normalized Euclidean distance from the hyperbolic point of the Lorenz equation to the present trajectory x(t), and the dashed line is the present residual power.

In the second computer simulation, a discrete chaotic dynamic equation is used. The dynamic function is called the Henon equation [5] defined by

$$y(n) = c + ay(n-1) + by(n-2) \tag{8}$$

By selecting different parameters of {a , b , c}, the above difference function can demonstrate periodic, unstable, or chaotic behaviors. The parameters are selected in our simulation as c=1, a=-1.4, and b=0.3 to place $y(n)$ into a chaotic region. Figure (5a) and (5b) show the dynamic trajectory $y(n)$ and its input vectors in an input vector space defined by $y(n-1)$ versus $y(n-2)$. In physics, this input vector space is also called a phase space, and the input vector plot in Figure (5b) is called the return map of the Henon equation. In the simulation, a linear forward predictor was used to develop the discrete trajectory $y(n)$. The orders used in the autoregressive model were 2, and 4. Both results demonstrated large prediction errors, whose relative variances were 0.7150, 0.6368 respectively. Here the relative variance is defined by the variance of residual divided by the variance of unknown process $y(n)$, it is a ratio that measures the percentage of unpredictable information. The results indicate that about 72% to 64% information in $y(n)$ is unpredictable, especially, increasing the order of the linear predictor does not improve its performance if the residual is caused by nonlinearty.

Next, a radial basis function nonlinear predictor was used to analyze the dynamic of the Henon equation. The number of the basis used was 11. The original y(n) and its estimation totally overlap. The relative variance of the residual was 9.6623×10^{-10}. Both the residual (Figure 6a) and its autocorrelation function (Figure 6b) show a white noise pattern. The future states of the

261

y(n) are almost predictable from the past, and the unknown process is deterministic despite the fact that the trajectory itself looks random.

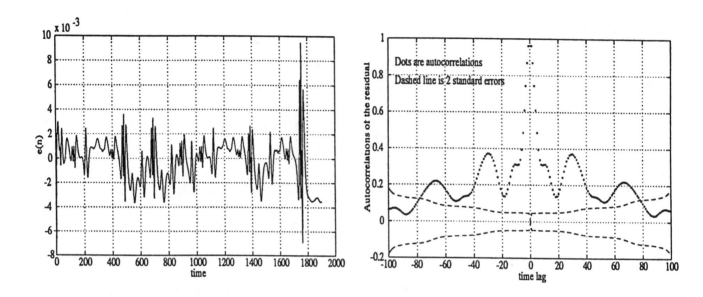

Figure 4. (4a) plots the forward prediction residual e(n) by using RBF network. In (4b), the dots are estimated autocorrelation coefficients of the residual in (4a), and, the dashed lines are the ± 2 times standard deviation of the estimation.

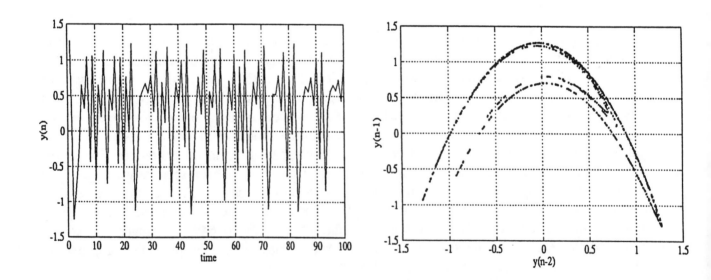

Figure 5. (5a) is the time series of the Henon equation. (5b) shows the input vectors of the Henon equation for training RBF network.

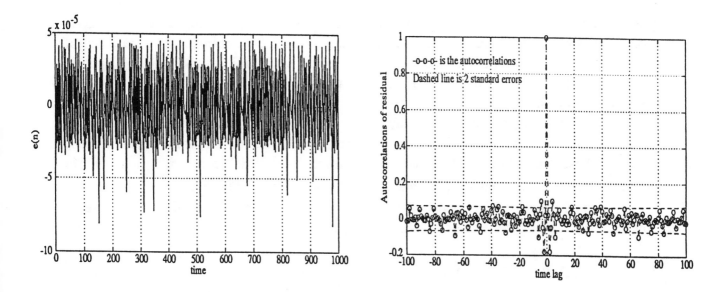

Figure 6.(6a) is the forward prediction residual of the Henon equation by using RBF network. In (6b), the dots are estimated autocorrelation coefficients of the residual in (6a), and the dashed lines are the ± 2 times standard deviation of the estimation.

IV. The analysis of the interspike intervals

In the previous sections, both the linear and nonlinear methods have been delineated for detecting a chaotic process. The computer simulations showed these methods to be promising in modeling chaotic processes. The structure embedded in the prediction error was shown especially useful in testing the low bound of the estimation. This estimation can, then, be further used to discriminate a stochastic process from chaotic dynamics. In this section, these techniques will be implemented in an analysis of interspike intervals. The experiments are designed to model the interspike interval both by linear and nonlinear methods. The questions to be answered are: First, whether or not the interspike interval can be modeled as being generated by a deterministic generator. Such a model would show (or not show) a short term predictability of the unknown process. Second, would such a model be linear or nonlinear? Only those processes which proved to be nonlinear and short term predictable would be classifiable as chaotic.

The raw data were collected from anesthetized (with barbiturate) rat somatosensory cortex and hippocampus. The records are of spontaneously firing neural units (there is no stimulus). Records of raw data were obtained by means of a Grass Model P5 preamplifier with an FET cathode follower. The recorded signal was band limited between 300 and 3000 Hz and amplified with a gain of 20,000. One hundred seconds of continuous voltages were sampled at a rate of 32 kHZ and stored by a BRAINWAVE system onto a PC-486 based computer. The raw data were then transferred for processing to a Silicon Graphics workstation. The units were sorted by a template matching program. The templates are histograms composed of the peak to peak

263

amplitude and descending slopes of all units in a recording. Individual units were matched to one of the several templates obtained in this fashion from each recording.

Records from 12 rats were used. Twenty three units were obtained from 7 hippocampal recording; 12 units were obtained from 5 somatosensory cortex recording. Figure (7a) gives a typical interspike interval record from somatosensory cortex. The mean value of the inter spike intervals is 115 ms , with a standard deviation of 86.65 ms .The interspike intervals appear to occur randomly but they also show a tendency to group at 50 to 125 ms. However, about every 15 to 20 intervals, the interval will suddenly increase to the level of 300 to 400 ms, and to oscillate a few times before returning to the lower base line. The autocorrelation functions (figure 7b) at lag =1, 2 are higher than the 95% confidence level. There are also some seasonal changes although these are below the 95% confidence level. The partial correlation function drops abruptly at lag >1, and   and it approximately equals to 95% level at lag 17.

A seasonal autoregressive model was constructed from one recording of the somatosensory spike-trains according to the autocorrelations and partial autocorrelations. The model equation is

$$(1-a_1 B)(1-a_2 B^{17})y(n)=e(n) \tag{9}$$

where B^k is a k steps delay operator, $e(n)$ is the excitation noise of the process or residual of the prediction, and $[a_1, a_2]$ are the unknown parameters of the model. The estimated results are

$$(1+0.5092B)(1+0.2924B^{17})y(n)=e(n) \tag{10a}$$

or

$$y(n)-0.5092y(n-1)-0.2924y(n-17)+0.1489y(n-18)=e(n) \tag{10b}$$

Figures (7c) and (7d) give the one step forward prediction error $e(n)$ and its autocorrelation function. The variance of the residual is 5425.9 (the stand deviation = 73.66). All the autocorrelation functions of the residual are below the 95 confidence level at lag > 0. The T ratio test for the estimated parameters in the equation (10a) are 5.87 and 2.7 respectively. Moreover, a sliding window of 100 interval points was applied to the interspike intervals; the estimated model parameters keep almost the same values as the window moves across the records.

Next, the nonlinear radial basis function estimator was applied to the same record. Fourteen bases were used in reconstructing the recorded interval train; the variance of the residual, and its autocorrelations were identical to the those obtained with the linear estimators.

The rest of the interspike intervals recorded from somatosensory cortex were processed using the same techniques. Most of them can be modeled as a first order autoregression function plus some seasonal effects at seasonal intervals of 7 to 17. Only 3 out of the 12 interval records from somatosensory cortex can be modeled as a first order autoregression model (AR(1)) or first order autoregression and first order moving-average model (ARMA(1,1)) without a seasonal period. The relative variance of the residual and the original interspike intervals was 0.914 in the linear prediction cases and 0.903 in the nonlinear cases, which means that less than 10 percent of the information in the interspike interval can be predicted according to previous observation.

The results indicate that the interspike intervals of the somatosensory cortex can be modeled as a time invariant (stationary) linear autoregression process under the condition of no stimulation. Only a very low percentage of the information at any interval can be predicted from previous intervals. Such a process is not chaotic but stochastic.

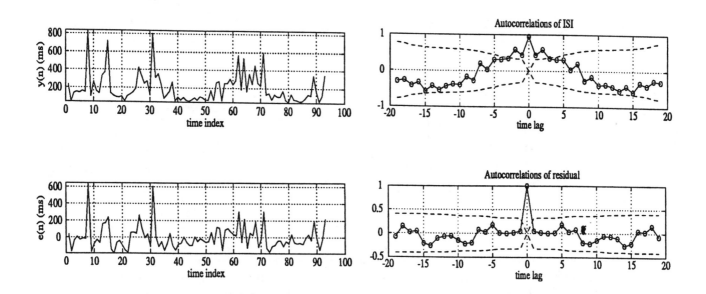

Figure 7. (7a [top left]) gives an example of interspike intervals recorded from somatosensory cortex. In (7b [top right]), the solid line is the estimated autocorrelation coefficients of interspike intervals in (7a), and dashed lines are the ± 2 times standard deviation of the estimation. (7c [bottom left]) is the residual of forward prediction of interspike intervals, and (7d [bottom right]) is the estimated autocorrelation coefficients of the residual and ± 2 times standard deviation of the estimation drawn as solid line and dashed lines respectively.

Figure (8a) gives an example of interspike intervals from hippocampus. As some units fire in bursts, only the first spike in a burst was sorted, so that the interspike interval becomes the inter burst interval (assuming that the unit is related to the burst). The same prediction methods as those used for analyzing the recordings made from somatosensory cortex were applied to the 20 different units obtained from the hippocampal records . The typical autocorrelation function (figure 8b) and partial autocorrelation functions were cut abruptly at lag = 1 or 2 , which is almost white noise. There is no seasonal tendency found in any of the hippocampal records. The first order or second order autoregression functions provide excellent models of the processes. The autocorrelations of prediction errors occur also as white noise. The relative variance of the residual and the interspike intervals *per se* are both about 0.974 for the linear estimator and 0.967 for the nonlinear one. These results indicate that the hippocampal interspike intervals are even more unpredictable than those recorded from somatosensory cortex. Both are stochastic.

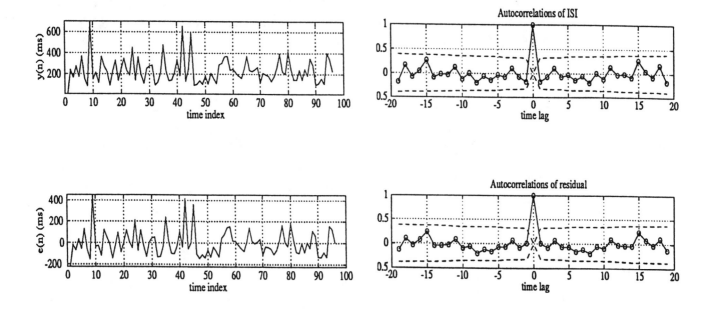

Figure 8. (8a [top left]) gives an example of interspike intervals recorded from hippocampus. In (8b [top right]), the solid line is the estimated autocorrelation coefficients of interspike intervals in (8a), and dashed lines are the ± 2 times standard deviation of the estimation. (8c [bottom left]) is the residual of forward prediction of interspike intervals, and (8d [bottom right]) is the estimated autocorrelation coefficients of the residual and ± 2 times standard deviation of the estimation drawn as solid line and dashed lines respectively.

V. Conclusion

1 Methods have been presented to distinguish chaotic from stochastic processes. These methods are based on short term predictions and the characteristic patterns of the prediction error. Computer simulations provided evaluations of the techniques when applied to known chaotic processes. When applied to real interspike intervals, the analysis showed that none of the interspike intervals could be modeled as a chaotic process generated by a deterministic function. Instead the results showed almost no predictability in the records, indicating the unstimulated interspike intervals to be essentially stochastic.

2 From an information transmission point of view, the more of a current process that can be predicted from previous observations, the less information can be contained in the current process. As the chaotic process is short term predictable from previous observations, the information obtained from any current sample would be small. If the train of interspike intervals were a carrier of information in the brain, the efficiency of information transmitted would be low in a chaotic mode. Only the less redundant stochastic process, i.e. a white-noise-like process can possible carry and transfer large amounts of information. Our data show spike trains to be open to such large amounts of information transmission.

References

[1]   D. Berger, K. Pribram, H. Wild, and C. Bridges "An analysis of neural spike-train distributions: determinants of the response of visual cortex neurons to changes in orientation and spatial frequency," Experimental Brain Research, 80 (1); pp. 129-134.

[2]   D. Berger and K. Pribram "The relationship between the Gabor elementary function and stochastic model of the inter-spike interval distribution in the responses of visual cortex neuron," Biological Cybernetics 67; 1991-1994.

[3]   D. Berger and K. Pribram "From Stochastic Resonance to Gabor Functions: An analysis of the probability function of interspike intervals recorded from visual cortical neurons," Rethinking Neural Networks: Quantum Fields and Biological Data, K. Pribram ed., Inns Press, Hillsdale, New Jersey, 1993

[4]   A. R. Bulsara and A.J. Maren "Coupled Neural-Dendritic Processes: Cooperative Stochastic Effects and Analysis of Spike Trains," Rethinking Neural Networks: Quantum Fields and Biological Data, K. Pribram ed., Inns Press, Hillsdale, New Jersey, 1993

[5]   T.S. Parker and L.O. Chua "Practical Numerical Algorithms for Chaotic System", Springer-Verlag, New York, 1989.

[6]   G.E.P. Box, and G. M. Jenkins, "Time Series Analysis: Forecasting and Control", Holden-Day, San Francisco, 1976.

[7]   M.J.D. Powell "Radial basis functions for multivariable interpolation: A review," in Algorithms for Approximation, J.C. Mason and M.G. Cox, eds. Oxford, pp. 143-167, 1987

[8]   D.S. Broomhead, D. Lowe, "Multivariable function interpolation and adaptive networks," Complex System, Vol. 2, pp. 321 - 355, 1988.

[9]   S. Chen, C.R.N. Cowan, P.M. Grant, "Orthogonal least square algorithm for radial basis function networks," IEEE tran. on Neural Networks, Vol. 2, No. 2, March, 1991.

[10]   Frank C. Hoppensteadt "Analysis and Simulation of Chaotic System" in Applied Mathematical Sciences, F. John, J.E. Marsden, L. Sirovich ed. Volume 94, chapter 2, Springer-Verlag , New York, 1993.

[11]   J.P. Burg, "Maximum Entropy Spectral Analysis, " Ph.D. dissertation, Stanford University, May 1975.

Chapter 11

Stochastic Model of Intensity Coding in Olfactory Neurons

Petr Lansky, Jean-Pierre Rospars

Stochastic Model of Intensity Coding in Olfactory Neurons

Petr Lánský[1] and Jean-Pierre Rospars[2]

[1] Institute of Physiology, Academy of Sciences of the Czech Republic, Vídeňská 1083, 142 20 Prague 4, Czech Republic

[2] Département de Zoologie and Laboratoire de Biométrie, Institut National de la Recherche Agronomique, 78026 Versailles Cedex, France

INTRODUCTION

Intensity of environmental stimulation is encoded in the nervous system by the frequency of action potentials [42], and the olfactory system is no exception to this rule. Electrophysiological investigations have shown that the frequency of action potentials increases with odor concentration in neuroreceptors ([6, 20, 23, 51] in insects; [11, 15, 41] in Amphibians). In most of these experimental recordings neurons do not fire perfectly regularly, which indicates that stochastic mechanisms are also present. Olfactory coding begins with transduction processes that take place in the dendritic cilia of specialized receptors (neuroreceptors) in the vertebrate olfactory mucosa and insect antennal sensilla. Odorant molecules bind to receptor proteins borne by the dendritic membrane, and a cascade of events follows that ultimately evokes a generator potential (see e.g., [1, 7, 8, 28]). When the generator potential is high enough, action potentials are generated and propagated to the second-order neurons. Each second-order neuron receives the excitatory terminals of a larger number (of the order of 10^3) of neuroreceptors and of inhibitory local neurons (see e.g., [46, 52]). These local neurons are excited by neuroreceptors, second-order neurons and neurons of higher centers. Thus, a second-order neuron can be inhibited as a result of its own activity (feedback inhibition) or from the activity of its neighbors (lateral inhibition). All this network activity is likely involved in intensity coding.

In parallel with the experimental studies, mathematical models were devised in an attempt to formalize the results of the experiments. Models of the neuroreceptor were based on physical properties of neurons [21, 22, 38] and global models relating directly the electrical (or behavioral) response to the concentration of odorant were proposed (see review in [12, 27]). In addition to these more or less specialized models, a whole range of mathematical models of neurons exists that were devised to take into account only the most basic and generic properties of neurons [58]. Most of these models describing the dynamics of interspike intervals (ISIs) are one dimensional, i.e. they model the time evolution of the neuronal membrane potential at only one point, the spike trigger zone. We term the membrane potential at the trigger zone the *axonal potential*. However, the stimulating actions impinging on the neuron take place on the dendrites (and soma in vertebrates), at points not located at the trigger zone. We term the sum of all dendritic contributions the *dendritic potential*.

The action potential (spike) is produced when the axonal potential exceeds a voltage threshold S. Formally, it corresponds to the first passage time (FPT) of a stochastic process X across the threshold S. The one-dimensional models are generally based on two assumptions. The first is that after spike generation, the axonal potential is reset to a constant $X(0) = x_0$ (reviewed in [58]) or to a random variable X_0 [32, 36]. The second assumption, implicitly contained in the fact that the models are unidimensional, is that the dendritic potential is also reset at the moment of spike generation. Consequently, the ISIs are independent random variables (for a stationary input they form a renewal process), whose probability density function is the only feature that differentiates the models that

269

generate them. The first assumption (axonal resetting) is physiologically well founded because the falling phase of the action potential is an active mechanism, due to opening of K^+ channels, that repolarizes the membrane and restores the resting potential. The second assumption (dendritic resetting) is questionable, and has been criticized [54].

A complete solution to this problem consists in describing the membrane potential at all points on the dendritic and somatic surface of the neuron. The resulting model would be too complicated, and not particularly useful. The cable models take into account the spatial extent of the neuron in a more tractable way, but even these models are difficult to handle, especially when the simultaneous activity of several of them is studied as in neural network applications. A simplified solution is to divide the neuron into two compartments, the somatodendritic part and the trigger zone, as proposed by [25]. A consequence of this division into two compartments is that it allows resetting the axonal potential without resetting the dendritic potential (for this reason compartmental or 2-point models can also be called *partial* reset models). The first compartment receives multiple synaptic inputs and its output is the input current to the second compartment (trigger zone). Kohn [25] described the trigger zone by the standard stochastic leaky integrator model (see below), and studied various models of the somatodendritic compartment with the objective of comparing the effects of different input noise currents on spiking activity. In our approach Kohn's method was modified to be more transparent and suitable for computation [47].

The goal of this contribution is to study theoretically how the concentration of an odorant is reflected in the activity of neuroreceptors and second-order neurons using a two-point description of these neurons. The models, based on a stochastic approach, describe not only the mean steady state of the variables, but also how they reach the steady state and what their amount of variability in the transient and steady states is.

TWO-POINT MODEL NEURON

Let A be the site of origin of action potentials and $Z = Z(t)$ the axonal potential at this point. Similarly D is a representative point of the dendritic membrane with dendritic potential, $Y = Y(t)$. The reference level for the membrane potential is taken at the resting potential, so that Y and Z reflect the membrane depolarization at their respective locations. We assume that Y depends only on the input to the neuron, not on Z, and we maintain the reset of the axonal potential (first assumption), but we no longer assume that the dendritic potential is also reset after spike emission (second assumption). Instead, the dendritic ionic channels are assumed to be unaffected, so that the evolution of the dendritic current and potential are independent of the spike generating mechanism. Our model aims at studying Z, whereas Y can be described by any of the models of the membrane potential.

Let us assume that the axonal membrane depolarization at A can be described by a circuit with a generator, a resistor, a capacitor, and a switch in parallel, which is the simplest realistic description of a neuron membrane. This model is usually called RC circuit or leaky integrator [49]. It is described by the following stochastic differential equation based on the principle of conservation of current

$$C dZ(t) + \frac{1}{R} Z(t) dt = I(t) dt, \quad Z(t_0) = z_0 \tag{1}$$

where R^{-1} is the membrane conductance, C the membrane capacitance, $I = I(t)$ the input and z_0 the resetting potential assumed throughout this paper to be equal to the resting level, $z_0 = 0$. The input I is in our two-compartment simplification the output from the dendritic part of the neuron. If a "slowly changing" stimulus is applied at time t_0 and the switch is open, the current I flows across the resistor and charges the condenser. According to (1) the depolarization Z is described by a convolution integral and can be further approximated in the form,

$$Z(t) = \frac{1}{C} \int_{t_0}^{t} \exp\left(-\frac{t-u}{\tau_A}\right) I(u) du \cong \frac{I(t)\tau_A}{C}\left(1 - \exp\left(-\frac{t-t_0}{\tau_A}\right)\right) \tag{2}$$

270

where $\tau_A = RC$ is the time constant of the axonal membrane. "Slowly changing" means that the variation of I has been small during the charging of the condenser, whose time scale is given by τ_A. The switch closes when Z exceeds the threshold S, which corresponds to the emission of a spike (opening of Na^+ channels). The condenser discharges and Z resets to 0, which corresponds to the opening of K^+ channels and the end of the spike. Then the switch opens and the condenser charges again, i.e. A is again submitted to the dendritic current and the process of activation and spike emission can continue. In the model (2), the voltage at A is reset after the spike and then exponentially tracks the depolarization at D. If $Z(t)$ does not exceed the threshold S for a long period, then the axonal and dendritic potentials become identical.

Let t_1, t_2, ..., t_k denote the moments when process $Z(t)$ reaches the threshold $S > 0$ and their differences, $\Delta_{k+1} = t_{k+1} - t_k$, the corresponding sequence of ISIs. The time dynamics of the axonal membrane potential Z follows from (2),

$$Z(t) = Y(t)\left(1 - \exp\left(-\frac{t - t_k}{\tau_A}\right)\right), \qquad t \in (t_k, t_{k+1}], \ k = 0, 1, \dots, \ Y(t_0) = y_0, \tag{3}$$

(the dendritic potential Y is assumed to be y_0 at time t_0 when its evolution begins). The moment of the next spike generation t_{k+1} is the realization of random variable

$$T_{k+1} = \inf\{t > t_k; \ Z(t) \geq S \mid Z(t_k) \geq S, \ Z(t_k + 0) = 0\} \tag{4}$$

which can be rewritten, by using (3), into the form

$$T_{k+1} = \inf\left\{t > t_k; \ Y(t)\left(1 - \exp\left(-\frac{t - t_k}{\tau_A}\right)\right) \geq S \mid Y(t_k) = \frac{S + \epsilon}{1 - \exp(-\Delta_k / \tau_A)}\right\}, \tag{5}$$

where $\epsilon > 0$ is a size of overcrossing the threshold S during the last spike. If Y has a continuous trajectory (diffusion process), then $\epsilon = 0$. It follows from (5) that the length of the next ISI depends on the actual value of the dendritic potential at the moment of last firing and thus on the length of the previous ISI. Therefore the ISIs form a time-homogeneous first-order Markov chain (Wold's Markov process) which is, in the case of stationary firing, characterized by the conditional density function $f(\Delta_2 \mid \Delta_1)$ for two consecutive ISIs, Δ_1 and Δ_2. Its marginal density $f(\Delta)$ (which in experimental works is estimated by ISI histograms) satisfies the equation

$$f(\Delta_2) = \int_0^\infty f(\Delta_2 \mid \Delta_1) f(\Delta_1) \mathrm{d}\Delta_1. \tag{6}$$

It is apparent from (5) that ISIs are not independent. This feature is the main difference between the *partial reset* (two-point) model and those with *total reset* (one-point). It follows from (5) that if $Y(t_k)$ is very high then Δ_k is very short. If Y changes slowly with respect to time constant τ_A, the next ISI, Δ_{k+1}, will be also short with high probability. On the other hand, if Δ_k is long, it follows from (5) that $Y(t_k) \cong S$ and consequently the next ISI will not be very short. For this reason we can expect that the model produces positively correlated sequences of ISIs.

The absolute refractory period t_{AR} is usually incorporated into the models by adding it to the generated ISIs. For the model presented above the solution is not so simple because the membrane potential at D evolves during this period and a new initial condition for Y at $t_k + t_{AR}$ needs to be considered; however, this feature may become important in the case of extremely fast firing.

COMPARISON OF ONE-POINT AND TWO-POINT DETERMINISTIC MODELS

The stochastic process X describing the axonal potential can also be singular (deterministic) with only one possible trajectory. The deterministic perfect (see below) and leaky integrator models have been used many times [3, 24, 49] for describing neuronal activity, mainly in sensory neurons. They offer description of the mean membrane potential only and are suitable mainly for studies of time-dependent input (e.g.,

[2]) for which the stochastic approach usually fails. The simplicity of these models permits a comparison between the classical one-point model and the two-point model introduced above. The lower case letters are used instead of capitals to stress the deterministic nature of the models in this section.

Perfect integrator

The perfect integrator models the membrane only by a condenser and a switch, so that the resistance R is infinitely large in (1). Let $i(t)$ be the input current, resulting for example from stimulation of a sensory neuron. Under the *one-point* assumptions the membrane potential x evolves between two spikes in accordance with differential equation

$$\mathrm{d}x = \mu(t)\mathrm{d}t, \quad x(t_k) = 0 \tag{8}$$

where $\mu(t) = i(t)/C$. Solving (8) we get,

$$x(t) = \int_{t_k}^{t} \mu(u)\mathrm{d}u \tag{9}$$

and next spike takes place at time t_{k+1} when $x(t_{k+1}) = S$. If $\mu(t)$ is equal to a constant μ, the interspike interval Δ is $\Delta = S/\mu$. The perfect integrator one-point neuron, when submitted to a constant stimulation, discharges spikes at a constant frequency $f = \mu/S$, proportional to stimulation and inversely proportional to threshold. This result can be found (in a limited range) in experimental measurements and thus, it seemingly supports the validity of the model.

Now, let us consider the *two-point* model, with the dendritic membrane at point D modelled by a perfect integrator. If the dendritic membrane generates a current $i(t)$, the dendritic potential $y(t)$ follows equation (9) in which t_k is replaced by the time onset of the stimulus, t_0, for which we assume $y(t_0) = y_0$. Solving (9) for constant stimulation, $\mu(t) = \mu$, the dendritic potential increases linearly with time without any limit, $y(t) = \mu t + y_0$. As a consequence, the axonal potential $z(t)$ following (3) takes for $t \in (t_k, t_{k+1}]$ the form

$$z(t) = \left(\mu t + y_0\right)\left(1 - \exp\left(-\frac{t - t_k}{\tau_A}\right)\right) \tag{10}$$

and the next spike takes place at time t_{k+1} such that $z(t_{k+1}) = S$ from which we obtain

$$\Delta_k = -\tau_A \ln\left(1 - \frac{S}{\mu t_{k+1} + y_0}\right). \tag{11}$$

Thus the ISIs are shorter and shorter for the constant input. This reveals that the dendritic reset assumption of model (8) helps perfect integration to look realistic (constant frequency of output). The absence of dendritic resetting shows why the perfect integrator model of the membrane is too simplified and merely phenomenological.

Leaky integrator

In the *one-point* leaky integrator, the membrane potential x evolves in accordance with the equation

$$\mathrm{d}x = (-x/\tau + 0(t))\,\mathrm{d}t, \quad x(t_k) = 0 \tag{12}$$

which is the deterministic counterpart of (1). Only one membrane constant τ appears in (12). The solution of (12) for $\mu(t) = \mu$ is

$$x(t) = \mu\tau\left(1 - \exp\left(-\frac{t - t_k}{\tau}\right)\right) \underset{t \to \infty}{=} \mu\tau \tag{13}$$

and under the condition $S < \mu\tau$ the model neuron fires regularly at intervals

272

$$\Delta = -\tau \ln\left(1 - \frac{S}{\mu\tau}\right). \tag{14}$$

For the *two-point* model, the equation for the axonal potential $z(t)$ can be derived from (3) and (13). Assuming that $y(t_0) = y_0$, then for $t > t_k$ we have,

$$z(t) = \left\{\mu\tau_D + (y_0 - \mu\tau_D)\exp\left(-\frac{t-t_0}{\tau_D}\right)\right\}\left\{1 - \exp\left(-\frac{t-t_k}{\tau_A}\right)\right\}. \tag{15}$$

where τ_D is the time constant of the dendritic membrane. If $t_0 \ll t_k$ then we can assume $y(t) = \mu\tau_D$ and (15) takes the form

$$z(t) = \mu\tau_D\left\{1 - \exp\left(-\frac{t-t_k}{\tau_A}\right)\right\}, \quad t > t_k. \tag{16}$$

This equation describes the same behavior as (13). Consequently, if the condition $S < \mu\tau_D$ is met, the model neuron also fires regularly with period

$$\Delta = -\tau_A \ln\left(1 - \frac{S}{\mu\tau_D}\right) \tag{17}$$

and the ISI depends on both constants τ_A and τ_D. Result (17) could be expected, as $\mu\tau_D$ is the asymptotic depolarization on the dendrite and following partial reset (3), the axonal depolarization exponentially (with time constant τ_A) approaches to level $\mu\tau_D$. The difference between the one- and two-point models becomes more apparent when the input is not constant. For example, if at time $t_k \gg t_0$ the input is set to zero ($\mu(t) = 0$ for $t > t_k$), then from (15) we have

$$z(t) = \mu\tau_D\exp\left(-\frac{t-t_k}{\tau_D}\right)\left(1 - \exp\left(-\frac{t-t_k}{\tau_A}\right)\right), \quad t > t_k \tag{18}$$

instead of $x(t) = 0$ yielded by classical model (13). Note that function (18) is not monotonic and, if the residual dendritic potential $y(t)$ is strong enough, a spike can be produced even after canceling the external input.

STOCHASTIC MODEL OF THE NEURORECEPTOR

The leaky integrator model presented in the previous section would be appropriate for the description of neuronal activity, if we were interested only in the regular generation of spikes. A stochastic approach has to be applied in order to mimic the variability of firing. In the present case, the stochastic feature results from the random bombardment of neuroreceptors by odor molecules.

Occupation and activation of receptor sites

Our model [34] is based in part on that proposed by Kaissling [21, 22; see Fig. 32] and is analogous to that employed by Tuckwell [57] for the description of the number of opened channels in a patch of neuronal membrane. We assume that there is only one odorant substance, that each receptor molecule possesses only one binding site and that the neuroreceptor bears n receptors. These n receptors can be either identical or belong to different classes. In both cases the receptor-odorant interaction is assumed to be a three-stage process; the receptor site is first occupied by the odorant molecule; then, if the interaction is strong enough the receptor is activated; finally the odorant molecule is released. In our simplification release is independent of activation.

Occupation and release. Let us assume that each receptor is occupied and released independently of others according to the stochastic reaction schemes $A + R \xrightarrow{\lambda} AR$ and $AR \xrightarrow{\mu} A + R$, where A is an unbound molecule of substance, R an unoccupied receptor, and AR a complex of the molecule and the receptor. The occupation parameter λ is an increasing function of the concentration and the release parameter μ is assumed to be specific to the site. This stochastic reaction scheme can be described by the following transition probabilities: a receptor site occupied at time t has a probability $\mu\Delta t + o(\Delta t)$ of being released in $(t, t + \Delta t]$, a site which is free at time t has a probability $\lambda \Delta t + o(\Delta t)$ of being occupied in $(t, t + \Delta t]$ and the probability of more than one event during this interval is $o(\Delta)$. The stochastic process giving the number of occupied sites, $X_n = \{X_n(t); \ t \geq 0\}$ defined by these transition probabilities, is a birth and death process with transition rates $\lambda_n(i) = \lambda(n - i)$ and $\mu_n(i) = \mu i$, for $i = 0$, 1, ..., n. This process is a continuous-time version of the Ehrenfest process and a stochastic generalization of the classical (deterministic) Michaelis-Menten model of enzymatic kinetics. The mean number of occupied sites is

$$E(X_n(t)) = n\lambda\alpha(1 - \exp(-t/\alpha)) + n_0\exp(-t/\alpha) \underset{t \to \infty}{=} n\lambda\alpha \qquad (19)$$

where n_0 is the number of occupied sites at time $t = 0$ and throughout the text $\alpha = (\lambda + \mu)^{-1}$. The variance of the number of occupied sites at time t is

$$\mathrm{Var}(X_n(t)) = n\mu\lambda\alpha^2 + \alpha(\mu - \lambda)(n_0 - n\lambda\alpha)\exp(-t/\alpha) + (\alpha n_0(\lambda - \mu) - n\lambda^2\alpha^2)\exp(-2t/\alpha) \qquad (20)$$

and its limiting value for $t \to \infty$ is,

$$\mathrm{Var}(X_n(\infty)) = n\mu\lambda\alpha^2 . \qquad (21)$$

For $\lambda = \mu$, the asymptotic variance (21) reaches its maximal value, $\mathrm{Var}(X_n(\infty)) = n/4$. The limits of the mean and variance in (19) and (21) for extremely high or low λ are obvious and they have a simple intuitive interpretation. The time variable t refers to the state that follows a step change of the concentration before a new steady state is achieved, whereas the behavior of the system under the steady state conditions is given by $t \to \infty$.

The approximation of a stochastic process with discontinuous trajectories by a stochastic diffusion process with similar statistical properties is often employed to simplify the computational problems [45]. Following Tuckwell [57], the process X_n can be approximated by the process $X_n^* = \{X_n^*(t); t \geq 0\}$ which is defined by the stochastic differential equation

$$X_n^*(t) = \lambda n\alpha + \sqrt{n}U(t) , \qquad (22)$$

where $U = \{U(t); t \geq 0\}$ is an Ornstein-Uhlenbeck process,

$$\mathrm{d}U(t) = -\frac{1}{\alpha}U(t)\mathrm{d}t + \sqrt{2\lambda\mu\alpha}\,\mathrm{d}W(t) , \qquad (23)$$

and $W = \{W(t); \ t \geq 0\}$ is a standard Wiener process. Process X_n^* is a Gaussian random process whose distribution at time t is normal. If $u_0 = (n_0 - \lambda n\alpha)/\sqrt{n}$ is taken as the initial value of process (23), its mean is (19) and its variance

$$\mathrm{Var}\ (X_n^*(t)) = n\mu\lambda\alpha^2\Big(1 - \exp(-2t/\alpha)\Big). \qquad (24)$$

The variances (20) and (24) become identical only with increasing time, $t \to \infty$. Then process $X_n^*(t)$ achieves a steady state which is governed by the normal distribution, $N(n\lambda\alpha, n\lambda\mu\alpha^2)$. It follows that the state space of X_n^* is not restricted like that of X_n. Therefore the diffusion approximation is advantageous mainly for the medium values of λ, whereas for extreme values some additional boundary conditions must be imposed.

Activation. We assume that an occupied receptor can be activated with probability p, independently of its past behavior and of the behavior of other receptors. The process describing the number of activated sites at time t is denoted by $Y_n = \{Y_n(t); t \geq 0\}$ and its properties can be derived directly from those for the process X_n. Analogously to (19), we can find that

$$E(Y_n(t)) = p\Big\{n\lambda\alpha(1 - \exp(-t/\alpha)) + n_0\exp(-t/\alpha)\Big\} \underset{t \to \infty}{=} pn\lambda\alpha . \qquad (25)$$

274

For the extreme values of the concentration, $E(Y_n(\infty)) \to pn$ as $\lambda \to \infty$ and $E(Y_n(\infty)) \to 0$ as $\lambda \to 0_+$. The variance of the process Y_n is given by

$$\text{Var}(Y_n(t)) = (1-p)E(Y_n(t)) + \tag{26}$$

$$+ \alpha p^2 \Big\{ n\mu\lambda\alpha + (\mu - \lambda)(n_0 - n\lambda\alpha)\exp(-t/\alpha) + (n_0(\lambda - \mu) - n\lambda^2\alpha)\exp(-2t/\alpha) \Big\}$$

and its limiting value as $t \to \infty$ is

$$\text{Var}(Y_n(\infty)) = (1-p)pn\lambda\alpha + p^2 n\mu\lambda\alpha^2 . \tag{27}$$

Asymptotic variance (27) is an increasing function of λ under the condition $p \leq 1/2$, otherwise it achieves its maximum, $n/4$, at $\lambda = \mu/(2p-1)$. Its limits are 0 as $\lambda \to 0_+$ and $(1-p)pn$ as $\lambda \to \infty$.

Multimodality of receptors. Uniformity of receptors applies to specialized neuroreceptors such as the pheromonal receptor cells of insects. However, most neuroreceptors are unspecialized and bear several types of receptor sites. Let us consider m types of receptors on a neuroreceptor with frequencies n_j, ($n_1 + \dots + n_m = n$). Each receptor site is characterized by the triplet $\{\lambda_j, \mu_j, p_j; j = 1, \dots, m\}$, with $\alpha_j = (\lambda_j + \mu_j)^{-1}$. The results for the jth subset can be derived directly from those for the process Y_n just by replacing λ, μ, p and n by λ_j, μ_j, p_j and n_j. The total number of activated sites at time t is the sum of the number of activated sites over all subsets. Therefore the mean value of the process Y_n can be directly written using (25),

$$E(Y_n(t)) = \sum_{j=1}^{m} p_j n_j \lambda_j \alpha_j (1 - \exp(-t/\alpha_j)) + \sum_{j=1}^{m} p_j n_{0j} \exp(-t/\alpha_j) \underset{t \to \infty}{=} \sum_{j=1}^{m} p_j n_j \lambda_j \alpha_j . \tag{28}$$

The asymptotic mean number of activated receptors under the condition that $\lambda_j \to \infty$ for each j can be defined as the saturation level, L; it is

$$L = \sum_{j=1}^{m} p_j n_j . \tag{29}$$

It follows from (29) that the saturation levels differ for neuroreceptors bearing different populations of receptor sites. This accounts, in part, for the variability in experimentally obtained input-output functions. This effect is enhanced by the variability in the process of activation of different receptor types as is apparent when comparing (21) and (27).

Finally, one may ask under which conditions our model coincides with the deterministic ones mentioned above. Equations (25) and (28) achieve the same mean as the deterministic leaky integrators (13) and (16) if the population of receptors is homogeneous ($m = 1$), and infinitely large, and if the transition rates are $\lambda(i) = \lambda$ and $\mu(i) = i\mu$. Moreover, to comply with the perfect integrator model we must additionally let $\mu(i) = 0$, which means that the odorant molecules are never released from the receptors.

Dendritic and axonal potentials

The *dendritic membrane potential* Y of the neuroreceptor is called a generator potential or receptor potential. It can be simulated by a stochastic process which is related to the number of activated receptors. If receptors only trigger the opening of nearby ionic channels, each activated receptor contributes to the dendritic potential by an amount that depends on its location over the neuroreceptor dendrites. Here, we assume that all contributions are equal, so that the process Y can be identified with either Y_n or Y_n^*. This assumption does not influence the qualitative behavior of the model. It should only be removed when parametrization of the model is performed to take into account the specific distribution of receptors on dendrites and the kind of second-messenger system to which they are linked.

The *axonal potential* Z_n is defined by (3) and its mean value in the time between two consecutive spikes, $t \in (t_k, t_{k+1}]$, is

$$\mathrm{E}(Z_n) = \left(1 - \exp\left(-\frac{t - t_k}{\tau_A}\right)\right) \sum_{j=1}^{m} \left\{ p_j n_j \lambda_j \alpha_j \left(1 - \exp\left(-\frac{t - t_0}{\alpha_j}\right)\right) + p_j n_{0j} \exp\left(-\frac{t - t_0}{\alpha_j}\right) \right\}. \quad (30)$$

This equation encompasses different types of activity, Poissonian or non-Poissonian with either regular or irregular ISIs, that correspond to three different levels of long-term stimulus concentration. These three main regions, without sharp boundaries, can be defined by the asymptotic mean dendritic potential.

If the asymptotic mean is high above the threshold,

$$\sum_{j=1}^{m} p_j n_j \lambda_j \alpha_j \gg S \quad (31)$$

which corresponds to a strong stimulation, the formula (30) can be used for the approximation of the ISI by solving the equation $\mathrm{E}(Z_n(t)) = S$. Then the ISI is approximated by the value

$$\tilde{\Delta} = -\tau_A \ln\left(1 - S / \sum_{j=1}^{m} p_j n_j \lambda_j \alpha_j\right) \quad (32)$$

which can be compared with that given by the deterministic leaky integrator (17). In this case the neuron fires rather regularly with fluctuations, related to those of Y_n around its mean, which are characterized by variance $\mathrm{Var}(Y_n(\infty))$. For example, (32) can be considered as a good approximation if there is no substantial difference between the solution of equation $\mathrm{E}(Z_n(t)) = S$ in which the asymptote is increased by $2\sqrt{\mathrm{Var}(Y_n(\infty))}$, and that in which it is decreased by the same amount.

The second region is characterized by condition

$$\sum_{j=1}^{m} p_j n_j \lambda_j \alpha_j \ll S. \quad (33)$$

In this case the firing pattern is Poissonian. Finally, in the intermediate region, which is a complement to (31) and (33) where the asymptotic mean is close to the threshold, the characteristics of firing are difficult to specify without simplification or simulations.

STOCHASTIC MODELS OF THE SECOND-ORDER NEURON

This neuron has all the features of central neurons and thus can be described by any model developed for them. If the second-order neuron receives no input except from the neuroreceptors which are connected to it, the simplest possibility would be to assume that each firing of a neuroreceptor causes firing of the second-order neuron (1:1 simplification, [59]). The same mechanism was proposed in [5] for describing the firing activity of a geniculate neuron excited by several retinal fibers. The output of the second-order neuron is then the superposition of all action potentials discharged by afferent neuroreceptors. However, the intensity (ω) of the superposed process could easily exceed the physiological characteristics of the second-order neuron because of its large number of neuroreceptors. Therefore this model is unrealistic.

A more advanced model assumes that each impulse in an afferent neuroreceptor causes a depolarizing jump in the second-order neuron and that these jumps are summed untill the threshold is crossed. Then ISIs follow either an Erlang (Gamma) distribution if the jumps are of fixed size or a randomized Gamma distribution if their sizes are different. Two kinds of objections can be raised against this model. First, experimentally observed ISIs do not often fit the theoretical distributions. Second, actual excitatory postsynaptic potentials (EPSPs) decay and this feature cannot be neglected when their summation is considered. The second objection is more serious since a simple fit is not a proof of any model's correctness. Both models mentioned up to now can be used only under the total reset assumptions and this is one more reason for considering them as biologically irrelevant.

276

Dendritic potential

The models that follow have been initially studied under the one-point scenario. However, they may equally well serve for describing the dendritic membrane potential of the two-point model.

The first realistic model is the "shot noise" process, i.e. Stein's model *without inhibition* [53]. It is characterized by a linear summation of EPSPs. Each EPSP is idealized as an abrupt depolarization followed by an exponential decay of the membrane potential to its resting level,

$$\mathrm{d}Y(t) = -\gamma Y(t)\mathrm{d}t + \sum_{i=1}^{r} a_i \mathrm{d}P_i(t), \quad Y(0) = y_0 \tag{34}$$

where $\gamma > 0$ is the time constant of the spontaneous decay, r is the number of neuroreceptors connected to the second-order neuron, $a_i \geq 0$ $(i = 1, ... , r)$ are the sizes of the EPSP evoked by a firing of the ith neuroreceptor and $P_i = \{P_i(t); t \geq 0\}$ $(i = 1, ... , r)$ are the point processes describing the activity of the ith neuroreceptor. The differences in values of a_i in (34) reflect the fact that the effect of the synapses from neuroreceptors depend on their location on the dendritic tree of the second-order neuron. The intensity ω_i of process P_i in (34) is the firing rate of the ith neuroreceptor; it is not only a function of λ_j (odor intensity) but also of the "configuration of receptors" of the ith neuroreceptor as given by μ_j, p_j and n_j. If the odor concentration is increased but the new concentration is low enough, both steady state levels fulfill condition (33) and the neuroreceptors fire according to Poisson processes. The increase in concentration results in a mere increase in the rate of these processes. This change can be very small and almost unnoticeable in a single neuroreceptor, but nonetheless it can evoke a substantially different activity in the second-order neuron due to the high convergence ratio r and the subsequent integration of the input rates following (34). To stress the non-constant character of EPSPs, equation (34) is changed to the form

$$Y(t) = -\gamma \int_0^t Y(s)\mathrm{d}s + \sum_{i=1}^{P(t)} A_i \tag{35}$$

where the intensity ω_a of the process P is the sum of the intensities of the neuroreceptor firings, and A_i are independent realizations of a positive random variable with a probability distribution proportional to the original ω_i and a_i. An exponential distribution of A_i would probably be realistic because more synapses are located on the distal part of the dendritic tree than on the proximal part.

To include *lateral inhibition* we can generalize model (35) to the basic form of Stein's model

$$Y(t) = -\gamma \int_0^t Y(s)\mathrm{d}s + \sum_{i=1}^{P(t)} A_i + \sum_{i=1}^{Q(t)} B_i \tag{36}$$

where the notations are the same as in (35), and $B_i \leq 0$ are inhibitory postsynaptic potentials (IPSPs) arriving in accordance with the point process Q of intensity ω_b. An enormous amount of literature is devoted to model (36) and its modifications. The most common is the diffusion approximation of (36) by the Ornstein-Uhlenbeck process (e.g., [30, 44]. This process $Y^* = \{Y^*(t); t \geq 0\}$ is defined by the stochastic differential equation generalizing equation (23),

$$\mathrm{d}Y^*(t) = (-\gamma Y^*(t) + \mu)\mathrm{d}t + \sigma\mathrm{d}W(t) \tag{37}$$

where $\sigma > 0$ and μ are the parameters related to the input processes as well as to the intrinsic neuronal properties.

The model (36) can be modified by taking into account reversal potentials (e.g., [31, 32, 56, 61]. One of these variants was studied by Lánský and Smith [37] in the form,

$$\mathrm{d}Y^*(t) = (-\gamma Y^* + \mu_1(V_E - Y^*) + \mu_2(Y^* - V_I))\mathrm{d}t + \sigma\sqrt{(V_E - Y^*)(Y^* - V_I)}\mathrm{d}W(t), \tag{38}$$

277

where $V_I < 0$ is a constant denoting the inhibitory reversal potential and $V_E > 0$ is another constant denoting the excitatory reversal potential, $\sigma > 0$, μ_1 and μ_2 are the parameters. Of course, these diffusion and discontinuous models can be combined within one model to reflect qualitative differences among synapses [39].

Fohlmeister [14] postulated two properties of the time course of *feedback inhibition*. First, in response to each impulse, the feedback, $H(t)$, is increased by a fixed amount h. Second, between the feedback increments, H declines exponentially with a time constant ν to some asymptotic level. The function $H(t)$ can be approximated by the solution of the differential equation

$$\mathrm{d}H(t) = -\nu H(t)\mathrm{d}t + hf(t - t_0) \tag{39}$$

where h is the unit effect of the inhibition, $f(t)$ describes the time course of the firing frequency and t_0 stands for a delay which we will neglect for simplicity. The feedback effect (39) changes (37) to the form,

$$\mathrm{d}Y^*(t) = (-\gamma Y^*(t) - H(t) + \mu)\mathrm{d}t + \sigma \mathrm{d}W(t) . \tag{40}$$

Axonal potential

Application of the partial reset to Stein's model (36) or any other model presented above is formally simple. However, the solution of the FPT problem in the modified models is even less tractable than in the original ones. Therefore, numerical methods or approximations must be used. As for the original models, the diffusion approximations help to solve the problem. So, consider now the Ornstein-Uhlenbeck model of the dendritic membrane potential given by (37). We can write its solution in the form, (with $\tau_D = 1/\gamma$),

$$Y^* = y_0\exp\left(-\frac{t - t_0}{\tau_D}\right) + \int_{t_0}^{t}\exp\left(-\frac{t - s}{\tau_D}\right)\sigma\mathrm{d}W(s) + \int_{t_0}^{t}\exp\left(-\frac{t - s}{\tau_D}\right)\mu\mathrm{d}s . \tag{41}$$

Under the assumption that the last spike appeared at time t_k and substituting (41) into (3), the axonal potential Z at time $t > t_k$ can be computed. It shows that the next ISI depends on the time evolution of the process W with decaying weight through the whole time period (t_0, t). For $t \gg t_0$, which corresponds to the situation in which process Y has reached a steady state, Z simplifies as

$$Z = \left\{\mu\tau_D + \int_{t_0}^{t}\exp\left(-\frac{t - s}{\tau_D}\right)\sigma\mathrm{d}W(s)\right\}\left\{1 - \exp\left(-\frac{t - t_k}{\tau_A}\right)\right\}. \tag{42}$$

The mean value of Z given by (42) is

$$\mathrm{E}(Z) = \mu\tau_D\left\{1 - \exp\left(-\frac{t - t_k}{\tau_A}\right)\right\}, \tag{43}$$

which can be directly identified with the deterministic leaky integrator (16). This is also the mean value of Stein's model (36) using notation $\mu = \mathrm{E}(A)\omega_a + \mathrm{E}(B)\omega_b$. The asymptotic variance of Z is

$$\mathrm{Var}(Z) = \frac{\sigma^2\tau_D}{2}\left\{1 - \exp\left(-\frac{t - t_k}{\tau_A}\right)\right\}^2 . \tag{44}$$

As for the neuroreceptor, three regimes of firing, depending on the relation between input μ and the threshold S, can be distinguished. The condition relating S to μ must be considered with respect to the variance (44), $\mathrm{Var}(Z) \cong \mathrm{Var}(Y(\infty)) = \sigma^2\tau_D/2$, which is controlled by σ^2.

For *high* levels of excitation, i.e. $S \ll \mu\tau_D$, the approximation (17) for the mean ISI can be applied. *Low* levels of excitation are defined by $S \gg \mu\tau_D$. In this case the present model is equivalent to that analysed in detail by Lánský and Smith [36, section 4] under the condition that the axonal potential will not reach the dendritic potential during the refractory period ($\tau_A \approx t_{AR}$) or a condition on the correlation time of process Y. Their model assumes that the axonal potential is reset to a random value which is here close to $\mu\tau_D$. It results in an activity characterized by CV ≥ 1 which tends to be Poissonian as S becomes higher; the coefficient of variation CV = standard deviation/mean, is used as an approximate measure of the Poissonian character of firing, in which case CV $= 1$. In the *medium* range, when the threshold is close to the asymptotic value of the process, $S \approx \mu\tau_D$, only approximations can be made.

DISCUSSION

Mean behavior of the neurons

Neuroreceptor. Equation (32) shows how the firing frequency of our neuroreceptor model varies with increasing odor concentration. The following discussion compares the properties of this equation with experimental results. It is based on the near proportionality between the mean number of activated sites (and consequently mean dendritic potential) and firing frequency, and on the proportionality between λ and odorant concentration. When odorant concentration is increased, the firing frequency given by (32) remains initially zero, because the validity of (32) is limited by condition (31). Then it rises to value f_s at concentration C_s for which the mean dendritic potential crosses the firing threshold. If we consider the first two terms of the polynomial approximation of (32) it can be seen than above C_s the firing frequency is linearly proportional to the dendritic potential, which is given by (25) or (28). However, below C_s spikes are also occasionally generated because of the random fluctuations of the dendritic potential. It can be shown by simulation that the firing frequency resulting from noise increases almost linearly from 0 to f_s [35].

(1) The first feature shown by experimental data that should be predicted by our model is that the plot of the firing frequency as a function of the logarithm of the odor concentration is of sigmoid shape. In the case of neuroreceptors bearing only one type of receptor site (unimodal), the asymptotic mean number of activated sites (25), in a semi-logarithmic plot, is sigmoidal. In the general case of neuroreceptors bearing m types of receptor sites (multimodal), the asymptotic mean number of occupied sites is given by a summation of m sigmoid curves, (28), which is again sigmoid. A sufficient condition for having one inflection point is linearity (or approximate linearity) of the second derivatives in the range of the original inflection points.

(2) The maximum number of activated sites which follows from (28) depends on the numbers n_j of receptor sites of each type and their affinities for the odorant molecule p_j. Obviously these may vary with the neuroreceptor, and thus the saturation levels are different in different neurons, as experimentally observed.

(3) Not only the saturation level but also the inflection point of the sigmoid curve varies. This point is at half the saturation level in equation (25). In the multimodal neuroreceptor model, (28), the ordinate of the inflection point may not be always at this half-way distance from the saturation level, and consequently it may vary from neuron to neuron.

(4) Another feature of experimental observations also found in our model is that the slope of the sigmoid curves at the inflection point is variable. The slope for the curve representing the number of activated sites (19) or dendritic potential (25) depends on n and p even if only one type of site is present.

(5) Finally, the sensitivity of different neuroreceptors is expected to vary. This sensitivity is related to the abscissa of the inflection point. In the case of a unimodal neuroreceptor where λ and μ are unique, this abscissa is such that $\lambda = \mu$. In multimodal neuroreceptors the introduction of different λ_j and μ_j breaks this symmetry because the concentrations that lead to $\lambda_j = \mu_j$ are different for different

receptor types. Therefore the model predicts that different populations of sites on neuroreceptors give different abscissae of the inflection point.

Second-order neuron. The model of second-order neuron depends on a greater number of parameters than that for the neuroreceptor, so that its behavior is both more flexible and more difficult to analyze. We restrict the discussion to some outstanding properties:

(1) The second-order neuron reacts in a lower range of concentrations than the neuroreceptor as can easily be verified numerically. This generalizes the theoretical result of van Drongelen et al. [59].

(2) The experimental observations indicate that the firing frequency of second-order neurons as a function of concentration is likely to be sigmoid again. The saturation of second-order neurons cannot generally be explained by the saturation of neuroreceptors because its sensitivity is higher to lower odorant concentrations (see above). What are the appropriate saturating mechanisms? A first possible mechanism is based on the refractory period T_R because for all models the firing frequency is a hyperbolic curve with an asymptote $1/T_R$. A second mechanism results from self-inhibition. It can be shown that the only non-contradictory solution to equation (40), when self-inhibition is taken into account, is that the firing frequency of the second-order neuron increases qualitatively more slowly than the excitatory input.

(3) Like neuroreceptors, second-order neurons differ in their response to the same odor. In the model this specificity can result from the characteristics of the neuroreceptors connected to a given second-order neuron. It can also result from a differential effect of lateral inhibition. Neglecting refractoriness and self-inhibition, while keeping lateral inhibition at a constant level, the position of the sensitivity range is shifted. However, excitatory input and lateral inhibition increase simultaneously with concentration; this competitive effect results in different slopes of the frequency curve at different concentrations. The input-output frequency characteristics are less and less steep with increasing frequency of inhibition in (36). We may conclude that the range of odor intensities coded by changes in firing frequency of the second-order neuron depends on the level of inhibition.

Stochastic behavior of the neurons

All the model features and experimental data mentioned above dealt exclusively with the mean behavior of the system. However our model predicts other statistical properties depending on the stimulus intensity. Those properties include characteristics such as specific firing laws, serial dependency, coefficient of variation greater than one, and bursting, that are useful to describe the olfactory system and other systems as well.

(1) For low asymptotic mean values of the dendritic potential, the neuroreceptor model generates spikes forming a Poisson process; i.e. ISI follows exponential distribution. If the rate of the process decreases, the neuroreceptor approaches the state of silence. Secondly, when odor concentration is such that the threshold, S, and the steady state of Z have approximately the same level, the model predicts that the distribution of ISIs becomes similar to Gamma, Inverse Gaussian or lognormal distributions. The specific type of the distribution of ISIs depends on the type of threshold and it is an open question whether these distributions are distinguishable. Finally, with increasing odorant concentration, i.e. with increasing stationary mean value of the process Y, the intervals between firings should become shorter and also more regular.

(2) Serial dependency, both positive and negative, has been often observed in real neurons (e.g., [9, 33]). The model predicts positive serial dependency of ISIs. This feature is not found in classical models with total reset which predict independent ISIs. Additional phenomena such as inhibitory feedback must be considered (e.g., [43]) to introduce a dependence of ISIs. The activity of the model does not depend on its entire history but it produces ISIs forming Wold's Markov process. This means that the stochastic properties of the current ISI are determined exclusively by the length of the previous one.

(3) Coefficients of variation larger than one have been found in most experimental studies mentioned up to now. This has also been also reported in several neuronal models whenever the reset

value is chosen above the resting potential [17, 32, 36]. This is not surprising because partial reset model emulates the persistent effect of the dendritic compartment on the trigger zone.

(4) Bursting is a very frequent type of neuronal behavior found in different experimental preparations (e.g., [4, 40, 48, 62]. Bursting, exceptionally long ISIs and high serial correlations are related phenomena. Theoretical models of bursting are often based on the assumption of two alternating states during which the spikes are either blocked or produced (e.g., [16]). A disadvantage of these models is that despite their close resemblance to the observed data, they are not based on biological reasoning. The other models for bursting utilize the concept of strong lateral inhibition [4] which is not acceptable, for example, in the case of olfactory neuroreceptors. Kohn [25] found for his two-compartment model that dendritic input created a tendency for random bursting. If the correlation time of dendritic process Y, i.e. the time after which the potential is no longer influenced by its previous values, is short, then Y can be regarded as a white noise and the membrane potential behaves like the Wiener process and no bursting can appear. On the other hand, if the correlation time (relatively to τ_A) is high, the trajectory of Y may be expected to change smoothly. Then, when Y is high above the threshold, it stays there for a certain time and the model produces a sequence of short ISIs which can be interpreted as a burst. Similarly, when Y falls below the threshold it yields an exceptionally long ISI.

(5) Spontaneous activity, i.e. spikes fired at random in the absence of overt stimulation, can be recorded from neurons in the olfactory system as well as in other sensory systems. We have shown that the second-order neuron spontaneously fires spikes, and the neuroreceptors bursts of spikes (not spikes), according to a Poisson process [48]. According to our model this means that the neuroreceptors alternate at rest between a state close to the resting potential (between burts) and a state close to the threshold (within bursts), whereas the dendritic potential of the second-order neuron remains far below the threshold.

Assumptions of the two-point model with partial reset

Information processing in the nervous system depends to a large extent on the transformation of the graded dendritic potential into a train of action potentials. The main characteristics of this transformation were established by extensive experimental investigations in sensory and central neurons (e.g., reviewed by [10, 26]) and neuron models should describe them adequately. Now, in most neuronal models in use, the dendritic membrane potential is assumed to return to the resting level following the action potential. This simplification (here termed total reset) is unrealistic because there is no active resetting mechanism in dendrites. The partial reset model provides a more realistic description of the functioning of a neuron, while keeping useful features of the previous models. The partial reset model and the total reset one behave differently in the transient states. In the model with total reset, a step change of the input induces an immediate change in the output frequency to a new constant firing level. On the other side, in the partial reset model the change to a new frequency is smooth.

In the model proposed, the axonal potential Z at point A depends on the dendritic potential Y at point D but not vice-versa, although D and A are infinitely close together. This asymmetry in the formulation of the model is the price to pay for having a simple (two-point) model which still retains the essential property that D is not reset. To formulate the model in more physiologically meaningful terms we may consider an elongated dendrite $D'D$, in contact with an axon by one of its ends D (as in insect neurons for example) and bearing odorant or neurotransmitter receptors on its other end D'. Then, depolarization at D (and consequently A) is only a fraction of the initial depolarization at D', but the repolarising current at A during the falling phase of the action potential may not be strong enough to yield repolarisation at D', which causes the aforementioned asymmetry. Of course, this is a simplification; actually an action potential can electrotonically invade dendrites and consequently modify the dendritic currents. This complication has been neglected to maintain simplicity.

Perspectives

The model presented assumes that a large number of receptors must be activated for producing one action potential. This simplification likely applies to the second-order neuron. However, it seems that it is not the case for neuroreceptors. First, it has been shown that highly sensitive "specialist" (unimodal) neuroreceptors such as the neuroreceptors detecting sexual pheromones in insects can trigger an action potential with only one activated receptor (see reviews [22, 50]). More recently, intracellular and patch-clamp recordings of "generalist" (multimodal) neuroreceptors have shown that the opening of only one or very few ionic channels were sufficient to initiate an action potential [13, 18, 38, 55]. If this is confirmed more importance should be given to small numbers of occupied sites (0, 1 and 2), and to the degree of maximum depolarization. The occupation of receptor sites, whether activated or not, is assumed to be an alternating Poisson process with rates λ and μ. This assumption yields an exponential distribution for all the sojourn periods. To generalize it, a distribution with density $g_0(t)$ and mean μ_0 for the occupation time, and another distribution with density $g_a(t)$ and mean μ_a for the activation time, could be considered. A suitable approach to follow for identifying the parameters of the model will depend on the type of experimental data available. If only ISIs are available then standard methods (for review see [58]) have to be used. If the trajectories of membrane potential are also available the methods introduced by Lánský [29] would be easily adaptable to this problem.

Several factors, presently under intensive experimental investigations, have not been explicitly taken into account in the present model. The hormonal and centrifugal influences, the turnover of neuroreceptors and the long term changes in synaptic plasticity have been neglected, so that the model applies only in short term conditions. These limitations are of no consequence because the concentration-response curves to be explained were also established in neurophysiological experiments of short duration. The presence of odorant transporter proteins [60] fits easily into the model because it acts only on the relationship (not specified in the model) between parameter λ (our main variable) and concentration of the odorant. The same remark applies for the mechanisms that eliminate the odorant (they act on μ). The detailed biochemical mechanisms of transduction have not been analyzed. We have assumed that the limiting step of the whole process is the odorant-receptor interaction. As discussed above this assumption leads to a basically correct account of the neuroreceptor behavior, which suggests that an essential feature of the real transduction process has been retained. Likewise, the fine structure of neuroreceptors, the complex neuronal circuitry of glomeruli [19, 46] and the distinction of different kinds of lateral inhibition acting at the input (periglomerular cells) and output (granule cells) levels of the second-order neurons [52] have not been considered in detail. However, these mechanisms do not call for a new model but for extensions and specifications of the present one.

Acknowledgements

This work has been partly supported by a grant #511101 from the Academy of Sciences of the Czech Republic, a fellowship from the Institut National de la Recherche Agronomique (to PL) and a grant "Sciences cognitives" from the Ministère de l'Enseignement Supérieur et de la Recherche (to JPR). The authors thank J. King for revising the manuscript.

References

[1] R.R.H. Anholt, "Odor recognition and olfactory transduction: the new frontier", *Chem. Senses*, vol. 16, pp. 421-427, 1991.

[2] C. Ascoli, M. Barbi, S. Chillemi and D. Petracchi, "Phase-locked responses in the *Limulus* lateral eye", *Biophys. J.*, vol. 19, pp. 219-240, 1977.

[3] M. Barbi, V. Carelli, C. Frediani and D. Petracchi, "The self-inhibited leaky integrator: Transfer function and steady state relations", *Biol. Cybern.*, vol. 20, pp. 51-59, 1975.

[4] M. Barbi and E.M. Ferdeghini, "Relevance of the single ommatidium performance in determining the oscillatory response of the *Limulus* retina", *Biol. Cybern.*, vol. 39, pp.45-51, 1980.

[5] P.O. Bishop, W.R. Levick and W.O. Williams, "Statistical analysis of the dark discharge of lateral geniculate neurons", *J. Physiol.*, vol. 170, pp. 598-612, 1964.

[6] J. Boeckh, K.D. Ernst, H. Sass and U. Waldow, "Anatomical and physiological characteristics of individual neurones in the central antennal pathway of insects", *J. Insect Physiol.*, vol. 30, pp. 15-26, 1984.

[7] L. Buck and R. Axel, "A novel multigene family may encode odorant receptors: a molecular basis for odor recognition", *Cell,* vol. 65, pp. 175-187, 1991.

[8] J. Carlson, "Olfaction in *Drosophila*: genetic and molecular analysis", *TINS,* vol. 14, pp. 520-524, 1991.

[9] M.J. Correia and J.P. Landolt, "A point process analysis of the spontaneous activity of anterior semicircular canal units in the anesthetized pigeon", *Biol. Cybern.,* vol. 27, pp. 199-213, 1977.

[10] H. Davis, "Some principles of sensory receptor action", *Physiol. Rev.,* vol. 41, pp. 391-416, 1961.

[11] P. Duchamp-Viret, A. Duchamp and M. Vigoroux, "Amplifying role of convergence in olfactory system. A comparative study of receptor cell and second order neuron sensitivities", *J. Neurophysiol.,* vol. 61, pp. 1085-1094, 1989.

[12] T. Engen, "Psychophysics", in *Experimental psychology,* J.W. Kling and L.A. Riggs (eds), New York: Rinehart and Winston, 1971.

[13] R. Fischmeister, R.K. Ayer and R.L. DeHaan, "Some limitations of the cell-attached patch clamp technique: a two-electrode analysis", *Pflüger Arch. Eur. J. Physiol.* vol. 406, pp. 73-82, 1986.

[14] J. Fohlmeister, "A theoretical study of neural adaptation and transient responses due to inhibitory feedback", *Bull. Math. Biol.,* vol. 41, pp. 257-282, 1979.

[15] T.V. Getchell and G.M. Shepherd, "Responses of olfactory receptor cells to step pulses of odour at different concentrations in the salamander", *J. Physiol.,* vol. 282, pp. 521-540, 1978.

[16] F. Grüneis, M. Nakao, M. Yamamoto, T. Musha and H. Nakahama, "An interpretation of $1/f$ fluctuation in neuronal spike trains during dream sleep", *Biol. Cybern.,* vol. 60, pp. 161-169, 1989.

[17] F.B. Hanson and H.C. Tuckwell, "Diffusion approximation for neuronal activity including synaptic reversal potentials", *J. Theor. Neurobiol.,* vol. 2, pp. 127-153, 1983.

[18] B. Hedlund, L.M. Masukawa and G.M. Shepherd, "Excitable properties of olfactory receptor neurons", *J. Neurosci.,* vol. 7, pp. 2338-2343, 1984.

[19] U. Homberg, T.A. Christensen and J.G. Hildebrand, "Structure and function of the deutocerebrum in insects", *Ann. Rev. Entomol.,* vol. 34, pp. 477-501, 1989.

[20] K.E. Kaissling, "Sensory transduction in insect olfactory receptors", in *Biochemistry of Sensory Functions,* L. Jaenicke (ed.), Berlin: Springer-Verlag, 1974.

[21] K.E. Kaissling, "Structure of odour molecules and multiple activities of receptor cells", in *Olfaction and Taste VI,* J. Le Magnen and P. Mac Leod (eds), London: IRL, 1977.

[22] K.E. Kaissling, *R.H. Wright Lectures on Insect Olfaction,* K. Colbow (ed), Burnaby, Canada: Simon Fraser University, 1987.

[23] K.E. Kaissling, C. Zack Strausfeld and E. Rumbo, "Adaptation processes in insect olfactory receptors: mechanisms and behavioral significance, *Olfaction and Taste IX, Ann. N.Y. Acad. Sci.,* 1987.

[24] B.W. Knight, "Dynamics of encoding in a population of neurons", *J. Gen. Physiol.,* vol. 59, pp. 734-766, 1972.

[25] A.F. Kohn, "Dendritic transformations on random synaptic inputs as measured from a neuron's spike train. Modeling and simulation", *IEEE Trans. Biomed. Engn.,* vol. 36, pp. 44-54, 1989.

[26] S.W. Kuffler, K.R. Nicholls and A.R. Martin, *From neuron to brain,* Sunderland: Sinauer, 1984.

[27] P. Laffort, "Communication olfactive et facettes de l'odorité", in *Odeurs et désodorisation dans l'environnement,* G. Martin and P. Laffort (eds), Paris: Lavoisier, 1990.

[28] D. Lancet, "Vertebrate olfactory reception", *Annu. Rev. Neurosci.,* vol. 9, pp. 329-355, 1986.

[29] P. Lánský, "Inference for the diffusion models of neuronal activity", *Math. Biosci.,* vol. 67, pp. 247-260, 1983.

[30] P. Lánský, "On approximations of Stein's neuronal model", *J. Theor. Biol.,* vol. 107, pp. 631-647, 1984.

[31] P. Lánský and V. Lánská, "Diffusion approximations of the neuronal model with synaptic reversal potentials", *Biol. Cybern.,* vol. 56, pp. 19-26, 1987.

[32] P. Lánský and M. Musila, "Variable initial depolarization in Stein's neuronal model with synaptic reversal potentials", *Biol. Cybern.,* vol. 64, pp. 285-291, 1991.

[33] P. Lánský and T. Radil, "Statistical inference on spontaneous neuronal discharge patterns", *Biol. Cybern.,* vol. 55, pp. 299-311, 1987.

[34] P. Lánský and J.P. Rospars , "Coding of odor intensity", *BioSystems,* vol. 31, pp. 15-38, 1993.

[35] P. Lánský and J.P. Rospars , "Ornstein-Uhlenbeck model neuron revisited", 1993 (submitted).

[36] P. Lánský and C.E. Smith, "The effect of a random initial condition in neural first-passage-time models", *Math. Biosci.*, vol. 93, pp. 191-215, 1989.

[37] P. Lánský and C.E. Smith, "A one-dimensional neuronal model diffusion model with reversal potentials", *J. Math. Phys. Sci.*, vol. 25, pp. 1-10, 1991.

[38] J.W. Lynch and P.H. Barry, "Action potentials initiated by single channels opening in a small neuron (rat olfactory receptor)", *Biophys. J.*, vol. 55, pp. 755-768, 1989.

[39] M. Musila and P. Lánský, "Generalized Stein's model for anatomically complex neurons", *BioSystems*, vol. 25, pp. 179-191, 1991.

[40] T. Nagai and K. Ueda, "Stochastic properties of gustatory impulse discharges in rat chorda tympani fibers", *J. Neurophysiol.*, vol. 45, pp. 574-592, 1981.

[41] R.J. O'Connel and M.M. Mozell, "Quantitative stimulation of frog olfactory receptors", *J. Neurophysiol.*, vol. 32, pp. 51-63, 1969.

[42] D.H. Perkel and T.H. Bullock, "Neural coding", *Neurosci. Res. Prog. Bull.*, vol. 6, pp. 221-350, 1968.

[43] D.H. Perkel and B. Mulloney, "Motor pattern production in reciprocally inhibitory neurons exhibiting postinhibitory rebound", *Science,* vol. 185, pp. 181-183, 1974.

[44] L.M. Ricciardi and L. Sacerdote, "The Ornstein-Uhlenbeck process as a model of neuronal activity", *Biol. Cybern.*, vol. 35, pp. 1-9, 1979.

[45] L.M. Ricciardi and S. Sato, "Diffusion processes and first-passage-time problems", in *Lectures in applied mathematics and informatics,* L.M. Ricciardi (ed), Manchester: Manchester Univ. Press, pp. 206-285, 1990.

[46] J.P. Rospars, "Structure and development of the insect antennodeutocerebral system", *Int. J. Insect Morphol. and Embryol.*, vol. 17, pp. 243-294, 1988.

[47] J.P. Rospars and P. Lánský, "Stochastic model neuron without resetting of dendritic potential: Application to the olfactory system", *Biol. Cybern.*, vol. 69, pp. 283-294, 1993.

[48] J.P. Rospars, P. Lánský, J. Vaillant, P. Duchamp-Viret and A. Duchamp, "Spontaneous activity of first- and second-order neurons in the olfactory system", 1993 (submitted).

[49] H. Scharstein, "Input-output relationship of the leaky-integrator neuron model", *J. Math. Biol.*, vol. 8, pp. 403-420, 1979.

[50] D. Schneider, "The sex-attractant receptor of moths", *Scientific Am.*, vol. 231, pp. 28-35, 1974.

[51] R. Selzer, "On the specificities of antennal olfactory receptor cells of *Periplaneta americana*", *Chem. Senses*, vol. 8, pp. 375-395, 1984.

[52] G.M. Shepherd, "Synaptic organization of the mammalian olfactory bulb", *Physiol. Rev.*, vol. 52, pp. 864-917, 1972.

[53] R.B. Stein, "A theoretical analysis of neuronal variability", *Biophys. J.*, vol. 5, pp. 173-195, 1965.

[54] C.F. Stevens, "Letter to the editor", *Biophys. J.*, vol. 4, pp. 417-419, 1964.

[55] D. Trotier, "A patch-clamp analysis of membrane currents in salamander olfactory cells", *Pflüger Arch. Eur. J. Physiol.*, vol. 407, pp. 589-595, 1986.

[56] H.C. Tuckwell, "Synaptic transmission in a model for stochastic neural activity", *J. theor. Biol.*, vol. 77, pp. 65-81, 1979.

[57] H.C. Tuckwell, "Diffusion approximation to conductance fluctuations and their effect on membrane potential", *J. theor. Biol.*, vol. 127, pp. 427-438, 1987.

[58] H.C. Tuckwell, *Introduction to theoretical neurobiology.* Cambridge: Cambridge University Press, 1988.

[59] W. Van Drongelen, A. Holley and K.B. Døving, "Convergence in the olfactory system: Quantitative aspects of odour sensitivity", *J. Theor. Biol.*, vol. 71, pp. 39-48, 1978.

[60] R.G. Vogt, G.D. Prestwich and M.R. Lerner, "Odorant binding protein subfamilies associated with distinct classes of olfactory receptor neurons in insects", *J. Neurobiol.*, vol. 22, pp. 74-84, 1991.

[61] A.J. Wilbur and J. Rinzel, "A theoretical basis for large coefficient of variation and bimodality in neuronal interspike interval distribution", *J. Theor. Biol.*, vol. 105, pp. 345-368, 1983.

[62] M. Yamamoto, H. Nakahama, K. Shima, T. Kodama and H. Mushiake, "Markov-dependency and spectral analysis on spike-counts in mesencephalic reticular neurons during sleep and attentive states", *Brain Res.*, vol. 366, pp. 279-298, 1986.

LIST OF KEYWORDS

Neuronal model
Membrane potential
Intensity coding
Olfactory system
Stochastic process
Sensory neuron

Chapter 12

Signal and Variability in Spike Trains

Michael Levine

Signal and Variability in Spike Trains

Michael W. Levine
University of Illinois at Chicago
Department of Psychology (M/C 285)
1007 West Harrison Street
Chicago, IL 60607-7137
U25216@uicvm.uic.edu

Intensive research over the past century has uncovered a wealth of information about ways the visual system works, and the principles by which a pattern of light and shade ultimately emerges into a perception of the world. Still, in 1993, we are not about to proclaim that we "understand" vision.

One relatively unexplored aspect of the visual system is its noise. The stable clarity of vision is remarkable in view of the noisiness of the channels that carry visual information. This noisiness, or variability, has been studied as a window into the mechanisms of the retina [e.g.: 2, 13, 14, 16, 27, 29, 30], and as a limit upon the ability of the system to detect weak stimuli [e.g.: 2, 12, 25, 26]. Variability is usually considered an unfortunate byproduct of the way nervous systems are built; few have considered the possible utility of variability. But lack of a function for variability would be surprising in view of the general economy of the nervous system. How might the signals due to visual stimuli interact with variability in the early visual pathway? After a brief review of the signal and noise encoded by the retina, I will concentrate on the transformations that occur in the *dorsal lateral geniculate nucleus* (**LGN**). The LGN is the major relay station that transfers the signal from the eyes to the central brain.

SIGNAL AND VARIABILITY IN THE RETINA

The retina, which is a piece of the brain stationed in the eyeball, performs considerable processing on the signal it transduces from the pattern of light and shade focussed upon it. The channel through which the rest of the brain receives this information is the optic nerve, comprising the myelinated axons of the ganglion cells of the retina. The only known way information can travel from retina to brain is to be encoded in the trains of action potentials, or *spikes* (also commonly called neural *impulses*), that propagate down these axons.

Codes for the Signal

One generally assumes that the neural code is frequency modulation: The rate at which spikes are produced is increased to indicate excitation. This concept is often simplified to assume the code is the rate of firing, or the average rate in some time window (e.g.: a count of spikes divided by the window width).

Other candidate codes have been suggested, and none ruled out. Rather than consider the rate of firing, one could consider the time intervals between successive spikes. Clearly, there is a 1:1 mapping between this and a frequency code; for a steady discharge, the mean interval is the inverse of the mean rate. But it is a nonlinear mapping, so one must attend to whether the intervals or rate are considered. The difference can be important when there is variance in the discharge, due either to temporal properties of the deterministic response or to stochastic variability superimposed on the deterministic response [20]. More complex codes that do not map directly to mean rate are also possible [e.g.: 9, 23, 40].

An additional complication is that there is not a single code sent in parallel along all the axons of the optic nerve. A variety of ganglion cell types have been identified that differ in anatomy, physiology, and pattern of response. Some act as opposite pairs (ON and OFF cells); others differ in the way they process spatial and temporal information (the X cells and Y cells); some lead to separate functional areas in the brain (the magnocellular and parvocellular systems of the primate; lower mammals lack this dichotomy, although Y cells may be part of the magnocellular system and X cells may provide higher resolution functions associated with the parvocellular system).

Variability of Firing

Variability expresses itself in two ways in the firing of ganglion cells. In the absence of any changing visual stimulation, the *sustained discharge* is not pacemaker-steady [24]. The first-order characterization of the sustained discharge is typically given by the first two moments of the intervals: the mean interval, μ, and the standard deviation of the intervals, σ. While some prefer to treat these as separate variables [19, 47], it is often convenient to consider the *coefficient of variation*, **CV**, which is the ratio of these quantities ($CV \equiv \sigma/\mu$). CV quantifies the relative noisiness of an interval based code [28].

A more complete description of the first-order statistics may be obtained by cumulating a histogram of the *interspike intervals* (**ISI**s), which presents the probability of obtaining intervals of each duration. There have been attempts to infer the nature of the causative stochastic process from the shape of the ISI histogram [e.g.: 3, 4, 5, 18, 32], but the results remain difficult to interpret because the shape of the ISI histogram is relatively insensitive to the distribution of the underlying variability [29, 30].

The second way variability is manifest is in the inconsistency of responses to identical stimuli. If the same stimulus is repeated many times, the average response may be estimated by cumulating a *peristimulus time histogram* (**PSTH**), which presents the average number of spikes obtained in bins of relatively narrow width subdividing the time before, during, and following each stimulus presentation. In this way, each bin represents the mean firing at some time relative to the stimulus events. If the stimulus is presented for a short time (on the order of one second) and then removed, the average firing pattern reveals a deterministic pattern. Some cells increase firing when the pattern is presented, typically relaxing to a plateau nearer the mean sustained discharge rate as the stimulus remains in place, and then show a temporary decline in rate at the removal of the stimulus; this is called an ON response. Cells that show such a response when a small increment of light is placed directly in the middle of their receptive fields are known as ON cells. There is also the possibility of the opposite response: a temporary decline in firing when the stimulus is first presented, and a temporary increase to well above sustained levels when it is withdrawn; this is an OFF response, and cells that show such a response when a small increment of light is placed directly in the middle of their receptive fields are OFF cells. There are many variants on these response patterns, and the particular response produced by a given cell depends on the nature of the stimulus.

The average responses are indicative of the stimulus that elicited them, but the individual responses that contribute to the average are often quite dissimilar [35, 31]. The total numbers of spikes, and their placement relative to the stimulus events, vary from presentation to presentation. This would appear to make the decoding task impossible, for the well-defined mapping from stimulus to response (or response pattern) will be blurred if each stimulus can engender a range of responses, apparently at random. Of course, there are many cells acting in parallel, so a more central processor could reduce the noise by averaging across cells with the same effect the PSTH achieves by averaging across time (assuming noise reduction is the goal).

It seems reasonable that the same variability responsible for the noisiness of the sustained discharge could also produce the inconsistency of responses. But if we assume that the mean level of sustained discharge is set by a signal analogous to (and in the same processing pathway as) the signal that produces the deterministic part of the responses to stimuli, an apparent contradiction emerges. The mean rate of sustained discharge may by changed by presenting temporally steady stimuli and waiting until all response to their introduction has abated. To a first approximation, CV declines as the reciprocal square root of the mean firing rate [28, 41]. For a renewal process, which ganglion cell discharges approximate (at least in cat [16]), the variance of rate, σ_R^2, is related to CV by

$$\sigma_R^2 = (CV)^2 \cdot \bar{r} / T_s \qquad (1)$$

where $\bar{r}$ is the mean rate, and T_s is the duration of the samples in which rate is measured. Equation (1), shows that if CV is proportional to the reciprocal square root of $\bar{r}$, σ_R^2 will be invariant with mean rate. This, however, is not the case: Studies of variance of rate with stimuli of various strengths presented to ganglion cells in goldfish [35] and in cat [31] show a clear increase in σ_R^2 with $\bar{r}$, for both ON and OFF cells.

As it happens, the disagreement is not as untenable as it might seem. The reciprocal square root is an approximation. The best power law fits for individual cells can be rather different from -0.5 [28, 47][1]. A reexamination of the data supporting a reciprocal square root relationship showed that a better description could be obtained by fitting a parabola to the logarithm of CV *versus* the logarithm of mean rate [34]. We presented a model that allows for a log parabolic relationship between CV and rate, and takes into account the temporal properties of the deterministic portion of the responses; the model accurately predicted the functions of variance of rate *versus* mean rate observed in ganglion cells of goldfish and of cat, while predicting a mean log parabolic relationship surprisingly close to the mean function obtained from a different group of cats [34].

If the variability of sustained discharges and the variance of responses may be explained by the same stochastic process, what is that process? Assume that random noise (the distribution is not critical) is simply added to the deterministic signal that adjusts mean rate. The signal plus noise is integrated, but the integral tends to decay to a resting level; when the integral exceeds some threshold level, a spike is produced and the integral resets to the resting level (leaky integrate-and-fire mechanism). This model reproduces the features of sustained discharges, including the log parabolic relationship between CV and mean rate [30]. Thus, the variability in the retina is consistent with simple random noise added to the deterministic signal; the net result is that variance of responses increases with mean response level, albeit less than proportionally.

THE TRANSFORMATION AT THE LGN

The lateral geniculate nucleus of the thalamus (LGN) is the major way-station from the retina to the more central brain. The *principal* or *relay cells* project to the visual cortex. Many (perhaps most) of the relay cells receive nearly all their monosynaptic retinal input from a single ganglion cell [11], but approximately half the synapses onto a relay cell are extraretinal in origin (coming from the brainstem [21, 36, 42], from thalamic interneurons [15], and as feedback from the cortex to which the LGN projects [1, 22]). The LGN appears to perform relatively mild processing of the deterministic signal, slightly increasing low spatial frequency attenuation [39], slightly increasing low temporal frequency attenuation [10, 33, 44], and slightly modifying velocity tuning [17]. The apparent price of this processing is a considerable increase in variability, which appears to be due to additional noise [33, 48]. The sustained discharges of LGN cells are generally at a lower rate than those of retina, with a higher CV; the discharge is about as good an approximation to a renewal process as is the retinal sustained discharge [33].

In preliminary reports [8, 30], we have indicated that the variance of rate of LGN cells also increases with the mean response rate. It appears that the relationship is more nearly linear (variance directly proportional to rate) than is the relationship for retinal ganglion cells. This implies that the LGN plays a role in a transformation by which variance is made proportional to rate, as it is in visual cortex [43, 45, 46]. The following is a more detailed examination of the variability of responses in LGN cells, compared to the variability of the one simultaneously recorded retinal afferent that is the principal driver of each LGN cell.

Methods for LGN Experiments

The data were recorded in the laboratory of Brian G. Cleland at the University of Sydney, Sydney, Australia. Dr. Cleland has refined a method for recording simultaneously from a single LGN neuron and a single retinal ganglion cell that is presynaptic to it [11]. Times of occurrence of spikes were recorded to the nearest 0.1 ms. Data were

---

[1]Troy and Robson [47] predicted reciprocal square root behavior from their observations on the power spectra of discharges. The disparity from reciprocal square root may be compensated for by temporal properties of the discharge (that is, it is not quite a renewal process [16]).

collected from paralyzed cats, anesthetized with a mixture of nitrous oxide (70%) and halothane (1-4%) in oxygen. A detailed description of the surgical procedures, including the monitoring that ensured the animals experienced no pain or discomfort, may be found in [11].

A microelectrode was advanced through a trephine hole in the cat's skull to the stereotaxic coordinates of the LGN. A light flashing on a tangent screen placed in front of the cat provided changing visual stimulation, so an LGN cell could be easily recognized by the modulation of its firing synchronized with the light. When a single LGN cell was isolated (by the usual criteria for an extracellular spike train from a single neuron: spikes of the same size and shape, and no two spikes occurring within less than a reasonable refractory period), its receptive field was localized on the screen. The cell was classified as ON or OFF, tested for possible motion or direction selectivity, and categorized as "brisk" or "sluggish," "sustained" or "transient," according to its responses to flashes of light [10]. The "brisk-sustained" cells were considered to be X cells, and the "brisk-transient" to be Y. Occasional checks of the spatial summation properties that properly define these classes attested to the validity of the classification. The more usual X/Y terminology will be used below.

When an LGN cell had been localized, a second extracellular electrode was advanced to the retina through a guide tube that punctured the sclera near the junction of the anterior and posterior chambers. This guide tube could be rotated about its entry point to locate the electrode tip at any position on the retina without disturbing the eye. Since ganglion cell receptive fields are generally concentric with their cell bodies, and it is near the cell body (or main dendritic trunk) that spikes are best recorded with an extracellular electrode, it was relatively simple to place the tip such that it recorded a ganglion cell whose receptive field was essentially coincident with that of the LGN cell isolated by the first electrode.

The ganglion cells in the appropriate region were explored individually to determine which of them provided monosynaptic input to the LGN cell. This was tested on-line by forming the cross-correlogram of the two spike trains. The cross-correlogram represents the firing by the LGN cell as a function of the time since each retinal spike. If the spike trains are unrelated, the cross-correlogram should be essentially flat; there is no reason for the LGN cell to fire more or less than its mean rate at any time relative to the ganglion cell spikes. When there is monosynaptic excitation, a sharp peak appears at a delay that represents the transmission time through the optic nerve plus the synaptic delay (see figure 1). When a single retinal cell drives the LGN cell, the peak is quite narrow (about 1 ms wide) and large; often, 90% of the LGN spikes fall within the peak during a strong, brief stimulus. Once the peak has been identified, it is simple to identify LGN spikes that are triggered by that retinal cell because each is preceded by a retinal spike within the narrow time window that includes the peak (these will be referred to as *triggered* spikes, and the retinal spike that presumably triggered each is deemed *successful*). The LGN spikes that fall outside the peak may be spontaneous spikes initiated by the LGN cell itself, or may be due to other excitatory synaptic influences on the LGN cell (other retinal cells with only a weak influence, or the corticofugal inputs, which are also excitatory [1]). LGN spikes for which a retinal spike is not present in the appropriate window are referred to as *anonymous* spikes (i.e.: due to an unknown source). In all the pairs reported here, the retinal ganglion cell

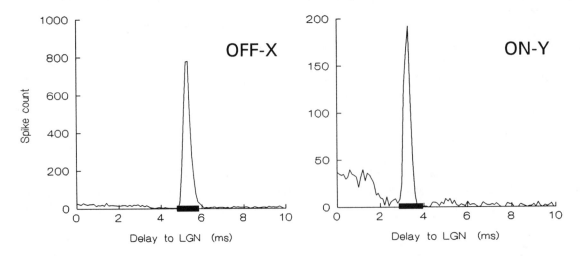

Figure 1: Cross-correlograms of Two Retina/LGN Pairs. OFF-X pair on left, ON-Y to right. Solid bar on x-axis indicates window in which LGN spikes were considered "triggered". Both in photopic conditions.

was considered the sole significant retinal input to the LGN cell. In all cases, the retinal cell was of the same type (ON or OFF, X or Y) as its partner LGN cell. The identification of X with "sustained" and Y with "transient" was further corroborated by the nonoverlapping ranges of delays to the peak observed for these types: 5.0-6.0 ms for the X pairs and 3.0-3.8 ms for the Y pairs.

Stimulation was of two types. In some cases, a spot approximately the diameter of the receptive field center (which was essentially identical for both members of a pair) flashed on the tangent screen at 1 Hz, superimposed on a white, mesopic background (1.8 cd/m²). The spot was flashed for nine to 60 cycles at each of four to 18 different luminances. For the second type of stimulation, the tangent screen was replaced with a white CRT monitor at a photopic mean luminance level (300 cd/m²). A cosine grating pattern of approximately the optimum spatial frequency for the pair was square-wave modulated in counterphase at 1 Hz. Thirty-nine cycles were repeated at each of 15 to 23 different contrasts, ranging from one to 60%. Twelve pairs were recorded: four ON-Y (three mesopic, one photopic), one OFF-Y (photopic), five ON-X (three mesopic, two photopic), and two OFF-X (both mesopic; one also recorded in photopic conditions, with no notable difference in its statistical properties).

LGN Results and Discussion

Variance of rate was evaluated by dividing each cycle of stimulation into two (1/2 sec) or four (1/4 sec) bins; the numbers of spikes in each bin of each cycle (divided by the bin duration) gave the rate. Mean rate and its variance were computed for corresponding bins across cycles. Data were presented as a plot of the logarithm of the variance *versus* the logarithm of the mean rate. There were thus about twice as many points representing 1/2 sec bins as stimulus strengths tested, and four times as many points representing 1/4 sec bins (there are actually slightly fewer points because bins representing periods with too few spikes were omitted). Two examples are shown in figure 2.

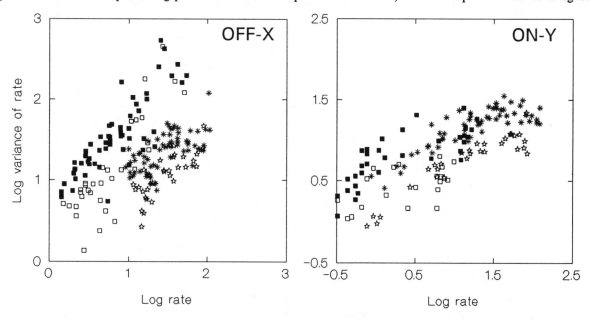

Figure 2: Log Variance of Rate *versus* Log Mean Rate in Response to Square-wave Modulated Cosine Grating. Simultaneously recorded retinal ganglion cell and LGN cell; same data as corresponding panels of figure 1. Retinal firing in 1/4 sec periods shown by asterisks, retinal firing in 1/2 sec periods by stars; LGN firing in 1/4 sec periods shown by solid squares, in 1/2 sec periods by open squares.

As may be seen in figure 2 by attending to any given symbol type, variance of rate increases with increased mean rate for both retinal and LGN cells, whether considered in 1/2 or 1/4 sec periods. The variance is greater in LGN cells (the points lie above the corresponding points for retina). Remember, these are responses to the same stimuli, recorded simultaneously, and the retinal cell is the principal, presumably sole, excitatory retinal driver of the corresponding LGN cell.

Although it is not the optimal way to characterize these functions, some idea of how nearly the variance of rate is directly proportional to mean rate may be obtained by finding the slopes of best-fit straight lines on double logarithmic plots like those in figure 2. We have observed that the distribution of the logarithms of slopes is more like a normal distribution than is the distribution of the slopes themselves [35], and so statistics are based on the log slopes (that is, the logarithms of the slopes on the double logarithmic plots).

LGN slopes are generally steeper than those for retina: Table 1 lists the geometric mean slopes for both 1/4 and 1/2 sec periods for LGN and retina (the geometric mean is the antilogarithm of the mean logarithm of slope). Both regression and principal component slopes are given. The differences between retina and LGN for 1/4 sec periods are significant for both regression and principal component slopes (regression: $t=3.92$, $p<0.005$; P.C.: $t=5.14$, $p<0.001$). For 1/2 sec periods only the principal component slopes are significantly different ($t=2.79$, $p<0.02$). All the retinal geometric mean slopes (both regression and principal component, 1/2 and 1/4 sec) differ significantly from unity (all $t>4.2$, $p<0.002$), but the only geometric mean LGN slope significantly different from unity is the regression fit for 1/4 sec ($t=4.75$, $p<0.001$).

Table 1: Geometric Mean Slopes

	All Pairs		X Cells (N=7)		Y Cells (N=5)	
	Retina	LGN	Retina	LGN	Retina	LGN
1/4 sec Regression	0.401	0.667	0.371	0.723	0.479	0.527
1/2 sec Regression	0.466	0.690	0.472	0.879	0.488	0.396
1/4 sec Principal Component	0.674	0.889	0.713	0.958	0.579	0.706
1/2 sec Principal Component	0.742	0.987	0.848	1.110	0.574	0.702

The differences in log slope between retina and LGN seemed to vary considerably among pairs, so the data set was sorted according to how much the log slope increased at the LGN (i.e.: the logarithm of the ratio of LGN slope/retinal slope). A remarkable finding emerged: Sorting for difference in log slope sorted according to whether the pairs were X or Y. The tendency for variance of rate to be more proportional to rate in the LGN than retina is largely a property of the X cell pathway. The means are separated by type in table 1. All the differences between retina and LGN (except 1/2 sec principal component) are significant for the X pairs (all $t>3.3$, $p<0.02$); only the 1/2 sec principal component difference is significant for the Y pairs ($t=3.23$, $p<0.05$). The differences in log regression slopes between retina and LGN show significant differences between X and Y pairs ($t>3.0$, $p<0.02$); that is, there is a significantly greater change in regression slope for X pairs than for Y pairs.

Comparison of the mean log slopes of X and Y cells shows the differences are all significant for LGN cells ($t>2.4$, $p<0.05$), but only the 1/2 sec log principal component slopes differ between X and Y cells in the retina ($t=3.52$, $p<0.01$). While the comparisons of X with Y must be evaluated cautiously because of the small sample size, it appears that retinal X and Y cells have similar functions relating variance of rate to rate; the relationship becomes steeper (more nearly directly proportional) in LGN X cells, but apparently not in LGN Y cells.

If the variance of rate is made more nearly proportional to rate in LGN X cells, how this is accomplished? Since we can identify which LGN spikes were directly triggered by the retinal spikes, and which retinal spikes triggered them, we may ask what manner of filtering is applied. A relatively straightforward answer may be found, at least for a first approximation: The probability of a retinal spike triggering an LGN spike is roughly a decaying exponential function of the time since the preceding retinal spike[2]. The shorter a retinal interspike interval, the more likely the second spike will succeed in triggering an LGN spike. This can be shown by plotting the ISI histogram of the entire retinal spike train, and the ISI histogram of only those intervals preceding spikes that are successful

---

[2]A decaying exponential function was first suggested by Dr. Brian Cleland based on his analyses of the sustained discharges of three retina/LGN pairs (ON-X, OFF-X, and ON-Y) [personal communication].

in triggering LGN spikes. The ratio of the two is the probability of success; it shows the shape of a decaying exponential in both X and Y pairs (see figure 3).

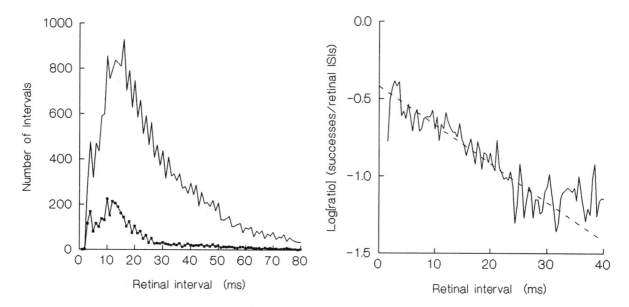

Figure 3: ISI Distributions and Success Ratio. Simultaneously recorded retinal ganglion cell and LGN cell; same data as left panel of figure 1 (OFF-X). **Left:** ISI distributions of all retinal spikes (plain line) and successes (line with points). **Right:** Logarithm of ratio of curves in left panel. Dashed line is regression fit to retinal ISI of 30 ms; it represents the relationship: **Ratio** $= 0.38\ e^{-\text{ISI}/17.37}$ (with ISI in ms).

A decaying exponential success function implies high-pass filtering of a frequency code, but does not obviously explain why variance of rate would be more linearly related to rate than in the input train. Nevertheless, the correlations between variance and mean rate of triggered spikes are quite high (>0.7), and the geometric mean slopes of log variance of rate *versus* rate for triggered spikes range from 0.81 for 1/4 sec regression lines to 0.94 for 1/2 sec principal component lines (see examples in figure 4). This is a significant increase over the slopes derived from retina (all $t>4.1$, $p<0.002$); the increase is significant in both X and Y pairs (except for 1/2 sec principal component lines in X pairs, all $t>3.2$, $p<0.05$). It is worth noting that the geometric mean slopes are greater for X than for Y pairs (except for 1/4 sec regression, all $t>2.4$, $p<0.05$).

The triggered LGN spikes may account for the effects observed, but what is the role of the anonymous LGN spikes? Just over 38% of the LGN spikes in these analyses were anonymous; the fraction was virtually identical for X and Y pairs. The rate of firing anonymous spikes (taken in 1/4 sec bins) was well correlated with the rate of retinal spikes for Y pairs (mean $r=0.66$), but not for X pairs (mean $r=0.06$); this difference in correlation between X and Y pairs was significant ($t=2.81$, $p<0.02$). It would appear the X LGN cells have about the same percentage of anonymous spikes, but, unlike LGN Y cells (for which the anonymous spikes parallel their retinal drive), the anonymous spikes in X cells are not well related to their retinal drive.

The log variance of the anonymous spikes shows strong correlation with the log mean rate of anonymous spikes, with geometric mean regression slopes of 0.79 (1/2 sec) and 0.86 (1/4 sec). The correlations between log variance of spike rate of anonymous spikes and log rate of anonymous spikes is not quite as strong as those for triggered spikes. The similarity to triggered spikes may be seen in the example in figure 4. There are no significant differences in anonymous spike variances between X and Y cells, except for a weaker correlation between log variance of spike rate of anonymous spikes and log rate of retinal spikes in X pairs than in Y ($t=2.50$, $p<0.05$).

There is a surprise in the PSTHs of triggered and anonymous LGN spikes. Since triggered spikes are the resultant of the direct retinal drive, they naturally should reproduce a filtered version of the deterministic response. Anonymous spikes, if they are not driven monosynaptically, should not be well related to the retinal drive. They might show increases concomitant with the retinal increases, but their responses would be expected to be sluggish or delayed as their driving signal passes through additional synapses and circuits.

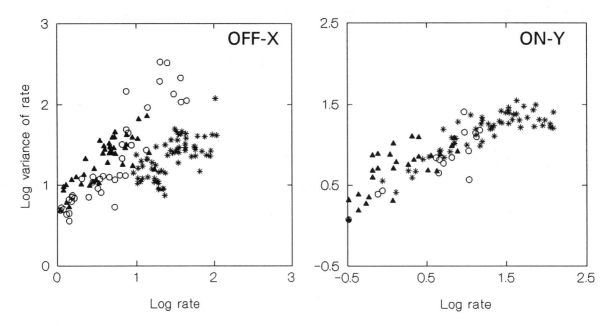

Figure 4: Log Variance of Rate *versus* Log Mean Rate for Triggered and Anonymous LGN Spikes. Simultaneously recorded retinal ganglion cell and LGN cell in each panel; same data as corresponding panels of figure 1, firing in 1/4 sec periods. Retinal firing shown by asterisks, triggered spikes by open circles, and anonymous spikes by solid triangles. Compare to figure 2.

This is not exactly the case. The PSTH of anonymous spikes during the "excitatory" phase of the responses (when the retinal spike rate is highest) is similar to that of the triggered spikes. Rather than being delayed, the initial responses of the anonymous spikes can precede the first signs of response by the triggered spikes. If these anonymous spikes are driven through an auxiliary pathway, that pathway must be fast, and parallel to the direct drive. It could not be corticofugal, for example, for the feedback could not precede the feed-forward pathway response. These anonymous spikes could be due to other direct retinal drivers, each of which is too weakly connected to produce significant peak in the cross-correlogram by itself but which in concert could provide sufficient excitation for a response[3].

In terms of simple response latency, X pairs show a slight tendency for the anonymous response to lead the triggered response (mean=0.45 ms, n.s.). In Y pairs, on the other hand, the tendency is for the anonymous response to lag the triggered response (mean=-2.01 ms, n.s.). This possible difference between X and Y pairs is not significant, only suggestive. For the anonymous spike responses to lead that of the triggered spikes for X pairs but not for Y pairs (if the finding can be verified) might suggest an input from the faster Y pathway to the X, perhaps through an interneuron that accounts for the close match of latencies.

While the anonymous spikes in the excitatory phase respond nearly in parallel to the retinal and triggered spikes, there is often a delayed discharge of anonymous spikes during the normally suppressed phase that corresponds to reduced firing in the retina. The discharge begins 100 to 200 ms after the stimulus event that signals suppression of the retinal, and therefore the triggered, firing (i.e.: following stimulus offset for ON cells, following stimulus onset for OFF cells). It builds gradually for another 50 to 100 ms, and then trails off. This discharge appears bursty, although there are often isolated spikes or long intervals between spikes. Delayed discharge was

---

[3]It is also possible that some of the anonymous spikes are actually the "low threshold" spikes that occur as a burst during a calcium spike generated in a hyperpolarized state [37]. Such bursts show a shorter latency than ordinary rate modulated spikes, but typically occur as a single burst per stimulus cycle following at least a 100 ms quiet period [38]. Since the anonymous spikes in the excitatory phase of the response show about as tonic a response as the triggered spikes, and there is generally no obvious quiet period, it is unlikely that many of these anonymous spikes are actually part of bursts due to calcium spikes during hyperpolarization.

observed in every X LGN cell; in all but one it accounted for about as many anonymous spikes as the discharge in the excitatory phase. No delayed discharge of anonymous spikes was ever observed in the Y LGN cells.

Since the delayed discharge of anonymous spikes is unique to X LGN cells, it is tempting to examine that discharge for an explanation of the difference between X and Y pairs in linearity of the variance of rate. However, some Y cell pairs show an increase in slope of log variance of rate *versus* log rate between retina and LGN, but nevertheless are devoid of this discharge. And a comparison of the strength of this discharge in X cells with the extent of their change in slope reveals no relationship. It is also is hard to imagine why an added discharge during the relatively low rate response phase would increase slope: It would increase variability (and rate), bringing the data points at the low end up toward those at the high end. Further analyses will be needed to explain how the variance of rate is made proportional to rate, and to define the role (if any) of the delayed burst in this process.

Finally, might the anonymous spikes actually be "learned" across the cycles of a repeated stimulus? Might they be an anticipatory response to the next cycle, such as has been observed even in retina [6]? To test for this, the PSTHs of triggered and anonymous spikes were plotted for the first three cycles and the last three cycles of stimulation. No differences could be discerned across cycles in the latencies to each response, or in the size of the delayed discharges of X cells. A simple spike count in the excitatory phase of the responses did show one significant effect: In both X and Y ganglion cells there was a tendency to fire fewer spikes in the final cycles than the first ($t=3.35$, $p<0.01$). This effect of fatigue or habituation was not significant in either the triggered or anonymous spikes of the LGN, although the tendency was in the same direction.

GENERAL DISCUSSION

It appears that the variance of rate is more nearly proportional to rate in the X cells of the LGN than in their corresponding retinal drivers; this is likely a step on the way to the direct proportionality reported for primary cortex [43, 45, 46] and the V4 "color and pattern" (parvocellular) area of primate higher cortex [43]. If this is truly an effect of the X system and not of the Y, as seems likely, it would seem that the features of the cortical variance are set more by X inputs than by Y. This could support the idea that the Y system plays a minor part in the main processing task of the cortex, the analysis of visual shape and form.

There is another possible implication to the finding that variance of rate is made proportional to rate: From equation (1), it may be seen that CV will be constant. That is, the signal to noise ratio will be independent of response strength if the <u>intervals</u> convey the neural code.

What advantage might be bestowed by having the signal to noise ratio held constant? If the function of the neural network (higher visual cortex) is to extract an image, or percept, the percept should not vary with the stimulus strength. The same solution should be found regardless of image quality, as long as the image is not too degraded to comprehend. We perceive that poorer images are "grayer" or "dirtier" than high quality images, but we still extract the same perception, recognize the same pattern in both. Lateral antagonism, light adaptation, contrast gain controls, and similar mechanisms known to function in the visual system serve to produce the constancy that permits us to see the same object regardless of lighting. Perhaps variability is part of an analogous process, and so must be similarly adjusted to maintain object constancy.

A role for noise has been postulated in terms of neural network problem solving: Variability is useful for preventing a problem-solving network from settling into a local minimum in the multidimensional solution space it is searching. Noise can be used to extricate the network from local minima, but the computational dilemma is how to keep the noise from dislodging the network from the correct solution [e.g.: 7]. Adjusting the amplitude of the variability to match the signal strength may be part of the answer. The variability is strong where the signal is strong, so there is sufficient dither to escape local minima (but the signal can still prevail). The variability weakens where the signal is weak, so there is minimal noise to prevent the network from taking account of subtle cues. It appears that a scaling of variability is precisely what the X system achieves.

Acknowledgments

I wish to thank Dr. Brian Cleland, who conducted all the retina/LGN pair experiments while I did what I could to assist. That work was supported by the NH&MRC of Australia, and by the Fogarty Center of NIH (TW01317). I am grateful to all the colleagues with whom I have worked over the years, especially to Drs. Laura Frishman and

Roger Zimmerman. Support for those endeavors came from NIH (R01EY00206, R01EY1951, R01EY6163, and F32EY05297), the Rush University Committee on Research, the Chicago Community Trust, and the Regenstein Foundation. The new analyses were supported by the University of Illinois at Chicago Research Board and Office of Social Science Research. Figures were prepared with SYGRAPH (SYSTAT, Inc., Evanston, IL., 1991). I also thank Dr. Karl Pribram for organizing this conference and inviting me to participate.

References

[1] G. Ahlsen, K. Grant, and S. Lindstrom, "Monosynaptic excitation of principal cells in the lateral geniculate nucleus by corticofugal fibers," *Brain Research*, vol. 234, pp. 454-458, 1982.

[2] H. B. Barlow and W. R. Levick, "Changes in the maintained discharge with adaptation level in the cat retina," *Journal of Physiology*, vol. 202, pp. 699-718, 1969.

[3] H. B. Barlow, W. R. Levick, and M. Yoon, "Responses to single quanta of light in retinal ganglion cells of the cat," *Vision Research*, Supplement No. 3, pp. 87-101, 1971.

[4] D. Berger, K. Pribram, H. Wild, and C. Bridges, "An analysis of neural spike-train distributions: determinants of the response of visual cortex neurons to changes in orientation and spatial frequency," *Experimental Brain Research*, vol. 80, pp. 129-134, 1990.

[5] P. O. Bishop, W. R. Levick, and W. O. Williams, "Statistical analysis of the dark discharge of lateral geniculate neurones," *Journal of Physiology*, vol. 170, pp. 598-612, 1964.

[6] T. H. Bullock, M. H. Hofmann, F. K. Nahm, J. G. New, and J. C. Prechtl, "Event-related potentials in the retina and optic tectum of fish," *Journal of Neurophysiology*, vol. 64, pp. 903-914, September 1990.

[7] R. M. Burton and G. J. Mpistos, "Event-dependent control of noise enhances learning in neural networks," *Neural Networks*, vol. 5, pp. 627-637, 1992.

[8] V. Carrión-Carire, B. G. Cleland, A. W. Freeman, M. W. Levine, and R. P. Zimmerman, "Variability of responses in retinal and geniculate cells," Presented at the Association for Research in Vision and Ophthalmology Spring Meeting, Sarasota, Florida, 1988. Abstract in *Investigative Ophthalmology & Visual Science*, vol. 29 supplement, p. 295, May 5, 1988.

[9] S.-H. Chung, S. A. Raymond, and J. Y. Lettvin, "Multiple meanings in single visual units," *Brain Behavior Evolution*, vol. 3, pp. 72-101, 1970.

[10] B. G. Cleland, M. W. Dubin, and W. R. Levick, "Sustained and transient neurones in the cat's retina and lateral geniculate nucleus," *Journal of Physiology*, vol. 217, pp. 473-496, 1971.

[11] B. G. Cleland and B. B. Lee, "A comparison of visual responses of cat lateral geniculate nucleus neurones with those of ganglion cells afferent to them," *Journal of Physiology*, vol. 369, pp. 249-268, 1985.

[12] T. E. Cohn, D. G. Green, and W. P. Tanner, "Receiver operating characteristic analysis: application to the study of quantum fluctuation effects in optic nerve of *Rana pipiens*," *Journal of General Physiology*, vol. 66, pp. 583-616, 1975.

[13] D. R. Copenhagen, K. Donner, and T. Reuter, "Ganglion cell performance at absolute threshold in toad retina: effects of dark events in rods," *Journal of Physiology*, vol. 393, pp. 667-680, 1987.

[14] K. Donner, D. R. Copenhagen, and T. Reuter, "Weber and noise adaptation in the retina of the toad *Bufo marinus*," *Journal of General Physiology*, vol 95, pp. 733-753, April 1990.

[15] M. W. Dubin and B. G. Cleland, "Organization of visual inputs to interneurons of lateral geniculate nucleus of cat," *Journal of Neurophysiology*, vol. 40, pp. 410-427, March 1977.

[16] L. J. Frishman and M. W. Levine, "Statistics of the maintained discharge of cat retinal ganglion cells," *Journal of Physiology*, vol. 339, pp. 475-494, 1983.

[17] L. J. Frishman, D. E. Schweitzer-Tong, and E. B. Goldstein, "Velocity tuning in dorsal lateral geniculate nucleus and retina of the cat," *Journal of Neurophysiology*, vol. 50, pp. 1393-1414, December 1983.

[18] G. L. Gerstein and B. Mandelbrot, "Random walk models for the spike activity of a single neuron," *Biophysical Journal*, vol. 4, pp. 41-68, 1964.

[19] G. Gestri, L. Maffei, and D. Petracchi, "Spatial and temporal organization in retinal units," *Kybernetik*, vol. 3, pp. 196-202, November 1966.

[20] G. Gestri, H. A. K. Mastebroek, and W. H. Zaagman, "Stochastic constancy, variability and adaptation of spike generation: performance of a giant neuron in the visual system of the fly," *Biological Cybernetics*, vol. 38, pp. 31-40, 1980.

[21] B. Hu, M. Steriade, and M. Deschênes, "The effects of brainstem peribrachial stimulation on neurons of the lateral geniculate nucleus," *Neuroscience*, vol. 31, pp. 13-24, January 1989.

[22] R. E. Kalil and R. Chase, "Corticofugal influence on the activity of lateral geniculate neurons in the cat," *Journal of Neurophysiology*, vol. 33, pp. 459-474, March 1970.

[23] J. Krüger and J. D. Becker, "Recognizing the visual stimulus from neuronal discharges," *Trends in Neurosciences*, vol. 14, pp. 282-286, July 1991.

[24] S. W. Kuffler, R. FitzHugh, and H. B. Barlow, "Maintained activity in the cat's retina in light and darkness," *Journal of General Physiology*, vol. 40, pp. 683-702, May 1957.

[25] P. Lennie, "Scotopic increment thresholds in retinal ganglion cells," *Vision Research*, vol. 19, pp. 425-443, 1979.

[26] W. R. Levick, L. N. Thibos, T. E. Cohn, D. Catanzaro, and H. B. Barlow, "Performance of cat retinal ganglion cells at low light levels," *Journal of General Physiology*, vol. 82, pp. 405-426, September 1983.

[27] M. W. Levine, "Retinal processing of intrinsic and extrinsic noise," *Journal of Neurophysiology*, vol. 48, pp. 992-1010, October 1982.

[28] M. W. Levine, "Variability in the maintained discharges of retinal ganglion cells," *Journal of the Optical Society of America* $\underline{A}$, vol. 4, pp. 2308-2320, December 1987.

[29] M. W. Levine, "The distribution of the intervals between neural impulses in the maintained discharges of retinal ganglion cells," *Biological Cybernetics*, vol. 65, pp. 459-467, 1991.

[30] M. W. Levine, "Modeling the variability of firing rate of retinal ganglion cells," *Mathematical Biosciences*, vol. 112, pp. 225-242, December 1992.

[31] M. W. Levine, B. G. Cleland, and R. P. Zimmerman, "Variability of responses of cat retinal ganglion cells," *Visual Neuroscience*, vol 8; pp. 277-279, 1992.

[32] M. W. Levine and J. M. Shefner, "A model for the variability of interspike intervals during sustained firing of a retinal neuron," *Biophysical Journal*, vol. 19, pp. 241-252, 1977.

[33] M. W. Levine and J. B. Troy, "The variability of the maintained discharge of cat dorsal lateral geniculate cells," *Journal of Physiology*, vol. 375, pp. 339-359, 1986.

[34] M. W. Levine and R. P. Zimmerman, "A model for the variability of maintained discharges and responses to flashes of light," *Biological Cybernetics*, vol. 65, pp. 469-477, 1991.

[35] M. W. Levine, R. P. Zimmerman, and V. Carrión-Carire, "Variability in responses of retinal ganglion cells," *Journal of the Optical Society of America A*, vol. 5, pp. 593-597, April 1988.

[36] S. Lindstrom, "Synaptic organization of inhibitory pathways to principal cells in the lateral geniculate nucleus of the cat," *Brain Research*, vol. 234, pp. 447-453, 1982.

[37] R. Llinás and H. Jahnsen, "Electrophysiology of mammalian thalamic neurones in vitro," *Nature*, vol. 297, pp. 406-408, June, 1982.

[38] S.-M. Lu, W. Guido, and S. M. Sherman, "Effects of membrane voltage on receptive field properties of lateral geniculate neurons in the cat: contributions of the low-threshold Ca^{+2} conductance," *Journal of Neurophysiology*, vol. 68, pp. 2185-2198, December, 1992.

[39] L. Maffei and A. Fiorentini, "Retinogeniculate convergence and analysis of contrast," *Journal of Neurophysiology*, vol. 35, pp. 65-72, 1972.

[40] B. J. Richmond and L. M. Optican, "Temporal encoding of two-dimensional patterns by single units in primate primary visual cortex II. information transmission," *Journal of Neurophysiology*, vol. 64, pp. 370-380, August 1990.

[41] J. G. Robson and J. B. Troy, "Nature of the maintained discharge of Q, X, and Y retinal ganglion cells of the cat," *Journal of the Optical Society of America A*, vol. 4, pp. 2301-2307, December 1987.

[42] W. Singer, "Control of thalamic transmission by corticofugal and ascending reticular pathways in the visual system," *Physiological Reviews*, vol. 57, pp. 386-420, 1977.

[43] R. J. Snowden, S. Treue, and R. A. Andersen, "The response of neurons in areas V1 and MT of the alert rhesus monkey to moving random dot patterns," *Experimental Brain Research*, vol. 88, pp. 389-400, 1992.

[44] Y. T. So and R. M. Shapley, "Spatial tuning of cells in and around lateral geniculate nucleus of the cat: X and Y relay cells and perigeniculate interneurons," *Journal of Neurophysiology*, vol. 45, pp. 107-120, January 1981.

[45] D. J. Tolhurst, J. A. Movshon, and A. F. Dean, "The statistical reliability of signals in single neurons in cat and monkey visual cortex," *Vision Research*, vol. 23, pp. 775-785, 1983.

[46] D. J. Tolhurst, J. A. Movshon, and I. D. Thompson, "The dependence of response amplitude and variance of cat visual cortical neurones on stimulus contrast," *Experimental Brain Research*, vol. 41, pp. 414-419, 1981.

[47] J. B. Troy and J. G. Robson, "Steady discharges of X and Y retinal ganglion cells of cat under photopic illuminance," *Visual Neuroscience*, vol. 9, pp. 535-553, 1992.

[48] J. R. Wilson, J. Bullier, and T. T. Norton, "Signal-to-noise comparisons for X and Y cells in the retina and lateral geniculate nucleus of the cat," *Experimental Brain Research*, vol. 70, pp. 399-405, 1988.

Chapter 13

Noise and the Neurosciences:
A Long History, a Recent Revival and Some Theory

J.P. Segundo, J.-F. Vibert, K. Pakdaman, M. Stiber, O. Diez Martinez

NOISE AND THE NEUROSCIENCES:

A LONG HISTORY, A RECENT REVIVAL AND SOME THEORY.

J.P. Segundo*, J.-F. Vibert**, K. Pakdaman**, M. Stiber*** and O. Diez Martínez****.
* Dept. of Anatomy and Cell Biology, Brain Research Institute; University of California; Los Angeles, Ca.,
90024-1763 U.S.A. (*iaqfjps@mvs.oac.ucla.edu*). Facultad de Ciencias, Universidad de la República,
Montevideo, Uruguay.
** Biomathémathiques, Biostatistique, Bioinformatique et Epidémiologie; INSERM U 263, Faculté de
Médecine Saint-Antoine; 27 rue Chaligny, 75571 Paris Cedex 12, FRANCE. (*vibert@b3e.jussieu.fr,
pakdaman@b3e.jussieu.fr*)
*** Dept. of Computer Science, Hong Kong University of Science and Technology, Clearwater Bay,
Kowloon, HONG KONG. (*stiber@uxmail.ust.hk*)
**** Universidad de las Américas, 72820 Cholula, Puebla, México. (*odiezm@udlaevms.pue.udlap.mx*)

"Fig. 4. The responses demonstrate the linearising effect of an auxiliary signal (first column), internal noise (second column) and spontaneous spike discharges (third column)."

Spekreijse, 1969 [63].

"...cycle histograms obtained with sinusoidal inputs are more sinusoidal and the form of the frequency response functions agrees with that predicted from the step response over a wider range of frequencies."

French et al., 1972 [26].

"Perturbations, often regarded as weak and inconsequential, are practically inevitable in nature and appear to have functional consequences: hence, they should not be ignored and perturbed behavior may be the rule in this system (as in others) with performance during jitter providing a more faithful picture of normal operation than the usual laboratory conditions where vibrations are avoided deliberately."

Macadar et al., 1975 [39].

INTRODUCTION

This chapter deals with the influence of noise on processing by nerve cells, as observed in sensory receptors and synapses and as revealed by the spikes trains they generate. The bulk of the chapter is a survey of the *publications that opened the field and provided its essential scaffolding;* namely, provided its rationale, plus the experimental demonstration of the influence, its many facets and its biological significance. Such publications are needed as take-off points and as frames of reference, to be used, critically of course, for the sake of economy, coherence and fairness. The list is not intended to be exhaustive. This survey is followed by a brief *outline of formal notions* about noise and its consequences, orienting within the conceptual background and providing guidelines for future research. Both the publications and the outline seem opportune and useful, given the importance of the topic and the renewed interest it elicits. The chapter closes with a *discussion* of general issues.

"Noise" has been assigned different meanings in earlier publications; furthermore, one or another of those meanings has been assigned also to "stochastic auxiliary signal," "dither," "jitter," and "perturbations." The main meanings follow. *a.* "Noise" (or its synonyms) are said to be present when some variable's dispersion around a central value (e.g., mean) is unsystematic. This dispersion usually implies some degree of unpredictability and may reflect known but neglected issues, and/or unknown ones. *b.* "Noise" is a waveform with many frequency components over a particular band, of similar amplitudes, and scattered phases. *c.* "Noise" is the un-interesting addition that distorts the interesting component referred to as "signal;" "un-interesting" and "interesting" refer to the observer's viewpoint. The signal delivered without noise is referred to as *"clean" or "non- perturbed.* Current uses of these terms are adopted, regardless of whether appropriate or not.

Mapping across receptors and synapses have remarkable similarities. These involve (see below) the type and clarity of non-linear distortions in clean drivings, the way fast noises influence slow signals, the relation between signal and noise features, and several formal underpinnings.

Trains of spikes generated by nerve cells –first order afferents at receptors and the connected neurons at the synapse- play an important role in this survey. Figures 1 and 13 illustrate the raw physiological data on which considerations are based. Recognition of the clear physiological implications of how spikes arise along ongoing time led to the traditional *assimilation of spike trains to point processes* [54] [56]. The instants when the individual spikes occur define what has been called the train's "timing;" it can be described equivalently by the ordered sets of either interspike intervals Ti or rates 1/Ti. The timing of a particular train implies jointly measures as *"time span", "spike number", "overall averages"* and *"pattern."* The averages are for interval "T$_2$+...+T$_n$)/(n-1)" and for rate "(n-1)/(T$_2$+...+T$_n$". The mean rates alluded to here are these and not those of the instantaneous rates. The relation between the statistics of the reciprocals interval T$_i$ and instantaneous rate 1/T$_i$ is not straightforward. Averages reflect whether spikes arise rarely and separated in time or often and close to each other. The pattern reflects whether spikes arise regularly with practically equal intervals as in pacemakers, in bursts, irregularly, and so forth. Patterns are measured by statistics reflecting dispersions (e.g., standard deviations, histograms) or correlations along the train (e.g., serial coefficients, auto-correlation histograms ACHs). This chapter refers often to average correlations between the output spike train from a nerve cell, and an input to the cell that is delivered several times. Correlations are measured by special cross-correlation histograms (CCHs) that display the average rate of the cell along the input. They are called "peri-stimulus histograms" generally, or "cycle histograms," when stimuli are periodic. The repeated input can arrive either periodically (e.g., sines for Figure 2-**I** or irregularly (rectangles for Figure 2- **II** or triangles for Figure 16). The input at sensory receptors is the stimulus itself, and at synapses the waveforms that modulate pre-synaptic rates. A natural way to analyze matchings between inputs and outputs is to look at the frequency components at each stage, individually and as they relate linearly or otherwise; i.e., looking at spectra, cross-spectra and coherences. At least one point process is involved in every case, be it at a receptor or a synapse. It is, in fact, an indispensable approach (e.g., [9] [8]). If this were to be discussed meaningfully, certain procedural issues should be clarified. We feel that this presentation would be exceeded by such a clarification, and that its essential purpose can be achieved without it.

TRANSDUCTION AT A SENSORY RECEPTOR

Transduction from clean sensory stimuli into spike trains in first order afferents involves, as is well known, a variety of features, including numerous and clear non-linear distortions. Their list is extensive and heterogeneous. Transduction of length in mechanoreceptors, for instance, involves an asymmetric sensitivity to change (greater to lengthening than to shortening), as well as hysteresis, saturations and special discharge forms (e.g., [13] [16] [18] [17] [22] [26] [39] [46] [52] [53] [70] [69] [78] [79]).

Figure 1 shows raw records of stimuli and of discharges in first order afferents. The experiment in **I** was on a crayfish fast adapting stretch receptor organ (FAO) submitted to sinusoidal length modulations. When sensory stimulation was without noise (**A**), i.e., clean or non-perturbed, the FAO fired during a narrow portion of the cycle and regularly; with noise (**B,C**), i.e., perturbed, it fired over more of the cycle and less regularly. Moreover, effects are apparent at both modulation frequencies and both noise amplitudes, though clearer with the stronger (**C**) than the weaker (**B**) noise. Extreme noise amplitudes either were ineffective when minor, or made the signal unrecognizable when major. The experiment in **II** was on isolated guitar-fish utricles maintained at two different orientations A and B relative to gravity, and switched from one to the other via step-like transitions. Without noise or jitter (upper part), the discharge of the smaller spike was somewhat slower and more regular than with (lower part, +J); it slowed during one transient (A-B), and accelerated during the other (B-A), and fired slower at B than at A. The large spike without jitter (upper part) fired exclusively at the transient; with jitter (lower part, +J), it fired at both orientations, faster at A.

a. Appropriate noise superimposed upon a clean signal attenuates non-linear distortions of sensory transduction; i.e., reduces departures from linearity (e.g., [13] [16] [26] [39] [63] [64]). Distortion reduction implies an increase in fidelity. Biologically, fidelity is important often [57]. The (retrospective) identification of length based upon the observed discharges becomes more straightforward to a human observer (though not necessarily more precise).[48]

We call *"fidelity"* the proportionate reproduction along time of the sensory or synaptic input profile (or of its mirror image) by the output discharge (usually judged by observing a single parameter). Increased fidelity means that the mapping is more straightforward, but not necessarily more accurate. Indeed, any mapping, simple or complex, is accurate if relations are one to one both ways. By the same token, fidelity does not mean more reliable identification of one member of the relation given the other (e.g., predicting the afferent discharge knowing the applied stimulus).

Fidelity improvement by noise during periodic stimulations is apparent when matching the average of the stimulus and the response. Figure 2-**I** shows observations in simulated cockroach mechano-receptors that mimicked correctly those in the living preparation. [26] A sinusoidal displacement is reproduced much better by the average, discharges, i.e., by cycle histograms, using perturbed (**B,C,D**) stimulations than using clean (**A**) ones. Improvement increased with noise amplitude from **B** to **D**, but deteriorated with very large amplitude noises (not illustrated). Figure 2-**II** with crayfish stretch receptor data shows two different maintained lengths A and B, switched from one to the other via step-like transitions; these constituted in effect rectangular stimuli. Also included are the corresponding peri-stimulus histograms (clean 1 or perturbed2), and their difference 3 (i.e., histogram 1 minus 2). [13]) The rate of the slowly adapting stretch receptor organ (SAO) with clean stimulation (**a-1**) overshoots with lengthening, adapts, reaches full- adaptation 35s later, undershoots with shortening, and again adapts. With noise (**2**), there is a joint reduction in the overshoot height (the difference **3** is positive), the time to full adaptation, and the undershoot duration. The rate of the fast adapting organ (FAO) with clean stimulation (**b-1**) is 0 (no firing) at length A, overshoots with lengthening, adapts, reaches full-adaptation at 0 48s later, and does not respond to shortening. With noise the FAO's behavior is very different (**2**); it fires when short, overshoots, adapts, reaches full-adaptation 40s later firing faster than when shorter, undershoots, and adapts. *The peri-stimulus histograms of both SAO and FAO with noise (2) depart less from the rectangles than with clean stimuli (1).* Noise increased fidelity, particularly in the FAO, reducing departures from rectangles (measured by least-square comparisons SE). The slowly-adapting (SAO) and the fast-adapting (FAO) receptor organs, when unperturbed, are prototypes of the classical categories of tonic and phasic behaviors, respectively. Figures 2- **II-a-1** and **b-1**, respectively, illustrate typical tonic and phasic responses to rectangular stimulation.

Classically, a *"tonic"* receptor or neuron responds to both invariant stimulus conditions and to transients; a *"phasic"* receptor or neuron responds only to transients. The tonic vs. phasic separation reflects preferential sensitivity to different input frequencies; it can arise at several levels including encoding at the output neuron.

Figure 3 corresponds to sinusoidal FAO stretchings. [16] The first and third rows exhibit the evolutions along the cycle of the average lengths (broken graphs) and the average rates, i.e., the cycle histograms (continuous): average lengths are the same for clean (left column) and perturbed (right) stimuli. *At both stimulus frequencies the matchings between stimulus and response are less close in the clean (left) than in the perturbed (right) cases.* This is obvious to the naked eye. In addition, the precise values of the stimulus-response differences (second and fourth rows) are generally larger in clean than in noisy modulations, in terms of both individual bin values (continuous graph) and overall average (broken horizontal graph).

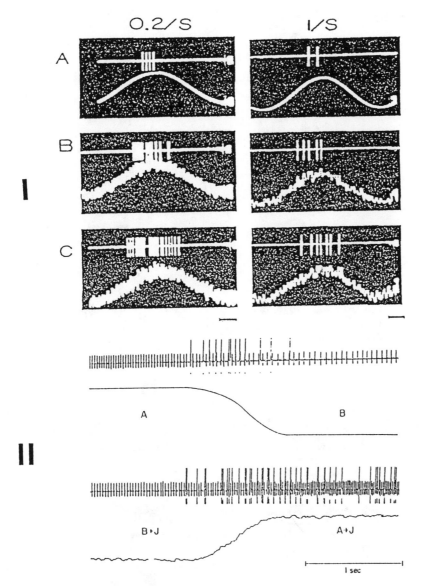

Figure 1: RAW EXPERIMENTAL DATA. SENSORY TRANSDUCTION. SPIKE TRAINS IN FIRST-ORDER AFFERENTS.

I. LENGTH MODULATION AT DIFFERENT FREQUENCIES. NOISE WITH DIFFERENT AMPLITUDES. INDIVIDUAL CYCLES. (Crayfish fast adapting stretch receptor organ FAO). As compared with the clean case (A), discharges with noise become less regular, occupy a larger portion of the cycle and show more spikes per cycle. This increases from weaker (B) to stronger (C) noise. Upper record from first order afferent. Lower record length: modulation depth 0.180mm (receptor length 6.0mm), frequency 0.2Hz and 1.0Hz (time calibrations 0.505s, 0.100s). [16] II. SPATIAL ORIENTATION MAINTAINED AND TRANSITIONS. NOISE. CHANGE IN RATES, IN VARIABILITIES, AND IN CHARACTER FROM PHASIC TO TONIC AFFERENT. (isolated guitar-fish utricle) Upper record, electrical activity from a single twig with action potentials from two cells. Lower record, orientations A and B; the representations of the transitions and of the noise or jitter J are only approximate. The small spike without jitter slows on passing from A to B, and its fully-adapted rate at B is lower than at A; with jitter (+J) it irregularized, accelerated on passing back from B to A and its fully-adapted rate is higher than at B. The large spike without jitter (upper part) is active only during the transition, and not otherwise. With jitter (+J) it fires during transitions; furthermore, shows a fully adapted discharge at both orientations, firing faster at A, than at B (where firing was very slow, and no spike appears in the figure), thus shifting its character from a phasic to a tonic.

303

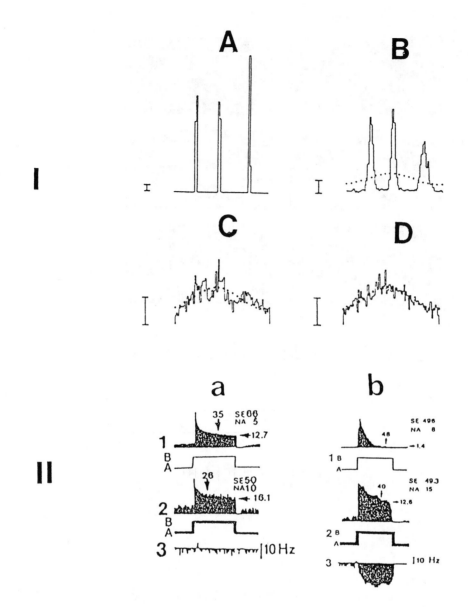

Figure 2: SENSORY TRANSDUCTION. NOISE. FIDELITY INCREASES. AVERAGES.
I. CLEAN vs. NOISY STIMULATION. Sinusoidal displacements (continuous line). Cycle histograms. Simulated cockroach mechanoreceptor. The average displacement is distorted much more with clean stimulations (A) than with perturbed ones (B, C, D). Improvement increased with noise amplitude from B to D; it deteriorated with very strong noises (not illustrated). [69]. II. RECEPTOR CONVERSION FROM THE PHASIC TO THE TONIC KIND. STIMULUS CONVERSION FROM SUB- TO SUPRA-THRESHOLD. Crayfish receptor organ a slowly adapting (SAO) b fast adapting (FAO). The SAO and the FAO are, respectively, tonic and phasic receptor prototypes. Cycle histograms during sensory stimuli consisting of periodic rectangular length changes, initially either lengthening a or shortening b. Receptor length is represented schematically under the histograms, shorter at A, longer at B; thicker lines indicate that noise was superimposed. NA: number of cycles averaged. SE: means squared error or difference between the cycle histogram and a rectangle of the same duration whose height was the average rate during the fully-adapted discharge at the corresponding length. The SE is given by the number at the horizontal arrow (arbitrary units). Number at vertical arrow: time from the step at which a fully-adapted discharge was achieved so the portion that followed is trend-free. Crayfish Procambarus clarkii; organs were isolated. [13]

Figure 4 shows Lissajous displays for sinusoidal stretching of the FAO. [16] *Noise attenuated non- linearities, and Lissajous shapes departed less from the ellipses that characterize linear mappings.* Each mark corresponds to a bin along the cycle, with average length as abscissae and average firing rate as ordinate; time (arrows) runs clockwise along all loops. Clean graphs (continuous) show the "loop-flat extension" Lissajous typical of SAOs and FAOs. [16] [17] [52] The loop at the greater lengths (right end) implies that for each of several lengths there were two FAO rates, higher or lower while the receptor was being stretched or shortened, respectively. This means double-valuedness, hysteresis, and a response that leads the stimulus. The flat extension implies a saturation where the receptor lengths were short and the afferent was silent. Perturbed Lissajous (dotted, open circles; dashed, small black circles) showed loops that were less angular and occupied more of the cycle; accordingly, flat extensions occupied less of the cycle.

Fidelity improvement by noise during periodic stimulations is apparent also when matching corresponding individual cycles in the clean and separately in the noisy situations. [16] This should be stressed since it is often ignored. In Figure 5 the naked eye reveals clearly that, though most cycles are distorted versions of the corresponding lengths, the perturbed cycles look more sinusoidal, particularly at the .2cps modulation. This impression was supported by the lower mean squared differences seen with individual noisy cycles.

Noise has other simplifying influences on sensory transduction. These are recognized when the periodic signal is characterized as a point process, and also are amplitude-related. [17] [53] *Noise smooths the relation between the average frequency of the stimulus and the average discharge rate or interspike interval of the afferent spike train.* The relation was obtained by delivering stimuli at different average frequencies (separated in time and in random order), then identifying the fully-adapted epochs and measuring the average afferent rates, and finally plotting one against the other. This procedure was carried out using stimuli with different degrees of variability, i.e. of noise. With very regular, i.e., clean, arrivals, relations had alternating positive and negative slopes; with increasingly irregular, i.e., noisy, stimulation, the zig-zag attenuates and converts to monotonicity.

Clean periodic stimuli whose frequencies differ elicit different discharge forms and patterns. **Noise attenuates these differences.** Discharge forms were analyzed for periodically delivered pulse-like lengthenings called "tugs." [18] Forms depended jointly on the frequency and the amplitude of the driver, as would be expected from such a non-linear couplings. At intermediate amplitudes, forms were either lockings or simple intermittencies reflecting quasi-periodicities. A preliminary exploration of greater amplitudes suggested more complex forms. An important question, as yet unexamined, is identifying the discharge forms that arise when a sine of given amplitude and frequency is superimposed with noises of different amplitudes. When noise was introduced by irregularizing the delivery of the tugs all frequencies produced the same irregular discharge pattern

Superimposing noise upon signals has other physiologically important consequences, besides fidelity improvement. **b. Noise either increases or does not change or decreases the overall average rates; average intervals behave of course oppositely.** [39] (see, respectively, Figures 1,2,6-a-3,4,7; or 6-b-3,4; or 6-c-3,4). Rate increases include cases where noise makes a spontaneously silent receptor cell fire uninterruptedly (Figure 1-II-large spike, 2-II-b, 7-FAO); this is discussed further below.

c. Noise usually increases dispersions around central values (e.g., mean, median). [16] [39] [78] For example, at a particular steady-state stimulus (e.g., fixed head orientation or length) and without noise, the discharge of tonic afferents often is regular and that of phasic afferents either regular, irregular or absent. Noise increases the wandering of intervals and rates. This is revealed by naked-eye examination of records (Figure 1), by the jaggedness of displays of the discharge, either averaged (Figure 2-a) or simply along running time (Figure 8), by interval standard deviations, coefficients of variation, and histograms (Figure 6). *When stimuli are low frequency sines, noise reduces the variability at most instants during the cycle, and makes it more uniform throughout [78] (Figure 9).* The dispersion's maximum is smaller, and the minimum either does not change or increases. *The regularity prevalent when stimulation is clean changes clearly when noise is superimposed.* In some afferents, though preserving its period, the prevalent regularity is much reduced as revealed by the autocorrelation histogram ACH (Figure 6a-3,4); in other afferents it is substituted by more complex periodicities (Figure 6b-3,4); in yet others, a new periodicity becomes prevalent (Figure 6-c-2,4).

d. Noise can influence sensory transduction by increasing, decreasing, or reversing its sensitivity (e.g., [13] [16] [22] [39] [46] [64]). Noise can also shift sensitivity from phasic to tonic. The *tonic sensitivity* of an afferent is to steady states and to low frequencies. It can be measured for,

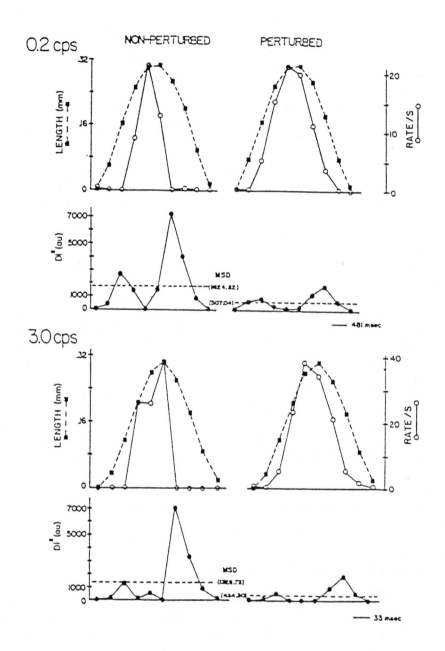

Figure 3: SENSORY TRANSDUCTION. FIDELITY INCREASE BY NOISE. I. INFLUENCE OF THE SAME NOISE UPON DIFFERENT STIMULUS FREQUENCIES. AVERAGE CYCLES. (Crayfish fast adapting stretch receptor organ FAO, Length stimulation sinusoidal.)

Stimulus frequencies 0.2 and 3.0Hz. **Left column** *non-perturbed, clean controls;* *right column perturbed by noise.* **First and third rows** *represent average cycles of length (broken graph, black circles, left axis mm) and cycle histograms (continuous, open circles, right axis /s). The maximum and minimum values of the length and of the rate do not always coincide because of the FAO's sensitivity to the velocity of the stretch.* **Second and fourth rows** *show mean squared deviations (arbitrary units) either in individual bins (continuous, black circles) or overall (horizontal broken line). Deviations were lower when the receptor was perturbed with both 0.2 and 3.0 cps [16].*

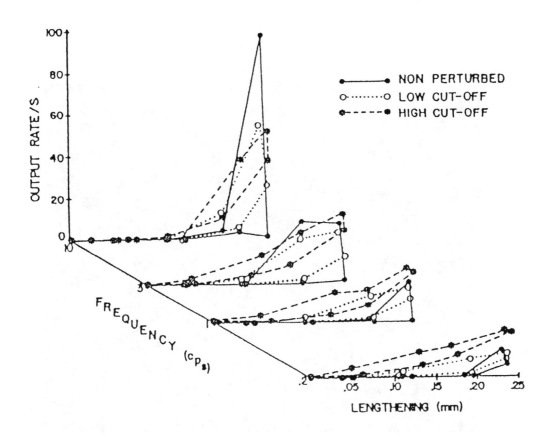

Figure 4: SENSORY TRANSDUCTION. FIDELITY INCREASE BY NOISE. II. INFLUENCE OF DIF-
FERENT NOISES UPON DIFFERENT STIMULUS FREQUENCIES. LISSAJOUS DIAGRAMS. (Crayfish
fast adapting stretch receptor organ FAO. Length stimulation sinusoidal.)
*To each bin along the cycle (i.e., the first, the second, etc.) corresponds a mark whose abscissae and ordinate
are, respectively, the average length and the average rate. Each display has a clockwise loop (arrow) at the
greater lengths and a flat extension on the abscissae at the shorter ones; they imply a discharge lead and a
saturation, respectively. When stimulation was* clean *(continuous line, small black circles),* Lissajous
plots were differed more from the ellipses of linear codings than when it was noisy *(dotted graphs, open
circles; dashed, large black circles). Improvement was better with the* modulation frequency *.2 Hz
and decreased through 1., 3. 10.Hz, displayed successively along the oblique axis. The consequences of the*
high frequency cut-off noise *(dashed, large black circles)* differed from those of the *low cut-off
noise (dotted, open circles),* particularly at the lower modulation frequencies [16].

307

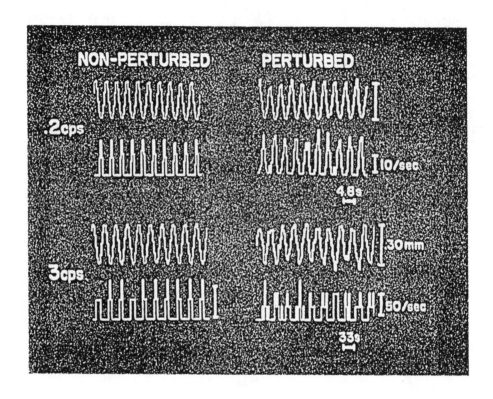

Figure 5: SENSORY TRANSDUCTION. FIDELITY INCREASE BY NOISE. III. INDIVIDUAL CYCLES. (Crayfish fast adapting stretch receptor organ FAO. Length stimulation sinusoidal.)
The naked eye examination of this figure suggests strongly that the resemblance between **discharges** (lower record in each entry) *and* **stimuli** (upper record) *was greater in the* **perturbed** (right) *than the* **clean** (left) *cases, and more so with .2 than with* 3Hz *[16].*

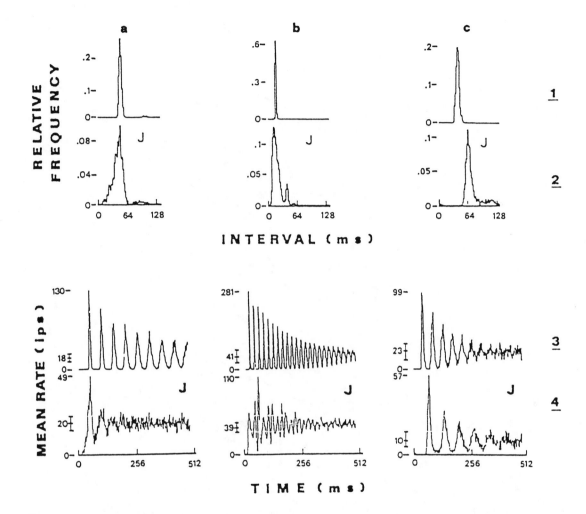

Figure 6: SENSORY TRANSDUCTION. NOISE, DISCHARGE STATISTICS. (Fish utricle. Stimulation maintained orientation relative to gravity).

Rows 1,3 clean controls *without noise;* rows 2,4 with noise *or jitter J.* Interval histograms (rows 1, 2): *abscissae, duration (ms); ordinate, relative frequency.* Auto- correlation histograms (3, 4): *abscissae, time after a spike; ordinate mean rate per sec per reference spike. The minimum, overall average and maximum rates are listed; empirically determined 95[39].*

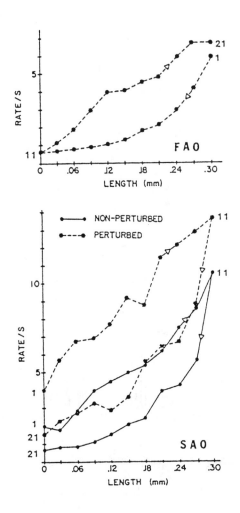

Figure 7: SENSORY TRANSDUCTION. NOISE, STEADY-STATE LENGTHS AND FULLY-ADAPTED RESPONSES. (Crayfish fast and slow adapting stretch receptor organs FAO, SAO. Stimulation maintained length.)

Relation between lengths (on abscissae) and average rates during fully adapted periods (on ordinates). **Clean (continuous graph, circles), perturbed (broken, asterisks).** *Step changes in length were applied successively starting from one extreme length at mark 1 (the longest in the FAO, the shortest in the SAO), following the order indicated by the arrowheads, reaching the other extreme length at mark 11, and returning to the first extreme at 21. Each plot shows hysteresis, i.e., at each length rates were higher when reached via stretching than via shortening. Furthermore, comparison in the SAO of the clean with the noisy graphs shows that clean marks were higher than the corresponding perturbed average. The FAO's fully-adapted rate differed from 0 only when perturbed [16].*

310

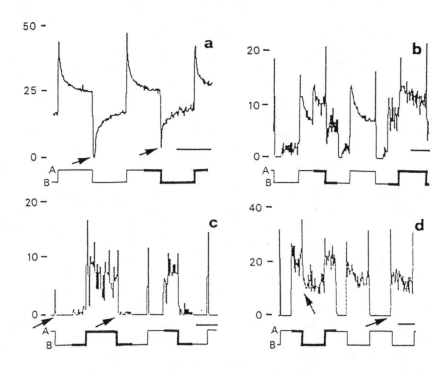

Figure 8: SENSORY TRANSDUCTION. NOISE AND SENSITIVITY. (Fish utricle. Stimulation maintained orientation relative to gravity, and transients from one to the other.)

Depending on the afferent fiber the sensitivity to maintained spatial orientation, is either unaffected (fibers a,b), revealed (c) or inverted (d) by noise. Abscissae, ongoing or running time; ordinate, average rates in successive bins. Bin-widths 1.5 (a,c,d), 2.0s (b); time calibration 1m. Lines underlying records represent spatial orientation, clean (light lines) or with noise (heavy lines); steps represent the double-parabolic transitions. Arrows are alluded to in the text. [39]

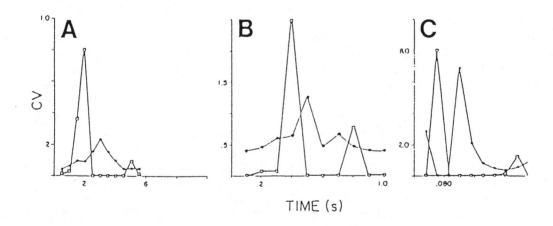

Figure 9: SENSORY TRANSDUCTION. NOISE AND DISCHARGE VARIABILITY. (Crayfish fast adapting stretch receptor organ FAO. Length stimulation sinusoidal at different frequencies).

The variability of the rate in each bin was measured by the coefficient of variation (CV), equal to the ratio of the rate standard deviation to the rate mean as estimated over all cycles. **Non-perturbed open squares; perturbed black circles. Abscissae, time along the cycle; ordinate, CV of the rate in that bin.** *Frequencies and periods: A (.17Hz, 5.731s), B (1.00, .994) and C (3.03, .330) [78].*

311

say, the SAO, by the difference between fully-adapted rates at specified receptor lengths. Noise will modify tonic sensitivity when changing one fully-adapted rate more than the other (e.g., if increasing it when the highest rate increases more; Figure 2-a, SAO). Noise does not modify sensitivity when it either does not alter rates (Figure 8-a) or changes them similarly (b). The statistical significance of the differences may decrease, however, because of increased variability. A special form of increase is that of a phasic receptor that, during clean stimulation and fully-adapted does not fire, but does when perturbed (Figures 1-II, 2-b, FAO; 8-c). *This means that noise moved the stimulus from below to above threshold. Thus, noise revealed an inapparent tonic sensitivity, and shifted the receptor's character from phasic to tonic.* It is possible also, though rare, that noise reverse the response polarity (compare transitions AB at the two arrows in Figure 8-d). The *phasic sensitivity*, i.e., that to higher frequencies and transients, also can be either increased or decreased; e.g. oblique arrows at transitions AB in Figure 8-c). *Changes induced by noise in a particular afferent are not necessarily of one same sign in the tonic and phasic responses, all increases for instance:* disparity is not surprising since different frequency components underlie transients and steady-states.

e. Practically the same stimuli can act upon several receptors simultaneously; this is commonplace in, say, skin, utricle, and retina. **Noise can influence the correlations between the afferent discharges from separate receptors [39]; furthermore, this influence may be stimulus-dependent. Correlations are read by neurons, and thus contribute meaningfully to sensory coding. [56]** The two utricular afferents whose cross- correlation histograms CCHs are in Figure 10 were uncorrelated during clean stimulation. During noisy stimulation and at both orientations A (a) and B (b), the histogram CCH had a periodic profile with evenly separated peaks and troughs, including a peak close to the origin; this reveals a strong tendency to fire periodically and synchronously. There were clear differences between both orientations, however. At orientation A (a), peaks and troughs were outstanding and the central peak was precisely at the origin; this revealed a strong tendency to fire periodically, and as well as a tight locking where spikes were fired simultaneously. Contrastingly, at orientation B (b), peaks and troughs were moderate and the central peak was to the origin's left; this revealed a weaker periodicity and a locking where one afferent led the other.

f. **Stability types.** The theoretical underpinnings of stability types in the utricle are provided by [46]; signals and perturbations were head orientations and loud clicks, respectively. Figure 11 shows that, when stays at a particular orientation where not perturbed (a), marks remained dispersed from the beginning to the end. Contrastingly, when perturbed (b) marks gradually became closer to each other. As explained at length by [46], the estimated boundaries of trajectory ensembles with clean stimulation revealed "simple" stability; i.e., one where trajectories remained bounded throughout. Contrastingly, perturbed ensembles revealed "contractive" stability; i.e., a special simple stability where bounds narrowed with time and at the end were narrower than initially.

The consequences of signal and noise superposition depend on the relation between the features of both. [16] [26] [69] [71] [78] *Fidelity improvement by a given noise, for instance, is greater for stimuli modulated at lower frequencies than for those at higher frequencies.* Modulation frequencies changed along the oblique axis in Figure 4; distortion attenuation was maximal at .2Hz, decreased for 1.0 and 3.0 Hz (see also Figures 1, 3), and deteriorated for 10.0Hz. *The susceptibility of a given signal to noise depends on the features of the latter.* Figure 4 illustrates also that noises whose *frequency components* have a higher cut-off (dashed graph, open circles) simplify sensory transduction more than noises with lower cut-offs (dashed, open circles). Indeed, the Lissajous shift from the clean loop-flat extension (continuous) towards an ellipse is greater and includes more of the cycle. Shifts are particularly noticeable at low stimulation frequencies (0.2, 1.0Hz; see above) at which with sinusoids, square waves, etc. noise can simplify non-linearities. [64]

Noises with different *amplitudes* influence differently the same signal. *Intermediate noise amplitudes are optimal in eliciting many consequences described here.* (e.g., [13] [14] [16] [22] [64] [69]). Indeed, when receptors were driven jointly by superimposed sines and noise, and noise amplitude increased, transduction distortions first decreased and then increased, i.e., fidelity increased to a maximum and then decreased. In Figure 1-I, for instance, noises were greater in C than in B. In Figure 2-I, as the noise superimposed upon the sinusoidal displacement approached an optimal intermediate amplitude along **A-D**, cycle histograms became more sinusoidal. In both series, signals were either not affected by weak noise, or swamped by very strong ones. Others have noted signal-to-noise ratios for several (input) noise amplitudes and found that it increased, peaked at an intermediate value and then decayed. [22] **In short, then, fidelity is enhanced optimally by certain perturbation spectra and amplitudes; we conjecture that this holds also**

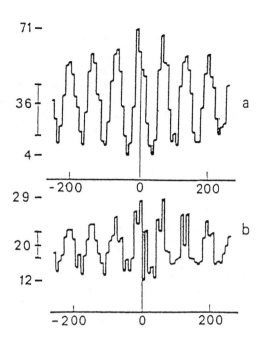

Figure 10: SENSORY TRANSDUCTION. NOISE AND DISCHARGE CORRELATIONS. STIMU-LUS-DEPENDENCY OF THE BETWEEN-DISCHARGE CORRELATION. (Fish utricle. Stimulation maintained orientation relative to gravity).

The two afferents were recorded from the same nerve twig. During the fully-adapted periods at maintained head orientations without noise, their discharges were not correlated. With noise J, discharges were correlated as demonstrated by the cross-correlation CCH peaks, troughs and periodicity. The correlation pattern varied at different orientations **a**, **b** *relative to gravity. CCHs: on abscissae, time from action potential in one cell (bin width 3ms); on ordinate, mean rate in the other cell (/s per reference spike); maximum, minimum and average values listed; vertical bars estimate empirically the 95*

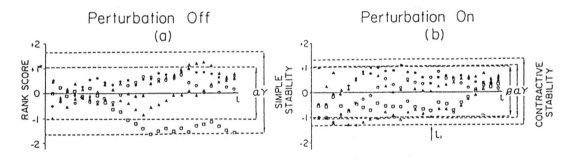

Figure 11: SENSORY TRANSDUCTION. NOISE INFLUENCE ON STABILITY BOUNDS AND TYPES. (Anesthetized cat. utricle. Tonic afferent).

Individually and as a group marks wander throughout the non-perturbed trajectories (a), but tend to cluster centrally in the perturbed one (b). (a) and (b) come from the same first-order sensory afferent. Signal: maintained head orientation in space. Perturbation: loud clicks delivered to the ear on the same side as the afferent. Abscissae: ongoing time from 0 to 28s. Ordinate: rank score based on a normalization of the non-parametric cumulative Kendal statistic for trend detection. Each mark (i.e., open squares, etc.) corresponds to a particular stay at a fixed head position; each mark sequence is referred to as "trajectory;" the fixed position was the same for all stays, clean or perturbed. Special stability boundaries are indicated: α refers to the initial boundaries at time 0; β to those at the "settling time" t_1, the earliest such that all rank scores thereafter had smaller absolute values than at t_1; γ to the maximum across all trajectories such that it included all rank scores. See Theory and Data analysis in [46]. Abscissae and ordinates represent pre- and post-synaptic rates; respectively [46].

for amplitude distributions (e.g., Gaussian vs. uniform). Hence, the kind of noise present in any situation must be always reckoned with.

The *"signal-to-noise ratio"* is the ratio of the magnitude of an interesting waveform to those of uninteresting ones. In this expression, "noise" refers to the entire uninteresting part (i.e., to sense c above), including any component of or reflecting the noise perturbation superimposed deliberately (sense b above),. Comparison of the ratio at the input and the output is an *index of fidelity* for that signal. The ratio can be estimated in several ways, some more meaningful and with wider applicability than others.

CODING ACROSS SYNAPSES

Coding of clean pre-synaptic spike trains into post-synaptic trains is characterized by transferring a broad and physiologically relevant frequency band, by an overall increasing or decreasing relation with E or IPSPs respectively, and by numerous marked distortions (e.g., Figures 12-15, [32] [43] [47] [49] [50] [51] [56] [57] [58] [60] [59]). Local distortions are due to opposite slopes, asymmetric sensitivities to the rate at which pre-synaptic discharges change, hysteresis and saturations at extreme rates. Yet other distortions reflect the fact that different discharge forms arise that are called "locked," "intermittent," "messy erratic" and "messy stammerings." A deterministic chaotic component is recognizable in both messy forms from simulations, but only in erratic forms from crayfish where stammering may be swamped by noise [65] [66] (Sugihara G., Grace D., Stiber M. and Segundo J.P., in preparation). The details of synaptic coding depend on numerous control parameters either pre- or post-synaptic; coding adopts several modes, each within a restricted domai.. defined by particular values of those variables.

Noise attenuates the distortions of synaptic coding, making the evolution along time of pre- and post-synaptic discharges more similar; i.e., noise increases fidelity. This will be discussed for steady-state, modulated discharges and transients.

a. Noise simplifies the relation between a steady-state pre- synaptic train and the corresponding post-synaptic output.

A *"steady-state discharge"* is stationary in the long-term and over many intervals, as well as in the intermediate and short terms over fewer intervals. A discharge is said to exhibit *"fast"* noise when its intervals are dispersed widely and each tells you nothing about the very next ones; it is unpredictable in the short term.

The influence of noise on steady-states was analyzed using pre- synaptic trains with the same averages but increasing degrees of variability, i.e., with increasing noise amplitudes. Specifically, the influence of noise was analyzed using trains whose interval distributions all with the same mean were gammas of orders that decreased from very high to 1 [56]) [32] [33] [47] [50] Thus, arrivals were at the same mean rate but went step by step practically from pacemaker to Poisson; their variabilities, i.e., noisiness, increased concomitantly. Simplification induced by noise involved two main consequences. They imply non trivial issues (e.g., [50]) out of place here. Firstly, noise *smooths the relation between pre- and post-synaptic averages*. Figure 12 illustrates relations (obtained as explained for sensory driving) for an inhibitory synapse. With clean arrivals (regular or pacemaker (**RG large black circles**), graphs have alternating positive and negative slopes; i.e. faster inhibition associates with faster inhibited. As the gamma order decreases and noise increases, the zig-zag attenuates and approaches monotonicity. The shift from zig-zag to monotonicity happens when the coefficient of variation is around .20 (**G.20 open triangles**). Finally when the inhibitory train is very noisy and irregular the relation is simple and monotonic (**P small open circles**). At each pre-synaptic rate, each degree of noise elicits a characteristic post-synaptic rate. All high rates tend to saturate, arresting the post-synaptic cell if inhibitory (as in Figure 12) or driving it maximally if excitatory; clean pacemaker arrivals are much more effective than noisy ones, however.

Simplification by noise involves also *the generalization to all rates of a similarity between pre- and post-synaptic patterns.* Figure 13 shows electrical records of raw experimental data. The spike trains –pre- and post-synaptic in the lower and upper records, respectively– illustrate this to the naked eye. With pre-synaptic noiseless pacemaker patterns, the similarity between corresponding trains depended on the rate. Their patterns were either identical when locked 1:1, or very similar at other locked ratios (Figure 13-**RG-A**) or contrasted clearly when intermittent or messy (**RG-B**); as patterns became noisier, all corresponding discharges became more alike, to the naked eye and statistically though of course not firing at identical

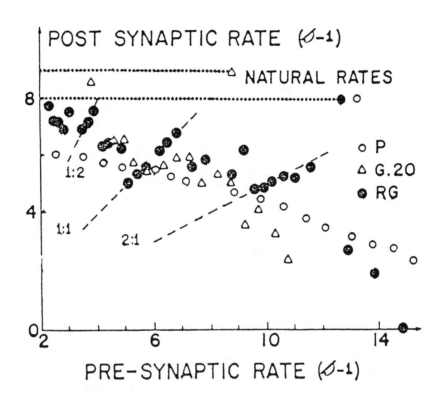

Figure 12: SYNAPTIC CODING. NOISE AND THE SIMPLIFICATION OF THE RELATION BETWEEN CORRESPONDING AVERAGE RATES DURING STEADY STATE INHIBITION. (Inhibitory synapse in crayfish slowly adapting stretch receptor organ SAO. Pre-synaptic discharge steady-state.)

Successive graphs illustrate the consequences of increasing the pre-synaptic noise, i.e., reducing the pre-synaptic periodicity, as measured by the corresponding interval coefficients of variation (standard deviation/average). RG large black circles, clean pacemaker with all intervals practically identical (CV almost 0); G.20 open traingles, intermediately noisy with gamma-distributed independent intervals (CVs .20, etc.); P small open circle, noisy Poisson-like with exponentially-distributed independent intervals. Abscissae pre-synaptic rate, ordinate post-synaptic rate. Horizontal dotted line post-synaptic rate without inhibition. Oblique broken lines indicate ratio of pre- to post- synaptic spikes; their reciprocals 2, 1, 1/2 are the slopes [32].

315

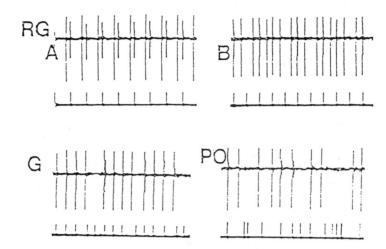

Figure 13: SYNAPTIC CODING. NOISE AND THE GENERALIZATION OF THE SIMILARITY BETWEEN CORRESPONDING DISCHARGES DURING STEADY-STATE INHIBITION (Inhibitory synapse in crayfish slowly adapting stretch receptor organ SAO. Pre-synaptic discharge steady-state.) *Frames provide brief samples of the* inhibitory (lower record) *and the* inhibited (upper record) *discharges.* Pre-synaptic discharges regular, clean or pacemaker RG; *each rate produces either (*A*) a locked 1:1 similar pattern (in this case identical), or (*B*) an irregular clearly different pattern.* Noisy patterns G, PO: *as arrivals became more irregular, all pairs of corresponding discharges became statistically more similar;* G, *gamma-distributed intervals whose coefficient of variation is 0.20;* PO, *exponentially distributed intervals coefficient of variation close to 1.0 [32].*

instants (G). With the quasi-Poisson arrivals pre- and post-synaptic discharges differed little, particularly when their rates were close (PO). Simplification was gradual: the non-monotonic relations and the lockings persisted up to coefficients of variation around 0.20 (Figures 12-G, 13-G).

b. **Noise simplifies the relation between a modulated pre- synaptic train and the corresponding post-synaptic output.** [59] [58] [57]

A *"modulated discharge,"* is stationary in the long-term, but its intervals fluctuate periodically so that many successive intervals correlate predictably; it thus is not stationary in the intermediate-term. Superposing fast noise upon modulated trains leads to short-term unpredictability plus predictability in the intermediate- and long-term.

Figure 14 includes slow modulations (1/30Hz). In the clean case (A the pre-synaptic marks (small dots) follow tightly the imposed sinusoidal form. The post-synaptic marks (triangles) do not, composing a highly distorted mapping that includes multiple groups, with several shapes, orientations and tightnesses, The noisy case B, on the other hand, displays pre- and post-synaptic marks both of which, though scattered, follow roughly sinusoidal profiles. Peaks in one coincide with troughs in the other (phase opposition). Pre-synaptic cycle histograms with sine forms are mapped, when modulations are clean, into distorted post-synaptic sines. Lissajous displays of average cycle histograms, pre-synaptic on abscissae and post-synaptic on ordinates, are non-monotonic and have loops (Figure 15-a). Different distortions are apparent with low A or high B modulation frequencies: "low" or "high" implies frequencies either much smaller or barely smaller than the usual average firing rates around 8/s. *Fidelity improvement is optimal with low frequency modulations, but deteriorates as frequency increases and disappears with high ones.* When modulations are noisy and at low frequencies, sines can map into acceptable sines (inverted). Lissajous (Figure 15-A-b) approximate the more or less flattened ellipses of linear mappings. Contrastingly, high frequency noisy modulations (B-b) retain the major distortions of the clean case.

c. **Noise simplifies the relation between pre-synaptic transients and the corresponding post-synaptic output.** [55] (Segundo J.P., Stiber M. Altshuler E. and Vibert J-F., unpublished) Transients pervade everyday life, arising at the beginning and the end or steady-states, along modulations, and so forth. Hence, they have undeniable physiological significance. A *transient* is a discharge with a trend [55]

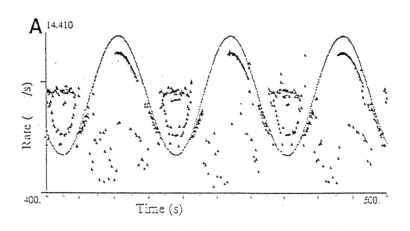

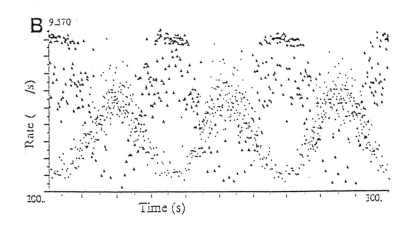

Figure 14: SYNAPTIC CODING. NOISE AND THE SIMPLIFICATION OF THE RELATION BETWEEN CORRESPONDING AVERAGE RATES DURING MODULATED INHIBITION. (Inhibitory synapse in crayfish slowly adapting stretch receptor organ SAO. Pre-synaptic discharge modulated sinusoidally.) A *CLEAN.* B *NOISY.* Each graph comes from a stationary portion; *each mark corresponds to a spike pre- (dots) or post- (triangles) synaptic (abscissae time of occurrence, ordinate preceding interval) [57].*

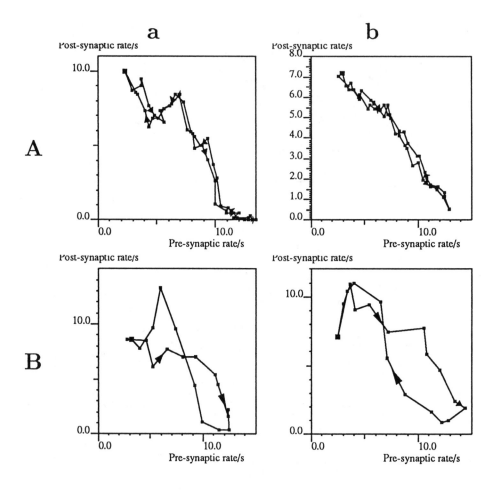

Figure 15: SYNAPTIC CODING. NOISE AND DIFFERENT MODULATION FREQUENCIES. LISSAJOUS DISPLAYS. (Inhibitory synapse in crayfish slowly adapting stretch receptor organ SAO. Pre-synaptic discharge modulated sinusoidally.)

Both post-synaptic **clean modulations (A,B-a)** *show an alternation of positive, negative and 0 slopes; the high frequency graph (*B-a*) has several hysteretic loops. The* **noisy low frequency modulation graph (A-b)** *suggests a practically linear in-phase mapping. The* **noisy high frequency modulation (B-b)** *retains its distortions, hysteretic loops included. Abscissae pre-synaptic cycle histogram; ordinate corresponding post-synaptic cycle histogram. The average pre- synaptic inhibitory modulation and the natural post-synaptic SAO discharges differed little between corresponding clean and noisy cases [59].*

(Segundo J.P., Stiber M. Altshuler E. and Vibert J.-F., unpublished). Figure 16 illustrates the post-synaptic consequences of a pre-synaptic transient in the form of a half- sine; both clean **I** and noisy **II** transients showed practically the same peri-stimulus histograms (**a**). The clean, transient was everywhere smooth, monotonic, and uniform; the noisy one had rapid ongoing fluctuationns. The post-synaptic response to the clean transient **I-b** had obvious non-monotonicites (arrows), absent in that to the noisy transient **II-b**, an acceptable average reproduction of the driver's mirror image.

When generated by many weak terminals converging upon a single neuron, synaptic noise assumes a particularly significant role; between-terminal correlations, important at any synaptic strength, become meaningful in a special manner [48] [54] [57]. Sets of weak converging terminals are found throughout the nervous system (e.g., Ia spindle afferents on motoneurons, parallel fibers on Purkinje cells). Figure 17 illustrates schematically the cases described below. Insets simply indicate general features by exaggerating them; e.g., the totally different insets in a. indicate that terminals have independent discharges, the identical ones in b. indicate synchronous discharges, etc. *The influence of a set of numerous weak terminals depends critically on the correlation between the individual discharges.* The conditions required by what follows are not unduly restrictive from a physiological viewpoint; conditions include comparable individual rates, moderate interactions, plus compensation of the individual weakness by the number of terminals (and vice-versa). *When the separate terminals show no correlations between their discharges, the joint influence of the set resembles a noise whose amplitude and frequencies depend on their synaptic strength, number and summed rates; the joint influence is largely independent of the pattern of the individual discharges (i.e., pacemaker, bursty, etc.).* If the individual terminals become weaker but their number increases, the average value of the noise changes little but its dispersion decreases; when terminals are sufficiently weak and numerous, the noise departs little from an invariant DC bias. The post-synaptic cell responds accordingly: e.g., if EPSPs are involved and the post-synaptic neuron is tonic, the output train will be less and less irregular, tending to a pacemaker discharge. Figure 17-**a** represents this schematically.

When the separate terminals tend to fire synchronously, the joint influence of the set resembles that of a single stronger terminal. Consequences depend on the arrival amplitudes, number, and rates, as well as on the patterns of the individual discharges. Resemblance increases as synchrony becomes tighter. E.g., a particular pre-synaptic modulation will have similar post-synaptic consequences when involving a set of weak terminals or a single powerful one, as illustrated by Figure 17-**b** and **c**; coding will be distorted similarly in both.

Distortions of clean low frequency modulations are simplified by superimposed fast noises. One set of terminals –either a single strong terminal or many correlated weak ones– may produce the low frequency signal. A separate set of many weak terminals firing independently may provide the noise (Figure 17-**d** and **e**). **We conjecture [57] that, in addition, both signal and noise may arise in one same terminal set where discharges are coherent at the low frequency but independent at the high ones that induce the noise (Figure 17-f).**

OUTLINE OF FORMAL NOTIONS.

Experimentalists and modelers are always confronted with noise from several sources. Certain general notions concerning noise are fundamental and must be kept in mind. For example, the term can have several meanings of which some were listed above. Furthermore, measurements performed on the same object at different times may not yield the same values, partly because measurement precision is finite, partly for other reasons. There is a close relation between "noise" in its several senses and the observer's knowledge of the system. This in turn relates to repercussions between the different levels at which observations are carried out. This level is implicit in the choice of target system and therefore of measurement and analysis tools.

In general, a system is a whole defined at one observation level and composed of sub-systems or parts at another level. Parts usually are in large numbers, and measurements on the system provide values in some sense integrated across those sub-systems. The variations of the individual sub-systems appear in the overall system as fluctuations that much of the time are small; this holds regardless of whether the variations of the parts are determined and predictable. When they are not, the integrated signal contains an unpredictable component; this component may be considered as noise, in the sense of an unsystematic, unpredictable dispersion (see *a.* above). ("Prediction" refers to our capacity to forecast the future evolution of a signal

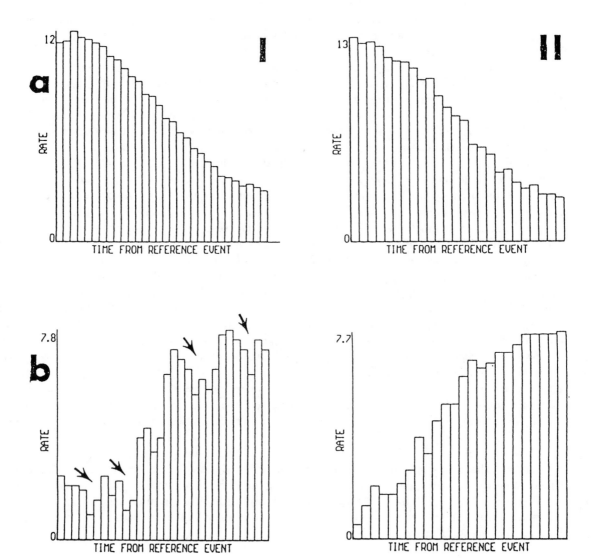

Figure 16: SYNAPTIC CODING. NOISE AND THE SIMPLIFICATION OF THE RELATION BETWEEN CORRESPONDING AVERAGE RATES DURING TRANSIENTS.

On the average, as illustrated by the peri-stimulus histograms, the pre-synaptic transients a *were the same practically the same slowing half-sines both clean* I-a *and with noise* II-a. *Individually, however, individual transients departed little from the average in the clean case and markedly in the noisy case. The corresponding average post-synaptic transients* b *had the opposite overall trends in both cases. The clean case* I-b *showed marked deviations from the driver half-sine, involving non- monotonicities indicated by arrows. The noisy case* II-b, *on the other hand was a good approximation to a mirror image of the half-sine. (Segundo, J.P., Stiber, M., and Vibert, J.-F., unpublished).*

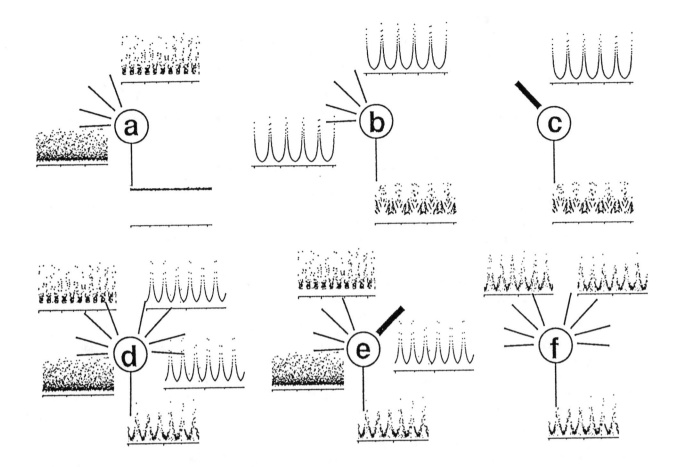

Figure 17: SYNAPTIC CODING. SET OF NUMEROUS WEAK TERMINALS CONVERGING UPON A SINGLE NEURON. CORRELATION BETWEEN DISCHARGES IN SEPARATE TERMINALS. NOISE. *See text. Schematic representation of a single post-synaptic neuron (circle), and its set of pre-synaptic terminals (converging lines). The set includes either many terminals (only four are represented) that individually have weak synaptic effects (thin lines, a,b,d-f) or a single one with intermediate effects (thick line c,e). The inserts are intended to represent spike discharges schematically; they are basic graphs with ongoing time on the abscissae and inter-spike intervals on the ordinate [50]. The pre-synaptic discharges are represented by the basic graphs in the upper part of each component portion. The weak terminals fire independently in the left-hand sets of d,e or dependently in b where all are modulated periodically; in f discharges correlate at low frequencies but are independent at high frequencies. The intermediate terminal is modulated periodically always. The output of the post-synaptic neuron is represented by the basic graph in the lower part of each component portion, close to the axon of the post-synaptic neuron.*

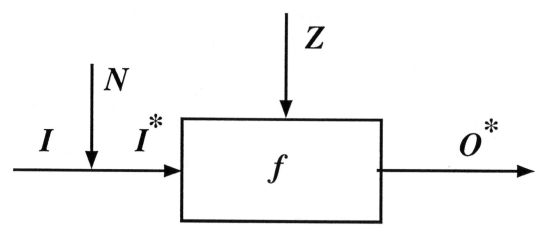

Figure 18: CODING A NOISY INPUT

I* represents the input to the system. It is the sum of a determined signal I and of a noise N. f is the transfer operator of the unit, it contains the influence of internal noise Z. The output O* is a stochastic variable. Information is extracted from this variable by various computation methods.

using knowledge about the past and present.) The experimenter targeting the whole system may discard, or ignore these fluctuations, judging them noise in the sense of an uninteresting part of the measurement (*c.* above).

As all others, scientists interested in the nervous system are confronted with noise and can approach their target at different levels. One level, for example, concerns membrane and their mechanisms (e.g. ions, pumps, gates, channels, receptors etc.). Patch clamp recordings have clarified a great deal about all this; however, transitions between closed and open channels and gates may involve intermediate molecular states not detected by the recordings. This lack of knowledge introduces a measure of uncertainty; models attempt to reflect it by appealing to Markov chains (probabilistic approach to uncertainty) or fractal concepts (deterministic approach) (e.g. [28][4]).

Experiments surveyed in this chapter were at the level of nerve cells, sensory receptors and synapses. Hence, at an observation level that differs from that just mentioned of membranes proper. *Figure 18 represents schematically the implicit conceptual context and experimental setup*, and thus will be useful for the present considerations.

The nerve cell is represented by a "black box" or system, considered essentially non- linear. It receives an *input* I on which an *external noise* N (see below) is superimposed. Z represents *internal noise* (see below). The *noisy input* I* and the *output* O* are studied by a variety of computational methods. The relation between them implies the *transfer function or operator f of the system in the presence of noise*.

Electrical events as receptor potentials, PSPs and spikes integrate and reflect the activity of the many entities involved in firing, transduction, and synaptic transmission and fluctuate because of them, as discussed above. For example, synaptic currents and PSPs will fluctuate because of the unpredictable switching of channels and gates and because of the random character of quantal neurotransmitter release that follows specific probabilistic laws (e.g., [23] [34]). All these fluctuations can be neglected when small compared to the targeted events. (One should keep in mind however, that even small causes may be influential when happening close to threshold.) These and other sources of noise at neuronal and lower levels affect spike discharge timings, adding a stochastic component to their dynamics. In 1977, Holden [29]] surveyed exhaustively and critically noises at these levels, as well as the relevant modelling approaches associated with each category. These fluctuations contribute to noise in either transduction, synaptic transmission or spike generation and are intrinsic to the preparation; hence, they are sources of an *"internal"* noise (Z in Figure 18).

The behavior of individual neurons (first-order afferent, post-synaptic) in the presence of external noise is the topic of this paper. It can can be studied formally using models; e.g., in integrate and fire and Hodgkin-Huxley models noise linearizes the transfer function between a constant depolarizing input and the mean stationary firing rate. [80] In living cells (see above), noise simplifies receptor and synaptic mappings.

In particular, *neurons in central networks* often integrate arrivals from many terminals; when moderately weak, numerous and uncorrelated they create a background noisy synaptic activity that contributes to the post-synaptic discharge (see above and Figure 17). It has been suggested [24] that such synaptic backgrounds generated by excitatory terminals are necessary for the ongoing activity of central networks involved in the control of, say, respiration and sleep-waking cycles. Modeled excitatory networks [77] where each neuron received some background noise can give rise to robust tonic or phasic activities of several kinds. In both cases noise provided a background excitatory bias that, when present in a network with a favorable connectivity, allowed certain outputs. Modeled results in particular showed that the specifics of the outputs reflected the properties of the component units and the overall connectivity, inter-neuronal delays being quite critical; they depended little on the details of the noise. Many workers have in fact modeled noisy network activity, including stochastic variation of synaptic weights [6]. Methods from statistical physics and field theory have been applied to analyze the behavior of networks made of simple stochastic units [2]. This paragraph offers a very brief view of the wide and active field of noise in a network.

It should be pointed out also that an external noise provides the basis of *procedures for non-linear system identification*. The Volterra-Wiener approach (e.g. [41]) imposes a Gaussian white-noise continuous input and estimates the orthogonal components of the transfer function. This was applied to receptors and nerve cells (e.g., [12] [10]). Noise in the form of pseudo-random binary sequences served to identify transduction in semicircular canals, as well as the mechanisms of vestibulo-ocular reflexes in experimental and clinical contexts. [45] [46] Auxiliary signals are useful for detection of operational characteristics in systems with static non-linearities. [63] A method comparable to the Volterra-Wiener's uses Poisson inputs for identification of point process systems, and has been applied to synaptic coding [7].

The single nerve cell –first-order afferent at a receptor, post- synaptic at a synapse– generates the output spike train that reflects inputs that are either a sensory stimulus or an arriving spike train. The corresponding input-output relation is the *sensory or synaptic "coding"*, and its rules constitute the "code". [56] Such codings are noisy, internally and externally. *Hence the nerve cell must be considered as a noisy, potentially imperfect signal-processing element that must be able to process noisy signals.* Noise can reduce the reliability of each unit, of course; that this is not always the case is the main theme of this chapter. "Reliability" refers to the capacity to discriminate between distinct inputs by the characteristics of their respective outputs.

The activities of neurons, receptors and synapses displays the complex dynamical features associated with non-linear systems. Methods originally developed for such dynamics are used more and more for the description and interpretation of physiological data and modelling. **Noisy perturbations affect the behavior of dynamical systems in many ways. The following lists some changes noise may induce in non-linear systems when delivered during stationary behaviors. It is an introduction to the background that the neurosciences must appeal to when looking for a formal context to understand past results and plan future lines of research. It is, we feel, a very significant part of this outline.**

1. The simplest stationary behavior is that whose attractor is an *asymptotically stable equilibrium point.* The latter is approached by all trajectories starting within a specific neighborhood that surrounds the point and is called its "basin". As long as perturbations do not dislodge trajectories from this basin, these remain around the equilibrium point; *noise of sufficiently low amplitude can therefore be neglected (theoretically at least though perhaps not in practice). 2.* Somewhat less simple behaviors involve attractors called *stable limit cycles.* As long as perturbations do not dislodge trajectories from the corresponding basin, they remain close to the limit cycle. However, and contrary to the former case, *low amplitude noise still can distort stable limit cycles, and thus cannot be neglected off-hand.* Kurrer and Shulten [35] analyzed the distortions induced by a weak Gaussian white noise in limit cycle trajectories of the Bonhoeffer-van der Pol model. The injected noise at any given time; i.e. at any given point on the limit cycle, had the same distribution in all directions around the corresponding point on the noise-free cycle; furthermore, noise distributions were the same at all points around the cycle. Result showed that at any given time the state of the perturbed system also followed a Gaussian distribution centered appropriately. Two striking differences were noted, however. First, at any given time, the amplitude distribution was not the same in all directions around the noise-free cycle. Second, these distributions were not the same at all points around the cycle. They call attention, for example, to a steady diffusion-like increase along the cycle in the dispersion of the perturbed trajectories around the corresponding points. Because of the attractor's stability, the average distribution of the trajectories remains the same on a plane orthogonal to the limit cycle. This was called quasi-stationary behavior. This is remindful of the point made earlier that just as meaningful may be the influence of the fast noise on the signal as the converse. In the system represented by the logistic map noise induces a *transition from a periodic state to a chaotic state.* [42]

3. Chaotic attractors are a third kind. Current investigations reveal different interactions between noise and chaotic dynamics. *a.* In the first place when examined also in the logistic map noise can simply *make chaos look more random* and disorderly (e.g. [42]) *b.* In other cases, noise has the opposite effect, referred to as "noise-induced order". In these cases noise has the following consequences. (e.g. [21]). *i.* A sharp peak appears in the power spectrum, i.e., a certain frequency component becomes outstanding. The similarity between the theoretical notion and the experimental data reviewed above, where noise enhanced slower signal fidelity is self-evident. *ii.* The positive Lyapounov exponent changes sign and becomes negative, another aspect of increased order. *iii.* Entropy decreases as the noise level increases. This entropy measures the uncertainty about the system being in a particular state. *iv.* The mutual information decreases exponentially as the lag increases. In the absence of noise it decreases in an oscillatory way. The mutual information refers to the prediction as to where the system will be in the future, after a particular lag, given its present state; it decreases as the future becomes more remote.

The following is one example that illustrates how noise can modify the global picture of system behavior and bifurcations, as represented in its bifurcation diagram. I.e., illustrates how noise changes the system's dependence on its control parameters. In this model, [38] the addition of a tiny amount of noise replaces a period doubling cascade to chaos by a noisy periodic orbit, stable across a wide range of parameters. *Interactions between chaos and noise have been reported for models of biological phenomena.* A model for population dynamics in interacting sub-populations [1] takes into account migration and perturbations; each segment evolves according to the logistic or Ricker equations. Without noise and when chaotic dynamics are present, sub-populations may reach low levels simultaneously, and thus imply the population's extinction. If appropriate noises were included, they combined with the segmentation to destroy correlations and avoid extinction. A model of vagal control of respiratory rhythms (applicable to synaptic driving) reproduced well observations on anesthetized cats. Respiration was driven by a ventilatory pump at several periods. When the animal was deeply anesthetized, the respiration was entrained with a 1:1 relationship between pump period and respiratory period, for a given pump period range. Outside this range a 2:1, 3:1, etc... locking were observed, and the graph of respiratory period versus pump period presented the charactistic zig-zag pattern observed in crayfish experiments shown in Fig. 12 (filled circles). When the anesthesia vanished, the locking was difficult to obtain, and the same graph presented a regular negative slope, as in Fig. 12 (open circles). Anesthesia decreases the number of active neurons in the central regions wherin is located a part of the respiratory centers, and thus decreases the respiration unrelated information representing noise arriving on respiratory related units [74]. A computer model developped to test this hypothesis confirmed the linearizing property of the noise in this given situation. [75]

When several basins are present and share boundaries, noise can produce complex behaviors, shifting the state of the system from one basin to another. Because of this several different stationary behaviors succeed one another under invariant drivings. This overall behaviors was called "hopping" [3]; it is encountered in periodically inhibited pacemaker neurons [50]. A special case of hopping arises when the system is bistable, that is has two stable equilibrium states.

"Stochastic resonance" refers to the noise-induced increase in the signal to noise ratio in a bistable system subject to sub-threshold modulation. The expression was first coined by in the study of climatic evolutions, [5], and compatible phenomena have been observed since in many physical systems. The theory and its applications to the neurosciences have been reviewed recently. [11] [44]

Up to this point only noise and stationary states have been considered. Non-equilibrium systems, and transient behaviors also display sensitivity to noise though studied much less frequently. (e.g. [36]), [55] More studies are needed to clarify these effects. Results obtained may be of high interest for the study of nervous systems, which operate in transitory regimes in a perturbed environment. All models presented in the previous paragraphs are deterministic under stochastic perturbations, and represent stochastic differential equations. It should be added that the numerical analysis of stochastic differential equations differs from that of ordinary differential equations. For a review and more details on this topic see [31]. A deterministic system is one where the trajectory in state space is completely determined by the initial conditions; trajectories not cross, merge or branch. This constraint on the dynamics can be removed, however, and the systems thus obtained are not rigorously deterministic in the above sense. The simplest case arises when there is a singular point in the state space. In one example, [20] all trajectories reach in finite time a singular point. At such a point, therefore, the entire history of any single trajectory is lost, and it becomes impossible to determine the initial condition from which it started. The singular point is not, however, an attracting point, and trajectories escape from it. The escape is controlled by noise and therefore gives rise to distinct trajectories. Such dynamics have also been applied to design artificial neural networks [81].

GENERAL CONSIDERATIONS.

The natural operation of sensory receptors and of synapses in vivo is perturbed by a variety of factors that are both unavoidable and unceasing. Important sources of perturbations are, among others, the multiplicity of the stimuli that act on each receptor (including those produced by displacements of the receptors themselves), and of the influences that impinge upon each neuron (including those from other pre-synaptic terminals). **The study of perturbed sensory and synaptic mappings thus has clearcut physiological implications.** It has always been obvious that noise in any context could be a nuisance, and often was. A long time ago it was considered invariably undesirable, unless it was weak and inconsequential. Several years ago, however, physiologists decided legitimately that the subject deserved more careful exploration. The only valid approach was empirical, of course, and therefore experiments where natural perturbations were mimicked by noise became an indispensable complement to the usual sterilized analyses where interferences are avoided.

From the very beginning –decades ago– it became obvious that noise was not always either deleterious or innocuous, and can in fact benefit signal transmission. Demonstrated first by communication engineers (e,g., [62]), the notion was extended immediately to processing by nerve cells. **A wave of biological publications of long standing has made explicit that natural perturbations are ubiquitous and therefore relevant to neural function, and has analyzed the essential biological consequences of noise, both theoretically and experimentally.** In sensory neurophysiology and in the late 'sixties, Spekreijse and collaborators were the first to demonstrate that noise benefitted sensory transduction, if matched appropriately to the signal; their initial study was in goldfish retinae and noise was referred to as "auxiliary stimulation. [63] [64] This seminal discovery was confirmed not long after when noise was tested successively on insect mechanoreceptors and fish utricles. [26] [39] In the 'seventies and 'eighties, a substantial number of publications extended knowledge about noise and sensory processing even further. In the field of synaptology, the influence of a fast noise on a slower signal was reported explicitly in 1976; [58] the issue of regularity vs. variability had been discussed for years (e.g., [43]). Theoretical notions are available in biological journals since the 'sixties (e.g., [64] [67] [68] [72]). **These publications demonstrated convincingly i. that striking differences exist between clean and noisy drivings of either receptors or synapses, ii. that the influence of noise assumes several forms, and iii. that such influences are contingent on the relation between the stimulus and the noise.** The actual list of relevant publications can start no later than the list included here, nor include fewer references.

A contemporary renewal of interest in experimental and theoretical analyses of noise in general and of its consequences includes relevant biological observations that deal with either receptors or synapses (e.g., [14] [22] [37] [61] [59] [57] [60] [73]). Some mutual neglect exists between publications; it is regrettable and should have been avoided. It becomes less forgivable as time spans lengthen and ignored lists become broaden, and priority claims explicit or implied are more fabricated.

As shown, noise has several significant consequences. Needless to say, each is contingent on many issues relating to the target preparation as well as to noise and signal. Their functional implications obviously depend on the entity and effect, and cannot be covered extensively. Noise can *improve fidelity;* i.e., increase the resemblance between sensory or synaptic inputs and the corresponding output discharges. This, as pointed out, has been known since the 'sixties. Hence, stating that traditionally noise was viewed as exclusively detrimental, [22] must refer to epochs prior to the abundant literature readily available since the 'sixties. It is useful to keep in mind that fidelity, though often important biologically, need not always be so [57]. Other significant consequences of noise are *altering averages, dispersions, stability types and correlations between terminals.* Noise also affects *the sensitivity of sensory transduction,* increasing, decreasing or reversing its tonic and/or phasic aspects, not necessarily both in the same way. In certain instances, a first-order afferent does not respond to certain stimuli when clean but does when perturbed by noise (e.g., Figures 1-II, 2-b, FAO; 8-c); sensitivity is thus enhanced and revealed, with sub-threshold stimuli becoming supra- threshold and thus detectable. This can imply the shift of the afferent's character from phasic to tonic.

Reiterated briefly will be certain **functional implications** Namely, that the induced changes in correlations between separate terminals are stimulus-dependent and, being legible to the single nerve cell, are important for neural coding, and ii. that noise in multiple converging weak terminals plays significant roles in network operation. [39] [54] Added will be two other implications. The first [26] [69] is based on demonstrations in living and simulated preparations that, for each range of sensory stimulus frequency and amplitude, there is an intermediate level of noise in the afferent neurons that minimizes distortions and optimizes transmission of information. This optimum is higher the closer the stimulus frequency is to the natural discharge of the afferent. Hence, high discharge variability is more useful in cells submitted to rapidly changing stimuli; this, the authors point out, is current in nature where cochlear and fast-adapting skin neurons have more irregular discharges than those of muscle spindles and slowly-adapting skin neurons. A similar notion is expressed by [64]. Other functional implications [14] involve noisily-modulated bistable systems, discharges in some sensory pathways (e.g., from fast-adapting neurons), their possible modulation of noisiness during sleep- wakefulness, and potential participation in interesting bistable psycho-physical phenomena.

Also beyond the scope of this paper is the detailed discussion of the *issues that underlie the influence of noise.* Noise can reflect input from other receptors or converging terminals, interferences at the level of transducer process, synapses proper or encoder, revealed by fluctuations in receptor potential, PSP magnitude, threshold, etc. [23][34] Some of these are reducible in principle but perhaps not easily in practice by experimental means (e.g., by eliminating or monitoring other inputs). Other perturbations (e.g., thermal agitation) hard to reduce even in principle, represent randomness in a more fundamental sense. Their identification in terms of specific physical variables in a particular receptor or synapse obviously is contingent on the entity, and cannot be identical for all receptors and synapses. The relevant literature is vast and disparate. In the utricle [46] [79], for instance, the jelly-like material supporting the otoliths and the wet-sand character of the latter can create non-linear mechanical forces that, as stiction and viscosity, induce multiple quasi-equilibrium states. The otolith membrane reinforces this, acting as a distributed system with separate non-linearly elastic elements moving somewhat independently. The function of the receptor hair-cells is anything but simple. [30] The utricle thus could reconcile the conflicting demands of an exquisite sensitivity required by skilled performance and a low sensitivity required by a large acceleration range. In formal terms, on the other hand, influential issues can be identified satisfactorily for many cases. For instance, simplification can be attributed to interactions between the high frequency components of the perturbation and the low ones of the signal, the respective powers being crucial. An asymmetric sensitivity to the rate of stimulus change with time is present often, and strongly influential; [16] [17] [46] [49] [58] its importance in general was postulated many years ago by Clynes. [15]

Practical and didactic considerations imposed upon this chapter yet other restrictions; two will be commented on briefly. First, noise in *networks more complicated than sensory receptors or synapse* –from the recurrent inhibitions or excitations to large ensembles– has a significance that needs no stressing (see above and [19] [25] [40] [76] [77]). Second, interest need not always concentrate on "slow signal, fast noise" interactions, but may target *the converse "fast signal, slow noise" situation.* E.g., when interested in the detection by the utricle of fast vibrations at different head orientations.

In short, noise is an inevitable and strongly influential aspect of the normal operation of nervous systems. Since attention was called to it in the 'sixties by Spekreijse and collaborators, [63] [64]) numerous publications have pointed out that sensory receptors and neurons are bombarded unavoidably in vivo by multiple stimuli; this justified the physiological importance of noise. Experimental and/or theoretical publications also demonstrated experimentally the following essentials. *i.* Noise does in fact influence sensory and synaptic coding. *ii.* Noise has several consequences; e..g, reducing non-linear distortions and improving fidelity in average and individual cycles, changing, revealing or inverting receptor sensitivities, etc. *iii.* Consequences are contingent on the relative features of the signal and the noise.

The biological reality mandates certain tenets that cannot be ignored when emitting value judgments, when searching for meaningful questions, and so forth For example, if sensory stimuli are involved, the range considered should include all those arising in everyday life, even if occasionally some subset or non- physiological ones may be relevant. [48] Stochastic resonance mimics well the discharges of cells whose intervals are integral multiples of a particular value, and the improvement of the signal-to-noise ratio of sub- threshold stimuli [11] [44] It also excludes explicitly supra-threshold stimuli (e.g., [11] [27]. From a biological viewpoint (i.e., physiological, psycho-physical, etc.) signal-to-noise ratio improvement is interesting always, both when revealing sub-liminal stimuli and regardless of the afferent discharges pattern (e.g. see Figures 1-**II**, 2-b, 8-c), and when making the no less significant supra-threshold ones more recognizable. *Therefore, the biological domain within which stochastic resonance can be applied does not cover entirely that where living receptors perform; furthermore, the excluded portion includes important situations. These two features impose bounds on the biological value of stochastic resonance.* A theory that covered the entire range of sub- and supra-threshold stimuli that pervade everyday life would have a broader, more meaningful domain of applicability, and be more valuable for physiologists. Even better yet in physiological terms would be theories that, in addition to fidelity improvement in the entire range, explained other noise-induced consequences (see above). So that this is not misinterpreted, we add our agreement with those who believe stochastic resonance to be an important theoretical construct with many significant applications in the practical sciences already, and more are to come.

Clearly, the role of noise in neural coding is a multi- disciplinary subject; it has attracted, and profited by, the joint contribution of several experimental and formal approaches. A balanced perspective, useful for any scientific endeavor, is particularly desirable (though it may be harder to achieve) when, as here, viewpoints are multiple and reflect disparate backgrounds. Needed, obviously, is a first evaluation based on the entire picture and all disciplines. This overall evaluation, though very necessary, is not sufficient. Just as important is one enunciated after extraction of the chapter from the multi-disciplinary context, and voiced in strictly biological terms. Indeed, when attempting a balanced perspective of noise and neural coding, evaluations based on strictly biological criteria are indispensable ingredients. Biologically, then, this research endeavor, finding a rationale in the natural history of everyday life, generating over decades a coherent set of experimental observations, and drawing sensible biological conclusions, has demonstrated a life of its own and delineated a clearcut identity. *Judged as such, detached from other viewpoints and independent of otherwise significant considerations, noise and neuronal processing stands by itself as a self contained, genuine and significant chapter in the Physiology of the Nervous System.* It goes without saying that parallel theoretical developments provided indispensable conceptual frameworks for understanding formal issues, for planning further experimental approaches, and so forth.

Acknowledgments

This work was supported by Trent H. Wells jr. Inc.

References

[1] J.C. Allen, W.M. Schaffer and D. Rosko, "Chaos reduces species extinction by amplifying local population noise", *Nature*, vol. 364, pp. 229–232, 1993.

[2] D.J. Amit, *Modelling Brain Function, The World of Attractor Neural Networks*, Cambridge: Cambridge University Press, 1989.

[3] F.T. Arecchi and A. Califano, "Low frequency hopping phenomena in a nonlinear system with many attractors", *Physics Letters A*, vol. 101, pp. 443–446,1984.

[4] F.G. Ball and J.A. Rice, "Stochastic models for ion channels", *Mathematical Biosciences*, vol. 112, pp. 189–206, 1992.

[5] R. Benzi, G. Parisi, A. Sutera and A. Vulpiani, "Stochastic resonance in climatic change", *Tellus*, vol. 34, pp. 10–16, 1982.

[6] P.C. Bressloff and J.G. Taylor, "Discrete time leaky integrator network with synaptic noise", *Neural Networks*, vol. 4, pp. 789–801, 1991.

[7] D.R. Brillinger, "The identification of point process systems", *Annals of Probability,*vol. 3, pp. 909–924, 1975.

[8] D.R. Brillinger, H.L. Bryant Jr. and J.P. Segundo, "Identification of synaptic operators", *Biological Cybernetics*, vol. 22, pp. 213–228, 1973.

[9] D.R. Brillinger and A. Villa, "Examples of the investigation of neural information processing by point process analysis", In *Advanced methods of physiological system modelling*, vol. 3, Ed. V. Marmarelis, New York: Plenum, in the press.

[10] H.L. Bryant and J.P. Segundo, "Spike initiation by transmembrane current: a white-noise analysis", *Journal of Physiology (London)*, vol. 260, pp 279–314, 1976.

[11] A.R. Bulsara, "Noise and nonlinearity in sensory neurons", in *Proceedings of the meeting on: Fluctuations and Order: New Synthesis*, Los-Alamos 09–12 September 1993, in press.

[12] W. Buño, J. Bustamante and J. Fuentes, "White-noise analysis of pace-maker response interrations and non-linearities in slowly adapting crayfish stretch receptors", *Journal of Physiology (London)*, vol. 350, pp. 55–80, 1984.

[13] W. Buño, J. Fuentes and J.P. Segundo, "Crayfish stretch receptor organs: effects of length steps with and without perturbations", *Biological Cybernetics*, vol. 31, pp. 99–110, 1978.

[14] D.R. Chialvo and A.V. Apkarian, "Modulated noisy biological dynamics: three examples", *Journal of Statistical Physics*, vol. 70, pp. 375–391, 1993.

[15] M. Clynes, "Unidirectional rate sensitivity: a biocybernetic law of reflex and humoral systems as physiologic channels of control and communications", *Annals of the New York Academy of Science*, vol. 92, pp. 946–969, 1961.

[16] O. Diez Martìnez, *Fast-adapting stretch receptor: periodic and steady-state stimulation with and without perturbation*, Thesis UCLA, 1981.

[17] O. Diez Martìnez, A.F. Kohn and J.P. Segundo,"Pervasive locking, saturation, asymmetric rate sensitivity and double-valuedness in crayfish stretch receptors", *Biological Cybernetics*, vol. 49, pp. 33–44, 1983.

[18] O. Diez Martìnez, R. Pérez, R. Budelli and J.P. Segundo, "Locking, intermittency and bifurcations in regularly driven pacemaker neurons. Poincaré mappings and biological implications", *Biological Cybernetics*, vol. 60, pp. 49–58, 1988.

[19] O. Diez Martìnez and J.P. Segundo, "Behavior of a single neuron in a recurrent excitatory loop", *Biological Cybernetics*, vol. 47, pp. 33–41, 1983.

[20] D.D. Dixon, F.W. Cummings and P.E. Kaus, "Continuous chaotic dynamics in two dimensions", *Physica D*, vol. 65, pp. 109–116, 1993.

[21] S. Doi, "A chaotic map with a flat segment can produce a noise-induced order", *Journal of Statistical Physics*, vol. 55, pp. 941–964, 1989.

[22] J.K. Douglass, L. Wilkens, E. Pantazelou and F. Moss, "Stochastic resonance: noise-enhanced information transfer in crayfish mechanoreceptors", *Nature*, submitted.

[23] P. Fatt and B. Katz, "An analysis of the end plate-potential recorded with an intra-cellular electrode", *Journal of Physiology (Lond.)*, vol. 115, pp. 320–370, 1951.

[24] G. Fortin and J. Champagnat, "Generation of synaptic activities in the solitary complex neurons of the rat in vitro", *submitted*.

[25] W.J. Freeman, "Tutorial on Neurobiology. From single neurons to brain chaos", *International Journal of Bifurcation and Chaos*, vol. 2, pp. 451–482, 1992.

[26] A. French, A.V. Holden and R.B. Stein, "The estimation of the frequency response function of a mechanoreceptor", *Kybernetik*, vol. 11, pp. 15–23, 1972.

[27] H. Gang, H. Haken and C.Z. Ning, "Nonlinear response effects in stochastic resonance", *Physical Review E*, vol. 47, pp. 2321–2325, 1993.

[28] B. Hille, *Ionic Channels of Excitable Membranes*, 2nd ed., Sunderland, Mass.: Sinauer, 1992.

[29] A.V. Holden, *Models of the Stochastic Activity of Neurones*, Lecture Notes in Biomathematics 12, Berlin–Heidelberg: Springer-Verlag, 1976.

[30] A.J. Hudspeth, "The hair cells of the inner ear", *Scientific American*, vol. 248, pp. 54–64, 1983.

[31] P.E. Kloeden and E. Platen, *The Numerical Solution of Stochastic Differential Equations*, Springer-Verlag, 1991.

[32] A.F. Kohn, A. Freitas da Rocha and J.P. Segundo, "Presynaptic irregularity and pacemaker Inhibition", *Biological Cybernetics*, vol. 41, pp. 5–18, 1981.

[33] A.F. Kohn and J.P. Segundo, "Neuromime computer simulations of synaptic interactions between pacemakers. Mathematical expansions of existing models". *Journal of Theoretical Neurobiology*, vol. 2, pp. 101–125, 1983.

[34] H. Korn and D.S. Faber, "Transmission at a central inhibitory synapse IV. Quantal structure of synaptic noise", *Journal of Neurophysiology*, vol. 63, pp. 198–222, 1991.

[35] C. Kurrer and K. Schulten, "Effect of noise and perturbations on limit cycle systems", *Physica D*, vol. 50, pp. 311–320, 1991.

[36] H.K. Leung and B.C. Lai, "Stochastic transient of a noise perturbed Haken-Zwanzig model", *Physical Review E*, vol. 47, pp. 3043–3047, 1993.

[37] A. Longtin, "Stochastic resonance in neuron models", *Journal of Statistical Physics*, vol. 70, pp. 309–327, 1993.

[38] G.D. Lythe and M.R.E. Proctor, "Noise and slow-fast dynamics in a three-wave resonance problem", *Physical review E*, vol. 47, pp. 3122–3127, 1993.

[39] O. Macadar, G. Wolfe, D.P. O'Leary and J.P. Segundo, "Response of the elasmobranch utricle to maintained spatial orientation, transitions and jitter", *Experimental Brain Research*, vol. 22, pp. 1–12, 1975.

[40] A.J. Mandell and K.A. Selz, " Brain stem neuronal noise and neocortical "resonance"", *Journal of Statistical Physics*, vol. 70, pp. 355–373, 1993.

[41] P.Z. Marmarelis and V.Z. Marmarelis, *Analysis of Physiological Systems: The White Noisae Approach*, New York: Plenum, 1978.

[42] G. Mayer-Kress and H. Haken, "The influence of noise on the logistic model", *Journal of Statistical Physics*, vol. 26, pp. 149–171, 1981.

[43] G.P. Moore, D.H. Perkel and J.P. Segundo, "Stability patterns in interneuronal pacemaker regulation". In: *Proceedings of the Third Annual San Diego Symposium on Biomedical Engineering, San Diego, California*, 1963, pp. 184–193.

[44] F. Moss, A. Bulsara and M. Schlesinger (eds.), "Stochastic resonance in Physics and Biology", *Journal of Statistical Physics*, vol. 70, pp. 1–515, 1993.

[45] D.P. O'Leary and L.L. Davis, "High-frequency autorotational testing of the vestibulo-ocular reflex", *Neurologic Clinics*, vol. 8, pp. 297–312, 1990.

[46] D.P. O'Leary, J.J. Vidal and J.P. Segundo, "Perturbation effects on stability of gravity receptors", *Biological Cybernetics*, vol. 17, pp. 99–108, 1975.

[47] D.H. Perkel, J. Schulman, T.H. Bullock, G.P. Moore and J.P. Segundo, "Pacemaker neurons: effects of regularly spaced synaptic input", *Science*, vol. 145, pp. 61–63, 1964.

[48] J.P. Segundo, "Communication and coding by nerve cells", in *The Neurosciences. Second Study Program*, G. C. Quarton, T.Melnechuk and F. O. Schmitt, (eds.), New York: Rockefeller University Press, 1970, pp. 569–586.

[49] J.P. Segundo, "Synaptic rate effects", in *Encyclopedia of Neuroscience*, G. Adelman (ed.), Boston: Birkhauser, 1987, pp. 1168-1170.

[50] J.P. Segundo, E. Altshuler, M. Stiber and A. Garfinkel, "Periodic inhibition of living pacemaker neurons (I) locked, intermittent, messy, and hopping behaviors", *International journal of Bifurcation and Chaos*, vol. 1, pp. 549–581, 1991.

[51] J.P. Segundo, E. Altshuler, M. Stiber and A. Garfinkel, "Periodic inhibition of living pacemaker neurons (II) influence of driver rates and transients and of non driven post-synaptic rates", *International journal of Bifurcation and Chaos*, vol. 1, pp. 873–890, 1991.

[52] J.P. Segundo and O. Diez Martìnez, "Dynamic and static hysteresis in crayfish mechano-receptors", *Biological Cybernetics*, vol. 52, pp. 291–296, 1985.

[53] J.P. Segundo, O. Diez Martìnez and H. Quijano, "Testing a model of excitatory interaction between pacemakers" *Biological Cybernetics*, vol. 55, pp. 355-3-65. 1987.

[54] J.P. Segundo, D.H. Perkel, H. Wyman, H. Hegstad and G.P. Moore, "Input-output relations in computer-simulated nerve cells. Influence of the statistical properties, number and interdependence of excitatory pre-synaptic terminals", *Kybernetik*, vol. 4, pp. 157–171, 1968.

[55] J.P. Segundo, M. Stiber, E. Altshuler and J.-F. Vibert, "Transients in the inhibitory driving of neurons and their postsynaptic consequences", *Neuroscience*, in press.

[56] J.P. Segundo, M. Stiber and J.-F. Vibert, " Synaptic coding of spike trains. In *The Handbook of Brain Theory and Neural Networks*. M. Arbib (ed.), in press.

[57] J.P. Segundo, M. Stiber, J.-F. Vibert and S. Hanneton, "Periodically modulated inhibition and its post-synaptic consequences. II. Influence of pre-synaptic slope, depth, range, noise and of post-synaptic natural discharges", submitted.

[58] J.P. Segundo, B.F. Tolkunov and G.W. Wolfe, "Relation between trains across an Inhibitory synapse. Influence of pre-synaptic irregularity", *Biological Cybernetics*, vol. 24, pp. 169–179, 1976.

[59] J.P. Segundo, J.-F. Vibert, M. Stiber and S. Hanneton, "Synaptic coding of periodically modulated spike trains", *Proceedings of the IEEE Meeting on Neural Networks, San Francisco*, vol. 1, 1993, pp. 58–63.

[60] J.P. Segundo, J.-F. Vibert, M. Stiber and S. Hanneton, "Periodically modulated inhibition and its post-synaptic consequences. I. General features. Influence of frequency", submitted.

[61] R.M. Siegel and H.L. Read, "Models of temporal dynamics of visual processing", *Journal of Statistical Physics*, vol. 70, pp. 297–309, 1993.

[62] R.J. Simpson, "Use of high frequency signals in identification of certain non-linear systems", *Int. J. Syst. Sci.*, vol. 4, pp. 121–127, 1973.

[63] H. Sperkeijse, "Rectification in the goldfish retina: analysis by sinusoidal and auxiliary stimulation", *Vision Research*, vol. 9, pp. 1461–1472, 1969.

[64] H. Spekreijse and H. Oosting, "Linearizing: a method for analyzing and synthesizing nonlinear systems", *Kybernetik*, vol. 7, pp. 22–31, 1970.

[65] M. Stiber, *Dynamics of synaptic interactions*, Thesis UCLA, 1992.

[66] M. Stiber and J.P. Segundo, "Dynamics of synaptic transfer in living and simulated neurons", in *Proceedings of the IEEE Internationa Conference on Neural Networks, San Francisco*, vol. 1, pp. 75–80, 1993.

[67] R.B. Stein, "A theoretical analysis of neuronal variability", *Biophys. J*, vol. 5, pp. 173–1943, 1965.

[68] R.B. Stein, "The information capacity of nerve cells using a frequency code", *Biophys. J.*, vol. 7, pp. 797–826, 1967.

[69] R.B. Stein, "The role of spike trains in transmitting and distorting sensory signals", in *The Neurosciences. Second Study Program*, G. C. Quarton, T. Melnechuk and F. O. Schmitt, eds., New York, Rockefeller University Press, 1970, ch. 53, pp. 597-604.

[70] R.B. Stein, "The stochastic properties of spike trains recorded from nerve cells", in *Stochastic point processes: statistical analysis, theory and applications*, P.A.W. Lewis (ed.), New York: Wiley Intersciences, 1972, pp. 700–731.

[71] R.B. Stein and A.S. French, "Models for the transmission of information by nerve cells", in *Excitatory synaptic mechamnims, Proceedings of the fifth International Meeting of Neurobiologists*, P. Andersen and J.K.S. Jansen (eds.), Oslo Universitetsforlaget, Sandejford Norway, 1970.

[72] R.B. Stein, A.S. French and A.V. Holden, "The frequency response, coherence and information capacity of two neuronal models", *Biophys. J.*, vol. 12, pp. 295–322, 1972.

[73] M.C. Teich, S.M. Khanna and P.C. Guiney, "Spectral characteristics and synchrony in primary auditory-nerve fibers in response to pure-tone acoustic swtimuli", *Journal of Statistical Physics*, vol. 70, pp. 257–279, 1993.

[74] J.-F. Vibert, D. Caille and J.P. Segundo, "Respiratory oscillator entrainment by periodic vagal afferents : an experimental test of a model", *Biol. Cybernetics*, vol 41, pp. 119–130, 1981.

[75] J.-F. Vibert, D. Caille, and J.P. Segundo, "Examination with a computer of how parameter changes and variabilities influence a model of oscillator entrainment" *Biological Cybernetics*, vol. 53, pp. 1–13, 1985.

[76] J.-F. Vibert, M. Davis and J.P. Segundo, "Recurrent inhibition; Its influence upon transduction and afferent discharges in slowly-adapting stretch receptor organs", *Biological Cybernetics*, vol. 33, pp. 167–178, 1979.

[77] J.-F. Vibert, K. Pakdaman and N. Azmy, "Inter-neural delay modification synchronizes biologically plausible neural networks", *Neural Networks*, in the press.

[78] J.-F. Vibert and J.P. Segundo, "Slowly adapting stretch-receptor organs: periodic stimulation with and without perturbations", *Biological Cybernetics*, vol. 33, pp. 81–92, 1979.

[79] J.J. Vidal, M. Jeannerod, W. Lifshitz, H. Levitan, J. Rosenberg and J.P. Segundo, "Static and dynamc properties of gravity sensitive receptors in the cat vestibular system", *Kybernetik*, vol. 9, pp. 205–215, 1971.

[80] X. Yu and E.R. Lewis, "Studies with spike initiators: linearization by noise allows continuous signal modulation in neural networks", *IEEE Transactions on Biomedical Engineering*, vol. 36, pp. 36–43, 1989.

[81] M. Zak, "Terminal attractors in neural networks", *Neural Networks*, vol. 2, pp. 259–274, 1989.

Chapter 14

Towards Simplicity: Noise and Cooperation in the "Perfect Integrator"

A. R. Bulsara

Towards Simplicity: Noise and Cooperation in the 'Perfect Integrator'

A. R. Bulsara

NCCOSC-RDT&E Division, Code 573, San Diego, CA 92152-5000

I. INTRODUCTION

Neuroscientists have known for decades that sensory information is encoded in the intervals between the action potentials or "spikes" characterizing neural firing events. Statistical analyses of experimentally obtained spike trains have shown the existence of a significant random component in the inter-spike intervals. There has been speculation, of late, that the noise may actually facilitate the transmission of sensory information; certainly there exists evidence that noise in networks of neurons can dynamically alter the properties of the membrane potential and the time constants [37,66]. The recent re-kindling of interest in the Stochastic Resonance phenomenon has lead to speculation that such nonlinear cooperative effects may occur naturally in living systems.

Stochastic resonance (SR) is a cooperative nonlinear phenomenon wherein the signal-to-noise ratio (SNR) at the output of a noisy nonlinear dynamic system driven by a weak deterministic modulation (which we shall take to be time-periodic), can actually be *enhanced* by increasing the noise. Given a bistable dynamic system, for example, information is transmitted through the system in the form of switching events between the stable states (attractors) of the potential function underlying the dynamics. Suppose a periodic signal is applied; its effect is to rock the potential, alternately raising and lowering the wells. However, should its amplitude be very low (compared to the height of the potential barrier), it will not be able to induce switching. In the presence of even small amounts of noise (assumed throughout this work to be Gaussian and delta-correlated) there will, however, always be a finite switching probability. Since the switching probability is greater when the system is in the 'elevated' well, which occurs when the signal is at its maximum, one realizes that the noise-induced switching events may acquire some degree of coherence with the deterministic signal as long as certain important system parameters (notably the potential barrier height and the locations of the fixed points) are appropriately adjusted. The power spectrum obtained from the time-series solution of this system shows a sharp signal, together with its weaker *odd* harmonics (for the case of a symmetric potential), superimposed on a Lorentzian-like noise background. Theoretically, the signal is represented as a δ-function spike; in practice, of course, the spike has a finite width and amplitude determined by the bandwidth of the measuring system [73,74]. Then, in order to compare theoretical results with experiments or simulations, one integrates over the line-shape of the signal function (at the fundamental frequency). If the signal feature is narrow and, in particular, falls entirely within one bin of the (discrete) experimental Fourier transform process, then one replaces the δ-function by $1/\Delta\omega$, the inverse of the width of a single frequency bin in the FFT. The area obtained by the integration represents the fraction of total switching events that are coherent with the stimulus. With increasing noise, the signal power spectral density, S (measured at the fundamental frequency ω), rises until, for a critical noise strength, the intra-well motion gives way to inter-well (or hopping) motion as the major contributor to the dynamics. At this point S decreases with noise; for very large noise strengths, the switching becomes noise-dominated and very rapid, with all coherence with the periodic signal being destroyed. For modulation frequencies comparable to the Kramers rate (the characteristic well-to-well switching rate in the noise-only case), the critical noise strength (at the maximum of the *signal-power* curve) corresponds to a matching between the modulation frequency and twice the Kramers rate, hence the somewhat misleading characterization of this effect as a 'resonance' in the physics literature. The noise power spectral density $N(\omega)$ is given by the background at the base of the signal feature and the SNR defined, in decibels, as $SNR \equiv 10\log_{10}(S/(N\,\Delta\omega))$. A plot of SNR vs. noise strength demonstrates a bell-shaped profile similar to that of the signal power spectral density; in the limit of very low (compared to the unperturbed Kramers rate) drive frequency, this curve and the signal power spectral density peak at approximately the same critical noise strength [27,50]. In the literature (and in this review), the SNR vs. input noise variance profile is sometimes taken to be the hallmark of SR, although the classical definition of the resonance involves the above-mentioned behavior of the signal feature in the output, rather than the SNR. The physics literature is replete with theories and examples of SR with good reviews available in forthcoming articles by Moss [52] and Jung [36] as well as the proceedings of a recent NATO workshop on the subject [53]. From a biological perspective, the recent work on SR in globally coupled arrays of nonlinear switching elements [8,35,54] is particularly significant.

It is important to point out that stochastic resonance (as characterized by the bell-shaped curve of SNR vs. noise) has not yet been directly observed in living systems with *internal* noise. One of its prime ingredients, noise-induced switching, has however been demonstrated in biological experiments [16,24,25]. In all such experiments, it is common to assemble an ensemble of firing events and fit a histogram to the refractory or reset intervals occurring between the "spikes". Such Inter-Spike-Interval Histograms (ISIHs) are ubiquitous in the neurophysiological literature and, as we shall see below, can be simply and elegantly explained by simple models of neurons as bistable dynamic switching devices subject to noise. The results have lead a few bold individuals to speculate on the possible beneficial role of noise (in particular, cooperative stochastic processes such as described in the preceeding paragraph) in the processing of sensory neural information [7-11,44-48]. Other researchers have speculated [40,61,62] that the experimentally observable background noise may be a natural phenomenon rather than a laboratory curiosity. Statistical analyses of experimentally obtained spike trains --the ISIH is obtained from experimental data, by assembling an ensemble of quiescent intervals (that separate firing events) into a histogram-- have also shown the existence of a significant random component in the inter-spike-intervals. These observations have lead neuroscientists to ponder the role of noise in sensory information processing for decades, usually relying on experimentally obtained spike trains and their associated ISIHs (both of which are ubiquitous in the neuroscience literature). It is impossible to exhaustively cite this vast body of prior work, but it must be pointed out that our efforts complement and extend conventional treatments by examining the response of our model neuron to a time-periodic external stimulus that is too small to induce firing by itself; in this case, the background noise nudges the system past its firing threshold (which, as we shall see in the next section, may actually be a function of the noise). Hence the noise, in some sense, mediates the response of the model neuron to the stimulus, an idea that will turn out to be central to our treatment of the ISIH.

The results of an investigation into some aspects of the role of noise in periodically modulated nonlinear systems in a neurophysiological context, constitutes the subject of this article. Our previous work [for a review, see e.g. refs. 11,12] consisted of modelling the sensory neuron as a noisy bistable (describable by a dynamics predicated on a "soft" potential) switching element. Such a model has been derived [8-10] from a fully coupled model of a cell body interacting (at the axon hillock), via a weak nonlinear coupling, with a dendritic "bath", the dendrites being represented as quasi-linear elements which, in general, would also be capable of "firing". Of course, the idea of bistability in this context is not new; it dates back to the seminal work of Landahl, McCullough and Pitts [41] who considered the neuron as a discrete (i.e. two-state) noisy threshold device. Today, their model while generally viewed as an over-simplification of real neurons, has served as a convenient starting point for the class of "connectionist" models of neural networks [2,17,18,20,30,32,33,49]. Although our model yields acceptable fits to experimental data and can provide a very elegant explanation of the salient features of experimentally observed ISIHs (these are summarized in the following section) it has become evident, recently, that it raises almost as many questions as it answers. For instance, it is generally accepted that neurons show bistability, of the type described above, only in certain restrictive regimes of parameter space. Different classes of neurons (even sensory neurons) are thought to exhibit different types of bistability, e.g., bistability between a fixed point and limit cycle that characterizes excitable oscillators such as those considered by Winfree [73]; the Fitzhugh-Nagumo model of excitable cells [26] belongs to this class. Experiments show [24] that background noise produces qualitatively similar cooperative behavior in this class of bistable models as well. Bistability of various kinds has been quantified in simplified Hodgkins-Huxley-type models [23] and postulated via theoretical arguments [1,57,72]. However, in other simple quasi-linear neural models e.g,. the "perfect" integrate-fire models, the results can be ambiguous. Here, noise introduces effects, in the ISIH, that closely resemble those observed in bistable models; the explanation of these effects cannot, however, be based on the same nonlinear stochastic-dynamic effects that underlie the response of bistable models. Recent results for this class of models are described in section III. Our fundamental characterization of bistable model neurons as threshold devices (no firing in the absence of noise) raises the issue of information loss during signal processing since only the firing events, that occur when a threshold is crossed, are recorded, with dynamical details regarding the passage to threshold being ignored. Of course, this must be weighed against experimental studies that demonstrate the existence of cooperative stochastic effects (e.g. SR) that cannot be explained by any form of linear filtering theory.

A final caveat: our approach lacks detailed "neurophysiological rigor". As physicists, we take a reductionist view by attempting to describe the global response of a complex system in terms of the response of a very few degrees of freedom that characterize the gross properties of the system (the renormalization group approach and the enormous success that it has enjoyed in treating complex systems is a classic example of this idea). As will become evident, in the following sections, noise introduces qualitatively similar effects in different dynamical models of stimulated neurons. These effects are visible at the level of the ISIH and the SNR, both of which are statistical (i.e. averaged) characterizations of the response. In addition to these measurements, other quantities that characterize the response (e.g. the mean firing rate and its variance) can be obtained via simple averages computed with respect to the ISIH; these quantities can also be directly measured in repeated trials in an experiment. Our approach is, therefore, quite adequate for describing the coupling between the noise and modulation in the neural dynamics on a statistical or *coarse-grained* level, as well as the mechanism whereby noise might actually enhance the flow of information through the system.

II. NEURONS AS BISTABLE ELEMENTS CHARACTERIZED BY A 'SOFT' POTENTIAL; STATISTICAL ANALYSIS OF SPIKE TRAINS

Recent work by Longtin, Bulsara and Moss (LBM) [44,45,48] has demonstrated how experimental ISIHs measured, for example, on the auditory nerve fibers of squirrel monkey [60] could be explained via a new interpretation of noise-driven bistable dynamics. They have introduced a simple bistable neuron model, a two-state system controlled by a double-well potential with neural firing events corresponding to transitions over the potential barrier (whose height is set such that the deterministic stimulus alone cannot cause transitions). The cell dynamics are described via a variable $x(t)$, loosely denoting the membrane potential, and evolving according to

$$\dot{x} = f(x) + q \sin \omega t + F(t), \tag{1}$$

where $f(x)$ is a hysteretic flow function (expressible as the gradient of a potential $U(x)$) and $F(t)$ is noise, taken to be Gaussian, delta-correlated, with zero mean. In the bistable description, the potential is taken to be the "soft" function $U(x) = ax^2/2 - b \ln(\cosh x)$. The system (1) has been numerically integrated, with the residence time in each potential well (these times represent the firing and quiescent intervals in our model) assembled into a histogram (the residence times density function $P(t)$), which displays a sequence of peaks with a characteristic spacing. Two unique sequences of temporal measurements are possible: the first measures the residence times in only one of the states of the potential and the histogram consists of peaks located at $t = n T_0/2$, T_0 being the period of the deterministic modulation and n an odd integer. The second sequence encompasses measurements of the total time spent in both potential wells, i.e. it includes the active *and* reset intervals; in the presence of noise, the reset intervals are of largely stochastic duration. The histogram corresponding to this sequence consists of peaks at locations $t = n T_0$ where n is any integer. The sequence of peaks implies a form of phase locking of the neural dynamics to the stimulus. Starting from its quiescent state, the neuron attempts to fire at the first maximum of the stimulus cycle. If it fails, it will try again at the next maximum, and so on. The latter sequence is the only one observable in an experiment; the former sequence, which corresponds to the refractory events is elegantly elucidated by the LBM theory. In addition to the peak spacing in the ISIH, most of the other substantive features of experimental ISIHs are explainable [47] via the simple model (1):

(a). Decreasing the noise intensity (keeping all other parameters fixed) leads to more peaks in the histogram since the "skipping" referred to above becomes more likely. Conversely, increasing the noise intensity tends to concentrate most of the probability in the first few peaks of the histogram.

(b). In general, the probability density of residence times is well approximated by a Gamma-like distribution of the form $P(T) = (T/<T>^2) \exp(-T/<T>)$, where $<T>$ is the mean of the ISIH. It is apparent that $P(T) \to 0$ and $\exp(-T/<T>)$ in the short and long time limits, respectively. For vanishingly small stimulus amplitude q, the distribution tends to a Gamma, conforming to experimental observations.

(c). Increasing the stimulus amplitude leads to an increase in the heights of the lower lying peaks in the ISIH.

(d). Memory effects (even within the framework of a description based on the theory of renewal processes) frequently occur, particularly at very low driving frequencies; they manifest themselves in deviations from an exponentially decaying envelope at low residence times (the first peak in the ISIH may not be the tallest one).

(e). The mean of the ISIH yields (through its inverse) the mean firing rate.

(f). The ISIH decay rate λ (the slope of the envelope on a semi-log scale) itself depends sensitively (exponentially) on the stimulus amplitude q for constant noise strength, and (again, exponentially) on the noise strength for fixed q.

Analog simulations of the dynamics yield an extremely good fit [44,48] to experimental data; the fit can be realized by changing only one parameter (the stimulus intensity or the noise intensity) and the results are almost independent of the functional form of the potential $U(x)$, depending critically on the ratio of barrier height to noise variance; this ratio determines the hopping rate between the basins of attraction in the absence of noise.

The LBM theory demonstrates that the peaks of the ISIH *cannot exist in the absence of noise*. In fact, one could speculate that, over a certain range of parameters, the noise and signal play interchangeable roles in determining the shape of the ISIH. All the stimulus and noise features are encoded in the ISIH, with the phase preference (we assume perfect phase locking to the stimulus throughout) encoded in the peak width; this assumptions seems to be consistent with experimental auditory nerve data at least. The noise may be used by the neuron to encode the stimulus features in the ISIH, while preserving a fine amplitude discrimination through the exponential dependence on λ. Other researchers [66] have shown that noise linearizes the mean firing rate-vs. current characteristic in neurons, producing a large dynamic range along with ISIH variations. This dynamic range is not found in noiseless Hodgkins-Huxley type models. Identifying the mean firing rate with the inverse of the mean of the ISIH seems to lead one naturally to this encoding. Although the LBM model provides an important first step in the understanding of the (possibly pivotal) role of noise in sensory information transfer, it is far from complete. The results do not appear to depend critically on the characteristics of the potential function $U(x)$ and the fundamental question: what aspects of the data are due to the statistical properties of noisy two-state systems as opposed to real (i.e. biological) properties of cells that transcend this simple description, has not been satisfactorily answered.

Bistable models of the type discussed above provide one of the simplest explanations of the possible mechanism underlying the processing and coding of sensory information in the nervous system. They elucidate the sequence of reset events that follow each neural firing, and noise is seen to play a pivotal role in the production of the ISIHs. The dynamics in a generic bistable system of the form (1) displays the N-shaped flow characteristic that is known to exist in exciteable cells [57]. In our derivation of the bistable model from the fully coupled neuro-dendritic model, the coefficients a and b in the potential function $U(x)$ are obtained in terms of the cell and bath parameters. Hence, the effect of the dendritic coupling is to modify the height of the potential barrier, thereby directly affecting the switching dynamics and the structure of the ISIH. The potential function for the system becomes bimodal above a critical value of b/a; this transition to bimodality is mediated by the noise in the dendritic bath; in fact, the theory introduces the concept of a noise-dependent firing threshold (defined as the barrier height). Stochastic resonance (as described in the preceeding section) is readily observable in these many-body models and the output SNR can be further enhanced (over its expected value for the isolated case) by the coupling to the dendritic bath. Since none of the cooperative effects that we have described here will occur in a monostable potential, the critical role of background noise is evident.

The physical model outlined above is striking for its simplicity and provides an elegant explanation for several features of experimentally computed ISIHs. Nonetheless, it can be criticized for lacking the neurophysiological rigor afforded by, say, the Hodgkins-Huxley equations and their derivants, including the class of "Integrate-and-Fire" models. We now consider some of the statistical properties of the simplest of these models.

III. THE 'PERFECT INTEGRATOR' REVISITED

In our work to date, we have confined our attention to nonlinear dynamic models of neuronal firing; the models rely on bistable firing characteristics to model the dynamics. However, the neurophysiological literature is replete with stochastic models of spontaneous and induced firing which are similar in spirit to the bistable models: firing takes place when the membrane voltage crosses a threshold. However, the models are not all characterized by hysteretic flow functions. The most ubiquitous of these models, the class of integrate-fire (IF) models, can be heuristically derived from single-neuron dynamics of the form (1), in the limit when the nonlinear term in the dynamics is very weak, so that the potential $U(x)$ is approximately parabolic, using stochastic linearization techniques [5,59]. In the most general case, the "leaky" integrator with threshold, one writes the dynamics in the form [65],

$$\dot{x} = \lambda (u_r - x) + \mu + F(t) + q \cos \omega t , \qquad (2)$$

which represents an Ornstein-Uhlenbeck process [15,69,71] in which μ is the (positive) drift to a firing threshold a, and λ is a decay constant governing the decay of the voltage variable $x(t)$ to an equilibrium or resting level u_r. $F(t)$ is taken to be white noise having zero mean and variance D. Equation (2), in the absence of the periodic stimulus, has been extensively studied [3,14,19,21,31,34,39,42,43,55,56,63,67,68] in the theoretical neuroscience literature. In these studies, it is generally assumed that the noise term $F(t)$ represents the net contribution from all the synaptic inputs to the cell. Deterministic IF models have been studied by Keener et. al. [38].

We consider now a simplification of the above model due originally to Gerstein and Mandelbrot (GM) [29] in which the $q=0, \lambda=0$ case was considered, the so-called "perfect integrator". Assuming the underlying dynamics to be time-stationary, a random walk description of the neural firing dynamics has been invoked by GM, based on the cornerstone requirement of a stable distribution function for the probability density of first passage times corresponding to the dynamics. The state variable x is assumed to execute a biased random walk to an absorbing threshold at which point a firing event is designated to have occurred and the membrane potential x is then instantaneously reset to its starting value (the reset mechanism being purely deterministic). It is this reset which renders the 'global' dynamics nonlinear. The distance between the origin and the threshold is the "barrier height" a, analogous to the height U_0 of the potential barrier in our bistable model. Further, it is assumed that the motion in phase space occurs under the influence of a positive drift coefficient μ which was defined by GM as roughly the difference between the drift velocities corresponding to excitatory and inhibitory synaptic inputs (it is neurophysiologically reasonable to assume these velocities to be different). For this model, the Wiener process with drift, one readily writes down the associated Fokker Planck Equation (FPE) [28,58,70]:

$$\frac{\partial}{\partial t} P(x,t) = -\mu \frac{\partial P}{\partial x} + \frac{D}{2} \frac{\partial^2 P}{\partial x^2},$$ (3)

whence the probability density function of first passage times is [22,29],

$$g_0(t) = \frac{a}{\sqrt{2\pi D t^3}} \exp\left\{ -\frac{(a - a_0 - \mu t)^2}{2Dt} \right\},$$ (4)

a_0 being the starting point of the random walk. The density function $g_0(t)$, often referred to in the statistical literature as the 'Inverse Gaussian', reproduces many of the properties of experimentally observed ISIHs for the spontaneous firing case. The mean first passage time $(a-a_0)/\mu$ to the absorbing threshold is calculated as the first moment of $g_0(t)$, and its reciprocal yields an average firing rate. The variance of the first passage time is $D(a-a_0)/\mu^3$. The model reproduces the salient features of the ISIHs obtained from spontaneous firing events reasonably well, including the long (exponential) tail in the first passage time density function $g(t)$. It also has numerous limitations (which have been ennumerated by GM), the most fundamental one being the assumption that the membrane potential is reset following each spike, with the random walk to the threshold restarting; nevertheless, the model provides a simple vehicle to explain the dynamics (on a grossly simplified level) that arise from the coupling of the noise and the periodic stimulus. A more rigorous (from a neurophysiological standpoint) grounding of the FPE (3) has been given by Stevens [64]. In order to make even better contact with experimental results, it is necessary to provide reasonably good numerical values for the drift coefficient μ, the "barrier height" a and the background noise variance D in the above model. A first attempt to do so (while simultaneously providing a test of the goodness of fit of the model to neurophysiological data) was carried out by Berger et. al. [4]. They carried out an experiment aimed at recording the inter-spike-interval distribution from extra-cellular recordings on the cat visual cortex. Having obtained the experimental ISIHs, they were able to compute the equivalent model quantities μ and a via the mean and standard deviation of the experimentally obtained ISIHs, assuming a fixed background noise variance D. While we do not give any further details of the experiment, it is noteworthy that, once these "self-consistent" values of μ, a and D were substituted into the first passage time probability density function, an excellent fit of the model to the experimental ISIHs resulted.

We now consider the GM model in the presence of a deterministic periodic stimulus $q \cos \omega t$, assuming the initial condition $a_0 = 0$. Once again we assume the phase-locked case. One can then write down and solve [13] the FPE to yield the probability density function $P(x, t)$. The first passage times density function is then computed via the prescription [22]:

$$g(t) = -\frac{d}{dt} \int_{-\infty}^{a} P(x, t) \, dx,$$

which yields, after some calculation,

$$g(t) = \frac{1}{\sqrt{2\pi D}} \frac{a}{t^{3/2}} e^{-h_1(a,t)} + \frac{aq}{Dt^2} \left(t \cos \omega t - \frac{1}{\omega} \sin \omega t \right) \Phi_c(h_3(a,t)) e^{h_2(t)}, \tag{5}$$

where $\Phi_c(x) \equiv 1 - \frac{2}{\sqrt{\pi}} \int_0^z e^{-t^2} dt$ is the Complementary Error function and we have defined,

$$h_1(a, t) \equiv \frac{\left(a - \mu t - \frac{q}{\omega} \sin \omega t \right)^2}{2Dt}$$

$$h_2(t) \equiv \frac{2a}{Dt} \left(\mu t + \frac{q}{\omega} \sin \omega t \right)$$

$$h_3(a, t) \equiv \frac{\left(a + \mu t + \frac{q}{\omega} \sin \omega t \right)}{\sqrt{2Dt}}.$$

We now discuss briefly some of the properties of the density functions (4) and (5). A plot of (5) yields an ISIH with the peaks at locations nT_0 where n is an integer and T_0 the stimulus period. The hidden or reset mechanism in this model is instantaneous (and deterministic), in contrast to the bistable models. However, the model differs from the bistable models in another very important respect. In the absence of noise and the periodic stimulus, the state-point *will* reach the threshold, provided the drift μ is positive; the model admits of the possibility of deterministic 'switching' or firing. For the $q \ll \mu$ case, a first-order perturbation solution (for t) of the dynamic equation $a = \mu t + \frac{q}{\omega} \sin \omega t$ yields the deterministic passage time,

$$\bar{T} = t_0 \left\{ 1 - \frac{\frac{q}{a\omega} \sin \omega t_0}{1 + \frac{q}{\mu} \cos \omega t_0} \right\}, \tag{6}$$

where $t_0 \equiv a/\mu$ is the mean first passage time (MFPT) in the presence of noise alone. Note that $\bar{T} \to t_0$ at high drive frequencies ω, as should be expected. The deterministic passage time (6) is also the MFPT in the presence of the noise and the periodic stimulus. For a long-tailed distribution of the form (3) however, possibly the more important quantity is the most probable time, or the mode. For the $q = 0$ case, this time is readily obtained by differentiation:

$$t_m = \frac{3D}{2\mu^2} \left\{ \sqrt{1 + \frac{4a^2\mu^2}{9D^2}} - 1 \right\}. \tag{7}$$

It is significant that the mode t_m depends on the noise. In experiments, firing times clustered about the mode are more probable. The mean of a large number of firing times may yield a MFPT t_0 which, depending on the physical characteristics of the density function (3) is close to the mode or far out in the tail. When analysing the properties of the ISIH the interplay of the three time-scales T_0, t_0, and t_m is crucial. With decreasing inhibition (represented as increasing drift μ for fixed excitation) or with decreasing noise strength (keeping the drift fixed), the ISIH approaches a more sharply peaked (Gaussian-like) density (in effect, the tail of the Gamma-like density (3) shrinks, with the mean

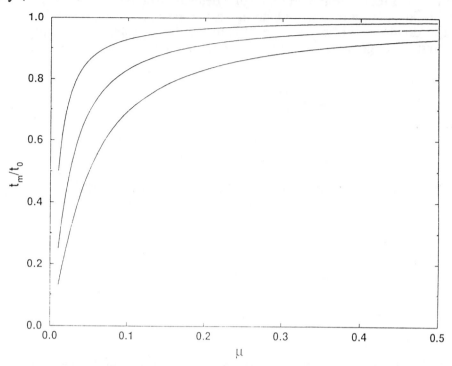

Fig 1. Mode of the noise-only density function (4), normalized to the mean, vs. the drift coefficient μ for $a=20$ and noise variance $D=0.1, 0.25, 0.5$ (top to bottom curves).

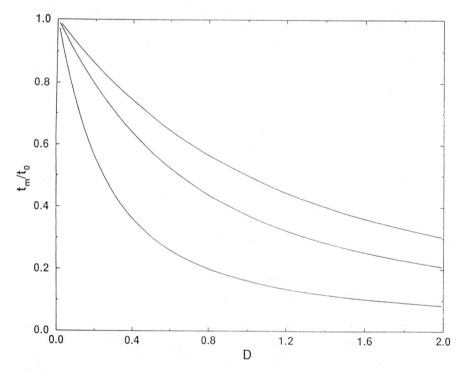

Fig 2. Mode of the noise only density function (4), normalized to the mean, vs. the noise variance D for $a=20$ and drift $\mu=0.1, 0.065, 0.025$ (top to bottom curves).

approaching the mode). This may be demonstrated via a Gram-Charlier expansion of the density function (3) and is depicted in figures 1 and 2 in which we plot the ratio t_m/t_0 vs. the drift μ and the noise variance D respectively. Increasing the drift leads to a more sharply peaked distribution (characterized by the rate at which $t_m/t_0 \to 1$) for a given noise

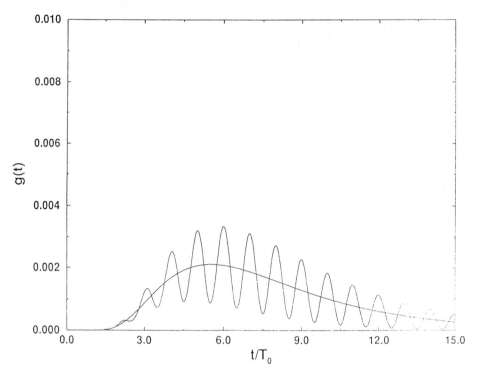

Fig 3. First passage time density function (5) and its $q=0$ counterpart (4) for $(a, \mu, q, \omega, D) \equiv (20, .04, .03, .1, .2)$.

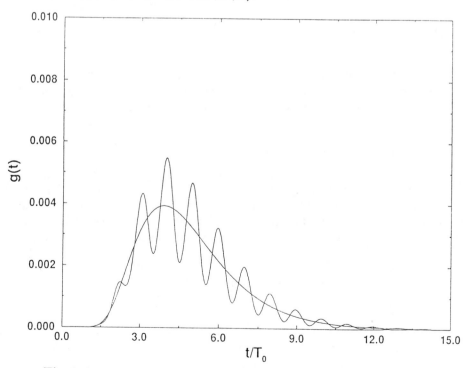

Fig 4. Same as figure 3 with $\mu = 0.065$.

variance; the approach to a very sharply peaked distribution is more rapid at lower noise strengths as seen in both figures. Figures 3-5 show the effect of increasing the drift μ on the ISIH; in these figures, the smooth curves represent the $q=0$ density function (3). Note that if we introduced a phase ϕ into the argument of the periodic stimulus and then defined a phase-averaged ISIH (the averaging being performed over a uniform distribution on $[0,2\pi]$), the two curves in each of the figures 3-5 would coincide; for the phase-locked case, one obtains an ISIH that is qualitatively similar to those observed for the

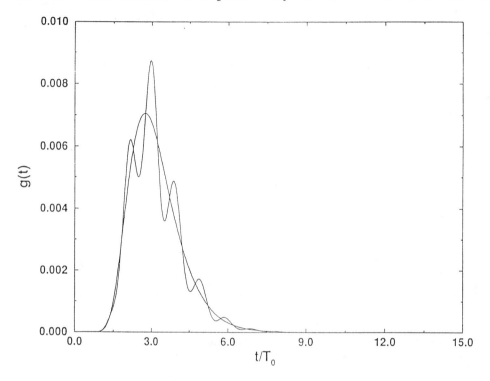

Fig 5. Same as figure 3 with $\mu=0.1$.

bistable models. The mean, variance, and mode of the ISIH (for small q) are seen to be extremely close to the corresponding quantities for the $q=0$ ISIH, as predicted above. It should be evident that if we adjust the stimulus and/or system parameters such that

$$t_m = nT_0,\tag{8}$$

then the nth peak in the ISIH will be the highest one.

The interesting feature about the ISIH (5) is that the peak heights go through maxima as functions of the noise variance D, all other parameters being held constant. This is demonstrated in figure 6 for a particular set of system and modulation parameters. One can calculate from (5) the critical noise D_c at which the nth peak passes through its maximum. Note that the peaks in (5) occur at times $t=nT_0$. Hence, the amplitude of the nth peak is given by

$$g_n = g_0 + g_1,\tag{9}$$

where

$$g_0 = \frac{a}{\sqrt{2\pi D t_n^3}} \exp\left[-(a-\mu t_n)^2/2D t_n\right],\tag{10a}$$

$$g_1 = \frac{aq}{D t_n} e^{2a\mu/D} \Phi_c\left[\frac{a+\mu t_n}{\sqrt{2D t_n}}\right],\tag{10b}$$

342

are the contributions from the $q=0$ and $q>0$ parts of the density function (7) (we set $t_n=nT_0=2n\pi/\omega$). Writing $D_c=D_{c0}+\delta$ where D_{c0} is the noise variance at which the expression (10a) is maximized and δ is the (much smaller) contribution from (10b), we easily find

$$D_{c0}=(a-\mu t_n)^2/t_n . \qquad (13)$$

The remaining contribution δ is found by setting the derivative of (9) equal to zero and then expanding to $O(\delta)$. This contribution is, however, much smaller than D_{c0} and can be neglected for the present. In figure 7, we focus our attention for a particular peak ($n=4$). We set $\mu\equiv\mu_c=0.159$ where, for this case, μ_c is found by setting $nT_0=t_0$. For a fixed noise variance D, this value of μ_c maximizes the height of this peak, although this does *not* imply that the peak in question is the highest one in the ISIH. Now, the noise variance is further decreased. This has the effect of moving the mode t_m such that the nth peak coincides with the mode ($t_m\approx nT_0$) and this peak becomes the highest one. Decreasing the noise further causes the peak to get taller and narrower; it becomes delta-function-like and attains its maximum height in the $t_m\rightarrow t_0\approx nT_0$ limit as discussed earlier.

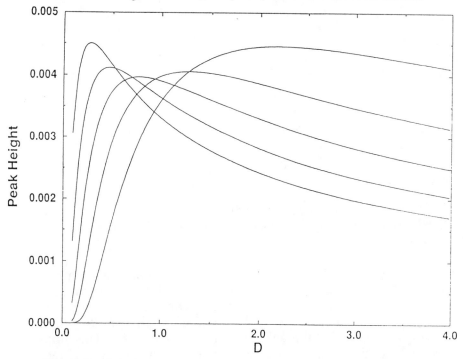

Fig 6. Peak heights vs. noise variance D for the density function (5) with $(a,\mu,q,\omega)\equiv(20,.055,.0475)$. Curves correspond to (reading from left to right) peak numbers $n=7,6,5,4,3$.

IV. DISCUSSION, CONCLUSIONS AND SPECULATION

It seems fitting to conclude this article with a question and some speculation. Clearly the question to be answered is: "Can the neuron indeed be characterized by a noisy nonlinear switching element, describeable by a bistable dynamics of the form (1) (with, say, a 'soft' potential $U(x)$) or a far simpler switching element described by the dynamics (2)?" Certainly, there is ample evidence that noise plays a critical role in the transmission and coding of information in the nervous system; most reasonable models of neural firing invoke some kind of diffusion process representation of the system on a statistical or coarse-grained level (in which the system is described via a probability density function rather than an individual trajectory solution). It seems reasonable then, that there should exist a form of self-regulatory mechanism such that the internal parameters

343

of the system (these parameters control, for instance, the height U_0 of the potential barrier) can be adjusted in response to the stimulus and noise characteristics. In our previous

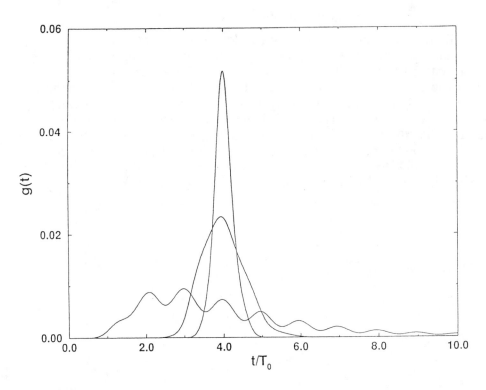

Fig 7. Height of peak no. 4 with $(a, q, \omega) \equiv (20, .0475, .2)$ and $\mu = 0.159$ (critical value...see text). Top curve: $D = 0.012$, middle curve: $D = 0.06$, bottom curve: $D = 1.0$.

work [8,9], in fact, we have been lead, in a simple way to the concept of a noise-dependent firing threshold. This is important because, for given stimulus and noise, one obtains well-defined histograms for only a small range of U_0. One may speculate further that the neuron (or the network) then *uses the background noise so that its response* (measured via the SNR or, equivalently, through the ISIH) *is optimized*. This implies that, for configurations that admit of stochastic resonance, the neuron (or network) operates close to the maximum of the stochastic resonance curve (SNR vs. noise variance) while simultaneously obtaining other information (e.g. amplitude, frequency, and phase) about the deterministic stimulus, via the ISIH. In effect, our construction and interpretation of the ISIH (together with the remarkable ability to explain most of the features of experimentally obtained ISIHs) as a natural outcome of our modelling the neuron as a noisy bistable switching element (in the LBM theory) or even via the extremely simple model of section III implies that *sensory neurons may measure the stimulus intensity by comparing it to the background noise, using the (internally adjusted) potential barrier height to mediate and optimize the measurement* [F. Moss 1992; private discussions]. In the perfect integrator model, the firing threshold is equivalent to a 'barrier' in the jargon of bistable dynamics; such models may be, in fact, derivable from more complex models such as those considered in the LBM studies. Our studies of collective behavior in large networks show that the coupling to other elements can enhance or degrade the SNR depending on the magnitudes *and* signs of the coupling coefficients, i.e., the excitatory or inhibitory nature of the interactions is critical. In the perfect integrator, the drift μ is controlled by the inhibition which, therefore, plays a critical role in even this simplest of descriptions of neural dynamics. What should be amply clear from this study and our previous work is that there is no single model that describes the dynamics of neurons everywhere in the nervous system; even the very simple model of section III has its drawbacks, but it serves to provide a simple description of the role of noise and inhibition in the firing dynamics of a single cell. In fact, a generalization of this model, the so-called 'leaky' integrator characterized by the full dynamics (2) may well provide a good model of the bursting that is so ubiquitous a feature of axonal firing.

The Inter-Spike-Interval Histograms are not, by themselves, necessarily an indicator of the presence of stochastic resonance as an underlying cooperative effect in neurophysiology. For bistable models having the general form (1) they are, however, a product of correlated (between the noise and deterministic modulation) switching and, as we have indicated in section I, there is some evidence that such switching processes do occur in neurophysiology (although the form of the bistability may be different from the potential systems defined by dynamics such as (1)). Various features of these histograms can, however, lend themselves to explanations based on stochastic resonance. Perhaps the most important of these features is that the heights of successive peaks pass through a maximum as a function of the noise strength. This has been demonstrated in section III for the simple 'perfect' integrator model and is also known to occur in bistable systems of the form (1) [47,76]. So far, attempts to quantify this "resonance" as a matching of two characteristic rates have been inconclusive, for the bistable case, largely because of the difficulty of (numerically) producing good ISIHs with low noise. For the simple IF model of section III, however, this connection (or lack of it) might be possible to establish, due to the analytical tractability of the problem; this is an area currently being actively investigated. Since these models admit of a deterministic switching (or firing) mechanism, in contrast with the fundamental precept of no deterministic switching that underlies the bistable models, the mechanism for the observed "resonances" of figure 6 may well differ from the corresponding mechanism in the bistable case.

What should be clear from this paper is that effects that, qualitatively at least, appear to be similar can occur in systems that are quite different. A simple observation of the ISIH or the resonance in the peak heights as a function of noise is not sufficient to establish a model for the underlying dynamics. In different terms, it is probable that simple models of the type discussed in section III may provide a good fit to experimental ISIHs just as we have seen [24,44,45,48] in various forms of bistable descriptions. In fact, we have shown that, for the bistable case, a good fit to experimental data is obtained using dynamics of the form (1) with different flow functions $f(x)$; the data shed no light on the precise form of the dynamics. This is a characteristic of our coarse-grained description of the dynamics in terms of probabilities and power spectra. In most theories of stochastic resonance in bistable systems, the quantity that critically mediates the dynamics is the ratio of the barrier height to the noise variance. This ratio, in fact, determines, as outlined in section II, the number and sizes of the peaks in the ISIH. So, one must end this review with the (by now) somewhat obvious question: "Which features of the ISIHs are due to underlying neurophysiological processes and which features are influenced by the statistics of the detection/measurement process or the statistics of the simple models such as (1) and (2) which have been invoked to explain the features of the ISIHs?"

ACKNOWLEDGEMENTS

It is a pleasure to acknowledge energizing conversations with Professor Karl Pribram (Radford Univ.) and Drs. Andre Longtin (Univ. of Ottawa), Frank Moss (Univ. of Missouri, St. Louis), Dante Chialvo and A. Vania Apkarian (Univ. of Syracuse), Stephen Schiff (Childrens' Hospital, Washington DC), Alianna Maren (Accurate Automation, Chattanooga, TN), Donatella Petracchi (Univ. of Pisa) and Bill Jacobs, Gabor Schmera and Mario Inchiosa (NCCOSC, San Diego). Support from the Physics and Life Sciences

345

Divisions of the Office of Naval Research is also gratefully acknowledged.

REFERENCES

1. L. Abbott, T. Kepler; Model neurons: from Hodgkin-Huxley to Hopfield. In *Statistical Mechanics of Neural Networks* edited by L. Garrido, Springer, Berlin 1989.

2. D. Amit; *Modeling Brain Function* Cambridge Univ. Press, Cambridge 1989.

3. C. Ascoli, M. Barbi, S. Chillemi, D. Petracchi; Phase-locked responses in the *limulus* lateral eye. *Biophys. J.* vol. 19, pp. 219-240, 1977.

4. D. Berger, K. Pribram, H. Wild, C. Bridges; An analysis of neural spike-train distributions: determinants of the response of visual cortex neurons to changes in orientation and spatial frequency. *Exp. Brain Res.* vol. 80, pp. 129-134, 1990.

5. A. Bulsara, K. Lindenberg, K. Shuler; Spectral analysis of a nonlinear oscillator driven by random and periodic forces. I. Linearized theory. *J. Stat. Phys.* vol. 27, pp. 787-808, 1982.

6. A. Bulsara, R. Boss, E. Jacobs; Noise effects in an electronic model of a single neuron. *Biol. Cyb.* vol. 61, pp. 211-222, 1989.

7. A. Bulsara, F. Moss; Cooperative stochastic processes in reduced neuron models. In *Proceedings of the International Conference on Noise in Physical Systems and 1/f Fluctuations, ICNF91* edited by T. Musha, S. Sato and Y. Yamamoto. Omsha, Tokyo, 1991.

8. A. Bulsara, A. Maren, G. Schmera ; Single effective neuron: dendritic coupling effects and stochastic resonance. *Biol. Cyb.* 1993 in press.

9. A. Bulsara, A. Maren; Coupled neuro-dendritic processes; cooperative stochastic effects and the statistical analysis of spike trains. In *Rethinking Neural Networks: Quantum Fields and Biological Data* edited by K. Pribram, L. Erlbaum Assoc., 1993.

10. A. Bulsara, G. Schmera; Stochastic resonance in globally coupled nonlinear oscillators. *Phys. Rev.* vol. E47, pp. 3734-38, 1993.

11. A. Bulsara, J. Douglass, F. Moss; Nonlinear resonance: noise-assisted information processing in physical and neurophysiological systems. *Naval Res. Rev.* vol. 45, pp. 23-67, 1993.

12. A. Bulsara; Noise and Nonlinearity in Sensory Neurons. In *Proceedings of the Los Alamos meeting on Fluctuations and Order: The New Synthesis* edited by M. Millonas, 1994 in press.

13. A. Bulsara, S. Lowen; Nonlinear Resonance in the Periodically Driven Wiener Process with Drift. 1994 Preprint.

14. R. Capocelli, L. Ricciardi; A continuous Markovian model for neuronal activity. *J. Theor. Biol.* vol. 40, pp. 369-387, 1973.

15. S. Chandrasekhar; Stochastic problems in physics and astronomy. *Rev. Mod. Phys.* vol. 15, pp. 1-89, 1943.

16. D. Chialvo, A. Apkarian; Modulated noisy biological dynamics: three examples. *J.*

Stat. Phys. vol. 70, pp. 375-392, 1993.

17. J. Clark; Statistical mechanics of neural networks. *Phys. Repts.* vol. 158, pp. 91-157, 1988.

18. J. Clark; Introduction to neural networks. In *Nonlinear Phenomena in Complex Systems* edited by A. Proto. North Holland, Amsterdam, 1989.

19. J. Clay, N. Goel; Diffusion models for the firing of a neuron with varying threshold. *J. Theor. Biol.* vol. 39, pp. 633-644, 1973.

20. J. Cowan; A statistical mechanics of nervous activity. In *Some Mathematical Questions in Biology* edited by M. Gerstenhaber, Amer. Math. Soc., Providence, RI, 1970.

21. J. Cowan; Stochastic models of neuro-electric activity. In *Statistical mechanics* edited by S. Rice, K. Freed, J. Light Univ. of Chicago Press, Chicago, 1974.

22. D. Cox, H. Miller; *Theory of Stochastic Processes.* Chapman and Hall, London, 1972.

23. J. Cronin J; *Mathematical Aspects of Hodgkins Huxley Neural Theory.* Cambridge Univ. Press, Cambridge, 1987.

24. J. Douglass, F. Moss, A. Longtin; Statistical and dynamical interpretation of ISIH data from periodically stimulated sensory neurons. In *Advances in Neural Information Processing Systems 4,* edited by S. Hanson, J. Cowan, L. Giles. Morgan Kaufmann, San Mateo, CA, 1993.

25. J. Douglass, L. Wilkens, E. Pantazelou, F. Moss; Stochastic resonance: noise-enhanced information transfer in crayfish mechanoreceptors. *Nature* vol. 365, pp. 337-340, 1993.

26. R. Fitzhugh; Mathematical models for excitation and propagation in nerve. In *Biological Engineering* edited by H. Schwan, McGraw Hill, NY, 1969.

27. R. Fox, Y. Lu; Stochastic resonance redux. *Phys. Rev. E* 1993, in press.

28. C. Gardiner; *Handbook of Stochastic Processes.* Springer, Berlin, 1985.

29. G. Gerstein, B. Mandelbrot; Random walk models for the spike activity of a single neuron. *Biophys. J.* vol. 4, pp. 41-68, 1964.

30. J. Hertz, A. Krogh, R. Palmer; *Introduction to the Theory of Neural Computation.* Addison-Wesley, Redwood City, CA, 1991.

31. A. Holden; *Models of the Stochastic Activity of Neurones;* Springer Verlag, Berlin 1976.

32. J. Hopfield; Neural networks and physical systems with emergent computational abilities. *Proc. Nat. Acad. Sci.* vol. 79, pp. 2554-58, 1982.

33. J. Hopfield; Neurons with graded response have collective computational properties like those of two-state neurons. *Proc. Natl. Acad. Sci.* vol. 81, pp. 3088-92, 1984.

34. P. Johannesma; Diffusion models for the stochastic activity of neurons. In *Neural Networks* edited by E. Caianello, Springer, Berlin, 1988.

35. P. Jung, U. Behn, E. Pantazelou, F. Moss; Collective response of globally coupled bistable oscillators. *Phys. Rev.* vol. A46, pp. R1709-1712, 1991.

36. P. Jung; Periodically driven stochastic systems. *Phys. Rept.* 1993, in press.

37. E. Kaplan, R. Barlow; Energy, quanta and *limulus* vision. *Vision Res.* vol. 16, pp. 745-751, 1976.

38. J.Keener, F. Hoppenstaedt, J. Rinzel; Integrate-and-fire models of nerve membrane response to oscillatory input. *SIAM J. Appl. Math.* vol. 41, pp. 503-517, 1981.

39. B. Knight; Dynamics of encoding in a population of neurons. *J. Gen. Physiol.* vol. 59, pp. 734-766, 1972.

40. A. Kohn, A. Freitas da Rocha, J. Segundo; Presynaptic irregularity and pacemaker inhibition. *Biol. Cyb.* vol. 41, pp. 5-18, 1981.

41. H. Landahl, W. McCullough, W. Pitts; A statistical consequence of the logical calculus of nervous nets. *Bull. Math. Biophys.* vol. 5, pp. 115-133, 1943.

42. P. Lansky; On approximations to Stein's neuronal model. *J. Theor. Biol.* vol. 107, pp. 631-647, 1984.

43. P. Lansky, T. Radil; Statistical inference on spontaneous neuronal discharge patterns. *Biol. Cyb.* vol. 55, pp. 299-311, 1987.

44. A. Longtin, A. Bulsara, F. Moss; Time-interval sequences in bistable systems and the noise-induced transmission of information by sensory neurons. *Phys. Rev. Lett.* vol. 67, pp. 656-659, 1991. See also *Nature* vol. 352, pp.469, 1991.

45. A. Longtin, A. Bulsara, F. Moss; Sensory information processing by noisy bistable neurons. *Mod. Phys. Lett.* vol. B6, pp. 1299-1308, 1992.

46. A. Longtin; Deterministic and stochastic dynamics of periodically forced sensory neurons. *Center Nonlin. Studies Newsl.* vol. 74 (Los Alamos Natl. Lab. preprint LA-UR-92-163), 1992.

47. A. Longtin; Stochastic resonance in neuron models. *J. Stat. Phys.* vol. 70, pp. 309-328, 1993.

48. A. Longtin, A. Bulsara, D. Pierson, F. Moss ; Bistability and dynamics of periodically forced sensory neurons. *Biol. Cyb.* 1993, in press.

49. A. Maren, C. Harston, R. Pap; *Handbook of Neural Computing Applications.* Academic Press, San Diego, CA, 1992.

50. B. McNamara, K. Wiesenfeld; Theory of stochastic resonance. *Phys. Rev.* vol. A39, pp.4854-4869, 1989.

51. G. Moore, D. Perkel, J. Segundo; Statistical analysis and functional interpretation of neuronal spike data. *Ann. Rev. Physiol.* vol. 28, pp. 493-522, 1966.

52. F. Moss F; Stochastic resonance; from the ice ages to the monkey's ear. In *Some Problems in Statistical Physics* edited by G. Weiss, SIAM, Philadelphia, 1993.

53. F. Moss, A. Bulsara, M. Shlesinger; Proceedings of the NATO Advanced Research Workshop: Stochastic Resonance in Physics and Biology. *J. Stat. Phys.* vol. 70, 1993.

54. E. Pantazelou, F. Moss, D. Chialvo; Noise-sampled signal transmission in an array of Schmitt triggers. *Noise in Physical Systems and 1/f Fluctuations,* edited by P. Handel and A. Chung, AIP Conference Proceedings Vol. 285, AIP Press, New York, 1993.

55. L. Ricciardi; *Diffusion Processes and Related Topics in Biology.* Springer, Berlin, 1977.

56. L. Ricciardi, S. Sato; First passage time density and moments of the Ornstein-Uhlenbeck process. *J. Appl. Prob.* vol. 25, pp. 43-57, 1988.

57. J. Rinzel, B. Ermentrout; Analysis of neuronal excitability and oscillations. In *Methods in Neuronal Modeling* edited by C. Koch, I. Segev. MIT Press, Cambridge, MA, 1989.

58. H. Risken; *The Fokker Planck Equation.* Springer, Berlin, 1984.

59. J. Roberts, P. Spanos; Stochastic averaging: An approximate method of solving random vibration problems". *Int. J. Non-Lin. Mech.* vol. 21, pp. 111-134, 1986.

60. J. Rose, J. Brugge, D. Anderson, J. Hind; Phase-locked response to low frequency tones in single auditory nerve fibres of squirrel monkey. *J. Neurophys.* vol. 30, pp. 769-793, 1967.

61. J. Segundo, B. Tolkunov, G. Wolfe G; Relation between trains of action potentials across an inhibitory synapse. Influence of presynaptic irregularity. *Biol. Cyb.* vol. 24, pp. 169-179, 1976.

62. J. Segundo, M. Stiber, J-F. Vibert, S. Hanneton; Periodically modulated inhibition and its post-synaptic consequences II. Influence of pre-synaptic slope, depth, range, noise and of post-synaptic natural discharges. 1993 Preprint

63. C. Smith; A heuristic approach to stochastic models of single neurons. In *Single Neuron Computation,* edited by T. McKenna, J. Davis, S. Zornetzer. Academic Press, NY, 1992.

64. C. Stevens; *Biophys. J.* vol. 4, pp. 417-419, 1964.

65. H. Sugiyama, G. Moore, D. Perkel; Solutions for a Stochastic Model of Neuronal Spike Production. *Math. Biosc.* vol. 8, pp. 323-341, 1970.

66. H. Treutlein, K. Schulten; Noise-induced limit cycles in the Bonhoeffer-van der Pol model of neural pulses. *Ber Bunsenges Phys. Chem.* vol. 89, pp. 710-718, 1985.

67. H. Tuckwell; *Stochastic Processes in the Neurosciences.* SIAM, Philadelphia, 1979.

68. H. Tuckwell; *Introduction to Theoretical Neurobiology, Vol. 2.* Cambridge Univ. Press, Cambridge, 1988.

69. G. Uhlenbeck, L. Ornstein; On the theory of the Brownian motion. *Phys. Rev.* vol. 36, pp. 823-841, 1930.

70. N. van Kampen; *Stochastic Processes in Physics and Chemistry*. North Holland, Amsterdam, 1983.

71. M. Wang, G. Uhlenbeck; On the theory of the Brownian motion II. *Rev. Mod. Phys.* vol. 17, pp. 323-342, 1945.

72. H. Wilson, J. Cowan; Excitatory and inhibitory interactions in localized populations of model neurons. *Biophys. J.* vol. 12, pp. 1-23, 1972.

73. A. Winfree; Biological rhythms and the behavior of populations of coupled oscillators. *J. Theor. Biol.* vol. 16, pp. 15-42, 1976.

74. T. Zhou, F. Moss; Remarks on stochastic resonance. *Phys. Rev.* vol. A39, pp. 4323-4326, 1989.

75. T. Zhou, F. Moss; Analog simulations of stochastic resonance. *Phys. Rev.* vol. A41, pp. 4255-4264, 1991.

76. T. Zhou, F. Moss, P. Jung; Escape-time Distributions of a Periodically Modulated Bistable System with Noise. *Phys. Rev.* vol. 42, pp. 3161-69, 1990.

Chapter 15

Cooperative Behavior in the Periodically Modulated Wiener Process

A.R. Bulsara, S.B. Lowen, C.D. Rees

COOPERATIVE BEHAVIOR IN THE PERIODICALLY MODULATED WIENER PROCESS

A. R. Bulsara

NCCOSC RDT&E Division, Code 573, San Diego, CA 92152-5000

S. B. Lowen

Dept. of Electrical Engineering, Columbia University, New York, NY 10027

C. D. Rees

NCCOSC RDT&E Division, Code 541, San Diego, CA 92152-5000

ABSTRACT

We consider a periodically modulated random walk (Wiener process) to an absorbing barrier with a deterministic reset to the starting point following each barrier crossing. Cooperative effects arising from the interplay between the noise and periodic modulation are analysed as they manifest themselves in two statistical measures of the response: the passage time statistics of the process and the power spectral density of the output. Simple relationships exist between the extrema that occur in these two characterizations. The spectral properties of the response are seen to bear a striking resemblance to the *stochastic resonance* phenomenon that is known to occur in periodically driven noisy nonlinear systems.

I. INTRODUCTION

The response of nonlinear dynamic systems to weak, deterministic, time-dependent stimuli in the presence of system noise has recently been of considerable interest to the statistical physics community. One of the most intriguing cooperative effects that arise out of the coupling between deterministic and random dynamics in a nonlinear system (usually taken to be bistable) is "Stochastic Resonance" (SR). This effect, originally reported by Benzi, Eckman and their co-workers [1] was proposed as a possible explanation for the Ice Ages [2]. It consists of a noise-induced enhancement of the response of a nonlinear system to a weak, external, time-periodic modulation in the presence of background noise. The signal strength, measured in the output power spectral density at the stimulus frequency, can actually be enhanced over its input value through a coherent transfer of energy between the noise and stimulus-dominated hopping dynamics between the stable attractors of the system. The mechanism of SR is simple. Given a bistable dynamic system, for example, information is transmitted through the system in the form of switching events between the stable states, or attractors, of the potential function underlying the dynamics. The effect of an applied time-periodic signal is then to rock the potential, alternately raising and lowering the wells. However, should its amplitude be very low (compared to the height of the potential barrier), it will not be able to induce switching. In the presence of even small amounts of noise (assumed throughout this work to be Gaussian and delta-correlated) there will, however, always be a finite switching probability. Since the switching probability is greater when the system is in the 'elevated' well, which occurs when the signal is at its maximum, one realizes that the noise-induced switching events may acquire some degree of coherence with the deterministic signal as long as certain important system parameters, notably the potential barrier height and the locations of the fixed points, are appropriately adjusted. With increasing noise, the component $S(\omega)$ of the output power spectral density at the stimulus frequency ω, rises until, for a critical noise strength, the intra-well motion gives way to inter-well (or hopping) motion as the major contributor to the dynamics. After this point $S(\omega)$ decreases with noise; for very large noise strengths, the switching becomes noise-dominated and very rapid, with all coherence with the periodic signal being destroyed. For modulation frequencies comparable to the Kramers rate (the characteristic well-to-well switching rate in the noise-only case), the critical noise strength (at the maximum of the signal-power curve) corresponds to a matching between the modulation frequency and twice the Kramers rate, hence the somewhat misleading characterization of this effect as a 'resonance' in the physics literature. The earliest theories of SR [3] embodied adiabatic assumptions wherein the modulation frequency was taken to be smaller than the Kramers rate of the system in the absence of the modulation. Later theories relied on systematic expansions of the response autocorrelation function in matrix continued fraction series [4] or linear response approaches [5]. The physics literature is also replete with demonstrations of SR in numerous experiments [6] and analog simulations [7]. A good overview of the phenomenon may be found in recent review articles by Moss [8] and Jung [9] as well as the proceedings of a NATO workshop on the subject [10]. Recent contributions to the field tend to focus on the role of multiplicative noise, i.e. fluctuations in the potential barrier height and locations of the minima [11], the extension of conventional theories of SR to new regimes of parameter space [12], and the interplay of noise and modulation in populations of globally coupled bistable elements [13,14]. In addition, there has been much recent speculation about the possible central role played by SR in the response of sensory neurons (modelled as bistable noise-controlled switching elements) in the mammalian nervous system [14,15].

The above paragraph provides a short survey of research carried out to date in this field, for the most part on bistable dynamic systems, i.e., systems whose dynamics can be underpinned by a double-welled "potential function". However, SR is by definition a threshold process. One assumes that the deterministic periodic modulation is too weak to cause transitions over the potential barrier in the absence of the noise; then even small amounts of added white noise will lead to noise-assisted barrier crossings, thereby enhancing the output signal-to-noise-ratio of the system. This, in turn, begs the question of whether similar cooperative effects can be seen in the response of a simpler system, quantified solely in terms of threshold crossing events. The fact that SR may indeed be a feature of signal processing by sensory neurons and that there exist simpler mathematical models of neural firing than the bistable models referred to above, provides further momentum to this question. A very recent paper by Wiesenfeld et. al. [16] describes SR in the response of a simple system, one in which a state point makes an excursion to a barrier, under the influence of white noise and a weak periodic signal; after surmounting the barrier (which is impossible without the noise) the state point is returned deterministically to its starting point. This system can be used as a prototype of a variety of "excitable systems", some of which are known to provide very good descriptions of certain properties of excitable cells. Indeed, Wiesenfeld et. al. are able to match the predictions of their generic theory quite well with analog simulations of a Fitzhugh-Nagummo model of the neuron, as well as experimental data from the mechano-receptor of the Missouri crayfish stimulated by external noise and a weak periodic modulation. The predictions match the simulations even though, unlike other single-state treatments of SR [17], they do not explicitly consider a system dynamics described by a monostable potential.

Motivated by recent work into the modeling of the response of sensory neurons to deterministic periodic signals embedded in a noise background [14,15], we wish to consider the response of simpler (compared to the plethora of bistable-system-based treatments to date) systems to such external stimuli. It seems fitting to consider continuous state space random walk models, since these embody some of the most fundamental concepts of statistical physics and can be used in modeling a wide variety of phenomena in areas as diverse as genetics and astronomy. In fact, the reponse of the simplest one-dimensional random walk to a time-periodic stimulus has already been described by Fletcher, Havlin and Weiss [18]; they show that the mean residence time is a minimum for certain characteristic frequencies. Excellent reviews of random walk dynamics exist [19], and rigorous theories of the first passage time in stationary one-dimensional random walks have been developed by Siegert and his co-workers [20] (see [21] for good reviews).

The model that we consider in this work is a special case of the periodically driven Ornstein-Uhlenbeck process [22]:

$$\dot{x} = \lambda(u_r - x) + \mu + F(t) + q \cos \omega t . \tag{1}$$

Equation (1), in the absence of the periodic stimulus, has been extensively studied in the theoretical neuroscience literature as a so-called "Integrate-Fire" (IF) model of neurons [23]. In these studies, $x(t)$ represents the cell membrane voltage, with μ being a positive drift to a firing threshold a while λ is a decay constant governing the decay of the voltage variable to a resting level u_r. The noise term $F(t)$ represents the net contribution from all the synaptic inputs to the cell; it is usually taken to be Gaussian and delta-correlated with zero mean and variance D. Deterministic IF models have been studied by Keener et. al. [24]. Excellent reviews of the applications of models such as (1) to neurophysiological modeling can be found in the works of Tuckwell [25].

In this work, we shall consider a simplification of the above model, the $\lambda = 0$ case; of course, the $\lambda = 0 = q = \mu$ case constitutes the celebrated free-particle problem studied by Einstein [22]. Before studying the effects of the periodic stimulus, however, it is instructive to review some of the results for the unmodulated ($q = 0$) case, the so-called Wiener Process [21,22]. Such a model was introduced by Gerstein and Mandelbrot (GM) [26] as a model of neural firing events subject to certain constraints. In their model, which they called the "perfect integrator", the underlying dynamics are assumed to be describable by a stationary random walk based on the cornerstone requirement of a stable distribution function, in the absence of drift, for the probability density of first passage times corresponding to the dynamics. The state variable $x(t)$, representing the membrane voltage, is assumed to execute a biased random walk to an absorbing threshold a at which point a firing event is designated to have occurred, and $x(t)$ is instantaneously reset to its starting value, the reset mechanism being purely deterministic. It is this reset which renders the 'global' dynamics nonlinear. It is also assumed that the motion occurs under the bias of a positive drift coefficient μ which was defined by GM as the suitably weighted difference between excitatory and inhibitory synaptic inputs (it is neurophysiologically reasonable to assume these inputs to be different [26]). For this model, the Wiener process with drift, one readily writes down the associated Fokker Planck Equation (FPE) [21,22],

$$\frac{\partial}{\partial t}P(x,t) = -\mu\frac{\partial P}{\partial x} + \frac{D}{2}\frac{\partial^2 P}{\partial x^2}. \tag{2}$$

From (2) the First Passage Times Density Function (FPTDF), also known in the neurophysiological literature as the Inter-Spike Interval Histogram (ISIH), is readily found to be [21],

$$g_0(t) = \frac{a}{\sqrt{2\pi D t^3}}\exp\left\{-\frac{(a-a_0-\mu t)^2}{2Dt}\right\}, \tag{3}$$

a_0 being the starting point of the random walk. The density function $g_0(t)$, often referred to in the statistical literature [27] as the Inverse Gaussian, reproduces many of the properties of experimentally observed FPTDFs (for spontaneous firings) reasonably well, including the long (exponential) tail in the FPTDF $g_0(t)$. However, the model also has numerous limitations (which have been enumerated by GM), the most fundamental one being the assumption that the membrane potential is deterministically reset following each firing event; nevertheless, it provides a simple vehicle to explain, on a grossly simplified level, the dynamics that arise from the coupling of the noise to the drift-driven dynamics in certain classes of neurons. A more rigorous (from a neurophysiological standpoint) grounding of the FPE (2) has been given by Stevens [28].

The first passage time statistics corresponding to the $q=0$ case are readily calculated from the FPTDF (3). In particular, the mean first passage time (MFPT) $\bar{t} \equiv t_0 = (a-a_0)/\mu$ to the absorbing threshold is calculated as the first moment of $g_0(t)$, and its reciprocal yields an average firing rate. The variance of the first passage time is $\overline{t^2} - \bar{t}^2 = D(a-a_0)/\mu^3$. For a long-tailed distribution of the form (3) however, possibly the more important quantity is the most probable time or mode, corresponding to the maximum of the FPTDF. For the $q=0$ case, this time is readily obtained by differentiation:

$$t_m = \frac{3D}{2\mu^2}\left\{\sqrt{1+\frac{4a^2\mu^2}{9D^2}} - 1\right\}. \tag{4}$$

It is significant that the mode t_m depends on the noise. In experiments, crossing or firing times clustered about the mode are more probable. The mean of a large number of firing times may yield a MFPT t_0 which, depending on the physical characteristics of the density function (3), is close to the mode or far out in the tail. When analysing the properties of the FPTDF, the interplay of the three time-scales $T_0 (=2\pi/\omega), t_0$, and t_m is crucial. With increasing drift μ (corresponding in a neurophysiological context to decreasing inhibition) or with decreasing noise strength, while keeping the drift fixed, the FPTDF approaches a more sharply peaked density; in effect, the tail of the density (3) shrinks, with the mean approaching the mode. This may be demonstrated via a Gram-Charlier expansion of the density function (3), and is depicted in figure 1 in which we plot the ratio t_m/t_0 vs. the drift μ and the noise variance D. Increasing the drift is seen to lead to a more sharply peaked distribution as $t_m/t_0 \to 1$ for a given noise variance; the approach to a very sharply peaked distribution is more rapid at lower noise strengths. In the $\mu \to 0$ limit, the mean t_0 increases without bound, corresponding to the long tail that emerges, in this limit, in the distribution function $g_0(t)$; the mode, however, approaches a limiting value $t_m = a^2/3D$. For this case, the moments of the FPTDF must be computed by invoking a cutoff t_c i.e., we re-define the FPTDF to be the probability density of reaching the barrier in some finite time t_c; this case is not considered in this work

In the following two sections, we detail the effects of including the periodic modulation term in the dynamics. The resulting FPTDFs are seen to be strikingly similar to and display many of the properties of Escape Time Distributions that have been studied in nonlinear systems with dynamics underpinned by a bistable potential. In fact, some of the noise-induced cooperative behavior that we will observe in the FPTDF and the power spectral density of the output $x(t)$ is seen to be strikingly similar to behavior in bistable systems that has been linked to the stochastic resonance phenomenon. A detailed discussion of these points is contained in the following sections.

II. WEAK PERIODIC STIMULUS AND THE FPTDF

We now consider the inclusion of the periodic modulation term in the dynamics: the $q > 0$ case of equation (1), but with $\lambda = 0$. We require that, following each crossing of the absorbing barrier at $x = a$, a particle described by the state variable $x(t)$ is reset to its starting point $a_0 = 0$. We also assume that the phase difference between the solution $x(t)$ and the periodic stimulus is reset to zero following each barrier crossing. This is an important point; if we allowed the phase to remain coherent across the reset times, there would be, after an initial transient, a preferred phase at which most of the threshold crossings occurred. Thus, the only effective difference between the coherent model and the full reset model would be a phase offset in the response statistics, merely a quantitative change. The FPE for our model is easily written down:

$$\frac{\partial}{\partial t} P(x,t) = -(\mu + q \cos \omega t)\frac{\partial P}{\partial x} + \frac{D}{2}\frac{\partial^2 P}{\partial x^2}. \tag{5}$$

The substitution $y = x - \mu t - \frac{q}{\omega}\sin \omega t$ enables us to solve the FPE, using the method of images, subject to the condition of the absorbing boundary at $x = a$,

$$\sqrt{2\pi Dt}\ P(x,t) = \exp\left[-\frac{(x - \mu t - \frac{q}{\omega}\sin\omega t)^2}{2Dt}\right]$$

$$-\exp\left[\frac{2a}{Dt}(\mu t + \frac{q}{\omega}\sin\omega t)\right]$$

$$\times \exp\left[-\frac{(x - 2a - \mu t - \frac{q}{\omega}\sin\omega t)^2}{2Dt}\right], \tag{6}$$

whence the FPTDF is computed via the prescription [21]

356

$$g(t) = -\frac{d}{dt}\int_{-\infty}^{a} P(x,t)\,dx,$$

which yields, after some calculation,

$$g(t) = \frac{1}{\sqrt{2\pi D}}\frac{a}{t^{3/2}}\exp(-f_1) + \frac{aq}{Dt^2}\left(t\cos\omega t - \frac{1}{\omega}\sin\omega t\right)\Phi_c(f_3)\exp(f_2), \qquad (7)$$

where $\Phi_c(z) \equiv \frac{2}{\sqrt{\pi}}\int_z^\infty e^{-t^2}\,dt$ is the Complementary Error Function and we have defined,

$$f_1 \equiv \frac{\left(a - \mu t - \frac{q}{\omega}\sin\omega t\right)^2}{2Dt}$$

$$f_2 \equiv \frac{2a}{Dt}\left(\mu t + \frac{q}{\omega}\sin\omega t\right)$$

$$f_3 \equiv \frac{\left(a + \mu t + \frac{q}{\omega}\sin\omega t\right)}{\sqrt{2Dt}}.$$

For future use, it is convenient to expand (7) to first order in q:

$$g(t) \approx g_0(t) + \frac{aq}{Dt^2}(t\cos\omega t - \omega^{-1}\sin\omega t)\Phi_c\left[\frac{a + \mu t}{\sqrt{2Dt}}\right]\exp(2a\mu/D). \qquad (8)$$

For the small values of q values considered in this work, this expression yields a FPTDF that is virtually identical to the exact expression (7).

We now briefly discuss some of the properties of the density function (7). The mean first passage time (MFPT) for the $q > 0$ case could be found directly from (7) by integration. It is, however, far simpler to note that the MFPT is simply the passage time to the boundary in the absence of noise. Then, since we assume the periodic motion to be simply a small perturbation to the drift dynamics, a first-order perturbation solution of the dynamic equation $a = \mu t + \frac{q}{\omega}\sin\omega t$ yields the deterministic passage time corresponding to the MFPT for the $\lambda = 0$ case of the process (1):

$$\bar{T} = t_0\left\{1 - \frac{\frac{q}{a\omega}\sin\omega t_0}{1 + \frac{q}{\mu}\cos\omega t_0}\right\}, \qquad (9)$$

where $t_0 \equiv a/\mu$ is the mean first passage time (MFPT) in the presence of noise alone. Note that $\bar{T} \to t_0$ at high drive frequencies ω, as expected. Also, in the absence of the drift, one obtains a MFPT $\bar{T} = \omega^{-1}\sin^{-1}(a\omega/q)$ which is defined only for $q > a\omega$; we do not consider this range of parameters in this work.

A plot of (7) exhibits peaks at locations nT_0 where n is a positive integer. Figure 2 shows the FPTDF for two choices of the drift μ; increasing the drift μ is seen to lead to a narrower FPTDF, as described in the preceeding section. The FPTDF (3) corresponding to the $q = 0$ case is seen to be the envelope of the more general FPTDF (7); in fact it is evident that if we adjust the stimulus and/or system parameters such that

$$t_m = n\,T_0, \qquad (10)$$

then the nth peak will be the highest one. This is shown in figure 2 (solid curves); here, the drift μ has been adjusted to make the peak at $n=4$ the highest one.

Peak Heights in the FPTDF

An interesting feature about the FPTDF (7) is that the peak heights go through maxima as functions of the noise variance D. This is demonstrated in figure 3 for a particular set of system and modulation parameters. One can calculate from (7) the critical noise D_c at which the nth peak passes through its maximum. Noting that the peaks in (7) occur at times $t = nT_0$, the amplitude of the nth peak is given by

$$h_n = h_0 + h_1, \tag{11}$$

where

$$h_0 = \frac{a}{\sqrt{2\pi D t_n^3}} \exp\left[-(a - \mu t_n)^2/2Dt_n\right], \tag{12a}$$

$$h_1 = \frac{aq}{Dt_n} e^{2a\mu/D} \Phi_c\left[\frac{a + \mu t_n}{\sqrt{2Dt_n}}\right], \tag{12b}$$

are the contributions from the $q=0$ and $q>0$ parts of the density function (7) (we set $t_n = nT_0 = 2n\pi/\omega$). Writing $D_c = D_{c0} + \delta$ where D_{c0} is the noise variance at which the expression (12a) is maximized and δ is the (much smaller) contribution from (12b), we easily find

$$D_{c0} = (a - \mu t_n)^2/t_n. \tag{13}$$

The remaining contribution δ is found by setting the derivative of (11) equal to zero and then expanding to $O(\delta)$. A somewhat tedious calculation yields:

$$\delta = -\frac{A_2}{A_1 + A_3} \tag{14}$$

where we have set

$$A_1 \equiv -\frac{a}{2\sqrt{2\pi e t_n^3 D_{c0}^5}},$$

$$A_2 \equiv -\frac{aq}{t_n} e^{2a\mu/D_{c0}}(a_1 b_1 - D_{c0}^{-5/2} z_1 e^{-p}),$$

$$A_3 \equiv \frac{aq}{t_n} e^{2a\mu/D_{c0}}\left\{\frac{2a\mu a_1 b_1}{D_{c0}} + a_1 b_2 + e^{-p}\left[z_1(D_{c0}^{-7/2} p + \frac{5}{2} D_{c0}^{-7/2}) - a_2 b_1 - 2a\mu D_{c0}^{-7/2} z_1\right]\right\},$$

$$p \equiv (a + \mu t_n)^2/(2D_{c0}t_n); \quad z_1 \equiv (a + \mu t_n)/\sqrt{2\pi t_n};$$

$$a_1 \equiv \Phi_c(p^{1/2}); \quad a_2 \equiv z_1/D_{c0}^{3/2};$$

$$b_1 \equiv D_{c0}^{-2} + 2a\mu D_{c0}^{-3}; \quad b_2 \equiv 2D_{c0}^{-3} + 6a\mu D_{c0}^{-4}.$$

For a fixed noise variance D, a particular peak tends to its maximum height for $\mu \to \mu_c$, where μ_c is defined by setting $nT_0 = t_0$. (Note that this does *not* imply that this peak is the highest one in the histogram). Thereafter, decreasing the noise variance further increases the height of the nth peak and, in the $D \to 0$ limit, the peak approaches a delta-function.

Hence, the $n^{th.}$ peak will have attained its maximum possible height in the singular limit $t_m \rightarrow t_0 \approx nT_0$, corresponding to the confluence of three characteristic times in the system. In this limit, the multi-peaked density function is supplanted by a single very narrow peak at nT_0. In practice these effects are somewhat difficult to observe because of the numerical problems encountered in plotting the FPTDF for extremely low noise variances. In figure 4 we plot the height of the fourth peak as a function of noise variance for different drift coefficients. As μ increases towards its critical value μ_c characterized by $t_0 = 4T_0$, the peak height increases and the critical noise strength (corresponding to the maximum in the peak height) approaches lower values. Figure 5 shows the effect of decreasing the noise, having set $\mu = \mu_c$. As the noise decreases, one approaches the $t_m = t_0$ limit. Since we already have set $t_0 = 4T_0$, the effect of decreasing the noise is to make the fourth peak the highest one in the FPTDF and, thereafter, to increase its height until it becomes a delta-function in the singular limit, $D \rightarrow 0$, in which the three time-scales coincide. The richness of behavior resulting from the coupling between the drift and noise-dominated motions is evident in this sub-section; we now demonstrate a somewhat different cooperative effect that is peculiar to this system.

Anti-Resonant Behavior

One final property of the density function (7) is worth describing: the height at the mode of the density function (3) goes through a minimum as a function of noise. This can be shown by direct differentiation and has appeared in the literature [27]. The effect also occurs for the $q > 0$ case. In figure 6 we plot this height as a function of noise variance D. The critical noise variance corresponding to the minimum turns out to be

$$D_m = \frac{a\mu}{2} + .3512 \, aq \, , \tag{15}$$

corresponding (for the $q = 0$ case) to a mode that is exactly half the mean ($t_m = \frac{1}{2} t_0$). The second term in (15) has been obtained numerically. The behavior can be interpreted as a separation of regimes in which the random walk is dominated by drift and diffusion effects. In fact, one readily observes that $g_0(t_m) \approx \left[\dfrac{\mu^3}{2\pi aD} \right]^{1/2}$ for $D \ll a\mu/2$ whereas $g_0(t_m) \approx \dfrac{3D}{2a^2} \left[\dfrac{6}{\pi e^3} \right]^{1/2}$ in the opposite limit, corresponding to noise-dominated motion; in the transition region ($D \approx a\mu/2$), no clear behavior pattern emerges. In the $q > 0$ case, one can set the parameters such that a particular peak is the highest. For a given drift and noise variance this amounts to setting the amplitude of the nth peak via expression (11) with nT_0 replaced by t_m, the mode, according to (10). This amplitude displays a minimum at a critical noise given by (15). Since the mode t_m depends on the noise, as we change D, we must change the frequency ω along with D if we desire the nth peak to be always the tallest one. Hence, for the modulated case, the above represents an adaptive change of parameters (the noise and frequency) such that the height of a given peak, always adjusted to be the tallest one in the FPTDF, passes through a minimum. This is shown in figure 7 in which the noise variance takes on three values, selected such that $g_0(t_m)$ passes through a minimum as a function of the noise. For each of these values the modulation frequency is adjusted, via the relation (10), so that the $n = 3$ peak is the highest. The height of the third peak in the FPTDF then passes through a minimum as a function of these noise values, although it remains the highest peak in the FPTDF. The FPTDF $g_0(t)$ follows the same behavior as the $n=3$ peak of $g(t)$ for these parameter choices; this is as expected since, in plotting the curves of figure 7, we have selected two noise variances about the minimum defined by (15), held the drift constant, and adjusted the modulation frequency such that the relation (10) is satisfied in each case with $n=3$.

We can compare the properties of the FPTDF (7) with existing results from modulated noisy bistable systems. The multi-peaked structure of the FPTDF, in the presence of the deterministic modulation, is well-known in noisy bistable dynamic systems. It was first observed by Gammaitoni et. al. in analog simulations [3] and has subsequently been described by numerous researchers in the nonlinear dynamics community [9,29]. Longtin, Bulsara and Moss (LBM) [15] pointed out that depending on the measurement process, two density functions were possible in driven bistable systems; these consisted of peaks at the locations nT_0 (n integer) and $nT_0/2$ (n odd-integer). They considered a 'soft'-potential model of neuron dynamics and speculated that the second density function corresponded to the 'hidden' or 'reset' events that follow every neural firing; such events cannot be directly observed in neurophysiological experiments. However, the random walk model under consideration in this work differs from all the above treatments of bistable models in a very important respect. In the bistable model treatments of SR, the potential barrier cannot be crossed in the absence of noise, since the amplitude of the periodic modulation is taken to be too small to allow deterministic switching. In the presence of a positive drift μ, however, the random walker considered in this work *will* reach the barrier in the absence of noise. This is reflected in a MFPT that does not depend on noise, in contrast with the Kramers rate that characterizes hopping events in bistable systems. However, this property also leads to the "anti-resonant" behavior in the FPTDF that has been described in the preceeding sub-section; such behavior, which reflects a competition between the noise and drift-dominated motion to the barrier, is not observed in bistable systems in which deterministic crossing events are forbidden. In bistable systems, the heights of peaks in the FPTDF display the same behavior that we observe in figure 3 [9,29]. Although there does not currently exist a precise frequency-matching condition that characterizes the "resonances" in the FPTDF peak heights, this effect has been espoused as a manifestation of SR at the level of the FPTDF in bistable systems, particular since the hopping rate in such systems is noise-dependent. No such significance can be attached to the behavior of figure 3 until we examine the spectral properties of the dynamics under consideration in this work; this is done in the following section.

III. SPECTRAL PROPERTIES OF THE DYNAMICS

The theory of the preceeding section, as well as the other theories of noise-induced switching referred to above, demonstrate that the multi-peaked structure of the FPTDF is a direct consequence of the noise. The LBM theory, in fact, invites speculation regarding the possible beneficial role of noise in sensory information processing. However SR, characterized by a maximum in the output SNR vs. noise-variance curve, has been demonstrated in a variety of physical experiments [6]. However, it has yet to be shown to play a fundamental role in sensory information processing in the nervous system, although there have been some experiments that show the characteristic SR behavior in neurons stimulated by periodic modulations superimposed on *externally* applied noise [30]. It is important to reiterate that the multi-peaked FPTDFs that are ubiquitous in the neurophysiological literature are not (by themselves) indicators of SR as an underlying cooperative stochastic effect. To obtain such density functions it is sufficient to have some form of optimization process whereby certain system parameters, e.g. the potential barrier height in a bistable system or the quantities a and μ in the noisy dynamics, can be adjusted in response to the applied stimulus. Such an adjustment optimizes the coherence between the stimulus, which is assumed to carry external information, and the system response (characterized by the output signal strength S or the signal-to-noise-ratio SNR). Although the peak heights in the FPTDF do display maxima as functions of the noise strength, attempts to quantify this "resonance" via a matching of two characteristic rates (as is the underlying precept in SR) have been largely inconclusive because of the practical difficulties associated with generating FPTDFs at low noise strengths.

The mathematical neurosciences literature contains several attempts to model neuron firing activity with an emphasis on stochastic point processes [25]. Generally, the focus has been on the FPTDF or ISIH. If the inter-spike-intervals are assumed to be independent and identically distributed, then the point process is a *renewal* process [21,25]. It is important to point out that the FPTDF (or the ISIH) that was described in the preceeding section is only one statistical measure of a point process; two different point processes may share identical FPTDFs. In addition, not all neurophysiological experiments yield FPTDFs that can be matched to the inverse gaussian. Most conventional considerations of the response of these systems are based on an analysis of the power spectral density (PSD) characterizing the output; hence, it seems reasonable to suppose that the two probabilistic measures of the response (the PSD and the FPTDF) should be related and in fact, for the case of a renewal process, they are known to be directly related. Accordingly, to understand better the cooperative behavior observed in the preceeding section, we now consider the PSD of our model. We treat our modulated random walk as a renewal process, since the crossing times are independent of one another. This is possible because of our assumption of the phase-resetting that accompanies the reset to the starting position, following each crossing of the barrier. Then, in terms of the FPTDF (8) we may write down the PSD at a frequency Ω [31]:

$$S(\Omega) = (\bar{T})^{-2} \delta(\Omega/2\pi) + (\bar{T})^{-1} \mathrm{Re} \left\{ \frac{1+\phi(\Omega)}{1-\phi(\Omega)} \right\}, \qquad (16)$$

where

$$\phi(\Omega) \equiv \int_0^\infty g(t) e^{i\Omega t} . dt \qquad (17)$$

is the characteristic function of the density function (7). At high frequencies, the PSD is seen to approach the limit $(\bar{T})^{-1}$ and at low frequencies, it approaches the limit $\{var(T)\}/(\bar{T})^3$ In the absence of modulation we have the characteristic function

$$\phi_0(\Omega) = \exp \left\{ \frac{a}{D} \left[\mu - \sqrt{\mu^2 - 2i\,\Omega D} \right] \right\}, \qquad (18)$$

which yields, combined with (15), the PSD at the frequency Ω corresponding to the $q=0$ case (the MFPT $\bar{T}$ is now replaced by t_0),

$$S_0(\Omega) = \frac{1 - e^{2A}}{1 + e^{2A} - 2e^A \cos B} t_0^{-1}, \qquad (19)$$

where we define,

$$A \equiv \frac{a\mu}{D} - a\left[\frac{\sqrt{\mu^4 + 4\Omega^2 D^2} + \mu^2}{2D^2}\right]^{1/2},$$ (20a)

$$B \equiv \frac{a}{\sqrt{2}D}\left[\sqrt{\mu^4 + 4\Omega^2 D^2} - \mu^2\right]^{1/2}$$ (20b)

The behavior of the expression (19) as a function of the noise variance D is effectively dominated by the behavior of the real part of the characteristic function ϕ_0. We can write the real part of ϕ_0 in the form

$$\phi_{0r} \equiv e^A \cos B,$$ (21)

which we now analyze in some detail. To begin with we note that $A \to 0$ in the $D \to 0$ and $D \to \infty$ limits; in between, it has a minimum at $D_e = \sqrt{2 + \sqrt{5}}\,\frac{\mu^2}{\Omega}$. We observe that $B(D=0) = a\Omega/\mu$; thereafter it decreases to zero for increasing D. Hence, the behavior of the relative maxima of ϕ_{0r} is determined by the parameter $\sigma = \frac{a\Omega}{2\pi\mu} \equiv t_0/T_0$, with $T_0 \equiv 2\pi/\Omega$ being the period corresponding to the frequency argument Ω in the PSD. A first-order expansion of ϕ_{0r} in D leads to the conclusion that for $\sigma < (\sqrt{2}\pi)^{-1}$, ϕ_{0r} is decreasing at the origin, so that the only relative maximum for this case occurs for $D=0$. For $(\sqrt{2}\pi)^{-1} < \sigma < 1/2$, there is no relative maximum. For $1/2 < \sigma < 1$ there is a relative maximum at $D=0$ since both terms in ϕ_{0r} are decreasing. For $\sigma \geq 1$, there is a relative maximum whenever $B = 2n\pi$ (n integer). In this case the number of relative maxima, N_m is given by $N_m = [\sigma]$, i.e., the greatest integer not greater than σ. For the case $N_m \geq 1$, the relative maxima of ϕ_{0r} are very closely located by setting $B = 2n\pi$, which yields the critical noise variance D_{max} at which the maxima occur

$$D_{max} = \frac{a^2}{4n^2\pi^2}\sqrt{\Omega^2 - n\Omega_0^2},$$ (22)

where $\Omega_0 \equiv 2\pi/t_0$. The actual maxima will be slightly displaced from these values because of the presence of the exponential in (19), but the displacement will be small since $0 \leq e^A \leq 1$. Note that, in (22), $n=1$ yields the "global" maximum, i.e. the one farthest from the origin. The actual maxima and minima can be easily found via expansion around D_{max} and D_e. Near the global maximum, characterized by $n=1$, the PSD (19) approaches the simple form,

$$S_0^{(m)} \equiv t_0^{-1}\frac{1 + \exp(A_m)}{1 - \exp(A_m)}$$ (23)

with A_m obtained by substituting (20a) into (18):

$$A_m = 2\pi\frac{\Omega_0 - \Omega}{\Omega_0 + \Omega}.$$ (24)

The height of this maximum decreases with increasing a or decreasing μ. At the maximum, the PSD is characterized by only the two frequencies Ω and Ω_0. In what follows, and in the figures, we shall replace the PSD frequency Ω by ω whenever we specifically refer to an applied periodic stimulus of frequency ω.

In figure 8 we show (top curves) the signal strength $S(\omega)$ vs. D, taken from the PSD for three modulation frequencies Ω. These curves are obtained numerically from full FPT density (8). The bottom curves show the same cases but with $q=0$; these curves are calculated directly from the theory of the preceeding paragraph. We note that the curves for $q>0$ are virtually identical (except for a vertical shift) to the $q=0$ case. For small q this is not surprising since, for the parameters considered in this work, the FPTDF is very well approximated by its first-order expansion in q. Hence, much of the analysis that follows can be carried out for the simpler $q=0$ case and extended, qualitatively at least, to the $0<q\ll\mu$ case. It is worth noting here that, in practice, we obtain very good results via the approximation (8) even for q approaching μ. The qualitative similarity in behavior of the spectral properties for the $q=0$ and $q>0$ cases is explicitly demonstrated in the figures. Decreasing the modulation frequency effectively makes the global maximum sharper and moves it to the left; these are characteristics of stochastic resonance as we know it in bistable systems. Note that if we take $\Omega=n\Omega_0$ there is a global maximum only at $D=0$ as shown by the analysis of the preceeding paragraph.

Can the critical noise value (at the maximum) be expressed in terms of characteristic frequencies of the system as in conventional SR? We consider R, defined as the ratio of the mode location, given by (4), of the noise-only FPTDF to the modulation period T_0; with the mode being evaluated at the critical noise strength D_{max} given by (20) that approximately locates the global maxima of the curves in figure 8. After some algebra R becomes

$$R \equiv \left[\frac{t_m}{T_0}\right]_{D_{max}} = \frac{3}{4\pi\Delta}\left[\left[1+\Delta\left[\frac{16}{9}\pi^2-1\right]\right]^{1/2}-(1-\Delta)^{1/2}\right], \qquad (25)$$

where we have introduced a parameter $\Delta \equiv \dfrac{\Omega_0^2}{\Omega^2} \equiv \dfrac{T_0^2}{t_0^2}$ that is related to the detuning. As expected, $R \to 1$ as $\Delta \to 1$. The parameter Δ thus defines the critical point at which the global maximum of the signal strength vs noise curve occurs. Recall that the actual global maximum occurs at a location somewhat displaced from that predicted by (20). It is tempting to assume that this ability to express R solely as a function of the ratio Δ at the global maximum is a manifestation of SR. However, this is not necesarily the case, because we can calculate the "SNR" at the drive frequency Ω as a function of D directly from the curves in figure 8; for this purpose, we define the SNR to be the ratio of the PSDs at the frequency Ω in the presence and absence of the periodic modulation at that frequency. The result is a monotonically decreasing function; it does not go through a maximum. Hence while the above-described effects may be an example of a nonlinear resonance that is controlled by noise, they need not be taken to be the same as SR as we know it in bistable systems. Finally, the gain in signal strength as a function of noise is, at least for all the parameters chosen here, quite small (less than 1dB). One can also plot the signal strength $S(\Omega)$ vs. noise variance for different drift values, although this is not shown. Increasing the drift is seen to lead to a more pronounced maximum. This should be expected since the signal strength at a given frequency in the PSD will increase with the number of barrier crossing events.

The effects of changing the drift μ while keeping the noise constant are shown in figure 9, wherein we plot the signal strength at the drive frequency vs the drift for four different drive frequencies. The curves all go through maxima at critical values of the drift. Once again, the $q=0$ case yields curves that are virtually identical to the the $q>0$ case except at very low μ, in which case the curves differ by a scale factor on the vertical axis. This is because with increasing μ the contribution of the second term in (8) to the FPTDF becomes increasingly negligible with the random walk becoming drift-dominated. Hence, it is far more convenient to carry out our analysis based on the $q=0$ case. Note that, as Ω increases, the signal strength at the maximum increases; this is contrary to the results depicted in figure 8, in which the noise strength is varied instead of the drift. We also find that the critical drift (at the maximum) of any of these curves corresponds to a *matching of the drive period T_0 with the deterministic switching rate t_0.* This condition closely resembles the frequency-matching conditions that define conventional SR. In figure 10 we plot the ratios t_m/T_0 and t_m/t_0 vs the drift, keeping the noise variance D constant. The intersections of the curves yield the critical μ values at which the peaks in figure 8 occur. A far more interesting situation is shown in figure 11. Here we plot the signal strength at a given frequency $\Omega=\omega$ vs. drift, and change the noise variance. Once again we obtain global maxima for μ values corresponding to $T_0=t_0$. However, we also notice the appearance of an additional peak in the signal strength for low applied noise which occurs at $T_0=t_0/2$. This effect can be explained by returning to eqn. (22) and inverting to obtain the dependence of μ on D. We readily find that

$$\Omega_0 = \frac{1}{n}\sqrt{\Omega^2 - \frac{16n^4\pi^4D^2}{a^4}}, \tag{26}$$

where we recall that $\Omega_0 = 2\pi\mu/a$. This expression will have a real root for $D < \frac{a^2\Omega}{4n^2\pi^2}$. For the case when $\Omega > 4\pi^2 D/a^2$, one can always find an $n \geq 1$ such that the argument of the square root in (26) is positive. Then $n=1$ defines the global or *dominant* maximum of the signal strength, corresponding to the largest μ value. For large a, the second term in the square root can be neglected (for small n) and we have the dominant maximum occurring at $\Omega_0 = \Omega$, i.e. $T_0 = t_0$; this is also the maximum that corresponds to the largest μ value. The next lower maximum occurs for $n=2$ ($T_0 = t_0/2$) and so on. In fact, one obtains a local maximum for all integer n values until the argument of the square root turns negative. Interestingly, the function $\cos B$ in (19), and therefore also the real part ϕ_{0r} of the characteristic function, both have maxima at the same n values. For large a, the first few maxima correspond very well to the condition $nT_0 = t_0$ (given by the first term in the square root of (26)) which was precisely the condition for the $n^{th.}$ peak in the FPTDF to attain its maximum height for a fixed noise variance D. However, as n increases, the second term in the square root of (26) becomes non-negligible and the maxima are determined via the full condition (26). In figure 12 we show a case with multiple maxima. Here $a=60$ and one expects to find $n=9$ maxima. However, the amplitudes of the maxima decrease rapidly with increasing n and the low-lying ones cannot be resolved on the scale of the figure. These curves are computed directly from eqn. (19) for the signal strength in the absence of the modulation; however a full numerical simulation of the dynamics of (1) with a small modulation amplitude q (compared to the drift μ) yields qualitatively similar behavior. The small differences between the $q=0$ and $q>0$ cases are evidenced solely in a vertical scale factor as stated earlier. The values of the drift μ corresponding to the maxima of figure 12 are well approximated by the condition

(26) with the second term in the square root neglected for small n. From the foregoing discussion, it is evident that the dominant maximum (the farthest one) occurs at $T_0/t_0 \equiv T_0 \mu/a = 1$; thereafter the maxima occur approximately at $T_0/t_0 = 1/2, 1/3, 1/4.....$ The effect of changing the noise variance is also shown in this figure; lowering D leads to the appearance of more peaks together with an increase in the peak amplitude. In fact, a given peak, in figure 12, attains its maximum possible height in the $D \rightarrow 0$ limit corresponding to the $t_m \rightarrow t_0$ case; this is precisely the limit, discussed in the preceeding section, in which the nth peak in the FPTDF approaches a delta-function. For both noise values, the dominant maxima occur for the same μ value; they correspond to $n=1$ and $T_0 \approx t_0$, a condition that is basically independent of the noise variance. As n increases, the second term in (26) becomes increasingly important in computing the critical values of μ, and the peak locations are no longer determined via the condition $\Omega_0 = \Omega/n$. We can compute exactly the signal strength $S_0^{(n)}$ for any discrete value of n, yielding the signal strength at the peaks in figure 12, by substituting (22) into (17). After some calculation we obtain

$$S_0^{(n)} \equiv t_0^{-1} \frac{1+\exp(A_n)}{1-\exp(A_n)} \tag{27}$$

where

$$A_n = \frac{a^2 \Omega}{2n \pi D} \left[\sqrt{1 - \frac{16n^4 \pi^4 D^2}{a^4 \Omega^2}} - 1 \right]. \tag{28}$$

The $n=1$ peak is the highest one. Also, $S_0^{(n)}$ increases with increasing frequency Ω, as was observed in figure 9. For large D values such that the square root in (26) is imaginary for $n=1$, we *still* observe a (single) maximum in the signal strength. Two such cases are shown in figure 11 ($D=2,4$). For these higher D values, the factor $\cos B$ in (19) has only a single, global, minimum and both the factors in (21) determine the location of the extrema of $S(\Omega)$, in contrast to the cases discussed above wherein the extrema of $\cos B$ yield the extrema of $S(\Omega)$ to a high degree of accuracy. As D increases with a and Ω held constant the peak becomes noticeably less sharp and the signal strength approaches a plateau.

To summarize, the preceeding paragraph has established a connection between the limiting behavior of the peaks in the signal strength and the FPTDF (8). If we consider the FPTDF as a function of the drift μ, then for $\mu = \mu_c \equiv a\Omega/2n\pi$ it consists of a single, very sharp peak located at $t/T_0 = n$. For small deviations from μ_c, this peak is shifted from this location and its height decreases. In fact, we have already seen, that for a given a, q, Ω, and D, the nth peak in the FPTDF attains its maximum height at a drift determined by $t_0 (=a/\mu) = nT_0$, in connection with figure 4. This condition sets the location of the mean of the FPTDF, which is precisely the condition for determining the locations of the peaks in figures 11 and 12. Having fixed the value of μ, the effect of changing the noise variance D is to render the FPTDF peak sharper and taller for decreasing D which ultimately leads to the singular limit $t_0 = nT_0 \approx t_m$ discussed in the preceeding section, or broader and lower for increasing D. Precisely this behavior is observed in the signal strength as shown in figure 12 for two D values. We have thus established a connection between the FPTDF (8) and the behavior of the signal strength $S(\Omega)$ which is obtained directly from the PSD. Changing the frequency yields curves that are qualitatively similar to figures 11 and 12 except that the locations and numbers of the peaks change. The maximum number of peaks allowed for a given Ω is contingent on the argument of the square root being non-negative. On a graph with T_0/t_0 as the abscissa, the resolvable or visible peaks occur at identical locations. Although the number of peaks may differ for different Ω values, the lower lying peaks are not resolvable on the scale of the figure; their amplitudes may, however, be different for different Ω values.

IV. CONCLUDING REMARKS

The behavior described in this work certainly has the flavor of stochastic resonance; however, we are reluctant to assign these effects to the same class as the cooperative behavior that is seen in driven bistable systems, although it may have much in common with existing observations on SR in simple systems as described in section one. Certainly major differences exist between the characterization of our problem and of bistable systems in the study of noise-induced cooperative behavior. One such difference is the introduction of a positive drift in our problem; this effectively removes the restrictive lack of deterministic switching that is commonly used to constrain bistable systems. We do, however, impose a constraint, the assumption that the periodic-stimulus-induced motion is a small perturbation to the drift-driven dynamics, which may be regarded as the counterpart of the proscription against deterministic switching in bistable model treatments. Despite this assumption, a passage to the boundary is guaranteed in our problem, even in the absence of noise, because of the positive drift. In fact, we observe that the drift significantly affects the response of the system, and the competition between the drift and noise-dominated motion introduces some very interesting behavior. The simplicity of this model (most of the calculations can be done analytically) permits us to establish a connection between the rich cooperative behavior observed at the level of the FPTDF and the PSD; a precise connection of this kind has not been possible in bistable systems because of the difficulty in performing simulations at low noise strengths. That the critical quantity R (eqn. (25)) can be expressed solely in terms of the frequencies Ω and Ω_0, points to the cooperative effects as being strongly frequency dependent, and it is important to note that no approximation similar to the adiabatic approximation [3], that is frequently made in bistable dynamics, has been made here. Nonetheless, the fact that we obtain qualitatively similar behavior to SR as it is commonly observed in bistable systems when we consider the output signal strength, but do not see the SNR (defined in section two) passing through a maximum, gives us reason to treat this effect as a somewhat different type of "resonance".

With regard to the neurophysiological ramifications of this work, it is important to observe that the FPTDFs of section two, for the $q > 0$ case, cannot exist in the absence of noise. The results of that section seem to point to the existence of a selection mechanism whereby the response to a deterministic periodic stimulus, whose frequency is its most important aspect, is enhanced by background noise, using the distance to the firing threshold (the absorbing boundary in our current system) as a 'control parameter' that can be internally adjusted. To obtain well-defined multi-peaked histograms such as we show in figure 2, one must have the system and stimulus parameters constrained within certain well-defined ranges. Then, increasing the drift or decreasing the noise variance leads to a dominant response at a particular harmonic; the response is a maximum at the confluence of the three times t_m, t_0, and nT_0, as described in section two. This model and other,

366

bistable, models embodying SR are open to the criticism that information may be lost in our consideration of these models as purely threshold devices, with all details regarding the passage to the threshold being neglected. Nevertheless these models reproduce (qualitatively, at least) remarkably similar behavior, in the FPTDF, to what is observed in experiments; in fact, the model (1) with $\lambda=0$, has been shown to reproduce some of the salient features observed in recordings from periodically stimulated cortical neurons [32].

ACKNOWLEDGEMENTS

We warmly acknowledge discussions with Drs. C. Hicks, R. Boss and E. Jacobs (NCCOSC) as well as Drs. L. Gammaitoni (Perugia), P. Jung (Augsburg and Illinois), R. Fox and K. Wiesenfeld (Georgia Tech.), L. Kiss (Uppsala), F. Moss (St. Louis), K. Pribram (Radford), H. Tuckwell (Canberra), P. Lansky (Prague), and K. Pakdaman (Paris). The work would not have been possible without support from the Physics Division of the Office of Naval Research; this support is gratefully acknowledged.

REFERENCES

1. R. Benzi, A. Sutera, A. Vulpiani; J. Phys. A14, L453 (1981). J-P. Eckmann, L. Thomas, P. Wittwer; J. Phys. A14, 3153 (1981). J-P. Eckmann, L. Thomas; J. Phys. A15, L261 (1982).

2. C. Nicolis, G. Nicolis; Tellus 33, 225 (1981). C. Nicolis; Tellus 34, 1 (1982). R. Benzi, G. Parisi, A. Sutera, A. Vulpiani; Tellus 34, 10 (1982); SIAM J. Appl. Math. 43, 565 (1983).

3. B. McNamara, K. Wiesenfeld; Phys. Rev. A39, 4854 (1989). L. Gammaitoni, F. Marchesoni, E. Menichaella-Saetta, S. Santucci; Phys. Rev. Lett. 62, 349 (1989); Phys. Rev. A40, 2114 (1989).

4. P. Jung, P. Hanggi; Europhys. Lett. 8, 505 (1989); Phys. Rev. A44, 8032 (1991).

5. M. Dykman, P. McClintock, R. Manella, N. Stocks; JETP Lett. 52, 141 (1990).

6. S. Fauve, F. Heslot; Phys. Lett. 97A, 5 (1983). B. McNamara, K. Wiesenfeld, R. Roy; Phys. Rev. Lett. 60, 2626 (1988). G. Vemuri, R. Roy; Phys. Rev. A39, 4668 (1989). L. Gammaitoni, F. Marchesoni, M. Martinelli, L. Pardi, S. Santucci; Phys. Lett. A158, 449 (1991). V. Anischenko, M. Safanova, L. Chua; Int. J. Bifurc. Chaos; 2, 392 (1992). M. Spano, M. Wun-Fogle, W. Ditto; Phys. Rev. A46, 5253 (1992). A. Hibbs, E. Jacobs, J. Bekkedahl, A. Bulsara, F. Moss; in, Noise in Physical Systems and 1/f Fluctuations, eds. P. Handel, A. Chung (AIP press, New York 1993). J. Grohs, S. Apanasevich, P. Jung, H. Isler, D. Burak, C. Klingshirn; "Noise Induced Switching and Stochastic Resonance in Optically Nonlinear CdS Crystals", Phys. Rev. E (1994), in press.

7. T. Zhou, F. Moss; Phys. Rev. A39, 4323 (1989). G. De-chun, H. Gang; Phys. Rev. 46, 3243 (1992).

8. F. Moss; in "An Introduction to Some Contemporary Problems in Statistical Physical

Physics", ed. G. Weiss (SIAM, Philadelphia 1994).

9. P. Jung; "Periodically Modulated Stochastic Systems", Phys. Rept. (1994), in press.

10. F. Moss, A. Bulsara, M. Shlesinger; Proceedings of the NATO Advanced Research Workshop on Stochastic Resonance in Physics and Biology, J. Stat. Phys. 70, (1993).

11. A. Bulsara, E. Jacobs, T. Zhou, F. Moss, L. Kiss; J. Theor. Biol. 152, 531 (1991). C. Doering, J. Gadoua; Phys. Rev. Lett. 69, 2318 (1992). R. Bartussek, P. Jung, P. Hanggi; in Noise in Physical Systems and 1/f Fluctuations, eds. P. Handel, A. Chung (AIP Press, New York 1993). U. Zurcher, C. Doering; Phys. Rev. E47, 3862 (1993). L. Gammaitoni, F. Marchesoni, E. Menichaella-Saetta, S. Santucci; "Multiplicative Stochastic Resonance", (1994) preprint. P. Hanggi; "Surmounting Fluctuating Barriers", (1994) preprint. R. Bartussek, P. Hanggi, P. Jung; "Stochastic Resonance in Optical Bistable Systems", (1994) preprint.

12. H. Gang, H. Haken, C. Ning; Phys. Lett. A172, 21 (1992). H. Gang, H. Haken, C. Ning; Phys. Rev. E47, 2321 (1993). T. Carroll, L. Pecora; Phys. Rev. Lett. 70, 576 (1993). T. Carroll, L. Pecora; Phys. Rev. E47, 3941 (1993). H. Gang, T. Ditzinger, C. Ning, H. Haken; Phys. Rev. Lett. 71, 807 (1993). L. Gammaitoni, F. Marchesoni, E. Menichaella-Saetta, S. Santucci; Phys. Rev. Lett. 71, 3625 (1993).

13. P. Jung, U. Behn, E. Pantazelou, F. Moss; Phys. Rev. A46, R1709 (1991). L. Kiss, Z. Gingl, Z. Marton, J. Kertesz, F. Moss, G. Schmera, A. Bulsara; J. Stat. Phys. 70, 451 (1993). E. Pantazelou, F. Moss, D. Chialvo; in Noise in Physical Systems and 1/f Fluctuations, eds. P. Handel, A. Chung (AIP Press, New York 1993).

14. A. Bulsara, G. Schmera; Phys. Rev. E47, 3734 (1993). A. Bulsara, A. Maren; Biol. Cyb. 70, 145 (1993). A. Bulsara, A. Maren; in Rethinking Neural Networks: Quantum Fields and Biological Data, ed. K. H. Pribram (L. Erlbaum Assoc. 1993).

15. A. Longtin, A. Bulsara, F. Moss; Phys. Rev. Lett. 67, 656 (1991) (see also Nature 352, 469 (1991)). A. Bulsara, F. Moss; in Proceedings of the Meeting on Noise in Physical Systems and 1/f Fluctuations ICNF91, eds. T. Musha, S. Sato, Y. Yamamoto (Omsha, Tokyo 1991). A. Longtin, A. Bulsara, F. Moss; Mod. Phys. Lett. B6, 1299 (1992). A. Longtin; Center Nonlin. Studies Newsl. 74, (1992) (Los Alamos Natl. Lab. preprint LA-UR-92-163). A. Longtin; J. Stat. Phys. 70, 309 (1993). A. Longtin, A. Bulsara, D. Pierson, F. Moss; Biol. Cyb. (1993), in press.

16. K. Wiesenfeld, D. Pierson, E. Pantazelou, C. Dames, F. Moss; "Stochastic Resonance on a Circle", (1994) preprint.

17. M. Gitterman, G. Weiss; J. Stat. Phys. 70, 107 (1993). N. Stocks, N. Stein, P. McClintock; J. Phys. A26, L85 (1993).

18. E. Fletcher, S. Havlin, G. Weiss; J. Stat. Phys. 51, 215 (1988).

19. See e.g. E. Montroll; in Proceedings of Symposia in Applied Mathematics, Vol. 26 (Amer. Math. Soc., Providence, RI 1964). E. Montroll and M. Shlesinger; in Studies in Statistical Mechanics, Vol 11, eds. E. Montroll and J.Lebowitz (North Holland, Amsterdam 1984) and references therein.

20. A. Siegert; Phys. Rev. $\underline{81}$, 617 (1951). D. Darling, A. Siegert; Ann. Math. Statist. $\underline{24}$, 624 (1953).

21. A. Bharucha-Reid; "Elements of the Theory of Markov Processes and their Applications", (McGraw Hill, N.Y. 1960). D. Cox, H. Miller; "The Theory of Stochastic Processe", (Chapman and Hall, London, 1965). W. Feller; "An Introduction to Probability Theory and its Applications" Vol. 2 (J. Wiley, New York, 1971). I. Blake, W. Lindsey; IEE Trans. Info. Th. $\underline{IT-19}$, 295 (1973).

22. G. Uhlenbeck, L. Ornstein; Phys. Rev. $\underline{36}$, 823 (1930). S. Chandrasekhar; Rev. Mod. Phys. $\underline{15}$, 1 (1943). M. Wang, G. Uhlenbeck; Rev. Mod. Phys. $\underline{17}$, 323 (1945). M. Kac; in Selected Papers on Noise and Stochastic Processes, ed. N. Wax (Dover, N.Y. 1954).

23. B. Knight; J. Gen. Physiol. $\underline{59}$, 734 (1972). R. Cappocelli, L. Ricciardi; J. Theor. Biol. $\underline{40}$, 369 (1973). J. Clay, N. Goel; J. Theor. Biol. $\underline{39}$, 633 (1973). J. Cowan; in Statistical Mechanics, eds. S. Rice, K. Freed, J. Light (Univ. of Chicago Press 1974). A. Holden; Models of the Stochastic Activity of Neurones (Springer Verlag, Berlin 1976). L. Ricciardi; Diffusion Processes and Related Topics in Biology (Springer Verlag, Berlin 1977). C. Ascoli, M. Barbi, S. Chilemmi, D. Petracchi; Biophys. J. $\underline{19}$, 219 (1977). P. Lansky; J. Theor. Biol. $\underline{107}$, 631 (1984). P. Lansky, T. Radil; Biol. Cyb. $\underline{55}$, 299 (1987). L. Ricciardi, S. Sato; J. Appl. Prob. $\underline{25}$, 43 (1988). P. Johannesma; in Neural Networks, ed. E. Caianello (Springer Verlag, Berlin 1988). C. Smith; in Single Neuron Computation, eds. T. McKenna, J. Davis, S. Zornetzer (Academic Press, NY 1992).

24. J. Keener, F. Hoppenstaedt, J. Rinzel; SIAM J. Appl. Math. $\underline{41}$, 503 (1981).

25. H. Tuckwell; "Stochastic Processes in the Neurosciences" (SIAM, Philadelphia 1979). "Introduction to Theoretical Neurobiology" Vol. 2 (Cambridge Univ. Press, 1988).

26. G. Gerstein, B. Mandelbrot; Biophys. J. $\underline{4}$, 41 (1964).

27. R. Chikara, L. Folks; "The Inverse Gaussian Distribution", (Marcel Dekker, N.Y. 1989).

28. C. Stevens; Biophys. J. $\underline{4}$, 417 (1964).

29. T. Zhou, F. Moss, P. Jung; Phys. Rev. $\underline{A42}$, 3161 (1990).

30. J. Douglass, F. Moss, A. Longtin; in Advances in Neural Information Processing Systems Vol 4, eds. S. Hanson, J. Cowan, L. Giles (Morgan Kauffman San Mateo, CA 1993). D. Chialvo, A. Apkarian; J. Stat. Phys. $\underline{70}$, 375 (1993). A. Bulsara, J. Douglas,

F. Moss; Naval Res. Rev. <u>45</u>, 23 (1993). J. Douglass, L. Wilkens, E. Pantezelou, F. Moss; Nature <u>365</u>, 337 (1993).

31. T. Lukes; Proc. Phys. Soc. London. <u>78</u>, 153 (1961). S. Lowen; Ph.D. dissertation, Columbia Univ., (1992) Ch. 3. S. Lowen and M. Teich; Phys. Rev. <u>E47</u>, 992 (1993).

32. R. Siegal and H. Read; J. Stat. Phys. <u>70</u>, 297 (1993).

FIGURE CAPTIONS

1. Mode-to-mean ratio of the FPTDF (3) vs. drift μ with noise variance (reading from top-to-bottom curves) $D=0.1, 0.25, 0.5$ and (inset) vs. noise variance D for (reading from top-to-bottom curves) $\mu=0.1, 0.0625, 0.025$. $a=20$ and $q=0$ for all curves.

2. FPTDF (7) vs. normalized time t/T_0 for $q=0$ cases (smooth curves) and $q=0.03$, with drift $\mu=0.065$ (solid curves) and 0.1 (dashed curves). $a=20, \omega=0.1$, and $D=0.2$ for all curves.

3. FPTDF peak heights vs. noise variance D corresponding to the density function (7) for peak numbers $n=7, 6, 5, 4, 3$ reading from left to right. $a=20, q=0.04753$, and $\omega=0.02$ for all curves.

4. FPTDF peak height of the $n=4$ peak vs. noise variance D for drift $\mu=0.085, 0.075, 0.065, 0.055$ (top to bottom curves, observed at the maxima). $a=20, q=0.0475$, and $\omega=0.2$ for all curves.

5. FPTDF (7) showing increase in height of $n=4$ peak with decreasing noise variance. $\mu=0.159$ (critical value, see text) and $D=1.0$ (bottom curve), 0.06 (middle curve), and 0.012 (top curve). $a=20, q=0.0475$, and $\omega=0.2$ for all curves.

6. Height of the FPTDF (7) at the mode vs. noise variance for periodic stimulus amplitude $q=0$ (bottom curve), 0.01 (middle curve), and 0.05 (top curve). $a=20$ and $\mu=0.065$ for all curves.

7. "Anti-resonant" behavior (see text) in the $n=3$ peak of the FPTDF. $D=0.195$ (dotted curve), 0.959 (solid curve; critical D as determined by (15)), and 2.702 (dashed curve). $a=20, \mu=0.065$, and $q=0.05$ for all curves, and modulation frequency ω is set, via the condition $t_m=3T_0$, such that $n=3$ peak is the highest in each case.

8. Signal strength $S(\omega)$ of the PSD for three modulation frequencies ω, plotted as function of the noise variance D, with $q=0.025$ (top three curves), and 0 (bottom curves). $\omega=0.12566$ (solid curves), 0.16 (open circles), and 0.2 (dashed curves). $a=20$ and $\mu=0.2$ for all curves.

9. Signal strength $S(\omega)$ vs. drift μ for (reading the sets of curves from bottom to top) $\omega=0.075, 0.1, 0.15, 0.2$. Solid and dashed curves in each set correspond to $q=0.025$ and $q=0$ respectively. $a=20$ and $D=1$ for all curves.

10. Ratios t_m/T_0 (solid curves) for $\omega=0.075, 0.1, 0.15, 0.2$ reading from bottom to top and t_m/t_0 (dashed curve), vs. drift μ. The intersections yield locations of the maxima in figure 9. $a=20, q=0.025$, and $D=1$ for all curves.

11. Signal strength $S(\omega)$ vs. μ for noise variance $D=0.15$ (solid curve), 0.5 (large dashes), 1.0 (dots), 2.0 (filled circles) and 4.0 (open circles). $a=20, q=0.025$, and $\omega=0.1$ for all curves.

12. Signal strength $S(\omega)$ vs. μ calculated directly from (19) with $q=0$. $D=1.0$ (solid curve) and 0.3 (dashed curve). $a=60$ and $\Omega=1.0$ for both curves.

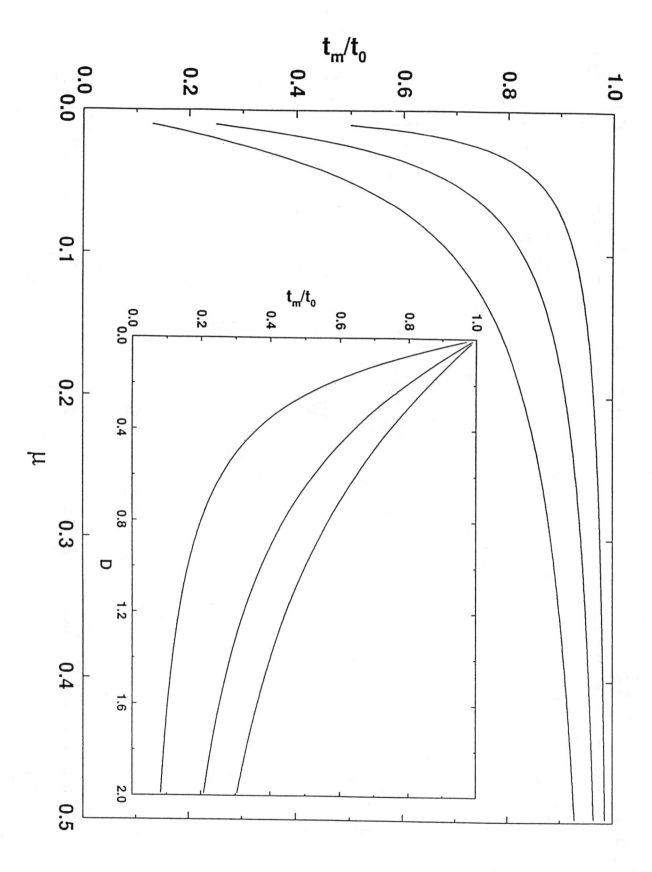

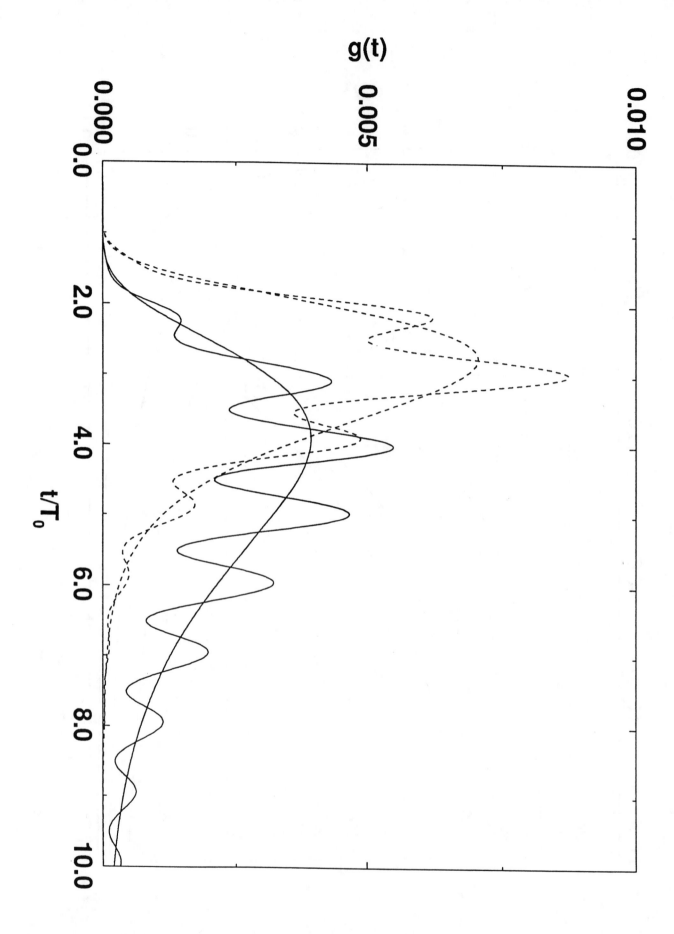

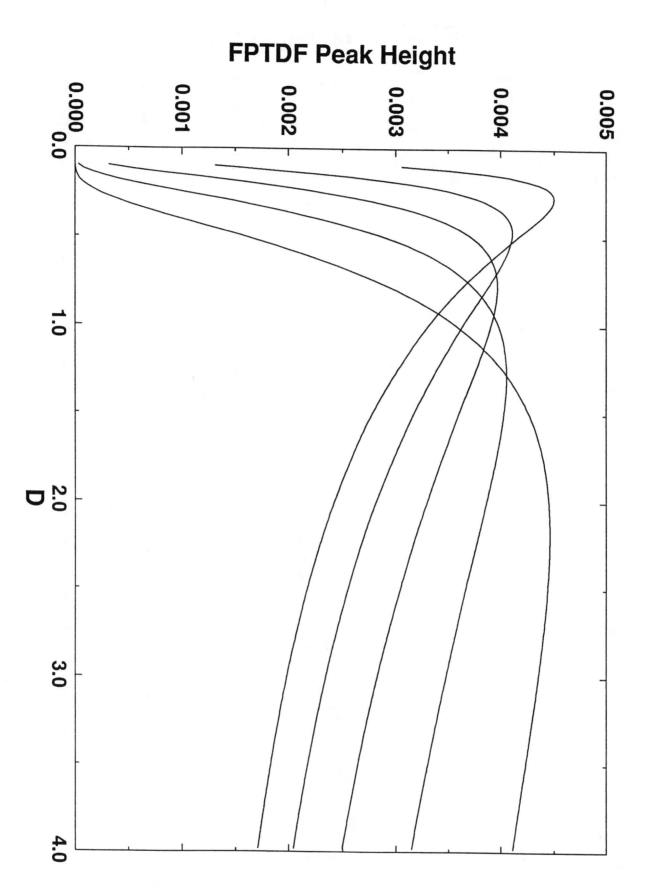

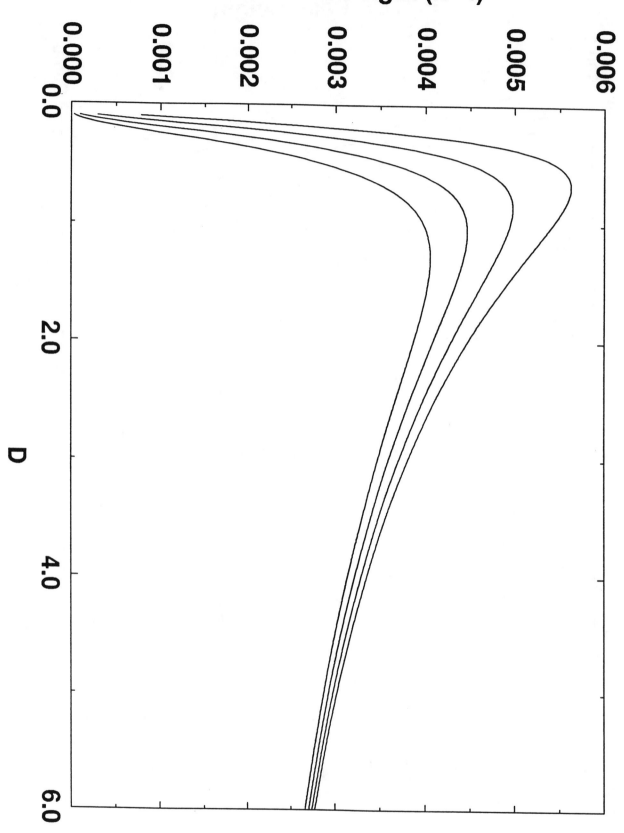

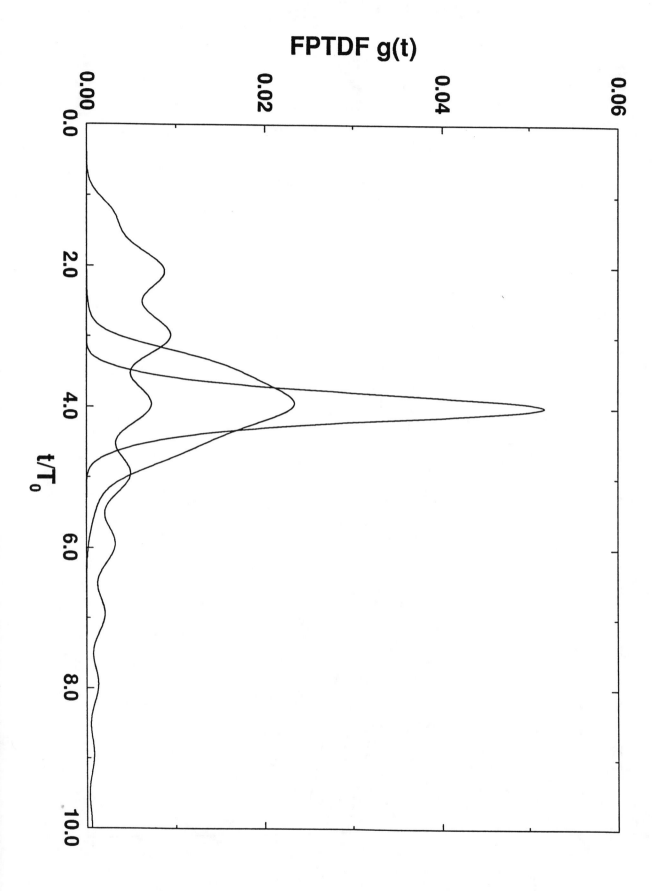

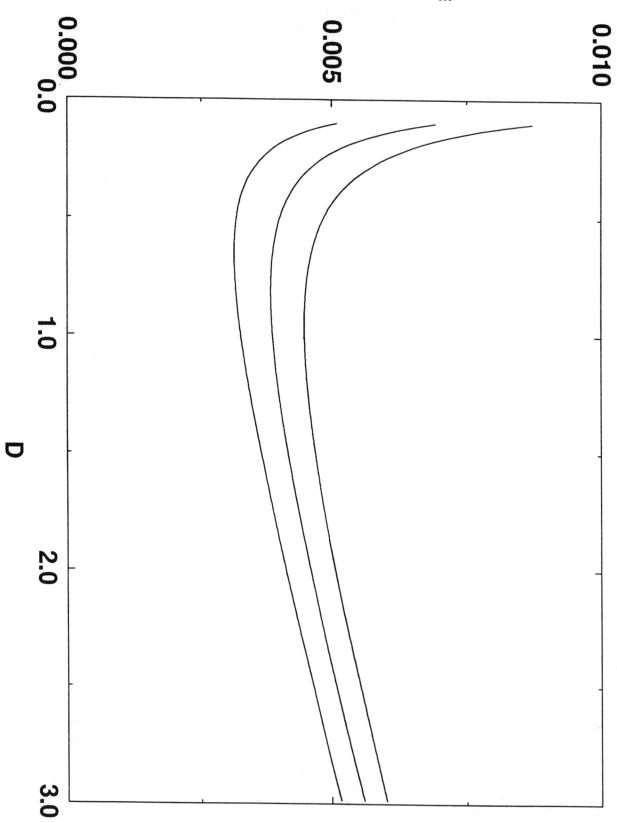

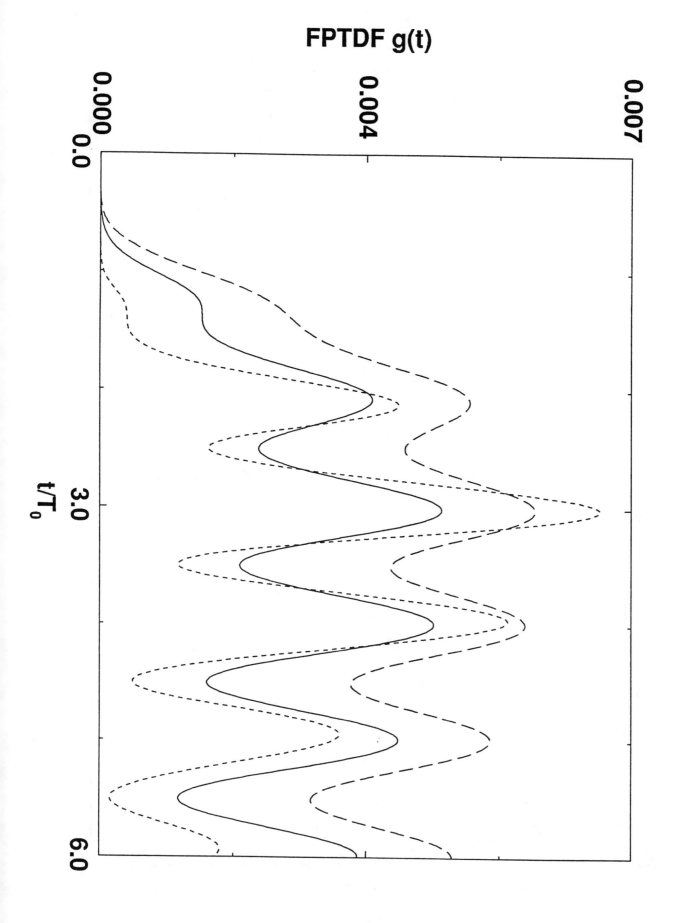

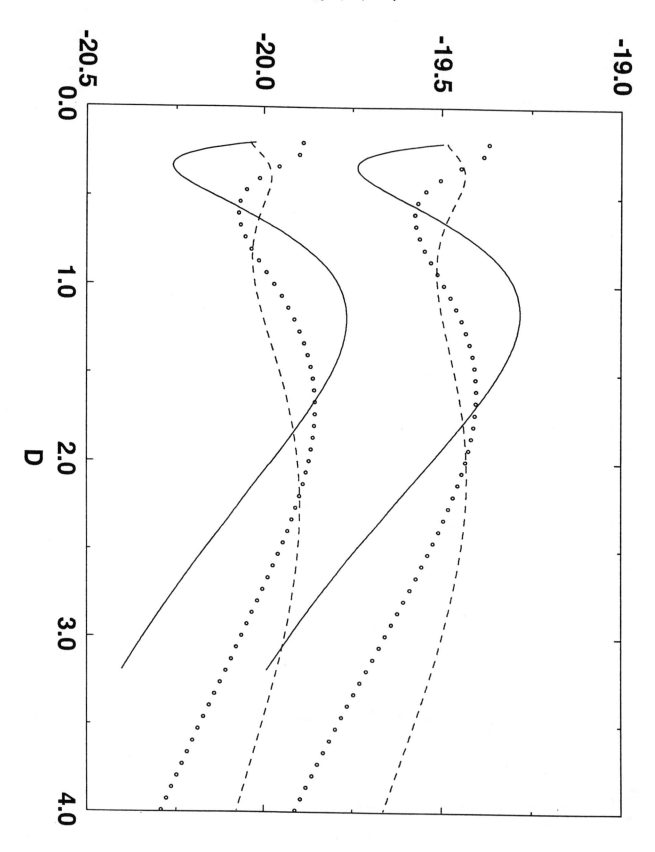

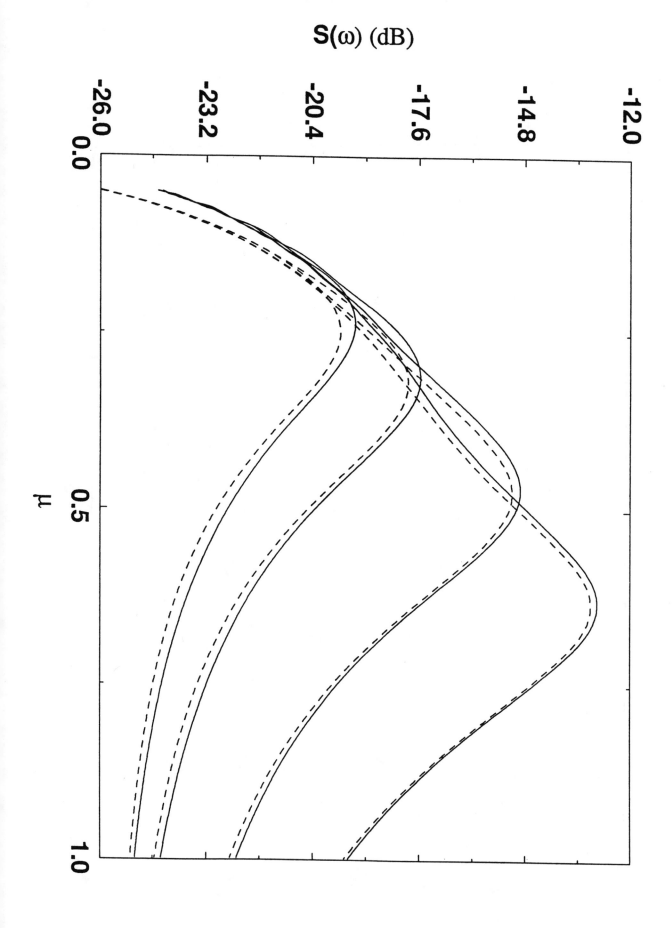

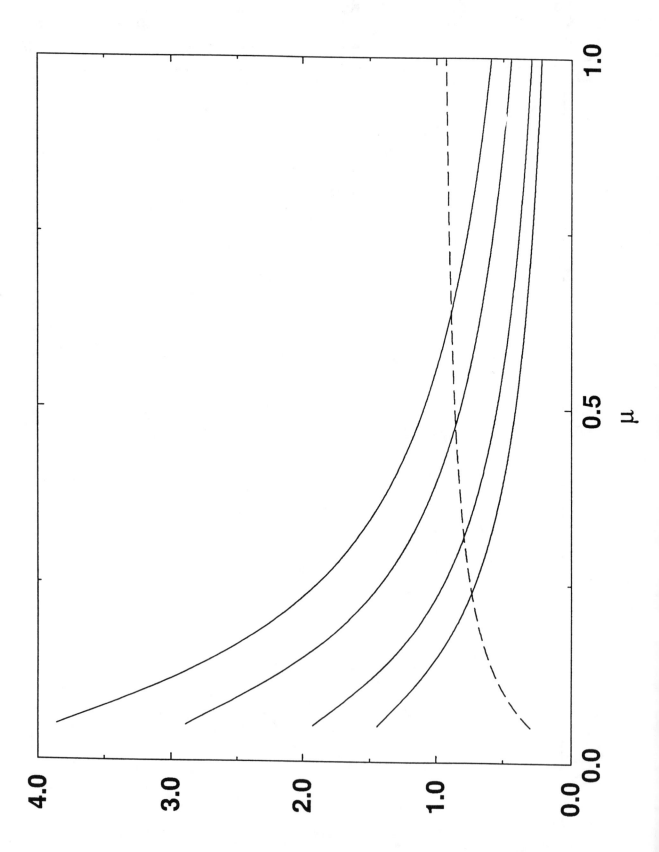

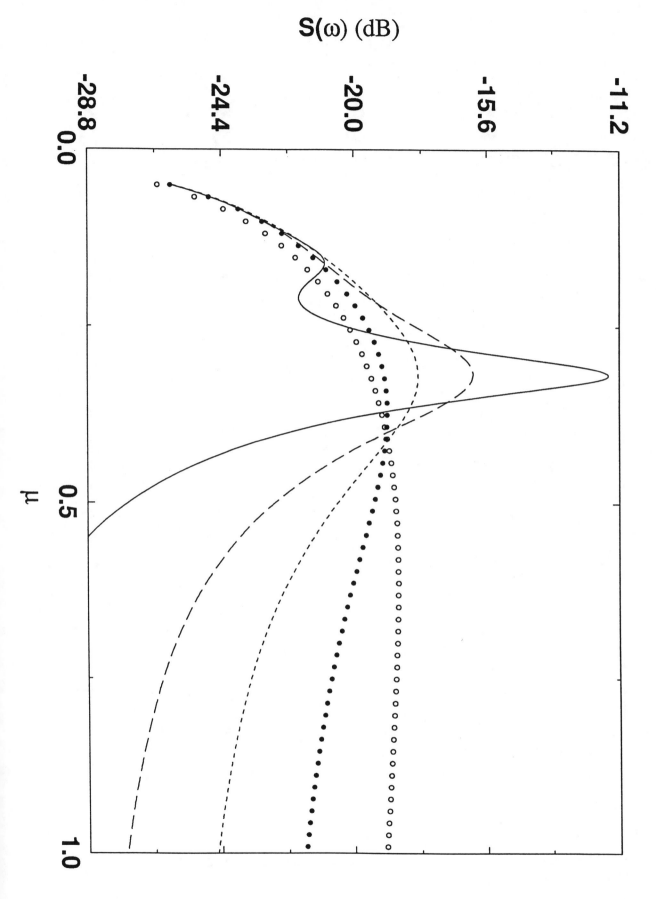

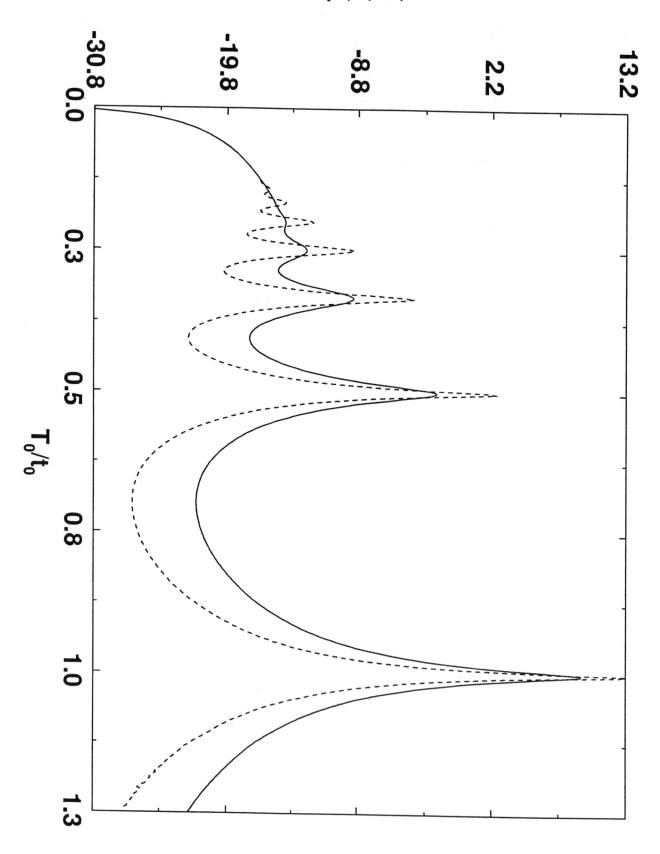

Chapter 16

Bistability and the Dynamics of Periodically Forced Sensory Neurons

André Longtin, Adi Bulsara, David Pierson, Frank Moss

Bistability and the dynamics of periodically forced sensory neurons

André Longtin [1], **Adi Bulsara** [2], **David Pierson** [3], **Frank Moss** [3]

[1] Département de Physique, University of Ottawa, 150 Louis Pasteur, Ottawa, Ont., Canada K1N 6N5
[2] NCCOSC–RDT&E Division, Materials Research Branch, San Diego, CA 92152, USA
[3] Department of Physics, University of Missouri at St. Louis, St. Louis, MO 63121, USA

Abstract. Many neurons at the sensory periphery receive periodic input, and their activity exhibits entrainment to this input in the form of a preferred phase for firing. This article describes a modeling study of neurons which skip a random number of cycles of the stimulus between firings over a large range of input intensities. This behavior was investigated using analog and digital simulations of the motion of a particle in a double-well with noise and sinusoidal forcing. Well residence-time distributions were found to exhibit the main features of the interspike interval histograms (ISIH) measured on real sensory neurons. The conditions under which it is useful to view neurons as simple bistable systems subject to noise are examined by identifying the features of the data which are expected to arise for such systems. This approach is complementary to previous studies of such data based, e.g., on nonhomogeneous point processes. Apart from looking at models which form the backbone of excitable models, our work allows us to speculate on the role that stochastic resonance, which can arise in this context, may play in the transmission of sensory information.

1 Introduction

This article examines the conditions under which periodically stimulated neurons can be modeled as bistable systems embedded in noise. The motivation for this work lies in experimental studies of phase locking in neurons of various sensory modalities. The auditory fibers of the squirrel monkey (Rose et al. 1967) and of the cat (Kiang 1984), cat retinal ganglion cells (Ogawa et al. 1966) and primary visual cortex (Siegel 1990), and mechanoreceptors of the macaque monkey (Talbot et al. 1968) are examples of cells which exhibit multimodal interspike interval histograms (ISIHs) when subjected to periodic forcing. The peaks of these ISIHs are located at integer multiples of the driving period T_0 and, except for the first few peaks, the envelope of the ISIH decays exponentially. Further, this behaviour is often seen across a large range of stimulus intensities. Apart from the phase preference, the firing of action potentials in these systems is aperiodic, as a random number of stimulus cycles can be 'skipped' between successive spikes.

Modeling of this kind of spike activity has focussed primarily on stochastic point processes (especially in the auditory literature: see, e.g., Weiss 1966; Johnson 1974; Kiang 1984; Gummer 1991; Lowen and Teich 1992). In the presence of a time-varying stimulus, these model processes are typically nonhomogeneous, i.e., their instantaneous rate is time-dependent (see Tuckwell 1989 for a review of stochastic modeling). Although these models can account for many features of the data, they do not have a spiking mechanism per se, as do the Hodgkin-Huxley equations and other excitable models. Recently, these ISIH data have been shown to be similar in many respects to histograms of residence times in the wells of noisy bistable systems (Fig. 1a) with periodic forcing (Longtin et al. 1991). Such potentials have been used to model a wide variety of systems, including the channel dynamics of auditory hair cells (Corey and Hudspeth 1983). Noisy bistable models have a long history in the fields of neural modeling and neural networks, especially as a powerful conceptual tool (Landahl et al. 1943; Hopfield 1982). Apart from being relevant for the study of genuinely bistable neural dynamics (see Sect. 3), they form the backbone of many excitable models. The "noisy bistability" point of view can help bridge the gap between point-process and excitable models, e.g., by allowing one to investigate how noise is coupled to the excitable dynamics. Further, this point of view raises the following question which is addressed in this article. What aspects of the data are due to the statistical properties of noisy two-state systems? This description could further benefit from the extensive literature on periodically forced noisy bistable systems (see, e.g., McNamara and Wiesenfeld 1989). It can shed new light on the mechanisms of sensory encoding and on a positive role for noise, traditionally known for, e.g., imposing limits on stimulus discrimination

(Siebert 1965). In particular, it is a highly exciting possibility that signal amplification by noise, an effect known as stochastic resonance (SR) (see Sect. 3), may play a role at different stages along afferent sensory pathways. While our study does not focus on this effect, it does lay the ground work for exploring SR in real neural systems. Recent work has in fact shown that excitable systems can exhibit SR (Chialvo and Apkarian 1993; Douglass et al. 1993; Longtin 1993), and the present work focusses on the related class of bistable models, which are simpler (and thus more tractable), yet still biologically relevant.

Section 2 gives a brief review of the existing literature on stochastic phase-locking. Section 3 presents the bistable models of interest and elaborates on aspects of the theory of periodically forced bistable systems which are useful to understand the skipping phenomenon. Analog computer simulations of the standard quartic and neuron models are presented in Sect. 4. They are compared to recently obtained cat auditory nerve data to illustrate how easily bistable models can reproduce the major statistical and temporal features of the data. Section 5 is a numerical study of a bistable model with 'soft potential' which examines the effects of noise bandwidth on ISIHs and return maps, as well as the amplitude dependence of the ISIH decay rate. The article closes with a discussion in Sect. 6.

2 Background

To our knowledge, the earliest attempt to model the skipping phenomenon can be found in the seminal work of Gerstein and Mandelbrot (1964). Their random walk integrate-and-fire (IF) model could generate peaks at integer multiples of the driving period when the parameter controlling the deterministic drift toward threshold was periodically modulated, simulating the action of auditory tone bursts (clicks) on the auditory fibers. Weiss (1966) has also proposed, as part of a model of the auditory periphery, a model neuron (intended to represent VIIIth nerve neurons) which is driven by the output of the transducer (i.e., the hair cell generator potential) as well as by gaussian noise. This model has a refractory period but no spiking mechanism per se (i.e., it is an IF model). It reproduces some of the features of multimodal ISIHs in response to fast auditory clicks (≈ 0.1 ms) presented at a slow rate. The intervals between peaks were determined by the oscillatory impulse response functions of the cochlear partition at the location of the hair cell which connects to the fiber. Below we focus on a general simple model of sensory neurons with sinusoidal stimulation (rather than periodic clicks) at various driving periods (greater than the refractory period) where skipping is observed. The phase-locking dynamics of biological oscillators has attracted much attention, especially when a steady entrainment pattern (e.g., m firings occurring during n cycles of the stimulus) is observed experimentally. However, Glass et al. (1980) have studied the phase-locking dynamics of a simple IF model with noise and have found unstable zones with no phase-locking in between regions of phase space with stable phase-locking

patterns. For low-amplitude periodic inputs, their model yielded quasi-periodic dynamics, while patterns with irregular skipped or intercalated beats were seen at higher amplitudes.

Another popular approach involves estimating the parameters of a stochastic point-process model to reproduce statistics of first order (such as the ISIH) and higher. Point processes in which the instantaneous rate is a fractal noise (Lowen and Teich 1992) are able to further account for slight correlations between spikes (i.e., "nonrenewability") which have been hypothesized to underlie spike clustering in spontaneous and driven auditory nerve data from certain species. The pure tone case has received special attention in the auditory literature and has led to the definition of an index of synchronization of the spiking to a harmonic of the stimulus (Johnson 1974). Modulation of a point process leads to time-dependent transition rates (ie., nonhomogeneity); yet it remains a Poisson point process as long as the spontaneous or modulation-induced transition rates between the states of the underlying system are slower than the internal relaxation times of the system. In this sense, the bistable models below generate switching events which obey the statistics of nonhomogeneous Poisson point processes (except for slight memory effects, see Sect. 4). A complementary approach to stochastic point processes lies in recent work on stochastic neural models incorporating a spiking mechanism to reproduce, e.g., current-firing rate characteristics (see, e.g., Treutlein and Schulten 1985). These models involve stochastic differential equations and thus have a deterministic component. This is interesting because, for certain data (e.g., Talbot et al. 1968), deterministic phase-locking can be seen at higher frequencies, suggesting an interplay between deterministic and stochastic processes.

3 The model

We focus on systems in the limit of large damping (which makes the acceleration term negligible) governed by the equation

$$\frac{dx}{dt} = -\frac{dU(x)}{dx} + \xi(t) + \varepsilon \sin(\omega t) \qquad (1)$$

where $U(x)$ is a double-well potential (Fig. 1a) and $\xi(t)$ is a gaussian-distributed white noise process of zero mean. White noise has a flat power spectrum; its autocorrelation is given by $\langle \xi(t)\xi(s) \rangle = 2D\delta(t-s)$. For our purposes here, the state variable $x(t)$ can be viewed as the soma potential. The right-hand side is the sum of all the forces acting on the "particle": the force arising from the potential $U(x)$, the modulation force and the stochastic force. Intuitively, the relaxation rate back to the resting potential is proportional to the steepness of the slope of the potential in the vicinity of the state identified with the resting state. Various approximate analytical expressions have been obtained (Zhou et al. 1990) for the distribution of residence times T (Fig. 1b) within a given well. This approach is interesting because it relates ISIH features

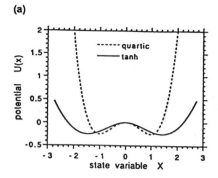

(a)

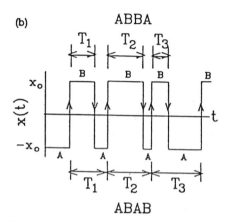

(b)

ABBA

ABAB

Fig. 1. a Double-well potentials used in our study: hyperbolic tangent (*solid line*) and standard quartic (*dotted line*). State *A* corresponds to $x(t) < 0$, and state *B* to $x(t) > 0$. b Signal obtained by applying a two-state filter to the time series corresponding to a particular realization of the stochastic process given by (1). The two symmetries of interest refer to ABBA events (*upper labels*) and ABAB events (*lower labels*). Equation (4) was used with a stimulus period of 4

(widths of peaks, etc.) to basic parameters of the 'potential' in which the soma voltage evolves. This theory further has the advantage over certain point-process models of always yielding positive probability values.

Although the identification of 'states' in the model with those of the neural system is not obvious, we expect that the eventual significance of our results will not depend on such a precise identification. One can readily identify the resting state of the neuron with the equilibrium point of the left well (Fig. 1a) as both are stable in the absence of forcing (the neurons of interest here fire spontaneously and randomly in the absence of forcing). The other state may correspond to an excited state (above threshold, with or without repetitive firing) which does not immediately reset to the resting state (certain excitable cells are known to exhibit such "long plateaus", see Rinzel and Ermentrout 1989); alternatively, it may correspond to a recovery state characterized by hyperpolarization, due either to the intrinsic ionic current dynamics of the cell or to the effect of inputs from other neurons, or both. In either case, the model assumes a stochastic reset from this state back to the resting state. It should be mentioned that our results are qualitatively similar when the reset has a weak or strong deterministic component (the latter occurring in excitable models: see,

e.g., Chialvo and Apkarian 1993; Douglass et al. 1993; Longtin 1993). An excitable cell such as a neuron has a characteristic current-voltage relation which is N-shaped (see, e.g., Rinzel and Ermentrout 1989), as does the negative gradient of a bistable potential; in other words, the N-shaped nonlinearity we investigated can be viewed as the backbone of excitability. While this fact in itself justifies our study of (1), it is important to note that bistability of various forms has been observed in simplified Hodgkin-Huxley-type neuron models as well as in vivo (see Rinzel and Ermentrout 1989 for a review). For example, bistability between a fixed point (no spiking) and a limit cycle (periodic spiking) in the squid giant axon has been observed. Bistability between two fixed points has also been found in models. It is possible, thus, that the main features of the data, and in particular signal enhancement by noise, are captured by the bistability feature per se, regardless of the kinds of states involved. For example, multimodal ISIHs could arise when noise kicks the system between a fixed point and a low-frequency limit cycle (it is thus likely that only one firing would be observed during a mean residence time on the limit cycle).

In this article, the "standard quartic model" and the Schmitt trigger are studied using simulations on an analog computer, while the softer potential of the "neuron model" is studied via both analog and digital simulations. The neuron model is described by the following nonlinear dynamic equation for the membrane potential $x(t)$:

$$\dot{x} = -ax + b \tanh x + F(t) + \varepsilon \sin \omega t \qquad (2)$$

We now assume (and from now on), however, that $F(t)$ is a zero mean gaussian noise with finite spectral bandwidth, i.e., with non-zero correlation time τ_c (equal to the inverse of its bandwidth). Its autocorrelation is $\langle F(t)F(s) \rangle = \dfrac{D}{\tau_c} \exp(-|t-s|/\tau_c)$, and its variance is simply D/τ_c. In the limit $\tau_c \to 0$ we recover gaussian delta-correlated noise (i.e., white noise) with variance $2D$. The stochastic process $F(t)$ (known as an Ornstein-Uhlenbeck process) is governed by $\dfrac{dF}{dt} = -\lambda F(t) + \lambda \xi(t)$ where $\lambda^{-1} \equiv \tau_c$. In the analog simulations below, $F(t)$ is generated by low-pass filtering quasi-white noise from a noise generator, the resulting bandwidth being equal to λ. The stochastic numerical simulations reported below were carried out using the algorithm of Manella and Palleschi (1989).

The potential function corresponding to the flow in (2) is shown in Fig. 1a. The barrier maximum is at $x = 0$ and the minima are located at $c \approx \pm b \tanh(b)$, the approximation holding for large b (we set $a = 1$ throughout this work). The potential is bistable for $b > 1$. When the mean residence time (for $\varepsilon = 0$) in a stable steady state is long compared with the internal relaxation time within the wells (local equilibrium assumption), and the noise is white and of low intensity, the rate of interwell switching is well described by the Kramer's rate (see Gardiner 1983)

$$r_0 \approx (2\pi)^{-1} [\,|U^{(2)}(O)|\,U^{(2)}(c)] \exp(-U_0/D) \qquad (3)$$

388

where U_0 is the height of the potential barrier and $U^{(2)}(x) \equiv \mathrm{d}^2 U/\mathrm{d}x^2$. Kramer's rate is found to decrease monotonically with increasing τ_c (Jung et al. 1989). When $D = 0$, interwell transitions are coherent with harmonic driving only if ε is sufficiently large. In the presence of both noise and modulation, the transition rates become time-dependent, due to the raising and lowering of the wells with respect to the barrier. A logical extension of Kramer's theory to this case has led to postulating (when $\varepsilon \ll U_0$ and $\omega < r_0$; see, e.g., McNamara and Wiesenfeld 1989) a Kramer's rate given by (3) with U_0 replaced by $U_0 + \varepsilon \sin \omega t$. An effect known as 'stochastic resonance' (SR) occurs when the r_0 is commensurate with the switching rate imposed by the external forcing, even though this forcing by itself cannot produce switchings (McNamara and Wiesenfeld 1989). The particle then has a high probability of switching at each stimulus half-cycle, i.e., the switchings correlate highly with the modulation. The signal-to-noise ratio (SNR) of $x(t)$ measured at ω exhibits a maximum ("resonance") as a function of D. SR thus leads to the counter intuitive notion that adding noise can enhance the observability of the impressed signal. The switching dynamics can also be studied using the distributions of residence times in the wells (or, equivalently, of transition times between wells). A resonance appears as the peak heights go through maxima as a function of D (Zhou et al. 1990); this has been linked to SR, although the matching of the aforementioned time scales has not yet been clearly established. It is an interesting prospect that SR is at work helping the sensory neurons respond to weak periodic signals. We did not study SR here even though it is a property (Bulsara et al. 1991) of the bistable models which, we will show, fit the data so well.

4 Analog simulations

Electronic analog computation is much faster than digital computation for studying stochastic problems. Further, analog computers are "real systems" with their own imperfections and nonlinearities, and their behavior can be seen as generic. This section discusses analog simulations of (2) as well as of the dynamics of the 'standard quartic' potential $U(x) = -\dfrac{x^2}{2} + \dfrac{x^4}{4}$:

$$\dot{x} = x - x^3 + F(t) + \varepsilon \sin(\omega t) \tag{4}$$

Here $U(x)$ (Fig. 1a) has a barrier height $U_0 = 1/4$ and minima located at $c = \pm 1.0$. The design and operation of these simulators have been described previously (Bulsara et al. 1991). The Schmitt trigger has also been used in a preliminary study of these ISIH data (Longtin et al. 1991). The "neuron" model of (2) is a "soft" potential, since it goes to infinity linearly in x. The standard quartic is "harder", going to infinity as x^4, while the Schmitt trigger can be seen as a potential with infinitely hard walls located at thresholds $\pm c$. Our goal is to show that while these three potentials are radically different as regards their stiffness, they are able to satisfactorily re-

produce the ISIH data. The conclusion to be drawn from this observation is that matching physiological data to such model potentials is not likely to reveal much about the "potentials" in which the soma voltage evolves. However, that the observed behaviors of real neurons are so easily mimicked by such simple bistable models strongly suggests that their dominant characteristics are describable by two-state dynamics.

Let AB represent a transition of the system state point from well A to well B. A time interval between an AB event and its following BA "reset" event will be referred to as an ABBA event (Fig. 1b). Such intervals are the statistical escape times from well B. One can, as we do below, assemble these escape times (or "residence times") into a histogram called the "probability density of escape times" or the "residence time histogram". Such a histogram has been previously investigated for (4) both theoretically and with analog and digital simulations (Zhou et al. 1990). It was found that the ABBA symmetry leads to a series of peaks in the escape time probability density located at the odd integer multiples of $T_0/2$. A time interval between an AB event and the next AB event, ignoring the time of the reset event BA, will be referred to as an ABAB event. Here the escape times from both wells are involved. The total escape time' is not, because of memory effects, simply the sum of the two independently determined escape times. Nor is the peak sequence the same. This symmetry leads to a sequence of peaks in the probability of escape times located at all integer multiples of T_0 (Longtin et al. 1991). In the physiological data only the ABAB sequence is observed, since ISIs are the times between sequential firing events. The reset event, which can be associated with membrane repolarization, is hidden from this measurement. Thus, only the ABAB symmetry is experimentally accessible. In the following, only the ABAB symmetry is used.

4.1 Aligning model and observed ISIHs

The probability density of ABBA escape times from a bistable system is well approximated by a gamma-like distribution

$$P(T) = \frac{T}{\langle T \rangle^2} \exp - \frac{T}{\langle T \rangle} \tag{5}$$

where $\langle T \rangle$ is the mean time spent in one well. The major features of the gamma distribution are $\lim_{T \to 0} P(T) = 0$, and $\lim_{T \to \infty} P(T) \simeq \exp(- T/\langle T \rangle)$. The density of ABAB events also has this general form, as do spontaneous ISIHs from those cells which exhibit multimodal ISIHs in the presence of a stimulus. One limiting case of this distribution is the decaying exponential which is the theoretical distribution of escape times for the "random telegraph signal" (which is derived from a Poisson point process, see Gardiner 1983). This density is approximated by the escape time distribution (for both symmetries) when $\tau_c \to 0$, and the switching time between the wells is short compared with $\langle T \rangle$. In analog simulations, the switching time is determined by the integration time constant τ_i (i.e., the actual coefficient of $\dot{x}$ in (2) and (4), determined by the RC value of the electronic integrator), while $\langle T \rangle$ is mainly determined by $U(x)$.

Figure 2a shows an ISIH obtained from the primary auditory nerve of a cat with an 800 Hz, 60 dB sound pressure level (SPL) stimulus to the ear. We note the sequence of decaying peaks located at all integer multiples of $T_0 \equiv 1.25$ ms characteristic of the ABAB symmetry. Figure 2c shows an analog simulation of the physiological data at 800 Hz, using the standard quartic (solid line) and the "neuron" [(2), dashed line] potentials. What is remarkable is that only one adjustable parameter is necessary to fit the experimental data. We can adjust either D or ε, save only that the other parameter lies within some range not very different from the barrier height U_0. If we had plotted the simulated ISIHs on top of the physiological data, the three curves would have become indistinguishable. We note, however, that the value $\tau_i = 10^{-4}$ in the circuit is of the same order of magnitude as a neural membrane time constant, e.g., 0.3–0.8 ms for guinea pig inner hair cells as measured by Russell and Sellick (1978) (hair cells produce the "recep-

tor potential" which induces the action potential in the postsynaptic axon from which the spikes trains are recorded). If τ_i were different by a few orders of magnitude, the fits would not be as good. Further, the noise used in these simulations has a correlation time of at most 0.1 τ_i, simulating the typically higher bandwidth of membrane noise or input noise (Calvin and Stevens 1968).

4.2 Nonmonotonicity of the ISIH envelope

When the stimulus intensity is small or its frequency high, the first peak of the ISIH is not the highest, as shown in Fig. 2b (Rose et al. 1967; Talbot et al. 1968). This represents cat auditory data at 800 Hz as in Fig. 2a, but at the weaker sound intensity of 30 dB SPL. The second peak is the highest, and the decay of the ISIH envelope is exponential after the third peak (not shown). Figure 2d shows that this effect is also exhibited by our bistable analog simulators when ε or D are reduced from their values in Fig. 2c. Once again, the analog results lie virtually on top of the neurophysiological data (not

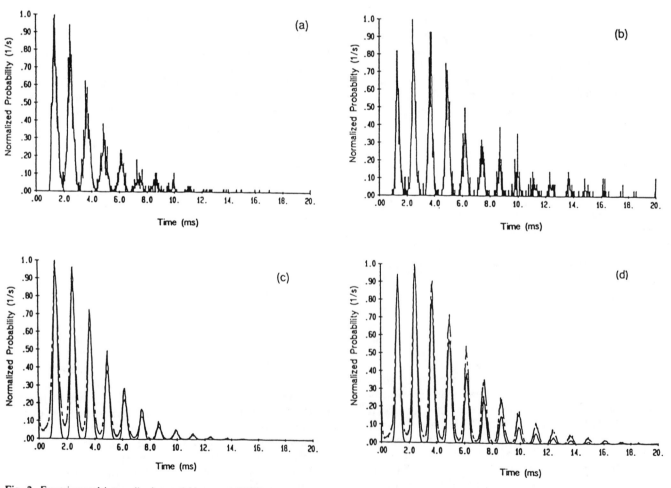

Fig. 2. Experimental interspike interval histogram (ISIH) data from cat primary auditory nerve with an 800-Hz stimulus: 60 dB SPL (a) and 30 dB SPL (b) (after Rhode). c. ISIHs from analog simulations at 800 Hz: the standard quartic with $\varepsilon = 0.209$ V and $2D = 0.0576$ V^2 (solid line) and the neuron model with $\varepsilon = 0.209$ V and $2D = 0.0756$ V^2 (broken line). The noise intensities have been adjusted to achieve the fits and are different because the barrier heights of the two potentials are different. Note that D was changed rather than ε, as both play similar roles: see Fig. 4. d. Analog simulations in the reduced amplitude case corresponding to b. The parameters for the standard quartic (solid line) are $\varepsilon = 0.209$ V and $2D = 0.0425$ V^2, and for the neuron model (broken line), $\varepsilon = 0.209$ V and $2D = 0.0602$ V^2. The integration time constant is $\tau_i = 10^{-4}$ and $\tau_c = 10^{-5}$

shown). While it is tempting to associate this nonmonotonicity with nonrenewability, one must remember that a renewal process can have any ISIH. The following discussion illustrates this point in the context of simple models of skipping.

The nonmonotonicity of the residence time density occurs in both the ABBA and ABAB sequences but is more evident in the latter (and is minimized for the ABBA sequence if the noise is white, as explained earlier in Sect. 4). It can be understood on simple statistical grounds. For a bistable system with periodic modulation, let us denote by p the probability of an AB transition during the half of the modulation period where this transition is favored (the probability of a BA transition during the other half being also p). Then the probability of an AB transition during the ith cycle of the stimulus (since the last BA event) is

$$P_i(AB) = p(1 - p)^{i-1} \qquad (6)$$

The probability of an ABAB event being complete after the ith cycle is given by

$$P_i(ABAB) = p^2 i(1 - p)^{i-1} \qquad (7)$$

This follows from (6) because an extra BA event (of probability p) is required; the factor i accounts for the different possible times at which the first AB transition can occur. Also, $\ln P_i(ABAB)$ does not depend linearly on i for small i, due to the factor $(\ln i)$. However, after the first few spikes, (7) does indeed become linear in i on a logarithmic scale, since the $(1 - p)^{i-1}$ factor dominates. In this simple model, (6) is a straight line on a log-lin scale, as in Zhou et al. (1990). This simple model also predicts that the maximum of the ISIH occurs at $i_{max} = -[\ln(1 - p)]^{-1}$. Thus, as $p \to 0$, $i_{max} \to \infty$; and as $p \to 1$, $i_{max} \to 0$. This is observed in neural data and our simulations: as the amplitude increases, p increases, and the probability shifts towards the first peaks. The proper behavior as a function of frequency also ensues by making p proportional to the stimulus period. Note that in this description the process is still considered renewal, since the probability p does not depend on i, the cycle number. The nonmonotonicity can thus arise from the simple statistics of counting the two events that make up an ABAB event.

It is also conceivable that a nonrenewal process underlies the nonmonotonicity. This would not be surprising given that correlations are suspected to account for the cluster shapes the return maps (Sect. 5). For example, the firing probability during one cycle might depend upon the last firing time. This is evident if one considers an even simpler model of the skipping behavior, in which p is now the probability of a "firing" (or completion of an ABAB event) occurring during a given cycle of the stimulus. Then the probability of firing in the ith cycle since the last firing is given by $P_i = p(1 - p)^{i-1}$, for which $\ln P_i = ai + b$ where a, b are constants. In this model, exponential decay is a signature of the independence of successive firing events, and nonmonotonicity arises only when $p = p(i)$, i.e., when p depends on the cycle number (the constants a and b could now depend

on i). But here there is only one way to fire after i cycles, while in the preceeding discussion, nonmonotonicity arose because of the multiple ways to make up a "firing after i cycles" event. In the present picture where p has a memory of past cycles, each successive cycle of the stimulus brings the soma voltage closer to crossing the metastable point, until finally one cycle kicks it over. This image is helpful when the frequency of the modulation is too high or the amplitude is too low; in both cases, the "particle" does not have time to exit on the first cycle. It is probable that some aspects of the nonmonotonicity can be understood in terms of renewal processes, and others in terms of memory effects. In fact, it seems that (7) may apply to a genuinely bistable neuron, while this last model (for which nonexponential decay implies ISI correlation) may be more appropriate for IF or excitable dynamics (or any with a large deterministic reset component).

5 Return maps, noise, and scaling

We now discuss in greater detail the finer aspects of the ISIHs. The numerical simulations in this section are of (2) with $b = 1.6056$ corresponding to a barrier height $U_0 = 0.25$ and minima located at ± 1.44. The range of signal and noise intensities must be appropriately selected in order to obtain a well-defined ISIH peak sequence. Too high a noise intensity will destroy the peak structure, leading to a single large peak with a maximum near $t = 0$. Too small a noise intensity results in a large number of well-defined peaks; however, the switching frequency drops considerably so that digital simulations take an unacceptable length of time. For the signal and noise values used here, the simulations (carried out on a HP-Apollo DN-425 workstation) took about 36 h to perform and involved 40 000 switching events for each histogram using a step size of 0.001. For simulation purposes, the white noise case corresponds to selecting an integration step size that is much greater than τ_c. For colored noise, τ_c exceeds the step size. Only ISIHs *corresponding to the ABAB symmetry* are considered here.

5.1 Return maps

In the absence of modulation ($\varepsilon = 0$), the simulated ISIHs, and often the neural spontaneous ISIH, are of gamma-type (Sect. 4.1); the dot density in the associated return map (a scatter plot of interval I_{i+1} vs I_i) first increases and then dies off exponentially with distance along the horizontal and vertical directions. Successive intervals are not significantly correlated (in either the $\varepsilon = 0$ or $\varepsilon \neq 0$ case), as lines connecting successive points show no obvious patterns and assume random orientations (not shown). This is also the case for the auditory data of interest here (although nonrenewal properties such as correlations over long time scales or between firing phases have been reported, see, e.g., Lowen and Teich 1992; Longtin 1993). Figure 3b shows a return map of the auditory data used in Fig. 2a. The tendency of the dots to cluster on a lattice with intersections at all integer multiples of T_0 ($= 1.25$ ms) indicates the ABAB symmetry. Moreover, there is a definite diagonal symmetry of slope -1 as indicated by the elongations of the individual clusters (this is often seen at frequencies below 1000 Hz). Similar scatter plots (including the elongation of the clusters) are obtained by plotting the successive ISIs from the model data used to generate Fig. 2c (not shown, although similar features appear in Fig. 3d discussed below). The lattice and negatively sloped clusters are thus basic properties of a periodically modulated noisy bistable system. The negative slopes bespeak some form of memory between successive ISIs such that if interval $I_i < mT_0$, then $I_{i+1} > nT_0$, where m, n are integers. Because there is skipping, however, this does not imply a relationship between the duration of successive ISIs. Nevertheless, this noticeable temporal structure is a manifestation of nonrenewal dynamics. This negative slope is enhanced by increasing τ_c as shown in the next section.

5.2 Effect of the noise correlation time

This section focusses on the effect of the bandwidth of the noise on the ISIH and return maps. The solid curve of Fig. 3a shows the ISIH from (2) in the quasi-white noise case ($\tau_c = 0.0001$). The striking feature is that, for this soft potential, the dominant peaks lie at $nT_0/2$ with n odd, even though the ABAB symmetry is being considered.

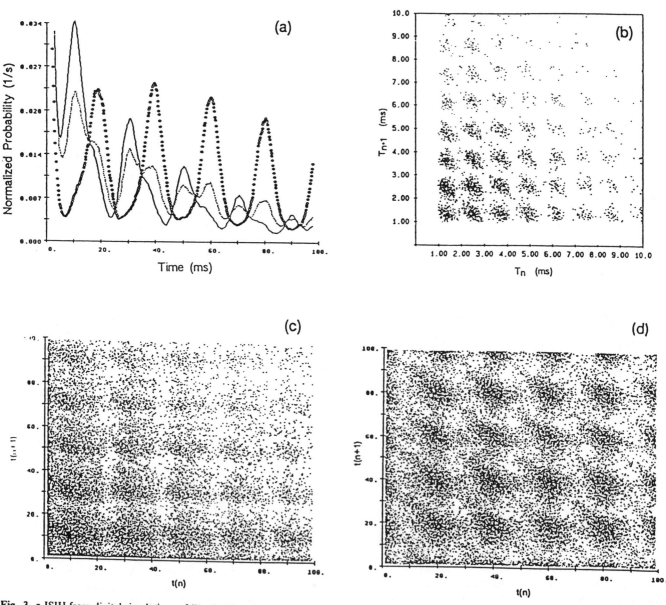

Fig. 3. **a** ISIH from digital simulations of (2) with $(b, \varepsilon, \omega, D) = (1.6056, 0.304, \pi/10, 0.067)$ and $\tau_c = 0.0001$ (*solid curve*), 0.05 (*dotted curve*), and 0.5 (*open circles*). **b** Experimental return map from the cat data used to generate Fig. 2a. **c** Return map corresponding to the ISIH in **a** with $\tau_c = 0.0001$ (quasi-white noise case), for which the points fall within clusters occurring at $nT_0/2$ where n is odd. **d** Same as **c** but with $\tau_c = 0.5$. The clusters occur here at mT_0 where m is an integer

392

The dotted curve ($\tau_c = 0.05$) shows the peak sequence at $nT_0/2$ with n odd transitioning to the sequence at mT_0 with m an integer; for $\tau_c = 0.5$, the normal ABAB sequence of peaks is recovered. The peaks in the quasi-white case may be explained by observing that, even though the potential is being rocked on a timescale $T_0/2$, there is always a finite probability of $x(t)$ sojourning about the metastable point longer than half a forcing period. A rapid back-and-forth transition at this point will, for example, cut a usual ABAB interval into two smaller ABAB intervals, with the result that the first peak now lies at $T_0/2$. These rapid crossings are emphasized by white noise. The correlations in the noise are passed on to the dynamics of $x(t)$, and the switchings are more compelled to follow the rocking of the potential. Figure 3c shows the associated return map for the quasi-white noise case and Fig. 3d, for the more colored case $\tau_c = 0.5$ (the value of τ_c used for the analog simulations in Fig. 2 are scaled differently than in these digital simulations and is similar to the value used here in the more colored case). The greatest aggregations of points in Fig. 3c are at locations $nT_0/2$ on the time axis, while for the more colored noise case, they occur at locations nT_0. The point clusters are thus seen to gain the negative slope feature as τ_c increases, i.e., as the memory of the noise and thus the autocorrelation of $x(t)$ increases. Finally, the model return maps are mirror symmetric with respect to the $I_{i+1} = I_i$ diagonal because the potential is symmetric about $x = 0$.

Similar results hold if we introduce a coarseness Δt into our measurement of the residence times (or, alternately, a coarseness Δx into our measurement of the position of the particle relative to the barrier). Crossings of the barrier midpoint occurring in rapid succession will then not contribute to ABAB events. Peaks occurring at multiples of $T_0/2$, as seen here for soft potentials (only) with quasi-white noise and/or too finely sampled dynamics, are sometimes observed in the neuron data (Rose et al. 1967; Talbot et al. 1968; Siegel, personal communication). If the neurons reset deterministically, then it is difficult to interpret these "out-of-phase" peaks in the context of a bistable model. On the other hand, our analysis so far has shown that many features of the data can be explained in this context, and it then becomes important to know that different potentials lead to different peak structures. Although the existence of two preferred firing phases (during one cycle), which these peaks imply, has been reported in the auditory literature at higher intensities ("peak splitting", see Johnson 1980), no direct relation to this effect is intended at this time. Also, the number of fast events (in the first bins) decreases as τ_c increases. Accordingly, the ISIH mean increases, implying a decrease in the Kramer's rate, as expected for colored noise (Sect. 3). Finally, in Fig. 3 τ_c was varied without changing D. This implies that the noise power (the integral of the power spectrum, equal to D/τ_c) decreases as τ_c increases. If D is decreased, the peaks are sharper (troughs are lower), and the probability spreads out from the origin to the other peaks (the same effect occurs if ε is decreased). This is difficult to illustrate in practice because low D simulations are prohibitively long to carry out.

5.3 Scaling of the ISIH decay rate

Here we investigate the dependence of the ISIH decay rate λ on ε. This rate can be suitably defined when the ISIH is almost exponential (i.e., for higher amplitude or lower frequency stimuli). Figure 4a plots λ as a function of ε at two noise variances D/τ_c. These results are from analog simulations of the Schmitt trigger. The interesting feature is that over a range of amplitudes, λ itself depends sensitively (exponentially) on ε. By comparison, a sensitive power-law-type dependence of λ on ε has been reported in Talbot et al. (1968) and Siegel (1990). Furthermore, we have measured the dependence of λ on D at two values of ε. The results are shown in Fig. 4b and are strikingly similar to those in Fig. 4a. This is not too surprising since the noise and the signal are additive terms on an equal footing in (1). Thus, over a certain range of parameters, noise and signal seem to play interchangeable roles in the determination of ISIH shape. Their roles are not completely reciprocal, however, since peak widths grow with D. It is also interesting to note that the stimulus features are encoded in the ISIH: ω determines the position of the peaks; ε, ω, and D determine the ISIH envelope; and the phase preference is reflected in the width of the peaks. Noise may be used by the neuron to encode the stimulus features in such an ISIH, all the while preserving a fine amplitude discrimination through an exponential dependence of λ on ε.

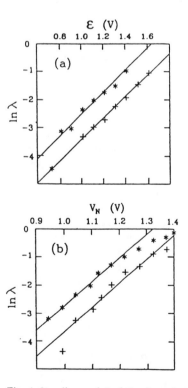

Fig. 4. Log-linear plot of the dependence of the ISIH decay rate on (a) ε at two values of D ($\ast$: $V_n = 1.0$; $+$: $V_n = 0.90$) and on (b) D at two values of ε ($\ast$: $\varepsilon = 1.0$; $+$: $\varepsilon = 0.80$). The results are obtained from analog simulations on a Schmitt trigger. The value of D is obtained from a measurement of $V_n^2 \equiv \langle V^2(t) \rangle \equiv (D/\tau_c)$ at the output of the noise generator

393

6 Discussion

Our study has described the features of the ISIH data from sensory neurons which arise from two-state dynamics: the ISIH shape, the return maps, the nonrenewal effects, the noise bandwidth effects, and the scaling of the ISIH decay rate with amplitude. Our results are general and apply to any form of bistability driven by deterministic and stochastic forces, be it in the electrical activity of single cells, cell populations, membrane channels, etc. Whatever the state variable, it is important to realize that the noise may be used advantageously, for example, by enhancing signal detection through stochastic resonance. Our results are also expected to hold when the stimulus is not sinusoidal as e.g., in Siegel's recordings (1990) where the amplitude is driven by a square wave. Our intuition is based on results (e.g., Zheng 1991) which show that SR with nonharmonic forcing can be similar to that with harmonic forcing. It is not known whether, as $\varepsilon \to 0$, the multimodal ISIHs converge to the spontaneous ISIHs in the same way in both the model and the real system. In the context of models described by (1), this would imply that the noise level is input-independent. The spontaneous data were not available at the time of our study, and this question will be pursued elsewhere.

There is a certain symmetry between bistable and IF models. IF models can be deterministic (these can fire periodically), stochastic, or both. In the latter case, the "voltage" performs a random walk with drift to an absorbing barrier, at which point it is reset to a resting value. The barrier of the bistable model is not absorbing, and the particle evolves in a similar potential on the other side of it. The effect of asymmetry, in which the transition back to the resting state is more favorable than the opposite transition, should be investigated (preliminary results indicate no major qualitative differences). A mean first passage time (MFPT) to the absorbing threshold is a natural quantity for the IF model and can be estimated as the ISIH mean. The equivalent quantity for the bistable model is the mean duration of an ABAB event (the ISIH mean also). It is not exact (because of correlation effects) to say that an ABAB event consists of two IF-type events, but the two intervals may be roughly similar. The bistable model also has no absolute refractoriness, since successive crossings of the metastable point arbitrarily close in time can occur (see Sect. 5). However, the noiseless IF model can have absolute refractoriness if there is a drift to threshold. This property disappears as soon as there is noise.

A crucial question is whether, in the presence of a periodic stimulus, the noise is always needed for firings to occur, as it is in our simplified models. The answer may be different for different sensory cells. In fact, skipping is seen over a large range of amplitudes in auditory neurons (Rose et al. 1967), but not in the mechano receptors of the skin (Talbot et al. 1968; Chialvo and Apkarian 1993). In our model, the ISIH collapses quickly to the first peak as deterministic switching becomes possible. Thus, to produce skipping with noisy bistability, the dynamic range of the periodic input to the cell must somehow be compressed to a range near or below the level at which deterministic firing occurs. This may be accomplished by nonlinear compression or by automatic gain control, which in the auditory case could occur at the cochlear mechanics level (see, e.g., Weiss 1966; Lyon 1990). Future investigations will hopefully clarify whether noise is used to enhance signal detection and extend the encoding capabilities in the way our study suggests.

Acknowledgements. We acknowledge helpful discussions with Vania Apkarian, Dante Chialvo, Valerie Gremillion, William Rhode, John Rinzel, Ralph Siegel, and Malvin Teich. Many thanks are due to W. Rhode of the University of Wisconsin for providing the cat auditory data. Support from A.L. from Los Alamos National Laboratory and NSERC (Canada) is gratefully acknowledged. This work was done under the auspices of the National Institute of Mental Health through grant 1-R01-MH47184-01, the Office of Naval Research through grants no. N00014-90-J-1327 and no. N00014-90-AF-001, and the US Department of Energy.

References

Bulsara A, Jacobs E, Zhou T, Moss F, Kiss L (1991) Stochastic resonance in a single neuron model: theory and analog simulation. J Theor Biol 154:531–555

Calvin W, Stevens CF (1968) Synaptic noise and other sources of randomness in motorneuron interspike interval. J Neurophysiol 31:574–587

Chialvo DR, Apkarian V (1993) Modulated noisy biological dynamics: three examples. J Stat Phys 70:375–391

Corey DP, Hudspeth AJ (1983) Kinetics of the receptor current in bullfrog saccular hair cells. J Neurosci 3:962–976

Douglass JK, Moss F, Longtin A (1993) Statistical and dynamical interpretation of ISIH data from periodically stimulated sensory neurons. In: Hanson SJ, Cowan J, Giles L (eds) Proceedings of the fifth neural information processing systems conference, Denver. Morgan Kaufmann, San Francisco

Gammaitoni L, Marchesoni F, Menichella-Saetta E, Santucci S (1989) Stochastic resonance in bistable systems. Phys Rev Lett 62: 349–352

Gardiner C (1983) Handbook of stochastic methods. Springer, Berlin Heidelberg New York

Gerstein GL, Mandelbrot B (1964) Random walk models for the spike activity of a single neuron. Biophys J 4:41–68

Glass L, Graves C, Petrillo GA, Mackey MC (1980) Unstable dynamics of a periodically driven oscillator in the presence of noise. J Theor Biol 86:455–475

Hopfield JJ (1982) Neural networks and physical systems with emergent collective computational abilities. Proc Nat Acad Sci USA 79:2554–2558

Johnson DH (1974) The response of single auditory-nerve fibers in the cat to single tones: synchrony and average discharge rate. PhD thesis, Massachusetts Institute of Technology, Cambridge, Mass

Johnson DH (1980) The relationship between spike rate and synchrony in responses of auditory-nerve fibers to single tones. J. Acoust Soc Am 68:1115–1122

Jung P, Hanggi P, Marchesoni F (1989) Colored-noise-driven bistable systems. Phys Rev A 40:5447–5450

Kiang NYS (1984) Peripheral neural processing of auditory information. In: Handbook of physiology, Vol III. Sensory processes. American Physiological Society, Part 2, Chap 15, pp 639–674

Landahl H, McCulloch WS, Pitts W (1943) A statistical consequence of the logical calculus of nervous nets. Bull Math Biophys 5:135–137

Longtin A (1993a) Stochastic resonance in neuron models. J Stat Phys 70:309–327

Longtin A (1993b) Nonlinear forecasting of spike trains from sensory neurons. Int J Bifurc Chaos (in press)

Longtin A, Bulsara A, Moss F (1991) Time interval sequences in bistable systems and the noise-induced transmission of information by sensory neurons. Phys Rev Lett 67:656–659

Lowen SB, Teich MC (1992) Auditory-nerve action potentials form a nonrenewal point process over short as well as long time scales. J Acoust Soc Am 92:803–806

Lyon RF (1990) Automatic gain control in cochlear mechanics. In: The mechanics and biophysics of hearing. (Lecture notes in biomathematics, Vol 87) pp 395–402

Mannella R, Palleschi V (1989) Fast and precise algorithm for computer simulation of stochastic differential equations. Phys Rev A 40:3381–3386

McNamara B, Wiesenfeld K (1989) Theory of stochastic resonance. Phys Rev A 39:4854–4875

Ogawa T, Bishop PO, Levick WR (1966) Temporal characteristics of responses to photic stimulation by single ganglion cells in the unopened eye of the cat. J Neurophysiol 6:2–30

Rinzel J, Ermentrout B (1989) Analysis of neural excitability and oscillations. In: Koch C, Segev I (eds) Methods in neuronal modeling. MIT Press, Cambridge, Mass

Rose J, Brugge J, Anderson D, Hind J (1967) Phase-locked response to low-frequency tones in single auditory nerve fibers of the squirrel monkey. J Neurophysiol 30:769–793

Russell IJ, Sellick PM (1978) Intracellular studies of hair cells in the mammalian cochlea. J Physiol 284:261–290

Siebert WM (1965) Some implications of the stochastic behavior of primary auditory neurons. Kybernetik 2:206–215

Siegel R (1990) Nonlinear dynamical system theory and primary visual cortical processing. Physica 42 D:385–395

Talbot W, Darian-Smith I, Kornhuber H, Mountcastle V (1968) The sense of flutter-vibration: comparison of the human capacity with response patterns of mechanoreceptive afferents for the monkey hand. J Neurophysiol 31:301–334

Treutlein H, Schulten K (1985) Noise induced limit cycles of the Bonhoeffer-Van der Pol model of neural pulses. Ber Bunsenges Phys Chem 89:710–718

Tuckwell HC (1989) Stochastic processes in the neurosciences. SIAM, Philadelphia

Weiss TF (1966) A model of the peripheral auditory system. Kybernetik 3:153–175

Zheng W (1991) Square-wave-driven stochastic resonance. Phys Rev A 44:6443–6447

Zhou T, Moss F, Jung P (1990) Escape-time distributions of a periodically modulated bistable system with noise. Phys Rev A 42: 3161–3169

Chapter 17

A Bifurcation Model of Neuronal of Spike Train Patterns:
A Nonlinear Dynamic Systems Approach

N.H. Farhat, M. Eldefrawy, S-Y. Lin

A BIFURCATION MODEL OF NEURONAL SPIKE TRAIN PATTERNS: A NONLINEAR DYNAMIC SYSTEMS APPROACH

N.H. Farhat, M. Eldefrawy and S-Y. Lin
University of Pennsylvania
Electrical Engineering Department
Philadelphia, PA 19104

ABSTRACT. A deterministic nonlinear dynamic systems approach to mathematical analysis of the integrate-and-fire (I & F) model neuron*, a monoionic simplification of the Hodgkin-Huxley model for action potential generation in the excitable biological membrane, is presented. It is shown that under periodic activation (driving signal), the firing behavior is described by an iterative map of the interval $[0, 2\pi]$ onto itself which we call *phase-transition map* (PTM). Periodic activation of the I & F model neuron occurs when its dendrites receive correlated incident patterns percipitated by certain sensory stimulus or when a network of such dendritic patterns enters a synchronized (phase-locked) state. Like other maps of the interval onto itself, the PTM is studied employing the tools of nonlinear dynamics. This furnishes a novel way of viewing the microneurodynamics of neural networks and shows, that despite the simplifications made in the I & F model neuron*, it exhibits, in its spiking behavior, a high degree of functional complexity approaching that of the living neuron. This is manifested by a variety of firing modalities depending on parameters of the periodic activation, which include regular firing phase-locked to the periodic activation or a subharmonic of it, quasi-periodic firing, bursting, and possibly erratic firing, and can bifurcate (rapidly switch) between these firing modalities as the parameters of the periodic activation are altered, hence the name *bifurcation model*. Illustrative examples of this complex behavior are given in the form of *bifurcation diagram*, *Arnold Tongues* diagram and the *Devil's Staircase* diagram. These show the neuron is able to detect coherent episodes in its *incident spike wavefront*, the aggregate of spike trains incident on its synaptic inputs, and encodes such coherent activity whenever it occurs, in a complex manner depending on the parameters of the periodic activation potential produced by dendritic-tree processing of the incident wavefront. When the activation potential is not periodic, the bifurcation model reverts to the usual sigmoidal response and shows an upper limit on firing frequency which serves the useful function of containing the maximum firing activity in a network of such neurons in a manner analogous, but not exactly equivalent, to a similar limit imposed by refractoriness in the living neuron.

The theory and characterization of the bifurcation model presented here could offer: (a) basis for *neuroholography* in that coherence effects and locally generated reference for phase definition can be identified, and (b) basis for explaining the way transient correlations may arise between local field potentials and single cell activity observed at different and widely separated cortical areas of cat and monkey in a series of important neurophysiological experiments reported by several investigators in the past five years.

Because it combines functional complexity with structural simplicity and low power consumption (because of its spiking nature), the bifurcation spike train model is ideal for use in simulation, or hardware implementation of a new generation of neurocomputers in which synchronicity, bifurcation, and chaos, and their possible role in higher-level cortical functions, can be studied.

---

* In this paper, when not referring to biological neurons, the term neuron is used to describe an artificial neuromime, a neuron-like processing element.

INTRODUCTION. Most neural net models assume sigmoidal activation of neurons and therefore cannot account for the relative timing of action potentials (spike train patterns) impinging on the dendritic-tree of a neuron from presynaptic neurons. The bifurcating model [1] is an outcome of using the tools of nonlinear dynamics to characterize the behavior of the neuron's excitable (axonal) membrane in a manner that accounts naturally for temporal effects. It combines functional complexity paralleling that of the living neuron with structural simplicity and low power consumption which makes it an attractive building-block for a new generation of neural networks specially suited for modeling higher-level cortical functions such as feature-binding, cognition, inferencing, attention, reasoning, etc.

There is increasing evidence in the literature encouraging speculation that such higher-level functions may involve synchronicity, phase-locking, bifurcations, erratic (chaotic firing for possible adaptive annealing), and dynamic signal dependent (adaptive) partitioning through which populations of cortical neurons may fleetingly divide into sub-populations or assemblies, each with a prescribed relative-phase pattern between its spiking neurons, that act in parallel in solving complex tasks with each sub-population acting collectively. Thus dynamic adaptive partitioning is the means by which cortical networks may carry out collective computations in several sub-populations of neurons in parallel. The significance of collective/parallel processing was recently discussed by Zak [2] in the context of *Nonlipschitzian* neural networks with unpredictable dynamics.

The relative timing and synchronicity in firing of neurons as a mechanism for feature-binding was predicted by Marlsburg [3] and Abeles [4] on theoretical grounds. Recently, synchronization effects have been observed in local field potentials and neuronal activity at different recording locations in the cat's visual cortex upon suitable visual stimulus [5]-[11], and more recently in several cortical areas of maqaque monkeys performing visual discrimination tasks [39], raising thereby intriguing speculation about the nature of cortical processing, and stimulating wide spread interest. Temporal effects in the olfactory bulb have also been studied extensively by Freeman [12] and claims regarding the implications of rythmic firing activity in consciousness have been covered by the media [13]. Further discussion of synchronization effects in temporal neural networks is given in [14]-[16]. It is now conjectured that synchronized firing of neurons in the visual cortex, for example, might : (a) label spatially coherent or common features in the visual data such as motion, contrast, texture, or color, (b) play a role in feature-binding, cognition, and other higher-level cortical functions, (c) could play a role in information absorption (learning) optimization in biological systems. Obviously, judging the validity of this conjecture requires thorough understanding of the mechanisms that can cause neurons at separate locations to synchronize their firings including, computer simulations aimed at studying and understanding the collective dynamics of spiking neural networks whose neurons are not simple processing element but possess functional complexity, like that of the bifurcating neuron model, that would reflect itself ultimately in the computing power of the network as a whole.

In this paper we present the results of a formulation of a bifurcation model which enables applying the power and the tools of nonlinear dynamics to characterizing its behavior in a manner that permits greater insight in neurodynamics and to possible utilization of synchronization, bifurcation and chaos in the design of a new generation of powerful neurocomputers.

The goal is to develop a bifurcation model that is <u>descriptive</u>, <u>predictive</u> and <u>quantitative</u>. Descriptive in the sense that it should give true physical insight into the complicated processes involved. In the words of P.M. Koch [17], "a useful theory describes the essential physics of a process simply, preferably with figures and simple equations whose behavior with variation of parameters can be explored. The theory must be predictive because unless it can raise new questions and predict answers, it will likely be a dead end". Experimenters warm-up to theories that say "if you do such-and-such, then you will observe thus-and-so". The theory needs to be also quantitative because something is missing if it cannot be reduced to calculations that "get the numbers right".

All these goals are achieved in the theory presented here. To them we need to add, from the outset, the essential features we seek in a neuron model evolving from any developed theory. These features are:

- Production of an action potential or spike

- Existence of a refractory period to limit the maximum firing frequency to conserve energy and eliminate reverberations and reflections in a network

- Ability to integrate incoming synaptic inputs and to account for passive and/or active spatio-temporal processing carried out by the neuron's dendritic-tree

- Ability to respond to external signals in a manner that resembles that of the living (biological) neuron, i.e., production of spiking activity similar to that observed in the biological neuron under different forms of stimulus.

- Be structurally simple and possess low power consumption in order to facilitate hardware implementation of neurocomputering structures.

The starting point is the Hodgkin and Huxley model of the biological membrane [18] which describes excitable membrane dynamics and spiking, the production of action potentials, in terms of three ionic currents. The shape of the action potential (spike) produced by this model resembles faithfully that observed in the living (biological) neuron and exhibits refractoriness. The distinct shape of the action potential is determined by the interplay between the dynamics of the three ionic currents in the model. Because the shape of all action potentials in biological networks is more or less the same, one can argue that the shape does not convey information and that only the interspike interval (the interval between action potentials) and/or the relative timing between action potentials in a network) are important in neuroprocessing of information. This argument has prompted us to simplify the H-H model to a monoionic current model in order to facilitate its analysis as a dynamical system. This is done in Section 2 for two types of activation: nonperiodic, which is shown to lead to the usual sigmoidal response, and periodic which is assumed to arise when the dendritic-tree receives correlated spike trains, i.e., coherent spike wavefronts and is shown to lead to functional complexity far exceeding that of the sigmoidal neuron model. Unlike the traditional treatment of spontaneous neuronal firing, fluctuations in membrane potential caused by spontaneous release of neurotransmitters in synaptic gaps are ignored here. This may not be a severe simplification when one considers the large number of spike trains impinging on a neuron and its dendritic-tree at any time, the large increase in the number of neurotransmitters released immediately following the arrival of an action potential at a synapse as compared to their spontaneous rate of release, and the high degree of correlation between arriving spike trains which could produce smooth periodically varying activation. In Section 2 we also present examples of applying the bifurcation model theory, specifically the PTM, to characterizing the behavior of two versions that illustrate the complex behavior of the model. Concluding remarks and implications of such functional complexity and other properties of the bifurcation model are discussed in Section 4.

2. ANALYSIS. Figure 1(a) shows an equivalent circuit of the monoionic model. In it I is the monoionic membrane currently representing an energy source for restoring the membrane potential after firing, R and C are the membrane resistance and capacitance respectively, v is the capacitor voltage, $i = \phi(v')$ represents the membrane nonlinearity, assumed to be S-shaped and u(t) is the activation potential of the membrane. u(t) represents the effect produced at the biological neurons hillock by synaptic inputs to the neuron. A piece-wise linear approximation of the S-shaped nonlinearity is shown in Fig. 2 after inclusion of the effect of the activation potential u(t) which represents the modulation in membrane potential produced by integration of action potentials (input spike trains) arriving at the neuron's dendritic-tree from its presynaptic neurons. The circuit in Fig. 1(b) is equivalent to that in Fig. 1(a) when the voltage source E is set equal to $E = IR$. It represents the circuit diagram of an integrate-and-fire neuron or relaxation oscillator neuron whose dynamics we will study here in detail. Despite its simplicity, this circuit will be shown to exhibit complex behavior, specially when u(t) is periodic. In Fig. 2, v_{th} and v_{ext} are related respectively to the breakdown or threshold voltage v_1 and the extinction voltage v_2 of the S-shaped nonlinearity $\phi(v)$. Notice that in the absence of activation potential or (driving signal) u(t), v' coincides with v and v_{th} reduces to v_1 while v_{ext} reduces to v_2.

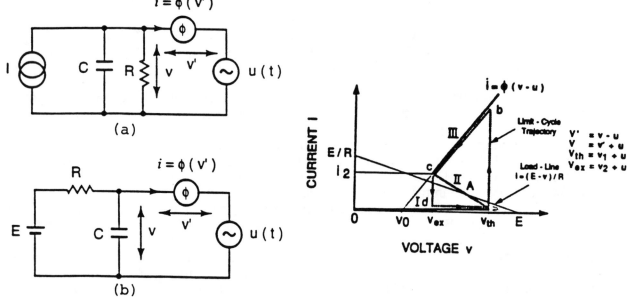

Fig. 1. Equivalent circuit of monoionic model of the excitable membrane.

Fig. 2. Piece-wise linear approximation of the S-shaped nonlinearity of the neurons membrane.

In the absence of the driving signal u(t) and when $E > v_1$, the circuit of Fig. 1(b) behaves as a nonlinear relaxation oscillator. The S-shaped i-v (current-voltage) characteristic $i = \phi(v')$ shown in Fig. 2 reduces to that shown in Fig. 3, i.e., $i = \phi(v)$ curve with a negative resistance region, a breakdown or threshold voltage v_1 and extinction voltage v_2. This i-v characteristic $i = \phi(v)$ is seen to consist of three distinct regions I, II and III. Regions I and III are positive resistance regions corresponding to the resistance of nonlinear element $i = \phi(v)$ in the off and on states respectively, while region II is a negative resistance region. The distance $\overline{cd}$ in this plot is exaggerated in comparison to that in actual i-v characteristics in order to delineate the negative resistance region of the plot. The behavior of the circuit in Fig. 1(b) is governed by the nonlinear differential equation,

400

$$C\frac{dv}{dt} + \phi(v) = \frac{E - v}{R} \tag{1}$$

The steady state, $\frac{dv}{dt} = 0$, of eq. (1) is defined by

$$\phi(v) = \frac{E - v}{R} \tag{2}$$

in which $i = (E-v)/R$ defines a load-line in the i-v plane as shown in Fig. 3 and the intersection point between the load-line and $\phi(v)$ defines the operating point A.

When $E > v_1$ and the load-line $i(v) = (E-v)/R$ intersects the i-v characteristics in the negative resistance region i.e., the operating point A falls in region II as shown in Fig. 3, the circuit of Fig. 1(b) exhibits the *limit-cycle* oscillations indicated by the closed dotted line trajectory $\overline{abcda}$. The portion $\overline{abcd}$ of the trajectory corresponds to the conduction of a current spike through the nonlinear element when the capacitor voltage v(t) reaches the breakdown value v_1, while the portion $\overline{da}$ corresponds to the interspike interval during which the charge in capacitor C is being restored and the nonlinear element is in off state. Changes in the values of E, v, and/or R, cause the load-line and operating point A to shift. Shifting the location of A within the negative resistance regions alters the speed of motion along the limit-cycle trajectory and this alters the firing frequency. Limit-cycle oscillations cease to exist when the operating point A enters either of regions I or III. When A is in region III, the nonlinear element remains on while for an A falling in region I, the nonlinear element remains off. The simple circuit dynamics described qualitatively above become considerably more complicated in the presence of a time varying or periodic driving signal u(t). Then we need to modify eq. (1) by replacing $\phi(v)$ with $\phi(v - u(t))$ which means that the limit-cycle dynamics are complicated by time dependent displacement of the ϕ curve in the horizontal direction vis-a-vis the stationary load line. This and the interplay between u(t) and the capacitor voltage v(t) is the underlying cause of the complex dynamics of the bifurcating neuron circuit and the observation of complex firing sequences for certain values of parameters of the periodic driving signal u(t) as will be shown later.

The limit-cycle trajectory can be readily displayed on a CRO by driving the x-axis of the CRO with the voltage drop proportional to i(t) in Fig. 3 and the Y-axis with the voltage $v = v(t)$ appearing across the nonlinear element. An example of such a display is given in the photograph of Fig. 4 which represents the *limit-cycle trajectory* in the i-v phase-space of the circuit of Fig. 1(b) and is seen to be similar to the idealized limit-cycle trajectory marked in Fig. 3. The apparent uneven brightness of the trajectory in the photograph, reflects the uneven speed with which the electron beam traces the trajectory on the CRO's phosphor screen as dictated by the time variation of i(t) and v(t)..

The current waveform i(t) corresponding to limit-cycle oscillations consists of a train of narrow fixed-shape impulses, or spikes, of fixed peak amplitude i_0 and duration T_1 corresponding to the $a \rightarrow b$, $b \rightarrow c \rightarrow d$ portions of the trajectory. The interspike interval T_2 corresponds to the $d \rightarrow a$ interval of the trajectory. The spikes in i(t) represent *action potentials* so to speak, of the bifurcating neuron. Expressions for T_1 and T_2 can be readily derived when the nonlinear element in Fig. 1 is assumed to have the idealized S-shaped characteristic of Fig. 3. The results are given by [19],

$$T_1 = RC \ln \left(\frac{E - v_2}{E - v_1} \right) \tag{3}$$

$$T2 = \rho C \ln \left(\frac{(v_1 - v_2)R - (E - v_1)R_i}{(v_2 - v_0)R - (E - v_2)R_i} \right) \tag{4}$$

where $\rho = RR_i/(R + R_i)$, with R_i being the nonlinear element's resistance in segment III of the i-v characteristics, and v_0 is the voltage value at the point of intersection of the extension of segment III of the characteristic with the v axis as shown in Fig. 3. All other quantities in eqs. (3) and (4) are as defined earlier. Note that eqs. (3) and (4) are meaningful only when $E > v_1$. When this condition is not satisfied the arguments of the ln (....) term in eq. (3) becomes negative precluding thereby physically meaningful solutions and disruption of limit-cycle oscillations. In accordance to eqs. (3) and (4) the interspike-interval or period of the bifurcating neuron's oscillation is $T = T_1 + T_2$ and the instantaneous firing frequency is $f = 1/T = 1/(T_1 + T_2)$. Because, in normal operation, $R_i \ll R$, we find that the spike width T_2 is much less than the interspike interval T_1 and therefore $T \cdot T1$ becomes a good approximation.

It is convenient to consider two regimes of operation when $u(t) \neq 0$. One is the none self-oscillatory regime, and the other is the self-oscillatory regime. We consider next the regime when the supply voltage E is slightly less than the breakdown voltage v_1, so that the nonlinear element is normally in extinguished state and the limit-cycle oscillations are not triggered spontaneously. The subthreshold value of E in this case is such that the addition of the driving signal is sufficient to trigger the limit-cycle oscillation whenever the voltage across the nonlinear element exceeds threshold. Thus, in the presence of u(t) and specially when u(t) is sufficiently slowly varying, that is the scale of its time-variations is large compared to the natural oscillation period T of the circuit we discussed earlier, the effect of u(t) on the circuit can be shown to be reproduced by suitably changing the supply voltage E. In this regime, our bifurcating neuron exhibits nearly sigmoidal dependence of firing frequency on activation i.e., on the effective voltage across the nonlinear element.

To show this we proceed as follows: Because the spike width T_2 is very narrow, we approximate the spike portion abcd of the limit-cycle oscillation of the S-shaped nonlinearity in Fig. 3 or Fig. 2 by,

$$i = \phi(v) = \phi(v') = \begin{cases} 0 & v' < v_1 \\ i_0 \delta(t) & v \geq v_1 \end{cases} \tag{5}$$

Since,

$$v' = v - u$$

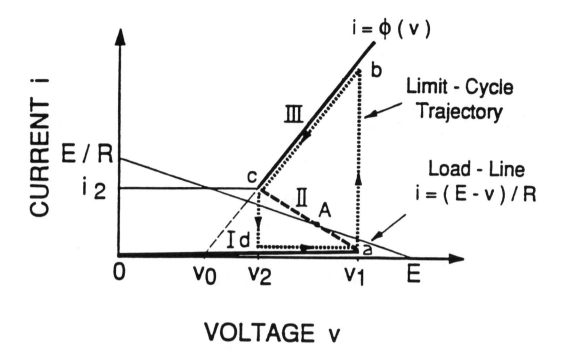

Fig. 3.   Idealized piece-wise linear approximation of the i-v (current-voltage) characteristic of the glow-lamp (glow-discharge tube) consisting of three segments: I, II and III and showing the limit-cycle trajectory abcd (dotted line) referred to in the text.

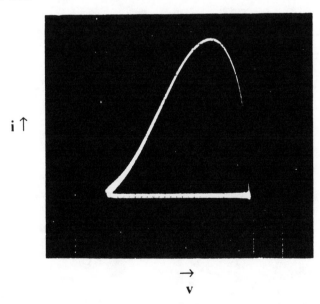

Fig. 4.   Limit cycle trajectory in the i-v phase-space of the circuit of Fig. 1 associated with the natural oscillations of the bifurcating neuron assuming glow-lamp S-shaped nonlinearity (E = 160 [V], R = 100 [KΩ], C = .1[μF], R_s = 10 [Ω]).   Vertical scale: 10 [mA/div.], horizontal scale: 10 [V/div.]).   A.C. coupled CRO display is shown.

403

we have,

$$v_1 = v_{th} - u \quad \rightarrow \quad v_{th} = v_1 + u$$

$$\tag{6}$$

$$v_2 = v_{ex} - u \quad \rightarrow \quad v_{ex} = v_2 + u.$$

The spike amplitude i_0 in eq. (5) is determined by considering the change ΔQ in the charge stored in the capacitor C because of a single firing of the neuron, i.e., the discharge of the capacitor during the $\overline{abcd}$ portion of a limit-cycle oscillation. This is,

$$\Delta Q = C \quad \Delta v$$

or,

$$\int i dt = C(v_{th} - v_{ex}) = C(v_1 - v_2)$$

or by using eq. (5)

$$\int i_0 \delta(t) \, dt = C(v_1 - v_2)$$

$$i_0 = C(v_1 - v_2). \tag{7}$$

which is seen to be determined by the capacitance C and the parameters v_1 and v_2 of the nonlinear S-shaped nonlinearity.

Now when $v < v_{th}$, $\phi(v - u) = 0$, eq. (1) reduces to,

$$C \frac{dv}{dt} = \frac{E - v}{R}$$

whose solution is,

$$v(t) = E - (E - v_2 - v(o)) \, Exp \, (-\frac{t}{RC}) \tag{8}$$

which represents the capacitor voltage build-up in the d$\rightarrow$ a region of the limit-cycle trajectory in Fig. 2.

The interspike interval T is found from eq. (8) by letting $t = T$ and $v(T) = v_{th}(T) = v_1 +$

u(T). This yields,

$$T = RC\ln\frac{E - v_2 - u(o)}{E - v_1 - u(T)} = RC\ln\frac{E - v_{ex(o)}}{E - v_{th(T)}} \qquad (9)$$

This analytical model is known as the *integrate and fire* model of the spiking neuron.

We see from comparing eqs. (9) and (6) that the effect of the activation potential (the neuron's driving signal) u is to horizontally shift the curve $\phi(v - u)$ in Fig. 2 to the left or to the right by an amount that depends on the magnitude and sign of u. Because the load line is stationary, this horizontal shifting causes a migration of the operating point A on the ϕ curve.

When u is positive and is increasing, $\phi(v - u)$ would be shifted to the right until $v_{th} \geq E$ at which instant the operating point A enters segment I of the ϕ curve and limit-cycle oscillations are halted or extinguished in agreement with the prediction of eq. (9) when $v_{th} \geq E$. This is analogous to complete inhibition of the firing of a biological neuron when a sufficient inhibitory activation potential u is present. Thus a positive u in our neuron model corresponds to inhibitory signal.

When u is negative and is gradually decreased, $\phi(v - u)$ shifts gradually to the left. This has the effect of increasing the firing frequency. A negative u in our neuron circuit (Fig. 1(b)) is therefore equivalent to an exitatory input. As the value of u is made more negative (increased excitation) the shift of $\phi(v')$ to the left continues until the operating point A leaves the negative resistance segment II and enters the positive resistance segment III of the ϕ curve. When this happens, the nonlinear element ϕ remains on (conducting state) and limit-cycle oscillations are again extinguished. Limit-cycle oscillations can not be triggered then no matter how strong an exitatory signal is received. This has the effect of limiting the maximum possible firing frequency and is analogous to the limiting of the maximum firing frequency in the biological neuron by the presence of an absolute refractory period.

We examine next two cases of u(t). In one case $u(t) = -V_m$ where V_m is a positive real constant whose value is changed gradually to determine how T and hence the firing frequency $f = \frac{1}{T}$ changes. This case leads to conventional sigmoidal response with an upper limit on the firing frequency. In the second case u(t) is assumed to be periodic. It leads to complex firing modalities of the neuron and includes bifurcation between them depending on parameters of the periodic activation.

Case I

Let $u(t) = -V_m$, then eq. (9) becomes,

$$T = RC\ln \frac{E - v_2 + V_m}{E - v_1 + V_m} \qquad (10)$$

and $\phi(v - u) = \phi(v + V_m)$. Thus a positive increasing V_m corresponds to increased inhibition and a lowering of the firing frequency $f = \frac{1}{T}$, while a negative decreasing V_m corresponds to increased excitation. The value of the maximum firing frequency f_{max} and the value of V_m at which the maximum firing frequency occurs are determined from Fig. 2 in the following manner:

When ϕ shifts to the left so that the load line passes through point C we have,

$$\frac{\overline{cd}}{E - v_{ex}} = \frac{E/R}{E}$$

or,

$$\frac{\overline{cd}}{E - v_2 - V_m} = \frac{1}{R}$$

which yields the maximum value of V_m for which firing stops,

$$V_{m_{max}} = E - v_2 - cdR \qquad (11)$$

by combining eqs. (8) and (7) one obtains an expression for the maximum firing frequency of our neuron.

$$f_{max} = \frac{1}{T_{min}} \qquad (12)$$

where

$$T_{min} = RC\ln \frac{2E - 2v_2 - cdR}{2E - (v_1 + v_2) - cdR} \qquad (13)$$

Thus the circuit in Fig. 1(b) is seen to have, when $u(t) = - V_m$, an upper limit on the firing frequency determined by the value of V_m. The upper bound on firing frequency is imposed by the nonlinear element remaining in the on state which stops limit-cycle oscillations. In contrast the maximum firing frequency of a biological neuron is imposed by the absolute refractory period immediately following each action potential (spike firing) during which the neuron is incapable of firing again no matter how strong an exitary stimulus it receives. In limiting the maximum firing frequency, refractoriness in the living neuron helps conserve energy and eliminate reverbrations.

The dependence of firing frequency $f = \frac{1}{T}$ on V_m where T is given by eq. (10) is shown in Fig. 5 (solid line curve marked $T_r = 0$) together with the measured firing frequency (dotted line curve). The two curves are for the case when the S-shaped nonlinearity ϕ is that of a glow-lamp. The circuit parameters and glow-lamp parameters are given in the figure caption. Verification of eq. (12) for an example of glow-lamp S-shaped nonlinearity with following parameters:

$$E = 160 \text{ [V]} \quad , \quad v_1 = 141 \text{ [V]} \quad , \quad v_2 = 125 \text{ [V]}$$
$$R = 10^5 \text{ [}\Omega\text{]} \quad , \quad C = 10^{-7} \text{ [F]} \quad , \quad \overline{cd} = 4 \ 10^{-4} \text{ [A]}$$

yields,

$$T_{min} = 7.6 \ 10^{-3} \text{ [sec]}$$

and therefore

$$f_{max} = \frac{1}{T_{min}} = 131 \text{ [Hz]}$$

which is in agreement with the experimental cutoff frequency observed in the preceding figure. Figure 5 also shows the effect of arbitrarily adding an absolute refractory interval T_r [msec] to the right-hand side of eq. (10). Such ad hoc inclusion of T_r is seen to accelerate saturation of the firing frequency.

Case II

The preceding analysis shows basically the bifurcation model can exhibit usual sigmoidal response. We show next however, that when the activation potential u(t) is periodic, the neuron alters its behavior and is able to phase-lock its firing to the frequency of the periodic activation or a sub-harmonic of it, or can fire quasiperiodically, erratically, or in bursts, all depending on the amplitude and frequency of the activation potential. Periodic activation at the neuron's hillock is assumed to arise whenever the spike trains (action potentials) incident on the neuron's dendritic-tree are correlated. If we refer to the aggregate of all spike trains incident, *at any time*, on the dendritric-tree as the *incident spike wavefront*, then a coherent incident wavefront produces a periodic activation potential, i.e., a periodic driving signal for the neuron. Thus we examine now the behavior of the circuit of Fig. 1(b) when the activation potential u(t) is periodic. The main result of the analysis is a Phase-Transition Map (PTM) which relates the phase θ_{n+1} of the n+1 spike produced by the neuron to θ_n, the phase of the n-th (preceding) spike. In our formulation, the phase of a spike is always measured relative to the immediately preceding peak (or some other selected feature) of the periodic activation potential. The PTM is a nonlinear iterative map on the (0 - 2π) interval, and as such, it lends itself to further analysis and treatment as is usually done in nonlinear dynamics with other maps of the interval onto itself like the *logistic* and the *circle map* for example.

For simplicity we assume the periodic activation or driving signal of the neuron (essentially the membrane potential at the hillock) is cosinusoidal of amplitude a, radian frequency ω_s and fixed phase θ, i.e.,

$$u(t) = a \cos(\omega_s t + \theta)$$

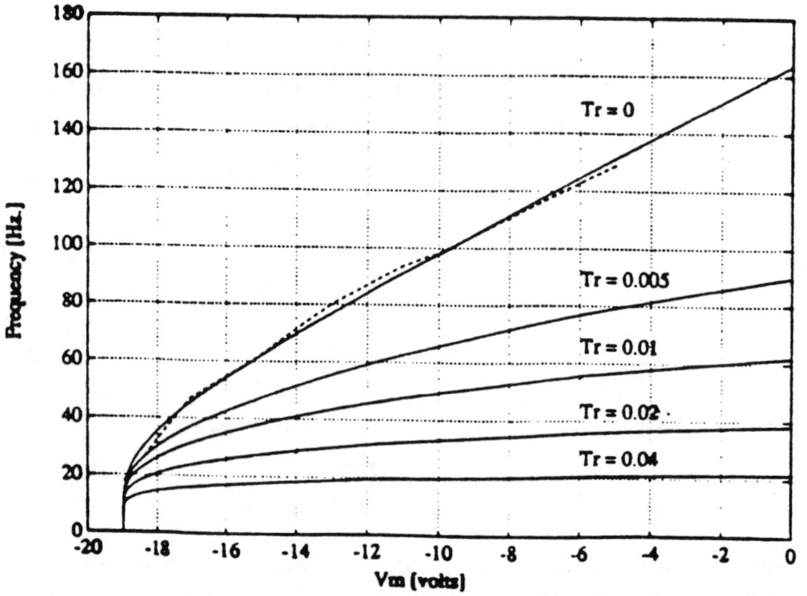

Fig. 5. Dependence of Firing frequency on activation potential Vm. Example of glow-lamp S-shaped nonlinearity with the following fixed parameters: V1 = 141 [volts] V2 = 125 [volts], RC = 0.01 [sec.], E = 160 [volts]. (solid) computed, (- - -) measured.

Then starting from the expression for the capacitor voltage in Fig. 1(b) we derived earlier (eq. 8),

$$v(t) = E - (E - v_2 - u(o)) \, Exp \, (-\frac{t}{RC}) \tag{14}$$

and by referring to Fig. 6 we see that

$$v(t) = v_{th}(t) \qquad at \qquad t = T \tag{15}$$

where

$$v_{th}(t) = v_1 + a \cos(\omega_s t + \theta) \tag{16}$$

408

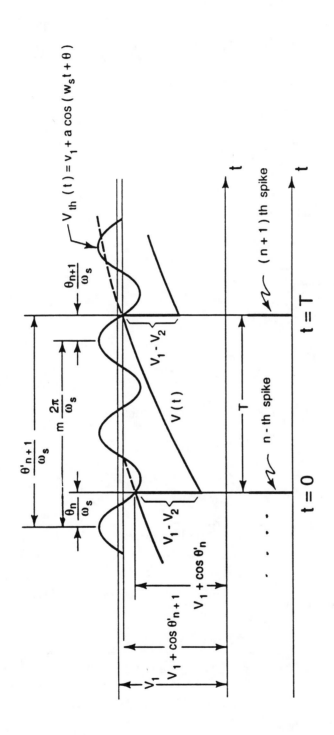

Fig. 6. Relation between the periodic driving signal (activation potential) appearing in $V_{th}(t)$, the capacitor voltage $V(t)$, and the spike pattern produced by the neuron (only two spikes are shown) referred to in the accompanying analysis. Note the relation between θ_n, θ'_{n+1} and θ_{n+1}.

409

Therefore from eqs. (14) and (15),

$$E - v_1 - a \cos (\omega_s T + \theta) = (E - v_2 - a \cos\theta) \, \mathrm{Exp} \left(- \frac{T}{RC}\right) \tag{17}$$

$$\omega_s T + \theta_n = \theta'_{n+1} \tag{18}$$

or,

$$\omega_s T = \theta'_{n+1} - \theta_n \tag{19}$$

$$T = \frac{\theta'_{n+1} - \theta_n}{\omega_s} \tag{20}$$

and letting

$$\theta'_{n+1} = \theta_{n+1} \, m + 2\pi \qquad m = \text{integer} \tag{21}$$

we have,

$$\theta_{n+1} = \theta'_{n+1} - m2\pi = [\theta'_{n+1}] \, \mathrm{mod.}2\pi \tag{22}$$

Therefore from eqs. (14) and (17),

$$E - v_1 - a \cos\theta'_{n+1} = (E - v_2 - a \cos\theta_n) \, \mathrm{Exp} \left(- \frac{\theta'_{n+1} - \theta_n}{\omega_s RC}\right) \tag{23}$$

or, in terms of normalized variables,

410

$$(1 - v'_1 - a' \cos\theta'_{n+1}) \, \mathrm{Exp} \frac{\theta'_{n+1}}{x} = (1 - v'_2 - a' \cos\theta_n) \, \mathrm{Exp} \frac{\theta_n}{x} \qquad (24)$$

where,

$$v'_1 = v_1/E \quad , \quad v'_2 = v_2/E \quad , \quad a' = a/E \quad , \quad x = \omega_s RC$$

Therefore finally from (24) and (22),

$$\theta'_{n+1} = \theta_n + x \ln \left(\frac{1 - v'_2 - a' \cos\theta_n}{1 - v'_1 - a' \cos\theta'_{n+1}} \right) \qquad (25)$$

and

$$\theta_{n+1} = [\theta'_{n+1}]_{\mathrm{mod}.2\pi} \qquad (26)$$

Equations (25) and (26) are the main results of this analysis. Taken together they form the relationship or mapping between θ_n, the phase of the n-th spike and θ_{n+1}, the phase of the (n+1)th spike in the firing activity of the neuron under cosinusoidal activation. Note the phase of a spike is always measured from the immediately preceding peak of the cosinusoidal drive signal (see Fig. 6). Equations (25) and (26) can be expressed symbolically in the form

$$\theta_{n+1} = g(\theta_n) \qquad (27)$$

where the function g(.) is defined by the mapping in eqs. (25) and (26). Note that eq. (25) is a transcendental equation in θ_{n+1} that must be solved first given θ_n, the system parameters, and those of the periodic driving signal. Having obtained θ'_{n+1} its modulus 2π is computed to obtain θ_{n+1}. We call the mapping in eq. (27) *Phase-Transition Map* (PTM). The PTM is a nonlinear iterative map of the interval $[0, 2\pi]$ onto itself. Like other iterative maps of interval onto itself, such as the Logistic Map and the Circle Map, the PTM can be studied using the tools of nonlinear dynamical systems.

For example, Fig. 7 shows the steps involved in obtaining a plot for the PTM of the bifurcating neuron using eq. (25) assuming a glow-lamp S-shaped nonlinearity and a periodic cosinusoidal driving signal activation of amplitude a = 1 [V] and frequency $f_s = \dfrac{\omega_s}{2\pi} = 190$ [Hz].

The PTM for this case, shown in Fig. 7 (c), can be iterated graphically as illustrated in Fig. 8(a). Entering the abscissa of this figure from an initial value θ_0 one draws a vertical line that intersects the plot giving the value of θ_1 which can be re-entered on the abscissa and the process repeated to find θ_2 and so forth. This procedure is greatly simplified by using the 45° line $\theta_{n+1} = \theta_n$ in performing the iterations. From θ_0 one moves vertically to intersect the PTM plot, then moves horizontally to intersect the 45° line, at a point whose abscissa gives the value of θ_1, then move vertically to intersect the plot again and move from there horizontally to meet the 45° line and obtain θ_2 and so forth. Starting from any initial value θ_0 the resulting sequence of phase values θ_n n=1,2,3... eventually settles into a regular pattern (orbit) or seemingly an erratic one depending on the parameters of the plot. The values of θ_n vs. n where n is the iteration number is shown in Fig. 8(b) for 1000 iterations. This plot clearly shows the firing pattern of the neuron for this case is quite complex but regular. Figure 8(c) shows the Lyapunov exponent [20],

$$\lambda = \lim_{N \to \infty} \left[\frac{1}{N} \sum_{n=1}^{N} \log | g'(\theta n) | \right] \qquad (28)$$

where $g'(\theta_n)$ is the derivitive or slope of the PTM at the iteration points, the values of θ_n produced by the map, or the periodically driven bifurcating neuron it represents. The Lyapunov exponent is a measure of regularity, or lack of it, in iterative maps. A value of $\lambda > 0$ is usually taken as an indication of irregularity or chaos. Because the θ_n pattern in Fig. 8(b) is regular, the corresponding Lyapunov exponent is seen to stabilize to zero after few hundred iterations when transients die out. The shape of the PTM changes markedly when the parameters (a, f_s) of the cosinusoidal driving signal are altered. This is demonstrated in the PTM plots and associated θ_n orbits which show period three (left) and period six (right) firing modalities shown in Fig. 9. Again because the θ_n patterns are ordered the Lyaponov exponents of the two plots are negative. It is worth noting that period-N firing modality covers the case when the neuron is bursting.

Qualitatively, similar results are obtained for bifurcating neurons employing solid-state nonlinear elements with S-shaped nonlinearity such as the unijunction transistor (UJT) and the programmable unijunction transistor (PUT) which are solid-state equivalents of the glow lamp.

A more encompassing view of bifurcating neuron dynamics, is provided by the *bifurcation diagram*. This is an intensity plot of the resulting phase orbit or sequence θ_n, after transients are allowed to die down. The values of θ_n are entered as points along the vertical above each frequency point as shown in the example of the measured bifurcation diagram for a programmable unijunction transistor neuron (PUTON) embodiment of the neuron shown in Fig. 10(a) for a fixed driving signal amplitude a = 0.6 [V]. The circuit diagram of the PUTON is shown in

412

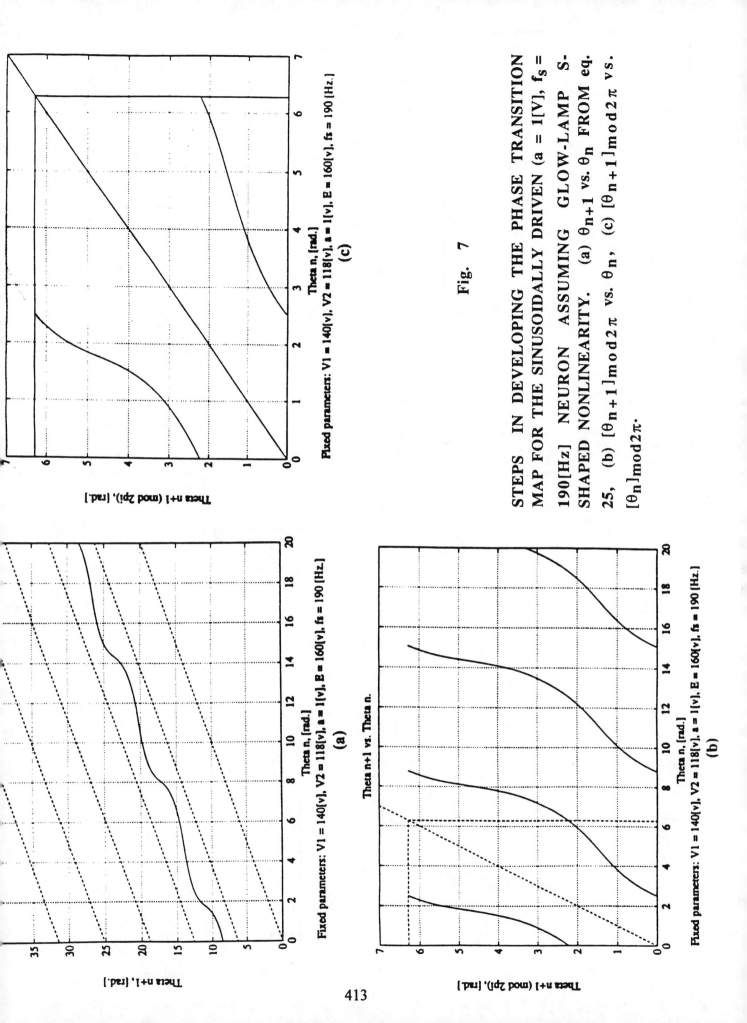

Theta n+1 vs. Theta n.

Fixed parameters: V1 = 140[v], V2 = 118[v], a = 1[v], E = 160[v], fs = 190 [Hz.]

(a)

Fixed parameters: V1 = 140[v], V2 = 118[v], a = 1[v], E = 160[v], fs = 190 [Hz.]

(b)

Fixed parameters: V1 = 140[v], V2 = 118[v], a = 1[v], E = 160[v], fs = 190 [Hz.]

(c)

Fig. 7

STEPS IN DEVELOPING THE PHASE TRANSITION MAP FOR THE SINUSOIDALLY DRIVEN (a = 1[V], f_s = 190[Hz] NEURON ASSUMING GLOW-LAMP S-SHAPED NONLINEARITY. (a) θ_{n+1} vs. θ_n FROM eq. 25, (b) $[\theta_{n+1}] \bmod 2\pi$ vs. θ_n, (c) $[\theta_{n+1}] \bmod 2\pi$ vs. $[\theta_n] \bmod 2\pi$.

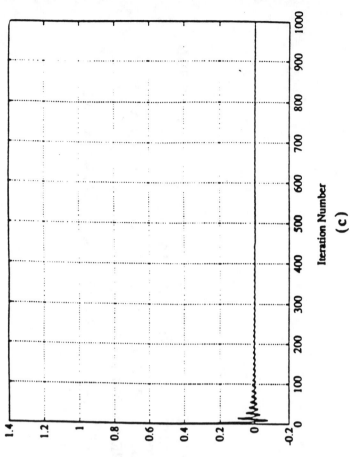

First 10 iterations

Fixed parameters: V1 = 140[v]. V2 = 118[v]. a = 1[v]. E = 160[v]. fs = 190 [Hz.]

(a)

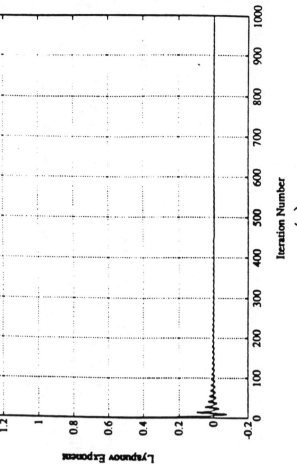

(c)

Fig. 8

RESULTS OF NUMERICAL ITERATION OF THE PHASE-TRANSITION MAP OF THE CO-SINUSOIDALLY DRIVEN (a = 1[V], f_s = 190[Hz]) NEURON: (a) FIRST 10 ITERATIONS. (b) θ_n vs. ITERATION NUMBER n, (c) LYAPUNOVE EXPONENT.

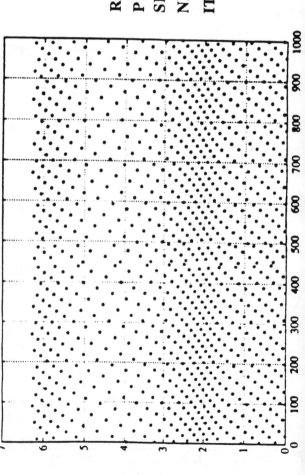

414

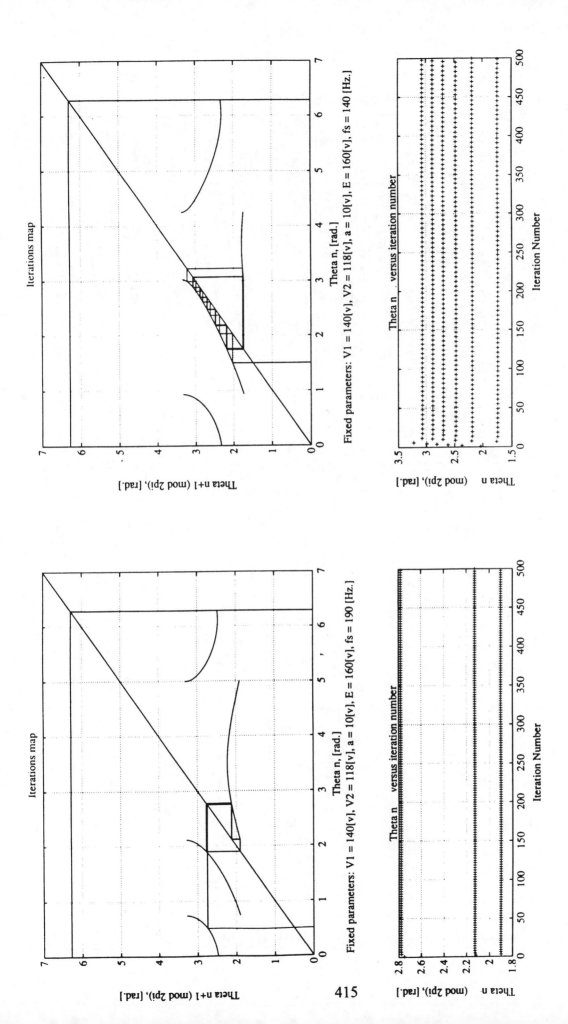

Iterations map

Fixed parameters: V1 = 140[v], V2 = 118[v], a = 10[v], E = 160[v], fs = 140 [Hz.]

Theta n   versus iteration number

Iterations map

Fixed parameters: V1 = 140[v], V2 = 118[v], a = 10[v], E = 160[v], fs = 190 [Hz.]

Theta n   versus iteration number

415

Fig. 9.   Two examples illustrating how the Phase Transition Map and, the resulting θ_n sequence, are altered when the driving signal parameter f_S is changed.

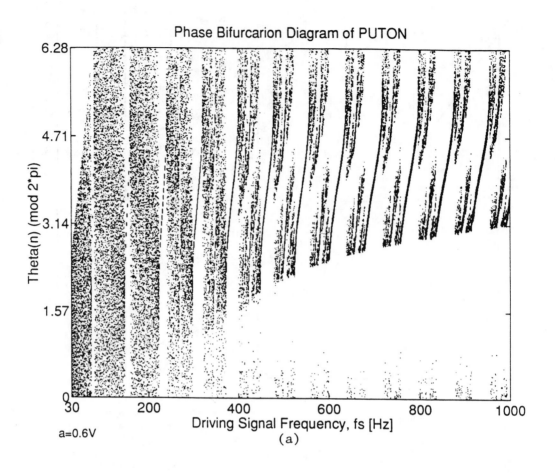

Phase Bifurcarion Diagram of PUTON

a=0.6V

(a)

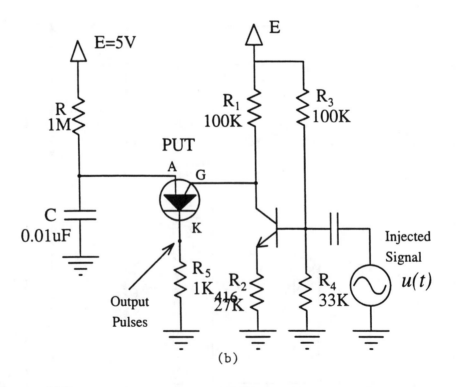

(b)

Fig. 10. Measured bifurcation diagram (a) of PUTON embodiment of the neuron shown in (b).

416

Fig. 10(b). The phase sequence θ_n is obtained by measuring the time delay between the n-th pulse or spike fired by the PUTON (observed at K) and the immediately preceding peak of the periodic injected signal (the immediately preceding zero crossing can also be used as time reference). Note the values of θ_n in the Fig. 10(a) are shown normalized to 2π. The figure demonstrates clearly, and at one glance, the rich variety of firing modalities the PUTON goes through as the frequency of periodic activation (driving signal) is altered.

The information in the bifurcation diagram can also be presented in a somewhat different format, that of a *Sawtooth Phase-lock diagram* or its equivalent the *Devil's Staircase diagram*. Since θ_n is the relative phase between the n-th spike fired by the neuron and the immediately preceding peak of its cosinusoidal activation potential or driving signal, the timing of the spikes can be determined and therefore also the interspike interval or its inverse: the instantaneous firing frequency f. Plots of the firing frequency f vs. driving frequency f_s or of the *phase-lock ratio* $\rho = \frac{f_s}{f}$ vs. f_s, also called the *rotation ratio*, computed from the θ_n sequences are shown in Fig. 11 for a neuron assuming a glow-lamp nonlinearity. Note both phase lock diagrams show presence of driving signal frequency windows over which perfect phase-locking with negligible standard deviation in firing frequency occur. These regions are separated by regimes of more complex firing modalities including quasi-periodic and perhaps erratic firing for which the standard deviation of the firing frequency is finite. The saw-tooth shape and distribution of the integer phase-lock regions in Fig. 11(a) resembles closely the plots of mean firing frequency vs. driving frequency observed by Perkel and Moore [37] in the monosynaptically periodically inhibited sensory neurons in the sea slug (Aplesia Californica) and the crayfish (Procambarus Clarkii).

The Devil's Staircase diagram measured for an embodiment employing a PUT nonlinearity is shown in Fig. 12(a) with a high resolution (expanded) plot of one of the segments lying between two phase-lock regions given in Fig. 12(b). This latter plot shows clearly the self-similar or fractal nature of the diagram where a staircase structure is easily discerned in the mean and the mean plus and mean minus standard deviation branches of the diagram. Note however that the finer rungs of the staircase appear to be blurred by noise in the PUTON circuit used in making the measurement. The transistion from a phase-lock region where the standard deviation of firing frequency (or rotation number) is negligible, to a region where the standard deviation is finite is seen to be quite abrupt attesting to the rapid switching of behavior of the bifurcating neuron as the value of the bifurcation parameter, f_s in this case, is altered. Again the plots of Figs. 11 and 12 are for a fixed value of driving signal amplitude. These plots can be regarded as the *phase-lock frequency response* of the bifurcation model at fixed driving signal amplitude. Phase-lock frequency response plots at different discrete values of driving signal amplitude can be obtained in a similar fashion. The data contained in such a series of plots can be presented compactly in the form of the *Arnold Tongues' diagram* shown in Fig. 13. This diagram can be interpreted as the frequency response of an active nonlinear processing element (e.g,. the bifurcation model), that is capable of phase-locking its firing to the driving signal. The horizontal lines in this plot give the width of the periodic phase-lock firing regions at each driving signal amplitude as the frequency is swept.

(a)

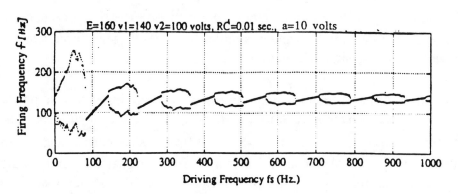

(b)

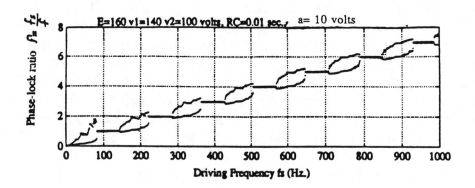

Fig. 11

Computed *phase-lock frequency response* of bifurcation model employing glow-lamp S-shaped nonlinearity. Driving cosinusoidal signal is $u(t) = a\cos(2\pi f_s t)$. Plots shown are for $a = 10[V]$ and operation conditions: supply voltage $E = 160[V]$, glow-lamp breakdown and extinction voltages $V_1 = 140[V]$, and $V_2 = 100[V]$ respectively. a) Sawtooth phase-lock diagram and b) corresponding staircase phase-lock diagram. In both diagrams the upper branches are the mean plus standard deviation of the firing frequency and the lower branches are the mean minus the standard deviation of the firing frequency. In the phase-lock regions the standard deviation is zero. The mean and standard deviation at each driving frequency f_s are calculated from a 200 msec record of the firing activity. Note in both plots the integer phase-lock regions (where the phase-lock ratio $\rho = f_s/f = 1,2,3 \ldots$) are separated by regions of irregular firing where the standard deviation in firing frequency is finite. These regions of erratic firing furnish adaptive "noise" that could play a role in "annealing" bifurcating neuron networks, i.e., drive them into entrained (phase-locked) states.

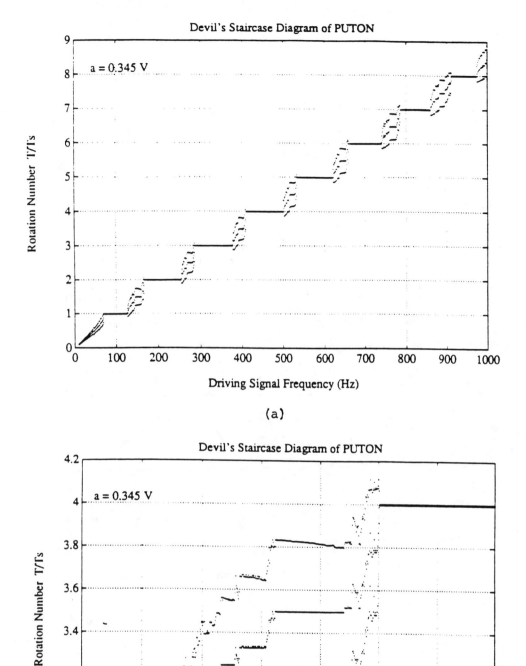

Fig. 12. Measured Devil's Staircase diagram of the periodically driven PUTON embodiment employing a programmable unijunction transistor (PUT) furnishing the S-shaped membrane nonlinearity (a), and expanded region of the diagram illustrating the self-similar or fractal nature of the Devil's Staircase diagram (b).

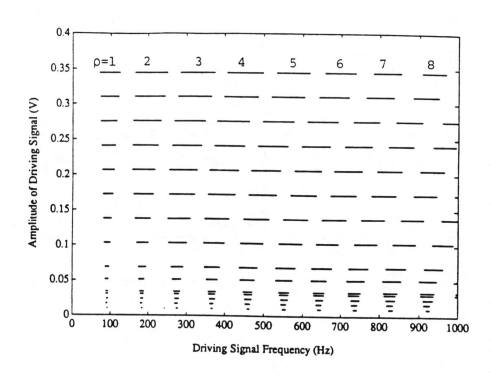

Fig. 13. The Arnold Tongues' diagram of the PUTON representing the phase-lock regions of the periodically driven PUTON (horizontal bars) for selected driving signal amplitude. If standard deviation of the interspike interval is below .04 [ms] a horizontal bar is plotted. In the regions between the horizontal bars, which form the tongues, the firing is quasi-periodic or erratic.

Outside these regions, which are shaped like wedges or tongues pointed downward, the firing can be period-N, quasi-periodic or even erratic. The tongues represent phase-lock regions with, starting from the left, integer phase-lock ratio $\rho = 1,2,3,....,$. It is noted the width of these integer phase-lock regions decreases as the amplitude of the driving signal is made smaller.

In deriving the PTM, we assumed cosinusoidal periodic activation or driving signal of the neuron to make the analysis tractable. We believe the complex behavior of the bifurcating model neuron observed for cosinusoidal activation does persist for arbitrary periodic activation. Replacing the cosinusoidal driving signal in Fig. 6 by an arbitrary periodic signal hints that this should be so and preliminary simulation results for an I & F neuron driven by a periodic signal composed of several sinusoidal components shows interspike sequences with similar complexity as when it is driven by a pure cosinusoidal signal. An interesting question in this regard is whether the bifurcation model phase-locks its firing to the strongest spectral component of the arbitrary periodic signal or not. This question is under investigation.

3. IMPLICATIONS AND SIGNIFICANCE OF THE BIFURCATING SPIKE TRAIN PATTERN CONCEPT.

The results presented so far show that the model neuron we consider has much more complex behavior than simple sigmoidal response employed widely in neural modeling today, where the state of the neuron is represented by its firing frequency, and the firing frequency is a nonlinear (sigmoidal shaped) function of the activation potential. In this mode of operation, and when the activation potential is above threshold, the spike train can be viewed as a VCO (voltage controlled oscillator) with a highly nonlinear (spike) output waveform. We have seen, however, when the activation potential becomes periodic, the spike train can alter its behavior (bifurcate) to a variety of phase-locked regular or erratic firing modalities depending on the parameters (amplitude and frequency) of the activation potential. Hence our use of the term *bifurcating spike train pattern*. Thus the neuron can act not only sigmoidally, as when its activation potential is slowly varying and is not periodic, but also can act as a detector/encoder of episodes of coherent incident spike wavefronts at its dendritic-tree that give rise to periodic activation.

The PTM, which is derived in the form given here for the first time, provides a powerful tool for modeling and studying the dynamics of neurons and neural networks using the customary tools of nonlinear dynamics such as: bifurcation diagram, Lyapanov exponent, entropy of the firing patterns or phase orbits, Devil's staircase diagram, and Arnold Tongues' diagram, all tools that provide a novel and useful approach to modeling, characterizing, and better understanding of cortical networks, higher-level cortical functions, and of how to ultimately incorporate feature-binding and cognition and other higher-level cortical functions in man-made systems.

In the above analysis a clear relation between a spike or action potential fired by a neuron and the limit-cycle trajectory in the i-v plane of the S-shaped nonlinearity used to represent the neuron's excitable membrane was established. It is interesting to speculate as to why use of limit-cycle oscillations and spiking neurons has evolved in biological systems. We offer the following reasons for such use:

421

(a) Stability of the limit-cycle oscillation, and hence its robustness and immunity while it persists to noise: The shape of spikes fired by the neuron is nearly invariant.

(b) Rapid entrainment and synchronization of systems possessing limit-cycle oscillations such as the bifurcating neuron which would allow coherent states to evolve rapidly within a coupled population of bifurcating neurons comprising a bifurcating neural network. A coherent or synchronized state is manifested by fixed relative-phase pattern (vector) between the firings of neurons in the network and by coherent incident spike wavefronts received by each neuron from other neurons in the network.

(c) The relative-phase vector of a synchronized network of N neurons is defined by an N-vector $\bar{\phi}$ with elements ϕ_i i=1,2,...N where $0 \le \phi_i < 2\pi$ is the phase between a spike fired by the i-th neuron and the immediately preceding spike of an arbitrarily selected reference neuron. If the i-th neuron fires τ_i [sec] after the reference neuron, then $\phi_i = \frac{\tau_i}{T} 2\pi$ where T is the interspike interval of the reference neuron. By this definition, the reference neuron's phase would be zero. If, because of measuring accuracy, the phase of each neuron can be distinguished over L levels then the total number of possible distinguishable permutations or states the network can assume is (NL)!. In contrast, a network of N binary neurons has a total of 2^N possible states while a network of N sigmoidal neurons whose outputs are distinguishable over L levels has a total of L^N possible states. If we take for the sake of illustration, N=3 and L=3, then the bifurcating neuron network can have a total of (3x3)! = 362,880 possible states. This exceeds by far the 2^3=8 states possible had the network been of binary neurons or the 3^3=27 states had it used sigmoidal neurons. These simple considerations serve to illustrate that in their making use of phase information, temporal networks, possess far denser state-space available for accessing by network dynamics than conventional sigmoidal or binary neuron networks. Accordingly one can intuitively expect that bifurcating neural networks would exhibit richer state-space behavior than sigmoidal networks or their binary cousins and to be capable, in general, of carrying out more complex signal processing operations and computations.

It is interesting to note, in connection with the above remarks that a possible advantage of multilevel sigmoidal neuron networks demonstrated in handling a gray-level image processing application is that the number of neurons and number of interconnections are reduced compared to binary neuron networks [21] which is an important concern in VLSI implementations of neural network. In the referenced work each neuron's response was represented by a multilevel sigmoidal function of L=16 levels. The results suggest that the smaller the slope of the staircase nonlinearity for each neuron, i.e., the larger is the value of L, the larger is the domain of attraction of each desired equilibrium point. The complexity of VLSI realization of multilevel threshold elements can neutralize however the advantage of reduced number of neurons and interconnections in such networks. Since the number of possible state levels (relative phase values) that can be naturally and automatically assumed by a neuron in a synchronized bifurcating or spiking neural network can be quite large, such networks could possess a distinct advantage, over multilevel threshold neural networks, in reducing the number of neurons and interconnections needed to handle information processing tasks. This is an interesting subject for further study of the practical advantages of bifurcating neural networks.

(d)   If we adopt the relative-phase vector, as the state variable for temporal networks, it would be tempting to speculate that relative-phase patterns in cortical networks serve as substrates for cognition and other higher-level cortical functions. A relative-phase vector can be represented as a point in a "relative-phase" state-space of the population or network. Periodic changes in the relative-phase pattern or vector in such networks can then be represented by a closed trajectory or limit-cycle in relative-phase state-space of the network. Similarly a chaotic or erratic sequence of relative-phase vectors can be associated with a chaotic trajectory in the relative-phase state-space of the network. The relative-phase state-space of bifurcating neural networks could thus exhibit point, periodic, and chaotic attractors. In this picture, chaos and the possibility of rapid bifurcation between such attractors, as induced by external signals, is of interest as means for rapidly searching the state-space of the network for coherent states that are meaningful for cognition, feature-binding, and other kinds of higher-level processing operations believed to be carried out by the cortex.

Defining the relative-phase pattern of a synchronized network of spiking neurons in the above manner is ambiguous because of the arbitriness of choosing the reference neuron. To remove this ambiguity we recall that in the analysis of Section 2, the relative-phase of the spikes fired by the individual neuron in a synchronized network was defined relative to the peak, or some other feature, e.g. zero-crossing, of the periodic activation signal driving it. Thus the periodic activation signals produced at the hillock of each neuron in a synchronized network can furnish a natural self-reference for determining the relative phase of spikes produced by each neuron and hence the relative-phase distribution of the network at any time without ambiguity. Of course, the self-reference signals exist only when the

network is in synchronized state. Accordingly the relative phase vector is $\bar{\theta}(t)$ whose components $0 \leq \theta_i(t) < 2\pi$, $i=1,2,...,N$ with N being the number of neurons of the network, are the relative-phase vs. iteration number, i.e., the orbits, produced by the

neurons. The relative-phase vector $\bar{\theta}(t)$ represents now the state of the network

unambiguously. At any instant of time, $\bar{\theta}(t)$ describes the position vector of a point in an N-dimensional relative-phase state-space of the network whose coordinates span the [0, 2π] range.

Thus when the orbit or sequence θ_n n=1,2,3,...for each neuron is fixed i.e., the relative-phase pattern of the synchronized network will be fixed i.e., $\bar{\theta}(t)$ is constant and the behavior of the network is represented by a fixed point in relative state-space.

In this case the network is both phase-locked and frequency locked. When $\bar{\theta}(t) = \bar{\theta}(t + T)$ i.e., the state vector evolution in time is periodic, the behavior is represented by closed state-space trajectory. The network assumes the same value of the relative-phase vector every T seconds. In this condition, every neuron can be in a period-m firing modality with the ratios of the values of m for the various neurons being related by integer numbers. The neurons in the network are then phase-locked but not frequency locked.

A network of neurons which can exhibit quasi-periodic or erratic firing for certain parameters of their periodic activation signals, could exhibit more complicated state-space trajectories. Such a network would contain neurons with erratic firing whose number and identity can change in time producing therefore quasi-periodic and chaotic state-space trajectories that could visit large regions of the state space. This suggests that such chaotic states or trajectories could serve as means for searching the relative-phase state-space of the network for point or periodic attractors that could represent meaningful cognitive states or could, as proposed by Zak [22], represent higher-level cognitive processes such as formation of new logical forms based upon generalization and abstraction.

(e) Dynamic Partitioning: There is mounting evidence at present that the signal processing function of the dendritic-tree of a living neuron is not confined to merely integrating the post synaptic potentials produced by its synaptic inputs (incident spike wavefront) in order to form the activation potential at the neuron's hillock, but could also include more complex nonlinear signal processing operations [23,24]. These operations are believed to stem from the action of excitable membranes at some spines on the dendritic-tree which makes for an active rather than passive dendritic-tree. This could give rise, in a coupled population of such dendritic-neurons, to stimulus driven synchronization and feature linking capabilities [25], and stimulus driven dynamic partitioning of a network into weakly interacting subpopulations [15],[26]-[28] that can perform collective computations in parallel which is significant for forming Non Lipschitzian networks with unpredictable dynamics. It is suggested [2] that Non Lipschitzian represent cortical networks better than conventional neural networks whose dynamics obey the Lipschitz condition. Dendritic-tree processing is meaningful in spiking neuron networks and therefore it is not an issue in sigmoidal neuron networks. Therefore consideration of spatiotemporal processing operations in dendritic-trees does not arise in sigmoidal networks.

(f) The spiking nature of the bifurcating neuron and the complexity of phase orbits (θ_n values associated with the spike trains) it produces under changing input conditions enables viewing the bifurcating neuron as an *information source*. It also enables defining the *entropy* and *mutual information* of the θ_n sequences or firing patterns produced. Specifically, we can view the bifurcating neuron as an information source with sequential output of symbols or events from the set $S = \{S_1, S_2, ...S_q\}$ with each symbol occurring with fixed probability $P(S_i)$ i=1,2,...,q. If the probability of a symbol occurring is independent of previous symbols we say the neuron is a <u>zero-memory source</u>. The information gained or received when the i-th symbol or event occurs is then by definition [29],

$$I(S_i) = \log_2 \frac{1}{P(S_i)} \tag{29}$$

The average amount of information received per symbol is

$$\langle I \rangle = \sum_{i=1}^{q} P(S_i) \ I(S_i) \tag{30}$$

$$= - \sum_{i=1}^{q} P(S_i) \ \log_2 \ P(S_i) = H \tag{31}$$

where H is the entropy.

We need to be more specific about what is meant by symbol when we view the bifurcating neuron as an information source. Consider the plot θ_n vs. n shown in Fig. 14 where n=1,2,...,N.

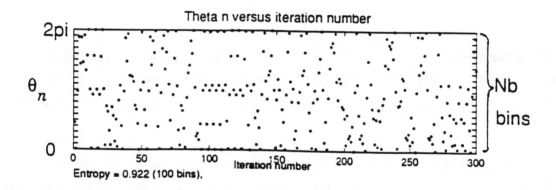

Fig. 14. Plot of typical θ_n vs. iteration number n referred to in entropy calculations.

There are N points in the plot and we assume N is sufficiently large. The θ_n axis, spanning the 0-2π interval, is divided into N_b bins. Then, by counting how many points fall in the i-th bin and dividing the outcome by N, we obtain the probability P_i of θ_n falling in bin i. This is also the frequency histogram of θ_n.

The entropy, which is a measure of disorder, is in accordance to eq. (31),

$$H \equiv - \sum_{i=1}^{N_b} P_i \ \log \ P_i$$

The maximum entropy or disorder occurs when the probability of θ_n falling in the i-th bin (i=1,2,3,...,N_b) is constant. The number of events per bin in this case is $\frac{N}{N_b}$ and $P_i = (\frac{N}{N_b}) \times (\frac{1}{N}) = \frac{1}{N_b}$. Thus

$$H_{max} = - P_i \log (P_i) \sum_{i=1}^{N_b} 1 = (- \frac{1}{N_b}) \log \frac{1}{N_b} \times N_b = \log N_b$$

Therefore the normalized Entropy

$$H_n = \frac{H}{H_{max}} = - \frac{1}{\log N_b} \sum_{i=1}^{N_b} P_i \log P_i \qquad (32)$$

provides a normalized measure of the degree of disorder in the orbits θ_n and therefore in spike trains produced by the bifurcating neuron. An $H_n = 1$ indicates chaotic firing. The computed normalized entropy of the θ_n sequence in Fig. 14 for example, assuming $N_b = 100$ bins is $H_n = .922$.

We have seen in the above that the neuron can be viewed as an information source producing symbols θ_n n=1,2,... with symbol probability $P(\theta_n)$. Because the orbit θ_n depends on the neuron's input (activation potential), the symbol probability changes as the input to the neuron, or the incident spike wavefront giving rise to it, changes. Different inputs produce therefore different symbols and corresponding symbol probabilities. The neuron can therefore also be viewed as a complex *encoder* of incident spike wavefronts.

The above observations may enable speculating on possible learning in bifurcating neural network in terms of reducing the *Cross-Entropy*,

$$G = \sum_{i=1}^{N} P(\theta_n) \log \frac{P'(\theta_n)}{P(\theta_n)} \qquad (33)$$

where $P(\theta_n)$ is the symbol probability produced by the neuron for certain input (incident spike wavefront) and $P'(\theta_n)$ is a target symbol probability we wish the neuron to produce for that input. The learning task then is how to modify the synaptic responses (synaptic weights and possibly time constants or synaptic delays) of the neuron so that G is minimized. Note that $G \rightarrow o$ when $P'(\theta_n) \rightarrow P(\theta_n)$. The goal then is to determine the synaptic responses of neurons in a population or pool of interconnected bifurcating neurons in which a portion of the neurons receive external inputs such that given input patterns which can be spatial or spatio-temporal, end up producing desired distinct relative phase patterns when the network gets synchronized. The learning algorithm developed must obey the usual minimal perturbation principle, i.e., reoccurrence of input patterns that have already been learned would not alter the synaptic weights and only novel inputs would produce synaptic response changes that minimally perturb the information already stored.

(g)   Although in preceding sections we refer to erratic firing of our bifurcation model under certain conditions of periodic activation, the Lyapunov exponents associated with values of a and f_s in the Arnold Tongues' diagram falling between the phase-lock regions have never been found to be positive which rules out the occurrence of chaotic firing. The seemingly erratic firing regions in the bifurcation diagram of Fig. 10(a) would therefore be representing period-m firing with long periods, i.e., large m or equivalently firing modalities where a long sequence of non-repeating values of θ_n occurs before the value of θ_n is repeated. This observation is supported by the Poincare-Bendixon theorem [30] which says that a system whose nonlinear dynamics are governed by two autonomous first-order ordinary differential equations containing nonlinear coupling terms cannot exhibit chaotic behavior (see also pages 2-5 of reference 20). The behavior of the cosinusoidally driven bifurcation model analyzed in Section 2 is governed by two differential equations:

$$\frac{dv}{dt} = \frac{E - v}{R} - \phi(v - u) \tag{34}$$

and

$$\frac{d\varphi}{dt} = \omega \tag{35}$$

where $u = a\cos\varphi$ and $\varphi = \omega t + \theta_o$, θ_o being an arbitrary constant phase and action potentials are produced whenever v reaches threshold (see eq. 5). According to the Poincare Bendixon theorem this system of equations cannot exhibit chaotic solutions i.e., chaotic sequences of firing phases θ_n. It is capable of producing as we stated long sequences of period-m that appear erratic to an observer if m is very large but are not strictly chaotic. Therefore in order to exhibit chaos, our bifurcating neuron model must be modified in such a way as to make its dynamics governed by at least three autonomous first-order differential equations with nonlinear coupling terms. This could occur when, for example, the threshold level v_1 of the S-shaped nonlinearity $i = \phi(v)$ is not constant, as assumed in the analysis of Section 2, but obeys a differential equation of its own like,

$$\frac{dv_1}{dt} = -\alpha v_1 + f(v) \tag{36}$$

where α is a constant and $f(\ )$ is a nonlinear function of v. Equation (36) adds *accommodation* to our bifurcation model making it resemble more biological neurons which are known to exhibit accommodation. It is worth noting that the Hodgkin-Huxley model of the biological membrane [18] and the MacGregor and Oliver version of it [31] consist of $N \geq 3$ autonomous first-order differential equations with nonlinear coupling terms. They are expected therefore to exhibit chaotic solutions for certain regions of their parameter spaces. It would seem therefore that under suitable conditions of periodic activation, biological neurons in the cortex would exhibit chaotic firing. Indeed chaotic firing regimes have been observed experimentally in the periodically driven biological membrane (the squid's giant axon) and the Molluscan neuron [33]-[37].

Inclusion of adaptive thresholding or accommodation in the analysis of the bifurcating model neuron described in this paper, although analytically challenging, is likely to lead to complex firing modalities under periodic activation that could include full blown chaotic firing. Two additional methods for introducing full blown chaos in the behavior of the circuit of Fig. 1 are under investigation. One involves adding a membrane inductance in parallel with the capacitor in Fig. 1(b) which would make the circuit obey a second order nonlinear differential equation resembling that of the nonlinear pendulum. The second method involves time-delay modulation of the restoring source (E or I) that represents a form of depletion of ionic pools available for restoring membrane potential by the firing of an action potential.

One may well ask at this point why is chaotic firing important? The following is an attempt to answer this question.

Chaos describes a strange intermediate state lying between rigid organization, i.e., order, and complete disorganization, i.e., disorder or randomness. It also connotes something between predictability and chance, between a deterministic signal and noise.

Chaos in neurodynamics could have beneficial consequences because decision making processes that show chaos mix consistency with unpredictibility and could overcome the limitations of both.

Understanding chaos and learning to use it in the design of in man-made systems in general and in neurodynamics in particular could be the key for increasing the power of neurocomputing by extending functional capabilities to higher-level processing like cognition, feature and concept binding, inferencing, reasoning, attention focusing, and possibly improved learning and optimization.

Possible roles for chaos are:

• Efficient search of state-space of a network that is neither systematic or random, but is driven by the dynamics of the network itself.

- As inherent (self-generated) adaptive (signal dependent) source of "noise" in a network, chaos could possibly furnish a mechanism for "self-annealing" the network into phase-locked states of "energy" minima that are cognitively meaningful.

4. CONCLUSIONS. The study of bifurcation in spiking neural networks and the roles of synchronicity, bifurcation and chaos in such networks is still in its infancy. It is however rapidly growing because of its promise for providing better understanding of higher-level cortical functions and of how to incorporate them in artificial neural networks to enhance the power of neurocomputing. Recent developments [25],[39] are examples of this trend. The study of the dynamics of the bifurcating model presented here is a step towards understanding how the functional complexity of the individual processing element governs the dynamics of bifurcating patterns in neural networks specially when they enter synchronized states and towards learning how to use synchronicity bifurcation and chaos in the design of a new generation of computing structures.

The ability to <u>design</u> bifurcation models and embodiments that exhibit, under periodic activation, truly chaotic firing in addition to all the other firing modalities (e.g., phase-locked, regular firing at integer phase-lock ratios, period-m firing including bursting) makes available, for the first time, a processing element with functional complexity far exceeding that of conventional model neurons employed in neural networks today. An opportunity for building and studying a new generation of neural networks consisting of processing elements that are rich in functional complexity presents itself. The roles of synchronicity, bifurcation and chaos in dynamical neural networks that emulate cortical functions such as feature-binding, separation of figure from ground, cognition, inferencing, reasoning and other higher-level functions can be studied. Indeed such studies have been started [40].

In-depth understanding of the dynamics of spiking neurons and their collective behavior is also important for the emerging field of *neuroprothsesis* [41] where it is envisioned that implantable artificial neurochips would be employed to compensate deficit or impairment in the human nervous system especially in motor control and the auditory and visual systems. It is very likely that such chips would be of the spiking variety to conserve energy and to be more morphic with biological neurons. In depth understanding of the dynamics of the model neurons used and their interaction is then of critical importance for achieving the desired functionality and ensuring reliable dynamics.

The dynamical systems approach presented here and the resulting bifurcating neuron model do not explicitly take into consideration the fluctuations in the membrane potential of biological neurons produced by the random gating of ionic channels in the membrane or by any other noise causes. The effect of such fluctuations can however be investigated by incorporating noise in the iteration process. This is readily done by adding a random number from a given distribution with prescribed variance to each iteration of the PTM. This procedure shows that although fine detail in the bifurcation diagram gets washed out by the added noise, gross features of the diagram are structurally stable under such perturbation.

The dynamics of the bifurcation model, and in particular its ability to produce phase-locked firing activity when it finds itself subjected to episodes of coherent incident spike wavefronts, offers a plausible explanation of the mechanism subserving the relatively recent physiological observations [5]-[11],[39] of stimulus induced synchronized firings and associated correlated LFPs observed at widely separated cortical regions sharing the same receptive field. One classical (nonquantum) way in which stimulus induced synchronization at widely spaced noninteracting regions of the cortex can occur is that: (a) such regions participate in encoding features of the same object through shared receptive field, and (b) pools of neurons in the two regions be receiving coherent incident spike wavefronts that are precipitated by the stimulus. This hypothesis is supported by the suggestion [42] that phase-locking of firing activity of central neurons engaged in the encoding of vibrotactile information is "probably due to temporal coherence in the impulse activity arriving over converging input fibers".

The ability of the bifurcation model to phase-lock its firing to periodic episodes in its activation potential that were precipitated by sensory inputs, suggests that the holographic metaphor of the brain [43]-[45] can be discussed in more specific terms than before. We are now able to point, for the first time, to a specific locally generated reference signal, namely the precipitated periodic activation, that can *cohere* the firing of selected neurons in a seething sea of cortical neurons. Which neurons are cohered depends on the sensory inputs and on connection (synaptic) weights between neurons i.e., on learned past experience. The selected population of cohered neurons would be constantly changing in space, time, and size by the changing sensory environment. One can speculate then that while a selected cohered population persists, the sensory-induced synchronized firing of the neurons represent a cognitive state or precept, analogous to a reconstructed wavefront and associated image in holography, that is ultimately viewed and interpreted by the "mind's-eye", in a yet unknown manner that is at the heart of the ever present mind-matter debate.

Finally one of the advantages of artificial spiking neurons is their low power consumption [46] as compared to sigmoidal neurons. The power consumption of the PUTON circuit of Fig. 10(b) for example is ~ 300 μw, and this is mostly consumed by the grid bias and signal injection part of the circuit; only about 20 μw are consumed by the actual firing or spiking of the PUT. An optoelectronic integrated circuit (OEIC) implementation of the circuit of Fig. 10(b) is expected however to provide the desirable levels of further reduced power consumption.

5. ACKNOWLEDGEMENT: The research described was supported by SDIO/IST under Office of Naval Research management and by the Army Research Office.

6. REFERENCES.

1. N. Farhat and M. Eldefrawy, "The Bifurcating Neuron: Characterization and Dynamics", Proc., *SPIE*, vol. 1773, pp. 23-34, 1993.

2. M. Zak, "An Unpredictable-Dynamics Approach to Neural Intelligence", *IEEE Expert*, vol. 7, pp. 4-10, August 1991.

3. Chr. v.d. Marlsberg, Internal Report 81-2, MPI Biophys. Chem. Gotingen, 1981.

4. M. Abeles, <u>Local Cortical Circuits</u>, Springer Verlag, Berlin, 1982.

5. C.M. Gray and W. Singer, *Soc. Neuroscience Abstract* 12404.3, 1987.

6. C.M. Gray, et. al., *Europ. J. Neurosc.*, vol. 2, pp. 607-619, 1990.

7. A.K. Engel, et. al., *Europ. J. Neurosc.*, vol. 2, pp. 588-606, 1990.

8. C.M. Gray, et. al., *Nature*, vol. 338, pp. 334-337, 1989.

9. R. Eckhorn, et. al., *Biol. Cybern.*, vol. 60, pp. 121-130, 1988.

10. P. Konig and T. Schillen, *Neural Computation*, vol. 3, pp. 133-166, 1991.

11. P. Konig and T. Schillen, *Neural Computation*, vol. 3, pp. 167-178, 1991.

12. W. Freeman, "The Physiology of Perception," *Sci. Am.*, pp. 78-85, Feb., 1991.

13. S. Blackeslee, "Nerve Cell Rythm may be Key to Consciousness," *The New York Times* (Science Times Section), Oct. 27, 1992.

14. K. Delaney, et. al., "Waves and Stimulus-Modulated Dynamics in an Oscillating Olfactory Network", (Private comm.)

15. E.R. Grannan, D. Kleinfeld, and H. Sompolinsky, "Stimulus-Dependent Synchronization of Neural Assemblies", *Neural Computation* vol. 5, pp. 550-569, July 1993.

16. L. Shastri and V. Ajjanagadde, "From Simple Associations to Systematic Reasoning", *Behavioral and Brain Sciences*", (To be published, September, 1993).

17. P.M. Koch, "Microwave Ionization of Excited Hydrogen Atoms: What We Do Not Understand", in Chaos, D.K. Campbell (Ed.), AIP, New York, p. 445, 1990.

18. A.L. Hodgkin and A.F. Huxley, "The Components of the Membrane Conductances in the Giant Axon of *Loligo*", *J. Physiol.*, vol. 116, pp. 473-496, 1952.

19. A.A. Andronow and C.E. Chaikin, Theory of Oscillations, Princeton University Press, Princeton, NJ, p. 171, 1949.

20. G.L. Baker and J.P. Gollub, Chaotic Dynamics, Cambridge University Press, Cambridge, pp. 85-89, 1990.

21. J. Si and A. Michel, "Analysis and Synthesis of Discrete-Time Neural Networks with Multilevel Threshold Functions", Proc. 1991 IEEE Int. Symp. on Circuits and Systems, vol. 3 (of 5) on Analog Circuits and Neural Networks, IEEE Publication # 91 CH3006-4, 1991.

22. M. Zak, "Chaos as a Part of Logical Structure in Neurodynamics", App. Math. Lett., vol. 2, pp. 175-177, 1989.

23. W. Rall and I. Segv, "Excitable Dendritic Spine Clusters: Nonlinear Synaptic Processing", in Computer Simulation in Brain Science, R.M.J. Cotterill (Ed.), Cambridge Univ. Press, Cambridge, pp. 26-43, 1988.

24. John G. Elias, "Artificial Dendritic-Trees", Neural Computation, vol. 5, pp. 648-664, July, 1993.

25. R. Eckhorn, H.J. Reitboek, M. Arndt, and P. Dike, "Feature Linking via Synchronization among Distributed Assemblies: Simulations of Results from the Cat Visual Cortex", Neural Computation, vol. 2, pp. 293-307, Fall, 1990.

26. A. Nischwitz, H. Glunder, A. van Oertzen and P. Klausner, "Synchronization and Label-Switching in Networks of Laterally Coupled Neurons", Artificial Neural Networks, 2, I. Aleksander and J. Taylor (Eds.), Elsevier Science Publishers, B.V., pp. 851-854, 1991.

27. I. Segev, "Computer Study of Presynaptic Inhibition Controlling the Spread of Action Potentials into Axonal Terminals", J. of Neurophysiology, vol. 63, pp. 987-998, May, 1990.

28. M. Usher, H.G. Schuster, E. Niebur, "Dynamics of Populations of Integrate-and-Fire Neurons, Partial Synchronization, and Memory", Neural Computation, vol. 5, pp. 570-586, July, 1993.

29. J.A. Freeman and D.M. Skapura, Neural Networks, Addison-Wesley, Reading, MA, (Section 5.1), 1991. See also, P.M. Woodward, Probability and Information Theory with Applications to Radar, (Second edition), Pergamon Press, Oxford, (Chapter 3), 1953.

30. F.C. Hoppensteadt, Analysis and Simulation of Chaotic Systems, Springer-Verlag, New York, pp. 31-32, 1992.

31. R. MacGregor and R. Oliver, "A Model for Repetitive Firing in Neurons", Kybernetik, vol. 16, pp. 53-64, 1974.

32. R. Guttman, L. Feldman and E. Jacobsson, "Frequency Entrainment of Squid Axon Membrane", J. Membrane Biology, vol. 56, pp. 9-18, 1980.

33. A.V. Holden and S.M. Ramadan, "The Response of a Molluscan Neurone to Cyclic Input: Entrainment and Phase-Locking", Biol. Cybern., vol. 43, pp. 157-163, 1981.

34. A.V. Holden, et. al., "The Induction of Periodic and Chaotic Activity in a Molluscan Neurone", Biol. Cybern., vol. 43, pp. 169-173, 1982.

35. G. Matsumoto, K. Aihara, M. Ichikawa, and A. Tasaki, "Periodic and Nonperiodic Responses of Membrane Potential in Squid Giant Axon Under Sinusoidal Current Stimulation", J. Theor. Neurobiol., vol. 3, pp. 1-14, 1983.

36. K. Aihara and G. Matsumoto, "Chaotic Oscillations and Bifurcation in Squid Giant Axon", in Chaos, A.V. Holden (Ed.), Princeton Univ. Press, Princeton, NJ, pp. 257-269, 1986.

37. D. Perkel and G. Moore, "Pacemaker Neurons: Effects of Regularly Spaced Synaptic Inputs", Science, vol. 145, pp. 61-63, July 1964.

38. J.L. Johnson, "Pulse-Coupled Neural Nets: Translation, Rotation, Scale, and Intensity Signal Invariant for Images", (Submitted to App. Optics, July 13, 1993).

39. S. Bressler, R. Coppola and R. Nakamura, "Episodic Multiregional Cortical Coherence at Multiple Frequencies during Visual Task Performance", Nature, vol. 366, pp. 153-156, Nov. 1993.

40. H. Szu, et. al., "Spatiotemporal Chaos Information Processing in Neural Networks: Electronic Implementation", in Rethinking Neural Networks, K.H. Pribram, ed., pp. 445-461, L. Erlbaum Associates Publishrs, Hillsdale, NJ, 1993.

41. R. Eckmiller, "Concerning the Challenge of Neurotechnology", in Neurobionics, H.-W. Bothe, M. Samii and R. Eckmiller, eds., pp. 21-28, Elsevier Science Publishers, Amsterdam, 1993.

42. M. Rowe, "Impulse Patterning in Central Neurons for Vibrotactile Coding", in Information Processing in the Mammalian Auditory and Tactile Systems, M. Rowe and L. Aitken, eds., pp. 111-115, Wiley-Liss, New York, 1990.

43. K.H. Pribram, "Some Dimensions of Remembering: Steps Toward Neuro-Physiological Model of Memory", in Macromolecules and Memory, J. Gaito, ed., Appleton-Century-Croft, New York, 1966.

44. P.R. Westlake, "The Possibilities of Neural Holographic Process Within the Brain", Kybernetik, vol. 7, pp. 129-153, 1970.

45. K. Wilber, The Holographic Paradigm, New Science Library, Shambala/Boston & London, 1985.

46. M. Mahowald and R. Douglas, "The Silicon Neuron", Nature, vol. 354, pp. 515-518, 1991.

Chapter 18

Neural Network Models for Chaotic-Fuzzy Information Processing

Harold Szu, Joe Garcia, Lotfi Zadeh, Charles C. Hsu, Joseph DeWitte, Jr., Gyu Moon, Desa Gobovic, Mona Zaghloul

Neural Network Models for Chaotic-Fuzzy Information Processing

Harold Szu, Joe Garcia, G. Rogers, Lotfi Zadeh[#], NSWC, Silver Spring MD 20903
Charles C. Hsu, Joseph DeWitte, Jr., Gyu Moon[*], Desa Gobovic, Mona Zaghloul
EE&CS GWU, Wash. DC 20052
[*]Dept. of Electronics, Hallym Univ., Choonchun, Korea
[#]Dept. of EE &CS., Univ. of California-Berkeley, Berkeley CA 94720

Abstract: A model of chaotic neural networks (CNN) is defined as follows: (i) a fixed-point Hebbian synaptic weight dynamic: $dW_{ij}/dt = -(W_{ij} - [x_i x_j - \delta_{ij}])$ with $x_i \equiv 2v_i - 1$; (ii) an instantaneous input $u_i = \Sigma_j W_{ij} v_j$; and (iii) a piecewise negative slope logic $v_i = \sigma_N(u_i)$ (if the total input happens at the threshold, then for more input the chaotic neuron produces a less output according to the mapping). Such a neuron has a N-shaped sigmoidal function. The feedback from other neurons gives a variable iteration slope of the output v_i versus the input u_i (which for no learning (i) would be fixed at 45°). This is how self-control of the collective chaos.

Two applications are given. The average synaptic weights plays an important role for the average feedback slopes useful for collective feature extraction and pattern recognition. Examples of habituation and novelty detection are resulted from hundred thousands σ_N neurons, but not from σ neurons. Another novel usage of the CNN is that of a bifurcation bridge between neural learning and Learnable Fuzzy Logic.

Keywords: Chaos, Chaotic Neuron, Chaotic Neural Networks, Feigenbaum, Bifurcation, Habituation, Novelty, Chips, SPICE

1. Onset of Fuzzy Logic via the Bifurcation of Non-overlapping Membership Functions to Overlapping Membership Functions

The field of Artificial Neural Networks (ANNs) is becoming a part of the rich field of nonlinear dynamics [1, 2]. Recently the two have been combined into Chaotic Neural Networks (CNNs) [3-16]. A motivation for chaotic fuzzy neural networks is to develop systems that can efficiently represent or predict events in chaotic processes. For biological reasons given by us [17, 18, 19] and by Freeman et al. [20], we wish to study a biologically meaningful neuron model that is "simple enough but not any simpler (A. Einstein)" yet can produce a bifurcation cascade toward chaos. The model must be able to be massively fabricated as a learnable neural network on electronic chips. Therefore, such an implementable neuron model should have no delay in neuron input-output, should not require

435

expensive sample-hold circuitry and should not have any inductance coil elements (this would allow magnetic field cross talk in a closely packed fabrication). Indeed, such a CNN has been designed [16,28] based on the 1-D N-

shaped sigmoidal function σ_N that has a small section near the input threshold value where a negative-slope logic is derived for a Markovian mean field approximation of the Cainainello refractory delay model (see Appendix A) [19] . It was further pointed out by Zadeh et al. [29] that chaos may provide a dynamical basis for fuzzy reasoning. In this paper we explore such a practical bridge between a CNN and fuzzy logic and hope to achieve a learnable fuzzy membership function (FMF).

For instance, to those who can vaguely recollect from the past decades (in the spirit of L. Zadeh, "exploiting the tolerance of imprecision"), the Japanese Embassy and the Washington D. C. Government seem to fail in predicting the peak weekend for the annual Cherry Blossoms (CB). Since Washington D. C. is located close to the Appalachian ridge in an unstable region where weather systems from Canada and the Gulf of Mexico converge, the weather chaotically fluctuates from year to year. Compounding this is the modulation by the 11-year period solar cycle. For Japanese and American tourists, Cherry trees are not cooperating with the embassy planning, but with Mother Nature---the species genetics and the weather (conceivably the Winter snowfall, the Spring rainfall, and the Solar activity play some roles). These complex conditions drive the underlying chaotic dynamics of the CB making long range forecasting especially difficult for this part of the United States. Since the full CB does not last long (having a life span Δt about five to ten days), it is difficult to predict the exact peak. How does one then treat such a chaotic time series?

It is intuitively clear that chaos provides a deterministic possibility useful for fuzzy logic. A basis of fuzzy logic is the FMF which is often chosen in the shape of a triangle for a clear centroid at its tip t =0 shown in Fig. 1 (a):

$$\Phi(t) = 1 - |t|; \qquad 0 \le |t| \le 1, \qquad (1)$$

$$0; \qquad \text{otherwise.}$$

It turns out that the triangle is equivalent to a low-pass scaling function used for the multiple resolution high-pass wavelet analysis:

$$\Phi(t) = \Phi(2t+1)/2 + \Phi(2t) + \Phi(2t-1)/2 \qquad (2)$$

shown in Fig. 1 (b) for the two-scale scaling relationship illustrating a special case of the Collage Theorem[34].

If the underlying fuzzy dynamics are the bifurcation route toward chaos, then we can expand the chaotic data set efficiently on this set of nesting triangular membership functions (MF), regressing from an non-overlapping crisp MF becoming overlapping fuzzy MF as schematically shown in Fig. 2. The Analogy between the bifurcation route to chaos (left of Fig. 2) and the crisp route to fuzzy overlapping membership function (right of Fig. 2). Note that Fig. 2 has taken into account of the standard FMF overlapping & complementing characteristics, but without the details of the CB ratio $\Delta T/\Delta t$ shown in next Fig. 3.

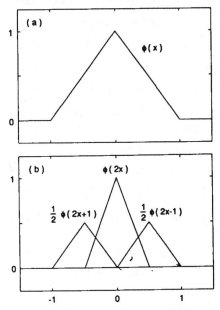

Fig. 1) A Hat Scaling Function Relation Useful for Fuzzy Membership Functions

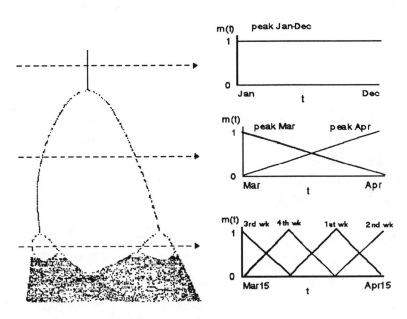

Fig. 2) Analogy between the bifurcation route to chaos (left) and the crisp route to fuzzy overlapping membership function (right)

437

If we assume [28] the triangle envelop covering a typical bifurcation cascade spectrum as the Fuzzy Membership Function (FMF), then the bifurcation to chaos suggests a multi-resolution FMF analysis as follows. We introduce an average life span of the cherry blossoms Δt, say

$$< \Delta t > = 7 \text{ days},$$

with a standard deviation σ_t of 3 days. We also introduce the time resolution scale length ΔT in the analysis of the periodic CB event. One can trivially forecast every year with the absolute certainty, "crisp or sharp" that the CB will surely peak sometime during the $\Delta T^{(0)}$ = Spring time of the year. A factor 2 increase in the precision, $\Delta T^{(1)} = \Delta T^{(0)}/2$, corresponds to a decrease in the certainty of the event: CB peak during March or April. Likewise, for $\Delta T^{(2)} = \Delta T^{(1)}/2$, still less certainty in the unit of a two week period at the end of March or at the beginning of April. However, this non-overlapping membership function can not be extended indefinitely. This is because of $\Delta T^{(3)} = \Delta T^{(2)}/2$ the sub-triangle becomes overlapping, thus marking the onset of the FMF when the resolution scale $\Delta T^{(3)}$ for a week approaches the average CB event span $<\Delta t >$.

Eq(2) gives the contribution due to the sharpening of the uncertainty FMF indicated by the dashed triangle having a narrowed range as shown in Fig. 3.

$$\Phi(2t) = \Phi(t) - \Phi(2t+1)/2 - \Phi(2t-1)/2 \qquad (3)$$

When actual data of the CB becomes available, we can apply the standard discrete wavelet analysis via Quadrature Mirror Filter Bank [31],

$$t \to t' = t - b / a$$
$$b = I; \quad I = 0, \pm 1, \pm 2, \pm 3,$$

where b is the shift parameter by days to catch the exact CB day defined with a FMF of width $\Delta T^{(3)}$ to train a classical ANN to predict the CB event. A more efficient way is to combine a wavelet network with an ANN into a so-called "wavenet"[32], of which each neuron assumes a daughter wavelet transfer function having a single value of $a = 2^I$.

In this paper, we wish to emphasize that a CNN has intrinsically combined an ANN with the multiresolution scale analysis via bifurcations. Since the bifurcation output of a σ_N neuron realizes a member of the FMF, then such cooperative chaotic neurodynamics determines a collective resolution scale $<\Delta T>$ which in turn may provide us with the possibility of a learnable fuzzy logic reasoning concerning when a quasi-periodic event will occur with respect to the dyadic scale.

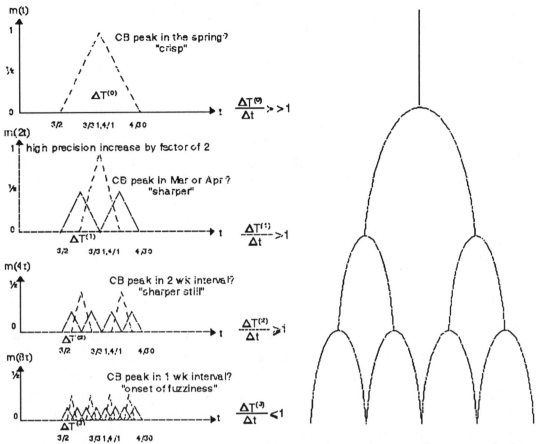

Fig. 3) The dashed triangles indicate the differences between two adjacent resolutions of the bifurcated membership functions in terms of the resolution scales $\Delta T^{(n)}$ toward overlap with the mean event life span $\langle \Delta t \rangle$.

We have pointed out the parallel route from "crisp" to "fuzzy" as "bifurcation" to "chaos". It is thus interesting to exam how a minimum change of the traditional sigmoidal neuron transfer function can generate the bifurcation to chaos in Sect. 2.

2. Review of Single Chaotic Neuron σ_N Models

The Nagumo-Sato (1972) model [12] of a neuron was originally biologically motivated by Fitzhugh (1961) [11], developed mathematically by Caianiello (1961)[10] and implemented with tunneling diodes and an inductance element by Harmon(1961) [13]. The inductor has a magnetic field which produces cross talk in an IC implementation. Recently, this challenge has been circumvented by Chua's Circuit[1], implemented by Yamakawa's chip [14] and Aihara's circuit.[9,15]. Various mathematical models of chaotic neurons are: (i) one-dimensional (1-D) recursive maps without delay; the single neuron via

439

Feigenbaum-like cascaded bifurcation spectrum that was demonstrated mathematically for the first time by Szu et. al. (ii) 1-D class of delayed maps include Caianiello & Nagumo models, and Aihara, and Yamakawa which is shown to be 2-D map without the delay. This class of 1-D delayed map can map 2-D (x_n, y_n) to 2-D (x_{n+1}, y_{n+1}) without any delay.

$$X_{n+1} = f(X_n) - aY_n$$
$$Y_{n+1} = X_n$$

In the sense of Poincare chaos, the sensitivity to the initial condition might be due to the fact that in this delayed map, all the previous data history is required to determine the present value , so that a slight change in data will perturb the outcome. This conjecture is easily seen by solving Eq(1a,b) formally as follows:

$$X_{n+1} = \Sigma^{\infty}_{k=0} (-a)^k \ f(X_{n-2k});$$

or, an equivalent recursion formula:

$$X_{n+1} = f(X_n) - aX_{n-1}$$

where $f(X_n)$ is the piecewise-linear discrete function in the cases of Yamakawa and Aihara, and is a smooth quadratic function, $f(X_n) = X_n^2 -1$ for the Henon map. Thus we have demonstrated that the set of 1-D delayed maps is mathematically equivalent to a 2-D map without delay of the Henon type attractor. Then the question remains what is computationally efficient while truly being a 1-D map without the delay?

To stay within the time scale of the classical McCulloch-Pitts (M-P) model of ANN we have modified the instantaneous input-output mapping:

$$v_i(t_{n+1}) = \sigma(u_i(t_n)) = (1+\exp(-u_i(t_n)))^{-1} \tag{4}$$

The net neuron input is an instantaneously weighted sum from other neurons,

$$u_i(t_n) = \Sigma_{j \neq i} W_{ij}(t_n) v_j(t_n) + \theta_i(t_n) \tag{5}$$

which is the original M-P model. The modification is, similar to a squid axon [7] but differs in the delay, given by Szu et. al. [17-20] as a piecewise negative logic (i.e. an abnormal or sick neuron having less output with more input near the threshold) which is chosen to be zero threshold value shown in Fig. 4a. This single neuron model is called σ_N and contains a piecewise negative logic section[17-20]. It was measured on the giant axons of squid under normal physiological conditions [21,22,23]. The negative slope region represents axonal

440

fatigue. In other words, the neuron support (housekeeping) functions cannot maintain a constant threshold, θ, due to the high output pulse rate. Therefore, θ is proportional to how rapid the output changes: $\theta \approx d\sigma/du = 4\lambda v(1-v)$, which is the chaotic logistic function [17,18,19, 20].

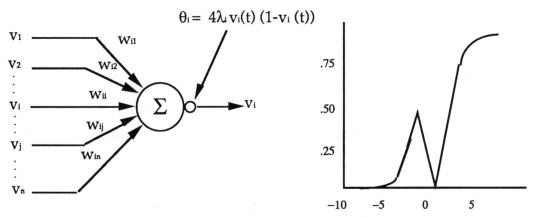

$$\theta_i = 4\lambda_i v_i(t)(1-v_i(t))$$

Fig. 4 a) Biological Conjecture for Piecewise Negative Logic σ_N Neuron Model.

In the linear region of σ, $v = \sigma(u-\theta) \approx \sigma(u-4\lambda v(1-v)) \approx \sigma(u) - \sigma(4\lambda v(1-v)) \approx \sigma_N(u)$. The subtraction of θ from the input is the source of the dip in the σ_N function. In Appendix A, we present a geometric series proof of bifurcations. The chaotic neuron models are spatiotemporal variations of the M-P sigmoidal model $v_i(t_{n+1})=\sigma(u_i(t_{n+1}))$ of which a mean field approximation of the net input u_i satisfies a recursion relationship $u_i(t_{n+1}) = k u_i(t_n)+[a(t_n) -\alpha \sigma(u_i(t_n))]$ for the refractory delay. The net input $u_i(t_{n+1})$ depends only on the current state $u_i(t_n)$ and no longer on the entire past history, which indicates a *Markovian* chain. In this paper, we are able to sum up the refractory delay effect and construct, a pre-squashed N-shape sigmoidal function $v_i(t_{n+1})=\sigma_N(u_i(t_{n+1}))$ with *no delay*, by means of a graphical method. This yields directly a Feigenbaum-like bifurcation cascade toward chaos precluding the need for excessive sample-hold circuitry for unnecessary delay time steps. The function σ_N is numerically modeled as follows (see Fig. 3)

if ($u_i <= -1.0$)	return $(1/(1+\exp(-(u_i+1))))$
else if ($u_i < 1.0$)	return $(-(u_i-1)/4)$
else	return $(2/(1+\exp(-(u_i-1))))$. (6)

To avoid the discontinuity points of σ_N, we have approximated σ_N as a cubic map (Fig. 4b):

$$v_n \quad = \quad P_3(u_n) = u_n \, (u_n + a) \, (u_n - b)(1/c^2) \qquad \text{(7a)}$$
$$u_{n+1} = v_n \qquad\qquad\qquad\qquad\qquad\qquad\qquad \text{(7b)}.$$

The cubic map has one attractor at u=0, and <u>two</u> repellers of positive slopes at u= − a, u= + b. It differs the quadratic logistic or Feigenbaum map of one attractor at and one repeller defined as

$$v_n = P_2(u_n) = 4\lambda \, u_n \, (1 - u_n) \qquad\qquad \text{(8a)}$$
$$u_{n+1} = v_n. \qquad\qquad\qquad\qquad\qquad\qquad \text{(8b)}$$

A class of polynomials P_N similar to Eqs(4,5) can be considered as the complexity increases. In the a=b case, Feigenbaum's peak value at u_n=1/2, the λ-knob, is related to the cubic roots (u=±a, u=0) at its maximum location: u=-a/√3 and λ=a³/√3.

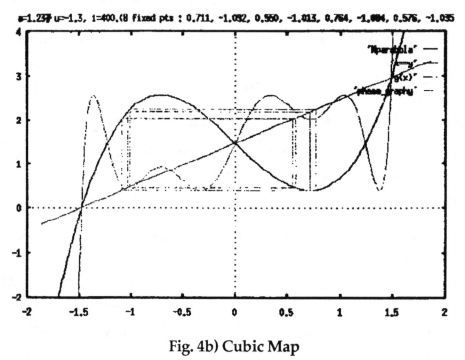

Fig. 4b) Cubic Map

Bifurcation Theorem: Bifurcation occurs when the geometric series ratio, that is the negative logic slope of σ_N versus the feedback baseline slope ω, is greater than one,

$$|\text{slope } \sigma_N| / \omega \quad \geq \quad 1 \qquad (9)$$

which means that as ω gets flatten the iteration series divergent. In other words, the critical angle Θ_{bf} for bifurcation is the angle between the feedback baseline and the negative logic line that must be bounded above by the slope of the negative logic

$$\Theta_{bf} \leq 2 \tan^{-1} |\text{slope } \sigma_N| \qquad (10)$$

Proof:

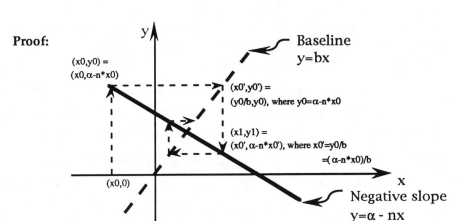

Analysis :

Iteration 0 ==> $y0 = \alpha - n*x0$

Iteration 1 ==> $y1 = \alpha - n*(\alpha-n*x0)/b$
$= \alpha - n/b*\alpha + n^2/b*x0$

Iteration 2 ==> $y2 = \alpha - n*(\alpha - n/b*\alpha + n^2/b*x0)/b$
$= \alpha - n/b*\alpha + n^2/b^2*\alpha - n^3/b^2*x0$

Iteration 3 ==> $y3 = \alpha - n*(\alpha - n/b*\alpha + n^2/b^2*\alpha - n^3/b^2*x0)/b$
$= \alpha - n/b*\alpha + n^2/b^2*\alpha - n^3/b^3*\alpha + n^4/b^3*xC$

Iteration 4 ==> ....

In the case of n=b:

The sequence will be $\alpha - n*x0, n*x0, \alpha - n*x0, n*x0,$
$\alpha - n*x0, n*x0,.....,$ which is a square dance.

In the case of n < b and n > b:

The sequence can be written as the following:
which is $\alpha - n/b*\alpha + n^2/b^2*\alpha - n^3/b^3*\alpha +-...+-....+n^{N+1}/b^N*x0$.
Then the result of this sequence will become
(1). $(r^{N+1} + 1)/(r+1)$; where N is the even number of the
iteration, and r is equal to n/b.
(2). $(1 - r^{N+1})/(r+1)$; where N is the odd number of the
iteration, and r is equal to n/b.
If n < b, then $0 < r < 1$. The result will converge.
If n > b, then $r > 1$. The result will diverge which could
produce chaos.
When b increases under the condition of n < b, the
convergent value, $\alpha/(r+1)+K$, will also increase, where K is the
constant of the last term of the sequence.

Our goal is to follow the M-P neuron model, while maintaining simplicity to allow chip fabrication of CNNs. The bifurcation route to chaos is through the so-called "square dance"[20]. This is shown in the four plots in Fig. 5. Fig. 5a describes the single neuron output as a function of the baseline slope ω. It is clear from the Theorem that the onset at $\omega = 0.25$, and iteration escapes to $v_n=1$ at $\omega = 0.165$ where the baseline passes the intersection point where the second branch of $\sigma_N = 0.25$. Fig. 5b depicts the "square dance" evolution for the σ_N with a baseline slope equal to 0.2. Fig. 5c shows the bifurcation behavior (output versus baseline slope) for a piecewise linear approximation to the σ_N. Finally, the cubic approximation function to σ_N is used in the bifurcation map in Fig. 5d. Here, the neuron output is plotted versus the left cubic root, a, and b=0.9, $1/c^2=3/2$. The first bifurcation occurs for a>0.72. From these displays, we conclude that the 1-D map without delay can produce chaos via bifurcation cascade. This fact is due to the instability of the feedback baseline intersecting the σ_N curve when the slope of the baseline changes. As the feedback gain ω increases beyond the absolute value of the slope of the function σ_N, i.e. 1/4, the system becomes chaotic.

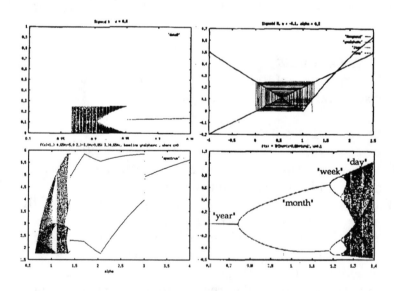

Fig. 5) Chaotic Bifurcation Cascade toward Chaos (Fig.5a & 5b over 5c &5d).

We have demonstrated, by SPICE simulation, an inductorless integrated circuit (Fig. 6a), that a simple 1-D chaotic mapping is achieved with a *delayless* N-

shape sigmoidal function. We show hardware design features of Piecewise Linear
N-shape Chaos Neuron in Appendix B.

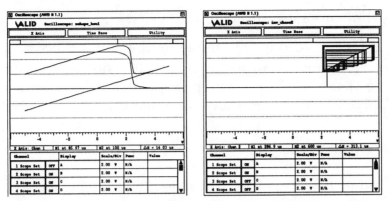

**Fig. 6a SPICE design for Piecewise linear N-shape Neuron for Chaos (Left : Piece-
wise Linear N-shape neuron; Right : "Square dance" evolution)**

Aihara et al. changed the shape of σ_N (denoted by a smaller letter before the
sigmoidal squash) in the parameter space of k and a, and then squashed it further
with the sigmoidal σ after a delay, i.e. $\sigma(\sigma_N) \equiv \sigma_N$ after a delay , in order to
produce the chaos. For comparison, we change our notation to Aihara in Fig.6b.

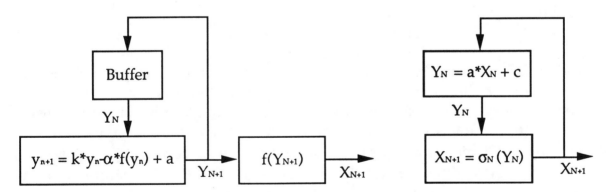

Fig. 6b) Different Delay Characteristics for Chaos Generations

Our model has nevertheless produced a Feigenbaum-like bifurcation
cascade, which will be shown to belong to the infinite-value, or fuzzy, logic. Our
model can learn the synaptic weights, via fixed-point Hebbian dynamics that
determine the "mean-weight" governing the iterative feedback between Eq(8a)
and Eq(8b).

Rather than a single neuron with direct feedback (y=x, or $v_i=u_i$), which
behaves like a dog that bites its own tail, a modification of the baseline slope y≠x
occurs because the main input u_i must be weighted by the synaptic junctions of
all neuron outputs as shown in Sect. 3. Thus, the mean weight and its variance

characterize an "average" baseline, that can provide insight about *collective* chaos.

3. Learning of Spatiotemporal Information by a CNN

The unique feature of our σ_N model is that the collective output can be learned adaptively in a neurochip as follows. The result is instantaneous within the resolution time step and always bounded within one unit for any unbounded input u_i collected from other synaptically weighted outputs v_j

$$u_i(t_n) = \Sigma_{i \neq j} W_{ij} v_j(t_n) - \theta_i = \Sigma_j W_{ij} v_j(t_n) \tag{11}$$

where, without losing the generality, we have defined the self-weight feedback $W_{ii} v_i = -\theta_i$, as the threshold value. Furthermore, we have demonstrated numerically for a single neuron the following bifurcation cascade to chaos with the gain coefficient $[\omega] = [W_{ii}]^{-1} \leq 1/4$ for the piecewise negative logic N-shaped sigmoidal logic.

In summary, we rewrite the model as a matrix-vector: $[W]\,v$ mapping, and the inverse matrix $[W]^{-1}$ determines baseline slope:

$$v(t_n) \quad = \quad \sigma_N(u(t_n)) \tag{12}$$
$$u(t_n) \quad = \quad [W]\,v(t_n); \tag{13}$$
$$v(t_n) \quad = \quad [W]^{-1}\,u(t_n) \quad = \quad [\omega]\,u(t_n) \tag{14}$$

However, for a massive CNN, we allow the feedback baseline slope to change by the learning weight, where the change of the baseline slope is related to the inverse of the synaptic weight matrix, $[W]^{-1}$. The weight adjustment is learned according to the first order fixed-point attractor equation. Since the firing rate outer product $v_i v_j$ is always positive, the memory outer product $(2v_i-1)(2v_j-1)$ can be positive for the excitatory and negative for the inhibitory and the Kronecker delta δ_{ij} is used to insure no diagonal self-memory. Thus

$$dW_{ij}/dt \quad = \quad -\beta\,(\,W_{ij} - \{x(v)_i x(v)_j\}\,) \tag{15}$$

of which the Hebbian matrix learning rule is the bipolar outer product:

$$W_{ij} \quad = \quad \{x(v)_i x(v)_j\} \equiv x(v)_i x(v)_j - \delta_{ij} x(v)_i^2. \tag{16}$$

For reasons of positive excitation and negative inhibition, the positive firing v_i is mapped to bipolar x_i:

$$x(v)_i \quad \equiv \quad 2v_i - 1 \tag{17}$$

The Kronecker delta term Eq(8) is not crucial and is introduced for optical implementations to eliminate the intensity saturation due to the self-interest memory $W_{ii} = 0(\varepsilon)$ for avoiding the recurrence fixed point along the unit diagonal.

The class of 1-D maps with an arbitrary feedback baseline slope, but without the time step delay, is new, simple and different from the Aihara circuit and Yamakawa chip. A large neural network with 10^5 neurons showed collective chaos with images. Smaller networks were studied numerically to investigate the first appearance of chaos in a network. A Hebbian network was used with a transfer function base on biological models. Networks of different sizes were studied ranging from 2 to 25 and up to 10^4 neurons. Chaos was found in each network. Fig. 6 illustrates our CNN a of hundred thousand σ_N neurons, in terms of visual image impression in the cortex. Our CNN model is meaningful for fuzzy information processing and provides through a neural network, the underlying dynamics for fuzzy logic. Furthermore, since this model is implemented without the sample-hold circuitry, it is suitable for implementation in a massively parallel neurochip.

We close this section by summarizing the potential of ANNs and CNNs to Fuzzy logic. Fuzzy Logic (FL) is useful in industrial engineering because it is simple (if-then rule-based) and provides us with the capability to "explore the tolerance of imprecision", according to L. Zadeh [35]. But just "like any other mathematical or computer model, FL falls prey to the 'curse of dimensionality'" [36]. We wish to point out that ANN have helped the FL in four areas, and where and when the CNN can do it more efficiently.

(1) Determination of Fuzzy Rule Set: ANNs have been used to learn the classifier variances having major and minor axes with respect to the (If-Input, Then-Output) rule domain, which when projected along the output and input axses give respectively the Fuzzy Membership Functions (FMF) [37]. To change the rule is more important to change FMF [38].

(2) Determination of the FMF: For example, it is often assumed that such membership functions are described by triangles with obvious centroids (rather than a crisp rectangle for numerical value)[39,40]. Automatic optimal splitting and combing of membership functions, as well as the shape of those functions, can be determined from data fed into a neural network. This paper addresses such a possibility via bifurcation.

(3) Determination of Fuzzy Inference Engine: A system is a distribution of parameters, of which an ANN is one that is useful for fuzzy logic control (Yamakawa[41]), e. g., truck-backing [42].

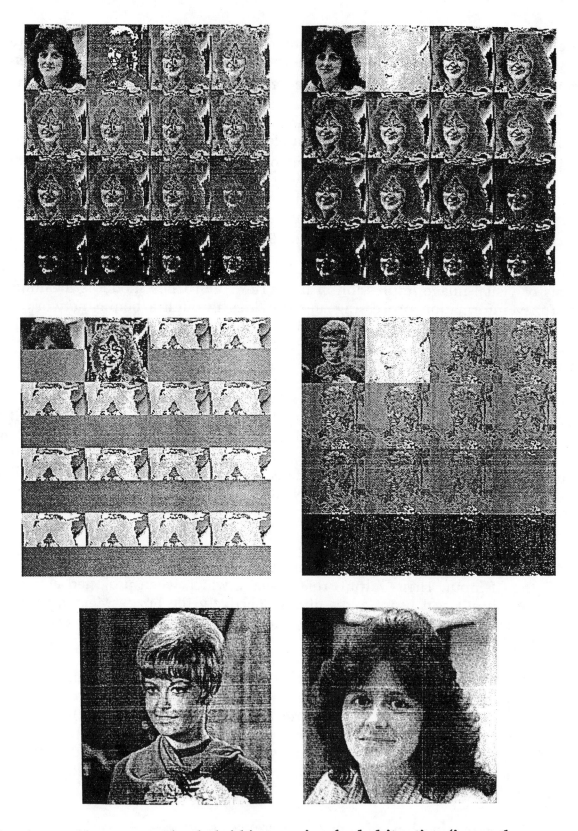

Fig. 6) Two faces, successive hybrid impression for habituation (ignored memory in white) and novelty (fast associative recall & then new memory) .

(4) Contribution to fast learning of ANN: Applying the Min-Max operations respectively for Fuzzy rule and defuzzification, both Carpenter et al [43] and Simpson [44] have achieved fast learning.

(5) Determination of Efficient Representation of Fuzzy Dynamics: Recently, a self-reference fuzzy liar paradox dynamics [29] and nonlinear spatiotemporal phenomena are efficiently described by chaotic maps or flows. This paper touches upon whether or not the underlying choatic maps are useful for some applications of the FL via the CNN [45].

4. Further Examples of Chaotic-Fuzzy Logic: the Fuzzy Liar and the Chaotic Liar

From the previous sections we envision that CNNs can be used to embed such compact descriptions into fuzzy logic inference engines. Why chaos? Only chaos is exponentially fast in switching from one attractor basin to another in terms of the CNN energy landscape, and yet the unpredictable outcome is always bounded within the possible membership set. Such a set is an open set of possibly infinite logic values, as opposed to binary logic, and therefore escapes the normalization requirement of traditional probability theory. Consider the following classical Liar logic, which can be transformed into a well-known Fuzzy Liar logic as follows:

Assertion (1):
This statement (e.g., she is his wife) is false.
If true, (1) must be false, i.e. she is not his wife.
If false--since he, the Liar, says it's false--it must be true.

Consequently, the semantical dynamics are due to a self-reference (is she his wife or isn't she?) which is an oscillation of cycle one between binary Truth (T) and False (F):

$$T, F, T, F, T, F, \tag{18}$$

Fuzzy Liar web dynamics become

$$x_{n+1} = 1 - x_n \tag{19}$$

where the word *web* refers to the iteration, as shown in Fig. 7a. This map has the appearance of a spider web. In case of an "emphatic liar", the negation (1-x) is nonlinear. For example, the equation of quadratic order is

$$x_{n+1} = (1 - x_n)^2 \tag{20}$$

which is plotted in Fig. 7b

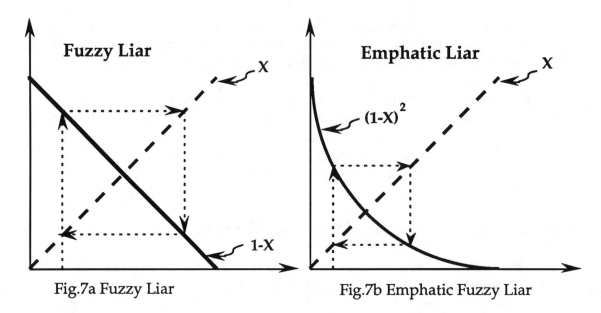

Fig.7a Fuzzy Liar   Fig.7b Emphatic Fuzzy Liar

We can analytically continue the emphatic liar to a chaotic liar (with infinite-value logic) through Feigenbaum's bifurcation cascade map as follows. Denote the fuzzy liar in x'-y' coordinates on a 1 by 1 domain, we obtain the old fuzzy liar

$$y' \quad = \quad (1-x')^2 \tag{21}$$

We can analytically extend it into a 2 by 2 domain, and then linearly transform back to a unit square, yielding

$$y' \quad = \quad 1-(y/\lambda). \tag{22a}$$
$$x' \quad = \quad 2-2x; \tag{22b}$$

Solving for the non-prime coordinates yields

$$y \quad = \quad \lambda\,(1-y') \tag{23a}$$
$$x \quad = \quad (2-x')/2 \tag{23b}$$

To transform the Emphatic Fuzzy Liar into a Chaotic Liar, simply substitute equations (12) and (13b) into (14a) which yields a Chaotic Liar:

$$y \quad = \quad 4\lambda\, x(1-x). \tag{24}$$

In recurrence form, the equation can be written as

$$x_{n+1} \quad = \quad 4\lambda\, x_n(1-x_n) \tag{25}$$

which is the chaotic logistic equation and induces a bifurcation cascade which begins at the peak value or the scaling factor $\lambda \geq 3/4$, where $\lambda = 3/4$ will produce exact one square dance, according to that the slope of the curve (N) and the slope of the baseline (B) are identical. Show as Fig. 8.

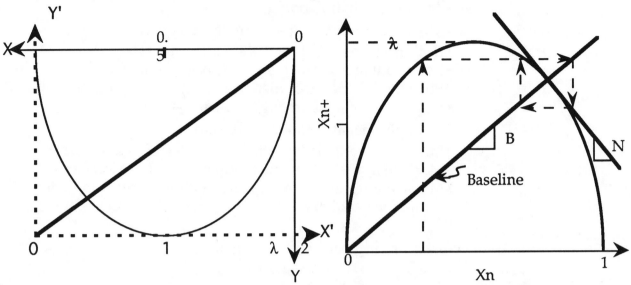

Fig. 8a Transformation Geometry for Chaos Liar

Fig. 8b Bifurcation Square Dance for Chaos Liar

The above discussion reveals the link between fuzzy logic and chaos theory. Based on this link, we hypothesize that the introduction of chaotic neurons into neural nets provides a natural way to endow neural nets with the ability to perform fuzzy logic reasoning. The face recognition experiments in section 3 show the importance of this sort of processing relative to classical associative memory performance.

The learning dynamics for both associative memory and CNNs are based on the Hebbian outer product and fixed point dynamics. However, the introduction of the σ_N function in the CNN exploits the advantages of nonlinear dynamics for efficient feature extraction for pattern recognition. This is in contrast to the classical associative memory, where fault tolerance of sharp image recall is the guiding design principal. From this and the earlier discussions, we believe that chaotic dynamics is the bridge between neural networks and fuzzy logic disciplines.

5. Comparisons among ANNs, BNNs, and CNNs

We wish to place our CNN model between a classical ANN and a typical Biological Neural Network (BNN). We compare them from the viewpoint of (i) neuron models, (ii) network architecture, (iii) learning methodologies, and (iv) memory mechanisms as follows:

- **Neuron Models**
  - ANN
    - Simplicity for stable engineering
    - Analog or Binary coding
    - M.-P. monotonic single-value logic $v_i = \sigma(u_i)$
  - BNN
    - Exploring noise and instability advantages
    - Pulse coding for long distance broadcasting,
    - Potentiation for short distance synaptic junction
    - Refractory delay, bursting, plateau, rebound
  - CNN
    - Piecewise negative logic $v_i = \sigma_N(u_i)$
    - Infinite value logic but with a bounded range of outputs
    - Markovian instantaneous mapping without refractory delay
    - Massive Parallel Chip Implementation without inductors
    - Neural chaos dictates fuzzy reasoning dynamics

- **Network Architectures: net input $u_i = \Sigma_j W_{ij}v_j - \theta_i$**
  - ANN
    - Fixed & Layered Architectures
  - BNN
    - Dynamical interconnect networks
  - CNN
    - Global interconnection within a functional unit.

- **Learning Methodologies**
  - ANN
    - Fixed-point (f.p.) dynamics & small perturbation learning:
    - Energy landscape concept
    - (1) Input dynamics (Hopfield)
      $$du_i/dt = -\partial H/\partial v_i = -(u_i - \Sigma_j W_{ij}v_j + \theta_i) = 0 \ (f.p.) \Rightarrow M.-P.$$
    - (2) Output dynamics(Cohen-Grossberg)
      $$dv_i/dt = -(v_i - \sigma(u_i)) = 0 \ (f.p.) \Rightarrow M.-P.$$
    - (3) Gradient descent dynamics (weight error Backprop.)
      $$\partial W_{ij}/\partial t = -\partial E/\partial W_{ij}$$
  - BNN
    - Coherence for adaptation & Synchronicity for consciousness
  - CNN
    - Fuzzy dynamics exploring the tolerance of imprecision.

- **Memory Mechanism**
  - ANN
    - Outer Products, Neighbor Classifiers, Adaptive Resonances
  - BNN
    - Long Term, & Short Term Traces Matched Filtering
  - CNN
    - Habituation pattern formation and fast Novelty storage.

There is a plenty of room for discussion in such a cursory comparison. Our goal is to stimulate interest in the cooparison among ANN, BNN, and CNN, e.g.:

• **Collective Behaviors in Biological NN and Artificial NN**	BNN,	ANN
• Consciousness to mind---Simultaneity to Coherence	yes?	not yet
• Associative Memory---Attractor Basins	yes	yes
• Habituation to Novelty ---Bifurcation to Chaotic Orbits	yes ?	yes?

• Noisy effects----correlation enhancement for optimization yes ?   yes

where question marks to yes imply no consensus about the details.

6.   Conclusion

In order to make systematically departure to the classical McCulloch-Pitts neuron model that have already extensively used in the ANN community with chips designed, we have previously produced with minimum change, a pulse coding for periodic and quasi periodic spikes, as well as irregular to chaotic spikes trains [17,18, 19].

We have shown for an arbitrary feedback baseline slope in a single σ_N neuron that Feigenbaum cascade avalanches when the feedback synaptic W_{ii} increases beyond the baseline slope $dv_i/du_i=1/W_{ii}$ as the gain ω passes the negative logic slope (1/4 in Fig.3.a). A large (10^5) chaotic ANN demonstrated collective image dynamics for the psychological effects of habituation and fast novelty pattern detection capability. Recently, Yanai-Amari showed an increased memory capacity for non-monotonic neurons [22]. For CNNs, this is not meant to increase the associative memory capacity, but rather to implement pattern recognition dynamics that can efficiently explore the tolerance of imprecision.

In summary, for biological single neuron relationships, we consider incoherence or coherence phenomena, but the community still needs to quantify the degree of synchronicity such as those of partial coherence measure in optics. For collective behaviors, we wish to differentiate the bounded measure of chaotic nonlinear dynamics versus those linear unbounded stochastic noise effects. It is known by the name of central limit theorem in probability theory that any noise distribution, constant density or not, so long as the second moment is bounded, in the limit of large sampling, it becomes a Gaussian distribution (which is extended to the finite domain). For example, a drunken sailor executing such a Brownian motion will be drifting to the infinite and never return back to the home. While linear noise may be good for the global optimization by the simulated annealing strategy [26,27], nonlinear chaos may be useful for fuzzy reasoning.

Lastly, we speculate about a Learnable Fuzzy Logic (LFL) by changing the degree of fuzziness through the CNN, because of two intrinsic attributes of CNN:

(i) All chaotic outputs (of such a single σ_N-neuron up to 10^5 σ_N-neurons) are unpredictable but always bounded. The open chaotic set forms a naturally Fuzzy Membership Function (FMF) of which its time evolution governs by CNN. The chaotic output states., unlike the unbounded noise effect, can be dynamically evolving through learning in time.

(ii) The fuzzy characteristics are just the statistical aspect of dynamical chaos that can change the fuzziness by input data to CNN given a desirable imprecision. As an example, the classical self-reference Liar Logic is transformed, via the Fuzzy Liar, to a Chaotic Liar.

If the LFL is implemented, the CNN can provide a dynamic Fuzzy Logic learning and reasoning.

Acknowledgement:

The authors (Szu & Garcia) wish to acknowledge the financial support of NSWCDD Seed & Venture Fund, and (Szu & Rogers) for NSWCDD IR Fund. Useful discussion with M. Feigenbaum at the Rockefeller University is acknowledged

Appendix A:
Hardware Design Features of PWL N-shape Chaos Neuron
Design Principles:
No Inductance
Simplicity for massive ANN Chip
Components: Inverter, Hold & Sample , and Op Amplifier

Mathematical Background:
PWL(PieceWise Linear) N Shape consists of an **inverter** and a **linear** function.

Example :

Mathematicl Models: *Circuit Models:*

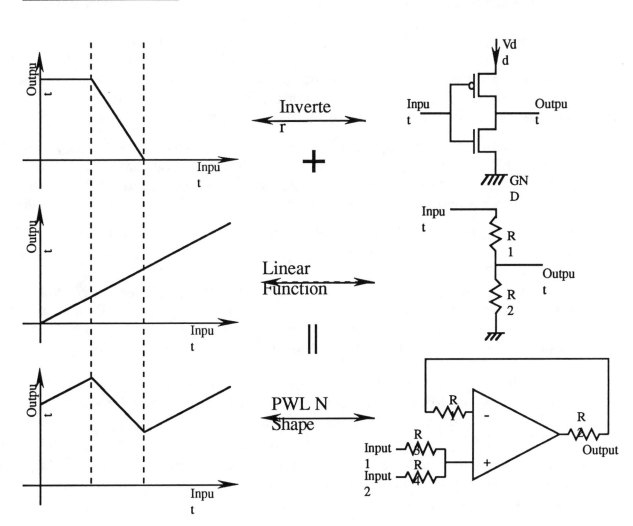

Appendix B: Derivation of σ_N

Based on mathematical chaotic elements [1,2], ANNs have been proposed [3-9] whose biological basis and information processing capabilities have not yet fully explored. Historically speaking, Caianiello (1961)[10], inspired by Hodgkin-Huxley (1952), Fitzhugh (1961)[11], and Harmon(1961) [13], generalized the McCulloch-Pitts (M-P) sigmoidal model, defined with the threshold θ by

$$v_i \quad = \quad \sigma(u_i - \theta) \quad \equiv \quad [1 + \exp(- \{u_i - \theta\})]^{-1}, \quad (B1),$$

to include a time-delayed refractory effect:

$$v_i(t_{n+1}) = \sigma(\Sigma_j \int_0^{t_n} W_{ij}(t_s) \, v_j(t_n - t_s) \, dt_s - \theta) \quad (B2)$$

where the time-dependent synaptic weight $W_{ij}(t_s)$ has a convolution integral.

Although the refractory delay is biologically meaningful; the delay increases the complexity of hardware fabrication. Fortunately, due to the Markovian approximation of the discrete time series, the Caianiello, FitzHugh, Harmon, Nagumo, Sato, and Aihara models can be summed as a nonlinear modification of the shape of the sigmoidal function, i.e. a pre-squashed N-shape

sigmoidal function $v_i = \sigma_N (u_i)$ as shown in the following graphic construction of a simple 1-D mapping *without* delay. We further show that it can generate a bifurcation cascade to chaos by either changing the shape or the feedback baseline slope. In other words, these Markovian delays can be entirely eliminated by

transforming the M-P σ to an N-shape or piecewise negative logic σ_N. Consequently, a simple CNN neurochip is designed with a synaptic learning capability.

The Caianiello's model of refractory pulses was simplified by Nagumo and Sato [12] by means of a Markovian mean field approximation as follows. In terms of a discrete-time geometric progression series of a space-uniform memory damping constant k (≤ 1), the net input to ith neuron is denoted by u_i

$$u_i(t_{n+1}) \quad \equiv \quad A(t_n) - \alpha \Sigma^{t_n}_{t_s=0} k^{t_s} v_i(t_n - t_s) - \theta, \quad (B3)$$

where the average input from the other neurons is abbreviated by A(t), and the net input u_i is equivalent to Aihara's internal state y(t+1). We prefer Hopfield's alphabetical-order notation, i. e., that input u_i follows output v_i which is consistent with the voltage/current notation. Furthermore, instead of Nagumo-Sato's unit step approximation for firing or not, Aihara et al. prefer the original analog sigmoidal mapping

$$v_i(t_{n+1}) \quad = \quad \sigma(u_i(t_{n+1})) \quad (B4)$$

A simple recurrence formula was derived, by Nagumo-Sato [12], by subtracting from Eq(2a) the following net input:

$$k u_i(t_n) \quad = \quad k A(t_{n-1}) - \alpha\, k \sum\nolimits_{t_s=0}^{t_{n-1}} k^{t_s}\, v_i(t_{n-1} - t_s) - k\theta,$$

which gives the extra term, $\alpha\, v_i(t_n)$, that by definition in Eq(B4), is $\alpha\sigma(u_i(t_n))$,

$$u_i(t_{n+1}) \quad = \quad k\, u_i(t_n) + a(t_n) - \alpha\sigma(u_i(t_n)) \qquad\qquad (B5)$$

where $a(t) \equiv A(t) - k\, A(t-1) - (1-k)\, \theta$ is usually positive for $k \le 1$ and $\theta = 0$. Eq(B5) says that the net input (or Aihara's internal state) $u_i(t_{n+1})$ depends only on the previous state of net input $u_i(t_n)$, and not on the early history, as it might appear at first glance in Eq(B3). Namely, the discrete mean field approximation is indeed a Markovian chain.

A simple graphical construction shown in the Figs. B1a,b,c, and d, shows that the Markovian chain recurrence formula in Eq(B5) is reduced, after a further squash, to the N-shape sigmoidal function model $\sigma_N \equiv \sigma(\sigma_N)$ by substituting Eq(B5) into Eq(B4) [17,18,19]. Fig. B1a shows the constant slope $k u_i$ in Eq(B5), and the inverted sigmoidal $[a - \alpha\sigma(u_i)]$ is shown in Fig. B1b. The sum of both of these terms, σ_N, is shown in Fig. B1c. The final result, the squashed σ_N, is depicted in Fig. B1d. This non-linear result involves *no delay*,

$$v_i(t_n) \quad = \quad \sigma_N(u_i(t_n)), \qquad\qquad (B6)$$

where σ_N is a piecewise (sick neuron) negative logic (i.e. more input, less output).

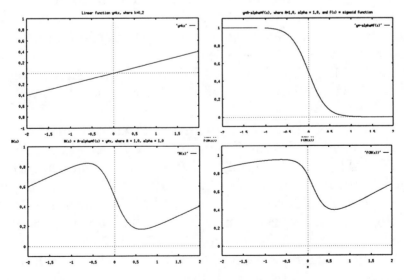

Fig. B1 Graphical Construction of σ_N from σ (steps a and b over c and d)

References:

[1] John Guckenheimer and Philip Holmes, Nonlinear Oscillations, Dynamical Systems, and Bifurcations of Vector Fields, Springer-Verlag, New York, 1983.

[2] Leon O. Chua, editor of special issue on"Chaotic Systems," Proc. IEEE, V. 75, no.8, 1987; e. g., A. Rodriguez-Vazquez, et al, "Chaos from switched-capacitor circuits: discrete maps," Proc. IEEE v. 75, pp.1109-1106, 1987.

[3] M.Y. Choi, "Dynamic Model of Neural Networks,"Phys. Rev. Lett. V. 61, 2809,1988.

[4] Lipo Wang, E. Pichler, J. Ross,"Oscillations and Chaos in neural networks: An Exactly solvable model," Proc. Natl, Acad. Sci. USA, Vol. 87, pp 9467-9471, 1990

[5] D. Hansel, H. Sompolinky, "Synchronization and Computation in a Chaotic Neural Network," Phys. R. Lett. 68, pp718-721, 92.

[6] E. K. Blum and Xin Wang, "Stability of Fixed Points and Periodic Orbits and Bifurcations in Analog Neural Networks," Neural Networks, V.5, pp. 557-587, 1992.

[7] G. Basti, A. Perrone, V. Cimagalli, M.Giona,E. Pasero, G. Morgavi,"A Dynamic Approach to invariant Feature Extraction from Time-Varying Inputs by Using Chaos in Neural Networks,"IJCNN-91 San Diego,-92 Vol. III, pp505-510.

[8] J. C. Principle, P. Lo."Chaotic Dynamics of Time-Delay Neural Networks," IJCNN-91 San Diego, Vol. II, pp403-409.

[9] K. Aihara, T. Takabe, M Yoyoda,"Chaotic Neural Network,"Phys. Lett A.144,333,1990

[10] E. R. Caianiello,A. Deluca, "Decision equation for binary systems. Application to neural behavior,"Kybernetik Vol. 3 , pp.33-40,1966.

[11] R. Fitzhugh, "Impulses and Physiological states in theoretical models of nerve membrane", Biophysics Vol. 1, pp. 445-466, 1961.

[12] J.Nagumo, S. Sato, "On a response characteristic of a mathematical neuron model," Kybernetik V. 10, pp. 155, 1972

[13] L.D.Harmon,"Studies with artificial neuron I: Propertied and functions of an artificial neuron"Kybernetik V.1,89-101,1961

[14] T. Yamakawa, T. Miki, E. Uchino,"A Chaotic Chip for Analyzing Nonlinear Discrete Dynamica Network Systems," Proc. 2nd. Int'l Conf. Fuzzy Logic & Neural Networks, Iizuka, Japan, 1992, pp563-566.

[15] N. Kanou, Y. Herio, K. Aihara, S. Nakamura,"A current-mode circuit of a chaotic neuron model," IEEE Circuit & System Conf. Proceedings, 1993

[16] D. Gobovic, C.C. Hsu, M. Zaghloul, H. Szu, "Chaotic Neuron Models and Their Electronic Circuit Implementation," submitted to Trans IEEE Circuit.

[17] H. Szu, G. Rogers,"Single Neuron Chaos," IJCNNBaltimore, V.III,pp103-108.

[18] H. Szu, G. Rogers,"Generalized McCullouch-Pitts Neuron Model with Threshold Dynamics,"IJCNN-92 Baltimore, Vol. III, pp535-540 (June 7-11,92)

[19] H. Szu, B. Telfer, G Rogers, Kyoung Lee, Gyu Moon, M.Zaghloul, M. Loew," Collective Chaos in Neural,Networks," Int'l Joint Conf. Neural Networks, IJCNN-92 Beijing China, Nov 1-6, 1992.

[20] H. Szu, B. Telfer, G. Rogers, D. Gobovic, C. Hsu,M. Zaghloul, W. Freeman, "Spatiotemporal Chaos Information Processing in Neural Networks -- Electric

Implementation," World Congress of Neural Networks, WCNN-93, Portland OR, July 12-16, 1993.

[21] S.Yoshizawa, H. Osada, J. Nagumo,"Pulse sequence generated by a degenerate Analog neuron model," Bio Cyb. Vol. 45, pp.23-33, 1982.

[22] K. Aihara, G. Matsumoto,"Chaotic oscillations and bifurcations in squid giant axons,"In; Chaos, A.V. Holden (ed), In: Princeton Univ . Press, Ch. 12, p. 257 1986

[23] Gen Matsumoto, K. Aihara, Y. Hanyu, N. Takahashi, S. Yoshizawa, J. Nagumo,"Chaos and Phase Locking in Normal Squid Axons,"Phys. Lett. A123, 162-166, 1987.

[24] D.R. Hofstadter, "Metamagical Themas:Questing for the Essence of Mind and Pattern," Chapter 16 ("Mathematical Chaos and Strange Attractors"), Basic Books : N.Y. 1985, pp364-395

[25] H. Yanai,S. Amari, "A Theory on Neural Networks with Non-monotone Neurons,"ICNN-93,1385

[26] H. Szu, R. Hartley, "Fast Simulated Annealing," Physics Letters Vol. A22, pp.157-162, June 8, 1987.

[27] H. Szu, R. Hartley," Nonconvex Optimization by Simulated Annealing," Proc. IEEE, Vol. 75, pp. 1538-1540, 1987.

[28] H. Szu, ..., IJCNN-93 Nagoya

[29] P. Grim, "Self-Reference and Chaos in Fuzzy Logic", Trans. IEEE Fuzzy Sys. V.1, pp.32-45, Feb 1993.

[30] H. Szu, L. Zadeh, C. Hsu, J. DeWitte, Jr., G. Moon, D. Gobovi, M. Zaghloul," Chaotic Neurochips for Fuzzy Computing," SPIE Prooceedings, Vol. 2037, (Chaos/Nonlinear Dynamics--Methods and Commercialization, ed. H. Wisniewski), pp. , 11-16 July, San Diego 1993.

[31] H. Szu & B, Telfer, "Mathematical Theorems of Adaptive Wavelet Transforms," to appear in: Adaptive Wavelet Transforms, 2nd special issue of Optical Engineering, June 1994.

[32] H. Szu, B. Telfer, S. Kadame, "Neural Network Adaptive Wavelets for Signal representation and Classification," In: Wavelet Transforms, special issue of Optical Engineering, Vol. 31, pp. 1907-1916, Sept. 1992.

[33] G. Matsumoto, K. Aihara, Y. Hanyu, N. Takahashi, S. Yoshizawa, J. Nagumo, " Chaos and Phase Locking in Normal Squid Axons," Phys. Letters A 123, 162-166, 1987.

[34] M. Barnsley, L. Hurd, "Fractal Image Compression,"AK Peters, Wellesley MA 1993. p. 100

[35]L. Zadeh, "Fuzzy Sets," Info & Control , V. 8, pp338-353, 1965.

[36] B. Kosko & S. Isaka, "Fuzzy Logic,"Sci. Am. ,pp. 76-81, July 1993.

[37] J. Dickerson, B. Kosko, "Fuzzy Function Approximation with Supervised Ellipsoidal Learning, WCNN-93 Vol. II, pp.9-17, Portland July 1993.

[38] P. Werbos, "Elastic Fuzzy Logic : A better way to combine Neural and Fuzzy Capabilities,"WCNN, V.II, pp.623-626, 1993.

[39] E. Cox, "Fuzzy Fundamantals,"IEEE Spectrum, pp. 58-61, Ocb. 1992.

[40] E. Cox, "Adaptive Fuzzzy Systems,"IEEE Spectrum, pp. 27-31, Feb 1993.

[41] T. Yamakawa, "A Fuzzy Inference Engine in nonlinear analog mode and its application to a fuzzy logic control""Trans IEEE NN V.4, pp.496-522, May 1993.

[42] S. Kong, B. Kosko, "Adap. Fuz. Sys. for Backing up a truck-&-tailer," T. IEEE V.3, 211-223, 1992.

[43] G. Carpenter, S. Grossberg, D. B. Rosen,"Fuzzy ART: Fast Learning & Categorization of Analog Patterns by An Adaptive Resonanc Systems, V. 4, p. 759-771, 1991.

[44] P. Simpson, "Fuzzy Min-Max N.N.--Part 1: Classification," Trans. IEEE NN, V.3, pp. 776-786, Sep. 1992;"Fuzzy Min-Max N.N.--P. 2: Clustering,"TRans IEEE Fuzzy Sys. V.1, pp32-45, Feb 1993.

[45] H. Szu, L. Zadeh, C. Hsu, J. DeWitte, Jr., G. Moon, D. Gobovi, M. Zaghloul," Chaotic Neurochips for Fuzzy Computing," SPIE Prooceedings, Vol. 2037, (Wisniewski), pp. 11-16 , July, San Diego 1993.

III. IMAGE PROCESSING

Chapter 19

Vector Coding in Neuronal Nets: Color Vision

Eugene M. Sokolov

VECTOR CODING IN NEURONAL NETS:

COLOR VISION[1]

E. N. Sokolov

Lomonosov Moscow State University

Moscow, 1993

(Abstract)

Factor analysis of a matrix of probabilities of instrumental conditioned reflexes to color stimuli in rhesus monkeys revealed four principle components that correspond to red-green, blue-yellow, brightness and darkness vectors. The lengths of the four orthogonal vectors representing colors are of a constant magnitude. This suggests that color stimuli are located on a hypersphere in four-dimensional space. Three polar coordinates (angles) of the hypersphere correspond to hue, lightness and saturation similar to those found in humans. Local patches of the hypersphere that correspond to response areas of color selective neurons in V4 of the monkey are suggestive of a color map as a mechanism of colortopic projection analogous to retinotopic, tonotopic and somatotopic projection maps. Under reinforcement, as in the process of associative learning, the color selector map induces modifications in plastic synapses of command neurons such that synaptic weight vectors become collinear with an input excitation vector generated by the conditional stimulus on the color map.

Vector Coding In Neuronal Nets: Color Vision

The coding of information in neuronal nets is closely related to the process of mapping. The cortical maps of receptive surfaces revealed in somatotopic and retinotopic projections serve as examples. In so far as different sound frequencies are systematically positioned along the Organ of Corti, the tonotopic cortical projection can be regarded as a subtype of the somatotopic one. The shift of a stimulus along the receptive surface results in a corresponding dislocation of the excitation maximum with respect to the cortical map. A problem arises concerning neuronal representations of stimuli that, being modified, are not shifted along a receptive surface, such as color change by local stimulation of the retina. The main hypothesis under consideration in this paper states that local stationary stimuli are also represented topically on maps composed from feature-selective neurons. The realization of such a representation is achieved by the generation, at the receptor level, of a

---

[1]   This study is fulfilled by financial support of The Russian Foundation of Fundamental Investigations (grant No. 93-04-20511)

combination of excitations in a local ensemble of receptors having overlapping response characteristics with respect to the stimulus parameter.

The local ensemble of receptors corresponds to a local ensemble of preselector neurons that in a parallel manner activate an array of feature-selectors, thus building up a selector map. Each feature-selective neuron of the map is characterized by a specific set of synapses constituting its weight vector that is of a constant length. The response of a feature-selector neuron is determined by an inner product of its weight vector and the input excitation vector generated by preselectors. Because the length of the excitation vector is also of a constant value, the excitation maximum in such a feature neuron of the selector map is reached when the input excitation vector is collinear with that neuron's weight vector (Sokolov and Vaitkyavichus, 1989). The change of a local stimulus results in a modification of the receptor excitation vector and the corresponding preselector excitation vector. This change is responsible for a translocation of the excitation maximum onto another neuron of the selector map possessing a weight vector collinear with the modified excitation vector. Thus, a change of a local stimulus that remains stationary on the receptor surface results in a shift of the excitation maximum with respect to the feature selector map in a manner similar to that which occurs for somatotopic, retinotopic and tonotopic projections. The distribution of excitations of neurons on a feature-selector map constitutes a selection excitation vector with components composed from inner products of the preselector excitation vector and the weight vectors of respective neurons of the selector map.

The neurons of the feature-selector map are linked via plastic (Hebbian) synapses with command neurons responsible for different behavioral acts (Sokolov, 1991). Reinforcement acts on the command neuron through non-plastic synapses. The plastic synapses between neurons of the selector map and a command neuron are enhanced if such neural excitation is followed by a reinforcement acting on the command neuron. The synaptic weights between stimulated neurons and non-reinforced command neurons are weakened. In this way a selective association between the conditional stimulus and reinforced behavior is established. At the initial stage of learning the weights of plastic synapses are equal to each other and weak. Consequently, the postsynaptic potentials to applied stimuli do not reach the firing threshold. In the process of associative learning when reinforcement follows activation of neurons of feature-selector maps, their synaptic weights gradually increase, and the weight vector of the command neuron becomes collinear with the input excitation vector. This is due to the fact that excitation of the command neuron is equal to the inner product of its weight and excitation vectors.

Modification of the weight vector of a command neuron is due to changes in plastic synapses under the influence of reinforcement of a conditional stimulus or non-reinforcement of a differential one. This modification can be expressed as a vector sum of the initial weight vector with the weight vector of synaptic change:

$$W_{k+1} = W_k +/- W_d$$

where, W_k - initial weight vector, W_{k+1} - modified weight vector, W_d - weight vector of synaptic changes under the influence of reinforcement (+) or non-reinforcement (-).

The weight vector of synaptic changes, in turn, is determined by the excitation vector generated by a particular stimulus in a degree of the command neuron excitation and coefficient of learning efficiency:

$$W_d = C*(F,W_k)*F$$

where, C - coefficient of learning efficiency, F - excitation vector, (F,W_k) - inner product of the command neuron's excitation vector and its initial weight vector.

Under the influence of a reinforcement the length of the command neuron's weight vector increases, and it rotates in a direction towards the reinforced excitation vector. Through non-reinforcement of a differential stimulus, the length of the command neuron's weight vector decreases, and it rotates away from the non-reinforced excitation vector produced by the differential stimulus (Fig. 1). At the final stage of learning the weight vector, being normalized, remains a constant length. When the excitation vector evoked by a stimulus and the weight vector of a command neuron are collinear, the excitation of the command neuron reaches maximum.

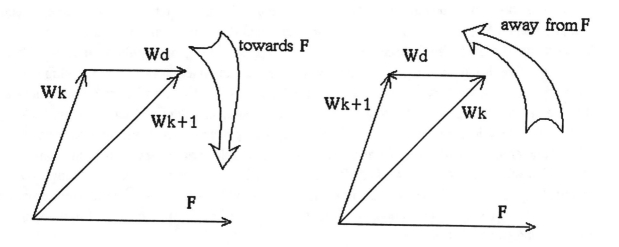

REINFORCEMENT   NON-REINFORCEMENT

Figure 1. Modification of a weight vector of a command neuron.

Response Probability

The behavioral act triggered by a command neuron is realized by a set of motor neurons in a "Yes" or No" manner that is due to fluctuations of the firing threshold of the command neuron. The excitation of the command neuron determines the response probability that, in turn, can be used as a measure of command neuron excitation. The conditional stimulus generating a feature excitation vector that is collinear with the elaborated weight vector of the command neuron evokes a maximum of its excitation, and accordingly, the highest level of response probability. The probabilities of motor responses to differential stimuli are inversely related to their distances from the position of the conditional stimulus on the feature map. This suggests that the probabilities of motor responses at the final stage of learning implicitly contain information concerning input excitation vectors and organization of the feature-selector map.

The Color Mapping Hypothesis

The main hypothesis concerning the role of vector codes in neuronal mapping of stimuli stationary with respect to a receptor surface was tested using colors as conditional and differential stimuli through associative instrumental learning in monkeys (Latanov, Polyanski, and Sokolov, 1991). It was assumed that a color map as an analogue of somatotopic, retinotopic and tonotopic projection is a colortopic structure. The choice of color stimuli was based on the fact that a change of color is occurring without spatial shift of the local stimulus against the retina. The experiments in monkeys replicated data obtained earlier in human\s (Sokolov and Izmailov, 1984).

Spherical Model of Color Vision in Humans

It is shown by a multidimensional scaling procedure in humans that colors of different spectral compositions are represented in the four-dimensional Euclidean space on the surface of a hypersphere. The Euclidean distances between points representing colors highly positively correlated with subjective differences between respective colors were obtained in experiments using a paired comparison procedure (Izmailov and Sokolov, 1991). It was also found that a spherical structure of the perceptual color space is present in color-deficient subjects (Paramei, Izmailov and Sokolov, 1991). The spherical model of color vision integrates psychophysical and neuronal aspects of information processing. The four Cartesian coordinates of color points represent excitations of red-green, blue-yellow, and brightness and darkness neurons. Three spherical coordinates (angles) of the hypersphere having radii corresponding to hue, saturation, and lightness. At the same time local patches of the hypersphere correspond to response areas of color-selective neurons found in the area V4 of monkeys (Zeki, 1990).

Color specific verbal responses acquired in childhood or elaborated in adults in experiments with artificial color names (Izmailov and Sokolov, 1992) strongly suggests that in the process of associative learning, selective color maps become specifically connected with command neurons responsible for the generation of verbal responses to particular color stimuli. The probabilities of behavioral responses are directly proportional to respective excitations of the command neurons responsible for generation of color names. The command neuron excitation in turn, depends on the inner product of an excitation vector composed of excitations of color selector maps and a learning-induced link vector composed of synaptic weights of neurons composing color-selector maps on the command neuron. Thus, the probability of verbal responses to color stimuli intrinsically contain information about color space (Sokolov and Izmailov, 1984). This was demonstrated by a reconstruction of color space from probabilities of color names used to categorize the colors. In the present study, it was hypothesized that these principles of color coding are operating in conditional reflexes to color stimuli in the monkey.

Color Coding in Monkeys

The prediction concerning probabilities of behavioral conditioned responses to color stimuli as a variable dependent on color excitation vectors was tested by instrumental conditioning in rhesus monkeys using computer-generated color stimuli (Latanov, Polyanski and Sokolov, 1991). The experiment consisted of random presentations of seven different colors. The pressings of the lever in response to a particular color serving as a conditional stimulus was reinforced by juice. The responses to other color stimuli were not reinforced. When the plateau level for one color stimulus was reached, another color was used as a conditional stimulus and the relearning was conducted until a plateau level was reached again. The power spectra of color stimuli were obtained by objective spectral analysis (Fig. 2A). These spectra were used for the estimation of X and Y coordinates (Fig 2A, B) and equivalent wavelengths (Fig. 2B).

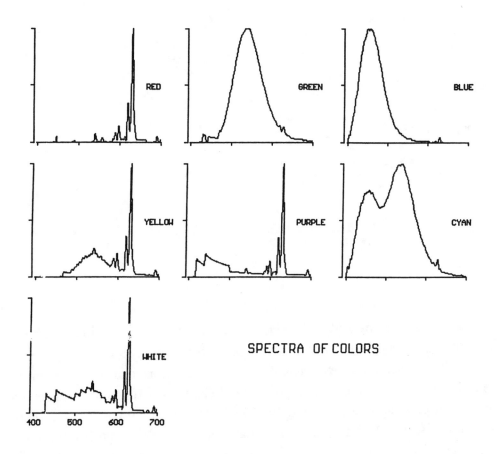

Figure 2A. Power spectrum of color stimuli. Horizontal axis - wave length (nm), vertical axis power (normalized to maximal level). Total power in mcw: red-7, green-10, yellow-4, blue-8, purple-17, cyan-21, white-65.

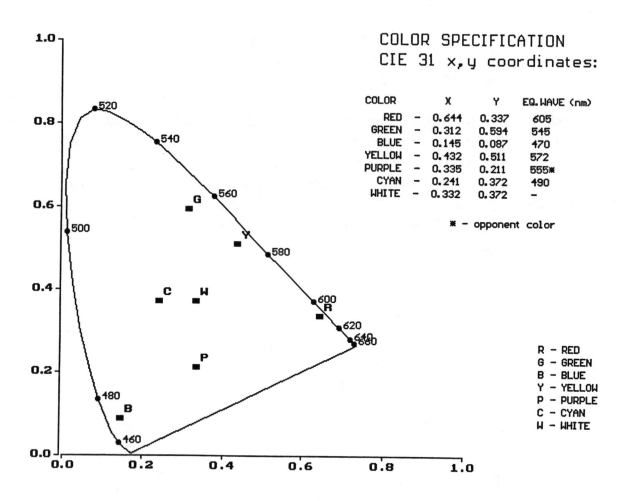

Figure 2B. The position of Color Stimuli on the XY plane of a color triangle.

The curves reaching plateau level during ten experimental sessions can be approximated by hyperbolic functions (Fig. 3A). An example of such a fitting by hyperbolic function of the form (Fig. 3A) $y = A + B/x$ is given for the experiment when blue color was reinforced as a conditional stimulus, and the other colors were not reinforced (3B and C). Such a function assumes that the variable y (response probability) approaches asymptotic value "A" as x (number of trials) increases to infinity. The magnitude $A \pm B$ corresponds to initial level of response probabilities at the start of the experiment (x=1).

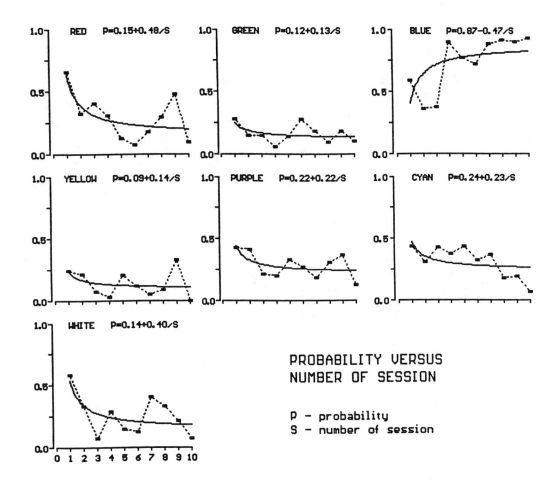

Figure 3A. Learning curves and their approximation to hyperbolic functions for seven colors. Horizontal axis-number of session; vertical axis-response probability. The ascent of curves corresponds to conditional stimuli, descent of curves to differential stimuli.

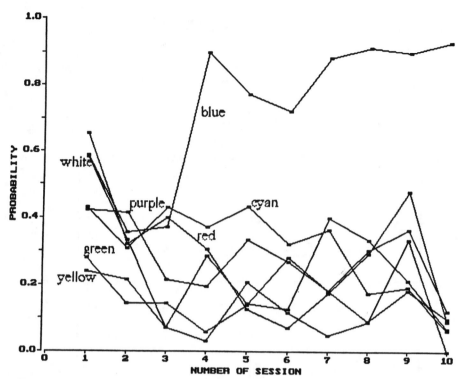

Figure 3B. The details of learning when blue color was reinforced. The asymptotic values of probabilities to different stimuli are directly related to their similarity with respect to the conditional stimulus. Axes same as Fig. 3A. the response probabilities approach plateau levels.

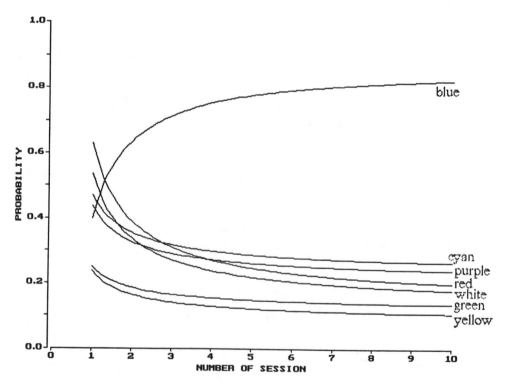

Figure 3C. The hyperbolic approximation of learning curves when blue color was reinforced. The asymptotic values of probabilities to different stimuli are directly related to their similarity to the conditional stimulus.

COLOR	HYPERBOLIC FUNCTIONS	PLATEAU LEVEL (%)	INITIAL LEVEL (%)
Blue	87.21 - 47.13/X	86	40.08
Red	15.07 + 47.96/X	21	63.03
Green	12.19 + 12.78/X	14	24.97
Yellow	9.19 + 14.43/X	11	23.62
Purple	23.73 + 22.03/X	24	43.76
Cyan	24.14 + 22.83/X	28	46.97
White	17.86 + 32.82/X	21	46.68

Table 1. The hyperbolic functions, plateau levels and initial levels of response probabilities.

It is evident from the data (Table 1) that asymptotic values for different stimuli are the greater the more similar (for a human observer) was the respective differential color stimulus (cyan) to the reinforced conditional color (blue). At the same time, the yellow color opponent to blue (and most distinct from it) is characterized by the low asymptotic value of probability. The plateau levels of response probabilities found directly by calculation of average number of responses at the end of the experiment highly correlate with the asymptotic values extracted from hyperbolic functions. This is evidence that the average response probabilities found at the end of the experiment truly have reached asymptotic values, and will not change by prolongation of the experiment. The initial levels of response probabilities given by A +/- B demonstrate that, at the start of the experiment, red color has the highest response probability due to the fact that it was used as a conditional stimulus in a preceding session. Green, as an opponent color to red, has with yellow the lowest response probabilities.

Thus, the plateau level of response probabilities for different color stimuli differ, and are greater the more similar the differential colors are to the conditional ones. The set of probabilities of responses to the conditional stimulus and the differential stimuli taken at plateau level constitutes a probability vector that is characteristic for a particular reinforced color. The matrix composed of all response probabilities for all seven colors sequentially used as conditional stimuli was constructed (Table 2). The probability matrix of instrumental responses is characterized by greatest values of probabilities on the main diagonal that correspond to conditional stimuli. It is evident from the matrix that opponent colors (red versus green, blue versus yellow) are characterized by the greatest differences in response probabilities used as conditioned and differential stimuli, respectively. The white color as a conditional stimulus differs mainly from the most saturated color (red). The data suggest that the excitation vector generated by a conditional stimulus produces, in the process of learning, a collinear vector of plastic synapses on the command neuron.

Reinforced Color	Red	Green	Yellow	Blue	Purple	Cyan	White
Red	82	12	18	21	24	20	12
Green	9	78	14	31	18	23	16
Yellow	26	37	91	24	32	33	31
Blue	21	14	11	86	24	28	21
Purple	27	23	25	32	86	25	29
Cyan	23	38	43	39	42	82	41
White	13	20	14	33	19	29	72

Table 2.   The matrix of response probabilities. Each row score corresponds to a probability vector characteristic for a specific conditional stimulus. The probabilities are smaller the more distinct are the conditional and differential stimuli.

One can say that probabilities of conditioned reflexes to differential stimuli are directly proportional to the inner products of their excitation vectors and the excitation vector of the conditional stimulus. The correlation matrix obtained from the probability matrix corresponds to the matrix of cosines of angles between excitation vectors of all color stimuli under investigation. The principle components of the correlation matrix have to be the basic excitation vectors of the color space. This conclusion was proved by factor analysis of the probability matrix which reveals four orthogonal principle components corresponding to red-green, blue-yellow, brightness and darkness neurons (Tables 3 and 4). The lengths of the excitation vectors with components given by four factors for all color stimuli are close to a constant value with variance equal to 0.095. This means that color stimuli are not distributed randomly in the four-dimensional space, rather they occupy a thin layer on the hypersphere.

Colors	Cartesian Coordinates				
	Factor X1	Factor X2	Factor X3	Factor X4	Length of Radius
Red	0.742	0.318	-0.487	-0.064	0.945
Green	-0.925	0.242	-0.177	-0.141	0.983
Yellow	-0.161	0.674	0.179	0.356	0.800
Blue	-0.046	-0.912	0.058	0.097	0.920
Purple	0.143	0.039	-0.076	0.868	0.884
Cyan	-0.224	0.113	0.547	0.457	0.756
White	0.086	0.034	0.944	-0.133	0.958

Mean of radii	0.892+/-0.032
Variance	0.095

Table 3.   The four factors characterizing color stimuli in perceptual space on the surface of the hypersphere.

Cartesian Coordinates

Colors	Factor X1	Factor X2	Factor X3	Factor X4	$\sqrt{x_1^2 + x_2^2}$	$\sqrt{x_3^2 + x_4^2}$
Red	0.979	0.172	0.017	0.112	0.994	0.113
Green	-0.922	0.205	0.327	0.009	0.945	0.327
Yellow	-0.109	0.552	0.663	0.494	0.563	0.827
Blue	-0.113	-0.853	0.466	0.206	0.860	0.510
Purple	0.122	-0.084	0.380	0.913	0.148	0.989
Cyan	-0.182	0.010	0.851	0.493	0.182	0.983
White	0.054	-0.065	0.996	0.012	0.085	0.996

Table 4.   Cartesian coordinates of color poins after normalization of data given in Table 3.

The projection of the four-dimensional vectors representing colors on the X_1X_2 (red-green, blue-yellow) plane demonstrates that the colors are located on it in a circular order according to their hue, with white color in the center (Fig 4A). The projection of points on the X_3X_4 (brightness, darkness) plane shows that colors are located in accordance with their lightness (Fig 4B). The projection of colors on the plane constructed from combined axes for hue $\sqrt{x_1^2 + x_2^2}$, and brightness $\sqrt{x_3^2 + x_4^2}$, demonstrates that colors are located on the arc in accordance with their saturation (Figure 4C).

Thus, each color point on the hypersphere is characterized by three angles corresponding to subjective aspects of colors and saturation. The inner products of four-dimensional vectors calculated from results in multidimensional scaling (Table 4) closely match the experimental response probabilities (Table 3).

Colortopic Projection

The reconstruction of a spherical color space for the monkey from the matrix of probabilities of instrumental responses estimated at the final stage of associative learning for a set of colors sequentially used as conditional stimuli supports the hypothesis concerning vector coding in neural nets. The excitation vectors present at receptor, preselector and selector map levels makes it possible to code colors by their positions on the color selector map. In line with the somatotopic, retinotopic and tonotopic projections, a colortopic projection is suggested.

The colortopic map of color-selective neurons as a hypersphere in the four-dimensional space correspond to the color-specific V4 area where color-selective neurons are located in the monkey (Zeki, 1990). One of the possible ways to build in the four-dimensional color map into a three-dimensional brain structure is to use columnar organization. It might be assumed that neurons within hue-saturation specific columns differ with respect to lightness. The most important point for information processing refers to the organization of a spherical structure that requires a normalization

473

of the excitation vector at the predetector level. It is proposed that such a normalization of excitation vectors at the predetector level is achieved by lateral inhibition between spatially neighboring identical preselector neurons. This normalization of excitation vectors is a key non-linearity in the information processing that makes possible the resulting linear operations at the level of color selective neurons, and at the stage of plastic synapses of a command neuron.

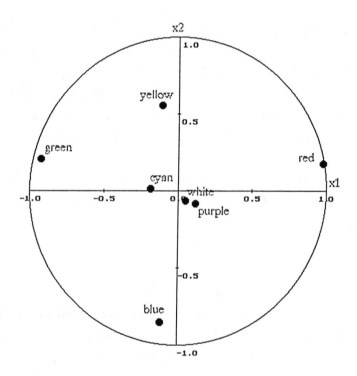

Figure 4A. The projection of color points on the X_1X_2 (red-green); (blue-yellow) plane. The white color is located close to the center. The saturated colors constitute a circle with angular measure of hue.

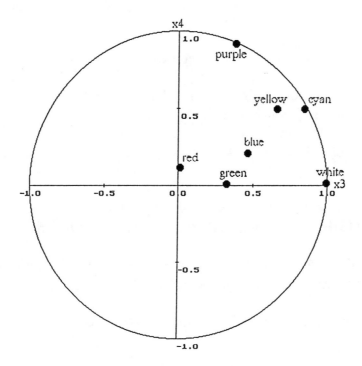

Figure 4B.   The projection of color points on the X_3X_4
(brightness-darkness) plane.   The saturated colors are close to
the center.   The angular measure corresponds to lightness.

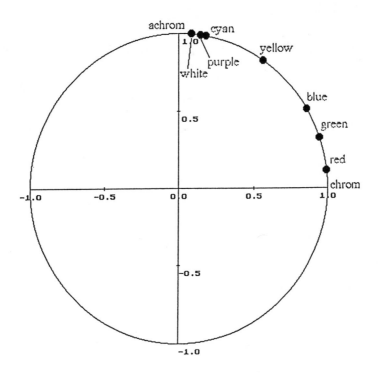

Figure 4C. The projection of color points on the $\sqrt{X_1^2+X_2^2}$; $\sqrt{X_3^2+X_4^2}$ or
hue-lightness plane. The color points are located on the
circumference in accordance with saturation.

References

Izmailov, Ch.A. and Sokolov, E.N. (1991) Spherical model of color and brightness discrimination. **Psychological Science**, **2**, 249-259.

Izmailov, Ch.A. and Sokolov, E.N. (1992) A semantic space of color names, **Psychological Science**, **3**, 105-110.

Latanov, A.V., Polansky, V.B., and Sokolov, E.N. (1991) Four-dimensional spherical color space of monkey. **Journal of Higher Nervous Activity**, Moscow, **41**, 636-646.

Paramei, G.V., Izmailov, Ch.A. and Sokolov, E.N. (1991) Multidimensional Scaling of large chromatic differences by normal and color-deficient subjects. **Psychological Science**, **2**, 244-248.

Sokolov, E.N. and Izmailov, Ch.A. (1984) **Tsvetovoe zrenie** (Color Vision), Moskva, Izdatelstvo MGU.

Sokolov, E.N., Vaitkyavichus, H.H. (1989) **Neurointelligence: From Neuron to Neurocomputer.** Moscow:Nauka.

Sokolov, E.N. (1991) Local plasticity in neuronal learning. In: **Memory: Organization and Locus of Change** (Eds. L.R. Squire, N.M. Weinberger, G.Lynch, and J.L. McGaugh), Oxford University Press, New York: Oxford, 364-392.

Zeki, S. (1990) Colour Vision and functional specialization in the visual cortex. **Discussions in Neuroscience**, **VI**(2), Elsevier: Amsterdam, 1-64.

Chapter 20

The Perception of Visual Form

Vadim Glezer

The Perception of Visual Form

Vadim Glezer
I.P.Pavlov Institute of Physiology
Sanct-Petersburg, Russia

IMAGING. MODEL OF MODULES AND QUANTUM THEORY OF INFORMATION.

The present paper reviews a number of studies on the neural mechanisms of visual pattern recognition carried out in the Laboratory of Vision of Pavlov Institute of Physiology and mostly unknown to the western reader. The paper contains the data and discussion concerning the organization of modules of visual cortex as creating premises for visual pattern recognition and how these premises are used in higher visual centers. We faced with the fact of great order in construction of neural organization of Visual Cortex (VC), when investigating the spatial and spatial frequency characteristics (SFCs) of simple cells of cat striate cortex.

In Fig.1 is shown the scheme of usual mapping of the receptive field (RF) with the aid of light and dark bars optimally oriented and moving or flickering in RF. Algebraic sum of responses in cell is suggested to be the weighting function (WF) of cell. Such spatial characteristic as size of RF and number of subfields are important for following discussion. As we will see later such method is not sufficient and does not reflect the true WF of the cell.

SFC obtained with the aid of sinusoidal grating of different spatial frequency is also shown. Important parameters here are: optimal frequency and bandwidth measured as the frequency range over which the response is greater than half of the maximum amplitude.

According to the most adopted point of view the module or hypercolumn of visual cortex is comprised by cells, RFs of which are bar or edge detectors (Fig.2a). The RFs have different width and orientation. On the scheme are shown the WFs of the cells in direction orthogonal to optimal orientation. The response of the cell is suggested to be equal to integral of product of two

dimensional WF and distribution of luminance in RF.
There is an alternative hypothesis (F i g. 2b) according to

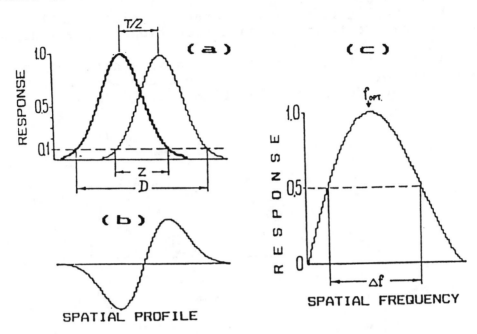

Fig.1. Diagram showing how the WF (b), SFC and bandwidth (c) were measured. Explanations in text. From [14].

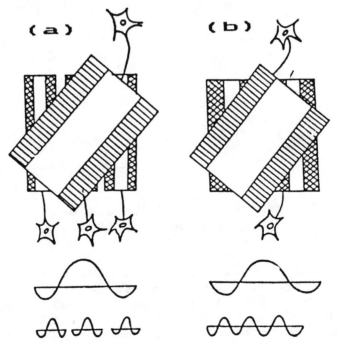

Fig.2   Two models of a module of VC. From [14].

which the narrow width elements in module are united and form a grating filter. In this case the module is a device performing piece wise Fourier-analysis of the image and harmonic basis functions must exist. Note that the sizes of filters must have the same value.

We investigated the parameters of simple cells as only they are capable to transmit the information on image without loss of it.

The first fact in favour of an alternative hypothesis (piece wise-Fourier analysis) is that we found the cells which can have up to 4 periods in profile of activity (Fig.3).

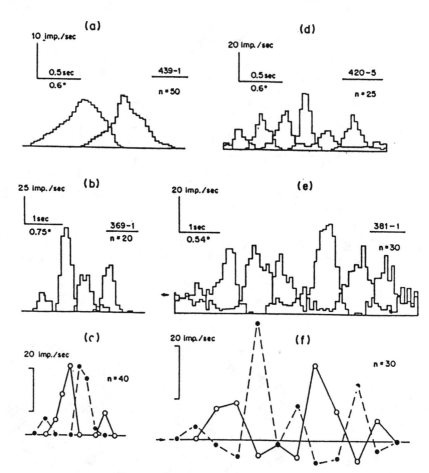

Fig.3 The responses of 4 striate cells to moving bars (a,b,d,e). In (c,f) - response of cells (b,e) to flickering bars. From [13].

This result was obtained with moving and flickering bars. The existence of such cells was shown also by other authors [23].

The next fact is that in some cells which had one or one and half periods in profile of activity real RF can have more periods. We used method of conditioning by Movshon et al.[21].

This cell responds to bars as bar detector (Fig.4,a,b). We used the method of conditioning (c). Two light or two dark bars were flashed simultaneously. One bar was in the on- or off-zone, the other was displaced with every probe.

This result may be explained as follows. In part of the subfields the single bar evokes membrane potential which is under the threshold of impulse response (dashed line in d). When two bars are applied the summed potential is above the impulse threshold. However as would be shown later the process of facilitation is also involved.

It is interesting to note that to stimulus of opposite polarity the inhibition is seen as must be in a linear cell.

Below is shown the WF obtained by inverse Fourier transformation of SFC (e,f).

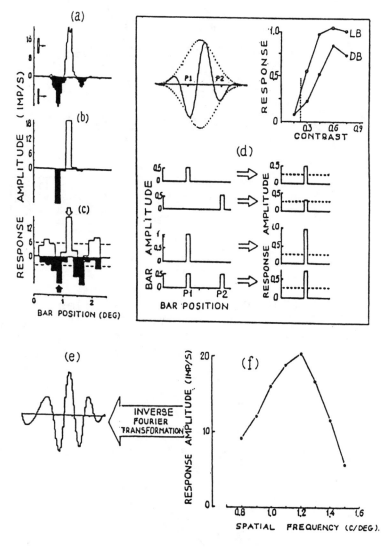

Fig.4. The subthreshold subfields are revealed by method of conditioning. Explanations in text.

At last we used the patches of grating of optimal frequency with one, two or more cycles in grating patch (Fig.5). This method used by different authors showed identical results

[2, 12, 13]. When we increased the number of cycles in grating the response was increased up to a point and then did not changed or declined. This point according to the law of superposition indicates the number of cycles in WF. The result is important for the following discussion, evidencing that the linear part of the

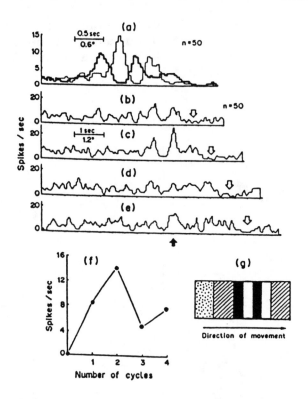

Fig.5. The summation of the responses in simple cell to increasing number of cycles in grating patch (b-e). In (g) - white and black rectangles are on- and off zones, hatched - inhibitory, stippled-disinhibitory. From [13].

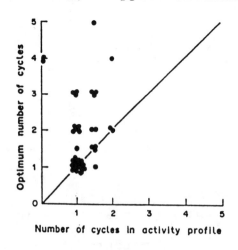

Fig.6. Scatter diagram. From [13].

RF is surrounded by inhibitory zone.

In the scatter diagram (Fig.6) the optimal number of cycles versus a number of cycles obtained with aid of bars is shown. Only in a half of cells they coincide. In other half of cells the number of cycles in WF is greater than can be shown with the aid of bars.

These data evidence in favour of a hypothesis of basis harmonic functions serving for expansion of the image.

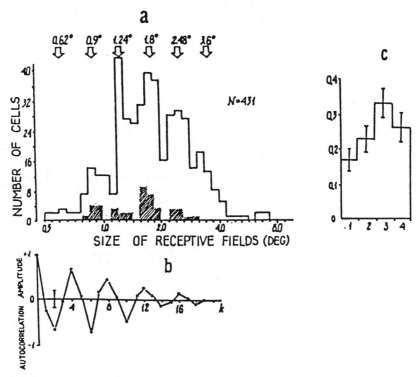

Fig.7. The distribution of RF sizes. From [14]

We tried to evaluate the basis quantitatively. In Fig.7a is shown the distribution of sizes of RFs of simple cells at eccentricity 0-6° and 0-1°(hatched rectangles). The RF sizes are clustered at half-octaves intervals and form a discrete distribution.The results are highly statistically significant as is shown by auto correlation function (b) and summed histogram.(c − the distribution was sampled by intervals , taken from the auto correlation function).

In Fig.8 is shown the distribution of optimal frequencies to which the simple cells are tuned. This result was obtained by Fourier-transformation of WF of cells. The distribution is also multimodale and frequencies are also clustered at half-octaves intervals. Black arrows show the results obtained by Pollen and Feldon [24]. Below optimal frequencies are obtained directly from SFCs.

Let us perform a simple operation (Fig.9). If we divide the value of size of the RF by value of the period of optimal frequency we obtain the index of complexity or the number of cycles in WF. We used the values from two distributions. When we divided the values of peaks in distribution of sizes and frequencies we obtained the following series which reflects the average values of harmonics irrespective of size of RF. The series was: 1, 1,41, 2, 2,9, 4,15. This result may have two interpretations of the type of harmonic basis functions.

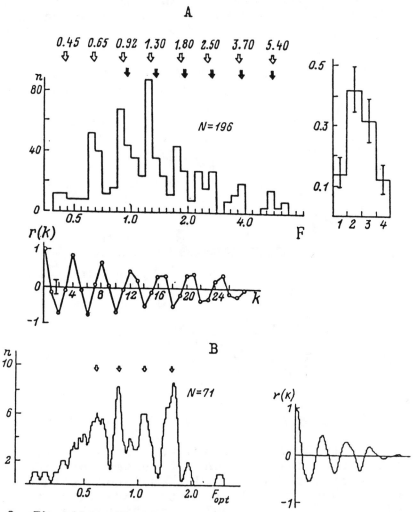

Fig.8 The distribution of optimal spatial frequencies. Explanations in text. From [14].

If we represent the result by two dimensional spatial frequency plane then there exist harmonics 1, 2, 3, 4 and also an additional term 1,41 - the first harmonic in diagonal orientation. The other terms in non vertical or horizontal orientations are near to the terms 1, 2, 3, 4 (Fig.9).

According to the second interpretation we can assume the local polar log frequency analysis. The two dimensional spatial frequency plane is shown here. We cannot choose now between these two alternatives. There are pro and con to both hypotheses. However the results obtained with the algorithm of invariant description where we used both alternatives do not show serious difference.

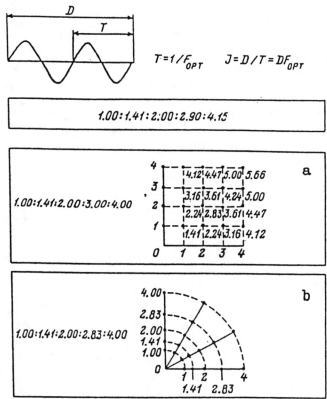

$$T = 1/F_{OPT} \qquad J = D/T = DF_{OPT}$$

1.00 : 1.41 : 2.00 : 2.90 : 4.15

Fig.9. Linear and polar log frequency Fourier - transformation.

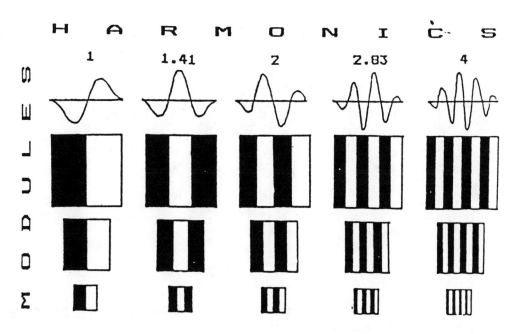

Fig.10. Model of module. (Only sinusoidal components and one orientation are shown).

These data allow to suggest the model of modules (Fig.10)
[9]. The module is formed by cells RFs of which have identical
size, different tuning and orientation and are projected in the
same region of visual field. The WF of cells of module form
harmonical series. The WFs of each harmonic are out of phase at
0°, 90°, 180° and 270° [25]. The WFs are described as
sinusoids or cosinusoids modulated by Gaussian [5, 17, 23].

Another fact evidences both in favour of model of modules and
in favour of high order of organization of nervous nets. The
distribution of relative bandwidth of SFCs of cells is also
discrete and clustered at half-octaves intervals (Fig.11).

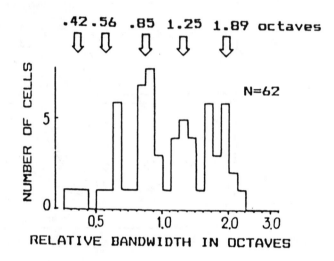

Fig.11. The distribution of relative bandwidths of simple cells.

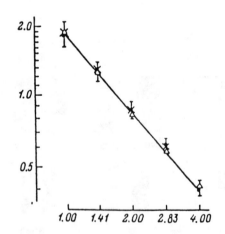

Fig.12. The dependence of relative bandwidth from number of
   harmonic.

In Fig.12 is shown the dependence of relative bandwidth from
number of harmonic. It is interesting to note that Daugman [4]

wrote that such basis functions are improbable as too severe restrictions on the elementary functions must exist. He wrote: "...in particular, they all must share the same windowing function. This entails that the spatial frequency bandwidth (in octave terms) ... will be inversely proportional to center frequencies.." (p.1175). However, as we can see this is really the case.

Let us consider now model of modules from the point of view of quantum theory of information proposed by Gabor [7].

Two additional facts are important here.
The WF of simple cell is a Gabor element - sinusoid modulated by Gaussian. It was shown by many authors [5, 17, 23] and confirmed in our laboratory [8]. The second fact is that the principle of uncertainty is performed in visual cortex, reflecting as Pribram wrought [28,p.27] "Fourier duality between space... and spectrum".

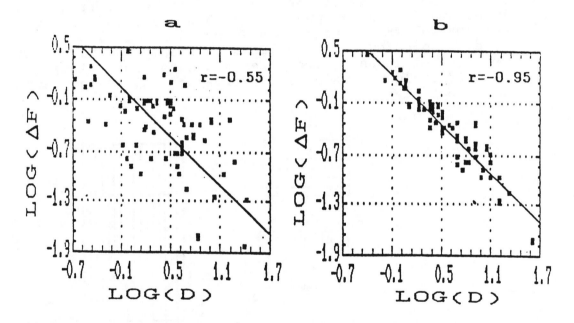

Fig.13. The dependence of relative bandwidth from size of RF. Explanations in text.

The product of bandwidth by size of RF is a constant The slope is equal to -1. Result is statistically significant but the dispersion is rather great, r=-0.55 (Fig.13,a). But as was shown before in about 50% of simple cells the measurement of size by usual method is incorrect. If we correct the size of RF by methods mentioned above then the slope is the same but coefficient of correlation is significantly increased up to -0,95 (b).

Let us now compare model of modules and quantum theory of information (Fig.14). According to the theory of information the signals may be described by three methods. Here the methods are shown for simplicity for unidimensional case, that is rather the line of receptors is discussed than two-dimensional retina.

Let us suppose that in a two-dimensional space rectangle $F_N d$ exist where F_N is Nyquist frequency. According to sampling method of Shannon the signal in interval d can be described by values in discrete intervals d equal to unit divided by doubled Nyquist frequency (b).

According to global Fourier-method the signal is described by set of filters each of which overlap all the retina (a). However such organization does not correspond to our knowledge about organization of nervous nets in visual system. Gabor [7] divided the rectangle on units which he named logons (c). Area occupied by logon is equal to product ΔF by d. The minimum area is achieved if the sinusoidal and cosinusoidal elements of logon are Gabor elements. In this case the optimal conditions for transmission of information are achieved.

Such scheme corresponds to the model of modules (d). The column corresponds to one module. The spatial frequency in logons in column increases upwards. The bandwidth and size of cells do not change. WFs of cells are Gabor elements. The field of vision is overlapped by set of columns or modules of different size. But the area of logon is the same in all columns. Thus the central part of field of vision is overlapped by nets of modules of different size.

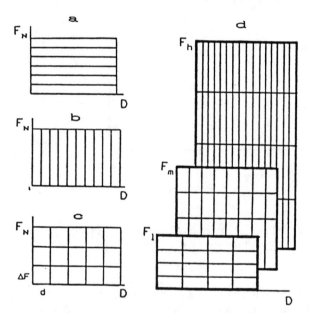

Fig.14. Scheme of possible methods of representations of signal. Explanations in text.

Gabor elements are optimal for transmission of information, the resulting image codes are very compact. But the elementary expansion functions are not orthogonal. As Gabor wrought himself only 67% of information are transmitted rightly.

However judging from our perception the image is restored fully. There are theoretical approaches to the problem [1, 3].Our experiment give following results.

Let us demonstrate it on one cell where we used method of conditioning and testing stimuli [21]. On the Fig.15 the

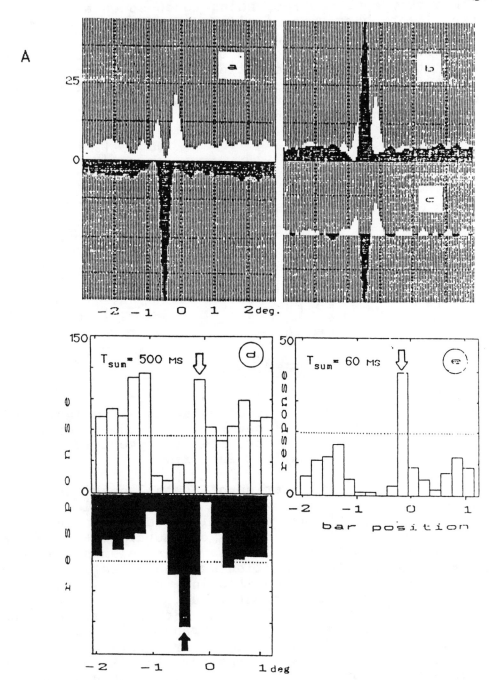

Fig.15. The quasi change of WF of a cell when it is measured by two bars extended in RF.

responses to moving light and dark bars (a, b, c) on background activity evoked by visual noise are shown.

In (d, below) two dark bars were applied. The conditioning
stimulus was in off-zone. Testing stimulus was displaced. Two
inhibitory zones corresponding to on-zones are seen. In (d, above)
two light bars were applied. The main result is that the
responses to doubled dark bar (we worked in linear part of
contrast characteristic) in off-zone, to double light bar in on-
zone at right and to conditioned bar plus testing bar in right
and left on-zones are equal. It is interesting for next
discussion that if we take only the beginning of response the
responses in the on-zones are not equal (e).

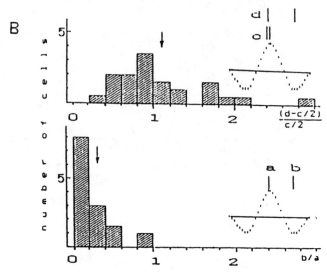

Fig.16. The distributions of relation of weights of peripheral
peak to central one when one (below) or two (above) bars
are applied. Arrows mean the averages of distributions.
Other explanations in text.

The diagram of relation of central peak to peripheral ones
for 27 cells is shown in Fig.16. Below is shown the
distribution, obtained using single bars, above - two bars. In
the second case the value of peripheral peak was calculated in
supposition that the cell is a linear element. We subtracted from
the response to conditioning plus testing stimuli half of
response to doubled conditioning stimulus and divided it by
response to conditioning stimulus. It is clear that the cells
behave like nonlinear elements. We can assume that when the
stimulus is extended in RF, expansion is performed rather by
sinusoid (cosinusoid) modulated by square wave impulse than by
Gaussian. We do not state however that it is really so and that
basis is now orthogonal. May be we should speak only about
improvement of expansion coefficients. But at the surface it
looks like the orthogonalization of basis with the aid of
facilitation.
We tried to understand in computer simulation how the process
of orthogonalization is achieved. We used for this purpose
modification of algorithm proposed by Daugman [3].
If the elementary function do not form complete orthogonal

set the desired set of coefficients (a_i) must be determined by optimization criterion. Daugman used such criterion as minimizing the squared norm of the difference-vector:

$$E=\| I(x,y)-C(x,y)\|^2 \qquad (1)$$

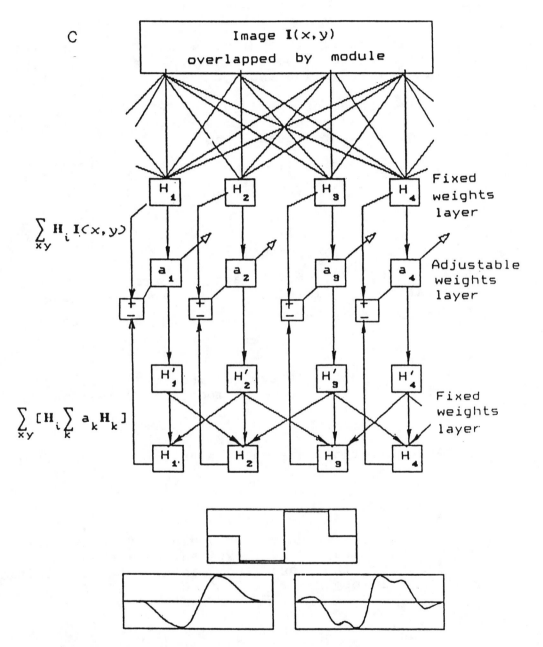

Fig.17. Scheme of neural nets in the module for finding of optimal coefficients. Results of computer simulation are shown below. See text.

491

The final state is when all $\Delta_i=0$. The modulation of this algorithm in our scheme is that the nervous net corresponds rather to one module than to all retina.

Below are shown the results of representation of square wave grating before the iterative process and after it. It is interesting to note that in final state Mach bands appear.

The Algorithm

1) For removal of constant component the stimulus is convolved with overlapped linear DOGs. As a result the stimulus is described as negative and positive values relatively to zero level.

2) Processing of the image $I'(x,y)$ by modules. Outputs of central excitatory part and peripheral inhibitory parts of RF of k-th module are represented as

$$I^{cen,c(s)}_{KNL} = \iint\limits_{x^2+y^2<(T_k/2)^2} I'(x,y)\ w^{cen,c(s)}_{KNL}dxdy \qquad (3)$$

$$I^{sur,c(s)}_{KNL} = \iint\limits_{(T_k/2)^2<x^2+y^2<T_k^2} I'(x,y)\ w^{sur,c(s)}_{KNL}dxdy \qquad (4)$$

where w is WF; K,N,L are numbers of module, harmonic, orientation; T_k is size of RFs of the k-th module. The output signal of k-th module is calculated as

$$f^{c(s)}_{KNL} = |I^{cen}| - |I^{sur}| \qquad (5)$$

3) A group of most excited modules is selected in following way. The excitation of k-th module is determined as follows:

$$R_k = \sum_{NL} |f^c_{KNL}| + |f^s_{KNL}| \qquad (6)$$

4) Convolutions are calculated for each interpolating neuron i

$$\sum_k g_i(k)\ R_k, \qquad i=1,\ 1.125,\ 1.25\dots,$$

where $g_i(k) = \exp(-(2/3(i-k)))^2$.

The number of WF i where the value of convolution is maximum defines the group of most excited modules.

5) Finally the image code invariant to position and size (position in depth) $(f^c_{NL},\ f^s_{NL})$, $N = 1,\dots,5$, $L = 1,\dots6$, is defined as

$$f^c_{NL} = \sum_k (g_{i_{max}}(k)\ f^c_{KNL}); \qquad f^s_{NL} = \sum_k (g_{i_{max}}(k)\ f^s_{KNL}) \qquad (7)$$

In computer simulation the algorithm was proved on letters and halftone images. As a criterion of nearness the correlation coefficients between image codes were calculated. The code of a

492

E will be minimized when its partial derivatives with respect to all of the n coefficients (a) equal zero.

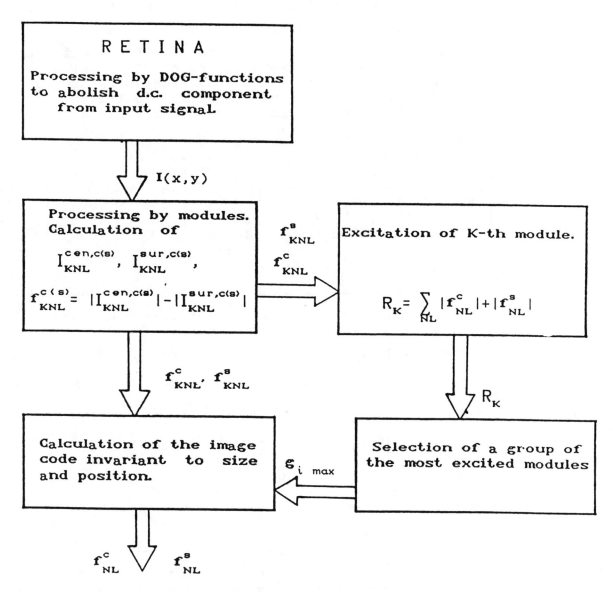

Fig.18 Scheme of the algorithm.

Daugman suggested neural net which calculates the weight adjustment Δ_i:

$$\Delta_i = \sum_{xy}(H_i(x,y) \, I(x,y)) - \sum_{xy}(H_i(x,y)(\sum_{k=1}^{n} a_k H_k(x,y))) \qquad (2)$$

The iterative rule for adjusting the value of each coefficient is $a_i \rightarrow a_i + \Delta_i$.

pattern does not change if the size of image is increased in $\sqrt{2}$ times. So we must check cases when the size is changed less then at the $\sqrt{2}$ points. To confirm that the code is invariant the initial pattern was increased according to the scale factor

$$x_i = 1 + [(\sqrt{2} - 1)/4] \cdot i, \quad i = 0, 1, 2, 3, 4.$$

The correlation coefficients between different images (Tables 1 and 3) and between images of different size (Tables 2 and 4) were calculated. The correlation is near to 1 for the image of different size and low between different images. Thus in principle the algorithm may be used for pattern recognition.

Table 1.

	К	Б	Т
К	1	-.50	.57
Б	-.50	1	-.29
Т	.57	-.29	1

Table 2.

	x_0	x_1	x_2	x_3	x_4
К	1	.996	.997	.999	.999
Б	1	.996	.998	.997	.999
Т	1	.998	.997	.996	.999

Table 3.

	Cup	Deer	Receiver	Elephant	Tiger
Cup	1	0.57	0.73	0.67	0.85
Deer	0.57	1	0.64	0.53	0.54
Receiver	0.73	0.64	1	0.82	0.61
Elephant	0.67	0.53	0.82	1	0.51
Tiger	0.85	0.54	0.61	0.51	1

Table 4.

	x_0	x_1	x_2	x_3	x_4
x_0	1	0.997	0.970	0.994	0.999
x_1	0.997	1	0.996	0.996	0.997
x_2	0.970	0.996	1	0.994	0.970
x_3	0.994	0.996	0.994	1	0.994
x_4	0.999	0.997	0.970	0.994	1

Chapter 21

Visually-triggered Neuronal Oscillations in the Pigeon: An Autocorrelation Study of Tectal Activity

Sergio Neuenschwander, Francisco Varela

Visually-triggered neuronal oscillations in the pigeon: an autocorrelation study of tectal activity

Sergio Neuenschwander* and Francisco J. Varela

*Institut des Neurosciences
9, quai St. Bernard, 75005 - Paris*

Running title: Visual oscillations in the avian optic tectum.

Number of pages: 28
Number of tables: 1
Number of figures: 11

Key words: temporal binding, neuronal assemblies, oscillatory activity, local field potential, multi-unit activity, avian optic tectum

* Present address: Max-Planck-Institut für Hirnforschung, Deutschordenstraße 46, 6000 - Frankfurt 71, Germany.

....
Correspondence should be sent to:
Sergio Neuenschwander
Max-Planck-Institut für Hirnforschung
Deutschordenstraße 46
6000 - Frankfurt - 71
Germany

Abstract

In this study we describe visually-triggered gamma oscillations in the optic tectum of awake pigeons. This study was motivated by the potential relevance of synchronous oscillatory responses in perceptual binding, in a laminated structure other than the mammalian neocortex. Tectal responses were recorded as local field potential and multi-unit activity by differential filtering. The local field potential was analyzed by computing its autocorrelation function and spectral power with a moving window applied to single response sweeps. The temporal structure of the spike trains was evaluated by computing averaged autocorrelograms. A damped sine wave function was fitted to the autocorrelograms in order to quantify the degree of oscillation of both signals. Epochs of significant oscillatory activity were observed in the local field potential in 60% of the trials (n=39). In all trials, significant oscillations occupied about 10% of the time the stimulus was present. The oscillatory events in both the local field potential and the multi-unit activity had frequencies in the range of 20-50 Hz. It is important to emphasize the great variability in the frequency and in the probability of occurrence of the oscillatory responses from trial to trial, which makes the oscillatory behavior of the tectal activity highly non-stationary. The oscillatory activity we describe in the avian tectum has characteristics similar to those reported in the mammalian neocortex. These findings from a fully awake animal strengthen the universality of oscillations as a possible carrier for synchronization of activity in the constitution of neuronal assemblies.

Introduction

Comparative physiology has much to contribute to the understanding of the neural mechanisms underlying perceptual cognitive processes, such as visual recognition and categorization, since cross-species comparisons provide important constraints for an unified explanation. If a neuronal mechanism proves to be universal across species, it is likely to be a fundamental process. In this study we apply this reasoning to the hypothesis that neuronal synchronization in sensory systems acts as a mechanism to link local features into a global percept.

The interest for exploring this hypothesis came from theoretical models that try to account for integrative processes without relying on single neuron responses, but instead, by taking the activity of a population of cells as fundamental (Abeles, 1982; Palm, 1982; von der Malsburg, 1983; von der Malsburg and Schneider, 1986). These models use synchronization of neuronal activity as a marker for an ensemble of cells. Neurons transiently linked by synchronous firing are thought to form a cell assembly, that could be viewed as a dynamical unit relevant to integrative processes, such as the segmentation of visual scenes. Synchronization may result, for example, from phase-coupling of oscillators, so that neurons belonging to a transient sub-network share a rhythmic activity. Thus the phase relationship between oscillating neurons could serve as a label for distinct transient cell assemblies that may be spatially interleaved; phase synchronization allows cells to switch from an assembly to another (for a review, see Singer, 1990; Engel *et al.*, 1991a; Engel *et al.*, 1992).

These ideas have became attractive because they provide a dynamical mechanism of linking, in contrast to the rigidity of other models, based solely on the wiring of neuronal populations. Perception, in all its richness, requires a highly flexible mechanism, that sustains a large-scale coordination of widely distributed neural activity in various areas. Given its basic nature, such an integrative mechanism should be similar in different neural systems and not confined to a particular species.

Synchronization of activity was first demonstrated within a behavioral context in the olfactory system of the rabbit, where macro potentials showed coherent oscillations in response to odor stimuli (Freeman, 1975).

Synchronized neuronal responses have subsequently been demonstrated in other structures such as the visual cortex of the cat (Gray and Singer, 1989; Eckhorn *et al.*, 1988; Gray *et al.*, 1990a; Engel *et al.*, 1990; Frégnac, 1991), and the visual and sensorimotor cortex of monkeys (Livingstone, 1991; Kreiter and Singer, 1992; Murthy and Fetz, 1991). Other reports have questioned the pertinence of these observations, since oscillations were less frequently found in the visual cortex (Young et al., 1992) and the inferotemporal cortext of the monkey (Gawne et al, 1991; Rolls and Tovee, 1992).

We have studied oscillatory activity in the avian visual system, and compared it with data collected from the mammalian neocortex. We have selected the pigeon, because it has amazing visual performances. For instance, pigeons are able to pass tests of visual pattern recognition with better scores than humans in a situation that involves recognition of patterns independent of their orientation (Delius and Hollard, 1982; Delius, 1985). Regarding more complex cognitive functions, pigeons are capable of perceptual categorization and generalization, as has been demonstrated with a behavioral paradigm that uses different types of leaves as a test (Cerella, 1979). Another example is their color vision ability. It has been shown that the color space of diurnal birds is of higher dimensionality than that of primates (Varela *et al.*, 1992). On the other hand, the visual pathways in birds have a strikingly different organization.

In the work reported here, we have recorded from a single electrode placed in the optic tectum (OT) of awake pigeons. The OT has a distinct laminar organization and is highly developed in birds (Holden, 1971). It is an ideal experimental choice since it plays a role not only in spatial vision (homologous to the superior colliculus in mammals) but in form and color vision as well. Correspondingly, tectal lesions produce severe deficit in discrimination tasks (Jarvis, 1974; Jassik-Gerschenfeld and Hardy, 1984). In view of the topographic organization of the OT, basic processes in form perception, for instance the identification of the contours of an object, demand a coordination of activity of neurons localized far apart. It is plausible that synchronization of oscillatory activity may mediate such integrative processes, as has been suggested for the visual cortex of the cat (Gray *et al.*, 1989, Engel *et al.*, 1990, Engel *et al.*, 1991b).

We recorded from awake animals to eliminate potential effects of anesthetics on stimulus-induced oscillatory activity. In addition, we have used an anesthetized preparation to evaluate how halothane anesthesia may affect stimulus-triggered oscillatory activity. Our analysis consisted in obtaining various quantitative indicators of oscillatory activity in successive epochs in both the spike responses and the local field potential in order to follow the emergence and decay of the oscillatory phenomena in a dynamic manner.

Some of this results have been presented in abstract form (Neuenschwander and Varela, 1990; 1992).

Methods

Animal preparation and recording

A total of 13 pigeons (*Columbia livia*) in three sets of experiments were used in this study. In a first group, the recordings were performed with awake animals, having the head fixed and body movements slightly restrained (n=8). In a second experimental group, the recordings were performed with animals under halothane anesthesia (n=2). In addition, we have recorded from paralyzed and lightly anesthetized animals (n=3) as a control for eye movements.

In all sets of experiments, prior to the recording sessions, a bolt for holding the head and a recording chamber were implanted onto the skull under inhalation anesthesia (Bilo *et al.*, 1972). First the animals were restrained by intramuscular injection of ketamine hydrochloride (Imalgène, Rhône Mérieux, 50 mg/kg) and then intubated and artificially ventilated with a mixture of 70% of nitrous oxide and 30% of oxygen to which 0.7% halothane (Hoechst) was added. The heart rate was continuously monitored during the surgical procedures, and the body temperature was kept constant at 40°.

In the experiments with halothane anesthetized and the control of lightly anesthetized and paralyzed animals, recording was resumed immediately after the implantation surgery. The stereotaxic ear bars and mouth piece were removed and the animal was maintained under 70% of nitrous oxide and 30% of oxygen. In the second experimental group, 0.5-1.5% halothane was supplemented to the inhalation mixture. In the control group, muscular relaxation was obtained by gallamine sulfate (Flaxédil, Specia, 5 mg/kg/hr) administered by continuous infusion into the subclavian vein, while the animal was kept under 70% of nitrous oxide and 30% of oxygen, as before. A local anesthetic (Lidocain 2%, Braun) was infiltrated in wound edges.

In the awake preparation, the tectal activity was recorded during 3-4 successive recording sessions at intervals of 1-2 days. The recording sessions started 2 days after the implantation. During the recordings, which lasted for 4-6 hours, the head was held fixed and the pigeon kept in a jacket to restrain body movements. The tectum was accessed by removing the cover lid of the recording chamber.

In each recording session, 3-4 successive penetrations of a single electrode were made into the optic tectum in the central visual field representation. The penetrations were made through the intact *dura*, roughly perpendicular to the tectal surface. Glass-coated tungsten electrodes with tapered tips were used to record extracellular multi-unit activity, except in 8 cases where single units were studied under the same methods.

Visual stimuli

A hand-held projector was used to determine the location and size of the receptive fields. For data collection, stimuli were generated with an optomechanical stimulator and consisted of a moving light bar passing over the receptive field in the forward and after a delay of 400-700 msec in the backwards direction. The stimuli were projected onto a translucent screen located 57 cm from the contralateral eye, extending over the lateral visual field. Movement was produced by a mirror galvanometer controlled by a computer that generated ramp waveforms with steps of 1-5 msec. The velocity of the stimulus was identical for the forward and backward movements (3-20 deg/sec) and the bar length was in general three times the receptive field size (approximately 7-10 deg). Each trial was 1.0-4.0 sec in duration, and was repeated 10 times. Because of the nature of the preparation, eye movements were not controlled; since pigeons make saccades of relatively small amplitude (Lemeignan *et al.*, 1992) it was possible to have the receptive field in study always inside the much larger zone of stimulation. The sharpness of the post-stimulus time histograms served as control for potential artifacts from eye saccades.

Data acquisition and analysis

A microcomputer (Macintosh IIci) with a LabView 2.0 interface (National Instruments, Austin) was used for the acquisition of data and the control of the optical bench. After amplification (X 10000) the signals were bandpass filtered in two different envelopes. The local field potential (LFP) was obtained after digitally filtering the original signal from 1 to 100 Hz (sampling frequency of 5 kHz), and multi-unit activity (MUA) was obtained after analog filtering from 0.5 to 3 kHz, followed by an amplitude threshold trigger to detect spike events. A computer count of the trigger output was made with a time resolution of 0.2 ms.

Analysis was performed on a trial by trial basis. First the spike trains were plotted in relation to the recorded LFP and cell activity was correlated with the ongoing LFP by calculating the spike-triggered average of the LFP (Gray and Singer, 1989). This was obtained by first normalizing the LFP activity for each trial (subtracting its mean over one sweep, and dividing it by its standard deviation), and then computing an average for the signal preceding and following each spike by 50 msec.

A key element in our analysis is that the autocorrelation function and the spectral power (FFT) of the LFP were calculated with a moving window algorithm. This consisted in a systematic application of a 200 msec analysis window on the signal every 100 msec steps. The power spectra and autocorrelation functions for each window were than plotted as two dimensional arrays, in which the amplitudes were normalized to unity.

The temporal structure of the spike trains were evaluated by computing the autorenewal density (autocorrelogram) within a 200-500 msec window over single sweeps. Since single sweeps did not always contain enough spikes to yield a robust autocorrelogram, we have calculated cumulative autocorrelograms over the 10 trials.

In order to ascertain that the relationship between multi-unit activity and LFP was not a mere artifact introduced by the digital filtering, a simulated train of spikes was treated in the same manner than the real data. We observed that, as expected, the simulated data reatained no oscillatory component in the LFP frequency band.

Quantification of oscillatory responses

In order to facilitate comparisons across species, we have followed closely the parameters used by Engel *et al.* (1990) for the quantification of oscillatory events in the cat visual cortex.

A Gabor function (a cosine function damped by a gaussian) was fitted to each autocorrelation function by means of the Levenberg-Marquardt algorithm

(Press *et al.*, 1986). The fitted Gabor function provided the descriptors for a quantitative classification of the oscillatory responses by means of four parameters: its period (T), amplitude (A), decay constant (τ), and the offset from the abscissa (B). In the case of the LFP autocorrelation function, the fitting algorithm could be simplified by subtracting the mean from the correlation function and a null value was assigned to the offset. The correlation coefficient between the fitted Gabor function and the raw data was calculated to evaluate the significance of the fit. Only the cases with correlation coefficients greater than 0.8 were analyzed further as discussed in Young *et al.* (1992).

The criteria for the classification of the autocorrelation functions were based on the following parameters: (1) the ratio τ/T of the fitted Gabor functions, (2) the ratio A_{stim}/A_{spont} of the Gabor function amplitude for the responses epoch under analysis and the Gabor function amplitude for an epoch of activity without stimulation or "spontaneous" (taken as the first 200-700 msec preceding the onset of the stimulus).

In the case of the MUA, the Gabor function was fitted to the cumulative autocorrelograms. In addition to the ratio τ/T, we have calculated the ratio of the amplitude over the offset of the Gabor function. This ratio was taken as the second criterion for classification.

In the LFP signal, activity within a window was considered as oscillatory when the fitted Gabor function had a τ/T greater than 1.0 and the amplitude ratio A_{stim}/A_{spont} greater than 1.5. For the MUA the rating criteria were slightly different: the autocorrelograms were classified as oscillatory if the fitted Gabor function had a τ/T ratio greater than 0.8 and the ratio A/B greater than 1.0. The basis for this choice of criteria is empirical and discussed in Engel *et al.* (1990).

These rating criteria were then applied to the moving window algorithm for the LFP and the results were displayed so that the epochs of oscillatory activity are indicated with a rectangle covering their duration (see figure 6 for an example). A distribution of frequencies (computed as the inverse of the period) was obtained for the Gabor functions that had significant scores. The probability of occurrence of an oscillation for the entire LFP response was estimated by counting the windows that were classified as oscillatory, and expressed as percentage with a temporal resolution of the step used in the moving window algorithm. The duration of the response was defined on basis of the firing of the neuron (as seen in the PSTH, peri-stimulus time histogram).

In selected cases, we have applied the moving window algorithm to the multi-unit responses as well on a trial by trial basis to study in detail the relations between oscillatory events in both the LFP and the MUA.

Results

We have studied the LFP and multi-unit activity from 86 recording sites at different tectal depths. Tectal cells recorded in the awake pigeon typically show burst responses to a moving light bar presented in their receptive fields. An oscillatory pattern in the responses could be observed as burst firings from several units lasting 3-10 msec, followed by silent periods of 25-40 msecs (Fig.1). Although primarily studied in the multi-unit activity, bursting could be observed in single units (n=8). In addition, oscillatory epochs in the LFP were occasionally seen in the ongoing activity independent of the visual stimulus.

LFP Responses

Oscillatory activity was readily observed in single sweeps of the local field potential in response to the forward or backward movement of the stimulus. As the bar crossed the receptive field the amplitude of the LFP increased at the same time, as it started to become oscillatory (Figs. 1 and 2). During epochs of spontaneous activity LFP amplitudes were comparatively small. Nevertheless, high amplitude oscillations could be observed in some trials just after the bar had crossed the receptive field, at times when the stimulus had already disappeared (Fig.2).

The dynamics of the LFP oscillations in a given trial are clearly seen in the compressed arrays of the autocorrelation functions and power spectra. In the example shown in Fig. 3, an epoch of oscillatory activity is seen in the autocorrelation function after the stimulus had crossed the receptive field in the forward direction. The observed oscillatory period is T= 29 msec. It has a frequency peak at about 34 Hz in the power spectrum, but contains a number of additional components in neighboring frequencies. In this case, the oscillatory modulation was weaker for the backward movement of the stimulus.

If one compares the cumulative power spectra for all trials, a clear difference is observed between the epochs of spontaneous activity and those where a visual stimulus was present (Fig. 4). The relative energy content at the

20-40 frequency range was approximately two times greater for the epochs of stimulation than for spontaneous activity. The power spectra of the LFP showed peaks at low frequencies, but the onset of an oscillatory response was always characterized by a shift to higher frequencies. Nevertheless, this increase is not reflected in a single peak, but in a rather broad increase comprising multiple peaks in the gamma range (between 20-60 Hz). This arises from the important inter- and intra-trial variation of the dominant LFP frequencies.

Temporal analysis of the LFP

We have studied the time course of oscillatory responses by moving an analysis window over single sweeps in all trials. The modulation of the LFP autocorrelation functions calculated for each successive window was quantified by computing the ratio of the fitted Gabor function decay constant over its period (τ/T, see Methods). The examples shown in Figure 5 illustrate how this approach describes the spectral content of the signal. On the one hand, there were oscillations with a rather regular period, lasting many cycles (Fig. 5, A). In these cases the signal has a narrow frequency spectrum; the power of the fitted Gabor function is a sharp gaussian, and its median coincides with the peak frequency of the signal. On the other hand, there were oscillations with a rather broad spectrum (Fig.5, C). We have used $\tau/T= 1.0$ as level of significance to flag the oscillatory events. At this level, there is a considerable jitter in frequency, which is reflected by the relatively broad spectrum of the corresponding Gabor function (a case rated as borderline is shown in Fig.5, B).

The frequency of occurrence of oscillatory events triggered by the stimulus was estimated by counting the windows where oscillations were rated as significant; an example is shown in Fig.6. In a total of 39 recording sites analyzed in this manner, 60% of the trials contained at least one significant window; and the total time during which significant oscillations were present (over the entire response time as given by the PSTH) was 10%. Significant oscillations in the LFP occurred as single or multiple events. They had variable latencies relative to the stimulus onset, variable durations (between 50 and 400 msec) and frequencies (between 18-60 Hz; overall frequency peak centered at 26 ± 8 Hz). The mean τ/T ratio was 1.5. In the control group for eye movements, recordings were made with the lightly anesthetized and paralyzed animal. The occurrence of oscillatory events and their distribution of frequencies (26 ± 5 Hz) were similar to those observed in the recordings with the awake animal.

Multi-unit spike responses

Oscillations were more clearly visible in multi-unit than in single cell responses. Nevertheless the rasters of isolated cells displayed unequivocal burst activities compatible with an oscillatory activity (not shown).

There was a considerable variation in the frequency and amplitude modulation between the autocorrelograms computed from individual trials (Figure 7). These variations was not related with the strength of the responses (number of spikes per second). Even with equally strong responses of the cells, oscillations could be either present (Figure 7 B, trial 8) or absent (trial 3). In all cases a negative going trough flanked the peak of the autocorrelogram (at 0 time lag), reflecting a grouped cell firing. As a result of the high variability of frequencies, the summed autocorrelation functions showed a weaker modulation than those of individual trials (Figure 7, D). In 17 recordings studied in this way, the Gabor functions fitted to the averaged autocorrelograms had a mean frequency of 35± 4 Hz and a τ/T ratio of 0.95. As a control, the autocorrelograms of the MUA calculated from responses shuffled by one stimulus period (shift predictor) showed no significant modulation (Figure 7, C).

In the great majority of the multi-unit activity recordings it was not possible to assign a preference of responses to the forward or backward movement of the stimulus, or to establish a dependency of the oscillatory modulation on the strength of the responses for one particular direction or velocity. This finding is consistent with single unit studies (Jassik-Gerschenfeld *et al.*, 1970), which demonstrate that most of tectal cells are non-selective to the direction of movement.

Relations between LFP and MUA oscillations

Typically, a rhythmic response in the multi-unit activity occurred in correspondence with a high amplitude oscillation of the recorded local field potential. This correspondence was clearly expressed in the spike-triggered average of the LFP, which shows that the spikes coincide with the negative-going phase of the LFP (Fig. 8). If the analysis window was centered on the response of a single trial (i.e., the response to the forward moving stimulus in Fig. 8) the oscillatory modulation in the spike-triggered average of the LFP was more pronounced than if the entire trial time was used (*i.e.*, the interstimulus interval and the response to the backward movement). Very large negative peaks in LFP were always observed in relation with a burst activity of the cells.

A further analysis of the relations between the LFP oscillations and the corresponding multi-unit activity was made for selected recording sites (n=4). In these cases we have applied the moving window algorithm to both the LFP and the MUA response. Examples of pairs of autocorrelation functions computed within the same window for both the LFP and the MUA are shown in Fig. 9. The power spectra of the LFP are also depicted and can be compared to the spectra computed for the MUA autocorrelograms. In most of the windows, there was a close match between the oscillation frequencies of the LFP and of MUA, as revealed by the Gabor functions fitted to the autocorrelograms and by the power spectra (Fig. 9, A). Moreover, in some cases the power spectra showed rather comparable peaks even though the frequencies of the fitted Gabor functions exhibited large differences (Fig. 9, B). Another example of seeming mismatch between the MUA and LFP oscillations is shown in Fig. 9, C. In this case, the oscillation in the LFP was rated as non-significant and displayed a broad spectrum of frequencies, but the peaks may have corresponded to those seen in the MUA power spectrum.

In another approach, we have plotted the frequencies of the LFP oscillations versus those of the MUA, by applying the moving window algorithm to both signals (Fig. 10). The cases of matched frequencies, excluding the ones with mismatch (as in Fig 9, B and C) represented 40% of the windows (n=76). The mean oscillation frequencies obtained in this group were 33.6± 5 Hz for the LFP and 33.9± 6 Hz for the MUA. There was a mismatch in 14% of the cases; in most of them the MUA autocorrelograms had no oscillatory modulation. The windows not containing enough spikes to fit a Gabor function into the MUA autocorrelogram comprised 30% of the total (Fig. 10, represented by dots). In the cases with mismatch, the frequencies of LFP oscillations were most often below or close to 20 Hz.

Effects of halothane anesthesia

In the second experimental group, the animals (n=2) were anesthetized with halothane (0.5-1.5%). During anesthesia the probability of oscillatory activity dropped (on the average) to less than 2%, and the Gabor functions fitted to the LFP autocorrelograms showed very low decay/period (τ/T) ratios (Fig. 11). However, a full recovery of the bursting behavior of the cells occurred within a few minutes after lowering the halothane concentration (less than 0.5 %). The samples recorded under high halothane, the power spectrum calculated for the LFP showed no stimulus-induced increase in the energy content at the gamma range, in contrast to the awake animals or after recovery (Fig.11).

Discussion

Our results show that a visual stimulus triggers oscillatory field potentials in the tectum of awake birds, indicating that a population of neighboring cells must have synchronized their discharges and engaged rhythmic activity in the respective frequency ranges. These oscillations resemble qualitatively those observed in the visual cortex of lightly anesthetized cats or awake monkeys: frequencies are in the gamma range, they are not unimodal but broad banded, and they present a significant intra- and inter-trial variability (Gray and Singer, 1987; Eckhorn *et al.*, 1988; Gray and Singer, 1989; Gray *et al.*,1990a; Kreiter and Singer, 1992).

In awake pigeons the oscillatory events were shorter (mean= 210 msec) than in the anesthetized cat (425 msec, see Table 1), but of similar duration as in the awake monkey (100-300 msec, Kreiter and Singer, 1992). Another difference is that the amplitude modulation (as measured by the ratio τ/T over 10 trials) of both LFP and MUA autocorrelograms was less pronounced in our data than in those from anesthetized cats (Table 1).

Comparison of frequency ranges

The oscillatory activities of the OT, as seen in both the LFP and the MUA, have frequencies in the range of 20-50 Hz. This represents a shift to lower frequencies if compared to the mean obtained in the visual cortex of light-anesthetized cats within similar conditions of stimulation (55± 10 Hz; Gray *et al.*, 1990a). The same frequency range as in the pigeon OT was seen in recordings from awake kittens in one brief report (Raether *et al.*, 1989). In a study of the striate cortex of anesthetized squirrel monkeys oscillatory responses were observed over a frequency range of 40-90 Hz (Livingstone, 1991). In the superior temporal sulcus of the awake macaque monkey this range is between 30-60 Hz (46± 9 Hz; Kreiter and Singer, 1992). It is clear then, that there is no unique or fixed frequency for these oscillations, and they are likely to reflect the species, the neural structure, as well as the experimental conditions in which they are measured; and probably the depth of anesthesia.

Feature dependencies

In our study the velocities of the stimuli ranged from 3 to 20 deg/sec. Although we did not study the feature dependence of oscillations in a systematic way, our data provide no clear evidence for a correlation between the velocity of the stimulus and the strength or frequency of the oscillatory responses. This contrasts with the observation in the cat that the mean frequency of the cortical oscillations increases monotonically with the velocity of the stimulus (Gray *et al.*, 1990a, Table 6). One possible explanation for this could be that tectal neurons in the pigeon respond alike to a great range of velocities (Hughes and Pearlman, 1974; Frost and Di Franco, 1976) and that most cells in the OT exhibit a spatial frequency selectivity to moving sine-wave gratings independently of the temporal modulation of the stimulus (Hardy and Jassik-Gerschenfeld, 1979).

Temporal Analysis

Moving a window in the LFP signal for a more detailed single trial analysis permitted a comparison of the time course of the oscillations as recently demonstrated also in the cat (Gray *et al.*, 1992). In fact, when our results are compared with those from the cat after applying the same algorithms to the raw data (Table 1), it is quite clear that in the lightly anesthetized adult cat the oscillations are significantly more regular and of greater duration.

We have used $\tau/T = 1.0$ as level of significance to flag oscillatory events in the LFP. By applying this criterion some jitter in the period of the oscillations is allowed, as reflected in the relatively broad power spectrum of the fitted Gabor functions (Fig. 5, B). Nevertheless, it is possible that the occurrence of oscillatory activity is somehow underestimated in our results, since at lower τ/T ratios a broader spectrum, though clearly within the gamma range, is also likely to occur (Fig. 5, C, rated as non-oscillatory). Synchronization may be achieved by patterns of activity far from being strictly periodic (Engel et *al.*, 1991c). If this is the case in the OT, our analysis quantitative analysis may underestimate the oscillatory activity that permits a binding mechanism.

In this study, most of the recordings were made with the animal awake, with no recordings of eye movements. Pigeons, however, make most often only small saccades (mean horizontal amplitude 2.2 deg, Lemeignan *et al.*, 1992) and therefore responses had quite stable latencies across the trials. Moreover, pigeons, as other birds, typically show a particular type of eye movement that consists in brief cyclotorsional oscillations of a frequency in the 25-30 Hz range that occur concurrently. It was suggested that these eye oscillations could mechanically boost the diffusions from the pecten into the vitreous chamber (Pettigrew et al., 1990), which is particularly relevant since the avian retina has no direct vascular supply. It may considered therefore that image slips caused by these eye oscillations introduced artifacts in our results. We consider this unlikely for several reasons. First, we have demonstrated that the tectal oscillations are clearly stimulus-triggered (Fig. 2); second, spontaneous eye movements containing eye oscillations are relatively rare compared to the repetition rate of our stimuli (14-23 saccades per min, Lemeignan *et al.*, 1992) . Third, the recordings made with the animal paralyzed and lightly anesthetized showed no significant differences in the occurrence of oscillatory episodes if compared to the awake preparation.

Relations between LFP and spike trains

The occurrence of a spike was tightly correlated with the LFP signal. However, the central negative peak in the spike triggered averages persisted in epochs classified as non-oscillatory as well. In other words, the correlation between the LFP and the spike trains was independent of the occurrence of an oscillation. As the LFP expresses the compound electrical changes of a cluster of neurons, this may indicate that larger groups of tectal cells discharge in synchrony also during spontaneous activity.

It has been postulated (Gray and Singer, 1989; Gray *et al.*, 1990b) that the LFP oscillations in the cortex reflect the synchronization of cells within the same cortical column. In fact, the studies in the cat prove that the orientation tuning curves of the MUA responses match those of the LFP, plotted as the relative amplitude of power spectra in the range of 25-65 Hz. It is rather surprising, then, that is more difficult to see an unequivocal oscillation in the MUA than in the corresponding LFP (Gray *at al.*, 1990a). This was particularly striking in our data. Typically, a clear oscillatory pattern seen in the MUA corresponded to a well modulated oscillatory activity in the LFP. In many instances, however, the occurrence of a non-oscillatory MUA was coincident to an oscillatory event of the LFP (14% of the cases, Fig. 10). Similar findings have been reported in other neural structures. In the prepyriform cortex of cats, oscillatory macro potentials were recorded in correspondence to non periodic firings of single cells (Freeman, 1968). In the hippocampus, it has been shown that synchronized cell activity may occur in correspondence to an oscillatory LFP, although the autocorrelation functions of individual spike trains have frequencies different from that of the population (Buzsáki, 1992). An important contribution for the field potential may come from subthreshold synaptic activity (see discussion in Gray *et al.*, 1992). The MUA, then, may reflects only a small subpopulation of cells contributing for the LFP.

In addition, we have observed a clear difference in the distribution of the oscillation frequencies of the LFP in relation to the MUA. The LFP oscillations, analyzed in a trial per trial basis, displayed a bias to low frequencies (mean of 26 Hz) in comparison to the averaged autocorrelograms of the MUA (mean frequency of 35 Hz). A discrepancy in the frequency distributions was seen as well in the cases studied by applying a moving window to both signals. In particular, most of the cases of mismatch as *e.g.* when the MUA autocorrelogram was non-oscillatory the frequencies of the LFP oscillations tended to be relatively low, around 20 Hz (Fig. 10).

Laminar vs. columnar organization

We have observed no dependence of oscillatory responses on the laminar position of the recordings. The OT has a well developed laminar organization, with evidences of some differentiation in functional characteristics of the cells across the layers (Hughes and Pearlman, 1974). Deeper in the tectum, the receptive field size increases, the responses to static stimuli vanish, and the surround inhibitory effect diminishes. On the other hand, neurons from different layers respond to the same range of velocity and are unlikely to be selective for the same direction of movement (Jassik-Gerschenfeld and Hardy, 1984).

Although the retino-tectal projections are topographically organized (Hamdi and Whitteridge, 1954), and the tectum is highly laminated there is no evidence in favor of a columnar organization of the OT. A tangential penetration does not detect any bias in the directional selectivity of the cells. To what extent the tectal intrinsic connections or its reciprocal projections to the nucleus rotundus or the Wulst participate in oscillatory activity is a completely open question. In any case, tectal LFP oscillations described here cannot be understood on the basis of columnarity in the same way as it has been proposed for the visual cortex of the cat (Gray *et al.*, 1990b; Eckhorn *et al.*, 1990). Our contention is, then, that neuronal oscillations may be characteristic of laminated neural structures, not being confined to structures possessing a columnar organization as the mammalian neocortex.

Effects of anesthesia

Oscillatory activities in the visual cortex of the cat were studied mainly using light anesthesia (nitrous oxide supplemented with 0.2-0.5% halothane). In our control experiments, we have used 0.5-1.5% halothane in 70% nitrous oxide. At higher concentration levels of halothane (above 1.0%) the visually evoked oscillations are impaired, although it was possible to record some activity of the cells. The fact that in the anesthetized cat (0.2-0.5% halothane; Gray *et al.*, 1990a) the oscillatory activity is quite robust, and not diminished, remains to be explained by more detailed studies, but they may simply be due to the differences in concentration levels proper to the species being used.

Conclusion

In this study we have been concerned with establishing and quantifying the oscillatory activity present in visual responses in the avian OT. In order to ascertain that this oscillatory activity has a similar functional role in perceptual binding as it has been postulated in mammals, it is imperative to study their synchronizations with multiple electrodes and the dependence of synchronization probability on stimulus configurations as it has been found in cat and monkey visual cortex (Gray *et al.*, 1989; Kreiter *et al.*, 1992). The present results give evidence for local synchronization of a group of neurons. We have already gathered evidence for the synchronization of spatially separated neurons in the avian OT; these results will be reported in a following publication.

Acknowledgements

We are grateful to our colleagues A. K. Engel, P. König (Max-Planck-Institut für Hirnforschung, Frankfurt) and B. Renault and J. Martiniere, (LENA, CNRS, Paris), for the continued support and many discussions. Thanks are also due to W. Singer, Y. Frégnac and V. Bringuier for helpful comments on the manuscript; J. P. Soutterrand for assistance in the mechanical setup, and Renate Ruhl in the preparation of the figures. This research was supported by a grant to FV from the MRT, France; SN was supported by CAPES, Brazil.

Abbreviations

LFP	local field potential
MUA	multi-unit activity
OT	optic tectum
PSTH	peri-stimulus time histogram

References

Abeles, M. (1982) Local Cortical Circuits. Spriger-Verlag, Berlin.

Bilo, D., Gerhard, B., Schönenberger I. and Nachtigall, W. (1972) Zur Methode der Halothan-Inhalationsnarkose bei Vögeln (Taube und Wellensittich). J. comp Physiol. 79: 137-152.

Cerella, J. (1979) Visual classes and natural categories in the pigeon. J. Exp. Psych: Hum Percep Perfor 5: 68-77.

Delius, J. (1985) Cognitive processes in pigeons. In: G. d'Ydewalle, Cognition, Information Processing and Motivation pp. 3-18. Elsevier Science Publishers B. V. (North-Holland).

Delius, J. and Hollard, V. D. (1982) Rotational invariance in visual pattern recognition by pigeons and humans. Science 218: 804-806.

Eckhorn R., Bauer R. , Jordan W., Brosch M, Kruse W., Munk M. and Reitboeck H.J. (1988) Coherent oscillations: a mechanism of feature linking in the visual cortex ? Biol. Cybern. 60 : 121-130.

Eckhorn, R., Reitboeck, H.J., Arndt, M. and Dicke, P. (1990) Feature linking via synchronization among distributed assemblies: simulations of results from cat visual cortex. Neural Comp. 2: 293-307.

Engel, A., König, P., Gray, C. and Singer, W. (1990) Stimulus-dependent neuronal oscillations in cat visual cortex: inter-columnar interaction as determined by cross-correlation analysis. Eur. J. Neurosci. 2: 588-606.

Engel, A., König, P., Kreiter, A., Gray, C. and Singer, W. (1991a) Temporal coding by coherent oscillations as a potential solution to the binding problem: physiological evidence. In: Schuster, and Weinheim, H.G. Nonlinear Dynamics and Neural Networks pp. 3-25, VCH Verlagsgesellschaft.

Engel, A. K., König, P., Kreiter, A. K. and Singer, W. (1991b) Interhemispheric synchronization of oscillatory responses in cat visual cortex. Science 252: 1177-1179.

Engel, A. K., König, P. and Singer, W. (1991c) Direct physiological evidence for scene segmentation by temporal coding. Proc. Natl. Acad. Sci. USA 88: 9136-9140.

Engel, A. K., König, P., Kreiter, A. K., Schillen, T. B. and Singer, W. (1992) Temporal coding in the visual cortex: new vistas on integration in the nervous system. Trends in Neurosci. 5(6):218-226.

Freeman, W. J. (1975) Mass Action in the Nervous System. Academic Press, New York.

Frégnac, Y. (1991) How many cycles make an oscillation? In: Gorea, A., Frégnac, Y., Kapoula, Z. and Finlay, J. Representations of Vision: Trends and Tacit Assumptions, pp. 97-109. Cambridge University Press.

Frost, B. J. and Di Franco, D. E. (1976) Motion characteristics of single units in the pigeon optic tectum. Vision research 16: 1229-1234.

Gray, C. M. and Singer, W. (1987) Stimulus-specific neuronal oscillations in the cat visual cortex: a cortical functional unit. Soc Neurosci. Abstr. 13: 404.3.

Gray, C. M. and Singer, W. (1989) Stimulus-specific neuronal oscillations in orientation columns of cat visual cortex. Proc. Natl. Acad. Sci. USA 86: 1689-1702.

Gray, C. M., König, P., Engel, A.K. and Singer, W. (1989) Oscillatory responses in cat visual cortex exhibit inter-columnar synchronization which reflects global stimulus properties. Nature 338:334-337.

Gray, C. M., König, P., Engel, A.K. and Singer, W. (1990a) Stimulus-dependent neuronal oscillations in cat cortex: receptive field properties and feature dependence. Eur. J. Neurosci. 2: 607-619.

Gray, C. M., König, P., Engel, A.K. and Singer, W. (1990b). Temporal properties of synchronous oscillatory neuronal interactions in cat striate cortex. In: Schuster, and Weinheim, H.G. Nonlinear Dynamics and Neural Networks, VCH Verlagsgesellschaft.

Gray, C. M., Engel, A.K., König, P. and Singer, W. (1992) Synchronization of oscillatory neuronal response in cat striate cortex: temporal properties. Visual Neurosci, 8:337-347.

Hamdi, F.A. and Whitteridge, D. (1954) The representation of the retina on the optic tectum of the pigeon. Quart. J. Exp. Physiol., 39, 111-119.

Hardy, O. and Jassik-Gerschenfeld, D. (1979) Spatial frequency and temporal frequency selectivity of single cells in the pigeon optic tectum. Vision Res. 19: 1001-1004.

Holden, A. L. (1971) The laminar organization of the pigeon optic tectum. J. Physiol. (London), 214: 44-45.

Hughes, C. P. and Pearlman, A. L. (1974) Single unit receptive fields and the cellular layers of the optic tectum. Brain Res. 80: 365-377.

Jarvis, C. D. (1974) Visual discrimination and spatial localization deficits after lesions of the tecto-fugal pathways in pigeons. Brain Behav. Evol. 9: 195-228.

Jassik-Gerschenfeld, D., Minois, F. and Condé-Courtine, F. (1970) Receptive fields properties of directionally selective units in the pigeon's optic tectum. Brain Res 24: 407-421.

Jassik-Gerschenfeld, D. and Hardy, O. (1984) The avian optic tectum: neurophysiology and behavioral correlations. In: Vanegas, H. Comparative Neurology of the Optic Tectum pp. 649-685. Plenum Publishing Corporation.

Kreiter, A. K. and Singer, W. (1992) Oscillatory neuronal responses in the visual cortex of the awake macaque monkey. Eur. J. Neurosci. 4: 369-375.

Kreiter, A.K., Engel, A.K. and Singer, W. (1992) Stimulus dependent synchronization in the caudal superior temporal sulcus of macaque monkeys. Soc. Neurosci. Abstracts, submitted.

Lemeignan, M., Sansonetti, A. and Gioanni, H. (1992) Spontaneous saccades under different visual conditions in the pigeon. NeuroReport 3: 17-20.

Livingstone, M. S. (1991) Visually-evoked oscillations in monkey striate cortex. Soc. Neurosci. Abstr. 17: 73.3.

Murthy, V. N. and Fetz, E. E. (1991) Synchronized 25-35 Hz oscillations in sensorimotor cortex of awake monkeys. Soc. Neurosci. Abstr. 17: 126.11.

Neuenschwander, S. and Varela, F. J. (1990) Sensory-triggered oscillatory activity in the avian tectum. Soc. Neurosci. Abstr. 16: 47.6.

Neuenschwander, S. and Varela, F. J. (1992) A quantitative study of oscillatory activity in the optic tectum of the awake pigeon. Eur. Neurosci. Assoc. Abstr. (submitted).

Palm, G. (1982) Neural Assemblies, an alternative approach to artificial intelligence. Springer-Verlag, Berlin.

Pettigrew, J., Wallman, J. and Wildsoet, C. F. (1990) Saccadic oscillations facilitate ocular perfusion from the avian pecten. Nature (343): 362-363.

Press, W. H., Flannery, B. P.m Teukolsky, S. A. and Vetterling, W. T. (1986) Numerical recipes. Cambridge Univ. Press, Cambridge.

Raether, A., Gray, C. M. and Singer, W. (1989) Intercolumnar interaction of oscillatory neuronal responses in the visual cortex of alert cats. Eur. J. Neurosci. Suppl. 2: 72.5.

Singer, W. (1990) Search for coherence: a basic principle of cortical self-organization. Concepts in Neurosci. 1(1):1-26.

Varela, F.J., Palacios, A. and Thompson, E. (1992) Ways of colouring. Behav. and Brain. Sci. 15(1):1-74.

von der Malsburg, C. (1983) How are nervous structures organized? In: Basar E., Flohr H., Hahen H., Mandell AJ. Synergetics of the Brain pp. 238-249. Springer, Berlin.

von der Malsburg, C. and Schneider, W. (1986) A neural cocktail-party processor. Biol. Cybern. 54: 29-40.

Legends

Table 1 Comparison between the LFP oscillatory activity in the avian OT and in the cat visual cortex. The same moving window method was applied to the LFP in both cases (we are grateful to A. Engel and P. König, Max-Planck-Institut für Hirnforschung, Frankfurt, for kindly providing the raw data of the cat).

Fig. 1 LFP and MUA traces recorded simultaneously in response to a light bar stimulus. The lower traces display at an expanded time scale the epoch delimited by the box in the upper traces. Tectal neurons show a burst firing behavior as seen in the lower traces, firing 1-4 spikes at cycles around 30 msec. The LFP and the cell activity are tightly related as bursting activities covary evenly with the negative-going phase of the LFP.

Fig. 2 LFP traces recorded in 10 successive trials from a single electrode. The signal was bandpass filtered at 10-80 Hz. The stimulus consisted in a moving light bar crossing the receptive field in one direction and in the opposite direction after a 400 msec delay. In most of the responses evoked by the stimulus a clear oscillatory pattern is seen. Upper box shows the peri-stimulus time histogram of the recorded multi-unit activity.

Fig. 3 Compressed arrays of LFP power spectra (A) and autocorrelation function (B) in a single trial. In both analysis a 512 msec window was moved at steps of 200 msec on the LFP signal, and the amplitudes were normalized to the maxima. In the autocorrelation function array the x-axis expresses time lag. The observed peak in the distribution of frequencies for the forward movement of the stimulus (34 Hz) coincides with the 29 msec period of the autocorrelation function. For the backward movement of the stimulus there was no leading frequency, and this is reflected in an attenuated autocorrelation function. Frequency resolution: 2.5 Hz.

Fig. 4 Cumulative power spectra of LFP in 10 sweeps in a recording from the awake animal. The thick line plot corresponds to the epoch of response to the forward movement of the stimulus and the thin line to the spontaneous activity before and between responses. The analysis window was of 300 msec in both cases. Frequency resolution: 3.3 Hz.

Fig. 5 Illustration of the criteria used to quantify the oscillatory episodes of the LFP. Examples of autocorrelation functions of the LFP and their respective fitted Gabor functions (thick line), computed within a 200 msec window, are shown to the left. The autocorrelation functions calculated for the spontaneous activity are depicted as dotted lines. At right, the respective power spectra computed for the signal and for the fitted Gabor function (thick line) are shown. The arrows mark the Gabor function frequencies (as indicated in the right corner of the autocorrelation boxes). The two criteria used for rating the oscillatory modulation of the LFP autocorrelation functions, the τ/T and ratio A_{stim}/A_{spont} ratios, are displayed at the left. The windows A and B were classified as oscillatory; in contrast, the window C was rated as non-oscillatory, since its τ/T ratio was below 1.0. For details see text. Frequency resolution of power spectra: 5 Hz.

Fig. 6 Significant oscillatory events in function of time for the LFP in a set of trials. (A) The steps in the graph depict the epochs in which at least one window (200 msec) was flagged as oscillatory (for the criteria of significance, see Methods). Notice the increase in the probability of occurrence of an oscillation in correspondence to the timing of the stimulus. The oscillation probability was estimated by first dividing the epoch of response in units of 100 msec and then computing those qualified as oscillatory. The epoch of response was defined on basis of the MUA response distribution (PSTH shown in B). (C) Distribution of frequencies of the fitted Gabor function for all the windows that succeeded to score. Mean frequency: 25 ±8 Hz.

Fig. 7 Variability in the oscillatory responses. (A) Spike trains plotted at high temporal resolution. (B) Autocorrelation functions computed for each trial within a 400 msec as in the spike rasters. Observe the considerable variation in the oscillatory responses in each trial, as much in the frequencies as in the decay of the oscillatory modulation. (C) The autocorrelograms calculated for each trial were summed up. The result is a much more attenuated autocorrelogram, what reveals the importance of variability in the oscillatory events. (D) Shuffled correlogram.

Fig. 8 Spike triggered average of the LFP. The average distribution of the LFP voltage was computed within a ± 50 msec window centered on the occurrence of each spike, and normalized by the trial mean. (A) Average calculated only for the epoch of response to the forward movement of the stimulus, as indicated by the box on the LFP and MUA traces. (B) Average calculated for the whole trial. The average of the LFP that was oscillatory for the selected epoch is much attenuated in the whole trial analysis.

Fig. 9 Comparison between the oscillations of the LFP and of the MUA. Three pairs of autocorrelation functions of both the LFP and the MUA, within the same analysis window, are presented in rows (A, B, C). The autocorrelations of the LFP (left, left column) and their fitted Gabor functions (thick lines) are shown, and also the power spectra of the signal (left, right column), calculated within the same window. The corresponding MUA autocorrelation functions and their fitted Gabor functions are shown to the right (left column), and also the power spectra of the MUA autocorrelograms (right, right column). Conventions and symbols as in Fig. 5. The autocorrelation functions in A exemplify the cases in which the frequencies of both the LFP and the MUA oscillatory episodes were matched. The autocorrelation functions in B and C give examples of an apparent mismatch; the period of the fitted Gabor functions are largely unequal, although the power spectra peaks are comparable. Analysis window in all correlograms: 200 msec. Frequency resolution of power spectra: 5 Hz.

Fig. 10 Plot of the frequencies of LFP oscillations versus the frequencies of MUA. The cases of matched and mismatched frequencies are denoted with filled and unfilled symbols respectively. The crossed symbols (Ø) were considered ambiguous, since although there was a difference in the frequencies of the fitted Gabor functions, the power spectra of the two signals displayed corresponding peaks. The dots denotes the cases in which the MUA autocorrelogram contained only a few spikes or none. The examples shown in the Fig. 9 are indicated by the letters A, B and C.

Fig. 11 Halothane anesthesia effects on the modulation of the oscillatory activity. (A) Histogram of MUA responses for the forward and backward movement of the stimulus after recovering from the anesthesia. (B) Ratio decay/period (τ/T) of the fitted Gabor functions cumulated in 10 trials (window: 200 msec, moving step: 100 msec), with 1.5% halothane anesthesia (thin line) and after recovering from the anesthesia (thick line), at the same recording site. Notice that the profiles of the MUA response histogram and of the cumulative τ/T ratio plot are similar. (C) Averaged power spectra calculated during the anesthesia (shaded line), and after recovery, for both the epoch without the stimulus (thin line) and for the epoch when the stimulus was present (thick line).

	pigeon (n=39)	cat (n=11)
average duration	210 msec	425 msec
frequency variability	26 ± 8 Hz	46 ± 5 Hz
τ/T	1.5 ± 0.4	2.7 ± 0.9
probability of occurrence	10 %	45 %

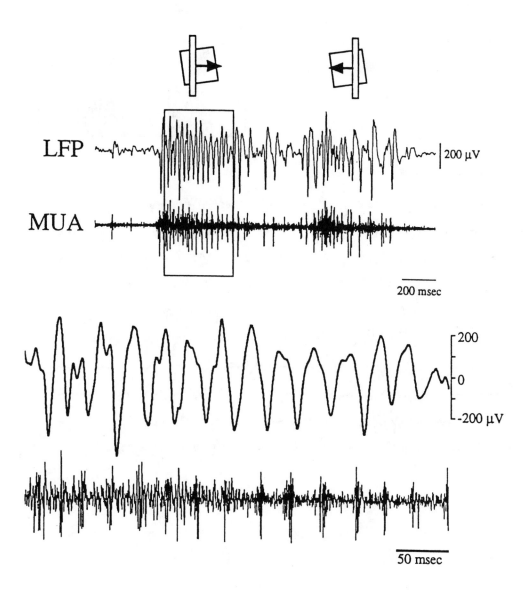

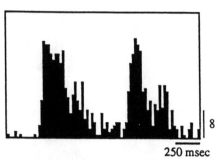

LFP

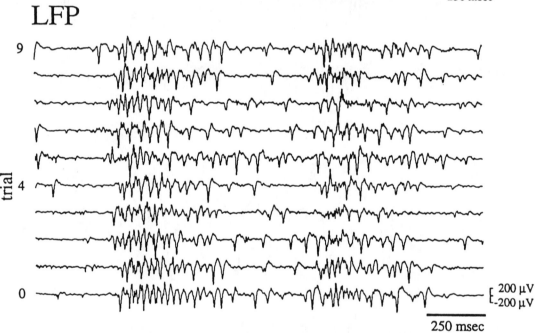

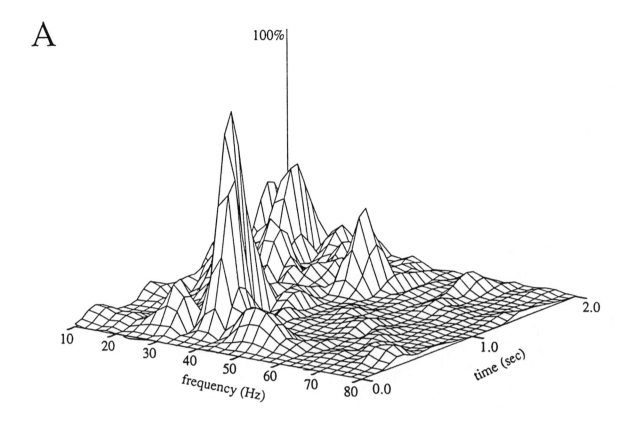

A

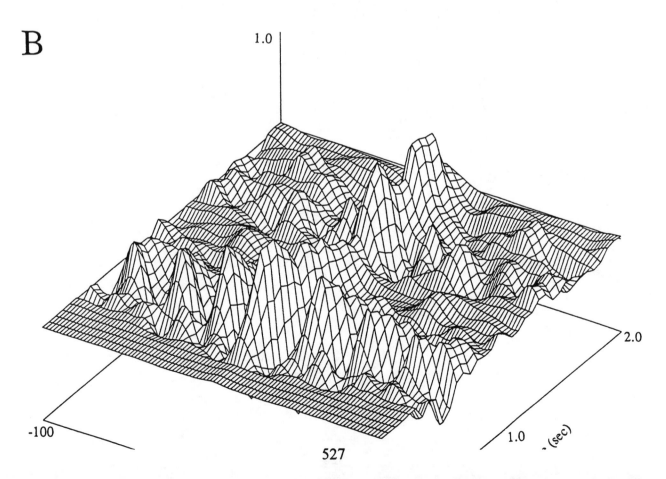

B

527

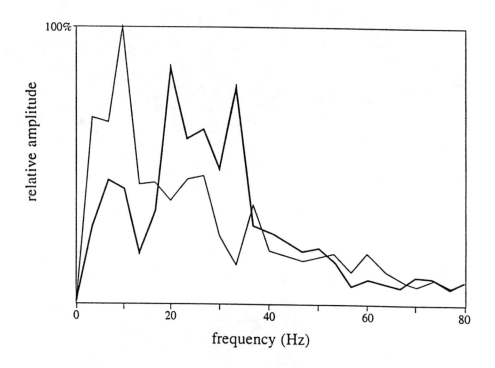

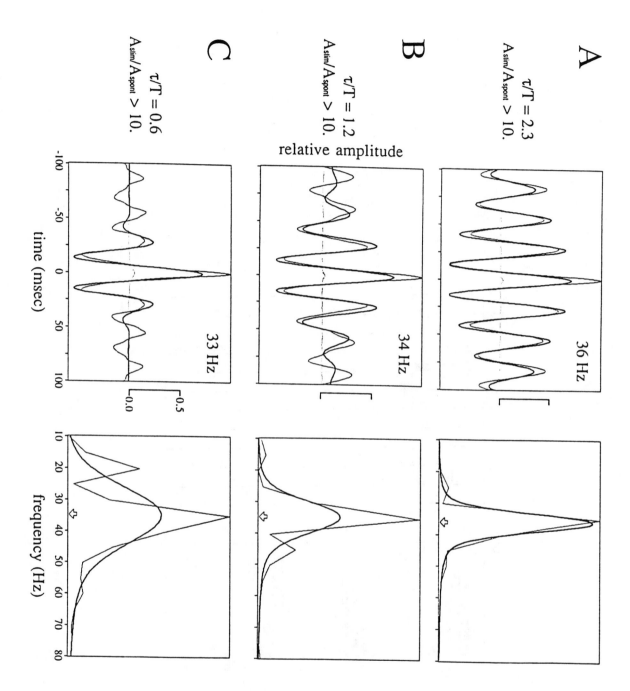

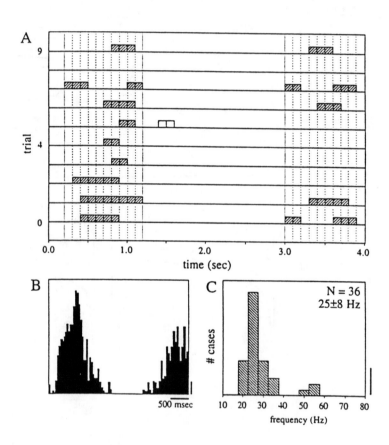

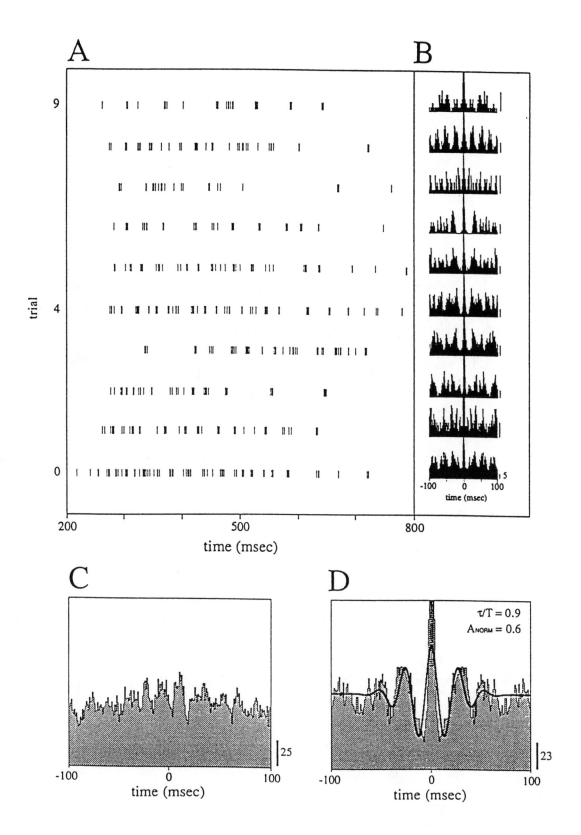

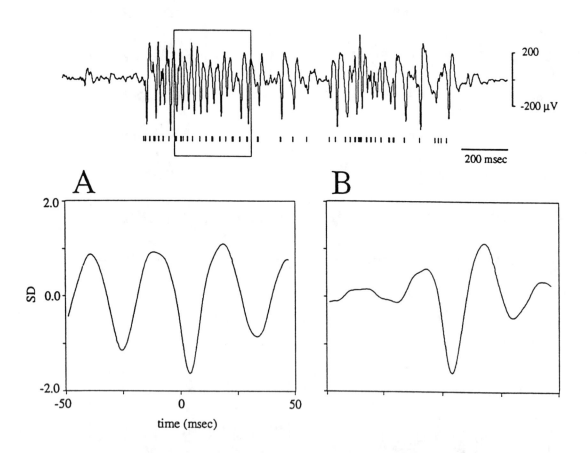

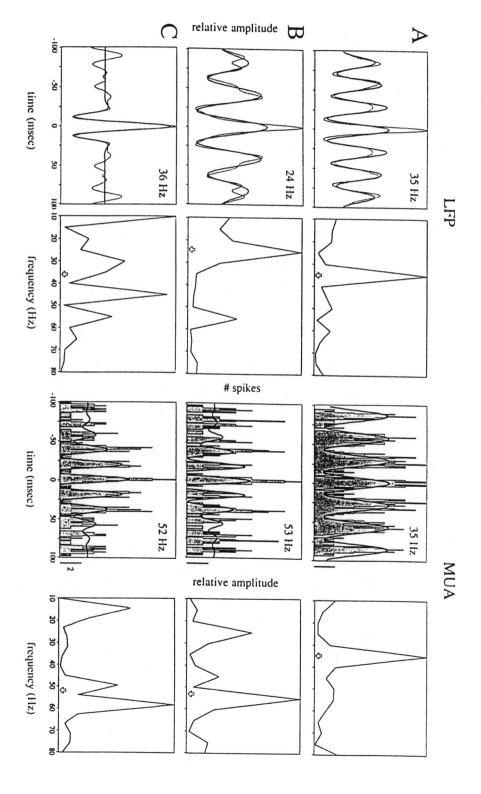

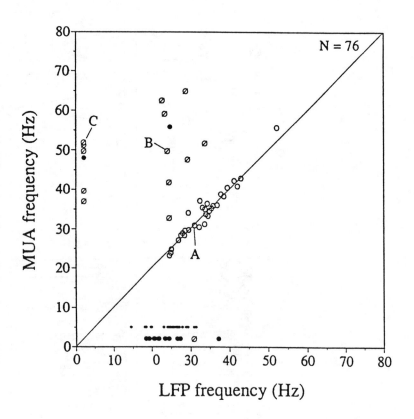

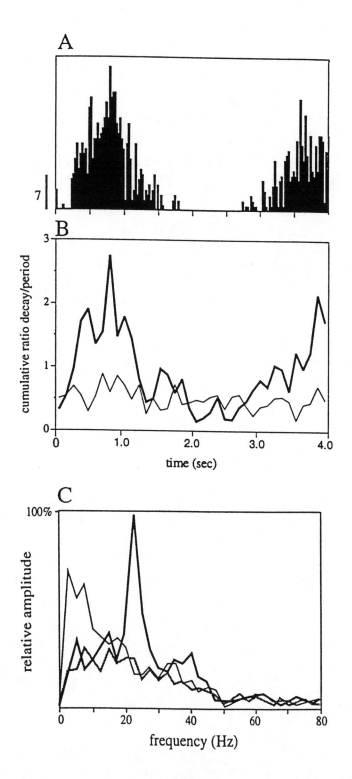

Chapter 22

Dynamic Self-Organization in the Brain as Observed by Transient Cortical Coherence

Steven Bressler

Dynamic Self-Organization in the Brain
as Observed by Transient Cortical Coherence

Steven L. Bressler
Center for Complex Systems
Florida Atlantic University
500 N.W. 20th Street
Boca Raton, FL 33431

The cerebral cortex is a structurally complex system, having a vast number of elementary units, even if consideration is restricted just to its neurons. Besides the huge number of elements is the extreme density of the interconnections among them. Each cortical neuron receives synaptic contacts from, and projects to, thousands of others. Cortical neurons are connected over a range of spatial scales from microns to tens of centimeters, and are likewise organized into groupings at multiple hierarchical levels, from microcolumns to global systems. Many cortical neurons are also embedded in long-range loops involving subcortical structures. Structural order is achieved within this complexity by cooperative processes at work in the brain. These processes, which are self-organizing, operate at every spatial scale, and include such phenomena as the development of cytoarchitectonic regions and the establishment of topographic maps [1].

Self-organization in the brain occurs on multiple time scales as well as spatial scales. In addition to the relatively slow developmental processes, there is evidence that the brain self-organizes during behavior on a faster, fraction-of-a-second time scale corresponding to higher cortical functions such as perception and motor control [2-5]. Since self-organization at this scale manifests patterns of cortical activity that metamorphose from moment to moment, it may be called "dynamic" self-organization. These patterns appear only transiently, making them difficult to observe unless specific steps are taken to capture them. Here, I will use the findings from a recent study of behaving macaque monkeys [2] to demonstrate a procedure for characterizing certain aspects of the dynamics of self-organization in cortical function.

CORTICAL CORRELATION

The presence of large-scale order in a system suggests that statistically reproducible relations, or correlations, should exist between activity in distant parts of the system [6]. However, correlations may only exist when the system is in particular states. In the case of the cerebral cortex, a structural basis for the establishment of correlations between widespread cortical locations exists both directly through the interconnection of many distant parts [7], and indirectly through subcortical structures [8]. Of all the correlations that are anatomically possible, though, only a limited subset may exist during any particular functional state. Furthermore, as brain systems undergo self-organization during behavior, each change of state may bring with it a corresponding change in the configuration of correlated cortical sites. Since the brain states corresponding to higher cortical functions are fleeting, to track this changing configuration requires that correlations be measured in brief intervals of time.

The question of how cortical correlation is manifested is one that is actively being explored by the neuroscience community. There has recently been a growing realization of the importance of temporal relations, and particularly in the crucial role played by temporal correlation, or synchronization [9-12]. Synchronization can be observed by measuring the similarity of temporal activity patterns, or cross-correlation, between different cortical sites. Since both neuronal pulse discharges and local field potentials (LFPs) can index the functional state of the cortex at a given site by their temporal pattern, synchronization between cortical sites has been studied by cross-correlation both of pulses [13-15] and LFPs [16-19]. The cross-correlation function is an adequate measure of the joint activity at two sites being tested when there are strong periodicities in common. However, it cannot be assumed in general that cortical synchronization will necessarily occur by way of periodic signals. Broad-band synchronization, involving correlation between two essentially aperiodic signals (i.e. containing a range of frequencies), is a distinct possibility. Cross-spectral techniques provide a general method for evaluating multi-frequency synchronization. In the work presented here, the coherence spectrum, which is the normalized cross-spectrum of two time series [20], is used for measuring synchronization of LFPs over a range of frequencies.

SPATIAL SAMPLING

Obviously, recording pulses or LFPs from a single site is insufficient to measure synchronization. Minimally, activity from a pair of sites must be recorded. As the number of recording sites is increased, spatial sampling improves, and the spatial patterning of large-scale cortical correlation can be better characterized. In the present study, LFPs were recorded simultaneously from up to 15 sites in one hemisphere of macaque monkeys (Figure 1). At each site the transcortical field potential was localized by differential recording with a surface-to-depth bipolar electrode. Common contributions to the two electrode tips were reduced by more that 10,000 times, thus eliminating fields propagated from a distance. The precision of localization was demonstrated in LFP averages which showed visual receptive field specificity in striate and prestriate regions but not in others. The LFPs were amplified (-6 dB at 10 and 100 Hz, 6 dB/octave falloff), digitized at 200 samples/sec, and stored as 12-bit words.

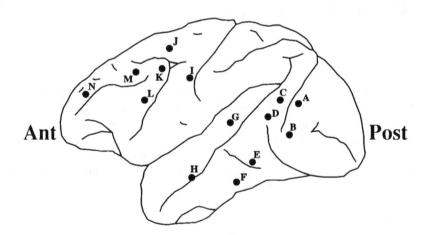

Figure 1: Map of Left Hemisphere of Monkey TI Showing Positions of Recording Sites.

BEHAVIORAL CONDITIONING

Characterization of dynamic self-organization during high-level cortical processing requires that subjects repeatedly perform a task that engages cortical functions of interest. Visuomotor function was studied by training macaque monkeys to perform a visual pattern discrimination task with a GO/NO-GO response paradigm. Experiments were performed by Dr. Richard Nakamura at the Laboratory of Neuropsychology of the National Institute of Mental Health. Experimental details have previously been reported [2].

The monkey initiated each trial by holding down a lever with the preferred hand (contralateral to the implanted hemisphere). Visual stimuli were presented for 100 msec beginning approximately 115 msec after the start of data collection. The stimulus set consisted of four diagonal patterns, each formed by four dots. Two dots were at opposite corners of an outer square, and two dots at opposite corners of a concentric inner square. Right- and left-slanted diagonal lines were formed when the outer and inner dots were slanted in the same direction, diagonal diamonds when they were slanted in opposite directions. No single dot could be used to discriminate between lines and diamonds.

On GO trials, the monkey responded to one pattern type (line or diamond) by lifting his hand from the lever before 500 msec after stimulus onset. If this was performed correctly, a water reward was provided at 500 msec. On NO-GO trials, when the other pattern type was presented, the monkey was required to keep the lever down for 500 msec. The analysis period extended from approximately 115 msec before stimulus onset until 500 msec after the stimulus onset, when the reward was delivered in the GO condition and the monkey was free to release the lever in the NO-GO condition. GO and NO-GO trials were randomly presented with equal probability in 1000-trial sessions lasting approximately 35 minutes. The intertrial interval was randomly varied between 0.5 and 1.25 seconds. Six sessions, two from each of three monkeys, have thus far been analyzed. Results from monkey TI are presented here.

TEMPORAL PATTERNS OF CORTICAL COHERENCE

Coherence spectra (Figure 2) were computed for every pairwise combination of sites in each of a series of 80-msec computation intervals which moved point by point (i.e. in 5 msec steps) across the analysis period. Thus, as the computation interval slid across the analysis period, coherence time-series were created for each frequency bin in the spectrum. In this way, the change in coherence with time could be observed for each frequency bin. The frequency resolution, inversely proportional to the length of the computation interval, was 12.5 Hz. Coherence time-series were computed for every pairwise combination of recording sites in GO and NO-GO conditions. All GO or NO-GO trials from a session were used to estimate each site pair's coherence. For statistical evaluation, the Fisher z-transform was first applied to the bounded coherence distribution to produce an approximately normal one. The 95% confidence limit for the mean coherence was computed over all site pairs from both conditions in the analysis period. Coherence values which exceeded that limit were considered significant.

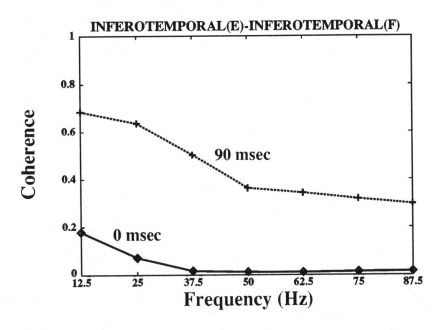

Figure 2: Coherence Spectra Computed Between Two Inferotemporal Cortical Sites (E and F in Figure 1) in Two 80-msec-wide Computation Intervals Centered at the Time of Stimulus Onset (0 msec) and 90 Msec Later in the GO Condition.

Multiple episodes of elevated coherence, lasting on the order of 50-100 msec and involving the entire range of observable frequencies, followed the stimulus. In monkey TI, coherence was significantly above baseline at some time during the analysis period in one or more frequency bins for 93% of the site pairs, and in all bins for 56%. In an illustrative session, with 500 GO and 488 NO-GO trials, recordings were made from 14 sites in TI, yielding 91 site pairs. Figure 3 shows the time-series of coherence between the two inferotemporal cortical sites (E and F in Figure 1). Following the stimulus are a series of episodes of elevated coherence, with peaks from 80 to 165 msec, that are significantly above baseline. The temporal patterns are similar, but not identical, for the GO (left) and NO-GO (right) conditions. The change in coherence generally follows the same pattern for all frequency bins. The spectra from Figure 2 appear as two time points (0 and 90 msec) in the GO time-series.

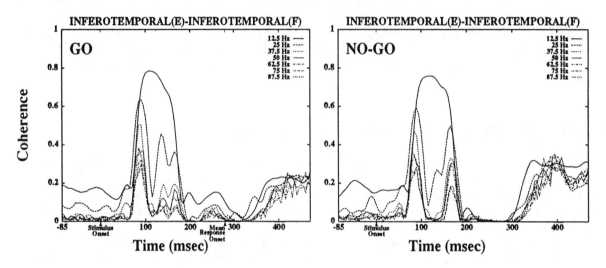

Figure 3: Coherence Time-Series of Two Inferotemporal Sites for the GO (Left) and NO-GO (Right) Conditions. Traces of the 7 Frequency Bins are Superimposed.

In Figure 4 we see the coherence relation between one of the inferotemporal cortical sites (E) from Figure 3 and a striate cortical site (B). Again, coherence largely follows the same pattern for all frequency bins, but there are differences between the two site pairs in the number, latency, duration, and size of the episodes. Thus, although a cortical site may be coherent with more than one other site, the temporal pattern of the change in coherence may be different for different site pairs.

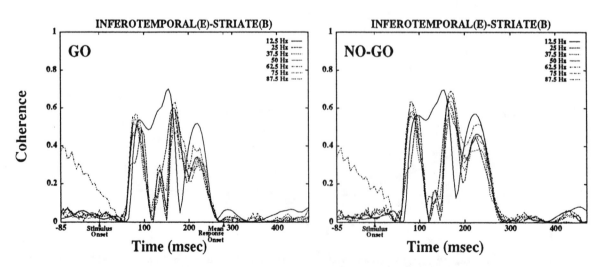

Figure 4: Coherence Time-Series of Inferotemporal Site E and Striate Site B.

Elevated coherence develops not only between sites within the posterior cortical areas, but also between widespread cortical sites. As illustrated in Figure 5, significant post-stimulus coherence develops between inferotemporal site E and a site in frontal cortex (J). This pair shows yet another temporal coherence pattern. Also, the difference between conditions is significant, with the maximum between-condition difference occurring approximately 50 msec before the mean response onset in the GO condition.

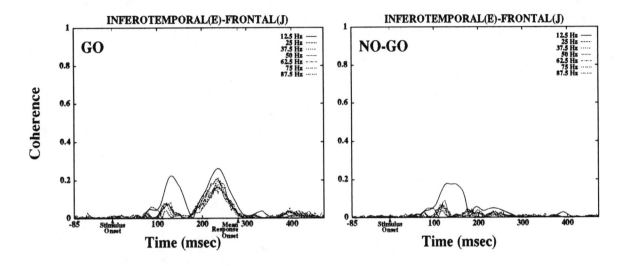

Figure 5: Coherence Time-Series of Inferotemporal Site E and Frontal Site J.

Other site pairs did not develop significant coherence, or only developed minimally significant coherence. For example, Figure 6 shows the coherence time-series between striate cortical site B and a site in the superotemporal cortex (G), in which coherence does not reach significance following the stimulus in either condition. This demonstrates that, although coherence develops between widespread cortical sites, it is nonetheless spatially specific, and does not involve all locations.

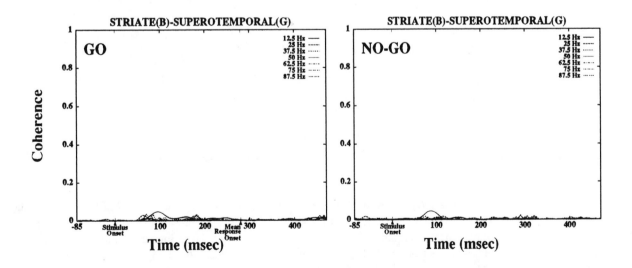

Figure 6: Coherence Time-Series of Striate Site B and Superotemporal Site G.

SPATIAL PATTERNS OF CORTICAL COHERENCE

In the preceding section, we saw that task-related, broad-band cortical coherence develops in transient episodes between sites in the same and different cortical areas, even when those areas are widely separated. That coherence between these sites emerges at specific times with respect to task events indicates that the coherence represents functional correlation. Although coherence is widespread, it is spatially selective. Thus, widely distributed sites become coherent without involving other intervening sites.

Consider now the constellation of cortical sites which are functionally correlated at any given time. For the collection of sampled sites, this constellation may be characterized by the spatial pattern of significant coherence. Following a procedure established in earlier studies [3-5], coherence is displayed on maps (e.g. Figure 1) in the form of lines connecting pairs of electrode sites that show significant coherence, with line width corresponding to the magnitude of coherence. In Figure 7, patterns of significant coherence are displayed in this manner for TI in the GO condition. Coherence was computed in 80-msec-wide intervals centered at four different times, and significance was determined with p < 0.001. Since the coherence at all observable frequencies generally rose and fell together, patterns for only one frequency bin, 50 Hz, are presented as an example.

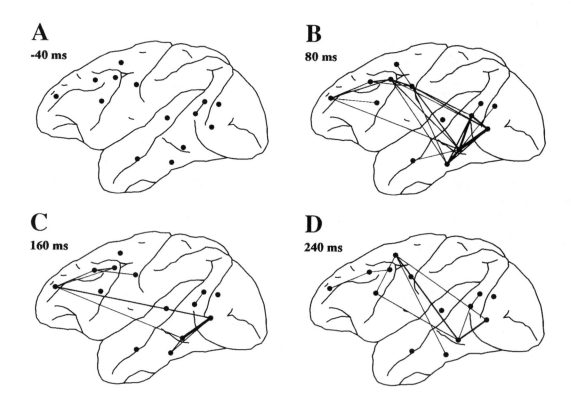

Figure 7: Spatial Patterns of Coherence (with Significance of P < 0.001) in the GO condition for the 50-Hz Frequency Bin.

Prior to the stimulus onset (7A), there is only one line having low coherence, indicating that appreciable widespread coherence does not exist among these electrode sites before stimulus presentation. This map represents the baseline state. At 80 msec post-stimulus (7B), corresponding to the first large increase in coherence seen in Figures 3 and 4, coherence is observed among multiple sites in striate, prestriate, inferotemporal, and frontal cortices. This pattern is marked by particularly strong coherences among striate, prestriate, and inferotemporal sites, i.e. visual areas. There are also prominent coherences among frontal sites, and between frontal and visual sites. Again, at 160 msec (7C), there are strong coherences among visual sites, among frontal sites, and between visual and frontal sites. However, the pattern has shifted its focus from that at 80 msec. For example, whereas frontal site K is involved with several visual sites at 80 msec, only frontal site N remains involved with visual sites at 160 msec. By 240 msec (7D), the pattern has again shifted, and frontal sites J and L are involved with visual sites. In summary, dynamic self-organization in the brain during execution of this visuomotor pattern discrimination task may be characterized by patterns of significant between-sites coherence, which change on a fraction-of-a-second basis.

DYNAMIC SELF-ORGANIZATION AND CORTICAL INFORMATION PROCESSING

These results do not afford an exact description of the spatial patterning of task-related coherence in the cortex in terms of the functionality of the participating sites. However, they are suggestive of a general functional scheme for cortical information processing at the systems level. Every cognitive task may be considered as a complex set of micro-steps, each with its own processing contingencies [21]. The cerebral cortex may then be viewed as a self-organizing network of high dimensionality which processes these cognitive micro-steps. The wide range of possible processing requirements mandates the need for a flexible system that is capable of spontaneous and rapid reorganization. The processing demands of each micro-step may be viewed as imposing a unique set of constraints on the system, restricting it to a particular network configuration, and thereby reducing its degrees of freedom.

If integration of the participating network nodes occurs by temporal correlation, then the spatial pattern of coherence among cortical sites may represent the particular network configuration imposed by the immediate processing contingencies. The changing spatial pattern of coherence may then reflect the underlying change in network configuration that corresponds to the evolution of the cognitive micro-steps necessary for task execution.

One way to test these ideas would be with more specific task manipulations and more functionally localized electrode placements. Thus, for example, electrodes could be placed in visual areas that are functionally identified as corresponding to particular aspects of visual function. e.g. color, shape, or movement. Then, tasks which specifically manipulate a given visual dimension would be expected to engage processing networks selectively involving the sites corresponding to that dimension. As another example, a recently identified area in frontal cortex that specifically subserves feature identification, and another that subserves spatial localization [22], would be expected to selectively participate in processing networks when tasks differentially require one or the other function.

It has been shown elsewhere [2] that transient elevated cortical coherence is indicative of intermittent synchronization in single-trial LFP waveforms, and it has been suggested that synchronization may be a neural mechanism for cortical binding. Binding has been proposed by Damasio [23] as a general mechanism for the integration of processing components in distributed cortical regions during perception, recall, and behavior. According to Damasio, posterior cortical areas require communication with anterior areas in order to "guide the pattern of multiregional activations necessary to reconstitute an event". The spatial patterns of coherence in Figure 7 are certainly consistent with this view. In this framework, then, dynamic self-organization in the brain, reflected in spatial patterns of transient cortical coherence, may actually represent a fundamental neurocognitive operation that gives each individual a coherent sense of reality.

Acknowledgments

Supported by NIMH grants MH43370 to the EEG Systems Laboratory, San Francisco, and MH42900 to the Center for Complex Systems.

References

[1] M. P. Stryker et al., "Principles of cortical self-organization", in *Neurobiology of Neocortex*, P. Rakic and W. Singer (Eds.), New York: Wiley, 1988, pp. 115-136.

[2] S. L. Bressler, R. Coppola, and R. Nakamura, "Episodic multi-regional cortical coherence at multiple frequencies during visual task performance by the macaque monkey", *Nature*, In press.

[3] A. S. Gevins and S. L. Bressler, "Functional topography of the human brain", in *Functional Brain Imaging*, G. Pfurtscheller and F. Lopes da Silva (Eds.), Bern: Hans Huber, 1988, pp. 99-116.

[4] A. S. Gevins, S. L. Bressler, N. H. Morgan, B. A. Cutillo, R. M. White, D. Greer, and J. Illes, "Event-related covariances during a bimanual visuomotor task. I. Methods and analysis of stimulus- and response-locked data", *Electroencephalography and Clinical Neurophysiology*, vol. 74, pp. 58-75, 1989.

[5] A. S. Gevins, B. A. Cutillo, S. L. Bressler, N. H. Morgan, R. M. White, J. Illes, and D. Greer, "Event-related covariances during a bimanual visuomotor task. II. Preparation and feedback", *Electroencephalography and Clinical Neurophysiology*, vol. 74, pp. 147-160, 1989.

[6] G. Nicolis and I. Prigogine, *Exploring Complexity: An Introduction*, New York: W. H. Freeman, 1989, ch. 1, p. 13.

[7] D. J. Felleman and D. C. Van Essen, "Distributed hierarchical processing in the primate cerebral cortex", *Cerebral Cortex*, vol. 1, pp. 1-47, 1991.

[8] P. Goldman-Rakic, "Topography of cognition: parallel distributed networks in primate association cortex", *Annual Review of Neuroscience*, vol. 11, pp. 137-156, 1988.

[9] J. G. Taylor, "Temporal processing in brain activity", in *Neural Network Dynamics*, J. Taylor, E. Caianiello, R. Cotterill and J Clark (Eds.), Berlin: Springer-Verlag, 1992, pp. 258-290.

[10] A. K. Engel, P. Konig, A. K. Kreiter, T. B. Schillen, and W. Singer, "Temporal coding in the visual cortex: new vistas on integration in the nervous system", *Trends in Neurosciences*, vol. 15, pp. 218-226, 1992.

[11] J. Kruger and J. D. Becker, "Recognizing the visual stimulus from neuronal discharges", *Trends in Neurosciences*, vol. 14, pp. 282-286, 1991.

[12] J. E. Cook, "Correlated activity in the CNS: a role on every timescale?", *Trends in Neurosciences*, vol. 14, pp. 397-401, 1991.

[13] E. Vaadia, E. Ahissar, H. Bergman, and Y. Lavner, "Correlated activity of neurons: a neural code for higher brain functions?", in *Neuronal Cooperativity*, J. Kruger (Ed.), Berlin: Springer-Verlag, 1991, pp. 249-279.

[14] A. Aertsen and G. Gerstein, "Evaluation of neuronal connectivity: sensitivity of cross-correlation", *Brain Research*, vol. 340, pp. 341-354, 1985.

[15] K. Toyama, "Functional connections of the visual cortex studied by cross-correlation techniques", in *Neurobiology of Neocortex*, P. Rakic and W. Singer (Eds.), New York: Wiley, 1988, pp. 203-217.

[16] V. N. Dumenko, "Electroencephalographic investigation of cortical relationships in dogs during formation of a conditioned reflex stereotype", in *Electrophysiology of the Central Nervous System*, V. Rusinov (Ed.), New York: Plenum, 1970, pp. 107-117.

[17] T. M. Efremova and V. D. Trush, "Power spectra of cortical electric activity in the rabbit in relation to conditioned reflexes", *Acta Neurobiologiae Experimentalis*, vol. 33, pp. 743-755, 1973.

[18] R. Eckhorn, R. Bauer, W. Jordan, M. Brosch, W. Kruse, M. Munk, and H. J. Reitboeck, "Coherent oscillations: a mechanism of feature linking in the visual cortex?", *Biological Cybernetics*, vol. 60, pp. 121-130, 1988.

[19] C. M. Gray, A. K. Engel, P. Konig, and W. Singer, "Synchronization of oscillatory neuronal responses in cat striate cortex: temporal properties", *Visual Neuroscience*, vol. 8, pp. 337-347, 1992.

[20] E. M. Glaser, and D. S. Ruchkin, *Principles of Neurobiological Signal Analysis*, New York: Academic, 1976, pp. 174-176.

[21] D. E. Rumelhart, G. E. Hinton, and J. L. McClelland, "A general framework for parallel distributed processing", in *Parallel Distributed Processing*, D. Rumelhart and J. McClelland (Eds.), Cambridge: MIT, 1986, pp. 45-76.

[22] F. A. Wilson, S. P. Ó Scalaidhe, and P. S. Goldman-Rakic, "Dissociation of object and spatial processing domains in primate prefrontal cortex", *Science*, vol. 260, pp. 1955-1958, 1993.

[23] A. R. Damasio, "The brain binds entities and events by multiregional activation from convergence zones", *Neural Computation*, vol. 1, pp. 123-132, 1989.

Chapter 23

**The Application of Katchalsky Network Models to
Radar Pattern Classification**

Harry R. Erwin

The Application of Katchalsky Network Models to Radar Pattern Classification

Harry R. Erwin
TRW GISD

Abstract:

Yong Yao's and Walter Freeman's KII and KIII models of the olfactory system (Yao and Freeman, 1990; Yao, Freeman, Burke, and Yang, 1991; Freeman, 1992) describe neural network architectures based on the olfactory system that use chaotic dynamics to perform rapid feature-classification and novelty-detection. Engineering application of these KI, KII, and KIII ('Katchalsky'[1]) networks has been slowed by a number of issues:

- Extension of the published results to practical problems has been difficult due to the limited background of most computer engineers in the neurophysiology of olfaction.
- Training methods for these networks remain poorly understood.
- Lack of invariance in biological Katchalsky networks makes data encoding for engineering applications unclear.

This paper describes the lessons learned in investigating a KIII Katchalsky network for an aircraft radar application.

Background

One area where the rapid pattern/feature-classification and novelty-detection seen in Katchalsky networks would be of great value is sensor signal processing for collision avoidance. Currently, the capacity of air and ground traffic control systems is limited by the skill of individual human controllers at managing movement in a complex environment. Since it takes about 500 milliseconds for a human controller to become consciously aware of an emergency and another 250-500 milliseconds to react, the vehicle spacings built into these systems must allow for a delayed initial reaction to an emergency. This requirement—often violated to some degree in practice—establishes a fundamental limit on road and airway capacity. Automation could improve traffic flow by providing more precise control over relative position and more rapid response to emergencies, but rapid identification and classification of vehicles is required, a non-trivial problem in real environments. This paper provides the qualitative background for a better understanding of the pattern-classification performance of Katchalsky networks. A quantitative assessment of their performance in realistic situations is a current goal of this research.

Biological Networks

The fundamental difference between an artificial neural network and a biological network lies in their computational model of the neuron. A neuron in an artificial network is usually modeled as a synchronous, time-stepped device—at each step, a collection of synaptic inputs is collected and transformed linearly, the resulting dynamics are allowed to settle, and a non-linear transformation of the net dendritic output is produced. Synaptic inputs in artificial networks can be positive or negative scalars, neurons are undifferentiated, and between-layer neuronal connectivity is extensive. A biological neuron, on the other hand, generates a frequency modulated signal that reports non-linearly on the current level of activation of its dendritic arbor. Synapses and neurons in biological networks specialize in function, connectivity is much more sparse and structured,

Acknowledgements: This research was funded by the TRW Systems Integration Group. The simulation used was based on code provided by Joseph Nardelli and Dr. Thomas J. McAvoy of the University of Maryland at College Park. My thanks to Walter Freeman, Leslie Kay, Neil W. Rickert, and James Scheppan for their comments.

Requests for reprints should be addressed to Harry R. Erwin, TRW GISD, P.O. Box 10400, Fairfax, VA 22031. The author can be contacted at herwin@gmu.edu or (703)734-6189.

[1]Named for A. Katchalsky, who originally identified the analogy between diffusion-coupled reactions and mass action in neuronal systems. See Freeman (1975) for background information on Katchalsky networks.

and locally there are within-layer connections. These differences allow biological networks to have more robust dynamics than artificial networks, with spatially distributed data signals often modulating a cyclic or chaotic carrier signal to identify the object of interest.

Chaotic dynamics in neural networks were first predicted in 1983 by Bernardo Huberman (*Physical Review* A28, 1204). More recently, Walter Freeman identified chaotic processing dynamics in the olfactory bulb of rabbits (see his 1991 paper in *Scientific American*, and his 1993 paper). These results are intriguing since a chaotic process can be efficient at exploring a search space and can converge exponentially fast to a terminal state once a pattern is identified.

Freeman's Work from an Engineer's Perspective

Some specifics on the biology of olfaction: The ensemble of sensory neurons can identify between 1000 and 10000 different odors, with most sensory cells sensitive to multiple odors. These feed into the olfactory processing system, which shows distributed activity—the 'gamma' wave with neurons synchronized in large numbers—that appears to reflect priming of the system to detect specific odors. With each breath, the system goes unstable (a state transition) and chaotically evolves to a conclusion as to the known or already learned odors present in the afferent (input) signal. The resulting efferent (output) data are distributed to the cortical systems in parallel. When an unknown odor is detected, a reafferent (feedback) signal sensitizes the system, which reverses habituation to the current environment and allows the new odor to be learned and associated with information provided by other senses.

The olfactory processing system consists of the sensory neurons, the olfactory bulb (OB), the anterior olfactory nucleus (AON), and the pyriform cortex (PC). The axons of the sensory neurons synapse in glomeruli in the OB, where they connect directly and indirectly with excitatory mitral and tufted cells. These are densely interconnected by excitatory synapses and connect with inhibitory granule cells by reciprocal dendrodentritic synapses[2]. The OB appears to function as a content addressable memory (CoAM) array, with groups of mitral/tufted cells competing to respond to the patterns of sensory data input. The fundamental dynamics of the OB are nonlinear and periodic, with the mitral/tufted cells outputting to pyramidal cells in the AON and PC. The OB output to the AON appears to preserve neighborhoods, while the output to the PC is thoroughly mixed (spatially integrated). The AON and PC are structured similarly to the OB, with densely interconnected networks of excitatory and inhibitory cells interacting nonlinearly to produce periodic outputs. The AON feeds back to the glomeruli and granule cells in the OB, and forward to the PC. The deepest layer of the PC is the primary interface to the rest of the brain.

Freeman has found that the activation patterns in the nucleus of the olfactory bulb are not invariant functions of the sensory stimuli, but instead appear to reflect the *meaning* of the stimuli. There is also a similar lack of invariance in the storage of mental images of past experience, with changes in stimulus or expectation changing the spatial pattern of activation. This suggests (in engineering terms) that the cortex loads the olfactory system (in real time) with a meaningful (semantic) representation of the environment, which is then the basis for reports back to the cortex classifying external events. This biological system provides a conceptual design for an intelligent system for stimulus identification and classification based on limited sensor data.

Chaos and Pattern Classification

Although automatic pattern-classification algorithms have been effective in a number of well-defined applications, the heterogeneous pattern-classification problem remains extremely difficult. Pattern-classification using a chaotic process is a possible solution to this problem. There are a number of reasons for this, including:

---

[2]See Hayashi, et al., 1992, for an interesting result on the mechanism of these synapses.

—Speed of search: In a chaotic dissipative system, the largest Lyapunov exponent is positive. This implies that the process diverges and converges exponentially, and in particular, can quickly leave a previously identified attractor in response to a stimulus. Conservative chaotic systems do not have this property, and non-chaotic dissipative processes tend to converge to stable low-energy limit cycles and fixed points characteristic of the process rather than of the pattern.

—Search coverage: Dissipative processes provide better coverage of a state space than conservative processes since they are not restricted to a submanifold of constant energy. This increases the volume investigated during the search process.

—Optimality: Effective search strategies must involve some combination of local and global search processes. The local search process should be a hill-climbing algorithm that searches for and finds local optima. The global search process then moves between local searches to avoid being trapped into a poor local optimum. Kauffman (1993) provides the following insight into such search processes[3]:

- The global search process should generate some "long-jump mutations" with a mean distance in character space beyond the correlation distance. Global search is initially very efficient, however as the best candidate found so far improves, the time needed to find a better candidate grows exponentially.
- Local search uses smaller search steps (less than the correlation distance) so that a hill-climbing algorithm can be used to locate the local optimum.
- An appropriate mix of global and local search steps and search termination criteria should be chosen so that the system is neither frozen on a poor local optimum nor floating in pattern space with no convergence. Fractal dynamics provide one mechanism for gaining this mix of search processes.

Since chaotic processes can be designed to meet these requirements, these considerations have led to our investigation of them as efficient tools for classification.

The Model System

The following figure illustrates the system model under study (with the 'nose' end to the left):

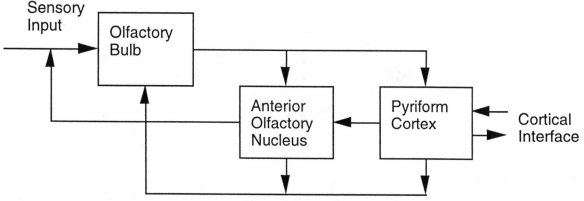

Figure 1, Model System Architecture

This system consists of three content-addressable memory (CoAM) units, corresponding to the olfactory bulb (OB), anterior olfactory nucleus (AON), and pyriform cortex (PC), and connected by arrays of delay lines. This is a modified version of the KIII model studied by Yao and Freeman. The primary differences are that the AON and PC CoAMs are not lumped and instead contain multiple (N-channel) column models, and the delay lines between CoAMs and the deep

---

[3]Note Kaufmann's "edge of chaos" concept is of unclear validity here.

pyramidal (C) cells at the cortical interface are also multiple (N-channel). This multiplicity has been introduced to allow training mechanisms to be studied in more detail.

According to Freeman (personal communications, 1993-94), the OB and PC are trainable *in vivo*—their excitatory elements are linked by modifiable connections into groups corresponding to the patterns potentially classified by the system, while the AON is not trainable. This training involves a combination of Hebbian and non-Hebbian learning. After a novel stimulus, the biological system automatically carries out habituation or association. Finally, it would be desirable if the model system were able to respond in turn to two consecutive known stimuli without returning to a null state.

Hebbian learning includes short- and long-term potentiation (discussed in Bliss and Collingwood, 1993), while non-Hebbian learning involves short- and long-term habituation and sensitization. Learning in the OB appears to be controlled by signals transmitted by the AON and originating in the PC and deeper cortices, with the subnetworks associated with 'interesting' features in the OB 'painted' by a reafferent excitatory signal that triggers potentiation if the detecting network is restimulated. Detecting networks in the OB for features 'not of interest' become habituated[4] and the linking synapses cease signaling. Sensitization and arousal, involving norepinephrine interneurons (McGaugh, 1991; Aston-Jones, et al, 1991; Aston-Jones, Chiang, and Alexinsky, 1991; and Aston-Jones, Rajkowski, Kubiak, and Alexinsky, 1994), will reverse this habituation if a feature later becomes 'interesting.'

Modeling the Content-Addressable Memories (CoAMs)

The three CoAMs consist of arrays of standard KII modules (Freeman, 1975). In the OB model, for example, the two excitatory elements (above and to the left in Figure 2) correspond to tufted/mitral cell populations, and the two inhibitory elements (below and to the right in the figure) correspond to granule cell populations. These interact non-linearly to produce oscillations in the activation levels of the individual elements. The KII modules making up each CoAM are interconnected by their front and back units to compete in response to incoming signals. Each KII module also connects with other CoAM arrays through delay lines resulting in relatively chaotic activation levels.

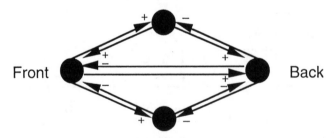

Figure 2, KII Module Structure

CoAM Interconnections

The OB, AON, and PC are interconnected by a system of delay lines (see Figure 1, above). The OB interfaces to the excitatory elements of both the AON and the PC; the AON interfaces to the inhibitory elements of the OB and provides what appear to be synthetic sensory signals to the excitatory elements of the OB; and the PC interfaces to the inhibitory elements of the AON (identifying patterns for detection), the OB (signaling the taking of a breath), and to deeper cor-

---

[4]Short term habituation appears to reflect depletion of transmitter vesicles in the presynaptic active zone of excitatory synapses (Bailey, 1991). The retrograde tranmitters associated with potentiation (see Barinaga, 1992, for a discussion of recent results) appear to facilitate movement of vesicles into the active zone, hence preventing habituation during conditioning.

tices (both efferent and reafferent signals). The simulation work reported here is unrealistic for the PC, since signals from the OB to the PC are not mixed (spatially integrated), but otherwise corresponds to the biology.

Sensory Data Preprocessing

The results reported here apply to a model of the olfactory processing system, which receives positionally and orientationally invariant sensory signals. Sensory data for the visual and auditory systems are not positionally and orientationally invariant and must be preprocessed into independent distance, orientation, and pattern channels before being presented to a pattern recognition network. Research into wavelet transform theory (cf. Simoncelli, et al., *IEEE Trans Inf Theory*, **38**, #2, Part II) indicates that this is not in general feasible—changes in orientation and position necessarily result in changes in the pattern signal. What can be done is a separation of the signal into independent components of fixed signal power, but pattern processing still requires hints about orientation and distance. This is an area under investigation.

Search Strategies

The search strategy used by the model system appears to involve three levels of exploration:
- The lowest level reflects the competition between groups of modules to classify a pattern. This corresponds to a hill-climbing process. If a feature is recognized, the portion of the system that recognized the feature drops into a near-limit cycle and terminates search.
- The second level involves the chaotic perturbation of the sensory input by the AON. This is an example of stochastic resonance (see Carroll and Pecora, 1993) and continues as long as the OB fails to recognize the sensory input pattern.
- The third level is mediated by the cortex, which designates patterns to the olfactory system for comparison to the sensory data. This is under investigation.

Engineering Results

The simulation experiments produced some extremely interesting results. The dynamic relationships between the various elements in the CoAMs are nominally chaotic (See Figure 3 for example); however, if the simulated olfactory bulb (OB) has been initialized to classify a specific pattern occurring in the afferent signal, elements corresponding to the pattern can become synchronized, with the other elements remaining in chaotic relationships. Figure 4 illustrates the synchronization observed when a pattern is recognized, and Figure 5 illustrates the pattern seen when the pattern is ambiguous. The ambiguity of this last figure implies the inherent dimensionality of the OB must be much greater than the number of input sensory channels, so that individual features can be represented by independent groups of modules. Studies are underway to help in understanding this better.

The coupled OB and AON form a modified Hebb-Marr (HM) autoassociative system (See McNaughton and Smolensky, 1991). The inhibitory divide signal in the standard H-M system is replaced here by a combination of normalized input signal (by the periglomular neurons) and non-linear thresholds applied to the output of the OB. Stochastic resonance involving chaotic signals generated by the interaction of the OB, AON, and PC appears to be involved in avoiding local energy minima (See Carroll and Pecora, 1993, for a discussion of the application of chaos to stochastic resonance). These signals also appear to be involved in allowing the system to simultaneously classify multiple independent features, since they support reporting in parallel.

The PC may be a component of a similar system processing the output of the OB+AON for a second layer of pattern classification. Note that in standard H-M autoassociators, ambiguous and unknown signals go to zero, while this system is more robust, converging either to a nearby known pattern or to a chaotic signal that denotes an unknown pattern.

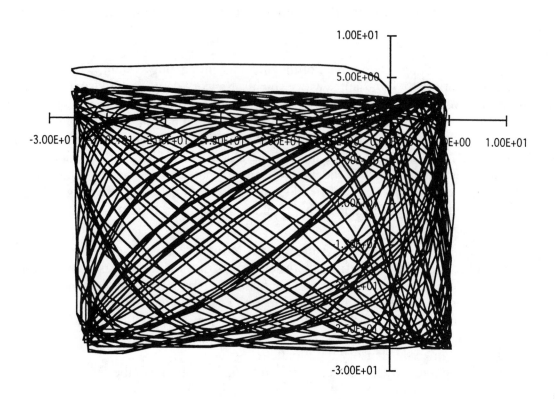

Figure 3, Activation Relationships for Unknown Data

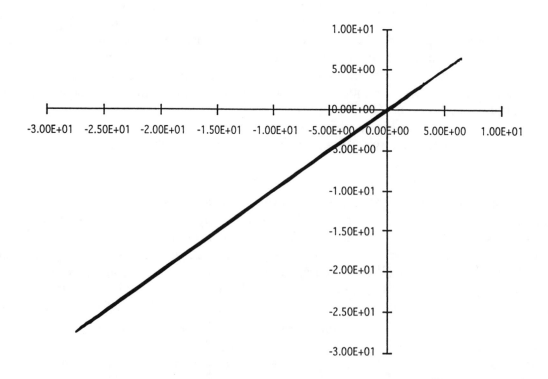

Figure 4, Activation Relationships for Unambiguous Data

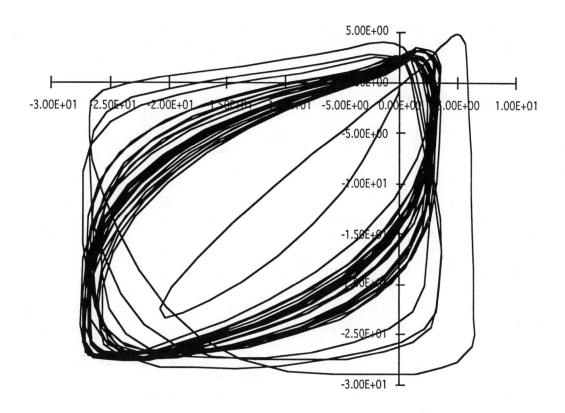

Figure 5, Activation Relationships for Ambiguous Data

Conclusions

1. If semantics correspond to patterns or features, it appears they can be carried by spatial synchronizations between element activations. Objects (and semantic concepts) can then be recognized when distributed activations become correlated. Individual pulse trains would carry no semantics—it is when multiple pulse trains have the same "carrier wave" that semantics appear. This relates to Bressler, Coppola, and Nakamura's recent (1993) result.

2. Raw sensory data from the olfactory receptors must be forwarded to the deeper cortices in some form to permit higher direction of pattern classification. Those data should probably be invariant and encoded in some simple manner.

3. The olfactory system appears to be an early processing point that serves to classify patterns of sensory stimuli for immediate action. One possible way to implement this architecture would be to pass the sensory data through to the deeper cortices as invariant signals, while superimposing in-band signaling (by synchronizing the pattern of specific components of the sensory data) when the sensory pattern is known. Lack of invariance would be specifically associated with this semantic signalling. Note this interpretation does not fit the biological data but does provide a potential engineering model.

4. This model suggests mechanisms for data processing in the cortex that are consistent with Barry Richmond's results (see Richmond, et al., 1993).

5. Further study is required to understand how the olfactory system is trained. The data provided by Simmons (1990) and Spence, et al. (1989, 1990) concerning bat and owl echolocation suggest that heuristic tuning can be very accurate in biological systems that are critical to the survival of the animal.

References

- Aston-Jones, G., et al., "Afferent regulation of locus cœruleus neurons: anatomy, physiology, and pharmacology," ch. 4 in *Progress in Brain Research,* Barnes, C. D., and Pompeiano, O., ed., Elsevier, 1991.
- Aston-Jones, G., Chiang, C., and Alexinsky, T., "Discharge of noradrenergic locus cœruleus neurons in behaving rats and monkeys suggests a role in vigilance," ch. 35 in *Progress in Brain Research,* Barnes, C. D., and Pompeiano, O., ed., Elsevier, 1991.
- Aston-Jones, G., Rajkowski, J., Kubiak, P., and Alexinsky, T., "Locus cœruleus neurons in monkey are selectively activated by attended cues in a vigilance task," *J. Neuroscience,* in press (1994).
- Bailey, C., "Morphological Basis of Short- and Long-Term Memory in *Aplysia,*" in *Perspectives on Cognitive Neuroscience*, Lister, R. G., and Weingartner, H., J., ed., Oxford, 1991.
- Barinaga, M., "New Accomplices in Cell Death," *Science,* 262:1211-1212, 19 November 1993, reporting on presentations by Sakire Pogun and Michael Kuhar, and Andrea Volterra, at the 1993 Society for Neuroscience meeting, with additional comments by Jeff Rothstein.
- Bliss and Collingridge, "A synaptic model of memory: long-term potentiation in the hippocampus," *Nature,* 361:31-39, 7 January 1993.
- Bressler, S. L., Coppola, R., and Nakamura, R., "Episodic multiregional cortical coherence at multiple frequencies during visual task performance," *Nature,* 366:153-156, 11 November 1993.
- Carroll, T. L., and Pecora, L. M., "Stochastic Resonance and Crises," *Physical Review Letters*, volume 70, number 5, pages 576-579, 1 February 1993.
- Freeman, W., *Mass Action in the Nervous System,* Academic Press, 1975.
- Freeman, W., "The Physiology of Perception," *Scientific American*, 264:78-85, February 1991.
- Freeman, W., "Neural Networks and Chaos," *INNS Above Threshold*, Fall 1992, 8-10.
- Freeman, W., "The Emergence of Chaotic Dynamics as a Basis for Comprehending Intentionality in Experimental Subjects," ch. 16 in *Rethinking Neural Networks: Quantum Fields and Biological Data*, Pribram, K., (ed.), INNS Press, LEA, 1993. Papers presented at the First Appalachian Conference on Behavioral Neurodynamics, September 1992.
- Hayashi, T., et al., "Role of a metabotrophic glutamate receptor in synaptic modulation in the accessory olfactory bulb," *Nature,* 366:687-690, 16 December 1993.
- Kauffman, S. A., *The Origins of Order,* Oxford, 1993.
- McNaughton, B. L., and Smolensky, P., "Connectionist and Neural Modeling: Converging in the Hippocampus," in *Perspectives on Cognitive Neuroscience*, Lister, R. G., and Weingartner, H., J., ed., Oxford, 1991.
- McGaugh, J. L., "Neuromodulation and the Storage of Information: Involvement of the Amygdaloid Complex," in *Perspectives on Cognitive Neuroscience*, Lister, R. G., and Weingartner, H., J., ed., Oxford, 1991.
- Richmond, B. J., Gawne, T. J., Kjaer, T. W., and Hertz, J. A., "Neuronal Encoding of Information Related to Visual Perception, Memory and Motivation," ch. 14 in *Rethinking Neural Networks: Quantum Fields and Biological Data*, Pribram, K., (ed.), INNS Press, LEA, 1993. Papers presented at the First Appalachian Conference on Behavioral Neurodynamics, September 1992.
- Simmons, J. A., 1990, "Acoustic-Imaging Computations by Echolocating Bats: Unification of Diversely-Represented Stimulus Features into Whole Images," pp. 2-9 in *Advances in neural information processing systems 2 (NIPS 2)*, Touretzky, David S., ed., Morgan Kaufmann, 1990.

- Spence, C. D., Pearson, J. C., Gelfand, J. J., Peterson, R. M., and Sullivan, W. E., "Neuronal Maps for Sensory-Motor Control in the Barn Owl," pp. 366-374 in *Advances in neural information processing systems 1 (NIPS 1)*, Touretzky, David S., ed., Morgan Kaufmann, 1989.
- Spence, C. D., "The Computation of Sound Source Elevation in the Barn Owl," pp. 10-17 in *Advances in neural information processing systems 2 (NIPS 2)*, Touretzky, David S., ed., Morgan Kaufmann, 1990.
- Yao and Freeman, "Model of Biological Pattern Recognition with Spatially Chaotic Dynamics," Neural Networks, **3:**153-170, 1990.
- Yao, Freeman, Burke, and Yang, "Pattern Recognition by a Distributed Neural Network: An Industrial Application," Neural Networks, **4:**103-121, 1991.

Chapter 24

Spectral Density Maps of Receptive Fields in the Rat's Somatosensory Cortex

Joseph King, Min Xie, Bibo Zheng, Karl Pribram

Spectral Density Maps of Receptive Fields

in the

Rat's Somatosensory Cortex

Joseph King, Min Xie, Bibo Zheng and Karl Pribram

Center for Brain Research and Informational Sciences
and Department of Psychology

Radford University, Radford, VA 24142

Abstract

To extend findings from visual neurophysiology we plotted responses for 48 locations in the somatosensory "barrel cortex" of the rat to spatial and temporal frequency stimulation of their vibrissae. The recordings obtained from bursts of spikes were plotted as response manifolds resembling field potentials such as those recorded with small macroelectrodes. The burst manifolds were shown to be composed of those obtained from single spikes, demonstrating continuity between two levels of analysis (single spikes and bursts).

A computer simulation of our results showed that, according to the principles of signal processing, the somatosensoty receptive fields can be readily described by Gabor-like functions much as in the visual system. Further, changes with respect to direction of whisker stimulation could be described in terms of spatiotemporal (vectorial?) shifts among these functions.

As late as the 1950's, the structure of memory storage and the brain processes leading to perception remained enigmatic. Thus Karl Lashley (1950) could exclaim that his lifelong search for an encoded memory trace had been in vain, and Gary Boring (1929) could indicate in his *History of Experimental Psychology* that little was to be gained, at this stage of knowledge, by psychologists studying brain function.

All this was dramatically changed when engineers, in the early 1960's, found ways to produce optical holograms using the mathematical formulation proposed by Dennis Gabor (1948). The mathematics of holography and physical properties of holograms provided a palpable instantiation of distributed memory and how percepts (images) could be retrieved from such a distributed store. Engineers, (e.g. Van Heerden, 1963) psychophysicists, (e.g. Julez and Pennington, 1965); and neuroscientists, (e.g. Pribram, 1966; and Pollen, Lee and Taylor, 1971) saw the relevance of holography to the hitherto intractable issues of brain function in memory and perception (Barrett, 1969; Campbell & Robson, 1968; and Pribram, Nuwer and Barron, 1974).

However, this early promise failed, for a variety of reasons, to take hold in the scientific community. The fact that neurophysiologically the holographic spread function is limited to single, albeit overlapping, receptive fields (patches) was not recognized by psychophysicists who, therefore, spent considerable energy in disproving globally conceived distributed functions. However, engineers, e.g. Bracewell (see review, 1969), soon showed that such patch holography could and did produce correlated three-dimensional images when inverse transformed, a technique that became the basis of optical image processing in tomography. The application of this principle to the receptive field structure (Robson 1975) overcame the psychophysical problem.

Further, it was unclear just how the principles involved in holography related to ordinary measures of brain physiology. For instance, the brain waves recorded with scalp electrodes are too slow to carry the required amount of information. Also, there seemed to be little evidence that the quadrature relation basic to performing a Fourier holographic transform could be found in the receptive field properties of the cerebral cortex. Finally, there was considerable confusion regarding just what needed to be encoded to provide a neural holographic process. These objections have, to a large measure, been met. The nanocircuitry of neural microtubles provides an adequately high frequency wave form for microprocessing in synaptodendritic receptive fields (e.g. Hammeroff, 1987). Quadriture has been shown in receptive fields within columns of the visual cortex (Pollen and Ronner, 1980). And, encoding of coefficients of intersections among waves, not of waves per se, was shown critical to the process (Pribram, 1991).

Despite this evidence, Churchland (1986), reflecting the received opinion of the neuroscience community, noted that: "the brain is like a hologram inasmuch as information appears to be distributed over a collection of neurons. However, beyond that, the holographic idea did not really manage to explain storage and retrieval phenomena. Although significant effort went into developing the analogy (see, for example, Longuet-Higgins, 1966) it did not flower into a creditable account of the processes in virtue of which data are stored, retrieved, forgotten, and so forth. Nor does the mathematics of the hologram appear to unlock the door to the mathematics of neural ensembles. The metaphor did, nonetheless, inspire research in parallel modelling of brain function" (pp. 407-408). In the same vein, Arbib (1969) states: " . . . we note that the Cambridge school of psychophysics (see Campbell, 1974 for an early review of their work) has psychophysical data showing that the visual cortex has cells that respond not so much to edges as to bars of a particular width or gratings of a certain spatial frequency. The cells of the visual cortex tuned for spatial frequency can be seen as falling into different channels depending on their spatial tuning. This might seem to support the contention that the brain extracts a spatial Fourier transform of the visual image, and then uses this for holographic storage or for position-independent recognition (Pribram, 1971). However, there is no evidence that the neural system has either the fine discrimination of spatial frequencies or the preservation of spatial phase information for such Fourier transformations to be computed with sufficient accuracy to be useful" (p. 134-135).

This view has also made its way into the popular literature on the subject. For example, Crick (1994) states "This analogy between the brain and a hologram has often been enthusiastically embraced by those who know rather little about either subject. It is almost certainly unrewarding, for two reasons. A detailed methematical analysis has shown that neural networks and holograms are mathematically distinct. More to the point, although neural networks are built from units that have some resemblance to real neurons, there is no trace in the brain of the apparatus or processes required for holograms." (p185).

That such statements can be made in view of so much evidence to the contrary -- see, for example, the volumes by Devalois and Devalois (1988) and by Pribram (1991) -- shows that something basic is at odds between the received view and those who have provided the evidence for the alternate view. We believe that the failure of holographic principles to take hold in neurophysiology is due to what is held to be the cerebral processing medium: ensembles of neurons or overlapping (receptive) fields of synaptodendritic arborizations. The distinction is a subtle one and concerns the level or scale at which processing is conceived to take place. Ensembles of neurons operating as systems (the current nomenclature is "modules"), communicating via axons, indeed have an important role to play: for instance, in information retrieval as indicated by localized clinical disabilities. Nonetheles, within modules, processing relies on distributed architectures such as those used in neural network simulations. It is our contention that, at this level of processing, the ensembles consist, not of neurons, but of patches of synaptodendritic networks.

What is needed is a method for mapping the activity of the overlapping synaptodendritic receptive fields in such a way as to convince the scientific community that something like a holographic process is indeed operating at the synaptodendritic level. Kuffler (1953), provided us with a major breakthrough when he showed that he could map patches of the dendritic field of a retinal ganglion cell by recording from its axon in the optic nerve. Kuffler's is a simple technique for making receptive field maps, which is now standard in neurophysiology. By stimulating a receptor or a set of receptors in a variety of dimensions and using the density of unit responses recorded from axons, a map of the functional organizarion of the synaptodentritic receptive field of that axon can be obtained. (See e.g. reviews by Bekesy, 1967 and Connor and Johnson, 1992 for somesthesis; and by Enroth-Kugel and Robson, 1966; and Rodiek and Stone, 1965 for vision).

Experiments by Barlow (1986) and by Gilbert and Wiesel, (1990) have shown that sensory stimulation beyond the reach of a particular neuron's receptive field can, under certain conditions, change that neuron's axonal response. Synaptodendritic patches are thus subject to changes produced in a more extended field of potentials occuring in neighboring synaptodendritic fields.

What is seldom recognized is that the Kuffler technique maps relations among local field potentials occurring in such extended overlapping dendritic arbors. The axon(s) from which the records are being made, sample a limited patch of this extended domain of overlapping receptive fields. Recently, Varella (1993) called attention to this relationship by demonstrating the correlation between burst activity recorded from an axon and the local field potentials generated in the synaptodendritic receptive field of that axon.

The current study also aims to explore the relations among local field potentials by mapping receptive field organization using the Kuffler technique. The specific questions posed and answered in the affirmative are 1) whether this technique can map the spectral properties of synaptodendritic receptive field potentials, and 2) whether such maps of receptive fields in the somatosensory cortex show properties of patch (quantum) holography (that is, of Gabor elementary functions) similar to those recorded from the visual cortex.

Methods and Results

The rat somatosensory system was chosen for convenience and because the relation between whisker stimulation and central neural pathways has been extensively studied (see review by Gustafson and Felbain-Keramidas, 1977). Whiskers were stimulated by a set of rotating cylinders, each grooved with equally spaced steps, the step width and adjacent grooves subtending equal angles. Three cylinders were used with their steps measuring 30 deg., 15 deg., and 7.5 deg., respectively. The cylinders were rotated at 8 different speeds, varying from 22.5 deg./sec. to 360 deg./sec. (The rotating cylinders were meant to mimic the drifting of gratings across the retinal receptors in vision.)

In most of our experiments an entire array of whiskers was subjected to contact with the rotating cylinders. This was done in order to bring the results of these somatosensory experiments into register with those performed in the visual system where an entire array of receptors is stimulated by the drifting grating.

Electrodes were teflon-coated stainless steel (Hare) ranging from 1-3 megohms impedance. Recordings were made from 48 locations using 23 different rats weighing 250-300 grams. Surgery was performed under pentobarbital anesthesia (50 mg/kg body weight, intra-peritoneally) supplemented with 0.05 cc atropine sulfate to inhibit excess respiratory tract accumulation of fluid. The rat was placed in a stereotaxic headholder (Kopf), and using a Zeiss surgical microscope, a small .25cm^2 round opening was made in the skull approximately 4 mm posterior and 4-5 mm lateral to bregma. An electrode was lowered slowly through the opening by means of a hydraulic micromanipulator until good responses were recorded, usually at a depth of 600-700 micra.

Records of raw data were obtained by means of an FET cathode follower which matched the impedance of the microelectrode to the input impedance of a Grass Model P5 preamplifier. The recorded signal was band limited between 300 and 3000 Hz and amplified with a gain of 20,000. One hundred seconds of continuous voltages were sampled at a rate of 32 KHZ and stored by a BRAINWAVE system onto a pc-486 computer. The raw data were then transferred for processing on a Silicon Graphics workstation. Approximately 1/3 to 1/2 gigabytes of data representing both single spikes and bursts of spikes were recorded during approximately one hour at each cortical location (Figures 1a-d).

Our data include both single spikes and bursts of spikes. When single spikes were used, their origin from a single neuron was assumed by a sorting procedure using template matching (based upon spike amplitude and recovery slope). More often we used bursts of spikes, especially during whisker stimulation (Figures 1a and c). The reason for this is that our records show a great deal of superposition of spikes during such bursts (Figures 1b and d). Also, the number of bursts increases dramatically during stimulation. On the average, during a 100 second record, the baseline has about 350 single spikes, 152 bursts, and 26 superpositions, while the stimulation record has about 265 spikes, 218 bursts, and 307 superpositions. Note that the spikes are relatively independent during baseline (Figure 1a), but fire in bursts during stimulation (Figure 1b). Also, note that the burst rate during stimulation is not synchronized to whisker stimulation (figure 1b); actual whisker stimulation is occurring at about 3 stimulations (flicks) per second, while the burst rate is about 8 bursts per second. We believe that bursts of such overlapping multi-spike records reflect the activity of closely

560

related neurons and, therefore, are useful tools for mapping overlapping receptive field characteristics. One way to sample the synaptodendritic receptive field potential manifold is from spike train

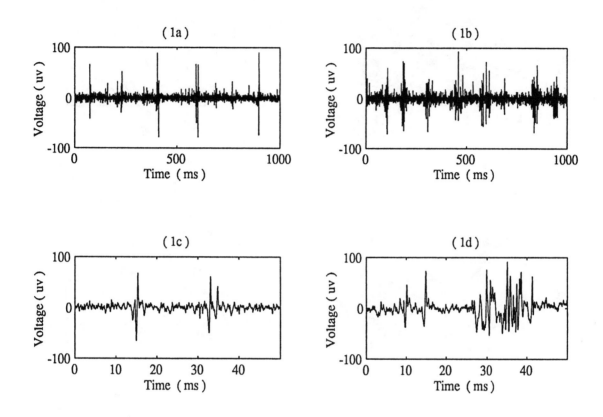

Figures 1a-d. Figure 1a presents one second of a typical recording with no whisker stimulation (baseline). Figure 1b presents data from the same location during one second of whisker stimulation (spatial frequency = 24 grooves/rev.; temporal freq. = 0.125 rps). Figures 1c and 1d show individual units during 50msecs of baseline (1c) and the superposition of units during whisker stimulation.

recordings made with multi-electrode arrays. This approach was taken by Nicolelis et. al, (1993) to map the spatial distribution of responses in the ventral posterior medialis nucleus (VPM) of the thalamus to a vibromechanical stimulus of 1 Hz for 100 msec. to various sites on the mystacial pad of the rat. As they used only one frequency of stimulation, they described their receptive field configurations in classical spatial terms. Nonetheless, interesting from our standpoint is their finding that : "These quantitative representations revealed that receptive fields in the VPM are much larger and spatiotemporally complex than [heretofore] reported." In their study they used temporary local (lidocaine) anesthesia of a small area of the mystacial pad, and showed a dramatic reorganization of the receptive field manifold (the extent and relations among receptive fields) while the anesthesia was in effect. After the anesthetic wore off, the manifold returned to its original configuration.

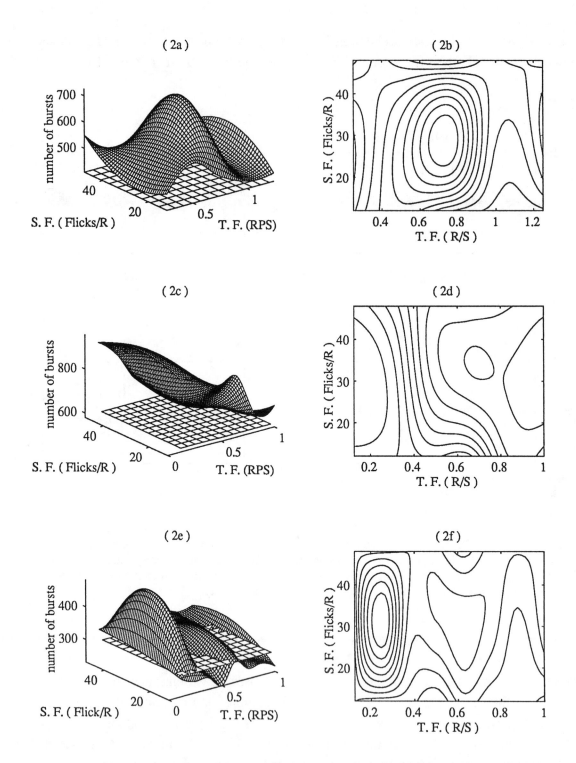

Figures 2a-f. Examples of receptive field manifolds and their associated contour maps derived by an interpolation (spline) procedure from recorded whisker stimulation. The contour map was abstracted from the manifold by plotting contours in terms of equal numbers of bursts per recording interval (100secs.). Each figure shows baseline activity (no whisker stimulation) at a given electrode location as a gr-plane located in terms of number of bursts per 100 secs.

The stability of the receptive field manifold for a particular set of stimulus values makes it possible to map using a single electrode location as was done in our experiments. There are two ways to access a manifold. One can either move the electrode (or use an array of electrodes) and sample various potions of the manifold using a constant set of stimulus parameters, or one can keep the electrode in the same location and shift the manifold by systematically changing the stimulation parameters. Both methods require that the configuration of the manifold remain stable for any particular values tested. Evidence from the VPM study indicates that this requirement can reasonably assumed to be met.

Axonal spike trains recored from single electrodes can be attributed to three separable processes: 1) those due to the sensory input per se, 2) those that are intrinsic to the operations of the synaptodendritic field potentials and 3) those that reflect the output of the axon hillock. (Pribram et al 1981; Berger and Pribram, 1992). In our experiments, sensory influences are generated by the frequency (spectrum) of the stimulus as modulated by the spacings of the grooves on the cylinders and the speed with which the cylinders are rotated. The results thus provide maps of the number of bursts or spikes generated at each spectral location as determined by the spatial and temporal parameters of the sensory input. (Figures 2a-f). The activity above or below baseline which resulted from whisker stimulation is plotted as a manifold describing total number of bursts (or spikes) per 100 secs. of stimulation. Spatial frequencies are scaled in terms of grooves per revolution, while temporal frequencies are scaled in terms of revolutions per socond. Thus, the density of stimulation of a whisker (or set of whiskers) is a function of both the spacings of the cylinder grooves and the speed with which the cylinder rotates. It is this density *per se* which composes the spectral domain.

In 27 experiments single whiskers were isolated and stimulated. Whiskers were identified according to accepted nomenclature as described by Simons (1978). The receptive field potential manifolds derived from such stimulations were irregular and poorly tuned to either spatial or temporal frequency. The intrinsic operations governing the configuration of the synaptodendritic field potentials are constrained by parameters such as the anatomical extent of each receptive field and the functional inhibitory and excitatory relationships among such fields. Our analyses were derived from both bursts of unit activity and from single units. We therefore sought to determine the relationships between the manifolds (field potential maps) derived from bursts and those derived from single units composing the bursts.

A manifold (Figure 3) constructed from bursts is shown to encompass those of the individual units composing the bursts: Figures 4a-d illustrate manifolds from the four single units which compose the bursts. These units were identified using a template constructed from a spike sorting procedure that discriminated the shape of the action potential (spike) on the basis of spike amplitude and recovery slope. The four single unit manifolds show a gradual change in shape corresponding to slight changes in location within the burst manifold: Figures 4a and b illustrate two peaks which progressively become combined into a single broad peak in the manifolds of Figures 4c and d. This demonstration of continuity between two levels of analysis (bursts and single units) strongly supports the view proposed by Pribram (1991) that extended networks of synaptodendritic fields serve as the processing medium, and therefore, single neurons are sampling from overlapping areas of the synaptodendritic network.

Simulation

According to signal processing theory, the general shape of a field potential manifold is the same for each combination of spatial and temporal frequencies (e.g.Fig. 5a). However, a central peak, reflecting the density of response for that spectral location in the manifold, will be shifted within the field according to the particular spatial and temporal stimulation values.

In order to discern whether, indeed, our data fit the requirements of signal processing theory, a simulation of the procedure was executed. The first stage of the simulation was to construct a putative truncated field potential manifold. Any extent of manifold is best described formally by a

(3a)

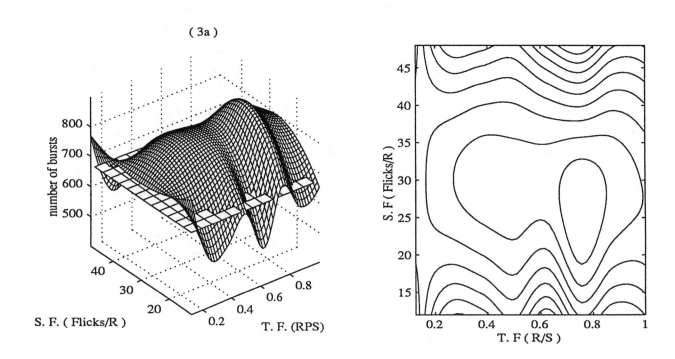

Figures 3a and b. Lateral (3a) view of an empirically derived burst manifold and its associated contour map (3b).

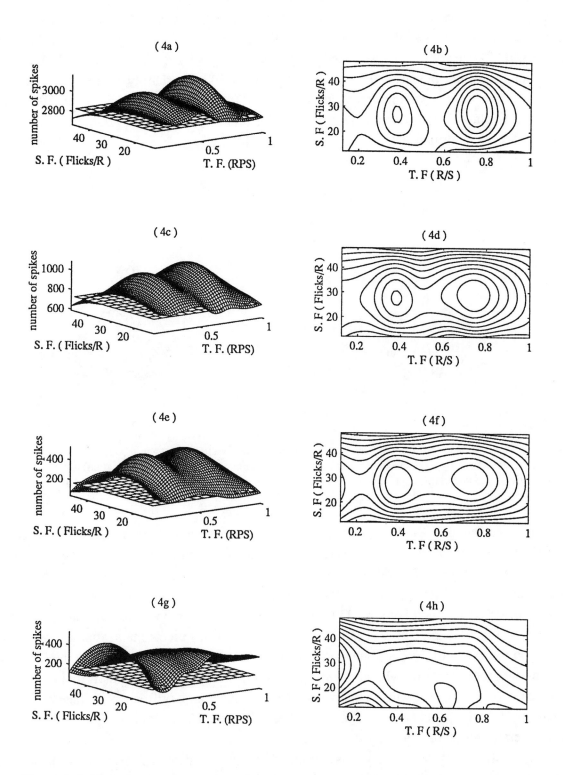

Figures 4a-h. These figures illustrate manifolds and their associated contour maps from four single units which compose the bursts used to construct the manifold in Figure3.

truncated spectral function such as a constrained Fourier representation. Gabor (1946 p.431) defined such a function as follows: "Let us now tentatively adopt the view that both time and frequency are legitimate references for describing a signal and illustrate this . . . by taking them as orthogonal coordinates. Its frequency is exactly defined [only] while its epoch is entirely undefined. A sudden surge or `delta function' (also called a `unit impulse function') has a sharply defined epoch, but its energy is distributed over the whole frequency spectrum" Daugman (1990), McLennon (1993) and Pribram and Carlton (1986), have extended this illustration to include, in addition to the time parameter, two spatial dimensions.

(5a)   (5b)

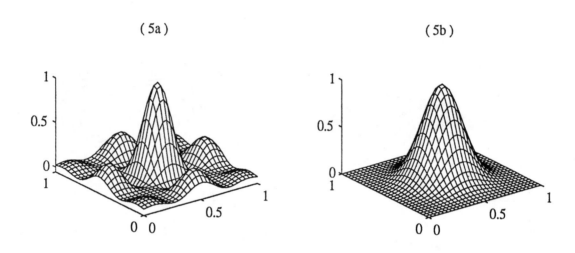

Figures 5a and b. 5a presents a simulated manifold (mexican hat function) representing a spectral distribution induced by a single external stimulus (spatial and temporal frequency combination) across the cortical synaptodendritic field. 5b presents the second stage of the simulation as a probe consisting of a band-pass filter formed by a Gaussian (exponential) function.

We chose a rectangular window in the spatiotemporal domain to constrain the two dimensional siusoidal signal. The reasons for this choice are: First, that the resulting spectrum generates a number of side lobes surrounding a central peak. In the visual system a number of side lobes has been observed at the lateral geniculate nucleus, (Hammond, 1972; Pribram, personal observation, 1974) and at the cortex (Pollen and Feldon 1979; Pollen and Pribram, personal observation 1972). The second reason for the choice of a rectangular window is that it reflects the spatial and temporal constraints on the extent of the distribution of the signal: the spatial constraint reflects the limits on spacings of the grooves on our cylinders; its temporal constraint, the limits on their rotation speed.

In addition, the rectangular window allows for maximum resolution of frequencies (see Zeevi and Daugman 1981; and Oppenheim and Shafer 1989 esp. Chapter 11, for review). The use of such a window generates a sinc function in the spectral domain.

In our simulations (Figure 6) each plot is a manifold of a spectral density function of a rectangular windowed continuous two-dimensional sinusoidal signal. When, in other experiments, only a single frequency of stimulation is used, a spatiotemporal "connection" matrix can be constructed from recordings made with multiple electrode arrays to represent the data (Barcala, Nicolelis and Chapin 1993). Our version of such a matrix represents the variety of spatially and temporally constrained spectral data gathered in our experiments as a sinc function, centered at the frequency of each stimulation pair, i.e.

$$F(\omega_1, \omega_2) = A \operatorname{sinc}(\omega_1 - \omega_{01}) \operatorname{sinc}(\omega_2 - \omega_{02})$$

where A is a scaling constant, ω_1 and ω_2 are spatial and temporal frequencies of the spectrum, and ω_{01} and ω_{02} are the spatial and temporal frequencies of the stimulation. The function $\operatorname{sinc}(\omega)$ is defined as :

$$\operatorname{sinc}(\omega) = \frac{\sin(\omega)}{\omega}$$

The second stage of the simulation uses as a probe, a Gaussian (exponential) function (Figure 5b). When this probe represents a single neuron it is limited by the spatial extent of the local field potentials fluctuating among that neuron's dendrites. When a burst manifold is modelled, the spatial constraint is assumed to portray a greater reach and is limited by the barrel (columnar) arrangement of the somatosensory cortex. Sampling is performed by the generative activity of the axon hillock, which, due to the upper and lower temporal limits of spike generation, functions as a bandpass filter which is the response of the sensory system. This filter is multiplied with the sinc function to yield a display of the manifold. Figures 6a-f depict manifolds and contours derived from these simulations. Note the close fit to the experimentally derived manifolds and contours shown in Figures 2a-f. A total of 48 manifolds were experimentally generated. Of those, three were essentially flat. Of the remaining 45, we simulated six; all but two of the remaining 39 have a shape that can be seen to be successfully simulatable with the technique described.

Discussion

The similarity of these manifolds obtained from recordings made from the somatosensory cortex to the receptive field characteristics demonstrated in the primary visual cortex (DeValois and DeValois, 1988; Pollen, and Taylor, 1974; Pribram and Carlton, 1986; Daugman, 1990) suggests that this processing medium is ubiquitous in the cortical synaptodendritic network.

The manifolds derived from our data are constructed of two orthogonal dimensions: one dimension reflects the spatial frequency of the stimulus and the other its temporal frequency. Because spatial and temporal variables constrain the spectral density response, a Gabor-like rather than a simple Fourier representation describes our results. Thus the results of our experiments can be interpreted in terms of an information field composed of Gabor-like elementary functions, that is, of truncated two dimensional sinusoids.

An unconstrained spectral representation is globally holographic; the constrained spectral domain, as in patch or multiplex holography, is termed holonomic. (For the derivation of this nomenclature,

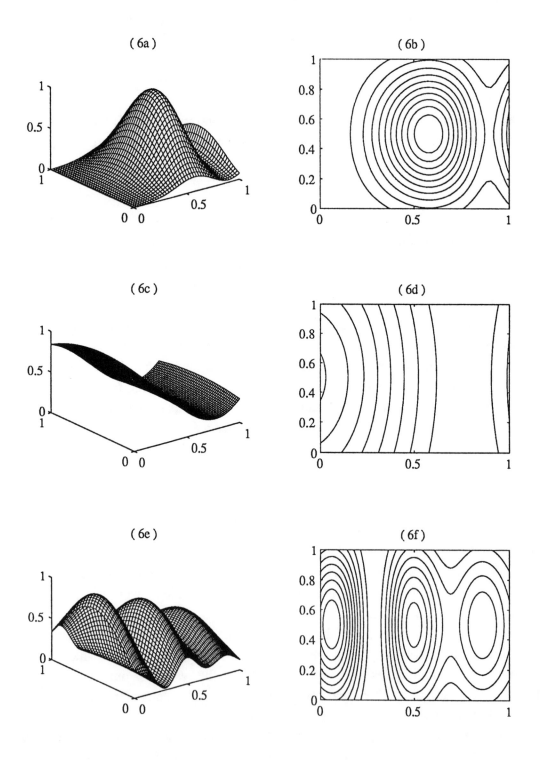

Figures 6a-f. Examples of simulated receptive field manifolds and their associated contour maps to be compared with the empirically derived maps presented in Figures 2a-f. Axes are normalized from 0 to 1.

originated by Hertz, see Pribram, 1991 p. 27.). Holonomic constraints quantize an essentially spectral process. Gabor called the elementary function described by the intersection of his spectral and time parameters a "quantum of information." His reason was that he could address the problem of the efficiency of communication accross the Atlantic cable in terms of " the formulation of Heisenberg's principle of indeterminacy in 1927. This discovery led to a great simplification in the mathematical apparatus of quantum theory which was recast in a form of which use will be made in the present paper" (1946, p. 432).

A possible resolution to the "binding problem" presents itself on the basis of these results. Processing of field potentials appears to be correctly described by patch holography: a manifold composed of Gabor-like elementary functions. Such descriptions are thus consistent with a quantum-type formulation. Non-local synchronization is a feature of quantum-type processes, and evidence has been presented that action-at-a-distance (saltation) is characteristic of processing in synaptodendritic arborizations (Shepherd et. al., 1985; Perkel and Perkel, 1985). Thus, spike trains recorded from axonal probes sampling isopotential loci within synaptodendritic manifolds would be expected to show synchronization.

The results of the experiments reported by Engel, Koenig, Kreiter and Singer (1991) support the conclusions presented here. Synchronization of frequencies was shown by them in records made from corresponding areas of the right and left visual corteces. Synchronization was disrupted by sectioning of the corpus callosum. As they note, the axonal transmission delay across the corpus callosum is approximately 6-8 msec. Reciprocal synchronization of frequencies within any single cycle of oscillation would, therefore, be difficult to achieve. Processing in the spectral domain, however, utilizes convolution-correlation algorithms, with the result that, over iterated cycles, phase coherence would come to be established. And, in fact, phase locking is what is reported by Engel et al to occur.

REFERENCES

Barcala, L.A., Nicolelis, M.A.L., and Chapin. J.K. (1993) Quantifying the connectivity properties underlying the dynamics of the rodent trigeminal network (Abstract), *Society For Neuroscience Abstracts: 23rd Annual Meeting, Vol. 19, Part 1.*

Barlow, H.B. (1986) Why Have Multiple Cortical Areas? *Vision Research*, 26, 81-90.

Barrett, T.W. (1969). The cortex as inferferometer: The transmission of amplitude, frequency, and phase in cortical structures. *Neuropsychologia, 7*, 135-148.

Bekesey, G. von (1967). *Sensory inhibition.* Princeton: Princeton University Press.

Berger & Pribram (1993) From Stochastic Resonance to Gabor Functions: An analysis of the probability density fubction of interspike untervals recorded from visual cortical neurons. In K.H. Pribram, Rethinking Neural Networks: Quantum Fields and Biological Data. INNS Publications. Lawrence Erlbaum Associates, Hillsdale, New Jersey.

Boring, E.G. (1929). *A history of experimental psychology.* New York: Appleton.

Campbell, F.W., & Robson, J.G. (1968). Application of Fourier analysis to the visibility of gratings. *Journal of Physiology, 197,* 551-566.

Conner, C.E. and Johnson, K.O. (1992) Neural Coding of Tactile Texture: Comparison of Spatial and Temporal Mechanisms for Roughness Perception. *Vision Research,* 12, 3414-3426.

Crick, F.H.C. (1994) *The Astonishing Hypothesis: The Scientific Search for the Soul,* New York: Charles Scribner's Sons.

Crick, F.H.C., & Asanuma, C. (1986). Certain aspects of the anatomy and physiology of the cerebral cortex. In J.L. McClelland & D.E. Rumelhart (Eds.), *Parallel distributed processing: Explorations in the microstructure of cognition, Vol. II: Psychological and biological models.* Cambridge, MA: MIT Press .

Daugman, J.G. (1990). An information-theoretic view of analog representation in striate cortex. In E. Schwartz (Ed.), *Computational neuroscience.* Cambridge, MA: MIT Press.

Engel, A.K. Koenig, P., Kreiter, A.K. and Singer, W. (1991). Interhemispheric Synchronization of Oscillatory Neural Responses in Cat Visual Cortex. Science, Vol. 252 pp 1177-1178. Washington, D.C.

DeValois, R.L., DeValois, K.K. (1988). *Spatial vision* Oxford psychology series No. 14). New York: Oxford University Press.

Enroth-Cugell, C., Robson, J.G. (1966). The contrast sensitivity of retinal ganglion cells of the cat. *Journal of Physiology, 198,* 517-552.

Gabor, D., (1946). Theory of communication. In *Journal of the Institute of Electrical Engineers, 93,* 429-441.

Gabor, D. (1948) A new microscopic principle. Nature, 161, 777-778

Gabor, D. (1968). Improved holographic model of temporal recall. *Nature, 217,* 1288-1289.

Gilbert, C.D., Wiesel, T.N. (1990) The influence of contextual stimuli on the orientation selectivity of cells in primary visual cortex of the cat, *Vision Research,* 30, 1689-1701.

Gray, C.M. et al., (1989). Oscillatory responses in cat visual cortex exhibit inter-columnar synchronization which reflects global stimulus properties. In *Nature, 338* (6213), 334-337.

Gustafson, J.W. and Felbain-Kermadias, S.L. (1977). Behavioral and neural approaches to the function of the mystacial vibrissae. In *Psychol. Bull. 84,* 477-488.

Hammond, P. (1972) Spatial Organization of Receptive Fields of LGN Neurons. Journal of Neurophysiology, 222, 53-54

Julez, B., & Pennington, K.S. (1965). Equidistributed information mapping: An analogy to holograms and memory. *Journal of the Optical Society of America, 55,* 605.

Kuffler, S.W. (1953), Discharge patterns and functional organization of mammalian retina. In *Journal of Neurophysiology, 16,* 37-69.

Lashley, K.S., (1950), In search of the engram. In Society for Experimental Biology (Grt. Britain) *Physiological Mechanisms in Animal Behavior, pp. 454-82.* New York: Academic.

MacLennon, B. (1993). Information Processing in the Dendritic Net. In Pribram (Ed.) *Rethinking Neural Networks: Quantum Fields and Biological Data . INNS Publications* New Jersey: Lawrence Erlbaum Associates.

Nicolelis, M.A.L., et al. (1993). Induction of immediate spatiotemporal changes in thalamic networks by peripheral block of ascending cutaneous information. In *Nature, 361*, 533-536.

Oppenheim, A.V., and Schafer, R.W. (1989) *Discrete Time Signal Processing*. Englewood Cliffs: Prentice Hall.

Perkel, D.H. & Perkel, D.J. (1985). Dendritic spines - role of active membrane in modulating synaptic efficacy. In *Brain Research, 525*, 331-335.

Pollen, D.A. , Lee, J.R., & Taylor, J.H. (1971). How does striate cortex begin reconstruction of the visual world? *Science, 173*, 74-77.

Pollen, D.A., & Taylor, J.H. (1974). The striate cortex and the spatial analysis of visual space. In F. O. Schmitt & F.G. Worden (Eds.), *The Neurosciences Third Study Program* (pp. 239-247). Cambridge, MA: The MIT Press.

Pribram, K.H. (1966). Some dimensions of remembering: Steps toward a neuropsychological model of memory. In J. Gaito (Ed.), *Macromolecules and behavior* (pp. 165-187). New York, NY: Academic Press.

Pribram, K.H. (1991). *Brain and Perception: Holonomy and Structure in Figural Processing*. New Jersey: Lawrence Erlbaum Associates.

Pribram, K.H., Blehart, S.R., & Spinelli, D.N. (1966). Effects on visual discrimination of crosshatching and undercutting the inferotemporal cortex of monkeys. In *Journal of Comparative and Physiological Psychology, 62*, 358-364 (1966).

Pribram, K.H. & Carlton, E.H. (1986). Holonomic brain theory in imaging and object perception. *Acta Psychologica, 63*, 175-210.

Pribram, K.H., Lassonde, M.C. and Ptito, M. (1981). Classification of Receptive Field Properties in Cat Visual Cortex. *Experimental Brain Research*. 43, 119-130.

Pribram, K.H., Nuwer, M., & Baron, R. (1974). The holographic hypotesis of memory structure in brain function and perception. In R. C. Atkinson, K.H. Krantz, R.C. Luce, & P. Suppes (Eds.), *Contemporary Developments in Mathematical Psychology* (pp. 416-467). San Francisco, CA: W.H. Freeman.

Rodieck, R.W., & Stone, J. (1965). Response of cat retinal ganglion cells to moving visual patterns. *Journal of Neurophysiology, 28*, 833-850.

Shepherd, G.M., Brayton, R.K., Miller, J.P., Segey, I., Rindsel, J., & Rall, W. (1985). Signal enhancement in distal cortical dendrites by means of interactions between active dendritic spines. In *Proceedings of the National Academy of Science, 82*, 2192-2195.

Simons, D.J. (1978). Response properties of vibrissa units in rat SI somatosensory neocortex. In *Journal of Neurophysiology, Vol. 41, No. 3*, .

Singer, W. (1993). Synchronization of cortical activity and its putative role in information processing and learning. In *Annual Review of Physiology, 55*, 349-74.

Sperry, R.W. (1947). Cerebral regulation of motor coordination in monkeys following multiple transection of sensorimotor cortex. In *Journal of Neurophysiology , 10*, 275-294.

Van Heerden, P.J. (1963). A new method of storing and retrieving information. *Applied Optics, 2*, 387-392.

IV. THE BRAIN AS CONTROLLER

Chapter 25

Perception. Double Dichotomy of Visual Brain

Vadim Glezer

PERCEPTION. DOUBLE DICHOTOMY OF VISUAL BRAIN.

The module organization of the visual brain creates premises for invariant description of the image. However such organization is important also for concrete description of the object.

Our investigations were based on a great series of papers where was shown that the object vision is localized in infero-temporal cortex (ITC) and spatial vision in post-parietal cortex (PPC) [Reviews: 16,19,20,27,28]. Our results show that the invariant description of the pattern is localized in ITC and in PPC are localized the mechanisms of concretization of the image and descriptions of spatial relations [9, 11, 22, 26, 31]. Weiscrantz [30] also suggested the existence of two such mechanisms.

In Fig.19 are shown the results of experiments carried out on monkeys. The animals were taught to find a positive image among a group of six ones presented simultaneously (b). After learning all images were identically transformed in every probe: changed in size or rotated. In this case the mechanism of invariant description should indicate that it is the same figure, whereas the mechanism of concretization should discern difference. Visual system of the animal does not know (is not taught) what is required from it. Therefore it is natural to expect that the more is deviation from original image the lesser is the probability of choosing of the positive figure. This was really obtained in the group of normal monkeys (c,d-curve 1). After extirpation of ITC in other group of monkeys (c,d-curve 3) the animals responded mostly to initial image and did not recognize it when it was transformed. We can conclude that the mechanism of invariant description is localized in ITC. In other group of monkeys the PPC was extirpated and results were directly opposite. The animals chose the image irrespectively of its transformations much better than normal monkeys (c,d-curve 2). We may conclude that the mechanism of invariant description remains.

The experiments were repeated on cats. If the intact monkeys are characterized by preponderance of invariant mechanism, in some cats the mechanism of concrete description can prevail. The cats are nearer to detector behaviour, which we define as behaviour based on using some detected spatial characteristics of objects, in distinction from the behaviour based on perception of object.

In those cats with absolute prevailing of invariance - on all stimuli the percent of correct responses was equal - the ablation of 21 field results in the same manner as extirpation of ITC in monkeys (Fig.20A,Da). The ablation of field 7 (B,Dc) in animals, which before the operation behaved themselves in the opposite manner, results in full invariance. We chose specially the polar types of behaviour, demonstrating distinctly the existence of two basic mechanisms. Of course in part of intact animals the intermediate initial modus of behaviour was observed.

It was obtained that in cats the mechanism of invariance is localized not only in field 21, but also in dorso-lateral and ventro-lateral Supra-Sylvian Sulcus (DLS-VLS).The lesion of these zones leads to the same results as the lesion of 21 field (C,Db).The same is evidenced also by following experiments [26] The extirpation of 21 field or DLS-VLS leads to disappearance of

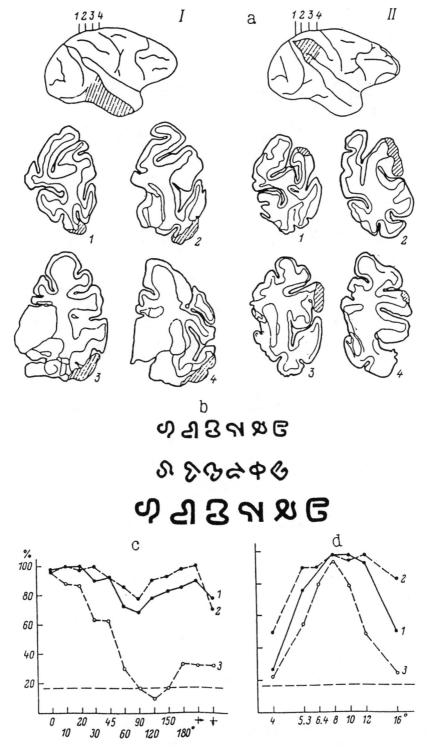

Fig.19 The role of ITC and PPC in visual recognition. Explanation in text. From [31].

responses to transformed stimuli. The additional lesion of the field 7 in both cases restored the invariance. This allows to state that both areas participate in creating of invariant

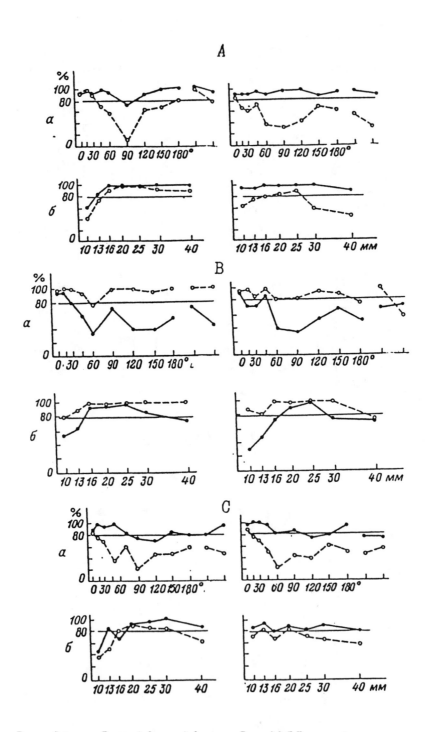

Fig.20. Results of extirpation of different areas in cat VC. Continuous line - norm, dashed line - after operation. Other explanations in text. From [3]

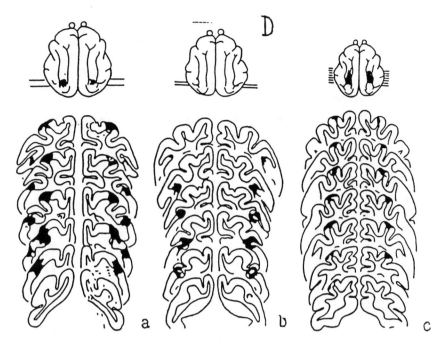

Fig.20.(*continuation*)

description. The disturbance of one of them leads to prevailing of the spatial mechanism , but after the lesion of the last the retained area comes into operation.

How the animals recognize the image when the mechanism of invariant description, which by definition is the mechanism of pattern recognition, is destroyed? It is interesting to discuss some clinical studies of brain lesions. Patients suffering from object agnosia caused by lesion of the ITC cannot recognize an object presented to them. For example, if shown a pen or a comb, they cannot recognized them. Instead, they said that this is a long narrow object [29]. Tonkonogii and Meerson observed in the clinic of the Bechterev Psychoneurological Institute a patient suffering from total object agnosia. Despite the severity of her condition, she oriented quite well in the external world, to the points where doubts were expressed as to whether she was faking or exaggerating her symptoms. In fact she was an intelligent woman , who was learned to use information supplied by the remaining mechanism . It was possible to judge about it on the basis of the following case. The researchers pointed to a portrait of Bechterev and asked what it is. She answered correctly. When asked to explain how she do it, she said: "It flows". That is she perceived the beard as something flowing. From this she concluded that it was a portrait of a man with a beard - and whose portrait might hang on the wall of the Bechterev Institute.

The following fact evidences also that the discrimination of form can be performed without the elaboration of visual pattern as description of the object. In all experiments described above the same alphabet of images was used. However when the alphabet consisted of very simple images, differing in orientations, angles and number of them, then the elaboration of

577

discrimination was fulfilled very quickly and the extirpation of 21 field does not decrease the level of invariance. It may be suggested that in these cases simple features (like curvature, orientation and so on) are used for discrimination , and patterns are not elaborated.

Besides dichotomy ITC - PPC the second type of dichotomy can

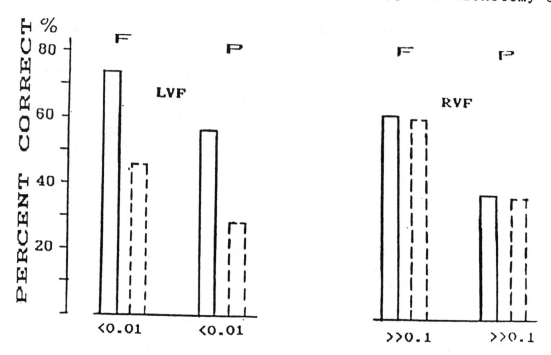

Fig.21. The dependence of recognition of form (F) and position (P) in LVF and RVF when the other dimension was estimated correctly (continuous lines) or incorrectly (dashed line). From [22].

be described. If one and the same visual object is presented to the right or to the left visual hemifield (RVF, LVF) of a man, being so addressed to the right or to the left hemispheres (RHS, LHS) the mild differences in its perception can be found. These differences allow to suggest different organization and function of higher visual centers in RHS and LHS.

It was shown before [review: 9, 11] that such parameters of the figure as form, size, position are described by separate independent channels. It was established in experiments when the stimuli were exposed in the center of the visual field. In experiments on Fig.20 the stimulus was one of two forms presented in 4 possible positions at eccentricity 3° from point of fixation. The subject had to report both characteristics of each stimulus. The exposure duration was too short for errorless recognition. We compared form recognition in cases when stimulus position was reported correctly or incorrectly for the LVF and the RVF separately; analogous comparison was done for position estimation in cases of correct and incorrect form recognition. In the LVF (RHS) the form of a stimulus can be recognized only if its position is correctly estimated. In the cases of incorrect estimation the recognition is at chance level (50% for form and 25% for position). However in the RVF (LHS) estimation of the form and position does not depend from correct or incorrect recognition of position and form correspondingly.

Analogous results were obtained when we analyzed the recognition of the stimuli varying in other dimensions. The conclusion is that independent channels exist only in LHS: one channel gives description of form invariant to position, size and orientation of the object, the other channels describe these parameters. In the RHS information about all stimuli dimensions is combined in one common code, there is no invariance here. But after training the RHS also becomes capable to invariant description (Fig.22A) and in final stage the invariance in RHS even exceeds the one in LHS. Quite analogous curves were obtained in cat with ablated left or right hemisphere (Fig.22B) That means that learned invariance which appears according to Hebb [15] as a result of uniting of different transformations of the form exist in RHS.

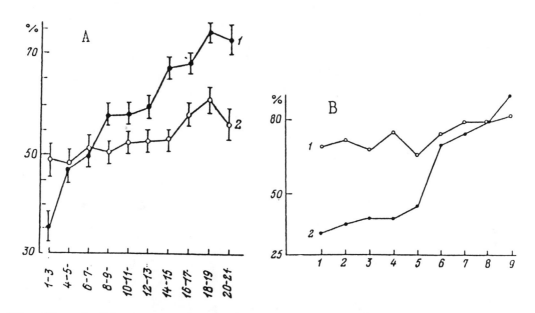

Fig.22. The influence of training on recognition of rotated forms in man in LHS (1) and in RHS (2) and in cat with ablated LHS (2) and RHS (1). From [22].

Many experiments were performed using pictures which were spatial frequency filtrated. In one experiment the photographs of objects of different size in which spatial harmonics exceeding one of the 5 possible levels had been removed, were presented in LVF or RVF. Note that we speak rather about harmonics per image than cycles per degree and consequently the size of image (7° or 1°55´) is not important. The subject's task was to report where a stimulus was presented, what was its form and what was its sharpness (the level of erosion). There were less errors in stimulus localization in the RVF (Fig.23), and the stimulus erosion has no influence on its detection. That means that only lowest harmonics can be used by the LHS in this task. The stimuli in the LVF were detected with less probability, especially those maintaining only lowest harmonics. So the RHS has difficulties when dealing with low harmonics. Great differences were observed in evaluation of sharpness. In the LHS sharpness was underestimated. The observer sees the images as

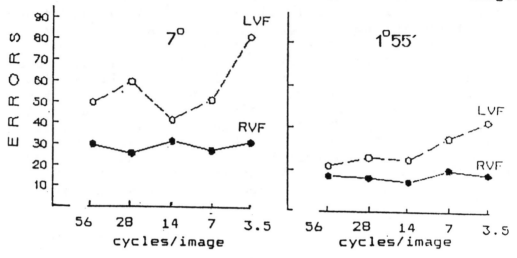

Fig.23. The number of errors in stimulus localization in LVF and RVF as a function of the level of stimulus spatial frequency filtration. Explanations in text. From [22].

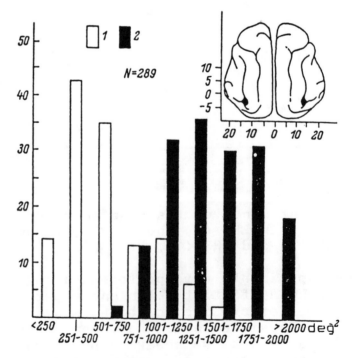

Fig.24. The distribution of sizes of RFs in 21 field in RHS (1) and LHS (2). From [6].

more blurred than it is really as if he does not see the high harmonics. The RHS is more realistic. These and other similar facts from the point of view of model of modules mean that the LHS uses the modules in a fashion as it was shown in the 1-st part of this paper. The group of modules coding the image corresponds to its size. The description of image. in RHS is comprised by several groups of modules of lesser size. Really it was shown in the cat that the RFs in RHS have lesser size than in LHS (Fig. 24). In this case the mechanism which connects several images in one entity must act. The mechanism of description of spatial relations in PPC is well suited for this role. There are clinical data which support this suggestion [18]. The description of image in this case is more precise and concrete, but it lacks invariance. In theory of recognition such method is named structural.

The method used by LHS may be named as discriminant method. The data evidencing that the visual system uses the method of discriminant functions for recognition were published long ago [Review: 9, 11 .] According to this method the discriminant functions extract in multidimensional invariant space (see Part I) an area corresponding to a pattern. The results of experiment (Fig 25) allow to suggest that the LHS uses this method for

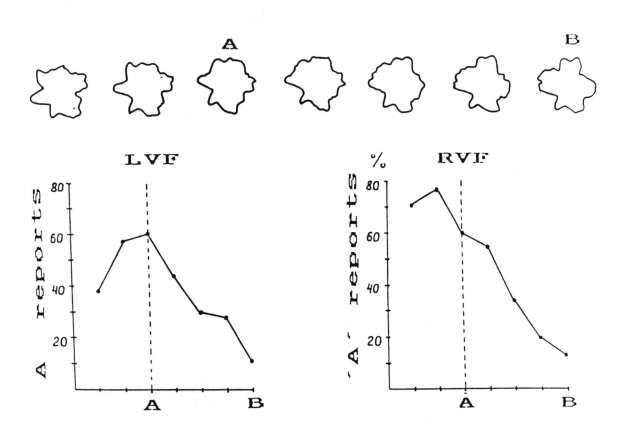

Fig.25. The classification of images forming a transitional row between two learned images "A" and "B". From [22].

recognition. The observers were trained to recognize two images A and B. After training the images A or B were exposed to the observer and besides them images which formed transitional row between A and B and to the left from A were also shown. The observers did not know about the row. They must answer only A or B. The amount of received information for every image in LHS and RHS was calculated. The LHS acts according to the predictions of multidimensional space theory. The more the image is displaced from the discriminant function in space the better is recognition. In the RHS the amount of information decreases to both sides from the learned image. It means that the RHS memorizes the concrete image in full detail without the connection with other images. This conclusion was confirmed in other form of experiment.

Thus the mutual functioning of both dichotomies allows the visual brain to create the model of the visual world. The information kept in model is highly ordered. It facilitates the process of extraction of information from the model and comparing it with the coming information. This process may be termed visual thinking.

The right PPC combines in concrete image the elements of image described by right ITC .The left PPC constructs the scene. from the invariant description of the patterns in left ITC. Thus as a result of mutual functioning of basic visual mechanisms. both generalized abstract and concrete descriptions of an object appear. Usually this categories are related to more highly psychic functions.

References.

[1] M.J.Bastiaan, Gabor's expansion of a signal into Gaussian elementary signals. Proc. of the IEEE, vol.68, pp.538-9, 1980.

[2] V.F.Danilova, V.I.Meshkenaite, N.V.Prazdnikova. Localization of two mechanisms of visual recognition in cat visual cortex. Sensornye sistemy. vol.1, pp. 93-102, 1987.(In Russian).

[3] R.L. De-Valois, L.G.Thorell, D.Y.Albrecht. Periodicity of striate-cortex cell receptive fields. J.Opt. Soc. Amer., vol.2, pp. 1115-23, 1985.

[4] J.G.Daugman. Complete discrete 2-D Gabor transforms by neural networks for image analysis and compression. IEEE Transactions, vol.36, pp.1169-79, 1988.

[5] D.J.Field and D,J.Tolhurst, The structure and symmetry of simple-cell RF profile in cat visual cortex. Proc.Roy.Soc. London. Ser.B,vol.228, pp.379-400, 1986.

[6] I.M.Gabibov and V.D Glezer. Asymmetry of sizes of receptive fields in 21 field of cat cortex. Doklady Akademii Nauk SSSR, vol.284, pp.1014-15, 1985. (In Russian)

[7] D.Gabor. Theory of communication. IEEE, vol.93, pp.429-59, 1946.

[8] V.E.Gauzelman, A.A.Pleskachauskas, V.D.Glezer, V.V.Yakovlev, Model of simple cells of cat striate cortex. Perception,

vol.19, p.38, 1990.

[9] V.D.Glezer, Mechanisms of visual recognition. Leningrad, Nauka, 1965, p.204. (In Russian).

[10] V.D.Glezer, Spatial and spatial-frequency characteristics of RFs of the visual cortex and piecewise Fourier-analysis. Models of the visual cortex. London, pp.265-272, 1985.

[11] V.D.Glezer. Vision and mind. Nauka, Sanct-Petersburg, 1993, p.284. (In Russian).

[12] V.D.Glezer,V.A.Ivanov, T.A.Tscherbach, Investigation of complex and hypercomplex RFs of visual cortex of the cat as spatial frequency filters. Vision Res., vol.13, pp.1875-1904, 1973

[13] V.D.Glezer, V.E.Gauzelman, V.V.Yakovlev, Spatial organization of subfields in RFs of cells in cat striate cortex. Vision Res., vol.29, pp.777-88, 1989

[14] V.D.Glezer, V.V.Yakovlev, V.E.Gauzelman, Harmonic basis functions for spatial coding in the cat striate cortex. Visual. Neurosci., vol.3, pp.351-63, 1989.

[15] D.O.Hebb, The organization of behaviour. New York, 1949, p.335.

[16] J.C.Lynch, The functional organization of posterior parietal association cortex. Behav.Brain Sci., vol.3, pp.485-534, 1980.

[17] S.Marcelja, Mathematical description of the responses of simple cortical cells. J.Opt.Soc.Am., vol.70, pp.1297-1300, 1980.

[18] Y.A.Meerson, Higher visual functions. Leningrad, 1989, p.163

[19] M.Mishkin, Cortical visual areas and their interaction. Brain human behavior. New York,,1972, p.187-208.

[20] M.Mishkin, A memory system in the monkey. Philos. Trans. Roy. Soc., London, vol.298, pp.85-95,1982.

[21] J.A.Movshon, I.D.Thompson, D.Y.Tolhurst, The receptive field organization of complex cells in the cat's striate cortex. J.Physiol., London, vol.283,pp.79-99, 1978.

[22] A.A.Nevskaya and L.I.Leushina, Asymmetry of hemispheres and visual recognition.Leningrad, 1990, p.152. (in Russian).

[23] L.A.Palmer, J.P.Jones, W.H.Mullikin, Functional organization of simple RFs. Models of the visual cortex, London, 1985, pp.273-280.

[24] D.A.Pollen and S.E.Feldon, Spatial periodicities of periodic complex cells in the visual cortex cluster at one half octaves intervals. Investig. Ophthalmol. Vis. Sci.,vol. 18, pp.429-34, 1979.

[25] D.A.Pollen and S.E.Ronner, Phase relationships between adjacent simple cells in the visual cortex. Science, vol.212, 1409-11, 1981

[26] N.V.Prazdnikova, V.F.Danilova, V.I.Meshkenaite, The role of the fields 21 and 7 and dorsal and ventral zones of lateral Supra-Sylvian areas of cat brain. Sensornye Sistemy, vol. 3, pp.292-301, 1989. (In Russian).

[27] K.H.Pribram, Languages of the brain. Russian edition 1975, p.464.

[28] K.H.Pribram, Brain and perception. Lawrence Erlbaum

Chapter 26

Visual Pathways Supporting Perception and Action in the Primate Cerebral Cortex

Melvyn Goodale

Visual pathways supporting perception and action in the primate cerebral cortex

Melvyn A. Goodale

University of Western Ontario, London, Canada

Behavioral and electrophysiological evidence suggests a new interpretation of the division of labor between the ventral and dorsal streams of visual processing in primate cerebral cortex. It is suggested that the ventral stream mediates the perception of objects while the dorsal stream mediates the on-line control of skilled actions directed at those objects.

Introduction

Ungerleider and Mishkin [1] first suggested the possibility that the visual pathways projecting from striate cortex to other cortical regions could be divided into two relatively independent 'streams' of visual processing. According to their original account, a ventral stream, arising in striate cortex and eventually terminating in the inferotemporal region, plays a critical role in the identification and recognition of objects, while a dorsal stream, projecting from striate cortex to the posterior parietal cortex, mediates the localization of those same objects. Since its introduction just over ten years ago, this distinction between object vision and spatial vision ('what' versus 'where') has become one of the most familiar functional dichotomies in visual neuroscience.

With the discovery that the retinal projections to the parvocellular (P) and magnocellular (M) layers of the dorsal lateral geniculate nucleus (LGNd) have different response properties and that these cytologically-defined channels remain segregated at the level of primary visual cortex and perhaps beyond (for review, see [2,3••]), attempts were made [4,5] to relate the differences in the properties of these channels to the distinction between two streams of processing made earlier by Ungerleider and Mishkin. According to at least one account [5], the P pathway, which had been linked to color and form vision, was thought to be the main contributor to the ventral stream (and thus object vision), while the M pathway, which was believed to be responsible for motion perception and stereopsis, was thought to provide the main input to the dorsal stream (and thus spatial vision). If such an account were true, then the primate visual system (within the geniculostriate route, at least) would consist of two independent and parallel sets of inputs that arise in the retina and remain segregated even at the highest levels of visual processing.

Although empirical support for this idea was initially quite compelling, recent evidence from a broad range of studies has challenged this simple account of visual processing. The results of psychophysical studies in monkeys with discrete lesions of the parvo- and magnocellular layers of LGNd [6–8] suggest that the distinctions between the kinds of visual processing carried out by these two pathways are not as sharp as was originally thought (with the exception of color vision which appears to depend almost entirely on the P pathway [6,7]). In fact, even the earlier electrophysiological studies of the responses of ganglion and geniculate cells had shown considerable overlap in the range of effective stimuli (for review, see [3••]). The current consensus is that the difference between the two channels is largely one of relative sensitivity within the temporal and spatial domains, with the M pathway favoring high temporal and low spatial frequencies, and the P pathway, low temporal and high spatial frequencies. In summary, the specializations of the parvo and magno pathways are perhaps best understood in terms of a trade-off amongst the different requirements of spatial, wavelength, and temporal processing [2,3••] and thus it is difficult to argue that one channel is specialized for object vision and the other for spatial vision.

Recent electrophysiological studies by John Maunsell and his colleagues [9,10••,11] suggest that the anatomical segregation of the magno and parvo inputs to the dorsal and ventral streams is also much less clear-cut than was originally thought. Thus, while inactivation of the magnocellular layers of the LGNd almost always reduces the responsivity of cells in the middle temporal area (MT), some cells in this dorsal stream area are also affected by inactivation of the parvocelluar layers, although to a lesser degree [9]. In V4, however, which is part of the ventral stream, most neurons are affected equally by inactivation of either the parvocellular or magnocellular layers of the LGNd [10••], a result which is consistent with the earlier observation that inputs from both of these cytological subdivisions are present in the blob and interblob regions of V1 [11]. In summary then, both the ventral and

---

Abbreviations

LGNd—dorsal lateral geniculate nucleus; LIP—lateral intraparietal sulcus; M—magnocellular; MST—medial superior temporal area; MT—middle temporal area; P—parvocellular.

the dorsal streams of processing appear to receive inputs from the M and P pathways (although the preponderance of input to the dorsal stream is from the M pathway), and the earlier suggestion [4,5] that there is a one-to-one correspondence between these input channels and the two visual streams appears to have been incorrect.

The original claim of Ungerleider and Mishkin, however, is not directly challenged by this evidence. Even the most recent studies of interconnectivity of the visual areas beyond V1 continue to show evidence for a dorsal and a ventral stream [12,13•]. Thus, it could still be the case that although each stream receives input from both the M and the P pathways, the dorsal stream uses its array of inputs to compute the spatial location of an object, while the ventral stream uses its array of inputs to compute the identity of that object. Recently, however, we have re-examined the nature of this functional distinction and proposed a radical new interpretation of the division of labor between the two streams — one which emphasizes the different transformational requirements of the output systems served by these two streams of visual processing [14,15••]. According to this new account, which is illustrated in Fig. 1, the ventral stream of projections is critical to the visual perception of objects while the

dorsal stream mediates the required sensorimotor transformations for visually guided actions directed at those objects. Thus, both streams process information about orientation and shape, and about spatial relationships, including depth; and both are subject to the modulatory influences of attention. Each stream, however, uses visual information in different ways. Transformations carried out in the ventral stream permit the formation of perceptual and cognitive representations which embody the enduring characteristics of objects and their spatial relations with each other; those carried out in the dorsal stream, which utilize the instantaneous and egocentric features of objects, mediate the control of goal-directed actions. I will now review some of the recent findings in visual neuropsychology and electrophysiology in light of this proposal.

Perception versus action

The initial evidence for this re-interpretation of the functional distinction between the dorsal and ventral streams came from a series of neuropsychological studies. It was

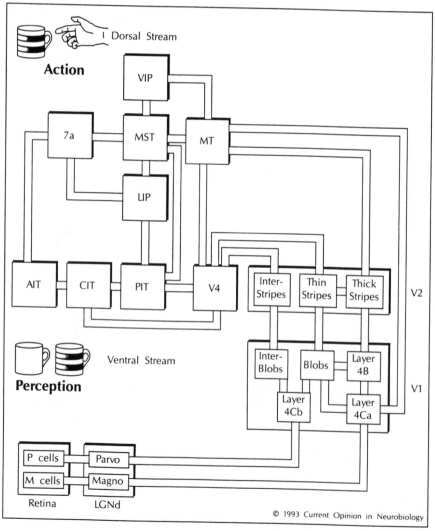

Fig.1. Schematic diagram illustrating the main pathways of the dorsal and ventral streams. Not all of the visual areas are illustrated here. The areas that are depicted, however, have been well studied in a number of different anatomical, electrophysiological, and behavioural investigations. Notice that while the P and M pathways remain segregated until they reach V1, they become heavily intermingled after that. Notice too that, even though two main streams of processing can be identified, they are heavily interconnected. AIT — anterior inferotemporal cortex; CIT — central inferotemporal cortex; PIT — posterior inferotemporal cortex; VIP — ventral intraparietal sulcus. This diagram is based on material discussed in [3••,10••,12,13•].

© 1993 Current Opinion in Neurobiology

noted, for example, that some patients with optic ataxia following damage to the posterior parietal region (the dorsal stream) not only fail to reach in the correct direction toward an object placed in their contra-lesional field, but they also fail to shape the posture of their hand and fingers to reflect the local orientation [16] or size [17] of the target object. At the same time, they have no trouble identifying such objects, or describing their relative location and local orientation [18]. In short, such patients are able to 'perceive' the features of objects, including their location, size, and local orientation, even though they cannot use this same information to guide their grasping movements.

Similar, but reciprocal, dissociations have recently been observed in a patient (D.F.) with visual form agnosia who, despite a profound inability to recognize the size and local orientation of objects, could nevertheless use

this information to calibrate her grasp and orient her hand when she attempted to pick up these same objects [19]. In addition, even though D.F. could not discriminate between objects with different outline shapes, she was as good as normal subjects at placing her index finger and thumb under visual control on appropriately opposed 'grasp' points on the object perimeter (Fig. 2) [20•]. Thus, D.F. remains capable of using the structural features of objects to control her visually guided grasping movements, despite her inability to 'perceive' these same object features.

It is difficult to explain these findings by appealing to the idea of separate streams of processing for object vision and spatial vision [1]. Such dissociations, however, are quite consistent with the idea that the ventral stream is specialized for the transformations underlying visual perception while the dorsal stream is specialized for the vi-

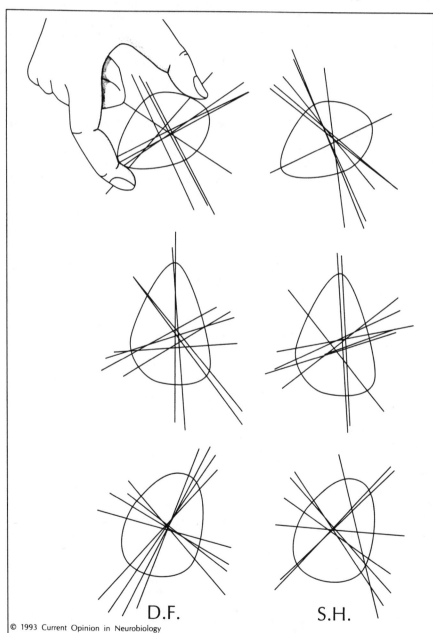

D.F.   S.H.

Fig. 2. Representative 'grasping' axes for three different shapes for a patient (D.F.) with visual form agnosia and a control subject (S.H.). Each line passes through the points where the index finger and thumb first made contact with the perimeter of the shape on individual trials in which the subjects were instructed to pick up the shape. Notice that D.F., who is unable to discriminate between any of these shapes when they are presented as pairs in a same-different task, places her finger and thumb on appropriately opposed points on either side of the shape. Her performance appears to differ little from that of the control subject. Thus, even though D.F cannot 'perceive' the shape of an object, she is able to use information about shape to control the posture and position of her fingers as she picks up the object [20•].

sual control of skilled action [14,15••]. But why should the brain require different transformations for perception and action?

Visual perception, which permits us to attach meaning and significance to objects and events in the world, tends to be 'object-centered' [21]. It is largely concerned with the enduring characteristics of objects (and their relations) so that objects can be recognized when they are encountered again in different visual contexts or from different vantage points, i.e., constancies of size, shape, color, lightness, and relative location need to be maintained across different viewing conditions. This is not the case for the visuomotor mechanisms that support actions, such as manual grasping movements, directed at objects. Here, the underlying visuomotor transformations have to be 'viewer-centered' [21]. In other words, the location of a goal object and its local orientation and motion must be encoded relative to the observer. In addition, because the position and local orientation of a goal object in the action space of an observer is rarely constant, such computations must take place *de novo* every time an action occurs. Thus, perception and action systems will require very different coding of visual information within the cortical visual pathways.

The dorsal action system

Electrophysiological studies of the dorsal and ventral streams provide clear evidence for this difference in coding (for a recent review, see [15••]). The responses of neurons in the dorsal stream, in contrast to those in the ventral stream, are greatly dependent on the concurrent behavior of the animal with respect to the visual stimulus. Since the pioneering work of Mountcastle (for review, see [22]) and Hyvärinen [23], separate subsets of cells in the posterior parietal cortex, which is the major terminus for projections in the dorsal stream, have been shown to be implicated in visual fixation, pursuit and saccadic eye movements, visually guided reaching, and the manipulation of objects. Indeed, in a recent review, Andersen [24] pointed out that most neurons in these areas "exhibit both sensory-related and movement-related activity". For example, the visual responses of a number of cells in posterior parietal cortex, are modulated by the gaze-direction of the monkey [25]. Recent work by Duhamel, Colby and Goldberg [26••] has shown that some cells in the lateral intraparietal sulcus (LIP), which lies in the posterior parietal region, show transient shifts in their receptive field just before the animal makes a saccadic eye movement, so that stimuli that will fall within the receptive field after the eye movement is completed will begin to modulate the cell's activity before the eye movement occurs. In addition, many cells will respond when an eye movement brings the site of a previously flashed stimulus into the cell's receptive field. These results suggest that networks of cells in the posterior parietal cortex anticipate the retinal consequences of saccadic eye movements and update the cortical representation of visual space to provide a continuously accu-

rate representation of the location of objects in the world with respect to the observer. The ego-centric coding provided by these and other movement-modulated visual cells in posterior parietal cortex is extremely short-term and would be updated every time the animal moved. Such coding would be of little use in establishing the relative (or allocentric) position of objects in space. But short-term coding of the ego-centric position of objects is just the sort of information that is critical for the programming and on-line control of skilled movements such as goal-directed grasping. Indeed, there is a long history of work showing deficits in visually guided reaching movements following damage to parietal cortex in the monkey (for review, see [15••]).

Other cells in the posterior parietal region, which have been shown to fire when the monkey manipulates an object, appear to be visually sensitive to the structural features of that object, such as its size and orientation — features that determine the posture of the hand and fingers during the grasping movement [27,28••]. Thus, these neurons, which are located in a region in posterior parietal cortex close to and overlapping area LIP, are tied both to object properties and to the movements of the hands and fingers that are appropriate for those properties. The source of the information required for the visual coding in these cells is unknown. It is unlikely, however, that the shape coding in these cells is dependent on input from the high-level modules in the ventral stream that support perceptual report since monkeys with massive deficits in object recognition following damage to inferotemporal cortex seem as capable as normal animals at reaching out and picking up objects [29,30].

Many of the motion sensitive cells in the dorsal pathway are well-suited to providing inputs for continually updating information about the disposition and structural features of objects in three-dimensional ego-space (see [31]). Also, a subset of these cells seem capable of monitoring limb position during manual prehension [22], while motion-sensitive cells in the temporal lobe have been reported not to respond to such self-produced visual motion [32•]. Some motion-sensitive cells in the medial superior temporal area (MST), which lies adjacent to area MT in the dorsal stream, are both disparity- and direction-selective, and have properties suggesting that they play a role in coding the direction of self-motion through the environment [33•]. Other cells in this region that appear to be involved in pursuit tracking of visual targets are modulated by both head and eye movements [34•].

The posterior parietal region is strongly linked with those premotor regions of the frontal cortex directly implicated in ocular control, reaching movements of the limb, and grasping actions of the hand and fingers, and to areas that have been implicated in short-term coding of spatial location (for reviews, see [15••,35•]). Moreover, the different networks in the posterior parietal area that are modulated by different motor outputs (saccades, pursuit eye movements, fixation, reaching, and manipulation) appear to be linked to corresponding functional areas in the premotor region [15••,35•]. It has been suggested that different combinations of these networks might be recruited for the production of different visuomotor acts [15••,36•].

Finally, it should be noted that the dorsal stream receives visual inputs from both the geniculostriate pathway and the superior colliculus (via the pulvinar and/or the lateral geniculate nucleus) [37]. Most of these inputs originate from the M pathway projections to LGNd or the superior colliculus. The fact that there is a large input from the superior colliculus, a structure known to be intimately involved in the control of saccadic eye movements [38], again speaks to the important role of the dorsal stream in the visual control of motor output.

The ventral perceptual system

In contrast to the dorsal stream, the primary source of visual input to the ventral stream comes from the geniculostriate pathway [37]. This input, as was mentioned earlier, is about equally divided between the M and the P pathways [10••]. In addition, unlike the cells in the posterior parietal cortex, visually-sensitive cells in inferotemporal cortex, the major terminus of the ventral stream, are unaffected by anesthesia and the concurrent behavior of the animal.

Many of the cells in inferotemporal cortex and in neighbouring areas of the superior temporal sulcus show remarkable categorical specificity for visual stimuli [39,40,41••,42••] and some of them maintain their selectivity irrespective of viewpoint, retinal image size, and even color [43,44,45•]. Cells in the anterior region of inferotemporal cortex also show a columnar arrangement (much like the columns in primary visual cortex) in which cells responsive to similar visual features of objects are clustered together [46••]. There is also evidence that color-sensitive cells in the inferotemporal cortex (IT) are organized systematically within a standard psychophysically-defined color space [47•]. These and other cells in inferotemporal cortex typically have exceptionally large receptive fields, usually including the fovea and often extending across the vertical meridian.

It is well-known that bilateral lesions of inferotemporal cortex typically produce severe deficits in visual recognition and discrimination learning [1, 48]. More recent studies have shown that lesions confined to visual areas that represent earlier stages of visual processing in the ventral stream, such as area V4, also result in marked deficits in the learning of discriminations based on the orientation and form of visual stimuli [49•,50•]. Surprisingly, V4 lesions produce only mild deficits in the learning of discriminations based on differences in color or hue [49•–52•]. There is some suggestion, however, that some aspects of color constancy mechanisms may depend on the integrity of V4 [52•].

These electrophysiological and behavioral observations are entirely consistent with the idea that networks of cells in the ventral stream, in sharp contrast to the action systems of the dorsal stream, are more concerned with the enduring characteristics of objects than they are with the moment-to-moment changes in the visual array [14,15••]. Indeed, the object-centered descriptions that the ventral stream delivers would appear to form the basic raw material for recognition memory and other long-term representations of the visual world. There is extensive evidence for the neural encoding of such visual memories in the neighbouring regions of the medial temporal lobe and related limbic areas (see [53,54]). In addition, within inferotemporal cortex itself, there is evidence to suggest that the responsivity of cells can be modulated by the reinforcement history of the stimuli employed to study them (see [55,56]). There is also recent evidence that cells in this region may play a role in comparing current visual inputs with internal representations of recalled images, which are themselves presumably stored in other regions [57••,58•].

Some modulation by behavioral context is apparent even earlier in the ventral stream. Thus, orientation-sensitive cells in V4 have been found to be modulated by the orientation of the sample stimulus in a delayed match-to-sample task [59]. Similar modulation was observed in V4 cells when either color or direction of motion was used as the matching criterion; little modulation, however, was found when this paradigm was used to study directionally-selective cells in area MT, which is traditionally described as the 'motion' area (VP Ferrera, JHR Maunsell, *Soc Neurosci Abstr* 1992, 18:592). In short, the behavioral context of the visual stimulus seems to affect the activity of units in the ventral stream more strongly than those in the dorsal stream.

Some remaining puzzles

Although the distinction between perception and action that we have put forward [14,15••] can account rather well for the neuropsychological and electrophysiological findings outlined above, a number of questions remain unanswered. One of these concerns the way in which visual motion is handled by the dorsal and ventral streams. I have already pointed out how the processing of motion information in the dorsal stream is particularly well-suited for the dynamic control of action. But motion can also play an important role in the perception of objects. Both humans and monkeys can recognize shapes defined entirely by motion, and there is evidence that cells in inferotemporal cortex also respond to boundaries defined by relative direction of motion [60•]. While it is not known whether the input to these cells arises from MT or from some other visual area that codes motion, it is likely that area MT provides critical input to the higher levels of both the ventral and the dorsal stream. Certainly, both monkeys [61•] and humans [62] have difficulty with a variety of motion perception tasks, including the recognition of motion-defined form, following lesions of area MT (or its putative human homolog) as well as deficits in the control of pursuit eye movements [62,63]. Nevertheless, recent observations have shown that it is possible to have lesions in the parietotemporal region of humans which result in deficits in the recognition of motion-defined form without deficits in the detection of motion or the perception of the direction of motion [64•].

An even more difficult set of problems concerns the role of attention and consciousness in the two streams of processing (for a discussion of these issues, see [14,15••]). Are the attentional mechanisms that operate during perception different from those that operate during the performance of skilled visuomotor acts? What is the nature of the distinction between 'conscious' perceptual experience and the apparently 'automatic' control of action? What are the neural substrates for these differences? While the answers to these and related questions will not come easily, the re-casting of the division of labor between the ventral and dorsal streams into a distinction between perception and action may provide a useful theoretical framework for exploring the role of attention and consciousness in visual processing.

Conclusions

In summary, there is a good deal of electrophysiological and behavioral evidence supporting the idea that two very different sets of transformations are carried out in the primate cerebral cortex and the characteristics of these transformations reflect the requirements of the different output systems that they serve. The two streams of visual processing that emanate from primary visual cortex appear to reflect this distinction: the ventral stream delivers the visual representations underlying long-term knowledge of objects and events in the world, and the dorsal stream, which utilizes the instantaneous and egocentric features of objects, mediates the on-line visual control of goal-directed actions.

Acknowledgements

Research in the author's laboratory is supported by a grant from the Medical Research Council of Canada.

References and recommended reading

Papers of particular interest, published within the annual period of review, have been highlighted as:
•   of special interest
••   of outstanding interest

1.   UNGERLEIDER LG, MISHKIN M: **Two Cortical Visual Systems.** In *Analysis of Visual Behavior.* Edited by Ingle DJ, Goodale MA, Mansfield RJW. Cambridge, Massachusetts: MIT Press; 1982:549–585.

2.   SCHILLER PH, LOGOTHETIS NK: **The Color-Opponent and Broad-band Channels of the Primate Visual System.** *Trends Neurosci* 1990, 13:392–398.

3.   MERIGAN WH, MAUNSELL JRH: **How Parallel are the Primate**
••   **Visual Pathways?** *Annu Rev Neurosci* 1993, 16:369–402.
An excellent review of the recent electrophysiological and behavioral work on the functional differences between the M and P pathways in the primate visual system.

4.   MAUNSELL JHR: **Physiological Evidence for Two Visual Subsystems.** In *Matters of Intelligence.* Edited by Vaina L. Dordrecht, Holland: Reidel Press; 1987:59–87.

5.   LIVINGSTONE MS, HUBEL DH: **Segregation of Form, Color, Movement and Depth: Anatomy, Physiology, and Perception.** *Science* 1988, 240:740–749.

6.   MERIGAN WH, KATZ LM, MAUNSELL JHR: **The Effects of Parvocellular Lateral Geniculate Lesions on the Acuity and Contrast Sensitivity of Macaque Monkeys.** *J Neurosci* 1991, 11:994–1001.

7.   SCHILLER PH, LOGOTHETIS NK, CHARLES ER: **Role of the Color Opponent and Broad-Band Channels in Vision.** *Visual Neurosci* 1990, 5:321–346.

8.   LYNCH JJ, SILVEIRA CL, PERRY VH, MERIGAN WH: **Visual Effects of Damage to P Ganglion Cells in Macaques.** *Visual Neurosci* 1992, 8:575–583.

9.   MAUNSELL JHR, NEALEY TA, DePRIEST DD: **Magnocellular and Parvocellular Contributions to Responses in the Middle Temporal Visual Area (MT) of the Macaque Monkey.** *J Neurosci* 1990, 10:3323–3334.

10.   FERRERA VP, NEALEY TA, MAUNSELL JHR: **Mixed Parvocellu-**
••   **lar and Magnocellular Geniculate Signals in Visual Area 4.** *Nature* 1992, 358:756–758.
This study describes experiments showing that selective inactivation of either the M or P pathway at the level of the LGNd can affect the responsivity of cells in V4. These results indicate that the both the M and the P pathways make significant contributions to the ventral stream.

11.   NEALY TA, MAUNSELL JHR: **Magnocellular Contributions to the Superfical Layers of Macaque Striate Cortex.** *Invest Ophthalmol Vis Sci* 1991, 32:1117.

12.   VAN ESSEN DC, ANDERSON CH, FELLEMAN DJ: **Information Processing in the Primate Visual System: An Integrated Systems Perspective.** *Science* 1992, 255:419–423.

13.   YOUNG MP: **Objective Analysis of the Topological Organi-**
•   **zation of the Primate Cortical Visual System.** *Nature* 1992, 358:152–154.
The author used a mathematical optimization technique to examine the topological organization of the visual projections in the primate cerebral cortex. This analysis revealed that the different pathways could be dichotomized into two streams of processing and that the two streams reconverged in the anterior region of the superior temporal polysensory area and in area 46 in prefrontal cortex.

14.   GOODALE MA, MILNER AD: **Separate Visual Pathways for Perception and Action.** *Trends Neurosci* 1992, 15:20–25.

15.   MILNER AD, GOODALE, MA: **Visual Pathways to Perception**
••   **and Action.** In *The Visually Responsive Neuron: From Basic Neurophysiology to Behavior. Prog Brain Res. Vol 95.* Edited by Hicks TP, Molotchnikoff S, Ono T. Amsterdam: Elsevier; 1993:317–338.
Both this paper and the earlier version by Goodale and Milner [14] propose a new account of the division of labor between the ventral and dorsal stream of visual processing in primate cerebral cortex. Evidence is presented to suggest that the ventral stream plays the major role in the perception of objects, while the dorsal stream mediates actions directed at those objects.

16.   PERENIN M-T, VIGHETTO A: **Optic Ataxia: A Specific Disruption in Visuomotor Mechanisms. I. Different Aspects of the Deficit in Reaching for Objects.** *Brain* 1988, 111:643–674.

17.   JAKOBSON LS, ARCHIBALD YM, CAREY DP, GOODALE MA: **A Kinematic Analysis of Reaching and Grasping Movements in a Patient Recovering from Optic Ataxia.** *Neuropsychologia* 1991, 29:803–809.

18.   JEANNEROD M: *The Neural and Behavioural Organization of Goal-Directed Movements.* Oxford: Oxford University Press; 1988.

19.   GOODALE MA, MILNER AD, JAKOBSON LS, CAREY DP: **A Neurological Dissociation Between Perceiving Objects and Grasping Them.** *Nature* 1991, 349:154–156.

20. MEENAN J-P, GOODALE MA, BÜLTHOFF HH: **Precision Grasping**
• **in a Visual Form Agnosic.** *Invest Ophthalmol Vis Sci* 1993,
34:1131.
This brief report describes a sharp dissociation between the perception of object shape and the use of this object feature in the control of grasping movements. A patient with visual form agnosia, who cannot discriminate between objects with different outline shapes, can nevertheless grasp such objects correctly under visual control.

21. MARR D: *Vision.* San Francisco: Freeman; 1982.

22. MOUNTCASTLE VB, MOTTER BC, STEINMETZ MA, DUFFY CJ: **Looking and Seeing: the Visual Functions of the Parietal Lobe.** In *Dynamic Aspects of Neocortical Function.* Edited by Edelman G, Gall WE, Cowan WM. New York: Wiley; 1984:160–193.

23. HYVÄRINEN J, PORANEN A: **Function of the Parietal Associative Area 7 as Revealed from Cellular Discharges in Alert Monkeys.** *Brain* 1974, 97:673–692.

24. ANDERSEN RA: **Inferior Parietal Lobule Function in Spatial Perception and Visuomotor Integration.** In *Handbook of Physiology. Section 1: The Nervous System. Vol V: Higher Functions of the Brain, Part 2.* Edited by Mountcastle VB, Plum F, Geiger SR. Bethesda: American Physiological Society; 1987:483–518.

25. ANDERSEN RA, ESSICK GK, SIEGEL RM: **The Encoding of Spatial Location by Posterior Parietal Neurons.** *Science* 1985, 230:456–458.

26. DUHAMEL J-R, COLBY CL, GOLDBERG ME: **The Updating of the**
•• **Representation of Visual Space in Parietal Cortex by Intended Eye Movements.** *Science* 1992, 255:90–92.
This report describes several elegant electrophysiological experiments showing that neurons in the posterior parietal cortex anticipate the retinal consequences of saccadic eye movements and update the retinal coordinates of remembered stimuli to generate a continuously accurate representation of visual space. Such cells could provide critical information about the egocentric location of objects for the on-line control of grasping movements and other actions.

27. TAIRA M, MINE S, GEORGOPOULOS AP, MURATA A, SAKATA H: **Parietal Cortex Neurons of the Monkey Related to the Visual Guidance of Hand Movement.** *Exp Brain Res* 1990, 83:29–36.

28. SAKATA H, TAIRA M, MINE S, MURATA A: **Hand-Movement-Re-**
•• **lated Neurons of the Posterior Parietal Cortex of the Monkey: Their Role in Visual Guidance of Hand Movements.** In *Control of Arm Movement in Space: Neurophysiological and Computational Approaches.* Edited by Caminiti R, Johnson PB, Burnod Y. Berlin: Springer-Verlag; 1992:185–198.
This article and an earlier report [27] provides electrophysiological evidence that some cells in the posterior parietal region, which fire when the monkey manipulates an object, are also visually sensitive to the size and orientation of that object.

29. KLÜVER H, BUCY PC: **Preliminary Analysis of Functions of the Temporal Lobes of Monkeys.** *Arch Neurol Psychiatr (Chicago)* 1939, 42:979–1000.

30. PRIBRAM KH: **Memory and the Organization of Attention.** In *Brain Function. Vol IV. UCLA Forum in Medical Sciences 6.* Edited by Lindsley DB, Lumsdaine AA. Berkeley: University of California Press; 1967:79–112.

31. NEWSOME WT, WURTZ RH, KOMATSU H: **Relation of Cortical Areas MT and MSR to Pursuit Eye Movements. II. Differentiation of Retinal from Extraretinal Inputs.** *J Neurophsiol* 1988, 60:604–620.

32. HIETANEN JK, PERRETT DI: **Motion Sensitive Cells in the**
• **Macaque Superior Temporal Polysensory Area. I. Lack of Response to the Sight of the Monkey's Own Limb Movement.** *Exp Brain Res* 1993, 93:117–128.
This report shows that cells in the anterior region of the dorsal superior temporal sulcus of the monkey which are sensitive to any visual movement produced by the experimenter are quite insensitive to the sight of the monkey's own movements. The authors suggest that it might be the predictability of the moving visual stimulus rather than the specific visual characteristics of the stimulus that determines the responsivity of these cells.

33. ROY J-P, KOMATSU H, WURTZ, RH: **Disparity Sensitivity of Neu-**
• **rons in Monkey Extrastriate Area MST.** *J Neurosci* 1992, 12:2478–2492.
The authors argue that the correlation between direction selectivity and disparity sensitivity in some MST neurons suggest a role for these cells in coding the direction of self-motion of the observer through the environment.

34. THIER P, ERICKSON RG: **Responses of Visual-Tracking Neu-**
• **rons from Cortical Area MST-I to Visual, Eye and Head Motion.** *Eur J Neurosci* 1992, 4:539–553.
The experiments described in this report demonstrate that some cells in the lateral part of area MST, which exhibit pursuit-related activity, are modulated by both head and eye movements as well as the moving visual stimulus. Moreover, in many of these cells, the preferred directions for the moving visual stimulus were closely correlated with the preferred direction of movement for the eyes and head.

35. CAVADA C, GOLDMAN-RAKIC PS: **Multiple Visual Areas in the**
• **Posterior Parietal Cortex of Primates.** In *The Visually Responsive Neuron: From Basic Neurophysiology to Behavior. Prog Brain Res. Vol 95.* Edited by Hicks TP, Molotchnikoff S, Ono T. Amsterdam: Elsevier; 1993:123–138.
A useful review of the pattern of connectivity between the posterior parietal cortex and other cortical regions such as prefrontal and premotor cortex.

36. STEIN JF: **The Representation of Egocentric Space in the**
• **Posterior Parietal Cortex.** *Behav Brain Sci* 1992, 15:691–700.
This theoretical paper suggests that posterior parietal cortex does not contain a 'map' of space but instead a distributed network of transformational algorithms for converting various sets of sensory vectors into other sensory reference frames or motor coordinates. While the emphasis is largely on spatial location rather than the actions required to deal with objects, the author recognizes that the dorsal stream must deal with multiple coordinate systems to control the range of different motor outputs that primates produce.

37. GROSS CG: **Contribution of Striate Cortex and the Superior Colliculus to Visual Function in Area MT, the Superior Temporal Polysensory Area and Inferotemporal Cortex.** *Neuropsychologia* 1991, 29:497–415.

38. SPARKS DL, MAYS LE: **Signal Transformations Required for the Generation of Saccadic Eye Movements.** *Annu Rev Neurosci* 1990, 13:3309–3336.

39. GROSS CG: **Visual Functions of Inferotemporal Cortex.** In *Handbook of Sensory Physiology. Vol 7. Part 3B.* Berlin: Springer-Verlag; 1973:451–482.

40. TANAKA K, SAITO H, FUKADA Y, MORIYA M: **Coding Visual Images of Objects in the Inferotemporal Cortex of the Macaque Monkey.** *J Neurophysiol* 1991, 66:170–189.

41. TANAKA K: **Inferotemporal Cortex and Higher Visual Func-**
•• **tions.** *Curr Opin Neurobiol* 1992, 2:502–505.
A brief but useful review of recent work on the coding of visual images in the inferotemporal cortex in the monkey. See also [40].

42. PERRETT DI, HIETANEN JK, ORAM MW, BENSON PJ: **Organization**
•• **and Functions of Cells Responsive to Faces in the Temporal Cortex.** *Philos Trans R Soc Lond [Biol]* 1992, 335:23–30.
The authors review the work on face-sensitive cells in the temporal cortex of monkeys and relate these findings to the human neuropsychological deficit, prosopagnosia. They suggest that some face-sensitive cells may be important components in circuitry supporting 'social attention' while others may play a role in the identification of faces.

43. HASSELMO ME, ROLLS ET, BAYLIS GC, NALWA V: **Object-Centred Encoding by Face-Selective Neurons in the Cortex in the Superior Temporal Sulcus of the Monkey.** *Exp Brain Res* 1989, 75:417–429.

44. PERRETT DI, ORAM MW, HARRIES MH, BEVAN R, BENSON PJ, THOMAS S: **Viewer-Centred and Object-Centred Coding of Heads in the Macaque Temporal Cortex.** *Exp Brain Res* 1991, 86:159–173.

45. HIETANEN JK, PERRETT DI, ORAM MW, BENSON PJ, DITTRICH
• WH: **The Effects of Lighting Conditions on Responses of Cells Selective for Face Views in the Macaque Temporal Cortex.** *Exp Brain Res* 1992, 89:157–171.

The aggregate responses of individual cells in monkey temporal cortex selective for the face and other views of the head remained largely unchanged under different light conditions, even though the responsivity of individual cells might change. Some cells showed remarkable 'lighting constancy' and continued to discriminate between different views of a face or head despite changes in the direction of lighting falling on the preferred head.

46. FUJITA I, TANAKA K, ITO M, CHENG K: **Columns for Visual Fea-**
•• **tures of Objects in Monkey Inferotemporal Cortex.** *Nature* 1992, 360:343–346.

This exciting report shows that neurons in the inferotemporal cortex that are tuned to particular visual stimuli are arranged in columns, in which cells with similar or related stimulus selectivity are grouped together.

47. KOMATSU H, IDEURA Y, KAJI S, YAMANE S: **Color Selectivity**
• **of Neurons in the Inferior Temporal Cortex of the Awake Macaque Monkey.** *J Neurosci* 1992, 12:408–424.

The authors show that color is an important factor determining the responsivity of inferotemporal cells and that the population of cells sensitive to color in this region of the ventral stream cover nearly all of the standard color space of the CIE chromaticity diagram.

48. DEAN P: **Visual Behavior in Monkeys with Inferotemporal Lesions.** In *Analysis of Visual Behavior.* Edited by Ingle DJ, Goodale MA, Mansfield RJW. Cambridge, Massachusetts: MIT Press; 1982:587–628.

49. HEYWOOD CA, GADOTTI A, COWEY A: **Cortical Area V4 and**
• **Its Role in the Perception of Color.** *J Neurosci* 1992, 12:4056–4065.

Monkeys with lesions of area V4 show little disturbance in their ability to perform a number of color discriminations which are typically failed by patients with achromatopsia. These same monkeys, however, showed a conspicuous deficit in form discriminations.

50. WALSH V, BUTLER SR, CARDEN D, KULIKOWSKI JJ: **The Effects**
• **of V4 Lesions on the Visual Abilities of Macaques: Shape Discrimination.** *Behav Brain Res* 1992, 50:115–126.

Monkeys with V4 lesions showed a deficit on relearning visual discriminations between different shapes or the orientation of identical shapes.

51. WALSH V, KULIKOWSKI JJ, BUTLER SR, CARDEN D: **The Effects**
• **of Lesions of Area V4 on the Visual Abilities of Macaques: Colour Categorization.** *Behav Brain Res* 1992, 52:81–89.

Although monkeys with V4 lesions took slightly longer than control animals to learn different color categories, the pattern of their categorization was essentially normal.

52. WALSH V, CARDEN D, BUTLER SR, KULIKOWSKI JJ: **The effects of**
• **V4 Lesions on the Visual Abilities of Macaques: Hue Discrimination and Colour Constancy.** *Behav Brain Res* 1993, 53:51–62.

Monkeys with lesions of V4 showed no evidence for a deficit in hue discrimination although their color constancy mechanisms were disturbed. This result together with the results of [49•] and [51•] suggest that V4 is not essential for hue or colour perception but may play a critical role in color constancy.

53. FAHY FL, RICHES IP, BROWN MW: **Neuronal Signals of Importance to the Performance of Visual Recognition Memory Tasks: Evidence from Recordings of Single Neurones in the Medial Thalamus of Primates.** In *The Visually Responsive Neuron: From Basic Neurophysiology to Behavior.* *Prog Brain Res, Vol 95.* Edited by Hicks TP, Molotchnikoff S, Ono T. Amsterdam: Elsevier; 1993:401–416.

54. NISHIJO H, ONO T, TAMURA R, NAKAMURA K: **Amygdalar and Hippocampal Neuron Responses Related to Recognition**
and Memory in Monkey. In *The Visually Responsive Neuron: From Basic Neurophysiology to Behavior. Prog Brain Res, Vol 95.* Edited by Hicks TP, Molotchnikoff S, Ono T. Amsterdam: Elsevier; 1993:339–358.

55. RICHMOND BJ, SATO T: **Enhancement of Inferior Temporal Neurons during Visual Discrimination.** *J Neurophysiol* 1987, 58:1292–1306.

56. SAKAI K, MIYASHITA Y: **Neural Organization for the Long-Term Memory of Paired Associates.** *Nature* 1992, 354:152–155.

57. ESKANDAR EM, RICHMOND BJ, OPTICAN LM: **Role of Inferior**
•• **Temporal Neurons in Visual Memory I. Temporal Encoding of Information About Visual Images, Recalled Images, and Behavioral Context.** *J Neurophysiol* 1992, 68:1277–1295.

On the basis of a complex analysis of the spike density functions of neurons in inferotemporal cortex as monkeys performed a sequential visual matching task, the authors conclude that neurons in this region compare internal representations of current visual images with the internal representation of recalled images.

58. ESKANDAR EM, OPTICAN LM, RICHMOND BJ: **Role of Inferior**
• **Temporal Neurons in Visual Memory II. Multiplying Temporal Waveforms Related to Vision and Memory.** *J Neurophysiol* 1992, 68:1296–1306.

This paper presents a model of how neurons in inferotemporal cortex might code information about current and previous visual input.

59. MAUNSELL JHR, NEALEY TA, SCLAR G, DE PRIEST DD: **Representation of Extraretinal Information in Monkey Visual Cortex.** In *Neural Mechanisms of Visual Perception.* Edited by Man-Kit Lam D, Gilbert CD. Texas: Portfolio Publishing; 1989:223–235.

60. SARY G, VOGELS R, ORBAN GA: **Cue-Invariant Shape Selectiv-**
• **ity of Macaque Inferior Temporal Neurons.** *Science* 1993, 260:995–997.

This report describes neurons in inferotemporal cortex that code for motion-defined contours. Some cells respond to contours that are defined by differences in either motion, luminance, or texture.

61. MARCAR VL, COWEY A: **The Effect of Removing Superior Tem-**
• **poral Cortical Motion Areas in the Macaque Monkey: II. Motion Discrimination Using Random Dot Displays.** *Eur J Neurosci* 1992, 4:1228–1238.

Lesions of area MT in the monkey resulted in deficits in their ability to discriminate certain kinds of motion-defined shapes. This result suggests that MT may contribute to the mechanisms underlying the perception of structure-from-motion.

62. ZIHL J, VON CRAMON D, MAI N: **Selective Disturbance of Movement Vision after Bilateral Brain Damage.** *Brain* 1983, 106:313–340.

63. NEWSOME WT, WURTZ RH, KOMATSU H: **Relation of Cortical Areas MT and MST to Pursuit Eye Movements. II. Differentiation of Retinal from Extraretinal Inputs.** *J Neurophysiol* 1988, 60:604–620.

64. REGAN D, GIASCHI D, SHARPE JA, HONG XH: **Visual Processing**
• **of Motion-Defined Form: Selective Failure in Patients with Parietotemporal Lesions.** *J Neurosci* 1992, 12:2198–2210.

This paper presents evidence that patients with cortical lesions in the parietotemporal region can show deficits in the recognition of motion-defined shapes without deficits in the detection of motion or the perception of direction of motion. The implications of these findings for understanding the interconnections between the dorsal and ventral streams of processing are discussed.

MA Goodale, Department of Psychology, University of Western Ontario, London, Ontario N6A 5C2, Canada.

Chapter 27

Auditory "Objects:"
The Role of Motor Activity in Auditory Perception and Speech Perception

Carol Fowler

Auditory "objects:" The role of motor activity in auditory perception and speech perception

Carol A. Fowler
Haskins Laboratories
270 Crown Street
New Haven, CT 06511
Fowler@Yalehask.bitnet

My topic is perception of events that are specified acoustically; within that topic, I will speculate on the possible role of the motor system in auditory event perception including, in particular, speech perception. A reason to address this latter issue in the context of the present conference is to consider the extent to which a viable theory of auditory perception can be developed that is closely parallel to the theory of visual perception proposed by Karl Pribram [20]. In his holonomic brain theory, as I understand it, successive transformations of visual stimulus input yield successive "re-presentations" of the input in the brain, initially representations of structures in light, but ultimately representations of real-world objects, classified into conceptual categories. His example of successive views of a California scene illustrates the last three representations that he proposes underlie visual perception of a layout:

> The upper part of the scene forms a curved deep blue surface that becomes less saturated at its juncture with a deep violet-green surface with undulating margins. In the foreground are splotches of tile-red interspersed with splotches of dark green....The same scene can be described in a different way: a blue hemisphere sitting astride a circular plane from which arise large undulating masses and smaller masses topped with three-dimensional shapes at various angles with one another and covered with semicylinders. Interspersed with these shapes are others, more rounded and composed of swaying round and elongated shimmering small objects. What I am looking at are, of course, the sky, the Santa Cruz hills, the roof tops of the quadrangle of buildings intermingled with trees. (p. 66).

The first description above is of a representation called an image, the second of a representation called an "object," and the final one is a representation that results from classification of object representations into conceptual categories.

In Pribram's theory, the motor system plays an important role in the transformation from image to object. Exploratory head and eye movements provide successive images of a scene from a variety of vantage points. These different vantage points permit discrimination of properties of the scene that vary over vantage points (such as the occlusion of part of an object by another) from those (such as object coherence and object shape) that do not. In this way, objects are recovered from images.

For researchers in the specific domain of speech perception, rather than auditory perception more generally, a suggestion that the motor system may be involved in perception is familiar. Liberman and his colleagues [e.g., 12, 15,16] have proposed and developed a "motor theory of speech perception" in which the listener's own speech motor system is involved in a central way in the perception of speech. It may be instructive, therefore, to see whether this theory offers sufficient parallels to Pribram's theory to provide the basis for development of a theory of auditory perception in which the motor system plays a role in the transformation of an image-like representation to an object-like representation. I suggest below that it will not do the job.

THE MOTOR THEORY OF SPEECH PERCEPTION

The motor theory of speech perception was developed to account for some unexpected experimental findings. These findings suggested that speech percepts correspond more closely to the vocal tract actions that gave rise to acoustic speech signals than they do to the signals themselves. A striking and venerable finding [13] is provided by the synthetic-speech syllables /di/ and /du/ depicted in Figure 1. The information that the initial consonant is /d/, rather than /b/ or /g/ is provided by the transition of the second formant (the upper resonance frequency in each syllable). Remarkably, in /di/, the transition begins high in frequency and rises whereas, in /du/, it begins lower and falls. Isolated from their contexts, the transitions sound as they look like they should sound, namely like pitch glides, the one high and rising in pitch, and the other lower and falling. That is, the transitions do not sound alike, and neither sounds like /d/. In context, the transitions are indistinguishable and sound like /d/. In these syllables, although there is apparently nothing invariant in the acoustic signal to explain the invariant percept, there is the same gesture of the tongue tip that is shared when the two syllables are produced by a human talker.

Why do invariant actions of the tongue tip give rise to different acoustic signals when the actions are produced in the context of different following vowels? The reason why they do is that talkers "coarticulate" successive phonetic segments when they speak--that is, they produce successive phonetic segments in overlapping time frames rather than producing them discretely in time. This makes the acoustic speech signal virtually everywhere context-sensitive.

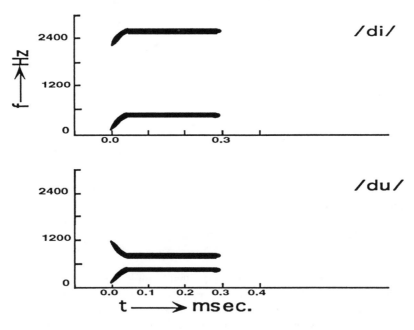

Figure 1: Synthetic-speech syllables /di/ and /du/ showing their different second formant transitions

A complementary finding, equally venerable [14,21] shows that invariance in the acoustic signal does not, necessarily, give rise to invariance in the corresponding percept. In particular, it does not when, to get invariance in the signal, articulatory gestures for a consonant coarticulated with different vowels, have to be distinct. In this case, the same stop consonant burst centered at 1440 Hz is heard as /p/ placed before formants for the vowel /i/, but as /k/ placed before the formants for the vowel /a/ as shown. It happens that to produce acoustically the same bursts in the contexts of these distinct vowels requires on the one hand a constriction at the lips and on the other a constriction by the tongue against the soft palate. Here again, the listener's percept appears to track the articulation rather than the acoustic speech signal. Figure 2 displays the findings from the two studies in a schematic way that makes the motivation to develop a motor theory clear.

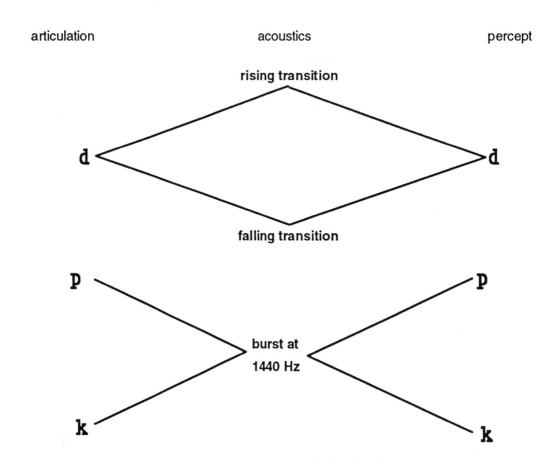

Figure 2: Schematic representation of the findings with /di/ and /du/ and /pi/ and /ka/ suggesting to motor theorists that the percept follows articulation more closely than it follows the acoustic signal

In the case of /di/ and /du/, the schema shows that an invariant articulatory gesture for /d/ gives rise, because it is coarticulated with different vowels, to distinct acoustic segments. The consonantal percept, however, like the articulation, is invariant. In the case of /pi/ and /ka/, different articulations give rise, because of coarticulation with gestures for different vowels, to the same stop burst in the acoustic signal. The same burst, however, is heard differently by listeners whose percepts, again, map onto the articulatory actions that caused them in a one-to-one fashion.

Of course, these are just two findings among many others that inspired the original development of the motor theory [12] or that fostered the later revised version of the theory [15,16]. The whole array of findings required that theorists explain why the speech percept has a motor character. Based in part on the contrast in the sounds of the two /d/ transitions of Figure 1 out of and in a speech context, the theorists concluded that auditory perception in general yields perception of the structure in the acoustic signal itself whereas speech perception does not. Generally, for example, frequency transitions are heard as pitch glides, but in speech perception they are not. If nonspeech auditory perception and speech perception do differ in that, in the one case, we hear the acoustic signal and, in the other, we do not, then speech perception must involve a distinct perceptual system in the brain from the system that renders perception, for example, of slamming doors, singing birds and bouncing balls. Further, the special perceptual system for speech must somehow give the speech percept a motor character.

Liberman and colleagues proposed that the speech percept acquires its motor character, because listeners use their own speech motor systems in perceiving the speech of others. They do so, and indeed, must do so (according to the motor theory), because of the complex mapping between the consonants and vowels that talkers intend to say and the acoustic signals they generate. Because talkers coarticulate consonants and vowels when they speak, there are no boundaries in the acoustic signal that constitute at once the end of information for one phonetic segment and the beginning of information for a following one. In addition, because of the temporal overlap of successive segments in articulation, the acoustic structure in the signal at virtually every point in time has been influenced by more than one phonetic segment. Therefore, the acoustic information that signals a consonant or vowel is highly context-sensitive as we have seen for the effect of /i/ and /u/ on the information for /d/ in Figure 1. Although, in consequence, there may be no invariant structure in an acoustic signal to specify a phonetic segment in all of the contexts in which it might occur, there is invariance in production. In production of /d/, there is always a gesture of the tongue tip that forms a constriction in the vocal tract at the alveolar ridge of the palate. Coarticulation affects what else is happening in the vocal tract at the same time, but the tongue tip gesture always occurs when /d/ is produced. If listeners could use the highly "encoded" (Liberman et al, 1967) acoustic speech signal somehow to recover the invariant actions of the vocal tract that produced it, their percept could be invariant across different contexts in which the same phonetic segment is produced.

In the revised motor theory [15], the objects (better, the "events"; see below) of speech perception are "intended phonetic gestures." The qualifier "intended" reflects Liberman and Mattingly's view that what is invariant about the production of phonetic segments will not, because of coarticulation, always be found in the actions of the vocal tract themselves. Instead they will be found at a level of implementation of a speech plan before coarticulatory overlap has occurred. Intended phonetic gestures are perceived by involving the speech motor system in the form of an "innate vocal tract synthesizer" in the recovery of phonetic information from acoustic speech signals. Effectively, the listener hears the output of the vocal-tract synthesizer, not the acoustic signal that inspired its output.

In the motor theory, there is another advantage to the involvement of production processes in perception beyond that of unravelling effects of coarticulation on phonetic segments. For any communication system to work, the messages produced by talkers must be recovered by listeners. Messages are generated by some sound producing system, but must be recovered by a sound receiving system. Somehow those distinct systems must maintain "parity"--that is, messages produced in the one modality must be recovered, more-or-less intact, in the other. One way to assure parity, perhaps, is to have essentially just one system--the production system--bear responsibilty both for production and for reception of the message. The requirement of parity may help to explain why there is evidence of production-perception linkages in the communication systems of other species as well [10,26].

COMPARISON BETWEEN THE MOTOR THEORY AND THE HOLONOMIC BRAIN THEORY

There are some superficial similarities between the motor theory of speech perception and Pribram's proposals [20] regarding the role of the motor system in constructing objects from images. In the motor theory of speech perception, the motor system has an intimate link to the perceptual system, and it is used in perception to recover a "distal" speech event from a "proximal" acoustic signal. In the holonomic brain theory, the motor system is used to recover a distal visible object in the environment from a representation of structure in reflected light. Thus, in the two theories, the motor system mediates a transformation between representations of structure in a sensed medium, air in the case of audition and light in the case of vision, to perception of an object or event.

However, there are fundamental differences in the theories as well. In the holonomic brain theory, the motor system initiates actions that provide successive images from a variety of vantage points permitting extraction of invariant object properties. The motor system does not have an analogous role in the motor theory. That is, the function of the motor involvement in speech perception is not to explore acoustic structure from multiple vantage points or to provide multiple images from which invariants can be discovered. Rather, it is, in a sense, to mimic covertly the intended motor actions of the speaker, and thereby to recreate in the listener's head the invariants of speech production that originated in the talker's head. Further, looked at from the perspective of the motor theory, "reasons" for motor involvement in perception are to handle destructive consequences of coarticulation on information in the acoustic speech signal and to preserve parity between talker and listener. Neither of these rationales for motor involvement has an analogue in the holonomic brain theory. Finally, in the motor theory, motor involvement is not a general characteristic of systems that perceive, but, rather, one special to speech perception or perhaps to communication systems generally where parity must be preserved.

Does this negative conclusion imply that a realistic theory of speech perception specifically, or of auditory perception more generally, cannot be developed that is analogous to Pribram's theory of visual perception? I do not think that it does. I will go on to suggest that the data leading to the motor theory of speech perception have a different interpretation than that put on it by the motor theorists. This alternative interpretation permits embedding the theory of speech perception in the context of the universal theory of perception developed by James Gibson [7,8]. As I will show, in that theory, there is a central role in perception generally of exploratory activity by perceivers.

AN ALTERNATIVE THEORY OF SPEECH PERCEPTION AND ITS POSSIBLE RELATION TO HOLONOMIC BRAIN THEORY

Gibson's theory of direct perception is a theory about "public" rather than covert aspects of perceiving. For many researchers, the goal of a theory of perception is to develop an account of the events that take place inside a perceiver beginning with stimulation at the sense organ and ending with achievement of a percept. Such theories are theories of covert aspects of perceiving. Gibson's aims were different in that all of the aims focused on perception in its publically observable aspects. One of his aims was to develop a characterization of the ecological niche of a perceiver--that is, of the set of "affordances" (possibilities for action) that the niche offered a perceiver. This characterization reveals what perceivers must come to know if they are to act felicitously in their niche--if they are to find food, avoid predators, locomote only on surfaces that afford locomotion, attempt to pass only through apertures that afford passage and so on. A second aim of Gibson's theory was to describe the information in structured media, such as light and air, that permit the environment to be known. As Gibson recognized, light, air and the surface of a perceiver's own body are causally structured by objects and events in the environment. Generally, idiosyncratic properties of an event will structure one or more of these media in idiosyncratic ways, and, therefore, structure in the media can specify the source of their structuring in the environment to a sensitive perceiver. Accordingly, a third of Gibson's aims was to determine experimentally whether structure in media such as light or air that specifies event properties is picked up by perceivers and used by them to recover the distal cause of their structure in the environment. Generally the results of research of this sort are positive. Whether the structure is in light [e.g., 24], air [e.g., 22]or on the surfaces and joints of the perceivers' bodies [e.g., 23], perceivers register structure in these proximal media, and, rather than perceiving that structure, they use it to recover affordances of the environment that were the distal causes of the structure.

Exploratory motor activity by the perceiver plays a central role in Gibson's theory of perception. In some cases, invariant information in reflected light to specify object or event properties may be unavailable at a fixed station point in the environment. When the perceiver moves around an object or event, additional information in light is revealed or created. Thus, in Gibson's theory, as in Pribram's, exploratory activity by a perceiver may be required for extraction of real-world object or event properties.

what's real	stimulation at the sense organ	what's perceived
1. environment of objects and events	optic array	environment of objects and events
2. graspable/palpable objects	skin deformations	graspable/palpable objects
3. sounding events	acoustic signal	sounding events
4. linguistic actions of the vocal tract	acoustic signal	linguistic actions of the vocal tract

Figure 3: Gibson's theory of public aspects of perceiving and its implications for theories of speech perception and general auditory perception

Figure 3 is meant to illustrate the implications of this public theory of perception for a theory of speech perception and of auditory perception more generally. In particular, a theory of speech perception as direct [1,5] proposes, in contrast to the motor theory, that speech perception is not special and that the speech percept would have a motor character whether or not the listener's speech motor system is involved in perception. If speech perception, in its public aspect, works like visual perception, then the auditory system of speech perceivers should certainly register the structure in the acoustic signal; however, they should not, therefore, experience hearing the

598

acoustic speech signal, but, rather they should use structure in the signal as information for its distal causal source in the environment. The causal source of an acoustic speech signal, of course, is the set of linguistically significant actions of the vocal tract that constitute the talker's utterance. In short, it is the univeral fact that perceivers use structure in media that has been caused by affordances of the environment as information for the affordances themselves that explains why the speech percept has a motor character. We perceive actions of the vocal tract, because that is what the structure in the acoustic signal informs us about.

From the perspective of this theory, auditory perception in general should work in the same way as speech perception. Listeners to slamming doors, bouncing balls and rustling leaves should hear, respectively, slamming doors, bouncing balls and rustling leaves, not the acoustic signals those events cause.

EVIDENCE DISTINGUISHING THE MOTOR THEORY FROM A THEORY OF DIRECT PERCEPTION OF SPEECH

There is, as yet, very little evidence that distinguishes predictions of the motor theory from those of a theory of direct perception of speech. One reason, of course, is that the two theories make many of the same predictions. The theories differ on the question whether the speech motor system is involved in speech perception, the motor theory proposing that it does and the direct theory (a theory of public, not of covert, aspects of perception) argues that the speech percept would have a motor character whether or not the speech motor system were involved. More generally, the motor theory predicts that evidence should be obtained for separate perceptual systems subsuming speech perception and general auditory perception. Finally, the theories differ in their predictions about nonspeech auditory perception: The motor theory predicts that it is, in general, "homomorphic" with (that is, the same in form as [16]) the acoustic signal whereas the theory of perception as direct predicts that it will always be homomorphic the signal's distal cause.

The McGurk effect

It is difficult to get any direct evidence on the first prediction. However, there is indirect behavioral evidence that I interpret as favoring the theory of direct perception. When subjects in an experiment are confronted with a dubbed videotape in which, for example, a speaker mouths the syllable /da/ at the same time that the sound track plays /ma/, listeners most frequently report hearing /na/--a blend of sight and sound [e.g., 17]. This result is called the "McGurk" effect.

For motor theorists [e.g., 11,15] this was a welcome finding, because it provided a further indication that listeners to speech are recovering vocal tract gestures, which, the findings showed, could be recovered from optical as well as acoustic information. It should perhaps not be surprising that, in the evolution of a specialized module for speech perception designed to recover gestures of the vocal tract, optical as well as acoustic information for gestures might be accepted by the module. After all, we frequently both see and hear speakers talk.

The finding is compatible with the theory of perception as direct also (as well as with other theories not considered here, such as Massaro's Fuzzy Logical Model of Perception [19]. In that theory, listeners perceive the affordances of the environment, which may be specified in any medium that has been causally structured by the event and that can impart its structure to a perceiver's sense organs.

The two theories appear to differ on the question whether haptic information for phonetic gestures should give rise to a McGurk effect. That is, should the haptic feel of a face mouthing /da/, simultaneous with acoustic /ma/, give rise to judgments that the heard syllable was /na/? Dekle and I [3] guessed that the motor theorists would predict no effect, because evolution would not have anticipated a use for haptically-provided information for gestures. In contrast, the theory of direct perception does predict an effect. Structure in any medium that has been lawfully caused by an event and that can be imparted to a perceptual system can specify the event to a perceiver.

In brief, Fowler and Dekle found a highly reliable effect of felt syllables on judgments of heard syllables even though subjects were told, accurately, that felt syllables were independently and randomly paired with acoustic syllables.

Duplex perception

A finding taken by the motor theorists to provide strong evidence that speech is perceived by a distinct perceptual system from that responsible for general auditory perception is the phenomenon known as "duplex perception." The usual procedure [e.g., 18] for obtaining duplex perception is to present most of a CV syllable (the "base") to one ear and its remainder (usually a third-formant transition) to the other ear. The direction of frequency change of the transition determines whether the whole syllable, base plus transition, is heard as /da/ or /ga/. Remarkably, listeners who receive the base in one ear and the transition in the other hear either /da/ or /ga/ in the ear receiving the base, and they hear whichever consonant is signaled by the transition. In addition, however, listeners also hear a "chirp" sound in the ear receiving the transition. Perception, thus, is duplex, because the transition apparently is heard in two ways at the same time--in one ear, as part of a consonant-vowel syllable and, in the other, as a stray nonspeech sound. That the two percepts exist simultaneously seems to require an interpretation that two distinct perceptual systems are responsible for the distinct percepts. Further, since one percept is phonetic--/d/ or /g/--and the other is homomorphic with the acoustic signal (that is, the transition, a frequency glide, sounds like a pitch glide), likely candidates, from the motor theory's perspective, for the contributing perceptual systems are the speech module and the general auditory system.

A hint that the findings can be intepreted differently is provided by a finding of Whalen and Liberman [25]. In that study, base CV fragments were presented to both ears along with sinewave caricatures of the F3 transition. The sinewave transitions (sounding now more like whistles than chirps) were presented at various intensities. At the lowest intensities, listeners heard just the base CV, which most of them identified as /da/. At intermediate intensities, they heard /da/ or /ga/ depending on which sinewave transition was provided, but perception was not duplex. At higher intensities still, perception was duplex. Whalen and Liberman's interpretation of this finding was that, not only is the speech perceptual system distinct from that responsible for general auditory perception, in addition, it is "preemptive" with respect to it. That is, the speech module serves almost as a filter on any incoming acoustic signal, taking for itself any phonetic information therein. Anything left over after the filtering is perceived homomorphically by the general auditory system.

Rosenblum and I [4,5] proposed a different interpretation. It was that base CVs are, for the perceptual system, almost like a jigsaw puzzle with just one piece missing. The formant transitions, usually presented to the other ear, are very tempting pattern completers, because they do, almost perfectly fill the hole in the CV pattern. Perception is duplex, we suggested, when the transition fills the pattern with something left over--for example, when its intensity is more than required to fit the intensity patterning in the base.

If our interpretation is correct, then duplex perception does not provide evidence for two distinct perceptual systems in the brain, but rather for pattern completion that could take place in just one system. If that is correct, then it should be possible to get duplex perception for stimuli that no one would expect to be perceived by a specialized perceptual module.

We chose the sound of a metal door slamming. To create an analogue to the syllable "base", we low-pass filtered the door sound. This eliminated the metalic sound of the door slam, and so we instructed our listeners to label that sound a "wooden door." We then high-pass filtered the original signal at the same frequency at which we had low pass filtered it before to get an analogue of the third formant transition. Listeners tended to guess that this sound was the sound of a baby rattle or of castinets, so we instructed them to label it a "shaking sound."

With these stimuli, we were able to obtain most of the effects associated with duplex perception of speech. Presenting the wooden door base and the shaking sound either to the same or to different ears at various intensities we found that subjects heard the "wooden door" most frequently at low intensities and the metal door plus the shaking sound (a duplex percept) at high intensities. At intermediate intensities with binaural presentation of the two sounds, subjects reported hearing the "metal door" most frequently--a finding analogous to Whalen and Liberman's findings of with CV syllables. These were the findings that led Whalen and Liberman to conclude that the speech module is preemptive with respect to the general auditory system. However, our findings cannot have that interpretation, because it is not plausible that there is a slamming door module separate from the perceptual system that handles other acoustic signals.

With dichotic presentation of base and shaking sound, duplex percepts were most common with intermediate intensities. We speculated that the reason that the duplex response comes in at lower intensities with dichotic than with binaural presentation is that perceivers have good information, in the distinct spatial locations of base and chirp or base and shaking sound for there being two distinct sound sources in the environment.

There are limitations to our study and hence to its convincingness to motor theorists. The most serious limitation is that we could not find an analogue to the sinewave transitions used by Whalen and Liberman. Accordingly, with binaural presentation, the door-sound fragments were integrated in a sense before they reached the perceiver's ear. In contrast, integration of the acoustically discrepant bases and sinewaves of Whalen and Liberman was truly perceptual.

We do believe, however, that the strategy of looking for duplex perception in signals that could not plausibly involve a specialized perceptual module [cf. 9] is a good way to test the motor theorists' interpretation that duplex perception reveals the existence of perceptual modules.

We always hear distal events

A final distinction between the motor theory and the theory of direct perception concerns nonspeech auditory perception. According to the motor theorists, in general auditory perception, the percept is of the acoustic signal; it is only in speech perception and sound localization that we hear the environmental cause of the signal. According to Gibson's theory of perception as direct, perceptual systems are the only means by which perceivers can know their environment, and they always function to yield perception of environmental affordances, not of their proximate effects in stimulation.

To my knowledge, no direct attempt has been made to distinguish the theories on these grounds. However, evidence in the literature does show at least that listeners can recover properties of distal events from acoustic signals [e.g., 2,6,22].

Conclusions from a comparison of the motor theory and the theory of direct perception of speech.

On two grounds, I conclude that the theory of speech perception as direct is favored over the motor theory. First, the preponderance of evidence favors it. Second, in the direct theory, the motor character of the speech percept is expected given that, universally, perception is the means by which perceivers come to know their world. In contrast to the motor theory, in this theory, the motor character of the speech percept does not imply that speech perception is special.

In the theory of speech perception as direct, there is no special role of any motor system in perception. Thus, what are the implications of adopting this account of speech perception for the development of a general theory of auditory perception consistent with Pribram's theory of visual perception? My view, in brief, is that, generally, Gibson's theory of public aspects of perceiving offers a way of complementing and completing the holonomic brain theory. It can be the public "front end" to that theory. However, I will suggest some modifications to the latter theory that will improve the fit of the theories one to the other.

Some revisions to holonomic brain theory?

In the holonomic brain theory, the motor system plays a necessary role in the transformation from image to object. In particular, head and eye movements provide a succession of images such that, across the images, information for the separateness of objects from their background and for object constancies is provided.

In Gibson's theory, exploratory activity by a perceiver can be essential to his or her detection of a real-world property. It is essential, as explained earlier, if, say, the structure in light from one vantage point does not specify the property in question, but structure revealed over the perceiver's exploratory movements does. Sometimes, however, specifying information is available from a single vantage point. This may be the case, sometimes, because movement in the world, not movement by the perceiver, provides specifying structure. For example, information for the separateness of a car from the pavement or its background is made available if the car is in motion.

The importance of exploratory movement by the perceiver in revealing informative structure in stimulation to the sense organs may differ across sensory modalities. Haptic exploration often is crucial to discovery of object properties. If the exploration is by hand, the hand may itself cover just a small portion of the explored object, and, typically things we explore by hand are not themselves in motion relative to the hand. In contrast, exploratory movement may be less important for auditory perception. I suggest this because, as Gaver [6] points out, acoustic signals can only be created by interactions among materials. So, in general, movement in the environment is the causal source of structure in acoustic signals. Exploratory movement by the perceiver may be less necessary, therefore, for revealing invariant acoustic information for sounding objects than it is for haptic or visual perception.

These considerations suggest, as one revision to Pribram's theory, that motor activity be seen as one possible, but not always essential, mediator between image and object. Other suggested revisions are to the concepts of image and object themselves.

Pribram suggests that head and eye movements generate a "set" of images over time. He does not claim that images are of static perspectives on a scene. However, it is difficult to see how else head movements, for example, could create a set of images. Generally head movements (and pursuit eyemovements) generate continuous change in optical structure that is intercepted by the eye. In auditory perception, even in the absence of exploratory movement by the listener, information is *only* conveyed by continuous changes in acoustic structure. Accordingly, a second suggested revision to the theory is to abandon the characterization of the initial cortical representations as sets of discrete images. One adjustment is to recognize that there is information in continuous changes in optical structure that is made available as a perceiver makes exploratory movements. Another might be to suggest that the representation at this stage is of structure in the light, whereas eventually, the perceiver must extract from light structure knowledge of the environmental objects and events that caused it. A remarkable, yet essential, feat in perception is the recovery of object and event properties despite the fact that our perceptual systems are sensitive, rather, to structure in light, in air and on the surfaces of the body. Accordingly, a transformation that takes place somehow is that structure in these media, registered by the sense organs, is used for the extraction of object and event properties. Because this sometimes necessitates exploratory activity on the part of the perceiver, I tentatively identify Pribram's image-to-object transformation with this transformation from a continuous representation of light structure to recovery from it of environmental event structure. In auditory perception and speech perception more specifically, the transformation is from a continuous representation of structure in the air registered first in perception to recovery of sounding-event properties.

A final revision I propose is simply a generalization of the concept of object. In auditory perception, there is a real sense in which the irreduceable perceivable is an event, not an object. As Gaver [6] puts it: "Sounds indicate that something has happened, that an event has occurred, that there as been an interaction of materials" (p. 22). In his taxonomy of events involving, for example, interactions of solid materials, basic level events are identified as deformations, impacts, scrapings and rolling. In short, there are no auditory objects, only auditory events.

Acknowledgments

Preparation of the manuscript was supported by NICHD Grant HD-01994 to Haskins Laboratories. I thank Michele Sancier for researching evidence for motor involvement in songbird and cricket communication.

References

[1] C. A. Fowler, "An event approach to the study of speech perception from a direct-realist perspective," *Journal of Phonetics*, vol. 14, pp. 3-28, 1986.

[2] C. A. Fowler, "Sound-producing sources as objects of speech perception: Rate normalization and nonspeech perception," *Journal of the Acoustical Society of America*, vol. 88, pp. 1236-1249, 1990.

[3] C. A. Fowler, and D.J. Dekle, "Listening with eye and hand: Crossmodal contributions to speech perception," *Journal of Experimental Psychology: Human Perception and Performance,* vol. 17, pp. 816-828, 1991.

[4] C. A. Fowler, and L.D. Rosenblum, "Duplex perception: A comparison of monosyllables and slamming doors," *Journal of Experimental Psychology: Human Perception and Performance,* vol. 16, pp. 742-754.

[5] C. A. Fowler, and L.D. Rosenblum, "The perception of phonetic gestures," in *Modularity and the motor theory of speech perception,* I.G. Mattingly and M. Studdert-Kennedy, Editors, Lawrence Erlbaum Associates: Hillsdale, N. J., pp. 33-59, 1993.

[6] W. W. Gaver, "What in the world do we hear? An ecological approach to auditory event perception," *Ecological Psychology*, vol. 5, pp. 1-29, 1993.

[7] J.J. Gibson,*The senses considered as perceptual systems*. Boston, MA: Houghton Mifflin, 1966.

[8] J.J. Gibson, *The ecological approach to visual perception.*, Boston: Houghton Mifflin, 1979.

[9] M. D. Hall and R. E. Pastore, "Musical duplex perception: Perception of figurally-good chords with subliminal distinguishing cues," *Journal of Experimental Psychology: Human Perception and Performance,* vol. 18, pp. 752-762, 1992.

[10] R. R. Hoy, J. Hahn and R. C. Paul, "Hybrid cricket auditory behavior: Evidence for genetic coupling in animal communication." *Science*, vol. 195, pp. 82-83, 1977.

[11] A. M. Liberman, "On finding that speech is special," *American Psychologist,* vol. 37, pp. 148-167, 1982.

[12] A. M. Liberman, F. S. Cooper, D. P. Shankweiler, M. G. Studdert-Kennedy, "Perception of the speech code," *Psycholgical Review*, vol. 74, pp. 431-461, 1967.

[13] A. M. Liberman, P. Delattre, F. S. Cooper and L. Gerstman, "The role of consonant-vowel transitions in the perception of the stop and nasal consonants." *Journal of Experimental Psychology,* vol. 68 (whole number 379), 1954.

[14] A. M. Liberman, P. Delattre and F. S. Cooper, "The role of selected stimulus variables in the perception of stop and nasal consonants," *American Journal of Psychology*, vol. 65, pp. 497-516, 1952.

[15] A. M. Liberman, and I. Mattingly, "The motor theory revised," *Cognition*, vol . 21, pp. 1-36, 1985.

[16] A. M. Liberman, and I. Mattingly, "A specialization for speech perception," *Science*, vol. 243, pp. 489-494.

[17] J. MacDonald, and H. McGurk, "Visual influences on speech perception," *Perception and Psychophysics* , vol. 24, pp 253-257., 1978.

[18] V., Mann, and A. Liberman, "Some differences between phonetic and auditory modes of perception," *Cognition*, vol. 14, pp. 211-235, 1983.

[19] Massaro, D., *Speech perception by ear and eye: A paradigm for psychological inquiry.* Hillsdale, N.J.: Lawrence Erlbaum Associates, 1987.

[20] K. Pribram, *Brain and Perception: Holonomy and structure in figural processing.* Hillsdale, N.J.: Lawrence Erlbaum Associates, 1991.

[21] C. Schatz, "The role of context in the perception of stops," *Language*, vol. 30, pp. 47-56, 1954.

[22] W. Schiff, and R. Oldak, "Accuracy of judging time to arrival: Effects of modality, trajectory and gender," *Journal of Experimental Psychology: Human Perception and Performance*, vol. 16, pp. 303-316, 1990.

[23] Solomon, H.Y. and M.T. Turvey, "Haptically perceiving the distances reachable with hand-held objects," *Journal of Experimental Psychology: Human Perception and Performance*, vol. 14, pp. 404-427, 1988.

[24] W. H. Warren, "Perceiving affordances: Visual guidance of stair climbing," *Journal of Experimental Psychology: Human Perception and Performance,* vol. 10, pp. 683-703, 1984.

[25] D. Whalen and A. M. Liberman, "Speech perception takes precedence over nonspeech perception," *Science,* vol. 237, pp. 169-171, 1987.

[26] H. Williams and F. Nottebohm, "Auditory responses in avian vocal motor neurons: A motor theory for song perception in birds," *Science*, vol. 229, pp. 279-282, 1985.

Chapter 28

Entities and Brain Organization:
Logogenesis of Meaningful Time-Forms

Manfred Clynes

Entities and Brain Organization:
Logogenesis of Meaningful Time-Forms

Manfred Clynes

19181 Mesquite Court, Sonoma Ca 95476

Abstract

The central nervous system function of time-form entities are examined. The term *Logogenesis* is introduced as a concept to denote genetically programmed development of mental concepts and time form-entities, as a counterpart to morphogenesis which concerns development of structure. Special attention is given to the time-form logogenesis of natural language entities of emotion communication, and their natural syntax. How time-forms are used in music to generate living, meaningful performances from written scores is described and proved with computer generated classical music, in the context of four modes of time experience, t1, t2, t3, and t4. The modes apply to different time scales and use different natural data processing properties. Models of appropriate peptide dynamics are suggested for some of these amygda-related processes. Some properties of modified time consciousness in relation to these modes are also discussed.

Time Entities and Space Entities

The questions are very simple: Nerve activity within the brain consists of continuing streams of firing nerve cells, of myriads of synaptic potentials and fields. In this sea of seemingly overwhelming activity how can entities arise? Where are they to be found?

Somewhere within the myriads of substreams of neural activity perceived entities and thoughts make their appearance. We shall try as far as we can to consider through what processes entities may be formed.   We will consider entities in *space* like a table, called objects, and entities in *time,* for which there is no common name. Most particularly, and perhaps somewhat uncommonly unfortunately, we will examine the nature of entities in time which we pervasively use in our daily life - in thoughts about our feelings, in communicating emotions and in our musical thought and activities.

An entity must have boundaries.   For a table, however, not only the boundaries but also the space beneath the table may be considered as part of the entity. What are the patterns of neuronal activity that include both the table and the space in which it exists?

Neuronal activities of the visual cortex and a number of separate areas of brain functioning cooperate in creating the concept of table, both in its perceived and imagined processes.   What defines a table in experience is created mentally.   The retina knows nothing of "table", in spite of its differential, analytic sensing.   To know that there is an entity, and that that entity moreover is a common object, and furthermore, is called "table" requires interactive processing of several involved brain areas whose interconnections are still only cursorily understood.   From these interactions somehow, a unitary experience, an entity, is assembled and some agency of the brain in effect "says (to itself)", this is a table. Mystery upon mysteries (here bravely tackled by Karl Pribram) -- and we are not even yet including this "table" in a *flow* of thought, as occurs spontaneously.   As soon as we are considering a flow of thought, time processes extraneous to the percept of the object 'table' are immediately involved.   The perception of the 'table' is immersed in the perception of time, though the object itself is in space and may be considered as stationary.

But when you move your gaze, or turn your head, or both, the image on the retina and in the mental screen upon which the retinal image is projected, move. Yet we know even when this image is moving in this manner, that the table is stationary. If that same table is actually moving with respect to the observer, who is not turning his head or moving the eyes, then that moving retinal image is directly experienced as moving. Even when the observer's head and eyes are also turning and moving, the table can also be experienced as moving. In nearly all these cases, the brain is able to distinguish the object 'table' from its motion and obtain a combined percept that includes both the object and its kind of motion, regardless of turning of head and eyes. Since it includes motion, it includes experience of time. And since change is preferentially sensed by the nervous system, movement actually facilitates the recognition of an object-*entity*.

Genetic basis for entity recognition: Logogenesis

The mother's face and smile are meaningfully perceived virtually as early as this can be measured, i.e. in a few-weeks-old infant. Animal studies suggest that some objects like a mother's teat are perceived so early and readily that it can be assumed that there is a genetic basis for such recognition. The capacity for recognizing faces in humans, and the animal's ability to recognize conspecifics of either sex are genetically programmed. Thus some entities "live" in us by virtue of our genetic program; their recognition may be compared to Plato's *idea*, with the proviso that here the "idea" arrives from biology rather than from pre-existing harmony - from the harmony of DNA functions, a consequence of natural law. The genetic processes responsible for this function should teach us greatly about the how the brain accomplishes this, once the appropriate genes and their corresponding proteins are known.

It is already gradually becoming clear how structural entities are being built by the genetic apparatus, i.e. the processes of morphogenesis. Logogenesis -- the genetic development in the individual of entities in consciousness: genetically developed entities of meaning, of feelings and concepts, and genetically programmed interpretations of conscious percepts -- should yield to similar approaches. For example, a suitable mutation (or several) could conceivably change an animal's recognition of a conspecific to that of another species. If this occurs it would allow the pursuit of the detailed neuronal processes that have been *changed* by the mutation. We may expect to learn more about the functioning of the brain by such means than by observing brain function itself in detail with electrodes and other sensors, or even by imaging techniques. When *logogenesis* will be understood through molecular biology, it should permit us to track down the difference between entities of learned and innate knowledge.

In recognition of entities as objects, there is interplay between the innate and the learned. But no matter what the interplay, the game is played out in the experience of time.

Logogenesis of time forms   -   sentic forms.

Curiously, we know rather more about logogenesis in the production and recognition of time-entities or objects, than we do about space-object logogenesis.

Objects with trajectories in time but not in space are rarely named. Since they seem to lack "solidity", they are seldom given names even though they appear frequently and often recurringly. Their boundaries are not defined through the visual, nor the tactile systems. How do we know their boundaries, then? When something ends in *time*, how do we know what has ended? In hearing sound, silence may mark an end, or on the other hand, it may merely indicate an "interval", a time analogous to the space between the lattices of a fence. Yet we frequently know when such an entity has ended. What is the nature of that something and how do we know if it is an entity?

t1, t2, t3, t4, Four time processes of time-form communication

Time for a physicist is a line where time goes from left to right, and the present is a point along that line. Any process in physics occurs from t1 to t2, two points along that line. The speed at which the point representing the present travels along that line is unspecified, and unspecifiable, a circumstance which does not worry a physicist. But the brain processes involved in time-consciousness are more particular. Different aspects of time experience involve different functionalities: there is more than one time-sensitive agency involved in our various experiences that involve time.

Here we shall be concerned with four different processing and experiential ways, operative on different time scales. A time object or entity has its invariance that makes it an entity, just as a space object has. What is the nature of that invariance?

An object in space includes its boundaries and is perceived in time. An object in time, however, has its own span of time, but is additionally experienced in the larger time-flow in the same direction, along with other perceptions, in a similar way as is a space object. We call this t1.

Time processing *within* a time-entity or object is a <u>second time process</u> superimposed: The time-object has a beginning, a middle and an end as it extends extension in time, and may also be experienced with memory and anticipation. Time scans across the time object and as it does so *memory* accumulates of its extension, and *anticipation* is gradually satisfied.

A <u>third temporal process</u> recognizes the speed at which the trajectory is traversed, or what is commonly called *tempo* in music (analogous to scale of a spatial entity).

A <u>fourth temporal process occurs in the millisecond range</u>, where durations are not perceived as time durations, and yet act to form characteristic perceived patterns, patterns which we note particularly in music rhythms and pulse, and in the shaping of speech, intrasyllabically.

Unlike the space object which we normally experience in the flow of time t1, a temporal entity is perceived through at least four distinct temporal processes. Instead of three dimensions of space and one of time with the experience of a spatial entity, plus the other sensory variables such as color, we are dealing with four dimensions of time in the experience of a time-entity, plus the dimensions of the sensed variables, e.g. sound.

Let us take an example. A person sighs. The sigh occurs in the flow of time-experience, say on a Saturday afternoon (t 1). Another person perceiving the sigh, and the person sighing, both know that the sigh began, took its course, and ended (process t2), i.e. had a particular trajectory in time, how the loudness and pitch rose and fell precisely, say. After the sigh there was no sigh and before the sigh there was no sigh. And further they know, let us say, that it was a medium long sigh, neither a very short sigh nor a very long one (time process t3). We can independently vary each of these dimensions. To a first approximation, distortion will not occur as the first dimension is varied, ie. whether the sigh is on Saturday afternoon, or morning. A

609

time entity has an invariance, just as 'table' has. To understand its specific shape, it needs to be experienced in time dimension 2 as an entity, with recognition of its particular trajectory (analogous to the shape of a table). Thirdly, a limited degree of vriation is possible in time dimension 3, the tempo, analogous to the spatial scale of a table. Time dimensions 2 and 3 interact similarly in the way how a table might be distorted by compression or expansion in one dimension, ie elongated or squeezed together. If it squeezed or elongated too much it will not be recognizable as a table any more. (Interestingly, with some biologically programmed time entities, the latitude of variation in this third time dimension is comparatively narrow, say +- 50 %. This is analogous to a narrow band spatial filter.)

The fourth process (t4) may be illustrated by considering the gait of a person. Seeing such persons from behind, we may able to recognize them quite readily: the pattern of the gait is seen as uniquely their own. This is a subtle pattern in time, and the nervous system resolves this with a millisecond range resolution that permits the entire pattern to be selectively experienced and classified. It works regardless of the exact tempo of the walk. It is "relative" pattern.

A similar process takes place *within* the beat in music, and we shall discuss this further, in a later section. Recently, neurons have been identified that selectively respond to duration, at such time scales (Cassaday, Ehrlich and Covey (1994)).

Let us now return to the example of a sigh. As one hears a sigh, fairly early during its course one already knows it is a sigh (the fragment is compared with *memory*, either innate or learned, very likely innate in the case of a sigh) , and thus one *anticipates* its continuing course - in this one is either correct, in which case a degree of satisfaction occurs, or not - in which case one registers a degree of surprise, or of irritation, a sense of a *mistake* having been made in the execution of the sigh; or less often, in having been induced into wrong anticipation. A sense of toying with one's emotions may also be felt, something in fact "unnatural". What is this naturalness which is being violated here?

The crux of the matter is that these entities in time can have "*meaning*". Logogenesis of such specific time-entities provide a natural dictionary of emotional meaning - meaning which is innately programmed, and innately understood and communicated.

We have called such time-form entities used in the communication and generation of emotions *essentic forms,* or more briefly, *sentic forms,* and have isolated these forms for a number of emotions, in particular for anger, grief, love, sexual desire, joy, hate and reverence (Clynes 1973, 1977,1988).

Such time entities have a contagious function. Their syntax is described in a later section.

Laughter and yawning may be taken as well known examples.

Serial Processing

In the memory process, serial order is an important factor. The direction of time is constant (unlike spatial orientation) so that what was *before* a particular event always remains that way in short-term memory (backward masking excepted, which occurs in the range of 30-50 milliseconds). Only in long-term memory is it easy to make mistakes concerning the order in which events have happened. Short-term events such as a pattern of speech maintains its order in time effortlessly. People do not normally reverse the order of syllables when they perceive a word, or even a sentence, nor do they reverse the order of notes within musical phrases. To do so in fact involves a special effort. *Reordering* the serial events is an *unnatural* process per se. The *natural* process is the placing of these events in the *correct serial order* - although we are so used to this that we do not easily see how extraordinary it is! We achieve this automatically in speech, music and many other events in daily life. The remarkableness of this ability is virtually completely neglected.

We don't know by what agency words remain (or are placed!) in the order they are "laid down". In a computer, there is no inherent requirement to keep the elements of the storage in a single order; only if they are given time labels is that order uniquely determined. A series of elements stored in an array may be read out as easily from left to right as from right to left, say, but they can easily be read out in random sequence also. A spoken sentence, however, necessarily remains in its proper order in memory, and is much more difficult to reproduce in reverse order, if at all possible. Actually, even if one attempts to reproduce a sentence in reverse order, one will tend to reproduce each of the constituent syllables as they were heard, and not themselves reversed in order. Finally, even if we could reverse each syllable, the actual sound involved in the syllables would still not be properly reversed. So we may say that *it is virtually impossible for any conscious person and presumably animal to simply reverse the temporal order in which an experience is stored.* This means that the beginning, middle, and end of a temporal object are nonarbitrary.

> Although we can look at an object in space at all angles, left to right or up
> and down, we can look at a temporal object only in the direction in which
> it was experienced - an important property that seems trivial unjustly.

Temporal forms have a shape which is determined by at least one sensory variable in addition to time. For example, sound volume. Because time has only one physical dimension, while space has three, the combination of time and sensory experience has a smaller dimensionality than the corresponding combination of a space object. Consider for example, sound, which in addition to duration has attributes of pitch, of loudness, of tone color, all of which may have their own trajectories. An object in space, however, may show a great many more attributes in addition to the three spatial dimensions with its virtually limitless variety of spatial shapes: space objects can have color and texture in all their variety, it may have smell, taste, and tactile qualities. With the relative impoverishment of shapes within sound it might seem surprising how great a variety of experience they can nevertheless provide. In fact, it may be the very economy of dimensionality which helps it to focus more directly into the reaches of emotion than the overabundant dimensional variety with which the visual system is constantly bombarded. (Because it is part of the function of the emotional code of dynamic shapes, that if any variable simultaneously expresses a dynamic form inimical to the meaning, the other variables that well express the meaning are diminished in their expressive and communicative power.)

The evolving nervous system has an option of treating inputs as parallel or as serial. Parallel inputs such as the visual system are suitable for spatial experience. Time forms necessarily require serial processing, but they also can accommodate a great deal of parallel processing. A single sound, for example, carries with it simultaneous information concerning pitch, loudness, direction, and even tone quality. Several sounds occurring together can be perceived relatively clearly, and better if they are spatially separated. Parallel processing is carried out simultaneously with serial ordering such as that of syllables and of a series of tones in music. And it is accomplished relatively effortlessly, without effort of consciously separating serial and parallel processes.

Just as there are innate and learned aspects to the recognition of spatial forms, there appear to be also both innate and learned aspects in the recognition of temporal forms. The brain is programmed genetically to produce and perceive certain patterns of sounds, for example the various cries of newly born babies, and many of the cries of birds and other animals. The invariant temporal direction of such time forms make them very suitable as signals, and provide special advantages. Living organisms have developed specific time forms which they use to communicate - assured that these signals will be likely to be understood. Such forms have arisen in evolution especially to generate and communicate internal states we have come to call emotions. Though quite a number of psychologists in the past doubted that emotions "exist" because they are not "things", that is, objects in space, nature has given their expression a status in certain ways more notable and powerful than that of spatial objects.

Body-mind windows in the action of time entities.

A person's gait is a time-entity. We easily recognize someone we know even from behind, seeing only his/her gait. Like facial recognition, for which separate brain structures exist, gait recognition involves highly sophisticated data processing, with millisecond range resolution, and memory for that time-entity. It is possible that specialized brain structures like those for facial recognition may exist for the perception of such time-entities and their storage in memory. Certainly, each animal species too tends to have its own unique gait, which we readily "know". Perhaps it is because of its evolutionary advantage in distinguishing among animals that we (and probably other animals) have developed this ability. Dynamic aspects tend always to be more impressive than static ones, since they are excite receptors to a greater extent. (It would be interesting to do an experiment say with cats, to see whether they will recognize a cat-like walk in an otherwise uncatlike model.)

A different aspect is invoked if we consider that a particular feeling may be generated by such a time-form entity. The connection between the form and the feeling, genetically based, becomes then an inherent 'window' across the mind- body barrier. A one-one relation existing between them, within given circumstances, gives us to understand that these forms are not arbitrary, and that our minds are hardly free to respond to them other than as the inherent connection ordains. That there is such a connection is most obvious for the various forms of laughter, for yawning, and perhaps also for crying, all of which cannot be taught at school, nor eradicated by dictators. Nor could one explain to a visitor from another galaxy say, who did not have such an inherent program, what these time form patterns feel like. As to *why* they feel like this, we cannot even explain to ourselves.

The interaction of the mind and body in executing action (Clynes 1969,1970) whether expressive or nonexpressive is hardly understood, but is clearly experienced even in lifting of a single finger. But we should draw attention to the possibility that action can be precisely controlled without kinesthetic feedback: as it happens continuingly in the muscularly mediated adjustment of the focus of the lens of the eye, merely by our intention to look somewhere; or in the regulation of blood flow to those parts of the brain engaged in a particular thought process. There may exist time form entities which are not consciously experienced, yet originate from mental requirements.

Our new, non-elitist understanding of the language of music

As the gait readily reveals an individual within the human species, or a species among non-human species (some humans who are very well acquainted with a group of lions, say, may even be able to distinguish individuals among them by their specific gait) so we have found that in music such repeated patterns are similarly able to communicate identity.

We have found that the *Composer's Pulse* is such a time-entity. It is described, like a gait would be, as a specific time-amplitude function. To explain: in the case of music one begins with an even grid pattern of time-slots where notes could be found, a kind of temporal lattice. The Composer's Pulse then represents a *combined* time and amplitude warp of that pattern, a warp that distorts the equal temporal grid on which notes can be placed, and also provides a substantial amplitude pattern imprint across a group of notes. Such a combined twofold warp pattern is applied recursively throughout the music piece, as if the composer were "walking" (or perhaps, on occasion, storming or meandering) through the piece. Additionally, in the case of music, this warping time-entity *is active on several levels of organization*, simultaneously, in a hierarchical manner. Perhaps it is somewhat as if an individual who was walking were also *talking* at the same time in his/her particular, individual manner, and that the pattern of the speech reflected, on a different scale, the pattern of the gait - but with the proviso that the talking pattern be coordinated with the walking pattern.

With the Composer's Pulse we have an example of *meaning* carried through millisecond modulation of sound patterns. The meaning is also evident in the muscular gestures in which the Pulse can be evident motorically (eg. conducting).. There is a one-one correspondence between the warp of the Pulse matrix and the form of the muscular repeated gesture (although the latter is dimensionally poorer). The warp predicts the gesture although the gesture cannot itself predict the warp, having less number of variables - the warp has 6 degrees of freedom, with a four-element Pulse. (If one were to measure several muscle tensions of the arm within the dynamic gesture however, there would be more variables available for this reverse prediction.)

Typical examples of meaning might be the strength and ethical restraint of the Beethoven pulse, the non-sexual longing of the Schubert pulse, the natural piety and enthusiasm of the Haydn pulse, the enveloping security of the Brahms pulse.

Ethnic pulses too carry emotionally oriented meaning: The feisty enthusiasm, the vital energy and temperament of the Hungarian Pulse of a Csardas, the sexual tension and macho-ness of Spanish music, the floating, joyfully sensuous lightness of the Viennese Waltz pulse, the pride and elan of the Polish Polonaise pulse, the joyful serenity of the pulse of certain Northern Indian music (Ragopati), the varieties of energy flow and feeling in African music, and so on. The nature of the meaning, as may be evident, tends always to be more precise than can be rendered in words.

Folk music today is not anymore even an endangered species: it is already extinct. No more folk music is being composed - it takes generations of refining and honing of the melodies for a beautiful folk song to arise through social nurturing. The Rock music of today is generated commercially and represents mostly the lowest common denominator, ie. emotional qualities that *sell* best, not that best express ethnic character. To a great extent, Music has ceased to be a muse and has become a whore. That has resulted in classical music becoming an endangered species.

But the new understanding of the language of music that we have now makes it possible to stage a rescue operation, to rescue classical music, because we can now make its expressive process and meaning readily available to anyone, not just to a strangely selected elite. No longer are athletics and coordination indispensable parts of learning music. They are abolished from music, to which they never belonged, except through dire necessity.

In this new way, we can chose the natural time-entities per se, creatively, without producing them with our bodies, have them pass through our mind-body windows, and activate our feelings, emotions, and insights in the way only music can. The entrance to a "better world", as Schubert said in his song 'An die Musik', a world in a sense our true home, is now open to essentially all of us - not merely as passive consumers, but as creative interpreters, as participants.

Molecular Basis of Logogenesis.

The basis of spatial entities in morphogenesis is mediated by the specific forms of proteins, and their folding. *Clocks may be regarded as converters of space forms to time forms.* Logogenesis of time-forms is most likely carried out by similar mechanisms as morphogenesis, with the mediation of specific molecular clocks to translate from space form to time form. Some molecular geneticists regard the genetic molecular apparatus as a language process with meaning. In logogenesis this carries across the body-mind barrier into genetically built inherent meaning: Meaning which finds its roots in specific proteins and how they fold, and in specific DNA sequences of genes, and one would presume developmentally in the action of neurotropic factors, and trk receptors, such as the recently discovered trkB and trkC, and their corresponding genes and gene regulators, a machinery basically similar to that of morphogenesis. It is probable that when the genes for laughter are found we may rather soon thereafter have our first relatively detailed description of logogenetic processes.

Continuity.

A central problem (though one that is rarely a subject of scientific concern) is how from discontinuous events in time and discontinuous entities in space - molecules, electrons - continuous experience can be generated.

Continuity in space can be generated in two ways: 1. through superposition of individual effects, a property of a field. For example, the needle of a meter may have a stable position on space - a continuity - because its coil automatically summates the individual effects of the billions of electrons that generate the "field"; nature's superposition principle makes this possible. Or, the earth swings around the sun because the gravitational effects of separate particles of sun matter are superimposed. The superposition is perfect, one may add.

The effect of summation of individual events may be sensed by a sensor sensitive to the field at some point(s) in space.

The second way continuity is achieved in nature is through structure, eg. a crystal, a leaf. Sensing structure however means making a model, whether it is a lock and key fit of a special part, or a re-creation of some aspect of the structure elsewhere in the brain, as a "model". This model of course has to be sensed further, perhaps as a key and lock situation, or eventually as a combination of field with key and lock (otherwise an endless chain of "models" ensues).

Computer memory, a chain of ones and zeros, represents a special case of structure. In the brain memory is frequently accompanied by a time categorization that gives us information about *when* this memory was acquired. And how is this "when" represented? Nobody knows.

Continuity *in time* is a separate problem about which even less is known. How do we know the beginning, middle, and end of a specific time course? How can the brain make a model of this? Are there field effects that specifically allow recognition of a particular time course of a variable?

We may of course consider that clocks with settable flags - interrupts - acting like alarm clocks that let us know when "time is up". We can imagine some agency setting the alarm. But the problem is far more demanding than that. While some timing aspects of the brain appears well to work like that (e.g. deciding before falling asleep when to wake up), the sensing of logogenetic timeform entities clearly does *not* work like that.

At the very beginning of a logogenetic time form (such as a sigh, a yawn , laughter, a love expression, an anger, grief, hate , sexual, joy, or reverence expression, to name most of those that we have studied) we do not know *what* is sensed. The sense of "what" develops in the course of the time form. But after 300-400 milliseconds we already know "what" is being expressed. "What" has already become conscious. But the expression continues on. Only as it continues for 1 - 4 seconds depending on the particular emotion or quality, does the feeling itself *accumulate*. The first recognition is mental only. The time form has to complete itself in order for the *quality* of feeling to be experienced. If it is terminated prematurely, chopped off, then the feeling - built up to that point of the single expression - tends to be actually blocked from that point on.

We may explain the process as follows: At the beginning, a key-lock molecular operation starts a clock, with an "on " signal, a particular logogenetic time form is selected and cumulative receptor binding begins. This cumulative receptor binding is sensed as a developing feeling. (This may involve some kind of cumulative field effect, on the "other side" of the receptors.) At the end, a second key-lock is activated shutting off further accumulation. Before further receptor binding can take place, another "on" signal needs to happen.

Thus if the off signal is not permitted to happen, or if it is not given sufficient time to act, there will be no possibility of a second expression accumulating further feeling.

Confusion can occur if the interval of time (and its time form) between an off signal and the next on signal is attempted to be interpreted as an expression in its own right instead of a 'reset', i.e. a separation between two successive expressions. In this case the sensing process may attempt to find some expressive meaning in a reset, a time slot necessarily devoid of such meaning. The lack of clear endpoints therefore can cause confusion. This can be seen in music, dance, a hallmark of poor performances, as well as in human and animal communication (musicians talk of the phrasing in music needing to "breathe").

At the second key-lock operation marking the end of a logogenetic time form "satisfaction" is experienced, in a degree largely independent of the particular emotion, but related to the success of expressing the time form "well".   Repeated expression will result in increase in accumulation at the receptor sites, and intensity of feeling, provided adequate time is left for 'reset' between successive expressions. (Generally fractions of a second to 1.5 seconds, depending on the emotion. Imagine one laughter merging into another, of the same person, without any break, and you will see what is meant;   it is felt as "mechanical").

The clocks and shaping of the logogenetic time forms appears to be largely done through the amygdala, the "gateway" to expression and perception of expression of emotion (Aggleton and Mishkin 1986).

Thus, the time-form entity gives rise to a *continuity* within itself, mediated by receptor binding processes. They result in the generation of "feeling", a feeling which can be blocked if the time-form cannot complete itself. Unlike a table, which can be partially visible and still be considered a table, a logogenetic time-form can fulfil its function only in complete temporal form. While an incomplete form may be mentally recognized as belonging to a particular emotion, it will be experienced as sterile, "intellectual", without the satisfying appendage of its own feeling.

Such a time-form, once begun, induces anticipation - as mentioned before -   an expectation of completion within its time-frame of 1.5 - 8 seconds, say (depending on which emotion is expressed).   A conscious, or preconscious, image is formed sometime (300 -500 millisecond) after it is is begun, and thereafter both expectation and memory are active (experiential time process t2). When completed, the satisfaction nulls out expectation, and memory comprises a single entity, the completed form with its feeling.

A successive expression of similar kind will then *automatically* be compared with the previous one as an entity: if it is in sound, it will be noted if it is louder or softer than the previous one, slower or faster, or a combination of these. Also noted would be a relative change in the time form itself, should it occur, apart from those transformations, for example the relative harshness of the sound. These automatic comparisons generally are part of the biological language process of these logogenetic forms, and add to meaning. One sigh, one peal of laughter is either louder or softer than another. In terms of touch, correspondingly the general pressure is greater or less, and greater or smaller areas of the body are being touched.

Similar comparisons occur willy-nilly in the expression and perception of music, where the time form entities are musical phrases or motifs.

Sameness in all these respects results in boredom, in dropping of the "story", and even irritation. (Boredom has been far too little studied as a quality of experience). This of course rests on the ability to perceive the sameness, ie. precise, effortless memory, and partly on anticipation. (Note: Minimalists have used this property to make ever smaller changes, that consequently can sharpen alertness)

This time experience process (t2) notes the *relative changes* in time-form entities.

There is a further time-experience process t3 which is aware of the general tempo of the entire sequence of entities, the unrolling of the 'canvas' in time. This is independent of the relative perception process of t2 in comparing time-forms, to a first order, ie. the comparisons work quite as well at different t3 tempos. t3 however is remembered independently of t2 aspects.

The entire experience is placed and remembered in t1, the life-line of the individual, e.g. it occurred last week on Tuesday afternoon.

Natural Syntax of Logogenetic Time- Forms.

The natural language of these time-forms that operate in t2 (2 - 10 seconds, forms having beginning, middle and end, involving memory and anticipation) works as follows:

1. **Gain:** The gain of transmission of such a time-form-entity or "word" is a function of the perfection of the dynamic form. The effectiveness of generating the quality of feeling expressed is greater the more authentic the form of the "word".

2. Symbiosis: The generation process may be similar in the individual who expresses the form (the sender) as in the receiver.

3. Iteration. Appropriate repetition of the "words" augments the generating effect. Appropriate repetition allows a duration of that language element time-form plus a random duration of the order of a small fraction (about 10-20%) of that duration, somewhat like intervals of silence between spoken words, but on a rather slower time scale.

4. Autosemantic: The meaning of the "word" is contained in the transmitted form itself.

5. Filters: What kind of error messages may be tolerated in t2 forms? What causes distortion of meaning? The kind of processing that t2 forms require is quite different from that we are used to in signal processing, such as frequency response, FFT, and time domain analysis or even wavelet analysis, their combination. Certain errors are quite tolerable, while others, seemingly of similar quantitative aspect are not.

Accordingly a new form of mathematics needs to be created to accommodate these functions. It is the hope of the author to embark on such development in collaboration with mathematicians in the coming years. To illustrate the requirements we may give a two examples: in visual sentic form processing, a work of art may have small parts missing, scratches that interrupt the expressive line, or even entire parts may be missing. The 'eye' will tent to smooth over the missing gaps and *complete* the form as if no gaps were there. However, even a relatively slight distortion of the shape of the form will be sensed as an obtrusive distortion of meaning. Yet small scaling factors will not materially affect the result. Least squares and other statistical analyses fail to distinguish between acceptable and non-acceptable faults and errors. The problem is to mathematically define the invariance that needs to be preserved. As a second example, in sound we may cite the phenomenon that an old 78 record of Schnabel for example contains far more musical content of meaning than a similar HI FI version that conserves the full frequency spectrum and has little noise background. What, again, is the invariance that is preserved in the 78 record but is absent in the new CD recording, and how can it be mathematically defined with respect to noise? While we actually have quantitative solutions to the appropriate microstructure that is essential and may be missing in the new CD version, we need to develop a relevant signal-to-noise theory in mathematics which could be generally applicable to biologically evolved logogenetic time forms, and take into account their special communicative properties, not present in sinusoidal signals and their combinations.

Thus the code of transmission and meaning are not independent as in humanly designed systems, such as Morse Code or PCM, but are unified in the elegant natural design. Sender, receiver, and message are codesigned by nature as a single system. The meaning *is* the analog form of the transmission. It is demodulated by the amygdala, it appears, the very structure that is also involved in its modulation (hence aptly called by Mishkin the "gateway" to emotional communication). The analog form may be produced in various sensory outputs e.g. sound and touch. The information arrives in discrete bundles, as separate time form entities, but each entity is analog. There thus can be a *chain of such discrete analog forms, the stream of emotional expression.*

The stream may tell an emotional 'story'; it does so in music for example, forming one stream of the double stream of music.

The form becomes experienced as meaning when it passes through the amygdala and activates the appropriate emotional brain circuitry. There is a natural interpretation function of these forms built in to our nervous systems, the converse of the natural the function that originates their expression. Gene systems that symbiotically produce such forms and empower their recognition have been identified for some mating song patterns in cicadas, for example, and effects of their mutation observed.

Music involves a second stream in addition to the one above: an invention of a repetitive pattern in time, a continuing selfrepeating pattern of consistent form we call the "beat". It is the "beat" that goes to the feet, causing them to move in a dynamic manner related to the character of the beat, and that character involves the musical microstructure *within* the beat, patterns within t4, with time warps of the order of 10 milliseconds, and limens of 1-2 milliseconds.

These are sensed not as time functions but qualitatively, as strong, massive, or light, elastic or sodden, energizing or braking, or, emotionally: confident, detached, ironic, hopeful, cheerful, sexually exciting, longing, gentle, engulfing, as a result of a combined amplitude and time warp, the warp being with respect to the grid of nominal numerical proportions of duration.

In ethnic music the character often relates to the rhythms of the language. With composer's pulses, the characteristic combined time and amplitude warps of a particular composer is significant in representing the identity of *who* is telling the musical story.

Music thus has two streams, both of which are decoded by the nervous system in real time, and involve time-form-entities of different kinds: one stream the unfolding emotional 'story' of the music, the other the repetitive signature, or the gait, figuratively, of the 'storyteller'. This second stream, even more than the real gait, carries implied personality structure with it.

In different historic periods, from Gregorian chant to rock music, one or the other stream may dominate; in the classic period of Bach, Beethoven and Mozart a fine balance is achieved.

Is the Composer's Pulse logogenetic?

The composer's pulse matrix, as far as experience has shown so far, remains rather invariant throughout his life, as it appears to fit in relation to his compositions of different periods. Even Beethoven's third period, when his style of composing underwent a radical and unparalleled change requires at most a minor modification of the pulse matrix. Accordingly, it seems not improbable that the pulse of a composer is something he inherits as a personal pattern, something that is part of his essential constitution, and is not the result of choice, nor probably of experience. It may be that individuals all have such characteristic dynamic patterns, but that only great composers have succeeded in embodying this in their music. That it is not a matter of style is evident from the great difference in the pulse matrices of Haydn and Mozart, who share a similar style, or from the differences of those of Schumann, Mendelssohn and Chopin for example.

At any rate, in the Composer's pulses we have time-form-entities that serve a distinct function, and are processed by the brain as meaningful entities. To what extent these entities derive from biological determining factors will need to be determined further. Studies with identical twin and non-identical twin subjects suggest themselves, if it were not for the scarcity of great composers among them! However, there may be methods other than though composed music that would allow one to estimate an individual's particular pulse pattern. One such study is being carried out by the author with "neutral" music which allows any pulse matrix to be superimposed, to see if individual preferences are consistent with other observable motoric characteristics of that person. Such music may contain distributed scale passages for example.

[Composers whose pulse have been identified so far are Bach, Beethoven, Brahms, Chopin, Franck, Haydn, Mendelssohn, Mozart, Scarlatti, Schubert, Schumann]

Precision as a function of t4, and of t3.

We may see two very different sources of temporal precision in music:

1. Sensitivity of the nervous system to time differences of the order of milliseconds in the duration of the elements within the beat, that affect the vitality of the beat, and of the music as a consequence. this sensitivity is not experienced as overtly relating to duration and time, but is experienced as other qualities, that have no known relation to time per se.

2. The stability of tempo, the t3 factor, has been measured to be of the order of 1 in 500 (Clynes and Walker, 1986, 1982). The tempo is in effect the repetition rate of the beat. But that rate is also modulated by the musical structure, such as the four bars of four bar phrases, which tend to superimpose a small but systematic and characteristic modulation on this tempo (of about 1 %). The composer's pulse operates on several hierarchical levels, but its effect is evened out over larger stretches of the music. That means that for a given musical piece, the tempo t3 is a stable time-form entity, if a piece has been well studied. It is the canvas on which the music is rolled out. The music unfurls in the present moment, but at a rate given by the canvas as it unfolds. The tempo is clearly linked to time in our experience: Faster and slower need no explanation. An interval greater than about .5 secs is experienced as partaking of time.

Yet the time of tempo is very different from the time taken by a phrase, by a sentic form of the expression of a particular emotion. Here, in t2, we are aware not of durations, or of repetition rates that also go to the feet, but of beginnings, anticipation and memory. On the 3 - 10 second level, there is structure within the time entity: it has a beginning, a middle, and an end.

So we see that music teaches us about time and time-entities, how we experience these in different temporal processes and modes, each involving different physiologic and psychophysiologic aspects, clocks, and neuronal circuitry: t4, t3, and t2. Finally, there is evidence (Clynes and Walker, 1986) that the *integral* of t3, over the entire piece, even of several movements, has a notable stability of its own.

Whether this stability is basically a function of t1 is an interesting question. It is well known that some people can wake up at very precise times after sleeping an entire night. How long-term time entities operate with precision is also evident in music as just mentioned, and appears to be related to an appreciation of the total invariant temporal size of a meaningful music-object entity, a major composition of the duration of the order of an hour. The stability appears to be independent of the environment, e.g. temperature, humidity, even it seems time of day. Further studies on this large scale stability promise to be fruitful.

Creation of 'Living' Music performances by computer.

In creating meaningful and moving performances with a computer, we use t4, t3 and t2 processes. But the use of t4 goes far beyond the warp of the pulse matrix we have already described. It also includes the shaping of each tone, and the vibrato that organically enriches it. As in the shaping of syllables in speech, music requires each tone to have an organic shape, a shape related to the shape of the phrase and its meaning. The shape of a note, as its amplitude contour (envelope is the technical term) follows the principle of <u>predictive amplitude shaping</u>: the shape of the 'present' note is governed by *what* the next note is *going to be* and *when*. (The shape is skewed forward if the tangent of the pitch time-curve to the next note is positive, backwards if negative). Mostly, except for longer notes, the shaping lies within t4, that is the shape is not experienced as having a beginning, middle and end, but is experienced as a single entity.

The principles of *predictive amplitude shaping* and of *hierarchical pulse* together provide most of the microscore that, combined with the score, creates living, meaningful music (Clynes, in preparation, 1983, 1985, 1986, 1987, 1990, 1992). It shapes music in t4 and t2 (the higher levels - at slower time scale - of the pulse being active in t2). It has no effect on t3, the tempo, which, as a first approximation, is independent of both.

These two principles of musicality - largely unconscious hitherto -- have provided means when programmed into a computer of adequate power (a high power PC), to allow musical individuals to readily create music interpretations of highest quality, without any of the usual technical skill of playing an instrument. That is, the ability to subtly shape music in time is independent of the muscular skill and coordination hitherto required to achieve this. This musical thinking ability actually surpasses in AI terms what has been possible in verbal expressive communication so far. It replaces the old machines that required detailed muscular control, with a more direct link between musical thought and its realization in sound: only the "mind and heart" is involved now in creating musical meaning, not the foibles, efforts and limitations, the athletics of muscular coordination and breath control requiring practically endless training, which are bypassed. Yet it preserves the instrumental sound with which the music speaks.

[Editor's note: the audience was delighted with music played extensively illustrating this at the conference, and saw that it indeed worked]

The extent to which this has become possible is ascribable to increased understanding of the nature and function of timeform entities.

Determinants of t3

An interesting question is what determines t3, the tempo? The choice is one of high precision (Clynes and Walker 1982,1986), as much as 1 part in 500. How is this choice arrived at? A feeling of "rightness" is involved that develops over time, as one knows the piece better.

Part of this rightness links with the integral of t3: the total time for the piece is implicit in the choice of t3,. But there are other factors at work. The entities at t2 level are sufficiently elastic so that variations of say +-8% in the overall t3, other things being equal, can be accommodated without considerable loss of meaning on the t2 level. More than that however would be a more serious matter. We need to look for different qualities of experience than t2 forms to account for the stability. The repetition rate of the pulse at the t4 level may provide some clues for this: Here we

626

are encountering aspects of "energy", of "flexibility" and "inflexibility". The "energy" of the repetitive pulse, or the 'beat' will tend to increase with increasing tempo (t3) but diminish after after a point, becoming "hurried". Diminishing the tempo will give more relaxation, as a slow walk becomes envisioned, then even contemplative exploration, eventually a stillness. Breathing replaces walking as the motoric analog.

We may note that the same piece when played with a different composer's pulse will acquire a different t3 depending on which composer's is used. For example a Mendelssohn Scherzo will have a faster t3 as a Mendelssohn piece, than if it would be played with the Beethoven pulse in a Beethovenian way. The precise tempo of a Mozart Allegro, such as the first movement of the piano concerto in C major K467 for example, is given by the concept of a moderate but determined march, a stepping out. Such a motoric mental analog has a strong influence on the tempo: gradations between running and walking, the imagined size and body constitution of the individual running or walking (vigor and massiveness for Beethoven, little elves in the case of Mendelssohn Scherzi for example). Over and above this there is the question of viewing the musical edifice. Each t3 choice gives a different view point. The relationship of these various influences in fixing a precise value for t3, independent of the environment, as was found in Clynes and Walker 1986, needs considerably more study. Different interpreters have their own preferred values of t3, which tend to cluster however, so that one can speak of a normative value of t3; although the mean value should *not* be taken as the optimal, most meaningful value unlike Repp has suggested. Faster values of t3, other things being equal, tend to promote a better overview of the large scale features of the piece, as might be expected. Slow t3 values in slow movements will promote the switch to breathing as the motoric analog. This may be relevant to Arthur Schnabel's expressed view that one within a given leeway, one should tend to play fast movements as fast as can be accommodated, and slow movements as slow as possible, thereby increasing the contrast.

The best estimate that can be given at this time is that the t3 value chosen by any individual interpreter is closely linked to his/her *concept* of the piece, an entity, like a seed, with overall significance for the entire piece, which, like the agency that generates a dream, is outside the scope of the present chapter.

Logogenetic Time Forms in Sentic Cycles.

In a sentic cycle, an emotional exercise form developed by the author that has been used therapeutically and as a preventive by thousands of subjects over two decades, a subject expresses and generates a series of emotions, by repeated finger pressure expression. Each expression has the duration of the time form entity for that emotion, plus a small quasi-random interval, before he/she initiates another expression of that emotion. The randomness insures that even after years of practise, the user does not know when the next expression will start, so an effect of dialog is created; the subject waits a bit before initiating the next expression, but is all ready to do so. Each emotion is repeated 23-40 times depending on the emotion, and each emotion phase lasts about 2-4 minutes, again depending on the emotion. The repeated expression helps to build up the intensity of the emotion, and is not so long that it satiates the process appreciably, in most cases. The entire cycle takes 27 minutes. While longer periods than 4 minutes for one emotion would tend to satiate that emotion generating process, by switching to the next emotion, a subject feels fresh with regard to that next emotion. This implies a differential receptor satiation for each of the emotions (the sequence of emotions in a sentic cycle is: no emotion, anger, hate, grief, love, sex, joy, reverence).

Two curious phenomena with respect to time experience are systematically observed in conjunction with doing sentic cycles. One is that frequently the time experience for the entire cycle is considerably misjudged: it is shortened systematically; the estimate being, and largely in agreement, that it took about 10 minutes (variance about +2 minutes, estimate is never below 10 minutes!). The shortening of time occurs especially when the cycle is "done well", i.e. the emotions are fluidly and moderately experienced. The experience has some dream-like aspects, in that a person, while sitting quietly, becomes involved in imagination, but there is no sleep at all.

The second phenomenon, probably related to the first, is that the longer expressions, like those of grief for example, which are of the order of 8-9 seconds, get to feel to have a faster repetition rate than they actually have, one gets 'into' that state and it 'flows' in a way that is different than starting out 'cold'. There is a trancelike state quite specific to the process. The time entities are shortened in experience, though not in reality. There appears to be a transformation of the time scale, t2. The total estimate of time seems correspondingly to be reduced perhaps as a consequence of shortening $t2$ experience. It is possible that something like this can occur with music too, in particular performances in which one is as it were "transported", but no systematic observation of this is known. Certainly actual performances of music do not show any such change in $t2$ under conditions of unusually fine performance; the $t3$ stability may override that, should it tend to occur. In any case, if it were similar to what happens in sentic cycles, the *actual* $t2$ expression would still be as long as usual, it would only *seem* to flow faster.

This paradigm offers a unique way to study a transformation of the sense of time, while still marking time with experiential time form entities that do not change their recorded form in time.

A further effect often observed in relation to sentic cycles is that after doing them there seems to be more time, for the next few hours, to accomplish whatever needs to be done, there seems to be a time expansion of sorts.

Human time consciousness is entirely relative to being human (Clynes 1992). [The author has suggested for specific processing reasons (Clynes 1992) that consciousness itself may be a genetically originated function, rather than a graded one requiring complexity; an all or nothing function like being pregnant rather than a gradually developing one, and one that may be shared with even lower-form animals who like us have no problems with simultaneous (and presumably conscious) sensing of sound, vision, smell and touch, and pain]. Time in physics does not define the present, which is an infinitesimal point traveling along the time axis at an unspecified and unspecifiable rate, according to physics. Therefore, conveniently physics does not and never has to deal with the present; it only considers movement from a T1 to a T2, two points on the time axis. Yet the present is all that exists, the past is gone, and the future is not yet here. To a stone a million years is neither a short nor a long time. The rate of our own timeconsciousness is undoubtedly a function of our genes, and may be changeable with increased understanding of molecular biology. The aspects discussed here could constitute a small step towards understanding what the present is in our experience, how past and future are reflected in it, a process very different from that encompassed by our notion of physical time, which strangely succeeds by leaving out the present from its picture of reality.

Conclusion

The precision of time form entities is made especially evident in music, where a tempo stability of 1 part in 500 and a 1-2 millisecond limen in event perception is evident. Clocks that transform form spatial into temporal form need to be postulated to account for this. The experience of time in the waking condition is seen to exist in at least four different modes, called t1 ,t2, t3, t4. Of these, t2 is concerned with the generation and communication of emotional qualities. t4 is manifest in the pulse microstructure of music, where 'syllabic' chunks of time rather than temporal entities having beginnings , middle and end as in t2 are experienced. t3 as a determinant of tempo is a mental function that integrates larger structures, and presents a 'canvas' on which temporal events unfurl. The various modes would seem to be represented in the brain by different functions, with different types of clocks. t2 may be active through the amygdala, t3 as a cortical function, t4 as a property of sound processing, and t1 as the general process of time consciousness of daily life. Memory and anticipation is especially adduced for t2 processes, is not present in t4 itself, and is employed only as a highly stable repetition engine, with a content bound memory for rate, in t3. Successful creation of living music performances through global adjustment of newly discovered principles of musicality enlarges our understanding of the language of music. They and the theory of music as a double stream, help us understand the nature of music, but also can elucidate, to a degree, the varied brain functions of time experience with time form entities.

Logogenesis may also be a conceptual tool to obtain better understanding of 'instinctive' behavior in the larger sense, in its relation between conscious and unconscious programming.

References

Aggleton, J.P. and Mishkin, M. (1986). "The amygdala: sensory gateway to the emotions", in *Emotion: Theory, Research and Experience*, edited by R. Plutchik and H. Kellerman, Vol 3, (Academic Press, New York).

Becking, G. (1928). *Der musikalische Rhythmus als Erkenntnisquelle* (Filser, Augsburg, Germany).

Cassaday, J.H., D. Ehrlich, E. Covey (1994)."Neural tuning in sound duration", Science Vol 264, pp. 847-850.

Clynes, M. (1969). "Precision of essentic form in living communication," in *Information processing in the nervous system,* edited by K.N. Leibovic and J.C. Eccles, (Springer, New York), pp. 177-206.

Clynes, M. (1970). "Towards a view of Man", in *Biomedical Engineering Systems,* edited by M. Clynes and J. Milsum , (McGraw-Hill, New York), pp. 272-358.

Clynes, M. (1972). "Sentography: Dynamic forms of communication of emotion and qualities", Comput. Biol. Med., 3, pp. 119-130.

Clynes, M. (1973). "Sentics: biocybernetics of emotion communication", Annals of the New York Academy of Sciences, 220, 3, 55-131.

Clynes, M. (1977). *Sentics, the touch of emotion.* (Doubleday Anchor, New York.)

Clynes, M. (1980). "The communication of emotion: theory of sentics", in *Theories of Emotion Vol. 1,* edited by R. Plutchik and H. Kellerman, (Academic Press. New York) pp. 171-216.

Clynes, M. (1983). "Expressive microstructure linked to living qualities" in *Publications of the Royal Swedish Academy of Music, No. 39* edited by J. Sundberg pp.76-181.

Clynes, M. (1985a). "Secrets of life in music" in *Analytica, Studies in the description oand analysis of music in honour of Ingmar Bengtsson. Publication of the Royal Swedish Academy of Music, No 47* pp. 3-15.

Clynes, M. (1985b). "Music beyond the score", Communication and Cognit., 19, 2, 169-194.

Clynes, M. (1986). "Generative principles of musical thought: Integration of microstructure with structure", Comm. and Cognition, CCAI, Vol. 3, 185-223.

Clynes, M., (1987). "What a musician can learn about music performance from newly discovered microstructure principles, P.M. and P.A.M", in *Action and Perception of Music,* edited by A. Gabrielsson (Publications of the Royal Swedish Academy of Music, No. 55, Stockholm) pp. 201-233.

Clynes, M. (1988). "Generalised emotion, how it is produced and sentic cycle therapy" in *Emotions and Psychopathology* edited by M.Clynes and J. Panksepp, (Plenum Press, New York) pp. 107-170.

Clynes, M. (1990a). "Some guidelines for the synthesis and testing of Pulse Microstructure in relation to musical meaning", Music Perception, 7, 4, 403-422.

Clynes M. (1990b). "Mind-body windows and music", Musikpaedagogische Forschung, Vol. 11, pp. 19-42, Essen, Germany: Verlag Die Blaue Eule.

631

Clynes, M. (1992). "Time-forms, nature's generators and communicators of emotion", *Proc. IEEE Int. Workshop on Robot and Human Communication*, Tokyo Sept. 1992, pp.18-31.

Clynes, M. (1993). Program of the Annual Meeting of American Association for the Advancement of Science, (AAAS,) Boston, February 1993 pp.. 58-59.

Clynes, M. (in press) Composer's Pulses as language elements in music, a study of groups of graded musical standing. *Cognition*.

Clynes, M. Interpretation of Music (Book and CD) MIT Press, Cambridge, in preparation.

Clynes M., and Nettheim, N., (1982). "The living quality of music, neurobiologic patterns of communicating feeling", in *Music, Mind and Brain: the Neuropsychology of Music* edited by M.Clynes, (Plenum, New York) pp. 47-82.

Clynes, M., and Walker,J. (1982). "Neurobiologic functions of rhythm, time and pulse in music", in *Music, Mind And Brain: the Neuropsychology of Music* edited by M. Clynes, (Plenum New York) pp. 171-216.

Clynes, M. and J. Walker (1986). "Music as Time's Measure", Music Perception 4,1,85-120.

Clynes, M., S. Jurisevic, and M. Rynn (1990). "Inherent cognitive substrates of specific emotions: Love is blocked by lying but Anger is not", Perceptual and Motor Skills, 70. pp 195-206.

Gabrielsson, A. (1986). Rhythm in Music. In J.Evans & M. Clynes (Eds.), *Rhythm in Psychologic, Linguistic and Musical Processes* (pp.131-167), Springfield,Ill.: Charles. C. Thomas

Hama, H. and Tsuda, K., (1990). "Finger-pressure waveforms measured on Clynes' sentograph distinguish among emotions". Perceptual and Motor Skills, 70, 371-376

Laban, R. (1958). *The mastery of movement*, London: Macdonald and Evans.

Minsky, M., (1987). *The Society of Mind*, Simon and Schuster, NewYork

Repp, B.H. (1989). "Expressive microstructure in music: Preliminary perceptual assessment of four composer's "pulses"", Music Perception, 6, 3, 243-274.

Sessions, Roger, (1970). *Questions About Music*, Harvard Uni. Press, Cambridge, Mass.

Thompson, W.F. (1989). "Composer-specific aspects of musical performance: an evaluation of Clynes' theory of pulse for performances of Mozart and Beethoven", Music Perception, 7,1,15-42.

Trusalit, A, (1938). Gestaltung und Bewegung in der Musik, Vierweg, Berlin-Lichterfelde, also synopsized in English by B. Repp in Psychology of Music, 21, 48-72, (1993).

Chapter 29

Role of the Frontal and Temporal Lobes in Scanning Visual Features

R. Bruce Bolster

Role of the frontal and temporal lobes
in scanning visual features

R. Bruce Bolster

Department of Psychology
University of Winnipeg
515 Portage Ave.
Winnipeg, Manitoba
Canada R3B 2E9

The perception of objects in vision is highly context
sensitive. A distinct physical object may or may not be
apprehended as such, depending on the characteristics that it
shares with the visual background. The survival of zebras
hinges implicitly on the failure of figure/ground processing in
the lion - on the predator's inability to distinguish it from its
visual surround. Life is harder for the Wildebeest. It was
never issued camouflaged clothing. It seems condemned to
permanent status as a visual object, a dark blob on a flat grassy
plain. Nonetheless its survival may hinge on failure of a more
subtle form of visual analysis. When chased by a lion, it will
run toward the center of the herd, and may may escape its pursuer
by "hiding" among a large number of highly similar objects -
other wildebeest - darting this way and that in the ensuing
visual confusion.

Successful visual discrimination of one wildebeest, or
indeed one person from the next, may be seen in the abstract as a
problem in combining attributes. This individual might have a
particular shape of horn, that one a particular colour of hair,

and still another a scar on its flank, but only one in the whole herd will possess all three in combination. Unfortunately for the lion, and indeed for monkey and human research subjects, the limitations on visual discrimination for combinations of visual features are rather stark.

Treisman (1977, 1988) has shown that even simple combinations of two visual attributes, such as colour and orientation, can be effectively "camouflaged" if they are presented among nonidentical stimuli that differ only in the combination of attributes they contain. For example, a green square will be difficult to find if it appears among red squares, green diamonds, and red diamonds. Under these conditions, the parallel processing capacity of the visual brain which causes feature discontinuities to "pop out" of the background fails to isolate the correct conjunction of features. Faced with this failure, the organism must resort to a time consuming search wherein "focal attention" (Treisman, 1977) is serially or sequentially swept across the various alternative stimuli until the target combination is located.

Reaction time studies have shown that, for both monkeys (Bolster & Pribram, 1993) and human observers (Treisman, Sykes & Gelade, 1977, Treisman & Patterson, 1984), identification of feature-combination targets in featurally similar context requires a fixed amount of search time for each additional feature-combination distractor which is added to the array. Visual attention under these conditions is swept from location to location under control of a central process that Effron (1990) has labelled "scan".

Electrophysiological experiments on monkeys have implicated several regions of visually responsive extrastriate cortex in the executive control of visual scan. Mountcastle et al (1975) and Robinson et al (1978) have shown that neurons in the inferoparietal cortex of macaque monkeys control saccadic eye movements and eye fixations in terms of specific local regions of the contralateral hemispace. Posner (1984) has shown that damage to parietal cortex in humans impairs the allocation of attention in the hemispace contralateral to the damaged hemisphere. This damage affects overt shifts of attention, involving eye movements, as well as covert attention shifts which do not require eye movement.

But what happens when scan is directed at specific *objects*, as opposed to locations. As noted above, scan is not ordinarily required to detect distinct features, such as a unique color or contour. But it is required for *combinations* of features when these are combined to form a visual "object" or target. Do different cortical regions control scan under these conditions? To answer this question for monkeys, we (Bolster & Pribram, 1993) implanted transcortical electrodes in a number of cortical regions, and then compared local-field potentials evoked by feature-combination targets presented with or without similar-feature distractors. Evoked potential differences related to the distracting feature context were prominent in two extrastriate cortical areas - the inferotemporal cortex and the inferior dorsolateral frontal region, as shown in Figure 1.

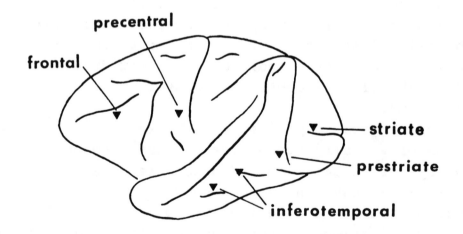

Figure 1

To what extent would these conclusions generalize to the human brain? Harter & Aine (1984) recorded scalp-evoked ERP's during visual conjunction search in humans, and reported significant event-related activity from frontal and temporal electrodes. This pattern was consistent with the neuroanatomical distribution of ERP's we observed in the monkey. It follows that localized damage to the critical zones of frontal and temporal cortex might be expected to impair conjunction search in humans.

EFFECTS OF FOCAL FOREBRAIN INJURY ON CONJUNCTION-SEARCH IN NEUROSURGICAL PATIENTS: A pilot experiment

As a first approach to the problem, we sought to identify neurosurgical patients who had sustained relatively focal cortical damage. We (Bolster & Birk, 1988) did this by recruiting volunteer subjects from the neurosurgical wards of the two university teaching hospitals in Winnipeg. Since localized cortical damage may occur in a variety of ways, such as infarction, trauma, or resection of cerebral tissue for treatment of neoplasm, we did not restrict our sample to any single pathology, but instead imposed some exclusionary criteria to eliminate possible confounds. We excluded patients who had a history of neurological illness prior to the event that led to their admission to the neurosurgical ward, or a history of mental retardation, psychiatric illness, drug or substance abuse, or dementia. The extent and location of cortical damage was assessed by examining pre- and postoperative CT scans and operative reports. Examination of CT scans also enabled us to eliminate patients who presented with more than one cerebral lesion, due to conditions such as multiple or serial CVA's and multiple metastatic tumours. Qualifying, consenting patients were then asked to visit the laboratory and perform our visual search tasks approximately one month following their discharge from hospital.

Control subjects, with no history of neurological illness, were recruited from the introductory psychology subject pool at the University of Winnipeg. These subjects also had to meet the exclusionary criteria listed above, and were matched in age to the neurosurgical cases.

Method

The basic task for each subject was to search a computer-generated array (Cutcomb, Bolster, & Pribram, 1981) of colored shapes to find a green square target. These targets were presented somewhere within a 3 X 3 array, and contained distracting stimuli which differed as to the features they shared with the target. Two array types were used - a "distinct feature" array, in which the distractors were all red diamonds, and thus shared neither color nor shape with the target, and a "shared feature" array, in which some distractors - red squares and green diamonds, shared one feature with the target. Examples of these stimulus arrays are shown in Figure 2.

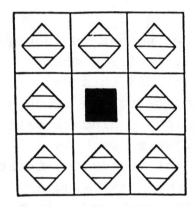

Distinct-feature array

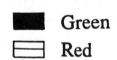

Green
Red

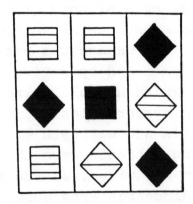

Shared-feature array

Figure 2

The arrays were presented behind clear, hinged plexiglas panels, for 100 msec, and subjects were instructed to

638

press the panel where the target appeared, as quickly as they could after the display came on. Responses were registered on-line, and scored for position, latency, and the stimulus which was chosen. This task was identical to that performed by monkeys in our previous experiments, except that subjects were "rewarded" by a beep from the computer for correct responses, instead of a banana pellet. The two array types were presented with equal frequency, in psuedorandom order. Target position was counterbalanced so that targets appeared with equal frequency in each position in the array. When subjects made errors by pressing a nontarget stimulus, the trial was repeated until the subject either responded correctly or made three successive errors. Testing continued until subjects made 27 correct responses to each array type.

Results

Over a period of approximately six months, we were able to recruit and test fourteen patients. Of these, eleven had lesions of the right cerebral hemisphere, and only three were left hemisphere cases, due principally to the difficulties inherent in obtaining informed consent from aphasic patients.

Performance data from control and patient groups are presented in the following three figures. Figure 3 depicts response latency for "hits" (reponses to the green square target) in each of the two array types.

Note that for all subjects, controls as well as patients, the presence of "shared feature" distractors produced longer response latencies, and thus more distraction, than "distinct feature" distractors, proving that featurally similar context helps to "camouflage" a feature conjunction target, making it more difficult to extract from its background. Note also that both brain-injured groups took longer than controls to respond to targets in either array type, but that their response latencies still reflect a strong difference between distinct and shared-feature context, with the latter always producing longer response latencies.

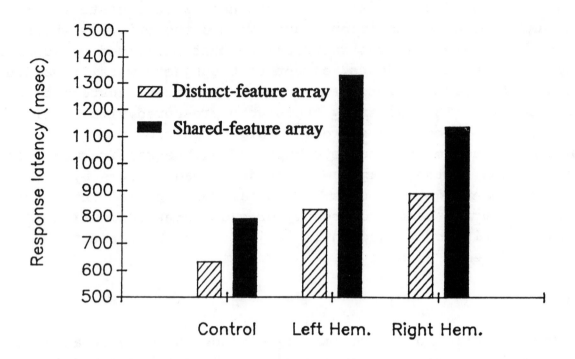

Figure 3

Figure 4 depicts the number of errors made by these subjects, that is to say instances when they chose one of the distractors instead of the target stimulus.

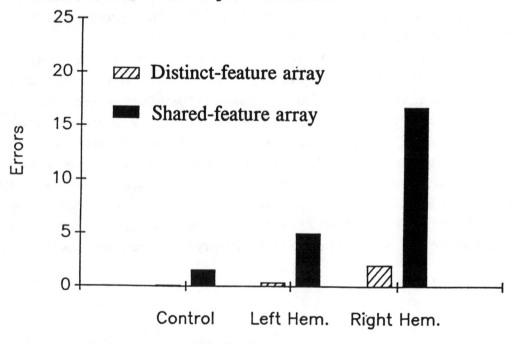

Figure 4

All subjects made more errors to shared-feature arrays. However patients with *right* hemisphere damage made substantially more errors than left hemisphere patients, with the effect most pronounced for "shared feature" arrays. These eleven patients made an average of 18 errors each, producing a total of 11 X 18 = 198 responses to distractors in shared-feature arrays. Of these, exactly 3 were directed to red diamonds, 4 to red squares, and the remaining *191* to green diamonds.

It is worthwhile to consider changes in processing competence that might give rise to such a pattern of performance. One possibility is that right hemisphere patients have lost the absolute capacity to focus attention on form as opposed to color. However all subjects, including controls, showed a strong tendency to choose green diamonds when selecting nontarget item. Note also that all subjects, including the right hemisphere cases, achieved the criterion of 27 correct responses to targets in shared-feature arrays. Right hemisphere patients therefore did not suffer from an absolute inability to process shared-feature arrays, nor did they fail to comprehend the demands of the conjunction search task. They were just more prone to a certain type of error. Bolster & Pribram (1993) noted that monkeys displayed a preference for color over form in performing an identical search task. The evidence indicates that, in both species, the tendency to make errors on the form dimension this relates to the relative difficulty of visual discrimination for the colors and shapes we have used. Recall that we used displays of 100 msec duration. Red vs. green is demonstrably easier than square vs. diamond, for extrafoveal stimuli, and the displays are too brief to permit refixation. This means that stimuli in the shared feature array may be processed "at a glance" - in parallel - for color, but not for shape. By attending to "green" at the time of stimulus presentation, subjects could deploy a parallel filter which would extract a subset of "green blobs" which could then be serially processed for shape.

Patients with right hemisphere damage showed little impairment in color discrimination in shared-feature arrays. If the model developed above is correct, this means there has been no damage to the parallel filter which enables items to be sorted on the basis of color. Adverse effects on processing were confined to the treatment of form information. Reaction time experiments have shown that, for shared-feature arrays, processing of this second feature dimension is *serial*, since reaction time increases linearly as shared-feature distractors are added to the array. Thus the impact of right hemisphere injury appears to be confined primarily to the *serial* operation that are required to locate targets in conjunction search.

With only three left hemisphere cases it is really impossible to place great confidence in the left hemisphere group as representative of left hemisphere damage generally - injuries in these cases might have missed the critical cortical regions entirely. Indeed the difficulty in recruiting suitable "focal injury" patients led us to focus on a different and more homogeneous clinical population as described in the next experiment. Nonetheless were intrigued by what seemed to us a counterintuitive result - namely that search for conjunction targets in "shared feature" context, which has been described repeatedly in the literature as a serial or sequential process, would be more affected by right than left hemisphere injury. The anomaly of course is that descriptions of hemispheric specialization in cognitive operations - including visual search - have traditionally allocated serial, analytic processing competence to the left hemisphere, whereas the right hemisphere competence has been characterized as "holistic" or parallel. (Gazzaniga, 1970; Patterson & Bradshaw, 1977; Moscovitch, 1979; Polich, 1978, 1980).

We began this experiment, however, not with the intention of focusing on hemispheric speciality, but instead on the issue of where, <u>within</u> the hemispheres, damage might debilitate feature-based, context-sensitive visual search. On this issue, we at least had enough cases of right hemisphere injury to draw some tentative conclusions. Since the error data seemed more telling in terms of processing competence, we elected to break down the sample as to location of damage, and then measure the relative impact on error rates on the two search tasks. These data are presented in the next figure.

Note that the greatest impact on error rates was produced by damage to the temporal lobe, parietal lobe, and dorsolateral, but not orbital, frontal lobe injury, and once again that the principal impact is on conjunction targets presented in "shared-feature" context. The orbitofrontal case is particularly striking for the absence of impact on accuracy, demonstrating that the effect is due neither to right hemisphere damage alone, nor to frontal lobe damage alone, but instead seems confined to the hemispheric convexity that includes the dorsolateral frontal, temporal and parietal cortices. These of course were the regions that Bolster & Pribram (1993) identified as critical to conjunction search in the monkey on the basis of transcortical ERP's.

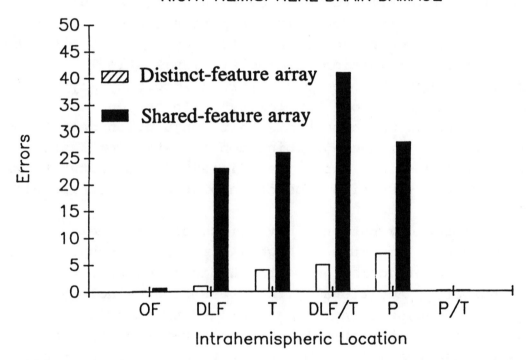

Figure 5

IMPACT OF TEMPORAL LOBECTOMY ON FEATURE BASED VISUAL SEARCH:

Following completion of the pilot experiment, Nicole Lanthier and I were fortunate to obtain the collaboration of a neurosurgeon, Dr. Garnette Sutherland, who specialized in the surgical treatment of epilepsy. Epileptic foci within the temporal lobes are notoriously refractory to pharmacological control, and surgery conducted on such patients normally involves unilateral resection of temporal lobe, including both lateral and medial aspects.

Patients with right, but not left, temporal lobectomy have been reported by Milner (1968) to suffer from deficits in visual memory, relating primarily to the retention of perceived material, and "a mild impairment in the perception of complex patterns" (pg. 191). Nonetheless Meier & French (1965) reported deficits in the discrimination of complex visual stimuli following right temporal lobectomy. This discrepancy may well devolve on the definition of "complexity". In the current experiment we explore the hypothesis that conjunction search - the discrimination of feature combination targets from featurally similar distractors - is a task of sufficient "complexity" to be adversely affected by surgical resection of the right temporal lobe.

Temporal lobectomy patients have circumscribed, well documented, and most importantly highly similar lesions from case to case, differing of course as to the hemisphere which was removed at surgery. Additionally the presenting pathology is similar in all cases, eliminating a confound present in our pilot experiment, which is the ambiguity of interpretation that arises when one attempts to compare a patient with a ischaemic infarct in region "A" with a patient with a resected meningioma from region "B". We undertook to recruit a relatively large sample of temporal lobe cases, and have to date tested twenty-two such individuals (ten left and twelve right hemisphere cases), together with an additional twenty-one age-matched nonpatient controls.

Method

The main task for each patient was the conjunction-search task, exactly as described above. However we wished at the same time to compare performance on another, previously developed visual task that has proven sensitive to the effects of temporal lobe resection. Therefore we administered the Complex Visual Discrimination Task of Meier & French, (1965). Representative discriminanda from this tasks are depicted in figure 6 below.

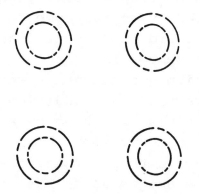

Example 1:   Problem providing a rotational cue

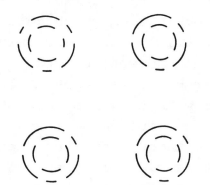

Example 2:   Problem providing a structural cue

Stimulus items from the Complex Visual Discrimination test (Meier & French, 1965).

Figure 6

This task incorporates an aspect which has proven critical to performance in our conjunction search task - namely that nontarget stimuli may share at least some attributes of the target, and thus act as potent distractors. However the Meier & French task differs from our own in that it does not involve search of a set of alternatives in order to identify a known target. Instead it is an "oddity" problem, in which the target is not only embedded in, but defined by, the featural context in which it appears. This is a different application of contextual information from the "known target" case, which might at least potentially place different demands on the brain and the way that temporal lobe structures are engaged in task solution.

We thought that this was possibility was sufficiently intriguing to justify modifying our computer-based conjunction search task so that it could be presented as an oddity problem. Having done this, we presented each patient with the oddity version of the conjunction search task - which we have labelled the "variable target" version, in addition to the green-square search task described aboves, which we have labelled the "fixed target" version, to avoid confusion. Displays in the variable target task were similar to those of the green square problem in that the target item was unique as to the combination of colour-form features, whereas there was always more than one of each alternative distractor. In the variable target version, however, the feature combination which defined the target shifted randomly from trial to trial, and could only be deduced by systematic inspection of the entire array. Examples of variable target conjunction search arrays appear below in figure 7.

Pilot experiments with the this version of the conjunction search task demonstrated a much higher degree of difficulty as compared with the fixed target version, such that when arrays were presented for 100 msec, as in previous experiments, subjects could no longer locate the target. Indeed, even a ten-fold increase in exposure time, to a full second, proved difficult for most neurologically intact subjects, including the experimenters.

Interpretation of "errors" as to the feature combination which was chosen, was no longer terribly meaningful, since it was unclear in the case of an error what the subject was "looking for" when s/he made a mistake. Therefore we adopted a different strategy in presenting and scoring this task. We began each

 Green

Red

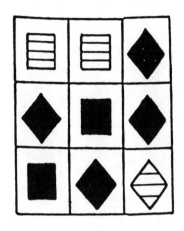

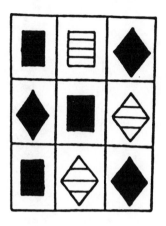

Example 1

Target: Red Diamond

Example 2

Target: Red Square

Variable Target Conjunction Search Task Arrays.

Figure 7

block of trials with a relatively long exposure duration of 5000
msec, hopefully within the capacity of even our most impaired
neurosurgical patients, and then reduced the exposure duration by
20% after every three trials. We then asked the question "at
what exposure duration will subjects begin to have difficulty
identifying the target". Difficulty" was defined operationally
as a failure criterion, reached when subjects made a given number
of consecutive errors.

Results

Response latency data for the fixed target, green-square
version of the conjunction search task are presented in Figure 8.

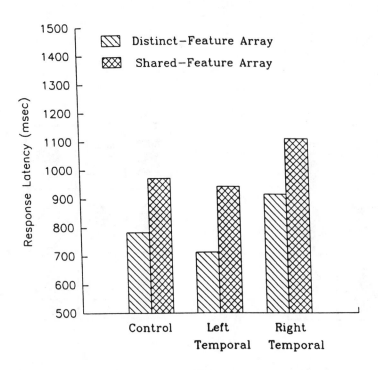

Figure 8

Unlike the data of the previous experiment, right, rather than left hemisphere damage produced the largest apparent elevation of response latency. Response latency was significantly longer in right lobectomy cases, as compared to controls, for both array types. There were no significant latency differences between the left hemishpere and control groups for either array type. Once again for controls and both lobectomy groups, response latencies were elevated (significantly) by the presence of shared-feature distractors.

Figure 9 shows the errors made by each group.

Once again, all subjects, regardless of neurological status, made significantly more errors when targets appeared among "shared feature" distractors. Although left temporal lobectomy appeared to increase error rates above control levels, this effect was not statistically significant. By contrast, resection of the right temporal lobe dramatically increased error rates, particularly for targets presented in "shared feature" context. Analysis revealed statistically significant elevation of error rates for the right lobectomy group as compared to either the left lobectomy group or control subjects. By contrast there were no statistically significant between-group differences in error rate for the targets presented in "distinct feature" context.

FIXED TARGET CONJUNCTION SEARCH TASK

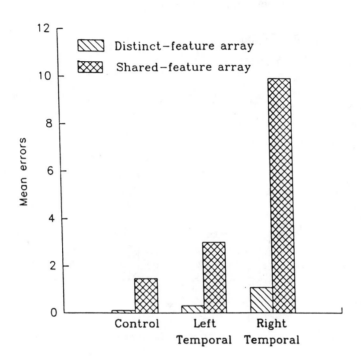

Figure 9

Performance data for the variable target "oddity" version of the conjunction-search task are presented in figure 10.

Once again it is apparent that right, but not left temporal lobectomy had a dramatic effect on performance, producing a significantly elevated "performance-limiting exposure duration", for the right hemisphere group as compared to either the left lobectomy or control group. This was true whether we applied "three successive" or a more stringent "five successive" error criterion as a determinant of task failure. Note that subjects with right lobectomy failed (to either criterion) at stimulus exposures that were at least twice as long as either of the other two groups. This result demonstrates that right temporal lobectomy not only impairs accuracy in discriminating conjunction targets from "shared feature context" but also limits the *rate* at which featural context can be processed for meaningful information.

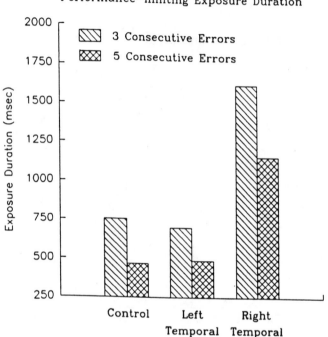

VARIABLE TARGET CONJUNCTION SEARCH TASK
Performance-limiting Exposure Duration

Figure 10

This observation is interesting in the light of Spinelli and Pribram's (1966) discovery that electrical stimulation applied (at the inferotemporal cortex) to the temporal lobe of monkeys changed the time constant of the visual recovery cycle - the time it took the visual cortex to recover from the refractory effects of a previous flash. Pribram (1971) noted that such effects reflect changes in the redundancy of fibres within a sensory channel, and thus the rate at which "information, a greater number of different signals, can be processed" (pg. 211).

To our surprise, the Complex Visual Discrimination task failed to discriminate lobectomy patients from controls. This is an anomalous result, since Meier and French (1965) found patients with right temporal lobectomy to be impaired on target identification this task. In our sample, there were no significant differences between the three subject groups on discrimination accuracy, and in fact the highest number of errors was made by control subjects (mean: 2.97), as opposed to mean values of 1.5 and 1.33 errors for the left and right temporal groups, respectively.

In their 1965 experiment, Meier & French presented the discriminanda on slides, at durations of 4, 8, and 16 seconds. However in the present experiment, stimuli were presented on photocopied sheets, and subjects were allowed to look at the discriminanda until they made a response. It is possible that by changing the task in this way we unwittingly removed a constraint on exposure duration which was critical to task performance. There would be no impairment on a self-paced task if right temporal lobectomy limits the rate of processing as opposed to the absolute amount of featural information that can be extracted from complex displays.

Response latency data from performance of the Complex Visual Discrimination task in the present sample reinforce this conclusion, although the magnitude of the effect did not achieve statistical significance. Given unlimited time to view the stimuli, right temporal lobe patients took longer (mean: 11.4 seconds) than either left temporal patients (mean: 8.63 seconds) or controls (mean: 8.9 seconds). Recall that right temporal patients performed as well as controls in discrimination accuracy. It is possible that they accomplished this by compensating for a reduced rate of information extraction with an increase in the duration of scan.

Discussion

I hope the experiments reviewed above have convinced you that, in people as well as monkeys, both the temporal and dorsolateral frontal cortex are critically involved in the business of extracting objects from potentially distracting featural context, apparently with right hemisphere superiority superimposed upon this competence in our own species. The interesting question is why these brain regions, which are after all relatively far removed from the primary geniculostriate projection, are involved in this demanding form of visual search.

Mishkin, Ungerleider, & Macko (1983) reviewed evidence for the differential involvement of monkey extrastriate cortex in the

extraction of information from visual input. They note that, as
the work of Mountcastle and his colleagues demonstrates, a dorsal
pathway converging on the inferoparietal cortex can be described
as a "spatial vision" channel, extracting information as to where
stimuli are located in extrapersonal visual space. A second,
ventral pathway, converging on the inferotemporal cortex, is
concerned with "object vision", the extraction of information
which makes object identification possible.

Degeneration labelling experiments by Jones & Powell (1970)
established that the inferoparietal and inferotemporal cortex are
each reciprocally connected with an anatomically circumscribed
zone of the dorsolateral frontal cortex. In the macaque monkey,
the frontal projection from the inferotemporal area is located in
the region inferior to the principle sulcus. Bolster & Pribram
(1993) found that strong activity was evoked in both
inferotemporal and inferior principalis region by the presence of
shared-feature distractors. Thus inferolateral frontal and
inferotemporal cortex acted as a functional unit during
conjunction search, as would be expected from the anatomical
connectivity. We proposed an extension of the ventral
extrastriate circuit into the frontal lobe to include inferior
portion of the dorsolateral frontal cortex.

Results from our human population support this model.
Several patients sustained damage to the frontal regions
presumed homologous to the inferolateral frontal regions which is
involved in conjunction search in monkeys. These patients
exhibited the expected impairment in detecting conjunction
targets in the presence of "shared'feature" distractors.

Converging research on two primate species has shown that
the lateral frontal cortex is involved in visual conjunction
search. Let me now try to persuade you that this task is
relevant to "object vision" - the competence which Ungerleider,
Macko & Mishkin have ascribed to the ventral extrastriate
pathway.

Intrinsic to the problem of object identification is the
discrimination of a particular thing from others which resemble
it. Hyundai automobiles, for me, are no longer clearly
discriminable for Hondas, or indeed a constantly increasing set
of new vehicles whose names I could not recite. Thus Hyundais as
a class of visual objects are incompletely specified and poorly
differentiated in my mind. Probably the same statements can be

made concerning the representation of Hyundais by my brain. No doubt this situation could be rectified by the application of focal visual attention to the stream of traffic passing beneath my office window. Some visual attributes, such as colour, will certainly prove irrelevant to the problem, but some distinct feature, akin to the prominent fins on a 50's era cadillac, may turn up which will allow Hyundais to "pop out" of traffic without the need for concentrated attention. I am not overly optimistic on this score, however. Instead I believe that the solution lies, like the wildebeest problem, in the operation of combining attributes into a superordinate percept. By this argument, Hyundais will prove to be unique only in terms of some combination or configuration of headlights, bumpers, windows, rooflines, and so on. Note that I do not for a minute believe that the cars I am watching are "assembled" by my visual brain from primary elements corresponding to those named above, rather that they will have to be analyzed into such components before I can learn to tell them apart.

By this argument, the role of the ventral extrastriate pathway has more to do with object *discrimination* than with object "vision" per se, and has more to do with the act of *recognition* than with passive representation.

We have shown that frontal and temporal damage makes subjects vulnerable to distraction by featurally similar context. In visual search tasks, the critical features of the target stimulus are defined by another type of context which determines what the subject is searching <u>for</u>. In our computer-based tasks this was experimentally defined as the feature conjunction which was rewarded with a "beep". The meaning of the stimuli to the subject was thus defined in terms of what was to be <u>done</u> with them, that is by their relevance to ongoing behaviour. This is what shaped discrimination, and defined "targets" as a class of "objects.

Thus the executive control of focal attention during discrimination learning depends intrinsically upon the subject's *intentions*, which depends in turn upon the potential effects of actions on the objects in view. One might therefore expect limbic and motoric structures of the forebrain to be intimately involved in the control of attention, and indeed McGuinnes & Pribram (1975) have incorporated the large body of evidence for such involvement into a comprehensive model. In this model, motor structures in the frontal lobe, including the basal ganglia and frontal neocortex act to modulate "activation", which imposes "readiness" on the control of responses. Basal ganglia and frontal cortex act reciprocally, respectively raising and lowering the threshold of response to a particular stimulus. Patients with dorsolateral frontal lesions in the current experiment were vulnerable to distraction by shared feature context, and it is possible to interpret this as an inhibitory failure, producing an increase in readiness to respond to either reinforced feature. Responses could then be triggered by a single feature instead of additively by the appropriate feature combination.

Patients with frontal lobe injury have been shown to have difficulty on other visual tasks which require constrained attention to visual features. The Wisconsin Card Sort test, which requires the flexible redeployment of attention from one feature (e.g. colour) to another (shape) in order to categorize multidimensional stimuli, has proven highly sensitive to dorsolateral frontal lobe damage (Milner, 1964). Kolb & Whishaw (1990) reported that some frontal patients continue to *respond* to the previously rewarded feature (e.g. colour) following a shift in reinforcing contingencies, while *verbally* acknowledging the shift to the newly reinforced feature dimension (e.g. form). Such dissociated behaviour shows that the problem for frontal patients is not with initiating a response, since the patients can perform the sorting task on the initial stimulus dimension, nor on the visual capacity to perceptually isolate a single stimulus attribute. Rather the difficulty is in inhibiting the response once it has become conditionaly linked to the appearance of a particular stimulus.

Unilateral temporal lobectomy typically involves removal of both lateral and medial cortex, including a major portion of the the hippocampus, as well as complete removal of the ipsilateral amygdala. Patients with right hemisphere temporal lobectomy were significantly impaired on both versions of the conjunction search task. Some degree of impairment would have been expected from the removal of lateral neocortex alone, since resection for lobectomy likely includes tissue homologous to the inferotemporal cortex in monkey, an area which our ERP evidence (Bolster & Pribram, 1993) indicates is strongly engaged in conjunction search. However there is reason to suppose that removal of amygdala and hippocampus may also contribute, perhaps in an additive way, to the observed performance deficit.

Pribram & McGuinness (1975) note that these structures each make distinct contributions to the control of attention. In their model, the amygdala modulates *arousal*, which determines whether an object is encoded as novel or familiar.

Shiffrin and Schneider (1977) identified two distinct types of attention which can be brought to bear on attentional tasks. *Automatic* processing enables parallel processing of visual stimuli and the effortless detection of target items. This leads to "pop out" phenomena in perception wherein the target is instantly recognized as distinct from its background. Treisman has shown that "pop out" occurs for visual stimuli that differ from background items on a single visual attribute (e.g. colour, shape, motion), as was the case for targets in our search task when they were presented in distinct-feature context. According to Pribram & McGuinness, "pop out" is accompanied by behavioral orienting toward the novel item, and phasic visceroautonomic activity which enables habituation to occur to the repetitive or invariant components of the stimulus situation, so that they come to be encoded as familiar. The visceroautonomic components of the orienting response are attenuated following amygdala resection, so the organism fails to habituate and treats even recurring stimuli as novel. Patients in the second experiment who underwent right temporal lobectomy were slower to respond to targets in distinct-feature arrays, and responded more frequently to "background" or distractor items. Note that these items had no features in common with the target stimulus. This pattern of behavior is consistent with defective orienting which may be due to amygdala resection. This is admittedly speculative, since we tested no patients who had damage confined to amygdala alone, unaccompanied by hippocampal and neocortical removal. It must be also be noted that left temporal patients actually performed slightly better than controls on detecting targets in distinct-feature arrays. Therefore anything said about amygdala in the context of visual processing needs to be qualified by saying something about hemisphericity - specifically that subcortical structures may be as strongly lateralized as cortical regions as regards their contribution to visual scan and discrimination learning.

The performance impairment produced by right temporal lobectomy was by no means confined to distinct-feature arrays - indeed it was much more pronounced for shared-feature arrays. Remember that target detection for arrays of this type entails a serial, centrally-directed search. Shiffrin & Schneider (1977) also reported serial search functions for shared-feature arrays, however their explanation of the central process which controlled search devolved on the ways in which responses were mapped onto stimulus features. When mapping was inconsistent from trial to trial, for example when a stimulus feature that appeared on a distractor turned up on a target on a subsequent trial, subjects were forced to use central, serial search. They labelled this *controlled processing*.

Controlled processing entails the expenditure of cognitive *effort* (Kahnemann, 1973). McGuinness & Pribram have linked hippocampal activity with effort in attentional processing. Conjunction search problems cannot be solved using automatic detection, in part because of the mapping problem identified by Shiffrin & Schneider. There are no consistent links between the correct response and any single feature, so that reflexive response habits that do develop are inappropriate to problem solution. For Pribram & McGuinness, the expenditure of *effort* represents the work of the hippocampus in uncoupling of overlearned stimulus-response connections so that new habits can be established. This requires the "opening up" of attention to sample new, previously unreinforced, stimuli.

If we examine the implications of this model as regards conjunction search, it follows that impaired performance on shared-feature arrays might arise following resection of the hippocampus, but in a way which is opposite to that produced by frontal damage. The "readiness" argument developed above predicts that frontal patients would tend to respond impulsively - that is to be fast, but inaccurate, as a result of attentional overinclusion. Hippocampal damage, by contrast, has been shown by Douglas, Barrett, Pribram & Cerny (1969) to produce *overexclusion* during visual discrimination in monkeys, due to a failure to sample a sufficiently large number of items or features in the stimulus array, and to shift response bias toward caution, as opposed to risk (Spevak & Pribram, 1973). For briefly presented arrays, errors would arise due to limitations on processing span, but performance might benefit from increased time to sample and respond to items that were initially unattended. This of course is what we observed for right temporal lobe patients in the second experiment. Although we have as yet been unable to test frontal patients under similar conditions, the prediction is that they would benefit much less than temporal patients from increased exposure duration during conjunction search.

Acknowledgements

1. The author wishes to thank Dr. Manfred Meier, who generously supplied a complete set of materials for the Complex Visual Discrimination test.

2. Data from temporal lobectomy cases were collected by Nicole Lanthier, and have been presented in her Honours undergraduate thesis, "Anterior temporal control of attention to visual features", University of Winnipeg, 1993.

3. We wish to thank the neurosurgical patients and students who consented to perform these perceptual tasks, for their willing participation and valuable contribution.

4. We wish to thank the members of the departments of neurosurgery, neurology, and radiology, Faculty of Medicine, University of Manitoba, who referred patients into these experiments, and the administrative staff of the Health Sciences Centre and St. Boniface hospital in Winnipeg for their support of this project.

References

Bolster, R.B & Birk, P. (1988) Effects of focal forebrain injury on feature-based visual search. Society for Neuroscience Abstracts, 14 (1) 218.

Bolster, R.B., & Pribram, K.H. (1993) Cortical involvement in visual scan in the monkey. Perception & Psychophysics, 53 (5), 505-518.

Cutcomb, S.D., Bolster, R.B, & Pribram, K.H. (1981). DADTA-VI: A minicomputer-based video control system for the analysis of behavioral and electrophysiological data. Behavior Research Methods and Instrumentation, 13, 337-340.

Douglas, R.J.; Barrett, T.W., Pribram, K.H. & Cerny, M.C. (1969). Limbic lesions and error reduction. Journal of Comparative and Physiological Psychology, 69, 473-480

Effron, Robert (1990) The decline and fall of hemispheric specialization. Hillsdale, N.J.: Lawrence Erlbaum.

Gazzaniga, M.S.   The Bisected Brain. (1970). New York: Appleton-Century Crofts.

Harter, M.R. & Aine, C.J. (1984).   Brain mechanisms of visual selective attention.   In R. Parasuraman & R. Davies (Eds) Varieties of Attention, pp. 293-321. New York: Academic Press.

Jones, E.C, & Powell, T.P.S. (1970).   An anatomical study of the converging sensory pathways within the cerebral cortex of the monkey.   Brain, 93, 793-820.

Kolb, B & Whishaw, I.Q. (1990).   Fundamentals of Human Neuropsychology. New York: W.H. Freeman & Co.

McGuinness, D. & Pribram, K.H. (1975)   Arousal, activation and effort in the control of attention.   Psychological Review, 82, 116-149

Meier, M.J & French, L.A. (1965).   Lateralized deficits in complex visual discrimination and bilateral transfer of reminiscence following unilateral temporal lobectomy. Neuropsychologia, 5, 261-262.

Mishkin, M., Ungerleider, L.G & Macko, K.A., (1983). Object vision and spatial vision: Two cortical pathways. Trends in Neuroscience, 6, 414-417.

Milner, B. (1964).   Some effects of frontal lobectomy in man.   In J.M. Warren and K. Akert, eds. The Frontal Granular Cortex and Behavior.   New York: McGraw-Hill.

Milner, B. (1968). Visual recognition and recall after right temporal-lobe excision in man.   Neuropsychologia, 6, 191-209.

Moscovitch, M.   (1979).   Information processing and the cerebral hemispheres.   In Handbook of Behavioral Neurobiology: Volume 2, Neuropsychology.   M.S. Gazzaniga (Ed).   New York: Plenum Press

Mountcastle, V.B., Lynch, J.C., Georgopolous, A., Sakata, H. & Acuna, C. (1975).   Posterior parietal association cortex of the monkey: command functions for operations within extrapersonal space.   Journal of Neurophysiology , 38, 871-908.

Patterson, K. & Bradshaw, J.L.   (1975).   Differential hemispheric mediation of nonverbal visual stimuli.   J. Exper. Psychol. Human Perception & Performance. 1, 246-252.

Polich, J.M. (1978) Hemisphereic differences in stimulus identification.   Perception & Psychophysics. 24, 49-57.

Polich, J.M. (1980).   Left hemisphere superiority for visual search.   Cortex, 16, 39-50

Posner, M.I, Walker, J.A., Friedrich, F.J., & Rafal, R.D. (1984). Effects of parietal lobe injury on covert orienting of visual attention. <u>Journal of Neuroscience</u>, 4, 1863-1874.

Pribram, Karl H. (1971). <u>Languages of the brain</u>. Englewood Cliffs, N.J.: Prentice-Hall.

Robinson, D.L.; Goldberg, M.E. & Stanton, G.B. (1978). Parietal association cortex in the primate: Sensory mechanisms and behavioral modulations. <u>J. Neurophysiol.</u> 41 (4), 910-932.

Spevack, A. & Pribram, K.H. (1973). A decisional analysis of the effects of limbic lesions in monkeys. <u>Journal of Comparative and Physiological Psychology</u>, 82, 211-226.

Spinelli, D.N. & Pribram, K.H. (1966) Changes in visual recovery functions produced by temporal lobe stimulation in the monkey. <u>Electroenceph. Clin. Neurophysiol.</u>, 20: 44-49.

Treisman, Anne (1977). Focused attention in the perception and retrieval of multidimensional stimuli. <u>Perception & Psychophysics</u>, 22 (1), 1-11.

Treisman, Anne (1988). Features and Objects: The fourteenth Bartlett Memorial Lecture. <u>Quarterly Journal of Experimental Psychology</u>, 40a (2), 201-237.

Treisman, A.M., Sykes, M., & Gelade, G. (1980). Selective attention and stimulus integration. in: <u>Attention and Performance VI</u>. Potomoc, Md.: Lawrence Erlbaum.

Treisman, A.M., & Patterson, R. (1984). Emergent features, attention, and object perception. <u>Journal of Experimental Psychology</u>, 10, 10-32.

Treisman, A,M., & Sato, S. (1990). Conjunction search revisited. <u>Journal of Experimental Psychology: Human Perception and Performance</u>. 16, 459-478.

FIGURE CAPTIONS

Figure 1:   Lateral view of monkey cerebral hemisphere, showing implant sites for transcortical electrodes (Bolster & Pribram, 1993)

Figure 2:   Stimulus arrays containing "distinct feature" and "shared feature" distractors. The task for the subject was to locate and press the green square target.

Figure 3:   Conjunction search task: group mean response latencies for "hits" (responses to green square targets)

Figure 4:   Conjunction search task: group mean error rates (responses to nontarget stimuli)

Figure 5:   Conjunction search task: effect of lesion site on error rate.

Figure 6:   Two stimulus items from the Complex Visual Discrimination task (Meier & French, 1965)

Figure 7:   Examples of stimulus arrays from the "oddity" version of the conjunction-search task.

Figure 8:   Conjunction search task - "known-target" (green square) version: effects of temporal lobectomy on group mean response latency.

Figure 9:   Conjunction search task - "known-target (green square) version: effects of temporal lobectomy on group mean error rate.

Figure 10: Conjunction search task - "oddity" version. Data are group mean values for performance-limiting exposure duration.

Chapter 30

Brain Systems Involved in Attention and Disattention (Hypnotic Analgesia) to Pain

Helen Crawford

Brain Systems Involved in Attention and Disattention (Hypnotic Analgesia) to Pain

Helen J. Crawford, Ph.D.
Department of Psychology
Virginia Polytechnic Institute and State University
Blacksburg, VA 24061

Abstract

Data are reviewed from regional cerebral blood flow, EEG, and somatosensory event-related potential (SERP; both scalp and intracranial) studies of attention to and disattention (hypnotic analgesia) of painful stimuli to provide further evidence for two neurophysiological systems of pain involving the cortex: (1) the epicritic, sensory system of pain associated with the parietal, posterior region, and (2) the protocritic, distress, comfort-discomfort system of pain associated with the far fronto-limbic region. Studies of neurophysiological changes accompanying suggested hypnotic analgesia support the hypothesis that the executive controller of the far frontal cortex, via the far fronto-limbic attentional system, acts as a gate against the ascent of painful stimuli into conscious awareness by "directing" downward the inhibition of incoming somatosensory information coming from the thalamic region. In hypnotically responsive individuals who could eliminate the perception of pain, reviewed studies demonstrated increased regional cerebral blood in the frontal and somatosensory regions, shifts in hemispheric dominance of EEG theta power, differential surface SERP topographical patterns in the anterior and posterior regions of the brain, and reduction of the intracranial SERP P160 waveform in the gyrus cingulus.

Pain is an alerter to us: it tells us that something biologically harmful may be happening to us. It can be a friend to us, but it also can be considered our enemy when it is overwhelming and prolonged. Unless we are one of the few misfortunate individuals who have been born with congenital insensitivity to pain (Sternbach, 1968), it has probably enveloped us all at some time or another in our lives, and led to decreased cognitive functioning, increased irritability, sleeplessness, and withdrawal from social interactions. Over 70 million people have chronic pain (Brena & Chapman, 1983), the most frequent symptom presented to the primary care physician. In the United States alone, an estimated 700 million work days are lost per year (Bonica, 1985), and the total cost of health care associated with pain is estimated to be 60 to 90 billion dollars annually.

In the United States, the most common treatment strategies for chronic pain are medications, surgery, or supportive talk -- yet, often they fail (Margolis, Zimny, Miller, & Taylor, 1964). Somewhat surprising to the medical community are recent findings from a national survey (Eisenberg, Kessler, Foster, Norlock, Calkins, & Delbanco, 1993): 34% of Americans reported seeking out unconventional medical therapies in the prior year, often for enduring, debilitating pain. While relaxation (including hypnosis) techniques have been shown to be effective for pain control (e.g., Hilgard & Hilgard, 1983) and are commonly sought out as possible alternative treatments, they are not consistently incorporated into mainstream medical treatments. Many recent advances have been made in understanding the basic mechanisms of pain (e.g., for review, see Price, 1988), yet we are far from understanding the neuropsychophysiology of pain and how these alternative treatments reduce or eliminate pain perception.

It is the search for understanding how hypnosis and hypnotic analgesia works at a neurophysiological level that has led me to conduct some exciting interdisciplinary, neuropsychophysiological research with my students and colleagues at Virginia Polytechnic Institute and State University, the BRAIN Center at Radford University, the University of Pennsylvania, and most recently at the Institute of the Brain in St. Petersburg, Russia. Our research questions include the following: What processes within the brain system permit us to reduce or eliminate the perception of pain? Where in the brain system are these inhibitory processes occurring? Why is it that highly hypnotizable individuals can more easily reduce or eliminate the perception of pain? Are there underlying psychological and neurophysiological differences between low and highly hypnotizable individuals that contribute to their ability or inability, respectively, to eliminate pain perception?

This paper reviews some of our published research (Crawford, 1989, 1990, 1994; Crawford & Gruzeler, 1992; Crawford, Gur, Skolnick, Gur & Benson, 1993) as well as ongoing research endeavors (e.g., Crawford, Pribram, Kugler, Xie, Zheng, & Knebel, 1993; Crawford, Pribram, Xie, & Zheng, 1993a, 1993b; Kropotov, Crawford, & Polyakov, 1994), that suggests that (a) highly hypnotizable individuals possess stronger attentional filtering abilities that may be associated with the fronto-limbic attentional system; and (b) hypnotic analgesia involves the far frontal cortex in the "directing" downward the inhibition of incoming painful sensations in a topographically specific inhibitory feedback circuit that cooperates in the regulation of thalamocortical activities.

The Paradox of Hypnotic Analgesia

Hypnotic analgesia is one of the best documented psychological treatments for controlling acute and chronic pain (for a review, see Hilgard & Hilgard, 1983). About 10% of the general population could go through open heart surgery or a thyroidectory using no anesthetic whatsoever, but rather using only hypnotically suggested analgesia. Many more can use it to reduce or modify the perception of pain and keep it under control. One or more cognitive strategies may be employed: denial (e.g., telling self the pain is not there), redefinition (e.g., redefining the pain as something else, such as painful pulses become the pulsing movement of arms while swimming), distraction (e.g., removing awareness of pain and becoming deeply involved in inner thoughts of being elsewhere), and/or dissociation (e.g., elimination of the perception of the arm and thinking it is no longer connected to the body).

From the many laboratory studies of hypnotic analgesia using experimental pain (e.g., cold pressor test, ischemic pain, or painful somatosensory electrical stimulations) there emerges an interesting paradox noted by the Hilgards (e.g., Hilgard & Hilgard, 1983) that interfaces cognitive psychology with neurophysiology. A highly hypnotizable person can sit with his or her hand in very cold water and report "I feel nothing whatsoever. I feel relaxed and comfortable. I am at the beach watching the waves and birds, and feeling the warmth of the sun." Or, this person may even look directly at the hand and say, "Oh, I know my hand is in the cold water, but I don't feel anything." The paradox noted is that while at the conscious level there is no awareness of pain or discomfort, at a physiological level there is reactivity. The autonomic system is showing reactivity: typically, there are increases in galvanic skin responses and cardiovascular changes such as blood pressure and heart rate increases (e.g., Olesko, Crawford, & Arany, 1989; Hilgard & Hilgard, 1983). There is a continuation of the sensory components of the evoked potential, although there is often a diminution of those components occurring 100 msec poststimulus (for review, see Crawford & Gruzelier, 1992). How can we resolve this paradox?

663

Attention and Pain

Several models of attention assist us in understanding the paradox of hypnotic analgesia. Posner and his colleagues (e.g., Posner & Dehaene, 1994; Posner & Petersen, 1990; Posner, Petersen, Fox, & Raichle, 1988) proposed that there are two major attentional systems: (a) one that is located in the posterior region of the brain and is involved with engaging and disengaging attention; and (b) another that is located in the anterior region of the brain and is involved in "attention for action" or effortful attention. Pribram and McGuinness (1975, 1992; see also Pribram, 1987, 1991) differentiated between arousal-familiarization (amygdala; orbito-frontal far frontal cortex), activation-readiness (basal ganglia; medio-frontal far frontal cortex), and effort (hippocampus; dorso-frontal far frontal cortex) circuits in the control of effortful attention (see Figure 1). The classical neurophysiological models of attention have been linear and hierarchical, yet recent evidence argues for the processing of information to be not only linear but also bidirectional, interactive and recursive (e.g., Pribram, 1991).

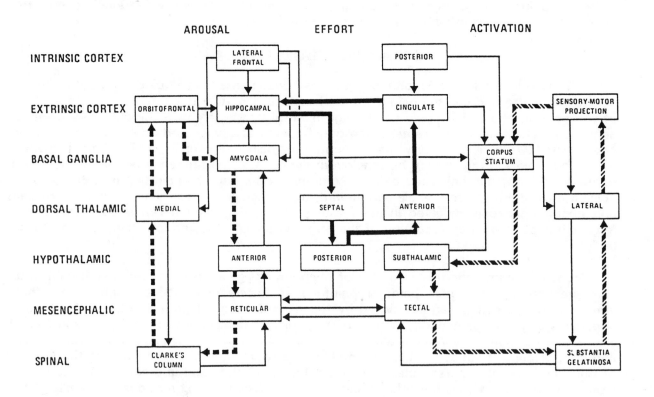

Figure 1. An oversimplified diagram of the connections involved in the arousal-familarization (amygdala), activation-readiness (basal ganglia), and the effort (hippocampal)) circuits. From: Pribram, 1991, p. 237.

While selective attention is a function of the posterior cerebral cortex, neurophysiological evidence shows that effortful attention, inhibition and resistance to distraction is a function of the fronto-limbic attentional system (for reviews, see Luria, 1966; Pribrim, 1973, 1986, 1991; Stuss & Benson, 1986). The executive controller (Hilgard, 1986; Pribram, 1973, 1991) or supervisory attentional system (SAS; Norman & Shallice, 1986; Shallice, 1988) of the far frontal cortex is involved with sequential actions and behaviors, sustained and focused attention, and inhibitory processes. Thus, this executive or SAS is hypothesized to modulate "lower-level systems (other parts of the brain) by activating or inhibiting particular schemata" (Frith, 1991, p. 186).

Turning to the neurophysiology of pain, we know much about the complex interactions between primary sensory afferents and neuronal responses within the dorsal horn of the spinal cord and the subcortical structures, but much less is known about the cortical-subcortical involvement (for a review, see Price, 1988). Anatomical studies have linked the monosynaptic and multisynaptic pain pathways from the thalamus to the posterior cortex and to the anterior cortex (particularly the amygdala and related limbic-cortical structures, as well as the orbito-frontal cortex) (e.g., Price, 1988; Pribram, 1991; Roland, 1992). Pain and temperature use a similar system (Pribram, 1991). Thus, the posterior region of the brain is involved in space and time, the epicritic processes, whereas the anterior region is involved in comfort- discomfort, the protocritic processes (Pribram, 1991). The interplay between cortical and subcortical brain dynamics, involving both the descending inhibitory pathways from the far frontal cortex and the paralleling ascending sensory systems is of utmost importance if we are to understand the perception and inhibition of painful stimuli.

Recent positron emission tomography research in humans has provided direct evidence for two neurophysiological systems of pain involving the cortex (Jones, Brown, Friston, Qi, & Frackowiak, 1991; Talbot, Marrett, Evans, Meyer, Bushnell, & Duncan, 1991). Mild, non-painful warmth was evaluated in terms of its temporal and spatial features, showing only increased cerebral activation in the posterior primary and secondary somatosensory cortex. When thermal heat became painful, Talbot et al. (1991) found an increased activation of the anterior cingulate cortex, and concluded that "the unilateral cingulate activation indicates that this forebrain area, thought to regulate emotions, contains an unexpectedly specific representation of pain" (p. 1355). Jones et al. (1991) found that painful thermal stimuli in comparison to nonpainful heat, as applied to the forearm, led to significant increases in blood flow in the contralateral cingulate cortex, thalamus, and lenticular nucleus.

Had Talbot et al. known of Pribram's (Chiu, Pribram, Drake, & Greene, 1976; reviewed by Pribram, 1991) seminal work, they would not have interpreted these as "unexpected" results. The frontal lobes are involved in the interpretation of discomfort-comfort (Pribram, 1991), and the anterior cingulate cortex is activated during lactate-induced panic (for a review, see Raichle, 1990). In rats, neurons that respond to noxious skin stimulation have been found in the far frontal cortex (e.g., Mantz, Milla, Glowinski, & Thierry, 1988). Removal of the frontal or cingulate cortex in patients with intractable pain leads to the amelioration of distress while not eliminating sensory pain (Bouckoms, 1989). Thus, the frontal cortex and the cingulate are implicated in the mediation of thalamic pain input.

Neuropsychophysiology of Hypnotic Analgesia

The question now arises as to what happens in these above discussed brain structures and processes during the ignoring of pain and the successful production of hypnotic analgesia. Our research is guided by Hilgard's (1986) neodissociation theory of hypnosis, as well as Pribram and McGuinness' (1975, 1992) attention model discussed earlier. Hilgard proposed that there is an executive ego or central control system that deals with the "planning, monitoring, and managing functions" of cognitive subsystems. During hypnosis this executive control system shifts attention from one cognitive control system to another so that information is processed and perceived in manners different than normal consciousness. If this is the case, then during suggested hypnotic analgesia the executive control system shifts cognitive gears and changes the hierarchical arrangement of the subsystems so that pain is no longer perceived at a conscious level. We would propose that Hilgard's executive control system is the far frontal cortex "directing" the inhibition of incoming painful stimuli. If so, we would anticipate neurophysiological changes in the anterior attentional system -- including the far frontal cortex, the anterior cingulum, the hippocampus and other structures, that would differ from the posterior attentional system.

Highly hypnotizable individuals ("highs") have greater attentional and disattentional abilities than low hypnotizable individuals ("lows") (e.g., Crawford, 1982, 1994; Crawford, Brown & Moon, 1993). We have argued elsewhere (Crawford, 1989, 1990, 1994; Crawford & Gruzelier, 1992; Crawford, Gur, et al., 1993) that highly hypnotizable persons possess a stronger filtering system associated with the fronto-limbic attentional system. We (Sabourin, Cutcomb, Crawford, & Pribram, 1990) and others (for reviews, see Crawford, 1994; Crawford & Gruzelier, 1992; Schacter, 1977) have shown that highly hypnotizable individuals generate, both in waking and hypnosis, more EEG theta power, hypothesized to be associated with focused attention and possibly generated within the hippocampal attentional system (for review, see Schacter, 1977), than lows. Recent neuroimaging techniques (PET, SPECT, CBF) that assess regional brain metabolism have found no differences in waking conditions between low and highly hypnotizable individuals, but have consistently reported that only highs show increased cerebral blood flow during hypnosis, suggestive of enhanced cognitive effort (Crawford, Gur et al., 1993; Halama, 1989; Meyer, Diehl, Ulrich, & Meinig, 1989; Walter, 1992).

Turning now to hypnotic analgesia per se, we have

    hypothesized that the far frontal cortex appears to be involved in a topographically specific inhibitory feedback circuit that cooperates in the regulation of thalamocortical activities (e.g., Birbaumer et al., 1990) during hypnotic analgesia. Thus, when hypnotic analgesia is produced, the far frontal cortex "determines" that the incoming painful events are irrelevant and inhibits somatosensory information coming from the thalamic region. Only the highly hypnotizable person appears to be able to learn to "disattend" and not experience pain (Crawford, Gur, et al., 1993, p. 183).

Regional Cerebral Blood Flow Differences during Pain and Hypnotic Analgesia

Crawford, Gur et al. (1993) is the first study to provide evidence of different regional cerebral blood flow (CBF) activation patterns during hypnotic analgesia, using the 133Xenon inhalation method during attention and disattention to ischemic pain as moderated by hypnotic level. Unlike many prior hypnotic analgesia studies, the subjects were stringently screened for hypnotic susceptibility and were given extensive preliminary training in controlling pain during cold pressor and ischemic pain sessions. Only those highs who could completely eliminate the perception of pain were studied in comparison to lows who could often reduce but not eliminate the perception of pain. Ischemic pain was administered to both arms during two counterbalanced conditions in waking and hypnosis: attend to pain and suggested analgesia. Similar imagery techniques to control pain were reported by lows and highs, but only the highs were successful in eliminating all perception of pain during hypnosis.

As anticipated, ischemic pain produced CBF increases in the somatosensory region. Of major theoretical interest was the finding that only the highs showed even further CBF increases during hypnotic analgesia: first, in the somatosensory region, and second, in the far frontal cortex (see Figure 2). Pet studies have shown increased activity during the performance of willed actions (for a review, see Frith, 1991). Thus, the increased CBF in the frontal cortex, particularly the fronto-orbital region, suggests mental effort occurring during the inhibition of painful stimuli. The increased CBF of the somatosensory cortex may be the result of this inhibitory process since fibers do lead from the frontal lobes to the more posterior regions, both cortico- cortical and cortico-subcortico-cortical (Pribram, 1991). PET and SPECT studies, as well as intracranial evoked potential studies as discussed below, will be able to elucidate the subcortical structures and processes involved in hypnotic analgesia.

Theta Power Shifts during Pain and Hypnotic Analgesia

Based upon animal (e.g., Crowne, Konow, Drake & Pribram, 1972; Isaacson, 1982, Isaacson & Pribram, 1986; R. Miller, 1991; Pribram, 1991) and human (e.g., Arnolds et al., 1980) studies, the hippocampus is implicated in selective attention as a sensory gating center -- one of filtering, inhibiting or gating irrelevant stimuli during selective attention processes. Theta (3-7 Hz) bursts are generated in the hippocampal area when animals are actively engaged in exploratory and other attentional behaviors, suggesting that the hippocampus through a cortico-hippocampal relay transmits information by theta wave modulation and Hebbian synaptic modification so that there is selective disattention (R. Miller, 1989, 1991). "It is as if these systems were processing 'don't look there' rather than 'look-here' (Pribram, 1991. p. 224). Thus, the willing of attention to and away from something, such as pain, may be correlated with theta activity as measured at the scalp, given that Michel, Lehmann, Henngeler, and Brandeis (1992) reported evidence of cortical surface theta being of a bihemispheric origin from the hippocampal region of the human brain.

As noted earlier, highly hypnotizable individuals generate more theta power than lows in waking and hypnosis, (for reviews, see Schacter, 1977; Crawford, 1994; Crawford & Gruzelier, 1992). In studies of epileptic patients with implanted intracranial electrodes, De Benedittus and Sironi (1986, 1988) proposed that "hypnotic behavior is mediated, at least in part, by a dynamic balance of antagonizing effects of discrete limbic structure - the amygdala and the hippocampus. In fact, the trance state is associated with hippocampal activity, concomitant with a partial amgdaloid complex functional inhibition" (1988, p. 104).

Shifts in theta and alpha power occurred in one patient undergoing dental surgery with successful hypnotic analgesia (Chen, Dworkin, & Bloomquist, 1981). Enhanced theta power at parietal, but not central, midline derivations was found in fakirs who demonstrated pain control while hanging from hooks or putting needles through their skin or tongue (Larbig, Elbert, Lutzenberger, Rockstroh, Schneer, & Birbaumer, 1982). During hypnosis, Crawford (1990) found that highs showed differential theta power patterns during attention to pain and hypnotic analgesia in one minute dips of the left hand into painfully cold water from those shown by the low hypnotizables. In all measured brain regions (F3, F4, T3, T4, P3, P4, O1, O2), highs showed significantly more theta (5.5 - 7.5 Hz) power than did lows. In the anterior temporal region (T3, T4), during pain and hypnotic analgesia conditions, low hypnotizables showed no significant asymmetries in theta power between the left and right hemispheres. By contrast, in high theta, the highs were significantly more left hemisphere dominant in the pain dip and showed a dramatic reversal in hemispheric dominance during successful suggested analgesia. Left hemisphere theta power decreased significantly while right hemisphere theta power increased in the anterior temporal region (T3, T4). These theta power shifts may reflect shifts in subcortical processing during hypnotic analgesia.

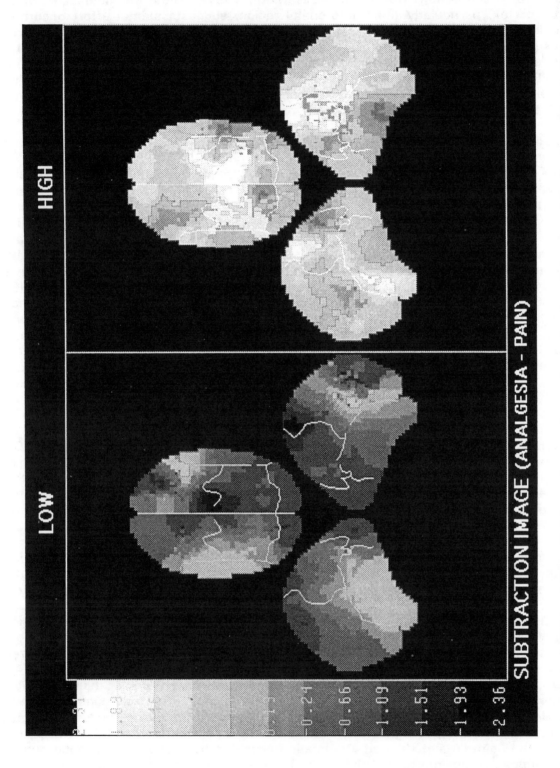

HIGH

LOW

SUBTRACTION IMAGE (ANALGESIA – PAIN)

Figure 2. Regional cerebral blood flow activity unique to hypnotic analgesia after subtraction of pain condition during hypnosis. Low hypnotizables are on the left and high hypnotizables are on the right. Increased to decreased CBF is coded, respectively, from light to dark shading. From Crawford, Gur, et al., 1993, p. 190. Copyright 1993 by Elsevier Science Publishers. Reprinted by permission.

Surface SERP Topographical Brain Maps during Pain and Hypnotic Analgesia

Turning now to somatosensory evoked-related potentials (SERPs) as another window into brain dynamics, my colleagues (Karl Pribram, Min Xie, Bibo Zheng) at the BRAIN Center, graduate students (Timothy Knebel, Jennifer Coplin) and I have initiated a major study of SERPs to painful electrical stimuli during conditions of attention and disattention. Only data from healthy college students are reported in this paper, but it should be noted that we are also studying a group of chronic low back pain patients. Past research has demonstrated that pain-associated SERPs occur at least by 160 ms after stimulation and SERP amplitudes correlate with perceived pain level (e.g., Chen, Chapman, & Harkins, 1979; for a review, see Stowell, 1984). During suggested analgesia in highly hypnotizable subjects, Mészáros, Bányai, and Greguss (1980) found decreases in the amplitude of P200 to short electrical impulses to the median nerve, while De Pascalis, Crawford, and Marucci (1992a, 1992b) found decreases of the N100-P200 component in the left hemisphere. Spiegel, Bierre, and Rootenberg (1989) reported greater reductions in later SERP components to suggested reduced pain, particularly in the right occipital region. Earlier SERP work, often confounded by poor assessments of hypnotic responsiveness and pain reduction, has led to mixed findings (for review, see Crawford & Gruzelier, 1992). None of these prior studies considered the differential SERP involvement of the frontal and posterior regions of the brain as demonstrated by Desmedt and Bourguet (1985). Yet, given the above discussion of anterior descending inhibitory pathways hypothesized to be involved in disattention to pain, we expected that successful hypnotic analgesia would be accompanied by a greater amplitude decrease in SERPs in the far frontal region (Fp1, Fp2) with a lesser reduction in SERP amplitudes in the more sensory, posterior regions.

Like our other hypnosis studies, subjects were first stringently screened for hypnotic susceptibility level on both the Harvard Group Scale of Hypnotic Susceptibility (Shor & Orne, 1962) and the Stanford Hypnotic Susceptibility Scale, Form C (SHSS:C; Weitzenhoffer & Hilgard, 1962). Healthy, right-handed low (0-4 SHSS:C) and highly (9-12 SHSS:C) hypnotizable persons were invited to participate in a cold pressor pain study. They participated in two hours of training which involved dipping their hands into very cold water for 60 second dips while attending to the pain and subsequently while learning to disattend the pain with hypnotic analgesia suggestions of denial, redefinition, distraction and/or dissociation. To continue in our research, highs had to meet the criteria of being able to eliminate completely the perception of sensory pain and distress in the cold water dips during hypnotically suggested analgesia.

At the BRAIN Center, while sitting in a comfortable reclining chair with eyes closed, subjects participated in an A-B-A (waking-hypnosis-waking) design. During the two waking conditions, subjects were instructed to attend to 30 noxious electrical stimuli of 0.2 msec duration, with an ISI of 3 seconds, delivered to the 3rd finger of the left hand by a Grass stimulator through an isolating transformer. During hypnosis, blocks of 30 stimuli were administered in the following order: (1) attend to the stimuli, (2) disattend the stimuli by producing analgesia of the hand, and (3) attend to the stimuli once again. At least five minutes of time separated each block. At the beginning of the research, the intensity of the shock stimuli was titrated for each subject to where it was moderately uncomfortable/painful (usually rated a 7 or 8 on a 0-10 point scale). At present we have run seven lows and 15 highs through this procedure; our preliminary results reported herein are based upon these subjects.

Brain electrical activity was recorded using an ElectroCap with recordings at far frontal (Fp1, Fp2), frontal (Fz, F3, F4, F7, F8), central (Cz, C3, C4), temporal (T3, T4, T5, T6), parietal (Pz, P3, P4), and occipital (O1, O2) derivations, all referenced to linked earlobes and grounded to a location directly above the nasion. Eye movements were recorded on another channel so that we could subsequently remove all epochs with artifacts. The averaging epoch was two seconds, including 500 msec of prestimulus baseline and 1500 msec poststimulus.

The Brain Scope developed by Min Xie and Bibo Zheng permits us to view the SERPs as they are evolving. Thus, we the researchers can have a window into our subjects' brains as they are reacting to the painful stimuli in the various conditions. There is a very dynamic movement of the SERPs across the 30 trials which is lost when one only examines the averaged SERP. For some subjects, there is a very strong response in the first few trials during attend conditions. Habituation occurs at differing rates across subjects; for some habituation occurs within five trials, and for others there is almost no habituation. In addition, there are large individual differences in the amplitude, latency and morphologies of the SERPs.

Only results of the three conditions (attend, hypnotic analgesia, attend) during hypnosis, with data from individual subjects rather than averages across subjects, are reported in this paper. Topographical brain maps of the averaged SERPs for attend to and hypnotic analgesia conditions for several low and high hypnotizables are provided in the accompanying figures. During attend to pain conditions, low hypnotizables consistently showed relatively little far frontal activation in comparison to the posterior regions (Figure 3), but over 50% of the highly hypnotizable subjects showed great SERP reactivity in all regions. The differential SERP involvement of the far frontal region during attention to pain between low and high hypnotizables was not anticipated, but may reflect neurophysiological differences in focal attention. We are now examining personality and cognitive variables which may correlate with SERP amplitudes and differential habituation rates in the far frontal region.

During hypnotic analgesia, highly hypnotizable subjects demonstrated substantial SERP component reductions as early as the N100-P120 that were evident over the whole SERP topographical brain map (Figures 4-5). By contrast, as anticipated, low hypnotizables subjects showed minor reductions in their SERPs (Figure 3).

As anticipated, there appears to be a dissociation between the far frontal and posterior regions of the brain. Desmedt and Bourguet (1985) demonstrated differential SERPs in the frontal and posterior regions of the brain suggestive of separate somatosensory systems. Our data demonstrated this too. In over half of the high hypnotizable subjects the far frontal region (Fp1, Fp2) showed strong arousal during attention to pain, but during hypnotic analgesia there was a flattening out of the SERPs to the point they are hard to measure. By contrast, the more posterior SERPs (including F3 and F4), while reduced in amplitude, were still evident. The other half of highs showed little SERP activity in the far frontal region in either attend or disattend conditions, but substantial reductions of SERPs at all locations during hypnotic analgesia. This data suggests that there are at least two types of highly hypnotizable subjects, both of which can eliminate the perception of pain, that have differential SERP topographical patterns particularly in the far frontal region. Overall, hypnotic analgesia is accompanied by SERP reductions in the posterior pain system and by even greater SERP diminutions or ameliorations in the far frontal region.

Anticipation of the stimuli out of awareness may have occurred in some highly hypnotizable subjects who experienced no conscious awareness of pain. We observed either a pre-stimulus contingent negative variation (CNV) or a late 400-500 msec negativity in the far frontal region of a few highs (Figure 5). The CNV is usually associated with the preparation to respond or inhibit responses. Preparation during temporal processing results in a CNV or CNV- like slow cortical potential that can be considered a measure of cortical excitability or inhibition, a preparation for a response or for an inhibition of a response (e.g.,

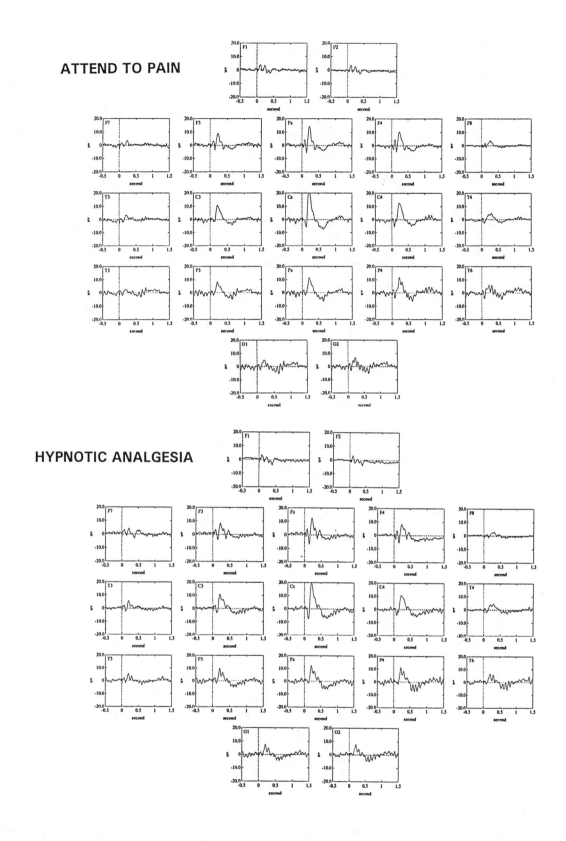

Figure 3. Low hypnotizable subject: Topographical map of somatosensory evoked-related potentials (500 msec pre-stimulus and 1500 msec post-stimulus across 30 trials at 19 electrode sites during hypnosis conditions of (1) attend to pain and (2) disattend (unsuccessfully suggested analgesia).

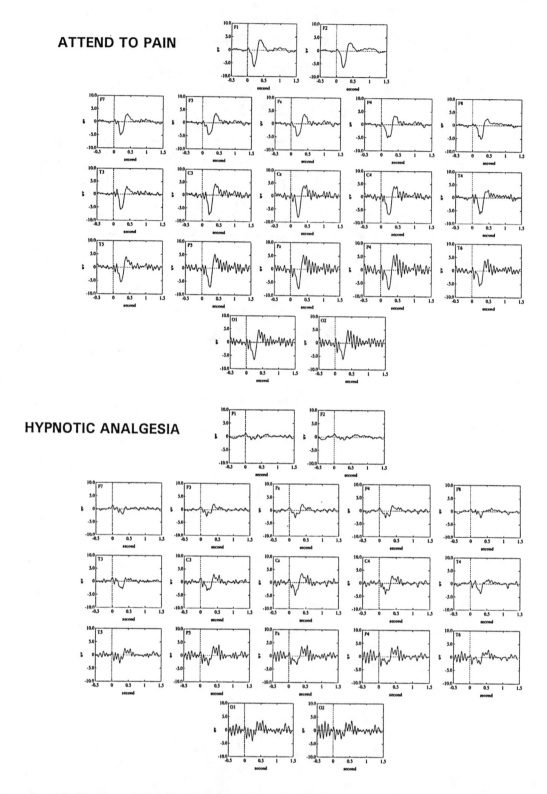

ATTEND TO PAIN

HYPNOTIC ANALGESIA

Figure 4. Highly hypnotizable subject #1: Topographical map of somatosensory evoked-related potentials (500 msec pre-stimulus and 1500 msec post-stimulus) averaged across 30 trials at 19 electrode sites during hypnosis conditions of (1) attend to pain and (2) disattend (successful suggested analgesia with no awareness of the pain). During hypnotic analgesia, note the more dramatic diminution of SERPs at the far frontal region (Fp1, Fp2) that is of a different pattern than the diminished SERP amplitudes in the posterior region.

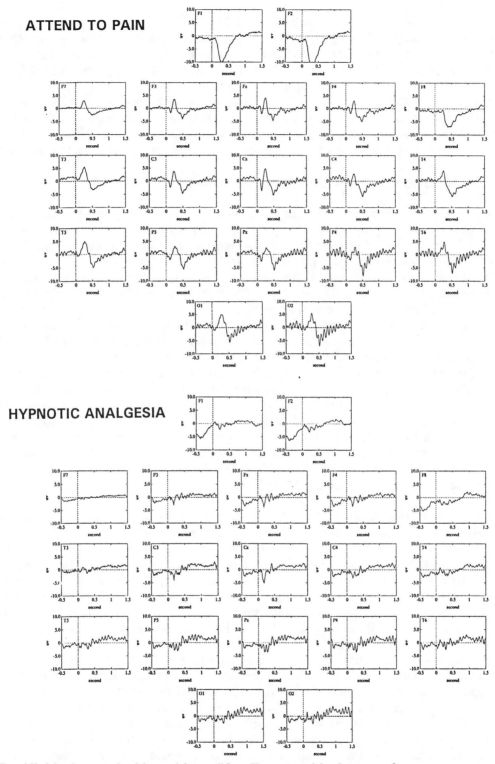

ATTEND TO PAIN

HYPNOTIC ANALGESIA

Figure 5. Highly hypnotizable subject #2: Topographical map of somatosensory evoked-related potentials (500 msec pre-stimulus and 1500 msec post-stimulus) averaged across 30 trials at 19 electrode sites during hypnosis conditions of (1) attend to pain and (2) disattend (successful suggested analgesia with no awareness of the pain). During hypnotic analgesia, note the more dramatic diminution of SERPs accompanied by a pre-stimulus CNV-like preparatory wave at the far frontal region (Fp1, Fp2) that is of a different pattern than the diminished SERPs in the posterior region.

Birbaumer, Elbert, Canavan, & Rochstroh, 1990). The occurrence of a far frontal CNV during hypnotic analgesia suggests that the far frontal cortex is involved in a topographically specific inhibitory feedback circuit that cooperates in the regulation of thalamo-cortical activities. For some highly hypnotizable subjects, at some level of consciousness there may be an anticipation of not responding to the painful stimuli, much like the monkeys of Crowne et al. (1972) who showed hippocampal theta bursts during inhibitory, no-go conditions. If this is the case, the hypnotic analgesia condition may be like a no-go condition for some subjects. We are now evaluating the relationships between the presence or absence of these CNVs and reported cognitive strategies to control pain.

Intracranial SERPs during Pain and Hypnotic Analgesia

Recently I conducted a collaborative project with Juri Kropotov and Yuri Polyakov (Kropotov, Crawford, & Polyakov, 1994) at the Institute of the Human Brain, Russian Academy of Sciences, St. Petersburg, Russia, where they investigate subcortical neuronal correlates of cognitive processing in patients with certain brain disorders. These patients were unresponsive to conventional treatment and consequently recommended to have intracranial electrodes implanted temporarily for further evaluation and possible treatment. Recent research (Kropotov, Etlinger, Ponomarev, & Savastyanov, 1992) showed that the strio-pallido-thalamic system of the human brain is involved in selective attention processes. We wished to evaluate subcortical processing of painful stimuli in certain brain structures hypothesized to be involved in directed attention. In particular, we were interested in the gyrus cingulus which recently has been shown to be activated during directed attention (attend to auditory tones) but not during non-directed attention (read a book and ignore the tones) (Kropotov, Näätänen, Sevastianov, Alho, Reinikainen, & Dubrovskaya, 1994). It was anticipated that if a patient was able to successfully reduce the perception of pain with hypnotic analgesia suggestions, then there would be a reduction of certain SERP components in those regions involved in directed attention. One such region we were able to evaluate was the gyrus cingulus, already identified in the normal processing of painful stimuli (Jones et al., 1991; Talbot et al., 1991).

Using the same task paradigm developed for the study of surface SERPs at the BRAIN Center, SERPs were recorded from scalp and intracranial electrodes in two female patients with obsessive-compulsive disorder. Both had intracranial electrodes implanted in the left gyrus cingulus and the left parieto-temporal cortex (Broadman area 21) as well as other regions. In addition, scalp electrodes were placed at Fz, Cz, and Pz. Patients had the procedure explained and signed informed consent forms. SERPs were recorded while patients were administered 30 moderately painful stimuli to the left middle finger in the following sequential conditions: active attention during waking, suggested hypnotic analgesia after hypnotic induction, and active attention during hypnosis. One patient was highly hypnotizable by the criteria of catalepsy of the arm during hypnosis; the other was not hypnotizable. Only the hypnotizable patient reported dramatic reductions in pain perception during suggested analgesia of the hand and arm. As is seen in Figure 6, reduced pain perception was accompanied by a significant reduction of the SERP at P160 waveform in the gyrus cingulus, but with no other significant changes there or at the other recording sites. Subsequent to the hypnotic analgesia, when the pain was attended to again during waking this patient showed a significant enhancement of the same positivity wave at Fz, as if there was a rebound effect (something we have also observed in some of our SERP subjects at the BRAINS Center). The nonresponsive patient showed no SERP changes across the conditions. These data provide further evidence for the decreased involvement of the gyrus cingulus during the ignoring of painful stimuli.

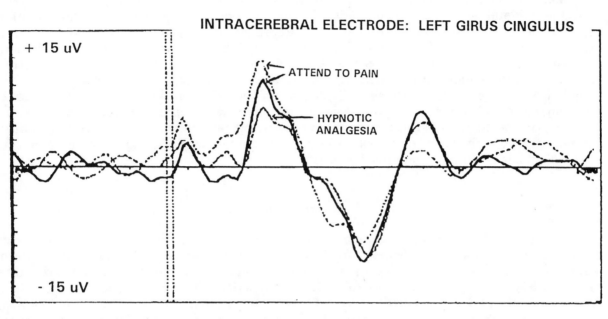

INTRACEREBRAL ELECTRODE: LEFT GIRUS CINGULUS

+ 15 uV

ATTEND TO PAIN

HYPNOTIC ANALGESIA

- 15 uV

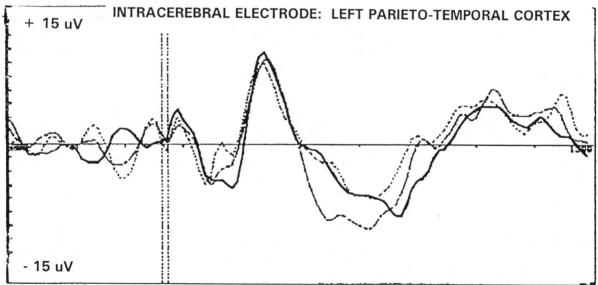

INTRACEREBRAL ELECTRODE: LEFT PARIETO-TEMPORAL CORTEX

+ 15 uV

- 15 uV

Figure 6. Highly hypnotizable obsessive-compulsive patient: somatosensory evoked-related potentials (200 msec pre-stimulus and 600 msec post-stimulus) averaged across 30 trials at two intracranial sites: left girus cingulus (Shaltenbrandt atlas: 29.12/ -7.42/32.41) and left parieto-temporal cortex (broadman area 21). In the left girus cingulus the P160 waveform is significantly lower in amplitude during hypnotically suggested analgesia than either of the conditions when the patient was asked to attend to the pain. From Kropotov, Crawford, & Poilyakov (in prep).

Summary

There is a very good accordance between the reviewed data from regional cerebral blood flow, EEG, and somatsensory event-related potential studies of attention and disattention (hypnotic analgesia) to painful stimuli to support the hypothesized existence of two pain systems in the cortex: (1) the epicritic, sensory aspects of pain more associated with the parietal, posterior region, and (2) the protocritic, distress, comfort-discomfort aspects of pain associated with the far fronto-limbic region. Our studies of the neuropsychophysiology of hypnotic analgesia during various experimental pain regimens consistently support the hypothesis that the executive controller of the far frontal cortex, via the far fronto-limbic attentional system, acts as a gate against the ascent of painful stimuli into conscious awareness. Evidence presented argues for the importance of studying individual differences in sustained and focused attention at both cognitive and neurophysiological levels. The puzzling neurophysiological differences observed, and often ignored, across individuals may well be clarified if only neurophysiologists would consider how individuals differ at a cognitive level.

Acknowledgments

The writing of this chapter was supported by a National Institutes of Health grant from the Office of Alternative Medicine (I R2 RR0958) to the author. Earlier research reported herein was supported by The Spencer Foundation, National Institutes of Health Biomedical Research Support grants, and intramural College of Arts and Sciences and Creative Match grants, Virginia Polytechnic Institute and State University, to the author. The following colleagues contributed actively to research projects discussed herein: Karl Pribram, Director of the BRAIN Center; Min Xie and Bibo Zheng, BRAIN Center electrical engineers who wrote the Brain Scope programs for the recording, storage and analyses of evoked potentials and EEG; Timothy Knebel and Jennifer Coplin, graduate students, at Virginia Tech who worked on all aspects of recent studies; Ruben Gur, Brett Skolnick, and Raquel Gur, of the University of Pennsylvania, who provided the opportunity to conduct the CBF study in their facilities; and Juri Kropotov, Head of the Laboratory for Neurobiology of Action Programming, Human Brain Institute of Russian Academy of Sciences, St. Petersburg, Russia, who provided the opportunity to work with their patients. These interdisciplinary collaborations have led to lively discussions and research endeavors, and I am greatly appreciative of my colleagues' contributions to the work and ideas presented in this paper.

References

Arnolds, D., Lopes Da Silva, F. H., Aitink, J. W., Kamp, A., & Boeijinga, P. (1980). The spectral properties of hippocampal EEG related to behavior in man. EEG and Clinical Neurophysiology, 50, 324-328.

Birbaumer, N., Elbert, T., Canavan, A. G. M., & Rockstroh, B. (1990). Slow potentials of the cerebral cortex and behavior. Physiological Reviews, 70, 1-41.

Bouckoms, A. J. (1989). Psychosurgery for pain. In P. D. Wall & R. Melzack (Eds.), Textbook of Pain, 2nd ed. (pp. 868-881). Edinburgh: Churchill Livingstone.

Brena, S. F., & Chapman, S. L. (1983). Management of patients with chronic pain. New York: S.P. Medical and Scientific Books.

Chen, A. C. N., Chapman, C. R., & Harkins, S. W. (1979). Brain evoked potentials are functional correlates of induced pain in man. Pain, 6, 305-314.

Chen, A. C. N., Dworkin, S. F., & Bloomquist, D. S. (1981). Cortical power spectrum analysis of hypnotic pain control in surgery. International Journal of Neuroscience, 13, 127-136.

Chiu, J. H., Pribram, K. H., Drake, K., & Greene, L. O., Jr. (1976). Disruption of temperature discrimination during limbic forebrain stimulation in monkeys. Neuropsychologia, 14, 293-310.

Crawford, H. J. (1982). Hypnotizability, daydreaming styles, imagery vividness, and absorption: A multidimensional study. Journal of Personality and Social Psychology, 42, 915-926.

Crawford, H. J. (1989). Cognitive and physiological flexibility: Multiple pathways to hypnotic responsiveness. In V. Gheorghui, P. Netter, H. Eysenck, and R. Rosenthal (Eds.), Suggestion and suggestibility: Theory and research (pp. 155-168). New York: Springer-Verlag.

Crawford, H. J. (1990). Cognitive and psychophysiological correlates of hypnotic responsiveness and hypnosis. In M. L. Fass & D. Brown (Eds.), Creative mastery in hypnosis and hypnoanalysis: A festschrift for Erika Fromm (pp. 47-54). Hillsdale, New Jersey: Lawrence Erlbaum Associates.

Crawford, H. J. (1994). Brain dynamics and hypnosis: Attentional and disattentional processes. International Journal of Clinical and Experimental Hypnosis, 42, 204-232.

Crawford, H. J., Brown, A., & Moon, C. (1993). Sustained attentional and disattentional abilities: Differences between low and highly hypnotizable persons. Journal of Abnormal Psychology, 102, 534-543.

Crawford, H. J., & Gruzelier, J. (1992). A midstream view of the neuropsychophysiology of hypnosis: Recent research and future directions. In E. Fromm and M. Nash (Eds.), Hypnosis: Research developments and perspectives (pp. 227-266). New York: Guilford Press.

Crawford, H. J., Gur, R. C., Skolnick, B., Gur, R. E., & Benson, D. (1993). Effects of hypnosis on regional cerebral blood flow during ischemic pain with and without suggested hypnotic analgesia. International Journal of Psychophysiology, 15, 181-195.

Crawford, H. J., Pribram, K., Kugler, P., Xie, M., Zheng, B., & Knebel, T. (1993). EEG and somatosensory evoked potential brain topographical changes during suggested hypnotic anesthesia. International Journal of Psychophysiology, 14, 118.

Crawford, H. J., Pribram, K., Xie, M., & Zheng, B. (1993a October). Far frontal "executive" control over disattention to pain during hypnotic analgesia: Evidence from somatosensory event-related potential research. Paper presented at the annual scientific meeting of the Society for Clinical and Experimental Hypnosis, Chicago, IL.

Crawford, H. J., Pribram, K., Xie, M., & Zheng, B. (1993b). Somatosensory event-related potentials and preparatory processing to painful stimuli: Effects of hypnotically suggested analgesia as moderated by hypnotic level. Paper presented at the annual meeting of the Society for Psychophysiological Research, Rottach-Egern, Germany.

Crowne, D. P., Konow, A., Drake, K. J., & Pribram, K. H. (1972). Hip pocampal electrical activity in the monkey during delayed alternation problems. Journal of EEG and clinical neurophysiology, 33, 567-577.

De Benedittus, G., & Siron, V. A. (1986). Deep cerebral electrical activity in man during hypnosis. International Journal of Clinical and Experimental Hypnosis, 34, 63-70.

De Benedittus, G., & Sironi, V. A. (1988). Arousal effects of electrical deep brain stimulation in hypnosis. International Journal of Clinical and Experimental Hypnosis, 36, 96-101.

De Pascalis, V., Crawford, H. J., & Marucci, F. S. (September 1992a). Effects of hypnosis and hypnotic analgesia on somatosensory evoked potentials during painful stimulations. Paper presented at the 6th International Congress of Psychophysiology. Berlin, Germany.

De Pascalis, V., Crawford, H. J., & Marucci, F. S. (1992). Analgesia ipnotica nella modulazione del dolore: Effeti sui potenziali somatosensoriali. <u>Comunicazioni Scientifice di Psicologie Generale</u>, 71-89.

Desmedt, J. E., & Bourguet, M. (1985). Color imaging of scalp topography of parietal and frontal components of somatosensory evoked potentials to stimulation of median or posterior tibial nerve in man. <u>EEG and Clinical Neurophysiology</u>, <u>62</u>, 1-17.

Eisenberg, D. M., Kessler, R. C., Foster, C., Norlock, F. E., Calkins, D. R., & Delbanco, T. L. (1993). Unconventional medicine in the United States. <u>New England Journal of Medicine</u>, <u>328</u>, 246-252.

Frith, C. D. (1991). Positron emission tomography studies of frontal lobe function: Relevance to psychiatric disease. In D. H. Chadwick & J. Whelan (Eds), <u>Exploring brain functional anatomy with positron tomography</u> (pp. 181-197). New York: Wiley (Ciba Foundation Symposium 163).

Halama, P. (1989). Die Veranderung der corticalen Durchblutung vor under in Hypnose. <u>Experimentelle und Klikische Hypnose</u>, <u>5</u>, 19-26.

Hilgard, E. R. (1986). <u>Divided consciousness: Multiple controls in human thought and action</u> (revised edition). New York: John Wiley & Sons.

Hilgard, E. R., & Hilgard, J. R. (1983). <u>Hypnosis in the relief of pain</u>. Palo Alto, CA: Kaufmann.

Isaacson, R. L. (1982). <u>The limbic system.</u> New York: Plenum Press.

Isaacson, R. L., & Pribram, K. H. (Eds.). (1986). <u>The hippocampus. Volume 4</u>. New York and London: Plenum Press.

Jones, A. K. P., Brown, W. D., Friston, K. R., Qi, L. J., & Frackowiak, R. S. J. (1991). Cortical and subcortical localization of response to pain in man using positron emission tomography. <u>Proceedings of the Royal Society of London, Series B, Biological Sciences</u>, <u>244</u>, 39-44.

Kropotov, J. D., Crawford, H. J., & Polyakov, Y. I. (1994). <u>Somatosensory pain and attention: Intracranial and scalp SERP recordings during suggested hypnotic analgesia in obsessive-compulsive patients</u>. Manuscript under preparation.

Kropotov, J. D., Etlinger, S. C., Ponomarev, V. A., & Sevastyanov, A.V. (1992). Event-related neuronal responses in the human strio-pallido-thalamic system. I. Sensory and motor functions. <u>EEG and Clinical Neurophysiology</u>, <u>84</u>, 373-385.

Kropotov, J. D., Näätänen, R., Sevastianov, A. V., Albo, K., Reinikainen, K., & Dubrovskaya, O. V. (1994). <u>Responses to stimulus change recorded from cortical and subcortical structures of the human brain</u>. Manuscript under editorial review.

Larbig, W., Elbert, T., Lutzenberger, W., Rockstroh, B., Schneer, G., & Birbaumer, N. (1982). EEG and slow brain potentials during anticipation and control of painful stimulation. <u>EEG and Clinical Neurophysiology</u>, <u>53</u>, 298- 309.

Luria, A. R. (1966). <u>Higher cortical functions in man</u>. New York: Basic Books (original publication by Moscow University Press in 1962).

Margolis, R. B., Zimny, G. H., Miller, D., & Taylor, J. M. (1984). Internists and the chronic pain patient. <u>Pain</u>, <u>20</u>, 151-156.

Mészáros, I., Bányai, E. I., & Greguss, A. C. (1980). Hypnosis, EEG and evoked potential. In M. Phantar, E. Rosquar, & M. Lavric (Eds.), <u>Hypnosis in psychotherapy and psychosomatic medicine</u>. Brang.

Meyer, H. K., Diehl, B. J., Ulrich, P. T., & Meinig, G. (1989). Anderungen der regionalen kortikalen durchblutung unter hypnose. <u>Zeitschrift fur Psychosomatische Medizin und Psychoanalyse</u>, <u>35</u>, 48-58.

Michel, C. M., Lehmann, D., Henggeler, B., & Brandeis, D. (1992). Localization of the sources of EEG delta, theta alpha and beta frequency bands using the FFT dipole approximation. <u>EEG and Clinical Neurophysiology</u>, <u>82</u>, 38-44.

Miller, R. (1989). Cortico-hippocampal interplay: Self-organizing phase-locked loops for indexing memory. <u>Psychobiology</u>, <u>17</u>, 115-128.

Miller, R. (1991). Cortico-hippocampal interplay and the representation of contexts in the brain. Berlin: Springer-Verlag.

Norman, D. A., & Shallice, T. (1986). Attention to action: Willed and automatic control of behavior. In R. J. Davidson, G. E., Schwartz, and D. Shapiro (Eds)., Consciousness and self-regulation: Advances in research and theory, Vol 4 (pp. 1-18). New York: Plenum Press.

Olesko, B., Arany, C., & Crawford, H. J. (1989 June). Cold pressor pain in high hypnotizables: Hypnotic analgesia versus waking. Paper presented at the American Psychological Society, Alexandria, VA.

Posner, M. I., & Dehaene, S. (1994). Attentional networks. Trends in Neurosciences, 17, 75-79

Posner, M. I., & Petersen, S. E. (1990). The attention span of the brain. Annual Review of Neuroscience, 13, 23-42.

Posner, M. I., Petersen, S. E., Fox, P. R., & Raichle, M. E. (1988). Localization of cognitive operations in the human brain. Science, 240, 1627-1631.

Pribram, K. H. (1973). The primate frontal cortex executive of the brain. In K.. H. Pribram, & A. R. Iuria (Eds)., Psychophysiology of the frontal lobes (pp. 293-314). New York: Academic Press.

Pribram, K. H. (1987). Subdivisions of the frontal cortex revisited. In E. Brown and E. Perecman (Eds.), The frontal lobes revisited (pp. 11-29). IRBN Press.

Pribram, K. H. (1986). The hippocampal system and recombinant processing. In R. Isaacson & K. H. Pribram (Eds.), The hippocampus, Vol. 4 (p. 329-370). New York: Plenum.

Pribram, K. H. (1991). Brain and perception: Holonomy and structure in figural processing. Hillsdale, New Jersey: Erlbaum Associates.

Pribram, K. H., & McGuinness, D. (1975). Arousal, activation, and effort in the control of attention. Psychological Review, 82, 116-149.

Pribram, K. H., & McGuinness, D. (1992). Attention and para-attentional processing: Event-related brain potentials as tests of a model. Annals of the New York Academy of Sciences, 658, 65-92.

Price, D. D. (1988). Psychological and neural mechanisms of pain. NY: Raven.

Roland, P. (1992). Cortical representation of pain. Trends in Neurosciences, 15, 3-5.

Sabourin, M. E., Cutcomb, S. D., Crawford, H. J., & Pribram, K. (1990) EEG correlates of hypnotic susceptibility and hypnotic trance: Spectral analysis and coherence. International Journal of Psychophysiology, 10, 125-142.

Schacter, D. L. (1977). EEG theta waves and psychological phenomena: A review and analysis. Biological Psychology, 5, 47-82.

Shallice, T. (1988). From neuropsychology to mental structure. Cambridge: Cambridge University Press.

Shor, R. E., & Orne, M. C. (1962). Harvard Group Scale of Hypnotic Susceptibility, Form A. Palo Alto: Consulting Psychologists Press.

Spiegel, D., Bierre, P., & Rootenberg, J. (1989). Hypnotic alteration of somatosensory perception. American Journal of Psychiatry, 146, 749-754.

Sternbach, R.A. (1968). Pain: A psychophysiological analysis. New York: Academic Press.

Stowell, H. (1984). Event related brain potentials and human pain: A first objective overview. International Journal of Psychophysiology, 1, 137-151.

Stuss, D.T., & Benson, D.F. (1986). The frontal lobes. New York: Raven Press.

Talbot, J. D., Marrett, S., Evans, A. C., Meyer, E., Bushnell, M. C., & Duncan, G. H. (1991). Multiple representations of pain in human cerebral cortex. Science, 251, 1355-1358.

Walter, H. (1992). Hypnose: Theorien, neurophysiologische Korrelate und praktische Hinweise zur Hypnosetherapie. Stuttgart: Georg Thieme Verlag.

Weitzenhoffer, A. M., & Hilgard, E. R. (1962) Stanford Hypnotic Susceptibility Scale, Form C. Palo Alto, CA: Consulting Psychologists Press.

Chapter 31

The Brain as a Neurocontroller:
New Hypotheses and New Experimental Possibilities

Paul Werbos

The Brain as a Neurocontroller:
New Hypotheses and New Experimental Possibilities

Paul J. Werbos
Room 675, National Science Foundation[*]
Arlington, Virginia, USA 22230
pwerbos@nsf.gov

This paper will describe how a new body of mathematics -- initially <u>motivated</u> by neuroscience but <u>developed</u> in recent years through engineering applications -- can begin to yield a <u>predictive</u>, <u>empirical</u> understanding of the phenomenon of intelligence in the brain. The paper is mainly written for neuroscientists, or for engineers working with neuroscientists; it tries to describe crucial new experiments which need to be performed in order to test and refine this new understanding.

The biggest single obstacle to the full use of mathematics in real neuroscience is the sheer difficulty of the relevant mathematics. The brain is far more complex than today's computers; therefore to understand it, one must use even more sophisticated mathematics than the average research engineer is familiar with. Because of this difficulty, a few "middle men" have presented oversimplified description of biology to the engineers, and oversimplified descriptions of the engineering to the biologists. These oversimplifications have often led to considerable misunderstanding and justified mistrust.

Because of these communications problems, this paper will be written in an extremely informal style. It will consist mainly of the transcript of a one-hour talk, edited for readability, with a few critical updates inserted. The first section will explain the fundamental approach, and move directly to the "bottom line" -- to some specific areas where new experiments are badly needed. The next two sections will discuss the underlying theory and mathematics in more detail. The second section will discuss the issue of supervised learning, which can shed light on <u>local circuits</u> within the brain. The final section will discuss the major concepts of neurocontrol, which can shed light on the <u>global organization</u> which unifies these local circuits into a truly intelligent system.

INTRODUCTION AND OVERVIEW

Goals of This Talk

I really am grateful to speak for once to an audience that is said to have a lot of physiologists in it. I wish I had more chances to do this, because I think that some of the things that we've learned on the engineering side lead to some very interesting experimental possibilities on the physiological side; if we had more chances to talk to

---

[*]The views herein are those of the author, not those of NSF; however, as government work, it is in the public domain conditional upon proper citation. This is an updated version of a paper in *Computational Neuroscience Symposium 1992*, edited by M.Penna, S.Chittajalu and P.G. Madhavan, available from Madhavan at the Electrical Engineering Department at IUPUI in Indianapolis, Indiana.

each other, we could learn a lot more about experiments which nobody is doing which could lead to some very exciting results in the future. That is what I would really like to talk about today.

Now, because it is late in the day, I figured it might be useful for me to summarize everything I am going to say in one list, so that you can see that it is finite, anyway. I'm basically going to try to make four major points today:

(1) First, I'm going to argue that we can understand intelligence or the brain in the same kind of mathematical way that we understand physics, as a real science. I'm not saying we're there yet, but I think it can be done.

(2) Second, I'm going to argue that neurocontrol gives us new mathematics, which is the mathematics we need in order to understand the brain mathematically.

(3) I'm going to argue that neurocontrol has made enormous progress in the last few years, in terms of new engineering applications, new mathematical designs and ideas, and new links to the brain. Jim Bower has described this process as a kind of convergent evolution. If you look at the simple-minded neural nets you see in a lot of the neural net conferences, they don't have much connection to biology. But when you look at people who have to solve really difficult, hard engineering control problems, they're driven to some of the same complexities we observe in the brain. So I would argue concretely there are signs of convergent evolution.

(4) Finally, most important, is that what we now have learned about what the brain might be doing suggests new opportunities for experiment. It suggests some surprising predictions. If the predictions are right, then you can use experiments to surprise a lot of people and have fun changing the culture, and if they're wrong, you can surprise a lot of mathematicians and come up with some new computational principles that people think are impossible. So either way, it's really important.

A caveat here is that as an NSF program director I'm not telling you that I've got a lot of money for this. In fact, I'm not allowed to spend money on things other than neuroengineering; my present budget is too small to allow anything more. I think that this is a very unfortunate situation, because if we're going to try to understand the human mind and human learning -- subjects of truly enormous importance -- then we have got to bring these things together; but right at the moment, there's essentially zero dollars available for the specific kind of two-way cooperation I'll be talking about today. I really wish somebody could fix that. (As this book goes to press, The Biology Directorate at NSF is preparing a Collaborative Research Initiative which could help fill this vacuum; however, the exact role of Engineering in that initiative is not yet clear.)

If this were an audience of policy people, or people who talk to their congressman, I would spend ninety percent of my time up here on items number one and two on my list. I could spend a good hour on this -- on the theory and the philosophy and all of that. If this were an engineering audience, I would talk about the applications and the designs; I have done that for about eight hours at a stretch. But here I am going to try to jump ahead to the brain stuff, but this is a little risky. You have to bear in mind that the kind of mathematics that's relevant to the brain is not the easy stuff. The kind of math you can totally understand in twenty minutes--that isn't what relates to the brain. The brain is a little more complicated, so I'm going to have to jump over some stuff and give some citations.

Can we Understand the Brain Mathematically?:
Prospects for a Newtonian Revolution

Before I get going, though, I really do want to say a little bit about the generalities here.

I suspect that a lot of the people in neuroscience started out by wanting to understand the human mind. They really wanted to understand something fundamental and important. But then they ran into a problem. Do you remember the old saying:"When you're up to your knees in alligators, it's hard to remember that your goal was to drain the swamp."? All of us have that problem, from time to time. I suspect that a lot of neuroscientists discover, as time goes on, that the brain is so complex that they lose hope of figuring it out in their own lifetimes. Some people have made a formal philosophy of that; they say, "look, the information content in any one brain is more complex than what I have spare neurons to understand, so by definition I cannot understand another brain, let alone everybody's brain."

But let us think about that idea a little more carefully.

If you try to know all of the synapse strengths, the connections, the state of all the networks in somebody's brain, and the reverberatory dynamics -- then of course, that is too complicated to ever understand in your life. There is no way that all of those details can be fully known scientifically. There will always be lots and lots of islands of understanding, and those islands are useful. We've seen good examples of studying connections even here today. But they don't tell you how intelligence works as a whole system. They're just little islands. And that is very discouraging.

But think back, how did physicists solve this problem, how did physics become a science? Basically there was this guy Isaac Newton, and what did he do? Instead of trying to describe every physical object in the universe, physics gave up on that, and they said "let us try to understand instead the simple underlying dynamics which <u>change</u> all of that complicated stuff over time." Maybe all of these complicated things are governed by something simple enough you can understand it. In physics, "simple enough" meant a page of equations and a thousand pages of explanation -- not trivial, but understandable.

My argument is that the same kind of approach could work on the brain <u>if</u> you think of learning as the dynamics. There is every reason to believe that underneath the complexity in the cerebral cortex and so on, there is a generalized, modular plasticity. Lashley has shown this, and I've heard of recent experiments where they've trained linguistic cortex to develop edge detectors just by wiring it up differently. It's very clear that there is a uniform, generalized modularity there in the interesting parts of the brain, which ought to be understandable if we focus on the learning, the plasticity[1]. Knowing the laws of learning would not immediately tell us a lot of specialized things about how we process specific sensory inputs in specific ways, but physicists have found that if you understand the underlying dynamic laws that control everything else, that's incredibly important later on when you try to do engineering.

So let us try to see if we can create -- I think we can create, in principle -- a Newtonian revolution, by focusing on the basic laws of learning in the high-level, modular organs like the cerebral cortex, the limbic lobes, the cerebellum, the olive, and so on. We won't ever understand the motor pools that way; they're like ad hoc preprocessors and postprocessors. But the really important stuff we <u>can</u> understand, in principle.

But of course you can't do that unless you have the right math. Newton had derivatives. Well, we too have a new flavor of derivatives; that's what backpropagation is really all about, at its base [2], but backpropagation is only one small part of this large area that I'm calling neurocontrol. Years ago, there was great work by David Robinson comparing conventional control theory with what goes on in the vestibular system. His early work was a really great example of cross-disciplinary collaboration, really applying mathematical concepts in detail, but it did not really focus on the issue of <u>learning</u> (unlike his newer work). It really scares me that the time delay between developing the necessary mathematics and control theory <u>in the engineering context</u> and <u>applying</u> it to the eye tracking system may have been something like a 20-40 year time delay. Our new math -- neurocontrol -- is only about two years old, in the engineering world. <u>I hope we don't have to wait 40 years before we start to apply it to the brain</u>! If we follow the normal course of government funding and human inertia, we might well wait 40 years; however, if we work a little hard to do what's unnatural, the mathematics is available today, if we have the will to go ahead with it.

I'll talk more about these issues later on, when I discuss recent progress in neurocontrol.

Neuroengineering and Neuroscience:
What is the Basis for Collaboration?

Let me move ahead now to the first slide (Figure 1 on the next page). This is again a generality slide. Like everybody else here I'm arguing that we need interdisciplinary cooperation, but I'd like to say a little bit about where the problem is, because we need to do more than just say interdisciplinary cooperation is needed; we need to have a concrete image in our heads of what it's about, or else we'll never be able to implement it.

A lot of people are excited because folks in the neuroscience side of the world studying the brain are now using neural network models. They are building up the field of computational neuroscience, which still belongs on the left-hand side of Figure 1. In computational neuroscience, we describe the brain by use of differential equations or other mathematical models, instead of just verbal anecdotes and whatnot. That's exciting. On the right-hand side of figure 1, in neuroengineering, we are using neural network systems to solve real-world engineering problems; that's also very exciting.

WHAT IS NEUROENGINEERING?

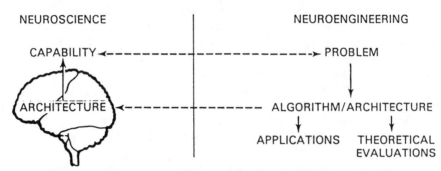

NEUROENGINEERING TRIES TO DEVELOP ALGORITHMS AND
ARCHITECTURES, INSPIRED BY WHAT IS KNOWN ABOUT
BRAIN FUNCTIONING, TO IMITATE BRAIN CAPABILITIES
WHICH ARE NOT YET ACHIEVED BY OTHER MEANS. BY
DEMONSTRATING ALGORITHM CAPABILITIES AND
PROPERTIES, IT MAY RAISE ISSUES WHICH FEED BACK TO
QUESTIONS OR HYPOTHESES FOR NEUROSCIENCE.

Figure 1. An NSF Definition of Neuroengineering

But the problem is this: what is the <u>connection</u> between the left and right sides of Figure 1? Even in today's symposium, which is very interdisciplinary, it is pretty easy to classify most of the talks into who is doing computational neuroscience and who is doing engineering applications. It's like a gulf. And what's the problem?

What's happening is that we're both using neural network models, but one group is using as its <u>standard of validation</u>: "Does the model fit the low-level circuit and the empirical data down at the low-level circuit?" Maybe more than that. But in engineering, the test is: "Does it work?" So we have two different communities, based on two different standards of validation. But in reality, <u>the brain itself meets both tests</u>. The real circuits not only fit their own biological data, they also work in solving very complex control challenges. Instead of having two communities, using two different standards of validation to inspire and to evaluate their work, we need to think of using both standards of validation together. And that's how we can get feedback back and forth here. I won't elaborate on this today; this is just a matter of general principles. As I said before, unfortunately, my tiny bit of money is entirely on the neuroengineering side, and that's something that needs to be changed.

Neural Nets and Neurocontrol:
Where Is the Right Mathematics?

A lot of people are worried that the artificial neural network (ANN) community, the engineering community, is itself caught in a kind of local minimum. It is true that 90% of the papers you see in a neural network conference these days talk about pattern recognition, and what are they actually doing? Usually, they are doing pattern classification, using associative memory or other simple systems. Usually they are "training" ANNs to match databases which contain definite targets for what the output of the ANN should be, for every single example in the database. There are lots of uses for this kind of task. But that's not intelligence. That's not consciousness, that's not what the mind does. We humans are not just simple classification machines! This really ought to be obvious to anyone.

This situation is kind of scary; you have to ask what is the relevance of that stuff? Now, I'm not going to talk today about consciousness or the mind/body problem; if I'm brave at SMC on Monday I'll talk about that[3,4,5], but here I'm going to focus on physiology.

If we agree that neuroengineering <u>has</u> been caught in a kind of local minimum or intellectual rut, then what is the way to get out of that local minimum? If you forgive a pun, I will argue that we can get out of that local minimum by <u>climbing out</u>, by climbing up a ladder -- and here's the ladder (Figure 2, on the next page), the ladder of designs of neurocontrol.

Again, let me warn you that this is just a quick overview; I'll be giving you citations to more detailed information later on. There are <u>many, many</u> designs in this emerging area of neurocontrol, which I define as the use

LADDER OF DESIGNS IN NEUROCONTROL

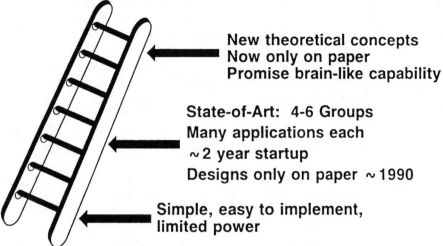

New theoretical concepts
Now only on paper
Promise brain-like capability

State-of-Art: 4-6 Groups
Many applications each
~2 year startup
Designs only on paper ~1990

Simple, easy to implement,
limited power

Figure 2. The Ladder of Designs in Neurocontrol

of well-specified neural nets -- either natural or artificial, just mathematically-defined neural nets -- to generate <u>control outputs</u>, which could be to motors, muscles, glands, stock transactions or whatever, but <u>real actions</u> in the real world.

In the neurocontrol field, we do have very simple designs, and these are the most popular. They're easy to do; they're a great start for people who want to get their students going, and start to build up software. This is the right place to start, but these designs do have very limited power, and they certainly are not like the brain.

In the middle level of the ladder, we have what I call the state-of-the-art group, and I'd say there are about four groups that are really in this category. It's curious that industry is here more than academia; I don't know why. Are university people scared to do new things? I don't know, but these state-of-the-art groups have mostly taken a couple of years to build up; maybe that's the problem, that you've got to keep your students around long enough, and build up modular software packages. After a couple of years of struggling, these groups have gotten real-world applications just this year, of things that were only on paper two or three years ago. And they have proven -- with really exciting, important applications -- that these more advanced, more brain-like methods are far more powerful in solving real-world problems. There are just incredibly important engineering problems that have been solved that are in the mill; again, today I won't talk about this a lot today, but I may make some reference to it.

After these methods on paper were used in real applications, it was a challenge to us theorists to move ahead of the applications people and come up with new methods to overcome the limits of the older ones, so that now on paper this year there are new methods which did not exist two or three years ago. And now, on paper, it looks as if these designs and ideas really have the potential to achieve true brain-like intelligence. So my bottom line is that at least on paper we now have the math we need to understand real intelligence. I'm not saying that these ideas are working yet on real systems, and that's what I try to pay people to do, to climb up this ladder with real engineering systems.

By the way, I'm saying that the bottom level of the ladder is a good place to start, but when I fund people, the higher they can go up the ladder, the higher the probability of funding. They may have to climb one step at a time, but they had better be moving upwards in a visible way. I'm trying to develop the engineering math that will be necessary to understand the brain. I'm using engineering as a <u>discipline</u> to get the math we need for what's really interesting, which is the mind and the brain.

Four New Empirical Possibilities: A Summary

Now before getting into the intricacies of neurocontrol, I would first like to give you my real bottom line. I would like to summarize four empirical areas where I think new experimental work could be really crucial. I will try to explain the reasoning behind all this in more detail later, but for now I will just give a summary:

(1) First, I'm going to argue that some form of backpropagation -- not the simple three-layer kind that most people have seen, but a more complicated, advanced form of backpropagation -- almost certainly must exist in the brain in order to explain some of the capabilities that we have observed there. That in turn suggests that we have to look for some novel mechanisms, to carry information backwards both within and between cells. Between cells, it is now well-known that nitric oxide (NO) acts as a backwards transmitter. In addition, a group of researchers including Timothy Bill -- one of the important pioneers in Long-Term Potentiation (LTP) [6] -- has discovered a new presynaptic receptor intimately related to LTP[7]. (The group speculates that this receptor may be involved in adapting the nearby synapse, but there is no reason to believe that this is its only function.) Back in 1974, after I had developed the backpropagation algorithm, I speculated that the cytoskeleton might take care of the backwards flows within cells [2]; this still appears to be a viable possibility [5,8,9,10], but there is new evidence that the usual kinds of field effects in membranes could also be involved[11]. David Gardner has shown that such backwards mechanisms are crucial to learning even at the level of aplysia[12,13]. Nevertheless, all of this is only just a beginning.

There is a lot of engineering work needed in this area, both in theory and in instrumentation. It's really frightening to me, when I look at how critical the cytoskeleton is in the nervous system (it is like half the nervous system!), to see that the amount of work that's been done understanding how the cytoskeleton relates computationally (or might relate) is negligible. We don't yet know that it's relevant, but we don't yet know that it's irrelevant either. It is amazing to me that we can just sit back and ignore it and give it maybe ten thousand a year, when we're spending a billion dollars on the other half, when we don't know what it does is. It's really frightening; we really need to be studying the cytoskeleton in any case, and backpropagation is just one of the things to look for when we do it.

In looking for backpropagation, you don't necessarily have to look at the cytoskeletal level. There are other kinds of experiments you can do, where region A has a forward fiber to region B (e.g., A might be a part of the limbic zone and you move on to something like the motor cortex), and sometimes you can find that the plasticity in A seems to depend on what happens in B. It would be interesting to see if you could cut the fiber from A to B and then see if you lose the plasticity in A. There's no way that could happen in a classical neuron model that's all feedforward and membrane-driven, but if it does happen then that means that you can unhinge the neuron model. I have tried to persuade Karl Pribram to look into experiments like that, and his (informal, not for scientific publication) response was "I've already done it, I've already proven this."

Pribram's response was really very interesting to me. If you ask a lot of the middlemen between the neural network field and biology, they'll tell you that this is impossible; however, when I ask Pribram he says it's already been proven, that there is a backpropagation there. I don't know whether to take his informal statements at face value yet; I think we need a lot closer collaboration to evaluate those experiments to see what they mean mathematically, but it's clear there is a lot to be done here.

(2) True reverse engineering of hippocampal and other slices. In the talk by Sclabassi earlier today, we heard some very exciting things about the hippocampus. It was particularly fascinating to hear that the kind of learning you get from LTP clearly doesn't represent the real nonlinearity of the system. I would speculate that appropriate slices through the brain can generate model systems that you can play with like artificial neural nets, where you can control the inputs and outputs. Why is it that when we do experiments in neural systems we try to always do them under natural conditions? If we think that biological neural circuits are general purpose learning machines, then let's play with them!

Let's see if we can use a slice of neural tissue to learn to recognize an
arbitrary pattern that hasn't been seen in nature. Let's find out what are the capabilities. Let's find out what the plasticity is in these more micro, more mathematical ways. And I would speculate, for example, that a slice through hippocampus and cerebral cortex that maintains those local recurrent links will have a better learning capability, in a sense I hope to have time to define, than any of the Hebbian or backpropagation, feedforward nets that are in use today.

In other words, there are two classes of nets people are using a lot -- the classic Hebbian, the Grossbergian nets, and then maybe the multi-layer perceptron (MLP) nets; I'm willing to bet that there are critical learning problems which I hope to talk about, which that kind of slice can solve better than any of the nets people now believe in, on the biological or the engineering side. Once you prove this, empirically, then I have some ideas for what is going on there, but the experiments are what's crucial for now. I think if you do the experiment, you will shake up a lot of people, and then they'll start thinking about those more powerful designs that we're just now starting to look at in engineering.

There is a whole lot to be done in this area. Once you have taken the first step -- demonstrating and describing plasticity on the slice -- you can then start looking for the learning mechanisms that underlie that plasticity. So in a way this might be a good place to begin before getting into some of the harder issues I discussed earlier.

Similar kinds of experiments could also be done in culture, if the right kinds of cells can be grown together in culture. Many biologists worry that cell cultures (and even slices) are very artificial. It can be dangerous to draw too many conclusions from what we see in culture, because the presence of other cell types and inputs in the brain could lead to very different kinds of behavior. Nevertheless, when groups of cells in culture do succeed in demonstrating certain kinds of engineering capabilities - such as the ability to learn to approximate mathematical functions more complex than those which Hebbian or MLP nets can learn -- then we probably can conclude that these cells possess these capabilities (or more) in nature, in the brain. There may be great value in figuring out what kinds of cells need to be present, as part of a culture, to generate what kinds of learning capabilities.

(3) A third area has to do with the inferior olive, which governs learning in the cerebellar system. I am told by Pellionisz that Llinas and his group have observed plasticity in the inferior olive, which is crucially related to the cerebellum and lower-level motor control. I haven't looked at the experiments myself, but based on a very careful examination of the cerebellum, working jointly with Pellionisz (not with tensor theory, working with Pellionisz on some new ideas), it is my conclusion that something unusual is going on[14].

There are two possibilities -- or rather, I'm predicting one of two possibilities. Both of them are very surprising. First of all, before doing the experiment proper, the first stage is to replicate the phenomenon of plasticity in the olive. Then you have to cut one of two fibers, and show that cutting those fibers eliminates the plasticity; this would narrow down the plasticity to one of two possible mechanisms. (The two fibers are: (1) the climbing fibers; (2) the collateral fibers from the deep cerebellar nuclei and vestibular nucleus to the olive.)

I hope that somebody can do this experiment soon. This may well be the most finite and do-able thing on this whole list here. So I really hope somebody looks at this. I have described that in more detail at the end of a recent paper[14]. This is an important experiment nobody has done--I don't think it should be that hard. And it is really critical to our next step in understanding what the cerebellum is doing.

After this talk was given, I found out that the first step -- of simply replicating plasticity in the olive -- itself a serious challenge. The original experiments by Llinas et al, reported in *Science* in 1975, are still highly controversial. Furthermore, there are certain learning tasks -- like those described by Richard Thompson -- which do not seem to elicit plasticity in the olive. (Just as most physical tasks only require the use of a few muscles, so too do many learning tasks exercise only a part of our learning abilities.) Hockberger and Alford at Northwestern University, working in communication with James Houk, in a small grant supported by NSF, have begun to explore learning mechanisms in olive cells, at a molecular level, in culture. It is predicted that olive cells can display plasticity in culture, but that it will be crucial to include enough other cell types (e.g. deep cerebellar nuclei cells) and to provide appropriate learning challenges through appropriate stimulation of the system; this may or may not be possible within the time-frame of this small start-up project. It is truly amazing that such a basic, important issue has been left unresolved for so many years. (Similar gaps exist in the present understanding of the nucleus basalis, another small but crucial piece of brain circuitry.)

A more technical issue, crucial to working out the fine points of this system, is the ability of the cerebellum to learn time sequences and delays [14]. This ability clearly depends on certain short-term memory capabilities of Purkinje cells, but it is very tricky to design a circuit which reproduces such capabilities. (See chapter 13 of [15].) Tam, at the University of North Texas, has begun some learning experiments in cultures which might shed light on this issue[16]; again, however, the efforts so far are only a crude beginning.

(4) Fourth, there is room for more true reverse engineering of the cerebellar motor system. Suzuki, Kawato et al[17] have done a magnificent job in getting this area started, but a lot more needs to be done. Suzuki et al have basically shown that the lower motor system is doing optimal control, not adaptive control in the classic sense, and not translation between different kinds of coordinate systems, but optimal control. I think that someone could play with that circuit a lot more than anyone has done so far. Suzuki et al, and Houk, think they know where the reward or utility functions are coming in from; if they are right, we could perturb these inputs and prove what the power is of this system in optimization, in adapting to new regimes. Again, we could play with the lower motor system, by

perturbing its inputs to see what capabilities it has as a general-purpose optimizer.

In brief, I have described four general areas where new kinds of experiments could be extremely useful. I don't know if I'm describing the tasks in exactly the right way. This is just an attempt to get the process started. I'm just a dumb engineer, as they often say. But I think that something
needs to be done to get us moving into these new kinds of areas, and there is some theory behind the ideas above.

SUPERVISED LEARNING: RECENT ANN RESULTS AND IMPLICATIONS FOR NEUROCONTROL AND BIOLOGY

Supervised Learning As A Neural Net Paradigm

A lot of people in neuroengineering get upset when I talk about control applications and control, because a lot of people in the artificial field really have this old idea (illustrated in Figure 3), that supervised learning is the same as neural network theory. They think that neural network theory is the same as learning a map from an input vector $\underline{X}$ to a target vector $\underline{Y}$, in hopes that in the future you'll be able to predict the right target vector. And you go through training sets and you learn over and over again what this mapping is.

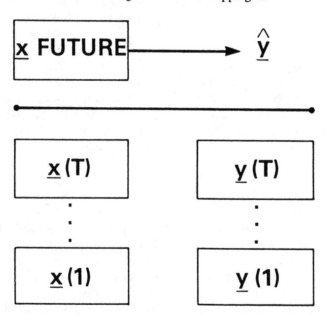

Figure 3. What Does Supervised Learning Do?

In fact, if you look at the Granger-Lynch model of the hippocampus (arguably the best existing model of the hippocampus as an associative memory) -- that's another form of supervised learning; it's just plain old pattern classification you're studying. Supervised learning tends to be an all-pervasive paradigm, even for biologically motivated research. Many people tend to think that supervised learning is fundamental theory, and that anything else is just dirty applications.

Supervised Learning versus Neurocontrol

Supervised learning is certainly useful, and it may well exist in subsystems of the brain, but it turns out that for really powerful control systems, you have to do stuff that is a lot harder.

What you have to do is stuff like this (see Figure 4 on the next page). When I'm giving a tutorial on how to do real neurocontrol in engineering, it turns out that I have to spend an hour or two on each one of the three main boxes in Figure 4. You do have supervised learning systems in these designs, but they're like little modules. And then you have a big system, a neurocontrol system, that takes these lower level modules and integrates them and links them. I often compare this situation to how we build computers: there's a lot of science to building the chip, but there's a lot of science to putting chips together to making a computer. Supervised learning is a general purpose concept, but neurocontrol is also general-purpose and fundamental; they simply address different general-purpose tasks.

It turns out that the work that's been done in neurocontrol at these multiple levels of organization has parallels to the brain, at multiple levels of organization. So the stuff we've learned down at the supervised learning level tends to be relevant to issues like what is the circuitry like <u>within</u> the cortex, <u>within</u> recurrent nets, or <u>within</u> the cerebellum, while the higher-level stuff is important when we try to figure out the organization that <u>connects</u> those systems. So that means I should talk about <u>both</u> of these levels and explain them before I talk about the brain. So I should spend eight hours before it all becomes crystal clear. Forgive me, it won't be quite as crystal clear as I like, because I don't have the eight hours.

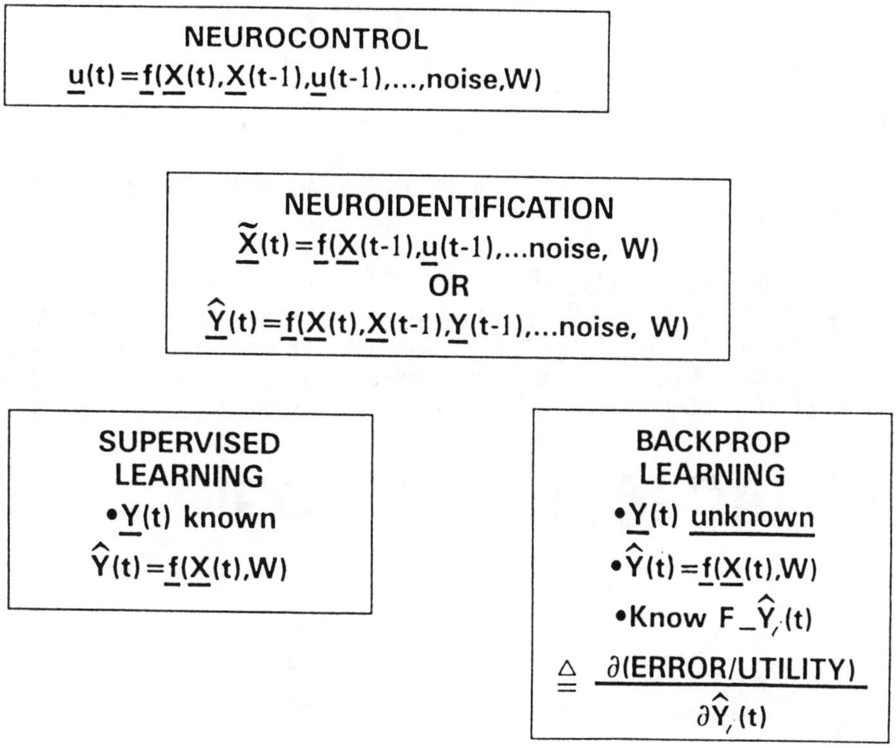

NEUROCONTROL
$$\underline{u}(t) = \underline{f}(\underline{X}(t), \underline{X}(t-1), \underline{u}(t-1), \dots, noise, W)$$

NEUROIDENTIFICATION
$$\tilde{X}(t) = \underline{f}(\underline{X}(t-1), \underline{u}(t-1), \dots noise, W)$$
OR
$$\hat{Y}(t) = \underline{f}(\underline{X}(t), \underline{X}(t-1), \underline{Y}(t-1), \dots noise, W)$$

SUPERVISED LEARNING
- $\underline{Y}(t)$ **known**
$$\hat{Y}(t) = \underline{f}(\underline{X}(t), W)$$

BACKPROP LEARNING
- $\underline{Y}(t)$ <u>**unknown**</u>
- $\hat{Y}(t) = \underline{f}(\underline{X}(t), W)$
- Know $F\_\hat{Y}_i(t)$
- $\triangleq \dfrac{\partial(\text{ERROR/UTILITY})}{\partial \hat{Y}_i(t)}$

Figure 4. Four Task Areas Critical to Neurocontrol

Three Supervised Learning Modules Used Today in Neurocontrol

First of all let me talk at the low level, at the supervised learning level. Little nets that learn pattern recognition. What has been useful in engineering?

Basically, there are three kinds of networks that people really use in real-world control applications:

(1) The most common is the multilayer perceptron (MLP). (See Figure 5 on the next page.)) <u>Please</u> don't call it a "backpropagation network"! The MLP is only one special case of what you can adapt with backpropagation. Furthermore, the MLP is a lot older than what I did in 1974. Bernie Widrow or Rosenblatt are the guys that should take credit for the MLP design itself.

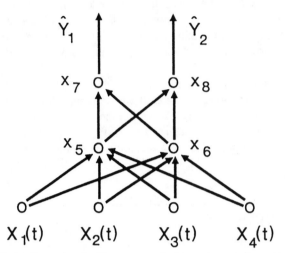

Figure 5. An Example of a Three-Layer Multilayer Perceptron (MLP)

The MLPs are basically the McCulloch-Pitts networks, the feedforward things. There have been some wonderful theorems about what they can do.

(2) and (3) Almost as common are the CMAC and the RBF designs. (Figure 6) These networks are examples of "local" learning systems. We have already heard about these designs from Nick DeClaris; for example, CMAC was first proposed by Albus, for a PhD thesis under DeClaris. There are many other local learning systems discussed in neural net meetings, but DeClaris' students happened to hit on what was useful more than most students. There are also many modified versions of the CMAC and the RBF, which give improved performance in control applications[15].

CMAC (RBF) NETWORK

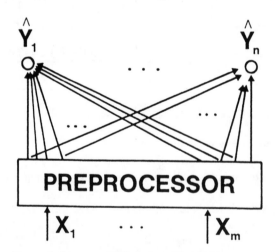

Figure 6. Structure of CMAC or RBF Network

Basically, these local learning rules perform forecasting by association. The MLP gives you a global model and is good for learning global functions, causal relations, etc. The local systems are more like forecasting by precedent. When you've got a new situation, you predict the result will be like what it was before when you had a similar situation. It's an associative memory, and this is what the Granger-Lynch stuff is, just another example of the same general principle.

So these are the things that most people use. These are feedforward nets, easy to implement and I'll show in a couple of charts how some people have used them. There are many other forms of associative memory, based on Hebbian learning, which have appeared in the biologically oriented literature; however, those kinds of nets are not used very often, for one reason or another. Most likely, people feel that the Hebbian nets now available are very similar in capability to the CMAC and RBF, because they are based on forecasting by precedent, while being harder to implement in real time. Why work harder to achieve the same capability? Another factor, however, is that people do tend to implement what is easiest first, not what is most powerful.

Local learning systems can be adapted in a variety of ways -- through least squares, through backpropagation (i.e. derivative-based learning), etc. No matter how they are adapted, they tend to be faster to adapt than global MLPs, because they do not have to "undo" what was learned in a previous region of space when they explore a new region of space. They are usually set up so that different weights are active in different regions of space. They tend to require many more weights, but learn faster. There may be ways to combine the best advantages of global and local networks together in one system[18], but no one has implemented the right kind of hybrid as yet.

What Kinds of Functions Can Such Modules Represent?

So what are the capabilities of these different kind of networks? Well, there are a lot of theorems. There's a guy named Andy Barron who has proven some beautiful theorems showing that those three-layer neural nets like MLPs are much better than Taylor series, polynomial expansions, or local learning rules even, to approximate any smooth function. It's beautiful.

In control applications, however, to really control an arm efficiently, sometimes you don't have a smooth function. Then you've got a problem and it often doesn't work, and a lot of control applications three layers won't work. So, a guy named Sontag at Rutgers has proven that it really can approximate the control functions you need if you've got two hidden layers.

But there's another problem. You can approximate any function, but you need to approximate it parsimoniously. MLPs are as good as any other feedforward net, but in general there are some functions which you cannot approximate parsimoniously with any feedforward net. This means that you need enormous numbers of hidden layers to approximate them, and enormous numbers of hidden neurons.

Marvin Minsky, years ago, gave an example of this in his famous book Perceptrons. He described the "connectedness" problem, which sounds at first like a very typical character-recognition, pixel-type problems, but it turns out to be a little different. Imagine that you've got a grid of 50x50 input pixels and that they're all either white or black, and that you're trying to recognize a desired pattern. What you're trying to do is to output a one if the blacks are all connected, and a zero if they're not.

Now it turns out that Minsky showed that the number of hidden units required for this task is just enormous. As the number of pixels grows, it becomes astronomical; no feedforward net of any kind is going to do a good job. But if you allow recurrence, recurrent feedback connections, what I call simultaneous recurrence (a special kind of feedback connection), then you can represent it parsimoniously.

I would argue that the kind of language-processing problem that Jim Anderson described earlier (from Fodor) is a problem in this family, where a feedforward net can't represent it parsimoniously, but a simultaneous recurrent net can represent it parsimoniously. And I've seen systems of that general sort, which so seem to work on that kind of problem, but I haven't studied Fodor's example in great detail.

It turns out that, if you want to deal with control problems like navigating a robot through a cluttered room where the clutter keeps moving and it's in a new position, you need to worry about finding a connected path. So there are good arguments[15,18] that higher-level intelligence has to use these kind of networks.

So that seems easy, but is it? Well, first of all, what happens if you have parts of the brain that have to make decisions quickly? Simultaneous-recurrent nets take time to settle down--what then? Then you've got to have a feedforward net, and what happens then?

Fast Feedforward Nets: The Cerebellum

Well, Figure 7 (on the next page) shows an example of a feedforward net with two hidden layers that is good for fast, general motor control. This comes from Nauta[1]; it is a diagram of the cerebellum. In the cerebellum, you start out with inputs along the mossy fibers (which some people would call an input "layer"). These inputs go to the granule cells, which operate as a first hidden layer, and you've got zillions of them. Some people say there are more granule cells than there are any other kind of cell in the brain, maybe ten times that number. That reinforces the point--you need a lot of hidden nodes if you try to do complex tasks with a (relatively local) feedforward net.

The next hidden layer in the cerebellum is the Purkinje cell layer. The output layer is basically the deep cerebellar layer and the vestibular nucleus (the FTN cells of the vestibular nucleus, to be precise); those two systems are basically together -- they're not right next to each other but they form one output layer, for functional purposes.

In summary, the cerebellum is not based on simultaneous-recurrence, which is slow but powerful. Strictly speaking, however, it is not just a static MLP, either. Above all, the Purkinje layer has some working memory capabilities[14], similar to well-known ANN designs. Such capabilities are tricky to adapt[15, chapter 13]; this, in turn, suggests that Purkinje cells might possibly be adapted by a combination of the well known olive-to-cerebellum mechanism, plus a local mechanism supporting the working memory effects. Also, because the Purkinje cells are large cells, and because continuity in output is very desirable at this level, it is conceivable that dendritic field effects, as described by Pribram, could occur within these cells[4,18].

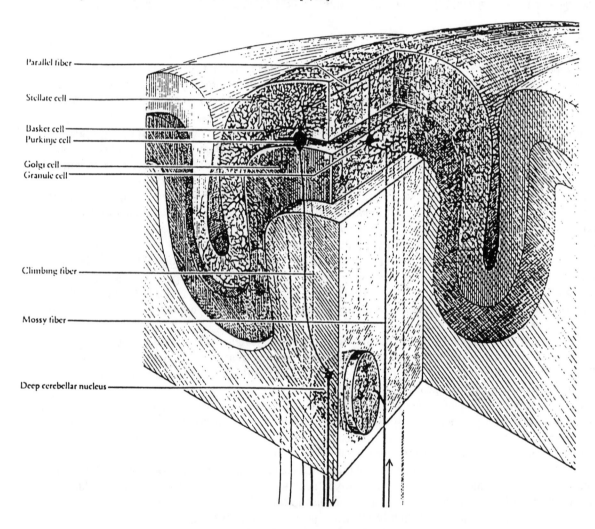

Figure 7. The cerebellum, from Nauta [1]

Slower, More Powerful Nets: The Cerebrum

But again, this kind of feedforward arrangement is not very good for the really higher-level kinds of functions like finding a connected path or connectedness. There are some kinds of functions you just can't expect the cerebellum to solve, because they require a more sophisticated processing. That leads to a prediction that somehow or other the higher levels, like the limbic lobes and the cerebral cortex, must form a kind of two-level system, where the low level is settling down...but first let me describe Figure 8, which shows what a simultaneous recurrent net (SRN) is.

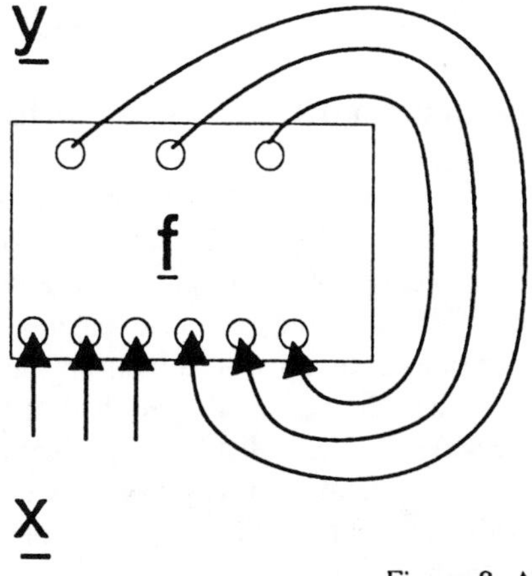

Figure 8. A Simultaneous Recurrent Network

Mathematically, an engineer would say that you plug in the inputs into any old feedforward structure (the net labelled $\underline{f}$ in Figure 8). But then you take the outputs of $\underline{f}$, and feed them back in as inputs to $\underline{f}$, and see how that changes the outputs. You keep feeding the outputs back in as inputs, again and again, until the values of the outputs settle down to some kind of equilibrium, $\underline{y}_\infty$. Now, to use a system like that... you have to plug in the inputs, wait through many cycles of the inner system $\underline{f}$ until the outputs settle down, and then that becomes just one cycle time of your bigger system. Now, when I first saw the engineering of this[15], I said this can't have anything to do with the brain, because you need really fast cycles inside of a longer cycle; how could that be biologically plausible? I knew that we needed all this to get intelligence in engineering, and I couldn't think of anything else; therefore, in the 1990 Decade of the Brain Symposium (sponsored by the National Federation for Brain Research and the INNS), I presented this from an Engineering point of view, without any notion of how the connection to the brain could be made.

Later that same day, Walter Freeman presented his model of the hippocampus, which involved exactly the same kind of loops within loops as in my model! He showed how very close inner recurrent loops operate at a very high cycle time, embedded within a larger, slower theta rhythm. For the inner loop, he said that the basic calculation cycle time is like 400 hertz, versus about 4 hertz -- quite enough to implement Figure 8. (Some people quote 80 hertz -- based on Fourier analysis rather than cycle times -- but that still would be enough for some functionality in this design. When I checked with Pribram, he assured me that fast, 1ms. synapses allow such high-frequency computation.) VonderMalsburg has convinced me that such dual-loop effects are even more certain to occur in the neocortex, but the neocortex contains additional capabilities and complexity which may make it harder to work with at present. I would speculate that SRN capabilities are crucial both to binocular vision and to the image segmentation capabilities of neocortex.

In brief, the biological data appears to fit the model beautifully. Now, if you look at Granger and Lynch's model of the hippocampus, it doesn't do that. In their model its like a feed forward, associative memory, and you only have an outer recurrence that's used to generate the associative memory. So what is that inner loop doing? Maybe the hippocampus is more powerful than associative memory. Maybe we need something more powerful than an associative memory to form emotions and make plans in our life, and maybe somebody can do an experiment proving it. I hope so.

Parenthetically, it should be noted that SRNs -- unlike feedforward networks -- can have problems in settling down to a stable equilibrium. In engineering, one can use a "tension" term [15,18] to reduce the probability of instability, but the possibility cannot be totally eliminated. The tension parameter is a global parameter, with an interesting analogy to the global level of adrenalin in the bloodstream. Karl Pribram has pointed out that there is a strong analogy between this "tension" term and the "unpleasure" principle of Freud[19], which plays a key role in understanding the possibility of instability in human brains. In the human limbic system, Pribram's empirical discussion [20] suggests that the hippocampus is an SRN, acting mainly as a "hidden layer" of the limbic network, a network in which the amygdala is the ultimate or penultimate output layer. (This suggests a kind of crude analogy between the hippocampus and the cerebellar cortex.)

Other Forms of Hebbian Learning

That covers most of what I really want to say about supervised learning. Again, please excuse my glossing over the many, many details; each one of these topics can be discussed in much more detail, and is so discussed in the papers cited.

For the sake of completeness, however, I should say a little about two forms of Hebbian learning which I did not mention above.

Most people who work with Hebbian learning would argue that there are really two different kinds of Hebbian learning system which could be used on supervised learning problems. There are local associative memory systems, which I discussed above. But there are also global systems, which are generally linear, and require that inputs be decorrelated before they enter the supervised learning system. A lot of decorrelating networks have been designed for use with such nets. However, after discussing this matter with Pribram, I am convinced that this latter class of network is not relevant to systems like the human brain. Pribram and others have shown again and again that biological representation systems have a great deal of redundancy (e.g., like wavelets but with a 1.5 amplification factor instead of 2, etc., as in the Simmons talk today). One would expect such redundancy, in any system which also has to have a high degree of fault tolerance. This is inconsistent with the mathematical requirement of orthogonality. In addition, the limitation to the linear case is not encouraging, either.

In 1992, I developed an alternative learning design which appears Hebbian in character, but has radically different properties[4,18]. It provides a mathematical representation of certain ideas by Pribram about dendritic field processing, which the talk today by Simmons provides strong empirical support for. It is closely linked to Chris Atkeson's experiments with locally-weighted regression, which has performed very well in robotics experiments at MIT. In retrospect, as I reconsider the issue of information flows around dendrites, I suspect that the design still needs to be revised, to account explicitly for the three-dimensional nature of local information flows, at least for biological modeling. In any case, the alternative design is still feedforward in terms of what it accomplishes; therefore, it might possibly be worth considering as a model of the innermost loop of the neocortex, but it does not obviate the need for simultaneous recurrence, and for the unusual kinds of nonHebbian feedback (as in Figure 8) required to adapt key parts of the neocortex and hippocampus -- if those systems are as powerful as I suspect.

Summary

In summary, I predict that the human brain contains some very complex circuitry, as required to solve some very complex adaptation problems. At present, most people would find it hard to believe that something that complicated is there, even though it does fit these new results of Freeman and so on. I think we need new experiments, based on living slices, to help get home to people that it's this kind of complexity that's in that system, and that the old models are simply not good enough. So that's the end of supervised learning.

THE HIGHER LEVEL OF ORGANIZATION: NEUROCONTROL

Now let me talk about neurocontrol. This is a subject I've talked about for eight hours at a stretch, so I will have to cut out a lot of important material here today. First, I want to talk about why this is crucial to understanding intelligence. I'll skip over my slides on engineering application areas. I will talk a little bit about the kind of designs that engineers are using today, but only a little. Mainly I will focus on the design concepts which relate directly to understanding the brain.

Why is Neurocontrol the Right Mathematics For Understanding the Brain?

This is a chart (Figure 9) that people look at and say, "I already know this." But if people could understand the implications of what they already know, this world would be a different place. There are some implications in what we already know that people haven't thought through. Now what I am going to talk about here is the reason why the human brain is a neurocontroller; let me give you the argument in a few stages.

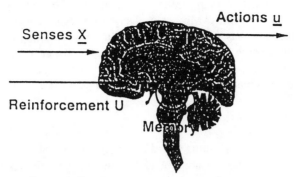

Figure 9. The Brain As a Neurocontroller

Step one: we know that the brain is an information processing system. I would call it a computer, except that people will think of sequential machines. But it's really a computer; it's an information processing system; its sole biological function is to be a computer. And what does it compute? It computes <u>actions</u> that control glands and muscles. So the point is that the function of the brain as a <u>whole system</u> is to perform control.

Some people think of control as something that's only in the cerebellum, just to control finger movements. That's not true. Nauta, in his classic text on neuroanatomy[1], stresses how you cannot separate what is the control system from the rest of the brain. Now that doesn't mean that the whole brain does tracking or pursuit movements; no, it doesn't do that; it does a higher order kind of control, of course. And you might use the term "sensorimotor control," if you will. But the point is that the brain as a <u>whole system</u> has the function of calculating these things. Everything in the brain is there to help it compute these outputs. So the function of the brain is to do that; if you want to understand the brain as a whole system, you have to understand the mathematics of what it takes to build a controller that has these kind of control capabilities, which again go far beyond mere trajectory tracking. (Those who <u>think</u> of control as trajectory planning may still have troubles with this; I urge them to reconsider the <u>definition</u> of control, and recognize that the overall mathematical literature on control has always been far wider than this in scope.)

Furthermore, you can't even understand a subsystem until you know how it fits into the whole system. Therefore, you can't even understand subsystems of the brain until you put them into this greater context, which is neurocontrol: the brain <u>is</u> a neurocontroller.

Capabilities of the Brain As a Controller

So, next slide (Figure 10). This slide shows what I regard as the most exciting and crucial capabilities of the brain as an intelligent controller. I should have added an extra line here about learning in real time; it's just so obvious, but it's something we've got to keep in mind.

BRAIN AS NEUROCONTROLLER:

- **Millions of Actuators**

- **Nonlinear Systems**

- **Noisy Systems**

- **Long-Term Horizon**

- **High-Speed Coordination**

Figure 10. Capabilities of the Brain As a Neurocontroller

695

The brain can control millions of actuators in parallel -- well, maybe only 900,000 -- it's the same principle, huge numbers. What about conventional controllers? Most control engineers regard one actuator as a normal problem and ten as a large problem. Thus the brain has an incredible capability, very exciting to engineers. It can handle nonlinearity and noise routinely, without being destabilized. And above all, most critical, it includes what you might call a long-term planning horizon. The AI people would say the long-term planning capability is the real intelligence. And the brain also has a high-speed coordination capability through the cerebellum, basically.

Brain Capabilities Versus ANN Capabilities

Now, how do these capabilities compare with anything we can conceive of in mathematics? Is there any hope of understanding them? Well, we presume there's a hope of understanding them, but is there a way that we can conceive of to understand them?

The next slide (Figue 11) provides a list of what's been done in Artificial Neural Networks in control. These are the basic kinds of capabilities that exist today. I've read hundreds of papers on this topic, but they all boil down to this. I've seen a lot of people try to wriggle out of my basic taxonomies, but these are basically the capabilities you've got. You've got people using neural nets in subsystems in control; that's not really neurocontrol. You've got people who have learned to clone experts, learned to copy a human movement. You've got people who

NEURAL NETWORKS (ANNs) IN CONTROL:

1. In Subsystems

2. Copy Experts
   Supervised Control

3. <u>Follow</u> Path, Setpoint, Ref. Model
   Direct Inverse Control
   Neural Adaptive Control

4. <u>Optimal</u> Control Over Time
   Backpropagation of Utility (Direct)
   Adaptive Critics

Figure 11. Four Tasks Performed by ANN Controllers
(Subsystem, Cloning, Tracking, Optimization)

do classical adaptive control, which is just a matter of trajectory tracking; for example, somebody tells you where to move your arm and you move it there. And then you've got systems that optimize over time.

Now, cloning or copying is definitely not what humans do. I admit that we may imitate our parents a little bit, but they don't tell us exactly what to do; they don't give us a complete vector of actions, and that's what the cloning designs require.

Likewise, we're not simple trajectory followers. We don't have somebody who tells us where to move our arm; maybe we have subsystems -- maybe, maybe not -- but that isn't what the human brain as a whole does.

So, that really leaves us only one choice, which has to do with optimization over time. Now, the notion of optimization over time is one people have taken seriously for centuries in studying human behavior. People have screamed at the idea for centuries as well, because it's clear that humans don't do a perfect job of optimization, but that's okay. If, in engineering, you do the best possible job of optimization, your system still won't be perfect. You don't have to worry about designing a system so perfect that it's implausible as a model of the human brain; in fact, that's the last thing you have to worry about, okay? There are a lot of imperfections in the engineering optimization systems quite close to those you see in biological systems.

Furthermore, the general concept of reinforcement learning is very pervasive in animal behavior. There's a guy named Harry Klopf who has recently shown that if you take some very simple optimization networks, they regenerate not only what's called Skinnerian conditioning (in other words, conditioning by reward and punishment); just incidentally, they replicate Pavlovian conditioning as well. So this concept really is powerful enough to cover the basic things we observe.

In summary, my argument here is that the optimizing designs are the only form of neural networks we know of, the only form of mathematics we can conceive of, which is really relevant to understanding brain-like intelligence. It seems to me that it's got to be what's going on in the brain.

If you look again at Figure 11, you will see that there are only two useful ways of doing the optimization over time (for large-scale problems). There is a thing called backpropagation of utility: I proposed this approach in my Ph.D. thesis in 1974; I invented it, so I have a vested interest in it, but I'll still tell you it's not biological. Flat out, it's not biological. I can explain why at length, if anybody's interested. I've written it up[2,15]; it's not biological. There's only one thing that's biological, and that's what I call adaptive critics, and I'm going to say that the brain is an adaptive critic system. I've got to explain what that means now.

ANN Control Designs Versus Brain Capabilities

Table 1 is a matrix comparing these designs against the capabilities of the brain. For the most part, this table simply reinforces what I just said, that the simple cloning stuff doesn't involve planning, that tracking

Table 1. Matrix of ANN Designs Versus Key Brain Capabilities

	Many Motors	Noise	Optimization Over Time	Real-time Learning
Supervised Control	X	X		X
Inverse Control	(X)	X		X
Neural Adaptive Control	?	?		?
Backprop Through Time	X		X	
Adaptive Critics:				
2-Net		X	X	X
Maximal	X	X	X	X

trajectories doesn't involve planning either, and that backpropagating utility is not brain-like because it can't handle noise and it's not so good for real time. But if you look at the table, you can see that it subdivides the world of adaptive critics a little further.

There was an old class of adaptive critics developed by Barto, Sutton and Anderson in 1983. It was a very useful first step in popularizing the idea. It can handle noise and optimization
over time and real time learning. A lot of people are having fun with it. It's good for a lot of engineering applications, but it won't handle many motors. And people have to understand it's very limited; it can't handle large problems. And when I say large, I mean like ten variables in an aircraft control problem. I mean that this is a really heavy limitation and that's been proven empirically now. (Tesauro has shown that a challenging AI problem -- playing backgammon -- yields very well to this design; that problem involves many theoretically possible states, but still involves a limited number of discrete action choices. Haykin's new book reviews the engineering experience -- which fits my summary here -- and White and Sofge, among others, have reported similar experience[15].)

On paper, in 1987 (actually before '87, in 1977), I proposed an alternative class of adaptive critics which combine backpropagation with adaptive critics. And let's call that Advanced Adaptive Critics. Combining backpropagation with adaptive critics in a fundamental way, not in a superficial way. And on paper, it looked to me that this approach solved the problem of handling many variables at once. And, as I said, I published that in 1977 as a solution to the slow convergence problem of the simpler critics. So that was actually before the Barto-Sutton-Anderson paper on the same kind of area.

In 1987 there were no working examples, but some people heard me present this in mid-1989 and now there are four working examples, at least, and two that are pretty close to real, and two of the examples are in large uses. There is one company that is a spinoff from McDonnell-Douglas (Neurodyne[15]) that has used these things to solve composite materials manufacturing problems that could never be solved before by any kind of neural network method, where the two nets would not work because they couldn't learn fast enough in real time. They have also used it in the control of an F-15 (providing real-time adaptation to aircraft damage in two seconds),

Direct Inverse Control (A Simple Approach to Trajectory Following)

Direct inverse control I've got to talk about because there are a lot of people who tacitly assume that this is what the brain does.

I was really glad to hear Dave Robinson talk at this workshop about how people think the brain is mapping from coordinate system A to coordinate system B, and about why this is a fundamentally misleading assumption. I agree with Dave very strongly that that is a bad way to describe what goes on in the cerebellum. And why?

People assume that the cerebellum is doing something like this (Figure 12). Suppose that you're trying to get a robot arm to follow a trajectory in physical space. You've got spatial coordinates X1 and X2. You control the

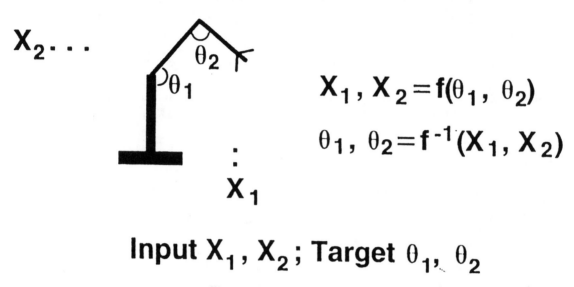

$$X_1, X_2 = f(\theta_1, \theta_2)$$

$$\theta_1, \theta_2 = f^{-1}(X_1, X_2)$$

Input X_1, X_2; Target θ_1, θ_2

Figure 12. Direct Inverse Control

thetas (joint angles). Somebody else is going to give you the X's, and you've got to figure out what are the thetas that get you to the right X's. Physically, you know that the position (X1,X2) is a function of the thetas. So if this function is invertible, then the thetas are a function of the X's, and what you can do is this: you can flail the arm around, get data on the thetas and the X's, real data, and then <u>learn</u> the mapping from the 's to the thetas. That's the basic idea. People like Kuperstein have taken this kind of approach, and people like Miller have done it, too. Kuperstein was an important pioneer in getting this approach started, but his reported error statistics (circa 3 percent) were too high to be useful in a practical way in robotics. Even in biology, we know that more accurate tracking is accomplished. I am puzzled why some people in neural nets go back so often to that early work, now that Kuperstein himself has moved on to other problems.

Now, Miller has shown that you can fix up the basic error statistics[15,17], but we still know that the human arm has many degrees of freedom. We know there are a lot of degrees of freedom in the human arm, more than there are in space; thus we know this mapping is not invertible for the human arm. So what is going on here?

Suzuki, Kawato and Uno have done a lot to explain this situation. They have lots of experiments proving that there is actually an <u>optimization</u> going on in this motor control system of the human arm. The details of that are in many places; for example, we have an MIT press book[17] where Kawato talks about that, and their experiments are unbelievable. I know that Hogan from MIT has recently questioned their conclusions, but neutral observers like Massone at Northwestern have looked over this controversy; it is my understanding that the empirical evidence is overwhelming that Suzuki et al are right on this particular point.

So we have a real optimizer down there in the cerebellum; we don't have the direct inverse coordinate-mapping kind of stuff; and that leads to some very interesting possibilities. Somebody should do some experiments to see how flexible and plastic that system is as an optimizer. Can they change what it optimizes? Can they use it to solve interesting optimization problems? And then the question is: how does it do it biologically? How does the cerebellum act as an optimizer?

By the way, there are a lot of engineering applications of direct inverse control.

698

For example, it has been used to control a simulator of the space shuttle main arm; you may be seeing the results on television in a few years, if all works as expected, but I don't have time to get into those kinds of details today. The bottom line is that direct inverse control has its uses, but is not relevant to the adaptive part of the human brain.

Adaptive Critics: A Way To Approximate Dynamic Programming

Now let's talk about adaptive critics.

One way of defining adaptive critics is to call them systems to approximate dynamic programming. When I give this definition to engineers, they say, "Oh, you're talking about something real. I thought it was garbage. You mentioned Freud and animal learning, so I assumed this can't work." But actually, you know that animal learning really does work; it is a powerful information processing system. Still, it is legitimate to look at it as an approximation to dynamic programming; that is one legitimate point of view.

In engineering, it is well-known that (for good mathematical reasons) there is only one set of techniques that is capable of finding the optimal strategy of action in a general, noisy nonlinear environment over time. There's only one that can do that in a general case, and that's called dynamic programming.

Figure 13 illustrates the basic idea of dynamic programming.

The way that dynamic programming works is that you give the system a utility function U or a performance function or primary reinforcement -- there are a thousand names for it; in other words, you tell it what you want to optimize <u>over time</u>, over the <u>future</u>. You also give it a stochastic model of the environment. Then, what dynamic programming does is that it comes out with something called the J function -- at least that's what Bryson and Ho

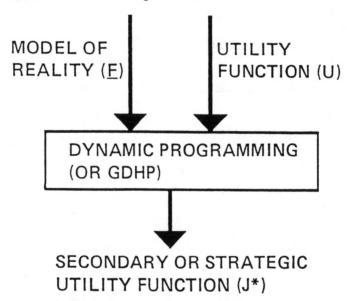

Figure 13. Inputs and Outputs of Dynamic Programming

call it. (To be more precise, in dynamic programming <u>you solve</u> an equation called the Bellman equation, in order to find this function J.) I like to call this function J a "strategic utility" function. It's just another utility function; it looks similar to U, in many ways.

The basic theorem of dynamic programming is this: if you maximize J in the short term, that will give you the strategy that optimizes U in the long term. So dynamic programming translates a difficult problem in planning or optimization over time into a problem in short term optimization. That is the essence of it.

And then the next question is: if there is only one exact way to do this, why don't we use dynamic programming for everything? In engineering and in biology, why don't we use it for everything, if it's the only exact and perfect thing? Well the reason is simple: it's too expensive. It may be the minimum-cost method, but the minimum cost is astronomical even when you have just a few variables. You can't do it exactly. A corollary of that is nobody will ever come up with a neural network that plays a perfect game of chess. So the next time a computer scientist tells you "gee, perfectly adapting a neural net is an NP-hard problem; therefore this isn't real and we've got to give up on it," ignore the computer scientist. The goal is not to play a perfect game of chess; that isn't what the brain does; and that isn't what our artificial systems can do, because it can't be done. That's one reason why the systems aren't perfectly optimal: it's not possible in a real- world engineering sense.

So what can you do? For a real-world, general purpose system that tries to optimize in the real world, we have to come up with a general purpose approximation to dynamic programming. That's what adaptive critics are. More precisely, adaptive critic systems are systems which contain networks whose job is to approximate either the J function of dynamic programming or its derivatives or something very close to it. That's what it is; you can call this "approximate dynamic programming" if you've got to sell it to a boss that doesn't like neural nets, and you'll be completely honest. You can call it adaptive critics among neural network people, or -- if you're talking to animal psychologists -- you can call it reinforcement learning, although that tends to understate what it's good for. Those are all legitimate names for what I am talking about here.

Intuitive Meaning of U and J

Now let me give you a little intuition about the meaning of all this, because once again, I'm saying the human brain is an adaptive critic system. So I am claiming we have a network in our brain that approximates the J function.

Table 2 gives us some intuition of what the J function is. If you're playing chess, the ultimate goal, at least in computer chess, is to win and not to lose. That's the intrinsic utility, U. But there's a famous rule of thumb, that a queen is worth nine points, a rook is worth five, etc.; people use that rule of thumb to see if they are making progress in the game. Beginners play to maximize points. Sophisticated people learn that holding the center is also worth something. And there are studies of Bobby-Fischer type people which argue that

Table 2. Examples of U and J

Domain	Basic Utility (U)	Strategic Utility (J)
Chess	Win/Lose	Queen = 9 points, etc.
Business Theory	Current Profit Cash Flow	Present Value of Strategic Assets (Performance Measures)
Human Thought	Pleasure/Pain Hunger	Hope/Fear Reaction to Job Loss
Behavioral Psychology	Primary Reinforcement	Secondary Reinforcement
Artificial Intelligence	Utility Function	Static Position Evaluator (Simon) Evaluation Function (Hayes-Roth)
Government Finance	National Values, Long-Term Goals	Cost/Benefit Measures
Physics	Lagrangian	Action Function
Economics	Current Value of Product to You	Market Price or Shadow Price ("Lagrange multipliers")

they don't really see ahead twenty moves -- even though they love to talk that way -- but that what they really do is to perform a very complex recurrent, strategic assessment to understand how well they're doing. And they really look ahead one move, but they do a complicated, strategic assessment of their options one move ahead.

In humanistic psychology you could think in terms of pleasure and pain, and hope and fear. In typical animal psychology, there's primary reinforcement and secondary reinforcement. This U/J concept occurs all over.

I don't think this concept is new to me; it's been hard-wired into our brains for years. But maybe we're just making it mathematical for the first time.

So when I say that the human brain is an adaptive critic, what does this theory really mean? In common-sense terms, all I'm saying is that we're governed by our hopes and fears, and these phenomena of hope and fear are irreducible things built into the human brain. I think that this is plausible. I don't think that it's a weird AI kind of theory, that hopes and fears are the fundamental grammar or representation wired into a big part of our intelligence.

The Barto/Sutton/Anderson Design

Figure 14 illustrates the 2-Net design I mentioned earlier. Because I don't have much time left today, let me explain very briefly the main reason why this design can be slow. The problem is that you've just one global reinforcement

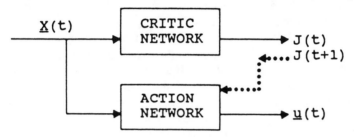

Figure 14. 2-Net Adaptive Critic of Barto, Sutton and Anderson

signal broadcasting to an action net. If you only have one action, then you know which action was wrong. But if you've got a hundred actions, and you made a mistake, then you don't know which one to change, in what direction. You don't have a sense of cause and effect; without cause and effect, it's kind of hard to learn. The ideas in this design may still be useful as part of a larger hybrid, but, by itself, this design could never describe a large-scale system like the brain. So now let's move on a little bit.

The Backpropagated Adaptive Critic: From Freud to Engineering

Figure 15 illustrates an idea I proposed in a journal article in 1977. Let me stress that this is only one of many advanced adaptive critic designs; you've got to go to the Handbook to get the complete list; this is only one. (I picked this one because it's the one case where there was a typo in the Handbook; the version here is correct.)

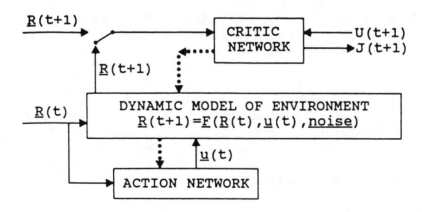

Figure 15. BAC (Version Which Uses J Output)

This is where the backpropagation algorithm really came from, originally, in unpublished reports I wrote in 1970-72. Later I learned how to simplify the idea of backpropagation, so people could copy it and reproduce it. That really happened in 1981[24], when I started playing the simple perceptron games with backpropagation and publishing that stuff, but Figure 15 is where I really came from in the first place.

And where did this idea come from? Believe it or not, I developed this idea as a mathematical translation of an idea from Freud. That's where backpropagation started. Freud had this idea. Freud was interested in neural nets. He had to make money later on, and he regretted that he had to make money doing stupid things, okay? That's on the record. He started out going to medical school, studying physiology, and what he really wanted to do was to build a neural network theory of the human mind. He felt that he _had_ developed a valid theory, and he came back to that theory later in life.

His model began with the idea that human behavior is governed by emotions. Does that sound weird? Not if you're a human, but sometimes I almost wonder who is and who isn't, when I see some of the theories floating around these days. At any rate, Freud had the idea that there was something called cathexis or psychic energy or emotional charge attached to things he called objects. According to his theory, people first of all learn cause-and-effect associations; for example, they may learn that "object" A is associated with "object" B at a later time. And his theory was that there is a _backwards_ flow of emotional energy. If A causes B, and B has emotional energy, then the emotional energy will flow from B back to A. And if A causes B to an extent W, then the backwards flow of emotional energy from B back to A will be proportional to the forwards rate. That really is backpropagation. That really is backpropagation, and my argument is that you have to have that. I cannot conceive of a way of using cause and effect information without doing what Freud said. If A causes B, then you have to find a way to credit A for B, directly. You have to exploit the fact that you know that A causes B to the extent W. So your flow of emotional energy has to use that number W that represents the forward association; you can't get out of that. I see no mathematical way to get out of it, and I've looked at a million attempts, by Grossberg and others; there's no way to get out of that. If you want to build a powerful system, you need a backwards flow.

Now, in mathematical terms, I can now give you a very different interpretation of Figure 15. In Figure 15, I am properly and dutifully following dynamic programming. (I figured this out later _after_ I had the design.) What I'm really doing is exactly what dynamic programming tells me to do, which is to pick an action vector **u** so as to maximize J. I maximize J directly and intelligently by calculating the derivatives of J with respect to action, any using those derivatives. This is _not_ error backpropagation. This is backpropagation as a way of calculating derivatives; I work back the derivatives with a special chain rule, the chain rule for ordered derivatives. I work backwards the derivatives of J with respect to U. And this is easy to implement, although you've got to read the _Handbook_ to get the details, since I don't have the time here today.

So the bottom line is this: because of this argument of Freud's, which is just about inescapable mathematically, nobody has found an alternative to this general approach. I would predict that there must be this kind of mechanism somewhere in the brain. I can't see any way you could do it otherwise; I haven't seen a contrary model that could work on that scale. And, as I mentioned before, my paper on the cytoskeleton[5] and other papers by Dayhoff and others describe plausible mechanisms that could implement it. It is very plausible.

On the engineering side, there are already a number of applications of Advanced Adaptive Critics (which I define as adaptive critic systems which adapt an Action network based at least in part on estimated derivatives of J with respect to **u**). There is an application to the continuous production of high-quality composite materials, which have a potential market worth many billions of dollars, et cetera. There is an F15 application I mentioned before. Again, I have no time for the details.

In the future, we might get into earth orbit at a much lower cost if we can solve certain control problems; they turn out to be optimal control problems, which classical control cannot handle very well. Again, dynamic programming -- the appropriate classical method -- is too expensive, but adaptive critics are not. The National Aerospace Plane office has recently given contracts to people to use adaptive critics, to solve optimization problems that can't be solved any other way. There is reason to believe we cannot reduce the cost of earth orbit without using this stuff, and it's being implemented today. A benchmark version of this control challenge is in [15].

Overall Architecture of the Brain

How does Figure 15 relate to the brain? Figure 16 on the next page is from a paper I published in 1987[25]. (That paper was the first to inform the Barto-Sutton-Anderson group about the dynamic interpretation here, and about my prior work; whatever its failings, it had a major influence on later developments.). This figure presented a very early approximation of what I think is going on.

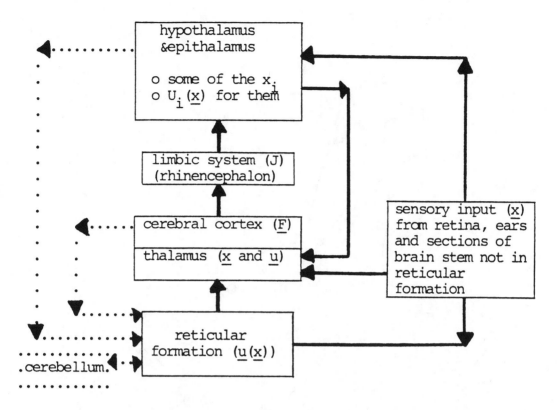

Figure 16. A First-Pass Neurocontrol Interpretation of the Brain (From [25])

I have argued that the hypothalamus (and maybe the epithalamus) are computing a built-in utility function. The hypothalamus is not the greatest center of plasticity, but it's a powerful source of primary reinforcement. I'm arguing that the primary function of the limbic lobes is as a critic network; we certainly know that there's secondary reinforcement in the limbic nodes, no surprise there. (See, for example, the classic work by Papez and by James Olds.)

I'm also arguing that the cerebral cortex includes the function of Model network; in other words, understanding cause-and-effect relations is its primary function. In engineering terms, that means that the cortex is performing system identification, which includes filtering or working memory (short-term memory) as a secondary function. This fits the recent studies demonstrating working memory capabilities in the temporal cortex (Goldman-Rakic) and in the frontal cortex, and the work by Barry Richmond demonstrating the relevant kinds of lagged recurrent effects even in visual cortex. (Because of plasticity studies, it would hard to imagine that a truly fundamental capability like working memory could be limited to any one architectonic area of the neocortex.)

Architecture of the Olive/Cerebellum System

Finally, in closing, I would like to come back to the cerebellum, which is the Action network within a complete multi-net lower-level control system. I would like to come back to the key question which I left open earlier in this section: "How could the lower motor system perform optimization? How could it be an adaptive critic system?" Here, I will summarize some thoughts from [14].

Houk has done a lot of work showing that the inferior olive sends training signals which adapt the Purkinje cells, in a way that looks like an adaptive critic arrangement. So this is consistent with the idea that the cerebellum is an Action net, and that the olive is a Critic directly adapting it. What Houk doesn't talk about is plasticity in the output layer of the network, which is a deep cerebellar array (plus FTN cells of the vestibular nucleus). Lisberger produced a flow chart of the FTN system for an excellent paper in Science which nevertheless confused some people in the neural net community, who apparently thought that the chart was a complete wiring diagram (even though Lisberger himself discussed other connections in the text); this has led to some nonempirical Hebbian models so unrealistic and so incomplete that the authors should not be mentioned.

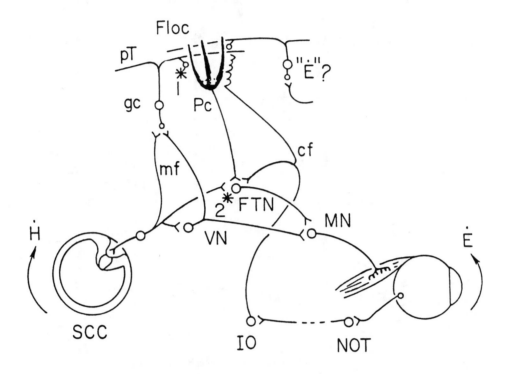

Figure 17. Flow Chart of the FTN System From David Robinson
IO=Inferior Olive; cf=Climbing Fiber;Pc=Purkinje Cell;gc=Granule Cell

Figure 17 is a better flow chart borrowed from Dave Robinson, who has a new paper that will explain this better. The bottom line is that there are cells of the vestibular nucleus (and presumably in the deep nuclei) that also get climbing fiber input from the olive, and there's good evidence that they train the output layer as well as the Purkinje layer. It turns out, if you look at this arrangement mathematically, this arrangement turns out to be equivalent to backpropagating through the action network, just like that adaptive critic architecture I was describing. And it's neat, because it's an electronic way of doing it that I wouldn't have thought of. The unique many-to-one architecture in the cerebellum makes this mathematically a valid implementation of backpropagation if you have the right training signal (a derivative signal) for the output layer. (Strictly speaking, the Purkinje-to-deep connectivity is more like 850-to-35, according to Pellionisz, rather than many-to-one in a precise sense; however, this is no problem, if we assume that the 35 related deep cells are representing a common variable, using multiple channels to permit greater precision.)

But how do you get this training signal from the olive? If you read things like Houk and Barto, they begin to be a little incoherent when it comes explaining how the olive learns to give a training signal specific to a given action variable. Now it turns out, on the neurocontrol side, that there is one and only one class of working design (we now know) that yields output in a powerful way that you can use to train individual action nodes. And it's this weird thing here (in Figure 18)...and you have this particular kind of critic network that outputs training signals to an action network, and what do these things represent? They represent the derivatives of J with respect to the individual, specific action variables.

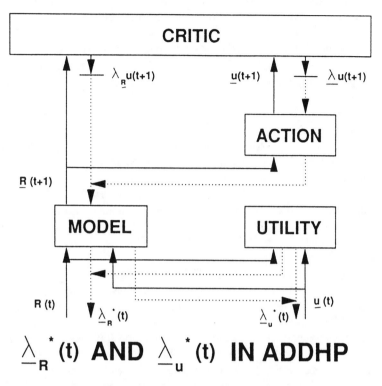

$$\underline{\lambda}_R^*(t) \text{ AND } \underline{\lambda}_u^*(t) \text{ IN ADDHP}$$

Figure 18. Example of an ANN Neurocontrol Design

Now, I don't think the cerebellum is doing this, I've matched Figure 18 to the cerebellar circuit and it doesn't fit. But it is very clear to me from what is going on here that those olive signals must represent the derivative of J with respect to **u**. Is there any way that that could happen?

Well, it turns out the cerebellum suggests a new design different from what we've had before, that is still understandable in terms of the same mathematics. The basic idea is that the olive output has to be trained in one of two ways:

either (1) there's a local target that tells each climbing fiber what the derivatives of J with respect to **u** are. In this arrangement, the point is that the olive is anticipating a slower system. The need for speed explains why it is good to have an olive; that's why you don't just use the target itself to train the cerebellum.

(2) The other hypothesis is that a lot of complicated learning is going on inside the olive (perhaps like Figure 18, for example). But you can't do that unless you have an efference copy of the action vector **u**.

So there are only two possible hypotheses. One is that there is some kind of backpropagation along the climbing fibers -- either in the climbing fibers or along them -- so that somehow a target which is local to the action region gets back to train the olive. That's one possibility; it's pretty crazy, but you could cut the fiber and find out. The other possibility is that the fibers that go from the deep nuclei back to the olive provide a complete efference copy which is used in training the olive. If that is true, then you cut those fibers and eliminate plasticity in the olive (or modify it substantially).

You can do the experiment. I can't. I hope that you do. Thank you.

References

[1] W.Nauta and M.Feirtag, *Fundamental Neuroanatomy*. W.H.Freeman, 1986.

[2] P.Werbos, *The Roots of Backpropagation: From Ordered Derivatives to Neural Networks and Political Forecasting*, Wiley, 1993.

[3] P.Werbos, "Neural networks and the human mind: new mathematics fits humanistic insight," in *Proc. Conf. SMC*, IEEE, 1992. An updated version is in [2].

[4] P.Werbos, "Quantum theory and neural systems: alternative approaches and a new design," in K.Pribram, ed.,

Rethinking Neural Networks: Quantum Fields an Biological Evidence, INNS Press/Erlbaum, 1993.

[5] P.Werbos, "The cytoskeleton: why it may be crucial to human learning and neurocontrol," *Nanobiology*, Vol.1, No.1, 1992.

[6] M.Baudry and J.Davis, eds, *Long-Term Potentiation: A Debate of Current Issues*, MIT Press, 1991.

[7] T.Smirnova, S.Laroche, M.Errington, A,Hicks, T.Bliss and J.Mallet, "Transsynaptic expression of a presynaptic glutamate receptor during hippocampal long-term potentiation," *Science*, Vol. 262, p.430-436, October 15, 1993.

[8] J.Dayhoff, S.Hameroff, R.Lahoz-Beltra and C.Swenborg,"Intracellular mechanisms in neuronal learning: adaptive models", *IJCNN92 Proceedings*, IEEE, 1992.

[9] F.Fukamauchi, C.Hough and D.Chuang, "m2- and m3-Muscarinic Acetylcholine receptor mRNAs have different responses to microtubule-affecting drugs," *Molecular and Cellular Neurosciences*, Vol. 2, p.315-319, 1991.

[10] C.Hough, F.Fukamauchi and D.Chuang, "Regulation of β-adrenergic receptor mRNA in rat C_6 glioma cells is sensitive to the state of microtubule assembly," *Journal of Neurochemistry*, Vol. 62, No.1, 1994.

[11] G.Stuart and B.Sakmann, "Active propagation of somatic action potentials into neocortical pyramidal cell dendrites," *Nature*, Vol. 367, No. 6458, p.69-72, Jan. 6, 1994.

[12] D.Gardner, "Backpropagation and neuromorphic plausibility," *WCNN93 Proceedings*, INNS Press/Erlbaum, 1993.

[13] D.Gardner, *The Neurobiology of Neural Networks*, MIT Press, 1993.

[14] P.Werbos and A.Pellionisz, "Neurocontrol and neurobiology," In *IJCNN Proceedings*, IEEE, 1992.

[15] D.White and D.Sofge,eds, *Handbook of Intelligent Control: Neural, Fuzzy and Adaptive Approaches*. Van Nostrand, 1992.

[16] D.C.Tam, personal communication and "A new conditional correlation statistics for detecting spatio-temporally correlated firing patterns in a biological neuronal network," *WCNN93 Proceedings*, INNS Press/Erlbaum, 1993.

[17] W.Miller,R.Sutton and P.Werbos,eds, *Neural Networks for Control*. MIT Press, 1990.

[18] P.Werbos, "Supervised learning," *WCNN93 Proceedings*, INNS Press/Erlbaum, 1993.

[19] P.Werbos, "Elastic fuzzy logic: a better fit to neurocontrol and true intelligence," *Journal of Intelligent and Fuzzy Systems*, Vol. 1, No. 4, 1993.

[20] K.Pribram and M.Gill, *Freud's Project Reassessed*, Basic Books, 1976.

[21] K.Pribram,"Familiarity and novelty: the contributions of the limbic forebrain to valuation and the processing of relevance," in D.Levine and S,Leven, eds, *Motivation, Emotion and Goal Direction in Neural Networks*, Erlbaum, 1992.

[22] P.Werbos, "Backpropagation through time: what it does and how to do it," *Proceedings of IEEE*, October 1990 issue. A slightly updated version is in [2].

[23] P.Werbos, "Neurocontrol: where it is going and why it is crucial," in I. Aleksander and J.Taylor, eds, *Artificial Neural Networks II*. North Holland, 1992. An updated version is in [2].

[24] P.Werbos, "Applications of advances in nonlinear sensitivity analysis," in R.Drenick and F.Kozin, eds, *Systems Modeling and Optimization: Proc. of the 1981 IFIP Conf.*, Springer-Verlag, 1982. Reprinted in [2].

[25] P.Werbos, "Building and understanding adaptive systems: a statistical/numerical approach to factory automation and brain research, *IEEE Trans. SMC*, Jan.-Feb. 1987.

AFTERWORD

By: Karl H. Pribram

As did Appalachian I, Appalachian II resolved, for me, certain hitherto intractable problems that plague the mind/brain relationship. In Appalachian I, the problem was: how can psychological processes reflect brain activity? Psychological processes such as language seem to be organized so differently from the recorded activity of the neurons and neural systems known to be critically involved. The answer came in the form of an identity at the subneuronal, synaptodendritic and cytoskeletal level. At that level, descriptions of the organization of the elementary neural process and descriptions of the organization of the elementary psychological process are identical: assuming that the brain is an information processing organ, the description of the organization of synaptodendritic cortical receptive fields is identical with the description of the organization of information processing in communication devices such as those that process language--e.g. telephony, and those that process images--e.g., tomography and television.

Appalachian II addressed a problem that emerges as a direct consequence of this identity. The form of the identity is symmetrical. The informational process is a two-way interaction: in a manner of speaking, the organization of the subneuronal process produces (causes) the organization of the elementary psychological process; but at the same time, this organization shapes (causes) the subneuronal process. The identity of organization, the information process involved, makes this way of speaking seem awkward and old fashioned, rooted in a pervasive Cartesian dualism. But it does call attention to the fact that identity implies symmetry.

Life and mind are not governed completely by the laws of symmetry. In fact, one might define an all important characteristic of life and mind is that symmetries become broken--especially time symmetry. In biology, birth, growth, procreation and death; in psychology, learning and memory, attention, intuition and thought are all time-symmetry breaking processes.

Prigogine's keynote addresses this issue and clarifies, for me, the "how" of time symmetry breaking. As I understand Prigogine's presentation (with help from Kunio Yasue and Mari Jibu), there are formulations in which spectral representations do not render both real and virtual "images" when Fourier transformed. Prigogine's discussion is restricted to certain quantum and/or classical systems driven by (non-self-adjoint) Hamiltonian operators (for quantum systems) and/or Liouville operators (for classical systems) which are "chosen" so that their time developments are kept contractive (i.e. loose information) and dissipative (i.e. loose energy). Thus, as Prigogine states in a letter to me in response to a question:

> The difference between real and complex spectrum is very simple. Take the Hamiltonian in Hilbert space, it has <u>real</u> eigenvalues E_1, E_2...

> Similarly the evolution operator $U_{(t)} = e^{-iHt}$ has complex eigenvalues such as $e^{-iE_1 t}$.

In generalized spaces, non square integrable eigen functions of H may be complex eigenvalues such as $E_1 = \alpha_1 - i\beta_1$. As a result the evolution operator has damping terms $e^{-i(\alpha_1 - i\beta_1)t} = e^{-i\alpha_1 t} e^{-\beta t}$. Then time symmetry is broken.

Critical to this formulation is the use of imaginary numbers. Equations that need complex numbers for their solution have an imaginary and real part. As indicated in the above equation in generalized (rather than Hilbert spaces) non square integrable eigen functions, though they have complex eigenvalues, their evolution operator (e.g. a Hamiltonian) has damping terms that essentially eliminate the imaginary component leaving only the component that falls on the real line. Thus, as a consequence of taking a path, time symmetry is broken. Is this also the mechanism whereby the virtual image produced (by means of a Fourier Transform) by the lens of the eye is suppressed?

In short undertaking a path, by explicit or implicit movement---whether as attention to input, as intending an action or as rummaging through memory (thought)---breaks time symmetry. The path not taken can never be retrieved.

Thus, Appalachian I and II have prepared the ground for future conferences. The topic for Appalachian III stems from the fact that undertaking a path lands us in a level, a scale, different from the terrain within which the path is located. The substrate, the landscape, of a psychological process such as consciousness may reside in the subneuronal architecture of the brain but the path taken through that landscape can configure very different "views" or scales. Appalachian III is therefore entitled "Scale in Conscious Experience: Is the Brain Too Important to Be Left to Biologists to Study?"

Further conferences are hoped for. The time is ripe, I believe, to tackle problems such as describing the brain processes involved in valuation (reinforcement and deterrence), in learning (self organization) and in making choices, with the same richness in technique and content as have characterized the first three conferences.

List of Authors Cited

5983-42P
5-29